THEOLOGICAL DICTIONARY

OF THE

OLD TESTAMENT

THEOLOGICAL DICTIONARY
OF THE
OLD TESTAMENT

EDITED BY

G. JOHANNES BOTTERWECK,
HELMER RINGGREN,
AND
HEINZ-JOSEF FABRY

VOLUME XVI
ARAMAIC DICTIONARY

EDITED BY

HOLGER GZELLA

Translated by

MARK E. BIDDLE

WILLIAM B. EERDMANS PUBLISHING COMPANY
GRAND RAPIDS, MICHIGAN

Wm. B. Eerdmans Publishing Co.
4035 Park East Court, SE, Grand Rapids, Michigan 49546
www.eerdmans.com

THEOLOGICAL DICTIONARY OF THE OLD TESTAMENT
Volume 16: ARAMAIC DICTIONARY
Translated from
THEOLOGISCHES WÖRTERBUCH ZUM ALTEN TESTAMENT
Band IX, ARAMÄISCHES WÖRTERBUCH
Published 2016 by
Verlag W. Kohlhammer GmbH, Stuttgart, Germany

Hardcover edition 2018
Paperback edition 2022

Library of Congress Cataloging-in-Publication Data

A catalog record for this book is available from the Library of Congress

Volume 16 ISBN 978-0-8028-8330-8

CONSULTING EDITOR

Holger Gzella, Leiden

PRIMARY CONTRIBUTORS

†K. Beyer, Heidelberg
S. Fassberg, Jerusalem
†D. N. Freedman, San Diego
A. Gianto, SJ, Rome
I. Gluska, Ramat Gan
V. Hug, Heidelberg
†M. Z. Kaddari, Ramat Gan
E. A. Knauf, Bern
I. Kottsieper, Göttingen
R. G. Kratz, Göttingen
R. J. Kuty, Liège
R. G. Lehmann, Mainz
E. Lipiński, Louvain
C. Martone, Torino
†H.-P. Müller, Münster
G. W. Nebe, Heidelberg
H.-D. Neef, Tübingen
H. Niehr, Tübingen
W. van Peursen, Amsterdam
D. Schwemer, Würzburg
D. Schwiderski, Heidelberg
C. Stadel, Beersheba
A. Steudel, Göttingen
E. J. C. Tigchelaar, Louvain
M. Waltisberg, Marburg
H. G. M. Williamson, Oxford

CONTENTS

Editor's Preface xix

Abbreviations xxi

Hints for Use xxxiii

Introduction xxxv

אב *ʾb*, אם (Beyer, Kottsieper) 1

אבד *ʾbd*, אבדן, שמד (Freedman/Yu, Kottsieper) 3

אבן *ʾbn* (Steudel/Maurer) 8

אזד *ʾzd* (Gzella) 9

אח *ʾḥ*, אחה (Beyer, Kottsieper) 10

אחידה *ʾḥydh*, אוחידו (Müller) 13

אחרי *ʾḥry*, אחר, אחרן, אחרין (Freedman/Yu, Kottsieper) 16

אילן *ʾjln*, אב, ענף, עפי, ארז (Freedman/Geoghegan) 21

אימה *ʾymh* (Gzella) 25

אכל *ʾkl*, זון, מזון, קרץ (Kaddari, Kottsieper) 26

אלה *ʾlh*, אל (Niehr) 31

אלף *ʾlp* (Steudel/Maurer) 45

אמן *ʾmn*, הימן, הימנו, מהימן (Beyer, Kottsieper) 47

אמר *ʾmr* (Freedman/Geoghegan, Kottsieper) 49

אנס *ʾns* (Kottsieper) 54

אנף *ʾnp* (Schwemer) 55

אנש *ʾnš* (Beyer, Kottsieper) 59

אנתה *ʾnth*, אנתו, נשין (Freedman/Levitt Kohn, Kottsieper) 63

אספרנה *ʾsprnh*, אדרזדה (Gzella) 66

אסר *ʾsr*, אסור, אסר (Kottsieper) 67

אע	*ʾʿ* (Freedman/Feliú, Kottsieper)	72
ארגון	*ʾrgwn* (Gzella)	74
ארח	*ʾrḥ* (Knauf)	75
אריה	*ʾryh* (Neef)	77
ארך	*ʾrk*, אריך, ארכה, ארך (Gzella)	79
ארק/ע	*ʾrq/ʾrʿ* (Kottsieper)	79
אש	*ʾš* (Schwemer)	85
אשה	*ʾšh*, יקד, יקדה, נור, שׂביב (Freedman/Homan, Kottsieper)	87
אשף	*ʾšp*, אסה, חרטם, כס/שׂדי (Niehr)	91
אשרן	*ʾšrn* (Gzella)	95
את	*ʾt*, תמה, תוה (Kottsieper)	95
אתה/י	*ʾtī* (Neef)	100
אתר	*ʾtr*, אשׁ/תרה (Lipiński)	103
באש	*bʾš*, ב(א)ישׁ, לחה, רשׁע, רשׁיע, שׁחיתה (Gluska, Kottsieper)	106
בדר	*bdr* (Schwemer)	113
בהל	*bhl*, בהילו (Lehmann)	116
בירת	*byrt* (Lipiński)	118
בית	*byt* (Freedman/Homan, Kottsieper)	119
בל	*bl* (Kaddari, Kottsieper)	126
בלי	*blī* (Gzella)	127
בנה/י	*bnī*, בנין (Kaddari, Kottsieper)	127
בעי	*bʿī*, בעו (Gzella)	131
בעל	*bʿl*, בעל (Niehr)	134
בקר	*bqr*, מבקר (Gzella)	139
בר	*br*, ברה (Martone)	141
בר	*br* /barr/, ברא, ברי (Gzella)	145
ברך	*brk*, ברכה, ברך, ארכבה (Kratz)	146
בשׂר	*bśr* (Tigchelaar)	153
גאי	*gʾī*, גאוה (Gzella)	155

גב *gb* (Gzella) 156
גבר *gbr*, גבר, גבורה, גבר, גברו (Gzella) 157
גו *gw*, גוי (Gzella) 161
גזר *gzr*, גזר, גזרה (Lipiński) 163
גלי I *glī* (Kratz) 166
גלי II *glī*, גלו, שבי (Kratz) 170
גלל *gll* (Williamson) 173
גנז *gnz*, גזבר, גנזך, גניזה (Lipiński) 175
גף *gp* (van Peursen) 177
גשם *gšm* (Gzella) 180
דב *db* (Lipiński) 181
דבח *dbḥ*, דבח, דבח, מדבח (Lipiński) 182
דבק *dbq* (Gzella) 186
דבר *dbr*, מדבר, דברת, דבר (Lipiński) 188
דהב *dhb* (Gzella) 193
דור *dūr*, דרה, דיר, מדר, דר, תדיר (Gzella) 196
דחל *dḥl*, דחיל, דחלה (Gzella) 199
דין *dīn*, דין, דין, מדינה, שפט (Niehr) 202
דכר *dkr* /dakar/ (Lipiński) 208
דכר *dkr*, דכיר, דכרן (Gzella) 210
דם *dm* (Tigchelaar) 214
דמי *dmī*, דמו (Gzella) 215
דקק *dqq* (Gzella) 217
דת *dt* (Gzella) 218
הדר *hdr*, הדר (Gzella) 219
הוי *hwī* (Gzella) 221
היכל *hykl* (Niehr) 224
הלך *hlk*, הוך, אזל, הלך (Gzella) 227
זבן *zbn*, זבון, זבן, זבנה, זבן (Lipiński) 232

זהר *zhr*, זהיר (Gzella) . . . 233
זיו *zyw* (Beyer) . . . 235
זכו *zkw*, זכי, זכי (Lipiński) . . . 236
זמן *zmn*, זמן (Schwiderski) . . . 238
זמר *zmr*, זמר, זמר (Gzella) . . . 241
זעק *z'q*, זעקה (Kuty) . . . 242
זרע *zr'*, זרע (Kuty) . . . 243
חבל *ḥbl*, חבל, חבולה (Gzella) . . . 245
חבר *ḥbr*, חבר, חבר (Nebe/Gzella) . . . 247
חדוה *ḥdwh*, חדי (Schwiderski) . . . 250
חוי *ḥwī* (Schwiderski) . . . 252
חור *ḥwr* (Beyer) . . . 255
חזי *ḥzī*, חזו, חזי, מחזה, חזו, חזון, חזיון, מחזי, חזה, רו (Gzella) . . . 256
חטא/חטי *ḥṭ'/ḥṭī*, חטא, חטי, זיד, חוב, חוב(ה), חיב, טעי, טעיה, טעו, עויה, עול (Gzella) . . . 261
חיי *ḥyī*, חי, חיין, חיוה (Gzella) . . . 266
חיל *ḥyl*, חיל (Gzella) . . . 271
חכם *ḥkm*, חכים, חכמה, ערם, ערמן, ערימו, סכל (Gzella) . . . 274
חלם *ḥlm*, חלם, חלם, הרהר II (Gzella) . . . 278
חלף *ḥlp*, חלף, חלפה (Stadel) . . . 283
חלק *ḥlq*, חלק, מחלקה (Gzella) . . . 285
חמה *ḥmh*, בנס, קצף, רגז (Kuty) . . . 288
חמר *ḥmr*, גפן, כרם, ענב (Gzella) . . . 291
חנטה *ḥnṭh* (Gzella) . . . 292
חנכה *ḥnkh* (Gzella) . . . 293
חנן *ḥnn*, חן, תחנונין (Gzella) . . . 294
חסן *ḥsn*, חסן, חסין (Gzella) . . . 296
חסף *ḥsp* (Gzella) . . . 299
חסר *ḥsr*, חסיר, חסרן (Gzella) . . . 300

חרב *ḥrb*, חרבן (Stadel) . . . 301
חרץ *ḥrṣ* (Stadel) . . . 303
חשב *ḥšb*, חשבן (Gzella) . . . 304
חשח *ḥšḥ*, חשחו (Gzella) . . . 307
חשך *ḥšk*, חשוך, חשיך (Gzella) . . . 309
חשל *ḥšl* (Gzella) . . . 312
חתם *ḥtm*, חתם (Gzella) . . . 313
טור *ṭwr*, כף (Gzella) . . . 315
טיב *ṭīb*, יטב, טאב, טב, טבו, טוב (Gzella) . . . 317
טל *ṭl* (Gzella) . . . 321
טלל *ṭll*, טל, טלל, טלול, מטלל (Gzella) . . . 322
טעם *ṭʿm*, טעם (Nebe) . . . 323
יד *yd*, כף, אצבע, דרע (Gzella) . . . 326
ידי *ydī* (Gzella) . . . 332
ידע *ydʿ*, מנדע (Gianto) . . . 335
יהב *yhb* (Gzella) . . . 341
יהוד *yhwd*, יהודי (Beyer) . . . 345
יום *ywm* (Gzella) . . . 346
יכל *ykl*, כהל, כבש (Gzella) . . . 349
ים *ym*, תחום (Gzella) . . . 351
ימא/ימי *ymʾ/ymī*, מומה (Niehr) . . . 353
יעט *yʿṭ*, עטה, יעט (Kuty) . . . 356
יצב *yṣb*, יציב, יצבה (Hug) . . . 357
יקר *yqr*, יקיר (Waltisberg) . . . 359
יתב *ytb*, מותב, תותב (Kuty) . . . 363
כדב *kdb*, כדב(ה), כדב (Gzella) . . . 366
כהן *khn*, כהנו, לוי, כמר (Gzella) . . . 367
כלל *kll*, כל, שיציא (Kuty) . . . 370
כנה *knh* (Gzella) . . . 372

כנש	*knš* (Fassberg)	374
כרסא	*krs'* (Lipiński)	375
כתב	*ktb*, כתב, כתבה, רשם (Gzella)	378
כתל	*ktl*, אגר (Gzella)	383
לבב	*lbb*, לב (Gzella)	384
לבש	*lbš*, לבוש, לבש (Gzella)	388
לחם	*lḥm* (Fassberg)	390
לחן	*lḥn*, לחנה (Gzella)	392
לילה	*lylh* (Beyer)	393
לשן	*lšn* (Gianto)	395
מאן	*m'n* (Gzella)	397
מגר	*mgr* (Gzella)	400
מדי	*mdy*, מדי, פרס, פרסי (Gzella)	401
מות	*mūt*, מית, מות, מותן (Gzella)	404
מחא/י	*mḥ'/mḥī* (Lipiński)	407
מטא/י	*mṭ'/mṭī* (Gzella)	410
מלאך	*ml'k* (Niehr)	413
מלח	*mlḥ*, מלח (Gzella)	415
מלא/י	*ml'/mlī*, מלה (Gzella)	417
מלך	*mlk*, מלכה, מלכו, מלך, מלך (Gzella)	420
מלל	*mll*, מלה, ממלל, אמר, לאמר, דברה (Gianto)	428
מנדה	*mndh* (Gzella)	434
מנחה	*mnḥh*, עלה, נסך, נחוח (Niehr)	435
מני	*mnī*, מנין, מנה, מנה, פרס (Gzella)	438
מרא	*mr'*, מראה (Niehr)	442
מרד	*mrd*, מרד, מרד (Stadel)	449
משח	*mšḥ*, משח, משיח (Gzella)	450
נביא	*nby'*, נבא, נבואה (Gzella)	453
נגד	*ngd*, נגד, נגוד, נגידו (Lipiński)	455

נגה	*ngh* (Gzella)	456
נדב	*ndb* (Nebe)	457
נדד	*ndd*, נוד, ערק (Gzella)	459
נדן	*ndn* (Gzella)	461
נהר	*nhr* /nahar/ (Gzella)	462
נהר	*nhr*, נהור, נהיר (Fassberg)	465
נור	*nūr*, נור (Gzella)	466
נזק	*nzq*, נזק (Gzella)	468
נחת	*nḥt* (Gzella)	470
נטל	*nṭl* (Gzella)	474
נטר	*nṭr*, מנטרה (Gzella)	475
נכסין	*nksyn* (Gzella)	478
נמר	*nmr* (Beyer)	481
נפל	*npl*, נפילין, מפלה (Gzella)	483
נפק	*npq*, נפקה, מפק (Gzella)	487
נצב	*nṣb*, נצבה (Fassberg)	492
נצח	*nṣḥ* (Gzella)	494
נצל	*nṣl*, פלט (Gzella)	495
נקה	*nqh*, נקי, נקה (Gzella)	499
נשא/י	*nś'/nśī*, נסב, לקח, טען, טעון (Gzella)	500
נשם	*nšm*, נשמה, נשם, נשב, נפש (Gzella)	505
נשר	*nšr* (Beyer)	510
נשתון	*nštwn* (Gzella)	511
נתן	*ntn*, נתין, מ(נ)תנ(ה), נבזבה (Gzella)	513
נתר	*ntr* (Gzella)	517
סבל	*sbl*, סבול, סמך (Gzella)	518
סגד	*sgd*, סגיד, סגדה, סגדו, מסגד (Lipiński)	521
סגן	*sgn* (Gzella)	523
סוף	*sūp*, סוף, סיפין, בטל (Gzella)	525

סלק	*slq* (Waltisberg)	528
סעד	*sʿd*, סעד, עדר (Gzella)	532
ספר	*spr*, ספר, אגרה (Gzella)	534
סרושׁי	*srwšy* (Gzella)	538
סרך	*srk* (Gzella)	539
סתר	*str*, סתר, מסתר, טמר, צפן (Gzella)	540
עבד	*ʿbd*, עבד, עבידה, עבד, מעבד, אמה (Gzella)	541
עבר	*ʿbr*, עבר, מעבר, עבור (Gzella)	547
עדי	*ʿdī*, עדי, עדינה (Gzella)	550
עדן	*ʿdn* (Gianto)	554
עור	*ʿwr*, אדר (Gzella)	556
עז	*ʿz*, צפיר (Hug)	557
עזקה	*ʿzqh* (Gzella)	560
עין	*ʿyn*, נבע, עור, שׁכן, בבה (Gzella)	561
עיר	*ʿyr* (Fassberg)	564
עלה	*ʿlh* (Gzella)	566
עלי	*ʿly*, עליון, עלי, עליה (Stadel)	566
עלים	*ʿlym* (Kuty)	569
עלל	*ʿll*, עלל, עללה, מעל, מעלין (Gzella)	571
עלם	*ʿlm* (Niehr)	576
עלע	*ʿlʿ* (Gzella)	580
עם	*ʿm*, אמה, ארם (Gzella)	581
עמק	*ʿmq*, עמק, עמיק (Gzella)	586
עני	I *ʿnī* (Gzella)	587
עני	II *ʿnī*, ענה, ענוה, עתר (Gzella)	590
ענן	*ʿnn*, ערפל, מטר, תלג (Gzella)	591
עצב	*ʿṣb*, עציב, אבל, בכי, כרי (Gzella)	593
עקר	*ʿqr*, עקר (Gzella)	594
ערד	*ʿrd* (Beyer)	596

ערר *ʿrr*, ער, ערר (Gzella) . . . 597
עשׂב *ʿśb*, דתא (Gzella) . . . 598
עשת *ʿšt* (Gzella) . . . 599
עתיק *ʿtyq* (Gzella) . . . 600
פחה *pḥh* (Gzella) . . . 602
פלג *plg*, פלג, פלגן, פלגן (Gzella) . . . 603
פלח *plḥ*, פלחן (Gzella) . . . 605
פם *pm* (Gzella) . . . 608
פרק *prq* (Gzella) . . . 611
פרשׁ *prš*, פרשׁ (Gzella) . . . 613
פרשגן *pršgn* (Gzella) . . . 616
פשׁר *pšr* (Tigchelaar) . . . 616
פתגם *ptgm* (Gzella) . . . 621
פתח *ptḥ* (Gzella) . . . 622
צבי *ṣbī*, צבו, צבין (Hug) . . . 626
צדק *ṣdq*, צדק, צדקה, צדיק (Gzella) . . . 630
צלח *ṣlḥ* (Gzella) . . . 635
צלי *ṣlī*, צלו, תצלו (Gzella) . . . 636
צלם *ṣlm*, נצב, נצבה, צורה (Gzella) . . . 640
צפר *ṣpr* (Hug) . . . 644
קבל *qbl*, קבל, קבילה (Gzella) . . . 646
קדם *qdm*, קדם, קדמה, קדמי, קדים (Stadel) . . . 650
קדשׁ *qdš*, קדשׁ, קדישׁ, מקדשׁ (Gzella) . . . 653
קום *qūm*, קים, מקם, קומה, קים (Gzella) . . . 659
קטל *qṭl*, קטל (Gzella) . . . 665
קטר *qṭr*, קטר (Nebe) . . . 668
קל *ql* (Gzella) . . . 670
קצץ *qṣṣ*, קצי, קצת, קצה, קץ (Nebe) . . . 672
קרא/י *qrʾ/qrī* (Hug) . . . 674

קרב	*qrb*, קרב, קרבן, קריב (Gzella)	677
קריה	*qryh*, קריה, קרי, קרתה, קיר (Lipiński)	682
קרן	*qrn* (Gzella)	686
קשט	*qšṭ* (Tigchelaar)	688
ראש	*r'š* (Stadel)	694
רב	*rb*, רבן, רבו, רבי, רבו, רבה (Gzella)	696
רגל	*rgl*, שק, ירך, מעין (Gzella)	701
רגש	*rgš* (Gzella)	703
רוח	*rwḥ* (Lipiński)	704
רז	*rz* (Nebe)	707
רחם	*rḥm*, רחם, רחים, רחם, רחמה, רחמן, חבב (Gzella)	710
רחץ	*rḥṣ*, רחצן (Kuty)	715
רחק	*rḥq*, רחיק (Gzella)	716
ריח	*ryḥ*, ריח (Gzella)	718
רים	*rīm*, רם, רמה, רום, מרום (Gzella)	719
רמי	*rmī* (Gzella)	723
רעי	*r'ī*, רעו, רעין (Gzella)	725
שׂב	*śb*, שׂיבה (Kuty)	727
שׂגא/י	*śg'/śgī*, שׂגי(א), שׂגא, משׂגה (Gzella)	729
שׂהד	*śhd*, שׂהד, שׂהדו (Lipiński)	732
שׂים	*śīm*, שׂימה (Gzella)	733
שׂכל	*śkl*, שׂכלתנו (Gzella)	738
שׂנא/י	*śn'/śnī*, שׂנאה, שׂנא (Lipiński)	739
שׂער	*ś'r* (Gzella)	740
שׁאל	*š'l*, שׁאלה (Gzella)	742
שׁאר	*š'r*, שׁאר, שׁארי (Gzella)	745
שׁבח	*šbḥ*, תשׁבחה (Gzella)	746
שׁבט	*šbṭ*, חטר (Gzella)	748
שׁבק	*šbq* (Gzella)	749

שבש *šbš* (Gzella). 753
שגל *šgl* (Gzella). 753
שוי *šwī*, שוה (Gzella) 754
שור *šwr* (Gzella) 756
שחת *šḥt* (Gzella). 757
שיזב *šyzb* (Lipiński) 757
שכב *škb*, משכב (Gzella) 759
שכח *škḥ*, שכחה (Gzella) 760
שכן *škn*, משכן (Gzella). 764
שלח *šlḥ*, שדר, אשתדור (Stadel) 766
שלט *šlṭ*, שליט, שלטן (Gianto) 769
שלי *šlī*, שלו, שלין, שלה, נוח, ניח (Gzella) 773
שלם *šlm*, שלם, שלם (Gzella). 775
שם *šm* (Gzella). 779
שמין *šmyn*, כוכב (Gzella) 785
שמע *šmʿ* (Waltisberg) 791
שמש *šmš* /šamš/ (Lipiński) 796
שמש *šmš* (Gzella) 801
שנה *šnh*, ירח, שבה (Gzella) 802
שני *šnī* (Gzella). 805
שעה *šʿh* (Gzella). 808
שפל *špl*, שפל, שפלו (Gzella). 809
שפר *špr*, שפיר, שפר, שפרפר (Gianto). 810
שרי *šrī*, משרי (Gzella) 813
שרש *šrš* (Gzella). 816
שתי *štī*, משתה, משתו, שקי, צבע (Gzella) 817
תבר *tbr* (Stadel). 820
תוב *tūb*, תוב(א) (Gzella). 821
תוה *twh* (Gzella) 824

תור *twr*, תורה, עגל (Beyer) . . . 825
תמה *tmh*, תמה (Gzella) . . . 827
תקל *tql*, תקל (שׁקל), מתקל (Gzella) . . . 828
תקן *tqn* (Gzella) . . . 830
תקף *tqp*, תקף, תקיף (Kuty) . . . 831
תרע *tr*ʿ, תרע, אסף, בב, דשׁ (Gzella) . . . 833

Iranian Official Titles in Biblical Aramaic . . . 836
Numbers . . . 841
Historical Outline of Aramaic Grammar . . . 849
Alphabetical Aramaic-English Word List . . . 863
English-Aramaic Glossary . . . 873

Editor's Preface

This volume completes the *Theological Dictionary of the Old Testament* (*TDOT*) after almost a half century. This final volume situates the vocabulary of the Aramaic sections of Ezra and Daniel in the context of its linguistic and cultural history and, thereby, frees Biblical Aramaic from its role as an appendix to the Hebrew Bible. Instead, it appears as what it is: part of an overarching literary tradition that spread in the course of the first millennium B.C.E. from Syria to Mesopotamia, Palestine, Egypt, Arabia, Anatolia, and even to Central Asia and, in various local forms, survived in literature, administration, and daily communication on into late antiquity. Even more than Hebrew, Aramaic attests the incorporation of the Old Testament in its broad cultural framework.

Because of its ambitious objective, the Aramaic dictionary in *TDOT* has its own history. Klaus Beyer (1929-2014) was enlisted as the first editor in January 1986; he declined, however, for various reasons, including that the state of research at the time could be easily understood as quite unfavorable for such a project. Ingo Kottsieper, responsible for the first fascicle in 2001, announced the volume a mere decade later in the *Zeitschrift für Althebraistik* 8 (1995), 80f. Yet it proved difficult to find authors who both possessed the necessary philological mastery over all the several dialects, corpora, and academic specialties involved in the widespread Aramaic material through which one could lay open the various connotations and layers of meaning of Biblical Aramaic, and could combine this expertise to answer the exegetical and religio-historical questions that a theological dictionary must address.

After years at a standstill, the enterprise was entrusted to the undersigned. Inititially, the difficulties continued unabated. At the moment of transfer, only a handful of articles, or at least articles in publishable form, for the second fascicle were on hand. Despite every effort, additional acceptances came rarely and did not always lead to submitted manuscripts. Torn between the thankless task and the aversion to quitting, the editor finally brought himself to write all the outstanding articles himself and is, therefore, more present here than one would usually expect. In any case, a broad unity in approach and presentation could be attained in this manner and more recent research could be incorporated directly. Special value was placed on the consideration of advances in the classification of the individual phases of the Aramaic language with their varying interrelationships, both Semitic philology and linguistic analysis, and the many recently discovered sources: the other manuscripts from the Dead Sea, the Clermont-Ganneau ostraca, all the Samaria Papyri, many Neo-Assyrian commercial documents, and the documents from the Bactrian provincial archive.

The changes in editor and approach from the first fascicle led to a few alterations in the format, beginning with the article on בעי (*b'ī*). With no change regarding theological relevance, efforts were made for greater philological depth of field through the examination of synonyms, the various nuances of grammatical constructions, and the various registers, and for tighter restriction to the varieties of Aramaic most closely related to Biblical Aramaic in linguistic and cultural terms, but within this framework, a presentation as complete and balanced as possible.

Thus, semantic fields and actual diction of older Aramaic find their first description on a broad basis. At the same time, a few essential transformations in the discipline of Old Testament since the first volumes of *TDOT* have received attention, especially the greater concentration on the immediate Syro-Palestinian environment of the literary tradition of ancient Israel, its transformation under Achaemenid rule, and its early reception mirrored in the documents from Qumran. In addition, references to the Aramaic of the Hellenistic-Roman period build a bridge to the environment of the New Testament and early Christianity. The selection of material could also be synchronized with the in-progress *Theologisches Wörterbuch zu den Qumrantexten* (*ThWQ*), whose editors have always willingly permitted insights into the current state of affairs.

The present English volume has introduced a few bibliographic additions but is otherwise a straightforward translation of the German original. The German edition of this volume was originally published in seven fascicles. A change in editorship and long time lapse between the first and the remaining fascicles (between the בנה and בעי entries) resulted in some inconsistencies in transcription style, linguistic preferences, and focus of the entries. These inconsistencies remain in the English volume, as it was impossible to remove them all during the translation.

Since no assistant, sabbatical, or other convenience facilitated the work on this book, expressions of gratitude can be omitted. One cannot keep silent, however, about the angelic patience of the publishing house, the authors, and the editor of *TDOT*, Heinz-Josef Fabry. He and Christian Stadel have also assisted energetically with the correction of the galley proofs and, thus, contributed to a good outcome. The mighty *manes* of Klaus Beyer patronized the completion through all the contrary circumstances of an ignorant higher education policy. In the end, it has returned to the hands that he once showed many a new skill.

It is easier for the undersigner to dedicate a book to the dead than to the living, for "the ever-silent, ever-pale never promise and never deny." On this point there must be an exception: The work is cordially dedicated to Georg Müller and Christian Wirz after more than fifteen years of true and deep friendship!

HOLGER GZELLA
Leiden, on the Feast of Saint Jerome 2018

Abbreviations

AAB	J. A. Fitzmeyer and S. A. Kaufman, *An Aramaic Bibliography*. Vol. I. Baltimore, 1992
AANL.R	*Atti dell'Accademia Nazionale dei Lincei-Rendiconti della Classe di Scienze Morali, Storiche e Filologiche*, Rome
AB	*Anchor Bible*, Garden City, NY
ABD	*Anchor Bible Dictionary*, ed. D. N. Freedman. 6 vols. New York, 1992
ABLAK	M. Noth, *Aufsätze zur biblischen Landes- und Altertumskunde*. 2 vols. Neukirchen, 1971
'Abod. Zar.	*'Abodah Zarah*
AbrN	*Abr-Nahrain*
AcScFen	*Acta Societatis scientiarum Fennicae*
adj.	adjective
abs.	absolute state
acc.	accusative
ADPV	*Abhandlungen des Deutschen Palästina-Vereins*, Wiesbaden
AEM	*Archives épistolaires de Mari*, Paris
AfO	*Archiv für Orientforschung*
AfOB	*Archiv für Orientforschung: Beiheft*, Graz
AGJU	*Arbeiten zur Geschichte des antiken Judentums und des Urchristentums*, Leiden
AH	*Achaemenid History*, Leiden
AHw	W. von Soden, *Akkadisches Handwörterbuch*. 3 vols. Wiesbaden, 1965-81
AIL	*Ancient Israel and Its Literature*, Atlanta
AJSL	*American Journal of Semitic Languages and Literatures*
Akk.	Akkadian
AKM	*Abhandlungen für die Kunde des Morgenlandes*, Wiesbaden
ALASP	*Abhandlungen zur Literatur Alt-Syrien-Palästinas*, Münster
ALD	H. Drawnel, *An Aramaic Wisdom Text from Qumran: A New Interpretation of the Levi Document*. *JSJSup* 86. Leiden, 2004
Amor.	Amorite
AnBib	*Analecta biblica*, Rome
ANEP	J. B. Pritchard, ed., *Ancient Near East in Pictures*. Princeton, 1954, ^{2}1969
ANESSup	*Ancient Near Eastern Studies Supplement*, Louvain
ANET	J. B. Pritchard, ed., *Ancient Near Eastern Texts Relating to the Old Testament*. Princeton, ^{3}1969

ANG	J. J. Stamm, *Die akkadische Namengebung*. Darmstadt, ^{2}1968
AnOr	*Analecta orientalia*, Rome
ANRW	*Aufstieg und Niedergang der römischen Welt*, Berlin, 1972–
AnSt	*Anatolian Studies*
Ant.	*Jewish Antiquities* (Josephus)
AOAT	*Alter Orient und Altes Testament*, Münster, Kevelaer, Neukirchen-Vluyn
AOB	H. Gressmann, ed., *Altorientalische Bilder zum AT*. Berlin, ^{2}1927
AOS	*American Oriental Series*, New Haven
AP	A. E. Cowley, *Aramaic Papyri of the Fifth Century B.C.* 1923, repr. Osnabrück, 1976
aph	aphel
APN	K. Tallqvist, *Assyrian Personal Names*. *AcScFen* 43/1. 1914, repr. Hildesheim, 1966
Arab.	Arabic
Aram	*Aram Society for Syro-Mesopotamian Studies*, Oxford
Aram.	Aramaic
AraSt	*Aramaic Studies*
ARE	J. H. Breasted, ed. *Ancient Records of Egypt*. 5 vols. Chicago, 1905-1907
ARM	*Archives royales de Mari*
ArOr	*Archív Orientální*
AS	*Assyriological Studies*, Chicago
ASAE	*Les Annales du service des antiquités de l'Égypte*
AsJT	*Asia Journal of Theology*
ATANT	*Abhandlungen zur Theologie des Alten und Neuen Testaments*, Zurich
ATTM	K. Beyer, *Die aramäischen Texte vom Toten Meer*. Göttingen, 1984-2004
ATTM.E	K. Beyer, *Die aramäischen Texte vom Toten Meer: Ergänzungsband*. Göttingen, 1994.
AuOr	*Aula orientalis*
AuS	G. Dalman, *Arbeit und Sitte in Palästina*. 7 vols. 1928-42, repr. Hildesheim, 1964
BA	*Biblical Archaeologist*
Bab.	Babylonian Talmud
BAH	*Bibliothèque archéologique et historique*, Paris
BaghM	*Baghdader Mitteilungen*
BASOR	*Bulletin of the American Schools for Oriental Research*
BASORSup	*Bulletin of the American Schools for Oriental Research Supplements*, New Haven
BATSH	*Berichte der Ausgrabung Tall Šēḫ Ḥamad / Dūr-Katlimmu*, Wiesbaden
B. Bab.	*Baba Batra*
BBB	*Bonner biblische Beiträge*, Berlin
BDB	F. Brown, S. R. Driver, and C. A. Briggs, *A Hebrew and English Lexicon of the Old Testament*. Oxford, 1907; Peabody, MA, ^{2}1979
BETL	*Bibliotheca ephemeridum theologicarum Lovaniensium*, Paris

BGMR	A. F. L. Beeston, M. 'A. Ghul, W. W. Müller, and J. Ryckman, *Dictionnaire sabéen (anglais-français-arabe)*. Louvain, 1982
BHK	*Biblia hebraica*. Ed. R. Kittel. Stuttgart, ³1929
BHS	*Biblia hebraica stuttgartensia*. Ed. K. Elliger and W. Rudolph. Stuttgart, 1966-77
bib.	bibliography
BibInt	*Biblical Interpretation*, Leiden
Bibl	*Biblica*
Biella	J. Biella, *Dictionary of Old South Arabic, Sabaean Dialect*. *HSS* 25. Winona Lake, IN, 1982
BietOr	*Biblica et Orientalia*, Rome
BiKi	*Bibel und Kirche*
BiOr	*Bibliotheca Orientalis*
B.J.	*Jewish War* (Josephus)
BK	*Biblischer Kommentar AT*, ed. M. Noth and H. W. Wolff. Neukirchen-Vluyn
BLA	H. Bauer and P. Leander, *Grammatik des Biblisch-Aramäischen*. Halle, 1927
BLe	H. Bauer and P. Leander, *Historische Grammatik der hebräischen Sprache des ATs*. 1918-22, repr. Hildesheim, 1991
BM	British Museum acquisition number
BMAP	E. G. Kraeling, *Brooklyn Museum Aramaic Papyri*. New Haven, 1953
BN	*Biblische Notizen*
BSOAS	*Bulletin of the School of Oriental and African Studies*
BTS	*Beiruter Texte und Studien*, Wiesbaden
BWL	W. G. Lambert, *Babylonian Wisdom Literature*. Oxford, 1959
BZABR	*Beihefte zur Zeitschrift für Altorientalische und Biblische Rechtsgeschichte*, Wiesbaden
BZAW	*Beihefte zur Zeitschrift für die alttestamentliche Wissenschaft*, Berlin
CAD	*Assyrian Dictionary of the Oriental Institute of the University of Chicago*. Chicago, 1956-2010
Can.	Canaanite
CBQ	*Catholic Biblical Quarterly*
CD	Damascus Document
CDA	J. Black, A. George, and N. Postgate, *A Concise Dictionary of Akkadian*. *SANTAG* 5. Wiesbaden, ²2012
CDG	W. Leslau, *Comparative Dictionary of Ge'ez*. Wiesbaden, 1987
CEJL	*Commentaries on Early Jewish Literature*, New York
CH	Code of Hammurabi
ch(s).	chapter(s)
CHANE	*Culture and History of the Ancient Near East*, Leiden
CIG	A. Boeckh, ed., *Corpus inscriptionum graecarum*. 4 vols. Berlin, 1828-77
CII	*Corpus inscriptionum Iranicarum*, London

CIISup	*Corpus inscriptionum Iranicarum Supplement Series*, London
CIS	*Corpus inscriptionum semiticarum*. Paris, 1881-
const.	construct
corr.	corrected, correction
COS	W. W. Hallo, ed., *The Context of Scripture*. Leiden, 1997-2002
CRAI	*Comptes rendus des séances de l'Académie des inscriptions et belles lettres*, Paris
CRRA	*Comptes rendus de la ... Rencontre Assyriologique Internationale*
CSF	*Collezione di studi fenici*, Rome
DaF	*Damaszener Forschungen*
DaM	*Damaszener Mitteilungen*
DBS	L. Pirot et. al, eds., *Dictionnaire de la Bible, Supplement*. Paris, 1926–
DCH	D. Clines, ed., *Dictionary of Classical Hebrew*. 9 vols. Sheffield, 1993-2014
DCLY	*Deuterocanonical and Cognate Literature Yearbook*, Berlin
DDD	K. van der Toorn, B. Becking, and P.-W. van der Horst, eds., *Dictionary of Deities and Demons in the Bible*. Leiden, ^{2}1999
det.	determinate state
Did.	Didache
DJBA	M. Sokoloff, *A Dictionary of Jewish Babylonian Aramaic of the Talmudic and Geonic Periods*. Baltimore, 2002
DJD	*Discoveries in the Judaean Desert*, Oxford
DJPA	M. Sokoloff, *A Dictionary of Jewish Palestinian Aramaic of the Byzantine Period*. Baltimore, 2002
DMOA	*Documenta et Monumenta Orientis Antiqui*, Leiden
DNSI	J. Hoftijzer and K. Jongeling, *Dictionary of North-West Semitic Inscriptions*. 2 vols. Leiden, 1995
DSA	A. Tal, *A Dictionary of Samaritan Aramaic*. Leiden, 2000-
DSD	*Dead Sea Discoveries*
DSSConc	M. Abegg, J. Bowley, and E. Cook, *The Dead Sea Scrolls Concordance*. 2 vols. Leiden, 2003, 2015
DSSStE	F. García Martínez and E. Tigchelaar, *The Dead Sea Scrolls: Study Edition*. 2 vols. Grand Rapids, 2000
Dtr.	Deuteronomistic (source)
DUL	G. del Olmo Lete and J. Sanmartín, *A Dictionary of the Ugaritic Language in the Alphabetic Tradition*. Trans. and ed. W. G. E. Watson. 2 vols. Leiden, ^{2}2004, ^{3}2015
EA	El Amarna
EANEC	*Explorations in Ancient Near Eastern Civilizations*, Winona Lake, IN
EdF	*Erträge der Forschung*, Darmstadt
EI	*Eretz-Israel*
emend.	emended
EMiqr	*Enṣiqlōpedyā miqrā'it (Encyclopedia Biblica)*. Jerusalem, 1950–
emph.	emphatic

EpAn	*Epigraphica Anatolica*
EPRO	*Études préliminaires aux religions orientales dans l'empire romain*, Leiden
ESE	M. Lidzbarski, *Ephemeris für semitische Epigraphik*. 3 vols. Giessen, 1900-1915
ÉtB	*Études bibliques*, Paris
Eth.	Ethiopic
ETL	*Ephemerides Theologicae Lovanienses*
Even-Shoshan	A. Even-Shoshan, *New Concordance of the Bible*. Jerusalem, ^{4}1983
ExpT	*Expository Times*
FAT	*Forschungen zum Alten Testament*, Tübingen
fem.	feminine
FF	*Forschungen und Fortschritte*, Berlin
FO	*Folia Orientalia*
Frahang	= B. Utas, H. S. Nyberg, and C. Toll, *Frahang i pahlavik*. Wiesbaden, 1988
fr(s).	fragment(s)
FRLANT	*Forschungen zur Religion und Literatur des Alten und Neuen Testaments*, Göttingen
FS	*Festschrift*
FSBP	*Fontes et Subsidia ad Bibliam Pertinentes*, Berlin
FTS	*Frankfurter theologische Studien*, Frankfurt am Main
FzB	*Forschungen zur Bibel*
GaG^{3}	W. von Soden, *Grundriss der akkadischen Grammatik*. *AnOr* 33. ^{3}1995 (with Erg., *AnOr* 47)
GesB	W. Gesenius and F. Buhl, *Hebräisches und aramäisches Handwörterbuch über das AT*. Berlin, ^{17}1921, ^{18}1987-2012
GesTh	W. Gesenius, *Thesaurus philologicus criticus linguae hebraeae et chaldaeae Veteris Testamenti*. 3 vols. Leipzig, 1829-58
GGA	*Göttingische Gelehrte Anzeigen*
Gilg.	Gilgamesh Epic
Giṭ	*Giṭṭin*
GN	geographical place name
GOF	*Göttinger Orientforschungen*, Wiesbaden
GOF.I	*Göttinger Orientforschung, Reihe 3: Iranica*, Wiesbaden
ha	haphel
Ḥag.	*Ḥagigah*
HANE/M	*History of the Ancient Near East/Monographs*, Padua
HAT	*Handbuch zum AT*, ser. 1, Tübingen
HBS	*Herders biblische Studien*, Freiburg im Breisgau
Heb.	Hebrew
HEO	*Hautes Études Orientales*, Paris
Herm	*Hermeneia*, Minneapolis
HKL	R. Borger, *Handbuch der Keilschriftliteratur*. 3 vols. Berlin, 1967-75

HO	*Handbuch der Orientalistik*, Leiden
HOS	*Heidelberger orientalistische Studien*, Heidelberg
HSAO	*Heidelberger Studien zum Alten Orient*, Heidelberg
HSK	*Handbücher zur Sprach- und Kommunikationswissenschaft*, Berlin
HSM	*Harvard Semitic Monographs*, Missoula, MT; Chico, CA; Atlanta; Winona Lake, IN
HSS	*Harvard Semitic Studies*, Missoula, MT; Chico, CA; Atlanta; Winona Lake, IN
HTR	*Harvard Theological Review*
ICC	*International Critical Commentary*, Edinburgh
IDB	G. A. Buttrick, ed., *Interpreter's Dictionary of the Bible*. 4 vols. Nashville, 1962; Supp. ed., K. Crim. Nashville, 1976
IEJ	*Israel Exploration Journal*
IF	*Indogermanische Forschungen*
impf.	imperfect
impv.	imperative
inf.	infinitive
itp	ithpeel
itpa	ithpaal
JA	*Journal Asiatique*
JANES	*Journal of the Ancient Near Eastern Society of Columbia University*
JAOS	*Journal of the American Oriental Society*
Jastrow	M. Jastrow, *Dictionary of the Targumim, the Talmud Babli and Yerushalmi, and the Midrashic Literature*. 1903; repr. 2 vols. in 1. Brooklyn, 1975
JBL	*Journal of Biblical Literature*
JBT	*Jahrbuch für Biblische Theologie*
JCS	*Journal of Cuneiform Studies*
JEOL	*Jaarbericht Ex Oriente Lux*
Jer.	Jerusalem Talmud
JESHO	*Journal of the Economic and Social History of the Orient*
JETS	*Journal of the Evangelical Theological Society*
JHNES	*Johns Hopkins Near Eastern Studies*, Baltimore
JJS	*Journal of Jewish Studies*
JNES	*Journal of Near Eastern Studies*
JNSL	*Journal of Northwest Semitic Languages*
JQR	*Jewish Quarterly Review*
JRAS	*Journal of the Royal Asiatic Society*
JS	A. Jaussen and M. R. Savignac inscriptions
JSHRZ	*Jüdische Schriften aus hellenistisch-römischer Zeit*, Gütersloh
JSJSup	*Journal for the Study of Judaism, Supplement*, Leiden
JSNTSup	*Journal for the Study of the NT, Supplement*, Sheffield
JSOTSup	*Journal for the Study of the OT, Supplement*, Sheffield
JSP	*Journal for the Study of the Pseudepigrapha*

JSPSup	*Journal for the Study of the Pseudepigrapha Supplements*, Sheffield
JSS	*Journal of Semitic Studies*
JSSSup	*Journal of Semitic Studies, Supplement*, Oxford
JTS	*Journal of Theological Studies*
K	*Ketib*
KAI	H. Donner and W. Röllig, *Kanaanäische und aramäische Inschriften*. 3 vols. Wiesbaden, ^{2}1966-69, ^{3}1971-76, ^{5}2002
KAT	*Kommentar zum AT*, Leipzig, Gütersloh
KBL	L. Koehler and W. Baumgartner, *Lexicon in Veteris Testamenti Libros*. Leiden, ^{1}1953, ^{2}1958, ^{3}1967–96
Ketub.	*Ketubbot*
König	E. König, *Hebräisches und aramäisches Wörterbuch zum AT*. Leipzig, 1910; $^{6/7}$1936
KTU	M. Dietrich, O. Loretz, and J. Sanmartín, eds., *Die keilalphabetischen Texte aus Ugarit. I*, AOAT 24. 1976
Lane	E. W. Lane, *An Arabic-English Lexicon*. 8 vols. London, 1863-93, repr. 1968
LAOS	*Leipziger altorientalistische Studien*, Wiesbaden
LAPO	*Littératures anciennes du Proche-Orient*, Paris
LexÄg	W. Helck and E. Otto, eds., *Lexikon der Ägyptologie*. Wiesbaden, 1975-
LexLingAeth	A. Dillmann, *Lexicon linguae aethiopicae*. Leipzig, 1865
LexLingAram	F. Zorell, *Lexicon hebraicum et aramaicum Veteris Testamenti*. Rome, 1958, repr. 1968
LexSyr	C. Brockelmann, *Lexicon syriacum*. Halle, 1928, ^{2}1968
LIMC	*Lexicon iconographicum mythologiae classicae*, H. C. Ackermann and J.-R. Gisler. 8 vols. Zurich, 1981-97
lit.	literally
l(l).	line(s)
LSJ	H. G. Liddell, R. Scott, and H. S. Jones, *A Greek-English Lexicon*. Oxford, ^{9}1940
LSP	F. Schulthess, *Lexicon Syropalaestinum*. Berlin, 1903
LSTS	*Library of Second Temple Studies*, London
m	*Mishnah* tractate
MAD	*Materials for the Assyrian Dictionary*. Chicago, 1952-1957
Mand.	Mandaic
Mandelkern	S. Mandelkern, *Veteris Testamenti concordantiae hebraicae atque chaldaicae*. Tel Aviv, 1971
MAOG	*Mitteilungen der Altorientalischen Gesellschaft*
masc.	masculine
MDAIA	*Mitteilungen des Deutschen Archäologischen Instituts, Athenische Abteilung*
MdD	E. S. Drower and R. Macuch, *Mandaic Dictionary*. Oxford, 1963
MEE	*Materiali epigrafici de Ebla*
MEOL	*Mémoires de la Société d'études orientales "Ex Oriente Lux,"* Leiden

Midr.	Midrash
MS(S)	manuscript(s)
Mus	*Le Muséon*
MUSJ	*Mélanges de l'Université St.-Joseph*
MVÄG	*Mitteilungen der Vorderasiatisch-Ägyptischen Gesellschaft*
Nabat.	Nabatean
NABU	*Nouvelles Assyriologiques Brèves et Utilitaires*
NBL	M. Görg, ed., *Neues Bibel-Lexikon*, Zurich, 1991
NEB	*Die Neue Echter-Bibel*, Würzburg
NEB.E	*Die Neue Echter-Bibel, Ergänzungsband*, Würzburg
NESE	R. Degen, W. W. Müller, and W. Röllig, *Neue Ephemeris für Semitische Epigraphik*. Wiesbaden, 1972-78
NICOT	*New International Commentary on the Old Testament*, Grand Rapids
NT	New Testament
NTOA	*Novum Testamentum et Orbis Antiquus*, Fribourg, Göttingen
NTS	*New Testament Studies*, Cambridge
NW	Northwest
obj.	object
OBO	*Orbis biblicus et orientalis*, Fribourg, Göttingen
OIP	*Oriental Institute Publications*, Chicago
OLA	*Orientalia lovaniensia analecta*, Louvain
OLP	*Orientalia lovaniensia periodica*
OLZ	*Orientalistische Literaturzeitung*
Or	*Orientalia* (NS)
OrAnt	*Oriens Antiquus*
OSA	Old South Arabic
OT	Old Testament
OTG	*Old Testament Guides*, Sheffield
pa	pael
Palmyr.	Palmyrene
pap.	papyrus
par.	parallel (passages)
pass.	passive
PAT	D. R. Hillers and E. Cussini, *Palmyrene Aramaic Texts*. Baltimore, 1996
pawl	pawlel
pe	peal
PEFQS	*Palestine Exploration Fund Quarterly Statement*
Pesaḥ.	*Pesaḥim*
pf.	perfect
Phoen.	Phoenician
PIHANS	*Publications de l'Institut historique-archéologique néerlandais de Stamboul*, Leiden
pl(s).	plural, plate(s)

PLO	*Porta Linguarum Orientalium*, Wiesbaden
PN	personal name
PNA	*The Prosopography of the Neo-Assyrian Empire*, Helsinki, 1998-
PNPI	J. K. Stark, *Personal Names in Palmyrene Inscriptions*. Oxford, 1971
ptcp.	participle
Pun.	Punic
PVTG	*Pseudepigrapha Veteris Testamenti Graece*, Leiden
Q	*Qere*
QD	*Quaestiones disputatae*, Freiburg im Breisgau
Qidd.	*Qiddušin*
RA	*Revue d'assyriologie et d'archéologie orientale*
Rab.	Rabbah (midrashic commentary)
RAC	T. Klauser et al., eds., *Reallexikon für Antike und Christentum*, Stuttgart, 1950-
RB	*Revue biblique*
RdM	*Die Religionen der Menschheit*, Stuttgart
RÉS	*Répertoire d'épigraphie sémitique*. Paris, 1900- (with number of text)
RevQ	*Revue de Qumrân*
RGG	H. Gunkel and L. Zscharnack, eds., *Die Religion in Geschichte und Gegenwart*, 5 vols. Tübingen, ^{2}1927-31; ed. K. Galling, 6 vols., ^{3}1957-65; ed. H. D. Betz et al., 9 vols., ^{4}1998-2007
RGRW	*Religions in the Graeco-Roman World*, Leiden
RHA	*Revue hittite et asianique*
RHPR	*Revue d'histoire et de philosophie religieuses*
RHR	*Revue de l'histoire des religions*
RLA	*Reallexikon der Assyriologie*. Berlin, 1932-
RSF	*Rivista di studi fenici*
RTP	H. Ingholt et al., *Recueil des tessères de Palmyre*. Paris, 1955
RVV	*Religionsgeschichtliche Versuche und Vorarbeiten*
SAA	*State Archives of Assyria*, Helsinki
SAAB	*State Archives of Assyria Bulletin*
SAAS	*State Archives of Assyria Studies*, Helsinki
Šabb.	*Shabbat*
SAIO	E. Lipiński, *Studies in Aramaic Inscriptions and Onomastics*. Louvain, 1975-2016
SAION	*Annali dell'Istituto Universitario Orientale di Napoli: Supplemento*, Naples
SAIS	*Studies in the Aramaic Interpretation of Scripture*, Leiden
Sam.	Samaritan
Sanh.	*Sanhedrin*
SBAW	*Sitzungsberichte der Bayerischen Akademie der Wissenschaften*, Munich
SBB	*Stuttgarter biblische Beiträge*, Stuttgart
SBFLA	*Studii Biblici Franciscani Liber Annuus*

SBLCS	*Society of Biblical Literature Commentary on the Septuagint*, Missoula, MT; Chico, CA; Atlanta
SBLDS	*Society of Biblical Literature Dissertation Series*, Missoula, MT; Chico, CA; Atlanta
SBLMS	*Society of Biblical Literature Monograph Series*, Missoula, MT; Chico, CA; Atlanta
SBS	*Stuttgarter Bibel-Studien*, Stuttgart
Segal	J. B. Segal, *Aramaic Texts from North Saqqara*. London, 1983
SEL	*Studi epigraphici e linguistici*
Sem	*Semitica*
ser.	series
sg.	singular
SHANE	*Studies in the History of the Ancient Near East*, Leiden
Sin.	Sinaiticus
SIr	*Studia Iranica*
SÖAW.PH	*Sitzungsberichte/Österreichische Akademie der Wissenschaften, Philosophisch-Historische Klasse*, Vienna
SS	*Studi Semitici*, Rome
SSLL	*Studies in Semitic Languages and Linguistics*, Leiden
SSN	*Studia Semitica Neerlandica*, Leiden
ST	*Studia Theologica*
STAR	*Studies in Theology and Religion*, Leiden
StAT	*Studien zu den Assur-Texten*, Saarbrücken
StBi	*Studi Biblici*, Brescia
STDJ	*Studies on the Texts of the Desert of Judah*, Leiden
StPohl	*Studia Pohl*, Rome
StSam	*Studia Samaritina*, Boston
StSem	*Studi Semitici*, Rome
SubBi	*Subsidia Biblica*, Rome
subj.	subject
subst.	substantive, substantival
suff.	suffix
SVT	*Supplements to Vetus Testamentum*, Leiden
SVTP	*Studia in Veteris Testamenti Pseudepigrapha*, Leiden
Syr	*Syria: Revue d'art oriental et d'archéologie*
TADAE	B. Porten and A. Yardeni, *Textbook of Aramaic Documents from Ancient Egypt*. 4 vols. Jerusalem, 1986-99
TAVO.B	*Beihefte zum Tübinger Atlas des Vorderen Orients*, Wiesbaden
TBN	*Themes in Biblical Narrative*, Leiden
TDNT	G. Kittel and G. Friedrich, eds., *Theological Dictionary of the New Testament*, 9 vols. plus index vol. Grand Rapids, 1964-76
TDOT	J. Botterweck et al., eds., *Theological Dictionary of the Old Testament*. 16 vols. Grand Rapids, 1974-

Tg.	Targum; Tg. Onq. = Targum Onqelos; Tg. Neof. = Targum Neofiti; Tg. Ps-J. = Targum Pseudo-Jonathan
THAT	E. Jenni and C. Westermann, eds., *Theologisches Handwörterbuch zum Alten Testament*. 2 vols. Zurich, Munich, 1971-76
ThDiss	*Theologische Dissertationen*, Basel
ThesSyr	R. Payne Smith, *Thesaurus Syriacus*. Oxford, 1897
ThesSyrSup	R. Payne Smith et al., *Thesaurus Syriacus: Supplement*. Oxford, 1927
ThQ	*Theologische Quartalschrift*
ThWQ	H.-J. Fabry and U. Dahmen, *Theologisches Wörterbuch zu den Qumrantexten*. 3 vols. Stuttgart, 2011-16
T.Fekh.	Tell Fekheriye
T. Levi	Testament of Levi
TLOT	E. Jenni and C. Westermann, eds., *Theological Lexicon of the Old Testament*. 3 vols. Peabody, Mass., 1997. English translation of *THAT*.
TM	Tell Mardikh-Ebla tablets
T.Qahat	Testament of Qahat
trans.	translated by
Transeu	*Transeuphratène*
TRE	G. Krause, G. Müller, and H. R. Balz, eds., *Theologische Realenzyklopädie*. 22 vols. Berlin, 1977-92
TRev	*Theologische Revue*
TSAJ	*Texts and Studies in Ancient Judaism*, Tübingen
TSSI	J. C. L. Gibson, *Textbook of Syrian Semitic Inscriptions*. Oxford, 1982
TStO	*Texte und Studien zur Orientalistik*, Hildesheim
TUAT	*Texte aus der Umwelt des ATs*, Gütersloh
TUAT.NF	*Texte aus der Umwelt des ATs, Neue Folge*, Gütersloh
TW	J. Levy, *Chaldäisches Wörterbuch über die Targumim*. Leipzig, ^{2}1881
TynB	*Tyndale Bulletin*
TZ	*Theologische Zeitschrift*
UBL	*Ugaritisch-biblische Literatur*, Münster
UCP	*University of California Publications*
UF	*Ugarit-Forschungen*
Ugar.	Ugaritic
UT	C. H. Gordon, *Ugaritic Textbook*. *AnOr* 38. 1965, ^{2}1967
v(v).	verse(s)
Vat.	Vaticanus
VOK	*Veröffentlichungen der Orientalischen Kommission*, Wiesbaden
VWGTh	*Veröffentlichungen der Wissenschaftlichen Gesellschaft für Theologie*, Gütersloh
WbÄS	A. Erman and H. Grapow, *Wörterbuch der ägyptischen Sprache*. 6 vols. Leipzig, 1926-31, repr. 1963
WBC	*Word Biblical Commentary*, Waco, TX; Dallas, Nashville

WDSP	*Wadi ed-Daliyeh Samaritan Papyri*
Wehr[5]	H. Wehr, *Arabisches Wörterbuch für die Schriftsprache der Gegenwart*. Wiesbaden, [5]1985
WO	*Die Welt des Orients*
WMANT	*Wissenschaftliche Monographien zum Alten und Neuen Testament*, Neukirchen-Vluyn
WTM	J. Levy, *Das Wörterbuch über die Talmudim und Midraschim*. 2nd ed. Berlin, 1924; repr. Darmstadt, 1963
WUNT	*Wissenschaftliche Untersuchungen zum Neuen Testament*, Tübingen
WUS	J. Aistleitner, *Wörterbuch der ugaritischen Sprache*. Berlin, [4]1974.
WZKM	*Wiener Zeitschrift für die Kunde des Morgenlandes*
YOS	*Yale Oriental Series Researches*, New Haven
ZA	*Zeitschrift für Assyriologie*
ZABR	*Zeitschrift für altorientalische und biblische Rechtsgeschichte*
ZAH	*Zeitschrift für Althebraistik*
ZÄS	*Zeitschrift für ägyptische Sprache und Altertumskunde*
ZAW	*Zeitschrift für die alttestamentliche Wissenschaft*
ZBK	*Zürcher Bibelkommentare*, Zurich
ZDMG	*Zeitschrift der Deutschen Morgenländischen Gesellschaft*
ZDPV	*Zeitschrift des Deutschen Palästina-Vereins*
ZNW	*Zeitschrift für neutestamentliche Wissenschaft*
ZS	*Zeitschrift für Semitistik*
ZThK	*Zeitschrift für Theologie und Kirche*

Hints for Use

Apart from the prepositions, conjunctions, pronouns, and particles, this dictionary incorporates almost the entire lexicon of Biblical Aramaic, including major and secondary lemmata, and at the same time, a major portion of the theologically relevant lexicon of all older Aramaic. The starting point, as in the Hebrew portion of the *TDOT*, consists of the canonical text of *BHS* so that, as a rule, only lexemes or roots that occur in Biblical Aramaic have independent lemmata. (The articles on *ymī* and *'lym* diverge from this principle. The first had already been commissioned by the editor of the first fascicle and was complete when the change of editors took place; the second was on the original lemma list, for reasons no longer evident, and belonged to the few that immediately found a contributor so that it, too, received an independent entry.)

Admittedly, the decision made at the outset and already executed in the first fascicle to establish the dictionary on the foundation of the lexicon of Biblical Aramaic resulted in the subordination of even otherwise frequent Aramaic lexemes that happened not to be attested in the not very extensive and generally very specific portions of Ezra and Daniel under semantically and substantively related terms. After the change of editors, the arrangement largely by functional groups in the first fascicle was assimilated to more of an alphabetic arrangement by Aramaic roots as has stood the test of time in classical Semitics, even if, in many instances, the sequence had already been interrupted (thus, e.g., *'mr* appears under *mll*). Through regular cross-references and the discussion of synonyms and antonyms, including the respective variations in nuance, attention has been given at least to shed initial light on the broader semantic field of the lexemes. The nuances important for any thorough involvement with literary texts, and, when possible, also the various levels of style and register (especially such as the often theologically adapted legal and administrative theology), should thereby be selectively differentiated. The complete alphabetic Word List and the English-Aramaic Glossary in the appendix should also make it easy for even those unpracticed in dealing with a root lexicon to find the word they seek.

Verbal roots and nominal forms in the absolute state are arranged according to their Imperial Aramaic spelling since it was also determinative for Biblical Aramaic. Roots ending in vowels are classified according to their form under *-ī*, not according to their spelling under *-h* (which is a pure vowel letter); for roots that end in -' in Imperial Aramaic, the older form is cited because it often continued to survive in historical spellings. The Imperial Aramaic pronunciation of nouns reconstructed according to the current state of research is given between slashes in the heading since this corresponds better to a historical perspective than the late (and certainly anachronistic with respect to circumstances in the first millennium B.C.E.) vocalization and permits a uniform treatment of both the Biblical Aramaic lexemes and those for which no canonical tradition of pronunciation has been preserved. The main text of the individual lemmata briefly treats phonetic developments before and after Achaemenid Imperial Aramaic, which was established here as the Archimedian point. The result is an approximate impression, based on today's knowledge, of pronunciation around 500 B.C.E. At the same time, words identical in the incomplete consonantal text can also be clearly distinguished. The transcription of vocalized Biblical Aramaic citations, in contrast to the mixture of transcription of pronunciation and transliteration employed in the first fascicle and elsewhere in *TDOT*, is made more precise (e.g., of vowel letters with the circumflex), and *š* and *ś* are consistently differentiated.

All entries begin with a brief overview containing information concerning etymology, the broader lexical field, and, where sensible, the various grammatical constructions (such as the usage of verbs with and without object, with various prepositions, or in various stems). The further structure generally follows a morphological classification with special treatment of verbal and nominal forms and of various verbal stems, but is usually arranged either in chronological phases of the language (Old, Imperial, Biblical, and Qumran Aramaic and sporadically later phases), that usually also indicate various contexts of usage (such as Imperial Aramaic legal and administrative terminology in contrast with a theological usage in the book of Daniel and at Qumran), or, in cases of largely unchanged meaning (as in the case of catch-all terms), various manners of usage (e.g., literal, figurative, technical). Instances are always cited according to the definitive editions, with full bibliographical information in the introduction and the list of abbreviations; where sensible, various readings or grammatical analyses in the scholarly discussion will be treated (as is often the case in the texts from Qumran).

Because of the much more heterogeneous body of sources in comparison to the Hebrew Bible, which, in addition to biblical and extrabiblical literary texts, also includes representative inscriptions, legal documents, commercial notes, and private letters, the depiction is primarily oriented toward the semantics of the individual terms themselves, not just to exegetical questions—this in keeping with the conviction that any responsible exegesis presupposes an understanding of the linguistic data as precise and nuanced as possible. At the center stands the Aramaic of the first millennium B.C.E., while the later literary languages will be treated more closely only in individual instances, but references to the common dictionaries will open a broader perspective in each case.

The first fascicle contained occasional interjections from its editor, Ingo Kottsieper, within the entries. In this translation, these interjections have been retained. Each is set off between bullets • • and concludes with the parenthetical signoff "(Ko.)" to indicate that this is the work of Kottsieper, not the author of the rest of the entry. The completed German edition contained supplementary material, which has been incorporated into the main text of this translation at the appropriate locations.

In passages where versification differs between the Aramaic or Hebrew text and the English—which occurs especially in the Aramaic chapters of Daniel 4 and 6—this volume follows the Aramaic/Hebrew. English readers may find the following list helpful. In Daniel, Aramaic 3:31-33 = English 4:1-3; Aram. 4:1-34 = Eng. 4:4-37; Aram. 6:1 = Eng. 5:31; and Aram. 6:2-29 = Eng. 6:1-28.

Introduction

When Aramaic was coming into increasingly wide use in Palestine after the fifth century B.C.E. under the influence of the Achaemenid dominance, it had already served for centuries as the language of state office, administration, and finally also literature in broad areas of the Near East. This "expansion" to an overarching lingua franca led in grand steps to the development of a differentiated, technical legal and commercial terminology with fixed documentary genres anchored in scribal education, genres such as certificates of debt, contracts, letters, as well as burial and memorial inscriptions, and to formal prose style. The administrative reform under Darius I (ca. 550-486 B.C.E.) and his successor Xerxes (515-465 B.C.E.) consolidated the use of Aramaic in the provinces of the Achaemenid Empire and homogenized spelling and the inventory of expressions. The Aramaic portions of the biblical text, the letters in official style in Ezr. 4:8-6:19 and 7:12-26, the court narratives and visions in Dnl. 2:4-7:28, also a brief clause in Jer. 10:11, and the translation of a place name in Gen. 31:47, rest on this literary tradition. It continues in post-Achaemenid times in the Aramaic of the texts from the Dead Sea—theological literature from Qumran, as well as letters and contracts from neighboring sites—and in the various Aramaic dialects of Syria, Arabia, and Mesopotamia which had already taken shape in the Hellenistic epoch and then served in mutually independent kingdoms under Roman dominion in the realms of law, administration, and public office. In late antiquity, when political loyalty as an identifying characteristic gave way to religious affiliation, a few of them developed further into literary languages of religio-cultural communities; subsequently, generation transmitted their rich literary corpora to generation. Thus, Biblical Aramaic is part of a body of Aramaic literature that developed over many centuries; its lexicon and idioms connect to a broad extrabiblical pattern of usage either, as in Ezra, by adopting existing legal and administrative terminology or, as in the apocalyptic visions of Daniel and later from Qumran, by adapting them theologically. The fine nuances of this often highly considered usage become apparent only if one also hears the historical connotations of the often heavily laden terminology.

A selective treatment of the Biblical Aramaic material within the history of older Aramaic language and culture, one of the chief objectives of this dictionary, presupposes, however, a more highly differentiated analysis of Aramaic itself, and of its complex development. This dictionary will outline it in chronological sequence.[1] One can distinguish the older Old Aramaic of the ninth and eighth centuries B.C.E. at the time of the independent Aramaic dialects of the Syrian principalities; the younger Old Aramaic

1. For a modern overview with information concerning the relevant primary and secondary literature, cf. H. Gzella, *A Cultural History of Aramaic: From the Beginnings to the Advent of Islam*. *HO* 111 (2015).

under, first, the Neo-Assyrian, and then, the Neo-Babylonian Empires in the seventh and sixth centuries B.C.E.; Achaemenid Imperial Aramaic as the administrative language of the Persian Empire in the fifth and fourth centuries B.C.E.; its locally independent offshoots in the Hellenistic-Roman period from about the third (very few texts from this period) century B.C.E. to the third century C.E.; finally, the Jewish, Christian, and other literary languages of late antiquity from the fourth century C.E. Thus, the common literary languages of the first millennium coincide with a geographical division perceptible since the beginning of the textual tradition in which the spoken dialects of neighboring regions intermix fluidly ("continuum of dialect"), but remain largely hidden in the shadows of official chancellery idioms. A thoroughgoing division of Aramaic into Eastern and Western dialects first becomes evident in Roman times. In the course of the expansion of Islam and, with it, of Arabic in the Near and Middle East, the once closely meshed network of Aramaic dialects and literary traditions was disrupted and Aramaic became the language of individual minorities, now scattered across the whole world. These historical periods, and later also the dialectical analysis, underlie the presentation of the material in the individual articles as a common frame of reference.

1. THE ARAMAIC OF THE IRON AGE SYRIAN PRINCIPALITIES

The first known witnesses to the Aramaic language are inscriptions with reports of royal deeds, the dedication of gifts to a deity, or treaties of state between allied princes from various parts of Syria in the ninth and eighth centuries B.C.E. Like Hebrew and a couple of Transjordanian languages with small literary corpora, Aramaic appears as a written language, already normed locally, with a scribal tradition that, among other things, finds expression in a fixed orthography and according to a standardized scheme of structured genres. All the Semitic languages of Syria-Palestine in the early Iron Age may have arisen from regional dialects under similar commercial, political, and cultural conditions, and can be assigned, from a historical-genealogical perspective, to the same subgroup, so-called "Northwest Semitic." Aramaic, alongside Canaanite (which further divides for the first millennium B.C.E. into Hebrew, Phoenician, Moabite, Ammonite, and perhaps Edomite) and Ugaritic (the literary language of the city-state of Ugarit on the Syrian coast that became extinct in the twelfth century B.C.E.), constitutes an independent branch within Northwest Semitic.[2] A few characteristic linguistic features distinguish it from all the other known languages of Syria-Palestine: a counterpart of the original Semitic phoneme */ṣ́/ (Canaanite /ṣ/) spelled with *q*; the definite article (det.) with /-ā/ (from an older */-āʾ/); the feminine plural in the absolute state with /-ān/; the 3ms suffix /-awhī/

2. See H. Gzella, "Northwest Semitic in General," in S. Weninger, ed., *The Semitic Languages: An International Handbook. HSK* 36 (2011), 425-51; for a broader panorama of the language situation of Syria-Palestine between the Late Bronze and the early Iron Ages, idem, "Peoples and Languages of the Levant During the Bronze and Iron Ages," in M. L. Steiner and A. E. Killebrew, eds., *The Oxford Handbook of the Archaeology of the Levant* (Oxford, 2014), 24-34, both with additional bibliography.

with a vocalic base (see the "Historical Outline of Aramaic Grammar" at the end of this volume); and various lexical elements such as /bar/ "son" (→ *br*), → *yhb* "to give," → *nḥt* "to descend," → *npq* "to exit," → *slq* "to ascend," → *ʻll* "to enter," and several more. In contrast to Canaanite, which can be traced back to the Late Bronze Age, the origins of Aramaic are imperceptible; consequently, the time and circumstances under which it assumed its later typical ground form are unknown. Aramaic rose to the level of a written language, however, exactly like the Phoenician dialects, Moabite, and Hebrew (which also divided into northern and southern dialects), after sometimes newly formed population groups consolidated after a period of economic and demographic collapse around 1000 B.C.E., and then grew in steps into more complex societies, and finally, developed into centralized forms of administrated areas oriented toward the respective chief city. This development also anchored the use of local standard languages in scribal education and early chancelleries.

Based on a few orthographic, morphological, and lexical characteristics in the earliest Old Aramaic inscriptions from the ninth and eighth centuries B.C.E. Syria, one can distinguish between the variety of the Tell Fekheriye inscription[3] from east Syria (ca. 850 B.C.E., and thus the oldest reasonably datable witness of the Aramaic language) and the standard variety, probably soon dispersed across the various small principalities of central Syria. The latter included a few royal and dedicatory inscriptions,[4] the relatively extensive treaties of state from Sefire,[5] and a few brief graffiti.[6] This variety found usage already circa 700 B.C.E., at least for official purposes, in Bukān in West Azerbaijan.[7] Despite this microvariation, however, both attest the characteristic features of Aramaic as a whole.[8] They are distinct linguistically from the local written language in Sam'al in north Syria, Sam'alian,[9] which has affinities with Aramaic in speech and idiom (and which, therefore, the dictionary regularly adduces in comparison) but which is not identical with it, given the clear divergences in the declension of nouns (between it and Aramaic stands the Kuttamuwa inscription known for only a few years).[10] With the encroachment of Assyrian dominion on Sam'al, the Aramaic of central Syria replaced it.[11] Similarly, the literary Deir ʻAlla inscription from the Transjordan (ca. 800 B.C.E.)[12] with a prophecy of disaster from the sagas associated with the seer Balaam does not belong

3. *KAI* 309.
4. *KAI* 201-202; 216-221; 231-232; 310-311.
5. *KAI* 222-224.
6. A selection is in *KAI* 203-213.
7. *KAI* 320.
8. A recent grammatical overview appears in H. Gzella, "Language and Script," in H. Niehr, ed., *The Aramaeans in Ancient Syria. HO* 106 (2014), 71-107; it also includes references to the still relevant sections of older literature.
9. *KAI* 214-215.
10. First published by D. G. Pardee, "A New Aramaic Inscription from Zinjirli," *BASOR* 356 (2009) 51-71; regarding the debated linguistic classification of Sam'alian, cf. the recent P. M. Noorlander, "Sam'alian in Its Northwest Semitic Setting: A Historical-Comparative Approach," *Or* 81 (2012) 202-38.
11. *KAI* 216-221.
12. The better reading of the first "combination" also appears in *KAI* 312.

to Old Aramaic in the stricter sense.[13] Nevertheless, in contrast to Sam'alian, it does not contain any independent characteristics, but combines a clearly Aramaic grammatical core with a few Canaanite words and stylistic phenomena (since all of these are limited to the realm of the lexicon, they cannot be adduced to classify the text as Canaanite). The best explanation so far traces the singular mixture of languages to the translation of a literary text from Canaanite into Aramaic; the assumption of a "national language" at Deir ʿAlla also lacks the otherwise expected historical preconditions since the archaeological findings evidence no traces whatsoever of any state structures. Because of its significance for scribal culture and as a witness to a tradition of religious literature, the dictionary deals with this inscription in relevant cases.

Thus, the first witnesses to the Aramaic language essentially stem from political office and illustrate the self-understanding of minor kings (→ *mlk*) competing with one another in power and prestige. At the same time, they attest the dispersal of legendary materials. Administrative texts from this early stage have not survived, presumably because of the perishable writing material. Nor is it possible for the earliest period to estimate the degree to which Aramaic may have been present further south in the region of the Hebrew language. Sporadic indications in the Old Testament of a common origin (Gen. 31:20,24,47; Dt. 26:5) find no further historical support. Similarly, there may have been regular contact and the corresponding linguistic influence in the Syro-Israelite border regions (the Tell Dan inscription documents directly,[14] and 1 K. 20:1-34; 22:1-36; 2 K. 6:8-23; 6:24-7:20 indirectly, the political conditions), to which a few plausible (but hardly demonstrably so) Aramaisms in archaic Hebrew passages such as Jgs. 5 may testify (→ *mḥī* I).

2. ARAMAIC ON THE WAY TO WORLD LANGUAGE

One can already conjecture the expansion of Aramaic in the older Old Aramaic period even in Mesopotamia by traders and artisans, and by the settlement of Aramaic-speaking tribes. Conversely, Assyrian advances toward Syria in the ninth century led to a growing reciprocal influence: the Tell Fekheriye inscription survives in a parallel Akkadian version in addition to the Aramaic, and various lexical borrowings on both sides can be identified from this time. After the expansion of the Neo-Assyrian Empire, which led to the incorporation of the previously independent principalities of Syria and of the northern kingdom of Israel by the end of the eighth century B.C.E., a phase of consolidation began, during which, alongside the uncontrolled spread of spoken dialects, the Assyrian administration increasingly included Aramaic. This process continued under the brief Neo-Babylonian rule in the sixth century. In addition, a few official letters demonstrate the role of Aramaic as a diplomatic language and even established a literary

13. The most important are treated briefly by K. Beyer, "The Languages of Transjordan," in H. Gzella, ed., *Languages from the World of the Bible* (New York, 2011), 111-27, esp. 123-26; for a discussion of classification, cf. also H. Gzella, "Deir ʿAllā," in G. Khan, ed., *Encyclopedia of Hebrew Language and Linguistics* (Leiden, 2013), 1:691-93.

14. *KAI* 310.

topos (2 K. 18:26).[15] Likewise, a few burial inscriptions (initially limited to prominent personalities) document its use in the private realm.[16] The magnitude of the preserved material, however, consists of hundreds of brief certificates of debt in Aramaic or Aramaic notes containing brief summaries on the corresponding Akkadian cuneiform tablets, mostly from the Assyrian epoch. Many of them have only become accessible in the last few years in official editions, which arrange by the respective archives to the extent that there is clarity concerning the circumstances of their discovery.[17] Additionally, an edict,[18] from Neo-Babylonian times, a certificate of debt or deposit from Syria,[19] and a couple of minor inscriptions are known. A contract and a pair of private letters from Egypt dated to the eve of the Achaemenid period belong linguistically to this later Old Aramaic and not yet to Achaemenid Imperial Aramaic.

Despite the rapid expansion of Aramaic in the Assyrian, and then in sequence, the Neo-Babylonian chancellery, the variation in the spelling, in the language itself, and in the structure of the administrative texts points to the continued absence of standardization. The remarkable differences from Achaemenid Imperial Aramaic speak for classifying the material of the seventh and sixth centuries to a later phase of Old Aramaic and not, as is sometimes the case (although with no linguistic justification), for extending the term Imperial Aramaic as a linguistic category to Neo-Assyrian and Neo-Babylonian times.[20] For linguistic reasons, one should link the proverbs of Aḥiqar preserved on an Imperial Aramaic papyrus with a later Old Aramaic variety, but their origins remain controversial.[21] In them, after the inscription from Deir ʿAlla that is not purely Aramaic, the usage of Aramaic for literary purposes is first evident; apparently, their roots are in a milieu of learned officials who assembled and catalogued traditional Syrian wisdom maxims in the context of scribal education. Because of their wealth of expression, the dictionary will discuss them regularly.

Admittedly, the preserved literature depicts the actual dispersal of Aramaic in this period only very partially because perishable writing materials may have often been used, but the evidence clearly demonstrates that the Aramaic language made a triumphal

15. *KAI* 233; 266.

16. *KAI* 225-226.

17. A summary compilation of the corresponding publications appears in A. Lemaire, "Remarks on the Aramaic of Upper Mesopotamia in the Seventh Century B.C.," in H. Gzella and M. L. Folmer, eds., *Aramaic in Its Historical and Linguistic Setting*. *VOK* 50 (2008), 77-92, esp. 77-80; meanwhile, one can add E. Lipiński, *SAIO* III (2010), and W. Röllig, *Die aramäischen Texte aus Tall Šēḫ Ḥamad / Dūr-Katlimmu / Magdalu*. *BATSH* 17/5 (2014). For the less numerous comments on Neo-Babylonian tablets (actual Aramaic tablets, in contrast, are largely lacking), see J. Oelsner, "Aramäische Beischriften auf neu- und spätbabylonischen Tontafeln," *WO* 36 (2006) 27-71.

18. *KAI* 317.

19. *KAI* 227.

20. The definitive grammar of the Aramaic of the Assyrian and Babylonian periods is V. Hug, *Altaramäische Grammatik der Texte des 7. und 6. Jh.s v.Chr. HSAO* 4 (1993), which includes the texts and translations of the material known at the time. Because of the highly formulaic character of the texts, subsequent new discoveries add only very little to the understanding of the grammar; for a few additions, cf. Gzella, *Cultural History*, 112-19.

21. For a discussion with literature, see Gzella, *Cultural History*, 150-53.

entry into the administration of the Neo-Assyrian Empire that long outlasted the initially independent Aramaic principalities of Syria in the ninth and eighth centuries. Since the end of the Neo-Assyrian period, "Arameans" as an ethnic category in its own right can no longer by identified (→ *'m*), in contrast to which, the language itself became a means of international communication. This process continued in the Neo-Babylonian period so that the old Semitic standard language of Mesopotamia, Akkadian, became increasingly restricted to the prestigious genre of royal inscriptions and the economic circle of the conservative temple and patrician families of Babylon. They constitute the overwhelming majority of the documentary material from the Neo-Babylonian period, just as indirect indications of various types suggest that in the sixth or, at the latest, the fifth century B.C.E., Aramaic had basically replaced Akkadian in everyday communication.[22]

During the Assyrian and Babylonian periods, Aramaic adopted a whole series of Akkadian loanwords or imitated originally Akkadian expressions using its own lexical means. At the same time, this created the preconditions for the use of a uniform Aramaic official diction standardized soon thereafter: terminology and formulas for different kinds of administrative notices, a formalized epistolary style, a complete inventory of juridical expressions, and a standard prose also suited for usages beyond the bureaucracy. Thus, exiles from Jerusalem came to a society in Babylonia that was already largely Aramaic-speaking and -writing. One cannot rule out the possibility that Aramaic had already spread following Assyrian dominion in the eighth and seventh centuries in the northern kingdom of Israel, whose own Hebrew chancellery tradition had fallen silent; in fact, it is even a likely assumption, although due to the lack of informative sources, it remains pure speculation. Consequently, the Achaemenid period first attests beyond doubt the expansion of Aramaic in Palestine.

3. ACHAEMENID IMPERIAL ARAMAIC AND BIBLICAL ARAMAIC

An administrative reform toward the beginning of Achaemenid rule, then, restricted the historically developed variation in written Aramaic and replaced it with a rigidly codified standard variety: Achaemenid Imperial Aramaic. It apparently rests on a Babylonian dialect and constitutes the foundation of a written tradition widespread as the lingua franca throughout the provincial chancelleries in the entire region between Egypt and Bactria that divided regionally after the demise of the Achaemenid dynasty and, in interaction with spoken Aramaic dialects, led to the development of various new local written languages.[23] Such a conscious codification formalized the already naturalized versions of Aramaic as a comprehensive means of communication. Typical features of orthography and grammar clearly distinguish Achaemenid Imperial Aramaic from older varieties: frequent "degeminating" orthography of /n/ in a contact position, 3s pronouns spelled

22. See P.-A. Beaulieu, "Aspects of Aramaic and Babylonian Linguistic Interaction in First Millennium BC Iraq," *Journal of Language Contact* 6 (2013) 358-78.

23. Cf. H. Gzella, "The Heritage of Imperial Aramaic in Eastern Aramaic," *AraSt* 6 (2008) 85-109; idem, *Cultural History*, 157-82.

hw and *hy*, the use of independent personal pronouns instead of suffixes for the 3p, and with the "perfect" the extension of the 3mp to the feminine. Historical spellings, such as, especially, *z* for /d/ which had arisen from an original */δ/ in some words were, meanwhile, adopted from older Aramaic written traditions. Because of this "expansion" to the standard language, regional variations are no longer perceptible; sporadic divergences from the norm result from the insular influence of other languages in the Achaemenid Empire. In some regions, such as Palestine and Egypt, the use of Aramaic as a written language, and sometimes even as a language of communication, expanded among the local population; in others, such as Anatolia, Arabia, and Iran, it came into a sometimes only superficial contact with the native languages. The populations of Syria and Mesopotamia also undoubtedly continued to speak Aramaic, as later evidence demonstrates (see below), but with regard to the textual documentation of the Achaemenid period, these regions continue to be blank spots for the time being.

In extent and breadth, the Imperial Aramaic corpus exceeds the attestation of all the preceding and, up to late antiquity, of all the subsequent Aramaic written languages. For this reason, and because of its linguistic and cultural proximity to Biblical Aramaic, which developed out of it, it constitutes the most important reference point for the material treated here. Dozens of legal documents, both official and private letters, commercial documents, memorial and burial inscriptions, an Aramaic translation of the Behistun Inscription of King Darius, and a few literary texts illustrate its geographically, socially, and functionally comprehensive usage.[24] Just as the literary production in all the ancient Near East has roots predominantly in the milieu of officials and priests, Imperial Aramaic administrative language also underlies the nonofficial writings: in Egypt

24. The numerous papyrus finds and a few inscriptions from Elephantine and other sites in Egypt are included in *TADAE* (as well as a couple pre-Imperial Aramaic ones, such as the private letters from Hermopolis), which now accompanies the roughly three hundred ostraca in the Clermont-Ganneau Collection by H. Lozachmeur, *La collection Clermont-Ganneau*, 2 vols. (Paris, 2006), supplemented by a few minor inscriptions in W. Röllig, "Neue phönizische und aramäische Krugaufschriften und Ostraka aus Elephantine," in D. Raue, S. J. Seidlmayer, and P. Speiser, eds., *The First Cataract of the Nile: One Region—Diverse Perspectives* (New York, 2013), 185-203. All the contracts from Samaria have been published in J. Dušek, *Les manuscrits araméens du Wadi Daliyeh et la Samarie vers 450-332 av. J.-C. CHANE* 30 (2007); ostraca from Idumea in D. Schwiderski, *Die alt- und reichsaramäischen Inschriften*, vol. II: *Texte und Bibliographie. FSBP* 4 (2004); and now B. Porten and A. Yardeni, *Textbook of Aramaic Ostraca from Idumea*, vol. 1: *Dossiers 1-10: 401 Commodity Chits* (Winona Lake, IN, 2014); and B. Porten and A. Yardeni, *Textbook of Aramaic Ostraca from Idumea*, vol. 2: *Dossiers 11-50: 263 Commodity Chits* (Winona Lake, IN, 2016). The uniformity of Imperial Aramaic has been confirmed, meanwhile, by an extensive archive with primarily official letters from the provincial administration of Bactria, accessible in J. Naveh and S. Shaked, *Aramaic Documents from Ancient Bactria (Fourth Century B.C.E.)* (London, 2012). Aramaic was also employed in the administration of justice. As addenda on objects (R. A. Bowman, *Aramaic Ritual Texts from Persepolis. OIP* 91 [1970]) and on a few, mostly unpublished, clay tables demonstrate, its role in relation to Elamite, which the bureaucratic centers of Iran typically employed in commercial texts, cannot yet be more precisely determined. Further, a few inscriptions from northern Arabia, Egypt (also in *TADAE*), and Asia Minor (*KAI* 228-230; 258-263; 267-272; 278; 318-319), and scattered minor inscriptions on weights, coins, vessels, seals, seal impressions, etc. (bibliography in *ATTM,* 29-32 and 2, 16f.) have survived.

a wisdom-influenced court novella about the fall and rehabilitation of the model advisor Aḥiqar, which, together with a collection of older proverbs (see above), was combined in a single papyrus, as well as minor fragments of other texts and, in Palestine, the Aramaic sections of Ezra and Daniel. A uniform scribal education in the provincial chancelleries and an efficient system of reporting stabilized the development of a standard variety employed empire-wide and of the legal and administrative terminology transmitted in it.[25] The numerous juridical documents and letters from high Achaemenid officials produce a variety of insights into the administrative practices that illuminate the socio-historical context in which the Old Testament acquired its transmitted form.

Since Achaemenid Imperial Aramaic was also introduced in Palestine as an administrative language and soon replaced Hebrew in this function, as evident in the change in Arad and Idumea between the sixth and fifth centuries B.C.E.,[26] it determines the language of the Aramaic passages in Ezra and Daniel.[27] Admittedly, scholars assess the precise nature of its relationship with Imperial Aramaic differently, but the fact that it arose from the Achaemenid written tradition is beyond doubt. Indications, in addition to the theologically adapted administrative terminology (such as, e.g., → *dt* for the divine law, → *ptgm* for a divine edit, the preposition → *qdm* "before" used of God, or → *šlṭ* for God's sovereign authority of all human dominion), include typical linguistic features such as degeminating spellings or the masculine instead of the feminine form for the "perfect" of the 3mp (see the grammatical outline in the appendix). Some even regard the letters in Ezra about the reconstruction of the temple as authentic Achaemenid documents.[28] In contrast, Daniel, whose Aramaic sections are now often dated to the period between ca. 320 B.C.E. and 200 B.C.E., exhibits what at least appear to be younger forms ending in /-n/ with certain pronominal elements and a verbal syntax that already preludes later phenomena. Consequently, in contrast to Ezra, some associate Daniel more closely with

25. Despite its importance, there is still no complete reference grammar for Imperial Aramaic, although a new overview is available in H. Gzella, "Imperial Aramaic," in Weninger, *Semitic Languages*, 574-86 (with a brief glance at Biblical Aramaic). The Egyptian subcorpus (include the pre-Imperial Aramaic texts), however, is the subject of the extensive, if primarily descriptive, grammar by T. Muraoka and B. Porten, *A Grammar of Egyptian Aramaic. HO* 32 (²2003).

26. *ATTM*, 2, 35.

27. Still indispensable as a reference grammar is *BLA*; as a dictionary, *LexLingAram* distinguishes itself in comparison to the Biblical Aramaic sections of Hebrew lexicons through its extreme precision in the rendering of syntactic constructions and its selection of Old and Imperial Aramaic parallels (the English translation J. A. Fitzmyer, *A Lexicon of Biblical Aramaic. SubBi* 42 [2011], adds as good as nothing and is typographically inferior). Commentaries regularly cited are H. G. M. Williamson, *Ezra, Nehemiah. WBC* (1985), for Ezra; and K. Koch, *Daniel 1–4. BK* XXII/1 (2005) (supplemented by J. J. Collins, *Daniel. Herm* [1993]) and J. A. Montgomery, *A Critical and Exegetical Commentary on the Book of Daniel. ICC* (1927), for Daniel.

28. So recently again H. G. M. Williamson, "The Aramaic Documents in Ezra Revisited," *JTS* 59 (2008) 41-62; critically, on the other hand, D. Schwiderski, *Handbuch des nordwestsemitischen Briefformulars: Ein Beitrag zur Echtheitsfrage der aramäischen Briefe des Esrabuches. BZAW* 295 (2000) (with a summary on pp. 381f.); and L. L. Grabbe, "The 'Persian' Documents in the Book of Ezra: Are They Authentic?" in O. Lipschits and M. Oeming, eds., *Judah and the Judaeans in the Persian Period* (Winona Lake, IN, 2006) 531-70.

somewhat later stages of development, such as, especially, the Aramaic from Qumran. The linguistic commonalities with Imperial Aramaic seem on the whole to balance with the differences (some of which can also be explained as orthographic modernizations),[29] but, especially given the focus of *TDOT* on the biblical text, Biblical Aramaic will be treated formally mostly as an independent category in the individual lemmata, thus acknowledging its variable categorization in the scholarship of the last century.

Along with the Imperial Aramaic written language, an Aramaic vernacular also spread in Achaemenid Palestine that is only indirectly evident at first, but which appears around the time of Jesus directly in a few private inscriptions on ossuaries, etc. It cannot be derived directly from Imperial Aramaic, but is apparently related to the Old Aramaic languages of Syria since, e.g., the object particle *yt* seems to reflect the older form *ʾyt* as in the inscriptions from Sefire instead of the Imperial Aramaic form *l-*. Thus, for not yet sufficiently explained reasons—although demographic developments such as the population decline in Babylonia and a resettlement of many regions in the former northern kingdom of Israel may have played an important role—local Aramaic dialects from western Syria and perhaps from the region of the former northern kingdom of Israel spread to Judea. They also underlie the various West Aramaic literary languages of Palestine in late antiquity. Hebrew continued in use, to be sure, mostly for the production of theological literature, but fell increasingly under the influence of Aramaic.[30] Of the Aramaisms in postexilic biblical books, at least official terms (to which the dictionary will refer briefly in the relevant lexemes) stem specifically from Imperial Aramaic. More profound alterations, such as word order and verbal syntax, of which the speaker is usually unaware, in contrast, probably derive from the Aramaic vernacular; in the meanwhile, it must have grown significantly among the population and especially among the learned. Thus, Aramaic in several forms in Achaemenid Palestine influenced Hebrew. At the same time, not every word that diverges from the Classical Hebrew written language, on the one hand, and exhibits points of agreement with Aramaic, on the other, is necessarily a borrowing from Aramaic; especially in poetic style it could also have preserved characteristics of an old Canaanite dialect.

After the Imperial Aramaic literary tradition gained additional footing in parts of the Achaemenid Empire and found usage for commerce, law, literature, private correspondence, and other purposes, it was able to survive for a long period in isolated regions even after the demise of Persian rule. In Syria and Palestine, it soon combined with the Aramaic dialects spoken there and, after the third century B.C.E., became the foundation of new literary languages. It is hardly possible, therefore, to establish the end of Imperial Aramaic chronologically.

29. For additional literature on the discussion, see H. Gzella, *Tempus, Aspekt und Modalität im Reichsaramäischen. VOK* 48 (2004), 42-44.

30. Cf. the recent overview in C. Stadel, "Aramaic Influence on Biblical Hebrew," in Khan, *Encyclopedia of Hebrew Language and Linguistics*, 1:162-65.

4. THE POST-ACHAEMENID LITERARY TRADITIONS

For the Hellenistic period, heralded by the conquests of Alexander the Great and consolidated under his successors, the use of Aramaic is hardly documented, but it continued initially without interruption at least in Egypt, Palestine (where Aramaic had sunk deep roots in the meanwhile), and Bactria after the fall of the Persian Empire. In Roman times, beginning with the first century B.C.E., independent local literary languages appear in Syria-Palestine, Arabia, and Mesopotamia that depend in varying degrees on the Achaemenid chancellery tradition: a Jewish Aramaic literary and administrative language ("Hasmonean") in theological and documentary texts from Qumran and other sites around the Dead Sea; Nabatean in northern Arabia; Palmyrene and Edessene ("Old Syriac") in Syria; and Hatrene in eastern Mesopotamia; plus a few scattered finds from other regions. They served mostly for public representation and administration in territorially limited Roman vassal kingdoms, and, at least in Palestine, also for a national religious literature. They distinguish themselves through varying combinations of the Imperial Aramaic tradition with the spoken Aramaic dialects that continued to develop in Aramaic-speaking areas (thus Syria-Palestine and Mesopotamia) beneath the surface of a uniform written language already during the Persian period; these were also subject in widely varying degrees to the influence of Greek. Because the Imperial Aramaic lingua franca was fading, regional peculiarities now also appear in textual witnesses to Aramaic. They surface in the post-Christian era as two clearly distinct strands of dialect, West Aramaic in Palestine and East Aramaic in Syria-Mesopotamia. Since the individual Aramaic literary languages attested roughly from the first century B.C.E. to the third century C.E. do not reflect the same stages of literary development, it is advisable to refrain from a uniform designation for this linguistic period (such as "Middle Aramaic" in the literature influenced by Anglophone scholarship).

Of these Aramaic languages from the Hellenistic and Roman periods, Hasmonean, the variety attested in texts from Qumran and its near vicinity, has the greatest significance for the *TDOT*. Especially the scrolls from Qumran with their visions, apocalypses, and court tales connect closely with the themes of the book of Daniel. At the same time, the discoveries from the Dead Sea as a whole can contribute to the understanding of New Testament concepts. The respective articles, therefore, take account of this material, when possible completely; when relevant, they will highlight especially the relationship with Biblical Aramaic (as at Qumran) and the Imperial Aramaic legal and administrative tradition (as in the private documents for the Dead Sea).[31] The relationship between

31. All of the Aramaic texts from the Dead Sea are most easily accessible in the convenient edition for the English-speaking realm, *DSSStE*, and for the German-speaking realm, *ATTM* and *ATTM*, 2. For the writings from Qumran, *DJD* is the often cited and internationally official edition; this dictionary also employs its sigla. Special editions of individual works such as 1QapGen, Enoch, 11QtgJob or *ALD* will be occasionally adduced. Many passages are controversial paleographically, however, so that the readings of *ATTM*, *DSSStE*, and *DJD* regularly differ. Where such differences are relevant for the explanation of the word usage, they will be briefly discussed. The original German text of this volume defaulted to *ATTM* and *ATTM, 2* for citing texts from the Dead Sea. For the English translation, these citations were changed to *DSSStE* where possible.

inherited Imperial Aramaic spellings and forms, on the one hand, and West Aramaic impacts, on the other, differ from manuscript to manuscript. Thus, a linguistic dating of the texts, some transmitted over a long period and sometimes reaching far into the Hellenistic period or even earlier, is hardly possible apart from paleography.[32] The Aramaic literature could also have originated outside of Qumran so that it is methodically sensible to establish their relationship to the other witnesses to written Aramaic from Palestine.[33] From roughly the birth of Christ, the local dialect of Jerusalem and Judea, Jewish Palestinian Aramaic, appears as a written language in increasing measure. In it, the Imperial Aramaic heritage faded further and the local color increased. With the disappearance of the Imperial Aramaic literary tradition of Palestine under Roman rule, the upper chronological limit of the dictionary has been attained; the lexicons of the rising West Aramaic literatures of late antiquity and especially of the rabbinic literature of Palestine are linked to the material treated here by references to *DJPA* (which then also cites additional information concerning the current dictionaries of Samaritan Aramaic and its Christian-Palestinian sister language).

This dictionary can only consider other varieties of Aramaic in the Hellenistic-Roman era selectively, especially if they illuminate the older diction or the cultural context (e.g., in the realm of religion). Nabatean in northern Arabia is still a close relative of Imperial Aramaic, presumably because it served only as a written language for legal documents and public representation, while the local population employed Arabic in daily communication. It occurs in numerous inscriptions; furthermore, near the Dead Sea a few extensive private contracts have been found.[34] From Syrian Palmyra, famed for its monumental architecture, substantially destroyed recently, a few honorary and grave inscriptions, in addition to a lengthy tax table, have survived, a series of them

In many cases, however, the *ATTM* and *DSSStE* differ slightly on the readings, so updating the citation would have rendered the article nonsensical. In these situations the original reference to *ATTM* has been retained.

32. Cf. H. Gzella, "Dating the Aramaic Texts from Qumran: Possibilities and Limits," *RevQ* 24 (2009) 61-78. An overview of the relevant characteristic of Imperial and West Aramaic appears in idem, *Cultural History*, 232f.

33. So the comparative-history-oriented phonetics, accidence, and glossary in *ATTM* (at the same time, the only complete scientific dictionary of the Aramaic texts from Qumran), similarly the synchronic (including the syntax) reference grammar by T. Muraoka, *A Grammar of Qumran Aramaic*. *ANESSup* 38 (2011). Select terms from the Aramaic texts from Qumran find extensive treatment in the respective articles by H.-J. Fabry and U. Dahmen, *Theologisches Wörterbuch zu den Qumrantexten* (2011-2016); in cases involving externally similar cognates in the Hebrew texts the cognates are included. In contrast, this dictionary is restricted to the Aramaic material and, in addition, places the accent somewhat more definitely on philology.

34. At the moment, there is no complete edition or modern grammar; for a selection of the most important inscriptions, see U. Hackl, H. Jenni, and C. Schneider, *Quellen zur Geschichte der Nabatäer: Textsammlung mit Übersetzung und Kommentar*. *NTOA* 51 (2003); private documents are included in *ATTM*, 2 and will be cited mostly following it. The only grammar, J. Cantineau, *Le Nabatéen*, 2 vols. (Paris, 1930-1932), does not yet take account of the discoveries from the Dead Sea. For a brief outline, cf. H. Gzella, "Late Imperial Aramaic," in Weninger, *Semitic Languages*, 598-609.

also with mostly Greek parallel versions. Many of them, following Hellenistic usage, served to honor leading citizens of the city publicly. Otherwise, expatriate Palmyrenes in various parts of the Roman Empire left behind shorter grave inscriptions that express a clear cultural self-consciousness (→ *dkr*; *ṣlm*). Palmyrene exhibits a mixture of Imperial Aramaic elements with East Aramaic imprints, which suggests that the Palmyrenes spoke Aramaic, because otherwise elements of dialect could hardly have found entry into the texts.[35] Edessene (or Old Syriac) also rests on a regional variety of East Aramaic that became a written language in the kingdom of Osrhoene sometime between Hellenistic and Roman times but has looser connections with Imperial Aramaic. From before the time of the Christianization of Edessa, a few brief building, grave, and memorial inscriptions survive, in addition to a few private documents from Dura Europos;[36] thereafter, Syriac developed into a richly attested and highly standardized theological normative language of the Christian Near East. In relevant cases, this dictionary will touch on its very extensive lexicon through references to *LexSyr* and, in this manner, connect to the older Aramaic tradition. The East Aramaic inscriptions from Hatra and the rest of east Mesopotamia demonstrate even more clearly that, in this region, too, Aramaic dialects developed continuously and then were elevated by the chancellery of a region's principality to a written language. As with the findings from Edessa, aside from a couple of decrees with legal decisions, they involve mostly private inscriptions that document construction, the memory of a member of the population, or personal piety.[37]

From Babylon in south Mesopotamia from pre-Christian times, only an Aramaic incantation text from Uruk dissociated from the established scribal traditions survives.[38] It, however, manifests several characteristic features of the later attested East Aramaic strand. Then in late antiquity, local dialects of Babylon produced the Jewish Babylonian and Mandean literary languages known from extensive sources, both of which no longer have direct relation to the Imperial Aramaic tradition. Because of their importance for the Aramaic lexicon in a diachronic perspective, this dictionary will take them into account

35. Almost all the texts appear in *PAT*, although, in contrast to the *editiones principes*, without translation and with only a glossary as aid. Grammars are still limited to J. Cantineau, *Grammaire du palmyrénien épigraphique* (Cairo, 1935); and F. Rosenthal, *Die Sprache der palmyrenischen Inschriften* (Leipzig, 1936), but must be replaced by newer depictions. For the transition, cf. the outline in Gzella, "Late Imperial Aramaic."

36. These inscriptions are newly collated and provided with a commentary, a grammatical outline, and a glossary by H. J. W. Drijvers and J. F. Healey, *The Old Syriac Inscriptions of Edessa and Osrhoene*. *HO* 32 (1999). The most important grammar for classical Syriac is T. Nöldeke, *Compendious Syriac Grammar*, trans. Peter T. Daniels (Winona Lake, IN, 2001). Nöldeke's grammar is still instructive, especially for Aramaic syntax. The standard dictionary *LexSyr* has also become available, meanwhile, in a new English version: M. Sokoloff, *A Syriac Lexicon* (Winona Lake, IN; Piscataway, NJ, 2009).

37. The most reliable edition is K. Beyer, *Die aramäischen Inschriften aus Assur, Hatra und dem übrigen Ostmesopotamien* (Göttingen, 1998), 28-114, with additions in idem, "Die aramäischen Inschriften aus Assur, Hatra und dem übrigen Ostmesopotamien," *WO* 43 (2013) 25-62 (along with a grammatical outline and a glossary, but without detailed commentary or bibliographical information).

38. *ATTM*, 2, 25-7.

through marginal references to *DJBA* and *MdD*. Important witnesses to the Aramaic dialectical landscape of Babylonia in late antiquity and the popular piety beyond theological orthodoxy are the numerous magical bowls; the dictionary will treat them, however, only in relevant individual cases, even though they document magical practices that may have already been customary in a much earlier period. Peripheral to the objective of this dictionary, finally, are a few public inscriptions in the Imperial Aramaic tradition from post-Achaemenid Afghanistan and Pakistan (the bilingual edict of Emperor Aśoka) and from Arsakidian Iran,[39] and the Aramaic material preserved as a relic of bureaucratic practice in Middle Persian ideograms (cf. *Frahang*).

The Achaemenid tradition, therefore, constitutes the most important linguistic and cultural history reference point for the first millennium B.C.E. and, thus, for Biblical Aramaic and indirectly for Biblical Hebrew, but, in the context of the totality of the linguistic witness, is only one manifestation of Aramaic among others even in antiquity. Common phonetic changes across the entire continuum of Aramaic dialects (see the "Historical Outline of Aramaic Grammar" at the end of this volume) demonstrate the widespread use of Aramaic for communication in many parts of the Near East between the three ancient Near Eastern empires and the expansion of Islam because such developments presuppose a network of neighboring groups of speakers. Thus, a dynamic interaction between the Imperial Aramaic written tradition and the local Aramaic vernaculars also characterizes the linguistic situation of Hellenistic and Roman times, which simultaneously constitutes the background of early Judaism, the New Testament, and the early church.[40]

5. ARRANGEMENT OF THE ARAMAIC DICTIONARY

A linguistically differentiated division of Aramaic undergirded by cultural history, as outlined here, produces the arrangement of the Aramaic dictionary in *TDOT*. Biblical Aramaic documents a local literary language, which itself arose from the Imperial Aramaic written tradition with its origin in the Achaemenid chancellery and which is best explained through it. This written tradition, for its part, has roots in Old Aramaic back to the beginning of the first written witnesses soon after 1000 B.C.E. and continues in post-Achaemenid Palestine in the religious literature of Qumran. Thus, the context of the Biblical Aramaic lexicon and the environment depicted in it is, in the first instance, Old and Imperial Aramaic and the Aramaic of the texts from the Dead Sea.

39. Bibliography concerning the Aśoka Edicts appears in Gzella, *Tempus*, 39-41; a new edition with commentary of the Arsakidic inscriptions in idem, "Aramaic in the Parthian Period: The Arsacid Inscriptions," in Gzella, *Aramaic in Its Historical and Linguistic Setting*, 103-30.

40. See, now, the extensive treatment in H. Gzella, *Cultural History*, 212-80, with additional, more recent bibliography.

אַב *'aḇ* /'ab/; אם *'m* /'emm/

I. Lexeme. II. Father, Ancestor. III. Figurative Use. IV. God as Father. V. *'em* "Mother." VI. Honoring Parents.

I. Lexeme. *'aḇ* "father" is a common Semitic babble word in which *-ū-* is inserted in the singular before the suffixes that begin with a consonant and *-āh-* is inserted in the plural before the feminine, rarely before the masculine ending.[1]

II. Father, Ancestor. The word usually designates the biological father (so also in Dnl. 5:2,11,13,18), rarely also a more distant male ancestor for which Aramaic has no unique expression, such as the paternal grandfather[2] (the maternal grandfather must be described as "father of the mother"); the great grandfather,[3] for which Nabatean[4] and the cuneiform of the upper Euphrates (ca. 1100 B.C.E.) have *'am(m)*;[5] the patriarchs Abraham or Jacob;[6] or stepfather.[7] In the plural, it denotes the male ancestors (Ezr. 4:15),[8] the male

F. Albrecht and R. Feldmeier, eds., *The Divine Father: Religious and Philosophical Concepts of Divine Parenthood in Antiquity. TBN* (2014); K. Beyer, *Die aramäischen Inschriften aus Assur, Hatra und dem übrigen Ostmesopotamien* (Göttingen, 1998); S. Brock, "'Come, Compassionate Mother . . ., Come, Holy Spirit'. A Forgotten Aspect of Early Eastern Christian Imagery," *Aram* 3 (1991) 249-57; G. Dalman, *The Words of Jesus*, trans. D. M. Kay (Edinburgh, 1902); H. J. W. Drijvers and J. F. Healey, *The Old Syriac Inscriptions of Edessa and Osrhoene. HO* I/42 (1999); E. Jenni, "אָב *'āb* father," *TLOT*, 1-13; M. L. Klein, *Genizah Manuscripts of Palestinian Targum to the Pentateuch I* (Cincinnati, 1986); W. Kornfeld, *Onomastica aramaica aus Ägypten. SÖAW. PH* 333 (1978); I. Kottsieper, "The Tel Dan Inscription (*KAI* 310) and the Political Relations between Aram-Damascus and Israel in the First Half of the First Millennium BCE," *Ahab Agonistes*. LHBOTS 421 (2007), 104-34; J. Kühlewein, "אֵם *'ēm* mother" *TLOT*, 130-33; M. Maraqten, *Die semitischen Personennamen in den alt- und reichsaramäischen Inschriften aus Vorderasien. TStO* 5 (1988); H. Ringgren, "אָב 'ābh," *TDOT*, I, 1-19; A. Strotmann, *Mein Vater bist du (Sir 51, 10). FTS* 39 (1991); G. Schelbert, *Abba: Der literarische Befund vom Altaramäischen bis zu den späten Midrasch- und Haggada-Werken. NTOA* (2011); R. Zadok, *On West Semites in Babylonia During the Chaldean and Achaemenian Periods* (Jerusalem, ²1978); C. Zimmermann, *Die Namen des Vaters* (Leiden, 2007), esp. 41ff.

1. *AP* 30.13 = 31.12.
2. CT. Levi Bodleian a:14; b:3,4 (T. Levi 33:14; 34:3,4; *DSSStE*, 50f.).
3. CT. Levi ar Bodleian b:3 (T. Levi 34:3; *DSSStE*, 50f.); 4Q542 1 1:8 (Testament of Qahat 1:8; *DSSStE*, 1082f.).
4. *DNSI*, 866f.
5. R. M. Whiting, "A Late Middle Assyrian Tablet from North Syria," *SAAB* 2 (1988) 99-101.
6. Palestinian Tg. of Gen. 35:9 C; Klein, 72f.
7. Hermopolis 4.13.
8. *AP* 30.13 = 31.12; 4Q534 1:7 (The Birth of Noah 1:7; *DSSStE*, 1070f.); 4Q542 1 1:5,12 (Testament of Qahat 1:5,12; *ATTM.E*, 83f.): the law as the "inheritance" of "your ancestors."

and female ancestors (Dnl. 2:23: "the God of my ancestors," Ezr. 5:12: "our ancestors angered the God of heaven").[9]

III. Figurative Use. Aḥiqar, the advisor of the Assyrian king Sennacherib, carries the designation the "father of all Assyria."[10]

• The fact that Hazael calls Hadadezer "my father" in Tg. Dnl. 3 although he was not his biological father indicates that *'b* has the sense of "predecessor" or "patron."[11] (Ko.) • The Aramaic in 11Q10 31:5 (Job 38:28) corresponds to "does the rain have a father?" of the Hebrew original.

IV. God as Father. Jewish Palestinian Aramaic first attests the form of address and tenderness of αββα as an address to God (Mk. 14:36; Rom. 8:15; Gal. 4:6), which takes the place of "my/our father" (attested since approximately the birth of Christ).[12] As a designation for God, "father" first appears in cuneiform Aramaic personal names.[13] Names of the type *'Abī-*,[14] which also appear in Aramaic, translate as "my adoptive father is (the deity). . ." (cf. the frequent counterpart *Bar-* "the adoptive son of the deity. . ."), since, as a rule, the name of the biological father is stated.[15]

V. *'em* "Mother." *'em*(*m*) "mother" is also a common Semitic babble word with an inserted -(*ā*)*h*- before the feminine and rarely also the masculine plural ending. It does not occur in Biblical Aramaic.

The word usually denotes the biological mother,[16] rarely also more distant female ancestors (if "grandmother" is not paraphrased "mother of father/mother"),[17] as in 4Q206 4:10 (1 En. 32:6) with a subsequent *rbt'* "the universal great grandmother" Eve.[18] In Nabatean, the goddess Allāt is "the mother of the gods."[19] The early Syriac church designated, not only the Holy Spirit, but also God as mother.[20] The second Old Syriac treaty line 5 first attests it in the meaning "major city" (240 C.E.).[21]

Beyer

---

9. 4Q213a 2:5 (T. Levi 48:5; *DSSStE,* 450f.): "the good reputation of their ancestors" (cf. also l. 3); 4Q550c 1:1 (Documents of Darius 4:1; *DSSStE,* 1098f.): "the sins of my ancestors"; 4Q545 1 2:12,17 (Testament of Amram 1:31; 2:3; *DSSStE,* 1090f.): burial of the "ancestors"; Graves from Jerusalem yJE 4:2; 5:1 (*ATTM,* 340): "(the bones) of our ancestors," and the parents (*DJPA*, 31b; *LexSyr*, la; in 4Q197 4 2:11 [Tob. 6:15; *DSSStE,* 390f.]) but "my father and mother" still occurs.

10. Aḥiqar 55.

11. Cf. Kottsieper, 119-20.

12. Cf. *ATTM,* 503; *ATTM.E,* 303.

13. Zadok, 53; first in old Syriac (unpublished); cf. *PNPI,* 63a with Beyer, 156,169.

14. Zadok, 54; Kornfeld, 37f.; *PNPI,* 1f.,63f.; Abbadi, 1f.,73f.

15. Regarding the post-Christian Aramaic "his/your/their father in heaven," cf. Dalman, 186-88.

16. So always in names, cf. *ATTM,* 513; *ATTM.E,* 308.

17. Cf. *DJPA*, 61b.

18. *DSSStE,* 426f.

19. *CIS* II 185.5f.

20. Cf. Brock, 249-57.

21. Cf. Drijvers-Healey, 238,240.

VI. Honoring Parents. The concept of honoring parents occurs in the sayings of Aḥiqar, although restricted to the aspect of respectful remembrance. It places father and mother on the same level. Thus, Aḥiqar 138 against boasting in the "name" (→ שׁם *šem*) of one's father and mother, i.e., not to derive one's own honor from that of one's parents. This implies the prohibition of undervaluing one's parents or even speaking badly about them in public. Aḥiqar 85 apparently presupposes the connection between one's esteem and the reputation of the family when it deals with the notion that one's reputation for a lack of self-control can also damage the reputation of one's father and descendants. A parallel appears in 4Q213a 2:3,5, which speaks of a woman desecrating her own reputation and, thus, the good reputation of her father and ancestors (and brothers), apparently through turpitude. Even a god can honor his father.[22]

Kottsieper

22. E.g., the sun god by building a temple; Hatra 107.7.

***אֵב** *'eḇ* → אִילָן *'îlān*

אבד *'bd*; אבדן *'bdn* /'abdān/; שׁמד *šmd*

I. Etymology. II. Older Aramaic Usage. II. Biblical Aramaic. IV. Qumran. V. *'bdn* "Destruction, Ruin." VI. *šmd*.

I. Etymology. The root *'bd* occurs with the meaning "to spoil" (G-stem) or "to destroy" (C-stem, D-stem) both in the eastern and western branches of the Semitic language family. Akkadian *abātu* means "to destroy" and Hebrew *'bd* "to perish." With this meaning, *'bd* also occurs in Syriac and Moabite.[1] Ugaritic also has the root *'bd* that means "to perish" both in the G- and the Gt-stems.[2] It appears once in a Phoenician inscription from Cyprus with the meaning "to destroy" (yiphil or piel).[3]

Freedman/Yu

J. Lewy, "Lexical and Grammatical Studies," *Or* NS 29 (1960) 20-45; N. Lohfink, "שׁמד *šmd*," TDOT, XV, 177-98; B. Otzen, "אָבַד 'ābhadh," TDOT, I, 19-23; J. Tropper, *Die Inschriften von Zincirli. ALASP* 6 (Münster, 1993), esp. 109f.

1. *KAI* 181.7.
2. *DUL*³, 7.
3. *KAI* 30.3.

The old Canaanite gloss EA 288.52 *a-ba-da-at* ("they [i.e., the nations] perish" = Akk. *ḫal-qa-at*) joins these instances. Since Arabic *'abida* occurs with the meaning "to be timid, prepared to flee" (said of animals, then of people in the meaning "to be timid, unapproachable, antisocial"), which corresponds, on the one hand, in the Ethiopic languages to "to be crazy, beside oneself",[4] and on the other hand, to Akkadian *abātu* "to flee,"[5] the root probably originally designated a state or a behavior in which the subject withdrew or was withdrawn from "normal" access. With respect to animate subjects, the connotation "to flee" (cf. Akk.) can result, or the statement that one behaves in a manner that renders social intercourse impossible, whether one is crazed (cf. the Ethiopic languages) or wandering or erratic; compare especially the Hebrew,[6] but also the Syriac and Arabic, whose connotation of "timidity" mediates between the two poles. With both animate and inanimate subjects, however, from the viewpoint of the speaker, the horizon of meaning also produces the connotation that something is "lost" or "perishes." East Semitic (Akk.) goes its own way by using this root, which largely corresponds in its intransitive meaning to *ḫalāqu*, primarily as a transitive.

Kottsieper

II. Older Aramaic Usage. Several Aramaic inscriptions, including the Old Aramaic ones from Zinçirli and Sefire, attest *'bd*. Despite the scarcity of specimens, several stems appear.

Many classify the language of the inscription *KAI* 215 from Zinçirli as Old Aramaic, but *DNSI* categorizes it as Sam'alian.[7] The authors follow the traditional classification, however, and, accordingly, assign it here to Aramaic. The instance in *KAI* 215.5 remains uncertain, however.[8]

Similarly, the haphel appears in an Imperial Aramaic inscription from Nerab and in the Greco-Aramaic diglot from Kandahar. Nerab has the haphel impf. 3mp. *wyh'bdw zr'k* "and they will destroy your seed."[9] The context is a grave inscription with the purpose of frightening wanton destroyers or robbers away from destroying the gravestone or the sarcophagus. The Kandahar inscription offers the form *hwbd*

4. *CDG*, 2f.

5. Cf. Lewy, 22-27; *CAD*, I/1, 45: *abātu* B; contra *AHw* I, 5: *abātu*.

6. Otzen, 21.

7. Cf. also Tropper, esp. 287ff.

8. • According to Tropper, 109f., *KAI* 215.5 may involve a pf. 3mp *qal* (*'bdw b'*[*rq*]) in the meaning "to wander around (in the country)." Yet, the reading *'bdt/n b'*[*rt*] is also possible, which would translate "the wells were destroyed." (*Ko.*) • The instances in the Sefire inscriptions, where *'bd* appears in the pael and the haphel, are more certain. *KAI* 222 B 36 offers [*l*]*'bdt* in a corrupt context. The same form also appears in *KAI* 223 B 7 *wl 'bdt 'šmhm* "in order to destroy their name." The haphel occurs twice in *KAI* 223 C 4f.: [*y*]*'mr 'h'bd spr*[*y*]*' wkm*[*l*]*n 'hbd 'yt ktk w'yt mlkh* ". . . he said: 'I will destroy the inscription'; and, in accordance with the words, I will destroy Ktk and his king."

9. *KAI* 225.11.

(haphel pf. 3ms), which omits the ': *wklhm 'dwšy' hwbd* "and he caused all hostile things (?) to disappear."[10]

A statement corresponding to *KAI* 225.11 also occurs in the second inscription from Nerab, which employs the peal, however: *w'ḥrth t'bd* "and his descendants will perish" (→ אחרי *'aḥ*[a]*rî* II).[11] This also involves a warning to those who could destroy the sarcophagus of the grave owner, hindering the act with severe curses and threats.

The peal also occurs in a papyrus from Elephantine in the context of the loss of the dowry.[12]

• In *AP* 15.27; 30.16 and perhaps *TADAE* B 1.1.13, *'bd* also denotes the loss of money or property as the result of a juristic action, in the event that one should not read *'dr* here instead. The connotation "to perish" also occurs in the Sabbath ostracon *TADAE* D7.16 obv. 3 (of vegetables that go bad?) and *TADAE* D7.5 obv. 5. Aḥiqar 94 speaks of the fact that the wisdom of a human being who omits the customary libation perishes. This figurative usage compares to *AP* 71.28 which overtly speaks of the fact that righteousness (*ṣdqt'*) disappears.[13] In *AD* 8.2,4, *'bd pe* denotes the disappearance of people during a revolution. (*Ko.*) •

III. Biblical Aramaic. Biblical Aramaic manifests *'bd* in the three stems peal, haphel, and hophal.

The sole instance of the peal occurs in Jer. 10:11, where Jeremiah describes the folly of the nations who venerate idols and admonishes the house of Israel to venerate Yahweh alone. After he has depicted the folly of those who worship idols, he proclaims that Yahweh is the God of truth and life and is the eternal King. Then follows the warning *'*[e]*lāhayyā' dî š*[e]*mayyā' w*[e]*'arqā' lā' '*[a]*ḇaḏû ye'ḇaḏû me'ar'ā' ûmin t*[e]*ḥôṯ š*[e]*mayyā' 'elleh* "they have not worshiped the God of heaven and earth; they will perish from the earth and beneath heaven."[14]

The haphel inf. occurs in Dnl. 2:12 in the description of how King Nebuchadnezzar decided to destroy all the sages living in Babylon (*l*[e]*hôḇāḏāh*, cf. also 2:24). Daniel reports this to his friends and presses them to ask God for his grace so that he and his friends may not perish with Babylon's sages: *dî lā' y*[e]*hoḇ*[e]*ḏûn dāniyye'l w*[e]*ḥaḇrôhî 'im š*[e]*'ār ḥakkîmê ḇāḇel* (Dnl. 2:18). Accordingly, Daniel responds to Arioch, the king's chief bodyguard: *l*[e]*ḥakkîmê ḇāḇel 'al t*[e]*hôḇeḏ* "Do not destroy the sages of Babylon" (Dnl. 2:24).

The sole instance of the hophal occurs in Dnl. 7:11 in the context of the vision of the fourth animal: *ḥāzeh h*[a]*wêṯ 'aḏ dî q*[e]*ṭîlaṯ ḥêwṯā' w*[e]*hûḇaḏ gišmah wîhîḇaṯ lîqeḏaṯ 'eššā'* "and I looked until the animal was killed and its body destroyed and given over to the flaming fire."

---

10. *KAI* 279.2.
11. *KAI* 226.10.
12. *BMAP* 7.25.
13. Cf. *TADAE* C1.2 v. II 21.
14. • If, however, one follows the traditional understanding of the passage, which LXX already presupposes, it is the gods, who did not create heaven and earth, who should perish. (*Ko.*) •

• Accordingly, then, the explanation of the vision (Dnl. 7:26) says the last king of the fourth empire, symbolized by the fourth animal, will be deprived of power in the judgment so that his dominion will be thoroughly annihilated (*lᵉhašmādāh ûlᵉhôḇādāh*). (*Ko.*) •

IV. Qumran. Various forms of the root *'bd* also appear in the literature from Qumran. A certain case of *y'bdwn* occurs in *wy'bdwn mn k*[*sl'*] "and they will perish because of [folly]" (11Q10 27:7 [Job 36:12]). Here, *wy'bdwn* renders the *wygw'w* of the Hebrew text.

Meanwhile, West Aramaic clearly employs the root *'bd* consistently with the meaning "to decay, to perish" in the G-stem and "to destroy, to annihilate" in the C-stem.

Freedman/Yu

The Enoch literature from Qumran also describes the demise of the giants produced by the angel marriages in the grand last judgment with *'bd*: *ybdwn bnyhwn* "their sons will perish" (4Q202 4:10 [1 En. 10:12]) and *'dyn y'bdwn lkw*[*l 'lmyn*] "then they will perish for all [eternity]" (4Q204 5:2 [1 En. 10:14]). This context probably also includes 4Q532 2:8, where *'bd wmyt* should be translated "he perished and died." Similarly, according to 4Q212 2:21 (1 En. 91:19), anyone who does injustice perishes irretrievably: *'bd lswp 'bdn'*. This corresponds to the use of *ybdh* in 6Q14 1:5 in the context of a proclamation of universal destruction (the flood?).

In 4Q550a, an account set in the time of Darius, *'bd* appears, but the context is not apocalyptic, unlike the previously mentioned passages. Line 2 offers the statement that a person's good name, i.e., one's reputation (→ שֵׁם *šem*), will not perish: *wl' ybd smh ṭb'*. This statement compares to a saying of Hillel in Midr. *'Abot*: *ngd šm' 'bd šm'* "The reputation spreads, the reputation perishes!"

V. *'bdn* "Destruction, Ruin." The nominal form *'bdn*, which should be vocalized *'abdān* according to the Syriac,[15] first occurs in the Qumran texts where, corresponding to the West Aramaic dialects, it consistently means "perdition, destruction." It occurs especially in the same contexts that also employ the verbal form *'bd*. Thus, one awaits the destruction of the sons of the angels in a "war of destruction" (*qrb 'bdn*, 4Q202 4:6 [1 En. 10:9]) or by a "[sword] of destruction" ([*ḥrb*] *'bdn*, 4Q204 6:17 [1 En. 14:6]).[16]

The passage concerning the destruction of evildoers already mentioned above, 4Q212 2:21 (1 En. 91:19), links *'bdn* directly with *'bd*; cf. also the "[year]s of your destruction" ([*šn*]*y 'bdnkn*), with which 4Q201 2:15 (1 En. 5:5) threatens the evildoers, as well as 4Q548 1:[4,]14; 2:1:12. The use of *'bdn* in 1 QapGen ar 12:17 refers to the destruction of the earth by the flood. Whether *'bdn*['] in 4Q203 8:12 intends the destruction of the angels who had intercourse with human daughters or rather

---

15. On the Judeo-Aramaic vocalization *'ô/obdān*, which is also attested, cf. *ATTM*, 504.

16. Cf. also *l'bd*[*n'*] as a designation for the destruction of the sons of the angels in the same context, 4Q202 6:8, and the likely emendation [*l'bd*]*n*, 4Q202 4:10 (1 En. 10:9).

the perdition that they thereby brought upon the world, cannot be determined with confidence.[17]

As an Aramaic loanword (as the ending *-ān* instead of *-ôn* already indicates), *'aḇdān* occurs along with *ḥereḇ* and *hereḡ* in Est. 9:5 in the description of the destruction of the enemies of the Jews. In contrast, in 11Q10 18:5 *'bdwn* directly renders the Hebrew *'aḇaddôn* (Job 31:12), which *DSSStE*, 1191f. correctly understands as a Hebrew loanword indicating the realm of the dead.

VI. *šmd*. In Dnl. 7:26, *lehašmāḏāh ûlehôḇāḏāh* joins *'bd* haphel with *šmd* haphel in a hendiadys, which, as the continuation *'aḏ sôpā'* "to the end" indicates, intends a statement of complete destruction. The object of the destruction is the "fourth horn," the symbol of Antiochus IV in the vision of Dnl. 7. This statement, intensified in this manner, impressively marks the final fate of the foreign realm hostile to God, which then introduces the eternal kingdom of the "people of the saints of the Most High" (v. 27).

This oldest instance of *šmd* in an Aramaic text employs the root entirely in the semantic realm of the Hebrew *šmd* hiphil "to eradicate, to remove." The analogy of *šmd* and *'bd* "to perish" in the OT becomes especially clear in that these two roots frequently appear together.[18] One should note here, especially, the similarly combination of *šmd* and *'bd* in Dt. 28:20,63.

The absence of *šmd* in the older Aramaic dialects (including Qumran) indicates that it is a Hebrew loanword.

The root, attested in prerabbinic times only in Hebrew, underwent a distinct development of meaning in rabbinic literature. Alongside the inherited meaning for *šmd* hiphil "to destroy, to eradicate," the piel, in particular, means "to force someone into apostasy," which is probably denominated from the noun *šemāḏ* "religious persecution." This derives, on the one hand, from the fact that Esther often designates the persecution by Haman with *šmd* hiphil (cf. Est. 3:6,13; 4:8; 7:4; 8:11), and, on the other, from the historical experience that the many persecutions had as their objective the eradication of Judaism through a powerful compulsion to apostasy. Jewish Aramaic then adopted *šmd* in this meaning. Since, from another perspective, the "eradication" of an apostate from his or her own people (cf. Ezk. 14:9) was tied to a curse or a ban (Dt. 28 already suggests this connection; cf. esp. v. 20), the noun *šammatt*,[19] which designates excommunication and then the ban generally, could also develop here. Then *šmt* "to excommunicate" and "to ban, to curse" derived from it. Finally, Jewish Aramaic then lent *šmd* to Syriac,[20] as well as *šmd* and *šmt* to Mandean.

Kottsieper

17. So *DSSStE,* 410f.; cf. the parallel statement *ḥbl' dy ḥbltwn bh* in 1:11.
18. Lohfink, 179.
19. *DJBA* 1163.
20. Cf. F. Schultheß, "Aramäisches," *ZA* 19 (1905/6), 132f.

אֶבֶן *ʾbn ʾeḇen*

I. Occurrences and General Usage. II. Biblical Usage. III. Qumran.

I. Occurrences and General Usage. “All Semitic languages with the exception of Arabic attest the root אֶבֶן for ‘rock.’”[1] Aramaic attests the feminine *qaṭl*-segholate in the singular absolute, construct, and determined, and in the plural construct, determined, and with suffix.

The word *ʾbn* denotes (1) an individual rock: “. . . he should smash him with a rock”;[2] (2) stone as a worked or rough material: “columns of stone,”[3] “*nʿbṣn* (supports?, inlaid work?) of stone,”[4] “gates of stone,”[5] “blocks hewn from stone,”[6] “*kpn* (vessels?) of stone,”[7] and “stones” as the construction material in sales contracts from Naḥal Ḥever;[8] (3) stone in the function of weights: *bʾbny mlkyʾ*,[9] [*bʾ*]*bny ptḥ*,[10] as a possible reading *ʾbny nbṭw* “Nabatean weight stone” and on a stone from Deir ʿAlla *ʾbn šrʿʾ*;[11] (4) a grave or memorial stone, a votive stele;[12] (5) a precious stone *ʾbnṣrp*;[13] (6) a stone in a figurative usage (“dumb as a rock”),[14] and, possibly, a ruler (“. . . and killed the stone of perdition [*ʾbn šḥt*] from the house of his father”).[15]

II. Biblical Usage. In ch. 2 of the book of Daniel, the dream of Nebuchadnezzar's statue of gold, silver, bronze, iron, and clay, *ʾeḇen* is the stone that breaks off the mountain with no human assistance, topples, and thus destroys, the statue. The stone itself then became a great mountain and filled the whole earth (Dnl. 2:34,35,45). The materials of the statue symbolize the Neo-Babylonian, Median, Persian, and Greek Empires in sequence through their destruction, the stone the eternal kingdom of God that makes an end of

---

A. Caquot and A. Lemaire, “Les Textes Araméens de Deir ʿAlla,” *Syr* 54 (1977) 189-208; J. Hoftijzer and K. van der Kooij, *Aramaic Texts from Deir ʿAlla. DMOA* 19 (1976); A. S. Kapelrud, “אֶבֶן *ʾebhen*,” *TDOT*, I, 48-51; M. L. Klein, *Genizah Manuscripts of Palestinian Targum to the Pentateuch I* (Cincinnati, 1986); J. A. Montgomery, “Notes on Early Aramaic Inscriptions,” *JAOS* 54 (1934) 421-25.

1. Kapelrud, 48.
2. *KAI* 214.31 (2×).
3. *AP* 30.9; [31.8].
4. *AP* 15.16; cf. *BMAP* 7.18.
5. *AP* 30.9f.
6. *AP* 30.10; 31.9.
7. *BMAP* 7.19.
8. See nV 45.7; 47.3; 81.4; cf. *ATTM*, 320; *ATTM.E*, 188,194; for the Phoenician and Punic examples, cf. *DNSI*, 6.
9. *AP* 5.7; 6.14; 8.14,21; 9.15; 10.4; 14.10; 15.5,6,9,10,14,34,36; [20.15]; 25.16; 43.3; 46.10; *BMAP* 3.6; 4.15,21; 5.8,15; 7.16,32; 9.20; 10.11,14; 12.30.
10. *AP* 11.2; in nV 22.33 (*ATTM.E*, 18; Nabatean).
11. Hoftijzer-van der Kooij, 267, tab. 19b; compare to Caquot-Lemaire, 190: “weight stone from *šrʿʾ*.”
12. For the Phoenician and Punic occurrences, cf. *DNSI*, 6.
13. *AP* 38.3; cf. *DNSI*, 976.
14. Tg. Neofiti and the Palestinian fragmentary Targum W on Ex. 15:16; Klein, 250f.
15. *KAI* 215.7; cf. *DNSI*, 7; contra Montgomery, 423: *bn* “son” with a prosthetic ʾ.

them and replaces them. In addition to idols of gold, silver, bronze, iron, and wood, Dnl. 5:4:23 mentions those of "stone." According to Dnl. 6:18, a stone closes the opening of the lion's den into which Daniel is thrown. Ezr. 5:8; 6:4 mentions *ʾbn gll* "ashlar rock" among the construction materials for the temple.

III. Qumran. Aramaic manuscripts from Qumran often mention stones. Although Qumran transmits all of these texts, all of them originated in pre-Qumran times. The Prayer of Nabonidus (4Q242 1–3:8) mentions "gods of stone" to whom Nabonidus prayed to no avail for seven years. In an uncertain context, the Testament of Qahat (4Q542 3 2:11) mentions stones that become heavy (burdens?). An altar of stone appears in the Visions of Amram (4Q547 2:2): ʾ]*mrt lkh ʿl mdb*[*ḥh*(?)]*dy ʾbny*[ʾ (or *ʾbn*ʾ[; cf. *ATTM.E,* 91: R 7:42). In the Tg. Job (11Q10), a "cornerstone" appears (11Q10 30,4 *ʾbn ḥzyth*; cf. Job 38:6); furthermore, water encrusted with ice becomes "hard as a rock" (11Q10 31,7; cf. Job 38:30), and a heart can be compared to a stone (11Q10 36:9; cf. Job 41:16). The Aramaic version of Tobit (4Q196 18:9) mentions stones whose nature and function can no longer be deduced from the preserved context; this passage in the LXX (Tob. 13:17) describes the streets of the future Jerusalem as paved with rubies and stones of Ophir. Similarly, the depiction of the New Jerusalem describes the streets of the holy city as paved with "white stones" (*ʾbn ḥwr*; 5Q15 1 1:6), which also compose the walls (2Q24 8:3), and the city gates are also of stone (5Q15 1 1:9). One reads in 11Q18 18:2:].*y wʿlyʾ šbʿʾ dwdyn tpyn ʿl ʾbny*[". . . and above it seven pots for cooking plated (?) also of stone." Two additional instances appear in an uncertain context in Fragment 10 1:5:] ʾ?*bn kwl ʾbnyhwn* and in Fragment 32 added above line 7:]*wyd*? *ʾbn dmʾ w*?[.

Steudel/Maurer

אֶדְרָע *ʾdrʿ ʾeḏrāʿ* → יַד *yd yaḏ*

אזד *ʾzd* /ʾazd/

I. Etymology and Lexical Field. II. Usage.

I. Etymology and Lexical Field. Traditional etymologies trace /ʾazd/ in Aramaic to an Old Persian adjective **azdā* "known."[1] Imperial Aramaic employs it as a noun "investi-

P. Huyse, "Quelques remarques sur deux mots iraniens," *SIr* 17 (1998) 31-40; J. Naveh and S. Shaked, *Aramaic Documents from Ancient Bactria (Fourth Century* B.C.E.*)* (London, 2012); J. Tavernier, *Iranica in the Achaemenid Period (ca. 550-330* B.C.*). OLA* 158 (2007).

1. See Huyse; Tavernier, 411, §4.4.4.2; older literature in *DNSI*, 25.

gation," in Daniel with the function of an adjective "known" or "established." In the first sense, it has affinities with the Gt-stem of → *šʾl* "to be heard," in the second with *yṣyb*.[2]

II. Usage. All three Imperial Aramaic instances seem to employ *ʾzd* as the object of the verb *ʿbd* "to make."[3] Because of the reference to *dyny*ʾ "judges"[4] and *typty*ʾ "police officers," *TADAE* A4.5:8 relates to a legal investigation (after the destruction of a well), which may also be assumed for the legal record in *TADAE* B8.11:4. In Naveh and Shaked, B1.3, however, to the extent that the preserved context provides clues, it seems to involve a communication and *TADAE* A4.5:9 probably mentions in the continuation an official report.[5] Dnl. 2:5,8 utilizes the term as a predicate of *mlh*[6] in the sense of the king's established decision. Meanwhile, *ʾzd* could indicate a communication so that various meanings need not necessarily be assumed for the various passages.

Gzella

2. → *yṣb*.

3. Clearly so in *TADAE* A4.5:8 and B8.11:4, consequently, the verb in Naveh and Shaked, B1.3 should probably be reconstructed as *tʿb*]*d*.

4. → *dyn*.

5. If the verb at the beginning of the line should, in fact, be reconstructed as *yty*[*d*ʿ].

6. → *mll*.

אזל *ʾzl* → הלך *hlk*

אָח *ʾḥ ʾaḥ*; אחה *ʾḥh ʾaḥā*

I. Lexeme. II. A Term of Relationship. III. Figurative Usage. IV. As a Divine Designation. V. *ʾḥh* "Sister." VI. Regarding the Relationship among Siblings.

R. Contini, "Fictive Use of the Kinship Terms 'Brother' and 'Sister'" *Solving Riddles and Untying Knots. FS J. C. Greenfield* (Winona Lake, IN, 1995), 60-64; K. Dijkstra, *Life and Loyalty. RGRW* 128 (1995), 315-18; E. Jenni, "אָח *ʾāḥ* brother," *TLOT*, 73-77; I. Kottsieper, "'We Have a Little Sister': Aspects of the Brother-Sister Relationship in Ancient Israel," in J. W. van Henten and A. Brenner, eds., *Families and Family Relations. STAR* 2 (2000), 49-80; W. Kornfeld, *Onomastica aramaica aus Ägypten. SÖAW.PH* 333 (1978); M. Maraqten, *Die semitischen Personennamen in den alt- und reichsaramäischen Inschriften aus Vorderasien, TStO* 5 (1988); H. Ringgren, "אָח ʾāch," *TDOT*, I, 188-93; R. C. Steiner and C. F. Nims, "Ashurbanipal and Shamash-shum-ukin," *RB* 92 (1985) 60-81; S. Vleeming and J. W. Wesselius, *Studies in Papyrus Amherst 63 I* (Amsterdam, 1985); R. Zadok, *On West Semites in Babylonia During the Chaldean and Achaemenian Periods: An Onomastic Study* (Jerusalem, ²1978).

I. Lexeme. The common Semitic *'aḫ* "brother" (with -*ū*- before singular suffixes beginning with a consonant)—with the derivative *'aḫāt* "sister" (pl. *'aḫawāt*)—became *'aḥ* around 200 B.C.E.[1]

II. A Term of Relationship. The word denotes the biological sons of the same man, although they need not have the same mother;[2] in T. Levi, etc., it is used of the twelve sons of Jacob;[3] the plural of the "siblings."[4] In addition, it may also occur in reference to the "cousin,"[5] yet "my brother" there is apparently addressed to the husband, just as, conversely, "my sister" in 4Q197 4 1:3 clearly means the wife;[6] in contrast, the designation "son of the uncle" occurs correctly.[7] Finally, "brother" can refer to the nephew,[8] for which, otherwise, the correct "son of one's brother" appears.[9]

With a subsequent *z'r* "small," it means "younger/youngest brother."[10]

III. Figurative Usage. The figurative meaning "member of the same tribe/nation, compatriot" is frequent.[11] The address "my brother!" appears frequently,[12] and "my brother" between Tobias and the angel.[13]

Through circumcision, foreigners become members of Israel,[14] yet the sage is never a foreigner.[15] The pious invite the needy and compatriots passing through.[16] Jews from Palestine and the diaspora follow the Jewish calendar.[17]

The meaning "(professional) colleague" occurs only in the addresses of letters from the seventh through fifth centuries B.C.E., in which "my brother" or "my brothers/sisters" always accompanies the name(s) of the recipient(s) and "your brother" the name of the

---

1. Cf. *ATTM,* 102.
2. Midr. *Ketub.* 4:10; cf. *ATTM,* 325.
3. E.g., CT. Levi Bodleian a:21 (T. Levi 33:22; *DSSStE,* 50f.); Cambridge d:3 (T. Levi 42:3; *DSSStE,* 54f.); 4Q213a 2:5 (T. Levi 48:5; *DSSStE,* 450f.); 4Q541 24 2:5 (T. Levi 2 5:5; *DSSStE,* 1080f.)
4. *LexSyr,* 10b.
5. 1 QapGen. ar 2:9 "my brother and lord"; 2:13 "my lord and brother"; cf. *DSSStE,* 28f.
6. Tob. 5:22; *DSSStE,* 388f.
7. E.g., in the Testament of Amram 2:1 (4Q545 1 2:14; *DSSStE,* 1090f.).
8. Babylonian Tg, Gen. 14:14,16 = the Heb. text.
9. E.g., 1 QapGen. ar 20:11,34; 21:7; 22:3,5,11.
10. 4Q545 1 1:5 = Testament of Amram 1:5; *DSSStE,* 1088f.
11. Outside T. Levi only forms with suffixes: Ezr. 7:18; 11Q18 15:3 (Heavenly Jerusalem 7:20; *DSSStE,* 1222f.); CT. Levi Cambridge a:19,23 (T. Levi 21:20; 22:1; *ATTM,* 195; *DSSStE,* 50f.); Cambridge f:7 (T. Levi 44:7; *ATTM,* 206f.); 4Q196 2:12 (Tob. 2:2; *DSSStE,* 384f.); 4Q196 14 2:5 = 4Q197 4 3:3 (Tob. 7:1; *DSSStE,* 386f.); missives from Rabbi Gamaliel II xyNG 1-3 (*ATTM,* 359).
12. 4Q196 14 2:5,8 = 4Q197 4 3:5 (Tob. 7:1,3; *DSSStE,* 386f.,392f.); letter of Kosiba ySK 11:2 (*ATTM.E,* 215).
13. 4Q197 4 1:12,16; 2:7,13 = 4Q196 14 1:9 (Tob. 6:7,11,14,16; *DSSStE,* 390f.); 4Q197 4 3:2,12 = 4Q196 14 2:5 (Tob. 7:1,9; *ATTM.E,* 142f.; *DSSStE* 386f.); 4Q197 5:9 (Tob. 9:2; *DSSStE,* 392f.).
14. CT. Levi Cambridge a 20,23 (T. Levi 21:20; 22:1; *ATTM,* 195; *DSSStE,* 50f.).
15. CT. Levi Cambridge a 7-12 + 1Q213 1 1:15-18 (T. Levi 44:7-12; *ATTM,* 206f. + *DSSStE,* 446).
16. 4Q196 2:12 (Tob. 2:2; *DSSStE,* 384f.); 14 2:7 = 4Q197 4 3:4 (Tob. 7:1; *DSSStE,* 386f., 392f.).
17. Missive of Rabbi Gamaliel II xyNG 1-3 (*ATTM,* 359).

sender,[18] even if it involves father and son,[19] mother and son,[20] and perhaps, indeed, under Egyptian influence, a married couple.[21]

In Nabatea, the prime minister carries the title "brother of the king" (from Milet)[22] or "brother of the regent" (from Petra),[23] as the geographer Strabo XVI 4:21 confirms.

IV. As a Divine Designation. As a divine designation, "brother" appears almost solely in cuneiform Aramaic personal names such as "(my) brother is (my) light/help/wall."[24] In addition to a divine designation, "(my) brother" is tantamount to "(the deity) is (my) patron deity,"[25] but otherwise also the biological brother as in the frequent name "(wholly) the brother of the father/mother!"[26]

V. *ʾḥh* "Sister." *ʾḥh* "sister," which does not occur in Biblical Aramaic, usually denotes the biological full or half-sister by the same father, rarely also relatives (to the sixth degree)[27] or the wife,[28] in the address of letters also the mother,[29] perhaps even the wife.[30] The frequent formulation "brother or sister" in the private contracts from Egypt demonstrates that here husband and wife had equal rights—which can be traced to Egyptian influence.[31] Nabatean designates the queen as "sister of the king."[32]

According to *KAI* 264 (circa 100 B.C.E.), in Arebsun/Cappadocia, the sister of the god Bēl is also his consort. In clearly Aramaic personal names, in contrast, it apparently always means the biological sister.[33]

Beyer

VI. Regarding the Relationship among Siblings. Frequently encountered, the figurative use of *ʾḥ* demonstrates the connotation of a connection between two people marked by togetherness and mutual responsibility. Accordingly, the literature manifests the motif that siblings vouch for one another or that the behavior of one also affects the situation of the other. Thus, the literary portrayal of Shamash-shum-ukin rising up against his brother

18. *KAI* 233; *AP* 21.1f.; 40.5; *RES* 1300.1f.
19. Padua 1.14.
20. Hermopolis 7.1,5.
21. Hermopolis 2.1; 4.1f.
22. *RÉS* 675.1.
23. *CIS* 2 351.1f.
24. Zadok, 54f.; Maraqten, 122-24; *PNPI*, 66.
25. Maraqten, 120-22; *PNPI*, 66f.
26. Zadok, 54; Maraqten, 118f.; Kornfeld 39; *ATTM*, 507.
27. 4Q197 4 3:13 (Tob. 7:9; *DSSStE*, 392f.).
28. 4Q197 4 2:19 (Tob. 6:19; *DSSStE*, 392f.); as address 4Q197 4 1:3 (Tob. 5:22; *DSSStE*, 388f.); cf. Abram's excuse in 1QapGen 20:27 = Gen. 12:19; 20:5.
29. Hermopolis 7.5.
30. Hermopolis 2.1; 4.1; cf. above.
31. *AP* 1.5, etc.; fifth century B.C.E.
32. *CIS* II 354.3, etc.
33. Maraqten, 124; *PNPI*, 67a.

Assurbanipal in Pap. Amherst 63 18-23 introduces the historically unsubstantiated motif that Assurbanipal tasked his sister with mediating between the brothers in the conflict.[34] In analogy to the notion that the behavior of the individual also affects the reputation of one's predecessors and descendants (→ אב *ʼaḇ* VI), 4Q213a 2:5 states that the incorrigible behavior of a woman damages the reputation of her brother.

Kottsieper

---

34. 19:15-21:13; cf. Vleeming-Wesselius, 34-36; Steiner-Nims, 73-76; cf. also Kottsieper, esp. 75-77.

אֲחִידָה *ʼḥydh ʼaḥîḏā*; אוחידו *ʼwḥydw*

I. Etymology. II. Biblical Aramaic. III. Qumran. IV. Palmyra.

I. Etymology. Following P. de Lagarde, who wanted to trace the Hebrew lexeme *ḥîḏāh* as a loanword to Aramaic *ªḥîḏāh*,[1] E. Kautzsch has suggested deriving *ʼªḥîḏāh* from the root *ʼḥd* (Semit. *ʼḫḏ*) "to take (into possession), to seize"[2] and presupposing a special meaning "to act, to close," as attested for the Hebrew *weʼāḥôz* in reference to city walls in Neh. 7:3 (2 MSS) and by Aramaic *pmy lʼ tʼḥz mn mln* in the Nerab Inscription (seventh century B.C.E.)[3] in reference to the mouth and its words;[4] *ʼªḥîḏāh* "riddle" would have then arisen metaphorically from a meaning "sealed."

In contrast, the Akkadian *aḫāzu* in the specialized meaning of the C-stem "to teach"[5] with the verbal noun *iḫzu* "teaching" is comparable;[6] in view of the former, G. Rinaldi wanted to explain *ʼªḥîḏāh* in the sense of *apprehendendum*. Accordingly, *ʼªḥîḏāh* would be a *qaṭīl*-form (peal pass. ptcp.) with a feminine ending. Morphologically similar derivatives of the same root would be *ʼ]ḥydyn* "captives"[7] and the pl.

V. Hamp, "חִידָה *chîdhāh*," *TDOT*, IV, 320-23; H.-P. Muller, "Der Begriff 'Rätsel' im AT," *VT* 20 (1970) 465-89); G. Rinaldi, "Alcuni termini ebraici relativi alia letteratura," *Bibl* 40 (1959) 274-276; M. Wagner, *Die lexikalischen und grammatikalischen Aramaismen im alttestamentlichen Hebräisch. BZAW* 96 (1966), 55f.

1. *Anmerkungen zur griechischen Übersetzung der Proverbien* (Leipzig, 1863), 73.
2. *Die Aramaismen im AT* (Halle, 1902), 30f.
3. *KAI* 226.4.
4. cf. *KBL*³, 1663.
5. *AHw*, I, 53; *CAD*, I/1, 177.
6. *GesB*¹⁸, 343: *ḥîḏāh.*
7. 11Q10 37:2 (Job 36:8).

const. *'ḥdy*, if, as is likely, *'ḥdy pmk* Aḥiqar 99 is to be translated "underhandedness of your mouth."[8]

First, the unlikely loss of *'a-* in the transition from Aramaic to Hebrew speaks against the suggestions of de Lagarde and Kautzsch; to the contrary, Hebrew *'eḥāḏ* "one" corresponds to Aramaic *ḥaḏ* (→ to count), Hebrew *'āḥôṯ* "sister" to Syriac *ḥāṯā*, etc.[9] Additionally, the semantic paths either from a meaning "to close (concretely)" or from a causative *aḫazu* Š-stem "to teach" and perhaps *iḫzu* "teaching" are both relatively broad; both "to teach" and "teaching" have no NW Semitic correspondence to *'ḥz*, especially since, as far as I know, *'ḥz* (*'ḫḏ*) does not occur here in the C-stem.

Instead of *'ḥd*, *'aḥîḏāh* may also be derived from a possible verb of speech **ḫīd*, which Akkadian attests as *ḫiādu* G-stem "to pronounce," Gt-stem "to speak out,"[10] and *ḫittu* II "statement,"[11] although admittedly only sparsely, but which may recur in the rare Arabic *ḫāta* (*i/u*), which according to Lane, 828c (820a.b) means "to produce a sound (of a bird with its wings)," with the derivative *ḫawāt*^{un} for the pertinent sound, etc. *'aḥîḏāh* would then be an action noun with a preformative /*'a-*/ and a feminine ending, a form relatively frequent also in Jewish Aramaic;[12] the form is comparable to the Akkadian masc. nouns of action on the pattern *ipris* such as *ikribu*(*m*) "prayer" or *išdiḫu*(*m*) "gain," and perhaps to a feminine on the *iprist* pattern such as *irnintum* → *irnittum* "objective."[13] Semantically, *'aḥîḏāh* "riddle" is easier to derive from a verb of speech if one assumes a specification of this meaning than from *'ḥd*. In any case, the metaphorical use of *'ḥd* "to close" or a causative use such as with *aḫāzu* Š "to teach" would have to be presupposed, both of which cease to be factors in the etymology suggested here.

Hebrew *ḥîdāh* is a substantivized inf. on the *qīlā* pattern like *bînāh* "insight," *qînāh* "lament," etc.; as such, *ḥîdāh* is a free allomorph of *'aḥîdāh* and, thus, not directly traceable to *'aḥîdāh*. The *ḥwd* encountered only in paranomastic combination with the object *ḥîdāh* (*ḥwd ḥîdāh* "to forfeit a riddle" Jgs. 14:12f.,16; Ezk. 17:2) is denominative. The character of the formation as a hollow root survives; the more common /*-ū-*/ replaces the internal vowel /*-ī-*/ because of the pressure toward systemization.

GesTh, I, 450, *BDB*, König 6/7, and G. Garbini[14] also wanted to derive *ḥîdāh* from a hollow root on the basis *ḥd*, *ḥḏ*, or the like.

II. Biblical Aramaic. The sole assured Biblical Aramaic occurrence of *'aḥîḏāh* is in Dnl. 5:12; it attributes Daniel with the capacity *'aḥ^{a}wāyaṯ 'aḥîdān* "to proclaim riddles," i.e., to solve them; the idea is of the enigmatic, i.e., mysteriously encrypted oracle mentioned earlier, the *mene tekel* written on the wall by a spectral finder. In this regard, the context presupposes the relationship of such mantic art to the dream interpretation and

8. Similarly, I. Kottsieper, *TUAT*, III/2, 336; contra Hamp, 870; J. M. Lindenberger, *The Aramaic Proverbs of Aḥiqar*. *JHNES* (1983), 77, who also think of "riddle" here, cf. *DNSI*, 32.

9. Cf. Müller, 484.

10. *AHw*, I, 342b; *CAD*, VI, 28a.

11. *AHw*, I, 350a; *CAD*, VI, 208b.

12. Citation in Müller, 485f., n. 7.

13. *GaG*^{3} §56a.

14. *Il Semitico di Nord-Ouest* (Naples, 1960), 195.

the "untying of magical knots (*qiṭrîn*)," although the action requires neither of the latter two; apparently, there is some phraseological relationship.

The fact that the oracle, like the dread and some apocalyptic visions of the future, encrypts the reality anticipated in a prediction is grounded, first, generally in the fact that, in view of the deterioration of the world in the latter times, everything tends to recede into the inaccessibility of mystery, as occurred in the two other metaphysical myths of the mantic sage Daniel, chs. 2 and 4f.[15] and in Dnl. 7–12.[16] The same rush of pessimism and skepticism brings a return to the archaic, as also occurs in the jargon of esoteric groups.[17] Various persons and things, assigned the same predicates, have a similar magical substance according to an archaic understanding of reality; the mantic sage can identify such persons and things and thus link the ciphers of dream, oracle, etc. with their counterparts in reality.[18]

If Daniel has such capacities, that is, he can "announce the mystery" (2:27), he merits the wages of the clever solver of puzzles;[19] socially disadvantaged groups in the Jewish diaspora in Babylon, in which stories like Dnl. (2,) 3–6 originally circulated, could identify with him and his social ascent to their compensatory satisfaction.

One also thinks of an enigmatic oracle with regard to the preceding apocalyptic statement of an angel in Dnl. 12:7 if one presupposes in 12:8bβ following the LXX καὶ τίνος αἱ παραβολαὶ αὗται the Hebrew *māh ᵓᵃḥîḏôṯ ᵓelleh* "what are (mean) these riddles?"[20] instead of the less meaningful Masoretic *māh ᵓaḥᵃrîṯ ᵓelleh* "what is the last (the outcome) of this?"[21] The preceding clause in the LXX is a competing interpretation of the phrase in the form of a paraphrase close to the MT. As a response, the cited phrase following the LXX promises the pseudepigraphical Daniel that the *hammaśkîlîm*, i.e., the apocalyptic "sages" at the time of the composition of the book of Daniel, will understand the words that "will remain hidden and sealed until the end time" (v. 9f.).

If Montgomery's retroversion is correct, Dnl. 12:8 provides the sole instance of *ᵓᵃḥîḏāh* in a Hebrew text; Dnl. 5:12 could certainly have influenced it. In contrast, *ḥîḏôṯ* appears in Dnl. 8:23.

III. Qumran. Attested twice in the fragmentary Aramaic version of T. Levi II, *ᵓwḥydw* also involves the nominal derivation of a verb of speech. The lexeme appears both times as an adverb modifying *mll* "to speak" (→ מלל *mll*): 4Q541 1+2:I:7 *m*]*llt ʿlwhy bᵓwḥydwᵓn* "and I spoke to them through. . . ."; 4Q541 2 2+3+4:1+5:6 *wmmll ᵓwḥydwᵓn* "and spoke. . . ." The text, copied around 100 B.C.E. although older, also permits one to

15. Cf. Müller, "Märchen, Legende und Enderwartung. Zum Verständnis des Buches Daniel," *VT* 26 (1976) 338-50.

16. Cf. Müller, "Mantische Weisheit und Apokalyptik," in P. A. H. Boer, ed., *Congress Volume Uppsala 1971. SVT* 22 (1972), 268-93.

17. Jolles, *Simple Forms*, trans. Peter J. Schwartz (London, 2017), 105,109ff.

18. Müller, 476f.

19. J. de Vries, *Die Märchen von klugen Rätsellösern* (Helsinki, 1928), 69ff., 84ff.

20. So J. A. Montgomery, *The Book of Daniel. ICC* 27 (^{2}1950), 478.

21. So, e.g., A. Bentzen, *Daniel. HAT* I/19 (1952), 86; O. Plöger, *Das Buch Daniel. KAT* 18 (1965), 169f.

think of "riddles" here;[22] the component ⟨-w-⟩ /-û-/ < */-ût-/ and the plural morpheme ⟨- 'n⟩ /-ān/ indicate feminine gender. The form has counterparts in Jewish Aramaic *'ûḥadṯā'* and Syriac *'ûḥdᵉṯā' 'ûhaḏtā'*, both "riddles," with by-forms.

IV. Palmyra. The Greco-Palmyrene diglot Inv X 115 attests *'ḥydw* in the meaning "matter" in the phrase *dy špr bkl 'ḥydw klh lmdynth* "who did the right thing in every matter for his city."[23] If πᾶσας λειτουργίας in the Greek paraphrase corresponds to *bkl 'ḥydw*; it may point to a connotation "matter" → "service."[24] The fact that a metonymy "riddle" → "matter" has an analogy in a similar shift of meaning for the Hebrew *dāḇār*, Aramaic *millāh*, Akkadian *awātu(m)*, etc. "word" → "matter" supports the derivation of *'ᵃḥîḏāh* et al from a verb of speech **ḥīd* (→ מלל *mll*).

Müller

22. Cf. *DSS*, 1079 (bib.).
23. D. R. Hillers and E. Cussini, *Palmyrene Aramaic Texts* (Baltimore, 1996), 208, cf. 337.
24. For similar Palmyrene expressions, cf. *DNSI*, 1184; regarding Inv X 115, J. Starcky, *Inventaire des inscriptions de Palmyre*, fasc. X (Damascus, 1949), 38 (bib.).

אַחֲרִי *'ḥry 'aḥᵃrî*; אַחַר *'ḥr 'aḥar*; אָחֳרָן *'ḥrn 'ŏḥᵒrān*; אחרין *'ḥryn*

I. Distribution and Etymology. II. Older Aramaic. III. Biblical Aramaic. IV. Qumran.

I. Distribution and Etymology. These words appear in the Bible only in the book of Daniel: *'aḥᵃrê* (pl. const. of *'aḥar*) "after" occurs twice (Dnl. 2:29,45), *'aḥᵃrî* "end" once (Dnl. 2:28), *'ŏḥrān* (fem. *'ŏḥrī*) "other" eleven times, and the textually dubious *'ḥryn* once (Dnl. 4:5). With the substantive *'āḥôr* in the sense of "back side," "back regions," Hebrew has a closely related word. As a substantive, *'aḥar* appears in the Hebrew section of the OT once in *bᵉ'aḥᵃrê haḥᵃnîṯ* "with the end of the spear" (2 S. 2:23). In Hebrew, the verb *'ḥr* means "to delay, to remain behind." Related words also occur in Arabic, Akkadian, Palmyrene, Syriac, and Ugaritic. Hebrew and the other Aramaic dialects attest the construct *'aḥᵃrê* employed prepositionally.

Freedman/Yu

'aḥar: G. W. Buchanan, "Eschatology and the 'End of Days,'" *JNES* 20 (1961) 188-93; S. Erlandsson, "אַחֵר *'achēr*," *TDOT*, I, 201-3; F. J. Helfmeyer, "אַחֲרֵי *'achᵃrê*," *TDOT*, I, 204-7; H. Seebaß, "אַחֲרִית *'achᵃrîth*," *TDOT*, I, 207-12.

Aramaic *'ḥr* traces back to the common Semitic root *'ḫr*; presumably, the ground form is the noun **'aḫar*. It generally designates that which comes later in a sequence. This sequential aspect explains its temporal meaning, which is its exclusive use in some languages. Thus, Ugaritic *aḫr* occurs only temporally as an adverb "then," "thereafter," "later,"[1] a conjunction "after,"[2] or a preposition "after."[3] The derivatives of the nominal stem *aḫr-* (< *aḫar-*,)[4] also have temporal meanings in Akkadian.[5] The sequential aspect also accounts for the local meaning "behind," "following," which occurs alongside the temporal especially in Hebrew, Aramaic, Arabic, and modern Semitic languages.[6]

Especially within the younger central Semitic languages like Hebrew, Aramaic, and Arabic, the root then underwent an independent development of meaning and assumed the additional connotation of the "other." This is probably because whatever appears to be additional seems thereby to be other. The deciding factor, meanwhile, lies not in the different character of the other, but in its secondary character in relation to the original.

The fact that the meaning "other" is secondary is also evident in the fact that the verbal stem *'ḫr*, employed mostly in the D-stem, denominalized from the noun *'aḫar*, with the connotations "to remain/place/keep behind, to linger" in the various languages only reflects the original meaning (cf. esp. Akk., Ugar., OSA, Heb., Aram., and Arab.).

The root occurs in Aramaic chiefly in the older dialects. In the later phases of the language, *b'tr* displaced *'ḥr* especially in the adverbial and prepositional function.

Kottsieper

II. Older Aramaic. The Old Aramaic texts already attest derivatives of the root *'ḥr*. Thus, *'ḥr* (*kn*) appears in the Tell Fekheriye inscription l. 10 as an adverbial modifier in the sense of "later" and *'ḥrn* in the Sefire inscription as a substantive in the sense of "other" in the clause *wkzy ḥbzw 'lhn byt* [*'by h' h*]*wt l'ḥrn* "and when the gods smote the house [of my father,] then [it] belonged to another."[7]

Since a larger corpus is accessible, the texts of so-called Imperial Aramaic attest several derivatives of the root: *'ḥr*, *'ḥrh*, *'ḥry*, and *'ḥrn; 'ḥr* appears in *KAI* 260 B 3.6; 262 and 264.4. Thus, one interprets *'ḥr KAI* 260 B 3.6 as an adverbial particle rendering Lydian *akad*. It is a simple, untranslatable introductory or transitional particle indicating the resumption of an issue.[8] *KAI* 262 has *'ḥd*, to be sure, but it could be a scribal error for *'ḥr* since *d* and *r* are easily confused for one another because of their graphic similarity.

---

1. J. Tropper, *Ugaritische Grammatik. AOAT* 273 ([1]2000), 743; cf. also *aḫrm* "consecutively," ibid., 747.
2. Ibid., 796.
3. Ibid., 771.
4. Cf. *GaG* §12b.
5. Cf. esp. *aḫrâtu* "future" (*CAD*, I/1, 194), *aḫrītis/aḫrâtaš* "for the future."
6. Cf. *CDG*, 13.
7. *KAI* 224.24.
8. Cf. *KAI* II 307.

The Arebsun inscription exhibits a certain example, however; it occurs in the clause *'ḥr byl kn 'mr ldynmzdysnš* "the Bēl spoke to DYNMZDYSNŠ."[9]

With the meaning "descendants," *'ḥrh* appears in the Nerab inscription: *w'ḥrth t'bd* "and his descendants should perish."[10] It attests *'ḥrh* in the meaning "henceforth."[11]

• The formulation *wyh'bdw zr 'k* "and they [i.e., the gods] will annihilate his descendants,"[12] also attested at Nerab, suggests the interpretation of *w'ḥrth t'bd* as "and his descendants will perish." Both are not only components of the curse portion of the inscriptions, but each follows the announcement of the death of the addressee. The *'ḥrh*, therefore, is that which follows the addressees temporally. This concretization in the sense of "descendents" finds an additional parallel in Nabatean *'ḥr(h)*[13] and in other languages such as Ugaritic *uḫry*[14] or Hebrew *'aḥ^a^rît* (e.g., Ps. 109:13; Jer. 31:17, Dnl. 11:4). (*Ko.*) •

The expression *'yš 'ḥrn* "another man" appears in the Imperial Aramaic inscription from Bahadirh, Cilicia.[15] It corresponds with *gbr 'ḥrn* in the texts from Elephantine.[16]

The papyri from Elephantine offer many Imperial Aramaic instances of derivatives of *'ḥr*. They attest *'ḥr* as an adverb "then, thereupon" and with suffixes in the sense of "after" as well as *'ḥrn* in the sense of "other." Thus, e.g., *'ḥr* appears once in a certificate of debt as the introduction to the determination of what the debtor must do in the future repayment,[17] and four times with regard to the case in which the conditions go unfulfilled: *whn l' šlmt . . . 'ḥr 'nh 'nny 'ḥwb. . .* "And I do not repay . . . , then I, Anani, will be guilty. . . ."[18]

With a nominal complement, *'ḥr* appears in the stipulations of a contract in the description of a house by a man and his wife in the expression *'ḥr mwtky* "after your death."[19] It also appears a few lines later, however, in the variant *'ḥry mwty* "after my death."[20]

'ḥryk is attested in *wbnyk šlyṭn 'ḥryk* "and your children shall have control after you,"[21] among other expressions.[22]

The adj. *'ḥrn* "other" (fem. mostly *'ḥrh*) occurs with equally frequency in the Elephantine papyri.[23] In the expression *ymn 'ḥrnn* "other days," however, *'ḥrn* has the meaning "later, future" (cf. Aḥiqar 52, etc.). In addition, it also appears with the preposition *'d*: *'d 'ḥrn* "until another time."[24]

---

9. *KAI* 264.4.
10. *KAI* 226.10.
11. *KAI* 225.13; cf. also *l'ḥrh*, *KAI* 226.8.
12. *KAI* 225.11, → אבד *'bd* 2.
13. Cf., e.g., *Atlal* 7, 105.3; *CIS* II 197.2; 200.2; 201.3, etc.
14. *KTU* 1.103+1.145:39f.
15. *KAI* 278.8.
16. See below.
17. *BMAP* 11.3.
18. *BMAP* 11.5f.; cf. ll. 7,8,10.
19. *BMAP* 4.17f.
20. *BMAP* 4.21.
21. *BMAP* 12.23.
22. Cf. *BMAP* 3.16,19; 9.19,21, etc.
23. Cf. e.g., *gbr 'ḥrn* "another man" in *BMAP* 3.19; 4.19, etc.
24. *BMAP* 10.10.

An example of *'ḥrn'* as an adverb derived from *'ḥr* occurs in *BMAP* 4.19: *hmw šlyṭn bḥlqy 'ḥrn'* "afterward, they shall have control over my portion."[25]

Freedman/Yu

The prepositional *'ḥry*, frequently attested in Imperial Aramaic, occasionally exhibits a local meaning (cf. esp. Aḥiqar 63 *šlḥ 'ḥry* "to send after") in addition to its typical temporal meaning.[26] In the contracts of Machseya from Elephantine, furthermore, it occurs twice in the context of the statement that a document "regarding" land being transferred will be written for someone.[27] That a legal document does not constitute a legal action but attests to its conclusion probably explains this unusual use in the framework of legal language. Thus, the transfer of land precedes the preparation and delivery of the document. Consequently, it was written for the recipient "afterward."

Another special usage in the juristo-economic realm apparently exists in *AP* 38.10 (= *TADAE* A4.3:10): *]lw ḥsrn šgy' šym 'ḥrwhy bbyt 'nny* "If the loss is large, there is reimbursement/compensation for him in the house Anania."[28] Here the pl. of *'ḥr* probably designates that which takes the place of lost goods, and, thus, follows in this sense. The by-form *'ḥry* common in Jewish Palestinian Aramaic probably derives from this usage of *'ḥr(y)*,[29] which, always in combination with *'rb* "pledge," "security," also designates to this or that individual the alternative that secondarily replaces a loss.

Finally, as a verb *'ḥr* (pael) occurs in the meaning "to hesitate," "to tarry."[30]

Kottsieper

III. Biblical Aramaic. In Biblical Aramaic, *'aḥar* has the basic meaning "after." Thus, the expression *māh dî lehᵉwe' 'ᵃḥrê ḏenāh* "what will be after this/in the future," occurs twice in Dnl. 2:29, 45 (the typical expression for this, in contrast, is *bā'ṯar* as in *bā'ṯar dᵉnāh* [Dnl. 7:6,7], cf. 1.). Dnl. 7:24 employs *'aḥᵃrê* in the description of the king who, according to Daniel's vision, will appear after the first ten kings: *'aśrāh malḵîn yᵉqumûn wᵉ'ŏḥᵒrān yᵉqûm 'aḥᵃrêhôn* "ten kings will arise and another will arise after them."

In Biblical Aramaic, both *'ŏḥᵒrān* and *'ŏḥᵒrî* mean "another"; in addition, *'ŏḥᵒrî* occurs as the feminine form of *ŏḥᵒrān*. The Biblical Hebrew expression *'ᵉlohîm 'aḥᵃrîm* "other gods" also occurs in Aramaic, although in the singular: *kôl qᵒḇel dî lā' 'îṯay 'ᵉlāh 'ŏḥᵒrān dî yikkul lᵉhaṣṣālāh kiḏnāh* "since there is no other God who can deliver like this one" (Dnl. 3:29). In Daniel, *'ŏḥᵒrān/î* can also refer to nations, kings,[31] individual persons, kingdoms, and animals. Thus, e.g., Daniel's speech to Nebuchadnezzar says of the coming messianic kingdom *ûmalḵûṯāh lᵉ'am 'ŏḥᵒrān lā' tišṯᵉbiq* "and the kingdom

25. Contrast the interpretation in *TADAE* B3.5, however.
26. See above.
27. *AP* 9.4; 13.7.
28. On the reading and interpretation, cf. *TADAE*; for other suggestions, cf. *DNSI*, 1129, s.v. *šjm*₂.
29. cf. *ATTM,* 508; *ATTM.E,* 306.
30. *AAB* B.1.23:3f.; I. Kottsieper, "Der Mann aus Babylonien," *Or* NS 69 (2000) 383.
31. Dnl. 7:24; see above.

will not be relinquished to another people" (Dnl. 2:44). In Dnl. 2:11 and 5:17, *'ŏḥºrān* means "another" human being.

In Dnl. 2:39, *malkû 'ŏḥºrî* refers twice to the two "other" kingdoms that will arise after the Babylonian. In 7:5 *ḥêwāh 'ŏḥºrî* describes the second animal that resembles a bear, while in 7:8 it refers to the small horn that grows after the ten horns of the fourth animal. Dnl. 7:6 then employs *'ŏḥºrî* as a substantive for the third animal that resembles a leopard and, thus, differs from the second. Thus, the substantive *'ŏḥºrî* here emphasizes the difference of the animals. In 7:20, too, *'ŏḥºri* has a corresponding function in reference to the small horn that grows between the eyes of the fourth animal. Here, it is not only a substantive again, but it clearly indicates that the new horn under discussion differs from all the previously mentioned horns of the animal.

Freedman/Yu

In addition, *'aḥªrî* also derives from the word stem *'aḥar*. Thus, in Dnl. 2:28 *bᵉ'aḥªrît yômayyā'* denotes the period for which the announcements in Nebuchadnezzar's dream are valid. One cannot distinguish this expression with certainty from *bᵉ'aḥªrît hayyāmîm*, which occurs thirteen times in the Hebrew OT, although the Qumran texts, Christian Palestinian Aramaic, and Syriac also know *'aḥªrî* in the meaning "last," "end." Therefore, *'aḥªrî* is probably not a Hebraism as such, but the whole phrase is a conscious adaptation of the marked Hebrew formulation. It belongs in the framework of prophetic speech announcing an intermediate future. This becomes particularly clear from considerations of the contexts of Dt. 4:30; 31:29; Isa. 2:2; Jer. 23:20; 30:24; 48:47; 49:39; Ezk. 38:16; Hos. 3:5; Mic. 4:1, and Dnl. 10:14. In Gen. 49:1, the expression marks the fact that the subsequent sayings about the nations refer first to the time after Israel became a people. Nu. 24:17 also identifies v. 14 as an announcement of the distant future. Therefore one should not translate the content of the phrase with "in the time to follow."[32] Instead, *'aḥªrît yômayyā'/hayyāmîm* denotes the "afterward" in relation to the day, i.e., the time that begins with the end of a specific period. In this regard, *hayyāmîm* in the sense of "a certain time" in, e.g., Gen. 26:8; 1 S. 1:20; 13:11; 18:26 is comparable.

If, therefore, the meaning "after a certain period" is likely for Dnl. 2:28, it stands in tension with vv. 29 and 45, where *'aḥªrê ḏᵉnāh* relates the vision to the immediate future, since *ḏᵉnāh* here means the "now." This also accords with the fact that the golden head of the statue seen in the vision is Nebuchadnezzar himself. This tension resolves when one assumes that v. 28aβγ.b represents a secondary addition that places the emphasis on the end of the vision, the announcement of the fourth kingdom and its ultimate divestiture as well as the establishment of the eternal kingdom.[33] The fact that the vision in its current form is not eschatological in the strict sense, but expects an eternal kingdom after a transition phase of various kingdoms, corresponds to the interpretation of *bᵉ'aḥªrît yômayyā'/hayyāmîm* given above that obviously does not denote the "end of (worldly) time," but

32. Contra Seebaß, 227.

33. Cf. e.g., R. G. Kratz, *Translatio imperii. WMANT* 63 (1987), 55-57.

an event at the end, dated after a specific time period. Whether this is eschatological in intention, therefore, the phrase itself does not express but only its context.[34]

With *ATTM,* 508, the *K 'ḥryn* in Dnl. 4:5 also probably derives from this word as a fem. pl., attested in the phrase *'aḏ 'ḥryn* with the meaning "finally, last," for which the Masora of Leningradensis suggests the reading *'ŏḥ°ren.*

Kottsieper

IV. Qumran. Most of the words with the root *'ḥr* attested in Old, Imperial, and Biblical Aramaic also occur with the corresponding meanings in the Qumran texts, including also the fem. of *'ḥrn,'ḥry* "other," which does not yet appear in pre-Biblical Aramaic texts.

The not yet identified Fragment 6Q23 2 *w'ḥr*["and thereafter" (?) attests *'ḥr* in the sense of "(there)after." The Genesis Apocryphon offers two instances of prepositional *'ḥr* with suffixes with the meaning "after, behind" (*'ḥrhwn* 1Q20 2:2; *'ḥryk* 1QapGen 21:14).

• In the meaning "other, future," *'ḥr* occurs as an adjective in the phrase *ldry' 'ḥry'* "the future generations" (4Q212 2:24 [1 En. 92:1]). (*Ko.*) •

4Q543 6.4 has *'ḥrn'* with the apparent meaning "the other," although the Elephantine papyri attest the same form with the meaning "furthermore."[35] Additional instances of the masc. form *'ḥrn* in the sense of "other" are, e.g., *wh' 'swp 'ḥrn* "and look, there was another gateway" (4Q554 1 3:16 = [*wh'*] *'sp 'wḥrn* 15 1:I:18) or *'d tr" 'ḥrn'* "up to the other gate" (5Q15 1 2:7). Two additional examples of the plural form of *'ḥrn* in adjectival and substantival usage are *ṭwryn 'ḥrnyn* "other, additional mountains" (4Q206 3:17 [1 En. 32:1]) and *'ḥrny' mn br* "the others from outside" (2Q24 8:4).

A few Qumran fragments also attest the fem. *'(w)ḥry*, e.g., *'wḥry* (2Q24 8:7) or *w'ḥryt' [y]hybt ltnynh* "and the other [i.e., bread] was given to the second [i.e., priest]" (2Q24 4:16).

Freedman/Yu

34. Cf. Buchanan, 190.
35. *BMAP* 4,19 → II.

אִילָן *'yln 'îlān*; אֵב *'b 'eḇ*; עֲנַף *'np ʿᵃnap*; עֳפִי *'py ʿᵒpî*; ארז *'rz* /'arz/

I. Etymology. II. 1. Hatra. 2. Elephantine. 3. Jewish Aramaic. III. Dnl. 4. IV. Qumran.

K.-H. Bernhardt, *Der alte Libanon* (Vienna, 1976), esp. 51-58; J. A. Fitzmyer and J. Harrington, *A Manual of Palestinian Aramaic Texts. BietOr* 34 (1978); I. Kottsieper, "Bäume als Kultort," in U. Neumann-Gorsolke and P. Riede, eds., *Das Kleid der Erde* (Stuttgart, 2002); M. Metzger, "Zeder, Weinstock und Weltenbaum," *Ernten, was man sät. FS K. Koch* (Neukirchen-Vluyn, 1991), 197-229; H. Ringgren, K. Nielsen, and H.-J. Fabry, "עֵץ *'eṣ*," *TDOT*, XI, 265-77.

I. Etymology. The Aramaic word for "tree," *'îlān*, corresponds to the Hebrew *'elôn* and *'elāh* "terebinth" or "oak." In addition, one finds Hebrew *'allôn* or *'allāh* "oak," Akkadian *allānu* "oak/acorn," Ugaritic *aln*, Arabic *'ilāl* in contrast to other counterparts for Aramaic *'îlān* such as Akkadian *aliānum/alânu/elânu* "tree," Phoenician *'ln*, Ugaritic *iln* and Akkadian *ilānu* "minor god," to the degree that the words for "oak" and "god" derive from the same root *'w/yl*. Despite the similarity between Hebrew *'elôn/'elāh* and *'allôn/allāh*, scholars normally assume two different roots, *'w/yl* and *'ll*.[1] A series of additional Aramaic words belong in the semantic field of *'îlān*, including *'ᵃnāp* (Syriac *'nāpā*) "branch" (cf. Hebrew *'ānāp*), *'pî* "foliage" (Syriac *'ûpyā;* cf. Hebrew *'pā'yim*, Ps. 104:12, which is apparently an Aramaic loanword in Hebrew;[2] perhaps also Akkadian *apu* "cane brake"). *'rz* "cedar" (Syriac *'arzā*; cf. Hebrew *'erez*, Ugaritic *arz*, Ethiopic *'rz*, Arabic *'arz* "cedar," "pine"), and **'eb̲* (cf. *'inbeh*, Dnl. 4:9,11,18) "fruit." The latter probably derives from the root *'bb* (cf. Jewish Aramaic *'bb* pael "to allow to ripen," Mandean *'byby'* "fruits') and is associated with Hebrew *'eb̲* "freshness," "greens," "blossom," "shoot" (cf. *bᵉ'ibbô* "in his freshness," Job 8:12, and *'ibbê hannāḥal* "blooms of the valley," Cant. 6:11), Ugaritic *ib* "fruit,"[3] Arabic *'abb* "grass," "meadow," Amharic *abbäbä* "to blossom,"[4] and perhaps Akkadian *ebēbu* "to be pure, clear" as well as Ugaritic *ib* "gem, brilliance" (*ib iqni* "a lapis lazuli-*ib*, brilliance of lapis lazuli")[5] or "moon goddess" (as a parallel for *nkl* = Ningal in *nkl wib*). If, however, **'eb̲* belongs to the root *'nb* (in which case, *'bb* may have derived from it secondarily), then one could point to Akkadian *inbu* (*enbu, imbu*) "fruit(tree)," "descendant." Ugaritic *ǵnb*(*m*) "grape(s)" or "fruits," Hebrew *'enāb̲* and Arabic *'inab* suggest the assumption, however, that Akkadian *inbu* belongs to this word-group.

II. 1. Hatra. An inscription on the lintel of a shrine in a palace in Hatra attests Aramaic *'rz* "cedar" or perhaps also "pine."[6] It seems to refer to the construction materials for a "house," apparently a temple since the word for "god" occurs after a gap in which the name of the god may have stood. However, this one-line inscription is not preserved well enough to permit an unequivocal interpretation.

2. Elephantine. The word *'rz* occurs frequently in the customs lists from Elephantine among the objects assembled and stored in the "house of the king." The cedar appears either as *'q 'rz sy* "cedar beams" (?) or *'q 'rz mlwt* "cedar plank" (?).[7] *AP* 20.10ff. attests it as material for ship construction.

Of particular interest, however, is the petition for the reconstruction of the Jewish temple on Elephantine of 11/26/407 B.C.E. which says that the roof of the earlier temple

1. Contra, however, W. F. Albright, "Albrecht Alt," *JBL* 75 (1956) 256.
2. Contra, however, M. Dahood, *Psalms III. AB* (1970), 38f.: "raven."
3. *KTU* 1.19:I:31.
4. Cf. W. Leslau, *Hebrew Cognates in Amharic* (Wiesbaden, 1969), 21.
5. *KTU* 1.14:III:43.
6. *KAI* 252.
7. Cf. *TADAE* C3.7, GR:3:24f.; FR:2:25f.; FV:2:17f.; 3:13f.; GV:2:21-4.

was built of cedar.[8] This has parallels in the construction of the Jerusalem temple (1 K. 6:9). Aḥiqar 175 attests *'rz'* in a saying preserved only fragmentarily that speaks of the protection of the cedar in which one can find oneself. This may be a metaphor for the protection one finds in the temple itself.

• Yet, this passage is hardly distinguishable from the instance of *'rz* in Pap. Amherst 63 18:1-4, which reports a lament ceremony by the Babylonian exiles between cedars (l. 2) at which one called upon El (l. 3). This not only constitutes a close parallel to Ps. 137:2, but also indicates that trees or groves functioned as cultic sites, but not as cultic objects. This not only corresponds to the biblical accusation that foreign cults were practiced "under every green tree" (cf., e.g., Dt. 12:2; 1 K. 14:23; 2 K. 16:4; 17:10; Isa. 57:5; Jer. 2:20; 3:6; Ezk. 6:13; 2 Ch. 28:4; similarly Jer. 17:2; Hos. 4:13), but also the many references to trees in the context of cultic site or places of sacrifice (cf. esp. Gen. 12:6f.; 13:18; 21:33; Josh. 24:26f.; Jgs. 6:11ff.; Ps. 92:14). The columns Jachin and Boaz, provided with floral décor, that stood in the temple probably trace back to the fact that trees could mark places suitable for the cult. In the background of this function of trees probably stands the fact that they served as symbols of the deity and thus could represent the deity's presence.[9] As the royal world-tree (cf. Ezk. 17:23; 31:1-9) that offers the animals protection, the cedar, in particular, stands in close connection with El, the king of the gods.[10] From this point, one can also suspect that the protection of the cedar in Aḥiqar 175 metaphorically represents the protection of El, the chief god of the sayings of Aḥiqar.[11] (*Ko.*) •

The word *'nb* may occur in the sayings of Aḥiqar in a dispute between the thornbush and the pomegranate. The thornbush asks the pomegranate what good its many thorns do for those "who touch your [fr]uit (*[b'/'n]byk*)." The pomegranate's response reminds the thornbush that it is only thorny for those who touch it (Aḥiqar 165f.).[12]

3. *Jewish Aramaic.* In the Targums, *'yln* normally translates the Hebrew *'eṣ* "tree,"[13] as well as *śîaḥ* "plant" (cf., e.g., Gen. 2:5; 21:15). It occurs only metaphorically, however. Thus, e.g., in Bab. *Pesaḥ.* 112a: "If you want to be hanged, have yourself hung in a large tree." This intends to express the idea that "if you must appeal to an authority, then be careful that it is a good one."

Apart from its normal meaning as "cedar," *'rz* also appears in the Talmud as a designation of outstanding people.[14] Instead of rendering it with the Aramaic equivalent, the Targum of Ezk. 31:3 translates Hebrew *'ānāp* with a form of *'py.* Finally, *'b* may occur as

---

8. *AP* 30.11; 31.10.
9. Cf. Kottsieper.
10. Cf. Ps. 80:11; Bernhardt, 53; Metzger, 212.
11. Cf. I. Kottsieper, "El—ferner oder naher Gott?," in R. Albertz and S. Otto, eds., *Religion und Gesellschaft. AOAT* 248 (1997), 27-34.
12. Cf. *TADAE* C1.1:7:101f.; contra *TUAT*, III/2, 332 (VII,7f.), which presupposes the emendation [*š*]*byk*.
13. Cf. e.g., Tg. Onq. of Gen. 1:11,12,29; 2:17; 3:1-3.
14. Bab. *Sabb.* 118b.

'byn in an ostracon from Masada; the context of the passage is destroyed, however, so that its reading remain uncertain.[15]

III. Dnl. 4. All six instances of *'îlān* occur in the report and interpretation of Nebuchadnezzar's dream (Dnl. 4:7,8,11,17,20,23). In them, *'îlān* refers to Nebuchadnezzar himself, and the towering height of the tree that offers protection to the animals of the field and a resting place in its branches to the birds symbolizes Nebuchadnezzar's power and dominion spreading "to the ends of the earth" (v. 19). Nevertheless, Daniel shares with him how he will be "cut down" and wander about like a wild animal until he acknowledges God's true dominion as the one who conveys dominion upon whom he will (v. 22).

In addition, the narrative in Dnl. 4 contains all the other terms examined here including *'rz* (cf. vv. 9,11,18). In Nebuchadnezzar's dream, a heavenly watchman commands: "Cut the tree (*'îlānā'*) down and cut off its branches (*'anpôhî*). Rip off its foliage (*'ŏpyeh*) and scatter its fruit (*'inbeh*)" (Dnl. 4:11a). The sequence in this list from largest (tree) to smallest (fruit) doubtlessly intends to express the totality of the fall of the "tree," i.e., of Nebuchadnezzar, and contrasts the destruction of the tree with its former mighty status: "Its foliage [*'ŏpyeh*] was beautiful, and its fruit [*'inbeh*] plentiful . . . and the birds of the heavens dwelt in its branches [*'anpôhî*]" (v. 9).

The theological statement of this passage is that all earthly dominion receives its authority ultimately from God and that no power—not even the mighty Babylonian Empire—can cancel God's plans. After he recovered his mind, Nebuchadnezzar acknowledges that God "deals with the host of heaven and inhabitants of the earth as he will" (v. 32).

• Obviously, the text thereby takes up the tradition motif of the world-tree that also occurs in Ezk. 17:22-24; 31:1-9.[16] Dnl. 4 shares with these two instances the fact that the protective character of the tree stands less at the center than does its world-encompassing power. The fact that, nonetheless, the motif of protection for living beings appears in all these passages demonstrates how closely linked it is with the world-tree. In this regard, the ideology that a true royal dominion is tied inseparably to the protection and preservation of those in the realm of the living lies in the background. Since the world-tree refers in the official realm consistently to a king (cf. also Ezk. 19:10f.) or in its adaptation in Ps. 80:9-11 to the stately, national Israel, it is not meant cosmologically, but as a fixed metaphor for the kingdom.[17] (*Ko.*) •

IV. Qumran. Parallel to the dream in Dnl. 4[18] and the four empires in Dnl. 7f., the trees (*'ylnyn*) in the "vision of the four trees" (4Q552/3; cf. *DSSStE,* 1102-5.) appear to represent four successive empires, of which Babylon is the first (4Q552 1 2:1ff.; 4Q553 6 2:1ff.). An additional agreement with the visions of the biblical book of Daniel is the fact that each of the nations in the Qumran texts apparently has its own angel (cf. Dnl. 10:13ff.).

---

15. Y. Yadin and J. Naveh, eds., *Masada I* (1989), 556:4; contra *ATTM.E,* 212.
16. Cf. above II.2; Metzger.
17. Cf. also IV on 4Q552/3.
18. See above III.

The Enoch literature utilizes trees and their fullness as an image for describing the idyllic nature of Enoch's revelation in which he goes to the garden of righteousness. These trees, especially "the tree of wisdom," are remarkably aromatic. Enoch encounters trees from which sap flows "called [balsam or galban]um" (4Q204 12:26f. [1 En. 32:1]), and which were "[fu]ll of resin [*nṭp*]" (4Q204 12:28 [1 En. 32:1]).[19] 4Q206 3:15 also mentions trees, but the text is very fragmentary. In the parallel 1 En. 31:3, it involves aloes that bear almond-like fruit.[20]

In 4Q530 3:11, [*ʾy*]*nyn* may occur[21] in a very corrupt context with no direct parallels in the other Enoch literature so that a more precise determination is not possible. Since, however, in the context of the "fallen," the text says that the trees come from heaven, it could be that the "trees" in this passage metaphorically represent the two hundred fallen angelic beings (?) who came from heaven and impregnated human women (cf. 1 En. 6:6-8; 64:2).

In an interesting section of the Genesis Apocryphon, Abraham relates a dream to Sara in which a date palm intervenes on behalf of a cedar (*ʾrz*) to save it from being felled. The interpretation of the dream is that Sara (the date palm) will save Abraham (the cedar) by claiming to the king of Egypt that she is Abraham's sister (1QapGen 19:14ff.). As in the biblical account (Gen. 12:10-20), her subterfuge succeeds and thereby Abraham attains great wealth.

Finally, T. Levi lists twelve varieties of wood considered suitable for sacrifice on the altar. The list mentions the cedar first.[22]

Freedman/Geoghegan

---

19. Reading with Fitzmyer-Harrington, 64.
20. M. A. Knibb, *The Ethiopic Book of Enoch 2* (Oxford, 1978), 119f.
21. So Fitzmyer-Harrington, 76.
22. CT. Levi ar Bodl. C:16; cf. 4Q214b 2-6:1(:4).

אימה *ʾymh* /ʾaymā/

I. Etymology. II. Usage.

I. Etymology. Feminine *ʾymh* /ʾaymā/ (> /ʾēmā/) "terror" occurs in Hebrew and Aramaic. The OT employs it often for the crippling fear of death that arises from war and violence. The older Aramaic instances may be influenced by it.

H.-J. Zobel, "אֵימָה *ʾēmāh*," *TDOT*, I, 219-21.

II. Usage. Aramaic first attests *'ymh* for the fourth, most horrible animal in the historical apocalypse of Dnl. 7, namely in the form of the derived adjective /'aymtānī/ "terrifying."[1] Together with *dḥyl* "frightful,"[2] it designates the visionary's initial impression, while the initial description of the appearance of the other three beings is more neutral. The noun itself appears in 1QapGen 11:17 for the fear that, according to Gen. 9:2, humans bring upon the animal world. There, it also parallels the corresponding form of *dḥl*, *dḥlh* "fear." Under the influence of this combination, the same dual expression outside MT occurs in 11Q10 33:2 (Job 39:20).[3]

Gzella

1. *ATTM*, 509; vocalized *'ēmṯānī.*
2. → *dḥl.*
3. → *dḥl* IV.

אכל *'kl*; זון *zwn*; מָזוֹן *mzwn māzôn*; קְרַץ *qrṣ qᵉraṣ*

I. Etymology. II. Biblical Aramaic. III. General Use in Aramaic and at Qumran. IV. (*'kl*) *qrṣ*. V. *zwn* 1. Basic Meaning. 2. Biblical Aramaic. 3. Regarding the Etymology.

I. Etymology. The root *'kl* "to eat" is common Semitic and occurs in all the Aramaic dialects. Biblical Aramaic attests it in Daniel.

II. Biblical Aramaic. In its concrete basic meaning, *'kl* appears only in the apocalyptic animal vision (Dnl. 7) and in a comparison regarding Nebuchadnezzar (Dnl. 4:30): *wᵉʿiśbā' kᵉṯôrîn ye'kul* "and he ate grass like cattle." Daniel says of the animal that resembles a bear: *qûmî 'ᵃkulî bᵉśar śaggî'* "Up, eat much flesh!" (Dnl. 7:5). The fourth animal, which differs from the others and has iron teeth, "devoured and crushed" (*'ākᵉlāh ûmaddqāh*, Dnl. 7:7,19).

The example in Dnl. 4:30 additionally exhibits the more general connotation "to take nourishment."

Contrariwise, in Dnl. 7 in the exposition of the vision, the root acquires the meaning "to destroy," with the fourth empire as subject. This corresponds to its paralleling *dqq aph*: *wᵉṯe'kul kōl 'arʿā' . . . wᵉṯaddeqinnah* "it will devour the whole earth . . . and crush it" (Dnl. 7:23).

W. Arnold, "The Roots *qrṭ* and *qrṣ* in Western Neo-Aramaic," in H. Gzella and M. L. Folmer, eds., *Aramaic in Its Historical and Linguistic Setting. VOK* 50 (2008), 305-11; S. A. Kaufman, *The Akkadian Influences on Aramaic. AS* 19 (1974), esp. 63; N. MacDonald, *Not Bread Alone* (Oxford, 2008); idem, *What Did the Ancient Israelites Eat?* (Grand Rapids, 2008); M. Ottosson, "אָכַל 'ākhal," *TDOT*, I, 236-41.

It occurs in the expression *'kl qrṣyn dy*, which literally means "to eat what has been pinched off someone" and idiomatically means "to denounce someone, to make accusations to the authorities because of alleged crime." The phrase originated in Akkadian (→ IV). Dnl. 3:8 says of a few Chaldeans *wa'ᵃḵalû qarṣêhôn dî yᵉhûḏāye'* "and they defamed the Jews," i.e., they accused them of refusing to prostrate themselves before the statue. The Chaldeans use the same expression to accuse Daniel: *wa'ᵃmar malkā' wᵉhayṯiw guḇrayyā' 'illeḵ dî 'ᵃḵalû qarṣôhî dî ḏāniyye'l* "and on the king's command, any men who had defamed Daniel were brought" (Dnl. 6:25).

Kaddari

III. General Use in Aramaic and at Qumran. Instances in Biblical Aramaic already demonstrate a double connotation for the root. On the one hand, from the perspective of the one eating it has the positive aspect of nourishment, on the other, from the perspective of what is eaten, that of destruction or consumption. This duality, which also accords with the use of the root in Hebrew and Akkadian, for example,[1] often reappears in the other Aramaic texts.

The aspect of consumption occurs e.g., in *AP* 13.4 where instead of *'plt* one should probably read *'klt* "I have consumed"[2] and refers to the goods that the speaker received from his daughter. One finds it at Qumran in the adaptation of Gen. 14:24 in reference to what Abraham's servants consumed in their campaign against the four kings.[3] While this still refers to nourishment and, accordingly, *'klw* can be translated there with "they have eaten," *'kl* in a letter from Masada probably refers to myrrh or a container for myrrh, so that the meaning "to consume" is clear here.[4]

The statement that the giants produced by relations between the angels and human women *'klyn 'ml kl bny 'nš'*[5] resonates with the elements both of consumption and of destruction: "they consumed the effort [i.e., the property gained thereby] of all people." Similarly, descriptions of the destructive power of the giants include the fact that they "wanted to eat much" (*wb'yn lm'kl śgy'*).[6] In the unequivocally negative sense of destruction, *'kl* already appears in the curses of the Sefire stele.[7] In the event of a treaty violation by Mati'el, it threatens that locust and worm will "devour" in his land for seven years (A 27), which, along with other catastrophes, leads to the destruction of the greenery of his land. A 30 describes not only the panther and the bear, but also the snake, the scorpion, the moth, and the flea—i.e., any animal that wreaks destruction with its mouth—as *'kl* acquires the general meaning "pest" here[8] and also has parallels in the description of

1. Ottosson, 253,254.
2. Cf. *TADAE* B2.7:4.
3. 1QapGen 22:23.
4. yMS 556:2f.; *ATTM.E,* 212.
5. 4Q201 3:17f. + 4Q202 2:21f. (1 En. 7:3).
6. 4Q531 5:6.
7. *KAI* 222.
8. So, e.g., *KAI* II 249.

demons as *aklm* in Ugaritic.[9] The statement *'šh 'klthm<w>* "a fire consumed her" unfortunately stands in a fragmentary context apparently in reference to a fugitive slave.[10] The concrete allusion is not entirely clear here, however.

"Eating" in the sense of "to take nourishment" plays a significant role in many contexts.[11] This versatility results, on one hand, from the fact that eating, along with drinking and sleeping, constitute the foundational actions of human life, defining the *conditio humana.* Thus, in CT. Levi ar Bodleian a:4f., along with the announcement of toil and rest, sleep and wakefulness, *zmnyn t'kwl wzmnyn tkpn* "sometimes you will eat, sometimes you will hunger" also appears. In contrast, a Jewish amulet from Turkey says that demons have hunger and thirst or are tired, to be sure, but nonetheless do not eat, drink, or sleep[12]—a motif already encountered, e.g., in 1 En. 15:11 or in the Arabic demon tradition.[13] This context also includes the fragmentary saying about the scorpion in Aḥiqar 85f., which apparently illustrates the peculiarity of this feared animal by its feeding behavior.

On the other hand, in primarily agrarian societies like those of the ancient Near East, whose supplies were continually threatened by droughts and/or bad harvests, the aspect of nourishment is much stronger in the consciousness of the individual than in modern welfare societies. This is reflected not only in the curses from Sefire mentioned above, but also in the fact that the realm of nourishment has central significance in such curses, even when they do not directly mention the root *'kl*. Here, along with the inscriptions from Sefire,[14] one should name especially the inscription from Tell Fekheriye.[15] In addition, in the Aramaic section, l. 2, it contains the explicit statement that upon the invocation of the curse, the men must eat barley from dung heaps. Conversely, the motif that people "eat and drink" in the Sam'alian inscription is a sign for the just, life-sustaining rule of the king.[16] Accordingly, the motif in 4Q537 3:1 that Israel will eat from the fruits and goods of the land may link directly with the statement that they will live:] *wtklwn pryh wkl ṭbth wtyḥwn* ["and you will eat fruits [i.e., of the land] and its goods and live."[17] In any case, the statement about eating expresses the aspect of the good life, which has parallels in Pap. Amherst 63 18.15-18. It describes the carefree life that Shamash-shum-ukin is supposed to lead in Babylonia in part with the motif that he will eat the bread of the land and drink its wine.[18]

---

9. *KTU* 1.12:I:26,36.

10. *KAI* 233.17; Asshur seventh century B.C.E.

11. Cf. e.g., Aḥiqar 127,129; nV 7:53 (*ATTM.E,* 168).

12. Seventh century C.E.; ggAG 1:17-22; *ATTM,* 372f.

13. Cf. J. Wellhausen, *Reste arabischen Heidentums* (^{2}1927), 149.

14. *KAI* 222 A 21ff.; 223 A 1ff.

15. Tell Fekheriye 18ff.; cf. the Akk. portion, ll. 30ff.

16. *KAI* 214.9; cf. also 215.9ff.; on the reading, cf. J. Tropper, *Die Inschriften von Zincirli. ALASP* 6 (1993), 116.

17. Contra K. Beyer, *ATTM.E,* 70f. (= B 5:21), who suggests *twḥwn* "and you will hurry."

18. Cf. R. C. Steiner and C. F. Nims, "Ashurbanipal and Shamash-shum-ukin," *RB* 92 (1985) 71 (17.15-18); S. P. Vleeming and J. W. Wesselius, *Studies in Papyrus Amherst 63 I* (Amsterdam, 1985), 34.

The close connection between life and eating also comes to expression in the fact that, for Panamuwa, the purpose of the cult of the dead is to enable him to eat in communion with the god Hadad. Thus, the invocation of the deceased king with the clause *t*[']*kl nbš pn*[*mw*] *'m hdd tšty nbš pnmw 'm h*[*d*]*d* "May the soul of Panamuwa eat with Hadad, may the soul of Panamuwa drink with Hadad" belongs in the context of the Hadad cult.[19] The eating (and drinking) of the deceased enabled through the cultic act simultaneously assures and symbolizes his life beyond death.

The last two passages mentioned also indicate an important broader social aspect of eating. In probably every culture, the common meal is one of the elements that constitutes, preserves, or gives expression to a community. Thence, unsurprisingly, the expression *'kl* (*'m*) "to eat (with someone)" occurs in contexts expressing community even if the eating per se possesses no active supporting function.[20] This social function of eating becomes especially clear in 4Q197 4 3:11-13 + 4Q199 (= Tob. 7:8ff.), where Raguel arranges a communal meal in honor of the coming Tobias, but which Tobias initially avoids until his wish to attain Sara as wife is fulfilled. This refusal to eat, which has a parallel (and proto-type?) in Gen. 24:33, definitely represents the refusal of undisturbed communion that can only exist if the concerns of both parties are settled.

Apparently, 1QapGen 21:20f. refers to the communal meal in the framework of the sacrificial feast. It configures the comment about the construction of Abraham's altar in Mamre (Gen. 13:18) to the effect that he also offers sacrifice there *w'klt w'štyt tmn 'nh wkwl 'nš byty* "and I ate and drank there, I and all the people of my house." Eating in the context of feasts as an expression of joy appears in 4Q545 1 1:7, while 4Q537 2:2 mentions the priests eating portions of the sacrifice as a fixed component of the sacrificial cult.

IV. (*'kl*) *qrṣ*. The expression *'kl qrṣ* (pl.) "to defame, to accuse (falsely)" occurs beyond Biblical Aramaic in most of the other Aramaic dialects (Jewish Aramaic, Syriac, Mandean).[21] Although difficult to distinguish with confidence from the Akkadian *akālu karṣī* "to defame," it is still noteworthy that the dissimilation of the original *q* present in Akkadian *karṣu* does not occur in most Aramaic dialects. The sole exception besides Mandean, in which this is to be expected based on internal phonetic developments of Mandean and need not derive from Akkadian,[22] occurs in *KAI* 269.2—a text, however, that exhibits Egyptian but no Akkadian influence.[23] Accordingly, it combines *krṣ* with *'mr* and thereby apparently attributes the aspect of defamation solely to *krṣ*. Already in Old Babylonian, however, *karṣu* alone can mean "defamation,"[24] which was then joined by derivatives such as *karriṣu* "defamatory" or *karāṣu* D-stem "to defame."[25]

19. *KAI* 214.21f.; similarly l. 17.

20. Cf. esp. 1QapGen 21:21f.; 4Q196 2:13 (= Tob. 2:2); 11Q10 38:5f. (= Job 42:11; cf. Heb. also Ex. 18:12; 1 S. 9:19; Job 1:4).

21. Cf. Kaufman, 63.

22. Cf. ibid., 121f.

23. Regarding the dissimilation of the *q*, cf. also the texts from Saqqara or the sayings of Aḥiqar (for which, see I. Kottsieper, *Die Sprache der Ahiqarspruche*. *BZAW* 194 [1990], 42,86).

24. Cf. *AHw*, II, 450: *karṣu*(*m*); EA 252,13f.

25. CH X r 66.

In Arabic, the common Semitic root *qrṣ* "to pinch (off), to tweak," however, also exhibits meanings such as "to speak in a hurtful, defamatory manner," especially in connection to the mouth.[26] Here, one should also compare Prov. 16:30 where *qoreṣ śᵉpātāyw* "who pinches with his lips" occurs in a section that deals with misrepresentations and perversions and the resulting contention and injuries. Therefore, it probably also involves the association of defamatory, damaging speech.

Consequently, if this connotation is not restricted to the Akkadian/Aramaic expression *akālu karṣī/'kl qrṣ*, one should proceed from the notion that the association of damaging, defamatory speech with the root was a distinctive of the root *qrṣ* in general—a ready assumption since pinching with mouth provides an image for hurtful speech. Only the connection with *'kl* seems to have been an independent Akkadian development,[27] which Aramaic then adopted as a coincidence, but not as a loanword.

One can regard the combination of *k/qrṣ* with *'kl* as a kind of intensification. The one who eats the "pinched off parts" of another is one who is not satisfied with harming his opponent with taunts and defamations, biting or pinching off with the mouth, but who employs them even further in order to demonstrate his advantage and so to destroy his opponent piece by piece. The proximity on the concrete level between *qrṣ* as a term for "to pinch," and thus with respect to the mouth also for "to bite" (cf. esp. Arab.), and *'kl* "to eat, to destroy" also comes to expression, e.g., in the parallelism of the two roots in *KTU* 1.12:I:10f., which describes the activity of the demons with "to devour" (*tikln*) and "to bite" (*tqrṣn*). If, then, on the level of reality, *'kl qrṣ* can definitely describe gradual destruction, this expression, based on the affinity of the root *qrṣ* with the aspect of defamation, can then also refer to the attempt to destroy one's opponent through defamation or false accusations.

V. *zwn*.

1. Basic Meaning. The broad horizon of meaning of *'kl* rests on the fact that the root originally denoted simply the act of "eating" and, consequently, can step in for the many aspects tied to it. With *zwn*, however, Aramaic has an independent root with the meaning "to take nourishment, to provide with nourishment." In contrast to *'kl*, *zwn*, attested in all Aramaic dialects since Imperial Aramaic, is largely restricted to this aspect. Only Syriac can also employ the root in the broader sense of "to donate, to give." This demonstrates that the aspect of giving is linked to this root along with that of nourishing and could become independent.

However, in the earlier period commercial texts, in particular, attest the root and demonstrate its primary connection with the realm of nourishment. Thus, *kl zwn* in a certificate of debt[28] obviously designates all kinds of foodstuff that would be required as compensation for outstanding interest payments (cf. also *zwn klh* "all the foodstuff" alongside silver, gold, and sacrificial offerings in a Nabatean legal text).[29] The ithpeel

26. Lane, 2514.

27. Cf. M. Held, "A Faithful Lover in an Old Babylonian Dialogue," *JCS* 15 (1961) 12.

28. *AP* 10.10,17.

29. P. C. Hammond, D. J. Johnson, and R. N. Jones, "A Religio-Legal Nabataean Inscription from the Atargatis/Al-'Uzza Temple at Petra," *BASOR* 263 (1986) 77.1; cf. R. N. Jones, "A New Reading of the Petra Temple Inscription," *BASOR* 275 (1989) 42.

participle *mztn* occurs in the juristic formulations of Jewish marriage contracts regulating the provision of the wife or daughters with food,[30] while *mzwn* in a Greco-Aramaic receipt denotes the food for provisioning a child and corresponds to Greek τ[ρο]φιων.[31]

2. *Biblical Aramaic.* The occurrences in the marriage contracts, especially, demonstrate that *zwn* can denote the fundamental, life-enabling provision with food. Therefore, this root was also suited for describing the life-giving and life-sustaining character of the world-tree with which Dnl. 4 compares Nebuchadnezzar.[32] It bears so many fruits that there is *māzôn lᵉḵollā' beh . . . ûminneh yittᵉzîn kŏl biśrā'* "food for all in him . . . and from him all flesh takes nourishment" (Dnl. 4:9; cf. v. 18).

3. *Regarding the Etymology.* Among the other Semitic languages, *zwn* occurs only in Hebrew, while Biblical Hebrew attests with certainty only the noun *māzôn* in Gen. 45:23 and 2 Ch. 11:23 in the meaning "provisions." The often-suggested conjecture of *yādîn* for *yāzôn* in Job 36:31 remains uncertain in view of the fact that 11Q10 28:8 already attests *ydyn*. If correct, it demonstrates that an earlier copyist obviously did not know what to make of *yzwn*.

Only then in Middle Hebrew does *zwn* occur with greater frequency. Therefore, one must regard *zwn* and *māzôn* in Hebrew[33] rather as an Aramaism and characterize the root as genuinely Aramaic. The etymological relationship to Akkadian *zanānu* "to equip, to provide" must be left open since this root can also be linked to *zyn/z'n* "to equip, to decorate."

Kottsieper

30. Cf. M 20:10 (*ATTM,* 309); 21:11,15 (*ATTM,* 311); *m. Ketub.* 4:11f. par. (cf. *ATTM,* 325f.).

31. nV 27:12; *ATTM.E,* 183f.

32. Cf. M. Metzger, "Zeder, Weinstock und Weltenbaum," *Ernten, was man sät. FS K. Koch* (1991), 200f.

33. Contra H. Bauer, "Bemerkungen zur VI. Tafel des Gilgamesch Epos," *OLZ* 10 (1926) 801; regarding the Aram./Syr. vocalization of *māzôn,* cf. *ATTM,* 568.

אֱלָהּ *'lh 'ᵉlāh;* אל *'l*

I. Etymology. II. Semantics. 1. Old Aramaic. 2. Imperial Aramaic. 3. Biblical Aramaic. III. Qumran. IV. LXX. V. Aramean Deities. 1. Upper Mesopotamia. 2. Northern Syria. 3. Central Syria. 4. Palmyra. 5. Hatra. 6. History of Reception.

On I: F. M. Cross, "אֵל *'ēl,*" *TDOT,* I, 242-61; J. M. Lindenberger, "The Gods of Ahiqar," *UF* 14 (1982) 10-117, esp. 107-11; D. Pardee, "Eloah," *DDD*², 285-88; H. Ringgren, "אֱלֹהִים *'ᵉlōhîm,*" *TDOT,* I, 267-84; J. Tropper, *Die Inschriften von Zincirli. ALASP* 6 (1993), esp. 62,197-205.

On II: D. K. Andrews, "Yahweh the God of the Heavens," *The Seed of Wisdom. FS T. J. Meek* (Toronto, 1964), 45-67; T. M. Bolin, "The Temple of יהו at Elephantine and Persian Religious Policy," in D. V. Edelman, ed., *The Triumph of Elohim* (Kampen, 1995), 127-42; E. G. Kraeling, *The Brooklyn Museum Aramaic Papyri* (New Haven, 1953), esp. 83-99; H. Niehr, *Der höchste Gott. BZAW* 190 (1990), esp. 43-60; idem, "JHWH in der Rolle des Ba'alšamem," in W. Dietrich and M. A. Klopfenstein, eds., *Ein Gott allein? OBO* 139 (1994), 307-26; idem, "God of Heaven," *DDD*², 370-72; B. Porten, *Archives from Elephantine* (Berkeley, 1968), esp. 103-86; M. H. Silverman, "Aramean Name-Types in the Elephantine Documents," *JAOS* 89 (1969) 691-709; idem, *Religious Values in the Jewish Proper Names at Elephantine. AOAT* 217 (1985), esp. 209-74; H. J. Stoebe, "Überlegungen zum Synkretismus der jüdischen Tempelgemeinde in Elephantine," *Beiträge zur Kulturgeschichte Vorderasiens. FS R. M. Boehmer* (Mainz, 1995), 619-26; K. van der Toorn, "Herem-Bethel and Elephantine Oath Procedure," *ZAW* 98 (1986) 282-85; idem, "Anat-Yahu, Some Other Deities, and the Jews of Elephantine," *Numen* 39 (1992) 80-101; A. Vincent, *La religion des Judéo-Araméens d'Eléphantine* (Paris, 1937), esp. 92-143; U. Winter, *Frau und Göttin. OBO* 53 (1983), esp. 494-508.

On III: H. Stegemann, "Religionsgeschichtliche Erwägungen zu den Gottesbezeichnungen in den Qumrantexten," in M. Delcor, ed., *Qumran. BETL* 46 (1978), 195-217.

On V.1-5: R. D. Barnett, "The Gods of Zinjirli," *CRRA* 11 (Leiden, 1964), 59-87; M. Cogan, "Ashima." *DDD*², 105f.; R. Comte du Mesnil du Buisson, *Les tessères et les monnaies de Palmyre* (Paris, 1962), esp. 167-439; M. Dietrich, *Die Aramäer Südbabyloniens in der Sargonidenzeit (700-648). AOAT* 7 (1970); L. Dirven, *The Palmyrenes of Dura-Europos. RGRW* 138 (1999); H. J. W. Drijvers, "Hatra, Palmyra und Edessa" *ANRW* II/8 (1978), 799-906; idem, *The Religion of Palmyra. Iconography of Religions* 15/15 (Leiden, 1976); idem, *Cults and Beliefs at Edessa. EPRO* 82 (1980), 76-121; idem, *Dea Syria. LIMC* III/1 (1986), 355-58; III/2, (1986), 263-66; idem, "Atargatis," *DDD*², 114-16; K. F. Euler, "Königtum und Götterwelt in den altaramäischen Inschriften Nordsyriens," *ZAW* 56 (1939) 272-313; M. Gawlikowski, "Les dieux de Palmyre," *ANRW* II/18.4 (1990), 2606-58; idem, "Hadad," *LIMC* IV/1 (1988), 365-67; *LIMC* IV/2 (1988), 209f.; H. Gese, *Die Religionen Altsyriens. RdM* 10,2 (1970), 216-29; T. Green, *The City of the Moon God. RGRW* 114 (1992); J. C. Greenfield, "The Aramaic God Rammān/Rimmōn," *IEJ* 26 (1976) 195-98; idem, *To Praise the Might of Hadad. FS P. Grelot* (Paris, 1987), 3-12; idem, "The Aramean God Hadad," *EI* 24 (1993) 54-61; idem, "Hadad," *DDD*², 377-82; P. Haider, M. Hutter, and S. Kreuzer, eds., *Religionsgeschichte Syriens* (Stuttgart, 1996), esp. 101-27; Y. Hajjar, *La triade d'Héliopolis-Baalbek. EPRO* 59 (1977); idem, "Jupiter Heliopolitanus," in M. J. Vermaseren, ed., *Die orientalischen Religionen im Römerreich. EPRO* 93 (1981), 213-40; idem, "Baalbek, grand centre religieux sous l'Empire," *ANRW* II/18.4 (1990), 2458-508; idem, "Dieux et cultes non héliopolitains de la Béqa', de l'Hermon et de l'Abilène à l'époque romaine," *ANRW* II/18.4 (1990), 2509-604; M. Hörig, *Dea Syria. AOAT* 208 (1979); idem, "Dea Syria—Atargatis," *ANRW* II/17.3 (1984), 1536-81; J. Hoftijzer, *Religio Aramaica. MEOL* 16 (1968); O. Keel, "Das Mondemblem von Harran auf Stelen und Siegelamuletten und der Kult der nächtlichen Gestirne bei den Aramäern," in O. Keel, *Studien zu den Stempelsiegeln aus Palästina/Israel IV. OBO* 135 (1994), 134-202; I. Kottsieper, "El—ferner oder naher Gott?," in R. Albertz, ed., *Religion und Gesellschaft. AOAT* 248 (1997), 25-74; B. Landsberger, *Sam'al* (Ankara, 1948), esp. 45-50; A. Lemaire, "Déesses et dieux de Syrie-Palestine d'après les inscriptions," in W. Dietrich and M. A. Klopfenstein, eds., *Ein Gott allein? OBO* 139 (1994), 127-58, esp. 135-42; J. M. Lindenberger, "The Gods of Ahiqar," *UF* 14 (1982) 105-17; E. Lipiński, "The God 'Arqu-Rashap in the Samallian Hadad Inscription," in M. Sokoloff, ed., *Arameans, Aramaic and the Aramaic Literary Tradition* (Ramat Gan, 1983), 15-21; idem, "The Moon-God of Harrān in Aramaean Cult and Onomastics," *SAIO* II (1994), 171-92; idem, "The Gods of the Skies in the Aramaean Pantheon," *SAIO* II (1994), 193-201; idem, "The 'Gods of the Land' in the Samalian Inscription of Panamuwa I," *SAIO* II (1994), 203-11; J. T. Milik, *Dédicaces faites par des dieux. BAH* 92 (1972); A. Moriya, "The Functions of the Gods in the Aramaic Inscriptions of Sefire," *Oriento* 25 (1980) 38-54 (in Japanese); M. J. Mulder, "Der

I. Etymology. The substantive *'lh* "god" is related etymologically with the common Semitic *ilu/'l* "god, deity" attested in the East, Northwest, and South Semitic languages with the exception of Ethiopic. It is presumably a primary noun. The form *'lh* as an appellative "god" characterizes Aramaic, while *'l* represents the divine name El.

II. Semantics.

1. Old Aramaic. The Old Aramaic inscriptions offer only a few instances of the sg. *'lh* designating a god. Mostly, they designate gods by name; *'lh* qualifies gods with epithets or mentions a god generally. Thus, in the stele inscription of Tell Fekheriye, Hadad appears as *'lh rḥmn* "merciful god" (l. 5).[1] The Hadad statue inscription of Panamuwa I from Sam'al mentions a "god of his father" (*'lh 'bh*).[2] The Asshur letter speaks in l. 19 of the "wrath of god" (*lbt 'lh*).[3]

The plural *'lhyn* usually refers to the entire pantheon of a locality or country, but it also represents groups of gods emphasized for various reasons. Thus, it covers the gods of the king,[4] the gods of a country,[5] or of a region.[6] Treaty gods are mentioned independently.[7]

The parallel reference to gods and humans on the stele inscription from Tell Fekheriye (l. 14) and in the memorial inscription for Panamuwa II[8] is a merism designating all those who populate heaven and earth. The qualification of the substantive *bt* "house" (→ בית *bayit*) with *'lhyn* as the *nomen regens* narrows the semantics of *bt* to "temple"[9] or "dwelling of the gods."[10]

Gott Hadad im nordwestsemitischen Raum," in J. G. P. Best and N. M. W. de Vries, eds., *Interaction and Acculturation in the Mediterranean 1* (Amsterdam, 1980), 69-83; H. Niehr, "Religion," in idem, ed., *The Aramaeans in Ancient Syria. HO* 106 (2014), 127-203; idem, *Religionen in Israels Umwelt. NEB.E* 5 (1998), esp. 148-94; J. Teixidor, *The Pantheon of Palmyra. EPRO* 79 (1979); G. Theuer, *Der Mondgott in den Religionen Syrien-Palästinas. OBO* 173 (2000), esp. 319-412; J. Tropper, *Die Inschriften von Zincirli. ALASP* 6 (1993), esp. 20-26; J. Tubach, *Im Schatten des Sonnengottes* (Wiesbaden, 1986); K. van der Toorn, "Anat-Yahu, Some Other Deities, and the Jews of Elephantine," *Numen* 39 (1992) 80-101; P. Xella, *Baal Hammon. CSF* 32 (1991), esp. 34-37,106-10; C. Zimmermann, *Die Namen des Vaters* (Leiden, 2007).

On V.6: H. J. W. Drijvers, *East of Antioch* (London, 1984); A. Feldtkeller, *Identitätssuche des syrischen Urchristentums. NTOA* 25 (1993); idem, *Im Reich der syrischen Göttin: Eine religiös plurale Kultur als Umwelt des frühen Christentums* (Gütersloh, 1994); P. W. Haider, "Spätantike und Christentum in Syrien," in E. M. Ruprechtsberger, ed., *Syrien* (Linz, 1993), 48-65; idem, M. Hutter and S. Kreuzer, eds., *Religionsgeschichte Syriens* (Stuttgart, 1996), esp. 145-299.

1. A. Abou-Assaf, P. Bordreuil, and A. R. Millard, *La statue de Tell Fekherye et son inscription bilingue assyro-araméenne* (Paris, 1982), 23f.
2. *KAI* 214.29.
3. *KAI* 233; V. Hug, *Altaramäische Grammatik der Texte des 7. und 6. Jh.s v. Chr. HSAO* 4 (1993), 21.
4. *KAI* 214.2,4,12,13,19; 217.3.
5. *KAI* 215.2,22; 222 A 12-13.
6. *KAI* 222 A 10.
7. *KAI* 222 A 12-13 (corr.); B 23.33; 223 B 9 (corr.); C 13; 224:4,14,17,23.
8. *KAI* 215.23.
9. *KAI* 202 B 9.
10. *KAI* 223 C 2f.,7.,9f.

Currently, the linguistic classification of the inscription from Tell Deir ʿAlla oscillates between non-Aramaic,[11] on the way to becoming Aramaic,[12] and Old Aramaic.[13] The inscription parallels *'lhn* and *šdyn* in I 1-6. One can assume a partial identity of the two groups of gods in which *'lhn* refers to the gods in general and *šdyn* to a specific group of gods.[14] The *'lhn* are subordinate to El as the highest god and function as mediators of revelation to the seer Balaam (I 1-2)[15] and as a heavenly council (I 5-6).[16]

In the sayings portion[17] of the Aḥiqar novella found at Elephantine (→ V.2), which is clearly older linguistically than the Imperial Aramaic texts from Elephantine,[18] one finds sometimes universally valid statements concerning the gods: Thus, the gods did not create evil (Aḥiqar 135); the gods honor wisdom which the "lord of the holy ones"[19] establishes in heaven (Aḥiqar 95). The following pertains to the relationship of humans to gods: To turn a weapon against a just person is a sin before the gods (Aḥiqar 128); the god of the one so threatened turns the weapon against the attacker (Aḥiqar 126); those whom the gods curse cannot save themselves by their own power (Aḥiqar 160); rejection by the gods destroys the sense of the nations (Aḥiqar 162); the gods change the lament to good for a lamenter whom they love (Aḥiqar 115); a human can do nothing without the gods (Aḥiqar 122); the gods will do ill to those whose mouths issue evil (Aḥiqar 124); if the eyes of the gods are on humans, they will live (Aḥiqar 124).

2. Imperial Aramaic. The salutations of the letters from Egypt petition the gods to care for the well-being of the letter's addressee.[20] This polytheistic salutation[21] also appears in letters written by Judeo-Arameans. In view of the fundamentally polytheistic Yahu religion of Elephantine, it can no longer be maintained that the writers thereby merely followed a scribal convention.[22]

---

11. P. K. McCarter in J. Hoftijzer and G. van der Kooij, eds., *The Balaam Text from Deir ʿAlla Re-Evaluated* (Leiden, 1991), 87-99; J. Huehnergard, ibid., 282-293; G. Rendsburg, "The Dialect of the Deir ʿAlla Inscription," *BiOr* 50 (1993) 309-28.

12. E.A. Knauf, review of J. Hackett, *The Balaam Text from Deir ʿAllā, ZDPV* 101 (1985) 191; idem, *Midian. ADPV* (1988), 64f. n. 313.

13. D. Pardee, "Response: The Linguistic Classification of the Deir ʿAlla Text Written on Plaster," in Hoftijzer-van der Kooij, *Balaam Text*, 100-105; J. Tropper, *Die Inschriften von Zincirli. ALASP* 6 (1993), 301-6,311; E. Lipiński, *SAIO II*, 104-10.

14. J. Hoftijzer and G. van der Kooij, *Aramaic Texts from Deir ʿAlla. DMOA* 19 (1976), 275f.; H. Niehr, *TDOT, XV*, 422-23; Lipiński, *SAIO II* (1994), 123; idem, "Shadday, Shadrapha et le dieu Satrape," *ZAH* 8 (1995) 247-59.

15. Text following Lipiński, *SAIO II*, 115f.

16. Ibid.

17. Cf. I. Kottsieper, *Die Sprache der Ahiqarspruche. BZAW* 194 (1990), 9-24.

18. Ibid., §292.

19. See below.

20. *AP* 17.lf.; 21:1; 37:lf. (corr.); 39:1; 41:1 (corr.); 54:10f. (corr., cf. *TADAE* A3.1 verso lf.); 56:1; 70:1 (corr.); *BMAP* 13.1; *TADAE* A3.10:1; A3.11:1 (corr.).

21. Regarding its age, cf. J. L. Cunchillos, "Le pronom démonstratif hn en ugaritique," *AuOr* 1, 1983, 61-66.

22. As e.g., Vincent contends (*Religion des Judéo-Araméens*).

Various Aramaic texts from Elephantine written by Judeo-Arameans provide Yahu with the title *'lh'* "the God."[23] Comparable is the formula *yhw 'lh' (zy) byb byrt'* "Yahu, the god in the fortification of Yeb,"[24] which also appears as *yhw 'lh' škn yb byrt'* "Yahu, the god who dwells in the fortification of Yeb" (→ שׁכן *škn*).[25] This formula refers to the presence of Yahi in his temple in Elephantine, i.e., a specific local manifestation of Yahweh distinct from the local manifestations of Yahweh from Palestine known from inscriptions that describe him as "Yahweh of Samaria/of Teman"[26] or as "God of Jerusalem."[27] Yahu's dwelling on Elephantine expresses his presence in the cultic image of the temple, perhaps in the form of a massebah. One can adduce as a counterpart from the Aramaic OT the formulation *'ᵉlāh yiśrā'el dî ḇîrûšᵉlem miškᵉneh* (Ezr. 7:15; cf. 7:19 *'ᵉlāh yᵉrûšᵉlaem*), and from the Hebrew OT the formulations *yhwh bᵉḥeḇrôn* (2 S. 15:7) and *yhwh bᵉṣiyyôn* (Ps. 99:2), as well as *dāḡôn bᵉ'ašdôḏ* (1 S. 5:5). Thereby, the formula from Elephantine takes its place in the poly-Yahwism known from Israel and Judah.[28]

The construct relation *'lh šmy'* related only to Yahu,[29] comparable also to the Yahu title *mr' šmy'* (→ מרא *māre'*; → שׁמין *šᵉmayin*), merits separate discussion. References to Phoenician[30] and Persian[31] influence have explained this title in terms of the history of religion. The second explanation, in particular, has enjoyed widespread acceptance, since interpreters have seen the reference to Yahu as "god (lord) of heaven" since the Persian period as an impact of the god Ahura Mazda and, on the part of the Judeo-Israelites, a *captatio benevolentiae* to the Persian overlords based on an identification of Yahu with Ahura Mazda. Contrariwise, however, one should probably point rather to the Aramaic history of the god Ba'alšamin. This reference to the Aramaic prehistory of the Yahu title "god (lord) of heaven" gains general plausibility in view of the Israelito-Aramaic character of the Yahu cult at Elephantine, as K. van der Toorn has demonstrated.[32] In the context of the reception of the Aramaic gods Bethel, Anat, and Ašima in Israel, their close relationship with Yahweh, and their transfer to Elephantine, one can also locate a reception of the god Ba'alšamin.

These considerations must be clarified in that Yahu is not simply identical with Ba'alšamin, as he is compared to Bethel in Israel and Elephantine. Rather, a divine name (Ba'alšamin) has become a divine epithet (*mr' šmy'*), which is assigned in apposition to the divine name Yahu or which can also represent this divine name. The addressing

23. *AP* 13.14; 22.1; 25.6; 38.1; 45:4; *BMAP* 3.10; 4.10; 6.2; 9.23; 10.17; 12.10f.,33; in contrast to *AP* 44.3, *TADAE* B7.3:3 complements Herem, not Yahu.

24. *AP* 6.4; *BMAP* 2.2; 4.2; 9.2; 10.2.

25. *BMAP* 12.2.

26. J. Renz and W. Röllig, *Handbuch der althebräischen Epigraphik I/1* (Darmstadt, 1995), 61f.,64.

27. Ibid., 245f.

28. K. van der Toorn, *DDD*², 910-19, esp. 918f.

29. *AP* 30.2 par. 31,2 (corr.); 38.2 (corr.); 40.1.

30. Vincent.

31. Bolin.

32. Cf. also R. C. Steiner, "Papyrus Amherst 63," in M. J. Geller, J. C. Greenfield, and M. Weitzman, eds., *Studia Aramaica. JSSSup* 4 (1995), 199-207, esp. 204-7.

of Yahu as *mr' šmy'* represents a translation of the originally Phoenician divine name Ba'alšamem. In Aramaic, this translation must involve the lexeme *mr'*, since it refers to the overlord (→ מרא *mārē'* II), while Aramaic *b'l* gives expression rather to the element of control, possession, and belonging (→ בעל *be'el* II).

For the religion of the Judeo-Israelites of Elephantine, the result is a polytheism with the deities Yahu, already identified in Israel with the Aramaic god Bethel who could also, consequently, appear in Elephantine under this name, and the goddesses Anatyahu (= Anatbethel) and Ašim-Bethel. The theophoric elements of proper names suggest additional deities such as Ḥerem.[33] Based on proximity with the Egyptians, *ḥnwm 'lh'* "the god Ḥnum" also appears frequently in the Elephantine texts via references to his temple or his priests.[34] *AP* 30.5 calls him *ḥnwb {'lh'} zy byb byrt'*, i.e., it emphasizes his connection with the temple of Elephantine. According to the ostracon Cl-G 70 (= *TADAE* D7.21) conc. 3,[35] one Judeo-Aramean blesses another by Yahu and Ḥn(um), thereby associating the two chief gods of Elephantine. Additional Egyptian gods encountered at Elephantine include Ptah[36] and Isis.[37] Sometimes the texts mention the gods of Egypt casually.[38]

The Arameans from Elephantine, who originated primarily from northern Syria, worshiped the gods Ašima, Banit, Bethel, and Nabu. The ostracon Cl-G 277 [=*TADAE* D7.30] mentions Bel, Šamaš, and Nergal.[39]

With regard to the function of the gods, because of the literary genres of the Elephantine papyri (contracts, letters, and lists), the cultic-ritual realm does not come to the fore, but the juristic. Thus, they frequently record oaths (→ ימא *ym'*) by the gods or declarations before the gods.[40] The god Yahu dominates among the Judeo-Arameans as the deity guaranteeing the oath. Moreover, there is also the case that a Judeo-Aramean married to an Egyptian swears to her husband by the goddess Sati.[41] Additional gods of the oath are Ḥerembetel[42] and Anatyahu.[43] Aspects of the cult of the god Yahu come into view in *AP* 30-32, the correspondence over the reestablishment of the Yahu temple on Elephantine (→ בית *bayiṯ*; → דבח *dbḥ*; → היכל *hêḵal*; → מנחה *minḥāh*).

The formulation of liberation for a god, attested only once, requires a separate explanation.[44] The prepositional phrase *l 'lh* does not mean "before the god,"[45] but should be

33. Silverman.

34. *AP* 13.15 (corr.); *BMAP* 3.8; 4.10; 6.8 (corr.); 9.10; 10.6.

35. A. Dupont-Sommer, "Le syncrétisme religieux des Juifs d'Éléphantine d'après un ostracon araméen inédit," *RHR* 130 (1945) 17-28; P. Grelot, *Documents araméens d'Egypte*. *LAPO* 5 (1972), no. 87.

36. *AP* 2.15f. (corr.; for the reading, cf. *TADAE* B4.4:15f.); 3.16f. (corr.; for the reading cf. *TADAE* B4.3:16f.); 72.15 (for the reading cf. *TADAE* C3.12:26).

37. *AP* 72.16 (= *TADAE* C3.12:27).

38. *AP* 7.2,8 (for the reading, cf. *TADAE* C1.2:19,25).

39. Dupont-Sommer, "Syncrétisme religieux," 28-39; Grelot, *Documents araméens d'Egypte*, no. 88.

40. *AP* 6.4; 7.7f.; 14.5; 44.1-3; 45.4.

41. *AP* 14.4-6.

42. *AP* 7.7f.

43. *AP* 44.3; along with Yahu (so AP) or Ḥerem (so *TADAE* B7.3).

44. *BMAP* 5.10.

45. Grelot, *Documents araméens d'Egypte*, no. 46.

understood literally as "for the god." It may represent an allusion to the temple or to the language of Babylonian release documents.[46]

For the further use of *'lh* in Palmyrene, cf. D. R. Hillers and E. Cussini, *Palmyrene Aramaic Texts* (Baltimore, 1996), 338; for the instances from Hatra and Nabatea, *DNSI*, 53-5.

3. Biblical Aramaic. For the use of *'ᵉlāh* in Biblical Aramaic, one must emphasize fundamentally that the plural *'ᵉlāhîn* or *'ᵉlāhayyā'* always means "(the) gods" and is not comparable to Hebrew *'ᵉlōhîm* "God."[47]

Jer. 10:11 contrasts the creator of the cosmos, Yahweh, with the gods (*'ᵉlāhayyā'*) who have not created heaven and earth. They should disappear from the earth and from under heaven.

From the perspective of the history of the text, Jer. 10:6-10 represents an addition to vv. 1-16 lacking in 4Q71 and the LXX.[48] Thus, v. 11 constitutes a reaction to the derision of the idol images in 10:1-5. If this reaction takes the form of a curse in Aramaic (gloss?), it receives additional commentary in vv. 12-15 in Hebrew.[49]

In the book of Daniel, on the one hand, *'ᵉlāhîn* denotes the Babylonian gods (Dnl. 2:11; 3:12,14,18) and their statues constructed of various materials (Dnl. 5:4,23). On the other, it can appear as a genitive of quality paraphrasing the adjective "divine." Thus, *rûaḥ 'ᵉlāhîn* denotes the "divine spirit" (Dnl. 5:14), *rûaḥ 'ᵉlāhîn qaddîšîn* a "holy divine spirit" (Dnl. 4:5f.,15; 5:11), *ḥoḵmaṯ 'ᵉlāhîn* the "divine wisdom" (Dnl. 5:11), and *bar 'ᵉlāhîn* a "divine one" (Dnl. 3:25; cf. 3:28: *mal'ᵃḵeh*). Comparable is the divine predication *'ᵉlāh 'ᵉlāhîn* "the God of gods," i.e., the supreme God (Dnl. 2:47; cf. *'ᵉlāhā' 'illāyā'* [*Q*: *'illā'āh*] in Dnl. 3:26,32; 5:18,21; *BLA* §89i). In essence, a polytheistic substratum may shimmer through these formulations, as well as those mentioned above, which acknowledges the *'ᵉlāhîn* as "divine beings."[50]

The sg. *'ᵉlāh(ā')* refers primarily to Yahweh, characterized as "God of Israel" (Ezr. 5:1; 6:14; 7:15) "God of my fathers" (Dnl. 2:23), "God of Jerusalem" (Ezr. 7:19), "living God" (Dnl. 6:21,27), "supreme God" (Dnl. 3:26,32; 5:18,21), and "great God" (Ezr. 5:8; Dnl. 2:45). He is also the God of Daniel and his companions (Dnl. 2:47; 3:17,28f.). As already in Elephantine, the Bible speaks of Yahweh as *'ᵉlāh šᵉmayyā'* (Ezr. 5:11 [+ *wᵉ'ar'ā'*],12; 6:9f.; 7:12,21,23; Dnl. 2:18f.,37,44; cf. 2:28). It can designate Yahweh's temple as *bêṯ 'ᵉlāhā'* (Ezr. 7:16f.,19f.; cf. Dnl. 5:3).

• Furthermore, the sg. *'ᵉlāh* also refers to the god of Nebuchadnezzar (Dnl. 4:5) or to an unspecified god (Dnl. 3:15; 6:8,13). Dnl. 6:8,13, with the phrase *kōl 'ᵉlāh waᵉ'ᵉnāš*, constitutes a parallel to the merism, also attested in the inscription from Tell Fekheriye and in *KAI* 215.23 (→ II.1), which denotes here everything besides the king that could come into question as venerable. (*Ko.*) •

46. B. Porten, *Archives from Elephantine* (Berkeley, 1968), 219-21.

47. *BLA* §87f.

48. P.-M. Bogaert, *Le livre de Jérémie. BETL* 54 (1981), 222-38; H.-J. Stipp, *Das masoretische und alexandrinische Sondergut des Jeremiabuches. OBO* 136 (1994), 92f.,133.

49. Bogaert, *Le livre de Jérémie*, 231.

50. K. Koch, *Das Buch Daniel. EdF* 144 (1980), 205-10.

With respect to the theological relevance of these observations, it is noteworthy that the book of Daniel consciously avoids the name Yahweh (attested only in 9:2,4,8,13f.,20) while preferring *'ᵉlāh* as a designation for God. It thereby avoids a restriction of the theological statements to the Jewish religion. Thus, it addresses Yahweh as a universal God, whose dominion dissolves the empires of all earthly rulers. This is especially evident where Daniel designates him as "God, Lord, or King of heaven."

III. Qumran. *ATTM,* 510f. and *ATTM.E,* 307 list the occurrences of the lexeme *'lh* "god" in the Aramaic texts from Qumran. In terms of semantics, these instances agree with the Old Aramaic, Imperial Aramaic, and Biblical Aramaic evidence. In Palestinian Judaism, on the evidence of the Hebrew and Aramaic texts from Qumran, *'lh'* or *'l* "god" replaced the Tetragrammaton.[51] In the Aramaic incantation texts from Palestine and Jordan, *'l* denotes El.[52]

IV. LXX. In the book of Ezra, LXX manifests essentially θεός as a rendering for *'ᵉlāh*. This is true in the book of Daniel primarily for the Θ-recension, while LXX, esp. in Dnl. 4–6, so differs from MT in configuration that MT could not have served as its prototype.[53]

V. Aramean Deities. It is essential to remark that there is no Aramaic religion. Rather, the starting-point is the existence of various local panthea and cults in the regions settled by Arameans. Characteristically, a weather god (mostly Hadad) stands at the head of these panthea and an Aramaic-speaking population practices the cult. Consequently, a regional approach to the depiction of the Aramaic panthea suggests itself over a purely diachronic one.

Aramaic panthea appear in a crescent-shaped region from upper Mesopotamia/northeast Syria in the east over southern Anatolia/northern Syria in the north, and Hamath, the Bekah, and the Antilebanon to Damascus and Palmyra in central Syria. Thus, Syria is the chief region for the distribution of Aramaic cults and deities. Substantially, the Arameans of the mid-Euphrates[54] and of southern Babylon,[55] concerning whose religion almost nothing is known with the exception of the proper names,[56] then the Arameans settled in Egypt and the aramaicization of Israel after 723/720 B.C.E.[57] must also be considered.

---

51. Stegemann, 200-202.

52. ggEM 1 (*ATTM,* 383; cf. however *ATTM.E,* 253); ooKA 2:4 (*ATTM,* 397f.); yyMA 2:9 (*ATTM.E,* 235f.) and gtAR 2:23 (*ATTM.E,* 250f.).

53. R. Albertz, *Der Gott des Daniel. SBS* 131 (1988).

54. P. Dion, "Les Araméens du Moyen-Euphrate au VIIIe Siècle à la Lumière des Inscriptions des Maîtres de Suhu et Mari," in J. A. Emerton, *Congress Volume: Paris 1992. SVT* 61 (1995), 53-73.

55. Dietrich; J. A. Brinkman, review of M. Dietrich, *Die Arama'er Sudbabyloniens in der Sargonidenzeit (700-648)*, *Or NS* 46 (1977) 304-25.

56. R. Zadok, *On West Semites in Babylonia During the Chaldean and Achaemenian Periods* (Jerusalem, ²1978); D. O. Edzard, "Kaldu (Chaldäer)," *RLA*, V (1976-1980), 291-97.

57. B. Becking, *The Fall of Samaria. SHANE* 2 (1992), 95-104; van der Toorn, "Anat-Yahu," 92-5; idem, "Migration and the Spread of Local Cults," in *Immigration and Emigration within the*

With respect to the chronological factor, the oldest evidence for the religion of the Arameans falls in the ninth century B.C.E. (statue inscription from Tell Fekheriye), while the latest reaches into the Christian era (Emesa, Palmyra, Hatra). Associated with this broad chronological span is a remarkable further development of religious concepts and practices.

1. Upper Mesopotamia. The statue inscription from Tell Fekheriye mentions by name the deities Hadad, Šala, and Nergal.[58] Hadad occupies the status of supreme god. He appears in his local manifestation as "Hadad (of) Sikan" (ll. 1,5f.,15f.) and "Lord of Khabur" (l. 16). The inscription describes him as the weather god responsible for the water of heaven and earth. He creates meadows, food, and sacrificial rations for all the gods and causes all lands to bloom (ll. 1-5). The goddess Šala (l. 18), of Hurrite origins, appears since old Babylonian times in Mesopotamia and North Syria as the paredra of weather gods such as Adad/Hadad and Dagan.[59] The third god named in this inscription, Nergal, whose scourge is designated as the plague (l. 23), is Babylonian in origin. The gods mentioned collectively in l. 4 constitute the pantheon of Sikan (Tell Fekheriye). The text also describes them as "brothers" (l. 4) of Hadad.[60]

2. Northern Syria. One can deduce the panthea of north Syria based on the steles and miniature art from Harran from the ninth to the sixth centuries B.C.E., the temple of Ain Dara between 1300 and 740 B.C.E., and the inscriptions and steles from Zincirli (Sam'al), Bit Agusi, and Hamath during the ninth and eighth centuries B.C.E.

Harran is the chief cultic site of the moon god Sin, later attested under the name Śahar. His cult reaches as far as Palestine. Alongside Sin, the lunar goddess Ningal is worshiped as his paredra, Nusku as his son, and the sun god.[61]

Based on its reliefs, the temple at Ain Dara evidences the cult of a mountain god and the goddess Ištar.[62]

Sam'al gives evidence of a distinction between the gods of the royal house of Sam'al and the more comprehensive pantheon of the kingdom. As gods of the royal house, one

---

Ancient Near East. FS. E. Lipiński. OLA 65 (1995), 356f.; idem, *Family Religion in Babylonia. SHANE* 7 (1996), 143,340f.

58. Abou-Assaf-Bordreuil-Millard, *Statue de Tell Fekherye.*

59. A. Archi, "Šalaš Consort of Dagan and Kumarbi," in *Studio Historiae Ardens. FS Ph.H.J. Houwink ten Cate* (Istanbul, 1995), 1-6.

60. Regarding the distribution of the Hadad cult as far as Bukan, cf. A. Lemaire, "Une inscription araméenne du VIII s. av. J.-C. trouvée à Bukân (Azerbaidjan iranien)," *SIr* 27 (1998) 15-30; idem, "L'inscription araméenne de Bukân et son intérêt historique," *CRAI* (1998), 293-300; I. Eph'al, "The Bukān Aramaic Inscription: Historical Considerations," *IEJ* 49 (1999) 116-21; J. Teixidor, "L'inscription araméenne de Bukân, relecture," *Sem* 49 (1999), 117-21.

61. Tubach, 129-31.

62. A. Abou Assaf, "Ein Relief der kriegerischen Göttin Ištar," *DaM* 1 (1983) 6f.; idem, "Der Tempel von 'Ain Dara," *DaF* 3 (1990); idem, "Der Tempel von 'Ain Dara in Nordsyrien," *Antike Welt* 24 (1993) 155-71; P. Werner, *Die Entwicklung der Sakralarchitektur in Nordsyrien und Kleinasien vom Neolithikum bis in das 1. Jt. B.C.E.* (Munich, 1994), 110-12.

finds Ba'al Ṣemed, Ba'al Hammon, and Rakib'el.[63] Hadad leads the gods of the pantheon of the kingdom.[64] Other gods mentioned by name are El, (Arq-)Rešef, and Šamaš.[65] They constitute the chief gods of the pantheon of Sam'al, which also includes the circle of the gods not mentioned by name.[66]

For kings Panamuwa I and Panamuwa II, Hadad, the supreme god of the pantheon, also occupied the status of personal god.[67] This close connection of the ruler with Hadad continues, as the royal cult of the dead discernible in Sam'al and in Tell Ḥalaf attests, beyond the king's death.[68]

Their successor, Barrakib, renames the dynastic god Rakib'el his lord,[69] thereby following older traditions.[70] *KAI* 218 attests a reception of the lunar god cult from Harran in Sam'al at the time of Barrakib, which may constitute an equation of the lunar god of Sam'al, already attested earlier in iconography, with the lunar god from Harran.[71]

Three Aramaic inscriptions, including one from Sam'al, mention the veneration of the goddess Kubaba.[72] Yet, this goddess does not appear in the Phoenician and Aramaic royal inscriptions from Sam'al so that, contrary to the widespread assumption about their status in Sam'al,[73] one should still probably think only of a very limited reception of the cult of the Hittite-Luwian goddess.[74]

Bit Agusi provides an instance of the veneration of Melqart as a personal god of King Barhadad.[75] This circumstance depends on politico-military and diplomatic relations between Tyre and Arpad.[76] The treaty steles from Sefire circa 750 B.C.E. demonstrate the pantheon of the kingdom of Bit Agusi by mentioning Hadad of Aleppo, the seven stars, El and Elyan, and the heaven and the earth, the depths of the sea and the sources, and day and night.[77] The veneration of Hadad of Aleppo merits particular emphasis as a reminiscence of the most important weather god in northern Syria since old Babylonian times.[78] His cult survived on into the first millennium B.C.E. in the kingdom of Bit Agusi,

---

63. *KAI* 24.15-16; cf. 216.5; 217.7-8.
64. *KAI* 214.2,11; 215.22.
65. *KAI* 214.2-3,11,18; 215.22.
66. *KAI* 215.22.
67. *KAI* 214; 215.
68. H. Niehr, "Zum Totenkult der Konige von Sam'al im 9. und 8. Jh. v. Chr.," *SEL* 11 (1994) 57-73; idem, "Ein weiterer Aspekt zum Totenkult der Könige von Sam'al," *SEL* 18 (2001) 83-97.
69. *KAI* 216.5; cf. 217.8; 218.
70. cf. *KAI* 24.16.
71. Tropper, 146.
72. J. D. Hawkins, "Kubaba," *RLA*, VI (1980-1983), 260.
73. Haider-Hutter-Kreuzer, 118f.
74. J. D. Hawkins, "Kubaba at Karkamis and Elsewhere," *AnSt* 31 (1981), 147-76; idem, "Kubaba," 257-61; Tropper, 23.
75. *KAI* 201.
76. W. T. Pitard, *Ancient Damascus* (Winona Lake, IN, 1987), 138-44; E. Puech, "Fragment d'une Apocalypse en Araméen (4Q246 = pseudo-Dan^{d}) et le Royaume de Dieu," *RB* 99 (1992) 311-34; C. Bonnet, *Or NS* 63 (1994) 291f.
77. *KAI* 222 A 10-12.
78. H. Klengel, "Der Wettergott von Halab," *JCS* 19 (1965) 87-93.

which also included Aleppo. In particular, the discovery of his temple on the citadel of the city demonstrates this.[79] Two inscribed grave steles from Nerab, which also belongs to the kingdom of Bit Agusi, manifest the veneration of additional deities in the seventh century B.C.E.: that of the lunar god Śahar from Harran, of the sun god Šamaš, the lunar goddess Nikkal, and the fire god Nusku.[80] It thereby becomes evident that the Aramaic religion adopted gods of Sumero-Babylonian origins.

Geographically in northern Syria, perhaps in the region of Aleppo, one can locate the veneration of the gods Bethel and Anatbethel, first mentioned in the treaty between Esarhaddon and Baal of Tyre.[81] Israel or Samaria identified Bethel with Yahweh and regarded Anat as his consort. Their cult reached beyond Israel to Elephantine where they appeared as Bethel and Anatyahu (=Anatbethel) in the Yahweh cult (→ II.2).

The Zakkur Inscription circa 800 B.C.E.[82] names as gods of the pantheon on Hamath and La'ash first Ba'alšamin, an originally Phoenician god,[83] first attested here in Aramaicized form (*b'lšmyn*, ll. A 3.11-13, etc.), who cares for the success of the kingdom. He is the national god of La'ash,[84] venerated in the capital city Hazrak. In addition, it mentions Iluwer, a Mesopotamian weather god, who represents the personal god of King Zakkur, as well as the sun god, the moon god, and the gods of heaven and the underworld.[85]

From additional inscriptions from Hamath, one can deduce the existence of a goddess Ba'alat,[86] perhaps of the god El and a goddess Elat.[87] Based on the OT (2 K. 17:30) and the inscriptions from Taima,[88] one can assume a goddess Ašima.

Aramaic religion attests the god El primarily in northern Syria. At Sam'al, El belongs among the chief gods of the pantheon, but does not head it nor belong among the dynastic gods.[89] The steles from Sefire mention El along with Elyan;[90] here, too, he does not head the pantheon.[91] Perhaps, El should be reconstructed in the Zakkur Inscription.[92] None of these northern Syrian panthea of Aramaic religion includes additional statements concerning the role and function of El.

---

79. Cf. K. Kohlmeyer, *Der Tempel des Wettergottes von Aleppo* (Münster, 2000).
80. *KAI* 225.9; 226.9.
81. S. Parpola and K. Watanabe, *Neo-Assyrian Treaties and Loyalty Oaths. SAA* II (1988), no. 5, IV 6′.
82. *KAI* 202.
83. Cf. *KAI* 4.3-6.
84. *ABLAK*, II, 1971, 138 n. 12.
85. *KAI* 202 B 23-26.
86. *KAI* 204.
87. Lemaire, 139f.
88. K. Beyer and A. Livingstone, "Die neuesten aramäischen Inschriften aus Taima," *ZDMG* 137 (1987) 286; A. Livingstone, "New Light on the Ancient Town of Taimā'," in Geller, *Studia Aramaica*, 133-43, esp. 142.
89. *KAI* 214.2,11,18; 215.22.
90. J. Fitzmyer, *The Aramaic Inscriptions of Sefire. BietOr* 19/A (^{2}1995), 75.
91. *KAI* 222 A 10-12.
92. *KAI* 202 B 23; Lemaire, 139 and n. 29.

The god El obtains a central role in the sayings of the Aḥiqar novella. For philological[93] and history of religions[94] reasons, the origins of the sayings of the Aḥiqar novella are more plausibly northern Syria than southern Syria/Palestine.[95] According to the sayings, El is with human beings (Aḥiqar 107,153,154,156,161,173).[96] The "Lord of the Holy Ones," i.e., the god Baʿalšamin, perhaps identical with El, occupies the supreme position in the pantheon of these sayings (Aḥiqar 95; → בעל *beʿel* II.2). The reference to the "daughter of El" (*bnt ʾl*) in a Palmyrene text from 63 C.E. represents one of the latest instances of El in Aramaic religion.[97]

It is essential in the evaluation of the position of El in Aramaic religion to warn against overemphasizing the importance of the Aramaic onomastica, since the theophoric element *ilu/ʾl* was used appellatively as "god" since the Late Bronze Age Amarna correspondence and generally the nonappellative usage cannot be identified in NW Semitic onomastica. A sidewise glance at contemporary Phoenician religion, which does not know the god El, confirms this.[98] Moreover, Judah and Israel merit attention. There, El appears neither in the epigraphy[99] nor in the OT[100] as a divine name, but only as an appellative.[101]

The question of the gods in Pap. Amherst 63 also merits treatment in the section on northern Syria. The Aramaic papyrus in Demotic script, found west of Thebes and to be associated with the Arameans of Syene stems from Mesopotamia with respect to its tradition, whence it came to Samerina.[102] Here, a veneration of the gods stemming from northern Syria and practiced in Samerina from 720[103] influences the world of the gods mentioned in this papyrus. In essence, the question of the gods is still in a controversial discussion since, depending on the transcription of the Demotic texts, individuals come to differing results. Thus, scholars have discovered the divine names Horus, Adonai, Sahar, Mar, El, Yah, El Bethel and Baal of heaven[104] or the divine names El, Adonai, Mar,

---

93. Tropper, 299,311.

94. J.M. Lindenberger, "The Gods of Ahiqar," *UF* 14 (1982) 106,116f.

95. I. Kottsieper, *Die Sprache der Ahiqarsprüche. BZAW* 194 (1990), 241-46; idem, "Die alttestamentliche Weisheit im Licht aramäischer Weisheitstraditionen," in B. Janowski, ed., *Weisheit außerhalb der kanonischen Weisheitsschriften. VWGTh* 10 (1996), 128-62, esp. 130-38.

96. Cf. Lindenberger, "Gods of Ahiqar," 109-11; Kottsieper, "El," 2-6.

97. Hillers-Cussini, *Palmyrene Aramaic Texts*, no. 0992.6.

98. W. Röllig, "El als Gottesbezeichnung im Phönizischen," *FS J. Friedrich* (Heidelberg, 1959), 403-16.

99. J. Renz and W. Röllig, *Handbuch der althebräischen Epigraphik I/1* (Darmstadt, 1995), 59,215; *II/1*, 93.

100. R. Rendtorff, "El als israelitische Gottesbezeichnung," *ZAW* 106 (1994) 4-21.

101. Regarding the discussion of El in Aramaic religions, cf. also C. Maier and J. Tropper, "El—ein aramäischer Gott?," *BN* 93 (1998) 77-88; and I. Kottsieper, "El—ein aramäischer Gott?—Eine Antwort," *BN* 94 (1998) 87-98.

102. So Steiner, "Papyrus Amherst 63," 205-7; contra e.g., I. Kottsieper, *Die Königpsalmen. UBL* 6 (1988), 64-72; idem, "Anmerkungen zu Pap. Amherst 63 Teil II-V," *UF* 29 (1997) 406-16.

103. R. C. Steiner, "The Aramaic Text in Demotic Script," *JAOS* 111 (1991) 362f.; idem, "Papyrus Amherst 65," 204-7 and, in general, van der Toorn, "Anat-Yahu."

104. C. F. Nims and R. C. Steiner, "A Paganized Version of Psalm 20:2-6 from the Aramaic Text in Demotic Script," *JAOS* 103 (1983) 261-74.

Ba'alšamin, and Bethel,[105] while the question of the possible identification of these gods essentially still remains. Another reading with a less clear identification of the divine figures assumes Horus as the god and understands *'dn* and *b'lšmn* as his epithets.[106] In essence, the clarification of such questions awaits the final publication of the papyrus.[107]

Beginning in the fourth/third centuries B.C.E., coins appear with the goddess Atargatis venerated in the cult of Hierapolis/Mambig, known later as Dea Syria. Together with Hadad, she stood at the head of the pantheon. The cult of Atargatis/Dea Syria spread in northern Mesopotamia and Syria as far as Hauran.

3. Central Syria. Data for the panthea of the Aramaic religion of central Syria are relatively meager. For the pantheon of Damascus in pre-Roman times, one can point to the stele inscription from Tell Dan that portrays Hadad as the god of the king and the victor in war and traces back to a king of Damascus from the second half of the ninth century B.C.E.[108] The Akkadian version of the treaty between Assurnerari V and Mati'el of Arpad mentions, although in an uncertain reading, "Hadad . . . and Ramman of (Damascus)."[109] Ramman was originally an epithet of the weather god Amurru/Martu. In the middle of the eighth century B.C.E., Ramman appears as an independent deity on the mid-Euphrates.[110] Thus, Hadad and Ramman are two different deities. The theophoric elements of the proper names of the kings of Damascus attest the deities Hadad and Ramman as well.[111] The OT identifies the two gods with one another; whether that was actually accurate for Damascus must remain open lacking evidence. 2 K. 5:18 mentions a temple of the god Rimmon, i.e., of Hadad Ramman (cf. also Zec. 12:11).[112] In Roman times, he was known as Jupiter Damascenus. As a pre-Roman deity from the Antilebanon, Ba'al Biqa' merits mention. His name was Hadad and he was worshiped in Roman times in Baalbek as Zeus

---

105. S. P. Vleeming and J. W. Wesselius, *Studies in Papyrus Amherst 63 I* (Amsterdam, 1985), 43-60; I. Kottsieper, "Anmerkungen zu Pap. Amherst 63," *ZAW* 100 (1988) 217-44; idem, *Königpsalmen*, 55-75; idem, "El," 9-11,18-21.

106. Z. Zevit, "The Common Origin of the Aramaicized Prayer to Horus and of Psalm 20," *JAOS* 110 (1990) 213-28.

107. A preliminary translation of the whole papyrus can be found in R. C. Steiner, "The Aramaic Text in Demotic Script," in W. W. Hallo, ed., *The Context of Scripture* I (Leiden, 1997), 309-27. Regarding the gods named in the New Year's ritual of this papyrus, cf. R. C. Steiner, "The Aramaic Text in Demotic Script: The Liturgy of a New Year's Festival Imported from Bethel to Syene by Exiles from Rash," *JAOS* 111 (1991) 362f.; idem, "Papyrus Amherst 63," 206.

108. A. Biran and J. Naveh, "An Aramaic Stele Fragment from Tel Dan," *IEJ* 43 (1993) 81-98; idem, "The Tel Dan Inscription: A New Fragment," *IEJ* 45 (1995) 1-18; H.-P. Müller, "Die aramäische Inschrift von Tel Dan," *ZAH* 8 (1995) 121-39; E. Lipiński, *SAIO II* (1994), 83-101; I. Kottsieper, "Die Inschrift von Tell Dan," in "*Und Mose schrieb dieses Lied auf.*" *FS O. Loretz. AOAT* 250 (1998), 475-500.

109. Parpola-Watanabe, *Neo-Assyrian Treaties*, no. 2 VI 24f.

110. A. Cavigneaux and B. K. Ismail, "Die Statthalter von Suhu und Mari im 8. Jh. v. Chr.," *BaghM* 21 (1990) 321-456, here 364 no. 5, Vs. 8; 379 no. 16, Vs. 8.

111. Pitard, *Ancient Damascus*, esp. 99-189; H. Sader, *Les états araméens de Syrie* (Beirut, 1987), 247-65; Kottsieper, "El," 44-46.

112. M. Mulder, *TDOT*, XIII, 507.

Helios or Jupiter Heliopolitanus. Additionally, the Bekah, Antilebanon, and Herman attest a further series of cults known only via Greek and Latin inscriptions.[113] The cult of Emesa (Homs) attests the god Elagabal whose name *ʾlh ʾgbl* means "the divine mountain."[114] The Arabic goddess al-Lāt appears as his paredra.[115]

4. Palmyra. Iconography[116] and, especially, inscriptions[117] facilitate the identification and characterization of the deities venerated in Palmyra. The Efca source with the god Yarḥibol worshiped there offers the oldest fixed point for the religion of Palmyra. Yarḥibol was originally a weather god who acquired lunar aspects. At Palmyra's height, however, he temporarily receded, then experienced a revival in the late period. The triad comprised of the god Bel and his satellite gods Aglibor (moon god) and Yarḥibol (sun god) dominated the religion of Palmyra. The god Bel owed his name, which actually traces to the NW Semitic *bʿl* and, according to transcriptions, was pronounced *bol*, to the influence of Marduk's title, *bēlum.* In Palmyra, Bel enjoyed veneration as a cosmic god to whom all other deities were subordinate. A second triad combined Baʿalšamin and his satellite gods Aglibol (moon god) and Malakbel (sun god). Only iconography and no inscriptions demonstrate this triad, and its influence on Palmyra's cult was clearly inferior to that of the Bel triad. In addition to these two triads, the cult exhibits a few other deities of Phoenician (e.g., Baal Hammon; Šadrapa), Mesopotamian (e.g., Apladad; Herta; Nabu; Nergal), and Arabic (e.g., Allat; Manawat; Raḥim) provenience. Besides the inscription, the tesserae of the *mrzḥ* associations mention their names as patron deities.[118] The cult of the so-called "anonymous god" in Palmyra's late period merits separate emphasis. One should decide the associated, much-discussed problem of the identity of the "anonymous god" in favor of the old local god of Palmyra Yarḥibol. The overwhelming majority of altars devoted to the "anonymous god" discovered are at his chief worship place, the Efca source.

In essence, it should also be emphasized with regard to divine iconography of Palmyra and Palmyrene that here a shift from fully plastic to relief cultic images took place, which indicates a shift in the cult from caring for the statue of the god to the veneration of the divine image as an icon.[119] In relation to Palmyra, the cult of Palmyrene gods in Dura Europos deserves mention.[120]

---

113. J. Hajjar, "Dieux et cultes non héliopolitains de la Béqaʿ," *ANRW*, II.18.4 (1990), 2509-604.

114. J. Starcky, "Stèle d'Elahagabal," *MUSJ* 49 (1975/76) 503-20.

115. Regarding her, cf. S. Krone, *Die altarabische Gottheit al-Lāt. HOS* 23 (1992).

116. Drijvers, *Religion.*

117. Hillers-Cussini, *Palmyrene Aramaic Texts.*

118. H. Ingholt, H. Seyrig, and J. Starcky, *Recueil des tessères de Palmyre. BAH* 58 (1955); C. Dunant, "Nouvelles tessères de Palmyre," *Syr* 36 (1959) 102-10; Comte du Mesnil du Buisson, 167-439.

119. M. Gawlikowski, "Aus dem syrischen Götterhimmel," in *1/2 Trierer Winckelmannsprogramm* (Mainz, 1979/80, 1981) 17-26.

120. R. Comte du Mesnil du Buisson, *Inventaire des inscriptions palmyréniennes de Doura-Europos* (Paris, 1939); Dirven.

5. Hatra. As evidenced by the inscriptions,[121] a triad, comprised of the deities Maran, Bar-Maren, and Martan, dominated the cult of Hatra. The god Maran ("our Lord") represents the chief god of Hatra identified with the sun god. As the moon goddess, Martan ("our Lady) is his paredra. Their son, Barmaren ("son of our Lord and Lady") exercises dominion over the earth and notably advances to become the most important God of Hatra. The cult of Baʿalšamin also pressed toward Hatra from Palmyra.[122] One can trace the cult of the triad of Hatra further in Asshur based on the Aramaic inscriptions and graffiti.[123]

6. History of Reception. The cult of the various Aramaic panthea and deities of Syria continued in practice in the Christian era up until the sixth century. The formation of early Christianity took place in Syria, especially in Damascus and Antioch, in the context of Aramaic religion so that one should regard it as formative for this epoch of Christianity. The reception of new, non-Aramaic gods such as Mithra, Dionysus, and Isis, and of the new philosophy of Neoplatonism, however, subjected the form of Aramaic religion in the Hellenistic-Roman era to sometimes serious innovations. The effects of Aramaic religion on early Christianity resulted, especially, from the propagation of divine epithets and the reception of Aramaic deities. The transformation of temples into churches (e.g., Damascus: Jupiter-Damascenus-Temple; Aleppo: Temple of the weather god; Palmyra: Temple of Bel and Baʿalšamin [?]) or the construction of churches in the temenoi of a few temples (e.g., Baalbek) affected the Christian cult.

Niehr

121. B. Aggoula, *Inventaire des inscriptions hatréennes. BAH* 139 (1991).
122. H. Niehr, "Ba'alsamem-Studien" *SEL* 13 (1996) 67-73.
123. B. Aggoula, *Inscriptions et graffites araméens d'Assour. SAION* 43 (1985).

אלף *'lp*

I. Occurrence and Etymology. II. General Usage. III. Biblical Usage. IV. Qumran.

I. Occurrence and Etymology. Aramaic texts attest the root *'lp* in the peal "to learn," "to be trusted," the pael "to teach," and the ithpael "to be learned" or (only Nabatean) "to assemble," "to compose."[1] Besides the verb, the derived substantive *'lpwn* "doctrine" occurs

B. Ego and H. Merkel, eds., *Religiöses Lernen in der biblischen, frühjüdischen und frühchristlichen Überlieferung. WUNT* 180 (Tübingen, 2005); A. S. Kapelrud, "לָמַד *lāmad*,' *TDOT*, VIII, 4-10; M. Wagner, *Die lexikalischen und grammatischen Aramaismen im alttestamentlichen Hebräisch. BZAW* 96 (1966).

1. Cf. also under *ylp* in *DJPA*, 241f.

at Qumran and *'wlpn* "doctrine," "learning" in later Aramaic.[2] Etymologically, it most likely derives from Akkadian *elēpu/alāpu* II "to sprout" (G-stem), "to grow together" (Gt-stem), "to cause to grow together" (Št-stem),[3] from which Hebrew *'allûp* "confidant" also derives. The specific meaning "to learn" and "to teach" characterizes Aramaic.

II. General Usage. A Sam'alian Zinçirli inscription already attests *'lp* in the meaning "to teach."[4] In Aḥiqar 80 (ithpael: *yt'lp*), the son is instructed and disciplined. • The parallel image of the son bound with a brick attached to his feet illustrates this. *'lp* stands here, however, in the context of a more repressive rearing and that of education. Nonetheless, the semantic horizon of *lmd* also demonstrates a similar breadth indicating "that in the old Semitic world, learning and teaching did not proceed entirely without chastisement."[5] (*Ko.*) • Hatra 106:b:4f. preserves *'lp* "to teach" again in an inscription: *dy 'lp' bḥlm' 'lp hnw* "whom god instructed in a dream." • Since it involves a building inscription by architects, the instruction by the deity may have consisted of inspiration concerning the configuration of the structure.[6] (*Ko.*) • The comparison of *'lp* with Persian *āmōxtan* "to teach" in *Frahang* XVIII.6 confirms the meaning "to teach," "to learn." *CIS* II 197:7; 217:10; 224:10 attest the meaning "to assemble," "to compose" for the ithpael in Nabatean.

III. Biblical Usage. The root *'lp* entered Biblical Hebrew as an Aramaic loanword with the meaning "to be trusted," "to learn (to know)" in the qal (Prov. 22:25) and "to instruct," "to make clever" in the piel (Job 15:5; 33:33; 35:11).[7] All specimens stem from wisdom contexts: Prov. 22:24f warns against keeping company with the wrathful in order not to become familiar with the lifestyle and thereby suffer injury. In his second discourse, Eliphaz accuses Job of speaking contemptuously of God: "For your misdeed teaches your mouth" (Job 15:5). Moreover, Elihu calls upon Job to be silent, for ". . . I will teach you wisdom" (Job 33:33). God makes a person more clever than the cattle of the earth and wiser than the birds of the heavens (Job 35:11).

IV. Qumran. The Enoch material transmitted in the Qumran discoveries and in the sectarian literature contains numerous instances of the root *'lp*. The fallen angels teach humans their knowledge (magic, incantation, soothsaying, etc.): 4Q201 3:15 (1 En. 7:1); 4:1,4 (1 En. 8:3); 4Q202 2:26 (1 En. 8:1); 3:1-4 (1 En. 8:3), cf. further 4Q531 9:4. The sectarian literature consistently employs *'lp* in wisdom contexts: 4Q213 1 1:10 (the one who learns wisdom receives honor), 1 1:13 (do not cease learning wisdom), 1 1:14 (a man who learns wisdom), 1 2:9 (to these passages, cf. also CT. Levi ar Cambridge e-f), 4Q541 2 2+3+4:1+5:6 (*lm '[lp]* "in order to learn," in connection with a sage who understands the depths and declares the mysteries), 7:6 (['*]lpw[nh. . .]* "his teaching"), 9 1:3 (in reference

2. Cf. *DJPA*, 39.
3. Cf. *AHw*, I, 199f., *CAD*, IV, 86-8 and Arabic *wālibat* "sapling" and *'alifa* "to be bound to something."
4. *KAI* 214.34; *t'lb* instead of *t'lp*, cf. J. Tropper, *Die Inschriften von Zincirli. ALASP* 6 (1993), 180f.
5. Kapelrud, 577.
6. Cf. J. T. Milik, "Dedicaces faites par des dieux," *BAH* 92 (1972) 388.
7. Cf. Wagner, 25.

to the priestly salvation figure at the end of time, whose teaching [*'lpwnh*] agrees with the will of God), CT. Levi ar Bodleian b:7,13 (Isaac teaches Levi the priestly law, cf. T. Levi 9:8f.), 4Q542 1 2:1 (Qahat's sons should behave in keeping with all the father left them and in keep with all that Qahat himself taught them). Also in a wisdom context, *'lp* appears in 4Q536 1 1:4 (*'lp*[*w*]*nh* "his teaching") and 4Q569 1:9 (*'lp bnykh* "teach your sons"). Furthermore, instances of the root *'lp* may occur in 1Q66 2:1 and 11Q10 13:4 (cf. Job 28:23; *ATTM,* 288: *y'*[*lp*], contra *DSSStE*, 1188f.: *yṣ*[. . .).[8]

Steudel/Maurer

8. Cf. M. Sokoloff, *The Targum to Job from Qumran Cave XI* (Ramat Gan, 1974), 52,120f.

אם *'m* /'emm/ → אַב *'b 'aḇ*

אֻמָּה *'mh 'ummāh* → עַם *'m 'am*

אמן *'mn*; הימן *hymn*; הימנו *hymnw*; מהימן *mhymn* /mahēman/

I. *'mn*. II. *hymn* and Derivatives.

I. *'mn*. The root *'mn* "reliable" occurs in Canaanite (especially Hebrew), Aramaic, and all of Arabic. In Aramaic, it occurs with certainty only in Syriac, Mandean, and at Hatra as *'ammīn* "reliable"[1] and the derived Syriac *'ammīnūṯā'* "stability" and the ithpeel "to remain." The instance of *'myn* assumed in *KAI* 266.3 (604/3 B.C.E.) is a misreading, however.[2] Because of the Hebrew and Arabic overlay, nothing clearly Aramaic is recognizable any longer in Samaritan (peal, pael, ithpael, *'mnw* "custom," *mmwn* "certainly").

II. *hymn* and Derivatives. At the latest by the ninth century B.C.E., the haphel I ' became I *w/y*.[3] Thereafter, throughout Aramaic (even outside the Hebrew sphere of in-

B. Aggoula, "Remarques sur les inscriptions hatréennes III," *Syr* 52 (1975) 181-206; A. Jepsen, "אָמַן *'aman*," *TDOT*, I, 292-323; H. Wildberger, "אמן *'mn* firm, secure," *TLOT*, 134-57.

1. *LexSyr*, 25a; *MdD*, 22b; Hatra 342.13.
2. Cf. *TADAE* Al.1:3: *wmyn* "and water."
3. *ATTM,* 105, n. 1.

fluence: Aḥiqar, Palmyrene, Hatra, Mandean, Christian Palestinian Aramaic) the haphel of *'mn* did not make the common transition to the aphel (eighth to sixth centuries B.C.E.)[4] and became an independent four consonant root *hymn*. In Dnl. 6:24, *be'lāheh* "in his God" follows the pf. *hêmin* "he trusted." The substantivized inf. const. *hymnwt* means "reliability," with a suffix *hymnwth* "his reliability,[5] from which, according to the evidence of the Babylonian Targum, the absolute *hymnw* was back-formed.[6]

The most frequently attested, and in all Aramaic languages, is the passive participle become an adjective *mhymn* "reliable": masc. sg. abs. *mhymn*;[7] fem. *mhymnh* (Nabatean) in the archive of Babata nV 1:51 (94 C.E.);[8] masc. pl. abs. *mhymnn* in Samaria Papyrus 1.12 (335 B.C.E.);[9] 4.13[10] or *mhymnyn*.[11] It refers mostly to persons, rarely also to a dream interpretation (Dnl. 2:45), vision[12] or a pledge.[13]

Beyer

In this regard, *mhymn* finds usage especially in the context of official business or tasks. Thus, the scribe of Hermopolis 4.9 seeks a "reliable man" apparently so that he can task him with something, and a Palmyrene inscription calls a person *gwy' mhymn'*,[14] apparently employed here as a title: "the reliable *gwy'*." Thus, *mhymn* also occurs as a title per se,[15] which should probably be grouped with the Syriac official designation *mhaiman* (traditionally "eunuch").[16] The *mhymn* here is the person one trusts and therefore tasks so that *mhymn* can then also have the sense of "commissioned."[17]

The semantic field of the world also includes, however, the aspect of truth. Thus, Aḥiqar 132 mentions as the opposite of the *hymnwt* of a person, the *kdbt špwth* "deceit of his lips." In this respect, according to this saying, the *hymnwt* permits human beings to find "esteem" (*ḥn*). The aspect of truth is also clear in the examples in the Samaria papyri that describe the witnesses to contracts as "reliable,"[18] which parallels Isa. 8:2 (*'eḏîm nae'emānîm*).[19] Finally, *hymnwt* or *mhymn* occurs in the immediate context of the word for "truth" (*qšwṭ*). Thus, 1QapGen 5:8 speaks of the *qšwṭ mhymn* "reliable

---

4. *ATTM*, 148; *ATTM.E*, 54.
5. Aḥiqar 132; 4Q550a 2; cf. also 4Q550b 3.
6. *TW*, 198b.
7. Hermopolis 4:9 (just before 500 B.C.E.), Dnl. 2:45; 6:5 (*mehêman*); 1QapGen 5:8; 1Q196 12:2 (Tob. 5:9; J. Fitzmyer, *DJD*, XIX [1995], 18).
8. *ATTM.E*, 166.
9. F. M. Cross, "Samaria Papyrus i," *IEJ* 18 (1985) 8*f.
10. D. M. Gropp, "The Samaria Papyri from Wâdi ed-Dâliyeh" (diss., Harvard, 1986), 83f.
11. Nabatean nV 1:6,34.
12. 1QapGen 5:8.
13. nV 1:6,34.
14. *CIS* II 4239.
15. Hatra 100.2; 139.3; 290.2.
16. *LexSyr*, 175a; Aggoula, 205f.
17. Hatra 232f.,4.
18. 1.12; 4.13.
19. Cross, "Samaria Papyrus i," 15*.

truth" and 4Q550b 3 of truthful and reliable service or behavior (*'bd mn qšwṭ wmn hy[mnw]*).

Kottsieper

אמר *'mr* → מלל *mll*

אִמַּר *'mr 'immer*

I. 1. Etymology. 2. Sheep and Shepherd Metaphor in the Ancient Near East and the OT. 3. Lamb as Sacrificial Animal. II. Old Aramaic. III. Biblical Aramaic. IV. LXX. V. Qumran. VI. Rabbinic Aramaic. VII. Regarding the Metaphorical Usage.

I. *1. Etymology.* The Aramaic word for "lamb" *'mr* (Biblical Aramaic *'immer*, cf. Syriac *'emmar*, Mandean *'mb*[']*r'*, both of which can also designate the astrological sign "Aries";[1] further Christian Palestinian Aramaic '[*y*]*mr*; cf. also Palmyrene *'mry'*, (pl. abs.)[2] has counterparts in most of the Semitic languages, including Ugaritic *imr*[3] and Arabic *'immar*. Akkadian *immeru* "sheep" also means "sheep and goat," "small livestock," and "ram."[4] It also appears in construct relations such as *immer šadi* "mountain sheep" or *immer ilī* "sheep of the gods." Apart perhaps from the personal name *'immer* (Jer. 20:1; Ezr. 2:37,59; 10:20; Neh. 3:29; 7:40,61; 11:13; 1 Ch. 9:12; 24:14),[5] Hebrew does not attest *'mr* in the meaning "lamb, sheep."

As a term for an individual animal in a flock, Hebrew utilizes instead *keḇeś* or its variant *keśeḇ* (cf. Akkadian *kabsu* "young ram," Arabic *kabš*, Syriac *kebšā'*) or *śeh* (cf. Akkadian *šūm*, *šu'u*, Arabic *šāt*, Ugaritic *š*, Aramaic *š't*) and *ṣo'n* to denote either an individual animal or the flock itself.[6]

In Jacob's Blessing (Gen. 49), however, *'imrê šāp̄er* may mean "beautiful young animals" (v. 21),[7] which would then be associated with this word. • The fact, however, that only Aramaic (although in all its major dialects), Akkadian, Ugaritic, and Phoenician-Punic[8] utilize the word, but Arabic only on the margins, Hebrew only with some question, and Southern Semitic not at all (as far as is now known), suggests that it involves

C. Dohmen, "כֶּבֶשׂ *keḇeś*," *TDOT*, VII, 43-52.

1. *ThesSyr*, 247; *MdD*, 352b.
2. *CIS* II 3913 II 42.
3. Cf. *KBL*[3], 65a.
4. *CAD*, VII, 129ff.
5. But cf. J. A. Thompson, "On Some Stamps and a Seal from Lachish," *BASOR* 86 (1942) 25f.
6. G. Waschke, *TDOT*, XII,197-207.
7. Cf. *KBL*[3], 65a.
8. *DNSI*, 78.

a cultural word at home in the Syro-Mesopotamian region that was then transmitted via Aramaic to Arabic.[9] The presumptive ground form is *immir whose *a* vocalization in later Aramaic dialects can be explained phonetically by the following *r*.[10] (*Ko.*) •

2. Sheep and Shepherd Metaphor in the Ancient Near East and the OT. The major significance that flocks had for the sustenance of communities leads to the fact that sheep and shepherd motifs are widespread in the literature of the ancient Near East.[11] Thus, Mesopotamian literature describes gods such as Enlil and Marduk as shepherds of the people[12] and kings such as Gilgamesh and Hammurabi as shepherds of their kingdoms.[13]

This motif also appears in Egypt, to be sure, but is much less common there. Thus, Merneptah in his Karnak inscription boasts that he is "the ruler. . .who tends as shepherd."[14] The common portrayal of Egyptian gods and kings with the crook in their hands is also interpreted to the effect that they are supposed to emphasize their function as shepherd.

The Bible describes God both as the shepherd of the people of Israel (e.g., Ps. 80:2; "Give ear, shepherd of Israel, who leads Jacob like a flock") and of the individual (e.g., Ps. 23:1; "the Lord is my shepherd, I shall not want"; cf. also Gen. 48:15). The shepherd motif also serves to describe God's liberating action in the context of the Exodus (e.g., Ps. 78:52: "He caused his people to break out like a flock and led them like sheep in the wilderness") and Israel's return from Exile (e.g., Jer. 23:3: "And I myself will gather the remnant of my flock from all nations where I have scattered them; and I will bring them back to their pasture, and they will be fruitful and multiply"; cf. also Isa. 40:11).

The Bible also compares Israel's leaders to a shepherd. The Israelites remind David that God told him that "you are to be the shepherd of my people Israel" (2 S. 5:2). Ps. 77:21 describes Moses and Aaron as mediators of God's shepherding ("You led your people like a shepherd by the hand of Moses and Aaron") and Jer. 23:1 designates Israel's rulers in general as shepherds—although bad ones ("Woe to the shepherds who destroy and scatter the flocks of my pasture! Saying of Yahweh").

3. Lamb as Sacrificial Animal. Lambs are among the most common sacrificial animals in the Bible. The *ʿôlāh* ("the burnt offering") of the *tāmîḏ*, i.e., the regular sacrifice, involved the daily offering of two lambs, one in the morning and one in the evening (Ex. 29:38-42). The more general *ʿôlāh* can also involve bulls and rams, however. A lamb seems to have been the primary sacrificial animal for Passover, even though a few biblical traditions also permit the offering of other domestic animals. Sacrificial animals must be a year old (*ben šᵉnāṯô*), flawless (*tāmîm*), and with no physical defects (*ʾašer bô mûm*; e.g., Lev 22:19f.; 23:12). Most sacrifices require a male lamb, although sometimes a female is also permitted (e.g., Lev 5:6; Num 6:14). The preference for male sacrificial

9. S. Fraenkel, *Die aramäischen Fremdwörter im Arabischen* (Leiden, 1886), 107f.
10. *ATTM,* 107,515.
11. Dohmen, 47ff.; G. Wallis, *TDOT*, XIV, 37-45.
12. E.g., EnEl VI:107; *ANET* 337 D (= IV R^2:23; cf. *HKL* I, 403) I 31.
13. E.g., Gilg II 24f.; CH I:22.
14. *ARE* 3:243.

animals is undoubtedly due to the necessity of preserving the flock since far fewer male than female animals were needed for that purpose.

II. Old Aramaic. *'mr* occurs in the middle of the eighth century B.C.E. in a Sefire inscription in the context of the curses against the king of Arpad, Mati'el, in the event that he should break the alliance with Barga'ya, the king of *Ktk*. They repeatedly employ the formulation, with slight variations, "may 7 X suckle one Y suckle and it will not be satisfied."[15] In such lists one also finds then "may seven mother sheep [*š'n*] suckle one lamb ['*mr*] and it will not be satisfied."[16]

The inscription from Tell Fekherye from the middle of the ninth century B.C.E. contains a similar, although harsher, curse. The author of the stele, the king of Gosan, threatens any who should erase his name from the stele with the words: "May a hundred mother sheep [*š'wn*] suckle one lamb ['*mr*] and it not be satisfied."[17]

Such curses underscore the importance of sheep for society since they produce both wool for clothing and shelter and milk and meat for nourishment.

In the sayings of Aḥiqar 120-122, *'mry'* occurs in a saying from the animal world that seems to give expression to the belief in divine determinism. In it a bear (*db*) turns to a group of lambs, apparently assuring them that he will do nothing harmful to them. The lambs responded: "Take what you want to take from us. . ., for it is not in the power of human[s] to lif[t] their feet and set them down with[out the god]s."

III. Biblical Aramaic. Biblical Aramaic attests *'immar* only three times in the book of Ezra, always in the plural *'immᵉrîn* and always in reference to sacrifice (Ezr. 6:9,17; 7:17).

The first instance appears in Darius's letter to the official of the province of Trans-Euphratene. According to Ezr. 5, Tattenai, the governor of Trans-Euphratene, and Shetar-Bosnai had sent a letter to Darius with the request to examine the Jews' claim that they had received permission under Cyrus to rebuild "the house of God that is in Jerusalem" (5:16). The Edict of Cyrus, which confirms the testimony of the Jewish elders, was found in Median Ekbatana (6:2). Thereupon, Darius placed it in force again not only determining that the Jews should be permitted to rebuild the temple, but also that all the costs should be paid from the royal treasury. Even the materials necessary for the daily sacrifice until the completion of the temple are included in these expenses: "whatever needed for the burnt offering for the God of heaven, whether young bulls, rams, and lambs ['*immᵉrîn*]" (6:9).

The next occurrence of "lambs" ('*immᵉrîn*) appears somewhat later in ch. 6 in a list of sacrifices offered at the ceremony consecrating the temple. The priest offers "one hundred bulls, two hundred rams, four hundred lambs, and twelve he-goats as a sin offering for all Israel according to the tribes of Israel" (Ezr. 6:17).

The last instance of our word occurs in the decree that Artaxerxes gave Ezra. Artaxerxes commanded Ezra to see to it that Judah and Jerusalem follow the law of God. Ar-

---

15. *KAI* 222 A 19-24; 223 A 1-3.
16. *KAI* 222 A 23; probably also to be emended in 223 A 2.
17. T.Fekh. 20.

taxerxes also commissioned him to acquire the animals for the sacrifice in the temple. As before, the list of sacrificial animals contains "young bulls, rams, and lambs" (Ezr. 7:17).

Freedman/Geoghegan

Ezr. 6:9, in particular, poses a historical problem in that at least the early Achaemenids, according to what appears to be known about their religion, fundamentally rejected animal sacrifice and, accordingly, did not support it among the peoples subject to them.[18] Consequently, it is dubious that the explicit arrangement of an official support of such sacrifices by Cyrus is historical. If one does not regard the whole letter fictitious,[19] then one must reckon here with a later revision. This view also finds support in the fact that the reference to animal sacrifice in Ezr. 6:9 is poorly integrated syntactically. The missive of Cyrus traces to an old source, however, that still knew, in keeping with Achaemenid practice, of no official support for animal sacrifice on the part of the Persians and into which secondarily, in assimilation to the Jewish sacrificial cult, the reference to the sacrificial animals for the burnt offering was inserted.

Kottsieper

IV. LXX. The LXX translates Biblical Aramaic *'immᵉrîn* with the Greek ἀμνός "lamb," also used mostly for the translation of Hebrew *keḇeś* (eighty-five times) or its variant *keśeḇ* (twice). In addition, Greek ἀρνός occurs less often, rendering *keḇeś* six times and *keśeḇ* five times, and least often πρόβατον (twice for *keḇeś* and six times for *keśeḇ*). Except for Lev. 14:10 (= πρόβατον), ἀμνός consistently renders the feminine forms *ka/iḇśāh* and *kiśbāh.*

V. Qumran. According to the Targum of Job from Cave 11, the friends of Job and his family members each gave him, in addition to the golden ring reported by MT (Job 42:11), a "female lamb" (*'mrh,* 11Q10 38:7).[20] *'mr* also appears in the fragments of the book of Enoch from Qumran that contain the report of Enoch's vision of Israel's sojourn in and Exodus from Egypt. This vision depicts Israel as "sheep" (*'mry'*), while the Egyptians appear as "wolves" (*dby'*; 4Q205 2 2:29; 4Q206 5 2:14ff.; cf. 1 En. 89:12-36). This image has parallels in the Hebrew Midr. Rab. Est. 9:2, e.g., where Israel also appears as a lamb (*kbś*), but the nations as wolves (→ VII).

18. H. Koch, *Die religiösen Verhältnisse der Dareioszeit. GOF.I* 4 (1977), 145f., 177f.; cf. also I. Kottsieper, "Die Religionspolitik der Achämeniden und die Juden von Elephantine," in R. G. Kratz, *Religion und Religionskontakte im Zeitalter der Achämeniden. VWGTh* 22 (2001), 150-78; idem, "Zum aramäischen Text der 'Trilingue' von Xanthos und ihrem historischen Hintergrund," *Ex Mesopotamia et Syria lux. FS M. Dietrich. AOAT* 281 (2001).

19. D. Schwiderski, *Handbuch des nordwestsemitischen Briefformulars. BZAW* 295 (2000), 381.

20. J. A. Fitzmyer and D. J. Harrington, *A Manual of Palestinian Aramaic Texts. BietOr* 34 (1978), 46.

VI. Rabbinic Aramaic. A letter from Rabban Gamaliel II (ca. 100 C.E.) addressed to "the exiles in Babylonia, Media, and Greece, and all the other exiles of Israel" determines that the current year should be lengthened by 30 days since, in addition to other signs, the lambs are still too tender (*'mry' rkykyn*) and the time of the grain harvest that marks the beginning of the year is not yet there.[21]

The Targums normally render both Hebrew *kebeś/keśeḇ* as well as *śeh* with *'mr* (*'immar*; cf. e.g., Tg. Onq. of Gen. 30:32; Ex. 29:39). The Palestinian Talmud employs *'mr* in a construct relation with *pysh'* to denote the paschal lamb.[22] It also appears in comparisons such as "May this be forbidden for me like the lamb (of the daily sacrifice)."[23] In a taunt about the Galilean pronunciation of the laryngeals and vowels, the Babylonian Talmud tells of a situation in which a Galilean cried out, "Who wants an *amar*?" which could be understood as "an ass" (*ḥamār*), as "wine" (*ḥᵃmar*), as "wool" (*ʿᵃmar*) or as "lamb" (*'immar*).[24]

This gives rise to the question of the relationship between Aramaic *'mr* "lamb" and *ʿmr* "wool." Although the two words are linked semantically, they come from different proto-Semitic roots, namely **'mr* and **ḍmr*. Old Aramaic rendered proto-Semitic *ḍ* with *q*, and later with ʿ. In Hebrew, the same *ḍ* became *ṣ* (cf. e.g., proto-Semitic **'arḍ* "earth," which became *'rq* or *'rʿ* in Aramaic, but *'ereṣ* in Hebrew, all forms of which Jer. 10:11-12 attest). Therefore, proto-Semitic **ḍmr* appears along with Aramaic *ʿᵃmar* (cf. Dnl. 7:9 "and the hair of his head was like pure wool") in Hebrew as *ṣmr* (cf. *ṣemmer* "wool" and Middle Hebrew as *ṣammār* "wool worker").

Freedman/Geoghegan

VII. Regarding the Metaphorical Usage. The figurative use in Aḥiqar 120-122 (→ II) and the Aramaic Enoch literature (→ V) demonstrates that *'mr*, like Hebrew *keḇeś*[25] appears to a special degree as a metaphor for helplessness or vulnerability. Thence, the corresponding shepherd metaphor (→ I.2) acquired a special anthropological meaning. Ancient Near Eastern and OT people experienced themselves more in the role of the "lamb" needing the protection and care of a heavenly (= god) and/or earthly (=king) shepherd. This documents a general experience of uncertainty and threat of (not just) ancient humans that led to a feeling of weakness and abandonment that corresponds to the experience or wish for concealment by a towering power.

Kottsieper

---

21. *ATTM,* 359f.
22. Jer. *Meg.* 72b; 74a; Jer. *Sanh.* 29c.
23. Midr. *Ned.* 1:3; Jer. *Ned.* 27a.
24. Bab. *'Erub.* 53b.
25. Dohmen, 52.

אנס *'ns*

I. Etymology and Distribution. II. Semantic Horizon. III. The Aramaic of the Babylonian Targum Tradition.

I. Etymology and Distribution. The genuinely Aramaic root *'ns* "to oppress," "to force" first occurs in Biblical Aramaic (Dnl. 4:6), thereafter especially in Jewish and Christian Palestinian Aramaic, less often also in Syriac. Outside the Aramaic language group, it occurs only in late Biblical Hebrew (Est. 1:8; Sir. 34:21 niphal; cf. *'wns* Sir. 20:4), in CD 16:13 and in Middle Hebrew in a usage corresponding to the Aramaic, so that it is rightly assumed to be an Aramaism.[1]

The etymological connection with Arabic *nassa* "to force" (said of a camel)[2] is dubious; it should probably be seen as a by-form of *nasaʾa* "to hold back" (< *nšʾ*; cf. Sabean ns_1ʾ).[3] The connection suggested by G. Hoffmann with *hns*,[4] which appears at Sefire (*wyhnsnh*)[5] and Nerab[6] should also be rejected. These passages involve the removal of a stele or a grave, or of its contents, which has nothing in common with the actual basic meaning of *'ns*. The Jewish Aramaic meaning of *'ns* in the sense of "to rob" adduced here[7] rests on a later dialectical semantic development (→ III) that one can hardly assume for these early inscriptions.

II. Semantic Horizon. The root *'ns* can denote any form of pressure or resistance that a thing or person can exert. This relative indeterminacy of the basic meaning accounts for the fact that the root, despite in few instances in the older texts, appears in various contexts with differing connotations. Thus, in Dnl. 4:6 Nebuchadnezzar assures Daniel, who can interpret dreams through the holy spirit indwelling him, that *kŏl rāz lāʾ 'ānes lāḵ* "no secret [is] an *'ānes* for you." The context makes it clear that *'ānes* (peal ptcp.) here should be understood in the sense of "difficulty," something that brings resistance or makes problems. The instance in 4Q531 17:9 points in a similar direction when a giant recounts his dream that "oppressed" (*ḥlmy 'nsn*[*y*]) him, while the parallel statement in l. 10 indicates that he could not sleep anymore. The aspect of the "oppressive" continues in the use of the noun *'wns* in the sense of "misfortune," "tragedy" that has befallen someone in Palestinian Jewish Aramaic.[8]

J. Barth, "Zur altaramäischen Inschrift des Königs Zkr," *OLZ* 12 (1909) 10-12; M. Wagner, *Die lexikalischen und grammatikalischen Aramaismen im alttestamentlichen Hebräisch. BZAW* 96 (1966).

1. Wagner, 27.
2. A. Guillaume, "Hebrew and Arabic Lexicography," *AbrN* 1 (1959) 6; *GesB*[18], 82a.
3. A. F. L. Beeston, et al, *Sabaic Dictionary* (Beirut, 1982), 98; cf. Lane, 2785b.
4. "Aramäische Inschriften aus Nerab bei Aleppo," *ZA* 11 (1896) 212.
5. *KAI* 202 B 20.
6. *KAI* 225.6: *thns*; 226.8: *lthns*; 226.9: *wthnsny*.
7. Cf. also Barth, 11.
8. E.g., Tg. Neof. of Lev. 10:19; *DJPA*, 40b.

In contrast, 1QapGen 11:13 speaks of Betenosh, who initially reacted very harshly to the suspicions of her husband Lamech that her child Noah was not his (l. 8), but finally responded to her husband. It describes this rehearsal with *'nst rwḥh'*: "she overcame her spirit," i.e., she controlled her emotions. Similarly, Bab. *B. Bat.* 57b expresses the aspect of self-control necessary in a situation of temptation with the phrase *'ns npšryh* "to overcome himself." While this connotes the pressure that one exerts on oneself in the restrictive aspect of control, conversely in Syriac *'ns* can also denote positive pressure with which one seeks to squeeze out the best from one's capacities. Thus, the Peshitta of Wisd. 14:19 describes the efforts of the artist to create a particularly beautiful image with *'ns 'wnwwrh* "he forced his art."

An essential aspect, however, is that of oppression or compulsion that one exerts on another in order to attain something. This aspect already occurs in *'wns* "compulsion," "force," which describes pharaoh's abduction of Sara in 1QapGen 20:11.[9] In addition, in a not entirely clear context, 4Q550 7 speaks of a "violent person and liar" (*'nws wšqr*).[10]

III. The Aramaic of the Babylonian Targum Tradition. From this point, finally, the aspect of violent robbery (but not of simple theft) could accrue to the root *'ns* in Babylonian-Targumic Aramaic, so that it was available to translate Hebrew *gzl*, too, which also denotes violent robbery.[11] Since the other dialects do not exhibit this,[12] it probably involves a unique semantic development within this dialect.

Kottsieper

---

9. Cf. also Jewish Aramaic *'wns*, *DJPA*, 40b; *TW*, I 42a.
10. Cf. Jewish Aramaic *'nws*, *TW*, 142a.
11. Cf. e.g., Tg. Onq. of Gen. 21:25; 31:31; Lev. 19:13; Dt. 28:31; *TW*, I 41f.; J. Schüpphaus, *TDOT*, II, 456-58.
12. Cf. *DJPA*, 40b,66; *LexSyr*, 30; *LSP*, 13b.

אֲנַף *'np* *ᵃnap̱*

I.1. Etymology and Occurrence. 2. Meanings. II. Instances in Aramaic. 1. Old Aramaic. 2. Imperial Aramaic. 3. Palmyrene. 4. Biblical Aramaic. 5. Qumran.

J. Cantineau, "Textes funéraires palmyréniens," *RB* 39 (1930) 520-51; A. Dupont-Sommer, "L'ostracon araméen du sabbat," *Sem* 2 (1949) 29-39; J. Bergman and E. Johnson, "אָנַף *'ānaph*," *TDOT*, I, 348-60; C. H. Kraeling, *The Excavations at Dura-Europos: Final Report VIII/1; The Synagogue* (New Haven, 1956); J. M. Lindenberger, *The Aramaic Proverbs of Ahiqar* (Baltimore, 1983); R. Comte Mesnil du Buisson, *Inventaire des inscriptions palmyréniennes de Doura-Europos* (Paris, 1939); B. Porten, "Une lettre araméenne conservée à l'Académie des Inscriptions et Belles-Lettres (AI 5-7): Une nouvelle reconstruction," *Sem* 33 (1983) 89-100; idem and J. C. Greenfield, *Jews of Elephantine and Arameans of Syene* (Jerusalem, 1984); W. Röllig, "Alte und neue Elfenbeininschriften," *NESE* 2 (1974) 37-64; M. Sznycer, "Trois fragments de papyri araméens d'Égypte d'époque perse," *Hommages à André Dupont-Sommer. FS. A. Dupont-Sommer* (Paris, 1971), 161-76.

I. *1. Etymology and Occurrence.* The common Semitic word for "nose" is *'anp* (*qatl*, masc.): Akk. *appu*,[1] Eblaite *a-bù*,[2] Arabic *'anf*,[3] Ethiopic *'anf*,[4] Ugaritic *ap*,[5] Hebrew *'ap*, Syriac *'appē* "face,"[6] and Mandean *'npy'*.[7] In addition to the form *'np*, which prevailed in the written younger languages (secondary geminate dissimilation),[8] Aramaic has the Old Aramaic form *'p* (*'ap*[*p*]) with assimilation of the preconsonantal /n/ that younger Aramaic also continues to attest alongside *'np*.

2. Meanings. As do most words denoting body parts, *'anp* carries many metaphorical meanings in the Semitic languages based either on the form of the nose itself (such as Akkadian *appu* "current of a stream") or its position as a body part protruding from the face (such as Aramaic "front side"; Akkadian "upper side," "peak"). Pars pro toto, Hebrew and the Aramaic family of languages can employ the word in the dual for "countenance." Consequently, Aramaic can also form expressions associated with *pānîm* "face" with *'pyn* (*'py 'rq* "face of the earthy" [→ II.2], *'npy myn* "face of the water" [→ II.5]; cf. in Heb. with *pānîm* Gen. 2:6; Isa. 14:21; Ps. 104:30; Job 38:30). This is also true for prepositional expressions with *'l*, *l*, *b*, and *mn*. Otherwise, it can denote a certain behavior specifically associated with the nose (such as Arabic *'anf* "arrogance," cf. Heb. Ps. 10:4: *rāšā' kᵉḡoḇah 'appô*). In Hebrew and in Ugaritic,[9] it established the meaning "wrath",[10] for which Hebrew and Moabite[11] formed a denominal verb *'np* "to be angry."[12] The dual of *'*(*n*)*p*, employed predominantly in Aramaic, originally denoted the two nostrils; in later Aramaic, however, "nostril" is *nḥyr* (*qatīl* < *nḥr* "to snuffle"),[13] as is also true of later Hebrew (*nᵉḥîr*, Job 41:12) and Akkadian (since Old Babylonian times).[14]

II. Instances in Aramaic.

1. Old Aramaic. The oldest examples in the inscriptions from Sefire[15] already offer almost the complete semantic spectrum of *'p*(*yn*): *KAI* 224.2 already evidences the basic

1. *AHw*, I, 60.
2. M. Krebernik, "Zu Syllabar und Orthographie der lexikalischen Texte aus Ebla," *ZA* 73 (1983) 9f.
3. Wehr[5], 48f.
4. *CDG*, 28.
5. *DUL*[3], 84f.
6. *LexSyr*, 39a.
7. *MdD*, 27a.
8. *ATTM*, 89-95; *ATTM.E*, 40f.
9. E.g., *KTU* 1.6:V21; *DUL*[3], 85; doubtful in Aramaic see II.2 on *AP* 37.9.
10. *GesB*[18], 87.
11. *DNSI*, 83 s.v. *'np*.
12. See Johnson in Bergman-Johnson, 379, cf. Arabic *'anifa* "to feel aversion."
13. 11Q10 33:2? = Job 39:20; so *ATTM*, 295. Regarding the difficulties in the reading, cf. J. P. M. van der Ploeg and A. S. van der Woude, *Le Targum de Job de la Grotte XI de Qumrân* (Leiden, 1971), 76 n. 2; M. Sokoloff, *The Targum to Job from Qumran Cave XI* (Ramat Gan, 1974), 155; XXXVI 5 (Job 41:12); *LexSyr*, 424a.
14. *AHw*, II, 714b: *naḫīru*.
15. *KAI* 222-224.

meaning "nose": *kl gbr zy yb'h rwḥ 'pwh* "anyone who seeks the breath of his nose (i.e., the breath of life)" (dual const. with 3ms suffix). The formulation designates the refugee who seeks asylum. The syntagma *rwḥ 'pyn* "breath (of life)" is not peculiar to Aramaic (cf. Heb. *rûaḥ 'appayim*, Lam. 4:20; Akk. *šār appī*).[16] *KAI* 222 A 42 exhibits the meaning "countenance": *wymḥ ' 'l 'pyh* "and one smote her face" (dual const. with 3fs suffix; → מחי *mḥī*). In *KAI* 222 A 28, *'pyn* serves to denote the earth's surface: *'l 'py 'rqh* (dual const.). The brief inscription on an ivory from Arslan Tash (Ḫadattu) for application to a throne designates with *'p* (sg. const.) either the front of a throne or a prominent (decorative) element of one: *'p krs'* "front (?) of the throne" (→ כרסא *karse'*).[17]

2. *Imperial Aramaic.* The blessing formulas of Imperial Aramaic letters regularly contain *'(n)pyn*: *brktky lptḥ zy yḥzny 'pyky bšlm* "I bless you by Ptah, may he let me see your face in well-being."[18] Dupont-Sommer 31 conv. 4-5[19] offers an unusual formulation: *tḥzyn 'npy w'ḥzh 'pyky* "You see my face and I see your face." Aḥiqar 134 in the context of a proverb also involves the meaning "face": *mkdb gzyr qdlh kbtwlh tymnh zy [tḥwh?] l'npyn* "The throat of a liar is slit like (that o)f a maiden who [shows] her face."[20] Aḥiqar 133 also says of the liar: *wyrwqn b'npwhy* "and one will spit in his face." The meaning "surface" occurs in the marriage contract *AP* 15.19: *'l 'npy 'r'* "on the surface of the earth." The combination involving the preposition *b* occurs frequently: *[b']npy m[lk] 'l tqwm* "Do not rise in the presence of a king."[21] The curse formula of *KAI* 228 A 13-15 (a stele from Taima) attests the combination with the preposition *mn* (cf. Heb. *me'al pᵉnê*): *'lhy tym' ynsḥwhy wzr'h wšmh mn 'npy tym'* "May the gods of Taima eradicate him and his descendants and his name from Taima!" The usage with the preposition *l* before an indication of the price appears only once: *l'npy kršn 10* "for the price of ten *krš*."[22] Similar expressions in Palmyrene (see II.3.) are comparable. The figurative meaning "wrath" is probably present in *AP* 37.9: *mhšdk 'npyn* "calming our wrath"; the context is too fragmentary, however, to give a certain interpretation.[23] • It may be, however, that *b'npwhy* in Aḥiqar 201 should be translated "(to die) in his wrath."[24] (*Ko.*) • In Pahlavi, *'p* survives as a punctuation mark.[25]

16. *AHw*, I, 60a.

17. Röllig, 40f., no. 3.

18. Hermopolis 2.2; cf. 1.2; 3.2; 4.2; 5.2; 6.2 (= *TADAE* A2.1-2.6); 8:2 (corr.; *TADAE* D1.1); *BMAP* 13.4; *TADAE* A5.1:4 (= Porten, 94:4; contra Sznycer, 168,172f); Padua 1.3 (*TADAE* A3.3:3).

19. *CIG* 152; *TADAE* D7.16.

20. Regarding the passage, see Lindenberger, 130f.; contra *TUAT*, III 329 [V 9]: "previously."

21. Aḥiqar 101; contra Lindenberger, 81: *['l ']npy* "against"; similarly *TUAT*, III 336 (X 7): *[b']npy* "against"; cf. *b'npwhy* Aḥiqar 201,202; later M 72:6 (*ATTM*, 318); xyNG 3 (= Jer. *San. 18d*; *ATTM*, 359).

22. Segal, 40.4.

23. Likewise *AP* 37.8; regarding the passages, see Porten-Greenfield, 81; *TADAE* A4.2 translates "our presence."

24. Cf. *TUAT*, III 341 (XV 10).

25. Cf. *Frahang* X.16; Kraeling, 300 (42.5); 301 (43.6-8); 311 (51.3).

3. *Palmyrene.* The professional designation *hdy nṭryn 'p bb'* "chief of the guards of the front of the gate" (*'p* sg. const)[26] stems from Dura Europos. A meaning that appears only in Palmyrene is *'py* (dual const.) before a currency designation in the sense of "to . . . (precisely)": *mks' dy kṣb' 'py dnr ḥyb lmtḥšbw* (// Greek 181: τὸ τοῦ σφάκτρου τέλος εἰς δηνάριον ὀφείλει λο[γεύεσθαι])[27] "The butcher's tax must be calculated to the denar (precisely)."[28] A further peculiarity of the Palmyrene inscriptions is *l'p'* "toward, against . . . thence" (adverbial accusative): Cantineau, 548 no. 14.6 *l'p' mdnḥ'* "toward the East."[29]

4. *Biblical Aramaic.* Just as in Imperial Aramaic, *'pyn* also means "countenance" in Biblical Aramaic—Dnl. 2:46: *be'ḏayin malkā' nᵉḇûkaḏneṣṣar nᵉpal 'al 'anpôhî* (LXX: ἐπὶ πρόσωπον) "Immediately, Nebuchadnezzar , the king, fell on his face";[30] Dnl. 3:19: *be'ḏayin nᵉḇûḵaḏneṣṣar hiṯmelî ḥᵉmā' ûṣᵉlem 'anpôhî 'eštannî* (*Q*; LXX: ἡ μορφὴ τοῦ προσώπου) "Immediately, Nebuchadnezzar was filled with wrath and his facial expression (lit. image of his countenance) was changed."[31]

5. *Qumran.* The Job Targum attests most of the meanings of *'(n)p(yn)*. "Nose" occurs in physiognomic descriptions (in the Heb. Job always *'ap̱*): 11Q10 10:10 (Job 27:3); 35:3.5 (Job 40:24,26, cf. 1QapGen 20:3; 4Q561 1 1:2); "countenance" (Heb. always *pānîm*): 11Q10 6:8 (Job 22:8); 23:4 (Job 33:26, face of God); 25:5 (Job 34:29; cf. 1QapGen 2:12,17; 20:2,4; 4Q203 3; 4Q543 6:5 = 4Q544 1:14 [paralleling *ḥzw* "appearance"]; 4Q544 1:9; 4Q196 5:8 [Tob. 3:12]; 4Q550d 3; 4Q531 9:3); "surface of the water": 11Q10 29:1 (Job 37:10; Heb. *roḥaḇ*); "surface of the primordial deep (?)": 31:7 (Job 38:30; Heb. *ûpᵉnê*); "surface of the earth": 29:3 (Job 37:12; Heb. *'al pᵉnê*). Additional prepositional expressions appear in 11Q10 33:3 (Job 39:21): *l'npy* "opposite" (Heb. *liqrā'ṯ*) and 33:4 (Job 39:22): *wl' ytwb mn 'npy ḥrb* "it (rope, wild cattle) does not turn back before a sword" (Heb. *mippᵉnê*).

Schwemer

26. Du Mesnil du Buisson 39.3 = Doura 39 in D. R. Hillers and E. Cussini, *Palmyrene Aramaic Texts* (Baltimore, 1996).

27. *CIS* II 3913 Palmyr. II 102f.

28. Cf. *CIS* II 3913 Palmyr. II 105f. // Greek 183f.; Palmyr. II 135.

29. cf. Cantineau, 526 no. 2B,3.

30. Cf. 4Q531 9:3.

31. Cf. 1QapGen 2:12:17; 20:2.

אֱנָשׁ *'nš 'ænāš*

I. Lexeme. II. Meaning. 1. As the Term for a Category. 2. "Humanity." 3. "Each," "All." 4. *br 'n(w)š*. III. The "Son of Man" in Dnl. 7. IV. Anthropology. 1. Human and Animal. 2. Human and God.

I. Lexeme. In Semitic, "human," from the root *'nš*, appears in the probably not deverbal, nominal forms *qiṭāl* (Can. and Aram.) or *quṭāl* (Arab.) and *qiṭl* (Arab.; Can. and Aram. only in the plural *'ᵃnāšîm/n* "people" of *'îš* "man"). The Aramaic word is increasingly spelled with *waw* from the end of the second century B.C.E. onward[1] since here dialectical Aramaic (and later under the influence of dialectical Arabic) *ā* sometimes became *ō*. In Aramaic, *'n*(*w*)*š* is the only word for "human," while it occurs in Hebrew (ca. 700 B.C.E. *ā* to *ō*), aside from the name of a patriarch and in Isa. 8:1, only in late poetry.

Aramaic *'n(w)s* "human" is usually construed as a masc. sg., but occasionally as a masc. pl.[2] The first datable forms with plural endings stem from the sixth century C.E.[3] Before that the word appears only in the three states of the singular and with suffixes.

II. Meaning.

1. As the Term for a Category. The word *'n(w)š* properly designates humans as a category, whether alongside God/a god (Dnl. 6:8.13),[4] in contrast to God/gods,[5] or in contrast

K. Beyer, "Der Menschensohn als Gott der Welt: Der Ursprung der hohen Christologie bei Jesus selbst," in *Der Christliche Orient und seine Umwelt. FS J. Tubachs* (Wiesbaden, 2007), 11-19; N. P. Bratsiotis, "אִישׁ *'îsh*," *TDOT*, I, 222-35; M. Casey, "Idiom and Translation: Some Aspects of the Son of Man Problem," *NTS* 41 (1995) 164-82; C. Colpe, "ὁ υἱὸς τοῦ ἀνθρώπου," *TDNT*, VIII, 400-477; J. Eggler, *Influences and Traditions Underlying the Vision of Daniel 7:2-14. OBO* 177 (2000); H. Haag, "בֶּן־אָדָם *ben 'ādhām*," *TDOT*, II, 159-65; M. Henze, *The Madness of King Nebuchadnezzar. JSJSup* 61. (1999); O. Keel, "Die Tiere und der Mensch in Daniel 7," in idem and U. Staub, *Hellenismus und Judentum. OBO* 178 (2000), 1-35; K. Koch, *Das Buch Daniel. EdF* 144 (1980), 216-34; idem, "Messias und Menschensohn," *JBT* 8 (1993) 73-102; idem, "Der "Menschensohn" in Daniel," *ZAW* 119 (2007) 369-85; idem, "Das Reich der Heiligen und des Menschensohns," in idem, *Die Reiche der Welt und der kommende Menschensohn* (Neukirchen-Vluyn, 1995), 140-72; J.-C. Loba Mkole, "Une synthèse d'opinions philologiques sur le Fils de l'homme," *JNSL* 22 (1996) 107-23; F. Maass, "אָדָם *'adhām*," *TDOT*, I, 75-87; idem, "אֱנוֹשׁ *'ᵉnôsh*,"*TDOT*, I, 345-48; T. B. Slater, "One Like a Son of Man in First-Century C.E. Judaism," *NTS* 41 (1995) 183-98; L. T. Stuckenbruck, "'One like a Son of Man as the Ancient of Days' in the Old Greek Recension of Daniel 7,13: Scribal Error or Theological Translation?" *ZNW* 86 (1995) 268-76; J. Tubach, *Im Schatten des Sonnengottes* (Wiesbaden, 1986), esp. 475-80; C. Westermann, "אָדָם *'ādām* person," *TLOT*, 31-42.

1. 4Q542 2:7 (*DSSStE*, 1084f.).
2. Aḥiqar (89),122,123f.; 1QapGen 20:32; 4Q548 3:3 (Testament of Amram 5:63; *DSSStE*, 1094f.); 11Q10 11:3 (Job 27:13); 28:2 (Job 36:25 = Heb.); letter of Simon bar Kosiba ySK 14:3-5 (*ATTM.E*, 216).
3. Jewish Galilean and Christian Palestinian Aramaic; *ATTM*, 517.
4. *KAI* 228 A 20 (Taima).
5. Aḥiqar 124: "The attention of the gods rests on [the] humans"; cf. also 162; Dnl. 4:14b,22b,29b; 5:21b: "The Most High is the ruler over all human kingdoms."

to the animals (Dnl. 4:13; 7:4,8).[6] Consequently, it also characterizes the human form,[7] the upright human stance (Dnl. 7:4), and human body parts (Dnl. 2:43 "human seed"; 4:13; 7:4 "human heart"; 5:5 "human hand"; 7:8 "human eyes").

2. *"Humanity."* From the category designation, it is only a small step via the meaning "(the) humanity"[8] to the collective "(the) humans,"[9] more concretely: "people,"[10] "inhabitants of" (Ezr. 4:11),[11] "members of"[12] specifically "members of his/my family,"[13] and "possessor of."[14]

3. *"Each," "All."* The phrase *kl ʾn(w)š* means "all," "each," "everyone" (Dnl. 3:10; 5:7; 6:13; Ezr. 6:11),[15] negated "no one,"[16] and even without *kl*.[17]

4. br ʾn(w)š. In order to express "individual person," "someone," Aramaic places *br* "son of" in the meaning "individual example of" (→ בר *bar*) before *ʾn(w)š*: *br ʾn(w)š*,[18] negated *lʾ . . . kwl br ʾnwš* "not a single person."[19] Its plural *bny ʾn(w)š(ʾ)* "(the) humans, people" (Dnl. 2:38; 5:21)[20] is synonymous with a simple *ʾn(w)š*, as the interchange between the two expressions in the same clause "he was driven out of the midst of humans" Dnl. 4:30 (*ʾᵃnāšāʾ*) and 5:21 (*bᵉnē ʾᵃnāšāʾ*) indicates. The combination with *bny* "sons," "children" can also include women, although there is also the combination with *brt* "daughter" in the sense of "female individual."[21]

III. The "son of man" in Dnl. 7. The best known and most controversial expression is *bar ʾᵉnāš* (LXX and Pseudo-Theod. υἱὸς ἀνθρώπου; → בר *bar* III) in Dnl. 7:13: "Together with (and like) the clouds in the sky (thus, not from the depths) came something (that looked) like an individual" human." This figure followed four animals that arose from the sea, images of the four emperors (7:17) or four empires (7:23f.) Thus, the human-like

6. 4Q204 4:10 (1 En. 89:36).
7. 4Q209 26:5 (1 En. 78:17); 4Q204 4:10 (1 En. 89:36).
8. 4Q534 1:8 (The Birth of Noah 1:8; *DSSStE,* 1070f.); 4Q536 1 1:7; 2:9 (The Birth of Noah 6:7; 7:9; *DSSStE,* 1072-75).
9. Aḥiqar 116,122; Dnl. 4:22,29,30; 4Q534 1:4 (The Birth of Noah 1:4; *DSSStE,* 1070f.).
10. 1QapGen 19:15; 20:32; 22:15; 11Q10 11:3 (Job 27:13).
11. yMS 556:2 (*ATTM.E,* 212).
12. *AP* 28.10; 1QapGen 21:19.
13. 1QapGen 20:16-19; 21:21.
14. 4Q545 3:5 (Testament of Amram 7:18; *DSSStE,* 1090f.): "human of his pleasure."
15. 4Q212 5:17,[20],22 (1 En. 93:12-14); 4Q197 4 2:5 (Tob. 6:13), etc.
16. 1QapGen 19:23; 4Q213b 3 (= CT. Levi Bodleian a 13; T. Levi 33:13); coffin from Jerusalem yJE 42 (*ATTM.E,* 207).
17. *AP* 28.8; *BMAP* 8.5,8; Dnl. 2:10; Letter of Simon bar Kosiba ySK 8:13 (*ATTM.E,* 214f.).
18. *KAI* 224.16 = TSSI II 9:16; Dnl. 7:13; 4Q206 2 2:4 (1 En. 22:5; regarding the reading, see *ATTM,* 241).
19. 1QapGen 21:13.
20. 1QapGen 19:15; 4Q201 3:18 (1 En. 7:3); 4Q206 2 2:1 (1 En. 22:3); 4Q209 23:8 (1 En. 77:3).
21. 1QapGen 6:20 *bnt ʾnw[š]*; Syr.

one symbolizes simultaneously both a rule and a realm ("corporate personality"). Only the interpretation as a person survived into the Christian era (NT; 1 En. 37-71; 4 Ezr. 13). It is entirely possible that an old (in which case probably Can.) myth of a shift of power in the divine realm, mitigated by the LXX and Rev. 1:13-16 through the equation of the human-like one with the ancient God, stands behind this symbol. The animal-human contrast may stem from the author of Dnl. 7 himself.

The shared lord and representative of the holy ones (of the Most High), i.e., of the angels (Dnl. 7:18,22,25; 7:21,22) and of the people of the holy ones of the Most High, i.e., of Israel (7:27)—each group includes the other (cf. the common shared cult and war of the Qumran community and of the angels)—can only be the archangel Michael as a new God, which also gave christology a framework. The NT ὁ υἱὸς τοῦ ἀνθρώπου "the Son of Man" must render a determined *br 'nš'*. Since a determined "the individual human," "the someone" is unusual,[22] it must be meant as a citation ("of the *bar 'enāš* known [from Dnl. 7:13]").

Beyer

IV. Anthropology.

1. Human and Animal. Aḥiqar 85b-89a contains proverbial units that describe the particular behaviors of real animals (scorpions, lions). The clause *h' kn pg' hm zy* [*'n*]*š'* "See, so is their fate!—That of humans!" that concludes each of these sayings, which obviously do not project human behavior on the animal or plant world like fables, indicates they operate on a fundamental comparability between human and animal life.

When, however, the interpretation of Nebuchadnezzar's dream in Dnl. 2 speaks of the fact that he has power over *b^enê 'anāšā' ḥêwaṯ bārā' w^e'ôp̱ š^emayyā'* "people, animals of the field, and birds of heaven" (v. 38), it may be due rather to a redactional connection to the world-tree motif in ch. 4 and not an additional reference to an essential similarity between the animal and human worlds. Thus, Dnl. 4 likewise compares Nebuchadnezzar as ruler of the world (v. 19) with the world-tree, whose "realm of dominion" includes, however, "the animals of the field" (*ḥêwaṯ bārā'*) and "the birds of heaven" (*ṣippare š^emayyā'*; vv. 9,18; cf. v. 11).

The relationship between animal and human in the tradition of Dnl. 4 is rather complex. Various motifs stand side-by-side here. The third-person account in vv. 22,29f. operates on the notion that Nebuchadnezzar was expelled from human society and lived with the wild animals. This applies, however, only to externalities: He will feed on grass, not live in a house, but in the wild, and he will appear outwardly as a brute. These depictions and the context imply that human life elevates itself from animal life through culture, which, in turn, signifies a debasement of the human being—just as, conversely, the cultivation of the wild Enkidu makes him a human being.[23] Because of his hubris (v. 27), Nebuchadnezzar stays in this animal existence until he acknowledges the true dominion of God (vv. 22,28). At the same time, this suggests a relationship between the capacity for recognition and

22. *ATTM,* 517f.; *ATTM.E,* 311.
23. Gilg PIII 105 (*TUAT,* III 651); Henze, 96.

human existence explicitly mentioned in the first-person account in vv 31,33. According to it, Nebuchadnezzar's animal existence was apparently tied to the loss of the capacity for recognition (*minda'*), whose return enabled both his acknowledgement of God's dominion and his return to the human world and to the throne. Keel (23-27) wants to see here an influence of Greek philosophy since the demarcation of the human from the animal precisely regarding the human capacity of understanding is an innovation of this tradition. Yet, for example, the twelve tablet version of the Gilgamesh Epic explicitly describes the cultivation of Enkidu, who was not an animal but only lived with animals,[24] as a broadening of his understanding (*ḫasīsu*).[25] Therefore, the fact that, among others, intellectual potentialities distinguish a human from an animal accords with the motif that human existence also expresses itself in the particular character of the human heart, the seat of thought and understanding. Thus, in addition to the motif of upright stance, the gift of a human heart depicts the humanization of the first animal in Dnl. 7:4. Conversely, when in Nebuchadnezzar's dream the world-tree loses its human heart and receives an animal heart (Dnl. 4:13), it is probably a later expansion that extends the idea of the first-person account that the king loses his capacity for understanding to a complete dehumanization of the king.

2. Human and God. Another important aspect of anthropology is the human potential to act self-determinedly. On the one side, this separates humans from animals in that humans can appear in this respect directly alongside the gods. This occurs in prohibitions addressed both to humans and to the gods,[26] and in the motif that one requests something of the gods or of humans (Dnl. 6:8,13). Both imply that human beings, just like gods—but not like animals—can determine their own actions. Thereby, however, the human being is, on the other side, also addressed as a responsible being, as recorded, e.g., in Aḥiqar 123f. There, one encounters the notion that the gods punish humans when they speak evil.

Aḥiqar 120b-123a points in another direction, however. It offers a fable in which a bear approaches lambs, apparently cordially, and receives the response that he should, indeed, take what he (usually) takes "for it is not in your power to lift your foot and to set it down again" (123). Without interruption, the fable applies the powerlessness of an animal even as powerful as the bear expressed here to human beings: "for it is not in the power of humans to lift their foot or to set it down without [the god]s" (cf. Jer. 10:23). With respect to their capacity to act, this fable once again links human beings closely with the animals. Just as they cannot act in their own power, so human beings cannot act in their own power, but only in agreement with the gods. The fact that the Aramaic sages append directly to this saying the saying mentioned above concerning the responsibility of humans in relation to the gods and then a saying, unfortunately not completely preserved, concerning what it means "if the eyes of the gods are on humans" demonstrates the thoroughgoing awareness of the irreducible complexity of human existence between impotence and responsibility.

Kottsieper

24. Contra Keel, 24.
25. Gilg I:iv:29; *TUAT*, III 678.
26. *KAI* 228 A 20.

אנתה *'nth* /'ettā/; **אנתו** *'ntw* /'ettū/; **נְשִׁין** *nšyn* *n^ešîn*

I. Etymology. II.1. Epigraphic Examples. 2. Elephantine. 3. Murabba'at. 4. Jewish Aramaic. III. Biblical Aramaic. IV. Qumran. V. *nš(y)n/nšwn.*

I. Etymology. The singular form of the word that means "woman" or "wife," *'nth*, traces back to the proto-Semitic root **'nṯ*. Contrariwise, the plural *nšyn* "women/wives" derives from the original root **nšw*.

The etymologies of both roots are uncertain. Although many scholars associate *'nth* with the root *'nš* (Aram. *'nš* "man"; → אנשׁ *'^enāš*), this seems unlikely because of the different final consonants. *'nš* can be linked to the verb *'nš* I "to be weak," possibly constituting an allusion to human mortality. Equally possible is the derivation from the root *'nš* II "to be genial, cordial" attested in Arabic, and South Semitic, which would link humans with the element of sociability.

Words related to the singular form appear in Ugar. (*aṯt*), Heb. (*'iššāh*), Phoen.-Pun. (*'št*, also plural), Akk. (*aššatu* [pl. *aššāti*] and *iššu*), Arab. (*'unṯā*), Ge'ez (*'anest*, pl. *'anestiyā* and *'a'nus*),[1] and OSA *'nṯ*. These many related words for "woman" in Semitic demonstrate, in fact, that the etymological relationship established in Gen. 2:23 between the Hebrew *'iššāh* "woman," which corresponds to Aram. *'nth*, and *'îš* "man" is false and that *'yš* does not belong to the same root.

Words corresponding to the plural *nšyn/nšwn* occur in Heb. (*nāšîm*) and Arab. (*nisā'*, *niswat*, *niswān*), cf. also Ugar. *nšm* and Akk. (*nišu*), which mean "people, men" however.

All Aramaic dialects attest *'nth/nšyn*.

Freedman/Levitt Kohn

With the plural form *nšwn*, the inscription from Tell Fekheriye[2] exhibits a peculiarity that, along with the Arabic forms, supports the derivation from **nšw*. Since, however, the plural form in Imperial Aramaic usually appears defectively as *nšn*, *nš(y)n* would then be traceable to a secondarily abbreviated base **niš* because a nominal derivative of **nšw nšyn* would be expected for the regular plural absolute. Conversely, it is also possible that one should assume a primary **niš* in the dialect of the inscription from Tell Fekheriye secondarily declined **niš-ūt* (if the Ugaritic and Akkadian words mentioned above are related to our word at the root level), or assimilated to a triradical root in the

N. P. Bratsiotis, "אִישׁ *'îsh*," *TDOT*, I, 222-35; É. Levine, *Marital Relations in Ancient Judaism. BZABR* 10 (2009); Y. Muffs, *Studies in the Aramaic Legal Papyri from Elephantine. HO* 66 (1969); B. Porten, *Archives from Elephantine* (Berkeley, 1968).

1. Cf. *CDG*, 32a; there also concerning the other Ethiopian languages.
2. T.Fekh. 21,22.

individual languages. Regarding the nominal form of *'nth* cf. I. Kottsieper, *Die Sprache der Ahiqarsprüche. BZAW* 194 (1990), 189.

Kottsieper

II. *1. Epigraphic Examples. 'nth* occurs in many Aramaic inscriptions, including legal texts (property and marriage contracts) and accounts, and usually denotes the "wife." The following forms appear: sg. abs. *'nth*, const. *'ntt*, *'tt*, emph. *'ntt'*, + 3ms suffix *'nšth*, *'ntth*, *'tth*, 2ms *'nttk* and 1cs *'ntty*. The inscriptions that exhibit the word include the one from Arebsun that describes the sister of the god Bel as his wife, too (*'ḥth w'ntth zy byl kn 'mr 'nh 'ntt zy byl mlk'* "The sister and wife of Bel said thus: 'I am the wife of the king, Bel'").[3] See further the statue of the woman from Hatra which describes the one depicted as *'ntt nšr'qb* "The wife of NŠR'QB" (l. 3),[4] the burial inscription for a woman from Armazi (*'ntt zy ywdmngn* "the wife of Yodmangan"),[5] or the texts from Saqqara.[6]

2. Elephantine. The word also appears frequently in the various contracts and documents found on Elephantine that attest the important and independent status of women in the Jewish colony of Elephantine. The fact that one of the two archives that contained all these Aramaic legal documents belonged to the woman Mibtaḥya testifies to the significant status of women.[7] The word *'nth*[8] occurs in documents concerning the possession of land[9] and real estate[10] and in marriage contracts.[11] It occurs additionally in a letter from Elephantine datable in the last decade of the fifth century B.C.E. that reports about the imprisonment of Jewish leaders, including several women.[12]

3. Murabba'at. A few passages in the Elephantine texts attest the word *'ntw* to express the status of a married woman or, perhaps, meaning "marriage": *l'ntw*.[13] The phrase *spr 'ntw*[14] apparently denotes a marriage contract.[15]

4. Jewish Aramaic. The word *'nth* also occurs, e.g. in several documents found in the Wadi Murabba'at stemming from the late first or early second centuries C.E. A marriage

3. *KAI* 264.2f.; cf. also l. 8.
4. *KAI* 249.
5. *KAI* 276.3.
6. J. Segal, 7.2; 29.8; 30b.4; 68.10; 98.3,4; 134.3.
7. Muffs, 55; Porten, 260f.; cf. e.g., also *AP* 28, which clearly indicates that Mibtaḥya possessed slaves.
8. Which except for *AP* 25.10-14 always means "wife."
9. *AP* 6.4.
10. *AP* 8.10; 9.4,6; 46.9,11; *BMAP* 4.2,25; 6.3; 12.2,11,24,33,35.
11. *AP* 15.4,18,27,32f.; *BMAP* 2.3,7; 7.4,21f.,25,29,36,38; cf. further *AP* 7.5.
12. *AP* 34.3.
13. *AP* 15.3; 48.3; *BMAP* 2.3; 7.3,37; 12.25.
14. *AP* 14.4; 35.5; *BMAP* 10.7,9f.; 12.18.
15. Muffs, 6.

contract between a man from the priestly family of Eliashib and his future wife, also from a priestly family,[16] attests the sentence [*'t*]*y thw' ly l'nth kdyn m*[*wšh*] "You shall be my wife according to the law of Moses" (l. 3).[17] The term also appears in a certificate of divorce granting the woman permission to remarry: *dy hwyt 'nty mn qdm dh dy 't ršy' bnpšky lmhk wlmhy 'nt<h> lkwl gbr yhwdy dy tṣbyn* "you who were my wife until now, so that you are now free for yourself to become the wife of another Jew whom you want."[18]

III. Biblical Aramaic. The sg. *'nth* does not occur in Biblical Aramaic. Dnl. 6:25 attests only the plural with the 3mp suffix *n^ešêhôn* denoting the wives of the officials who accused Daniel. These women were ultimately thrown into the lions' den with their husbands and children. The word occurs generally here with no particular theological significance.

IV. Qumran. A few Aramaic texts from Qumran attest *'nth* in the sense of "woman," "wife." Thus, it occurs in the Job Targum from Cave 11: *rwḥ hmkt l'ntty* "I have debased (my) spirit before my wife" (11Q10 11:6 [Job 19:17]), "[if] my heart was tempted by a wo[man] (*b[l'nth]*)" (11Q10 18:1f. [Job 31:9]). It appears frequently in the Genesis Apocryphon from Cave 1, including three times in reference to Lamech's wife Betenosh (*bt'nwš 'ntty* "my wife Betenosh," 1QapGen 2:3,8,12). In this section, Betenosh falls under suspicion of being pregnant by one of the fallen angels. Lamech journeys to paradise so that his grandfather Enoch can calm him over the matter. The word occurs elsewhere in reference to Sarai, Abram's wife, in the context of a journey to Egypt. Sarai is taken captive and transferred to the harem of Pharaoh Zoan. It attests the following forms: *lšry 'ntty* "my wife Sarai" (1QapGen 19:17); *wnsbh' lh l'nth* "and he took her as his wife" (20:9); *'ntty* "my wife" (19:24; 20:14,15); *wšry 'ntth* "and his wife Sarai"; *'ntth* "his wife" (20:23); *šry 'ntt 'brm* "Sarai, the wife of Abram" (20:25); *'nttk* "your wife" (20:27 [2×]); and *wnsbth' ly l'nth* "I took her as my wife." (20:27). Finally, the conclusion of the story reports that Lot took his wife from the daughters of Egypt (*wnsb lh 'nth mn bnt* [*mṣryn*]; 20:34). For additional instances, cf. *ATTM,* 518 and *ATTM.E,* 311.

Freedman/Levitt Kohn

V. *nš(y)n/nšwn.* The plural *nšyn/nšwn* denotes groups of women in general,[19] and, frequently wives as well when it does not involve multiple wives of one man.[20] An unequivocal example of *nšyn* in the context of real polygamy occurs only in *KAI* 222 A 41 (Sefire, eighth century B.C.E.), which speaks primarily of the wives (*nšy*) of King Mati'el. This evidence does not argue that monogamy was the norm in the communities from

16. M 20; *ATTM,* 309f.; J. A. Fitzmyer and D. J. Harrington, *A Manual of Palestinian Aramaic Texts*. *BietOr* 34 (1978), 140f.

17. Cf. a similar marriage contract from Egypt, yyZZ 36:8 (*ATTM.E,* 246).

18. M 19:5-7,16-19; *ATTM,* 307f.; Fitzmyer-Harrington, 138-41.

19. Esp. T.Fekh. 21,22; Uruk (12),37; 1QapGen 20:7; 4Q214 3:3 (*DJD,* XXII [1996], 49).

20. *AP* 30.20; 31.14; *BMAP* 7.38; 1QapGen 12:16, 4Q201:111,14 (=4Q202 2:18; ?) 4:5; 4Q203 8:7,8.

which our texts stem. Clauses in the marriage contracts that explicitly exclude it indicate that polygamy was absolutely still a real possibility in the Persian period.[21]

The fact that, meanwhile, both *ʾnth* and *nšyn* are relatively rare as generic terms for "woman"[22] finds an explanation in the social status of the woman, who was fundamentally subordinate to a man: as a young girl to her father, as a wife (*ʾnth*) then to her husband, so that the term for woman was normally a synonym for wife, usually contrasted with *bʿl* as the counter concept "husband" (→ בעל *beʿel*). Her appearance as an independent legal subject (esp. → II.2) indicates, however, that this classification is not to be understood as a deprival of rights. The designation of a woman as *ʾntt* of a man in such contexts apparently functions to identify her clearly, as recorded in the legal texts such as those from Naḥal Ḥever[23] or Murabbaʿat[24] and in grave inscriptions[25] or other simple references to names.[26] This close association of *ʾnth* in reference to a specific woman with her status as wife may also explain the peculiar Imperial Aramaic choice for the title "Lady, Dame," not *ʾnth*, but the pl. abs. *nš(y)n*,[27] from which the simple meaning "woman" also becomes attached to *nš(y)n*.[28] Especially, *TADAE* C3.9:3,0 makes it clear that *nš(y)n* does not mean wife in this usage since it follows *nšn rbh* "a great woman" by describing her as *ʾntth* "his wife." Accordingly, then, *Frahang* XI.5 equates *nyšh* with the Persian *zan* "woman."

Kottsieper

---

21. *AP* 15.31f.; *BMAP* 7.36f.

22. for *ʾnth* "woman" at Qumran, cf. in addition to 11Q10 18:2 (→ IV) esp. also 4Q197 4 1:13; 4Q213a 2:3; in 11Q10 36:2f. (Job 41:9), *ʾnth* in the formula *ʾnth lḥbrth* "one another" simply takes up a no-longer preserved feminine word for scale.

23. Cf. e.g., V 45:12 (*ATTM,* 320f.).

24. M 26:3 (*ATTM,* 313f.).

25. E.g., yJE9b (*ATTM,* 341).

26. E.g., yMS 399,402 (*ATTM.E,* 210); → II.1.

27. *AP* 8.2; 10.2; *BMAP* 3.2; 4.2; 5.2; 7.3; 9.2; 12.1.

28. *BMAP* 3.3; *TADAE* C.3.9:3,7,9,12,14.

אסה *ʾsh* → אָשַׁף *ʾāšap̱*

אספרנה *ʾsprnh* /ʾosparnā/; אדרזדה *ʾdrzdh* /ʾedrazdā/

I. Etymology and Lexical Field. II. Usage.

J. Naveh and S. Shaked, *Aramaic Documents from Ancient Bactria (Fourth Century B.C.E.)* (London, 2012); J. Tavernier, *Iranica in the Achaemenid Period (ca. 550-330 B.C.). OLA* 158 (2007).

I. Etymology and Lexical Field. The Aramaic adverb *'sprnh* /'osparnā/ "completely, exactly" traces to Old Persian **uspṛna*.[1] It belongs to Imperial Aramaic administrative terminology and also appears rather frequently in Ezra. Semantically, it has affinities with the adverb *'drzdh* /'edrazdā/ "diligently, exactly," also borrowed from Old Persian, in Ezr. 7:23. It refers there to the precise delivery of the goods allocated for the Jerusalem temple by royal command and corresponds with *'sprnh* in 7:21, etc.

II. Usage. In Achaemenid sources, *'sprnh* denotes the precise weight of a silver stater[2] and the complete (i.e., counted or weighed) delivery of grain to a barn of the Bactrian satrap;[3] this usage also explains the use in an Egyptian satrap's letter[4] for an undiminished delivery of something (revenues?). Accordingly, the word often refers in Ezra to the exact payment or provision of goods (6:8; 7:17,21) and execution of royal commands generally (6:12f.), sometimes generally for the careful execution of a commission or intention (the construction work on the temple in 5:8 and the procedure for lawbreakers in 7:26).

Gzella

1. Tavernier, 406f., §4.4.2.21.
2. *KAI* 263.
3. Naveh and Shaked, A6.8.
4. *TADAE* A6.13,4.

אֱסָר *'sr* *'esār; אֱסוּר *'swr* *'esûr; אסר *'sr*

I. *'sr:* Basic Meaning and Etymology. II. Older Aramaic. 1. "To Detain," "to Fasten." 2. *'sr* as a Legal Term. 3. Upbringing. 4. Summary. III. Biblical Aramaic. 1. *'esār*. 2. *'esûr*. IV. Qumran. V. Magic.

I. *'sr:* Basic Meaning and Etymology. One can hardly assign the root *'sr*, distributed throughout the entire Semitic linguistic realm, the basic meaning "to bind" in the technical sense: Akkadian does not attest this meaning whatsoever and *'sr* consistently

W. Boochs, "Strafen," *LexÄg* VI, 68-72; E. Ebeling, "Gefangener, Gefängnis," *RLA*, III (1957), 180-82; M. Henze, *The Madness of King Nebuchadnezzar*. *JSJSup* 61 (1999); K. Koch, "Gottes Herrschaft über das Reich des Menschen," in idem, *Die Reiche der Welt und der kommende Menschensohn* (Neukirchen-Vluyn, 1995), 83-116; G. Thür, "Desmoterion," *Brill's New Pauly*, Antiquity IV (2004), 318-19; M. Wagner, *Die lexikalischen und grammatikalischen Aramaismen im alttestamentlichen Hebräisch*. *BZAW* 96 (1966).

manifests a close relationship to imprisonment. If one takes into further consideration the fact that the Akkadian word exhibits the basic meaning "to include" and can designate canalization,[1] then one must assume that *'sr* originally denoted actions that hinder someone or something from moving freely. The canalization of waters can be just as easily derived from this basic meaning as Akkadian *esirtu* "concubine" can be from "enclosed one"[2] and the meaning "to harness (a wagon)" attested in Ugaritic,[3] Hebrew (e.g., Gen. 46:29), and Phoenician.[4] The latter meaning derives from the technique of attaching animals to a wagon (e.g., 1 S. 6:7,10), thereby—in analogy to canalizing water—restricting their freedom of movement and subjecting it to human will. Since, however, a process designated by *'sr* was very often associated with the technique of binding, shackling, one can easily understand how *'sr* in West Semitic then also accrued the connotation "to tether," "to tie up" and finally came to be employed in a diluted fashion for "to gird," etc. The fact that this involves a secondary and probably rather late development is evident in that Hebrew, e.g., attests this meaning only rarely (Job 12:18; similarly, but still clearly with the connotation "to tether," Neh. 4:12) and that older Aramaic does not know it at all (→ IV).

II. Older Aramaic.

1. "To Detain," "to Fasten." In both Old and Imperial Aramaic, the verbal root *'sr* first occurs in the meaning "to take prisoner," "to fasten." Thus, in the oldest instance from Sefire, it designates the capture of a ruler in the context of a putsch.[5] The antonym there is *šrh* "to set free" and the parallel act for removing a ruler is *qtl* "to kill."

In the legal diction of the Imperial Aramaic papyri from Egypt, to the degree that the pertinent preserved contexts permit a precise interpretation, *'sr* denotes detention in the context of legal cases. Thus, *AP* 38.3f. reports the detention of a Jew from Elephantine by the garrison commander because of a stolen stone found with merchants. A further text mentions persons who were detained, apparently also involving the important role played by theft (ll. 3-8).[6] Another text makes it clear that *'sr* means detention and not imprisonment.[7] Also in the context of a legal case, it speaks of *'ḥd* "to grab," "to seize," i.e., "to imprison," and *'sr* "to detain" in sequence. *AP* 66.5.4[8] also confirms this interpretation: *'ḥ[d]w 'srw bkbly*["they imprisoned, placed in chains of. . . ." The supplement with *bkbly* indicates that such a detention could also involve shackling. Finally, one can also refer to Segal 50.9, where one encounters a *by'sm*, which probably denotes a prison (cf. Heb. *bêṯ hā'esûr* [Jer. 37:15]; *bêṯ hā'ᵃsîrîm* [Jgs. 16:21,25, *K*]; Akk. *bīt esēri* "cage").[9]

1. *AHw*, I, 249b.
2. B. Landsberger, "Studien zu den Urkunden aus der Zeit des Ninurta—tukul—Assur," *AfO* 10 (1935-1936) 144f.
3. *KTU* 1.20:II:3; 1.22:II:22.
4. *DNSI*, 90f.
5. *KAI* 224.18.
6. Reconstructed by combining *AP* 56 and 34 (*TADAE* A4.4).
7. *AP* 69 A 3f. (= *TADAE* B8.5:7f.).
8. = *TADAE* A4.6:16.
9. *AHw*, I, 249b.

2. *'sr as a Legal Term.* The noun *'sr*, which denotes a contractual agreement, also belongs to Imperial Aramaic legal terminology. The slave contracts of the Samaria papyri designate as such agreements that are "established" (*qwm hiph;* 1.11; 3.9) and cannot be altered (*šnh b;* 2.6; 7.11; cf. further 2.4,10).[10] This noun also apparently occurs in Segal 8.10[11] and 3.1,[12] in association with words like *qym* "covenant," *ktb* "to write," *spr* "document," and *'bd* "to make," Here, *'sr* is a documented agreement governing the rights of the parties to the contract and thus restricting their discretion.

This usage of *'sr*, which cannot be distinguished from Biblical Aramaic *'ᵉsār* (→ III.1), has precursors in the designation of a legal agreement as *'sr'*, as attested as an Aramaic addendum on a clay tablet from the time of Nabonidus.[13]

This legal use may also be present in a Palmyrene inscription: *w'srw whqymw byny[hn]* "and they assumed obligations and arranged between [themselves]."[14] This usage gives rise, then, to the possibility of a new interpretation of the divine designation *rb'syr'* in the famed Palmyrene tariff schedule to whose temple the new tariff provisions were brought.[15] Thus, one may understand *'syr* as a designation for the obligation or the regulation that restricted even the customs collectors in their caprice, which apparently often led to contention (I:4ff.!). The "lord of the obligation/regulation," then, was the god who guaranteed this regulation; this designation corresponds in substance with the *'lhy 'dy'* "the gods of the contracts,"[16] whose temple apparently likewise houses the text of the contract.[17]

3. *Upbringing.* The specimen in Aḥiqar 80 does not belong to legal diction, however. Here, the hithpeel *ytsr* appears in the phrase *br' zy yt'lp wytsr wytšym 'rḥ' brglw[hy*, in which *br' zy yt'lp* means quite generally "the son who will be instructed/reared," while *wytšym 'rḥ' brglw[hy* "and to whose feet a brick will be fastened" rather drastically expresses the repressive character of education (→ אלף *'lp* II), which massively restricts the son's freedom of movement. In this context, *'sr* conforms very well to the horizon of meaning involving the restriction of someone's realm of action. It is noteworthy, however, if no scribal error is involved, that the assimilation of the ' in *ytsr*, which, as *yt'lp* already indicates, does not correspond with the diction of the sayings of Aḥiqar otherwise. Thus, it may be a later addition of the Imperial Aramaic scribe who wanted thereby to express the subsequent remarkable model of a restrictive method of education.[18]

10. Concerning the texts, see F. M. Cross, "Samaria Papyrus i," *EI* 18 (1985) 8*f.; D. M. Gropp, "The Samaria Papyri from Wâdi ed-Dâliyeh" (diss., Harvard, 1986), 1f.,38f.,63f.,105f.

11. = *TADAE* B5.6:10.

12. = *TADAE* B8.10:1.

13. A. T. Clay, *The Babylonian Expedition of the University of Pennsylvania VIII/1* (Philadelphia, 1908), no. 51.

14. J. Cantineau, "Tadmorea," *Syr* 17 (1936) 351.12; cf. D. R. Hillers and E. Cussini, *Palmyrene Aramaic Texts* (Baltimore, 1996), 342a.

15. *CIS* II 3913:I:10 (= Ραβασειρη Greek I:11).

16. *KAI* 222 B 23.33; 244.4,14,17,23.

17. *KAI* 223 C 2f.

18. I. Kottsieper, *Die Sprache der Ahiqarsprüche. BZAW* 194 (1990), §35,231.

4. *Summary.* The central texts of older Aramaic, therefore, manifest *'sr* in a broad spectrum of meaning that still largely reflects the original meaning of the root. The controversial instances from Kandahar[19] and Tang-I Sarvak,[20] i.e., from the outlying regions, remain unclear.[21]

III. Biblical Aramaic.

1. 'ᵉsār. In Dnl. 6:8-10,13f.,16, Biblical Aramaic *'ᵉsār* designates Darius's famed prohibition against addressing a request to anyone other than the king himself for thirty days. Thus, it does not involve a general law, but a situation-bound edict. The designation *'ᵉsār* apparently alludes to the noun *'sr* as a term for a restrictive legal agreement or determination (→ II.2). Accordingly, Dnl. 6 manifests the same lexical field also attested in the passages mentioned above. The description of the promulgation of the prohibition employs *qwm* hiphil, e.g., (6:9,16; cf. also v. 8), while its legal documentation plays a great role (6:9f.,13f.). *šnh* haphel expresses its (prohibited) alteration (6:9,16). Consequently, one can speak of *'ᵉsār* as a fixed legal term, which also survived in Nabatean *'sr* "restrictive order"[22] and Syriac *'esār* in the meaning "verdict," "penalty" or "abeyance,"[23] and probably also offered the foundation for Hebrew[24] *'ᵉsār/'issār* "vow of abstinence."[25]

2. 'ᵉsûr. The use of the plural form *'ᵉsûrîn* in Ezr. 7:26, where it represents detention in the context of penal law, also points to the legal realm. In this regard, it takes up the corresponding use of *'sr* in older Aramaic (→ II.1) and finds counterparts especially in Syriac *'asūr*, Mandean *'swr*, Christian Palestinian Aramaic *'swr* "shackle," "prison,"[26] which Jewish Aramaic[27] and Samaritan Aramaic[28] also attest.

Contrary to the common view, however, it is hardly correct to assume that *'ᵉsûrîn* designates imprisonment here. The observation that such a penalty rarely appears in ancient societies and is not common in biblical law argues against it; the detention of politically disagreeable persons (e.g., 2 K. 17:4; Jer. 37:15) naturally does not belong in the realm of the penal law addressed in Ezr. 7:26. Instead, detention in the framework of a legal proceeding serves, first, to hinder the flight of the suspected and convicted and to facilitate a punishment.[29] This observation also accords, however, with the fact that in Ezr. 7:26 *'ᵉsûrîn* falls syntactically outside the series of forms of punishment structured by a threefold *hen.* In contrast, *wᵉleʼᵉsûrîn* joins the series without *hen.* Thus, one may

19. *KAI* 279.7.
20. *Asia Major* NS II (1951-1952) 171:1:3; 2:2.
21. Cf. the discussion in the literature cited in *DNSI,* 90f.
22. nV 7:53,60,61; *ATTM.E,* 167-73.
23. *LexSyr,* 38a.
24. And Jewish Aramaic; *DJPA,* 68a; *WT,* I 51b.
25. Wagner, 28; cf. also Jewish Aramaic *'yswr* "prohibition," "prohibited" (*DJPA,* 51b) and Samaritan Aramaic *'yswr* "oath," "vow" (*LSP* A 55a).
26. *LexSyr,* 38a; *MdD,* 354; *LSP,* 15f.
27. Tg. of Prov. 7:22: "shackle."
28. "Prison," Tg. A of Gen. 51:10.
29. Boochs, 69; Thür, 318; Ebeling, 181f.

conjecture that *w^e^le'^e^sûrîn* did not stand in the text originally, but was added later by an editor who missed the aspect of detention, absolutely important not only in the context of penal law, and who wanted to express the fact that the Jewish self-administration in Ezr. 7 was, of course, authorized to detain people.

It is entirely unclear and disputed what Dnl. 4:12,20 means precisely by the "shackles of iron and bronze," in which the rootstock of the tree was placed after its destruction.[30] The author may take up here an ancient Near Eastern motif of trees provided with metal bands,[31] but then one must decide that he hardly understood it any longer[32] and interpreted here in the sense of a shackling of the tree or of the king.

IV. Qumran. The root *'sr* occurs at Qumran with a stronger connotation of binding. Thus, apart from 1Q20 1 1:4 where *'syryn* ("prisoner" [?]) occurs in a destroyed context, 11Q10 27:2 corresponding to Job 36:8 speaks of the *'syryn b*[of "those placed in [shackles]." The question is whether 4Q203 8:14 means a captive to be liberated (*šrw' 'syrkn* "set your prisoners free"),[33] or that the giants should loosen their bonds (*šrw' 'swrkn* "your shackles loosen").[34] In 11Q10 30:1 (Job 38:3) and 34:2 (Job 40:7), then, the oldest instance so far of Aramaic *'sr* in the faded meaning "to gird" appears. In view of the fact that it renders Hebrew *'zr*, it is likely that this further development of the meaning of *'sr* was assisted by similar sounding root *'zr* "to gird" so that no "relationship"[35] exists here at all, but, herein, *'sr* depends on *'zr*.

V. Magic. The restrictive meaning of the root in the sense of "to restrict someone's freedom of movement or possibilities" becomes especially evident in its use in the context of its power to lame or disable. This occurs both in respect to the defense against magical or demonic power and for themselves. Thus, in the incantation from Uruk *a-si-ir li-iš-šá-ni(-')* should be understood in the sense of "who lames the tongue."[36] Moreover, the Palestinian Targum tradition of Dt. 24:6 employs forms of *'sr* in the context of the enchantment of newlyweds.[37] Conversely, amulets exhibit *'sr* in the context of the banning of demonic powers.[38] When one encounters *'sr* in l. 9 after two terms for "to tie" or "to bind" (*mqṭrnh 'lyk wmqm 'n' 'lyk)* in an amulet from Egypt (fifth century C.E.)[39],

30. Cf. the overview in J. J. Collins, *Daniel. Herm* (Minneapolis, 1993), 226f.; Henze, 84-87.

31. Koch, 111-17; Henze, 87-89.

32. Henze, 89.

33. cf. *ATTM,* 261.

34. So e.g., J. T. *Milik, The Books of Enoch* (Oxford, 1976), 315f.; *DSSStE,* 410f. (*'swrkwn*); cf. also the *'swr tqy[p]* "a strong shackle" appearing in the corrupt context of 4Q532 2:14.

35. So *GesB*[18], 31b.

36. A Oppenheim, "Lexikalische Untersuchungen zu den 'Kappadokischen' Briefen," *AfO* 12 (1937-39), 106.5,8.

37. Tg. Neof.; Tg. Yer.; Tg. Jon.; *WT*, I 50b; *DJPA*, 68b.

38. ooXX 10:3 (*ATTM.E,* 264); gg(t)AR 2:35 (*ATTM.E,* 250f.).

39. R. Kotansky, J. Naveh, and S. Shaked, "A Greek-Aramaic Silver Amulet from Egypt in the Ashmolean Museum," *Mus* 105 (1992) 5-25.

then the scribe may have likewise associated "to bind" with *'srnh y'tyk*. Since, however, in contrast to the first two words for "to bind," constructed with *'l* "about," "against," *'sr* appears here with a direct object and connects to the statement that thereby the one adjured shall have no more power, just as in l. 16 *'sr* is apparently associated with the magical power of Solomon's ring, it is nonetheless more likely that *'sr* occurs here, not in the specific sense "to bind," but as a technical magical term for "to render powerless," "to inhibit in efficacy."

Kottsieper

אָע *'' 'āʻ*

I. Etymology and Forms. II. Horizon of Meaning. III. Biblical Aramaic. IV. Qumran. V. Rabbinic Literature.

For the discussion of the form → *'l'*.

I. Etymology and Forms. The Hebrew counterpart of *''* is *'eṣ*. The Imperial Aramaic texts from Egypt offer *'q* (sg. abs.)[1] and *'q'* (sg. det.).[2] In Biblical Aramaic and Jewish Aramaic, the sg. abs. and det. are *'āʻ* and *'āʻā'*, respectively.

Freedman/Feliú

Additional forms in older Aramaic are the pl. abs. *'qn*,[3] which appears in *AP* 30.11; 31.10 as *'qhn*. This accords with the shift in the forms of the pl. const. *'qy*[4] and *'qhy*.[5] In *AP* 26.18, the pl. det. is *'qy'*. Later, only the simple pl. form *''yn*, *''y*, and *''y'* still appear.[6]

The transitional form between *''* and *'q* to *''* occurs at Qumran: *''yn*[7] and *''y*,[8] for which CT. Levi ar Bodleian c, 13.19 has *''yn* or *''y*. Among the other Aramaic dialects, the word only occurs in Nabatean.[9] The later dialects such as Syriac, Christian Palestinian Aramaic,

H. Ringgren and K. Nielsem, "עֵץ *'eṣ*," *TDOT*, XI, 265-76.

1. *AP* 20.5; *BMAP* 7.19.
2. E.g., Ostracon Cl-G 228 (= *TADAE* D7.5) conv. 1.
3. Aḥiqar 104,125; Segal 41.5.
4. *AP* 26.10,12, etc.
5. Segal 40.4; on the form, cf. also Segal 57.
6. Cf. *ATTM*, 520.
7. 4Q214b 2-6 1:3.
8. 4Q214b 2-6 1:5.
9. J. Naveh, "A Nabatean Incantation Text," *IEJ* 29 (1979) 112.9.

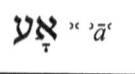

and Mandean employ, among other terms, *qys* (*qês*, *qays*), which also occurs in Jewish Aramaic, or → אילן *'îlān*.

The word traces to the common Semitic—apart from Modern South Arabian—primary noun *'*iḍ*, cf. in addition to Hebrew *'eṣ* also Phoen. *'ṣ*, Ugar. *'ṣ*, Akk. *iṣ(ṣ)u*, Arab. *'iḍat*, OSA *'ḍ*, and Eth. *'ᵉḍ*. Since in Aramaic, *ḍ* assimilated, via an intermediary step that approximated *q* and was accordingly spelled with this sign in older Aramaic, with *ġ* spelled with ' and underlying *aḫ-ḫu* "wood" in Uruk 2,[10] and finally transitioned fully to ', a word arose that consisted of a closed syllable with identical consonants. Since most Semitic languages avoid such a syllable or word structure, this led to a dissimilation of the open ' to '.

Kottsieper

II. Horizon of Meaning. The word exhibits three meanings: (1) "wood" in the general sense;[11] (2) certain objects consisting of wood, such as, e.g., "plank" or "beam";[12] (3) "tree."[13] Only the context in which the word occurs determines its exact meaning.

• In the sayings of Aḥiqar, the word "wood" occurs twice in a comparison. Thus, its destructibility alongside the vulnerability of flesh to a knife in Aḥiqar 104 serves as an image for a human being's defenselessness and lack of rights in contrast to the power of the king. Moreover, anyone who chops wood in the dark, being unable to see, is like a clumsy thief who gets caught.[14] (*Ko.*) •

III. Biblical Aramaic. *'ā'* occurs five times in the Bible either as a sg. abs. *'ā'* (Ezr. 5:8; 6:4,11) or det. *'ā'ā'* (e.g., Dnl. 5:4,23), each time in reference to concrete objects. In the three passages in Ezr., it is best translated "lumber" or "beams" and occurs each time in the context of the reconstruction of the Jerusalem temple. Thus, it denotes the lumber that the Persian King Cyrus donated for the reconstruction (Ezr. 6:4) and that was included in the structure of the walls of the temple (Ezr. 5:8; cf. 6:4). Ezr. 6:11 is particularly interesting since the word occurs here in the context of a curse. The Edict of Darius declares concerning any who may hinder the reconstruction: "that a beam (*'ā'*) will be ripped out of his house and, once reerected, he will be hanged on it." This curse acquires its full rhetorical significance only if one reads it in connection with the reference to building lumber in the preceding section (6:4). Thus, it appears as an ironic antithesis to Ezr. 6:4: Just as Cyrus and Darius finance the reconstruction of the "house of God" (6:3) by also supplying, among other things, the wood for its construction, so must any who oppose this project provide the wood for his gallows from his own house, which will ultimately destroy it. Thus, wood here becomes a sign both for blessing and for the fates of the various groups depending on the extent to which they agree with God's plan.

10. Contra A. Dupont-Sommer, "La Tablette Cuneiforme Arameenne de Warka," *RA* 39 (1942-44) 41f., who points to a nonetheless dubious Akk. "hunting net."

11. Cf. e.g., Ostracon Cl-G 228 (= *TADAE* D7.5) conv. 1.

12. Cf. e.g., *AP* 26.10,12-14,17f.,20.

13. Cf. e.g., CT. Levi ar Bodleian c,18f.

14. Aḥiqar 125.

The two instances in the book of Daniel also refer to an agreement, since both relate to idol images (Dnl. 5:4,23). Both passages involve gods of wood (ʾāʿāʾ) in a list alongside those of gold, silver, bronze, iron, and stone, which Belshazzar and his courtiers praise. Dnl. 5:23 expresses the contrast between these gods, who appear materially, and the true God, who does not and whom Belshazzar and his people do not honor. Thus, this verse describes God as "Lord of Heaven" (*mārē' šᵉmayyāʾ*), emphasizing his transcendence in contrast to the Babylonian gods produced from earthly materials.

IV. Qumran. The word appears only rarely in the Qumran texts. The fragment 4Q519 attests ʿʿ with no near context. Better preserved is 4Q242, the "Prayer of Nabonidus," which offers our word in the det. state as part of a construct chain naming the gods of gold, silver, wood, stone, and clay (l-3:7f.). Nabonidus had vainly sought redemption from his suffering from these gods before a Jew healed him. Therefore this text, as does the book of Daniel (to which 4Q242 exhibits close affinities), negatively contrasts gods produced from earthly material with the true God (of Israel).

• In addition, the word for wood as *ʿyn* or *ʿy* (→ I) occurs in the Aramaic tradition of T. Levi for the sacrificial wood that must be carefully chosen; cf. 4Q214b 2–6:I:3,5; and CT. Levi ar Bodleian c:9,13,18,19,22. Only twelve particularly aromatic species of tree are permissible (cedar, juniper, almond, tamarind, pine, ash, cypress, fig, olive, laurel, myrtle, and balsa), of which only the pieces that show no worm damage may be used. This tradition is attributed to Abraham. (*Ko.*) •

V. Rabbinic Literature. In rabbinic literature, ʿʿ can normally be translated simply "wood," cf. e.g., the three instances in the Tg. of Josh. 9:21,23,27, all of which refer to the Gibeonites as *lqṭy ʾʿyn* "wood gatherers." This construction represents MT *ḥoṭᵉḇê ʿeṣîm* "wood cutters." Frequently, however, the word denotes a particular species of wood such as cedar (*ʿyn dqdrynyn*, Tg. Neof. of Gen. 6:14) or acacia (*ʿyn d(y)šṭyn*, Tg. Neof. of Ex. 25:13; 27:6; 36:20; 38:6; Dt. 10:3; cf. also Tg. Onq. of Lev. 14:4; Jer. *Šabb.* 10c; Jer. *Pesaḥ.* 30d). One also encounters the plural form *ʾʿym*, e.g., Jer. *Eruvin* 19c; Jer. *Sukkah* 52a, where both instances stand in a context that suggests the translation "(cross) beam."

Freedman/Feliú

אֶצְבָּה *ʾṣbh* → יָד *yd yaḏ*

ארגון *ʾrgwn* /ʾargawān/

I. Etymology. II. Usage.

I. Etymology. The Aramaic form *ʾrgwn* /ʾargawān/ "purple wool" apparently developed secondarily from Akkadian *argamannu,*[1] whose ultimate origin can no longer be determined.[2] In this Aramaic form, the word also appears in 2 Ch. 2:6. It denotes reddish purple and differs from blue;[3] both were imported from Phoenicia[4] and, therefore, represented expensive luxury and royal splendor.

II. Usage. In older Aramaic, *ʾrgwn* always belongs among the gifts that kings make to those especially favored. Belshazzar promised purple garments[5] together with a golden chain[6] and a position as third in the kingdom to the one who could solve the puzzle of the flaming writing (Dnl. 5:7,16,29); according to 1QapGen 20:31 purple linen garments,[7] together with silver and gold, constitute the pharaoh's parting gifts for Abraham and Sarah; an instance in the court novella from Qumran without context[8] may have stood in a similar setting.

Gzella

1. With /m/ > /w/, see *ATTM,* 101.
2. Cf. P. Mankowski, *Akkadian Loanwords in Biblical Hebrew. HSS* 47 (2000), 38f.
3. /takilt/, also attested in Heb. in 2 C. 2:6 as *tᵉḵēlæṯ* and also in post-Christian Aram.
4. Cf. C. Bender, *Die Sprache der Textilien* (Stuttgart, 2008), 59f.
5. Here in the plur. det. *ʾrgwnʾ* for the concrete objects.
6. → *dhb.*
7. Here as an attributive in the sg. abs.
8. 4Q550 4:5.

ארז *ʾrz* → אִילָן *ʾyln ʾîlān*

אֲרַח *ʾrḥ ʾᵒraḥ*

I. Etymology. II.1. "Path." 2. In the Figurative Sense.

I. Etymology. The word **ʾurḥ* "path," attested in Aramaic from Old Aramaic to modern Aramaic,[1] occurs in the OT only in the plural with a suffix: *ʾorḥāṯāḵ* Dnl. 5:23; *ʾorḥāṯeh* Dnl. 4:34 (in Codex L always vocalized with *holem*, otherwise with *qamets khatuf*). The word *urḫum* "path" found since Old Akkadian[2] and the verb *arāḫum* "to

J. Bergman, A. Haldar, H. Ringgren, and K. Koch, "דֶּרֶךְ *dereḵ,*" *TDOT,* III, 270-93.

1. *KBL*³, 1673b.
2. *AHw*, III, 1429.

hurry" attested since Old Babylonian[3] demonstrate that the root *'rḫ* is at least Proto-Semitic.[4] Whether one is justified in assuming an *arāḫum* II "to consume," "to destroy"[5] is extremely questionable[6] in light of the Sabaean *'rḫ* "undertaking," "battle," "legal dispute."[7] In Hebrew, *'oraḥ* "path," "course" appears exclusively, apart from Gen. 18:11, in poetic texts along with and instead of *dereḵ*.

II. *1. "Path."* Sam'alian attests *'rḥ* in the sense of "military road"[8] and in Old Aramaic as the path that should remain open to diplomats.[9] At Elephantine, *'rḥ mlk'* ("king's street") denotes the public thoroughfare[10] in contrast to the neighborhood lane *šwq*.[11] 1QapGen 21:28 has in view with *'rḥ' dy mdbr'* ("wilderness road") the caravan, later Roman, road from the Euphrates via Palmyra to Damascus; 22:4 means by *'rḥ'* <*dy*> *ḥlt' rbt'* ("street of the great valley") the road through the Jordan Valley. For many, including admirers of Paul Gerhardt's famous hymn "Commit Thou All Thy Griefs," the "path" of the clouds in heaven in 11Q10 31:3 (Job 38:25) stands at the boundary to figurative use.

• From the connotation of the road that one can travel along on a journey to the use of the word for the course that one takes developed, i.e., for the "journey."[12] On the other hand, such a path that leads away from the secured living space or the social environment, also certainly has its dangers. Demons could lurk along it[13] and a demon can seduce a young man to sin on it.[14] *(Ko.)* •

2. In the Figurative Sense. Like Hebrew *dereḵ*, *'rḥ* can just as well denote "moral conduct": 11Q10 6:2 (Job 22:3 *dereḵ* with a divergent number); 15:2 (Job 29:25 *dereḵ*, with an altered suffix), and 23:6 (Job 33:27, where *wᵉlo' šāwāh lî* "he did not repay me for it" becomes in Aramaic *wl' k'rḥy hštlmt* "and it will not be repaid me according to my conduct"). 4Q213a 1 1:12 knows "paths of truth" (*'rḥt qšṭ*; cf. also 4Q212 2:18 [1 En. 91:18]; 4:22 [91:14]; 5:25 [94:1]; 4Q 213:3+4:9) or as the counter image, the "paths of error" (*'rḥt ṭ'w*; 4Q537 3:2).

In Dnl. 4:34, the praise of God "for all his deeds are truth and his paths (*wᵉ'orḥāṯeh*) are (upright) judgment (*dîn*)" in the mouth of Nebuchadnezzar[15] concludes the novella of the "king of Babylon in the wilderness" (Dnl. 3:31-4:34). Dnl. 5:18-22 cites this story in order to

3. *AHw*, I, 63.
4. For possible Hamitic parallels, however, cf. V. E. Orel and O. V. Stolbova, *Hamito-Semitic Etymological Dictionary*. *HO* I/18 (1995), 31f.
5. So *AHw*, I, 63b.
6. In Akkadian, the meaning "to attack" would be more likely in association with "to hurry" than "to consume" would be.
7. A. F. L. Beeston, et al., *Sabaic Dictionary* (Beirut, 1982), 7.
8. Zinçirli: *KAI* 215.18.
9. Sefire: *KAI* 224.9.
10. *AP* 25.6f.
11. *AP* 5.12,14; 13.14; cf. also the map in *TADAE* 2:178.
12. Cf. esp. the Papyrus Padua 1.2 (*TADAE* A3.3:2); *CIS* II 3913 II 60; 4Q197 4 1:4 (Tob. 5:22).
13. ggQN 1:38 (*ATTM.E*, 257).
14. ggXX 4:11 (*ATTM*, 395).
15. Originally involving Nabonidus, cf. 4Q242.

portray Belshazzar's arrogance all the more clearly in relation to Nebuchadnezzar's humility, and underscores the citation in 5:23 by the keyword connection of *'orḥāṯāḵ* with 4:34: "but the God, in whose hand the thread of your life [*nišmeṯāḵ*] lies and with whom are all your paths [*'orḥāṯāḵ*], you have not glorified." It is hardly accidental that the two keywords of this passage "path" (= Heb. *dereḵ*) and "breath" (= Heb. *nᵉšāmāh*) frame the Psalter (Ps. 1:1; 150:6).

Knauf

אַרְיֵה *'ryh 'aryeh*

I. Etymology. II. General Aramaic Usage. III. Biblical Aramaic Usage. IV. Qumran and Later Epigraphy.

I. Etymology. The noun *'aryeh* and related forms occur in Heb., Aram., Eth. (*'arwe* "[wild] animal"),[1] Berber, Nubian,[2] Akk. (*a/erû* "eagle"),[3] and Arab.[4] According to L. Köhler (122f.), one should note in relation to the question of the etymology of *'aryeh* that "lion" in Berber is *ar*, in pl. *iran,* and in Nubian *ārun*. Thus, the origin of the words leads via Egypt to the Nubian region. One can counter, however, that *'aryeh* occurs in Akkadian as *a/erû* "eagle" (the eagle as the "lion" of the sky)[5] and in Arab. as *'arwīyat* "ibex" (cf. also OSA *'rwy-n*).[6] Thus, one must begin by assuming that a common Semitic word for "large, wild animal" stands behind *'aryeh*.[7] The noun *'aryeh* arose from *'ary/way* and consequently counts among the quad-radical nouns.[8]

G. J. Botterweck, "אֲרִי *'ᵃrî*," *TDOT*, I, 374-88; I. Cornelius, "The Lion in the Art of the Ancient Near East," *JNSL* 15 (1989) 53-85; bib.; J. Eggler, *Influences and Traditions Underlying the Vision of Daniel 7:2-14*. *OBO* 177 (2000); J.-G. Heintz, "Löwe," *NBL*, II (1995), 656f.; O. Keel, *The Symbolism of the Biblical World*, trans. Timothy J. Hallett (Winona Lake, IN, 1997); idem and U. Staub, *Hellenismus und Judentum*. *OBO* 178 (2000); B. Lang, *Kein Aufstand in Jerusalem*. *SBB* 7 (1978), 93-101; F. Stolz, "אֲרִי *'ᵃrî* lion," *TLOT*, 170-72; B. A. Strawn, "Leonine Imagery in Early Jewish and Christian Literatures," *JSP* 17 (2007) 37-74; U. Worschech, "Der assyrisch-babylonische Löwenmensch und der 'menschliche' Löwe aus Daniel 7,4," *Ad bene et fideliter seminandum. FS K. Deller*. *AOAT* 220 (1988), 321-33.

1. *CDG*, 40.
2. L. Köhler, "Lexikologisch-geographisches 1," *ZDPV* 62 (1939), 123; cf. also V. O. Orel and O. V. Stolbova, *Hamito-Semitic Etymological Dictionary*. *HO* I/18 (1995), 16.
3. *AHw*, I, 72,247; W. von Soden and E.F. Weidner, "*aqrabu* und *našru*," *AfO* 18 (1957/58) 393.
4. Lane, 1196f.; cf. also *KBL*³, 84f.; Botterweck, 405f.
5. Von Soden, *AfO* 18, 393.
6. A. F. L. Beeston, et al., *Sabaic Dictionary* (Beirut, 1982), 7.
7. G. Bergsträsser, *Introduction to the Semitic Languages*, trans. Peter T. Daniels (Winona Lake, IN, 1983), 210-11.
8. *BLA*, §51m'''; I. Kottsieper, *Die Sprache der Ahiqarsprüche*. *BZAW* 194 (1990), §183b.

II. General Aramaic Usage. The noun occurs in Old Aramaic in the Sefire inscriptions[9] as a governing noun in the sg. abs.: *pm ʾryh* "the mouth of the lion." It appears here along with *nmrh* "panther." In the Aramaic ideograms in Middle Persian, it occurs in *Frahang* IX.4. The sayings of Aḥiqar describe how the lion (*ʾryʾ*, sg. det.) from the cover of its lair lies in ambush for the deer[10] and how he (*ʾryʾ* sg. det.) dialogues with the ass.[11] Aḥiqar 117 says there is no lion (*ʾryh*, sg. abs.) in the sea.

· The threat or the aggressivity of the lion has particular significance even in the last passage mentioned: Since no (real) *ʾryh* exists in the sea, one calls the flood, which springs on its victim like a lion, "lion" (*lbʾ*).[12] (*Ko.*) ·

In addition, a Palmyrene relief depicting a lion attests *ʾryʾ* (sg. det.).[13]

III. Biblical Aramaic Usage. The instances in Biblical Aramaic occur exclusively in the book of Daniel: 6:8,13,17,20f.,23,25,28; 7:4. The account of Daniel in the lion's den (Dnl. 6) employs *ʾaryeh* in the pl. det. *ʾaryāwāṯāʾ*. It appears here mostly as a governing noun in conjunction with *goḇ* "den" (6:8,13,25), *pum* "mouth" (6:23; → פם *pum*), and *yaḏ* "hand," "power" (6:28; → יד *yaḏ*). Dnl. 6 describes the lion as a dangerous, ravenous, and threatening animal. In this regard, *ʾaryeh* denotes the grown lion, both male and female. The lions' den consists of a declivity in the earth in which captive animals were kept as show objects.[14] Because this enclosure has the form of a cistern, it had overtones of a journey to Hades.[15] This interpretation is problematic, however, since Herodotus *Hist.* III:11 knows forms of punishment comparable to those in Dnl. 6 that he regarded as especially gruesome.[16] Dnl. 6:11ff. deals with guarding the body of the one who trusts God as his Lord. The enemy of God, contrariwise, must suffer death. The lions execute this death (6:25).

Dnl. 7:4 employs *ʾaryeh* in the sg. abs. in conjunction with the preposition *kᵉ*. Daniel sees four animals arise from the sea in a night vision; it describes the first animal lion-like, but with eagle's wings. This lion-like animal represents the Babylonian Empire.

IV. Qumran and Later Epigraphy. In the Aramaic texts from Qumran, *ʾryh* appears in an astrological brontology where it designates the constellation "Leo" (sg. det.; 4Q318 2 1:1,6; 2 2:2; *DSSStE,* 676f.). An amulet from Egypt employs the lion as an image of power and speed for the wolf must flee before it (l. 18).[17]

Neef

---

9. *KAI* 223 A 9.
10. Aḥiqar 88f.
11. Aḥiqar 110.
12. Cf. P. Grelot, *Documents arameens d'Égypte. LAPO* 5 (1972), 439; I. Kottsieper, "Die Religionspolitik der Achameniden und die Juden von Elephantine," in R. G. Kratz, *Religion und Religionskontakte im Zeitalter der Achämeniden. VWGTh* 10 (1996), 133.
13. PNO 61.1; cf. D. R. Hillers and E. Cussini, *Palmyrene Aramaic Texts* (Baltimore, 1996), 246a.
14. J.–C. Lebram, *Das Buch Daniel. ZBK* 23 (1994), 79.
15. A. Bentzen, "Daniel 6," *FS A. Bertholet* (Tübingen, 1950), 58-64.
16. Lebram, *Buch Daniel*, 82.
17. R. Kotansky, J. Naveh, and S. Shaked, "A Greek-Aramaic Silver Amulet from Egypt in the Ashmolean Museum," *Mus* 105 (1992) 5-24, esp. 9,11,17.

ארך *ʾrk*; ארך *ʾrk* /ʾork/; ארכה *ʾrkh* /ʾarakā/; אריך *ʾryk* /ʾarīk/

I. Etymology. II. Usage.

I. Etymology. Forms of the root *ʾrk* "to be long" have a common Semitic origin. The verb is rare in Aramaic. It occurs in the temporal sense in the wish for a long life,[1] figuratively in 4Q550 1:4 with *rwḥ* as subject and in the context for "to be bored" or "to be patient." Nouns are the masculine *ʾrk* /ʾork/ for spatial length and the feminine *ʾrkh* /ʾarakā/ for temporal duration; the adjective *ʾryk* /ʾarīk/ "long" can have either nuance.

II. Usage. *ʾrk* serves for dimensions: in Imperial Aramaic in descriptions of real estate,[2] clothes in the dowry,[3] and lumber;[4] at Qumran for the dimensions of the new Jerusalem.[5] In contrast, *ʾrkh* denotes a finite period of time.[6] *ʾryk* occurs in temporal[7] and spatial usages.[8]

Gzella

1. *KAI* 309.7,14; *TADAE* C2.1.72; likewise the C-stem in *KAI* 226.3.
2. *TADAE* B3.7:4; 3.12:7,15.
3. *TADAE* B2.6:8f.,11; 3.8:11f.
4. *TADAE* A6.2:18f.,19.
5. *ATTM*, 2, 355.
6. Dnl. 4:24; 7:12; 4Q530 7 2:3.
7. *TADAE* A4.7:3 par. 4.8:3; of life.
8. 1QapGen 20:5, of Sarah's pianist's fingers; 4Q561 3:3, without context.

אֲרַק/אֲרַע *ʾrq/ʾrʿ ʾaraq/ʾaraʿ*

I. Etymology and Forms. II. The Basic Dimensions of the Term for the Earth. III. Heaven and Earth. IV. The Earth as the Habitat of Humans. V. The Earth as a Cosmic Entity. VI. "Property," "Land." VII. The Earth as the Place for Plants. VIII. "Floor," "Bottom."

I. Etymology and Forms. The basic word *ʾarḍ* "earth" occurs in all Semitic languages with the exception of South Semitic, which attests it only in OSA. In accordance with

J. Bergman/M. Ottosson, "אֶרֶץ *ʾerets*," *TDOT*, I, 418-36; F. M. Fales, *Aramaic Epigraphs on Clay Tablets of the Neo-Assyrian Period. StSem* NS 2 (1986); W. Röllig, "El-Creator-Of-The-Earth," *DDD*², 280f.; H. H. Schmid, "אֶרֶץ *ʾereṣ* earth, land," *TLOT*, 172-79; J. Teixidor, *The Pantheon of Palmyra. EPRO* 79 (1979); S. Uemura, *Land or Earth? A Terminological Study of Hebrew* ʾereṣ *and Aramaic* ʾaraʿ *in the Graeco-Roman Period* (London, 2012).

the rendering of Proto-Semitic *ḍ* with *q* in Old Aramaic, beginning at the end of the sixth century B.C.E. increasingly represented by and ultimately replaced with ʿ, the word appears both as *ʾrq* and as *ʾrʿ*, while the transition from *ʾrq* to *ʾrʿ* is fluid—Jer. 10:11 even exhibits both spellings in one verse (→ III). Like Hebrew *ʾereṣ*, which represents the form of *ʾarḍ* that one would expect in Hebrew according to the laws of phonetics, *ʾrq/ʿ* is a feminine and, as a plural, manifests the feminine forms with *t*.[1]

II. The Basic Dimensions of the Term for the Earth. The basic meaning of the Semitic word *ʾarḍ* is "earth" in the sense that it designates the firm space under the feet of human beings. The earth, however, delimits not only the human habitat at the bottom, but simultaneously constitutes it—humans live on the earth, and it enables their spatial expansion in the horizontal. Wherever humans can go is "earth"—and therefore the habitat of humans is also the "earth" at the same time.

The fundament experience of humans produces the primary counterpart, "heaven" (→ שְׁמַיִן *šᵉmayin*), which contrasts with both aspects of the earth mentioned. On the one hand, it marks that which is above in contrast to that which is below (the earth), and on the other hand, that which is fundamentally inaccessible to humans. This dichotomy, which exhibits both a spatial and a functional dimension, reflects in the Aramaic use of the word for "earth."

III. Heaven and Earth. This dichotomy becomes particularly clear in the merism "heaven and earth" describing the whole world, the cosmos. The oldest Aramaic inscription known so far already designates Hadad as *gwgl šmyn wʾrq* "canal inspector of heaven and earth," which expresses his responsibility for the whole world.[2] This instance, which, after all, adopts a traditional Akkadian epithet,[3] compares to a series of Aramaic formulations. Thus, the curse formula of the stele of Zakur also mentions along with the gods specified by name the *ʾlhy šmy[n wʾlh]y ʾrq* "the gods of heaven and the gods of earth," denoting the totality of the gods,[4] and the introduction of the letter of Adon speaks of the [*ʾlhy*] *šmyn wʾrqʾ*, the "[gods] of heaven and earth."[5] Accordingly, a curse formula in the treaty texts from Sefire threatens the violator of the treaty that Hadad may pour on him *klmh lḥyh bʾrq wbšmyn* "everything that is bad on earth and in heaven," i.e., briefly, "everything evil."[6] Language about heaven and earth also appears frequently in the literary texts of Pap. Amherst 63,[7] in which, e.g., 11:1f. depicts the power of God through his activity on earth and in heaven.[8]

The language of "heaven and earth" continues in Biblical Aramaic. Thus, according to Dnl. 4:34, the all-surmounting dominion of God becomes clear in his unrestricted activity

---

1. *ESE* II 206:N,1: *ʾrqt* (const.); AD 12.6: *ʾrqtʾ* (det.); thus also then in the later Aramaic dialects.
2. T.Fekh. 2.
3. Cf. *AHw*, I, 296a.
4. *KAI* 202 B 25f.
5. *TADAE* A1.1:[1]f.
6. *KAI* 222 A 26.
7. S. P. Vleeming and J. W. Wesselius, *Studies in Papyrus Amherst 63 I* (Amsterdam, 1985), 25f.
8. S. P. Vleeming and J. W. Wesselius, *Studies in Papyrus Amherst 63 II* (Amsterdam, 1990), 54f.

among the "host of heaven and the inhabitants of the earth" and Dnl. 6:28 depicts it with the statement that he "does signs and wonders in heaven and on the earth." Likewise, the designation of Yahweh as "God of heaven and earth" (*'ᵉlāh šᵉmayyā' we'ar'ā'*) in Ezr. 5:11, which is otherwise singular in the OT except for Gen 24:3—v. 12 already returns to the widespread designation as "God of heaven"—intends to emphasize the "universality of the God of Israel."[9] When the Qumran texts simply adopting the designations as *qonê šāmayîm wā'āreṣ* in Gen. 14:19,22 call God *mrh šmy' w'r'* "Lord of heaven and earth,"[10] it, too, indicates the unusual character of the reference in Ezr. 5:11. The explanation of the fact that God is not the "God of the earth" involves the association of the designation "God of heaven" with God's transcendence and not with God's realm of power and activity, which would then be restricted to heaven—God belongs to another dimension than humans assigned to earth. Thus, Zeph. 2:11 probably does not speak accidentally of the "gods of the earth," whom Yahweh destroys, but signals thereby their ultimately nongodly nature.

In the bounds of the monotheistic attack on polytheism, Jer. 10:11 emphasizes that the gods made neither the heavens nor the earth (*'arqā'*)—thus, they made nothing. Consequently, they should disappear from the earth (*me'ar'ā'*) and from beneath heaven (*ûmin tᵉḥôṯ šᵉmayyā'*). Notably, the second statement not only now employs *'ᵃra'* instead of *'ᵃraq*, but also both parts of the statement actually say the same thing since the realm "under the heavens" corresponds to the earth. In addition, the statement alternates between the assimilated and the unassimilated forms of *min*. The unequivocal chiastic structure of the statement[11] makes it unadvisable to assume it is only a redaction unity so that the alternation in the spelling of *'ᵃraq/'* is probably due to the orthographical uncertainty of the later traditions with regard for the rendering of the word.[12] Nevertheless, one suspects that *min tᵉḥôṯ* represents an insertion and that the text originally spoke of the fact that these useless gods "of the earth and the heaven" should disappear (cf. Zeph. 2:11). Thus, this Aramaic insertion into a Hebrew text probably constitutes a citation that originally spoke of the fact that the gods, who created nothing, will also perish entirely—from earth and heaven! Whether it originally involved a monotheistic polemic against polytheism or the *dî*-clause was meant more restrictively in the sense of "only the gods, who. . ." cannot be decided without the original context. The current context explains the addition, however, since in it this statement refers to the idol images that exist only on earth. If the gods were to perish from heaven, it would presuppose the existence of such gods.

Heaven and earth also appear together in 4Q204 1:18ff. (1 En. 2:1ff.) in the call to regard the order of the whole cosmos as manifest in the phenomena in heaven and on earth.[13]

The dichotomy of heaven and earth also became clear in passages where heaven, as the divine world, confronts the earth. Thus, according to an inscription from Arebsun,[14]

---

9. A. H. J. Gunneweg, *Esra*. *KAT* XIX/1 (1985), 102.

10. 1QapGen 22:16,21.

11. J. Ferry, *Illusions et salut dans la prédication prophétique de Jérémie*. *BZAW* 269 (1999), 242.

12. Cf. e.g., also *AP* 6, which mostly employs *'rq* (ll. 5-7, etc.), but *'r'* stands in l. 16.

13. Cf. 4Q201 2:1ff.

14. *RÉS* 1785 B:4.

Bel turns attention to a land (→ V) by leaving heaven: *[by]l npq mn šmyʾ wḥzh bʾrqʾ zʾ* "[Be]l came out of heaven and looked at this land." The giant Uhiah sees in his dream that "the ruler of heaven descended to earth" (*šlṭn šmyʾ lʾrʿʾ nḥt*).[15]

IV. The Earth as the Habitat of Humans. Aḥiqar 108, where human action appears in the metaphor of walking on the earth, makes the connection between "earth" and the habitat of humans particularly clear. Accordingly, the Enoch literature from Qumran repeatedly describes the various events in the early history of humanity emphatically as happening on the earth.[16] 4Q204 5 1:21 (1 En. 105:1) and 4Q212 4:20 (1 En. 91:14) even describe all humanity as *bny ʾrʿʾ (klh)* "children of the (whole) earth." Finally, 4Q210 1 2:2 (1 En. 76:4) mentions winds that heal the earth and preserve life so that it personalizes the earth itself as habitat. Accordingly, other apocalyptic texts emphasize that the events they announce will take place on the earth.[17]

Language about dominion over the earth also has in view primarily power over human beings. It first appears in the description of Tiglath-pileser, borrowed from the Akkadian, as *mrʾ rbʿy ʾrqʾ* "Lord of the four regions of the world," which assumes the division of the inhabited earth into four regions.[18]

Dnl. 4 takes up the connection between "earth" and human habitat when it symbolizes Nebuchadnezzar's worldwide dominion with the world-tree planted in the center of the earth (v. 7), but having such height that it can be seen to the ends of the whole earth (vv. 8,17). Verse 19 then explicitly states that it symbolizes dominion over the entire earth. The fact that it means dominion over all humanity becomes clear in v. 32, which relates Nebuchadnezzar's dominion to the overarching dominion of God over the "inhabitations of the (entire) earth." Accordingly, Nebuchadnezzar addresses his letter proclaiming this dominion over all humanity "to all peoples, nations, and languages that dwell on the whole earth" (3:31; cf. also 6:26). Dnl. 2:39 also belongs in this context. It speaks of the dominion of the third empire over the whole earth, as does 2:33-35, where the stone that becomes a mountain and fills the whole earth refers to the final kingdom of God (vv. 44f.).[19] Finally, the statement in 7:23 that the fourth kingdom will devour and crush the whole earth refers not to a specific destruction of the earth, but to Alexander's empire.

V. The Earth as a Cosmic Entity. With no direct relation to humanity, but more as a cosmic entity, *ʾrq/ʿ* occurs in the statements about creation, e.g.—naturally, Jer. 10:11 also implies such a concept (→ III)—in Tg. Job from Qumran, which speaks much more clearly than its prototype of the fact that God "made" the earth. Thus, 11Q10 24:7 renders *mî p̄āqaḏ ʿālâw ʾarṣoh* (MT *ʾarṣāh*; cf. *BHS*) "who entrusted his earth to him" in Job 34:13 with *hwʾ ʾrʿʾ ʿbd* "he made the earth"; 30:2 likewise interprets the foundation of the

15. 4Q530 2:16.

16. E.g., 1Q23:9+14+15:3; 4Q201 4:5 (1 En. 8:4); 4Q202 3:8 (1 En. 9:1); 4Q203 8:9; 4Q204 5 2:28 (1 En. 107:1).

17. 4Q246 1:4.

18. *KAI* 216.3f.; 217.2.

19. Cf. the similar 4Q246 1:7.

earth (*ysd*) in 38:4 generally as creation: *'n hwyt bm 'bdy 'r'* "Where were you when I made the earth?"

It is questionable, however, whether the etymology of the Semitic divine name *'lq(w)nr'* for Poseidon[20] attested in Palmyrene texts was clear to Aramaic speakers and therefore whether they were aware that it originally spoke of "El, the creator/owner of the earth."[21] Since the ' of *'r'* essentially remains unwritten and the form *'lqwnr'* indicates a pronunciation of the central element as *qōnē*, whereas one would expect Aramaic *qānē*, it probably represents a mechanical adoption of the name along with the deity from the West. Regarding the assumption that Hatra 23:3 also attests this designation as *qnh dy r'/h*, cf. the new reading *qnh wzr 'h* "whose nest and descendants."[22]

VI. "Property," "Land." Language about the "whole earth" already presupposes a cosmology that, at least theoretically, can understand the earth as a closed entity. The fundamental experience of individual human beings or of a group, however, is that the earth, in the region that they can survey, constitutes their habitat that they develop, work, and cultivate. The use of *'rq/'* in the sense of "parcel of land," "field" probably derives from this relationship. By nature, it occurs with particular frequency in legal texts such as the Aramaic texts from Egypt.[23] Here, however, one can seek the roots of the meaning "territory," "land," which occurs in the older texts only in the construct state.[24] *KAI* 279 also makes clear the connection between the area called *'rq* and the group living in it. It states that as the result of the king's piety "all human beings" (*klhm 'nšn*, l. 2), probably a designation for all his subjects, and the "whole land" (*kl 'rq'*; l. 3), i.e., his land, do better. In this meaning, *'rq/'* may have originally designated the habitat of a group or clan, especially since the transition to state structures in the originally city-state regions of Syria-Palestine was certainly fluid. *KAI* 222 A 28 makes it clear that *'rq/'* was very much still known in its concrete meaning as the firm "earth" on which one finds oneself when *'py 'rqh* "the surface of his land" manifests both aspects of *'rq/'* at the same time.

The occurrences in Aramaic addenda from the Assyrian realm also belong in this context. Thus, the phrase *bzy 'rq'* (eighth century B.C.E.)[25] appears frequently on bronze weights from Nineveh, apparently an expression for the measurement of a mine. On the same pieces, (*zy*) *mlk* "royal mine" also indicates them.[26] On the other hand, *'rq* appears in *CIS* II 28 (Nineveh; seventh century B.C.E.) in *zy 'rq ḥm'* apparently in the meaning "city," "municipal area" as the origin of a person: "the one from the municipal area of Ḥame'."[27] Thus, one can take the statement *bzy 'rq'* in the sense of "according to the dimension of the city, of the municipal region" in which the addition of the (same) weight in royal

20. *DNSI*, 111; Teixidor, 25-27.

21. *DNSI*, 1015f.; Röllig.

22. K. Beyer, *Die aramäischen Inschriften aus Assur, Hatra und dem übrigen Ostmesopotamien* (Göttingen, 1998), 33.

23. Esp. *AP* 6; 8; 9; cf. also 15.19; *DNSI*, 112.

24. *KAI* 222 A 28; B 27; 223 A 8; 224:6; cf. also Sam'alian 215:5,7: *'rq y'dy* "the land of Yaudi."

25. *CIS* II 1a; 2a, 3a; 4a.

26. *CIS* II 1c; 2c; 3c; 4c; cf. also Akk. *ša šarri* in the Akkadian text of *CIS* II 2-4.

27. Fales, 187.

mine correlates this local data with the official, as it were. Here, too, then, *ʾrq* apparently still has the connotation of the manageable, local habitat. Accordingly, *š 30 (?) zy bnšyʾ* (Bab. from the time of Darius II)[28] should be translated "30 (?) shekels (according to the weight) of the region of the Bannešeans."

The Qumran texts first also attest *ʾrʿ* in the general meaning "region," "district," as 1QapGen 16:10, in particular, demonstrates: *kwl ʾrʿ ṣpwnʾ kwlhʾ* "the whole land of the north in entirety."[29] Thus instead of the Hebrew text that still parallels uninhabited land (*ʾereṣ loʾ ʾîš*) with the uninhabited wilderness, the Targum of Job 38:26[30] combines them into one expression and speaks of the "wilderness land in which there are no people" (*ʾrʿ mdbr dy lʾ ʾnš bh*). The original meaning as "land of someone" is still perceptible, however, in formulations such as *lʾrʿ bny ḥm lʾrʿ mṣryn* "to the land of the Hamites, to the land of Egypt."[31]

VII. The Earth as the Place for Plants. The aspect of the earth as the producer of plants appears only relatively rarely in the preserved texts. In Biblical Aramaic, only Dnl. 4 pertains here. It has the image of the roots of the world-tree being left in the earth after its destruction (vv. 12,20) and, in addition, mentions "the grass of the earth" (*ʿaśab̲ ʾarʿāʾ*; v. 12).

The fact, however, that the earth in this function has major significance for human beings becomes clear especially in the account of the rebellion of Shamash-shum-ukin in Pap. Amherst 63 18-23.[32] Thus, in the depiction of the catastrophic birth year of Shamash-shum-ukin, the author takes up the image, known also from Lev. 26:19, Dt. 28:23, and Asarhaddon's Succession Treaty §63,[33] that "the earth [*ʾrq*]" was "of bronze" (18.11), i.e., that it no longer bore fruit, as the continuation also demonstrates when it speaks of the fact that "the heavens were iron, the ground [*ʿpr*] destroyed by dryness, and the heavens a glowing brick" (18.11f.). Conversely, the treaty expresses the positive significance of his counterpart by saying that "the earth was healthy, the skinny roasted with fat" (l. 6).[34] A Samalian inscription also demonstrates the fact that a king who pleases god influences quite materially the fertility of the earth of his land since the gods give prosperity (→ VI).[35]

The war crime of sowing the earth with salt to hinder it from producing illustrates the dependence of human well-being on the fact that the earth can produce fruit. *TADAE* D23.1:Va:13 offers an example: *ʾrʿʾ ʾzrʿ mlḥ* "and I will sow the earth with salt."

---

28. *ESE* II 209:X:2.

29. Cf. also, e.g., 19:11.

30. 11Q10 31:3f.

31. 1QapGen 19:13; for additional texts, cf. *ATTM*, 524; *ATTM.E*, 314.

32. R. C. Steiner and C. F. Nims, "Ashurbanipal and Shamash-shum-ukin," *RB* 92 (1985) 60-81, which numbers the columns 17-22 and translates somewhat differently.

33. S. Parpola and K. Watanabe, *Neo-Assyrian Treaties and Loyalty Oaths. SAA* II (1988), 51.

34. I. Kottsieper, "Die literarische Aufnahme assyrischer Begebenheiten in frühen aramäischen Texten," in D. Charpin and F. Joannès, eds., *La circulation des biens, des personnes et des idées dans le Proche-Orient ancien* (Paris, 1992), 284f.

35. *KAI* 214.5-7 (cf. also 279.3).

VIII. "Floor," "Bottom." The spatial dimension that the earth acquires as the lower boundary of the human habitat manifests itself in the use of *'rq/'* as a term for the lowest area of something. Thus, e.g., in an Imperial Aramaic text *mn 'r'' w'd 'l'* can designate the extension of a wall from the floor upward,[36] while in Palmyrene, *'r' gwmḥ'* designates the lower portion of an alcove.[37] This usage has a counterpart in the *qaṭlīt*-form *'ar'ī* that designates the floor of the lion's den in Dnl. 6:25. The connotation "floor" also occurs in Dnl. 7:4 in the image of the first animal in the vision, depicted as being raised from the floor and erected like a human being. Thereby a metaphorical meaning also becomes clear: That which is found on the floor is lowly and powerless—in contrast to the world-tree, which demonstrates its power by towering over the whole earth and reaching as far as the heavens (Dnl. 4:7f.; → IV). This metaphor reappears in 7:17, which speaks of the fact that four kings "were raised from the earth" (*yᵉqûmûn min 'ar'ā'*) denoting the attainment of world dominion. Correspondingly, Dnl. 2:39 can describe a lesser power as *'ar'ā'* (*K*) *min*, literally "closer to the earth/floor."

Kottsieper

36. *AP* 5.5.
37. H. Ingholt, "Palmyrene Sculptures in Beirut," *Berytus* 1 (1934) 38,10f.

אֹשׁ *'š 'oš*

I.1. Etymology and Occurrence. 2. Equivalents. 3. Technical Backgrounds. II. Instances in Aramaic. 1. Biblical-Aramaic. 2. Qumran.

I. *1. Etymology and Occurrence.* *'oš*, attested in Aramaic since the Persian period and always used in the plural, has no Semitic etymology. The word was borrowed from

W. Baumgartner, "Untersuchungen zu den akkadischen Bauausdrücken," *ZA* 36 (1925) 219-53; M. Black, *Apocalypsis Henochi Graece. PVTG* III (1970), 1-50; G. Dalman, *Arbeit und Sitte in Palästina VII* (Gütersloh, 1942); A. Falkenstein, "Sumerische Bauausdrücke," *Or* NS 35 (1966) 229-46; V. Fritz, *The City in Ancient Israel*, trans. Jill Pittinger (Sheffield, 1995); A. H. J. Gunneweg, *Esra. KAT* XIX/1 (1985); S. A. Kaufman, *The Akkadian Influence on Aramaic. AS* 19 (1974); R. Macuch, *Grammatik des samaritanischen Aramäisch. StSam* IV (1982); B. Mosis, "יָסַד *yāsad*," *TDOT*, VI, 109-21; C. Müller-Kessler, *Grammatik des Christlich-Palästinisch-Aramäischen I. TStO* 6 (1991); W. Rudolph, *Esra und Nehemia, HAT* I/20 (1949); C. G. Tuland, "'Uššayyā' and 'Uššarnâ," *JNES* 17 (1958) 269-75; S. Uhlig, *Das äthiopische Henochbuch. JSHRZ* V/6 (1984); H. G. M. Williamson, *Ezra, Nehemia. WBC* 16 (1985); G. R. H. Wright, *Ancient Building in South Syria and Palestine. HO* VII/I,II B 3,1-2 (1985).

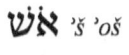

Akkadian (*uššu* "foundation," mostly pl. *uššū*, since old Akkadian).[1] In turn, Akk. *uššu* is probably a loanword from Sumerian (UŠ, $UŠ_8$ [APIN, formerly URU_4] "foundation slab," "foundation").[2] In addition to attestations in later Aramaic,[3] *'oš* survives in Middle Hebrew[4] and in Arab.[5] Some have posited a relationship to Samaritan Aramaic *āreš* (*'rš*), *ūreš* (*'wrš*) "chief," "root," "principle," but it is entirely uncertain.[6] Hebrew *'āšᵉyāh* "tower," "column" (< Akk. *asītu*, cf. Jewish Aram. *'āšîṯā'*) must be distinguished from *'oš*.

2\. *Equivalents*. Equivalents derive from the root *ysd* "to found" (Heb. *môsāḏ*), *šyt*, *šty* "to place" (Heb. *šeṯ*,[7] Syr. *'eštā'*)[8] or *smk* "to support" (Middle Heb. *sᵉmûḵôṯ* "columns," Jewish Aramaic *sāmeḵā'* "support").[9]

3\. *Technical Backgrounds*. The depth and configuration of a foundation depend on the respective subsoil (the natural foundation) and the construction materials available. In Palestine, stone foundations on which the clay brickwork rested were the rule. Only fortifications and large structures had hewn stone foundations, otherwise they were of field or broken stone. Frequently, the remnants of the walls of older structures were reused as foundations.[10]

II. Instances in Aramaic.

1. Biblical-Aramaic. In Biblical Aramaic, *'oš* occurs only in Ezra, which always employs it as a construction term designating the foundation of the city walls of Jerusalem and of the temple. The missive of Bishlam and his colleagues to Artaxerxes reports of the reconstruction of Jerusalem: *wᵉšûrayyā' šaḵlilû* (*Q*) *wᵉ'uššoyyā' yaḥîṭû* "they reerect the walls and improve the foundations" (Ezr. 4:12; → כלל *kll*).[11] Ezr. 5:16 addresses the foundations of the temple: *'ᵉḏayin šešbaṣṣar deḵ'ᵃṯā' yᵉhaḇ 'uššoyyā' dî bêṯ 'ᵉlāhā'* "Thereupon, one Sheshbazzar came and laid the foundations of the temple of God." The relationship with Ezr. 6:3 *wᵉ'uššôhî mᵉsôḇᵉlîn* is not certain. Some propose an emendation to *wᵉ'eššôhî* "and one brings one's burnt offering." Gunneweg (104) describes the passage as irreparably corrupt. In contrast, Williamson (68,71) maintains the derivation from *'oš*: "and let its foundations be retained" (→ סבל *sbl*). Rudolph's suggestion (54; likewise *BHS*) to emend to *ûmišḥôhî mittᵉḵilîn* "its dimensions are measured" remains uncertain.

1\. Cf. *AHw*, III, 1442a; Kaufman, 110.

2\. Falkenstein, 229-35; Baumgarten, 236-45.

3\. For Christian Palestinian Aramaic, cf. Müller-Kessler, 85,109 with n. 72; for Jewish Aramaic cf. *'ûššā'* "foundation," "column," *WTM*, I 176a.

4\. *'ûš*, Jastrow, 35b (in *WTM*, I 176a under Jewish Aramaic *'ûššā'*); *'šš* "to found," "to secure," *WTM*, I 182a.

5\. *'uss* "foundation" with derivatives, Wehr[5], 22.

6\. Macuch, 21-22.

7\. Relationship uncertain, cf. *KBL*[3], 1536b.

8\. *LexSyr*, 810b-11a.

9\. *WTM*, III 544b,546a.

10\. Dalman, 47ff.; Fritz, 136f.; Wright, 380-91.

11\. On *ḥw/yṭ* *KBL*[3], 1705.

2. *Qumran.* A figurative use appears in 4Q212 4:14 (1 En. 91:11): *ʿqryn ʾšy ḥmsʾ* "they will eradicate the foundations of injustice" (→ עקר *ʿqr*); the subsequent lines expand the construction metaphor by depicting the construction of the eschatological temple. This occurrence places *ʾš* in the lexical field of *šrš* "root" and *ʿqr* "root(stock)." 11Q10 30:4 (Job 38:6) mentions the foundations of the earth:[12] *ʿl mʾ ʾšyh ʾḥydyn* "What do their foundations rest on?" 4Q204 6:24 (1 En. 14:10) ascribes to the foundations of a heavenly house seen in a vision an appearance like snow:]x *tlg ʾš*[*why*.[13]

Schwemer

---

12. For the motif, see Mosis, 673f.
13. So *ATTM,* 239; *DSSStE*, 416f.: *d]y tlg ʾš*[*n*; Greek (Black, 28): καὶ ἐδάφη χιονικά "and foundations/floors of snow"; Eth.: "and its floors (were of) hail," Uhlig, 539.

אֶשָּׁא *ʾšʾ ʾeššāʾ*; יקד *yqd*; יְקֵדָה *yqdh yeqedāh*; נור *nwr nûr*; שְׁבִיב *šbyb šebîb*

I. Etymology. II. The Significance of Fire, Especially in the Hebrew OT. III. Usage in Non-biblical Aramaic. 1. Old Aramaic. 2. Uruk. 3. Jewish Aramaic. IV. Biblical Aramaic. V. Qumran.

I. Etymology. The Aramaic word for "fire," Biblical Aramaic *ʾeššāʾ* (Syr./Christian Palestinian Aramaic *ʾeššātāʾ* "fever"), is common to most Semitic languages. The related words include Hebrew *ʾeš*, Akkadian *išātu*, Ethiopic *ʾesāt*,[1] and Ugaritic *išt*. Arabic lacks it, however. All the languages mentioned employ the word as a feminine.

• Meanwhile, in analogy to the Hebrew *ʾeš*, Aramaic[2] and Christian Palestinian Aramaic also exhibit morphologically masculine forms, which may also be present in Biblical Aramaic if one relates *ʾeššāʾ* Dnl. 7:11 to the previously mentioned stream of fire (*nehar dî nûr*; v. 10). Then, this form would be masc. sg. det. (*Ko.*) •

J. Bergman, J. Krecher, V. Hamp, "אֵשׁ *ʾēsh*," *TDOT*, I, 418-28; P. de Lagarde, *Übersicht über die im Aramäischen, Arabischen und Hebräischen übliche Bildung der Nomina. AKGW* 35 (1888); D. N. Freedman and J. Lundbom, "יָקַד *yāqad*," *TDOT*, VI, 271-74; E. M. Good, "Fire," *IDB*, II, 268f.; M. Haran, *Temples and Temple-Service in Ancient Israel*, (Oxford, 1978); D. Kellermann, "נֵר *nēr*," *TDOT*, 10, 14-24; A. Lemaire and J.-M. Durand, *Les inscriptions araméennes de Sfiré. HEO* (Paris, 1984); C. Meyers, "Lampstand," *ABD*, IV, 141-43; C. Meyers and H.-J. Fabry, "מְנוֹרָה *menôrāh*, *TDOT*, VIII, 401-7; D. Wetzstein, "Ueber אנושה Ps. 69,21," in F. Delitzsch, *Die Psalmen. BC* IV/1 (Leipzig, [4]1883), 883-90.

1. *CDG*, 44b.
2. *Frahang* XIII.5.

The etymology is controversial with two directions defining the discussion. Some assume the root *ʾnš "to be social, friendly," so that "fire" would be the friendly, social element.[3] If this were correct, however, one would expect that the *n* in the middle of the root in Akkadian would manifest as germination. Others suspect an onomatopoeic root as the foundation,[4] in which case one can point to similar-sounding words for "fire" in non-Semitic languages such as, e.g., Sumerian IZI.

Aramaic *ʾeššāʾ/h* has many synonyms; *šeḇîḇ* (cf. Syr. *šbîbāʾ*, Mand. *šʾmbyby*ʾ "sparks") means "flame" and is related to Hebrew *šāḇîḇ*, Arabic *šabba* "to burn, to blaze," and Akkadian *šabādu* "to glow, to wither." Another Aramaic word for fire is *nûr*, which corresponds to Arabic *nār* "fire" or *nūr* "light" (cf. also "minaret"), Ugaritic *nr* "light" (cf. also *nrt* "lights"[5] or *nwr* "to shine"),[6] and Akkadian *nūru* "light" (cf. also *naw/māru* "to be bright, to shine"). The underlying root *nwr* also occurs in the Hebrew words *menôrāh* for "candleholder" or *ner/nîr* for "light," "lamp." Finally, the root *yqd* (< *wqd*) has the connotation "to burn." Very frequent in Aramaic, *yqd* or Biblical Aramaic *yeqḏāh* "burning" has linkages with Hebrew *yāqaḏ* and Arabic *waqada* "to burn," as well as Akkadian *qâdu* "to ignite."[7]

II. The Significance of Fire, Especially in the Hebrew OT. Fire appeared in many contexts throughout the ancient Near East. Both animal and plant sacrifices were usually offered through fire. To this end, priests maintained a continual fire on the altar (cf. Lev 6:5f. [MT]). The execution of a divine judgment often involved fire. Thus, fire destroyed the inhabitants of Sodom and Gomorrah (Gen. 19:24). Aaron's sons Nadab and Abihu died by fire according to Lev. 10:2. Fire also killed the 250 followers of Korah (Num. 16:35). It also served, however, as a medium for theophanies and divine appearances. Thus, the images of the smoking firepot and a flaming torch represent Yahweh in Abram's dream (Gen. 15:17) and God speaks to Moses from a burning bush (Ex. 3:2). Other passages speak of fire proceeding from Yahweh's mouth (Ps. 18:9; 2 S. 22:9). A pillar of fire leads the wandering Israelites by night (Ex. 13:21, etc.). Similarly, Dnl. 10:6 employs fire as a metaphor to describe the appearance of the angelic being: "His face looked like a lightning bolt [*bārāq*] and his eyes were like torches of fire [*kelappîḏê ʾeš*]." Finally, the seven-branched candlestand that stood both in the tent of meeting and in the temple symbolizes God's presence.[8]

Lamps also symbolize the Davidic dynasty, as the expression *nîr leḏāwîḏ* ("a lamp for David," 1 K. 11:36; cf. 15:4; 2 K. 8:19) suggests. 2 S. 21:17 describes David himself as "a light of Israel" (*ner yiśrāʾel*).

Freedman/Homan

3. E.g., Wetzstein, 888; cf. de Lagarde, 68.
4. E.g., Good, 268b.
5. J. Tropper, *Ugaritische Grammatik. AOAT* 273 (2000), 190.
6. Ibid., 648.
7. • For a possible connection with Geʿez *mogada* "to ignite" and corresponding Ethiopic derivatives, cf. W. Leslau, *Ethiopic and South Arabic Contributions to the Hebrew Lexicon. UCP* 20 (Berkeley, 1958), 24f. and *CDG*, 332a. (*Ko.*) •
8. Haran, 218,226; Meyers, "Lampstand," 142.

III. Usage in nonbiblical Aramaic.

1. Old Aramaic. The morphologically masc. form *'š* (→ I) occurs along with *yqd* "to burn" in the Sefire inscription (eighth century B.C.E.) in the context of a curse process in which wax is burned.[9] Just as it is "burned in fire" (*b'š tqd*), so also should Arpad (l. 35) or its king Mati'el "burn" (*t/yqd*).

It is debated whether l. 25 also attests the word. While the majority of editors assume here in this threat of consequences for a possible treaty violation on Mati'el's part the reading *zy ymlk 'šr* "(a land) that Assyria will rule," others read *zy yml k'š* "that will die out like fire."[10] In contrast, *DNSI* (121) suggests *zy ymlk 'š* "where fire will rule." In view of the connotation of the destructive power that *'š(h)* displays (see below), the latter seems to be the best interpretation. Moreover, the fact that this politically specific statement concerning Assyria does not suit the metaphorical language of the passage speaks against the first, and the fact that transience does not otherwise belong to the imagery associated with *'š(h)* speaks against the second.

Aḥiqar 101-104[11] is of particular interest for the metaphorical significance of fire. It obviously compares the king's wrath over the insubordination or recalcitrance of subordinates with a stroke of lightning (*brq*, 101) and a blazing fire (*'šh yqdh*, 103) that threatens them. The passage concludes with a saying that illustrates the absolute destructive power of the king by asserting that it is just as impossible to reconcile with him as it is for wood to reconcile with fire (*'šh*) or meat with the knife. In view of the fact that the destructive power of wrath appears in other texts (→ III.2), this massive adaptation of the fire metaphor is probably due to royal ideology that regarded the king as god's representative and entirely comparable to him (Aḥiqar 107f.; → מלך *melek*). Therefore, the fire metaphor attested in relation to the theophany and the judgment of God (→ II)[12] could obviously apply to the king.

The statement "she ignited a fire" (*'šh 'klth<m>*)[13] once again exhibits the connotation of destruction (→ אכל *'kl* III), but it stands in an unclear context so that the specific intention here is unclear. Similarly unclear is the mention in an inscription from Arebsun[14] of fire (*'št*) that is cloaked (?). This statement follows the statement that a sage stands before Bel and the gods; in light of the passages in Aḥiqar, the image offered here should be interpreted to the effect that the fire of divine wrath is calmed.

Kottsieper

2. Uruk. The incantation text from Uruk contains a phrase that employs the word for "fire" as an image for "wrath": "Who is angry? Who is enraged? Who is clothed with the clothing of wrath, (has) fire in his mouth?"[15]

---

9. *KAI* 222 A 35.37, For parallels cf. Krecher in Bergman-Krecher-Hamp, 455.

10. Cf. the overview in A. Lemaire-J.-M. Durand, 133.

11. For the reading, cf. I. Kottsieper, *Die Sprache der Ahiqarsprüche. BZAW* 194 (1990), 12,20 (= X 7-10).

12. Krecher and Hamp in Bergman-Krecher-Hamp, 455-58.

13. *KAI* 233.17.

14. *RÉS* 1785 A 3.

15. Uruk 19-21; cf. 22-24,32.

3. Jewish Aramaic. Later Jewish Aramaic frequently employs both *'š'* and *'št'* for "fire," and also frequently *nûr*. In addition, they also designate high temperatures and fevers.[16]

IV. Biblical Aramaic. The Aramaic sections of the OT employ *'eššā'* once. It occurs in Dnl. 7:11 along with *y^eqedāh* in a description of the cremation of the body of the fourth animal: "And I watched until the animal was killed and its body destroyed and given over to the burning fire (*lîqedat 'eššā'*)." The synonyms for *'eššā'* appear in Dnl. 3, the account of Nebuchadnezzar's attempt to incinerate Shadrach, Meshach, and Abednego as punishment for failing to bow down to the newly erected golden statue. The three were to be thrown into a "blazing oven" (*'attûn nûrā' yāqidtā'*). This expression occurs eight times in Dnl. 3 (vv. 6,11,15,17,20,21,23,26). Dnl. 3:22 reports that the oven was so hot that the "flames of the fire" (*š^ebîbā' dî nûrā'*) killed Nebuchadnezzar's servants who threw Shadrach, Meshach and Abednego into the oven; *nûrā'* occurs a further five times in Dnl. 3:24-27 in reference to the fire into which the three were thrown while, astonishingly, the "odor of fire" (*rêaḥ nûr*) did not cling to their clothing (v. 27).

Moreover, Dnl. 7:9b-10a employs the fire motif to describe God's throne: "His throne was flames of fire [*š^ebîbîn dî nûr*]; its wheels a burning fire [*nûr dāliq*]. A river of fire [*nûr*] burst out and flowed from it." The motif is comparable to the fiery wagon and being described in the vision in Ezk. 1 and perhaps also with the description of the throne in Isa. 6, where the prophet saw God on a throne with seraphim (cf. *śrp* "to burn" above it.

V. Qumran. Fire also plays a major role in the theology of Qumran. Thus, e.g., the words of the heavenly light say that God destroyed the land of Israel in his wrath (by the fire of your [i.e., God's] zeal" *b'š qn'tkh*; 4Q504 1-2 5:5). While the Heb. term occurs rather frequently in the Hebrew literature from Qumran,[17] *'šh* occurs only rarely in the Aramaic texts.

Freedman/Homan

Thus, besides 11Q10 23:2 and 36:5, it occurs with certainty in the incantation 4Q560 11:4 in reference to fever. This meaning may also be present in 11Q10 23:2, where, diverging from Job 33:24, in the context of the physical suffering of the sinner it speaks of fire or even fever tormenting him (*'šh yšnqnh*). In contrast, 36:5 *'šh* takes up Heb. *'š* in Job 41:11.

The instance in 4Q542 1 2:7, where *b'[y]š'* occurs in the context of punishment, may belong to → באשׁ *b'š*.[18]

More often, however, one encounters *nwr*, which can denote the sacrificial fire (11Q18 13:3; CT. Levi ar Bodleian c:23 [cf. 4Q214b 2-6:7]) and fiery phenomena that Enoch sees

16. E.g., Tg. Yer. of Gen. 21:15; Bab. *Yoma* 29:9; Bab. *Šabb.* 66b; Bab. *Yebam.* 71b; Jastrow 126b; *ATTM*, 524; *ATTM.E*, 314f.

17. In addition to K. G. Kuhn, *Konkordanz zu den Qumrantexten* (Göttingen, 1960), 23b, cf. also, e.g., 4Q487 1 2:4; 4Q504 6:10; 4Q510 2:4.

18. With *ATTM.E*, 84 (contra, e.g., *DSSStE*, 1083 "in the f[i]re").

on his heavenly journey (4Q204 6:22 [cf. 1 En. 14:9]; 4Q205 1 1:5 [cf. 1 En. 24:1]); cf. also the fragment from 4Q206,3,[19] that offers *bl*]*šny nwr*, which may correspond to 1 En. 21:3, as well as 4Q529 2 that stems from a vision report. Further, *nwr* also designates the destructive fire of judgment (4Q530 2:9f.). In Tg. Job, however, *nwr* occurs in passages where the Hebrew original has *'ôr* "light" (11Q10 8:3 [Job 24:13]; 29:2 [Job 37:11]; 36:4 [Job 41:10]).

This peculiarity finds its counterpart in the use of *nwr* aphel in the sense of "to shine" (in reference to the moon) in 4Q208 (e.g., 15:3) and 4Q209 (e.g., 1:5,7; 2:4). This variation between "fire" and "light" becomes especially clear also in 4Q541, which says of the eternal sun of the new priest that "it will shine" (*tnyr*; 9:I:3,4),[20] so that the darkness yields (ll. 4f.). This is linked to the image that its "fire" (*nwrh'*) will "burn" (*yzh*) everywhere (l. 4). Clearly, however, *nwr* does not mean "fire" in a destructive sense, but the fire that gives light and therefore illuminates.

Kottsieper

19. J. T. Milik, *The Books of Enoch* (Oxford, 1976), 228.

20. Cf. T. Levi 18:2-4; M. Philonenko, "Son soleil éternel brillera (4QTestLévi$^{c-d(?)}$ ii 9)," *RHPR* 73 (1993) 405-8.

אָשַׁף *'šp 'āšap*; אסה *'sh*; חַרְטֹם *ḥrṭm ḥarṭom*; כַּס/שְׂדָּי *ks/śdy kas/śdāy*

I. Etymology. II. Semantics. III. Lexical Field. 1. *'sh*. 2. *ḥarṭom*. 3. *kas/śdāy*. IV. LXX.

R. D. Biggs, "Medizin. A. In Mesopotamien," *RLA*, VII, 623-29; J. Bottéro, "Magie. A. In Mesopotamien," *RLA*, VII, 200-34; J. Brinkman, *A Political History of Post-Kassite Babylonia. AnOr* 43 (1968); idem, "Notes on Arameans and Chaldeans in Southern Babylonia in the Early Seventh Century B.C.," *Or* 46 (1977) 304-25, esp. 305-9; F. H. Cryer, *Divination in Ancient Israel and Its Near Eastern Environment. JSOTSup* 142 (1994); M. Dietrich, *Die Aramäer Südbabyloniens in der Sargonidenzeit. AOAT* 7 (1970); P.-E. Dion, "Medical Personnel in the Ancient Near East: *asu* and *āšipu* in Aramaic Garb," *Aram* 1 (1989) 206-16; J.-M. Durand, "Maladies et médecins," *AEM* I/1 (1988) 541-84; D. O. Edzard, "Kaldu," *RLA*, V (1976-1980), 291-97; M. J. Geller, "The Last Wedge," *ZA* 87 (1997) 43-96, esp. 60-64; H. Goedicke, "*ḥarṭummîm,*" *Or* NS 65 (1996) 24-30; T. L. Holm, *Of Courtiers and Kings. EANEC* 1 (2013), 104-14 (a summary of the discussion concerning the etymology and meaning of *ḥrṭm* /ḥarṭom/); B. Janowski, *Sühne als Heilsgeschehen. WMANT* 55 (1982), 33-57; A. Jeffers, *Magic and Divination in Ancient Palestine and Syria. SHANE* 8 (1996); S. A. Kaufman, *The Akkadian Influences on Aramaic. AS* 19 (1974), 37,38f.; H. Kees, "Der sog. oberste Vorlesepriester," *ZÄS* 87 (1962) 119-39; K. Koch, *Daniel. BK* XXII/1 (1986), 10f.,45-52,73-76; W. J. W. Koster, "Chaldäer," *RAC* 2 (1954) 1006-21; H. P. Müller, "Magisch-mantische Weisheit

I. Etymology. Aramaic *'āšap̱* is an Akkadian loanword derived from the verb *(w)ašāpu* "to conjure" or from the substantive *(w)āšipu* "incantation priest, evocator."[1] In Neo-Assyrian, and early and late Babylonian texts, the *(w)āšipu* appears as a ritual expert alongside the "physician" (*āsû*).[2] Similarly, Aramaic *'āšap̱* can be understood as "incantation priest." There are additional derivatives in Syriac and Mandean.[3]

II. Semantics. The oldest instances of *'āšap̱* (always L-stem; regarding the variants *'āšāp̱* and *'aššāp̱* in Dnl. 2:10, cf. *BHK*) appear in the Aramaic of the book of Daniel. The context of the lexeme paralleling *gāzer* (→ גזר *gzr*), *ḥakkîm* (→ חכים *ḥakkîm*), *ḥarṭom* and *kaśdāy* is nonspecific in Dnl. 2:10,27; 4:4. These passages involve the dream interpretation demanded by King Nebuchadnezzar that the mantics and sages could not produce. Dnl. 5:7,15 offers the same context for the activity of this group. According to it, *'āšap̱, ḥakkîm, kaśdāy*, and *gāzer* should interpret the writing on the wall, but they are not in a position to do so. According to Dnl. 5:11, Nebuchadnezzar installs Daniel as the chief (*raḇ*) of the *ḥarṭummîn, 'āšᵉpîn, kaśdā'în*, and *gāzᵉrîn*.

1QapGen 20:18-20 manifests another realm of activity for *'āšap̱*. There, physicians (*'sy'*), *'špt'*, and all the sages could not heal the king of Egypt (*l'sywth*, ll. 19,20).[4] In accordance with this, *'šp* appears in the context of the healing art in analogy to the Babylonian evidence[5] as conjurer of demons of illness.[6]

It must be fundamentally emphasized that the use of *'āšap̱* and the three other technical terms from its lexical field in the Aramaic book of Daniel (see below III) no longer stand in contact with Neo-Babylonian medical practice, for "old and new words for magicians and diviners are simply heaped up to suggest a totality, to the greater credit of the one man of God, whose genuine inspiration was able to put to shame this whole roster of evil know-how."[7]

---

und die Gestalt Daniels," *UF* 1 (1969) 79-94; idem, "*ḥarṭom*," *TDOT*, V, 176-79; E. Otto, "Cheriheb," *LexÄg*, 1, 940-43; J. Quaegebeur, "On the Egyptian Equivalent of Biblical *ḥarṭummîm*," in S. I. Groll, ed., *Pharaonic Egypt, the Bible and Christianity* (Jerusalem, 1985), 162-72; E. Reiner, *Astral Magic in Babylonia. Transactions of the American Philosophical Society* 8 (Philadelphia, 1995), esp. 43-60; E. K. Ritter, "Magical-Expert (= Ašipu) and Physician (= *Āsû*): Notes on Two Complementary Professions in Babylonian Medicine," *Studies in Honor of Benno Landsberger on His 75th Birthday. FS B. Landsberger. AS* 16 (1965), 299-321; H. H. Rowley, "The Chaldeans," *ExpT* 39 (1928) 188f.; J. Scurlock, "Physician, Exorcist, Conjurer, Magician: A Tale of Two Healing Professionals," in T. Abusch and K. van der Toorn, eds., *Mesopotamian Magic. Ancient Magic and Divination* 1 (Groningen, 1999), 69-79; W. Spiegelberg, *Demotica I/1. SBAW* (1925), 4-7; J. Vergote, *Joseph en Égypte. Orientalia et Biblica Lovaniensia* 3 (Leuven, 1959).

1. *AHw*, I, 1484a,1487f.; *CAD*, I/2, 431-35; Kaufman, 38f.
2. Ritter; *AHw*, III, 1488a.
3. Cf. *ThesSyr*, 409 and *MdD*, 41.
4. *ATTM*, 175f. *DSSStE*, 42f., reads *'špy'* "wizards."
5. Cf. Biggs; Bottéro.
6. Dion, 213f.
7. Ibid., 213.

III. Lexical Field.

1. ʾsh. The noun *ʾsh* "physician" and the denominated *ʾsh* "to heal" derive from Sumerian A.ZU, which came to Aramaic[8] via Akkadian *āsû* "physician."[9] It occurs as a professional designation in the Nabatean grave inscriptions from Mandarin Salish.[10] Additional examples come from Palmyra[11] and perhaps from Hatra,[12] Jewish Aramaic,[13] Mandean,[14] and Syriac.[15]

Furthermore, *ʾsy* also appears as a hypocoristic PN in Palmyra,[16] Asshur,[17] and among the Nabateans.[18]

The motif of Abraham, the physician (*ʾsyʾ*), in Syriac literature is particularly interesting for the reception history of the OT.[19]

2. ḥarṭom. Most scholars derive Heb. and Aram. *ḥarṭom* from Egyptian *ḥr.tp* "superior," which traces back to *ẖry-ḥb(.t) ḥry.tp* "chief lectionary priest," "magician," "soothsaying priest."[20] However, *ẖry-ḥb(t)* and *ḥry-tp* are two different titles.[21] Neo-Assyrian attests it as *ḫarṭibi* "dream interpreter."[22] In the reception of the title in the Semitic realm, the lectionary priest's competence in magic and the healing arts steps to the fore out of the original Egyptian tradition of the lectionary priest as the leader of rituals.

In the Hebrew story of Joseph the *ḥarṭummîm* parallel the *ḥāḵām* in the context of the interpretation of pharaoh's dream (Gen. 41:8), where they seem to be "mantics." In the plague narratives, *ḥarṭummîm* appear in Ex. 7:11,22; 8:3,14f; 9:11 where they represent Egyptian magicians.

In the Heb. introduction of the book of Daniel, the *ḥarṭummîm* are the mantics at the Babylonian royal court (Dnl. 1:20; 2:2). The Aramaic use in Dnl. 2:10,27; 4:4 corresponds to the Hebrew. The reference to a "chief of the mantics" in Dnl. 4:6; 5:11, a rank that

---

8. Kaufman, 37.

9. *AHw*, I, 76b; *CAD*, I/2, 344-47.

10. *CIS* II 206,1; cf. J. F. Healey, *The Nabataean Tomb Inscriptions of Mada'in Salih. JSSSup* 1 (1993), 166,167.

11. *DNSI*, 88; D. R. Hillers and E. Cussini, *Palmyrene Aramaic Texts* (Baltimore, 1996), 341.

12. Cf. B. Aggoula, *Inventaire des inscriptions hatréennes. BAH* 139 (1991), Nr. 92; *DNSI*, 88; contra K. Beyer, *Die aramäischen Inschriften aus Assur, Hatra und dem übrigen Obermesopotamien* (Göttingen, 1998), 50.

13. Jastrow, 92f.; *DJPA*, 67; *ATTM*, 519; *ATTM.E*, 312.

14. *MdD*, 27f.

15. *ThesSyr*, 288-90.

16. *PNPI*, 6,71.

17. E. Lipiński, *SAIO* I (1975), 109f.

18. F. al-Khraysheh, "Die Personennamen in den nabatäischen Inschriften des Corpus Inscriptionum Semiticarum" (diss., Marburg/Lahn, 1986), 44.

19. Cf. T. Kronholm, "Abraham, the Physician: The Image of Abraham the Patriarch in the Genuine Hymns of Ephraem Syrus," in *Solving Riddles and Untying Knots. FS J. C. Greenfield* (Winona Lake, IN, 1995), 107-15.

20. *WbÄS*, III, 140,395; Kees; Vergote; Otto; D. B. Redford, *A Study of the Biblical Story of Joseph (Genesis 37–50). SVT* 20 (1970), 203f.; Müller; Koch.

21. Quaegebeur.

22. *AHw*, I, 328; *CAD*, VI, 116.

Daniel held, indicates a hierarchical order of the *ḥarṭummîn*. The specific activity of these mantics will have primarily involved dream and oracle interpretation.

The Aramaic from Qumran also attests the abstract *ḥrṭmw* "soothsaying" (4Q201 4:2 [1 En. 8:3]). • Here, *ḥrṭmw* belongs to the arts of black magic, against which the magic that the angel Hermoni teaches humans is a protection. Consequently, the term here probably takes up the use of *ḥrṭm* in the realm of magic (Ex. 7–9) rather than of mantics. (*Ko.*) •

3. kas/śdāy. *kas/śdāy* traces back to Akk. *kaldu/kašdu*. It involves a term attested since the ninth century B.C.E. for a population in southern Babylon. It is debated whether the Kaldu as a population represent a segment of the Arameans of southern Babylon or a separate branch of Semites.[23] Most interpreters understand the reference in Dnl. 1:4 to the fact that those exiled along with Daniel receive instruction in the literature and language of the Chaldeans as a reference to Aramaic.[24] The narrative context, however, suggests that Akkadian in its late Babylonian form, and perhaps even Sumerian as a holy language, may be more likely.[25]. It is significant for the further development of the term that in Neo-Babylonian and early Persian times, the Chaldeans constituted the priesthood of the temple of Marduk in Babylon. The soothsaying priests and exorcists, in particular, were Chaldeans. Thus, *kas/śdāy* became a term designating experts in the interpretation of the future and of omens. This appears in Dnl. 2:2 (Heb.) which employs other technical terms for dream and omen interpreters in parallel. Thus, one gains the understanding of the lexeme as "scholar," "magician," "astrologer," "omen interpreter." Dnl. 2:4 (Heb.),5,10 has *kaśdāy* as an umbrella term for all magicians, mantics, and sages. Accordingly, one can observe a dual usage of *kaśdāy* in the Aramaic book of Daniel. As a gentilic, it denotes "Chaldean," "Babylonian." Thus, *gub̲rîn kaśdā'în* are "Babylonian men" (Dnl. 3:8) and Belshazzar as *malkā' kaśdāyā'* (*K*; *Q*: *kaśdā'āh*) is the "Babylonian king" (Dnl. 5:30). Comparable is the designation of Nebuchadnezzar as *melek̲ bābel kasdāyā'* (*K*; *Q*: *kasdā'āh*) "the king of Babel, of the Chaldeans" (Ezr. 5:12).

As a title, *kaśdāy* represents "astrologer," "omen interpreter" (Dnl. 2:5,10; 4:4; 5:7.11). The same situation may also pertain in Palmyr. (*kldy*).[26] Syriac and Mandean manifest still other derivatives.[27] For the reception history, cf. Geller, 60-64.

IV. LXX. The LXX and Θ translate *'āšap̲* with μάγος (Dnl. 2:10; 4:4 [= Θ 4:7]; 5:11 [Θ],15 [Θ]) or φαρμακός (2:27 [Θ: μάγος]; 5:7). In Dnl. 5:7 LXX differs from MT, but Θ agrees with MT and renders *'āšap̲* with μάγος here, too. For *ḥarṭom* one finds σόφος (Dnl. 2:10) and ἐπαοιδός (Dnl. 2:10 [Θ],27; 4:4 [= Θ 4:7]; 4:6 [= Θ 4:9]; 5:11 [Θ]). Καλδαῖος renders *kas/śdāy* (Dnl. 2:10; 4:4 [= Θ 4:7]; 5:7), which designates Babylonians in Greek literature, and since Herodotus also magicians.[28]

Niehr

23. Dietrich; Brinkman, "Notes"; Edzard, 29lf.
24. Edzard, 296.
25. Koch, 46f. with reference to Dnl. 2:26 LXX (Koch incorrectly attributes it to Θ).
26. *DNSI*, 510; Hillers-Cussini, 372.
27. *ThesSyr*, 1745; *MdD*, 197,216.
28. Edzard, 296.

אשרן *'šrn* /'āšarn/

I. Etymology. II. Usage.

I. Etymology. Among the very few Iranian loanwords from the lexical field of construction and architecture in Aramaic, one finds *'šrn* /'āšarn/ "wooden structure, woodwork"; it traces to **āçarna*.[1] Its exact meaning is disputed, however.[2]

II. Usage. The word first occurs in Imperial Aramaic documents from Egypt. It can designate either the mere construction material, as in *TADAE* A6.2:5,9,21 (permit for repairs to a ship with a list of the necessary raw materials)[3] and presumably B3.4:23 (sale of property), or an already completed wooden structure such as the Elephantine temple.[4] Ezra 5:3 also employs the word in this latter sense for the interior furnishings of the sanctuary in Jerusalem. In addition to the ceiling, wood was also incorporated into the walls (5:8).[5] It remains unclear, however, the exact phase of the construction work to which Ezr. 5:1-17 refers.[6]

Gzella

J. Tavernier, *Iranica in the Achaemenid Period (ca. 550–330 B.C.). OLA* 158 (2007).

1. Tavernier, 437, §4.4.8.1.
2. See *DNSI*, 129f. for bib.
3. Cf. without context *TADAE* D3.21:1, probably also a list.
4. *TADAE* 4.5:18; 4.7:11.
5. → *ktl.*
6. Cf. H. G. M. Williamson, *Ezra, Nehemiah. WBC* (1985), 70.

אָת *'t 'āṯ*; תְּמַהּ *tmh t^emah*; תוה *twh*

I. *'āṯ*. 1. Etymology. 2. General Use. II. *tmh/twh*. 1. Basic Meaning and Etymology. 2. The Noun *tmh*. III. *'āt* and *t^emah* in Biblical Aramaic.

U. Berges, "תָּמַהּ *tāmah, TDOT*, XV, 681-84; F. J. Helfmeyer, "אוֹת *'oth*," *TDOT*, I, 167-88; C. A. Keller, *Das Wort OTH als "Offenbarungszeichen Gottes"* (Basel, 1946), esp. 146f.; K. H. Rengstorf, σημεῖον, *TDNT*, VII, 199-261, esp. 216f.; S. Wagner, "מוֹפֵת *môpeṯ*," *TDOT*, VIII, 174-81; W. Weiß, *Zeichen und Wunder*. WMANT 67 (1995), esp. 15-17.

I. *'āṯ*.

1. Etymology. The word *'t* "sign," attested in Aramaic since Biblical Aramaic, has counterparts in Ugaritic *at*[1] and Heb. *'ôṯ*, which points to a *qāl* (*'āt*) as the common basis. The traditional vocalization of the word in Biblical Aramaic, Jewish Aramaic (along with *'aṯ*), and Syriac as *'āṯ* also suggests this. The Mandean *'t(')*[2] also points to a vocalization with an *a*-vowel.

Etymologically related is Akk. *ittu* II "sign,"[3] which is closely linked semantically with *ittu* I "the particular, characteristic." The latter, however, especially via the plural *idātu* in contrast to *ittātu*, proves to be an etymologically independent word. The plural form *ittātu* from *ittu* II corresponds to the fem. pl. form of the word in Ugar. (*att*),[4] Heb., Syr., and Mand. (*'twt'* [*'āṯwāṯā*], etc.).[5] In contrast to the NW Semitic specimens, however, the Akk. *ittu* seems to trace back to a *qill* form. Even if no decision can be made concerning how the Proto-Semitic form sounded (in the event that a single form stood at the beginning and two pronunciations of a basic word did not coexist), one can still operate on the assumption that it involved a primary word with the radicals ' and *t*.

Thence, the frequently suggested etymological connection to Arabic *'āya*^{tun} "sign" and the related derivation from an otherwise unattested root *'wy*[6] is to be rejected. It is also contradicted by the fact that both in Arabic, as well as in NW Semitic, such doubly weak roots normally treat the second radical as strong.

Just as ambiguous as the etymological evidence is the morphological categorization of the word. Syriac, like Akkadian, consistently treats the word as a fem., while in West Aramaic *'t*, as in Heb., is mostly a masc., but Syr. also manifests divergent masc. pl. forms. The Babylonian Targum tradition offers various mixed forms: The plural is usually constructed with masculine forms (fem. in Tg. Onq. e.g., only in Ex. 7:3; 10:2; Num. 2:2; 14:22) and in many passages the word also appears as a masc. (cf. e.g., Tg. Onq. of Ex. 4:8; 8:19), but in Tg. Jon. of Josh. 24:17 the masc. pl. form can also be understood as a fem.: *'tyh rbrbt'*. Since Babylonian Jewish Aramaic outside the Targums no longer attests the word, one can conclude that it was not native there, but traces to the Hasmonean substratum of the Babylonian Targum tradition,[7] so that in the course of the transmission of the text, these mixed forms could develop under the influence of the neighboring East Aramaic dialects.

These forms then also influenced the further transmission of the originally Palestinian textual tradition so that, e.g., instances of the masc. pl. in the Palestinian Mishnah tradition[8] also appear as fem. in later editions. The sole instance of *'t* in Samaritan Aramaic, which otherwise knows only the Hebraistic form *'wt*,[9] also involves such influence.

---

1. *DUL*^{3}, 117f.
2. *MdD*, 42b.
3. *AHw*, I, 406a.
4. *KTU* 1.103:1.
5. *LexSyr*, 53b; *MdD*, 42b.
6. Cf. *GesB*^{18}, 28.
7. *ATTM*, 36.
8. Cf. *DJPA*, 79a.
9. *DSA*, 14f.,70a.

2. General Use. In Aramaic, *'t* originally had a spectrum of meaning as broad as that of Hebrew *'ôṯ*, as Syriac and the fact that the Babylonian Targum consistently renders Hebrew *'ôṯ* with *'t* demonstrate. The Palestinian Targum tradition exhibits a somewhat different picture. Apart from the specimens in Deuteronomy, in which Hebrew *'ôṯ* stands alongside *môpeṯ* (Dt. 4:34; 6:22; 7:19; 13:2,3; 26:8; 28:46; 29:2; 34:11; but not Ex. 7:3), it occurs in Tg. Neof. and the related tradition of the Targum fragment only in Gen. 1:14 (the heavenly lights as signs) and in Tg. Neof. of Ex. 13:9 for the tefillin (in v. 16 then added in the margin). In the middle stands the Tg. Yer., which usually, although not always (e.g., Gen. 9:13; Ex. 3:12), renders *'ôṯ* with *'t*. Outside the Targum literature, Palestinian Jewish Aramaic attests it only in the meaning "letter," "character." A particular affinity to targumic diction is also evident in the older texts. Thus, it is hardly an accident that both the Biblical Aramaic instances (→ III) and 1QapGen 12:1 (cf. Gen. 9:13) employ *'t* in contexts that obviousliy depend on Hebrew statements with *'ôṯ*. In addition, *'t* occurs with certainty at Qumran only in 4Q5482 2:12 (*'twhy*), whose context is as unclear as it is in 1Q20 1 1:9, where it may be that one should also read *'twhy* with *ATTM,* 166. In the later magical texts, in analogy to the other nontargumic instances, *'t* designates written characters.[10]

One can rather easily explain this body of evidence by the fact that in Palestinian (Jewish) Aramaic, the meaning of *'t* as "sign" became increasingly narrowed to the written sign so that, finally, it acquired the predominant meaning "letter," "character." This probably accompanies an expansion of the capacity to write with a phonetic alphabet in which the individual characters no longer possess a general sign character. Such a sign no longer referred to something concrete and is, therefore, ultimately no longer a sign, which naturally had effects on diction. Only under the influence of Biblical Hebrew *'ôṯ* could Jewish Aramaic *'t* retain its old breadth of meaning. This interpretation accords with the fact that in Syriac, which did not also undergo this development of meaning (and perhaps then also gained influence on the Christian Palestinian Aramaic use of *'t*), *'tw* arose as an independent word for "letter," "character," i.e., this new area of meaning become decoupled form the original *'t*.

It is questionable whether such an *'tw* also appears in V 48:5 (*ATTM.E,* 189f.) = X Ḥev/Se 9:5.[11]

II. *tmh/twh*.

1. Basic Meaning and Etymology. Like Hebrew *tmh*, the root *tmh* (with a consonantal *h*; Mandean *thm* with metathesis),[12] attested in all Aramaic dialects since Biblical Aramaic, denotes the reaction to a surprising or extraordinary event. "To be astonished" is the most widespread meaning in Aramaic, as a glance into the pertinent lexica already indicates.[13] It also occurs frequently at Qumran. Thus, 1QapGen 20:9 expresses pharaoh's

10. Cf. esp. ggQN 1:9: *w'tyh qdyšyh dktybyn* "and the holy characters that are written" (*ATTM.E,* 256f.); in an unclear context also yyMA 3:12 (*ATTM.E,* 237).

11. Cf. A. Yardeni, *DJD,* XXVII (1997), 39,47.

12. *MdD,* 483a.

13. *ThesSyr*, 4455f; *TW*, I 542b; *DJPA*, 584a; *LSP*, 221a.

astonishment at Sara's beauty with *tmh* (ithpeel/ithpael; *wʾtmh ʿl kwl šqph* "and he was astonished at all her beauty"). In addition, CT. Levi ar Bodleian a:11f. expresses Levi's astonishment that his other dream confirmed his earlier dream with *ʾnh mtmh* (ithpeel/ithpael or pael?) "I am astonished." Finally, one may call attention to 4Q205 1 2:8, which can probably be emended based on the parallel 1 En. 26:6 *]mht* to *wt]mht*[14] or *wʾt]mht*[15] "and I was astonished" to denote Enoch's reaction to the mountains in his second vision journey.

The meaning "to be astonished" makes little sense, on the other hand, in the Job Targum 11Q10 10:2 (Job 26:11) where *wytmhwn* renders the Hebrew *wᵉyiṯmᵉhû* and describes the reaction of the pillars of heaven that God causes to shake. The nominal form *tmhʾ* joins this use. In 4:5 (Job 21:6), it renders the Hebrew *pallaṣûṯ* "to quake" → "to startle." Therefore, "to startle" also belongs to the root's horizon of meaning.

Later dialects manifest a more complex picture. Thus, Syriac also employs *tmh* with the connotation of "fright," comparable to the rendering of *yiśʿᵃrû ʿālêḵā śaʿar* in the (Bab.) Tg. Jon. of Ezk. 32:10 with *ytmhwn ʿlk tymh* (cf., on the other hand, 27:35, which translates the parallel statement *śāʿarû śaʿar* with *zʿw zyʿ*). The West Aramaic dialects widely exhibit the meaning "to be astonished" and employ for "to frighten," "to be horrified," etc., the root *twh*, which also exhibits a consonantal *h* and, furthermore, a consonantal *w*. Syriac also knows this root primarily in this negative meaning. "Fright," "to be horrified" also gives the best sense for *twh* in Dnl. 3:24 since "to be astonished" is hardly sufficient reason for the king suddenly to leap up (→ בהל *bhl* II).

In view of the broad semantic horizon of Hebrew *tmh* and the absence of *twh* beyond the realm of Aramaic, this evidence seems best explained in terms of *twh* as an inner-Aramaic rhyme for *tmh* that originally denoted all forms of reaction to an unusual or unexpected event, from astonishment to fear. In this regard, the use of *twh* in later dialects argues that it was originally limited to the realm of fright. Thence, the path was clear for secondarily narrowing the wide semantic realm covered by *tmh* to the element of astonishment since now a root for "to be frightened" was available in *twh*—a path taken mostly by the West Aramaic dialects.

2. *The Noun* tmh. The *qiṭl*-form that underlies Biblical Aramaic *tᵉmah* is also widespread in the later dialects. On the one hand, *tmh* can express the reaction of astonishment, wonder, or, in East Aramaic, also fright and, on the other, especially in West Aramaic dialects, it can also denote what this reaction produces. The restriction of *tmh* to the realm of astonishment brings with it the fact that the noun *tmh* can also occur as a term for "wonder."[16] For the Biblical Aramaic use (→ III), it is particularly significant that the Palestinian Targum tradition, as represented—although fragmentarily—in Tg. Yer. of the Pentateuch, Psalms, and 1 and 2 Chronicles, essentially renders Hebrew *môpeṯ* with *tmh*, while the Bab. Tg. Onq. of the Pentateuch, Tg. Jon. of the prophets, and the tradition represented by Tg. Neof. never have *tmh* in this function. Since, however, the

14. *DSSStE*, 422f.
15. *ATTM*, 241.
16. *WT*, I 542f.; *LSP*, 221b; *DSA*, 954a.

Christian Palestinian Aramaic tradition, e.g., of Isa. 8:18, renders *lᵉ'ôṯôṯ ûlᵉmôpᵉṯîm* with *'tyn wtmhyn*, one can assume here an independent Palestinian translation tradition for which *tmh* was a direct equivalent of *môpeṯ*, but which simultaneously also rendered *'ôṯ* with *'aṯ* (→ I.2).

III. *'āt* and *tᵉmah* in Biblical Aramaic. Based on these results, the mention of the *'āṯayyā' wᵉṯimhayyā'* or *'āṯîn wᵉṯimhîn* in Dnl. 3:32 and 6:28, the "signs and wonders" that God does, can rightly be understood as a direct adaptation of the especially Dtr. language of the signs (*'ôṯôṯ*) and wonders (*môpᵉṯîm*) that God performed in the context of the Exodus (Dt. 4:34; 6:22; 7:19; 26:8; 29:2; 34:11; cf. Jer. 32:20f.; Ps. 78:43; 105:27; 135:9; Neh. 9:10). Dnl. 3:33 strengthens this relationship when it emphasizes the grandeur and power of these signs and wonders. Here, the characterization of the signs of God as *raḇrᵉḇîn* corresponds to the targumic rendering of *gᵉḏôlîm* in the "credo" Dt. 6:22 and in the introduction of the covenant-making in Dt. 29:2. The fact that the author of this section appeals consciously here to traditional formulations also finds confirmation in the nearly literal rendering of Ps. 145:13 in 3:33b.[17]

Both Dnl. 3:32f. and 6:28 stand in fictive letters in which Nebuchadnezzar or Darius addresses all peoples and calls for the acknowledgment of God's dominion and that belong to an independent redactional layer of the Aramaic Daniel tradition.[18] In this regard, it is probably no accident that the signs and wonders in 3:32 relate specifically to God's action in relation to King Nebuchadnezzar whose fate teaches him to recognize God's power (Dnl. 4) and in 6:28, however, become evident in God's liberating activity on behalf of his pious Jews. Thereby, the texts take up both aspects linked with the signs and wonders in the torah tradition: first, God's treatment of pharaoh (Dt. 6:22; 29:2 [cf. v. 1!]; cf. also Ex. 7:3), and, second, the deliverance and guidance out of Egypt (Dt. 7:19; 26:8). At the same time, however, it becomes clear that the author thinks that the great signs and wonders that God does are neither limited to the exodus nor fundamentally justify a division between Israel and the nations, that is, must end a pagan superpower. Instead, as the accounts from the exile illustrate, they can also lead a pagan superpower to acknowledge the saving sovereignty of God—which, after all, corresponds fully to their intention (Dt. 4:35). Since the author of this layer appeals to a Palestinian translation tradition, he may belong to circles in Palestine who sought a path in the Hellenstic period for preserving their own religious tradition, on the one hand, and for avoiding conflict with the pagan superpower, on the other, and thereby appealed to accounts concerning the exilic period.

Kottsieper

17. W. S. Towner, "The Poetic Passages of Daniel 1-6," *CBQ* 31 (1969) 321.
18. R. G. Kratz, *Translatio imperii. WMANT* 63 (1991), 93f.,156-60.

אתה *'tī*

I. Etymology. II. General Aramaic Usage. III. Biblical Aramaic Usage. IV. Qumran and Later Jewish Aramaic Inscriptions.

I. Etymology. Ugaritic,[1] Punic, Palmyrene, Nabatean, the texts from Deir ʿAlla and Hatra,[2] Arabic, and OSA,[3] Ethiopic,[4] and Thamudic[5] attest the verb *'th* "to come." The verb occurs in the Hebrew of the OT as an Aramaism especially in Second Isaiah (41:25, etc.) and Job (16:22, etc.).[6] In Biblical Aramaic, it numbers simultaneously among the first *aleph* and the third guttural verbs. In the haphel "to bring" and hophal "to be brought," it joins the class of first *yod* verbs.[7]

II. General Aramaic Usage. In the Old Aramaic Sefire inscriptions,[8] the verb *'th* occurs exclusively in the imperfect. In all passages, it should be translated "to come." In *KAI* 222 B 31f., it is always linked to the prefixed negation *l* (= *l'*): *lt'th* = *l* + 2ms impf. peal; [*lt'*]*twn* = *l* + 2mp impf. peal; [*l*]*y'th* = *l* + 3ms impf. peal. To indicate direction, the verb combines with the preposition *'l*.[9] Subjects of *'th* include "one of the kings,"[10] "your son,"[11] "your grandson,"[12] or a fugitive.[13] The verb also has the meaning "to come" in an Aramaic inscription from Assyria, *KAI* 233.7 *'t't* "and I came" and l. 11 *y'th* "(Upāq-ana-Arba'il) will come." In the 3pl. pf. peal, *'th* occurs in an inscription from Saqqāra/Egypt: *'tw* "(the troops of the king of Babel) have come."[14] It is combined with the subject "the gods" (*'lhn*) and the preposition *'l* in the texts from Deir ʿAlla to describe

---

E. Jenni, "'Kommen' im theologischen Sprachgebrauch des Alten Testaments," *Wort-Gebot-Glaube. FS W. Eichrodt. ATANT* 59 (1970), 251-61; idem, "בוא *bô'* to come," *TLOT*, 201-4; K. G. Kuhn, μαρανα9ά, *TDNT*, IV, 466-72; H.-D. Preuß, "בּוֹא *bô'*; אָתָה *'āthāh*," *TDOT*, II, 20-49; F. Schnutenhaus, "Das Kommen und Erscheinen Gottes im Alten Testament," *ZAW* 76 (1964) 1-22; M. Wagner, *Die lexikalischen und grammatikalischen Aramaismen im alttestamentlichen Hebräisch. BZAW* 96 (1966).

1. *DUL*³, 119f.
2. *DNSI*, 133-36.
3. W. W. Müller, "Altsüdarabische Beiträge zum hebräischen Lexikon," *ZAW* 75 (1963) 307.
4. *CDG*, 46f.
5. A. van den Branden, *Les Inscriptions thamoudéens* (Louvain, 1950), 511.
6. Wagner, 31 [no. 31].
7. *BLA*, §49e-h.
8. *KAI* 222-224.
9. *KAI* 222 B 13.
10. *KAI* 222 B 28.
11. *KAI* 224.11.
12. *KAI* 224.12.
13. *KAI* 224.20.
14. *KAI* 266.4.

the appearance of the gods to the seer: *'lhn h'wy'tw 'lwh* "the gods came to him."[15] The interpretation of *'th* in II 14 is uncertain since the line is destroyed. Here one can read either a 3ms pf. peal or a ptcp. sg. abs. Additional specimens appear, e.g., in *AP* 5.3 (*'tyt*, 1s impf. peal); 30.8 (*'tw* 3pl pf. peal); 37.11 (*'th* 3ms pf. peal); Aḥiqar 118 (*'ty* fs impf.); *AP* 38.5 (*'tyn* ptcp. mpl. abs.); 82.11 (*y'th* 3s impf. peal); 24.36 (*hyty* 3ms pf. haphel); 27.14 (*lhytyh* inf. haphel).

· Here, too, the meanings "to come" for the peal and "to bring" for the haphel predominate. As a component of a fixed phrase, *'th* appears in *t'th ʿl blk* "may this come to your awareness,"[16] where the subject is a circumstance and not a specific person or thing (→ בל *bal* III). The connotation "to present" (of food sacrifices) for the haphel may be evident in *AP* 27.14 (*lhytyh mnḥ[h* "in order to bring food sacrifices"), although the context is too corrupt to permit an exact interpretation. Therefore, *'th* proves to be largely synonymous with Hebrew *bw'*. (*Ko.*) ·

III. Biblical Aramaic Usage. Biblical Aramaic attests the verb seven times in the peal in the meaning "to come" (Dnl. 3:2,26; 7:13,22; Ezr. 4:12; 5:3,16), seven times in the haphel "to bring" (Dnl. 3:13; 5:2,3,13,23; 6:17,25), and twice in the hophal "to be brought" (Dnl. 3:13; 6:18).

In the peal, one or several persons are consistently the subject of *'th*. Ezr. 5:3,16 mention Tattenai (v. 3), the governor of the region beyond the river, and Sheshbazzar (v. 16), who have come to the Jews because of the construction of the temple. The verb has a forensic undertone in Dnl. 7:22 where it speaks of the coming of the Ancient of Days to enforce justice for the holy ones of the Most High. In Ezr. 4:12 (*'ᵃṯô* 3mp pf. peal) it stands alongside the verb *slq* as a term for the return of the Jews to Jerusalem from the exile. In Daniel's vision of the four animals (Dnl. 7), Daniel sees one like a son of man who came with the clouds of heaven: *'āṯeh hᵃwā'* (Dnl. 7:13). Here, the auxiliary verb "to be" joins the participle of *'th* to emphasize the duration of the process in the past.[17] In Dnl. 3:2, *lemeṯe'* (< **me'ṯe'*; "in order to come")[18] as an infinitive depends on the verb *šlḥ* "to send." In Dnl. 3:26, *we'ᵉṯô* stands as a second-person imperative alongside *puqû*. The addressees are Shadrach, Meshach, and Abednego whom Nebuchadnezzar commands: "come out and come here (i.e., from the fiery furnace)!"

In the haphel, *'th* serves, first, as a term for the transportation of the Jews from Judah into exile (Dnl. 5:13), and, second, to describe bringing persons (Dnl. 3:13; 6:17,25) and things (Dnl. 5:2,3,23). In Dnl. 3:13, the haphel infinitive depends on the verb *'mr* "to say." The passage tells of the king's command to bring Shadrach, Meshach, and Abednego. Dnl. 6 speaks of bringing Daniel (6:17 with the preposition *l*ᵉ) and the men who had accused Daniel (6:25). In Dnl. 5:3,23, the golden vessels from the temple in Jerusalem are the objects of *'th* haphel.

---

15. J. Hoftijzer and G. van der Kooij, *Aramaic Texts from Deir ʿAlla. DMOA* 19 (1976), I 1.
16. Aḥiqar 97.
17. *BLA*, §81pq.
18. *KBL*³, 1676.

The two instances of the hophal (Dnl. 3:13; 6:18) have persons (3:13) or things (6:18) as subjects. In Dnl. 3:13, it describes the execution of the command to bring Shadrach, Meshach, and Abednego before the king, a command formulated with the haphel (see above). Dnl. 6:18 says that a stone was brought to cover the lion's den. The *ā* in the second (penultimate) syllable encountered in both verb forms should be changed to an *a*.[19] The analogy with the strong verb probably evokes the *-ay* that has appeared here.[20]

IV. Qumran and Later Jewish Aramaic Inscriptions. The instances of *'th* in the Aramaic texts from the Dead Sea and other later Jewish Aramaic inscriptions are numerous.[21] In the peal, the following distinctions in translation may be made:

1. The verb can be translated "to come" and, if linked with the preposition *l* as a particle of direction, "to come to." This usage appears in many passages in 1QapGen: 2:25 "I have come to Uruk" (*'tyt l'rk*);[22] 21:19 "and I came into my house" (*w'tyt . . . lbyty*). In the literature concerning the giants, 4Q530 2:21 says "and he (i.e., the giant Mahawai) came to . . ." (*w'th l. . .*).[23] In the Megillat Ta'anit transmitted in rabbinic tradition,[24] paragraph 35 links *'th* with *l* while in this case the subject of *'th* is not a person, but "the good news" (*bšwrt'*): "the good news came to the Jews" (*'tt bšwrt' ṭbt' lyjhwd'y*). Besides *l*, *'l* also expresses direction. Thus, e.g., 1QapGen 20:21 says: "Thereupon Harcanos came to me" (*b'dyn 'th 'ly ḥrqnwš*). One reads in 4Q204 4:5 (1 En. 89:33) that the lamb "came to the flock" (*w'th 'l 'n'*). The Testament of Amram combines *'th* with the double preposition *l'l* ("he came to him" *'th l'lwhy*).[25]

• Similarly, 4Q541 2 3+4 1+5:7 speaks of the discipline of wisdom that "will come to you": *mw[sr ḥk]mh y'th l'lykh*. The adversative significance of the *'l* as well as the convenient association of *'th* with future events and phenomena that are yet "to come" is evident in apocalyptic texts. Thus, 4Q246 1:4 says that the future affliction "will come upon the earth" (*tth 'l 'r'*; cf. similarly 4Q213 3+4:11; 4Q540 1). It is debatable whether *'th* in the phrase *wkl' 'th 'd 'lm'* (4Q246 1:3) should also be understood as "all that which will come until eternity"[26] or *'th* here taken as the personal pronoun "you."[27] The μαρανα θα from 1 Cor. 16:22 (cf. Did. 10:6) fits well in this eschatologico-apocalyptic context. For linguistic reasons,[28] it should probably be understood in the sense of "Come, our Lord!" In the connotations of approaching and arriving suited to the word for "to come," the concrete significance of the future for those awaiting and their surroundings comes to the fore with greater emphasis than in the alternative discussion of appearance. (*Ko.*) •

---

19. So *BHS*.
20. *BLA*, §49fg.
21. *ATTM*, 525; *ATTM.E*, 315.
22. Reading with *ATTM*, 169.
23. So *ATTM*, 265; *DSSStE*, 1064f. emends *l[hwn]* "to them."
24. Cf. *ATTM*, 354-58.
25. 4Q545 1:10; according to *ATTM.E*, 86.
26. So e.g., *DSSStE*, 492f.; F. M. Cross, in D. W. Parry and S. D. Ricks, eds., *Current Research and Technological Developments on the Dead Sea Scrolls*. *STDJ* 20 (1996), 6; F. García Martínez, 25.
27. So É. Puech, *DJD*, XXII, (1996), 171; *ATTM.E*, 112.
28. *ATTM*, 124.

Finally, the preposition *lwt* indicates direction toward a goal. Tg. Job of 42:11 (11Q10 38:4f.) says: "And Job came. . ." (*w'tyn lwt 'ywb. . .*). 4Q209 7 3:2 combines *'th* in the infinitive with the modal verb *twb* also in the infinitive and extends it with the preposition *b*: "it (i.e., the sun) began to come again . . . on the course" (*lmtb lmth . . . bḥrtyh*). In a letter from Simon bar Kosiba (134-135 C.E.), *'th* appears with the associative preposition *'m*: "he should come with you" (*wyth 'mkwn*).[29] Finally, one should mention the preposition *'d* which may accompany *'th* in Tg. Job of 38:11: "as far as here <you will come>" (*'d tn' <tt'>*).[30]

2. The meaning "to arrive" is evident in the astronomical book concerning the four cardinal directions (4Q209 23:4f.; 1 En. 77:2). The explanation of the different directions describes the west as the great direction "because the stars of heaven arrive there" (*bdy tmn 't[yn kw]kby šmy'*).

3. The translation of *'th* with "to go," "to journey" suits 1QapGen 19:9; 21:15,17. It also links the verb with the preposition *lyd* "to the side," "at." In the context of the depiction of Abram's journey, 21:15,17 says that he travelled beside the sea (21:15: *w'tyt lyd ym'*; 17: *whwyt 'th ly lyd ym' šmwq'*).

In the haphel, *'th* translates "to bring." Thus, Job's friends come to him to comfort him because of the misfortune that "God had brought upon him" (11Q10 38:7 [Job 42:11]: *hyty 'lh' 'lwhy*). Here, the preposition *'l* accompanies *'th* haphel.

The ossuary of King Uzziah of Judah (circa 50 C.E.) attests the verb in the hophal. The subject of *'th* is "the bones of Uzziah" that "were brought here . . ." (*lkh htyt . . .*).[31]

The verb *'th* appears as the name of a divine being on an amulet from Irbid/Jordan dated to the seventh century C.E. The name of the angel mentioned here is Ataya (*'thyh*).[32] It is named along with the divine beings Lelya, Qallat, Cherub, and Shamarya, the angel of Yahu. They are supposed to emit healing power for the pregnant Marin, the daughter of Sara.

Neef

---

29. ySK 1 1:6f.; *ATTM.E,* 215.

30. 11Q10 30:8. Cf. already M. Sokoloff, *The Targum to Job from Qumran Cave XI* (Ramat Gan, 1974), 148.

31. yJE 20:1; *ATTM,* 343.

32. ggAR 1:24; *ATTM,* 375.

אֲתַר *'tr* *ᵃṯar; אשרה/אתרה *'šrh/'trh*

I. Basic Meaning. II. Use of *'šrt-/'trt-* to Designate a Holy Place. III. Use of *'šr-/'tr-* to Designate Holy Place. 1. Palestinian Aramaic. 2. Nabatean and Palmyrene. 3. Assyrio-Babylonian Backgrounds.

I. Basic Meaning. The Aramaic word *'tr* (Biblical Aram. *'ᵃṯar*), like the Hebrew relative pronoun *'ᵃšer*, derives from the common Semitic root *'ṯr*, although, in contrast to Hebrew, Aramaic preserves the noun in its original meaning "place," "location"; it is widely attested in all Aramaic dialects, including Biblical Aramaic (cf. Ezr. 5:15; 6:3,5,7). Old Aramaic texts, in keeping with a widespread scribal tradition of consistently rendering *ṯ* with *š*, spell it *'šr* since the Phoenician alphabet employed for writing Aramaic had no specific sign for this phoneme. Only the inscription from Tell Fekheriye follows another system here in which *s* expresses *ṯ*.[1]

Occasionally, the word also has the meaning "trace," as, e.g., in Dnl. 2:35, and often appears in prepositional and adverbial phrases such as *lᵉ'aṯreh* "to his place" (Ezr. 6:5) or *'ᵃṯar dî* "where," literally "the place that" (Ezr. 6:3).

II. Use of *'šrt-/'trt-* to Designate a Holy Place. Old Aramaic and Imperial Aramaic attest the feminine derivative of *'ṯr* with the meaning "holy place" or "sanctuary," corresponding to Akk. *aširtu*,[2] Phoen. *'šrt*,[3] and Heb. *'ᵃšērāh*.[4] The earliest known instance occurs in the Sefire treaty from the middle of the eighth century B.C.E. where the context, however, is unfortunately incomplete: *[b]yt gš w'mh 'm 'šrthm* "Bet-Gush and its people with the holy sites."[5] The word appears later in the grave inscription from Sardis, a Lydo-Aramaic diglot from the middle of the fourth century B.C.E. It calls the burial place *'trt'* "the holy place." The presence of a holy tree, designated by the Old Persian load word *drḥt*, identical with the New Persian *diqaḫt* "tree," characterizes the sites: *znh stwn' wm'rt' drḥt 'trt' wprbr* "this is the stele and the grotto, the tree of the holy place and the foyer (dromos)."[6] The combination *drḥt 'trt'* finds an exact parallel in Hebrew *'ᵃṣê hā'ᵃšērāh* "the trees of the holy place" (Jgs. 6:26) and refers to the same religious element of a burial site as the "oaks" of the "region" in the Aramaic inscription from Keseçek Köyü, which also dates to the fourth century B.C.E.[7] The religious practice of planting shade trees at holy places explains the proper definition of the *'ᵃšērāh* offered

---

J. C. de Moor, "אֲשֵׁרָה *'ᵃshērāh*," *TDOT*, I, 438-44; F. G. Hüttenmeister, "The Aramaic Inscription from the Synagogue at Ḥ. 'Ammudim," *IEJ* 28 (1978) 109-12; idem, *Die jüdischen Synagogen, Lehrhäuser und Gerichtshöfe. TAVO.B* B 12/1 (1977); E. Lipiński, *Studies in Aramaic Inscriptions and Onomastics. OLA* 1 (1975), esp. 34,155-57; J. T. Milik, *Dédicaces faites par des dieux. BAH* 92 (1972), esp. 136,177; G. Reeg, *Die samaritanischen Synagogen. TAVO.B* B 12/2 (1977); J.-P. Rey-Coquais, *Inscriptions grecques et latines de la Syrie VI. BAH* 78 (1967), esp. 120,122; C. Roberts, T. C. Skeat, and A. D. Nock, "The Gild of Zeus Hypsistos," *HTR* 29 (1936) 39-88, esp. 45f.; M.-J. Seux, *Épithètes royales akkadiennes et sumériennes* (Paris 1967), esp. 323-25.

1. Cf. A. Abou-Assaf, P. Bordreuil, A. E. Millard, *La Statue de Tell Fekherye et son inscription bilingue assyro-araméenne* (Paris, 1982), 43f.
2. *AHw*, I, 80b; *CAD*, I/2, 436-39.
3. M. Dothan, "A Phoenician Inscription from 'Akko," *IEJ* 35 (1985) 86.
4. E. Lipiński, "The Goddess Atirat in Ancient Arabia, in Babylon, and in Ugarit," *OLP* 3 (1972) 112-16.
5. *KAI* 222 B 11.
6. *KAI* 260.2-3; for the reading and interpretation, cf. Lipiński, 155-57.
7. *KAI* 258.2; for the reading and interpretation, cf. Lipiński, 147f.; *DNSI*, 19 (bib.).

in the Mishnah (Midr. 'Abod. Zar. 3:7). It is "anything under which a foreign cult takes place" (*kl šyš tḥtyh 'bwdh zrh*).

III. Use of *'šr-/'tr-* to Designate Holy Place.

1. Palestinian Aramaic. Jewish Palestinian-Aramaic also employs the emphatic state *'tr'* or *'trh* of the word *'tr* to denote the synagogue.[8] Various inscriptions reaching back to the fourth century C.E. attest this usage, such as, e.g., in the synagogue of Umm el-'Amed (ca. 300 C.E.): *'bdw hdntr' dmry šwmy'* "they made this holy place of the Lord of Heaven."[9] The phonetic spelling *hdntr'* reflects the pronunciation *hadenatra* < *haden 'atrā'*. The plaster inscription of the Rehov Synagogue also omits the ': *'lyn ytrwn wrmwn btrh mṣw[t]h* "these (men) were generous and gave alms at the holy place."[10] In other passages, the adj. *qdyš* "holy" modifies the subst. *'tr*; so e.g., in the inscription of the mosaic floor in the synagoge at Hammat: *yhy šlmh 'l kl mn d'bd mṣwth bhdn 'trh qdyšh* "may peace be upon the one who gave alms at this holy place."[11] Similar phrases also occur in the later synagogue inscriptions from the fifth through the sixth centuries C.E., as in Christian Palestinian Aramaic texts that can designate a church simply as *'tr'* "(holy) place."[12] Greek renders these designations of the place of worship literally with ὁ ἅγιος τόπος, ὁ ἁγιώτατος τόπος[13] or simply ὁ τόπος.[14]

2. Nabatean and Palmyrene. The usage of the word *'tr* to designate a place of worship is not a Jewish innovation of the fourth century C.E. since Nabatean inscriptions from the first centuries B.C.E. and C.E. already attest it. The grand foundation inscription in Qabr et-Turkmān from Petra states, among other things, that *kl 'ṣl' dy b'try' 'lh ḥrm wḥrg dwšr' 'lh mr'n'* "all the goods located in this (holy) place are holy and the inviolable property of Dushara, the god of our Lord."[15] Even though the plural *'try'* can mean simply "places," "sites," the context makes it clear that the places meant here are holy for they belong to a royal burial site and are dedicated to the national god. In other Nabatean inscriptions *'tr'* also obviously means "holy place,"[16] a meaning that may also occur in Palmyrene: *dkyr 'gylw . . . dyhb 'tr' lkpt'* "may Ogeilu be remembered . . . who gave the (holy) place for the alcove."[17] This example is not entirely convincing, but a better example is *ḥmn' klh hw w'trh* "the whole incense altar, it itself and its (holy) place,"[18] as is *bkl 'tr klh* "in the entire holy place."[19]

---

8. *DJPA*, 82b.
9. Hüttenmeister, "Inscription," 109; *ATTM*, 399 (ooUA 1.3f.).
10. *ATTM*, 382 (ggBS 7.1).
11. *ATTM*, 386 (ggHM 1.1f.).
12. E.g., ccAM 1.5; *ATTM*, 402f.
13. E.g., Hüttenmeister, *Synagogen*, 129,133,136,171.
14. Roberts-Skeat-Nock; Milik, 136; Reeg, 631f.; Rey-Coquais.
15. *CIS* II 350.3.
16. *CIS* II 217.7; 235 A:2; RÉS 1110 A and C; 1119A; 1174 = *CIS* II 270.1.
17. J. Cantineau, "Tadmorea III," *Syr* 19 (1938) 159 = *PAT* 2791; Milik, 177.
18. *CIS* II 3917.3-4 = *PAT* 0263.
19. *PAT* 1929.5.

Furthermore, the Greek word τόπος, employed in Syria with the special meaning "set-apart, inaccessible region," translates *'tr'* in just this meaning as "holy place." Palmyra and Dura-Europos attest this meaning. An inscription from Palmyra mentions the εωνθας τόπου "the cultic service of the holy place,"[20] while εωνθας apparently translates Aramaic *'wnt'*. Moreover, in Dura-Europos, an inscription from the temple of Atargatus mentions the dedication of a "holy place for the goddess" (τὸν . . . τόπον τῆι θεᾶι).[21]

3. Assyrio-Babylonian Backgrounds. This Aramaic use of *'tr'* and the plural *'try'* is very likely linked to the Neo-Assyrian and Neo-Babylonian use of the plural *ašrāt* or *ašrē* to designate sanctuaries.[22] A frequent depiction of the Assyro-Babylonian kings is as "seeing after holy places (of the gods)."[23] E.g., Nabonidus commends himself to Marduk as *mušte"û ašrēka* "the one who sees after your holy places," while Neriglissar employs the fem. pl.: *mušte"û ašrātika*.[24] Since this expression already occurs in Middle Babylonian texts,[25] the transition from Old Aramaic *'šrt* to *'try'* und *'tr'* must be due to Assyro-Bablyonian influence.

Lipiński

20. H. Seyrig, "Textes relatifs à la garnison romaine de Palmyre," *Syr* 14 (1933) 276.4.
21. R. N. Frye, "Inscriptions from Dura-Europos," *Yale Classical Studies* 14 (1955) 129-31, no. 2.5f.
22. *AHw*, I, 83a (4d); *CAD*, I/2, 456-60.
23. Seux.
24. Seux, 325.
25. *AHw*, I, 83.

באשׁ *b'š*; באישׁ *b'yš ba'îš*; באישׁ *b'yš*; לחה *lḥī*; רשׁע *rš'*; רשׁיע *ršy' raššī'*; שְׁחִיתָה *šḥyth šᵉḥîṯāh*

I. Etymology. II. The Verb *b'š*. 1. Meaning and Occurrence. 2. Related and Antonymous Verbs. III. The Adjective *bîš*. 1. Meaning and Occurrence. 2. *šᵉḥîṯāh*. IV. Qumran. 1. The Verb *b'š*. 2. The Noun *b'š*. 3. The Adjective *b'yš*. 4. *šḥt–rš'/ršy'*.

I. Etymology. The Aramaic verb *b'š* (Biblical Aram. *bᵉ'eš*), which appears in Syriac as *bêš* "to be bad," "to displease" (peal; aphel "to make stinky, odious," "to sin," and "to

J. Conrad, "שָׁחַת *šāḥaṯ*," *TDOT*, XIV, 583-95; J. A. Montgomery, *The Book of Daniel. ICC* (1927), esp. 276; T. Nöldeke, *Kurzgefaßte syrische Grammatik* (Leipzig, 1898), esp. §171; H. Ringgren, "רָשַׁע *rāša'*," *TDOT*, XIV, 1-9.

tempt to sin," as well as ithpael "to be badly treated"),[1] in Christian Palestinian Aramaic as *bêš* "to be sick, unwell, weak" (peal),[2] and in Mandean as *byš* "to be bad, evil,"[3] corresponds to Akkadian *ba'āšu* (also *be'ēšu*) "to be bad, stinky,"[4] OSA *b's* "to be harmful" and *hb's* "to damage,"[5] Arabic *ba'isa* "to be in a miserable situation,"[6] and Hebrew *bā'aš* "to be stinky" (qal and the intransitive hiphil) as well as metaphorically "to be odious," "to discredit oneself" (niphal und hithpael), "to make odious" (transitive hiphil; Middle Hebrew attests *b'š* only in the hiphil "to make stinky" [transitive], "to smell bad" [intransitive]),[7] and Ethiopic *b*[e]*'sa* "to be bad, harmful," etc.[8]

• The previously assumed Ugaritic instances of this root[9] must be disregarded.[10] (*Ko.*) •

II. The Verb *b'š*. The verb *b'š*, rare in older Aramaic, appears more frequently in the texts of the later dialects, i.e., beginning in the second century C.E. Because of the elision of the ', the presumed ground form **ba'iš*, which appears as *be'eš* in Masoretic texts, became *bēš* in later Aramaic.[11]

1. Meaning and Occurrence. The basic meaning of the root is "to be bad," "to smell bad." It occurs in Biblical Aramaic, however, only once in the peal in an impersonal usage:[12] *'*[e]*dayin malkā' k*[e]*dî mill*[e]*ṯā' š*[e]*ma' śaggî' b*[e]*'eš '*[a]*lôhî* "When the king heard the matter, it displeased him very much" (Dnl. 6:15).

Later dialects employ it both fientically and as a status verb; cf. e.g., Syr. *b'šynn* (peal fientic) *mn ḥywt '* "we behaved worse than the animals"; *l' mb'šyn* (aphel) "they cause no harm, do nothing evil";[13] Christian Palestinian Aramaic e.g., *km' db'š lh* "such as displeases him";[14] Jewish Aramaic Tg. Onq. of Ex. 21:8 *'m byšt b 'yny rbwnh* "if they displease their master"; Jer. *Ter.* 45c *r 'yynyy 'yb'š* (ithpeel) "R. Jannai became ill"; Bab. *Ned.* 40a *rb ḥlbw b'yš* (peal) "Rab Helbo was sick"; and the aphel in the meaning "to behave badly"[15] and "to cause damage," "to do harm."[16]

---

1. *LexSyr*, 56f.

2. *LSP*, 21a; F. Schulthess, *Grammatik des christlich-palästinischen Aramäisch* (Tübingen, 1924), 130b; on the other stems, cf. C. Müller-Kessler, *Grammatik des Christlich-Palästinisch-Aramäischen 1* (Hildesheim, 1991), 269.

3. *MdD*, 63b.

4. *AHw*, I, 94a; *CAD*, II, 4b-6b.

5. W. W. Müller, "Altsüdarabische Beiträge zum hebräischen Lexikon," *ZAW* 75 (1963) 307.

6. Lane, 146a.

7. *WTM*, I 188b.

8. *CDG*, 82b.

9. Cf. e.g., *UT*, no. 439; *KBL*[3], 102a; *AHw*, I, 94a.

10. Cf. *KTU* 1.48:8; 2.4:19.

11. Cf. e.g., T. Nöldeke, *Kurzgefaßte syrische Grammatik* (Darmstadt, 1898), §171; Schulthess, *Grammatik*, §19.

12. Montgomery.

13. J. Payne Smith, *A Compendious Syriac Dictionary* (Oxford, 1903), 34a.

14. *LSP*, 21a.

15. E.g., Tg. of 1 S. 12:25.

16. E.g., Tg. Onq. of Gen. 19:9 or said of an evil spirit in ooKA 3:4 (*mb'šh, ATTM.E*, 260).

2. *Related and Antonymous Verbs*. A series of semantically related roots exist in Aramaic, of which, however, only *šḥt* "to ruin" still occurs in Biblical Aramaic in the derivative *šᵉḥîṯāh* (→ III.2). Biblical Aramaic does not attest *lḥh* "evil" and *rš*ʿ "to commit an outrage" at all (regarding *ʿᵃwāyāh* and *ḥṭ*ʾ and its derivatives, → חטי *ḥᵃṭāy*). Nonetheless, *lḥh* occurs often in Old and Imperial Aramaic. Thus, Waidrang, the opponent of the Jews of Elephantine, is described as *lḥy*ʾ "the evil one": ʾ*ḥr wydrng zk lḥy*ʾ ʾ*grt šlḥ* "then Waidrang, this evil one, sent a letter."[17]

Gluska

In addition to Segal 26.17, where ʿ*l lḥy*ʾ ʾ*lk* "because (?) of this evil one" occurs in a corrupt context, these are the only inscriptional instances of the word after 500 B.C.E. In contrast, it occurs with remarkable frequency in older texts, as particularly in the inscriptions from Sefire (eighth century B.C.E.) and in the sayings of Aḥiqar (ca. 700 B.C.E.).[18] In *KAI* 222 A 26, it denotes the evil that the weather god Hadad may pour out as punishment. *KAI* 222 C 6f. offers *lḥ[yh]* to designate the ills that a dynasty that does no good can experience (ll. 4f.). The juxtaposition with good also occurs then in ll. 19f.: ʾ*hpk ṭbt*ʾ *w*ʾ*šm [l]lḥyt* "I will topple the good and turn it to evil." Finally, *KAI* 224.2 employs the phrase *ymll mln lḥyt* "to speak evil words" probably in the sense of "to plot against someone."[19]

The sayings of Aḥiqar frequently attest a *gbr lḥh* "an evil man," while the contrasted person is called *gbr ṭb*. Thus, Aḥiqar 163f. states that, indeed, one cannot see into the heart of another, but as soon as a good man (*gbr ṭb*) sees "[the] ev[il]" (*l[ḥyth]*) of another, he will break off social contact with him.[20] Similarly, Aḥiqar 130 warns against borrowing from an "evil man," while l. 138 calls one who does not praise his parents an "evil man." The feminine *lḥyh* occurs in this text always with the meaning "wickedness," "evil" and, therefore, denotes the character or deeds of the *gbr lḥh*, as l. 163 already indicates (see above). Thus, l. 134, among others, parallels the deceiver (*mkdb*) with one who does evil (*zy y*ʿ*bd lḥyt*ʾ). The religio-ethical significance of the term then becomes especially clear in the sayings that depict the reaction of the gods to this evil. Shamash steps forward as judge against one who does his master evil (l. 198) and the gods do evil (*yḥwn*, l. 124) to people whose mouths issue evil (*lḥyh*). In addition, this is the only inscriptional instance of a verbal use of *lḥh*, probably a denominated pael.[21] The association of the mouth with *lḥyh* demonstrates that *lḥyh*, as in *KAI* 224.2, can also connote evil, conniving speech. This is probably also the case for Aḥiqar 139, as the parallel statements in 139f. express.

17. *AP* 30.6f.; 31.6; cf. 32.6; similarly *AD* 5.7.
18. Cf. I. Kottsieper, *Die Sprache der Ahiqarsprüche*. *BZAW* 194 (1990), §292.
19. Cf., e.g., H. Tawil, "The End of the Hadad Inscription in the Light of Akkadian," *JNES* 32 (1973) 478 n. 20.
20. Cf. Kottsieper, 10,17; *TUAT*, III, 332.
21. Cf. Kottsieper, 213.

A seventh century B.C.E. inscription from Nerab speaks of a "bad death" (*mwt lḥhy*),[22] while the phrase *ṭb' wlḥy'* "good and bad" (oo. 5f.) in a Bauer-Meissner Papyrus (515 B.C.E.) refers to harvest yields.[23]

In view of this evidence and the fact that in older inscriptional Aramaic *b'š* first appears sparsely in the seventh century B.C.E., but then frequently, one may surmise that *lḥh* was originally typical as the older Aramaic term for "bad" in both the ethical and concrete senses which then gave way to derivatives of the root *b'š*. Accordingly, it occurs in the transition phase in a direct exchange with instances of *lḥh* demonstrating its fundamental interchangeability. Thus, the statement in a stele from Nerab that the gods should make a graverobber undergo a bad death (*yhb'šw mmtth*),[24] which has later parallels in the grave inscription from Bet She'arim (*ymwt/yhy m'yt bswp byš* "may he die a bad death"),[25] corresponds to the threat of a bad death from the same period and also stemming from Nerab (see above).[26] The evil that the miscreant (*lḥh*) Waidrang and his associates did to the Jewish temple is described as *b'yš*[27] or *b'yšt'*.[28] Finally, the noun *b'yš* or its later form *bš* (see below) also occurs, like *lḥh*, in the context of defamation.[29]

Since the term *lḥh* consistently means "bad," an etymological relationship with Akkadian *lu''û* "to besmirch" and Arabic *laḥā* "to revile, to insult" is rather unlikely.[30] Should there be some etymological relationship, nonetheless, then one must assume that the older Aramaic, already very early on, made this term in a unique manner into its general word for "bad," "evil," thereby entirely obscuring its origin.

Kottsieper

Syriac, however, still attests the root in isolation in the meaning "to destroy," "to sever" with the adjective *lḥy'* "hostile."[31]

The root *rš'* occurs only rarely in Aramaic. Syriac attests it chiefly in the aphel in the meaning "to behave outrageously" and in nominal derivatives like *ršy'* "bad," "miscreant," and as a theological expression "worldly," "sacrilegious."[32] The derivative *ršy'* "evildoer," "miscreant" also dominates in Jewish and Christian Palestinian Aramaic, while verbal forms also appear mostly in the aphel.[33] Consequently, it may be a Hebrew loanword in Aramaic.

22. *KAI* 225.10.
23. *TADAE* B1.1.
24. *KAI* 226.9f.
25. ggNB 1:4; 2:4-6 (*ATTM,* 390).
26. *KAI* 225.10.
27. *AP* 30.17; 31.16.
28. *AP* 30.17.
29. *KAI* 269.2; Hatra 74.8.
30. E.g., *AD* 19b; D. Pardee, review of J. C. L. Gibson, *Textbook of Syrian Semitic Inscriptions,* vol. 2, *JNES* 37 (1978) 197.
31. *LexSyr*, 363b.
32. *LexSyr*, 746a.
33. Jastrow, 1500a,1501; *LSP*, 197b.

• Since, however, the sayings of Aḥiqar already attest *ršyʿ* twice (ll. 168,171), the borrowing must have taken place quite early on. In view of the observation that the sayings of Aḥiqar also exhibit Canaanite influence otherwise,[34] it is entirely conceivable. Common to both instances is the fact that they view the future bad fate of the evildoer in favor of his opponent. Thus, ll. 17f. advise the one whom the evildoer grabs by the seam of his clothing—an expression of covetousness[35]—to rely upon Shamash. He will give the victim the evildoer's good. Moreover, ll. 168f. speak of the city of the evildoer, which, on the "day of the wind," will begin to totter and become booty (cf. e.g., Prov. 10:25; Jer. 23:19; Isa. 27:8; 28:2). Unfortunately the identity of the despoiler has not been preserved, although the emendation *ṣdyq* "a righteous one" is entirely conceivable. If one compares this instance with those of *lḥh* in the sayings of Aḥiqar, the latter seems to describe more concretely the evil that he does, while *ršyʿ* describes a more fundamental behavior. (*Ko.*) •

Biblical Aramaic attests *ṭᵉʾeḇ* (→טאב *ṭʾb*) as an antonym of *bᵉʾeš*. The dichotomy of the two terms reflects, especially, in the fact that they occur in the same formula: *śaggîʾ ṭᵉʾeḇ ʿᵃlôhî* "it pleased him very much" (Dnl. 6:24) vs. *śaggîʾ bᵉʾeš ʿᵃlôhî* "it displeased him very much" (Dnl. 6:15).

III. The Adjective *bîš*. The *Q bîštāʾ* in contrast to the *K bᵉʾîštāʾ* (Ezr. 4:12; peal ptcp. pass. fem. sg. det.; cf. *bi-ʾi-šá-ti-ia* "the bad for me," Uruk 35) manifests a phonetic development similar to the vocalization of the verbal root (→ II). In addition to the Akkadian *biʾšu, bīšu* "bad,"[36] additional comparable forms of the adjective in the sense of "bad," "evil" appear in Imperial Aramaic (in addition to *bʾyš* also *byš*,[37] fem. *bʾyšh/tʾ*; → II.1), Palmyrene (*byšʾ/t*), and at Hatra (*bš*),[38] as well as, in the later dialects, Syriac *bîš*, Samaritan *byš*,[39] Mandean *byš*,[40] Christian Palestinian Aramaic *byš* and *bš*,[41] and Jewish Aramaic *bᵉʾîš*[42] alongside *bîš* "bad."[43]

1. Meaning and Occurrence. Biblical Aramaic attests the adjective only once: *qiryᵉṯāʾ mārāḏtāʾ ûḇîštāʾ bānayin* "they build the rebellious and evil city" (Ezr. 4:12). This statement also occurs in the letter that Rehum, the Persian governor, and the scribe Shimshai wrote to Artaxerxes concerning the Jews of Jerusalem.

---

34. Kottsieper, 244.

35. I. Kottsieper, "El—ferner oder naher Gott?," in R. Albertz and S. Otto, *Religion und Gesellschaft. AOAT* 248 (1997), 36f.

36. *AHw*, I, 131.

37. *KAI* 258.3.

38. *DNSI*, 142.

39. Z. Ben-Hayyim, *The Literary and Oral Tradition of Hebrew and Aramaic Amongst the Samaritans I/II* (Jerusalem, 1957), 591f.

40. *MdD*, 63a.

41. *LSP*, 21b.

42. Jastrow, 135b.

43. Jastrow, 167a.

As an example, Jewish Aramaic, which attests *bîš* "bad," "evil" in phrases like *hgyyn byš* "bad thoughts,"[44] but also *'pyhwn byšyn* "their face is sad,"[45] illustrates the semantic horizon of this adjective. It also appears often in contrast to *ṭb*.[46] Additional expressions include: Syriac *mwt' byš'* "gruesome death" or *byš gd'* "unfortunate"[47] (cf. already Palmyrene *byšt gd'*);[48] Jewish Aramaic *ḥyt' bšt'* "the wild animal"[49] and *šwm byš* "a bad reputation";[50] Palestinian Jewish Aramaic *'t' byš'* "an evil woman," *mylh byš*,[51] and *ptgm' byš'* "the evil matter"[52] describing apostasy from God. In the context of superstition, one also encounters the designation of the "evil eye" in Jewish Aramaic as *'yn' byš'*,[53] found on an amulet.[54] The synagogue inscription yyEN 3:2f., *hy'mr lšn byš ʿl ḥbryh lʿmmyh* "or defames another among the non-Jews,"[55] attests the connotation of defamation (→ II.2).

Along with this adjectival use, the word also appears as a substantive, e.g., Syriac and Jewish Aramaic *byš* "the evil one," which Syriac also uses for the devil, while in Jewish Aramaic, both the masculine and the feminine form can also mean "the evil," "the bad."[56] This is the basis for the derivation of Syriac, Christian Palestinian Aramaic, and Jewish Aramaic *byšw* "wickedness," "evil," "misfortune," "sorrow.

2. šᵉḥîṯāh. As a semantically related expression, Biblical Aramaic attests *šᵉḥîṯāh*, which means both "bad" and, as a substantive, "evil," and appears three times. As a noun, it appears in Dnl. 6:5 in *ʿillāh ûšᵉḥîṯāh* "grounds (i.e., of the accusation) and evil" and *šālû ûšᵉḥîṯāh* "negligence and evil," which Daniel's opponents seek in him to no avail. Dnl. 2:9 attests it adjectivally in a metaphor: *ûmillāh ḵiḏḇāh ûšᵉḥîṯāh* "a false and perverted word." The word then occurs occasionally in Jewish Aramaic, sometimes meaning "maimed,"[57] sometimes in the fem. as a substantive in the sense of "(moral) depravity," "a bad thing."[58] Syriac and Mandean know the root, however, only in the context of "rust," and the like; cf., e.g., Syriac *šwḥt'* "rust," "dirt,"[59] and Mandean *šwt'* "rust," "verdigris."[60]

---

44. Tg. Neof. of Gen. 6:5.
45. Tg. Neof. of Gen. 40:6; cf. further *DJPA*, 102a.
46. Jastrow, 167a.
47. Payne Smith, 43a.
48. *CIS* II 4486.3f.,7f.
49. Tg. Onq. of Gen. 37:20.
50. Tg. Onq. of Num. 13:32.
51. *DJPA*, 102a.
52. Tg. Onq. of Dt. 13:12.
53. Jastrow, 1071f.
54. E.g., ooKA 2.2f. *'ynh byšth*; *ATTM*, 398; *DNSI*, 142.
55. *ATTM*, 364.
56. Cf. e.g., Tg. Onq. of Gen. 26:29; ggAR 3:3 (*ATTM*, 376); in Syriac mostly feminine; *LexSyr*, 57a; Payne Smith, 43a.
57. Tg. Jon. of Lev. 22:24.
58. Tg. of Ps. 17:3 and Ruth 4:22.
59. *LexSyr*, 771.
60. *MdD*, 458a.

IV. Qumran.

1. The Verb b 'š. The verbal root *b'š* (peal) occurs at Qumran in the meaning "to displease" (1QapGen 21:7 w*b'š 'ly* "and it displeased me"), on the one hand, and also in the sense of "to be/become evil" (4Q204 5 2:27 *[d]r mn dr yb'š bkdn* "generation after generation will thereby become (more) evil"; cf. 1 En. 107:1), on the other. In the aphel, it means "to do evil" (4Q551 1:5 *'ḥy 'l tb'šw* "my brother, do nothing evil"; 4Q554 2 3:20 *wyb'šwn lzr'k* "and they will do evil to your descendants").

2. The Noun b 'š. As a noun, *b'š* (< *bo'š*) occurs in the sense of "something bad," which Christian Palestinian Aramaic[61] and late amulets[62] also attest as *bwš* in the meaning "weakness," "exhaustion," "sickness." Thus, the continuation of 4Q204 5 2:27 (1 En. 107:1; → IV.1) reads *wb'š lhw'* "and there will be evil."[63]

3. The Adjective b 'yš. *b'yš* occurs both as a masc. and as a fem. in the meaning "something bad," "misfortune," e.g., in 4Q203 8:14 *'lykwn lb'š* "against you for bad" and 4Q212 2:25 *bb'št'* "in misfortune."[64] As an adjective, it occurs in the expression *rwh b'yš'* "evil spirit": *šlḥ lh 'l 'lywn . . . rwḥ b'yš'* "God Most High sent him [i.e., pharaoh, who had taken Sara for himself] . . . an evil spirit."[65]

Gluska

The motif of the evil spirit that besets and tortures a person, occurs in later times frequently on amulets.[66]

Consequently, at Qumran, *b'yš* frequently denotes the misfortune or evil that one encounters;[67] or the designation of the ulcers that Nabonidus got as *b'yš'*[68] and *mlh [b'y]šh 'l* "an evil word against."[69] The word also appears in the ethical sense, however. 4Q213a 1 1:13 speaks of *b'yš' wznwt'* "the evil and the bawdiness" in a petition asking to be protected against them. Their opposites are the *'rḥt qšṭ* "the paths of truth" (l. 12), which accords with the juxtaposition of *qšṭ* and *rš'* (→ IV.5) also attested elsewhere. All three terms then occur together in 4Q204 5 2:28, which announces the *dry qwšṭ'* "generations of truth" on whose appearance *b'yšth wrš 'h yswp* "evil and iniquity end." Conversely, 4Q541 9 1:6 speaks of an "evil and perverse" generation (*drh b'yš w'pyk*), characterized particularly by dishonesty (ll. 5f.,7). Further, CT. Levi Cambridge e:14f.[70] cites a proverb that expresses the deed-consequence relationship, and may have a

61. *LSP*, 22a.
62. ggQN 1:13 (*ATTM.E,* 256); ooTI 6:[2,]18,31 (*ATTM.E,* 262).
63. *DSSStE*, 420f.
64. So *ATTM*, 246f.; *DSSStE*, 442f. reads in contrast *bbhšt'*; cf. 1 En. 92:2.
65. 1QapGen 20:16f.
66. cf. ggAG 1:6,12 (*ATTM,* 372); ggAR 1:4f.,19 (*ATTM,* 375); ooKA 3:4 (*ATTM.E,* 260).
67. Cf. e.g., 11Q10 16:3 (Job 30:14); 19:4 (31:29); 38:6 (42:11).
68. 4Q242 1-3:2.
69. 4Q550c 3:2; and 4Q550e 1.
70. Cf. 4Q213 1 1:8f.

parallel in 4Q550c 3:6f.: [*zr*]ʿ *dy zrʿ ṭ'b ṭ'b mhn ʿl wdy zrʿ byš ʿlwhy t'yb zrʿh* Whoever sows good, gathers good, but whoever sows evil, his seed falls back on him!"[71] Moreover, 4Q529 10 describes the sins of the flood generation as *kl dy b'yš qwdm rby mr*[' *ʿlm'*] "everything that is evil before my Lord, [the eternal] Lo[rd]." Finally, the reconstruction of fragments from 4Q537 suggested by *ATTM.E,* 70f. (ll.21-30) resembles an entire catalogue of terms for error, debauchery, and guilt, including *wb'yštkwn* "your wickedness."[72]

4. šḥt—ršʿ/ršyʿ. The root *šḥt* occurs with certainty only once at Qumran describing the damaged appearance of a person: *'npyk kdn' ʿlyk šn' wšḥt* "your face has so changed and been damaged."[73]

5. In contrast, Qumran attests the root *ršʿ* rather well, especially in its derivative *ršy'* "evildoer," "sacrilegious." Apart from the instances in the Targum of Job that merely render the Hebrew *rāšāʿ*,[74] Qumran texts apparently link the evildoer with the fool consistently. Thus, *ršyʿ* renders the Hebrew *'ᵉwîl* twice in the Targum of Job[75] and 4Q548 describes the sons of darkness as, among other things, *skl wrš*[*y*?ʿ] "fools and evildoers,"[76] while the sons of light appear as [*ḥky*]*m wqšyṭ* "[wis]e and truthful."[77] The juxtaposition of truth and iniquity also occurs then in 4Q542 1 2:8 (*b*[*d*]*ry qwšṭ' wy ʿdwn kwl bny ršʿ*[']) "in the generation of truth. And/but all the sons of iniquity will disappear") and in 4Q204 5 2:28 (→ IV.3). Finally, the apocalyptic text 4Q536 speaks of the "days of iniquity" (*ywmy ršʿ*', 1:II:11) or of the "time of the evildoers," which will "elapse forever" (*wʿdn ršyʿyn ydʿk lʿlmyn*, l. 13). The woe over a fool or a man whose mouth possesses folly that occurs between these two interrelated instances (l. 11) probably also indicates the close connection between evildoing and folly.

Kottsieper

71. Cf. *ATTM.E,* 116.
72. L. 23 = 4Q537 3:3.
73. 1QapGen 2:17.
74. 11Q10 3:6 (Job 20:5); 7:4 (22:18); 11:3 (27:13); 34:8 (40:12).
75. 4Q157 1 2:8 (Job 5:3); 11Q10 2:7 (19:18).
76. 4Q548 2:5.
77. 4Q548 1:12.

בדר *bdr*

I. Etymology and Occurrence. II Instances in Older Aramaic. 1. Imperial Aramaic. 2. Biblical Aramaic. 3. Qumran. 4. Nabatean.

I. Etymology and Occurrence. Beyond the Aramaic family of languages,[1] the root *bḏr* "to scatter" continues in Arabic *baḏara* "to sow," "to scatter out," "to distribute," "to dissipate" (II stem)[2] and Hebrew *pzr*.[3] Aramaic employs *bdr* in the pael in the meaning "to spread," and in the peal in the meaning "to scatter." Syriac knows the root *bdr* with a few nominal derivatives.[4] The root *bḏr* is also evident in Mandean *b'zr'* "drilling," "seed(time)," "seed grain" with its derivatives.[5]

• Traditionally, this Mandean word group is derived from a contraction of *br* and *zrʿ*,[6] which Syriac also attests (e.g., Peshitta of Lev. 11:37f.). Since, however, not only Jewish Aramaic and Syriac also know words for "seed" or "seed oil" based on *b(y)zr*,[7] but *Frahang* IV.5 also equates *bzr'* with Middle Persian *tōhm* "seed," this derivation is dubious. On the other hand, Aramaic does not otherwise employ the verbal root *bḏr* in the context of sowing. The simplest explanation of this complex body of evidence involves the assumption that a secondary differentiation in the use of the root *bḏr* occurred in Aramaic. Apparently under the influence of *zrʿ* (→ זרע *zᵉraʿ*), nominal forms referring to "seed" shifted to *bzr*, which then probably affected Arabic, which, in addition to the common *bḏr* (so also in Modern South Arabian and as an Arabic loanword in Geʿez),[8] also occasionally exhibits *bzr*. (*Ko.*) •

The root *bḏr* does not survive in Akkadian; the Akkadian equivalent is *sapāḫu*.[9]

II. Instances in Older Aramaic.

1. Imperial Aramaic. The curse formula of the Lydo-Aramaic diglot from Sardis, a grave inscription dating to the fourth or fifth century,[10] offers so far the only Imperial Aramaic specimen outside Biblical Aramaic of the verb *bdr*. (7) *'rtmw zy klw*

R. Degen, review of E. Lipiński, *Studies in Aramaic Inscriptions and Onomastics*, *WO* 9 (1977-78) 167-72; G. R. Driver, *Problems in Aramaic and Hebrew Texts. FS A. Deimel. AnOr* 12 (1935), 46-70, esp. 54; S. Gevirtz, "West-Semitic Curses and the Problem of the Origins of Hebrew Law," *VT* 11 (1961) 137-58, esp. 150; R. Gusmani, *Lydisches Wörterbuch* (Heidelberg, 1964); idem, *Lydisches Wörterbuch, Ergänzungsband 3* (Heidelberg, 1986); E. Lipiński, *Studies in Aramaic Inscriptions and Onomastics. OLA* 1 (1975); R. Macuch, *Handbook of Classical and Modern Mandaic* (Berlin, 1965); J. T. Milik, "'Prière de Nabonide' et autres écrits d'un cycle de Daniel," *RB* 63 (1956) 407-15; C. Müller-Kessler, *Grammatik des Christlich-Palästinisch-Aramäischen I. TStO* 6 (1991); T. Nöldeke, *Mandäische Grammatik* (Halle, 1875); H. Ringgren, "פוץ *pûṣ*," *TDOT*, XI, 509-12; M. Wagner, *Die lexikalischen und grammatikalischen Aramaismen im alttestamentlichen Hebräisch. BZAW* 96 (1966).

1. See below II; cf. also *WTM*, 195; *TW*, 83 s.v. *bᵉḏar bîddûr*; Müller-Kessler, 168.
2. Wehr[5], 74f. with derivatives.
3. Ringgren, 547; aramaizing *bzr* in Dnl. 11:24; Ps. 68:31, see Wagner, 33 (no. 37).
4. *LexSyr*, 60.
5. *MdD*, 47a.
6. Nöldeke, 55,140,183,187; Macuch, 204.
7. *WTM*, 1209a; *LexSyr*, 65.
8. *CDG*, 118a.
9. *AHw*, III, 1024f.
10. *KAI* 260.

w'pššy trbṣh bjth (8) *qnynh ṭyn wmyn wmnd'mth ybdrwnh wyr/pth* "the Artemis of Koloë and the (Artemis) of the Ephesians will destroy his flocks, his house, his property, ground and water and everything that belongs to him."[11] The Lydian equivalent of the Aramaic *bdr* is *vcbaqẽnt*,[12] which yields no further clues. The analysis of *ybdrwnh* encounters two difficulties: 1. The jussive expected in the curse formula must consist of the short form *ybdrw*; 2. The construction of *bdr* with a double accusative is unusual.

Lipiński (159f.) attempts a solution by separating *nh* as the particle "indeed";[13] the suggestion has not been received.[14] In fact, Lipiński's interpretation is rendered unlikely by the facts, first, that in the instances known to date the particle *nh/'* always follows the imperative, never the jussive or the imperfect, and, second, that it has only been identified since the first century B.C.E.

2. Biblical Aramaic. The account of Nebuchadnezzar's dream in Dnl. 4 employs *bdr* for the scattering of the fruits of the tree that appears to the king in the dream. It involves a meaning similar to that in *KAI* 260.8 insofar as the scattering signifies the loss of property or fruits: *ûḇaddarû 'inbeh* "and scattered its fruits!" (Dnl. 4:11; Θ 4:14 translates διασκορπίζειν—as does the LXX the otherwise frequent Hebrew *p/bzr*).

3. Qumran. 4Q244 13:1[15] offers in a fragmentary context *wbdr 'nwn* "and he scattered them."[16]

4. Nabatean. The Nabatean deed of gift nV 7 from the archive of Babata (Naḥal Ḥever, 120 C.E.) describes the trees planted in a dispersed pattern, indicating that *bdr* "to scatter" could be employed in a sense other than "to forfeit."[17]

Schwemer

---

11. Regarding *wyr/pth* see *DNSI*, 472 s.v. *jrt*$_2$ (bib.); Degen, review of Lipiński, 170.
12. 3p pres.-fut. of *vcbaqẽn-*, Gusmani, *Wörterbuch*, 223f.; idem, *Ergänzungsband*, 123f.
13. Cf. 1QapGen 20:25: *nh*; 11Q10 30:1 (Job 38:3); 34:3,6,7 (Job 40:7,10,11); 37:6 (Job 42:4); 4Q204 5 2:29: *n'*.
14. Degen, review of Lipiński, 170; *ATTM*, 529 s.v. *bdr*.
15. *DJD*, XXII (1996), 130.
16. Milik, 413.
17. nV 7:13; *ATTM.E*, 167-73.

בהל *bhl*; בְּהִילוּ *bhylw bᵉhîlû*

I. Etymology, Instances. II. "To Hurry." III. "To Be Frightened."

I. Etymology, Instances. So far, older Aramaic has not attested *bhl* and Biblical Aramaic has it only eleven times (in ten verses) in the book of Daniel. The substantive *bᵉhîlû* derived from it, for which Daniel has the inf. hithpeel *hiṯbᵉhālāh* (→ II), appears in the Bible only in Ezr. 4:23. The scope of its meaning, which lies between "to be frightened" and "to hurry," points the disputed etymology most likely to Arabic *bahara* (VII) "to be breathless" with the interchange of the liquids *r/l*, which may also explain the development of the meaning "to cease" for *bhl* in Syriac.[1] The notion that the meaning "to hurry," attested predominantly late in Hebrew, first arose under the influence of Aramaic[2] is not compelling in view of the body of citations in Aramaic and may just as well involve a general further semantic development of the word that even ultimately led to the Syriac meaning "to rest," "to cease." Specifically, the root appears in Biblical Aramaic seven times in the pael, three times in the hithpeel, and once in the hithpael.

The term *blh*, attested only once in Ezr. 4:4 "to scare off," and the derived, rare, and late Hebrew noun *ballāhāh* "terror" (Isaiah [1×], Ezekiel [3×], Psalms [1×], Job [4×]) arose from *bhl* through metathesis of the radicals; cf. Syriac *balhī* "to confound," "to disturb" and *būlhāyā*' "panic," "terror."

II. "To Hurry." In the hithpeel, the verb has apparently completely retained the reflexive meaning "to hurry oneself" < "to act breathlessly" proximal to the hypothesized base meaning. It appears in Biblical Aramaic only as the infinitive hithpeel *hiṯbᵉhālāh* in Dnl. 2:25; 3:24 and 6:20. In the same usage, Ezr. 4:23 has the noun *bᵉhîlû* "haste" attested biblically only here, but elsewhere also in the Targums[3] and in Samaritan Aramaic,[4] as an abstract of an otherwise unattested adjective *bahīl*. Since West Aramaic does not otherwise attest the G-stem peal of *bhl* (regarding Syriac with its different semantic development → I), the infinitive hithpeel may also involve a

---

J. Blau, "Etymologische Untersuchungen auf Grund des palaestinischen Arabisch," *VT* 5 (1955) 337-44; H. Gzella, *Tempus, Aspekt und Modalität im Reichsaramäischen. VOK* 48 (2004), 143f. (for the use of the suffixed imperfect of *bhl* among participles in Dnl. 5:6); A. Murtonen, *Hebrew in Its West Semitic Setting I. SSLL* 13 (1989), esp. 106; B. Otzen, "בהל *bhl*," *TDOT*, II, 3-5; J. Tropper, "Lexikographische Untersuchungen zum Biblisch-Aramäischen," *JNSL* 23 (1997) 105-28, esp. 107; M. Wagner, *Die lexikalischen und grammatikalischen Aramaismen im alttestamentlichen Hebräisch. BZAW* 96 (1966).

1. Blau, 339.
2. Wagner, 33.
3. *TW*, I 84a.
4. *DSA* 83b.

nominalization comparable to the adverbial function of the substantive *b*ᵉ*hîlû* in Ezr. 4:23, which still evidences the basic meaning of the root *bhl* "breathless," "to be agitated." This finds support in the usage, for in all the cases cited, it involves the expression, combined with the preposition *b*, of an agitated movement "with haste," "hurrying," always in a violent reaction to a previous event. The associated verbs are *'zl* "to go" (Ezr. 4:23; Dnl. 6:20), *'ll* haphel "to bring in" (Dnl. 2:24), and *qwm* "to stand up" (Dnl. 3:24).

Apart from the later targumic and Samaritan Aramaic usage, the sole instance of a finite form in the meaning "to hurry" appears from Qumran in 1QapGen 2:3 as an ithpeel pf. 1s *'tbhlt w'lt*. Admittedly, N. Avigad and Y. Yadin[5] and J.A. Fitzmyer[6] translate this passage assuming an ithpael,[7] with "Then I, Lamech, became frightened and I went,"[8] although fear appears here in the context somewhat too late and is by no means suited to the topic; here too, *bhl* accompanies a verb of movement (*'ll*), and this movement results, as in the OT occurrences, in a hasty reaction (*'tbhlt*) to an unexpected event. Consequently, one should retain here, too, the general meaning of the verb in the reflexive of the G-stem as "to hurry."[9]

III. "To Be Frightened." The remaining occurrences in the pael (Dnl. 4:2,16 [2×]; 5:6,10; 7:15,28, always in the impf. with suffix) and as a ptcp. hithpael (Dnl. 5:9) all appear in the semantic field of horror and can, as resultative paels "to cause breathlessness" > "to frighten" or (hithpael) "to be frightened," be derived with equal ease from the assumed basic meaning. The verb always parallels other expressions of horror or terror (*dḥl* pael "to frighten" [Dnl. 4:2], *šmm* ithpoel "to be paralyzed in fear" [4:16], *krh* ithpeel "to be distressed" [7:15], and frequently the change of the look on one's face [*zîw šnh*; 5:6,9,10; 7:28]). The frightened reactions relate to dreams and visions in which the announcement of what is to come intervenes in the present.

At Qumran, this meaning of *bhl* appears as a pael ptc. *mbhlh* in the Testament of Amram 4Q544 1:2[10] expressing horrifying reports of war.

Lehmann

---

5. *A Genesis Apocryphon* (Jerusalem, 1956), 40.
6. *The Genesis Apocryphon. BietOr* 18A (^{2}1971), 51.
7. Ibid., 82.
8. Cf. also *DSS*, 29.
9. Cf. *ATTM*, 168.
10. = 4Q545 1:II:16.

בִּירַת *byrt bîraṯ*

I.1. Etymology. 2. Aramaic Forms. II. Usage.

I. *1. Etymology.* The form *bîrāh* "fortification," employed in Hebrew as a loanword (Est. 1:2,5; 2:3,5,8; 3:15; 8:14; 9:6,11,12; Dnl. 8:2; Neh. 1:1; 2:8; 7:2; 1 Ch. 29:1,19; Wagner) is a back-formation from the Aramaic abs. *byrt*[1] due to the assumption that the *t* was a feminine ending. The same word was lent as *bīrat* into Elamite: *pír-ra-tam$_6$-ma* "in the fortification."[2] Nonetheless, in reality, the *t* belongs to the root, at least if it is Semitic. It seems to be present in the South Ethiopic adjective *b^{e}rtu* "strong" and in the verb *b^{ä}rätta, b^{e}rätä* "to be strong," which was then adopted even into Cushite.[3] From this root, which was originally pronounced **bt*ʿ[4] and exhibits the noun **bittu*ʿ, and which then became *birtu(*ʿ*)* in prehistoric times through dissimilation, only Akkadian retained the derivative *birtu* "fortification,"[5] to the extent that the suggested etymology is correct. The plural *birātu(m)*, which Mari attests frequently, indicates that the underlying root in Mesopotamia was already unknown in the Old Babylonian period. According to another hypothesis, however, *birtu* could also be regarded as a loanword from the old Indian *púr-* "wall," *púra-* "fortification" since the vowel *i* occurs in the place of *u* in Baltic languages; cf. Lithuanian *pilì(s)*, Latvian *pìl(s)* "fortification," "fortress."[6] This borrowing would date, then, to the time of the Indo-Aryan immigration into upper Mesopotamia. Nevertheless, based on the absence of unequivocal indications, it is questionable whether this immigration dates as early as the Old Babylonian period ca. 1800 B.C.E.[7]

2. Aramaic Forms. Aramaic borrowed the word at the latest by the beginning of the seventh century B.C.E. where it simultaneously appears in the new form **bīrān*, which is

---

G. G. Cameron, *Persepolis Treasury Tablets. OIP* 65 (1948), esp. 86,141; S. A. Kaufman, *The Akkadian Influences on Aramaic. AS* 19 (1974), esp. 44; A. Lemaire and H. Lozachmeur, "Bīrāh/Birtā' en araméen," *Syr* 64 (1987) 261-66; idem, "La *Birta* en Méditerranée orientale," *Sem* 43-44 (1995) 75-78; E. Lipiński, "Emprunts suméro-akkadiens en hébreu biblique," *ZAH* 1 (1988) 61-73, esp. 64f.; idem, "Origins and avatars of *birtu* 'stronghold,'" *ArOr* 67 (1999) 609-17; M. Wagner, *Die lexikalischen und grammatikalischen Aramaismen im alttestamentlichen Hebräisch. BZAW* 96 (1966), esp. 34f.

1. *AP* 13.4; R. A. Bowman, *Aramaic Ritual Texts from Persepolis. OIP* 91 (1970), no. 4.1;46.1; F. Altheim and R. Stiehl, *Die zweite (aramäische) Inschrift von Mchetʿa. FF* 35 (1961), 173.11.
2. Cameron, no. 36.2; 44.2; 44a.2; cf. *pír-tam$_6$*, R. T. Hallock, *Persepolis Fortification Tablets. OIP* 92 (1969), no. 423.4.
3. W. Leslau, *Etymological Dictionary of Gurage III* (Wiesbaden, 1979), 156b.
4. Cf. Tigrinya *bärt^{e}ʿe* ← **battiʿa* "to be strong."
5. *AHw*, I, 129b; *CAD*, II, 261-63.
6. M. Mayrhofer, *Kurzgefaßtes etymologisches Wörterbuch des Altindischen II* (Heidelberg, 1963), 327.
7. Cf. G. Wilhelm, *RLA*, VIII (1993–1997), 291-93.

not directly attested, however. The Neo-Babylonian plural form *bīranātu*, first encountered in the early phase of Asarhaddon's reign,[8] implies it. Based on the *ī* that the word exhibits, there is also the variant plural *bīranētu*,[9] attested indirectly in the late Aramaic loanword *byrnyt*.[10] Under the influence of colloquial Aramaic, as still attested in Neo-Aramaic,[11] Aramaic vocalized this form *bîrānyāt* and Hebrew *bîrāniyyôt* (2 Ch. 17:12; 27:4), while the consonantal spelling *byrnywt* with *w* indicates that this pronunciation traces to the Greco-Roman period. Instead, a derivative **bîrānît* never existed and the clearly written *-n* in *byrtn* in an inscription from Persepolis[12] indicates the Old Persian affix *-ana*, often appended to nouns designating a place.[13]

II. Usage. The construct *byrt* with a subsequent place name (e.g., *byrt yb*) or the determined state following a place name (e.g., *yb byrt'*) occurs frequently in the Persian period.[14] The two constructions apparently have the same meaning, expressing the notion that *bîrtā'* means the city itself, as is also true for Ezr. 6:2. The obvious conclusion to be drawn is that *bîrtā'* is not the citadel in a city, but the "wall-protected city" itself. This finds confirmation in the fact that, in Neo-Assyrian royal inscriptions, *birtu* corresponds to *āl dannūti* "fortified city" and the LXX normally renders *bîrāh/bîraṯ* with πόλις. Hebrew *bîrāh* in Neh. 2:8 and Dnl. 8:2 corresponds to βάρις in Flavius Josephus, Ant. 15.11.4 and in Θ Dnl. 8:2, however. Otherwise, in fact, the LXX utilizes this Greek word, whose etymology is problematic, to denote a palace or a fortress (Ps. 45[44]:9), but, apparently because of the similarity in sound, it was chosen in these cases to render *bîrāh*. In an expanded meaning, *byrt* can then denote a walled sanctuary. It occurs in this meaning in 1 Ch. 29:1,19 and in Nabatean *CIS* II 164:3, where *byrt'* corresponds to Greek τὸ ἱερόν. In an adaptation of 1 Ch. 29:1,19, the statement that "the whole temple mount was called *bîrāh*" appears in Jer. *Pesaḥ*.

Lipiński

8. I. Starr, *Queries to the Sungod. SAA* 4 (1990), 18.9,10; S. Parpola, *Letters from Assyrian and Babylonian Scholars. SAA* 10 (1993), 112.10.
9. GaG §10d.
10. Tg. of Am. 3:9.
11. K. G. Tsereteli, *The Modern Assyrian Language* (Moscow, 1978), 48.
12. Bowman, no. 77.2.
13. R. G. Kent, *Old Persian. AOS* 33 (1953), 51, §147.
14. *DNSI*, 155f.

בַּיִת *byt bayiṯ*

I. Etymology and Meanings in the Semitic Languages. II. General Aramaic Usage. III. Biblical Aramaic. IV. Qumran.

I. Etymology and Meanings in the Semitic Langauges. The Aramaic word for "house," *bayiṯ*, is common in most Semitic languages. The corresponding words include Hebrew *bayiṯ*, Akkadian *bītu*, Ugaritic *bt*, Ethiopic *bet*, Arabic *bait*, and Phoenician *bt*. Although, in most cases, the noun is masculine, the underlying root *byt* sometimes has a verbal use: Aramaic *bw/yt*, Arabic *bāta*, Akkadian *biāt/dum*, *bâtu*, Ethiopic *bēta*, and Ugaritic *by/wt*,[1] all of which mean "to spend the night."

The Semitic noun *byt* can usually be translated "house," but is by no means restricted to this meaning. In Ugaritic, *bt* can also mean "palace," "temple," "barn," "stall," or even "family."[2] In Arabic, the meanings of *bait* include "house," "tent," "chamber," "apartment," "toilet," "sanctuary," "ark," "container," and "palace.[3] Akkadian *bītu* renders "house," "dwelling," "animal pen," "temple," "palace," "room," "burial chamber," "container," "place," "region," "household," "estate," "family," and "nomadic camp."[4] Similarly, the many uses of *bayiṯ* in Biblical Hebrew also encompass "palace," "tent," "harem," "animal pen," "place," "container," "family," and "household matters."[5]

Consequently, in its broadest meaning, Semitic *byt* means places in which practically anything can live. Thus, e.g., the expression *bêṯ ʿakkāḇîš* "house of the spider" in Job 8:14 can best be translated "spider web," and Ps. 84:4 can even call a bird's nest a "house." Accordingly, the stone that Jacob anoints can become the dweling of God according to Gen 28:22 since it calls it *bêṯ ʾelohîm* "the house of God." This recalls the story that Philo of Byblos recounts offering the euhemeristic interpretation of the battle that Chronos waged against his father Uranus. For his part, he had constructed βαιτυλια which Philo regarded as animated rocks.[6] In any case, one finds in the use of the Semitic root *byt* an extensive breadth of different meanings, which, as we will see, pertains to Aramaic as well.

· The fact that the verbal derivative occurs in the various languages, apparently independently of one another, in the limited meaning "to spend the night," indicates that this arose at a very early phase of the Semitic languages. If this is true, then *byt* would have originally designated primarily the place where one spent the night. Especially in hunter-gatherer cultures, however, this is the "dwelling place," i.e., the place

---

W. Dietrich, "*dāwid, dôd* und *bjtdwd*," *TZ* 53 (1997) 17-32; P.-E. Dion, *Les Araméens à l'âge du fer: histoire politique et structures sociales. ÉtB* NS 34 (1997); H. Donner, "Zu Gen. 28,22," *ZAW* 74 (1962) 68-70; J. A. Fitzmyer and D. J. Harrington, *A Manual of Palestinian Aramaic Texts*. BietOr 34 (1978); D. N. Freedman and J. C. Geoghegan, "'House of David' Is There!" *BAR* 21/2 (1995) 78f.; H. A. Hoffner, "בַּיִת *bayith*," *TDOT*, II, 107-16; J. Hoftijzer and G. van der Kooij, *Aramaic Texts from Deir ʿAlla. DMOA* 19 (1976); T. Ishida, *The Royal Dynasties in Ancient Israel. BZAW* 142 (1977), esp. 100f.; A. Lemaire, "'House of David' Restored in Moabite Inscription," *BAR* 20/2 (1994) 30-37; idem and J.-M. Durand, *Les inscriptions araméennes de Sfiré. HEO* 20 (1984); H.-P. Müller, "Die aramäische Inschrift von Deir ʿAllā und die älteren Bileamsprüche," ZAW 94 (1982) 214-44; B. Porten, *Archives from Elephantine* (Berkeley, 1968).

1. *DUL*³, 241: b-t.
2. *UT* no. 463; *DUL*³, 243-47.
3. Lane, 280f.
4. *CAD*, II, 282-96.
5. *BDB*, 108-10.
6. A. I. Baumgarten, *The Phoenician History of Philo of Byblos. EPRO* 89 (1981), 202.

where one normally returns in the evening for the night and which is appropriately equipped. (*Ko.*) •

II. General Aramaic Usage. The general meaning "house" for *byt* appears in many Aramaic texts and inscriptions.[7] Aramaic inscriptions that employ the word *byt* "house" include *KAI* 222 B 40 (Sefire), T.Fekh. 17; *KAI* 216.7,13,16-19; *AP* 13.11.[8]

Freedman/Homan

In addition to instances in which *byt* designates "house" as a simple structure,[9] in some texts it refers to a luxurious palace structure.[10] The distinction between a *byt štw'* "winter palace" and a *byt kyṣ'* "summer palace" in this text (ll. 18f.) demonstrates that upper class people who could afford it could possess several houses suited to the different seasons of the year. The palace built by Barrakib and designated simply as *byt*, however, was apparently so well furnished and spacious that it could serve both purposes (cf. Jer. 36:22; Am. 3:15; Hoffner, 635).

In contrast, the designation *byt mlk(')* acquires the meaning "palace" in the sense of "seat of government." Thus, the treaty of state *KAI* 222 A 6 also names among the parties to the treaty *kl 'll byt mlk* "all who enter the palace," and apparently means thereby the political leadership, i.e., those who have access to the king in his residence. Entirely separate from the presence of the king, the term *byt mlk'* appears in the texts from Elephantine[11] as a designation for a local administrative building.[12]

The original meaning of *byt* as a resting or dwelling place still glimmers through in the Palmyrene, Nabatean, Jewish Aramaic, and Syriac designation of the grave as *byt 'lm* "house of eternity,"[13] for which now the second combination of the inscription from Deir 'Alla with *byt 'lmn* constitutes a very early parallel (l. 6).[14] H.-P. Müller points in this context correctly to the parallel designation *mškby 'lmyk* "your eternal resing places" in l. 11 of the same text, which, for its part, has parallels in Phoenician, Hebrew, and Syriac,[15] and to Akkadian *šubat dār(i)āti* "dwelling of duration."[16] Since the latter only appears beginning in the Neo-Assyrian period,[17] it could represent a transfer of the term, apparently common and in use quite early in Aramaic, into Akkadian. In any case, the parallels cited make it clear that *byt* does not denote the house in the architectural sense, but the place in

7. Cf. e.g., for Jewish Aramaic *DJPA*, 92.
8. Cf. *DNSI*, 156-63.
9. E.g., *AP* 5.3,13; 6.8; *KAI* 260.7.
10. E.g., *KAI* 216.13,15-17.
11. E.g., *AP* 2.12,14,16.
12. Cf. Porten, 60.
13. *DNSI*, 160; *DJPA*, 95a; *LexSyr*, 70b.
14. Hoftijzer-van der Kooij, 224; J. A. Hackett, *The Balaam Text from Deir 'Alla. HSM* 31 (1980), 59.
15. Cf. Hoftijzer-van der Kooj, 233.
16. Müller, 231.
17. *AHw*, I, 164a; *CAD*, III, 111a.

which the deceased "dwells" or rests. Nevertheless, one may speculate that this diction was a starting point alongside others for the rock grave design with facades resembling houses and temples that developed later, especially in the Nabatean realm.

In relation to deities, *byt* denotes the temple, often with *byt* in the construct preceding the name of the god.[18] The more general *'lh* can replace the name, however.[19] In the Sefire inscription *KAI* 223 C 2f.,7,9f., *bty 'lhy'* probably also designates the temple of the gods.[20] The context suggests that temples archived the texts of state treaties. This procedure accords with the statement that the treaties were sealed before (*qdm*) the gods[21] and that they were also considered treaties of the gods themselves.[22] Therefore, the oft proposed interpretation that the *bty 'lhy'* here means the steles themselves and, consequently, should be associated with the *bêt* *ᵉlohîm* in Gen. 28:22 (→ I)[23] should be rejected.

The Yahu temple at Elephantine, usually designated by the Akkadian loanword *'gwr* (< *ekurru*)[24] also appears in ll. 2f. of the ostracon edited by Aimé-Giron as *byt yhh*.[25] This text speaks of an article of clothing that the sender had left behind in the *byt byt yhh*. The reference to the "house of the Yahu temple" indicates that the temple at Elephantine did not consist simply of one building. It is unlikely that the first *byt* here denotes the Adyton[26] unless one wants to accuse the sender of the note with leaving his own clothing (*ktwny* "my garment" l. 1) in the holy of holies. Instead, the first *byt* here denotes the temple itself including the antechambers while the actual *byt yhh* refers to the entire temple complex. Accordingly, burnt sacrifices were also offered in the temple at Elephantine[27] and it could also be called *byt mdbh' zy 'lh' šmy'* "the altar house of the God of heaven."[28] For purely technical reasons, one can assume that an altar for burnt sacrifice was surely outside the temple structure proper (which, moreover, had a cedar wood roof).[29] Since the topographical data in the various Elephantine papyri indicate an elongated rectangle,[30] it is likely that the temple consisted of a building with an anterior courtyard that contained the altar for burnt sacrifice.

Kottsieper

---

18. E.g., T.Fekh. 17 *bt hdd* "temple of Hadad"; *KAI* 228 A 12 *byt ṣlm* "temple of Salm."

19. E.g., Old Aramaic *bty 'lhn* "temple of the gods" *KAI* 202 B 9; Palmyrene *'lhyhn* "temple of their gods" *CIS* II 3923.4.

20. J. C. Greenfield, review of J. Fitzmyer, *The Aramaic Inscriptions of Sefire*, *JBL* 87 (1968) 241; Lemaire-Durand, 142.

21. *KAI* 222 A 7ff.

22. *KAI* 222 B 5f.; 223 B 2.

23. E.g., Donner, 69; *KAI*, II 262.

24. S. A. Kaufman, *The Akkadian Influences on Aramaic*. *AS* 19 (1974), 48; e.g., *AP* 13.14; 25.6; 30.6,7; *BMAP* 4.10.

25. *Trois ostraca araméens d'Éléphantine*. *ASAE* 26 (1926), 27-29 (=*TADAE* D7.18).

26. So E. G., Kraeling in *BMAP* 96.

27. Cf. *AP* 30.21f.,25f.; 31.21,25.

28. *AP* 32.3f.

29. Cf. *AP* 30.11; 31.10.

30. For a reconstruction, cf. Porten, 109ff. and the charts in *TADAE* 2,176.

The word *byt* also refers to the Jerusalem temple, designated as "the holy house" (*byt mqdšh.*[31]

The word *byt* can also denote a dynasty; thus, both the inscription from Tell Dan (l. 9)[32] and the Moab stele (*KAI* 181.31)[33] designate the Judean royal house as *byt dwd*. Barrakib also links his rule with his father's "house" in *KAI* 216.7.

Freedman/Homan

KAI 217.3 lists the gods of the Sam'alian dynasty, including Barrakib, under the term *'lhy byt 'by* "the gods of my father's house," which contrasts with the simpler designation of Rakibel's dynastic god in a Sam'alian inscription as *bʿl byt* "lord of the house."[34] Thus, "dynasty" belongs to the semantic field "household, family," which *byt* also covers in Aramaic. Apparently, here, too, the local elements stand in the foreground since *byt* also designates the group assembled in a dwelling place. This could be both family members and other persons belonging to the household as the inscriptions that mention other family members besides the *byt* indicate.[35] In Aramaic, then, the term *byt* acquired great political significance. Thus, *byt* + PN could designate tribes and even smaller kingdoms while the name apparently refers to the progenitor of the tribe or of the ruling dynasty.[36] Therefore, it is entirely possible that *byt dwd* in the Dan inscription refers to the Judean kingdom or the Judeans, which also better conforms to the formulation [*ml*]*k byt dwd* "king of the house of David" and its parallel *mlk yšr'l* "king of Israel" (l. 8).[37] It may be, then, that the expression *byt 'b* designates not just a dynasty, but also a kingdom to the extent that the speaker related *'b* to the progenitor of the (ruling) tribe whose house encompasses not only his family members, but the entire region under his authority. At least the Sam'alian inscription *KAI* 215.7 operates accordingly on the assumption that one can be installed as king over the house of one's father.

Kottsieper

Similarly, adherents of a particular school of a sage are regarded as members of his house.[38]

Aramaic *byt*, however, also frequently means simply the place where something is located, such as, e.g., Jewish Aramaic demonstrates. This is the case with the expres-

---

31. Fitzmyer-Harrington, A50:8; A51:8; A52:8; cf. *ATTM,* 369f.; *DJPA*, 94.

32. Freedman-Geoghegan. For the discussion of this passage, cf. I. Kottsieper, "Die Inschrift vom Tell Dan und die politischen Beziehungen zwischen Aram-Damascus und Israel in der 1. Hälfte des 1. Jahrtausends vor Christus," "*Und Mose schrieb dieses Lied auf.*" *Fs. O. Loretz. AOAT* 250 (1998), 475f. and n. 2.

33. For the reading and interpretation, cf. Lemaire, 34-37.

34. *KAI* 215.22.

35. Cf. *KAI* 224.9f. (brothers, sons), and *DNSI*, 161.

36. Dion, 225-32.

37. Cf. Dietrich, esp. 27-29.

38. *DJPA*, 92b.

sion *byt mlkw* "house of the kingship," which can denote both the palace and the entire kingdom.[39] The treasury of a palace is called *byt gnzyn* "the house of gathering."[40] A farmer's land can be called *byt ḥql* "house of the field" and the synagogue is a *byt knyšh* "house of assembly."[41]

III. Biblical Aramaic. The Aramaic sections of the OT employ the noun *bayiṯ* forty-four times. The greater portion of these (thirty) refer to the temple in Jerusalem. A number of expressions designate this site, including *bayṯā'* "the house" (Ezr. 5:11; 6:3), *bayṯā' ḏᵉnāh* "this house" (Ezr. 5:3,9,12; 6:15), *bayṯeh* "his house" (Dnl. 5:23), *bêṯ 'ᵉlāhā'* "the house of God" (Dnl. 5:3; Ezr. 4:24; 5:2,13-17; 6:3,5 (2×),7 (2×),8,12,16,17; 7:24), *bêṯ 'ᵉlāhā' rabbā'* "the house of the great god" (Ezr. 5:8), *bêṯ 'ᵉlāh šᵉmayyā'* "the house of the God of heaven" (Ezr. 7:23), *bêṯ 'ᵉlāhᵃḵom/'ᵉlāhāḵ* "the house of your God" (Ezr. 7:17,19,20), and *bêṯ 'ᵉlāhᵃhom* "the house of their God" (Ezr. 7:16). Moreover, the parallel use of *bêṯ 'ᵉlāhā'* and *hêḵlā'* "temple" in Ezr. 5:14 and 6:5 indicates the connection between "house" and "temple" (→ היכל *hêḵal*). Thus, both the original temple before its destruction in 587 B.C.E. and the second temple were in no way simple structures. They served as God's earthly dwelling place. Ex. 25:9 indicates that God had at least two dwelling places, the original dwelling in heaven and its copy on earth constructed according to specifications as a model (*taḇnîṯ*).

Biblical Aramaic does not restrict the usage of *bayiṯ* to the temple, however, but can relate it to many other structures. Daniel goes to his house (*lᵉbayṯeh*, Dnl. 2:17; 6:11); the Persian royal treasury was stored in a *bêṯ ginzê malkā'* (Ezr. 7:20), which also archived documents (Ezr. 5:17: *bêṯ ginzayyā'*). Thus, the royal library was also called *bêṯ siprayyā'* (Ezr. 6:1). • The continuation with *dî ḡinzayyā' mᵉhaḥᵃṯîn tammāh* "where the treasures were stored" links the archive with the treasury, as does 5:17, although the text may be corrupt here and have originally spoken of the "treasury where the documents were stored."[42] (*Ko.*) • Dnl. 5:10 mentions a *bêṯ mišťᵉyā'* "the house of the feast/drinking," obviously a designation for the banquet hall. The word *bayiṯ* also refers to the palace, the house of the king (Ezr. 6:4 *bêṯ malkā'*; Dnl. 4:1 only *bayiṯ* along with *hêḵal*).

• In Ezr. 6:4, *bêṯ malkā'* takes on the connotation "royal household/court," which pays for the costs of the temple construction. Perhaps, however, this instance should also be associated with the *byt mlk'* of the Elephantine texts where it denotes the local administrative buildings of the Persian authorities (→ II). Then, Ezr. 6:4 would not only deal generally with the idea that the royal house will assume the costs, but would also indicate very concretely that the local Persian administration should make the means available from its income, which ultimately belong to the king. Finally, *beṯ malḵû* the "house of the kingdom" in Dnl. 4:27 designates Babel as the royal city. (*Ko.*) •

Three passages in the Aramaic portions of the OT employ *bayiṯ* in curses of kings to secure obedience in various situations. The Persian king Darius declares concerning the

39. *DJPA*, 94a.
40. *DJPA*, 93a.
41. *DJPA*, 93b; but cf. also e.g., *DNSI*, 160; *LexSyr*, 69-72.
42. Cf. e.g., J. Becker, *Esra, Nehemiah. NEB* 25 (1990), 37.

one who deviates from his decree that the Jerusalem temple should be reconstructed that "A beam shall be ripped from his house, and may he be impaled and hung on it. And may his house become a heap of ruins in exchange" (Ezr. 6:11). Similarly, Nebuchadnezzar threatens his subordinates with the destruction of their houses. This appears first in Dnl. 2:5, where the Babylonian king announces that if his dream interpreters cannot correctly interpret his dream, "their houses will be made heaps of ruins." This same threat occurs in Dnl. 3:29 in connection with the fact that Shadrach, Meshach, and Abednego had escaped the fiery furnace unscathed. Nebuchadnezzar announces that, if anyone were to speak evil of the God of Shadrach, Meshach, or Abednego, "his house will be made into a heap of ruins." The idea of destroying another's house is apparently timeless[43] and belongs among the most severe penalties a society can impose.

Biblical Aramaic employs the Semitic root *byt* only once as a verb; this usage obviously derives from the original noun. This usage of *byt* occurs in Dnl. 6:19 where the text states that, immediately after he had put Daniel into the lion's den, Darius went into his palace and spent the night (*ûḇaṯ*).

IV. Qumran. Aramaic *byt* also occurs frequently in the texts discovered at Qumran. Again, we also find *byt* in a verbal usage with the meaning "to dwell," "to spend the night." Thus, e.g., in the Aramaic Targum of Job found at Qumran, God asks Job whether an ox "would spend the night" (*hybyt*; 11Q10 32:8; cf. Job 39:9, which employs Heb. *lwn*) in Job's stall. • Aramaic *ybyt* also renders Hebrew *yālîn* in 11Q10 36:7 (Job 41:14), which here means simply "to dwell," however. It apparently constitutes a more mechanical translation based on the equation *lwn* "to stay overnight" = *byt*. (*Ko.*) •

The use of *byt* in the sense of "household" occurs in the Genesis Apocryphon from Cave 1, where Abraham asks God to raise his hand against the king of Egypt "and his whole house" (*wbkwl byth*, 1QapGen 20:15; cf. ll. 16,17,18,20,28). A similar usage occurs in 11Q10 19:7f., where Job speaks of the "men of my house" (*'nš byty*; cf. Job 31:31 *mᵉṯê 'ŏholî* "men of my tent"); cf. further, e.g., 11Q10 V:2; 1QapGen 21:21. By far the most frequent meaning of *byt* at Qumran is "house"; cf. e.g., 11Q10 2:4; 38:6; 1QapGen 21:6.

Freedman/Homan

Thus, the word also occurs frequently in the description of the city blocks of the new Jerusalem (5Q15 1 2:6ff.; 2:2). The Tg. of Lev. 16:20 describes the temple, adopting Hebrew *qoddæš* in 4Q156 2:4 as *byt qdš'*, while 4Q550c 3:4 attests the meaning "palace" (*byt mlk*[']).[44] Since this topic appears in the context of the inner court of the palace where a stele is erected, it is clear here, too, that *byt* describes the entire palace complex. A *byt mlk'* is, indeed, not primarily the "house of the king." Instead, the term designates the politically important residence of the king (→ II).

The connotation "dwelling place" also appears in 1QapGen 21:19 in the comment that, after his tour through the land of Israel, Abram returned to his "house," and unequivo-

43. Cf. e.g., also *KAI* 260.7.

44. Contra *ATTM.E,* 116: *byt mlk*[*wt*]', which is less likely for epigraphic reasons.

cally in 11Q10 32:5, which speaks of the steppe as *byt* (= Hebrew Job 39:6) for the wild ass. Qumran (4Q549 2:6) also probably attests the related designation of the grave as *byt ʿlm* (→ II).

Kottsieper

בָּל bl bāl

I. Etymology and Occurrence. II. Biblical Aramaic. III. General Aramaic Usage.

I. Etymology and Occurrence. Along with the early Aramaic instances in Aḥiqar 97, etc. (→ III), *bāl*, attested only in the absolute state, corresponds to Syriac *bāl* "soul, spirit," which also translates Hebrew *leḇ(āḇ)*, and Arabic *bāl* "attention." In terms of substance, the Mishnaic-Hebrew expression *ntn dʿtw l. . .* is comparable.

II. Biblical Aramaic. Biblical Aramaic exhibits the meaning "attention" as the object of *śym* in the expression *śām bāl l. . .* employed like the word *leḇ(āḇ)* in the corresponding Hebrew expression: *malkā . . . śaggî beʾeš ʿalôhî weʿal dānîyyeʾl śām bāl lešêzāḇûṯeh* "the king (i.e., Darius) was very agitated and gave (his) attention to saving Daniel" (Dnl. 6:15).

Kaddari

III. General Aramaic Usage. If, therefore, a close semantic relationship exists between Aramaic *bāl* and the lexical field "heart," it rests solely on the fact that *lb*(*b*) "heart," according to ancient Near Eastern anthropology the seat of understanding and attention (→ לבב *lebab*; Fabry, *TDOT*, VII, 399-438), can also assume meanings such as "attention," "mind." In the Aramaic languages, as in Arabic, *bāl* never occurs, however, for the concrete "heart." Thus, the Peshitta translates Hebrew *leḇ* only in the expressions *šyt leḇ* (Ex. 7:23; 1 S. 4:20; 2 S. 13:20) or *śym* (*ʿal*) *leḇ* (Ex. 9:21; Isa. 42:25; 57:1), that is, in contexts in which *leḇ* designates the mind or attention.

In the oldest specimen so far, which traces to a text tradition from the period around 700 B.C.E.,[1] *bl* occurs in the expression *ʾth ʿl bl*, also widespread in Syriac, that means "to consider, to take care of, to look after" (literally "to come to [his] *bl*).[2] In the later

---

S. Lieberman, *Greek in Jewish Palestine* (New York, ²1965).

1. Aḥiqar 97; I. Kottsieper, *Die Sprache der Ahiqarsprüche*. *BZAW* 194 (1990), §292.
2. *ThesSyr*, 529a.

Palestinian Aramaic dialects, in contrast, the phrase *yhb bl* "to give (his) *bl*" in the sense of "to pay attention" occurs frequently. It corresponds to *yhb lb*, *yb dʿt*, or *yhb hwn*.[3] Mandean consistently employs *b'l* in the meaning "mind, intention."[4]

Therefore, one can take *bl* as an independent term for the "mind" that one directs at something or into which something can come.

Kottsieper

3. Lieberman, 172-75.
4. *MdD*, 47b.

בלי *blī*

I. Etymology and Forms. II. Usage.

I. Etymology and Forms. In Aramaic, the Semitic root *blī* appears in the G-stem "to perish" and in the D-stem "to annihilate," as an adjective *blh* /balǣ/ "dissipated";[1] it also underlies the rare preposition *bly* "without."[2]

II. Usage. The verb appears in the D-stem in Dnl. 7:25 with the last secular ruler who oppresses the holy ones; in the G-stem in 4Q536 2 2:12 it denotes a perishable book; 4Q562 1 lacks context.

Gzella

J. Gamberoni, "בָּלָה *bālāh*," *TDOT*, II, 128-31.

1. *TADAE* B3.8:10,12, of a used garment.
2. 4Q157 1 2:5 (Job 4:20), as in the Heb. text.

בנה *bnī*; בִּנְיָן *bnyn binyān*

I. Etymology. II. Biblical Aramaic. 1. *bnh*. 2. *binyān*. III. Inscriptional Aramaic. 1. *bnh*. 2. *bnyn*. 3. *bnyt*/Banit. IV. Qumran. 1. *bnh*. 2. *bnyn*.

B. Aggoula, "Hatreana I: Construction, édifices, maçons et sculpteurs dans les inscriptions hatréennes," *Syr* 65 (1988) 197-216; S. Wagner, "בָּנָה *bānāh*," *TDOT*, II, 166-81.

I. Etymology. The root, attested in all Aramaic dialects, also occurs in Akkadian, Phoenician, Moabite, Hebrew, Arabic, and South Arabic, although not in the Ethiopic linguistic realm.

II. Biblical Aramaic.

1. bnh. Biblical Aramaic attests the peal of *bnh* "to build" with the house of God as object, e.g., Ezr. 5:2: *wᵉšāriw lᵉmiḇneʾ bêṯ ʾᵉlāhā* "and they began to build the house of God" (cf. also 5:3,9,11,13,17; 6:7,8).

• While these passages refer to the reconstruction of the destroyed temple, Ezr. 5:11 with *ûmeleḵ lᵉyiśrāʾel raḇ bᵉnāhî wᵉšaḵlᵉleh* "and a great king of Israel built and completed it" refers to a distinct construction under Solomon. The same verse also has the phrase *hᵃwāʾ ḇᵉneh miqqaḏmaṯ dᵉnāh šᵉnîn śaggîʾān* "and it was built many years earlier," which exhibits the pass. ptcp. of the peal in the meaning "to exist as a building." (*Ko.*) •

Once, the peal refers to the city of Babel *dî ʾᵃnāh ḇᵉnayṯah lᵉḇêṯ malḵû* "that I built as a royal residence" (Dnl. 4:27).

• Unless one wishes to begin with the notion that the author of Dnl. 4 assumed that Nebuchadnezzar built Babel, the passage attests *bnh* "to build" with the connotation "to expand," while, in analogy to the construction of the temple, Ezr. 4:12 speaks of the reconstruction of Jerusalem. In Ezr. 6:14 *bnh* peal occurs without a direct object as a general designation for construction activity. (*Ko.*) •

The hithpeel manifests the meaning "to be (re)constructed" and occurs both with the house of God (e.g., Ezr. 5:8 *wᵉhûʾ miṯbᵉneʾ ʾeḇen gᵉlāl* "it will be reconstructed of hewn stones"; cf. also 5:15,16; 6:3) and with the city of Jerusalem as subject (e.g., Ezr. 4:13 *hen qiryᵉṯāʾ ḏāḵ tiṯbᵉneʾ* "if this city is rebuilt"; cf. also vv. 16,21).

2. binyān. *binyān* is an action noun that denotes metonymically the result of the act of "building": *guḇrayyāʾ dî ḏᵉnāh ḇinyānāʾ bānayin* "the men who are busy in this construction" or literally "who build this building" (Ezr. 5:4). Here, *binyān* is the object of the result, the effected object of the verb *bnh*.

Kaddari

III. Inscriptional Aramaic.

1. bnh. The usage in the epigraphic texts demonstrates that *bnh* can refer to the erection of almost any building, especially of stone. Thus, the objects mentioned include a temple,[1] palaces,[2] graves,[3] walls,[4] as well as statues[5] and altar tables.[6] Therefore, *bnh*

1. E.g., *KAI* 202 B 9; oML 1:6 (*ATTM*, 406).
2. E.g., *KAI* 216:20.
3. E.g., *CIS* II 169.3; 4123.
4. *AP* 5.4,20.
5. *CIS* II 4193.1.
6. Hatra 62.1; cf. also *DNSI*, 176f.; Aggoula, 198-201.

appears here, as in Biblical Aramaic, as a construction term employed exclusively for stone construction. Thus, e.g., in relation to the preparation of a grave, *bn'* in the Palmyrene inscription Inv IV 13:1 designates the process that takes place after excavation (*ḥpr*) and before ornamentation (*ṣbt*),[7] therefore probably the architectural construction of the gravesite. The construction use of *bnh* corresponds to the fact that Herodian times knew the apparently honorific professional or functional designation *bnh/' hklh* "chief builder of the temple," as an ossuary inscription from Jerusalem attests.[8] Finally, *bnh* employed absolutely denotes the "cultivation" of a plot of ground with a building as a typical form of its usufruct.[9] The documents from Elephantine concerning the Jewish temple there, which had also been destroyed, exhibit close affinities with formulations referring to the reconstruction of the destroyed temple in Ezr. 5. Here, too, *bnh* means "to reconstruct," on one hand,[10] and refers to earlier construction, on the other,[11] while especially the peal pass. ptcp. indicates previous existence as a building as in Ezr. 5:11.[12]

2. bnyn. In this text corpus, *bnyn* designates that which is constructed (e.g., *bnyn' zy tbnh* "the building that you will build")[13] or the process of construction per se. Thus, the gates of the Jewish temple on Elephantine are described as *bnyn ps(y)lh zy 'bn* "a construction of quarried stones."[14] Finally, the word also connotes the process of building itself.[15] The precise meaning of *bnyn bl* or *bnyn' dy bl* on the Palmyrene Tesserae remains uncertain. Even if it clearly relates to the temple of Bel, it is still unclear whether it refers to specifications for its construction or instead to the construction shed.[16]

3. bnyt/*Banit.* Therefore, a technical use of the root and its derivatives persists throughout. Only Hatra I 34.3 would offer the sole instance of the use of *bnh* in the sense of "to create," if the reading *bnyt kwl* is correct,[17] in an epithet of the deity *'šrbl*: "the creatrix of all." Nonetheless, this may then be an adaptation from Akkadian since only there does *banû* also acquire the meaning "to create" and is the epithet *bānû* "creator" or *bānītu* "creatrix" well attested.[18]

---

7. Cf. D. R. Hillers and E. Cussini, *Palmyrene Aramaic Texts* (Baltimore, 1996), 178,347.
8. yJE 25a,b (*ATTM,* 344); cf. also Christian Palestinian Aramaic ccAD 1.2 (*ATTM,* 402).
9. *AP* 8.19; 9.5; nV 7:59 (*ATTM.E,* 168,171).
10. *AP* 30.23,25,27; 31.23,24,26; 32.8.
11. *AP* 30.13,25; 31.12.
12. *AP* 30.14; 31.13; 32.4f.
13. *BMAP* 3.22.
14. *AP* 30.10; 31.9.
15. E.g., Inv IX 11:4; Aggoula, 201f.
16. Cf. A. Caquot, *Recueil des tesseres de Palmyre. BAH* 58 (1955), 141.
17. Contra, however, e.g., A. Caquot, "Inscriptions et Graffites Hatreens de Doura-Europos," *Syr* 30 (1953) 239: *bt tkdm*; K. Beyer, *Die aramäischen Inschriften aus Assur, Hatra und dem übrigen Ostmesopotamien* (Göttingen, 1998), 37: *brt t*[. . .].
18. *CAD,* II, 94f.

This word probably also occurs in the name of the goddess *bnt*,[19] who had a temple in Syene.[20] The unequivocally Akkadian form of the name demonstrates that this, too, is an Akkadianism, which indicates that the root *bnh* was apparently not available in Aramaic in the meaning "to create" so that a corresponding aramaization of the term as *bnyh* or *bnyt'/h* was not possible.

IV. Qumran.

1. bnh. This technical diction also occurs consistently at Qumran. Thus, as objects of the construction one encounters here besides palaces (4Q212 4:18 [1 En. 91:13]) and cities (1QapGen 19:9) the altars that Abram erected (1QapGen 21:1,20) and the graves of Amram's ancestors (4Q544 1:1,3,4). The specifications of construction materials can also utilize this root, as the specifications concerning the city walls of the heavenly Jerusalem, which are "built" of gemstones, indicate (*bnyh bḥš*[*ml*] *wspyr kdkwd*, 4Q554 2 2:15). This motif, which traces back to Isa. 54:11f. and reaches to Rev. 21:18-21, also occurs in 4Q196 18:7f. (= Tob. 13:17). Finally, the archangel Michael describes the primeval Babel in Gen. 11 as *mtbnyh . . . lšmh dy rby* [*mr' 'lm'*] "built for the name of my lord, [the eternal lord]" (4Q529 9).

Only one passage probably speaks of God's direct construction activity, although here, too, *bnh* occurs clearly as a technical term for city construction. Thus, 4Q550e:2 offers the statement]*bnh ṣywn wbh ysttrwn kl 'ny 'mh* "]he built Zion, and all the poor of his people will find safety in it," which apparently adapts Isa. 14:32: *kî YHWH yissad ṣiyyôn ûḇāh yeḥ^e^sû ^ca^niyyê 'ammô* "for Yahweh founded Zion and on it the suffering of his people find safety." The rendering of *ysd* "to found" with *bnh* "to build" indicates that here *ṣywn* apparently refers to the city Jerusalem[21] and not to Zion as the mountain of God and the dwelling of Yahweh.[22]

2. bnyn. At Qumran, *bnyn* was used only for "building" (4Q243 10:3). In 4Q537 2:1 and 11Q18 9:4f. it probably refers to the temple or its buildings.

Kottsieper

19. M. Cogan, "Sukkoth-Benoth," *DDD*², 822.

20. Hermopolis 2:1 (*TADAE* A2.2,1): *byt bnt bswn* (= 3:1 [*TADAE* A2.4:1]); cf. also 1:7 (*TADAE* A2.3:7) and 2:12 (*TADAE* A2.2:12).

21. Cf. O. Kaiser, *Der Prophet Jesaja: Kapitel 13–39. ATD* 18 (³1983), 47.

22. H. Wildberger, *Isaiah 13-27*. Continental Commentaries, trans. Thomas H. Trapp (Minneapolis, 1991), 100.

בעי *b'ī*; בעו *b'w* /ba'ū/

I. Etymology, Semantic Field, and Grammatical Constructions. II. Old and Imperial Aramaic. III. Biblical Aramaic and Qumran. IV. Deverbal Noun "Request."

I. Etymology, Semantic Field, and Grammatical Constructions. A thoroughly productive use of the verbal root *b'ī* "to want, seek, request" distinguishes Aramaic from related languages;[1] the verb is usually associated with Arabic *bġī* "to want." Semantically, it corresponds to the root *bqš*[2] common in Hebrew and the other NW Semitic languages. In the connotation "to seek," → *škḥ* "to find" functions as an antonym.[3]

The verb regularly appears in the G-stem either as an intransitive[4] or a transitive with the abstract or concrete thing desired or requested as object (also with an internal object)[5] and can be supplemented by various prepositional expressions: quite often with *mn* in reference to the addressee;[6] rarely with *'l* "regarding, for" as a further addition (e.g., Dnl. 7:16). In legal diction, the Gt-passive "to be required" also appears.[7] The form *y^eḇa'ōn*, vocalized in unusual fashion as a D-stem in Dnl. 4:33 ("they search for"), is unique and suspect.[8] When used as a modal verb "to want," the full verb may appear either in the infinitive after *l-* (Dnl. 6:5; 1QapGen 19:15,19,21; 20:9) or, with a change of subject, in the object clause following *dy* (Dnl. 2:16; 1QapGen 20:21).

In the course of time, the modal use of *b'ī* "to wish that" grew into an expression for the immediate future "to be about to."[9] One can already observe an early phase of this development in Dnl. 2:13b: According to the enraged king's command to kill all the dream interpreters, "Daniel and his companions were also about to be killed" (*ūḇ^e'ō dānī'ēl w^eḥaḇrōhī l^ehiṯq^eṭālā*); this development resulted in forms of the root *b'ī* becoming an in-

J. A. Fitzmyer, *The Aramaic Inscriptions of Sefire. BietOr* 19A (²1995); H. Gzella, *Tempus, Aspekt und Modalität im Reichsaramäischen. VOK* 48 (2004); H. Lozachmeur, *La collection Clermont-Ganneau: Ostraca, épigraphes sur jarre, étiquettes de bois*, 2 vols. (Paris, 2006); B. Schlenke, "*b'h*" *ThWQ*, I, 480-83.

1. The very few Heb. instances are unusual: Ex. 24:4b is problematic from a text-critical perspective; Isa. 21:12 "to ask" (G-stem) and Ob. 6 "to be sought out" (N-stem) can be attributed to poetic diction.

2. From *bqθ*; cf. S. Wagner, "בִּקֵּשׁ *biqqēsh*," *TDOT*, II, 229-41.

3. The two appear together in *TADAE* C1.1,34 in reference to a place, and absolutely in Dnl. 6:5.

4. 1QapGen 20:12.

5. See IV below.

6. E.g., *TADAE* A4.3,6; Dnl. 2:23; 7:16; probably on the model of Achaemenid courtly style (cf. *ATTM*, 679f.; 2:471), in deferential address, such as in reference to God, also with *mn* → *qdm* as in Dnl. 2:18 or only *qdm* in 6:12.

7. As in the Palmyrene tax tables, *PAT* 0259 ii:70; and often in Nabatean contracts from the Dead Sea, nV 2:12; 3:38; 43:19 in *ATTM*, 2.

8. *BLA* §158n. *ATTM*, 534 subsumes it under the G-stem.

9. Gzella, 229f.

dication of the future in later Aramaic languages.[10] Furthermore, a related noun *bʿw* /baʿū/ "request" also appears sporadically, although it is less frequent than the verb and in both of the only certain instances from pre-Christian times in direct relation to it (Dnl. 6:8,14).[11]

II. Old and Imperial Aramaic. Many of the nuances established in the broad semantic spectrum of the verb *bʿī* already appear in the Imperial Aramaic period. The earliest instances, however, already occur in the Old Aramaic state treaties from Sefire in Syria. In any case, the expression *ybʿh rʾšy lhmtty* "to seek my head in order to kill me" in a revenge clause clearly has juridical connotations;[12] without sufficient context, other instances remain unclear[13] or are probably related to a homonymous root "to swell (in wrath)."[14] They all represent the original modal nuance "to want."

In the Imperial Aramaic texts from Elephantine and elsewhere in Egypt, the meaning "to seek for" also survives. With a likewise negative connotation, it appears in the similarly formal style of the request letter from the Jewish community concerning the reconstruction of the temple, which says that the opponents "seek evil for that temple" (*bʿw bʾyš lʾgwrʾ zk*).[15] In the everyday speech of the letters, however, the verb refers to a desire with the objective of remediating a lack, such as in the search for a buyer for a house.[16] Thus, already on the eve of the Imperial Aramaic tradition in Egypt, items "sought for" include a boat to transport a person (in the private letter from Hermopolis 6:9f.);[17] personnel suitable for the estate of the Satrap (in official documents);[18] or, quite generally, any kind of need.[19] This verb for "to seek, to need" also occurs regularly in the private letters on the Clermont-Ganneau ostraca from Elephantine, which document the ordering and delivery of all sorts of goods of daily life, although, unfortunately, mostly without sufficient context.[20] Occasionally, the nuance "to need, lack" comes to the fore without necessarily implying a finding.[21]

In certain cases, specifically juridical connotations in the sense of "to demand" also appear, as in the private contracts from Palymra[22] and Nabatean ones from the Dead Sea,[23] further, of the gods with reference to the penalty for a sacrilege, in curse formulas

---

10. A "prospective" use of verbs of desire is also common in other languages, as in Luther's translation of Matt. 26:58, "until he could see where it wanted to go."

11. See IV below.

12. *KAI* 224.11; so also perhaps in the lost, but presumably parallel expression in 223 B 8.

13. *KAI* 222 B 39, here with *nbšk* "you, yourself" as subject; 223 B 17.

14. *KAI* 224.2; cf. Fitzmyer, 143; and *DNSI*, 181.

15. *TADAE* A4.7,16f.

16. *TADAE* A3.8,6.

17. *TADAE* B2.6,9f.

18. *TADAE* A6.10,3,4,7,9.

19. *TADAE* A4.3,6, there with *mh ṣbw wmlh* "any desire or matter whatsoever" as object.

20. Nonetheless, nos. 36cc2; 67cv1; 179cv4; 228cv3 [with *gld* "skin"]; 244cc1 in Lozachmeur seem relatively certain, as do nos. 152cc6 according to *TADAE* D7.16 and 200cc4.

21. As in *TADAE* C1.1,53.

22. *PAT* 1981.4; in the passive, *PAT* 0259 ii.70.

23. nV 2:12,15; 3:13,37,45; 42:28; 43;18, etc., in *ATTM* 2, often in parallel with the passive. See I above.

in dedicatory and boundary inscriptions from Cilicia[24] and in the Xanthos stele.[25] These expressions apparently mirror a common Imperial Aramaic legal tradition. A few additional examples from this period are fragmentary.[26]

III. Biblical Aramaic and Qumran. The post-Imperial Aramaic religious literature from Palestine and, especially, the Biblical Aramaic book of Daniel, attest the meaning "to request" for *b'ī* very frequently, often with "from," occasionally, however, also the meaning "to search (for errors)" with a negative connotation (according to Dnl. 6:5, Daniel's enemies watched him continuously [a periphrastic construction with the participle after → *hwī*], in order to find some occasion to harm him), not unlike the expression "to seek"—which may have been restricted to elevated style—in Old and Imperial Aramaic.[27] In the sense of "to request," the verb refers in the Daniel narratives sometimes to the king (2:16,49), but usually to God (2:18,23; 6:8,12,13,14). Thus, it acquires the nuance "to pray."

As the Aramaic texts from Qumran show, this shading did not limit the broad semantic spectrum of the root, however. It appears often here, too, sometimes in direct connection with a form of the verb → *ḥnn* "to have mercy" and, consequently, clearly in the sense of "to pray for mercy";[28] moreover, it may underlie the masculine personal name *Ba'iyā(n)* "Requested (of God)" attested in the Bar-Kosiba Letters.[29] Yet, *b'ī* is used both for requests addressed to people[30] and for a demand, often with negative connotations.[31] In addition, it occurs in reference to the search for shade from (*mn qdm*) the sun[32] and, in a wisdom admonition, along with → *bqr* "to investigate," for the pursuit of knowledge.[33] If Beyer's reading of the corresponding object in the second half of the line of the last reference as *mh dyn' b''* "what justice requires"[34] is correct, and there are good reasons to think so,[35] this second occurrence of *b'ī* reflects an older juridical nuance, "to claim," that has evolved into a theological-ethical usage.[36] A few additional instances are too fragmentary for a more precise determination.

The broad usage of this verb already established in Imperial Aramaic survives in later Western and Eastern Aramaic.[37]

---

24. *KAI* 258.5; 259.2f.; cf. *DNSI*, 180.
25. *KAI* 319.26f.
26. See *DNSI*, 180 for an overview.
27. See II above.
28. 1QapGen 20:12; 4Q204 6:18 (1 En. 14:7).
29. *ATTM*, 534; cf. *Šā'ūl* in Heb.
30. 1QapGen 20:21.
31. Expressly for killing in 1QapGen 19:19 and 20:9; in 19:15 also for the felling of a cedar, which symbolizes Abraham and his destruction in a dream, however.
32. 4Q201 1 2:7 par. 4Q204 1 1:26 (1 En. 4:1).
33. 4Q541 24 2:4, T. Levi.
34. *ATTM*, 2:112.
35. Cf. H. Gzella, "*dyn*," *ThWQ*, I, 677.
36. See II above.
37. See *DJPA*, 107f.; *DJBA*, 224-26; *LexSyr*, 82; *MdD*, 44.

IV. Deverbal Noun "Request." In religious contexts, the feminine abstract noun *b'w* /ba'ū/ "request" (in Masoretic pointing, as in a few other words, the /a/ is retained through lengthening to *bā'ū*)[38] has the meaning "petitionary prayer," as in Dnl. 6:8,14, where it appears in each case in a *figura etymologica* as the direct object of the verb *b'ī*. Because of the consistently very fragmentary contexts of the few possible instances in the Aramaic texts from Qumran, it is not possible to say with certainty, however, the precise usage in which this noun was employed there: see, for example, *b'w[tkwn* in 4Q204 6:13 (1 En. 14:4), where, however, *ATTM*, 239 reads a *y* instead of *w* and thus posits a verbal form "you prayed"; in contrast, *ATTM*, 2:107f. (L 45:7) has *kl b'w* "each request" for 4Q213 1 2+2,7 (Hymn to Wisdom in the Levi text), while other editors suspect an instance of the verbal root here.

Outside Biblical Aramaic, consequently, assured examples occur only in post-Christian times, indeed, also in religious language: thus *bb'w mnkwn* "with a request for you" (thus, like the verb, with the preposition *mn* indicating the addressee) in a Jewish Palestinian magical text addressed to a long series of angels (probably sixth or seventh century C.E.)[39] and especially *b'wt'* "petitionary prayer" in a Palestinian Christian church inscription in memory of a donor (717/718 C.E. according to Beyer's reading).[40]

The expression *bb'w* with the preposition *b* was apparently also lexicalized as a particle of courtesy, "please!" It is first attested in this function, however, only later, although in both Western[41] and Eastern Aramaic,[42] which suggests that it was already widespread earlier in the vernacular. In Jewish Babylonian Aramaic, in contrast, the by-form of the noun, *ba^{ca}yā* "question, request" was productive.[43]

Gzella

38. Cf. *ATTM*, 133 n. 2.
39. ooXX 12:9f. in *ATTM.E*, 265.
40. ccAM 1:9 in *ATTM.E*, 270.
41. *DJPA*, 84a.
42. *LexSyr*, 83a.
43. *DJBA*, 266f.

בעל *b'l* /ba'l/; בעל *b'l*

I. Etymology. II. Semantics. 1. Sam'alian and Old Aramaic. 2. Aḥiqar. 3. Imperial Aramaic. 4. Biblical Aramaic. 5. Qumran. 6. Names of Deities. 7. Personal Names. III. LXX.

I. Etymology. The substantive *bʿl* occurs in East Semitic[1] and in several Northwest Semitic languages[2] for "lord," "owner," "member," "citizen." In addition, → *mr'* (/māre'/), which is semantically distinct from *bʿl*, also exists in Aramaic. Aramaic pantheons call the weather god, Baʿal, Hadad (→ *'lh* V). The Aramaic denominative verb *bʿl* (haphel) means "to make someone a husband = to marry" (→ II.3).[3] Syriac also attests it as *bʿl* (ithpeel) "to marry"[4] and Palestinian Jewish Aramaic as *bʿl* "to have sexual intercourse."[5]

II. Semantics.

1. Sam'alian and Old Aramaic. The inscriptions from Sam'al belong among the oldest instances of the lexeme.[6] In them, *bʿl* designates the owner of silver and gold[7] and the upper class of villages.[8] In the military sphere, *bʿl rkb*[9] refers to the cavalry. On the level of religion and royal ideology, the god Rakib-El is the *bʿl byt,* the "lord of the house."[10] Since *byt* denotes the royal house, *bʿl byt* is usually understood as "lord of the dynasty" (→ *byt* II).

The usage of *mr'* in the inscriptions from Sam'al contrasts with the usage of *bʿl.* This title is reserved for Tiglath-pileser III as the "lord of the four quarters of the world"[11] and

---

K.-A. Abraham, "Echtscheiding volgens de Elefantine huwe-lijkscontracten" (diss., Louvain, 1985); S. A. Kaufman, *The Akkadian Influences on Aramaic. AS* 19 (1974), 42f.; K. Koch, *Daniel 1–4. BK* XXII/1 (2005), 160-64; J. Kühlewein, "בַּעַל *baʿal* owner," *TLOT*, 247-51; E. Y. Kutscher, בעל טעם, *EMiqr* 2 (1954), 293f.; A. Lemaire, "Villes, rois et gouverneurs au Levant d'après les inscriptions monumentales ouest-sémitiques (IXᵉ-VIIᵉ siècles av. J.-C.)," *Sem* 43/44 (1995) 21-36; E. Lipiński, "Marriage and Divorce in the Judaism of the Persian Period," *Transeu* 4 (1973) 63-71; idem, "The Wife's Right to Divorce in the Light of an Ancient Near Eastern Tradition," *Jewish Law Annual* 4 (1981) 9-27; S. Mittmann, "Tobia, Sanballat und die persische Provinz Juda," *JNSL* 26 (2000) 1-50; J. C. de Moor and M. J. Mulder, "בַּעַל *baʿal*," *TDOT*, II, 181-200; H.-P. Müller, "Der Gottesname *BʿL* und seine Phraseologien im Hebräischen und im Phönizisch-Punischen," *JSS* 50 (2005) 281-96; H. Niehr, *Baʿalšamem. OLA* 123 (2003), 89-184; B. Porten, "Five Fragmentary Aramaic Marriage Documents: New Collations and Restorations," *Abr-Nahrain* 27 (1989) 80-105; B. H. Reynolds III, "*bʿl*," *ThWQ*, I, 483-86; D. Schwiderski, *Handbuch des nordwestsemitischen Briefformulars. BZAW* 295 (2000), 187-193, 357-59; M. W. Stolper, "The Governor of Babylon and Across-the-River in 486 B.C.," *JNES* 48 (1989) 283-305; R. Yaron, "Aramaic Marriage Contracts from Elephantine," *JSS* 3 (1958) 1-39; idem, *Introduction to the Law of the Aramaic Papyri* (Oxford 1961), 45-50.

1. *AHw*, I, 118-20; *CAD*, II, 191-98.
2. J. Cantineau, *Le Nabatéen II* (Paris 1932), 73; *DNSI*, 182-84; *ThesSyr*, 561-64; *MdD*, 60; *DUL*³, 203-6.
3. *DNSI*, 182.
4. *ThesSyr*, 561.
5. *DJPA*, 109.
6. Cf. H. Gzella, "Language and Script," in H. Niehr, ed., *The Aramaeans in Ancient Syria. HO* I/106 (2014), 71-107, esp. 74f.
7. *KAI* 215.11; 216.10f.
8. *KAI* 215.10.
9. *KAI* 215.3,10.
10. *KAI* 215.22; cf. 24.16.
11. *KAI* 216.3f.; 217.1f.

as the suzerain of Barrakib,[12] for the god Rakib-El as "lord of Barrakib,"[13] and for the god Ba'alḥaran, the "lord of Barrakib."[14] Thus, *b'l* has the connotation "possessor" "owner," while *mr'* denotes the overlord on both human and divine levels.

In the Sefire treaties, *b'l* describes the lords in the sense of the upper class[15] of Kitikka and Arpad.[16] They are named by dynasty and location as parties to the treaty and are not identical with the → *'m* "people."[17] In *KAI* 224.23,26 *b'l* refers to the upper class of Tal'ayim.[18]

2. Aḥiqar. The sayings of Aḥiqar[19] attest a divine epithet *b'l qdšn* "lord of the holy ones."[20] With respect to the identification of this epithet, some have thought of the god Ba'alšamin based on the use of *šmyn* in the parallel verse[21] or of the sun god Šamaš.[22] Since Hadad constitutes the head of the Aramaic pantheons of Syria, however, it is appropriate to see Hadad as the lord of a pantheon here, too.[23] Additionally, *b'l 'gr* occurs in the same corpus of texts as "employer."[24] This individual is advised against employing a poor worker along with a good one.

3. Imperial Aramaic. In the Elephantine papyri *b'l* appears in various usages that continue the semantics of the substantive already established for the Old Aramaic inscriptions.

On the one hand, *b'l* denotes the husband,[25] in which the element of authority over the wife still echoes. Derived from this substantive is the verb *b'l* (haphel) "to make husband," "to marry," with a woman as subject. In one text from Elephantine,[26] however, this translation makes little sense; instead it refers to marital relations.[27]

The documents *TADAE* B2.6; 3.3; 3.8; 6.1; 6.2; 6.3; 6.4 (cf. B2.5) reveal the legal steps in a marriage. First mentioned is the bridegroom's request for the permission of the father of the bride or her brother, lord, or mother. The formula spoken by the husband seals the marriage: *hy 'ntty w'nh b'lh mn ywm' znh w'd 'lm* "She is my wife and I am her husband

12. *KAI* 216.6,9; 217.3f.
13. *KAI* 216.5f.
14. *KAI* 218.
15. *ABLAK*, II, 1971, 172; J. Fitzmyer, *The Aramaic Inscriptions of Sefire. BietOr* 19/A (^{2}1995), 64.
16. *KAI* 222 A 4; B 4f.
17. *KAI* 222 A 29f; B 5.11; 223 B 3; C 16.
18. Cf. also the instance from Dur-Katlimmu in W. Röllig, *Die aramäischen Texte aus Tall Šēḫ Ḥamad / Dūr-Katlimmu / Magdalu. BATSH* 17/Texte 5 (2014), 34 no. D 7.2.
19. *TADAE* C1.1 and H. Niehr, *Aramäischer Aḥiqar* (Gütersloh, 2007), 42-52.
20. *TADAE* C1.1,6,79.
21. Cf. J. M. Lindenberger, "The Gods of Ahiqar," *UF* 14 (1982) 114-16; contra Niehr, *Ba'alšamem*, 98.
22. Cf. E. Lipiński, *The Aramaeans. OLA* 100 (2000), 625.
23. Cf. Niehr, *Aḥiqar*, 19.
24. *TADAE* C1.1,7,100.
25. E.g., in *TADAE* B2.3,7; 2.6,21,23; 3.3,9; 3.8,24,26,33,35,40.
26. *TADAE* B3.8,33.
27. P. Grelot, *Documents araméens d'Egypte. LAPO* 5 (1972), 237e; cf. also the discussion in *DNSI*, 182.

from this day to eternity."[28] Then follows the payment of the "bride gift" (*mhr*)[29] to the head of the bride's family. The *mhr* becomes part of the bride's dowry. Its full payment formalizes the marriage. The last step of the marriage ceremony consists of the formulation of a contract that may list the rights and duties of the couple, the extent of the *mhr*, and the personal property the woman brings with her into the marriage.

Divorce, which the woman can also initiate, is executed through the formula: *śn't l'ntty* PN/*l*PN *b'ly (l' thwh/yhwh ly 'ntt/b'l)* "I hate my wife PN/my husband PN; (she/he shall not be my wife/husband)."[30] The pronouncement of the divorce formula must take place in public (*b'dh*).[31] Whoever initiates the divorce must pay a "divorce fee."[32] If the woman initiates the divorce, she could forfeit her dowry,[33] but retain her property.[34] If the divorce results from the husband's initiative, he forfeits the *mhr* and must surrender to the wife all of her property.[35]

Regarding *b'l* as "husband" cf., among others, the grave inscription of a priest of Ba'al from Memphis, also dating to circa 500 B.C.E.,[36] *CIS* II 162 (Nabat.), 4518A,3 (Palmyr.),[37] the marriage contracts from Wadi Murabba'at[38] and the inscriptions from Hatra.[39]

The element of control inherent in the semantics of *b'l* also finds expression when the Aḥiqar novella describes Aḥiqar as "the lord of good counsel" (*b'l 'ṭt' ṭbt'*).[40]

In addition, *b'l* denotes the members of a political or military society. Since the inhabitants of Elephantine and Syene belonged as soldiers to a particular military unit (*dgl*) and as civilians to a city, the designation *b'l dgl w* (*b'l*) *qryh* refers to all inhabitants.[41] The terms *b'ly qryh* "inhabitants of the city"[42] and *b'ly yb* "inhabitants of Elephantine"[43] also occur. The trilingual text from Xanthos[44] also attests *b'l* in Imperial

28. *TADAE* B2.6,4; 3.3,3f.; 3.8,4; 6.1,3f. (corr.).

29. E. Lipiński, "מֹהַר *mōhar*," *TDOT*, VIII, 142-49; idem, "La donation matrimoniale dans l'ancient [*sic!*] droit hébraique," in *Šulmu*, ed. P. Vavroušek and V. Soucek (Prague, 1988), 173-93.

30. Cf. *TADAE* B2.6,23,27; 3.3,9; 3.8,21f.,24f.; E. Lipiński, "שָׂנֵא *śānē'*," *TDOT*, XIV 164-74; H. Gzella, *Tempus, Aspekt und Modalität im Reichsaramäischen. VOK* 48 (2004), 207.

31. *TADAE* B2.6,15,22f.,26f; 3.3,7; 3.8,21.

32. *TADAE* B2.6,23f.; 3.3,8f.; 3.8,22-26.

33. *TADAE* B3.8,24f.

34. *TADAE* B3.8,26-28.

35. *TADAE* B2.6,26-28.

36. A. Dupont-Sommer, "Une stèle araméenne d'un prêtre de Ba'al trouvée en Égypte," *Syr* 33 (1956) 79-87; Grelot, *Documents araméens*, no. 77; V. Hug, *Altaramäische Grammatik der Texte des 7. und 6. Jh.s v.Chr. HSAO* 4 (1993), 34f.; contra J. T. Milik, "Les papyrus araméens d'Hermoupolis et les cultes syro-phéniciens en Egypte perse," *Bibl* 48 (1967) 566 n. 3 "citizen of Anoth"; cf. *TADAE* D21.17,3.

37. Cf. also *PAT* 348b.

38. M 20.9; 21.12 (*ATTM*, 309-11).

39. H5.3, 30.4 and 35.6 in K. Beyer, *Die aramäischen Inschriften aus Assur, Hatra und dem übrigen Ostmesopotamien* (Göttingen, 1998).

40. *TADAE* C1.1,3,42.

41. *TADAE*, B2.1,9; 2.7,10; 6.3,7.

42. *TADAE*, B2.9,10f.; 6.3,7.

43. *TADAE* A4.7,22; 4.8,22; cf. H. Lozachmeur, "La birta en Méditerranée orientale," *Sem* 43/44 (1995) 69f.

44. *KAI* 319,6.11; cf. A. Lemaire, "The Xanthos Trilingual Revisited," in *Solving Riddles and Untying Knots. FS. J. C. Greenfield* (Winona Lake, IN, 1995), 424f.

Aramaic as an inhabitant or the upper class of a city, as do two other Aramaic texts from there.[45]

Then, the official title *bʿl* → *ṭʿm* ("commander") appears in the letters of the Egyptian Satrap Aršama and of the Satrap of Bactria. A scribe (→ *spr*) bore the title and, judging from the context, it refers to the manager of a chancellery.[46] The title was borrowed from the Akkadian *bēl ṭēmi*.[47]

Borrowed from the Akkadian *bēl piqitti* "commissioned,"[48] *bʿl pqt* constitutes another title that refers to a commissioner or supervisor.[49]

The self-designation by the inhabitants of Elephantine *bʿly ṭbtk wrḥmyk* "entitled to your benevolence"[50] paralleling *rḥmyk* ("your friends," → *rḥm*) evidences once again the semantics of *bʿl* "lord."[51]

4. *Biblical Aramaic.* The title *bʿl ṭʿm* "commander," already attested in Achaemenid official correspondence, appears in the Aramaic OT in Ezr. 4:8f.,17 (*beʿēl ṭeʿēm*; according to one manuscript and a few versions, also in 4:23; cf. *BHS*). With regard to the commander bearing the Hebrew PN Rehum, it refers to the head of a chancellery. Since it does not employ the title *pæḥā* (→ *pḥh*), it does not refer to the governor of Samaria.[52] Together with the scribe named in parallel, Rehum represents the chief administrator of the Satrapy of Transeuphratene.

5. *Qumran.* In texts from Palestine including Qumran, *bʿl* as husband appears in 1QapGen 20:23,25 as well as in marriage contracts[53] and other legal documents.[54] In addition, *bʿl* → *dyn* as "opponent before the court" is attested.[55] This legal technical term, borrowed from the Akk. *bēl dīni*,[56] appears in Aramaic first in Qumran and then frequently in Jewish Palestinian,[57] Syriac,[58] and Mandaic.[59]

---

45. A. Dupont-Sommer, *La stèle trilingue du Letoon. Fouilles de Xanthos* VI (Paris, 1979), 171,3; 173,5.

46. *TADAE*, A6.2,23 and A2.7 in J. Naveh and S. Shaked, *Aramaic Documents from Ancient Bactria* (London, 2012); cf. there, too, 23f. and Stolper, 299-303.

47. *AHw*, III, 1387.

48. *AHw*, I, 120.

49. A. Caquot, "Une inscription araméenne d'époque assyrienne," *Hommages à André Dupont-Sommer. FS. A. Dupont-Sommer* (Paris, 1971), 9-16; *SAIO* I (1975), 77-82; I. Kottsieper, "Der Mann aus Babylonien—Steuerhinterzieher, Flüchtling, Immigrant oder Agent?," *Or* 69 (2000) 368-92, esp. 376,386f.

50. *TADAE*, A4.7,23f.; 4.8,23; cf. D7.1,3f.: *bʿl ṭbtkm*.

51. Cf. *LexLingAram*, 30, *habentes gratiam tuam*, and *DNSI*, 417f. s.v. *ṭbḥ*$_1$.

52. Cf. A. H. J. Gunneweg, *Esra. KAT* XIX/1 (1985), 89; contra G. W. Ahlström, *The History of Ancient Palestine from the Palaeolithic Period to Alexander's Conquest. JSOTSup* 146 (1993), 848.

53. M 20:9; 21:12 (*ATTM*, 309f.); yyZZ 36:27 (corr.; *ATTM.E*, 245f.).

54. nV 7:25f.,68-71 (*ATTM*, 2, 219); nV 22:31 (*ATTM*, 2, 236); V 50:6 (*ATTM*, 191f.).

55. 4Q531 17:5 (*DSSStE*, 1066f.).

56. *AHw*, I, 119b; *CAD*, III, 155f.

57. *DJPA*, 109a.

58. *ThesSyr*, 562.

59. *MdD*, 60.

6. Names of Deities. In the Aramaic pantheons of Syria (→ *'lh* V), a variety of divine names formed with *bʿl* occur. Thus, in Sam'al, the gods Baʿal Ṣemed, Baʿal Ḥammon, and Baʿal Ḥarran are attested. Hamath has Baʿalšamin and a goddess Pahalatis, whose name traces to the goddess Baʿalat from Byblos. The place Baʿalbek traces its name to the "*bʿl* of the spring."[60] The majority of divine names containing *bʿl* stem from Palmyra. The divine names Yarḥibol and Aglibol trace to the preclassical era of the oasis city. Under the influence of *bēlum*, the Mesopotamian epithet for Marduk, the equally ancient divine name Bol became Bel; his satellite god, Malakbel is also comparable. The gods Baʿalšamin and Baʿal Hammon come from outside Palmyra. For Hatra, the god Baʿalšamin adopted from elsewhere merits attention; here, PNs such as Mar'elahe formed with the element *mr'* and others from the native pantheon dominate otherwise.

7. Personal Names. Regarding the PNs of the Old and Imperial Aramaic inscriptions, cf. M. Maraqten, *Die semitischen Personennamen in den alt- und reichsaramäischen Inschriften aus Vorderasien. TStO* 5 (1988), 48f.,224; regarding those from Elephantine with the theophoric element *bʿl*, M. H. Silverman, *Religious Values in the Jewish Proper Names at Elephantine. AOAT* 217 (1985), 137f.; and regarding the corresponding Nabatean, F. al-Khraysheh, "Die Personennamen in den nabatäischen Inschriften des Corpus Inscriptionum Semiticarum" (diss., Marburg, 1986), 28f.,56f.,126,128,179f.,184. In Palmyra, PNs with the theophoric elements *bwl, bl*, and *bʿl* are extant.[61] In Hatra, *bl* appears as a theophoric element of PNs.[62]

III. LXX, The LXX does not translate the title *b^{e}ʿēl ṭ^{e}ʿēm* in Ezr. 4:8f.,17, but transcribes it as βααλταμ (cf. LXX of 4:23) and probably misunderstands it as a PN.

Niehr

60. Cf. S. Wild, *Libanesische Ortsnamen. BTS* 9 (1973), 219-23.
61. *PNPI*, 74f.,76f.,78,116.
62. See S. Abbadi, *Die Personennamen der Inschriften aus Hatra. TStO* 1 (1983), 68.

בקר *bqr*; מבקר *mbqr* /mabaqqer/

I. Etymology and Grammatical Constructions. II. Biblical Aramaic. III. Qumran. IV. Uncertain *mbqr* "Overseer"(?).

B. Beck, "בָּקָר *bāqār*," *TDOT*, II, 209-16; R. C. Steiner, "The *mbqr* at Qumran, the *episkopos* in the Athenian Empire, and the Meaning of *lbqr'* in Ezra 7:14," *JBL* 120 (2001) 623-46.

I. Etymology and Grammatical Constructions. In Aramaic, the verb *bqr* has the meaning "to inquire, investigate" and occurs regularly in the D-stem; it probably derives from an identical common Semitic verbal root with the original meaning "to split, divide." The etymological relationships to the collective noun /baqar/ "(cow) herd" (Hebrew *bāqār*),[1] also widespread in Semitic languages, on the one hand, whether as "cloven hoofed" or as "animal for plowing" (= splitting the earth), and to the specifically Hebrew time designation *boqær* "morning," or the break of day,[2] on the other hand, remain enigmatic; on balance, here, then, all the research of herds of grammarians and lexicographers have still not led to a breakthrough and divided the truth from speculation.

Depending on the construction, the Aramaic verb *bqr* can take on a variety of nuances. The object of the investigation is usually introduced with the preposition *b-* or *l-*, sometimes in a subordinate clause following *hn* "of" (Ezr. 5:17), and can be defined more precisely with *ʿl* "concerning" (Ezr. 7:14). As a transitive with a direct object, *bqr* is employed in the sense of "to test" with an optional added adverbial phrase introduced with *mn* "for."[3] The Dt-stem functions as a passive. Due to the correspondence of *ybqr* in Ezr. 4:15 with *ytbqr* in 5:17, Beyer[4] posits an otherwise unattested passive of the D-stem for the first passage; others emend it to read *ytbqr* (cf. *BHS*; otherwise, it must involve an impersonal passive, "one should investigate").

II. Biblical Aramaic. The earlier instances all appear in Biblical Aramaic, namely in Ezr. 4:15,19; 5:17; 6:1; 7:14. They refer to official Persian investigations prompted by royal decree in the state archives where past decisions with the character of precedent were preserved (→ *dkr* III), or to Ezra himself (7:14) examining the inhabitants of Judah and their living conditions.[5]

III. Qumran. In later Aramaic languages, more general usages of this verb are also documented, beginning with the texts from Qumran: for the inventory of one's own property (1QapGen 22:29, here with *mnī* "to count"), for the inspection of a building (*bnyn*, 4Q243 10:3, → *bnh*; although absent a broader context), and in the wisdom admonition "Inquire after [*bqr*] and seek [*bʿy* → *bʿī*] and know [*dʿ*, → *ydʿ*], what justice [*dyn*ʾ][6] requires!" (4Q541 24 2:4 [T.Levi]). The Aramaic Levi Document employs the same verb for the inspection of wood for (*mn*) worm infestation in the preparation of a sacrifice.[7]

---

1. Later also attested in Western and Eastern Aramaic literature: *DJPA*, 110; *DJBA*, 231; *LexSyr*, 88a; *MdD*, 49, etc.

2. Cf. J Bergman, H. Ringgren, and C. Barth, *TDOT*, "בֹּקֶר *bōqer*," II, 217-28.

3. Cf. *ATTM*, 1, 535; 2, 363.

4. *ATTM*, 2, 363.

5. See Steiner, 624-626 for a discussion.

6. According to the reading in *ATTM*, 2, 112; see the more extensive discussion by H. Gzella, "*dyn*," *ThWQ*, I, 677.

7. *ALD* 22 according to the Geniza manuscript Bodl. c; the parallel in 4Q214b 2-6(:2) does not retain it, however.

This broad usage continued later,[8] expanding in Jewish Palestinian to include "to take care of"[9] and "to clean, to clear away."[10]

IV. Uncertain *mbqr* "Overseer"(?). The precise nuance of the priestly title or attributive *mbqr'* remains entirely obscure (probably a substantivized participle, thus perhaps "[sacrifice] examiner?") in a handful of Nabatean inscriptions[11] as does its possible relationship to the title *mbqr* "overseer" in the Hebrew Damascus Document and the Community Rule from Qumran.[12]

Gzella

8. *DSA*, 111; *LexSyr*, 87b; *MdD*, 68.
9. Esp. involving the sick, see *DJPA*, 110b.
10. *ATTM*, 2, 363.
11. See *DNSI*, 187 for the citations and the relevant discussion.
12. Cf. Steiner, 643-46.

בר *br* /bar/; ברה *brh* /barā/

I. Etymology. II. General Aramaic Usage. III. Biblical Aramaic Usage. IV. Qumran. V. *brh*.

J. J. Collins, *Daniel. Herm* (1993), esp. 304-10; C. Colpe, "ὁ υἱὸς τοῦ ἀνθρώπου," *TDNT*, VIII, 400-77; F. M. Cross, "Notes on the Doctrine of the Two Messiahs at Qumran and the Extra-canonical *Daniel Apocalypse* (4Q426)," in D. W. Parry and S. D. Ricks, eds., *Current Research and Technological Developments on the Dead Sea Scrolls. STDJ* 20 (1996), 1-13; J. Eggler, *Influences and Traditions Underlying the Vision of Daniel 7:2-14. OBO* 177 (2000); S. E. Fassberg, "The Forms of 'Son' and 'Daughter' in Aramaic," in H. Gzella and M. L. Folmer, eds., *Aramaic in Its Historical and Linguistic Setting. VOK* 50 (2008), 41-53; J. A. Fitzmyer, "The Contribution of Qumran Aramaic to the Study of the New Testament," in idem, *A Wandering Aramean: Collected Aramaic Essays. SBLMS* 25 (1979), 85-113; D. Flusser, "The Hubris of the Antichrist in a Fragment from Qumran," *Immanuel* 10 (1980) 31-37; F. García Martínez, "The Eschatological Figure of 4Q246," in idem, *Qumran and Apocalyptic. Studies on the Aramaic Texts from Qumran. STDJ* 9 (1992), 162-79; idem, "Two Messianic Figures in the Qumran Texts," in D. W. Parry and S. D. Ricks, eds., *Current Research and Technological Developments on the Dead Sea Scrolls. STDJ* 20 (1996), 14-40; esp. 25-30; H. Gzella, "Deir 'Allā," in G. Khan, ed., *Encyclopedia of Hebrew Language and Linguistics* (Leiden, 2013), 1:691-93; H. Haag, "בֵּן *bēn*," *TDOT*, II, 147-59; idem, "בֶּן־אָדָם *ben 'ādhām*," TDOT, II, 159-65; J. Jokiranta, "*bn*," *ThWQ*, I, 462-73; O. Keel, "Messias und Menschensohn. Die zweistufige Messianologie der jüngeren Apokalyptik," *JBT* 8 (1993) 73-102; esp. 80-83; idem, "Das Reich der Heiligen und des Menschensohns. Ein Kapitel politischer Theologie," in idem, *Die Reiche der Welt und der kommende Menschensohn* (Neukirchen-Vluyn, 1995), 140-72, esp. 156-72; idem, "Die Tiere und der Mensch in Daniel 7," in idem and U. Staub,

I. Etymology. The etymology of the word *bar* is uncertain. According to *BLA* §51f, one must assume a word **bir* derived from the Proto-Semitic **bin*, although the transition *n* > *r*, which also occurs in Modern South Arabian, has not yet been explained. The derivation of the word from the root *br'* "to create" is dubious. Most likely, one can consider *bar*, like *ben*, a primitive word.[1] Regarding the various forms (including names in cuneiform) that developed over the course of the history of the Aramaic language, see Fassberg. Scholars have sometimes explained the unstable vowel by an original form /br/ with a syllabic /r/.[2]

II. General Aramaic Usage. In general Aramaic usage, the word primarily denotes "son." The most ancient texts already attest the term.[3] In the inscriptions from Sefire (circa 750 B.C.E), the expression *br br* denotes the grandson.[4] In addition, the word *br* with the meaning "son" appears in the inscription from Deir 'Allā (circa 700 B.C.E.).[5]

Already in early texts, *bar* also occurs with the meaning "member of a certain group," which appears frequently in later Biblical Aramaic and in Qumran. Thus, the expression *br 'nš* "son of man" already appears in Old Aramaic[6] as a designation for a person, i.e., a "member of humanity." *KAI* 222 B 3 offers in *bny gš* an early instance of the meaning "inhabitant (of Gush)," which is comparable to the use of *br* at Palmyra as a designation for a tribal member.[7] Members of a caravan (*bny šyrt'*)[8] or a cultic association (*bny mrzḥ*)[9] could also be designated *br*, as, e.g., the "members of the holy community" (*bny ḥbwrth qdyšth*).[10] Later Aramaic languages also exhibit many corresponding constructions with *br*.[11] In *TADAE* A4.7 (408 B.C.E.) the senders wish for the Persian governor as recipient that God grant him the goodwill of King Darius and his royal house (l. 3: *bny byt'*).

Hellenismus und Judentum. OBO 178 (2000), 1-35; K. Koch, *Das Buch Daniel. EdF* 144 (1980), esp. 214-34; É. Puech, "Fragment d'une apocalypse en araméen (4Q246 = pseudo-Dan^{d}) et le 'Royaume de Dieu,'" *RB* 99 (1992) 98-131; idem, "Notes sur la fragment d'Apocalypse 4Q246: 'Les Fils de Dieu,'" *RB* 101 (1994) 533-58; esp. 547-56; P. Sacchi, *Storia del Secondo Tempio* (Torino, 1994); G. Vermes, "The Present State of the 'Son of Man' Debate," *JJS* 29 (1978) 123-34; R. Zadok, *On West Semites in Babylonia during the Chaldaean and Achaemenian Period* (Jerusalem, ^{2}1978).

1. Haag, "בֵּן *bēn*,"149.
2. R. D. Hoberman, "Initial Consonant Clusters in Hebrew and Aramaic," *JNES* 48 (1989) 25-29.
3. Ninth century B.C.E. Tell Fekheriye (*KAI* 309) 6; Tell Dan (*KAI* 310) 7,8; cf. *DNSI*, 188-95; for cuneiform occurrences, cf. Zadok, 106-8 and *ATTM*, 535.
4. *KAI* 223 C 14; 224.1,12,15,25; for later instances, cf. *DNSI*, 193f.
5. J. Hoftijzer and G. van der Kooij, *Aramaic Texts from Deir 'Alla. DMOA* 19 (1976) (*KAI* 320), I:2; VIIId 2; regarding their relationship to Aramaic, see Gzella (bib.).
6. *KAI* 224.16.
7. E.g., Inv XI 83:2; *CIS* II 3922.2.
8. *CIS* II 3916.2, etc.
9. RTP 301.1; cf. *PAT* 349a.
10. ggBS 1.1 (*ATTM*, 377).
11. Cf. *DJPA*, 97-101; *LexSyr*, 89-94.

III. Biblical Aramaic Usage. In Biblical Aramaic, *bar* primarily denotes the relationship between father and son. It can also express any other family relationship, as well a close relationship between two people or things. In reference to direct descent, i.e., to the son begotten by the father, one should note Dnl. 5:22 (*bᵉreh* "his son," said of Belshazzar, Nebuchadnezzar's son), 6:25 (*bᵉnēhōn* "their sons/children," i.e., the people who had accused Daniel), Ezr. 5:2 (Zerubbabel, Shealtiel's son, and Jeshua, the son of Jozadak); Ezr. 6:9, where *bᵉnē ṯōrīn* means young bulls, should be understood in the same sense. The term *bar* also denotes other relationships: in Ezr. 5:1; 6:14 in the expression *zᵉḵaryā bar ʿiddō* "Zechariah, 'son' of Iddo," *bar* apparently denotes "grandson" (cf. Zech 1:1). In Ezr. 6:10; 7:23, *ūḇᵉnōhī* in the phrase *malkā ūḇᵉnōhī* "the king and his sons" refers generally to the descendants of the king. The term *bar* also often designates people as members of a certain group (→ II) since the word connotes a close connection. This is the case in Ezr. 6:16 (*bᵉnē yiśrāʾēl . . . bᵉnē gālūṯā* "Israelites . . . the exiles"; cf. Dnl. 2:25; 5:13; 6:14); Dnl. 2:38 (*bᵉnē ʾᵃnāšā* "human beings"; cf. 5:21); 3:25 (*bar ʾᵉlāhīn* "a divine being").[12] Finally, when followed by the word *šᵉnā* "year" and a number, *bar* refers to age; cf. Dnl. 6:1 (*kᵉḇar šᵉnīn šittīn wᵉṯartēn* "when he was 62 years old").

Based on the few occurrences in Biblical Aramaic, it is not possible to determine a precise theological value for *bar* "son" (in contrast to the Heb. *ben*) in the human realm. The expression *kᵉḇar ʾᵉnāš* "like a son of man," which occurs in Dnl. 7:13, is particularly significant, however. Although it appears in this passage as a symbol of the chosen people (→ *ʾnš* III), it should be emphasized that its interpretation beyond the context of Dnl. 7:13f. in later reception exhibits a distinctively different development. In the dream visions of 1 En. 37–71, the son of man (identified with Enoch, sufficient evidence to rule out a Christian origin for the work, cf. 1 En. 71:14 and Sacchi 370) is the one who will execute final judgment, as also in the NT the son of man has a messianic function.

IV. Qumran. The same meanings as in Biblical Aramaic are attested in the texts from the Dead Sea. These texts, however, offer a greater differentiation in meanings and, therefore, permit a more precise interpretation of difficult biblical passages. Here, too, *br* chiefly means "son" (e.g., 4Q543 1), from which derive the designations for other degrees of relationships: *br br* "grandson" ("son's son," 1QapGen 12:16), *br ʾḥ* "nephew" ("brother's son") 1QapGen 20:11,34; 21:7,34; 22:3,5,11; 4Q196 2:9 [Tob. 1:22: ἐξάδελφος]), and *br dd* "cousin" ("uncle's son," cf. 4Q197 4 3:5 [Tob. 7:2: ἀνεψιός]). The possible use of simple *br* in the sense of "grandson," which is uncertain in Ezr. 5:1; 6:14, finds confirmation in the Aramaic T. Levi where Isaac calls Levi *bry*.[13]

For a theological understanding of the term "son," 1QapGen 22:33 (cf. Gen. 15:2f.) is important. This text involves the futility of a human life that cannot extend itself in sons.

The Qumran text most important for an analysis of the theological significance of the word *br*, however, is 4Q246.[14] The manuscript can be dated paleographically to the last

---

12. Cf. Haag, "בֵּן *bēn*," 157, who relates the expression "with the ancient Near Eastern concept of the community of divine or heavenly beings."

13. CTLevi, HS Bodl b 9.11.15.

14. *DJD*, XXII (1996), 165-84.

third of the first century B.C.E.; it reports how a nameless figure falls before the throne of a king, afraid because of dream visions, and explains the dream vision as referring to bloodshed in the regions of the kingdom because of a mighty king. Thereafter, however, a figure will appear whom all will serve called the "son of God" and "son of the Most High" (2 1: *brh dy ʾl ytʾmr wbr ʿlywn yqrwnh*). The realm of the mighty kings will fall and God's peace will reign for the people. Then there will be no more war; everyone will live in peace. All prayers will honor this "son of God" and "son of the Most High"; his power is the very God with whose help he will subject the nations for eternity.

The interpretation is controversial: according to J. T. Milik,[15] the interpretation of the dream vision relates to the Seleucid era and the mysterious figure called "son of God" and "son of the Most High" is probably Alexander Balas (150-145 B.C.E.), whom coin inscriptions called Theopator (Θεωπάτωρ). In contrast, Fitzmyer underscores the apocalyptic character of the text: the introduction of the heir to the Davidic throne begins in 1:8 and the titles mentioned are conveyed upon this heir. According to Flusser, the king whom all will serve is the demonic figure identified in Christian writings with the antichrist. García Martínez thinks that the mysterious figure may be an angel, perhaps Michael, Melchizedek, and the Prince of Light mentioned in other Qumran texts, and the kingdom of eternal peace that of the people of God that follows the final eschatological battle. One can assume with Puech ("Fragment d'une apocalypse," 126) that the figure displayed in the dream vision is Daniel; in contrast, it remains difficult to decide whether the figure called "son of God" and "son of the Most High" should be understood in a positive (possibly as the messiah)[16] or in a negative (Alexander Balas or Antiochus IV)[17] sense.

Here, too, the word *br* denotes a person as a member of a certain group, sometimes in theologically significant expressions.[18] In the Testament of Amram (4Q543–4Q548), whose earliest manuscript stems probably from the middle of the second century B.C.E. judging on paleographic grounds, Amram, the father of Moses and Aaron relates a vision to his sons in his hour of death. In this vision, a good and an evil angel struggle over possession of the soul of Amram.[19] The adherents of the two angels are called "sons of light" (e.g., 4Q548 1 2:2,16: *bny nhwrʾ*; cf. *bny brktʾ* "sons of blessing" [l. 5] or *bny ṣ[dqth]* "sons of righteousness" [l. 7]) and "sons of darkness" (e.g., 4Q548 1 2:2,11: *bny ḥšwkʾ*) or "sons of lying" (so 4Q548 1 2:2,8: *bny šqr*). In Qumran's predeterministic perspective, there is no doubt that this expression designations two groups of people whom God has destined for salvation (light) or damnation (darkness), cf. 4Q548 1 2:2,9f.: [. . . *kl bny nhwrʾ*] *nhyryn lhwwn* [*wkl bny*] *ḥšwkʾ ḥšykyn lhwwn* "[. . . All sons of light" will be bright and "all sons of] darkness will be dark"; similarly 4Q542 (Testament of Qahat) 1 ii 8: *wyʿdwn kwl bny ršʿ*[ʾ . . .]: "And all the sons of iniquity will vanish."

15. Cf. Fitzmyer, 92.
16. Cf. Cross.
17. Cf. *ATTM*, 2, 146f.
18. For additional instances, see *ATTM*, 536f.; 2, 363f.; Jokiranta, 472f.
19. Cf. H. Gzella, "*dyn*," *ThWQ*, I, 675f.

V. *brh*. The OT does not attest the lexeme *brh* "daughter." It is attested, however, as a neologism built on *bar*[20] since the eighth century B.C.E. on a seal.[21] Imperial Aramaic continued to spell the construct state *brt* for some time, even when transcriptions suggest the pronunciation /baṯ/.[22] Essentially, *brh* designates the daughter as begotten by her father, and the word appears often in this sense in contracts stemming from Elephantine where, in many cases, parties to contracts explain that the conditions of the contract also pertain to the sons and daughters.[23]

This basic meaning is also attested at Qumran: 4Q197 4 1:17.[18] (Tob. 6:1f.) employs *brh* to designate Sarah as Raguel's daughter (cf. 4Q197 4 2:5 [Tob. 6:13]), 4Q545 1 1:5 for Miriam as Qahat's daughter, and 1QapGen 12:16 for the daughters of the sons of Noah. A few specialized meanings of *br* also occur at Qumran for *brh*, cf. 1QapGen 20:34, where *bnt* [*mṣryn*] means "Egyptian," and 4Q545 1 1:6, where *brt tltyn šnyn* denotes a "thirty-year-old."

Martone

---

20. So already *ATTM*, 537; cf. Fassberg, 49f.
21. Cf. N. Avigad, "New Light on MSH. Seal Impressions," *IEJ* 8 (1958) 228-30.
22. *ATTM*, 537.
23. E.g., *BMAP* 3.4,15,17,18; 4.13; 5.5.

בר *br* /barr/; ברא *br* /barrā/; ברי *bry* /barrāy/

I. Noun "Open Field." II. Adverb "Out." III. Adjective of Affiliation "Outside."

I. Noun "Open Field." The noun *br* /barr/ "open field" (a *qal* formation with a different origin than → *br* /bar/ "son") occurs often in the fixed expression *ḥwyt br'* "the animals of the field" (Dnl. 2:38; 4:9,18,20,22,29; 1QapGen 13:8), sometimes also as a real estate term in the legal texts from the Dead Sea[1] and presumably in an entirely general sense as *bbr'* "in the field = outside" in a Clermont-Ganneau Ostracon.[2] Along with the adverbial ending /-ā/,[3] however, it is the basis of the common adverb *br'* "out" (→ II) and adjective *bry* "outer" (III). Its antonym is → *gw* /gaww/ "inner," which forms similar adverbial expressions and also forms a corresponding adjective of affiliation.

ATTM, 537f.; 2, 365; H. Lozachmeur, *La collection Clermont-Ganneau*, 2 vols. (Paris, 2006).

1. *ATTM*, 2, 365.
2. Lozachmeur, No. 97.4; two other instances in the same corpus, nos. 211 and X10, remain unclear.
3. *ATTM*, 537f.

II. Adverb "Out." As a lexicalized adverb *br'* /barrā/ "out," an original /barr/ already appears in the pre-Imperial Aramaic sayings of Aḥiqar.[4] It can be employed locally or logically and be combined with other prepositions. Since the Imperial Aramaic texts from Elephantine, *br(')* *mn* "out from" is attested quite often,[5] also at Qumran[6] and later.[7]

III. Adjective of Affiliation "Outside." The adverb of affiliation *bry* /barrāy/ "outside" is formed from the same root through the *nisbe* ending /-āy/. It occurs often in the vision of the new Jerusalem from Qumran; the feminine *bryt'* appears there in a substantive function "public place."[8] Additional instances occur at Hatra. Later, Jewish Babylonian usage, in particular, attests many prepositional combinations.[9]

Gzella

---

4. *TADAE* C1.1, 93: "out."
5. Cf. *DNSI*, 195 and recently supplemented with Clermont-Ganneau No. 35cv,4 and 68cc,3; according to *ATTM*, 537, *br* is a defective spelling.
6. 2Q24 8:7.
7. See *DJPA*, 110bf. for Palestinian Jewish usage; *DJBA*, 239f. for Babylonian; *LexSyr*, 88 for Syriac; and *MdD*, 228 for Mandaic.
8. 4Q554 2 2:14; 2 3:17.20; 5Q15 1 1:1; 1 2:2.
9. *DJBA*, 240f.

ברך *brk*; ברכה *brkh* /barakā/; ברך *brk* /berk/; ארכבה *'rkbh* /'arkobā/

I. Etymology. II. General Aramaic Usage. III. Biblical Aramaic. IV. Qumran. V. "Knee," "to Kneel."

I. Etymology. Most lexica distinguish two roots: *brk* I "knee, to kneel" and *brk* II "to bless, praise."[1] Others assume one root,[2] although it seems forced to derive both meanings

---

J. K. Aitken, *ThWQ*, "*brk*," I, 521-29; C. A. Keller and G. Wehmeier, "ברך *brk* pi. to bless," *TLOT*, 266-82; C. W. Mitchell, *The Meaning of BRK "To Bless" in the Old Testament. SBLDS* 95 (1987); J. Scharbert, "ברך *brk*," *TDOT*, II, 279-308; idem, "'Fluchen' und 'Segnen' im Alten Testament," *Bib* 39 (1958) 1-26; W. Schottroff, *Der altisraelitische Fluchspruch. WMANT* 30 (1969); G. Wehmeier, *Der Segen im Alten Testament: Eine semasiologische Untersuchung der Wurzel brk. ThDiss* VI (1970).

1. *GesB* and *GesB*[18], *KBL*[2] and *KBL*[3], *DCH*, in reverse order, also *DNSI*.
2. *BDB*, *WUS*, König, *TW*, *WTM*, Jastrow, and the Arabic lexica.

from a common origin.[3] Only NW Semitic and S Semitic[4] attest *brk* in the meaning "to bless, praise." In Old South Arabian[5] and Egyptian,[6] the lexeme occurs as a NW Semitic loanword; it occurs in cuneiform in proper names.[7] Moreover, an etymological relationship with the Akkadian equivalent *karābu(m)* "to pray, dedicate, bless, greet" has been posited.[8] The assumption of metathesis of the first and third radical is, however, uncertain.

II. General Aramaic Usage. Old Aramaic has not yet given evidence of the root. Occurrences begin with Imperial Aramaic and are represented thenceforth in all levels of the Aramaic language.[9] Beyond personal names,[10] it occurs primarily in two usages: 1. as a greeting formula in letters, and 2. as a wish for blessing in grave and dedicatory inscriptions. 3. The customary usage in Hebrew and Biblical Aramaic in the sense of "to praise (God)" constitutes an exception.

1. The finite verb (pael) appears as a greeting formula in the Hermopolis-Papyri from the fifth century B.C.E.,[11] usually in the 1cs perfect + a 2ms/2fs suffix *brktk(y) lptḥ* "I bless/greet you before Ptah"[12] and once in the 1cp perfect + 2fp suffix *brknkn lptḥ* "We bless/greet you before Ptah."[13] It involves a formula also attested in Phoenician and Hebrew.[14] In it, it is difficult to understand the preposition *l* instrumentally (synonymous with *b*), but only locally ("before Ptah") or in the sense of possession ("to make/declare the blessed of the deity").[15] The verbal construction presupposes the corresponding passive participle of the G-stem attested in Padua 1, l. 2: *brk 'nt [lyhw 'lh']* "Blessed be you [before Yahu, the God]."[16] The content of the greeting appears in the purpose clause that usually follows: *zy yḥzny/yḥwny'py(yn) bšlm* "so that I may see your countenance in salvation." Here as elsewhere, the direct wish for salvation and life [*šlm wḥ*]*yn šlḥt lky* "I send you salvation and life"[17] can appear in place of the greeting, which recommends the addressee to the deity and the deity's blessing.[18] A combination of the two appears in an ostracon from Elephantine,[19] ll. 2-3: *šlm wḥyn šlḥt lk brktk lyhh wlḥn^{w}m* "Salvation and life I send you,

3. Wehmeier, 8-17; Scharbert, "'Fluchen' und 'Segnen,'" 17f.; Mitchell, 8-16.
4. Ugar., Phoen.-Pun., Heb., Aram., Arab., Eth.
5. W. Müller, "Altsüdarabische Beiträge zum hebräischen Lexikon," *ZAW* 75 (1963) 307.
6. Wehmeier, 18-66; Schottroff, 178-98; Scharbert, "ברך *brk*," 283-84.
7. *ATTM*, 538; *KBL*³, 1683.
8. *AHw*, I, 369f. 445f.; *CAD*, VII, 62-66; VIII, 192-98; see also B. Landsberger, "Das 'Gute Wort,'" *MAOG* 4 (1928/29) 294-321; cf. OSA *krb* "to dedicate, sacrifice."
9. *KBL*³, 1683.
10. *AP*, *BMAP*.
11. *TSSI*, II no. 27 = *TADAE* A2.1-7, and D1.1.
12. Hermopolis 1.2; 2.2; 3.1f.; 4.2; 6.1f.; 8.1f.
13. Hermapolis 5.1f.; regarding the perfect in cases of coincidence, cf. H. Gzella, *Tempus, Aspekt und Modalität im Reichsaramäischen. VOK* 48 (2004), 212-14.
14. *KAI* 50; Renz-Röllig KAgr(9) 8.1-2; 9.4-6; Arad(8) 40.3; Arad(6) 16.2-3; 21.2.
15. Wehmeier, 54, etc.; Renz-Röllig II/1, 30f.
16. *TSSI*, II No. 28 = *TADAE* A3.3.
17. Herm 7.1.
18. Cf. Renz-Röllig II/1, 14f.
19. Clermont-Ganneau 70 = *TADAE* D7.21, text following *TADAE*.

I bless you [i.e.,: declare you hereby blessed] before Yahu and Chnum," if one should not read a suffixed noun.[20] An ostracon from Aswan,[21] whose formulation seems to be a contraction of the two (*brk*[*h*/*t*?] *šlḥt lky* "I send you the blessing/blessings [i.e., of the gods]"), may give evidence that the noun also found use in the greeting formula.

2. As a wish for blessing in burial and dedicatory inscriptions, one encounters mostly the passive participle of the G-stem (peal). Instances are widespread.[22] In the Imperial Aramaic texts from Egypt—burial inscriptions from Sakkara[23] and Memphis,[24] Karpentras Inscription,[25] Graffiti from Abydos[26] and others with various provenance[27]—the formula *bryk* PN *qdm* GN or *bryk* PN *l* + GN "Blessed be PN before DN" (in many variations) dominates. With it, a third party delivers the deceased or the author of the graffiti delivers him- or herself to the deity, usually Osiris, but also Isis, Horus, Chnum, Min, or Šamaš, and to the blessing emanating from the deity.

Occasionally, the abbreviated form *bryk* PN "Blessed be PN" with no mention of the deity occurs. In the Nabatean inscriptions from various locales, it is the rule.[28] The short form, in particular, indicates that the wish for blessing is not tied to certain deities and is not related to the time after death in every case. It combines often with other elements common otherwise in the Nabatean memorial inscriptions, elements such as *dkyr* PN "May PN be remembered" (→ *dkr*), → *šlm* "well-being" or *lṭb* "for the best" (→ *ṭyb*), and *lʿlm* "forever" (→ *ʿlm*), e.g., in the formula *dkyr wbryk* PN.[29] In turn, this formula is the rule in Assur and Hatra and appears here, as in the Imperial Aramaic texts from Egypt, along with reference to the deity: *dkyr wbryk* PN *qdm* . . . (*lṭb wlšnpyr*) "May PN be remembered and blessed before . . . (for the good and the beautiful)."[30] (In reference to the king, the passive participle appears once in the construct state: *bryk ʾlhʾ*, par. *plḥ ʾlhʾ* "Statue of the king . . ., of the votary, blessed of god").[31]

The passive participle of *brk* also appears occasionally in Palmyra, predominantly in the plural and, as in Assur and Hatra, in combination with *dkr* "to remember." Yet, as is typical in Akkadian and Phoenician-Punic inscriptions,[32] the finite verb form, in fact the impf. (pael), usually appears. The chief examples are the tesserae,[33] on which the following formula occurs often, for example: *bl* (*nbw*) *ybrk l* + PN "May Bel (Nebo)

20. Cf. Scharbert, "ברך *brk*," 283.
21. *TADAE* D7.1 ll. 1-2.
22. *DNSI*, 200f.; Wehmeier, 49-53,56-62; Schottroff, 185-88.
23. *CIS* II 122 = *KAI* 267 = TSSI II No. 23 = *TADAE* D20.3, cf. also 20.4.
24. *RÉS* 1788 = *TADAE* D20.2.
25. *CIS* II 141 = *KAI* 269 = *TSSI*, II No. 24 = *TADAE* D20.5.
26. *CIS* II 126-134/*RÉS* 1364-1377 and 607-610/*TADAE* D22.8,9-27.
27. *CIS* II 135-136/*RÉS* 960-962/*TADAE* D22.40-44, further 22.29-33.46-51.
28. *CIS* II 385; 590; 868, etc.
29. *CIS* II 346-347; 534, etc.
30. *KAI* 244; 246 = Hatra 23; 25, cf. further Assur 12?; 14; 27d, i; 28a; Hatra 12; 77; 81; 146; 225; 296; 1016.
31. *KAI* 243 = Hatra 21.
32. Schottroff, 179ff.
33. H. Ingholt, et al., *Recueil des Tessères de Palmyre*. *BAH* 58 (1955).

bless PN."[34] If the force of blessing is understood as an independent entity, a well can also "bless"[35] or "be blessed (and consequently rich in blessing)."[36] The pael impf. also appears in a papyrus in Demotic script (from Syria?),[37] in which a person addressed in the second-person singular is called to the attention of the blessing of Baal, Bel, and Nabu and their partners from their earthly dwellings (col. VII:3-6): *ybrk'k' b'l mn ṣ'p'n'* etc. "May Baal bless you from Zaphon, etc." If Porten-Yardeni[38] has correctly emended the Aramaic version of the Behistun Inscription Sachau pl. 56:4 rev., ll. 2-3,[39] the impf. of the root *qll* stands as the antonym: ("If you do not conceal the truth") *'hwrmzd yb[rkk* "Ahura Mazda will bless you"—("If you conceal it") *'hwrmzd yq[llk* "Ahura Mazda will curse you."

Schottroff[40] derives the rich formulaic material, especially the participial blessing formula limited to Aramaic and Hebrew, from the original *Sitz im Leben* of the greeting. The use of the finite verb form in letters and the thorough agreement in content with corresponding greeting formulas in the ancient Near East speak for this position. The nomad hypothesis built of the antagonism between cultivated land and wilderness is not necessary.

3. Only Palmyra attests to the application of the participial blessing formula to the gods, indeed usually the anonymous god as the grammatical subject so that the word assumes the meaning "to praise": *bryk šmh l'lm'* "Blessed/praised be his name forever" = "(the one), whose name be blessed/praised forever," etc.;[41] reference to the gods by name also occurs, however.[42]

Scholars have attributed this singular usage in Aramaic inscriptions to Jewish influence.[43] In Palestinian Jewish Aramaic, besides the passive participle of the G-stem and of the pael with humans as subject in the meaning "bless" or "praise (God"), the ithpael is also attested.[44] In rare instances, one finds finite verb forms in the peal.[45] The increasing use of the noun in the inscriptions stands out.[46] Otherwise, the later phases of the language exhibit no peculiarities.[47]

III. Biblical Aramaic. Biblical Aramaic attests the root exclusively in the book of Daniel: the passive participle of the G-stem (peal) in Dnl. 3:28, the pael in 2:19 (pf. 3ms),

34. *RTP* nos. 92b; 108a; 109a; 110a; 134b; 304; 305; cf. also 242, further the Old Syriac inscriptions in Wehmeier, 62f.
35. No. 722.
36. *CIS* II 3976.
37. R. A. Bowman, "An Aramaic Religious Text in Demotic Script," *JNES* 3 (1944) 219-31.
38. *TADAE* C2.1 col. XI, §13 = CII I/V col. 5, §10, ll. 72-73.
39. *AP* S. 266.
40. 188-98.
41. A list of texts and variants in *CIS* II/3 992; LidzNE 153; the texts in *PAT*, 256 and passim.
42. *RTP*, no. 244.
43. Wehmeier, 61f.; however Schottroff, 187 n. 5 expresses doubt.
44. *DJPA*, 113f., Nabat. perhaps in *RÉS* 529,2.
45. Wehmeier, 65.
46. Wehmeier, 63f.; *DNSI*, 201f.; *ATTM*, 538f.
47. Palestinian Jewish, Palestinian Christian, Samaritan, Babylonian Jewish, Syriac, Mandaic, and finally the modern Aramaic languages.

4:31 (pf. 1cs), and 2:20 (pass. ptcp.). The meaning is always the same "to laud/praise (God)"; the direct object is regularly introduced with the preposition *l*. Occurrences occupy prominent positions in the framework of the narratives in Dnl. 1–6, almost all of which, after Daniel's programmatic prayer in 2:19-23, end with a hymnic cadence in the mouth of the pagan king (2:47; 3:28f.; 4:31-34, cf. also 3:31-33; 6:27f.). In the prayer in 2:19-23 Daniel gives thanks for the revelation of a mystery, namely the dream and its interpretation for which Nebuchadnezzar had asked the wise men of Babylon and which the God of Heaven had revealed to Daniel in a night vision (cf. 2:28ff.) in response to his plea (2:19). The thanksgiving and with it the praise go to the "God of Heaven" (*bārīḵ lǣᵡᵉlāh šᵉmayyā*, 2:19), whose "name be praised from eternity to eternity" (*lœhᵉwē šᵉmeh dī-ᵡᵉlāhā mᵉḇārak min-ʿālmā wᵉʿaḏ-ʿālmā*, 2:20) and whom Daniel describes (2:23) as "God of my fathers," i.e., whom he identifies with the God of Daniel and his three Jewish companions who also live in the Babylonian court (Dnl. 1 and 2:17f.). Introduced by the relative particle *dy*, various epithets for this God follow the praise of God's name: wisdom and strength, dominion over times and kings, the granting of wisdom and insight (2:21f.). In 3:28 King Nebuchadnezzar himself addresses praise to this God (*bᵉrīḵ ᵡᵉlāhᵃhōn dī-*), namely because this God had sent an angel and saved the three youths from the fiery oven. Subsequently, Nebuchadnezzar issues an edict (3:29; → *ṭʿm*) that places their constant confession of the one God (3:17f.,28) —this God—under the formal protection of the king with the threat of the death penalty (cf. 6:27f.). In 4:31 the pagan king—healed from his hubris through divine intervention and now looking heavenward—addresses his praise to the "Most High," the "King of Heaven" (4:34) whose dominion and realm endure eternally and who can act as he will on earth as in heaven (4:31f., cf. 3:33; 6:27f.).

With the exception of the Palmyra inscriptions, the usage of *brk* in Dnl. has no parallel in general Aramaic diction, but all the more in Biblical Hebrew, and here, taking into account the synonyms and contextual connections, especially in the Psalms.[48] The fact that this markedly theological (Jewish) discourse is placed in the mouth of a pagan king, and especially of Nebuchadnezzar, is neither parody nor subversive agitation, but arises from the particular theological, more precisely the *golah*-oriented and theocratic, concept of the Daniel narratives that has affinities with the theology of the late psalms (Ps. 103; 145) and Chronicles and which knows nothing yet of the eschatological-apocalyptic hopes of the Aramaic and Hebrew visions of Daniel in Dnl. 7; 8–12.[49]

IV. Qumran. In the manuscripts from the Dead Sea, the root occurs in the pass. ptcp. of the peal, in the pf., impf., impv. (4Q196 17 2:3 [Tob. 13:7] emended), and ptcp. of the pael, and also as a noun.[50] It occurs in three syntactic usages: 1. with people as subj. and obj.; 2. with God as subj. and people or things as obj.; 3. with people as the subj. and God as the obj.; and 4. in an uncertain context.

---

48. *TLOT*, 270,273,281f.; Scharbert, "ברך *brk*," 291-92; idem, "'Fluchen' und 'Segnen,'" 18f.; Mitchell, 133-64.

49. Cf. R. G. Kratz, *Translatio imperii. WMANT* 63 (1991), esp. 161ff.

50. *ATTM*, 538f. and 2:365.

1. In the rendition of the text of Gen. 14, 1QapGen 22:15f. cite Melchizedek's greeting of Abraham with the formula *brk* PN *l* + GN, reminiscent of the letter formula, here with the pass. ptcp. of the G-stem, in the greeting: *wbrk l*[ʾ]*brm wʾmr bryk ʾbrm lʾl ʿlywn mrh šmyʾ wʾrʿ* "And he blessed Abram and said, 'Blessed be Abram before the God Most High, the Lord of heaven and earth.'" Also in the context of a greeting scene, Isaac blesses Levi alone in CTL Bodl. a, 14f. (4Q213b 4 emended), and Levi and his father in CTL Bodl. b, 4. Levi's blessing of his father and brothers and his father's and brothers' blessing of Levi in CTL Bodl. a, 21-23 occur in connection with the installation of Levi as the high priest of the eternal God. The construct state of the noun in 11Q10 14:7 (Job 29:13) also falls under the category of textual rendition. Following MT, it can be emended to read "the lost blessing came upon me" describing Job's just intervention on behalf of the weak. In the vision of the new Jerusalem (11Q18 16 2-17 i 1), the noun seems to designate a priestly procedure. Following the Ethiopic text, it is common to emend the superscription inspired by Deut. 33:1 in 4Q201 1:1 (1 En. 1:1) to read, "Words of blessing by which Enoch blessed the true elect, the. . . ."

2. The fact that God blessed Job again after his harsh fate appears in the textual rendition of Job 42:12 in 11Q10 38:9. The blessing includes a multitude of children, among other things, which also seems to be in mind in T.Lev. (4Q213a 1 2:6f.) with reference to the promises to Abraham and Sarah, if the emendations are correct. The noun in 4Q204 5:7 (1 En. 10:18) refers to the fertility of the earth after surviving the last judgment. Well-being and good conduct go hand in hand in this context. The planting of truth ([*n*]*ṣbt qwšṭʾ*) and the deliverance of the upright precede the sprouting of vegetation and the beginning of life in peace (5:4f.). This aspect of eschatological salvation stands in the foreground in the last testaments from Levi's family of priests: 4Q213 1 1:8 (T.Lev.[a]; emended following CTL Cambridge e, 14) promises a "blessed yield" (*ʿllh br*]*kh*) for those who act in justice and truth (1 1:6f.), for: Whoever sows good will reap good, but seed will fall back upon the one who reaps evil (1 1:8f.).[51] 4Q542 1 2:3 (T.Qahat) promises "eternal blessings" (*brkt ʿlmʾ*) and compares them to the "whole word of (eternal) truth" (1 2:1f.), the possession of which distinguishes the "families of the truth" from the "sons of evil" (1 2:8). Finally, 4Q548 1:5 (the Testament of Amram) speaks of the "sons of the blessing" (*bny brktʾ*), who are identical with the "sons of righteousness" and the "sons of the light" and are contrasted with the "sons of the lie" and the "sons of darkness" (1:7-16).

3. The root takes on the meaning "to laud, praise" in prayer and hymnic praise of God, which—on the trajectory from Dan. 1–6, late psalms, and Chronicles—stamps the theology of the (pre-Qumran) apocrypha and the genre of the rewritten Bible.[52] Thus, it comes as no surprise that in the Aramaic version of the book of Tobit, the praise of the holy name of God and other formulas appear in the prayer of Sarah in Tob. 3:11 (4Q196 6:7 emended), and in the great hymn in Tob. 13, preserved to a degree in v. 7 (4Q196 17 2:3 emended) and v. 18 (4Q196 18:11). Praise also appears in a certain frequency in 1QapGen: 5:23 in the preflood period (*mbrk lmrh kwlʾ*); 12:17 after the flood and in place

---

51. Cf. H. Gzella, "*ʿll*," III, *ThWQ*, III, 129.

52. See R. G. Kratz, *Das Judentum im Zeitalter des Zweiten Tempels. FAT* 42 (^{2}2013), 187-226,245-279,280-311.

of the blessings in Gen. 9:20-27 (*whwyt mbrk lmrh šmy' l'l 'lywn lqdyš' rb' dy plṭn' mn 'bdn'* "and I praise the Lord of heaven, God Most High, the great Holy One who saved us from perishing"); 20:12f. in Abraham's imploring night prayer concerning Sarah's fate in Egypt, which is transmitted elsewhere only in Philo and Josephus, and clearly recalls Dnl. 2:20-22 (*bryk 'nth 'l 'lywn mry lkwl 'lmym dy 'nth mrh wšlyṭ 'l kwl' wbkwl mlky 'r'' 'nth šlyṭ lm'bd bkwlhwn dyn wk'n* . . . "Praised be you, God Most High, my Lord, in all eternity, you who are Lord and powerful over all and are powerful over all the kings of the earth in order to hold judgment over them, and now . . ."); 21:1-4 in the sacrifice in Bethel after returning from Egypt in the fulfillment of Gen. 13:4 (*wqryt tmn bšm mrh 'lmy' whllt lšm 'lh' wbrkt 'lh' w'wdyt tmn qwdm 'lh' 'l kwl nksy' wṭbt' dy yhb ly wdy 'bd 'my ṭb wdy 'tybny l'r'' d' bšlm* "And I called there on the name of the eternal Lord and praised the name of God and praised God and there thanked God for all the riches and goods that he granted me, and for the goodness that he did for me, and for allowing me to return to this land safely"); 22:16f. as the second element in Melchizedek's greeting (*bryk 'brm l'l 'lywn* . . . *wbryk 'l 'lywn dy* "Blessed be Abram before God Most High . . . and praised by God Most High, who . . ."). Shifted into eschatology and in reference to circumstances in heaven, the same prayer formulas appear in some parts of the Enoch literature, although they are only poorly preserved. The reading is usually uncertain: 4Q205 1 1:2 (1 En. 22:14: *lhwh bryk dyn qwšṭ*[' "Praised be the true Judge"); further 1 En. 9:4;[53] 36:4;[54] 77:1;[55] Book of Giants 13:3.[56]

4. *ATTM*, 2, 126f. (4Q558) and 134 J 7.13 (11Q18) are uncertain instances with no clear context.

V. "Knee," "to Kneel." The verb "to kneel, to fall down (in prayer)" is denominated from the substantive *brk* /berk/ "knee," which occurs in most Semitic languages[57] and with which *'rkbh* /'arkobā/ (Arab. *rukba*) "knee" is usually associated.[58] Not only Aramaic,[59] but also Hebrew, Ugaritic, Arabic, and Ethiopic[60] attest the verb. Hebrew *b^e^rēḵā* "pool" did not appear in Aramaic originally (the Targums adopt the Heb. lexeme in the pertinent passages). Apart from an uncertain specimen of the root in middle Persian Pehlevi,[61] the oldest and easily unique Aramaic attestation of both the noun and the verb is Dnl. 6:11. Contrary to the edict of the king, Daniel prayed facing Jerusalem three times daily by opening the window of his house, falling on his knee (*bārēḵ 'al-birḵōhī*), and praying before his God (*ūm^e^ṣallē ūmōḏē q^o^ḏām ^ʾæ^lāheh*). Despite the semantic proximity, this passage does not permit one to construe an etymological relationship between *brk* "to bless, praise" and *brk* "knee, to kneel." The use of *'arkubā* "knee" in Dnl. 5:6 is

53. *ATTM*, 237f.
54. Milik, *The Books of Enoch* (Oxford, 1976), 4QEn^c^ 1 13:30, pp. 203, 351.
55. *ATTM*, 255.
56. *ATTM*, 266, contrast 4Q203 9:3; Milik, 316f.
57. *KBL*^{3}, 153f.,1683; *GesB*^{18}, 179.
58. *KBL*^{3}, 1674; *ATTM* 523.
59. *KBL*^{3}, 1683.
60. *KBL*^{3}, 152; *GesB*^{18}, 177.
61. DNSI, 202.

purely anatomical:[62] When he saw the *Menetekel*, Daniel's face grew pale and his knees knocked together (*wᵉʾarkubāṯeh dā lᵉḏā nāqᵉšān*). In 4Q534 1:6, *ATTM*, 2, 163 reads *lmʾth lh ʿl ʾrkwbth* "to go to his knees."

Kratz

62. On the form, see *BLA* §241q′.

בשׂר *bśr* /baśar/

I. Etymology and Meaning. II. General Aramaic Usage and Ancient Translations. III. Biblical Aramaic. IV. Qumran Aramaic.

I. Etymology and Meaning. Many Semitic languages attest the noun *bśr* with the meaning "flesh," the substance of a human or animal body: in Ugaritic (*bšr*), Hebrew (*bāśār*), Aramaic (*bśr*; *bisrā*; *besrō*), Old South Arabian (*bs₂r*), and in a few Ethiopic languages such as Harari and Gurage (*bäsär*), as well as Gafat (*bäsärä*); Old Ethiopic *bāśor* is a rare loanword. Arabic *bašara* "skin" is also related to the primary noun, as may be Punic *bšr*, which presumably means "child, descendant." The noun does not occur in East Semitic, although the rare *bišru* "small child" in Akkadian used to be associated with it. In a few languages, such as Ugaritic, Hebrew, and Aramaic, *bśr* can refer in an expanded sense to the whole human body and euphemistically to the male organ. Yet another use for living being, human (so also Arabic *bašar*) or animal, appears in Hebrew and Aramaic. Overall, the spectrum of meaning of *bśr* in Aramaic corresponds to that in Biblical Hebrew.

II. General Aramaic Usage and Ancient Translations. The earliest attestation of Aramaic *bśr* to date appears in Aḥiqar,[1] where it refers to flesh as the substance of the body. In l. 184 *ʾkl bśrh* "eat his (a deer's) flesh" stands in parallel with *ʾšd dmh* "to pour out his blood" (→ *dm*), and according to l. 88 the flesh cannot offer any resistance to a knife. Outside Biblical and Qumran Aramaic, the only other ancient attestations are pap. Amherst 63 6:6, again in the construction *ʾkl bśrh* "to each his (a lamb's) flesh" and in parallel with "to drink his blood," and a few Imperial Aramaic ostraca from Elephan-

P. Altmann, *Festive Meals in Ancient Israel*. *BZAW* 424 (2011), 72-132; N. P. Bratsiotis, "בָּשָׂר bāśār," *TDOT*, II, 317-32; E. Jenni, "בָּשָׂר bāśār flesh," *TLOT*, 283-85; H. Lozachmeur, *La collection Clermont-Ganneau: Ostraca, épigraphes sur jarre, étiquettes de bois*, 2 vols. (Paris, 2006); E. J. C. Tigchelaar, "*bśr*," *ThWQ*, I, 537-47.

1. *TADAE* C1.1,88 and 184.

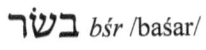

tine, there in relation to the delivery of food.[2] Later Aramaic languages exhibit greater attestation; it largely corresponds to the Hebrew findings, however (→ I). The ancient translations reflect this state of affairs: in Greek chiefly σάρξ, but also ζῷα[3] and σῶμα,[4] and in Frahang-i Pahlavīk 10:2 *gošt* "flesh."

III. Biblical Aramaic. In Biblical Aramaic, the noun appears in Dnl. 2:11, 4:9 and 7:5. According to 7:5, the second animal that arises from the sea in Daniel's vision (→ *db*) is commanded: "Eat much flesh!" (*'kly bśr śgy'*), apparently attributing to the Median kingdom the voracity of wild animals. In the Chaldeans' statement in 2:11, "flesh" refers to people in general and expressly in contrast to divine beings. The immediate context, however, produces no contrast between mortal humans and immortal deities, but between natural human knowledge and the divine knowledge of mysteries. In 4:9, the tree in the vision is said to nourish "all flesh" (*kl bśr*), which includes both the "animals of the earth" and the "birds of heaven" in the preceding lines, thus all living beings.

IV. Qumran Aramaic. In the Aramaic texts from the Dead Sea, *bśr*[5] occurs with the following meanings: 1. flesh, 2. body, 3. male member (?), and 4. humans or all living beings.

1. Twice *bśr* denotes flesh that is consumed: 4Q556a 5 1:9, in a fragmentary context, perhaps a prophecy *ex eventu* of the crisis under Antiochus, reads *'klyn bśr ḥzyr'* "eating pork flesh"; according to 4Q201 1 3:21 (*wlmkl bśr*[*hn*),[6] the giants eat each other's flesh. Sacrificial flesh appears in 1QapGen 10:15: *kwl bśrhwn ʿl mdbḥ' 'qṭrt* "I burned all their flesh on the altar," in a description of Noah's sacrifice after landing on Ararat. In 11Q18 13 6 (new Jerusalem), *bśr* serves as a designation of a bull's sacrificial flesh; in 11Q18 25 4, *bśrh* could be part of a section concerning the Passover sacrifice. Although *bśr* is usually distinguished from → *dm* "blood," in 4Q531 (4QGiants^{c}) 19 3 it stands in parallel with "bone": *l*['] *grmyn 'nḥn' wl' bśr* "we are neither bone nor flesh," in light of 19 4, presumably a description of the future state of the giants as bodiless evil spirits: *b*]*śr wntmḥh mn ṣwrtn'* "fl]esh, and we will be stripped of our form." The magical text 4Q560 1 1:3 mentions a male and a female poison that penetrates *bśr*, thus either into the flesh or into the body in general. In 11Q10 36:8 (Job 41:15), *bśrh* refers to the flesh of a crocodile.

2. In a pair of passages, *bśr* denotes the entire body, as in Aram. Levi 6:5:[7] *kʿn 'zdky bbśrk mn kl ṭwm't kl gbr* "Now, I consider you clean in your body from any uncleanness of any man" (→ *zkw*).[8] In 2Q24 1, *bśrhwn*, which appears out of context, could belong to a description of the cleansing of the bodies of priests.

---

2. S. Clermont-Ganneau, no. 233 and, in a partially destroyed context, perhaps 2 and 247.
3. OG Dnl. 4:9.
4. *ALD* Athos-HS.
5. Spelled phonetically in 4Q530 *bsr*.
6. See 1 En. 7:5 καὶ ἀλλήλων τὰς σάρκας κατεσθίειν.
7. The Aram. text is only preserved in MS Bodl. b.
8. γίνου καθαρὸς ἐν τῷ σώματί σου in the Athos MS.

3. In the Aramaic Levi 1:3,[9] *nzwrw ʿwrlt bśrkwn* "Trim the foreskin of your flesh!" may refer euphemistically to the male member, just as in comparable Hebrew expressions.

4. The expression *k(w)l bśr(')* "all flesh" consistently denotes humanity or all living beings. 4Q530 2 2+6-12,19 (4QGiants[b]) has the singular formulation *kl ḥy' wbsr'* "all living beings and (all) flesh"; the two expressions may have been chosen in order to include the giants and human beings. 4Q204 1 1:16 (*b*]*śr'*) preserves a part of 1 En. 1:9 καὶ ἐλέγξει πᾶσαν σάρκα, where "all flesh" stands in parallel with "all the evil" (πάντας τοὺς ἀσεβεῖς). In other passages, the context is fragmentary so that the precise referent of "all flesh" remains unclear. This applies to 1QapGen 1:25,29 (probably part of the flood account), 4Q213b 1 1,[10] 4Q214b 7 1, 4Q531 22 4, 4Q532 1 1:10 (a giant or watcher struggles against all flesh) and perhaps 4Q546 10 1. The state of the evidence demonstrates the "all flesh" is not a general designation for humanity and that the emphasis is not on fleshliness and thus on the mortality of living beings as such. This expression occurs especially in narratives about the flood or the Watchers or Giants; therefore, the frequent use of "all flesh" in Gen. 6–9 to distinguish people (and animals) from Watchers and Giants may influence its usage. At times, as in 1 En. 1:9 and perhaps in 1QapGen1, "all flesh" is associated with evil (as in Gen. 6:13 or Jer. 25:31) and with God's judgment.

Tigchelaar

9. MS Cambridge a.
10. The Aram. Levi text from Qumran reads *kl bśr*[', in contrast to the Geniza text's *kwlh*.

גאי *g'ī*; גאוה *g'wh* /ga'wā/

I. Etymology and Form. II. Meaning.

I. Etymology and Form. Although the root *g'ī* (probably from an older **g'ū*, as the /w/ in the noun *g'wh* indicates) "to be/become grand, haughty" is first attested in the literary Aramaic languages of late antiquity as a finite verb,[1] nominal derivatives already appear occasionally in earlier times. These include the feminine verbal noun *g'wh* /ga'wā/ "arrogance," which, after losing the glottal stop that closes the syllable with lengthening of the preceding /a/ in typical Aramaic fashion to /ē/,[2] can also be spelled phonetically

D. Kellermann, "גָּאָה *gā'āh*," *TDOT*, II, 344-50; J. Luzarraga, "El Magnificat (Lc 1:46-55) a través del arameo," *Gregorianum* 90 (2009) 5-27, esp. 19-21; H.-P. Stähli, "גאה *g'h* to be high," *TLOT*, 285-87; U. Thurnherr, "Stolz," *Historisches Wörterbuch der Philosophie* (Basel, 1998), 10:201-8.

1. In the Dt-stem, as in Palestinian Jewish Aramaic: *DJPA*, 118a; Syriac: *LexSyr*, 100.
2. See *ATTM*, 138f., with additional examples.

gwh[3] and appear in Masoretic pointing as *gēwā* (Dnl. 4:34); further the masculine adjective *g'h* /ga'æ/ "haughty" with retention of the original /'/.[4] Its usage largely corresponds to that of the Hebrew cognate *g'ī* and its various nominal derivatives.

II. Meaning. In usage, this root reflects the ambivalence of the feeling that it denotes. While in the Aristotelian doctrine of virtue, anyone who in his pride (μεγαλοψυχία) truly merits honor, the Judeo-Christian tradition usually emphasizes the vice of arrogance (*superbia*) as the dark side of pride; indeed, in view of the incomparable majesty of God (→ *hdr*), humility is more appropriate for human beings.

Thus, Nebuchadnezzar's hymnic praise of God in Dnl. 4:34 mentions in the same breath God's perfection and God's ability "to humble those who walk in pride" (*mhlkyn bgwh ykl lhšplh*). The three instances of *g'wh*/*gwh* and *g'h* in the Aramaic texts from Qumran also convey a negative connotation. All are in 11Q10 and all represent the corresponding Hebrew cognate with the same meaning in MT: in 34:6f. (Job 40:10f.) just as in Dnl. 4:34, they form a contrast to the majesty of God, who humbles the proud (with the verbal noun *gwh* in the first line probably as an *abstractum pro concreto* alongside *rm rwḥ* "arrogant of mind" and in parallel with the substantivized adjective *kl g'h* "every arrogant [person]" in the subsequent line), which is, in turn, represented by *lhšplh*. In 26:7 (Job 35:12), the construct form *g*]*'wt* appears in a genitive relationship with *b*]*'yšyn* "evil." According to a late Palestinian Jewish magical amulet from Egypt (probably fourth to sixth century C.E.), the serpent, the ancestor of the demon it charms, fell because of arrogance.[5]

In Palestinian-Jewish Aramaic, the verb *g'ī* also occurs, both for unjustified human arrogance and for justified grandeur;[6] since the seventh century C.E., the Hebrew noun *gā'ōn* has served as an honorific for rabbinic scholars.

Gzella

3. 11Q10 34:6 (Job 40:10).
4. 11Q10 34:7 (Job 40:11).
5. yyZZ 11:4 in *ATTM.E*, 242f.
6. *DJPA*, 118a.

גב *gb* /gobb/

I. General Usage. II. As a Lions' Den.

D. Helms, *Konfliktfelder der Diaspora und die Löwengrube. BZAW* 446 (2014), esp. 272ff.; J. A. Montgomery, *The Book of Daniel. ICC* (1927), esp. 268-81.

I. General Usage. The primary noun *gb* /gobb/ "den," related to the Arabic *ǧubb* "well, cistern, den," is distinct from the identically spelled *gb* for /gabb/ "side."[1] It appears in Nabatean in a combined building and dedicatory inscription for "water reservoir, cistern" alongside *ṣryḥy'* "the rock chamber."[2] Palmyrene also attests it, presumably with the same meaning, in the expression *bt gb'* "cistern building."[3] In this usage, it seems to overlap semantically with the noun *b'r*, also attested in Imperial Aramaic and in Nabatean.[4] As its usage in Dnl. 6 indicates, however, *gb* can also denote quite generally an apparently cistern-like, deep hole with a narrow opening, without necessarily assuming thereby the presence of water. The Hebrew equivalent *bōr* can also denote both "cistern" and "prison cell."[5]

II. As a Lions' Den. The other Aramaic instances stem from the story of Daniel in the lions' den in Dnl. 6 (*goḇ 'aryāwāṯā*, thus, determined and thereby already presupposing awareness of the first reference in 6:8) and appear there in high frequency: Dnl. 6:8,13,17f.,20f.,24a.b.,25 (→ also *'ryh*). Daniel, now in an exalted post, aroused the jealousy of other royal officials with his success at court; they conspired against him and succeeded in having him thrown into the lions' den because of his religion. There, however, he survived the night whereupon the king gave the slanderers over to the very death they had planned for Daniel.

In Mesopotamia, e.g., lions were indeed captured and kept;[6] but a realistic historical context for a royal lions' den for punishing the condemned outside of literary traditions cannot be demonstrated. Instead, this episode seems indebted to the topos, also widespread elsewhere, of the hero who survives being thrown into a hole (intensified sometimes with wild animals); cf., e.g., in the OT also Gen. 37:24 (Joseph) and Jer. 38:6 (Jeremiah). Both of these passages employ the term *bōr* (→ I).

Gzella

1. From an older */ganb/; cf. *ATTM*, 544.
2. RÉS 1432:1; the text with translation and commentary also in U. Hackl, H. Jenni, and C. Schneider, *Quellen zur Geschichte der Nabatäer*. *NTOA* 51 (2003), 219f.
3. *PAT* 1919.4; see *DNSI*, 207.
4. Cf. *DNSI*, 141f.
5. See *GesB*[18].
6. Cf. W. Heimpel, "Löwe," *RlA*, VII (1980-83), 81f.

גבר *gbr*; גבר *gbr* /gabar/; גבורה *gbwrh* /gabūrā/; גבר *gbr* /gabbār/; גברו *gbrw* /gabbārū/

I. Etymology and Forms. II. Noun "Man." 1. In the Full Sense. 2. As an Indefinite Expression. III. Noun "Strength." IV. Noun "Hero," "Giant." V. Noun "Powerful [One]."

I. Etymology and Forms. Forms of the root *gbr* "to be strong" belong to the common vocabulary of the Semitic languages. The verb seems to occur rather rarely in Aramaic and is unequivocally attested first at Qumran in texts,[1] but already appeared quite early as a component in West Semitic personal names *-ga-bar* and *-ga-ba-ri* in cuneiform texts from Muraššu around the middle of the first millennium B.C.E.;[2] thus, perhaps also in the name of the archangel Gabriel, if it is not a noun.

As a verbal root, *gbr* in older material at least twice in the G-stem with ingressive meaning (each supplemented with a prepositional phrase): once for an olive tree growing mightily in 1QapGen 13:13 (Noah's dream), *gbr brwmh* "it grew in stature";[3] finally, with a negative connotation of Abraham's increasing plagues in 1QapGen 20:18: *wgbrw ʿlwhy* "they became more intense for him." In contrast, the few other possible instances are uncertain. In 4Q531 22:3 (Book of Giants), occasionally a t-stem "to strengthen" is postulated with a prefix reconstructed in the lacuna; it is attested without doubt only later, however.[4]

Throughout Aramaic, however, the noun *gbr* /gabr/ "man" is very common. It can also function in the place of an indefinite pronoun (→ II); furthermore, /gabbār/ "hero" (→ IV) and the two related feminine abstracts *gbwrh* /gabūrā/ "strength" (→ III) and, rarer, *gbrw* /gabbārū/ "might" (→ IV) occur as well. Like the verb, they are neutral and could refer to power in the good or the evil sense.

II. Noun "Man."

1. In the Full Sense. If the noun *gbr* /gabr/[5] is used in the full sense of "grown man," it constitutes the antonym of /ʾettā/ "woman" (→ *ʾnth*).[6] The noun *gbr* can also distinguish the grown man from the child.[7] Men, women, and children fall under the categorical designation → *ʾnš* /ʾenāš/ "human being" alongside or in distinction to gods and animals.

H. Gzella, "Animacy," in G. Khan, ed., *Encyclopedia of Hebrew Language and Linguistics* (Leiden, 2013), 1:109f.; H. Kosmala, "גָּבַר *gābhar*," *TDOT*, II, 367-82; J. Kühlewein, "גבר *gbr* to be superior," *TLOT*, 299-302; T. Muraoka, *A Grammar of Qumran Aramaic. ANESSup* 38 (2011); E. D. Reymond, "*gbr*," *ThWQ*, I, 565-73; L. T. Stuckenbruck, *The Book of Giants from Qumran. TSAJ* 63 (1997).

1. A possible instance in the Old Aramaic state treaties from Sefire, *KAI* 223 B 19, continues to be disputed and could also be interpreted as a noun; cf. *DNSI*, 210.

2. *ATTM*, 540.

3. On the reading, see D. A. Machiela, *The Dead Sea Genesis Apocryphon. STDJ* 79 (2009), 58; *gbr* should probably be understood, with *ATTM*, 2, 367, as a perfect, not with J. Fitzmyer, *The Genesis Apocryphon. BietOr* 18/B (^{2}2004), 165 as an active ptcp.

4. *DJPA*, 120b; *DJBA*, 258, there also instances of the causative stem "to strengthen"; *LexSyr*, 102, which also lists a D-stem "to enliven."

5. Rarely also in the form /gubr/, e.g., in the pointing of the plural according to MT; see *ATTM*, 541 for additional instances.

6. Cf. *TADAE* B3.4,3 and 4Q197 4 1:13 (Tob. 6:8), where the Greek version renders the contrast with ἀνθρώπου ἢ γυναικός; if "woman" is used specifically for "wife," however, it contrasts with → *bʿl* /baʿl/ "husband."

7. So implicitly in 1QapGen 6:6; in contrast to *ʿlwmyn* "youths" in 11Q10 14:2 (Job 29:8), cf. II.2 below.

This very frequent nuance appears in Old Aramaic in the expression *gbr š‘wt’* “man of wax” in the description of a curse ritual in Sefire[8] and is very common throughout.[9] Indetermined, it evolves seamlessly into the general meaning “one of the. . .” (“a man of/in,” Dnl. 2:25; 5:11; 1QapGen 19:24; → II.2).

2. As an Indefinite Expression. Furthermore, *gbr* regularly appears in a faded sense for “someone” (with the negation *l’* “no one”: Dnl. 2:10) without specifically referring to a man; if necessary for additional precision, it can be juxtaposed with a form of *’nth* in order to explicitly include men and women together.[10] In this case, it assumes the role of an indefinite pronoun for indicating persons, for which Aramaic has no independent word.[11]

It is already attested with this gradation in Old Aramaic in the curse formula *kl gbr zy* “anyone who . . .”[12] and then regularly in Imperial Aramaic for “someone” in the legal diction of contracts: *gbr zy* “someone who/to whom”[13] or determined *gbr’ zy* “the one who,”[14] *gbr ’ḥrn* “someone else.”[15] A repetition as in *kwl gbr wgbr*[16] may represent a distributive “each person”;[17] for this Imperial Aramaic attests *lgbr lgbr*[18] or simply *gbr* with a verb in the first-person plural.[19] Similarly, *gbr . . . wgbr* denotes “one. . .another,”[20] for which one also later encounters *gbr . . .* → *ḥbr*.

Together with an adjective or participle, an adverbial complement or an apposition, *gbr* can represent an indetermined substantivized adjective “a/an. . .,” as in *gbr l’ lb*[*b*] “a heartless person,”[21] *gbr ṭb* “a good person” (ll. 99,100), *guḇrīn kaśdā’īn* “Chaldeans” in Dnl. 3:8 and *guḇrīn yᵉhūdā’īn* “Judeans” in Dnl. 3:12, *guḇrīn gibbārē-ḥayil* “elite soldiers” (Dnl. 3:20, → IV), *gbryn bḥryn lqrb* “the best for the war.”[22] It has the same function with indetermined numerical expressions.[23]

---

8. I A = *KAI* 222 A 39.

9. Cf., e.g., “those men” *TADAE* C1.1,56; Dnl. 3:12,13,22,23,27; 6:6, 12,16,25; Ezr. 4:21; 5:4,10; 6:8; often pejoratively for nameless enemies.

10. So in a legal text in *TADAE* B3.4,3 and in directions for an exorcism in 4Q197 4 1:13 (Tob. 6:8); → II.1.

11. Cf. Gzella; Muraoka, 155.

12. Sefire III = *KAI* 224,1f., similarly later *KAI* 228 A 12.

13. E.g., *TADAE* B2.10,11; so also in God’s verdict: 4Q536 2 2:13, further in a blessing formula in a Palmyrene inscription: *PAT* 1666.9.

14. *TADAE* B3.5,20.

15. *TADAE* B2.7,8,11; B3.5,19; it remains unclear in this case whether this expression differs from *’yš ’ḥrn* in B3.5,19f.

16. 2Q24 4:18.

17. See the translation of *DSSStE*, 218f.; the broader context is destroyed, however.

18. *TADAE* A6.9,4f.; B4.4,7.

19. *TADAE* B2.11,14.

20. 11Q10 38:7f. (Job 42:11).

21. Aḥiqar, *TADAE* C1.1,82.

22. 1QapGen 22:6.

23. Cf. *tltt gbryn mn* “three of” 1QapGen 19:24, determined, in contrast, *tltt gbry’* “the three men” in 22:23.

In 11Q10, *gbr* usually translates its homophonic Hebrew counterpart if used in the full sense of "grown man." A distributive expression, on the other hand, employs *'îš*.[24] It serves in 14:2 (Job 29:8), however, to render *yᵉšîšîm* "aged people."[25] Later Aramaic diction also corresponds overall with these findings.

III. Noun "Strength." The noun *gbwrh* /gabūrā/ "strength" occurs in Old Aramaic times in Sam'alian[26] in a partially destroyed curse formula with "bow" and "word,"[27] probably to express the various means forbidden for use to alter the inscription.

In the theological diction of the book of Daniel, the definite form *gbwrt'* "the strength" along with *ḥkmt'* "the wisdom" designates a characteristic attribute of God (Dnl. 2:20), who also grants these gifts, however, to select people like Daniel (2:23). The same combination continues to appear in later wisdom traditions such as the petitionary prayer of Levi;[28] as a divine and human attribute, *gbwrh* is also attested in Palestinian Jewish Aramaic.[29] The plural denotes "great deeds" in general,[30] the marvelous "mighty deeds" of God in the religious sense, thus first in the admonition to consider them in 11Q10 29:5 (Job 37:14, for the Hebrew *npl'wt*), but also later.[31]

IV. Noun "Hero," "Giant." The noun *gbr* /gabbār/ "hero"[32] exhibits the same *qattāl*-form as many designations for professions and persons who regularly perform certain procedures and, thus, as a characteristic.[33] Nonetheless, (although it is unattested in this meaning) it has also been derived from a denominal verb in the D-stem "to become a man" on the basis of /gabr/ "man."[34] As an epithet of the god Hadad, the Tell Fekheriye inscription[35] already attests it in Old Aramaic and it also appears in personal names.[36]

In Dnl. 3:20 the sole instance in the phrase *gibbārē-ḥayil* as a technical military term seems to mean "elite soldiers,"[37] in the context, probably members of the royal bodyguard who cast Daniel's friends into the oven. In the Aramaic texts from Qumran, the noun occurs only in the Book of Giants where it can only be distinguished from *gbr* /gabr/ "man," identical in the consonantal text, on the basis of its specific meaning. There it

24. 11Q10 38:7f. (Job 42:11).

25. For additional instances, see *DNSI*, 210f., *ATTM*, 541 and 2, 367.

26. Whose relationship to Aramaic is disputed, cf. H. Gzella, "Language and Script," in H. Niehr, ed., *The Aramaeans in Ancient Syria. HO* I/106 (2014), 71-107, esp. 74f.

27. *KAI* 214.32.

28. 4Q213a 1:14.

29. *DJPA*, 119a.

30. So also in a Palmyrene dedicatory inscription, *PAT* 1928.2, with the verb *'bd* "to do" and the prepositional phrase *'mhwn* "to/for them."

31. *DJPA*, ibid.

32. In Tiberian as in Hebrew vocalized *gibbōr* then /gibbār/; later also with orthographic dissimilation like Syriac *gnbr.*

33. Cf. *BLA* §51c'''.

34. So J. Fox, *Semitic Noun Patterns. HSS* 52 (2003), 260f.

35. *KAI* 309.12.

36. Cf. S. A. Kaufman, "Si'gabbar: Priest of Sahr in Nerab," *JAOS* 90 (1970) 270f.

37. Cf. *GesB*[18].

regularly refers to the giants who fathered the Watchers of human mothers,[38] often in the determined state of the plural *gbry'* "the giants." Yet it is not entirely clear whether the expression *gbryn wnpylyn* "giants and monsters"[39] refers to two distinct subgroups or the two terms are employed as synonyms.[40]

V. Noun "Powerful [One]." Instead of the more common nominal form *gbwrh* /gabūrā/, the likewise feminine abstract form *gbrw* /gabbārū/ occurs twice in the Book of Giants. Both passages refer to something supernatural, whether negative or positive. In 4Q531 22:3 (following another form of *gbr*, → I) *bḥsn gbrwty* "with the strength of my might" appears in the report of the leader of the fallen angels, Semyaza in parallel to the preceding *btqwp ḥyl dr'y* "with the violence of the might of my arm"; the concentration of synonyms for "power" reflects excess. In contrast, 4Q540 2 2+6-12:16 employs *gbrw'*[41] figuratively of a giant's impressive dream in which the ruler of heaven descends to earth, as in Dnl. 7:10, in order to pass judgment.[42] In later East Aramaic, this noun is employed generally for "mighty deed."[43]

Gzella

38. E.g., 4Q203 7a:7; 4Q530 1 1:8; 4Q530 2 2+6-12:3,13,15,20,21.
39. 4Q531 1:2.
40. Cf. Stuckenbruck, 111f.
41. With a purely orthographic ' to indicate the preceding long vowel.
42. Cf. H. Gzella, "*dyn*," *ThWQ*, I, 678.
43. *DJBA*, 259f.; *LexSyr*, 102; *MdD*, 72.

גו *gw* /gaww/; גוי *gwy* /gawwāy/

I. Etymology and Form. II. In Prepositional Expressions. III. Gentilic Adjective.

I. Etymology and Form. After the shortening of final long consonants in Aramaic, probably around 200-150 B.C.E.,[1] and the contraction of diphthongs,[2] the originally primary noun *gw* /gaww/ "interior" appears as /gō/.[3] The spelling *gw'* with a non-etymological ', which can mark a final long vowel especially in texts from Qumran but

ATTM, 541f.; 2, 368; *DNSI*, 215-17; H.-J. Fabry, "גְּוִיָּה *gᵉviyyāh*," *TDOT*, II, 433-38.

1. *ATTM*, 120-22.
2. Ibid., 116-20.
3. Rarely spelled phonetically *gh*, evidence of this phonetic rule; thus twice in a sales contract from the Dead Sea, V 45:4 in *ATTM*, 320f.

also sometimes in Biblical Aramaic,[4] is obviously secondary. Such spellings are not, however, clearly distinguishable from possible adverbial forms with an adverbial ending /-ā/.[5]

The original meaning as a noun, however, is hardly still in currency.[6] Usually *gw* occurs instead in lexicalized prepositional expressions, much like its antonym → *br* "outside."

II. In Prepositional Expressions. In combination with the prepositions *b-*, *l-*, and *min*, *gw* with a pronominal suffix or in construct state in nominal clauses and with verbs of movement[7] indicate either the place (*bgw* "in the interior of") or the direction (*lgw* "into" and *mn gw* "out of"). This usage is already attested in Old Aramaic;[8] in Imperial Aramaic, subsequently, not just in the local sense "upon, within," but also absolutely in the figurative "in this regard," as presumably first and foremost in the formal juridical diction of contracts.[9]

Later Aramaic follows the same usage; cf. Biblical Aramaic *lgw(ʾ)* "in . . . into" of the oven in Dnl. 3:6,11,15,21,23f., then *bgw(ʾ)* "in . . . within" (Dnl. 3:25)[10] and subsequently again *mn gw(ʾ)* "out . . . out of" (Dnl. 3:26). The scale has no significance; *bgw* can be used for "in the midst of a city" (Ezr. 4:15) or even "in the middle of the earth" (Dnl. 4:7; 1QapGen 19:12); in contrast, the difficult *bgwʾ ndnh* in Dnl. 7:15 should probably be emended following J. A. Montgomery to read *bgyn dnh* "hence."[11] Especially in the terminology of the chancellery, *bgw* is used for the interior of a letter or a document (Ezr. 5:7; 6:2).[12] It also appears in the frequency one could expect in the extensive architectural descriptions of the new Jerusalem from Qumran.[13]

Later, various additional combined prepositional phrases such as *lgw mn* "within" or *mn lgw* "inside" with a redundant *mn* appear,[14] while simple *lgw* is also used in the sense of "allotted to" (so in a synagogue inscription from the fifth century C.E. in the context of the donation of a sum of money for a mosaic).[15]

III. Gentilic Adjective. The adjective of affiliation *gwy* /gawwāy/ "located within" with a *nisbe* ending (analogous to its antonym *bry* /barrāy/ "outside," → *br* /barr/) is first

4. *ATTM*, 411.
5. Such as *brʾ* "outside"; cf. *ATTM*, 2, 368; → *br* /barr/.
6. The possible instance without a preposition *wgwʾ* in 1Q32 2:2 is a fragment without context, and the initial *w* is not entirely certain.
7. E.g., *ʿll* in 1QapGen 14:16,17.
8. *KAI* 202 B 3: *bgwh* "in its midst = among."
9. See, e.g., on the one hand, *TADAE* B2.4,6 *tb bgw ʿm ʾnttk* "live on it (i.e., on the previously described parcel of land) with your wife" and, on the other, B4.4,9 *wṭyb lbbn bgw* "our heart was satisfied with it."
10. Similarly 4Q206 4 1:14.17; 4 2:3 (1 En. 89:1,3,8).
11. *The Book of Daniel. ICC* (1927), 306.
12. Probably also *TADAE* B2.1,15 in reference to the list of witnesses and later still in contracts from the Dead Sea, which have roots in the same legal tradition: *ATTM*, 2, 368.
13. See, e.g., 4Q554 1 3:15.22; 5Q15 1 1:17 and 1 2:4; further examples in *ATTM*, 2, 368.
14. Cf. *ATTM*, 2, 368.
15. ggHA 4,4 in *ATTM*, 385f.

attested in the vision of the new Jerusalem[16] and demarcates there in the description of a block of houses an "inside" from an "outside" gate. It also occurs in Nabatean, Palmyrene, and the Aramaic from Hatra in the same meaning[17] and underlies only later attested nominal formation such as Syriac *gawwāyā* and *gawwāyūṯā* "inside."[18]

Gzella

16. 4Q554 2 3:16 par. 5Q15 1 1:18, in the immediate context with *bry*.
17. *DNSI*, 218.
18. *LexSyr*, 107.

גזר *gzr*; גזר *gzr* /gāzer/ or /gazzār/; גזרה *gzrh* /gazīrā/

I. Slaughter of Animals. II. Conclusion of a Contract. III. Circumcision. IV. Abscission. V. Fortune-telling. VI. "Determination," "Decision."

I. Slaughter of Animals. The basic meaning of the Aramaic verb *gzr* is "to cut," but its most frequent use seems indebted to a reference to the slaughter of animals for consumption by means of slitting the throat horizontally as in the ritual slaughter procedures of the Semitic peoples. In Arabic, too, *ğazara* means "to slaughter (an animal)," and *ğazzār* denotes the butcher. Thus, the Aramaic verb corresponds to the Hebrew *šḥṭ*.

The Sefire state treaties from the middle of the eighth century attest its use for the slaughter of animals. Here, *gzr* is often incorrectly translated "to cut into two parts." In the pertinent passages, one finds the (internal) passive: [*'yk zy*] *ygzr 'gl' znh kn ygzr mt''l wygzrn rbwh* "[just as] this calf is slaughtered, so may Mati'-'el be slaughtered, and may his nobles be slaughtered!"[1] An allusion to late-born lambs may yet occur in a fragmentary context, if *'pl'* there means the produce of the second harvest: *kn tgzr 'pl'*, "thus you will slaughter late-born."[2] In Aḥiqar[3] the metaphorical application of an everyday practice in the realm of wisdom indicates the precise nature of the slaughter: *mkdb gzyr*

ATTM, 542; 2, 368f.; *DNSI*, 220; A. Dupont-Sommer, *Exorcismes et guérisons dans les écrits de Qoumrân. SVT* 7 (1960), 246-61; M. Görg, "גָּזַר *gāzar*," *TDOT*, II, 459-61; E. Lipiński, "The Root *GZR* in Semitic," *AuOr* 17-18 (1999-2000) 493-97; idem, *Studies in Aramaic Inscriptions and Onomastics II. OLA* 57 (1994), esp. 72; D. J. McCarthy, *Treaty and Covenant. AnBib* 21a (²1978), esp. 92ff.; R. Polzin, "*Hwqy'* and Covenantal Institutions in Early Israel," *HTR* 62 (1969) 227-40, esp. 235ff.

1. Sefire IA = *KAI* 222 A 39f.
2. Sefire IB = *KAI* 222 B 43.
3. *TADAE* C1.1,134.

qdlh "a liar, his throat is slit." The dissimilated verb *ganzara* in Tigre, from the intensive **gazzara*, means "to cut into pieces."

II. Conclusion of a Contract. A blood rite seals the conclusion of a contract, usually the slaughter of an animal whose throat is cut. In the Amorite tradition of Mari, the expression *ḫayaram qatālum* "slaughter the foal of an ass" indicates the conclusion of a treaty, and a somewhat later text from Alalaḫ explicitly states that the throat of the sacrificial animal was cut while one pronounced the solemn oath formula.[4] The same practice also existed in ancient Greece, as indicated by formulations such as λαιμούς τινος τέμνειν[5] or τέμνειν σφάγια[6] "to slit the throat of a sacrificial animal." Thus, in Aramaic *gzr ʿdy'*, literally "to slaughter a contract,"[7] became the technical term for the conclusion of a compact. The same formula may appear in the inscription from Tell al-Qāḍi (*KAI* 309), l. 1′ (*wgzr*[.*ʿdy'*(?)])[8] and has parallels in the Hebrew *kāraṯ bᵉrîṯ*, in the Greek ὅρκια τέμνειν, or in the Latin *foedus ferire*. The Aramaic sources contain no trace, however, of a ritual in which one passed between the parts of a slaughtered animal or stood between them, although *gᵉzar qiyyām* in Targum Onqelos of Gen. 15:18 translates the Hebrew *kāraṯ bᵉrîṯ*.

III. Circumcision. Since circumcision was considered the sign of the covenant (Gen. 17:11f.) and consisted of the abscission of the foreskin (that covers the male organ) or a part of it, the Aramaic verb *gzr* could also be used in the sense of "circumcise" or "have oneself circumcised," like Classical Ethiopic *gazara*,[9] in Southern Ethiopic also *gär*(*r*) *äzä* with metathesis. This use of *gzr* corresponds, therefore, to the Hebrew *mûl*.[10] It appears in T.Lev. 21:21 referring to the account in Gen. 34:15: *gzrw ʿwrlt bśrkwn*, "circumcise the foreskin of your flesh." The same connotation of *gzr* is also widespread in Palestinian Jewish and Babylonian Jewish Aramaic, thus in Targum, Midrash, and the Talmud, but also in Mandaic[11] and in Syriac.[12] In addition, there are other corresponding verbal nouns, such as Syriac *gzārā*, which means "circumcision," while Syriac *gzūrtā* can denote either "circumcision," as in Mandaic,[13] or collectively "the circumcised." The *gāzūrā* is the "circumciser," but also the "butcher."

IV. Abscission. The use of *gzr* in the sense of "to circumcise" reflects its meaning "to cut off" (→ III). It is also attested in the state treaties from Sefire; there, the verb also refers to the possibility of deleting clauses of the treaty: *wlygr*[*zn m*]*lh mlky '*[*rpd*] *mnhm*,

4. See G. F. Hasel, "כָּרַת *kāraṯ*," *TDOT*, VII, 351.
5. Aristophanes, *Birds*, 1560.
6. Euripides, *Suppliants*, 1196.
7. E.g., Sefire IA = *KAI* 222 A 7.
8. See A. Biran and J. Naveh, "The Tel Dan Inscription: A New Fragment," *IEJ* 45 (1995) 12.
9. *CDG*, 211.
10. See G. Mayer, "מוּל *mûl*," *TDOT*, VIII, 158-62.
11. *MdD*, 87.
12. *ThesSyr*, 699f.
13. *MdD*, 86.

"and the kings of A[rpad] will not cut off a word from them."[14] Elsewhere, it appears in the reflexive-passive verb stems, as in the oldest known instance of the verb *gzr*, here still with a *t*-infix, in the Tell Fekheriye inscription: *wmwtn šbt zy nyrgl ʾl ygtzr mn mth*, "and may pestilence, the club of Nergal, not be cut off from his land."[15] Later, the stem with *t*-prefix replaced the older infixed form, as in Dnl. 2:34 and 2:45: "a stone became loose without the assistance of a hand."[16] A metaphorical use of the nuance "to cut off" appears in reference to the determination of time in 11Q10 5:3 (Job 21:21): [*mny*]*n yrhwḥy gzyryn*, "[the numbe]r of his months is cut off."

V. Fortune-telling. The slaughter of animals was also quite generally associated with the prediction of the future based on hepatoscopy and extispicy. A competent specialist who slaughtered an animal in order to obtain a look into future events was, consequently, not just a "butcher" in the sense of the corresponding derivative *ǧazzār* in Arabic, but also a "soothsayer." He appears in Dnl. 2:27; 4:4; 5:7,11, in each case in the absolute or determined plurals *gāzᵉrīn* or *gāzᵉrayyā*. Judging from the form, these instances involve an active participle, but the transliteration γαζαρηνοί in the LXX, presumably for an original *gazzārīn*, represents a much older pronunciation that does not rest on the formation of the active participle *qātil*,[17] but on the common Semitic *nomen professionis* according to the *qattāl* pattern. The same word also occurs in Nabonidus's Prayer from Qumran,[18] which says: *wḥṭʾy šbq lh gzr* "and a soothsayer reduced my sins." The passive construction *šbq lh*, borrowed in Aramaic from old Persian,[19] appears here without the expected internal vowel (*šbyq*).[20] This could indicate a comparably ancient spelling and, thus, presume an Imperial Aramaic origin for the text,[21] which attests to the Aramaic use of *gzr* "soothsayer" already in the fifth century B.C.E.

VI. "Determination," "Decision." It is very difficult to determine a priori whether the nuance of *gzr* in the sense of "to decide" (with a direct object or object clause) and the noun *gᵉzīrā* "determination, decision" derived from it traces to the activity of the soothsayer or quite simply to the semantic field of the verb in its basic meaning "to cut"; it can, in fact, take on the juridical connotation "to decide" with reference to a legal proceeding, like the Akkadian *parāsu* "to separate." Admittedly, the two alterna-

14. Sefire IB = *KAI* 222 B 41.

15. *KAI* 309.23.

16. Cf. also H. Gzella, "Voice in Classical Hebrew against Its Semitic Background," *Or* 78 (2009) 302.

17. So yet also *ATTM*, 108.

18. 4Q242 1:4.

19. Regarding this phenomenon, see also H. Gzella, "The Heritage of Imperial Aramaic in Eastern Aramaic," *AraSt* 6 (2008) 92f. (bib.).

20. Regarding the disputed construction in the passage, cf. H. Gzella, "*šbq*," I and III, *ThWQ*, III, 833-34 and 834-35, for the interpretation in context.

21. Regarding the question of dating, see also A. Lange and M. Sieker, "Gattung und Quellenwert des Gebets des Nabonid," in H.-J. Fabry, A. Lange, and H. Lichtenberger, eds., *Qumranstudien* (Göttingen, 1996), 3-34, esp. 6-8.

tives are not entirely mutually exclusive, since *parāsu* also occurs in the meaning "to decide" in the context of extispicy, in *bārû ina bīri arkat ul iprus*, "the practitioner of extispicy could not decide the case with this investigation.[22] In any case, the Akkadian phrase *dīna parāsu* means "to render a judgment," and this very expression has an exact parallel in Aramaic *ʿlyk dyn qšṭʾ gzr*, "he renders a just judgment for you" (→ *dyn* II.3).[23]

A legal background may also best explain this use of the verb *gzr* and suits the noun *gezīrā* in expressions such as *bgzyrn* [*ʿly*]*kwn* "through a judgment against you,"[24] *bgzrt ʿyryn*, "through the judgment of the Watchers" (Dnl. 4:14) or *gzrt ʿlyʾ hyʾ*, "it is a judgment of the Most High" (Dnl. 4:21). Furthermore, the *Megillat Taʿanit* mentions a "Book of Decrees," *spr gzrtʾ* (→ IV). Conjectures as to the identity of this reference include a Sadducean legal codex even older than the Mishnah.[25] The forensic connotations of the verb *gzr* and the noun *gᵉzīrā* are also known in late Palestinian Jewish[26] and Babylonian Jewish Aramaic,[27] Mandaic,[28] and Syriac.[29]

Lipiński

22. *BWL* 39.6.
23. 4Q196/7 6:13 (4QTob).
24. 4Q204 14,4 (4QEnᶜ).
25. Cf. *ATTM*, 356, with bib.
26. *DJPA*, 126.
27. *DJBA*, 276.
28. *MdD*, 87.
29. *ThesSyr*, 700f.

גלי I *glī*

I. Etymology and General Usage. II. Biblical Aramaic. III. Qumran.

I. Etymology and General Usage. The word *glī* is a III*w*/*y* root that can hardly be distinguished in accidence. In this case, however, it may be possible to differentiate two roots: *glī* I "to expose, show, reveal" and *glū* II "to go away, to go abroad, to emigrate."[1]

F. A. Gosling, "An Open Question Relating to the Hebrew Root *glh*," *ZAH* 11 (1998) 125-32; D. A. Machiela, "*glh*," *ThWQ*, I, 605-12; R. E. Price, "A Lexicographical Study of *glh*, *šbh* and *šwb* in Reference to Exile in the Tanach" (diss., Duke, 1977); C. Westermann and R. Albertz, "גלה *glh* to uncover," *TLOT*, 314-20; H.-J. Zobel, "גָּלָה *gālāh*," *TDOT*, II, 476-88.

1. I. Kottsieper, *Die Sprache der Aḥiqarsprüche*. *BZAW* 194 (1990), 160f.; Gosling; contra Price, 19-35.

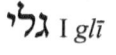

Usually, the two meanings are listed under one root[2] and an etymological relationship is assumed.[3] The semantic difference, however, reflected also in the distribution of examples, speaks in support of the distinction.[4] In Phoenician, the root (in the G-stem) has the transitive meaning "to uncover, disclose,"[5] which is tied in Hebrew (qal, niphal, piel/pual, and hithpael) and Aramaic (Imperial and Biblical Aram. only peal, in Qumran and thereafter also pael and ithpael) and in other Semitic languages (Syr., Eth., and Arab.) to the second, intransitive meaning. This phenomenon is first attested in Ugaritic, where *gly* is employed in parallel with *bʾ* "to come" in the sense of "to present oneself, make one's way, go."[6] From this meaning, in Hebrew (qal and hiphil/hophal) and Aramaic (Biblical Aram. only haphel, in Qumran and thereafter also qal) and in Ethiopic, here also with a distinction between the roots,[7] the special meaning "to go into exile, to be deported" developed. Aramaic also has it as a loanword.[8] The noun /galū/ "deportation, deported"[9] derives from *glī* II corresponding to *šbī* "to capture, deport" and /šebī/ (Biblical Aram. *šᵉḇī*) "captivity, captive" (see below). Both meanings survive in later phases of the language.[10]

The earliest (preserved) example of *glī* I in Aram. is Aḥiqar: *rz-/msthr/ḥṭʾ-*]*yk ʾl tgly qdm* [*rḥ*]*myk* . . . "Do not reveal your [secrets/misdeeds] to your friends so that they do not take your name lightly."[11] The wisdom use presupposes the profane use of the root in the sense of "to uncover, reveal," which characterized it from the outset, and gives no trace of a meaning with specific connotations for a theology of revelation. The same situation pertains to the second instance from Elephantine, a letter to the lords of Yeb, which complains of the continued absence of Aršama: *hnlw glyn ʾnpyn ʿl ʾršm* [added above the line: *qdmn*] *lkn lʾ kznh hw*[*h* . . .] "Had we revealed our countenance (showed ourselves) before Aršama, this would not [have happened. . .]."[12] The expression "to reveal the countenance" recalls the phrase, customary in Hebrew, "to open one's ear/eye,"[13] but implies a reflexive nuance "to show oneself, to reveal oneself, to apply to

2. *GesB* and *GesB*[18], *BDB*, *KBL*[2] and *KBL*[3], *DCH*, *DNSI*.

3. M. H. Pope, *El in the Ugaritic Texts*. *SVT* 2 (1955), 64; Zobel, 476-77.

4. Zorell, 151f.; *LexLingAram*, 35; Mandelkern, 262f., and Even-Shoshan, 234-36 for the Heb.; *TLOT*, 314f.; *ATTM*, 543.

5. *KAI* 1 = *TSSI*, III n. 4, l. 2: *wygl ʾrn zn* ". . . and opened this sarcophagus"; perhaps also *KAI* 10 = *TSSI*, III n. 25, l. 14f.: *wtgl mstrw* "and you open his hiding place."

6. *DUL*[3], 296.

7. Cf. *BDB* and Gosling.

8. *AHw*, I, 275b; 1555b; see W. von Soden, "Aramäische Wörter in neuassyrischen und neu- und spätbabylonischen Texten: Ein Vorbericht I (agâ -*mūš)," *Or* 35 (1966) 8 no. 21; idem, "Aramäische Wörter in neuassyrischen und neu- und spätbabylonischen Texten: Ein Vorbericht III," *Or* 46 (1977) 186 no. 21; and K. Deller, "The Neo-Assyrian Epigraphical Remains of Nimrud," *Or* 35 (1966) 194.

9. In the Masoretic pointing *gālū*, with lengthening of the /a/, cf. *ATTM*, 133 n. 2; Heb. *gālūṯ* and *gōlā*.

10. *ATTM*, 543; *ATTM*, 2, 369; *DJPA*, 129f.; TM, 140-2; *WTM* I, 332-4; Jastrow, 247f.; cf. Price, 83f.

11. *TADAE* C1.1,141.

12. *AP* 37 = *TADAE* A4.2,8.

13. *TLOT*, 316,319.

someone" (or middle "to appear"?), which may have served as a bridge for the association with *glī* II "to repair to" (or middle-passive of a change of location). In Biblical Aramaic and Qumran, the word assumes theological quality and serves as the epitome of eschatological revelation.

II. Biblical Aramaic. In Biblical Aramaic *glī* I occurs exclusively in Dnl. 2. Here, the root appears seven times in four passages (Dnl. 2:22,29,30,47); the manuscripts from Qumran also attest it.[14] As in the two instances from Elephantine (→ I), the verb is inflected in the G-stem (peal); the masc. sg. ptcp. (2:22,28f.,47), the inf. (2:47), and the internal passive of the peal stem (2:19,30) are attested. Counterparts are → *ḥwī* (pael or haphel) "to communicate" and → *ydʿ* (haphel) "to make known." With one exception (2:47), the subject everywhere is God, the object (with a pass. subject), a "secret" (*rāz*; → *rz*). Judging from the procedure, it refers to the puzzle that King Nebuchadnezzar had given the wise men of Babylonia, namely to make known not only (as in Dnl. 4) the interpretation of a dream, but the dream itself. This puzzle was revealed to Daniel in a dream (2:19), indeed, by the God who gives wisdom to the wise and understanding to those with understanding, who reveals the profound and concealed and knows what is in the darkness (2:12f.); a god who discloses secrets (*gālē rāzīn*) and would like for the king to experience what will happen "after him" or "at the end of days" (2:28-30). For which Daniel, the one to whom the "discloser of secrets" was revealed and the one to whom the secret was revealed in order to reveal it to the king, demonstrated gratitude (2:47). In terms of content, the "secret" refers to the dream of the statue and the stone (2:31ff.), which in its original version symbolized the Babylonian and Medo-Persian Empires in the succession of three empires (2:37-39*,45), in the final version of the text the four empires and the kingdom of God.[15] The process as such lives on profane, wisdom-influenced diction in the context of dream and puzzle interpretation and the transfer to God of the capacities for knowing hidden things and making them known. Only through the identification with the content of the dream does the disclosure gain the character of divine (eschatological) revelation. In the background stands the saying "betrayal of secrets" (*gālā sōḏ*, cf. Prov. 20:19; in the piel Prov. 11:13; 25:9; Aram. [*gly rzh*] in a synagogue inscription from En-Gedi),[16] which also refers to the revelation of the divine actions toward his servants, the prophets, in the secondary, late verse Am. 3:7, and which, in this sense, became part of the repertoire of apocalypticism.

III. Qumran. In the manuscripts from the Dead Sea as in Hebrew, *glī* I occurs both in the G-stem qal or peal and also in the D-stem pael and for the passive in the ithpael.[17] In two passages, the profane, wisdom usage survives. In CTL Bodl a, 13[18] Levi says of

14. 4Q112 3 1:17 and 7: *DJD*, XI (1998), 244,248.
15. Cf. R. G. Kratz, *Translatio imperii. WMANT* 63 (1991), 48ff.
16. Fifth century C.E., yyEN 3:4 in *ATTM*, 364.
17. *ATTM*, 543 and 2, 369.
18. 4Q213b 3f. (T.Lev.ᶜ).

his dream—which deals with the dominion of the priesthood and of the sword—that he has hidden it in his heart and revealed it to no one: *wkl ʾnš lʾ glyth*. 11Q10 27:3f. cites Job 36:10 and the traditional expression "opening the ear," with God as the subject and wisdom instruction as the objective: *wygl ʾdnyhwn lmwsr* "and he will open their ears to instruction." The continuation of the citation ("and he will say to them: if they will repent from their evil deeds, if they hear and do . . .") makes it clear that the expression has already been placed in a new, eschatological plane in the speeches of Elihu.

This plane is also presupposed when the subject involves the heavenly secrets that the fallen angels betray to humans or, used positively, that an angel or the primordial wise ones reveal. The Book of Watchers in 1 Enoch relates the former in an exegesis of Gen. 6:1-4 in order to explain how the depravity of humanity before the flood came about. In addition to the fornication and violence of the biblical text, 1 En. 8:3 mentions conjuration and astrology that the fallen angels provided to human beings: *wkwlhwn šryw lglyh* (inf. pael) *rzyn lnšyhwn* "and they began to betray secrets to their wives."[19] The secret concept can also refer to the other, positive, aspect, however: the revelation of proper heavenly knowledge, associated in 1 Enoch with the figure of Enoch. This is the case in the very fragmentary text 4Q536 1 1:8, which Beyer[20] places among the Noachide fragments: *yglʾ rzyn kʿlywnyn* "and he will reveal secrets as does the Most High."[21] In the same fragment, 1 1:3 already speaks of the fact that something (presumably the "lights," i.e., the stars)[22] would be revealed to someone (*lh ytglwn nhy*[*ryn*). The root *glī* I may also occur in the Noachide fragment 4Q534 2:21 ([*ytg*?]*lwn*), although the reading is not certain and the context unclear.

Another book in the Enoch literature, the ten week prophecy,[23] contains the example: *wq*[*šwṭ w*]*d*[*yn qšwṭ bh*] *ytglʾ lkl bny ʾrʿʾ klh* "and ri[ghteousness and just] judg[ment] will be revealed to all the children of the entire earth." The judgment of all the evildoers of the world takes place in the penultimate, ninth week (*wmn btrh šbwʿ tšʿy*), before judgment is passed on the Watchers (the angels), the first heaven vanishes, and a new heaven where eternal righteousness rules appears in the tenth and last week. The Ethiopic text is somewhat shorter than the Aramaic, but says the same thing: "And thereafter, in the ninth week, the judgment of the entire world will be revealed."[24] Beyer adduces a passage in the animal apocalypse, 1 En. 89:35[25] as an additional example in the Enoch literature. It discusses Moses and the golden calf following Ex. 32–34. Yet, neither the shorter Ethiopic text[26] nor Milik[27] and *DSSStE*[28] confirm the reconstructed reading (*lʾ mglʾ* "not to reveal"). They both read an inf. pael from *bgl* (*lʾ*[*y l*]*bglʾ* "set up reproaching,"

19. 4Q201 4:4f. par. 4Q202 3:5.
20. *ATTM*, 2, 162-65.
21. 4Q534,535,561.
22. Cf. *ATTM*, 2, 165.
23. 4Q212 4:19f.
24. *JSHRZ* V/6, 714.
25. *ATTM*, 245f.
26. *JSHRZ* V/6, 688f.
27. *The Books of Henoch* (Leiden, 1976), 204-6.
28. 4Q204 13:4 99.

"busied himself with scolding").[29] The reference to the "many" whom God will raise up and the "reveal" or "are revealed" (ptcp. pael *śg'yn mgly'n*) in the fragment 4Q541 24 2:3, which has been (conditionally) assigned to the Apocryphon or the Testament of Levi, has no perceptible context.

Kratz

29. Cf. also M. Black, *The Book of Enoch, or, I Enoch. SVTP* 7 (1985), 266,367.

גלי II *glī*; גלו *glw* /galū/; שׁבי *šbī*

I. Etymology and General Usage. II. Biblical Aramaic. III. Qumran.

I. Etymology and General Usage. For the etymology, see above → *glī* I. The inscriptional attestation of *glī* II "to go away, to be led away" is sparse and sometimes uncertain.[1] There are no early NW Semitic instances; apart from Ugarit, attestation begins only with Biblical Hebrew and Aramaic.[2] This phenomenon probably involves the fact that the root was originally a verb of locomotion and became the *terminus technicus* for the exile and the exiles only under the influence of the deportation in the Neo-Assyrian period and then solidly after the Babylonian era. Presumably, this influence also explains the derivatives *gālū* (Biblical Aram.), *gālūṯ*, and *gōlā* (Biblical Heb.), as well as the intrusion of the Aramaic loanword into Akkadian (→ *glī* I).

The root *šbī* with its derivatives underwent the same specification. From the outset, they covered the semantic field of "to lead into captivity, captivity, captive" in reference to gods (idols), people, animals, and objects, and later became, in Biblical Hebrew and in the Aramaic of Tobit, a fixed expression for the exile.[3] Particularly telling are instances that combine *šbī* and *glī* II (Ezk. 12:11; Nah. 3:10; Ezr. 2:1/ Neh. 7:6; Ezr. 8:35).

F. A. Gosling, "An Open Question Relating to the Hebrew Root *glh*," *ZAH* 11 (1998) 125-32; D. A. Machiela, "*glh*," *ThWQ*, I, 605-12; B. Otzen, "שָׁבָה šābāh," *TDOT*, XIV, 286-94; R. E. Price, "A Lexicographical Study of *glh*, *šbh* and *šwb* in Reference to Exile in the Tanach" (diss., Duke, 1977); C. Westermann and R. Albertz, "גלה *glh* to uncover," *TLOT*, 314-20; H.-J. Zobel, "גָּלָה *gālāh*," *TDOT*, II 476-88.

1. Cf. *DNSI*, 223f.; *ATTM*, 543; 2, 369; regarding *ngl* in H 95, entered in *DNSI*, 715, cf. Beyer, *Die aramäischen Inschriften aus Assur, Hatra und dem übrigen Ostmesopotamien* (Göttingen, 1998), Hatra 51, who reads a PN.

2. *TLOT*, 314f.

3. Cf. *KBL*³, 1286f.,1293f., 1295f.; Otzen, 286ff.; *TLOT*, 315f.; Price, 35-37,55ff. and loc. cit.; on Tob. → III.

The inscriptions[4] offer clues as to the circumstances in which this specification took place. *KAI* 215 = *TSSI*, II n. 14, l. 8 mentions the "captives of Ya'udi" (*šby y'dy*), who, on the installation of Panamuwas II as king over Ya'udi-Sam'al by Tiglath-pileser III, were released. Presumably, they represent political prisoners in their own land. The northern Syrian prince had left the anti-Assyrian coalition and offered himself to the Assyrian king as vassal in order to survive internal disputes surrounding the throne. Loyalty was good for him and his son and successor Barrakib. *KAI* 233 = *TSSI*, II no. 20, l. 15f. speaks of deportations of greater dimensions undertaken by famous Assyrian kings: *šby šbh tkltplsr mn byt'wkn* [*wšby*] *šbh 'lly mn byt 'dn wšby šbh šrkn mn drsn wšb*[*y šbh sn*]*hrb mn kšn* "Tiglath-pileser led a captivity/captives from Bit-'WKN [Akk. Bīt-Amukkāni], Ululay [Shalmaneser V] led a captivity from Bit-Adini, Sargon led a captivity from Dur-Sin, and Sennacherib led a captivity from KŠN/KŠW (Kish?)." An Assyrian official Bel-etir writes to his "brother" Pir'i-Amurri in the tense situation of the dispute between Assurbanipal and Šamaššumukin referring to the earlier practice of Assyrian kings. This practice becomes a literary topos in the Bar-Puneš text found among the Elephantine papyri: *wšby' zy šbyt bzy šnt'* "and the captives you took this year . . ." refers to the (Egyptian) king.[5] As in *KAI* 233, it employs the *figura etymologica* with the noun as internal object;[6] the difficult Heb. expression *šûḇ šḇûṯ* and the like could have arisen from this usage.[7] The example on an ostracon from Persian times[8] also stems from Elephantine. Line 5 offers a *y*]*wm šbh* "day of the Sabbath" or ". . . captured" and in l. 6 clearly the third plur. pf. qal: *k'n hn l' šbw lntn tmh* "Now, if they have not taken Natan captive there, may he move against me and I will crush. . . ." Biblical Aramaic does not attest the root, although it reappears with both the general and the specific meanings in Biblical Hebrew, in Qumran (see immediately below) and later Aramaic.[9]

II. Biblical Aramaic. In Biblical Aramaic *glī* II occurs only twice in the pf. haphel. One passage, Ezr. 4:10, recalls the retrospective in *KAI* 233.14f. It speaks of deportations by an Assyrian with the poorly transmitted name Asnapar, whom some versions identify with Shalmanassar and scholarship with Assurbanipal or the Asarhaddon mentioned in Ezr. 4:2.[10] The authors of the letter of accusation against Jerusalem claim to stem from the peoples whom the Assyrian king exiled and settled in Samaria and in the other territory beyond the river (Trans-Euphrates; cf. 2 K. 17:24ff.). They appeal vis-à-vis the Persian King Artaxerxes, the addressee of the letter, to the Assyrian king as a model and to their origins that grant them particular status. The "exile" by the Assyrian king is considered here a privilege to a degree. With the reverse value, this is also the case in the second

---

4. *DNSI*, 1000f.

5. *TADAE* C1.2,5; new edition in B. Porten, "The Prophecy of Ḥor bar Punesh and the Demise of Righteousness," in F. Hoffmann and H. J. Thissen, eds., *Res Severa Verum Gaudium. FS. K.-T. Zauzich* (Louvain, 2004), 427-66.

6. Cf. also 1QapGen 12:12 and Heb. Dt. 21:10; Jgs. 5:12; Ps. 68:19; 2 Ch. 28:17; with *min* Nu. 21:1; 2 Ch. 28:5,11.

7. Cf. *TDOT*, XIV, 294-302; Price, 89ff.

8. *TADAE* D7.10.

9. *ATTM*, 700; 2, 486; *DJPA*, 534f.; *WTM* IV, 496f.; Jastrow, 1513f.; Price, 84-86.

10. Cf. *KBL*³, 1671.

passage, Ezr. 5:12. It appears in the (proto-)chronistic historical summary in Ezr. 5:11-16 and recalls the Babylonian exile initiated by Yahweh. The elders of Judah, who justify the construction of the Second Temple under Darius in response to inquiries by the Persian governor, introduce the history of the temple implements, deported to Babel by the Babylonian King Nebuchadnezzar and supposed to be given over to Sheshbazzar by the Persian King Cyrus and returned to Jerusalem, with the explicit command to reconstruct the temple destroyed by the Babylonian king on its old site (cf. 2 Ch. 36/Ezr. 1). After the return, the "exile" also justifies special privilege, not just for the temple implements, but, as Ezr. 1–4 indicate, also for the returned Babylonian *golah*. This self-understanding on the part of the returnees expresses itself not least in the collective designation formed with the noun, *b^e nē gālûṯā (dī ye hûḏ)* "Exiled (from Judah)," which occurs in Dnl. 2:25;[11] 5:13; 6:14[12] and Ezr. 6:16 (Heb. Ezr. 4:1; 6:19f.; 8:35; 10:7,16). Whenever and whatever the actual number of those returned from Babylonian captivity may be, the *golah* considered it a privilege to contribute as leaders in the postexilic restoration of Judah. The chronistic theology, which had precursors and successors, including the chronicle of the construction of the temple in Ezr. 5–6 and the Aramaic narratives in Daniel,[13] at least suggest this.

III. Qumran. The historical reminiscences in 4Q244 12:1-4,[14] which recalls Ezr. 5:12, also call the exiles "sons of the exile," *bny glwt'*: Since the *bny yśr'l*, "the sons of Israel," have fallen away from God, he gave them into the hand of Nebuchadnezzar, and they become the "sons of the *golah*." In contrast to Ezr. 5, the outline of history in 4Q243-245 (psDan[a-c])[15] ends—it begins already with the primeval history (mentioning the flood and the tower of Babel)—not with the (chronistic) first year of Cyrus and the construction of the temple under Darius, but, like the visions in the book of Daniel and the ten weeks and animal apocalypses of 1 Enoch, with a prospective on the eschaton. A second instance of the noun[16] designates the exodus from Egypt, by which the Testament of Amram is dated, as "the exile of Israel to Egypt": *lglwt yśr'l lmṣryn*. The expression picks up on the basic meaning of the root *glī* II, "to go abroad, to emigrate," yet it vibrates with the experience of the Babylonian exile, by which the book of Ezekiel is dated, and probably also that of the Egyptian diaspora.

Qumran Aramaic also attests the root *šbī*. It appears in concentration in 1QapGen 21-22, the Aramaic rendition of Gen. 14, as a verb in the pf. and ptcp. (act. and pass.) of the G-stem (21:34; 22:3,4,10,12,19) and as a noun (12:12,25), once also in the *figura etymologica* (12:12). Catalysts for the concentration are, on the one hand, the fictive scene of Gen. 14, configured on the model of Assyrian (and Persian) punitive expeditions, and on the other, the text itself that employs the verb *šbī* (niphal) in Gen 14:14 for the capture of Lot by the Elamite coalition. This is the clue to the broad, Midrash-like depiction of the scene.

11. 4Q112 3 1:17 *bny glwt' dy yhwdy'*.
12. 4Q113 7 2:8 *y*]*hwd*.
13. R. G. Kratz, *Translatio imperi.*, *WMANT* 63 (1991), esp. 185,190ff.,260ff.; idem, *Kyros im Deuterojesaja-Buch. FAT* 1 (1991), 103-8.
14. Cf. 4Q243 13.
15. *DSSStE*, 488-92; critical edition and reconstruction in *DJD*, XVII (2005).
16. 4Q543 1:4 par. 4Q545 1 1:4.

The original meaning of the lexeme with military connotations may also be applicable to the fragment 4Q533 1:6 that speaks of taking captives in relation to a "new province" (. . .]*mdynt' ḥdt' dy šbh kl dy hw' b*[. . .) and invokes in favor a prophetic pronouncement (*'l dnh 'mr nbw" dy*). Closer to the root *glī* II stands the diction in the Aramaic. Its chief characters are those "of the sons of Naphtali who are captives in Nineveh": 4Q197 4 3:6 (Tob. 7:3) *mn bny nptly* [*dy*] *šbyn bnynwh*.[17] Reference to "the land of captivity" occurs twice in the prayer. The first is at the beginning in the petition in order to assert the integrity of Tobit and his family: 4Q196 6:10 (Tob. 3:15) *bkl 'r't šbyn'* "in all the lands of our captivity";[18] the other is in the thanksgiving prayer at the end of the book: 4Q196 17 2:3 (Tob. 13:8) *b'r*] *šby'*.[19] Here, then, the Assyrian *golah* from the former Northern Kingdom, to a degree the opposite of the nations transplanted in Samaria of Ezr. 4:10, are promised a diaspora identity comparable to the self-understanding of the Babylonian *golah*.

Kratz

17. G I ἐκ τῶν υἱῶν Νεφθαλεὶμ τῶν αἰχμαλώτων ἐν Νινευή, G II ἐκ τῶν υἱῶν Νεφθαλεὶμ ἡμεῖς τῶν αἰχμαλωτισθέντων ἐν Νινευή.

18. G I and II have here the sg. ἐν τῇ γῇ τῆς αἰχμαλωσίας μου.

19. Only G I has ἐν τῇ γῇ τῆς αἰχμαλωσίας μου.

גלל *gll* /galāl/

I. Distribution, Context, and Etymology. II. Traditional Interpretation. III. Usage in Aramaic Generally for "Special Stone." IV. Interpretation in the Context of Biblical Aramaic.

I. Distribution, Context, and Etymology. *g^e^lāl* occurs twice in Biblical Aramaic (Ezr. 5:8 and 6:4), in each case as an attribute of the preceding *'æḇæn* "stone." The context clearly indicates that each case involves construction material for the temple. It has long been unclear, however, precisely how these stones are obtained. The noun is generally associated with the root *gll* "to roll," which, however, is attested in West Aramaic as a verb only late,[1] but which already appears earlier in other nominal derivations,

R. A. Bowman, "אֶבֶן גְּלָל—*aban galâlu* (Ezra 5:8; 6:4)," in I. T. Naamani and D. Rudavsky, eds., *Dōrōn: Hebraic Studies. FS. A. I. Katsch* (New York, 1965), 64-74; F. C. Fensham, *The Books of Ezra and Nehemiah. NICOT* (1982); A. H. J. Gunneweg, *Esra. KAT* 19/1 (1985); R. T. Hallock, *Persepolis Fortification Tablets. OIP* 92 (1969); Z. Talshir, *1 Esdras: A Text Critical Commentary. SBLSCS* 50 (2001); H. G. M. Williamson, "'eben g^e^lāl (Ezra 5:8; 6:4) Again," *BASOR* 280 (1990) 83-88; idem, *Ezra and Nehemiah. OTG* (1987).

1. *DJPA*, 129a.

i.e., *glgl* /galgal/ "wheel,"[2] *mglh* /magallā/ "scroll of scripture" (Ezr. 6:2) and /golgolā/ "skull" in the well-known New Testament toponym Golgotha.[3]

II. Traditional Interpretation. Already in antiquity, disagreement concerning the exact meaning of the noun dominated, and the ancient translations often render the two passages differently. Thus, the LXX has "select stones" and "strong stones"; in contrast, 1 Esd. (6:8 and 24) reads "(precious) polished stones" (perhaps under the influence of 1 K. 5:31, 7:9 and Isa. 28:16)[4]; the Vulgate has "unpolished stone(s)" (which may reflect 1 K. 6:7); and, finally, the Peshitta translates "very large stones" and "building blocks."

The same uncertainty can also be found in modern translations and commentaries, even though the most widespread explanation of the word interprets the word in terms of its presumed etymological connection with *gll* "to roll" and on this basis translates *gᵉlāl* as "large stones," "building block," or the like, since "the stones were so large that they were rolled to the building site,"[5] although this does not offer unequivocal evidence for this interpretation.

III. Usage in Aramaic Generally for "Special Stone." Following Bowman, it is preferable, nonetheless, to understand *gᵉlāl* in relation to a use of *gll* in Aramaic that corresponds to the Akkadian *galālu* "stone(s)."[6] The Akkadian word is used for a series of different stone objects such as steles, columns, tableware, and much more, which has an exact parallel in the use of the Aramaic *gll* in ink inscriptions on objects such as pestles, mortars, and tablets found in the treasury of Persepolis.

In view of these texts, Bowman suggested that the word means simply "stone," so that he felt compelled to explain *ʾæḇæn* in the biblical text as a kind of determinative, although neither Aramaic nor Hebrew offers parallels. In any case, it seems clear that *gᵉlāl* describes a particular characteristic of a stone, for which there are indications in an Aramaic gloss of an Elamite text.[7] There, both the immediate and the broader context confirm that it involves a special kind of stone.[8] In the Greco-Aramaic tax scale from Palmyra[9] *gll* appears with the Greek counterpart στήλη λιθίνη "(stone) stele."[10] Although it is not possible to attain absolute certainty here, the best option for translating this expression in the biblical passages seems, nonetheless, to be "select stone."

IV. Interpretation in the Context of Biblical Aramaic. The noun *gᵉlāl* appears in the context of a letter from the satrap of "beyond the river" to King Darius and in his

2. Old Aramaic in *KAI* 216.8 of a chariot; 4Q209 6:9 for the moon.
3. With dissimilation in Greek transcription following Mt. 27:33; Mk. 15:22; Jn. 19:17: *ATTM*, 543f.; 2, 369.
4. Cf. Talshir, 334-36.
5. Fensham, 82; cf. Gunneweg, 101.
6. *CAD*, V, 11.
7. Hallock, 442.
8. Cf. Williamson, 1990 for the details; now adopted by *ATTM*, 2, 369: "especially desirable stone."
9. *PAT* 0259 i.9.
10. *DNSI*, 224.

response, which cites a decree of Cyrus. It is hardly astonishing that, precisely in such a context, a rare expression occurs that the biblical author probably retained because its distinctiveness made it seem suitable for an important building like the Jerusalem temple. In a later time, when the precise technical significance had already paled, it could easily be understood in the sense of the typological parallels between the First and Second Temples (→ II), as other texts that describe the construction of the Second Temple suggest.[11]

Williamson

11. Cf. Williamson, *Ezra and Nehemiah*, 82-83.

גנז *gnz* /ganza/; גזבר *gzbr* /ganzabār/; גנזך *gnzk* /ganzak/; גניזה *gnyzh* /ganīzā/

I. Etymology, Variants, and Derivates. II. Verb *gnz* and Geniza. III. Parthian Texts.

I. Etymology, Variants, and Derivates. The Aramaic noun *ginzā* is borrowed directly from the Persian **ganδa*- or Median **ganza* "depot, treasury."[1] The /n/ often assimilates with a subsequent /z/, as in Syriac *gazzā* alongside *ganzā*, Greek γάζα and Ethiopic *gaza*, further in the compound nouns *giddaḇār* (cf. Dnl. 3:2,3), *gizbār*, *gizzaḇār* (Ezr. 1:8; 7:21) and Syriac *gizzabrā* from **ganδa-bāra* "treasurer" or "depot master." It is preserved, however, in late Babylonian *gan-za-ba-ru*,[2] Mandaic *ganzibrā* (a priestly title), and Ethiopic *ganzab* "money," which apparently derives from *ganza-bāra* and was borrowed via Syriac.

The original Aramaic form of these loanwords surely had the vowel /a/ in the first syllable and no assimilation of the /n/. This vowel persists in the Hebrew *ganzaḵ* (1 Ch. 28:11), also

F. Altheim and R. Stiehl, *Geschichte Mittelasiens im Altertum* (Berlin, 1970), esp. 547, 558; F. Cumont, *Fouilles de Doura-Europos. BAH* 9 (1926), esp. 405f.; P. Gignoux, *Glossaire des inscriptions pehlevies et parthes. CIISup* 1 (1972), esp. 22,51; W. Hinz, "Achämenidische Hofverwaltung," *ZA* 61 (1971), 260-311, esp. 261, 266; idem, *Altiranisches Sprachgut der Nebenüberlieferungen. GOF* III/3 (1975), esp. 102; idem, *Neue Wege im Altpersischen. GOF* III/1 (1973), esp. 31; O. Klíma, review of M. Mayrhofer, *Die Rekonstruktion des Medischen*, *ArOr* 38 (1970) 89-94; E. Lipiński, "Median *ganza- as Loanword," *Anabasis* 5 (2014) 7-12; J. Naveh and S. Shaked, "Ritual Texts or Treasury Documents?," *Or* 42 (1973) 445-57; M. Sznycer, "Quelques observations sur les ostraca de Nisa," *Sem* 13 (1963) 31-37; J. Tavernier, *Iranica in the Achaemenid Period (ca. 550-330 B.C.): Lexicon of Old Iranian Proper Names and Loanwords Attested in Non-Iranian Texts. OLA* 158 (2007), esp. 422, §4.4.7.48f.; 443, §4.4.10.8; 553; M. Wagner, *Die lexikalischen und grammatikalischen Aramaismen im alttestamentlichen Hebräisch. BZAW* 96 (1966), esp. 41f.

1. See Klíma.
2. *AHw*, I, 281a.

"storehouse" or "treasury," which preserves the same word *ganδa- or *ganza with the very frequent Old Iranian suffix -ka-. In contrast to the Hebrew *haggizbār* in Ezr. 1:8, the transcription in the LXX as γασβαρηνου preserves the form *gazbarīn* "treasurer," as it sounded before the change of the /a/ to /i/. The synagogue inscription from Dura-Europos, dated to 245 C.E., first attests this vowel shift with certainty. In it, the "treasurer" bears the title *gynzbrh.*[3]

In contrast, the /n/ is almost never assimilated in the Aramaic documents from the Persian period, neither in *gnz'* nor in the compounds *gnzbr'* and *'pgnzbr'* from **upa-ganδa-bāra-* "deputy treasurer."[4] The sole possible exception is now a putative instance of *gzb[r'* in a small fragment of an official letter from Bactria form the late Achaemenid period,[5] used after a personal name and, thus, presumably a title. In any case, the word occurs at the end of a line with only the upper half of the first three letters legible at all, so that this interpretation cannot be considered assured. Consequently, the earliest indubitable attestation of the assimilated form of the word γάζα is in Theophrastus (ca. 370-288/5 B.C.E.), *Historia plantarum* VIII:11:5.

The occurrence of the spelling *gizzaḇrayyā* in Ezr. 7:21 after the expression *bēṯ ginzē malkā* in 7:20 is, thus, particularly noteworthy and confirms the results of a literary-critical analysis, according to which Ezr. 7:21-26 stems from a later time or was added by another hand. The word is correctly translated γαζοφύλαξ in 3 Esd. 2:8, a Greek derivation from γάζα, as is already attested in a citation from Phylarchus (third century B.C.E.) in Athenaeus, *Deipnosophistai* 261b and in Dura-Europos γαζζοφύ(λαξ) spelled with double ζ to render *nz*.[6] The second element of the compound, which is based on the Persian title, **-bāra-*, denotes the "bearer" or "keeper."[7]

II. Verb *gnz* and Geniza. In addition to the biblical use of *bēṯ ginzayyā* (Ezr. 5:17; 6:1), "treasury," or "storehouse," but also "archive," *bēṯ ginzē malkā* (Ezr. 7:20), "royal treasury," and *gizzaḇrayyā* (Ezr. 7:21 → I) or *g^{e}ḏāb^{e}rayyā* (Dnl. 3:2,3),[8] "treasurer" or "keeper of the storehouse," the verb *gnz* "to store," thus also "to hide,"[9] occur in Jewish Aramaic dialects, Mishnaic Hebrew, and in Syriac.[10] This verb derives from **ganzā* and is already attested in the Mishnah[11] and in the Tosefta.

Furthermore, a verbal noun *g^{e}nīzā* "store room, depot (of decommissioned sacral objects)" derives from the passive participle of the Aramaic form *g^{e}nīz* "stored." The same noun also occurs in the Mishnah,[12] which says that Holy Scriptures no longer suited for use *ṭ'wnym gnyzh* "require storage." The Babylonian Talmud[13] then employs the expression *bēṯ g^{e}nīzā* for precisely this purpose.

---

3. J. Naveh, *On Stone and Mosaic* (Jerusalem, 1978), no. 88, l. 6f.
4. See *DNSI*, 229 for index of occurrences.
5. J. Naveh and S. Shaked, *Aramaic Documents from Ancient Bactria* (London, 2012), no. B10.2.
6. See Cumont.
7. P. Horn, *Grundriss der neupersischen Etymologie* (Straßburg, 1893), no. 1073.
8. See *ATTM*, 415 on the form.
9. *DJPA*, 133; *DJBA*, 295.
10. *ThesSyr*, 750f.
11. *Šabb.* 9:6.
12. *Šabb.* 16:1.
13. *Pesaḥ.* 118.

III. Parthian Texts. The word *gnz'* occurs on the ostraca from Nisa from the first century B.C.E. It has been disputed, however, whether this is composed in Aramaic with many middle Persian loanwords or in Parthian employing Aramaic alphabet as heterograms. This question does not concern *gnz'* as such, because the corresponding middle Persian noun would have been written the same way alphabetically. In any case, "royal treasury" is regularly indicated by the phrase *gnz' mlk'*,[14] in the determined state with no determinative particle *zy*. This clearly non-Semitic construction indicates that the expression is Parthian and that *mlk'* must be as *šāh*. One could raise the same question concerning the derivation of "treasurer," *gnzbr*, in Nisa and in a Parthian ostracon from Dura-Europos or concerning *gznbr*, a form with metathesis also attested in Nisa.[15]

Lipiński

14. Ostraca 2007; Nov. 100+97:2.
15. Sznycer, 34.

גף *gp* /gapp/

I. Etymology and Distribution. 1. Semitic. 2. Aramaic. II. Biblical Aramaic. III. Enoch's Animal Vision. IV. Mesopotamian Texts. V. Iconography.

A. Caquot, review of M. Delcor, *Le livre de Daniel*, *VT* 23 (1973) 113-17; idem, "Sur les quatre bêtes de Daniel," *Sem* 5 (1955) 5-13; D. Cohen, *Dictionnaire des racines sémitiques ou attestées dans les langues sémitiques* (Paris, 1970-); J. J. Collins, *Daniel. Herm.* (1993); idem, "Stirring Up the Great Sea: The Religio-Historical Background of Daniel 7," in A. S. van der Woude, ed., *The Book of Daniel in the Light of New Findings. BETL* 106 (1993), 121-36; M. I. Delcor, *Le livre de Daniel. Sources Bibliques* 7 (Paris, 1971); J. E. Goldingay, *Daniel. WBC* 30 (1989); A. Green, "Ancient Mesopotamian Religious Iconography," in J. M. Sasson, ed., *Civilizations of the Ancient Near East* (New York, 1995), 3:1842-55; H. Gunkel, *Creation and Chaos in the Primeval Era and the Eschaton* (Grand Rapids, 2006), 205-14; L. F. Hartman and A. A. Di Lella, *The Book of Daniel. AB* 23 (1978); H. S. Kvanvig, "An Akkadian Vision as Background for Daniel 7?," *ST* 35 (1981) 85-89; idem, *Roots of Apocalyptic. The Mesopotamian Background of the Enoch Figure and of the Son of Man. WMANT* 61 (1988); M. Noth, "The Understanding of History in Old Testament Apocalyptic," in idem, *The Laws in the Pentateuch and Other Studies*, trans. D. R. Ap-Thomas (London, 1984), 194-214; F. Schultheß, *Homonyme Wurzeln im Syrischen* (Berlin, 1900); A. Spychet, "Reliefs, Statuary and Monumental Paintings," in J. M. Sasson, ed., *Civilizations of the Ancient Near East* (New York, 1995), 4:2583-2600; M. Wagner, *Die lexikalischen und grammatikalischen Aramaismen im alttestamentlichen Hebräisch. BZAW* 96 (1966); J. Walton, "The Anzu Myth as Relevant Background for Daniel 7," in J. J. Collins and P. W. Flint, eds., *The Book of Daniel* (Leiden, 2002), 1:69-89; O. Weber, *Altorientalische Siegelbilder* (Leipzig, 1920).

I. Etymology and Distribution.

1. Semitic. The feminine noun *gap(p)* derives from the Semitic root *gdp* with assimilation of the *d* to the subsequent *p* (**gadp- > gapp-*),[1] cf. Syriac *gdp* "to fly," Arabic *ğadafa*,[2] Akkadian *agappu, gappu*. According to *BDB*[3] it is related to Biblical Hebrew *ʾᵃgāp̄* "host, army" (with prosthetic *aleph*), which *BDB* considers an Akkadian loanword (independent of a possible Aramaic mediation), but according to *KBL*[3] and *GesB*[18],[4] it is more likely to be associated with the root *gpp*. It is debated, however, whether Biblical Hebrew *gdp* "to jeer, blaspheme" belongs to the same root.[5]

2. Aramaic. In Aramaic, *gap(p)* is well attested and appears in Palestinian Jewish,[6] Babylonian Jewish,[7] Samaritan,[8] and Palestinian Christian Aramaic,[9] as well as Syriac[10] and Mandaic.[11] Its use in a Nabatean incantation text,[12] however, is very uncertain.[13] The following related forms occur in the various Aramaic languages: (1) Retaining the *d*: Palestinian Jewish *gadpā*[14] and Mandaic *gadpa*.[15] (2) With a prosthetic glottal stop: Palestinian Jewish *ʾᵃgap̄*.[16] (3) With *n*: Mandaic *ganpa*,[17] that developed either through dissimilation of the geminate *pp > np* from *gappa*[18] or from *kanpa* (→ *knp*) with *k > g*.[19]

II. Biblical Aramaic. The vision of Dnl. 7 compares the first animal in 7:4 with a lion (→ *ʾryh*) with eagle's wings. The lion and the eagle, the kings of the land animals and of the skies, belong among the most mighty animals, cf. 2 S. 1:23; Jer. 49:19,22. The wings of the eagle symbolize strength and authority; cf. Ezk. 17:3-5 concerning the king of Babel. Hab. 1:8 describes the eagle as a ravenous predator. The two animals here epitomize the incomparable power of the Babylonian Empire.

1. So *BLA* §7j and *ATTM*, 541.
2. Cohen, 2:102.
3. *BDB*, 8.
4. Both following Schultheß, 16f.
5. Cf. Wagner, 39.
6. *DJPA*, 134b.
7. *DJBA*, 297a.
8. *DSA*, 156b.
9. *LSP*, 40a.
10. *LexSyr*, 128b; *ThesSyr*, 763a.
11. MdD, 77a.
12. J. Naveh, "A Nabatean Incantation Text," *IEJ* 29 (1979) 112f.
13. *DNSI*, 231.
14. *DJPA*, 121b.
15. *MdD*, 74a, yet, according to M. Sokoloff, review of L. Koehler and W. Baumgartner, *Hebräisches und aramäisches Lexikon zum Alten Testament*, *DSD* 7 (2000) 87, the form with *d* in Palestinian Jewish is secondary.
16. *DJPA*, 34b.
17. *MdD*, 77b.
18. *ATTM*, 93.541.
19. T. Nöldeke, *Mandäische Grammatik* (Halle, 1875), §43.

Nonetheless, according to Dnl. 7:4, the wings will be torn away from the animal, it will be set on its feet like a human being, and given a human heart. The "blessings"[20] of this scene is interpreted variously: as the humanization of Babylonian rule (cf. Dnl. 4:13), perhaps in reference to Nebuchadnezzar's successor Nabonidus,[21] or as in anticipation of the anthropomorphic figure in Dnl. 7:13f.[22] Nevertheless, such a positive interpretation does not take into account the significance of the eagle as a symbol of power and force.

The third animal in Dnl. 7:6 resembles a panther (→ *nmr*), has four bird wings, and four heads. In the biblical world of imagery, the panther is also a feared predator (cf. Isa. 11:6; Jer. 5:6; Hos. 13:7; Cant. 4:8) although this animal "is weaker than a lion, has smaller wings (merely those of a—presumably common, small—'bird') than the eagle's wings of the lion" and serves as "a suitable image for the Persian Empire that resembles the Babylonian Empire in the scope of its realm of influence but which was, at least from the Jewish perspective, less destructive than the Babylonian Empire."[23] The number four refers either to universal claims (as in expressions of totality) or to the four Persian kings according to Dnl. 11:2.

III. Enoch's Animal Vision. Lion, panther, and eagle also occur in a list (although not as chimeras) in Enoch's animal vision (1 En. 83–90) that stems from roughly the same time as the final redaction of the book of Daniel. In 1 En. 89:10,55 and 90:2 they belong among the wild animals that symbolize the pagans and threaten to devour the Israelite sheep.

IV. Mesopotamian Texts. Parallels to the winged chimeras of Daniel appear in Mesopotamian literature among others in the bird monsters which, according to the omen series *šumma izbu*, announce important events,[24] in chaos battle myths such as Enuma Eliš[25] and the Anzu myth,[26] the Vision of the Underworld[27] and astrological animal symbols.[28]

V. Iconography. Chimeras are also widely attested in Mesopotamian iconography.[29] Apotropaic figures, from monumental palace sculptures to small clay figurines, include human-headed winged lions (presumably to be identified with the *šēdu*, originally a patron deity, then, in Syriac literature, e.g., a demon), which are attested from the mid-Assyrian to the Neo-Assyrian times. The human-headed winged bull

20. Goldingay.
21. Caquot.
22. Kvanvig.
23. Hartman and Di Lella.
24. Porter.
25. Gunkel.
26. Walton.
27. Kvanvig.
28. Caquot.
29. *ANEP*, no. 644-666; *AOB* no. 367-403.

appears more frequently (apparently the *lamassu* or the *šēdu*), examples of which appear from the Early Dynastic to the Achaemenid period. A lion "set on its feet" is comparable to portrayals of a lion in upright posture.[30] The various chimeras of Hellenistic iconography also include winged lions and other combinations of lion, bird, and other animals.

van Peursen

30. *ANEP* no. 192; Weber, nos. 15, 17, 64, etc.

גשׁם *gšm* /gešm/

I. Etymology and Distribution. II. Usage.

I. Etymology and Distribution. In older Aramaic, only the book of Daniel attests the noun *gšm* /gešm/ "body,"[1] but it may be related to the synonymous Arabic *ǧism*. Later, it also occurs in isolated in Palestinian Jewish Aramaic[2] and in East Aramaic.[3]

II. Usage. In Biblical Aramaic, *gšm* designates the body as a concrete, material object and appears only in suffixed forms. It is thereby distinguished from → *bśr* as the term for the general substance of the body and constitutes a contrast with the entire male or female person (→ *ʼnš* "human being"; *ʼnth* "woman"; *gbr* "man") or some other living being (→ *ḥyī*). In four of the five instances, it represents the living human body, subjected to various elements or natural forces, but nonetheless suffering no lasting injury: the flames of the oven that could not harm the men protected by God in Dnl. 3:27f. and the dew of heaven that dampens the king expelled from human society in 4:30 and 5:21. Dnl. 7:11, however, also uses it once for the cadaver of the smitten apocalyptic animal committed to the fire and, thus, definitively destroyed.

Gzella

ATTM, 545; 2, 371.

1. For the *æ* in the first syllable in Tiberian pointing, see *BLA* §41s.
2. *DJPA*, 137b.
3. See *LexSyr* 136 for Syriac, where the by-form /gušm/ may have arisen secondarily through assimilation of the vowel to the /m/; cf. *MdD*, 92 for Mandaic.

דב *db* /dobb/

I. Form and Meaning. II. Usage.

I. Form and Meaning. The LXX translates the word employed in the comparison involving the second animal in Daniel's vision in Dnl. 7:5 (→ *dmī*) with ἄρκτος "bear." The Masoretes point it *doḇ* in agreement with the Hebrew and targumic Aramaic *doḇ* "bear." The usual Aramaic lexeme for "bear" is *dubb-* or *dubbā* with the feminine counterpart *dbbh*,[1] which exhibits the glide *h* between the two *ā*-vowels (**dubbāhā*[*h*]), as in *šmh'* "the memorial stone"[2] and in the plural of a few other nouns (e.g., *'immāhāṯā* "the mothers," *ᵃḇāhāṯāḵ* "your fathers," *šᵉmāhāṯ* "names").

Nevertheless, the author of Dnl. 7, as Abraham Ibn Esra (ca. 1090-1167) already correctly noted in his "long" commentary on Daniel, does not intend this word to refer to the bear, but the wolf.[3] In fact, the interpretation as bear contradicts the immediate context of Dnl. 7:5 since the description of "three ribs in its mouth" and the command "eat much flesh!" issued to the animal perfectly suits a wolf, known as a violent carnivore (Zeph. 3:3) that devours flesh whenever it can. These characteristics hardly suit the brown bear, however. It is, indeed, an omnivore, but especially values honey, not meat.

From the perspective of the history of literature, the authors of Mesopotamian animal fables knew well the carnivorous lifestyle of the "wolf who bites into the best of the meat"[4] and the *db* that follows the lion in Dnl. 7:4 seems to correspond to the pattern "lion and wolf" as in the Erra Epic I:85: "lions and wolves destroy Šakkan's herd." In addition, a Jewish Aramaic magic bowl with a text apparently influenced by Dnl. 7:4-6 or a common source exhibits the sequences "lion, wolf, panther" and "lions, wolves, panthers."[5]

ATTM, 546; A. Caquot, "דֹּב *dōbh*," *TDOT*, III, 70-71; idem, "Sur les quatre bêtes de Daniel," *Sem* 5 (1955) 5-13; J. A. Fitzmyer, *The Aramaic Inscriptions of Sefire*. *BietOr* 19A (²1995); R. M. Frank, "The Description of the Bear in Daniel 7.5," *CBQ* 21 (1959) 505-7; L. Keimer, "Altägyptische, griechisch-römische und byzantinisch-koptische Darstellungen des syrischen Bären," *AfO* 17 (1954-56) 336-46; S. Ḥ. Kook, "*H'rwt lšmwt b'lj ḥjjm*," *Sinai* 14 (1943-44) 343-46; E. Lipiński, "The Bear and the Wolf in Aramaic Sources," *Rocznik Orientalistyczny* 52/2 (1999) 21-25; idem, *Studies in Aramaic Inscriptions and Onomastics II*. *OLA* 57 (1994), esp. 225f.; D. Opitz, "Der Bär bei den Babyloniern und bei Berossus," *AfO* 8 (1933) 45-51; J. A. Rimbach, "Bears or Bees? Sefire IA 31 and Daniel 7," *JBL* 97 (1978) 565f.; H. B. Tristram, *Natural History of the Bible* (London, ⁵1877), esp. 40-49; T. Wittstruck, "The Influence of Treaty Curse Imagery on the Beast Imagery of Daniel 7," *JBL* 97 (1978) 100-102.

1. *KAI* 222 A 31.
2. A. Lemaire, "Deux nouvelles stèles funéraires araméennes de Cilicie orientale," *EpAn* 23 (1994) 27.
3. On the wolf in the world of biblical imagery, cf. G. J. Botterweck, "זְאֵב *ze'ēbh*," *TDOT*, III, 1-7.
4. *BWL* 207.13.
5. J. Naveh and S. Shaked, *Amulets and Magic Bowls* (Jerusalem, 1985), bowl no. 13.4-5,12.

It is, consequently, very likely that the author of Dnl. 7:5 has a wolf in mind. In Aramaic, the wolf was originally called *δiʾb*, but the assimilation *ʾb* > *bb* is already attested in seventh-century B.C.E. Aramaic personal names,[6] while the shift *δ* > *d* also already took place in the same, or at the latest in the following, century. Thus, the wolf was then called *dibb-* with the by-form *dīḇ-* in later Aramaic texts, in Syriac, and in Neo-Aramaic dialects in which the wolf is called *dīḇā*, *dēḇa*, or *deḇo*. Jewish texts interchange "wolf" and "bear,"[7] but one should interpret talmudic passages that allude to Dnl. 7:5 in the light of reliable manuscripts and magic bowls.

II. Usage. The authors of Isa. 11:6 and 65:25 also knew the animal fable of the wolf and the lamb. There, the Hebrew text with *dīḇā ʿim/wᵉ-ʾīmmᵉrā* "the wolf with/and the lamb" is translated into Aramaic. An allusion to this fable appears in the sayings of Aḥiqar:[8] *dbʾ ʾzl ʿl ʾmr[yʾ]* "the wolf went to [the] lamb[s]," where the common translation "bear" rests, once again, on a misunderstanding. The same fable also influenced the author of 1 En. 89, where in the Aramaic text of 4Q206 (1 En. 89:14,27) wolves appear as *dbyʾ* (**dibbayyā*), which, in the Old Ethiopic version, could also be correctly rendered *ʾazʾᵉbᵉt* "wolves."

In the Babylonian Talmud,[9] the wolf in Dnl. 7:5 symbolizes the Persian[10] or the Median Empire,[11] perhaps the Parthian dynasty of the Arsacides and especially Mithridates I, who became king in 176 B.C.E. and founded the Parthian Empire. The talmudic interpretation may be correct if *db* denotes the wolf. In fact, Iranian texts often link the wolf (*gurg*) with demonic powers and "wolves" (*dibia*) appear in Mandaic as bringers of death.[12] Nevertheless, other symbolic explanations of the animals in Dnl. 7 have also been suggested, including some astrological in nature.[13]

Lipiński

---

6. Lipiński, *Studies*, 225f.
7. Kook.
8. *TADAE* C1.1,168.
9. Cf. *DJBA*, 315, 326.
10. *Qidd.* 72a (31).
11. *Gen.Rab.* 99.
12. E. M. Yamauchi, *Mandaic Incantation Texts. AOS* 49 (1967), no. 33.11.
13. See Caquot.

דבח *dbḥ*; דבח *dbḥ* /debaḥ/; דבח *dbḥ* /dabbāḥ/ (or /dāḇōḥ/); מדבח *mdbḥ* /madbaḥ/

I. Etymology and Derivatives. II. Verb "to Sacrifice." III. Noun *dbḥ* "Sacrifice." IV. Noun *dbḥ* "Offerer." V. Noun *mdbḥ* "Altar." 1. Jewish. 2. Gentile.

I. Etymology and Derivatives. Aramaic *dbḥ* represents a later spelling of the Semitic root *δbḥ*, which appears in older Aramaic texts as *zbḥ*. It expresses the idea of slaughtering or sacrifice to a deity. In addition to the verb *dbḥ* Aramaic also has the nouns *d*ᵉ*ḇaḥ*/*deḇḥā* "sacrifice," *dabbāḥ*/*dabbūḥā* "offerer, sacrificial priest," *maḏbaḥ*/*maḏb*ᵉ*ḥā* "offering place, altar," as well as a few other derivatives. The same terms could also refer in a somewhat different meaning as *deḇḥā* for the (sacrificial) feast, especially the Passover Feast, and *maḏb*ᵉ*ḥā* for a prayer room, a site for venerating a deity, or the choir room of a church. The root *dbḥ* is identical with the Hebrew *zbḥ*,[1] but, at the same time, its widespread use among various Gentile, Jewish, and Christian population groups throughout the Near East led to a broader semantic field. The word *dbḥyt'* in the Palmyrene inscription *CIS* II, 4029.4,[2] however, is not related to *dbḥ* but denotes the origin of the donor of the inscription as *Bē(t)-Ḥt'* and should be analyzed as *d-By-Ḥt'*.[3]

II. Verb "to Sacrifice." Interestingly, the Frahang-i Pahlavīk 19.12 translates the Aramaic form *yzbḥwn* with the middle Iranian *yaštan* and *yaz-* "to venerate" although *dbḥ* in the trilingual Xanthos inscription[4] from the year 358 B.C.E. refers explicitly to the sacrifice of animals: *kmr' znh zbḥ lr'š yrḥ' nqwh l-kndws 'lh' wdbḥ šnh bšnh twr* "This priest will offer a sheep to the god Kandawats on the new moon and will offer a steer every year." Safaite graffiti[5] attests the same usage of *δbḥ*. Nevertheless, the Sam'alian inscription on the Hadad statue from the mid-eighth century B.C.E. already employs *zbḥ* with the name of the deity as direct object and seems, therefore, to use the verb in the sense of "to venerate": *wyzbḥ hdd zn* "and he will venerate this Hadad."[6]

Ezra 6:3 may indirectly confirm such a semantic development: *bayṯā yiṯb*ᵉ*nē* ᵓᵃ*ṯar dī-ḏāḇ*ᵉ*ḥīn diḇ*ᵉ*ḥīn* "the temple should be (re-)built as a site at which one sacrifices." The use of the internal object *diḇ*ᵉ*ḥīn* "sacrifice" indicates that the verb alone no longer expressed the idea of sacrifice. Moreover, 3 Esd. 6:23 reproduces the same passage in a manner that seems to avoid any mention of a bloody sacrifice: ὅπου ἐπιθύουσιν διὰ πυρὸς ἐνδελεχοῦς "where one presents sacrifice through a continual fire." The translator may have even alluded consciously to Iranian fire temples because he wanted to reproduce the command of the Persian king.

ATTM, 546; 2, 372; J. Bergman, H. Ringgren, and B. Lang, "זָבַח *zābhach*," *TDOT*, IV, 8-29; C. Dohmen, "מִזְבֵּחַ *mizbēaḥ*," *TDOT*, VIII, 209-25; S. Germany, "*mzbḥ*," *ThWQ*, II, 627-32; W. K. Gilders, "*zbḥ*," *ThWQ*, I, 824-27; V. Hamp, "טָבַח *ṭāḇaḥ*, *TDOT*, V, 283-87; L. Jalabert and R. Mouterde, *Inscriptions grecques et latines de la Syrie II. BAH* 32 (1939), 256-67; J. T. Milik, *Dédicaces faites par des dieux. BAH* 92 (1972), esp. 26, 152; idem, "Nouvelles inscriptions sémitiques et grecques du pays de Moab," *SBFLA* 9 (1958-59) 330-58, esp. 331-33; idem, "Les papyrus araméens d'Hermoupolis et les cultes syro-phéniciens en Égypte perse," *Bibl* 48 (1967) 546-622, esp. 577f.; B. Porten, *Archives from Elephantine* (Berkeley, 1968), esp. 113-15, 292-95.

1. See J. Bergman, H. Ringgren, and B. Lang; C. Dohmen.
2. *PAT* 0375.
3. Milik, *Dédicaces*, 152.
4. *KAI* 319.14-17.
5. *ESE*, II, 350, l. 30.
6. *KAI* 214.15-16,21.

III. Noun *dbḥ* "Sacrifice." The noun *dbḥ* "sacrifice" occurs in a pair of Aramaic texts from Persian era Egypt, but only in the two exemplars of the letter that the leaders of the Jewish community in Elephantine sent in the year 408 B.C.E. to Bagohi, the administrator of Judea, has a comprehensible context been preserved. The pertinent word appears in the clause *zy yqrb lh ʿlwh wdbḥn* "who offers (*Yhw*) holocaust and sacrifice,"[7] although the same letter also mentions earlier "the grain offering, incense, and the burnt offering," *m(n)ḥtʾ wlbnwtʾ wʿlwtʾ* (7,21,25; 8,21, 24f.); consequently, the question arises as to whether the following plural *dbḥn*, distinguished through the choice of words from the burnt offering, encompasses the grain and incense offering. The letter *TADAE* A4. 10,10f. confirms this assumption. It excludes the burnt offering and, thus, supports the interpretation of *dib̲ᵉḥīn* in Ezr. 6:3 through 3 Esd. 6:23 because Greek often employs ἐπιθύω for incense,[8] e.g., Diodorus XII:11, Aristophanes, *Plutos* 1116.

The suffixed form *zbḥh* "his sacrifice" appears in the Samʾalian inscription dedicated to Hadad,[9] but the context is fragmentary. This form ending in *-h* cannot, however, be interpreted as a feminine variant because such a variant is attested in Syriac as a noun exhibiting another pattern, *d̲b̲īḥūṯā* "sacrifice, slaughter."

An inscription from Mt. Gerizim from the third or second century B.C.E. mentions the *byt dbḥʾ*, the "slaughterhouse."[10]

IV. Noun *dbḥ* "Offerer." The professional designation *dbḥ* appears in a Palmyrene inscription on a small altar dedicated in the year 213 C.E. by *Mlkw dbḥ l-Bl ʾlhʾ ṭb*.[11] It occurs further in Hatra in the grave inscription of a *dbḥʾ d-mlkʾ* "royal sacrificial priest."[12] Later still Syriac texts attest to the function of the "offerer."[13]

V. Noun *mdbḥ* "Altar."

1. Jewish. The "sacrifice site" or the "altar" is called *mad̲baḥ* in Aramaic. In Ezr. 7:17 this term denotes the main altar of the Second Temple in Jerusalem. The proleptic suffix *-h* of *mdbḥh* there indicates an eastern construction in Imperial Aramaic.

Isolated fragments of the Aramaic vision of the new Jerusalem, inspired by the last chapters of the book of Ezekiel, contain references to an altar for bread sacrifice,[14] which is also mentioned in the *Megillat Taʿanit*,[15] and to the altar for burnt sacrifice,[16] precisely as

7. *TADAE* A4.7,28; 8,27.
8. Examples in *LSJ*, 635.
9. *KAI* 214.18?,22.
10. Y. Magen, H. Misgav, and L. Tsfania, *Mount Gerizim Excavations*, vol. 1 (Jerusalem, 2004), no. 199 (p. 171).
11. *PAT* 1625.8f.; cf. Milik, *Dédicaces*, 26.
12. H164:2; text in K. Beyer, *Die aramäischen Inschriften aus Assur, Hatra und dem übrigen Ostmesopotamien* (Göttingen, 1998), 61, who vocalizes *dāb̲ōḥā* following Syriac.
13. *LexSyr*, 138a; *ThesSyr*, 806f.
14. 2Q24 4:6.
15. Text in *ATTM*, 356f.
16. 2Q24 5-6:5; 7:2.

in Ezk. 43:13-27. A fragment of a Targum of Lev. 16[17] reports how "the horns of the altar" were smeared with goat blood, as in Lev. 16:18. The later Targums employ the word *mdbḥ* here in the same sense to translate the Hebrew *mizbēᵃḥ*. A constructed sacrificial altar is also the reference in 1QapGen where it says that Abraham erected an altar in Bethel (21:1) and in Mamre (21:20) in order to present a burnt offering and a grain offering (21:2. 20). Likewise, T. Levi 35:5,7,14,21,23 and 36:2 refer to a constructed sacrificial altar because lumber must be placed under "the burnt offering on the altar," *'lt' 'l mdbḥ'* (35:21) and the priest should sprinkle "the blood on the sides of the altar," *lmzrq dm' 'l kwtly mdbḥ'* (36:1-2). In contrast, 1QapGen 10:15 refers to an incense altar because there Noah says: *'l mdbḥ' 'qṭrt* "I presented incense on the altar." Indeed, *qṭr* is used in Aramaic, in contrast to Hebrew,[18] explicitly and exclusively for incense.[19] This circumstance means that 1QapGen 10:15 does not correspond to the biblical text of Gen. 8:20. Such an alteration is difficult to understand in the light of Gen. 9:3, however; there the text refers specifically to a later incident when God permitted people to eat meat.

The "altar of *Yahu*," *mdbḥ zy yhw 'lh'*, in the Jewish temple on Elephantine serves for "the grain offering, the incense, and the burnt offering" according to the letter of the community elders already cited,[20] but the brief memorandum that finally approved the reconstruction of the sanctuary (→ *dkr* III) prescribes that "one should present the grain offering and the incense on the altar as was formerly done," *mnḥt wlbnwt' yqrbwn 'l mdbḥ' zk lqbl zy lqdmyn hwh nt'bd*.[21] This document mentions no burnt offering, however, which implies that "the house of the altar of the God of heaven," like the sanctuary mentioned there (9:3f.), contains no sacrificial altar, but only an incense altar that also served for the presentation of grain offerings. The somewhat later letter *TADAE* A4.10,10f. expressly excludes burnt offerings.

2. *Gentile.* Non-Jewish Aramaic sources only rarely mention altars. However, the Aramaic grave inscription for a northern Arabic queen from the fourth or third century B.C.E. found near el-Kerak,[22] mentions a grave altar: *wgr sr' mlkt'* ['']*bd 'bdkmš ḥll br 'm' mdbḥ' dnh wnškth lzk b*[*y*]*t*['] "rock tomb of Sarra, the queen: 'Abdu-Kamosh Hillal, son of 'Amma, made this altar and its shrine for this building." The meaning of the Kerak inscription lies in the fact that it shows how the altar could transform from its function as a ritual object into a symbol of a deity hidden in a shrine. This transition comes to completion in the cult of Zeus Μαδβαχος, of the "altar," venerated in the sanctuary of Ğebel Šeiḫ Barakāt northwest of Aleppo. This place, described by Theodoret (Hist. Phil. 4:2), has produced several Greek inscriptions,[23] but has not yet been excavated. The same god is mentioned by the Greek version of his name Βωμός, likewise "altar," in an

17. 4Q156.
18. Cf. R. E. Clements, "קטר *qṭr*," *TDOT*, XIII, 9-16.
19. P. Heger, "קטר: נסק-סלק A Study of Two Different Verbs Used by Onkelos to Translate the Term קטר of the Masoretic Text," *ZAW* 107 (1995) 466-81.
20. *TADAE* A4.7, 25f.; 8,24f.; → III.
21. *TADAE* A4.9,9-11.
22. Milik, "Nouvelles inscriptions."
23. *IGLS* II, 465-74.

inscription from Burǧ Bāqirḥā;[24] the proximity to Antioch may explain why his cult was also established in Acco, as the name *Ndbḵh* (from *Maḏbaḥā*), which, according to the Talmud was given a local deity,[25] suggests. This name displays the same shift from *m* to *n* that appears in the prefix of words with a bilabial such as *b*. Instead of which, the presumably Aramaic personal name *ʾšm-mdbḥ* from Egypt belongs to an inscription that, in all likelihood, may be counterfeit.[26]

Lipiński

24. *IGLS* II, 569.
25. *ʾAbod. Zar.* 11b.
26. J. Naveh, "Aramaica Dubiosa," *JNES* 27 (1968) 321.

דבק *dbq*

I. Grammatical Constructions. II. Meaning "to Adhere to, to Adjoin." III. Meaning "Arrive."

I. Grammatical Constructions. In Aramaic as in Hebrew, the verbal root *dbq* regularly occurs in the intransitive G-stem "to cling to, to adhere," and is constructed with a variety of prepositional expressions, usually introduced with *l-*, rarely with *b-*[1] or *ʿm* (Dnl. 2:43), in some cases also with a further addition (→ II). This original meaning persists in Neo-Aramaic and Neo-Arabic languages that employ the same root as well as certain nominal derivatives for the capture of birds with birdlime.[2] The figurative use "to border on (*l-*)" in geographical descriptions is common, however (→ II), as is, in 1QapGen, the noteworthy use "to arrive."[3] In this apparently secondary meaning, the verb in Aramaic also forms a (relatively rare) causative stem "to bring to (*l-*)."[4] Later, the D-stem "to connect" and the corresponding Dt-stem for the passive "to be connected" are clearly attested.[5]

II. Meaning "to Adhere to, to Adjoin." The common literal meaning "to cling to, to adhere" as in Hebrew occurs once in Biblical Aramaic and frequently in the Aramaic texts

E. Jenni, "דבק *dbq* to hang on," *TLOT*, 324f.; B. Schlenke, "*dbq*," *ThWQ*, I, 628-33; G. Wallis, "דָּבַק *dābhaq*," TDOT, IV, 79-84.

1. 1QapGen 14:11,14.
2. Cf. S. Fraenkel, *Die aramäischen Fremdwörter im Arabischen* (Leiden, 1886), 120f.
3. Usually also constructed with *l-* to indicate the objective, in 1QapGen 21:6 also with *ʿd*; → III.
4. 4Q204 1 6:23 (1 En. 14:10).
5. *DJPA*, 138; *DJBA*, 312f.; *LexSyr*, 139; *MdD*, 101.

from Qumran. It seems to be negated in the interpretation of the vision of the colossus with clay feet (→ *dhb* II) in Dnl. 2:43 for empires that, despite a policy of intermarriage, do no intermix just as iron does not adhere to clay (periphrastic ptcp. with the imperfect of *hwī* to express duration in the future, supplemented with *dnh ʿm dnh* "the one with the other" to designate reciprocity).[6] 1QapGen 14:11,14 employs the verb in the interpretation of a dream image of a plant sprout that adheres firmly to (*b*) its stump;[7] 11Q10 14:4 (Job 29:10) uses it of the tongue sticking to the gums; 36:2 (Job 41:8) uses it for the airtight armor of Leviathan; and 36:8 (41:15) employs it for Leviathan's firmly jointed belly.

In Imperial Aramaic contracts, however, the figurative use of the participle or imperfect for "to border on (*l*-)" often appears in the description of the location of plots of land[8] or parts of buildings.[9] The same usage continues in the description of grave niches in Palmyrene burial inscriptions such as *PAT* 0053.4 to clarify the circumstances of possession (cession texts; they follow the Imperial Aramaic legal tradition) and in the geographic definition of land boundaries distributed to Noah's sons after the Flood in 1QapGen 16:10,11,19; 17:8,9,10,16.

Similarly, *dbq* is employed metaphorically for emotional attachment to something, as already in the pre-Imperial Aramaic Hermopolis Letters, here 4.5 (with *lbb* "heart" as subject and said of a robe), and perhaps *ʾl tdbq* "may he not hang on to" in 4Q197 4 1:1 (Tob. 5:19),[10] which *ATTM*, 2, 177 nevertheless interprets following the difficult Greek text ἀργύριον τῷ ἀργυρίῳ μὴ φθάσαι as "to be joined to."[11] Moreover, the verb in 4Q539 5:3 should probably be understood similarly in relation to being ruled by possessions.[12]

III. Meaning "Arrive." While the meaning "to cling, to adhere" in literal or figurative usage is attested across the entire history of the Aramaic language, a remarkable use of *dbq* for "to get to" appears in concentration in 1QapGen from Qumran in relation to other verbs of movement in Abraham's report of his journeys, usually in the first person singular: 19:8,9; 21:1,16,17,18,29; 22:7,10, always with *l*- indicating the objective; for Lot's arrival in Sodom according to 21:6 in contrast with *ʿd*, possibly for the nuance "right up to" indicating the extreme endpoint.[13] This usage presumably developed as an extension of the older meaning "to border on = to reach" into "to arrive at." Although it otherwise is typical only of 1QapGen, a corresponding caus-

6. On this passage, cf. H. Gzella, *Tempus, Aspekt und Modalität im Reichsaramäischen. VOK* 48 (2004), 263f.

7. Usually read as *gdm*, according to *ATTM*, 2, 97f., however, *grm*, literally "bones," here "self."

8. *TADAE* B2.3,6; B2.10,5; B3.4,9; B3.5,9,11; B3.10,9, here with the addition *ʾgr bʾgr* "wall to wall."

9. *TADAE* B2.1,5,4f.; B3.10,10.

10. Of money, according to DSSStE 389 and J. Fitzmyer, *Tobit. CEJL* (2003), 197.

11. Cf. in possible support now also *lmdbqt* "in order to join to" in Ostracon 156cc6 Clermont-Ganneau collection, but the interpretation is not certain, see H. Lozachmeur, *La collection Clermont-Ganneau*, vol. 1 (Paris, 2006), 309 with n. 326; thus, the meaning "to connect" of the D-stem only later clearly demonstrable could already appear here.

12. On the context of the passage, cf. H. Gzella, "*šlṭ*," III, *ThWQ*, III, 951.

13. Cf. J. Fitzmyer, *The Genesis Apocryphon. BietOr* 18/B (^{2}2004), 218: "as far as."

ative stem "to bring to" in the internal passive and also in the first-person singular *'dbqt lb'y r[b* "I was brought to a great house," appears in the report of Enoch's dream journey.[14]

Gzella

14. 4Q204 1 6:23 (1 En. 14:10).

דבר *dbr*; מדבר *mdbr* /madbar/; דברת *dbrt* /dabar(at)/; דבר *dbr* /dabbār/

I. Etymology. II. Meaning of the Ground Stem. 1. Intransitive. 2. Transitive "to Take." III. Meaning of the Doubled Stem. IV. Noun *madbar*. V. Other Nominal Derivatives. 1. "Run." 2. "Leader."

I. Etymology. The Aramaic root *dbr* essentially expresses departing or heading toward an objective. It belongs to the common Semitic basic lexicon and underlies the Akkadian *dap/bāru* "to go to," the Ugaritic *dbr* "to depart,"[1] the old Canaanite *dubburu* "to expel,"[2] the Arabic *dabara* "to turn one's back,"[3] and the classic Ethiopic *dabr* "mountain" or "pasture."[4] The latter corresponds to the later Aramaic *daḇrā*, which presumably appears as *dabru* in the Babylonian lexical list *Malku* = *šarru*.[5] In fact, *daḇr* is a "distant" location like the *d*ᵉ*ḇīr*, the "remote" back room of the temple,[6] unless it was originally the holy "mountain," much as Ge'ez calls a cloister *dabr* because holy sites can usually be found on hills. In any case, the term *d*ᵉ*ḇīr* belongs to the same root.

ATTM, 546f.; 2, 372; H. Gzella, "*dbr* I," *ThWQ*, I, 634-36; J. C. Greenfield, "The Prepositions *'ad - 'al* in Aramaic and Hebrew," *BSOAS* 40 (1977) 371f.; E. Lipiński, "'Leadership': The Roots *DBR* and *NGD* in Aramaic," in "*Und Mose schrieb dieses Lied auf.*" *FS O. Loretz. AOAT* 250 (1998), 501-14, esp. 501-8; W. L. Moran, "*duppuru* (*dubburu*)—*ṭuppuru* too?," *JCS* 33 (1981) 44-7; A. F. Rainey, *Canaanite in the Amarna Tablets*, vol. II. *HO* I/25 (1996), esp. 146-48, 309; A. Schoors, *The Preacher Sought to Find Pleasing Words I. Grammar. OLA* 41 (1991), esp. 123f., 147; W. von Soden, "Zum akkadischen Wörterbuch: 34. *duppuru* und *ṭuppuru*," *Or* 18 (1949) 393-95; B. Zuckerman, "'For your sake . . .': A Case Study in Aramaic Semantics," *JANES* 15 (1983) 119-29.

1. *DUL*³, 261.
2. EA 1394f.
3. H. Wehr, *A Dictionary of Modern Written Arabic* (Urbana, IL, ⁴1994), 312.
4. *CDG*, 121.
5. M. J. Geller, "A Vocabulary of Rare Words," *Or* 61 (1992) 206f.; new edition by I. Hrůša, *Die akkadische Synonymenliste malku = šarru. AOAT* 50 (2010), here VIII 157.
6. See M. Ottosson, "הֵיכָל *hêkhāl*," *TDOT*, III, 384-85.

The Akkadian verb usually appears as *duppuru,*[7] "to depart" or "to stay away," with the characteristic unvoiced allophone (*dbr*/*dpr*), while, in contrast, *ṭapāru*[8] very likely must be stricken from the lexicon[9] because the reading *dap*/*bāru* is equally possible, especially in Mari[10] and in the Amarna letters. In fact, the root *dbr* has an Afro-Asiatic etymology because it occurs in Cushitic, as Oromo *dabra* "he goes by" with the causative *dabar-sa* "he brings over here," and in Libyco-Berber with the verb *dfar* "to go along behind," "to take over there," as well as the noun *dᵉffīr* "back portion." It is related to the Egyptian *dbn* "to walk around," particularly since *n* and *r* could trace to allophones of the same phonemic liquid in Afro-Asiatic.

In contrast, Aramaic *dbr* has nothing to do with Hebrew *dbr* "to say"[11] that represents a dissimilated form of *dbb* "to speak."[12] In Aramaic, this root essentially has the meaning "to head toward," "to go to," "to lead to" (*dbr l-*), but also "to take," a nuance frequent in the G-stem in targumic and talmudic Aramaic.[13] The absent vocalization sometimes makes it difficult, however, to distinguish between the G-stem and the D-stem. One of the best-known nominal derivations of this root is *maḏbar*, a distant location, thus, "wilderness" or "steppe" (→ IV),[14] but *diḇr* "run" and *dabbār* "leader" should also be mentioned at this point (→ V).

II. Meaning of the Ground Stem.

1. Intransitive. The G-stem of *dbr* appears with certainty in a fifth century B.C.E. ostracon with an Aramaic letter from Elephantine in Egypt: *dbr ʿlwhy wyntnhy lkm* "go to him and he will give it to you."[15] The phrase *dbr l-* "to lead, guide" also presupposes the use of the G-stem because it is attested with the G-stem infinitive *lmdbr*: [*šryw* . . .] *lmdbr ʾln lʾln* "some [began. . .] to lead the others."[16] The same nuance also appears in 1QapGen 21:27: *dbr mlk ʿylm lkwl ḥbrwhy* "the king of Elam assumed leadership over all his allies." A further instance occurs in 4Q205/6 (1 En. 89:14), where the Classical Ethiopic text replaces the "ram" with the "lord": *wdbr dkrʾ lʾmryʾ kwlhwn* "and the goat assumed the leadership of all lambs." The G-stem infinitive *lmdbr* appears further in a passage in the astronomical book of Enoch that mentions the part of the earth that humanity chose as a dwelling: *ḥd mnhwn lmdbr bh bny ʾnšʾ* "one of them for the people to walk around in."[17] At the same time, the use of the verb *dbr* here seems to allude to an original nomadic lifestyle.

---

7. *AHw*, I, 177; *CAD*, III, 186-88.
8. *AHw*, III, 1380.
9. Moran.
10. *ARM* XV 199, 275.
11. See J. Bergman, H. Lutzmann, and W. H. Schmidt, "דָּבָר *dābhar*," *TDOT*, III, 84-125.
12. *AHw*, I, 146f.; *CAD*, III, 4-14, cf. 132-34.
13. *DJPA*, 138f.; *DJBA*, 313.
14. Cf. S. Talmon, "מִדְבָּר *miḏbār*," *TDOT*, VIII, 87-118.
15. *RÉS* 1295, 7-10; *ESE* III,120; *TADAE* D7.29,7-9.
16. 4Q205/6 (1 En. 89:1).
17. 4Q209 (1 En. 77:3).

2. *Transitive "to Take."* The transitive meaning "to take" appears in Maqqedah[18] and is frequent in the Targums, where *dbr* is usually vocalized as a G-stem, e.g., *qūm dᵉḇar yāṯ ʾīṯᵉṯāḵ wᵉyāṯ tartēn bᵉnāṯāḵ* "Stand up, take your wife and your two daughters!";[19] *ūḏḇar yāṯ kol gēṯūhī* "and he took all his flocks."[20] The same stem may, therefore, also be present in 11Q10 35:7 (Job 40:28): *wtdbrnh lʿbd ʿlm* "and will take him as a slave forever?". A G-stem must likewise be accepted for the corresponding specimen in a letter from Bar-Kosiba: *wtdbrwn yt tyrsws . . . wyth ʿmkwn* "and you will take Tirsos in . . . and he will come with you."[21] This nuance of *dbr* appears further in lines 3 and 9 of the same letters and frequently in 1QapGen in reference to Sara: *dbrhʾ wḥzhʾ* "he took her and saw her" (20:9); *hʾ ʾnttk dbrh* "here is your wife: take her!" (20:27). The internal passive of the G-stem occurs twice and thereby confirms that this stem and not the D-stem is used for the active diathesis: *kdy dbryt mny* "when she was taken from me" (20:11); *dbrt ʾntty mny* "my wife has been taken from me" (20:14). Finally, it seems that the G-stem must also be assumed in the letter from the elders of the Jewish community from Elephantine since the text refers to soldiers who would be led in and not out: *npyn (zk) dbr mṣryʾ ʿm ḥylʾ ʾḥrnn* "(that one) Naphaina took the Egyptians along with the other troops."[22]

III. Meaning of the Doubled Stem. Although *dbr* with the meaning "to lead" occurs both in the G- and the D-stem in Palestinian Jewish[23] and Babylonian Jewish[24] Aramaic, Syriac,[25] and Mandaic,[26] its use with the specific meaning "to lead something out" in Mandaic corresponds to the D-stem,[27] as also ensues from the Syriac *waw* amulet: *mdbryn myʾ wʿlmʾ bmʿbrtʾ* "leading the water and the world into the ford."[28] The figurative use of *dbr* in the Babylonian Talmud also confirms it: *ʿd kmh qʾ mdbrt ʾlmnwt ḥyyn* "how long will you continue to live the life of widow?"[29] This last expression has a parallel in a fragment of 1QapGen 6:2 (*kwl ywmy dbrt* "I spent all my days") and in a Palmyrene honorary inscription, *dbr ʿmrh škytyt* "he led his life in an honorable manner."[30] Taken together, these examples demonstrate that *dbr* should be identified in such contexts as a D-stem, *dabbar*, not as a G-stem.

This also seems to be the case when *dbr* means "to remove." Despite the Syriac parallels *dḇar baqtīrā* "to take with force,"[31] one should assume the imperfect of the D-stem

18. I. Ephʿal and J. Naveh, *Aramaic Ostraca of the Fourth Century BC from Idumaea* (Jerusalem, 1996), no 46, 1.
19. Tg. Onq. of Gen. 19:15.
20. Tg. Onq. of Gen. 31:18.
21. Pap. Yadin 56, 5-7.
22. *TADAE* A4.7,8; 8,7.
23. *DJPA*, 138f.
24. *DJBA*, 313.
25. *ThesSyr*, 811-13.
26. *MdD*, 102.
27. *MdD*, 102.
28. J. Naveh and S. Shaked, *Amulets and Magic Bowls* (Jerusalem, 1985), no. A6.5-6.
29. *Ketub.* 62b.
30. *CIS* II 3932.6; *PAT* 0278.6.
31. *ThesSyr*, 3589.

ldabbar for the sentence from an inscription from Hatra *l' ldbrhn . . . bqṭyr'*[32] "may he not remove her . . . with force" in contrast to the typical interpretation. In this context, one could also cite a passage from Targum Onqelos on Ex. 14:21 where the combination *dbr b-* also occurs: *weḏabbar yhy yāṯ yammā berūaḥ qiḏūmā* "and the Lord removed the sea with an east wind." Most likely, the D-stem of *dbr* also appears in 4Q210 78:7 where it refers to the moon: *wdbr* (or *ydbr*) *yrḥy' bplgy šby'yn* "he removed the moon in fourteenths."[33]

IV. Noun *madbar*. The noun *maḏbar* denotes the uncultivated, underused land, the wilderness and the steppe, where the shepherd can lead his flocks: *weḏabbar yāṯ 'ānā . . . le-maḏberā* "and Moses led the flocks . . . into the steppe.[34] It is uninhabited land;[35] it designates the boundary of a palm garden in a legal text from the Dead Sea.[36] The word *mdbr* also occurs in the Assur ostracon[37] and became a loanword in Akkadian.[38] In 4Q209 (1 En. 77:3), the *mdbryn* are a certain section of the earth; according to the Book of Giants, a few varieties of living beings dwell there.[39] According to the same text, Enoch, however, dwells beyond "the great wilderness, *mdbr' rb'*.[40] It is doubtful, however, whether this mythical wilderness is identical with the "great wilderness" in 1QapGen 21:11, which refers to the Syrian steppe that extends to the Euphrates and is known for its caravan routes, *'rḥ' dy mdbr'*.[41] The expression "El-Paran that is in the wilderness" in the same text[42] was taken from Gen. 14:6, but its location is unknown. In Greek Enoch *mdbr* is sometimes left untranslated, but interpreted as a place name: Μανδοβαρα (1 En. 26:1), Βαβδερα (1 En. 29:1).

V. Other Nominal Derivatives.

1. "Run." The astronomical book of Enoch seems to establish why the lunar month is shorter than the solar month by observing that the course of the moon "falls behind the course of the sun," *mḥsr mn dbr šmš*.[43] The noun *dbr* in its use in this passage reflects the basic meaning of the root and denotes the course of the stars in Targum Jonathan of Jgs. 5:20, which says that the stars battled against Sisera: *mikkiḇšē diḇrēhōn tammān 'itt^egaḥ q^erāḇā 'im Sīs^erā* "from the courses of their orbits, war was waged against Sisera." One may certainly vocalize *diḇr* here because this lexeme already turns up as a loanword

32. H79.12f.

33. This is the fundamental astronomical unit of measurement for night and day time, which are each divided into fourteen parts; cf. H. Gzella, "*dbr* I," *ThWQ*, I, 635f.

34. Tg. Onq. on Ex. 3:1.

35. 11Q10 31:4 (Job 38:26).

36. Pap.Yadin 7.5.

37. *KAI* 233.5.

38. *AHw*, II, 572a; *CAD*, X/1, 11f.

39. 4Q203 8:13.

40. 4Q530 3:5; cf. Gen. 5:24.

41. 1QapGen 21:28.

42. 1QapGen 21:29f.

43. 4Q209 (1 En. 79:5).

with the spelling *dybr* in the (Proto-)Mishnaic of the Copper Scroll:[44] *bdybr hšlyšy* "in the third course" (i.e., of the cave).[45]

The expression *'l dbr* or *'al dibraṯ*[46] was often used in Imperial Aramaic[47] and also occurs in Dnl. 2:30 and 4:14, in 11Q10 1:7 (Job 18:4) and 34:4 (Job 40:8), as well as in early Mishnaic Hebrew (Eccl. 3:18; 7:14; 8:2). It is not associated with the Hebrew *dāḇār* "word," however, but with the Aramaic *diḇr-* "course" and literally means "over the course of," "by reason of" or "because," "from," and "thereby." The occurrence of *'l dbr* in the sayings of Aḥiqar and in the Bar-Puneš text[48] certainly contradicts the hypothesis of a Hebrew origin, whereas there is no root *dbr* "to speak" in Aramaic. Conversely, this circumstance does not establish that the Hebrew use of the same expression must necessarily be an Aramaism because the root *dbr* "to lead" is present in Hebrew at least in its derivatives *d^eḇīr* and *miḏbar*. The form *'l dbrt* with a final *-t* must certainly have a dialectical origin. The substantive *dbrt* occurs in Job 5:8, where its basic meaning also appears clearly: *'æl-^{xe}lōhīm 'āśīm diḇrāṯī* "I will direct my course to God." Likewise, it found entry in Ps. 110:4: *'al-diḇrāṯī malkī-ṣædæq* "from a just king." The assimilated forms *'dbr* and *'d dbrt*[49] demonstrate that this expression became a fixed formula. After the fifth century B.C.E., Aramaic texts no longer attest its older variant *'l dbr*, and *'l dbrt* fell into disuse after the second century B.C.E.

2. "Leader." This noun *dibr(at)* must be distinguished, however, from *dabbār* "leader" or "wagon driver," as in Targum Jonathan of 2 K. 9:20, where the watchman recognizes Jehu's wagon driver: *dabbārā k^edabbārā d^eYehū* "the wagon driver is like the wagon driver of Jehu." The Deir 'Allā wall inscription may also attest the word. There, in contrast to the typical explanation following the Hebrew "to speak," *dbr* in *spr dbr* can also be understood either as the Aramaic verb or as the noun that more precisely defines the "scribe who leads (away)." Yet, an exact interpretation is not possible because the text is in a fragmentary condition. The same noun may also appear in a Palmyrene inscription where one reads *bdbry kl*[. . .] "among the leaders of all [. . .]."[50] In contrast, the title *mdwbr*, which very often designates the household servant in the Nisa ostraca,[51] is a Persian word that consists of the components *maδu-* "wine" and the root morpheme **-bāra-* "bearing, provided with" for the formation of professional designations.[52]

Lipiński

---

44. 3Q15 2:3.
45. *DSSStE*, 232: *brwbd.*
46. See W. H. Schmidt, "דָּבַר *dābhar*," *TDOT*, III, 106.
47. *DNSI*, 239f.
48. *TADAE* C1.1,201; 2,23.
49. *TADAE* B7.1,3; Dnl. 4:14.
50. C. Dunant, *Le sanctuaire de Baalshamin à Palmyre III* (Rome, 1971), no. 34:1; *PAT* 0187.1.
51. See *DNSI*, 596.
52. P. Horn, *Grundriss der neupersischen Etymologie* (Straßburg, 1893), no. 1073.

דהב *dhb* /dahab/

I. Etymology and General Usage. II. As a Symbol in the Golden Age Myth. III. As an Attribute of Idols.

I. Etymology and General Usage. As is also true in other Semitic languages, the Aramaic lexeme *dhb* /dahab/, developed from the older /δahab/ and consequently spelled *zhb* on into the Imperial Aramaic period, serves as a general designation for "gold." It can be supplemented with an addition such as *ṭb* /ṭāb/ "pure" (→ *ṭyb*).[1] A cognate of the substantive /ḫurāṣu/[2] common instead in Akkadian, Ugaritic, and Phoenician-Punic appears in Syriac as the adjective *ḥrā'ā* "blond, golden yellow,"[3] but the underlying noun is not productive in Aramaic.

Since the Old Aramaic period, *zhb*/*dhb* "gold" in the general sense is attested throughout, but was employed figuratively quite early on alongside *ksp* /kasp/ "silver" for power or high value. It occurs first in the royal epithet *b'ly ksp wb'ly zhb* "owner of silver and owner of gold" in inscriptions from Sam'al,[4] furthermore, probably figuratively for something valuable, in a fragmentary wisdom saying of Aḥiqar.[5]

It also appears once in Imperial Aramaic as the material of valuable temple implements.[6] The attribute *zy zhb'* "of gold," as in this passage, also continues to appear later, but is interchangeable with a construct phrase (as in Dnl. 5:2,3, also for cultic vessels; cf. the corresponding variation in Dnl. 3:1 and 3:5). Furthermore, insignia of authority employ it as in the golden chain in Dnl. 5:7,16,29, presumably a typical Persian symbol,[7] and commercial texts as a designation for material.[8] On the other hand, it is also used in a figurative sense for a person's merit before a god, which is worth more than a sacrifice of a thousand talents of silver and gold.[9]

J. J. Collins, *Daniel. Herm* (1993); B. Gregory, "*zhb*,"*ThWQ*, I, 830-33; B. Kedar-Klopfstein, "זָהָב *zāhābh*," *TDOT*, IV, 32-40; K. Koch, *Daniel 1–4. BK* XXII/1 (2005).

1. Dnl. 2:32; 11Q18 10 1:2; 11:4; literally "good" and corresponding to the Hebrew *ṭāhōr*.
2. Hebrew *ḥārûṣ*, employed in poetic texts as a synonym for *zāhāḇ*.
3. *LexSyr*, 257f.
4. *KAI* 215.11, composed in Sam'alian, which is closely related to Old Aramaic, then after the shift to Old Aramaic as the official language, once again in *KAI* 216.11; regarding the language situation, cf. H. Gzella, "Language and Script," in H. Niehr, ed., *The Aramaeans in Ancient Syria. HO* I/106 (2014), 71-107, esp. 74f.
5. *TADAE* C1.1,192.
6. *TADAE* A4.7,12 par. 4.8,11; Ezr. 5:14 and 6:5, similarly 7:15,16,18 for the "gold and silver" for new fixtures for the temple.
7. Cf. Collins, 247.
8. Very frequent in import and export lists *TADAE* C3.7.
9. *TADAE* A4.7,28, said here of the one who authorizes the reconstruction of the destroyed temple in Elephantine; the copy A4.8:27 transfers "silver" only.

Starting from such figurative expressions, "gold" came to be employed generally for "valuable objects" or "wealth" in combination, not just with silver, which continued to be a widespread combination and also occurs in various, mostly fragmentary, instances from Qumran,[10] but also with other noble metals of lesser value such as *nḥš* /noḥāš/ "copper, bronze" and *przl* /parzel/ "iron." This is already the case in an Imperial Aramaic contract concerning a silver credit[11] that names these four metals in the midst of an enumeration of distrainable objects that the creditor can take from the house of the debtor in the event of a delay in payment.[12]

This list, which is also traditional in biblical diction, is used in addition to differentiate by worthiness in the figurative language of the visions (→ II), or inclusively of idol images made and foolishly venerated by people in contrast to the living God (→ III).

An adjective of association *dhby* /dahabāy/ "golden" may be attested in 1QapGen 13:9 alongside *kspy* /kaspāy/ "of silver,"[13] but the context is very fragmentary.

II. As a Symbol in the Golden Age Myth. In the vision of the "colossus with clay feet" in Dnl. 2, the proverbial list "gold, silver, copper, and iron" (→ I) appears as a theological interpretation of world history. King Nebuchadnezzar dreamed of a giant statue with a golden head, a silver torso, a copper stomach, iron legs, and feet of iron and clay (Dnl. 2:31-33); it was smashed (→ *dqq*) by a stone that then grew into a great mountain that covered the entire world (2:34f.). In the interpretation, the metals are all associated with sequential and ever increasingly declining empires (2:36-45): the golden head, of the best metal, stands for Nebuchadnezzar himself; the silver upper body for a lesser empire after him, the copper stomach for a third, worldwide empire; the iron legs for a fourth, especially gruesome; and the feet of iron and clay, finally, for a divided empire that, despite its marriage policy, does not become mixed (just as iron and clay do not combine → *dbq*) and finally collapses with the arrival of the comprehensive kingdom of God that comes from the outside with no human assistance.

Attempts to identify these political entities precisely run throughout the entire history of the interpretation of the book of Daniel; according to the current dominant opinion, an older, originally three-leveled scheme with the empires Assyria, Media, and Persia was adapted through the alteration of Assyria in Babylonia and expanded with Alexander and/or the Hellenistic Diadochoi.[14] In any case the sequence of four metals with decreasing value recalls the ancient "Golden Age Myth," as it has appeared repeatedly since Hesiod's didactic epic *Works and Days* from the eighth or early seventh century B.C.E. in the literature and was received especially in Augustian poetry (Horace, Virgil, Tibullus and very extensively Ovid in the first book of his *Metamorphoses*).[15] Gold, silver, and

10. Cf. 1QapGen 20:31,33 with the enumeration of Abraham's property; 4Q529 1:15.

11. *TADAE* B3.1,9f.

12. Cf. later *ṣn't ksp wdhb* "artistic objects of silver and gold" in a similar context in a Nabatean contract from the Dead Sea concerned with securing a dowry, nV 1:25 in *ATTM*, 2, 205-8.

13. *ATTM*, 2, 373.

14. Cf. Collins, 166-70.

15. For an overview, cf. B. Gatz, *Weltalter, goldene Zeit und sinnverwandte Vorstellungen* (Hildesheim, 1967); Koch, 126-38 envisages an Iranian origin.

iron also appear in this sequence in a dream vision of Noah in 1QapGen 13:9f., but the context there remains obscure.

In another vision, of the new Jerusalem from Qumran, gates and the foundations of the walls appear to be of pure gold[16] and thereby represent the divine majesty.

III. As an Attribute of Idols. Because of their high value, gold and silver also serve for the production or decoration of statues of gods. Since around the time of Deutero-Isaiah (Isa. 44:9-20), their veneration has been repeatedly subject to a strict monotheistic and anti-image critique by which Judaism in the Hellenistic-Roman period distinguished itself from pagan cults. In fact, from this perspective, the less concrete term "paganism" can be defined for antiquity in the broadest sense as idolatry, thus, as the veneration of gods in the form of images or statues.[17]

The super-sized golden or gilded statue (*ṣᵉlēm dī-ḏᵉhaḇ*) in Dnl. 3 serves as a symbol of such a conflict. King Nebuchadnezzar commissioned it and obligated all the subjects of the empire to worship it under threat of the death penalty. In the course of the chapter, it is repeated in litany fashion that it involves a statue of god—grandiose but lifeless (Dnl. 3:1,5,7,10,12,14,18). As devotees of the true God, Daniel and his friends refused to obey, were denounced by their enemies, and cast into a fiery oven. Through loyalty to the invisible God who, in contrast to the idol images (as costly and impressive as they may be), proves to be efficacious, however, they survived, which is why even the king converted and placed their religion under special protection.

If Dnl. 3 emphasizes the contrast between lifeless idols and God, the veneration of "gods of gold, silver, iron, wood, and stone"—thus an expanded version of the traditional list of four metals (→ I and II)—at Belshazzar's banquet (Dnl. 5:4,23) appears not only senseless, but sacrilegious. The profanation of the Jewish temple's gold and silver vessels at a feast (5:2,3) made it even worse and, thus, would inevitably bring divine punishment. Nebuchadnezzar recognized God and was saved, his son "Belshazzar, however, was killed in the same night by his servants."

In the same tradition as Daniel's Aramaic court narratives stands the "Prayer of Nabonidus" from Qumran.[18] At the same time, it makes clear that the tradition of the insanity and salvation of Nebuchadnezzar in Dnl. 4 (and perhaps all of Dnl. 2–4) originally referred to Nabonidus. An expansion of the fixed list appears here, too, in the king's confession that he has prayed for years to the false gods: *ʾlhy ksp*ʾ *wdhb*ʾ [*nḥš*ʾ *przl*ʾ] ʿʾ *ʾbn*ʾ *ḥsp*ʾ "gods of silver and gold, [of bronze and iron,] of wood, of stone and of clay."[19] God, however, sent him a Jewish dream interpreter, who provided him a view of true worship and thereby healed the king physically and spiritually.

Gzella

16. 4Q554 2 2:15; 11Q18 10 1:2; 11:4; cf. Tob. 13:17.
17. Cf. generally M. Halbertal and A. Margalit, *Idolatry* (Cambridge, 1992).
18. 4Q242.
19. 4Q242 1-3:7f.; in *DSSStE*, 486f.

דור *dūr*; דרה *drh* /dārā/; דיר *dyr* /dayr/ (> /dēr/); מדר *mdr* /madār/; דר *dr* /dār/; תדיר *tdyr* /tadīr/

I. Etymology and Usage of the Verb. II. Deverbal Nouns of Dwelling. 1. "Court." 2. "Pen." 3. "Residence." III. Temporal Terms. 1. "Generation." 2. "Lasting."

I. Etymology and Usage of the Verb. The Semitic verbal root *dūr* appears throughout Aramaic with the meaning "to dwell," in accord with most of its nominal derivatives: /dārā/ "court," /dayr/ (> /dēr/) "pen, stable" and /madār/ "residence" (→ II). If, however, as is sometimes assumed, the temporal terms /dār/ "generation" and /tadīr/ "lasting" (→ III) can be linked to the same root[1] and not with another homonymous root,[2] a less specific common meaning such as "to circle (spatially or temporally)" may be on hand. In any case the two spectra of meaning, dwelling and the transition of generations, had already become clearly differentiated in Aramaic and in Hebrew in the known phases of the languages; cyclical being and fleeting becoming were probably seen as too contradictory. The verbal root, therefore, has no concretely demonstrable temporal connotations. They become clearly perceptible only in the post-Achaemenid offshoots of Imperial Aramaic.

The verb *dūr* "to dwell" is employed in the G-stem and is construed as an intransitive; a place designation can be added after a preposition: usually with *b-* "in," less often also *tḥt* "under" (Dnl. 4:18) or *ltmn* "there"[3] and later *ʿm* "with." It is first attested in the Biblical Aramaic of the book of Daniel where it indicates a stay of indefinite duration and can be used of people as well as animals: of people, animals, and birds in Nebuchadnezzar's empire, which is equated with the entire inhabited world in Dnl. 2:38 (*wbkl dy dʾryn bny-ʾnšʾ ḥywt brʾ wʿwp-šmyʾ* "everywhere where people, animals of the field, and birds of the air dwell") and both 3:31 and 6:26 (*ktb lkl-ʿmmyʾ ʾmyʾ wlšnyʾ dy dʾryn bkl-ʾrʿ* "and he wrote to all peoples, nations, and languages who live all over the earth"), but also figuratively for the living beings to whom the world tree described with a similar formulation offers home and protection according to Dnl. 4:9,18f. Thus, it corresponds to the ancient idea of the "world inhabited by people," the οἰκουμένη, as the LXX of 2:38 translates idiomatically and appropriately. 4Q209 23:3 (1 En. 77:1), however, uses the verb in the play on words involving *drwm* /darōm/ "south" and *dʾr* /dāʾar/ "dwelling" (the two lexemes are not related etymologically) for the habitation of God.

Thus, as a description of circumstance, *dūr* occurs regularly in the participle for the general (timeless) or in the imperfect for the current (immediate) present; their worldwide perspective can explain its relatively frequent occurrence in Daniel's court narratives. The substantivized participle *dʾryn* also stands for "inhabitant" and the combination "in-

U. Dahmen, "*dwr*," *ThWQ*, I, 665-67; C. Martone, "*dwr*," *ThWQ*, I, 667-71.

1. So e.g., *LexSyr*, 147; *ATTM*, 547f.
2. So, e.g., *GesB*[18], 1481f.,1484.
3. 4Q209 23:3 (1 En. 77:1).

habitant of earth" (Dnl. 4:32, here in their transience contrasted with the eternal God of heaven). Later Babylonian Jewish Aramaic, where the verb seems to remain especially productive, attests the causative stem "to provide someone a dwelling place" and the Gt-stem "to stay."[4]

II. Deverbal Nouns of Dwelling. Various nominal derivations for general or concrete concepts of dwelling appear more frequently than the verb itself. Under the influence of the cloistered lifestyle, many new forms developed later in Syriac literature, which, after all, originated for the most part in monasteries and scribal schools.[5]

1. "Court." The legal texts from the Dead Sea well attest the feminine *qāl*-noun *drh* /dārā/ "court" (and is thereby distinguishable from the masculine /dār/ "generation," → III.1) as part of a house purchase[6] or in relation to the right to inhabit in a donation[7] and is often mentioned alongside "houses" and "gates."[8] The encounter between Tobias and Raguel in Ekbatana takes place "before the gate of the court," likewise of a private house, in 4Q196 14 2:6 par. 4Q197 4 3:3 (Tob. 7:1) from Qumran. Otherwise, *drt mlk'* appears often in a figurative sense for the royal court: often as a standing expression in a diaspora novella set at the court of Darius,[9] in this case in order to emphasize the literary context. Finally, it occurs once in the astrological work 4Q318 8:7 in the announcement of "hardship for the provinces and destruction for the royal court" (*'ml lmdynt' wḥr[bn ld]rt mlk'*) with thunder in the sign of Taurus; here center and periphery probably serve as an expression of totality for the entire empire. In the *Megillat Ta'anit*, *drt'* also denotes the temple court (IX:20).[10]

2. "Pen." In contrast, *dyr* /dayr/ (> /dēr/)[11] is employed in a less specific, but still concrete sense. In Enoch's animal vision from Qumran, it stands for "pen, stable" of small livestock.[12] Elsewhere, however, *dyr* refers without doubt to a human "(household) community." It is attested in this meaning in Palmyrene[13] and in the East Mesopotamian of Hatra and Assur, here specifically for personnel, e.g., *dyr' klh gwyt' wbryt'* "the complete internal and external (temple) personnel" in H35.7, similarly *ḥy' dyr'* "the well-being of the personnel" in H290.6, and possibly also *bn' drhwn* "members of their (i.e., the royal)

4. *DJBA*, 321f.
5. Cf. *LexSyr*, 147.
6. E.g., V 49:4 in *ATTM*, 2, 252f.
7. E.g., nV 7,13.49 and 15.52 in *ATTM*, 2, 218-23.
8. Other texts in *ATTM*, 548 and 2, 373.
9. 4Q550 6+6a-c,6f. and 7+7a,4.
10. Text in *ATTM*, 357.
11. As a *qatl*-form developed from the older */dayr/.
12. 4Q204 4:6,8 (1 En. 89:34f.) and 4Q207 1:3 (1 En. 86:2); *ATTM*, 2, 247f. catalogs an additional instance in the contract for the sale of land nV 43:18, but the reading is uncertain and the context difficult.
13. *qšyš' dy dyr'* "the eldest of the community" in PAT 0862:2f. and *dyr' dy qryt'* "community of the city" in 2625:4f.

personnel" in H79.12 and the same combination for "household community" in H408.6 (if, in fact, the last two passages involve a defective spelling of /dayr/ (> /dēr/) and not the word /dār/ "generation" [→ III.1]).[14] The meaning "cloister" in Syriac, also preserved in many place names composed with "Dēr-," developed, then, from the same nuance.

3. "Residence." Finally, the third noun form, *mdr* /madār/, served quite generally for "dwelling place." A by-form *mdwr* /madōr/ with the identical meaning can be explained either as a secondary dialectical variant[15] or as a Canaanite loanword,[16] but the first explanation is the more likely.[17] It first occurs in Biblical Aramaic and there once designates the dwelling of the gods, which is not with human beings (Dnl. 2:11), as well as three times the dwelling among the wild animals of Nebuchadnezzar who had been cast out of society (4:22,29; 5:21). It also serves for "residence" generally in the Aramaic texts from Qumran.[18]

III. Temporal Terms. Even if they have a common etymology, the noun *dr* /dār/ "generation"[19] and the adjective *tdyr* /tadīr/ "lasting" are to be distinguished from the above.

1. "Generation." The first instances of *dr* "generation" occur in the Aramaic book of Daniel. They appear in a formulaic predication of the eternal power of God that endures from generation to generation (*'m dr wdr*; Dnl. 3:33 and 4:31, both times in the context of *mlkwt* "kingship" [→ *mlk*] and *šlṭn* "dominion" [→ *šlṭ*] and in parallel with → *'lm* "eternity").

In the roughly thirty instances in the Aramaic texts from Qumran, *dr* also serves mostly as a term for eternity, often in the traditional combination with *'lm* in the construct state *dry 'lm'* or *dry 'lmn* "eternal generation(s)" and even most emphatically *kl dry 'lmn*.[20] Near the Biblical Aramaic passage stands the usage in the hymnic praise of God, which will continue from generation to generation, in 4Q196 17 2:14 (Tob. 13:13), and in the praise of the eternal throne of God by the angels in 4Q202 1 3:15 (1 En. 9:4).

Additionally, *dr* also became a fixed term in apocalyptic theology of history. In the Testament of Amram, it appears for the continued existence of Israel[21] and in the Testament of

---

14. For text and translation cf. K. Beyer, *Die aramäischen Inschriften aus Assur, Hatra und dem übrigen Ostmesopotamien* (Göttingen, 1998).

15. *ATTM*, 548.

16. M. Sokoloff, review of *Die aramäischen Texte vom Toten Meer samt den Inschriften aus Palästina, dem Testament Levis aus der Kairoer Genisa, der Fastenrolle und den alten talmudischen Zitaten... Ergänzungsband* by K. Beyer, *DSD* 2 (1995) 222.

17. So correctly, C. Stadel, *Hebraismen in den aramäischen Texten vom Toten Meer* (Heidelberg, 2008), 48.

18. *mdwr* in 4Q540 1:4, Levi Apocryphon, and *'tr mdrh* "the place of his residence" as a translation of *tkwntw* "his location" in 11Q10 7A:4 (Job 23:3) and *mdrh* of *mšknwtyw* "his dwelling places" in 32:5 (Job 39:6).

19. Ca. 23 years: *ATTM*, 2, 373

20. So probably in the context of an eternal curse in T. Levi, 4Q213a 3-4,7; the same expression in a positive context for the majesty after the redemption of the word further in 4Q212 1 2:17 (1 En. 91:10) and 4Q212 1 4:18 (1 En. 91:13).

21. 4Q543 2a-b,2.7; 4Q545 4:17 and 4Q547 9:7 explicitly with reference to the priestly line; 4Q548 1 2:2:6: *kl dry yśr'l.*

Qahat for the transmission of religious-cultural heritage among those faithful to the law.[22] In contrast, in the Levi Apocryphon it denotes a specific, depraved generation.[23] Enoch's speech does not address the current, but a "distant (future) generation";[24] the giants are imprisoned for seventy generations until judgment day;[25] and the generations become ever more depraved (*dr mn dr yb'š*) until the "generations of the truth" will appear.[26]

In later Babylonian Jewish Aramaic the same noun is also attested in the meaning "series, line" (in the local as well as the genealogical senses).[27] Two instances of *dr* in the inscriptions from Hatra can also be interpreted as defective spellings of *dyr* "(household) community, personnel" instead of as /dār/ "generation" (→ II.2).

2. *"Lasting."* Finally, the noun "duration" also gave rise to the adjective *tdyr* "lasting." Daniel 6:17, 21 employ the feminine form *tdyr'* adverbially after the preposition *b-* as an epithet of Daniel who serves God without ceasing; as an adjective in a later Palestinian Jewish synagogue inscription, it denotes the constantly flowing (*tdyrn*) gifts of generous donors.[28] The situations in the other late Palestinian Jewish and Babylonian Jewish Aramaic are similar.[29]

Gzella

---

22. Here alongside *dry ʿlmn* in 4Q542 1 2:4 also *dry qwšṭ'* "generations of the truth": 4Q542 1 1:3; 1 2:8.

23. 4Q541 9 1:2.6.

24. *d[r r]ḥq*, 4Q201 1 1:4 (1 En. 1:2); similarly *dry' 'ḥry'* "future generations" in 4Q212 1 2:24 (1 En. 92:1).

25. 4Q202 1 4:10 (1 En. 10:12).

26. 4Q204 5 2:27f. (1 En. 107:1); see also H. Gzella, "*b'š*," *ThWQ*, I, 346 and cf. the related motif of the decay of the eras in the sequence of the empires of decreasing value, → *dhb* II.

27. *DJBA*, 349.

28. ggHA 1:4 in ATTM 384.

29. Cf. *DJPA*, 576a; *DJBA*, 1194.

דחל *dḥl*; דחיל *dḥyl* /daḥīl/; דחלה *dḥlh* /deḥlā/

I. Etymology, Grammatical Constructions, and Semantic Field. II. General Usage. III. Participle "Feared, Frightening." IV. Noun "Fear."

I. Etymology, Grammatical Constructions, and Semantic Field. The common Aramaic verbal root *dḥl* "to be afraid" traces back to the older **δḥl* and was therefore

---

H.-F. Fuhs, "יָרֵא *yārē'*," *TDOT*, VI, 290-315; H. Gzella, "*dḥl*," *ThWQ*, I, 671-74.

spelled *zḥl* on into the Imperial Aramaic period; only then did the spelling adapt to the phonetic shift */δ/ > /d/ that had already appeared earlier.[1] Although the perfect in the G-stem has the theme vowel */i/ (in Aramaic /e/) as is otherwise typical of stative roots, the verb can also be construed transitively with the object of fear as the direct object of the verb; the cause of the fear may optionally be added after the preposition *mn,* since the Imperial Aramaic period in respectful speech, that is, involving fear before divine beings or the king, also following *mn qdm,*[2] a manner of expression that originated in Achaemenid chancellery style.[3] A causal subordinate clause introduced by *bzy* "because" can also follow,[4] or an object clause following *dy l'*[5] or later *d(y)lm'*[6] "that," exactly like the Latin *timere ne.*

The perfect designates both the state of "having fear" as well as its incipience "to become afraid."[7] In contrast the D-stem expresses the factitive meaning "to frighten";[8] Palestinian Jewish Aramaic also attests for this meaning the causative stem with the related Dt-middle-passive "to get frightened."[9]

The semantic field includes along with → *bhl* in the D-stem "to frighten" (Dt-stem "to be frightened") the sometimes synonymously employed and similarly construed verb *zwʿ* "to tremble, be afraid";[10] the Hebrew counterparts are *yr'* and *pḥd.* The paling of the face (→ *zyw*) as a physical reaction to being frightened is also mentioned (Dnl. 5:6,9,10, here in context with verb *bhl*).

Among the nominal forms, the passive participle /daḥīl/ "feared, fearful" and the feminine verbal noun /deḥlā/ "fear" are already in usage in pre-Christian times. In the literary Aramaic of late antiquity, one also encounters many additional nominal derivations.[11]

II. General Usage. For the most part in the preserved material, *zḥl*/*dḥl* "to be afraid" refers to fear or reverence before the numinous. This connotation already shines through in one of the oldest known instances, a curse formula in an Old Aramaic treaty of state from Sefire:[12] It extends the divine punishment for the destruction of the inscription to the case in which someone fears executing this work and therefore commissions another to do so. Imperial Aramaic employs the verb in the framing storyline of Aḥiqar for fear in a life-threatening situation[13] and in a letter from the archive of the Elephantine community

1. *ATTM,* 100.
2. 4Q205 2 2:30; 4Q204 4:5f. (1 En. 89:31,34); Dnl. 6:27; before the king: Dnl. 5:19.
3. *ATTM,* 679f.
4. *TADAE* A4.2,7.
5. So possibly already in 1QapGen 19:23, but the verb at the beginning of the line is an emendation; similarly in Syriac: *LexSyr,* 148b.
6. Cf. *DJBA,* 324b; *LexSyr,* 148b.
7. So, e.g., in 4Q196 2:2 (Tob. 1:19): *dḥlt wʿrqt* "I became fearful and fled."
8. As in Dnl. 4:2, where it appears with *bhl,* and presumably also in 4Q545 7:2, see *ATTM,* 2, 124.
9. *DJPA,* 143a.
10. See *ATTM,* 568 for texts; employed in Dnl. 5:19 and 6:27 in parallelism with *dḥl.*
11. Cf. *LexSyr,* 149a.
12. II C = *KAI* 223 C 6.
13. *TADAE* C1.1,45.

for a fear, not further specified, of being in the minority in connection with a conflict with the Egyptians the nature of which is unclear.[14]

In Biblical Aramaic *dḥl* refers equally to fear of the king (Dnl. 5:19) and to fear of God (6:27); in both passages the verb is constructed with *mn qdm*. It appears further in the D-stem with an alarming dream as subject (4:2). For all these older usages, there are also examples in the Aramaic texts from Qumran. Reverence for God as an ethical stance belongs to the core of religious sentiment in the diaspora where one must manage without temple and king as pillars of cultural self-consciousness, and, thus, appears, hardly by accident, in Tobit[15] and a novella set at the court of Darius.[16] In addition, demons could instill fear,[17] as could dreams,[18] but, as in Aḥiqar, also fear of threatened execution.[19]

The active participle /dāḥel/ "fearing, revering" appears with a positive connotation in the sense of reverence for the gods in the royal titulature of Aramaic inscriptions from the Roman period. There, in the combination *dḥl ʾlhʾ* "god-fearing" it corresponds to the Hellenistic epithet εὐσεβής /dāḥel/ "pious" from Palmyra.[20] For the general background of this terminology, see especially H. Gzella, "Die Palmyrener in der griechisch-römischen Welt," *KLIO* 87 (2005) 450, and idem, "Das Aramaïsche in den römischen Ostprovinzen: Sprachsituationen in Arabien, Syrien und Mesopotamien zur Kaiserzeit," *BiOr* 63 (2006) 37.

The admonition *ʾl tzḥl/dḥl* "Fear not!" also already occurs in Old Aramaic and is placed in the mouth of a patron deity of a Syrian prince in a royal inscription.[21] In Imperial Aramaic, the framing storyline of Aḥiqar employs it to encourage the main character,[22] who fears for his life after an intrigue (l. 45: *dḥlt*). Both usages continue in the Aramaic texts from Qumran in religious speech as a revelation formula in theophanies and salvation oracles[23] as well as in the general sense as a stereotypical expression of encouragement.[24]

III. Participle "Feared, Frightening." Instead of "feared" in the purely passive sense, the passive participle *dḥyl* /daḥīl/ usually expresses the gerundive (referring to a possibility or necessity) nuance "frightful," to which nonactive participles lend themselves in any case.[25] In the Aramaic portions of the Bible and the writings from Qumran,

14. *TADAE* A4.2,7.
15. 4Q198 1:1 (Tob. 14:2).
16. 4Q550 7+7a,1.
17. 4Q197 4 2:9 (Tob. 6:15).
18. 1QapGen 19:18; 4Q530 2 2+6-12:20.
19. 4Q196 2:2 (Tob. 1:19).
20. Cf. H200.8 from Hatra and *PAT* 0260.3 and 0276.3 (in each case with a Greek counterpart; only Aramaic in *PAT* 1386.2).
21. *KAI* 202 A 13.
22. *TADAE* C1.1,54.
23. 1QapGen 11:15 and 22:30, dependent on Gen. 9:1 and 15:1.
24. 4Q197 4 1:2.3 (Tob. 5:21); 4 2:17 (Tob. 6:18); 5:6 (Tob. 8:1).
25. See H. Gzella, "Voice in Classical Hebrew against Its Semitic Background," *Or* 78 (2009) 306; cf. *BLA* §297c.

this form occurs in visions of superhuman figures in order to emphasize their extraordinary immensity: for the colossus with clay feet in Dnl. 2:31 and the fourth, most sinister animal in Dnl. 7:7,19 as well as for the "lord of the sheep" in Enoch's animal vision.[26] In these cases, it denotes either the object itself (Dnl. 7:7,19) or its appearance (Dnl. 2:31; 4Q205 2 2:29). Later it appears with both negative and positive connotations and can refer to God and his mighty acts.[27]

IV. Noun "Fear." The noun *dḥlh* /deḥlā/ is well-attested beginning with the Aramaic texts from Qumran. In 11Q10 33:3 (Job 39:22) it translates the Hebrew *pḥd* and is supplemented in 11Q10 33:2 (Job 39:20) by the synonym *ʾymh* "horror" of the original; it describes the boundless might of a horse eager for battle. In 1QapGen 11:17 the two terms appear side-by-side, apparently in the context of the power of postdiluvial human beings over all animals (*ʾymtkwn wdḥltkwn* "horror and fear of you"; cf. Gen. 9:2). Further, the astrological thunder doctrine employs *dḥlh* for the sequence of tribulations (*mrʿ*) announced by thunder in the sign of Gemini.[28] Later Aramaic also regularly employs *dḥlh* in agreement with the verb for fear of God.[29]

Gzella

26. 4Q205 2 2:29 (1 En. 89:30); an additional instance from Qumran, 1QapGen 2:26, has no context.
27. Cf. *DJPA*, 143; *DJBA*, 324b; *LexSyr*, 149a.
28. 4Q318 8:9.
29. See *DJPA*, 143 for Palestinian Jewish Aramaic and *LexSyr*, 149a for Syriac.

דין *dīn*; דין *dyn* /dīn/; דין *dyn* /dayyān/; מדינה *mdynh* /madīnā/; שפט *špṭ*

I. Etymology. II. Semantics. 1. Imperial Aramaic. 2. Biblical Aramaic. 3. Qumran. 4. Personal Names. 5. Excursus: *špṭ*. III. LXX.

K. Beyer, *Die aramäischen Inschriften aus Assur, Hatra und dem übrigen Ostmesopotamien* (Göttingen, 1998); F. Briquel-Chatonnet, "Palmyre, une cité pour les nomades," *Sem* 43/44 (1995) 123-34; J. Dušek, *Les manuscrits araméens du Wadi Daliyeh et la Samarie vers 450-332 av. J.-C. CHANE* 30 (2007); M. L. Folmer, *The Aramaic Language in the Achaemenid Period. OLA* 68 (1995), 649-52; L. Gardet, "din," *Encyclopédie de l'Islam* II:301-4; J. C. Greenfield, "The Aramaic Legal Texts of the Achaemenian Period," *Transeu* 3 (1990) 85-92; H.Gzella, "*dyn*," *ThWQ*, I, 674-80; V. Hamp and G. J. Botterweck, "דִּין *dîn*," TDOT, III, 187-194; S. Lackenbacher, "madinâtum," *NABU* 1987 no. 81; A. Lemaire and H. Lozachmeur, "La birta en méditerranée orientale," *Sem* 43/44 (1995) 75-8; G. Liedke, "דין *dîn* to judge," *TLOT*, 335f.; E. Lipiński, "Géographie linguistique de la

I. Etymology. The root first appears in Akkadian with the derivations *diānu* or *dânu* "to judge,"[1] *dayyānu, dayyānūtu* "judge, judgeship,"[2] and *dīnu* "legal decision, legal statute/case, lawsuit."[3] Ugaritic *dn* "to judge, to make right" and *dn* "legal case, lawsuit"[4] represent the oldest NW Semitic instance of the root *dīn* and its derivatives. In addition, Hebrew *dīn* "to judge, to make right" and Syriac *dwn* with its derivatives[5] merit attention. Whereas *špṭ*[6] clearly dominates in Hebrew, in Aramaic *dīn* does while *špṭ* only appears as a rarely attested loanword (→ II.5). Later, *dīn* attained the meaning "religion," as in Mandaic[7] and in Arabic.[8]

II. Semantics.

1. Imperial Aramaic. The Elephantine Papyri attest the substantive *dyn* (/dīn/) in a variety of usages in the legal sphere. One finds *qbl dyn ʿl* "to bring charges against";[9] *hlk bdyn* "to go before the court";[10] *ršī dyn (wdbb)* "to accuse";[11] *ʿbd dyn* "to hold a trial";[12] *rḥq mn dyn* "to forgo a trial";[13] *grī dyn wdbb* "to litigate";[14] and *ʿbd dyn spr' znh* "to proceed in accordance with this document";[15] *ʿbd dyn śn'h* "to execute the law of divorce."[16]

Transeuphratène à l'époque achéménide," *Transeu* 3 (1990) 95-107; H. Lozachmeur, "Un exemple de ville-garnison judéo-araméenne du Ve siècle: Yeb, la forteresse," *Sem* 43/44 (1995) 67-74; S. E. McEvenue, "The Political Structure in Judah from Cyrus to Nehemiah," *CBQ* 43 (1981) 353-64; J. Naveh and S. Shaked, *Aramaic Documents from Ancient Bactria (Fourth Century B.C.E.)* (London, 2012); H. Niehr, *Herrschen und Richten. FzB* 54 (1986), 60-63; R. North, "Civil Authority in Esra," *FS E. Volterra* (Milan, 1971), 377-404; B. Porten, *Archives from Elephantine* (Berkeley, 1968), 45-53; J. J. Rabinowitz, "The Aramaic Papyri, the Demotic Papyri from Gebelên and Talmudic Sources," *Bibl* 38 (1957), 269-74; J. B. Segal, *Aramaic Texts from North Saqqara* (London, 1983); C. C. Torrey, "Medina and ΠΟΛΙΣ, and Luke i.39," *HTR* 17 (1924) 83-91; D. Sperling, "The Akkadian Legal Term *dīnu u dabābu*," *JANES* 1 (1968/69) 35-40; J. J. Stamm, "Namen rechtlichen Inhalts," in idem, *Beiträge zur hebräischen und altorientalischen Namenkunde. OBO* 30 (1980), 159-77; A. Verger, *L'amministrazione della giustizia nei papiri aramaici de Elefantina. AANL.R* 8,19 (1964), 75-94; idem, *Ricerche giuridiche sui papiri aramaici di Elefantina. SS* 16 (1965).

1. *AHw*, I, 167f.; *CAD*, III, 100-103.
2. *AHw*, I, 151; *CAD*, III, 28-33.
3. *AHw*, I, 171f.; *CAD*, III, 150-56.
4. *KTU* 1.16 VI 33f.,46f.; 17 V 7f.
5. *ThesSyr*, 841-45.
6. H. Niehr, "שָׁפַט *šāpaṭ*," *TDOT*, XV, 411-31.
7. *MdD*, 108.
8. Gardet.
9. *TADAE* B2.2,16.
10. *TADAE* B2.3,22; 3.1,19; 3.11,15; 5.4,6f.(+*dbb*).
11. *TADAE* B2.3, 12.20; 2.4,13; 2.7,8f.; 2.9,11,14; 2.10,15; 2.11,8f.; 3.5,13; 3.10,18-19,19f.; 3.11,12; 3.12,25,27; 5.3,3 (corr.),4(corr.); 5.5,4,6(corr.).
12. *TADAE* B2.3,27; 2.8,3.
13. *TADAE* B2.2,15f.; 2.8,11; 2.11,11.
14. *TADAE* B2.2,12; 2.7,10 (*dyn wbb'*); 2.8,7,8f.; 2.10,10; 3.2,4f.; 3.4,12f.,14,17 (*dyn wzbb*); 3.5,13f.,16; 5.2,9(corr.).
15. *TADAE* B2.6,31; 3.8,32; 6.3,11(corr.).
16. *TADAE* B3.8,34(corr.),37(corr.); 6.4,2(corr.),6.

Should a matter be finally settled, it is announced with the formula *wl' dyn* (*wl' dbb*) "and there will be no trial (and no charge)."[17] Furthermore, *dyn* denotes the right over or to something.[18] The formulation *l' ʿbd dyn ḥdh wtrtyn mn nšy knwth* PN *ʾntth* "not to do the law of one or two wives of his colleague, in relation to PN, his wife"[19] refers to the husband's fulfillment of marital duty.[20] Otherwise, he should do *dyn śn'h,* i.e., finalize the divorce.[21] The same is also said of the woman.[22]

The title *dyn* (/dayyān/) "judge" sometimes parallels → *sgn* "governor,"[23] → *mr'* "lord,"[24] or both titles.[25] In addition, the judge parallels the *rbḥyl* "garrison commander."[26] The existence of "judges of the king"[27] and "judges of the province"[28] indicate a variety of classes of judges. The title *mr'* could refer to the *frataraka* or the garrison commander since they both perform judicial tasks. They had priority over the judges, some lay judges in honorary positions and not officials or officers. The idiom "PN + his colleagues, the judges"[29] points to this circumstance. The trials were held in Syene[30] and Elephantine.[31] The oath texts *TADAE* B7.1-4 and B2.2,4-7 (cf. 2.3,24; → *ym'*) convey insights into trial procedures.

As before, the philological and factual explanation of the formulations *bnp'*[32] and *bdyn np'*[33] remains open. Compare the variety of positions in *DNSI*, 740 s.v. *np'*$_2$. A third century B.C.E. papyrus from Edfu speaks of a college of judges from Abydos.[34]

The papyri from north Saqqara attest *dyn* "judge"[35] and *dynh* "lawsuit, legal case,"[36] both lexemes in mostly very fragmentary contexts, however. As at Elephantine and Abydos, a college of judges is mentioned often. On grounds of the papyri 1-18 that relate to the legal sphere, one can identify aspects of the legal practices of the Arameans of north Saqqara.[37]

---

17. *TADAE* B2.3,14,21f.; 2.6,25f. (*wl' ydyn wl' dbb*),29; 2.8,10; 2.9,16; 2.10,17; 2.11,12,14; 3.5,15,22; 3.6,15; 3.7,17(corr.); 3.8,32; 3.13,8,12; 4.7,3; 5.4,6(corr.) 6.3,12(corr.).
18. *TADAE* B5.6,8,13.
19. *TADAE* B3.8,38.
20. Rabinowitz, 269-271; P. Grelot, *Documents araméens d'Egypte. LAPO* 5 (1972), 237.
21. *TADAE* B3.8,39.
22. *TADAE* B3.8,39f.
23. *TADAE* B2.3,13; 3.1,13,18f.; regarding the title, cf. Lemaire and Lozachmeur, 77f.
24. *TADAE* B3.2,6.
25. *TADAE* B3.12,28; 4.6,14(corr.).
26. *TADAE* A5.2,7; B5.1,3.
27. *TADAE* B5.1,3.
28. *TADAE* A5.2,4(corr.),7.
29. *TADAE* B2.2,6; 8.4,2.
30. *TADAE* B2.2,17; 2.8,3.
31. *TADAE* B2.9; 2.10.
32. *TADAE* B7.2,4.
33. *TADAE* B2.9,4.
34. *AP* 82:1f.; cf. R. Degen, "Zu den aramäischen Texten aus Edfu," *NESE* 3 (1978) 60.
35. Segal nos. 16.2; 27.2; 30a2; 79.1 (corr.); 121.2,3 (corr.).
36. Segal no. 8.8,13.
37. Segal 5.8.

Similarly, the letters of the Achaemenid satraps from Bactria attest the professional designation or title *dyn*.[38]

In XIII 197[39] the wisdom sayings of Aḥiqar mention the sun god who in his classical role as judge-god regulates the relationship between lord and servant.[40] In a narrative context in pap. Amherst 63 3:6 the leader of a community is addressed as *dyn* "judge," in the ritual as *mlk* "king."[41]

The substantive *mdnh* (/madīnā/) "(judicial) precinct," first attested in Mari,[42] is formed based on the verbal root *dīn*. *TADAE* B3.13,10f. sets the province apart from Elephantine and Syene. *TADAE* C3.14,35 mentions the province of Thebes,[43] *TADAE* C3.14,38; A4.5,9 the province of the south, and C3.19,14 the expenditures of a province. *TADAE* A6.9,1f. mentions various provinces in Mesopotamia and Syria. The "province of the great marshes," i.e., the Fayyum, may be the reference of *ḥth rbʾ mdyntʾ*[44] from north Saqqara.[45]

The papyri from Wadi Daliyeh attest the formulation *šmryn byrtʾ zy bšmryn mdyntʾ* ("Samaria, the fortress that [lies] in the province of Samaria").[46]

Because of a narrowing of the concept, *mdnh* can also mean "city" in addition to "province" in Palestinian Jewish Aramaic,[47] Syriac, and Mandaic.[48] In Palmyra *mdnh* is to be understood as "city" (with surroundings), and less often as "town" and no longer as "province."[49] The characterization of a Palmyrene citizen as *rḥym mdyth* ("one who loves his homeland")[50] and of an inhabitant of Hatra as *ʿbyd ṭbʾ l*[*mdt*]*ʾ* ("benefactor of the [cit]y"),[51] further *šwr mdynt* "city wall" demonstrate this circumstance.[52]

2. Biblical Aramaic. Biblical Aramaic exhibits two instances of *dayyān*: Ezr. 7:25 and 4:9. In the edict of Artaxerxes, Ezra is commissioned to install judges (*šāp̄ṭīn wᵉdayyānīn*:

38. Naveh and Shaked nos. A1:1,2,8,13; A4:2.

39. H. Niehr, *Weisheitliche, magische und legendarische Erzählungen. JSHRZ* NS II/2 (2007), 51f.; M. Weigl, *Die aramäischen Achikar-Sprüche aus Elephantine und die alttestamentliche Weisheitsliteratur. BZAW* 399 (2010), 531.

40. J. Kutter, *nur ili. AOAT* 346 (2008), 337.

41. R. C. Steiner, *The Aramaic Text in Demotic Script. JAOS* 111 (1991), 362; idem, *COS* (1997), I:311.

42. Lackenbacher.

43. Cf. *TADAE* C3.14frag.e. 1,2; A 4.2,6.

44. Lipiński, 96.

45. Segal no. 103.

46. Cf. Dušek no. 1.1; 4.1; 5.1; 26.1.

47. *DJPA*, 291f.

48. *KBL*³, 1733.

49. Briquel-Chatonnet; *PAT*, 378.

50. Inv IX, 29.2.

51. R. Bertolini, "Une stèle inédite de Hatra," *Sem* 43 (1996) 143-46; Beyer, H1039; cf. H. Gzella, "Das Aramäische in den römischen Ostprovinzen," *BiOr* 63 (2006) 27,37.

52. H1056,2, Beyer, "Die aramäischen Inschriften aus Assur, Hatra und dem übrigen Ostmesopotamien (datiert 44 v. Chr. bis 238 n. Chr.): Nachträge," *WO* 43 (2013) 44.

hendiadys) who are to judge the people in the province Abār Nahara, all who know the law of God (→ *dt*; *qere*)[53] and to instruct those who do not know it (Ezr. 7:25). A legal proceeding (*dīnā*) with the consequences of death, expulsion, financial penalty, or imprisonment should be instituted against those who do not precisely follow the law of God and of the king (v. 26). One should read *dāyyānayyā* in Ezr. 4:9.[54] Thus, it does not represent a gentilic,[55] but, as in Elephantine and north Saqqara, a reference to a college of judges.[56] Already the LXX and the Masoretes have misunderstood the text based on the subsequent land names. The two texts do not suffice to yield information concerning the legal organization of the postexilic period in Palestine, especially since the dispensation of justice in this period did not lie in the hands of judges alone.[57]

The usage of *dīnā* as "legal proceeding" and "court" in Biblical Aramaic is comparable to that of the Elephantine texts. According to the vision of Dnl. 7:9-14, a royal council assembles around God Most High. This royal council functions as a court (*dīnā*) that sits to give counsel and (for whom) books were opened (v. 10). The evil of the fourth day against the Most High is answered by a court that sits (to give counsel; Dnl. 7:26).

Dnl. 7:22 presents a text-critical problem. Given the addition of *y^e^ṯīḇ w^e^šolṭāneh* after *dīnā* (*BHK*; *BHS*) undertaken by many based on vv. 10.26, *dīnā* is to be understood as court as in vv 10, 26. Otherwise, *dīnā* is the object of → *yhb* and will thus be understood as "might, gratification, regiment, decision."[58]

Similarly, *dīnā* denotes righteousness;[59] God's ways are *q^e^šoṭ* and *dīn* (Dnl. 4:34).

In Biblical Aramaic, too, *m^e^ḏīnā* can designate the province or a city and the surrounding province. Provinces are the intention in Ezr. 4:15; 5:8; 6:2; Dnl. 3:2f. One should assume *m^e^ḏīnā* as a city (and the surrounding province?) in cases involving a construct phrase + place name such as *m^e^ḏīnaṯ bāḇœl* (Ezr. 7:16; Dnl. 2:48f.; 3:1,12,30).[60]

3. Qumran. The Aramaic texts from Palestine including Qumran attest *dīn* as "to judge" and "to argue."[61] They apply the subst. *dyn* "judgment";[62] they mention judges in God's court.[63] The subst. *dyn* essentially denotes "right" and "justice." It forms formulaic expressions: *dyn wdbb* "legal proceeding,"[64] *dīn dyn* "to make judgment,"[65] *ʿbd dyn b/mn* "to pun-

53. Cf. *BLA* §13h.

54. Cf., e.g., *LexLingAram*, 43; R. Achenbach, "Der Titel der persischen Verwaltungsbeamten in Esra 4,9b (MT)," *ZAH* 13 (2000) 137f.

55. Contra MT; A. H. J. Gunneweg, *Esra. KAT* XIX/1, 82,84.

56. *KBL*³, 1693.

57. H. Niehr, *Rechtsprechung in Israel. SBS* 130 (1987), 101-17; idem, "שָׁפַט *šāpaṭ*," *TDOT*, XV, 420-21.

58. Cf. *KBL*³, 1692,

59. *LexLingAram*, 43.

60. Cf. E. M. Cook, "In the Plain of the Wall," *JBL* 108 (1989) 115f.

61. *ATTM*, 552; *ATTM*, 2, 377.

62. 4Q205 1 1:2 *DSSStE*, 422f.

63. F 3:12 *ATTM*, 2, 145.

64. nV 7:21,27,66 *ATTM*, 2, 218f.

65. 4Q542 1 2:5 *DSSStE*, 1082f.

ish, judge, do justice"[66] and *gzr dyn* "to decide a lawful right" (→ *gzr* VI).[67] In addition, one encounters the phrase *bʿl dyn* as "accuser."[68] This legal technical term, borrowed from the Akkaidan *bēl dīni*,[69] first appears in Aramaic in Qumran and then more frequently in Syriac[70] and Mandaic.[71] The last judgment appears as *dyn ʿlmʾ* "eternal judgment,"[72] *wqṣ dyn ʾrbʾ* "the moment of the great judgment,"[73] and *ywm dynʾ* "day of judgment."[74] As a further derivative based on *dyn*, one also finds *mdnh* as "province" or "region."

4. Personal Names. In PN the verbal base *dyn* means "to make right." Such PN are extant in *Daniel* ("God has made right"), a PN already attested in Ugarit,[75] and the PN [*h*]*dldn* "May Haddu judge" attested in a document from Tell Halaf.[76] Regarding the occurrences in Elephantine, cf. M. Silverman, *Religious Values in the Jewish Proper Names at Elephantine. AOAT* 217 (1985), 141. In Palmyra the PN *dywn, dynʾ* and *dynyʾ* are attested.[77] The Aramaic inscriptions from Assur know the PN *ʾsrbdyn* ("Assur-Bēl is judge"), *ʾsrdyn* ("Assur is judge"), and *nbwdyn* ("Nabū is judge").[78]

5. Excursus: špṭ. Derivatives of the root *špṭ* appear in Aramaic as loanwords. The Deir ʿAllā inscription 2.17 has a first-person plural whose semantics ("to argue" or "to judge")[79] remain unclear because of the difficult context. The sayings of Aḥiqar contain an additional form of the G-stem in the meaning "to quarrel, argue."[80] Otherwise, only the N-stem of *špṭ* in Hebrew has this meaning. A document from Elephantine exhibits the form *nšpṭ*[81] and in l. 7 [*š*]*pṭ ʿl*, although the fragmentary context permits no grammatical or semantic interpretation.[82] Ezr. 7:25 employs *šāpṭīn* "judges" as a synonym for *dayyānīn.*

66. 1QapGen 20:13f. *DSSStE*, 40f.; H 24:2 *ATTM*, 241; 91:11 (corr.) 12 *ATTM*, 248; CT. Levi Cambridge a:17 *DSSStE*, 50f.

67. 4Q197 4 2:2 *DSSStE*, 390f.

68. 4Q531 17:5 *DSSStE*, 1066f.

69. *AHw*, I, 119; *CAD*, III, 155f.

70. *ThesSyr*, 562.

71. *MdD*, 60.

72. 4Q212 4:23 *DSSStE*, 444f.

73. 4Q206 2 2:2-3 *DSSStE*, 424f.; 4Q212 4:23 *DSSStE*, 444f.

74. 4Q205 1 1:1 *DSSStE*, 420f.; cf. 10:12 *ATTM*, 238.

75. Cf. *KTU* 1.17-19.

76. *THU* 2:7; cf. V. Hug, *Altaramäische Grammatik der Texte des 7. und 6. Jh.s v.Chr. HSAO* 4 (1993), 26,153.

77. *PNPI* 14.83.

78. Beyer, 154,161.

79. Cf. J. Hoftijzer and G. van der Kooji, *Aramaic Texts from Deir ʿAlla. DMOA* 19 (1976), 181,244; H.-P. Müller, "Die aramäische Inschrift von Deir ʿAllā und die älteren Bileamsprüche," *ZAW* 94 (1982) 218.

80. *TADAE* C1.1,88; cf. R. Contini and C. Grottanelli, *Il saggio Ahiqar. StBi* 148 (2005), 123; H. Niehr, *Weisheitliche, magische und legendarische Erzählungen. JSHRZ* NS II/2 (2007), 43; M. Weigl, *Die aramäischen Achikar-Sprüche aus Elephantine und die alttestamentliche Weisheitsliteratur. BZAW* 399 (2010), 152-57.

81. *TADAE* C3.3,1,5.

82. Yet cf. Hug, 33,151.

III. LXX. The LXX renders *dayyān* in Ezr. 7:25 with κρίτης and *dīn* with κρίνειν. It understands the judges of Ezr. 4:9 as the gentilic Διναῖοι. It usually translates *m^e ḏīnā* with χώρα, although πόλις appears in Ezr. 6:2.

Niehr

דכר *dkr* /dakar/

I. General Meaning and in Personal Names. II. As Sacrificial Animals. III. Symbolic Usage. IV. As an Astronomical Sign.

I. General Meaning and in Personal Names. The substantive /dakar/, vocalized *d^e ḵar* in Tiberian pointing and spelled *zkr* in the oldest texts,[1] is a *qatal*, or perhaps *qitl*, noun of the root *δkr* "male" (in both the biological and the figurative senses). In Aramaic, it denotes a male person, as in Palmyrene[2] and in Targum Onqelos of Gen. 1:27, further the male animal of the flock, the ram, as in I En. 46:1 and in Targum Onqelos of Nu. 28:11, or the male member, as, e.g., in many Syriac texts[3] and perhaps already in 4Q560 1 1:3.5.[4] The books of Enoch call rams *dkr(yn) dy ʿn*, literally "the little men of the flock."[5] The river mentioned in pap.Yadin 7:9,40,42 was probably called "the Ram" *nhrʾ dkrʾ*.[6] To denote a person of the male sex, the *qatūl* or *qattūl* nominal forms can also be employed, as in *d^e kūrā* or *d^e kkūrā* in Targum Onqelos of Gen. 17:10,14; Ex. 23:17; 34:23; Dt. 16:16; 20:13, etc. Assyrian and Babylonian texts attest the intensive form *Zakkūr*(*u*)/

ATTM, 554f.; 2, 378; B. Adamczewski, "'Ten Jubilees of Years': Heptadic Calculations of the End of the Epoch of Inquiry and the Evolving Ideology of the Hasmoneans," *Qumran Chronicle* 16 (2008) 19-36, esp. 25-27; M. Albani, "Der Zodiakos in 4Q318 und die Henoch-Astronomie," *Mitteilungen und Beiträge. Forschungsstelle Judentum* 7 (1993) 1-42, esp. 27-32; J. A. Brinkman, "Dakkūru," *PNA* I/2 (1999), 370-72; R. E. Clements, "זָכָר *zākhār*," *TDOT*, IV, 82-87; H.-J. Fabry, "*zkr*," *ThWQ*, I, 849-52; J. C. Greenfield and M. Sokoloff, "An Astrological Text from Qumran (4Q318) and Reflections on Some Zodiacal Names," *RevQ* 16 (1995) 507-25, esp. 512; H. R. Jacobus, "The Zodiac Sign Names in the Dead Sea Scrolls (4Q318)," *ARAM* 24 (2012) 311-31; M. Metzger, *Vorderorientalische Ikonographie und Altes Testament: Gesammelte Aufsätze* (Münster, 2004), esp. 124-45; J. T. Milik, *The Books of Enoch* (Oxford, 1976), esp. 187, 222-25, 241, 302; B. L. van der Waerden, "History of the Zodiac," *AfO* 16 (1952/53) 216-30.

1. *DNSI*, 329f.
2. *PAT* 0024.2; *PAT* 0570.
3. *LexSyr*, 153b.
4. Cf. *DSSStE*, 1116f.
5. 1Q23 1+6:2-3; 4Q205 89:12,44.
6. Contra *ATTM*, 2, 220: "the Male [= wild] River."

Dakkūr(*u*) in personal names, especially as the eponymous ancestor of the Chaldean tribe, Bīt-Dakkūri.

II. As Sacrificial Animals. Ezr. 6:9,17 and 7:17 mention rams among the animals customarily slaughtered for burnt offerings. They appear in the decree that King Darius issued to have the temple in Jerusalem rebuilt (Ezr. 6:9); according to Ezr. 6:17, two hundred rams were to be offered during the dedication festivities for the Second Temple, and rams are also listed among the animals that King Artaxerxes had purchased with his royal contribution and the voluntary donations of the people for sacrifice in the Jerusalem temple (Ezr. 7:17). These accounts correspond to preexilic practice, but the specific type of sacrifice often goes unnamed.

III. Symbolic Usage. The books of Enoch contain highly detailed descriptions of Enoch's dream visions. According to one of them, it seems, every pair of animals saved from the flood is supposed to have birthed two hundred males. Thus, the sheep, too, would have two hundred rams.[7] In another dream, a white ram represents Israel/Jacob and fathers twelve lambs that symbolize the tribes of Israel.[8] The ram leads eleven of the twelve lambs to pasture alongside the wolves;[9] this is an allusion to the story of Joseph in Egypt, and the wolves represent the Egyptians. In another passage, however, the ram of the flock is no longer Israel/Jacob, but King Saul, who jabs foxes, wild pigs, and dogs with his horns.[10] The foxes represent the Ammonites of 1 S. 11:1-15, the wild pigs the Amalekites of 1 S. 15:1-9, and the dogs certainly the Philistines. Nevertheless, the ram of the flock went "en route into error" ([*šg*']$^?$ *b'rḥ*),[11] and another was placed at the head of the flock. This second passage (1 En. 89:45f.), which is not preserved among the fragments from Cave 4 at Qumran, alludes to Samuel's investiture of David (1 S. 16). In contrast, 1 En. 90:9-36, a passage that also has not been preserved in Aramaic, seems to allude to events from the early Hasmonean period: the horned rams would then represent the royal claims of the new leaders, indeed, while omitting the entire history from Solomon to the Hasmoneans.[12]

IV. As an Astronomical Sign. The Aramaic "Brontologion" (manual on divination by thunder) 4Q318 contains the traditional list with the names of the Zodiac, including the ram, *aries* (*dkr'*; 8 1:6). It is not, however, associated according to the traditional pattern with the month Nisan, but with Adar, the last month that begins and ends in the sign of the Ram.[13] This circumstance corresponds, then, to the sequence in the Babylonian MUL.APIN series I:iv:33-39,[14] that traces back to the early first millennium B.C.E.

7. 1Q23 1+6:2-3.
8. 4Q205 (1 En. 89:12).
9. 4Q205 (1 En. 89:14); in another interpretation: "bears," → *db*.
10. 4Q205 (1 En. 89:43).
11. 4Q205 (1 En. 89:44).
12. Adamczewski.
13. Albani; Greenfield and Sokoloff; cf. Jacobus.
14. H. Hunger and D. Pingree, *MUL.APIN: An Astronomical Compendium in Cuneiform. AfOB* 24 (1989), 68-9, 141.

and ends with the Ram. The Talmud does not mention the signs of the Zodiac, but their symbols appear often in early Jewish art, especially on the mosaic floors of the ancient synagogues of Palestine in Sepphoris, Bet Alfa, Hammath Tiberias, En-Gedi, Naarah (ʿAyn Dūk).[15] There, however, the Ram is consistently called *ṭāleh* "Lamb" in Hebrew,[16] as also in Mandaic where the first sign of the Zodiac is called *mbrʾ*,[17] a dissimilated form from *ʾimmerā*, "lamb." Consequently, it is hardly likely that *ṭāleh* refers to the paschal lamb although it is sacrificed in the month of Nisan.

Lipiński

15. Cf. recently R. Hachlili, *Ancient Synagogues:Archaeology and Art: New Discoveries and Current Research. HO* I/105 (2013).
16. Jacobus, 319.
17. J. C. Greenfield and J. Naveh, "A Mandaic Lead Amulet with Four Incantations," *EI* 18 (1985) 97-107; E. Lipiński, *Semitic Linguistics in Historical Perspective. OLA* 230 (2014), 251f.

דכר *dkr*; דכיר *dkyr* /dakīr/; דכרן *dkrn* /dokrān/

I. Etymology, Grammatical Constructions, and General Usage. II. Participle "to Be Remembered" in Memorial Inscriptions. III. Noun "Remembrance, Record."

I. Etymology, Grammatical Constructions, and General Usage. In the oldest known Aramaic spelling, the common Semitic verbal root **δkr* "to remember" first appears as *zkr*. Yet, after the fusion of the originally interdental */δ/ with the dental /d/ around 800 B.C.E. or somewhat earlier,[1] spelling also conformed to the new pronunciation so that this verb and its nominal derivatives appear increasingly from the Imperial Aramaic period onward as *dkr*. Some kind of connection with → *dkr* /dakar/ "male, ram" is possible, but not assured.

As a verb, *zkr*/*dkr* usually appears in the G-stem as a transitive with the thing recalled as a direct object, as clearly in *yzkrny wʿṭty ybʿh* "he will remember me and seek my ad-

K. Beyer, *Die aramäischen Inschriften aus Assur, Hatra und dem übrigen. Ostmesopotamien* (Göttingen, 1998); H. Eising, "זָכַר *zākhar*," *TDOT*, IV, 64-82; H. Gzella, "Das Aramäische in den römischen Ostprovinzen: Sprachsituationen in Arabien, Syrien und Mesopotamien zur Kaiserzeit," *BiOr* 63 (2006) 15-39; J. F. Healey, "May He Be Remembered for Good: An Aramaic Formula," in K. J. Cathcart and M. Maher, eds., *Targumic and Cognate Studies. FS M. McNamara. JSOTSup* 230 (1996), 177-86; L. Novakovic, "*zkr*," *ThWQ*, I, 840-49; W. Schottroff, "זכר *zkr* to remember," *TLOT*, 381-88; C. Stadel, "The 'Remembered for Good' Formula in Samaritan Aramaic and Early Hybrid Samaritan Hebrew," *JJS* 63 (2012), 285-306.

1. *ATTM*, 100.

vice" in the Imperial Aramaic story that frames Aḥiqar.[2] The reading of *TADAE* A4.4,8 is disputed, in contrast; instead of *dkrw*, some have suggested *dbrw*.[3] Further instances come from post-Achaemenid times, but correspond precisely to this older usage, cf. e.g., Hatra H13.3 and 23.5 with direct objects and H1015.9 without,[4] and at Qumran *dkwr ʿny* "Remember the poor of . . .";[5] in contrast, the text of 1QapGen 2:9, where some read *dkr lk ʿl* "recall . . .," is rather uncertain.[6] Moreover, religious diction knows of God's remembrance of his creation (*lbryth*),[7] perhaps also the remembrance of the holy ones in 4Q536 2 i+3:2, but the context of this passage is very fragmentary.

Additionally, later Aramaic languages attest the doubled transitive causative stem "to remind someone of something, mention"[8] and the middle-passive Gt-stem "to remember" or, less often, "to be remembered."[9]

Very often and in many variants, Aramaic memorial epigraphy, which began to assume its specific form in the Hellenistic period, utilizes the passive participle *dkyr* /dakīr/ (later /dḵīr/) "to be remembered" (→ II). In addition, Old Aramaic and onward attests the noun *dkrn* (in an old or more conservative spelling: *zkrn*) /dokrān/ "remembrance," in the official terminology of Imperial Aramaic "memorandum" (→ III); the form *diḵrōn* as pointed in Biblical Aramaic arose through the reduction of /ā/ to /ō/, as often occurs in the pronunciation of other words,[10] and subsequent dissimilation.

II. Participle "to Be Remembered" in Memorial Inscriptions. With the development of a private memorial epigraphy in various Aramaic languages since the Hellenistic epoch, which is attested in several Nabatean, Palmyrene, Edessene, as well as East Mesopotamian, Jewish Palestinian, and Samaritan inscriptions and which attained its apex in the Roman period, the passive participle of the G-stem *dkyr* "to be remembered" (in Hatra very often *bl dkyr* "to be truly remembered") remained a fixed component in this genre. As is otherwise common, in this usage it is also often supplemented with the name or names of the person or persons to be remembered. The pertinent addition and its placement in relation to the names differ in the various Aramaic corpora; *lṭb* "for good" in Jewish Palestinian and in Hatra and *bṭb* "in good" in Nabatean and Palmyrene are particularly frequent, but variants such as *bkl* "in all," *bšlm* "in peace" (or combinations thereof), *ʿd/lʿlm* "forever," *dkyr wbryk* "remembered and blessed," *qdm* "before/by" together with a divine name also occur, as an exception, even *lbyš* "for ill."[11]

---

2. *TADAE* C1.1,53; similarly in the still older Sam'alian, which is closely akin to Aramaic: *KAI* 214.17.

3. Cf. *DNSI*, 322.

4. Text and translation in Beyer.

5. 4Q569 1-2:8.

6. D. A. Machiela, *The Dead Sea Genesis Apocryphon. STDJ* 79 (2009), 35.

7. 4Q529 1:11, words of the archangel Michael.

8. In magical texts also "to pronounce," as in ooXX 8:20, *ATTM.E*, 262f.

9. *DJPA*, 149f.; *DJBA*, 337f.; *LexSyr*, 153; *MdD*, 110.

10. Cf. *ATTM*, 137.

11. See *DNSI*, 323-29 for an extensive collection and *ATTM*, 554 for a brief overview of the West Aramaic material.

It is uncertain whether, even given all their formal agreement, these inscriptions also always serve the same purpose. Some may address passers-by with the request to pronounce the name of the deceased and thereby to maintain his memory among the living.[12] In contrast, Jewish Palestinian and Samaritan synagogue inscriptions, in particular, perpetuate the memory of donors and their contributions to the construction or the furnishing of the pertinent sanctuaries that were erected in great numbers in the course of the consolidation of religious traditions beginning in the fourth century C.E., but not necessarily after the death of these people.[13] If one interprets the addition *qdm* with the name or names of a god or several gods in many inscriptions from Hatra not spatially "before," but in honorific discourse as "by," at least here, the request does not address the reader, but the gods themselves.[14] Public representation and private religiosity belong in equal measure to the determinative impulses of the Aramaic memorial epigraphy of the post-Achaemenid era.[15]

III. Noun "Remembrance, Record." The noun *zkrn*/*dkrn* also initially denoted "remembrance" quite generally. Official documents, already in the Old Aramaic period, however, use it for a definite obligation on the generations. This may already be the case in the oldest known specimen: the end of a state treaty from Sefire[16] between two princes explicitly describes the record on the stele as a memorial with legal consequences for subsequent generations (*mh ktbt lzkrn lbry* [*wlbr*] *bry* "what I have written is a reminder for my son [and the son] of my son. . .").

The same noun refers to the remembrance of private individuals in the Aramaic memorial inscriptions and is employed quite often in this sense in Palmyrene and Nabatean, in Hatra (although in isolation), and in Jewish Palestinian and Samaritan Aramaic. Just like the passive participle "to be remembered" (→ II), it can be supplemented with the attribute "good" (*ṭb*) or "the good" (*ṭb'*) and sometimes with other additions (such as *l'lm* "forever"),[17] in contrast to the mere *dkrn* from Hatra;[18] the two forms are also combined, e.g., in a Byzantine synagogue inscription from Jericho (*dkyrn lṭb yhwy dkrnhwn lṭb* "may you be remembered for good, may your memory be for good").[19] Especially in relation to the dedication of an altar or remembrance "before" (*qdm*, possibly "by" here, → II) the gods, a religious connotation is involved. It also underlies the use of *dkrn* for bread as a memorial sacrifice in the priestly ritual as described in the vision of the new Jerusalem from Qumran.[20]

---

12. So Healey.
13. Cf. Stadel.
14. Beyer, 9; *ATTM*, 2, 378.
15. See Gzella for an overview.
16. IC = *KAI* 222 C 2f.
17. Cf., e.g., for Palmyrene *PAT* 0060.1, 0346.1, or 1670A.1.
18. 0339.1 and H230.4 or H390.1.
19. ggJR 1 in *ATTM*, 388.
20. 11Q18 20:1 par. 2Q24 4; the few other instances form Qumran, such as 4Q550 4a:6, are too fragmentary for a precise interpretation.

In contrast, in the diction of the Achaemenid government, *zkrn*/*dkrn* became a legal technical term "minutes, memorandum." Thus, *zkrn* introduces a notice concerning the officially and legally effective decision of the provincial government to agree to the reconstruction of the Elephantine temple.[21] In this regard, it remains uncertain, however, whether the word *zkrn* here denotes the legally binding decision or only the document employed as an *aide-mémoire* for a mandate communicated orally.[22] According to Ezr. 6:2, the edict (*ṭᵉʿēm*; → *ṭʿm*) concerning the construction of the temple in 6:3–5 begins in the same fashion with the heading *diḵrōn*, but has the form of an official decree.[23] In the event that this text does not involve an authentic document but a literary fiction, it nonetheless imitates Achaemenid diction precisely.[24]

The technical administrative connotation is also at hand if the term *sᵉp̄ar doḵrānayyā* in Ezr. 4:15 is not to be understood simply as a descriptive chronicle, but as a collection of records of earlier royal edicts in the form of a scroll (*mglh*) that one could consult in the archive (according to Ezr. 5:17 and 6:1 in royal treasuries, → *gnz* II) for legal precedents (→ *bqr*).

Finally, the precise significance of *zkrn* at the beginning of the individual sections of a very fragmentary document collection from Elephantine with lists of various delivered goods and, perhaps, other services rendered[25] remains unclear, similar to the inventory in Ezr. 1:9-11, as does the significance of *lzkrn* in the likewise fragmentary harbor journal from Memphis.[26] If the paleographically ambiguous reading of *ldkrn* (thus, in a modern spelling) in a list from Bactria at the beginning of the Alexandrian period with goods for distribution is correct,[27] it may represent a comparable specimen from the other end of the Achaemenid sphere of influence. If the term in such lists has the same official connotation as in *TADAE* A4.9,1,2, *zkrn*/*dkrn* seems to refer to officially confirmed summaries.

Gzella

21. *TADAE* A4.9,1,2; the text itself contains a few corrections and may be only a copy of the original document for the community archive.

22. Cf. P. Grelot, *Documents araméens d'Égypte* (Paris, 1972), 415; J. C. Greenfield, "Aspects of Archives in the Achaemenid Period," in K. R. Veenhof, ed., *Cuneiform Archives and Libraries* (Leiden, 1986), 289-95, esp. 290.

23. Cf. H. G. M. Williamson, *Ezra, Nehemiah. WBC* (1985), 74f.

24. Concerning the still controversial question of authenticity, cf. recently pro H. G. M. Williamson, "The Aramaic Documents in Ezra Revisited," *JTS* 59 (2006) 41-62; and contra L. L. Grabbe, "The 'Persian' Documents in the Book of Ezra: Are They Authentic?," in O. Lipschits and M. Oeming, eds., *Judah and the Judeans in the Persian Period* (Winona Lake, IN, 2006), 531-70.

25. *TADAE* C3. 13,1,10,24,44,46,48,50,55.

26. *TADAE* C3.8, Rolle IIIB, ll. 16 and 34.

27. C4.52 in J. Naveh and S. Shaked, *Aramaic Documents from Ancient Bactria* (London, 2012), cf. 212.

דם *dm* /dam/

I. General Aramaic Usage. II. Qumran.

I. General Aramaic Usage. All Semitic languages know the biradical primary noun *dm* "blood." Biblical Aramaic does not attest it; the preserved older instances reaching to the Hellenistic-Roman period refer especially to the blood of slain or wounded humans and animals, but *dm* presumably also denotes blood quite generally as a component of the living body (cf. αἷμα in 1 En. 15:4, whose Aram. original has not been preserved, however). The most common combination is *ʾšd dm* "to shed blood,"[1] and spilling or drinking blood appears often in synonymous parallelism with eating meat (→ *bśr*; *ʾkl bśrh* in Aḥiqar).[2] In a revenge clause (*nqm*), an Old Aramaic state treaty from Sefire[3] mentions the blood of the slain; according to Aḥiqar,[4] predators shed (*ʾšd*) or suck (*ynq*) the blood of their victims. Pap. Amherst 63 6.6 employs the image of a lamb whose blood is drunk (*štī*).

The plural *dmn* "price, value"[5] is sometimes associated with *dm* "blood" (via "blood money."[6]

II. Qumran. The Aramaic texts from the Dead Sea employ *dm* "blood" in the following contexts: 1. description of antediluvian violence and sinfulness; 2. sacrifice and ritual; 3. in the prohibition of bloodshed; and 4. (perhaps) in reference to eschatological suffering.

1. Description of antediluvian violence and sinfulness. Like predators, the giants shed (*ʾšd*; 1QapGen 6:19) and drink (*štī*; 4Q202 1 2:25 [1 En. 7:5]) blood; they spilled much blood (*špk*; 4Q201 1 4:7 [1 En. 9:1, cf. 9:9]). The Book of Giants mentions blood only in fragmentary contexts: 4Q206 3 1:6 (*špk*), 4Q531 1 4, 28 2, 32 2 and perhaps 6Q8 12 2. First Enoch 6–11 associates the violence described in Gen. 6:11 with the blood that the giants had spill and that had stained the earth; it apparently regards the flood as cleansing water.

2. Sacrifice and ritual. The Targum 4Q156 1 7 of Lev 16:14 mentions the blood of a bull as an atoning sacrifice; 1QapGen 10:15 describes how Noah poured (*ʾšd*) the blood of the sacrificial animal at the foot of the altar, followed in l. 16 by the sacrifice of the dove and

J. Berman and B. Kedar-Kopfstein, "דָּם *dām*," *TDOT*, III, 234-50; G. Gerleman, "דָּם *dām* blood," *TLOT*, 337-39; M. J. Lynch, "*dm*," *ThWQ*, I, 689-95.

1. See below as well as the Palmyrene inscription *PAT* 1122.
2. *TADAE* C1.1,184 and pap. Amherst 63 6:6; cf. 1 En. 7:5.
3. *KAI* 224.11f.
4. *TADAE* C1.1,168,184.
5. Very often in legal texts in the Imperial Aramaic tradition, see *DNSI*, 252f.
6. Thus *ATTM*, 2, 379; *DJBA*, 343; cf. *AHw*, I, 158.

its blood on the altar itself. The Aramaic Levi text mentions blood in 8:1-3 (preserved in Geniza manuscripts), with reference to the sprinkling (*zrq*) of the sides of the altar, the washing (*rḥʿ*) of blood from hands and feet, and the commandment that the blood of the sacrificial animal may not be visible (on its head). The context of *dm* in 1QapGen 6:24 and 7:10,12 permits no more precise determination.

3. *In the prohibition of bloodshed.* 1QapGen 11:17 paraphrases Gen. 9:4 as a prohibition of any consumption of blood (*kwl dm lʾ tʾklwn*). Surprisingly, this section, at least in the extant text, lacks any explicit reference to the fact that Noah and his sons may eat meat.

4. *In reference to eschatological suffering.* Almost no context for *dmkh* "your blood" in 4Q541 4 2:4 has been preserved, but if one links the instance with 4Q541 6 3 "gashes of your wounds" (following Isa. 53:3f.), it could be part of a description of the suffering of the eschatological priest, although the fragmentary preservation gives no information whether it implies atonement through the blood and wounds of the priest.

Tigchelaar

דמי *dmī*; דמו *dmw* /damū/

I. Grammatical Constructions and General Usage. II. Vision Literature. III. Noun "Similarity."

I. Grammatical Constructions and General Usage. Instances of the verbal root *dmī* "to resemble, to be similar" occur only in Aramaic and Hebrew; the usage seems to be largely identical. The stative G-stem is employed intransitively and regularly supplemented with a prepositional expression following *l-* "to resemble someone," less often *mn* "to be similar to." It occurs in the general sense for, e.g., the resemblance among relatives[1] or of things (appearances of the moon;[2] possibly also sinews in flesh),[3] but also abstractly for a person's status[4] or for any kind of equivalence of goods.[5]

M. Becker, "*dmh*," *ThWQ*, I, 695-99; E. Jenni, "דמה *dmh* to be like," *TLOT*, 339-42; H. D. Preuss, "דָּמָה *dāmāh*," *TDOT*, III, 250-60.

1. 4Q197 4 3:5 (Tob. 7:2).
2. 4Q209 26:4f.
3. 4Q546 13:5; contra *ATTM*, 2, 124 (R 8:11).
4. Thus in 4Q213 1 1:16 (Aram. Levi text) for the appearance of the wise who is nowhere regarded a stranger.
5. *PAT* 0259 2.114.

The notion of incomparability can appear with either a negative or a positive connotation: the former in the hyperbole equating someone suffering a lack, not with just anyone (*l' ydmh lkwl gbr*), but with the great sea;[6] the second in the praise in a second century C.E. grave inscription for the prematurely deceased daughter of a royal official from Armazi in Georgia (*l' dm' yhwh mn ṭbwt* "no one was like [her] in excellence").[7]

In the D-stem, the verb generally has a transitive nuance "to compare, equate, imitate" and takes a direct object, here too with an optional complement following the prepositions *b*- or *l*-; in the meaning "to suppose," an object clause follows *dy* "that."[8] Occasionally, the Dt-stem "to be comparable"[9] is employed for "to appear to someone (*l*-) as (*b*-)," e.g., as said in a magical amulet from Palestine of a demon whom people encounter in various forms.[10] This use of the G- and D-stem continues without interruption in later West[11] and East Aramaic.[12]

II. Vision Literature. In the vision literature as extent in Daniel and various documents from Qumran, *dmī* (often in the ptcp. for the description of a situation and relation with forms of the root → *ḥzī* "to see") serves, with the help of a comparison, to make things that lie otherwise outside human experience and comprehension at least approaching comprehensible. Here, then, similarity rather than exact equality comes to the foreground. According to Dnl. 3:25, the figure of the enigmatic fourth man in the oven (according to 3:28, an angel), resembles that of a "son of God," thus of a divine being (*dmh lbr 'lhyn*, → *br*); Dnl. 7:5, the other instance in Biblical Aramaic, compares the third of the four supernatural animals with a → *db*, traditionally understood as a "bear," but the description does not correspond to that of a bear. In the report of Enoch's journey to heaven, the myrrh trees of an entire forest of fantastic trees are comparable to the bark of an almond tree.[13]

III. Noun "Similarity." In contrast to the verb, first attested in the Imperial Aramaic tradition, the noun derived from it, *dmw* /damū/ "similarity" is already attested in the oldest preserved Aramaic text, the inscription from Tell Fekheriye.[14] There it alternates with → *ṣlm* to describe the statue of the local king that is provided with this inscription.[15]

Beginning in Imperial Aramaic, *dmw* also appears with the lexicalized prepositional expressions *bdmwt*, *kdwmt*, or *ldmwt* "similar to" for a comparison of whatever sort, first

6. 4Q540 1:3, Levi Apocryphon.
7. *KAI* 276.9-11; in the Greek parallel version: τὸ κάλλος ἀμείμητον εἶχε.
8. 4Q197 4 2:18 (Tob. 6:18).
9. See *DJPA*, 151f. for instances.
10. ooXX 18:12f. in *ATTM.E*, 266f.; in *tdmyn* the infix /t-/ is probably assimilated as it consistently appears in a nonstandard spelling in post-Achaemenid Aramaic cf. *ATTM*, 2, 379.
11. *DJPA*, 151f.
12. *DJBA*, 341f.
13. 4Q204 1 12:28 (1 En. 31:2).
14. *KAI* 309.1,15.
15. Cf. W. R. Garr, *In His Own Image and Likeness: Humanity, Divinity, and Monotheism. CHANE* 5 (2003), 121f.

in the treaty *TADAE* B3.4, 21 (*byt ldmwt bytk* "a house like your house"), then in Qumran[16] and still later in West Aramaic.[17] Beyer[18] adds a by-form *dmy* /domī/ "similar" and notes two possible instances in 1 En. 78:17 and 79:6, but these are not entirely proven.

Gzella

16. 4Q209 26:4f. (1 En. 79:6).
17. *DJPA*, 151b.
18. *ATTM*, 555.

דקק *dqq*

I. Grammatical Constructions. II Usage.

I. Grammatical Constructions. The common Semitic verbal root *dqq* "to be crushed, to crush" occurs in Aramaic in the middle-passive G-stem "to be crushed = to become dust" (Dnl. 2:35)[1] and in the transitive active causative stem "to crush" with that which is crushed as the object (Dnl. 2:34,40,44,45; 6:25; 7:7,19,23; in Dnl. 2:34f. the passive G-stem and active causative stem meanings stand alongside one another), and further, once in the probably synonymous D-stem.[2] If *dqq* can be employed even in the G-stem both as an active and a middle-passive (the latter possibly to express a sudden change of situation), it would be a "labile" or "ambitransitive" root like Heb. *hpk* or *ṣpn*.[3]

II. Usage. As the distribution of examples indicates, *dqq* in older Aramaic appears primarily in the vision literature, especially in Daniel. It belongs among the rather numerous verbs of destruction (→ *ḥbl*) that describe the often immense images of this genre graphically and in detail; in this genre, thus, the vocabulary for various forms of destruction is very distinctive and includes both general and very specific lexemes. The verb can be employed expressly for the pulverization of very hard objects such as stone (Dnl. 2:34f.) or bones (6:25, here with lions as the subject), although also generally for

ATTM, 557; 2, 381; H. Lozachmeur, *La collection Clermont-Ganneau: Ostraca, épigraphes sur jarre, étiquettes de bois*, 2 vols. (Paris, 2006).

1. Cf. *BLA* §166d for the form; it is also attested as an active later: *DJPA*, 154; *DJBA*, 348f.
2. *mdqq* in 4Q206 1 26:16, corresponding to the form of the causative stem *mdqyn* in the parallel 4Q204 1 12:29 (1 En. 31:3).
3. Cf. H. Gzella, "Voice in Classical Hebrew against Its Semitic Background," *Or* 78 (2009) 295.

a total and complete destruction (thus Dnl. 2:40,44 and 7:7,19,23).[4] The adjective *dqyq* /daqqīq/ "small, tender, wasting (from fever)" derived from the verbal root is only certainly attested later in Aramaic;[5] in contrast, the alternative form *dq* /daq/ "thin" already appears at Qumran.[6] In the Imperial Aramaic ostraca in the Clermont-Ganneau collection, however, there has now been found an instance of *dqq* "finely ground" as a further description of *mlḥ* "salt."[7] The grammatical form is unclear in the consonantal text; in addition to an adjective, it could involve a participle of the middle-passive G-stem "to pound." Meanwhile, the word *dqdq'*[*t* in another ostracon[8] cannot be interpreted with certainty.

Gzella

4. In 1 En. 31:3 it is used of the pulverization of tree bark, but there also in the context of a vision; regarding the Qumran examples, → I.
5. Cf. *DJPA*, 154 for Jewish Palestinian.
6. 4Q561 1 1:1.4, of a beard; see further *ATTM*, 557; 2, 381.
7. No. 16cv3 in Lozachmeur, alongside *ḥsp* "rough"(?).
8. No. 106cc3; cf. H. Gzella, review of Lozachmeur, *BiOr* 70 (2013), 471, bottom.

דת *dt* /dāt/

I. Juridical Use. II. Religious Use.

I. Juridical Use. Like the other Iranian loanwords, the feminine *dt* /dāt/ "law, royal edict," was adopted into Aramaic in the Achaemenid period and is attested beginning in Biblical Aramaic. The original usage for "state law" occurs in Dnl. 6:9,13,16 expressly described as "the inalterable law of the Medes and Persians," and in Ezr. 7:26. It also appears in the sense of an ad hoc edict of the angry king in Dnl. 2:9,13,15 (cf. → *ṭ'm* in 3:29).

Older documentary texts, however, preserve only the compound *dtbr* /dātabar/ "judge" or "person with legal training" (from *dātabara*, literally "legal entity"),[1] namely the legal papyri from Saqqara.[2] It also appears in the context of a list of high officials in Biblical

J. B. Segal, *Aramaic Texts from North Saqqara* (London, 1983); J. Tavernier, *Iranica in the Achaemenid Period (ca. 550-330 B.C.). OLA* 158 (2007); C. J. Tuplin, "The Justice of Darius," in A. Fitzpatrick-McKinley, ed., *Assessing Biblical and Classical Sources for the Reconstruction of Perisan Influence, History, and Culture* (Wiesbaden, 2015), 73-126.

1. Tavernier, 418f.
2. Segal nos. 13.3, 14.5.

Aramaic (Dnl. 3:2f.). In the light of the preserved material, however, its specific nuance cannot be distinguished from → *dyn* /dayyān/, the usual word for "judge" in Aramaic.

II. Religious Use. The Aramaic religious literature of Palestine, as it appears in Biblical Aramaic and the texts from Qumran, appropriated various terms and expressions from Achaemenid administrative language theologically. Just as *ptgm* "decision, matter" appears in the secondary meaning "divine edict,"[3] so *dt* has also clearly acquired the nuance "law of God." Thus, Ezr. 7:26 places divine and royal law on one level; otherwise, this originally juridical expression often designates the "commandment of the God of heaven" (Ezr. 7:12,21) or the "commandments of your God" (Ezr. 7:25). These instances make no distinction terminologically between the law as a whole and the respective constitutive individual laws as the parallelism of plural (Ezr. 7:25) and singular (7:26) indicates.[4] The same usage continued in Qumran, where in the context of the marriage of Noah's sons and daughters one encounters the expression "according to the law of the eternal instruction" (*kdt ḥwq ʿlmʾ*).[5] In the standard form of the talmudic marriage contract, whose terminology was after all rooted in the Imperial Aramaic legal tradition, *dt* then expressly represents "the law of Moses and the Jews" (*kdt mšh wyhwdʾy*).[6]

Gzella

3. Cf. H. Gzella, "*ptgm*," *ThWQ*, III, 359-61.
4. An emendation to the singular in 7:25 is ultimately unnecessary, see H. G. M. Williamson, *Ezra, Nehemiah. WBC* (1985), 97, and xxxvii-xxxix on the controversial question of whether this law already originally referred quite specifically to the Pentateuch.
5. 1QapGen 6:8.
6. Text in *ATTM*, 325.

הדר *hdr* /hadar/; הדר *hdr*

I. Lexical Field. II. Usage. III. Denominal Verb.

I. Lexical Field. Even though West Semitic attests the noun *hdr* /hadar/ "majesty" rather well, its etymology remains obscure. In Aramaic, as in Hebrew, it denotes the visible epitome of a person's totality that goes far beyond normal proportions; hence, it combines beauty and honor. The range of synonyms in Aramaic seems much less distinctive in this area than does the Hebrew, which developed a rich vocabulary around

H. Macumber, "*hdr*," *ThWQ*, I, 746-9; G. Warmuth, "הָדָר *hādhār*,"*TDOT*, III, 335-41.

the central concept of divine honor (*kāḇōḏ*; attested in Aramaic probably only as a loan-word),[1] especially in liturgical diction.[2]

Nonetheless, Aramaic *hdr* has long appeared primarily in combination with → *yqr* "honor,"[3] less often with *tšbḥh* "praise" (→ *šbḥ*).[4] In Greek and Latin theological diction, the corresponding vocabulary was further concentrated on δόξα and *gloria*.

From the adjective *hdyr* /hadīr/ "glorious" already attested in pre-Imperial Aramaic,[5] a new abstract then developed secondarily in East Aramaic with the reconstructed ground form /hadīrūtā/ "majesty"[6] and apparently replaced *hdr* there.

II. Usage. The role of the concept *hdr* in royal typology is first perceptible in a pre-Imperial Aramaic saying of Aḥiqar: *špyr mlk lmḥzh kšmš wyqyr hdrh* "The king is as beautiful to look at as Šamaš/the sun and his majesty is honorable."[7] It continues in the book of Daniel, in which the three Biblical Aramaic instances of the noun appear, indeed, all in reference to King Nebuchadnezzar (twice in his self-conscious presentation in Dnl. 4:27,33, once in Daniel's payment of respect to Nebuchadnezzar's son Belshazzar in 5:18). The Aramaic texts from Qumran then apply it to the majesty of God; the word occurs there in Enoch's prayer to God, before whose majesty all tremble,[8] and in Enoch's description of blooming trees, whose leaves and fruits serve them for majesty and honor, whose behavior in compliance with the law in the course of the seasons points, however, to their eternal creator (cf. *hāḏār* in Lev. 23:40 and Isa. 35:2).[9]

III. Denominal Verb. The verb *hdr* "to ascribe majesty" may derive from the noun *hdr*. Consequently, the verb, as often with denominal roots, appears in the D-stem. In older Aramaic, it is attested only in Daniel. In contrast to the noun, however, all three instances (Dnl. 4:31,34; 5:23) refer to God as the indirect object introduced by *l-*. The verb consistently appears in direct, hymnic relationship to the verbs of praise → *brk*, → *šbḥ*, and → *rīm*; each instance involves the recognition of God as the Most High who also humbles the arrogant (thus, expressly, in Dnl. 4:34; → *g'ī*): King Nebuchadnezzar (Dnl. 4:31,34) did so and was delivered, his son Belshazzar did not (5:23), and that was his downfall.

Gzella

---

1. *ATTM*, 602.
2. Cf. Warmuth, 336.
3. Cf. *TADAE* C1.1,92; Dnl. 4:27,33; 5:18; 4Q203 9:2; 4Q204 1 1:29 (1 En. 5:1); 11Q10 34:6 (Job 40:10), where *wyqr* was apparently added to the *hdr* of MT precisely because of the frequency of this combination.
4. 4Q201 1 2:10.
5. *TADAE* C1.1,206, of a wealthy person who prided himself in his possessions.
6. *DJBA*, 81b, s.v. *'dyrwt'*; *LexSyr*, 172.
7. *TADAE* C1.1,92.
8. 4Q203 9:2; similarly probably also 1Q19 13-14:2, cf. *ATTM*, 229 n. 1 for an approximate reconstruction of this small fragment.
9. 4Q204 1 1:29 (1 En. 5:1).

הוי *hwī*

I. Etymology, Forms, and Grammatical Constructions. II. As an Indicator of Time. III. In the Full Sense of "to Exist, to Happen," and "to Turn Into" (*l-*). IV. With *l-* for "to Have." V. Other Prepositional Expressions.

I. Etymology, Forms, and Grammatical Constructions. Of the various lexemes for "to be" in the individual Semitic languages, the Aramaic *hwī* is closest to the Hebrew *hyī* in form and function. Contrariwise, there is no etymological relationship to Akkadian *bašû* or the root *kūn*, which means "to be" not only in Arabic and Ethiopic, but also in Ugaritic and Pheonician, while Aramaic and Hebrew employ it for "to stand firm." Thus, in terms of the geography of dialect, the etymologically obscure *hwī*/*hyī* for "to be" in the languages of central Syria and Palestine interrupts the corresponding use of *kūn* in northern Syria and the northern coastal strip, on one side, and northern Arabia, on the other.

Since a copula first developed in Aramaic in post-Christian times, *hwī* was employed either as an indicator of time, whose perfect or imperfect fixes the time reference of otherwise nominal clauses in relation either to the past or the future, or in the full sense of "to exist, to happen." Specific nuances result through the use of certain prepositions, especially *l-* for "to turn into" or in impersonal expressions for "to have," and other propositions for a variety of other usages. With the increasing integration of the participle into the Aramaic verbal system since Imperial Aramaic, the addition of *hwī* transposed the indeterminate duration, which by nature suits participles as an indicator of a state of being, into the past or future so that such periphrastic constructions then expressed the imperfect aspect of duration or repetition in addition to the time interval and became ever more frequent after Imperial Aramaic.[1] The later phases of the language largely agree.[2]

Some Aramaic languages developed unusual forms. First, the third-person imperfect of *hwī*, which otherwise has the preformative /y-/, is formed in Biblical Aramaic, Aramaic texts from Qumran, and sometimes in contracts from the Dead Sea instead with *l-*, which apparently arose from an old precative particle and in the course of time displaced /y-/ in all verb forms in East Aramaic. Thereby, *lhwh*/*lhw'* was distinguished graphically from the Tetragrammaton for the divine name of the biblical tradition employed with constantly increasing reticence.[3] It is not known, however, whether one pronounced the

---

S. Amsler, "היה *hyh* to be," *TLOT*, 359-65; J. Bergman, H. Ringgren, and K.-H. Bernhardt, "הָיָה *hāyāh*," *TDOT*, III, 369-81; K. Egger, "Die verbalen Funktionen des Partizips im Genesis Apocryphon," *KUSATU* 11 (2010) 43-108; H. Gzella, *Tempus, Aspekt und Modalität im Reichsaramäischen. VOK* 48 (2004).

1. An exhaustive overview of the older material appears in *DNSI*, 271-276 and (with a better classification of the individual usages) *ATTM*, 560f. and 2, 383f.

2. Cf. *DJPA*, 160f.; *DJBA*, 370-73; *LexSyr*, 173; *MdD*, 134.

3. Cf. H. Gzella, "The Heritage of Imperial Aramaic in Eastern Aramaic," *AraSt* 6 (2008) 103; *ATTM*, 98.

l- that was also extended to the plural. Second, in later Jewish Palestinian, the participle with an enclitic personal pronoun, that is *hwynh*/*hwyn'*, in the masculine /hāwē-nā/ and in the feminine /hāwiyānā/ replaced the first-person singular of the perfect of *hwī* (*hwyt*).[4]

II. As an Indicator of Time. Older Aramaic, like related languages, expressed relations between two nominal phrases through juxtaposition or a preposition to mark a spatial or logical relationship in the present through nominal clauses. In a clear narrative context, such as the book of Daniel, nominal clauses could also, in some cases, be employed in reference to the past (Dnl. 2:49; 4:9; 5:21). In contrast, should such a statement of condition be transposed into the past, the future, or the realm of possibility, Aramaic added the perfect, the (long) imperfect, the short imperfect (jussive, until it fell out of use), or the imperative of *hwī*. Thereby, the temporal or modal marking of this semantically "empty" verb indicated by the corresponding conjugation transferred to the circumstantial statement of the nominal clause.[5] Since it is naturally already open-ended, the present-future nuance dominates the long imperfect, which is associated with the semantically linked categories of present-future, imperfect aspect, and epistemic modality. Therefore, in Old and Imperial Aramaic one already encounters for the past, e.g., *zy hww b'gwr' zk* "that were in that temple" (perfect),[6] for the future *ṣdqh yhwh lk qdm yhw* "it will be to your credit before Yahweh" (imperfect),[7] and for a wish *šlm yhwy lk* "May peace be with you!" (jussive),[8] or *whwy ḥlph* "and be his successor!" (imperative).[9]

Thus, participial clauses, which also denote an open circumstance, could be supplemented with dynamic verbs and thereby depict even a nonstative verbal action as underway in periphrastic constructions involving *hwī*: first for the present (which, after all, is always underway); then once again through the addition of the perfect or imperfect of *hwī*, as an explicit marking of openness in the past in contrast to a pure perfect; or, less often, in the future, whereby the less clearly marked imperfect in terms of its temporal aspect is defined as future with an imperfective aspect; infrequently also with the imperative:[10] *hᵃwā miṯnaṣṣaḥ* "he took care to distinguish himself" (Dnl. 6:4), *zy 'hwh mšlm lk* "what I will tell you"[11] or *hwy šlḥ* "do you want to send?" (polite).[12]

The decision between a closed or unmarked and explicitly open-ended narrative perspective is often subjective and is most frequent in the depiction of past events (where elaboration can slow the narrative flow, as *whww' qṭl bhwn* "he murdered among

4. S. E. Fassberg, "Lamed-Yodh Verbs in Palestinian Targumic Aramaic," in M. J. Geller, J. C. Greenfield, and S. Weitzman, eds., *Studia Aramaica: New Sources and New Approaches* (Oxford, 1995), 43-52, esp. 47-50.

5. Gzella, 255-59.

6. *TADAE* A4.7,30.

7. *TADAE* A4.7,27.

8. *TADAE* C1.1,94.

9. Sefire III = *KAI* 224.22; cf. J. A. Fitzmyer, *The Aramaic Inscriptions of Sefire*. *BietOr* 19/A (^{2}1995), 158f.

10. See generally Gzella, 243-68; specifically regarding 1QapGen, see Egger.

11. *TADAE* B4.2,6f.; cf. Dnl. 2:43.

12. *TADAE* D7.6,10f.

them"),[13] but may also be additionally motivated by the context (cf. the change from the periphrastic construction with an indeterminate object to the pure perfect with a determinate in 1QapGen 21:28).[14] Since Imperial Aramaic, such constrictions increased in all the later varieties and stimulated an analogous development in postexilic Hebrew.[15] The few cases in which a periphrastic construction clearly indicates an ingressive or unique event ([ʿ]*nh hwwʾ* "he answered"),[16] still require closer investigation, as do the isolated later instances of the participle of *hwī* together with another participle.[17]

With the passive participle, *hwī* can be employed for impersonally formulated instructions (thus, esp., in *ydyʿ yhwy* "Let it be known")[18] or for a pluperfect since, as a rule, the passive participle presupposed a past event (*hww mtyldyn* "there had been born").[19]

III. In the Full Sense of "to Exist, to Happen," and "to Turn Into" (*l*-). Besides its frequent usage as an indication of time, *hwī* can also be used to mean "to exist, to happen," for which in relation to the present tense the particle of existence *ʾyty* /ʾītay/ "there is" was also available.[20] If, e.g., *hwh* in *KAI* 320,2f. is a perfect, it refers to "any plague there has ever been anywhere on the earth;[21] for the closed past one finds *ʾp hwh* "furthermore, it happened that. . ."[22] or *wśtwʾ hwh* "and it was/became winter";[23] for the future, e.g., *mā dī læhᵉʷē* "what will happen" (Dnl. 2:28,29,45) or *dī-lᵉmā læhᵉʷē qᵉṣap̄ ʿal* "so that wrath will not come against. . ." (Ezr. 7:23). The syntax of the verb gives rise to specific nuances, as, especially, with *l*- for the ingressive "to turn into" (which is imitated in the NT by γίνεσθαι εἰς), e.g., *hᵃwāṯ lᵉṭūr* "turn into a rock" (Dnl. 2:35), *whwʾt ly lʾt* "and it turned into a sign for me,"[24] less often with *k*-: *wahᵃwō kᵉʿūr* "and they became like chaff" (Dnl. 2:35).

The inalterable participle *hwh* is utilized in official style, in contracts, e.g., to define more precisely "what is,"[25] also later to indicate time more precisely.[26]

IV. With *l*- for "to Have." Often, *hwī* also appears with the preposition *l*- to indicate possession in the past, future, or in the realms of possibility or desirability. Thereby, this

---

13. 1QapGen 22:8f.; cf. H. Gzella, "*qṭl*," *ThWQ*, III, 521.
14. Gzella, 259f.
15. Cf. H. Gzella, "The Use of the Participle in the Hebrew Bar Kosiba Letters in the Light of Aramaic," *DSD* 14 (2007) 96-98.
16. 4Q530 2 2+6-12,15.
17. Cf. H. Gzella, "Zu den Verlaufsformen für die Gegenwart im Aramäischen," *Or* 75 (2006) 185f.
18. Cf. *TADAE* A6.10,8; Dnl. 3:18; Ezr. 4:12,13; 5:8.
19. 4Q201 1 3:17 (1 En. 7:2).
20. *DNSI*, 50f.; *ATTM*, 509 and 2, 345; it can also function as a copula, as in Dnl. 2:11, or with a participle to emphasize the actual present instead of the general, as in Dnl. 3:18; cf. Gzella, 218f.
21. Cf. Gzella 257f.
22. *TADAE* A4.7,9.
23. 4Q211 1 1:4 (1 En. 82:22).
24. 1QapGen 12:1; without *l*-: *hwyt ʾnʾ nwḥ gbr* "I, Noah, turned into a man," 6:6.
25. *TADAE* B2.3,3; 3.1,5.
26. Cf. H1030b,1 from Hatra, see K. Beyer, *Die aramäischen Inschriften aus Assur, Hatra und dem übrigen Ostmesopotamien* (Göttingen, 1998), 111.

construction replaces the preterit, future, and modal forms of a word for "to have" which is not extant in Semitic, cf. *mattᵉnāṯāḵ lāḵ læhæwyān* "your gifts should belong to you" (Dnl. 5:17),[27] *k]l d[y]hwh ly* "everything that I owned,"[28] sometimes in an ingressive sense "to be bestowed."[29]

V. Other Prepositional Expressions. In addition, other prepositional constructions in connection with *hwī* produce other specific nuances. Together with *ʿl* it is used once in the sense of "to need,"[30] but in the legal diction of contracts also for "to be incumbent on someone,"[31] which is otherwise expressed with *l-*.[32] In a partitive relationship, one encounters *mn*: *wlʾ thwh mn šn*ʾ "and you will not be one of the enemies (= not belong to the enemies)."[33] In all these and comparable cases, then, the semantically idle verb *hwī* anchors the logical relationship already marked by a preposition in a temporal or modal framework.

Gzella

27. Cf. nV 1:30 in *ATTM*, 2, 205-7: *wytwb wyhwʾ lh mn kʿn* "and from now on, it will belong to you again."

28. 4Q196 2:2 (Tob. 1:20).

29. As in 4Q197 4 2:18 (Tob. 6:18) of children; similarly in nV 7:25,66 of a widow who does not get another husband, text in *ATTM*, 2, 218-23.

30. *TADAE* C1.1,43,55f., here of Aḥiqar's counsel, which the king and the country need urgently.

31. nV 6:6,8 in *ATTM*, 2, 216f.

32. *TADAE* B2.4,11.

33. 4Q541 24 2:6, Levi Apocryphon.

היכל *hykl* /hēkal/

I. Etymology. II. Semantics. 1. Old Aramaic. 2. Imperial Aramaic. 3. Biblical Aramaic. 4. Qumran. III. LXX.

I. Etymology. Aramaic *hykl* "palace, temple" traces via Akkadian *ekallu*(*m*) "palace"[1] to Sumerian *E.GAL* "palace, temple." In the NW Semitic languages, in addition to Ar-

K. Beyer, *Die aramäischen Inschriften aus Assur, Hatra und dem übrigen Ostmesopotamien* (Göttingen, 1998); S. A. Kaufman, *The Akkadian Influences on Aramaic. AS* 19 (1974); E. Lipiński, "Emprunts suméro-akkadiens en hébreu biblique," *ZAH* 1 (1988) 61-73; P. V. Mankowski, *Akkadian Loanwords in Biblical Hebrew. HSS* 47 (2000); M. Ottosson, "הֵיכָל *hêkhāl*," *TDOT*, III, 382-88; B. A. Strawn, *hykl*," *ThWQ*, I, 779-81.

1. *AHw*, I, 191-93; *CAD*, IV, 52-62.

amaic *hyk* one also finds Ugaritic *hkl* "palace," Hebrew *hēḵāl* "temple (hall), palace," Syriac *hayklā* "palace, temple,"[2] and Mandaic *hykl'* "temple."[3]

II. Semantics. Besides *hykl* as a technical term for "temple," Aramaic also has *'gwrh/ 'kwrh*, → *byt* and *msgd* (→ *sgd*). For "palace" there is also *byt*.

1. Old Aramaic. The oldest Aramaic example of *hykl* exists in the reference to a business tax "for the palace" (*lhykl'*) on a Neo-Assyrian ostracon from Kalhu/Nimrud.[4]

2. Imperial Aramaic. Imperial Aramaic instances stem from the Aḥiqar novella where the narrative introduction employs *hykl'* for the palace.[5] More precisely, it involves the gate of the palace (*bb hykl'*; *tr' hykl'*), where Aḥiqar pursues his profession as chancellor and keeper of the seal and where he also establishes his nephew, Nadin, in this office. The reference intends an office in the entrance of the palace or, in a figurative sense, an activity in service of the palace (→ *plḥ*).[6]

In the Palmyrene inscriptions, *hykl* appears as a temple and denotes the temple of Bel and his satellite gods[7] and the temple of Baalšamin.[8] The parallelism of *hykl'* and *rbny 'wnt' dy bl* ("the head of the priesthood of Bel"), where *hykl'* refers to the temple as an institution,[9] merits particular reference. In *PAT* 0305.5f. the pronaos (*prn'*) and the ornamentation (*tṣby*) of the entire facility stand in parallel with *hykl'*. Here *hykl'* denotes the temple structure, i.e., the cella. *PAT* 1347.4f. elevates the *hykl* as the cella of the temple of Bel from the thalamoi (*qdšn*),[10] or from other related sanctuaries/chapels.[11] The Palmyrene inscriptions from Dura Europos mention the temple of Bel and Yarḥibol (*hykl' lbl wyrḥbwl*).[12] To date, there are two instances of *hykl* "temple" from Hatra. The inscription from Iwan 4 of the great temple mentions a *sgyl hykl' rb'*, i.e., "Esagila, the great temple."[13] The referent of *sgyl* "Esagila" is probably the temple complex of the sun god in Hatra.[14] A temple, not defined more precisely, appears in the building inscription

2. *ThesSyr*, 1003f.

3. *MdD*, 143; regarding pronunciation and the method of borrowing, see Kaufman, 27 and Lipiński, 65; cf. Mankowski, 51f.

4. A. R. Millard, "Some Aramaic Epigraphs," *Iraq* 34 (1972) 131f.; F. M. Fales, *Aramaic Epigraphs on Clay Tablets of the Neo-Assyrian Period. StSem* NS 2 (1986), no. 43.

5. *TADAE* C1.1,9,17,23,44.

6. *TADAE* C1.1,17.

7. *PAT* 1347.4; 2043.1.

8. *PAT* 0185.1; 0305.5.

9. *PAT* 2043.1-4.

10. So C.B. Costecalde, *DBS* (1985), X:1385f.

11. So A. Bounni and K. Assad, *Palmyre histoire, monuments, et Musée* (Damascus, 1982), 107. For other understandings of this passage, cf. *PAT*, 405 s.v. *qdš*.

12. R. Comte du Mesnil du Buisson, *Inventaire des inscriptions palmyréniennes de Doura Europos* (Paris, 1939), no. 1,6f.

13. H107.6.

14. Beyer, 168, s.v.

H192.2. An additional loanword attested in Hatra and Palmyra based on Akk. *arad ekalli* is *ʾrdklʾ* "mason."[15]

3. Biblical Aramaic. Biblical Aramaic knows *hyklʾ*, in both meanings as "temple" and "palace." Three passages stereotypically discuss the *hēḵᵉlā dī ḇīrūšᵉlæm* (Ezr. 5: 14f.; 6:5; Dnl. 5:2), meaning the temple of Yahweh, while the *hēḵᵉlā dī ḇāḇæl* (Ezr. 5:14) refers to the temple of Babylon's gods. The theme of these passages consists of the theft of the temple fixtures and their restitution (Ezr. 5:14f.; 6:5), or the misuse of these implements (Dnl. 5:2).

In both of the Ezra passages, the context casts significant light on the choice of the word for temple. The letter of Tatnai in Ezr. 5 designates the Yahweh temple in Jerusalem as *bayiṯ* (5:3,9,11,12), or as *bēṯ ʾᵆlāhā* (5:8,13,14,15,16,17). Only when the discussion deals with the temple implements and their theft and transfer to Babel does *hēḵal* refer to the temples in Jerusalem and in Babel (5:14). Ezra 6, where *bēṯ ʾᵆlāhā* appears in 6:3,5,7,8,12 and *hēḵal* only in the context of the temple utensils in 6:5, is comparable.

As "palace," *hykl* refers to the palace of the kings of Babylon (Dnl. 4:1,26; 5:5; 6:19) or of Persia (Ezr. 4:14). The context of the passages just mentioned is determined by the fact that the opponents of construction of the wall in Jerusalem turn to Artaxerxes with the following affirmation of loyalty: *mᵉlaḥ hēḵᵉlā mᵉlaḥnā* "we have salted the salt of the palace." This statement refers to the fact that these opponents stand in the service of the palace, a service remunerated with a salt ration. This usage continues on to the French *salaire* and English *salary*, terms that stand for "remuneration" and derive from the Roman state practice of allotting salt to its officials.[16]

4. Qumran. The Aramaic texts from Qumran attest *hykl* primarily as "temple," as in the Megillat Ta`anit from the period 67-70 C.E.;[17] furthermore, one can adduce an ossuary inscription from Jerusalem from the first half of the first century[18] that mentions a "temple architect" (*bnh hklh*). Regarding the examples from Ezr. 6:5 and Dnl. 6:19 as well as the new Jerusalem from Qumran, cf. *ATTM*, 2, 384. The twelve weeks apocalypse of the astrological book of Enoch 91:13[19] attests *hykl* in the sense of "palace."

III. LXX. In passages where *hēḵal* refers to a temple, the LXX translates with ναός (Ezr. 6:5; Dnl. 5:2 LXX), or with ὁ οἶκος ὁ ἐν Ιερουσαλημ (Ezr. 5:14f.), or ὁ οἶκος τοῦ Θεοῦ (Dnl. 5:2 LXX). When *hēḵal* refers to the royal palace, LXX has ὁ οἶκος (τοῦ βασιλέως) (Dnl. 5:5; 6:19 LXX) or ἡ βασίλεια (Dnl. 6:19 LXX).

Niehr

15. Index in Beyer, 170 and idem, "Die aramäischen Inschriften aus Assur, Hatra und dem übrigen Ostmesopotamien," *WO* 43 (2013) 56; cf. Kaufman, 35 and esp. B. Aggoula, *Inventaire des inscriptions hatréennes. BAH* 139 (1991), 1f.

16. E. Lipiński, *Dieux et déesses de l'univers phénicien et punique. OLA* 64 (1995), 114.

17. *ATTM*, 357f.

18. *ATTM*, 344.

19. *ATTM*, 248.

הלך *hlk* and הוך *hūk*; אזל *ʾzl*; הלך *hlk* /helk/

I. Etymology, Forms, Grammatical Constructions, and Lexical Field. II. G-stem *hūk* and *ʾzl* "to Go." III. D-stem *hlk* "to Walk." IV. Noun "Property or Income Tax."

I. Etymology, Forms, Grammatical Constructions, and Lexical Field. In Aramaic, the common Semitic verbal root *hlk* appears in the otherwise common meaning "to go" not in the G-stem but in the D-stem, indeed with the durative-iterative nuance "to walk around, stroll" indicated thereby (thus, similar to the hithpael in Hebrew), both in the literal and the figurative sense (→ III). In contrast, Old Aramaic already employed for the general meaning "to go" the likely hollow root *hūk*, which may have once constituted an allomorph of *hlk* but which became differentiated over time.[1]

In turn, in the older material, *hūk* stood mostly in a suppletive relationship with the typical Aramaic verb *ʾzl* "to go, to go away," so that the imperfect and infinitive are formed with *hūk* but the perfect, imperative, and participle were replaced with the corresponding forms of *ʾzl*. The reason for such a division could be a comparable frequency in usage given the lack of semantic differentiation whereby the paradigmatic differences diminished, although the roots themselves were initially retained (a suppletive paradigm from various lexemes for designating going arose, e.g., also in Romance languages, cf. French *aller*, *va* and *ira*). However, Old Aramaic attests an imperfect of *ʾzl*.[2] In post-Imperial Aramaic, *ʾzl* then replaced *hūk* (preserved only as an archaism) and developed its own forms of the imperfect and the infinitive.[3]

The two verbs are constructed virtually alike. As a rule, they appear with animate subjects or subjects experienced as animate (such as wisdom;[4] with inanimate subjects such as borders[5] or paths,[6] they denote their natural course) and could be supplemented

J. Dušek, *Les manuscrits araméens du Wadi Daliyeh et la Samarie vers 450-332 av. J.-C. CHANE* 30 (2007); H. Gzella, *Tempus, Aspekt und Modalität im Reichsaramäischen. VOK* 48 (2004); F. J. Helfmeyer, "הָלַךְ *hālakh*," *TDOT*, III, 388-403; E. Jenni, *Das hebräische Piʿel* (Zürich, 1968), esp. 151-54; S. A. Kaufman, *The Akkadian Influences on Aramaic. AS* 19 (1974); J. Naveh and S. Shaked, *Aramaic Documents from Ancient Bactria (Fourth Century* B.C.E.*)* (London, 2012); G. Sauer, "הלך *hlk* to go," *TLOT*, 365-70; J. B. Segal, *Aramaic Texts from North Saqqara* (London, 1983); C. Stadel, "*hlk*," *ThWQ*, I, 781-89.

1. So T. Nöldeke, "Die aramäischen Papyri von Assuan," *ZA* 20 (1907) 142, and *BLA* §144b, contra F. Rundgren, "Zum Lexikon des Alten Testaments," *AcOr* 21 (1953) 304-16; cf. *DNSI*, 281.
2. Sefire IB = *KAI* 222 B 39.
3. According to Beyer's reading in *ATTM*, 2, 90, an imperfect *tʾzl* "you will go" already appears again in 1QapGen 3:15, but this is uncertain because of the very unclear and fragmentary letters in this passage, cf. D. A. Machiela, *The Dead Sea Genesis Apocryphon. STDJ* 79 (2009), 38; *tʾzl* "she left" in H342,7 from Hatra is very clear, however.
4. 4Q534 1 1:8.
5. 1QapGen 16:17.
6. 1QapGen 6:3.

with *l-* "to" for places and persons in order to indicate the objective,[7] in cases of great distance less often also with *ʿd* "as far as"[8] or with persons "up to."[9] In addition, in some cases *hūk* appears with the object without preposition,[10] minimally transitive with the path traveled as object (in astronomical terminology for the sun that travels all its paths: *šmšʾ lmhk kl ḥrbyh*)[11] or following *b-* "in" (figuratively of walking in the paths of the truth).[12] The more common term in the older material, *ʾzl*, is also attested as a directive with the preposition *ʿl* "to" for persons[13] and with *ʿm* "together with."[14] An adverb of manner such as *bbhylw* "hurriedly" (Ezr. 4:23; cf. Dnl. 6:20) or another abstract such as *byšyrwtʾ* "in uprightness"[15] can also be added. Later, other prepositional supplements also appear.[16]

The range of synonyms for verbs of movement is well developed. To express the idea of coming, Aramaic employs *ʾtī* (→ *ʾth*). For going quickly, running, Aramaic, as other Semitic languages, has the root *rūṭ* (from an older *rūθ* and thus still spelled *rwṣ* in Old Aramaic), cf. e.g., already *KAI* 216.4 and later 1QapGen 2;19; in 11Q10 36:5 (Job 41:11) this term also translates Hebrew *hlk* once. "To enter, to go on" is *drk* (with a direct object or a prepositional expression following *ʿl*), "to go away" → *npq*, "to climb up here" → *slq*, "to enter" → *ʿll*, and "to crawl" *rḥš*. In East Aramaic, the root *sgī* in the G- or D-stem for "to go, to move" was also quite productive,[17] and occurs once already in the pre-Imperial Aramaic sayings of Aḥiqar (of the gods who come to help a righteous person under threat).[18]

The noun *hlk* /helk/ for a particular variety of tax that appears in Imperial Aramaic administrative terminology (→ IV) was borrowed from the Akkadian *ilku* and did not develop within Aramaic from *hlk*. In form, however, it was assimilated to the Aramaic root and, thereby, distinguished graphically from the demonstrative pronoun *ʾlk* "those."[19]

II. G-stem *hūk* and *ʾzl* "to Go." For forms such as *ʾhk* "I go"[20] or *yhkn* "they go,"[21] one can reconstruct with a likelihood bordering on certainty a root *hūk* in the G-stem,[22] not *hlk*[23]

7. 1QapGen 22:4; 4Q534 1 1:8.
8. 4Q204 5 2:29 (1 En. 107:2): *ʾzl*; 4Q568 1:1: *hūk*.
9. *KAI* 310.3.
10. Sefire III = *KAI* 224.5: *wyhkn ḥlb* "and they are going to Aleppo."
11. 4Q209 7 3:2 (1 En. 73); similarly 4Q209 23:6 (1 En. 77:3).
12. 4Q212 1 2:20 (1 En. 91:19).
13. *TADAE* A4.5,3; A4.7,5 par. 4.8,4; Dnl. 2:24; Ezr. 4:23.
14. Segal no. 29 2.2.
15. 4Q542 1 1:9.
16. Cf. *DJPA*, 43-45; *DJBA*, 100-102; *LexSyr*, 10; *MdD*, 12.
17. *DJBA*, 786f.; *LexSyr*, 457; *MdD*, 317.
18. *TADAE* C1.1,145.
19. With the standardization of Imperial Aramaic orthography, other disambiguating spellings were also created, cf. *hw* "he" and *hy* "she" for the personal pronoun instead of the older *hʾ*.
20. *KAI* 224.6.
21. *KAI* 222 A 24.
22. Cf. *BLA*, §46b; *ATTM*, 562.
23. Attested in Aram. only in the D-stem.

with assimilation of the /l/.[24] Vocalized Biblical Aramaic forms like *yᵉhāḵ* (Dnl. 2:13; Ezr. 6:5) or *limhāḵ* (Ezr. 7:13) correspond precisely to the Old and Imperial Aramaic evidence[25] and point to an imperfect thematic vowel /ā/ as is more frequently the case in Arabic and Hebrew in *bō'* from **bā'* "to come." The etymology of this root *hūk* remains unclear, however. Since there is partial semantic overlap with → *slq* "to ascend" or simply "to go,"[26] the otherwise atypical assimilation of /l/ for the imperfect of *slq* could stand under the influence of corresponding forms of *hūk*. For the etymologically likewise obscure *'zl* one can conceive of an original telic nuance "to go away,"[27] which may then explain the suppletive distribution of *'zl* for the perfect and *hūk* for the imperfect.

Old Aramaic already attests *'zl/hūk* with the literal meaning "to go." It is used there independently[28] or in conjunction with another main verb[29] that can also be joined asyndetically.[30] At the same time, the figurative meaning of "to go" already suggests itself here and subsequently in many languages as a common euphemism for "to die." In the Tell Dan inscription[31] the two usages appear together: the father of the narrator lay down and went to [his fathers] (l. 3: *wyškb 'by yhk 'l*[. . .]),[32] his own patron deity Hadad then went into battle and assured him the victory of the enemy kings of Israel (l. 5: *wyhk hdd qdmy*).

In Imperial Aramaic the literal meaning dominates and the suppletive division of *'zl* and *hūk* (→ I) is fully defined because of the documentary character of the texts. Hence, *'zl* in the perfect is used for events in the past. Thus, the verb refers to the provincial governor's visit with the king,[33] but also generally for an official or private journey[34] and in the Aramaic version of the Behistun Inscription often for friendly and enemy troop movements.[35] In a unique case, an infinitive can be added as a purpose clause (*'zl lmnś' m'kl* "he went to bring food").[36] The imperative of *'zl* with an asyndetically joined second imperative functions as an interjection "Go!" in commands of higher ranking officials.[37] Here, too, a second main verb may be added asyndetically;[38] the ethical dative marks ingressive action.[39] Sometimes, however, the use of *'zl/hūk* itself from the literal meaning

---

24. As earlier sometimes suggested, see the references in R. Degen, *Altaramäische Grammatik der Inschriften des 10.–8. Jh. v. Chr. AKM* 38/8 (1969), 79 with n. 83.
25. Thereafter *'zl* replaced *hūk*.
26. *KAI* 310.2; 317.1.
27. Thus following, e.g., Sabaean "to stay out," Biella, 10?
28. Sefire III = *KAI* 224.5 → I.
29. Sefire III = *KAI* 224.6: *'d 'hk 'nh w'rqhm* "until I go to calm her"; IA = *KAI* 222 A 24: *yhkn bšṭ lḥm* "they [hens] go in search of food."
30. *TADAE* C1.1,94, a pre-Imperial Aramaic saying of Aḥiqar.
31. *KAI* 310.
32. Regarding the construction, cf. Gzella, 323 n. 65.
33. *TADAE* A4.5,3; A4.7,5 par. 4.8,4; cf. C1.1,75; in each case with *'l* "to."
34. Naveh and Shaked no. A1,4; *TADAE* A3.6,2 and 4.4,2, both in fragmentary contexts.
35. *TADAE* C2.1,15,20,25,32,38,45, similarly Naveh and Shaked no. A2,5.
36. Segal no. 29 2.5.
37. *TADAE* C2.1,19,31,53; Ezr. 5:15; likewise later: 1QapGen 5:10; 20:23.
38. *TADAE* C.1.1,76; 1QapGen 20:24.
39. *TADAE* C1.1,22: *'zlt ly lbyty* "I set out to go home," cf. Gzella, 254.

"to go" shines through in ingressive action, as in *šbq yhkw ʿl ʿbydthm* "Let them go so that they can get to work."[40]

The same usage continued in post-Imperial Aramaic (for examples from the Aramaic texts from Qumran, → I).[41] The figurative meaning for "to die" is also attested again there;[42] similarly, *ʾzl/hūk* together with a word for "way" or "path" is employed in the ethical sense for the conduct of life,[43] much like *hlk* (→ III). Admittedly, now *ʾzl* increasingly displaces *hūk* (→ I).

III. D-stem *hlk* "to Walk." In contrast to the aspect neutral suppletive paradigm *ʾzl/hūk*, the D-stem of the root *hlk* is limited in Aramaic to the atelic shading of "to walk" as an expression of duration or reiteration. It can first be identified in Imperial Aramaic. The participle *mahleḵīn* in Dnl. 3:25 and 4:34 is indeed pointed as a causative in the Tiberian system, but, judging from other evidence in Aramaic including the corresponding form of the singular in Dnl. 4:26, should nevertheless be understood as a D-stem (**mᵉhallᵉḵīn*), as is also true in the Babylonian tradition.[44] The construction resembles that of *ʾzl/hūk*.

This verb is usually employed in the literal sense of "to walk around," as already in the earliest known specimens: in the narrative framework of Aḥiqar it appears in a participial circumstantial clause *wʾnh mhlk* "while I strolled"[45] as an expression of an occurrence described as ongoing; if the preceding text in the missing portion of the papyrus contained a punctual verb,[46] it represents an instance of an "incident scheme."[47] The participle of *hlk* also describes an ongoing action that plays out before the eyes of the speaker in a legal papyrus: *ḥzyt ʿbdʾ zk mhlk* "I saw that slave walking (around)."[48] King Nebuchadnezzar makes a similar statement in Dnl. 3:25, when he sees four men walking around in the oven. The verb in Dnl. 4:26 describes the king's movement on the roof of his palace, much as David went up to and down from the roof of his palace according to 2 S. 11:2 (*hlk* in the hithpael). Based on the widespread notion of life as a journey, *hlk* in the D-stem, just as *ʾzl/hūk* in the G-stem sometimes does, can also mean "to conduct a lifestyle," and be more closely defined by a prepositional expression such as *mhlkyn bgwh* "to walk in arrogance" Dnl. 4:34.

Both nuances are still attested in the Aramaic texts from Qumran. Here, the verb is used in the literal sense of traversing an entire country.[49] The figurative use appears in Noah's review of his life in 1QapGen 6:2 (here supplemented with *bšbyly ʾmt ʿlmʾ* "on paths of eternal truth") and in the praise in the Testament of Qahat for those who have

40. Naveh and Shaked no. A4,5.
41. More extensively, C. Stadel, 788.
42. 1QapGen 22:33; 4Q531 7:5.
43. 4Q212 1 2:20 (1 En. 91:19); 4Q537 5:2.
44. See, e.g., *BLA* §216s.
45. *TADAE* C1.1,40.
46. Such as "one found me" in the perfect as in C.1.1,76.
47. Cf. Gzella, 100,247.
48. *TADAE* B8.3,4; cf. also Gzella, 277.
49. 1QapGen 11:11; 21:13.

"walked in the heritage" (*hylktwn yrwt*[*t'*];[50] here probably with a direct object, but with a low degree of transitivity as one can expect of nonpunctual, atelic matters). In 4Q542 1 1:12, 1 2:13 (Dt-stem, apparently with the same meaning) and 4Q546 9:6, the root has been expanded secondarily with a /y/ between the first and second radicals instead of lengthening of the second radical.[51] A few additional instances are too fragmentary for precise interpretation. A couple of instances of the same verb in Palmyrene honorific inscriptions as praise for the integrity of the honoree are comparable, however.[52]

In later Aramaic the literal meaning predominates.[53] There, too, one finds examples of the Dt-stem since a reflexive or medial nuance suits verbs of going (around) by nature (like German "sich ergehen" or Greek ἔρχομαι).

IV. Noun "Property or Income Tax." The Akkadian loanword *hlk* /helk/, from *ilku* (Tiberian vocalization *hᵃlāḵ*),[54] is utilized as a collective singular and sometimes accompanies other Akkadian terms for taxes, especially *mndh* /maddā/ (from *maddattu*/*mandattu*;[55] Tiberian *middā*) "income tax" and *blw* /belō/ (from *biltu*;[56] Tiberian *bᵉlō*) "tribute," so throughout in Ezr. 4:13,20; 7:24. It appears further in a couple of Aramaic epigraphs on Neo-Babylonian clay tablets in cuneiform from the Achaemenid-era Muraššu archive[57] and in Imperial Aramaic documents from the entire region between Egypt and Bactria: in the confirmation of a hereditary tenure for a subordinate from the Aršamas archive,[58] in a contract fragment from Samaria,[59] and in a letter from the Bactrian satrap.[60] In official texts, *mndh*, too, is widely attested in the singular or plural.[61]

Normally, *hlk* is interpreted to mean a tax on land or the produce of a cultivated piece of land, but only in *TADAE* A6.11,5 is that also evident from the context. In the letter of the Bactrian satrap A1,2,14, it seems to relate to an unjustified demand at the expense of camel herders. In Ezr. 7:24, it belongs to the taxes from which the personnel of the new Jerusalem temple have been freed at the behest of the Persian king.[62]

Gzella

---

50. 4Q542 1 1:12.

51. Cf. *ATTM,* 2, 331, and more extensively C. Stadel, *Hebraismen in den aramäischen Texten vom Toten Meer* (Heidelberg, 2008), 56f., with a discussion of less convincing interpretations.

52. *PAT* 1375.3; 1381.5.

53. *DJPA*, 165b; *DJBA*, 384b; *LexSyr* 177a; *MdD*, 148.

54. *AHw*, II, 371f. and Kaufman, 58.

55. Kaufman, 67.

56. Kaufman, 44 and on the form *ATTM*, 137.

57. Citations in *DNSI*, 283.

58. *TADAE* A6.11,5.

59. *WDSP* 32 fr. 2,2 in Dušek; also H. Gzella, review of Dušek, *BiOr* 69 (2012) 610.

60. A1,2.14 in Naveh and Shaked, although also in a fragmentary context.

61. Egypt: *TADAE* A6.13,4; A6.14,3; B3.6; C3.5; C3.7; Bactria: A8,2 in Naveh and Shaked.

62. Regarding the theme in general, cf. also H. Klinkott, "Steuern, Zölle und Tribute im Achaimenidenreich," in H. Klinkott/S. Kubisch and R. Müller-Wollermann, eds., *Geschenke und Steuern, Zölle und Tribute* (Leiden, 2007), 263-90.

זבן *zbn*; זבון *zbwn* /zabbūn/; זבן *zbn* /zabīn/; זבנה *zbnh* /zabīnā/; זבן *zbn* /zabbīn/ or /zibbūn/

I. Basic Meaning. II. Figurative Use.

I. Basic Meaning. The Aramaic verb *zbn* in the G-stem means "to buy," in the D-stem "to sell." It occurs in Imperial Aramaic, among others, often in the papyrus contracts from the Wadi ed-Daliyeh where it consistently refers to the sale of slaves.[1] In addition, a Dt-stem for the passive "to be sold" is attested in the Nabatean tradition spelled *'tzbn*,[2] in the imperfect *ytzbn* or *yztbn*, thus with or without metathesis and without partial assimilation. The G-stem corresponds semantically to the Hebrew verb *qnī*, the D-stem, in contrast, to Hebrew *mkr*, like e.g., the infinitive *lzbnh* "in order to sell" in an Imperial Aramaic ostracon from Elephantine.[3]

Several nominal derivations of this root are attested, especially *zbwn* /zabbūn/ "seller,"[4] *zbn* /zabīn/,[5] or *zbnh* /zabīnā/ "purchase, market goods"[6] and *zbn* /zabbīn/ or /zibbūn/ "sale," in Syriac also *zubbānā* with the same meaning.[7] A well-attested male personal name *Zabīn(u)* or *Zabīnā(')* appeared beginning in the seventh century B.C.E. in cuneiform texts and underlies Aramaic and Hebrew *zbn*, *zbyn'* and *zb(y)nw* (Nabatean) and Greek and Latin Ζαβεινα(ς), Ζαβινας, Ζεβινας, *Zabinas* and *Zebinnas*.[8] By form, it is a passive participle of the G-stem with the original meaning "sold," thus "slave," like Syriac *zḇīnā*. This name seems not, however, to have the connotation "redeemed," and therefore does not allude to the practice of redeeming the firstborn son such as is attested in Ex. 13:13, 34:19f. and Nu. 3:46f. In such contexts, Biblical Hebrew employs the verb *pdī*, rendered in the passages cited in Targum Onqelos with *prq* "to redeem," a verb that also occurs in Aramaic in Dnl. 4:24.

II. Figurative Use. The sole biblical instance of *zbn* in Dnl. 2:8 has the figurative meaning "to gain time," literally "to buy time": *'iddānā 'antūn zāḇᵉnīn*. This use of the verbs seems to occur nowhere else, but one may compare it with the Hebrew *mṣ' 't* in Sir. 12:16: "to find an opportunity," literally "to find the (right) time." The expression

ATTM, 566f.; 2, 388f.; *DJBA*, 398f.; *DNSI*, 303-6; J. Dušek, *Les manuscrits araméens du Wadi Daliyeh et la Samarie vers 450-332 av. J.-C. CHANE* 30 (2007); G. F. Grassi, *Semitic Onomastics from Dura Europos* (Padua, 2012); W. Leslau, *Comparative Dictionary of Ge'ez* (Wiesbaden, 1987).

1. *WDSP* 4.9; 8.7; 20.4; 26.2.
2. Pap.Yadin 7,16.54.
3. *TADAE* D7.1,5.
4. EN 199.1.
5. Pap.Yadin 8,7.
6. EN 72.3; Beersheba Ostracon 6.
7. *LexSyr*, 187b.
8. See also Grassi, 195 (bib.).

ʿiddānā zᵉḇan "to buy time" may suggest an original wordplay (**zaḇnā zᵉḇan*), since *zaḇnā* means "time" in Syriac, Nabatean, Palmyrene, and Neo-Aramaic (*zōna*; → *zmn*); the situation is similar in several Ethiopic languages, such as Tigrinya, Tigre, Argobba, and Amharic (*zäbän*), whence it was even adopted in Cushitic as *daban* (with the change from /z/ to /d/).[9] There is no apparent etymological connection between the two lexemes, however.

Lipiński

9. See *CDG*, 638f.

זהר *zhr*; זהיר *zhyr* /zahīr/

I. Forms, Occurrences, and Grammatical Constructions. II. Verb "to Pay Attention." III. Adjective "Attentive."

I. Forms, Occurrences, and Grammatical Constructions. The typical Aramaic root *zhr* "to pay attention" is regularly attested beginning with the Hermopolis letters (ca. 500 B.C.E.). It is probably related etymologically to the homonymous verb *zhr* "to sparkle, shine."[1] In the Gt-stem (as indicated by later pointings; with the customary metathesis of sibilants at the beginning of the root and equalization of the degree of voicing [partial assimilation] of the stem morpheme /t/ to /d/), it generally has a medial meaning "to pay attention, to be on one's guard."[2] The quite rare t-forms with an initial /h-/ (of *zhr* only the imperative *hzdhry*)[3] are probably hypercorrect spellings;[4] *ʾzhr* with assimilation in *TADAE* C2.1,65 may be a phonetic spelling. In the course of time, Hebrew also borrowed the verb, where, as expected, the N-stem covers the medial nuance.[5]

A prepositional supplement with *b-* can designate more precisely the object of attention in the sense of "to pay attention to," which can then be further supplemented with *mn* "for." In addition, a verbal supplement following *dlʾ* with the imperfect "that . . .

H. Gzella, *Tempus, Aspekt und Modalität im Reichsaramäischen. VOK* 48 (2004); idem, "Voice in Classical Hebrew against Its Semitic Background," *Or* 78 (2009) 292-325; M. L. Klein, *Genizah Manuscripts of Palestinian Targum to the Pentateuch*, 2 vols. (Cincinnati, 1986); C. Stadel, *Hebraismen in den aramäischen Texten vom Toten Meer* (Heidelberg, 2008).

1. M. Görg, "זָהַר *zāhar*," *TDOT*, IV, 41-46.
2. Cf. Gzella, "Voice in Classical Hebrew against Its Semitic Background," *Or* 78 (2009) 305f.
3. *TADAE* D7.9,9.
4. On the problem, see Stadel, 79f.
5. Gzella, "Voice," 307f.

not" occurs frequently in Jewish Palestinian Aramaic.[6] Thus, *zhr* overlaps semantically with the verbal roots *nṭr* and *šmr* "to guard," but in contrast to them, was not originally employed in the G-stem. Occasionally, the causative stem "to warn someone" appears with a direct object and *mn* "against."

The *qaṭīl*-verbal adjective *zhyr* /zahīr/[7] "attentive, careful" is constructed similarly.

II. Verb "to Pay Attention." In older Aramaic, the verb occurs in the Gt-stem often in epistolary style and mostly in the imperative, either absolutely, as in *ʾzdhrw* "pay attention!,"[8] or with an indication of the person following *b*, as in *ʾzdhry bh* "pay attention to them!"[9] The precise significance of the supplement *mn* in Hermopolis 4.9 is disputed,[10] but in the light of later instances, "from" in the sense of "to protect someone from someone" seems plausible.[11] It is equally unclear, whether *ʾzhr* "guard yourself" in the Aramaic version of the Behistun Inscription[12] stands absolutely or with the preceding *mn kdbn śgʾyn* "from great lies." In the meaning "to pay attention to" and the addition of *byrwttʾ* "to the heritage," this everyday verb receives a theological nuance in the Testament of Qahat from Qumran.[13] The same usage continues in both West and East Aramaic.[14] This medial construction occurs occasionally in Jewish Babylonian Aramaic, but also reanalyzed as a transitive/active with an indication of a direct object following *l* "to guard something."[15]

The causative stem "to warn" is first attested in 1QapGen 6:3 *lʾzhrwtny mn* "to caution me against" (suffixed infinitive, probably functioning adverbially).[16] It was more productive in Jewish Babylonian Aramaic.[17] Syriac, however, preferred the D-stem for this nuance.[18]

III. Adjective "Attentive." The verbal adjective *zhyr* /zahīr/ is first attested in older Aramaic in Ezr. 4:22 and occurs there in the periphrastic construction with an infinitive as a verbal complement: *zhyryn hww šlw lmʿbd ʿl-dnh* "Be warned against being careless in this regard!"; similarly *zhyr b-* "attentive to" in 4Q563 1:5. It only appears later in Jewish Palestinian and Jewish Babylonian Aramaic as an adjective "cautious, clever, attentive," sometimes also supplemented with a prepositional phrase introduced with

6. *DJPA*, 173.
7. *ATTM*, 567.
8. *TADAE* A4.1,5.
9. Hermopolis 2.17; similarly 4.8f.; cf. *TADAE* D7.9,9.
10. Cf. *DNSI*, 307.
11. See instances of "to stay away from" in the Palestinian Targums in *DJPA*, 173a; cf. *DJBA*, 400a.
12. *TADAE* C2.1,65.
13. 4Q542 1 1:4.
14. *DJPA*, 173; *DJBA*, 400; *LexSyr*, 190.
15. Cf. the instance from the Babylonian Talmud Giṭ 69a(36) in *DJBA*, 400.
16. See the translation in *DSSStE*, 30f. and cf. in general Gzella, *Tempus*, 294.
17. *DJBA*, 400.
18. *LexSyr*, 190b.

b- or *l*- "attentive to," "careful with";[19] similarly, in Syriac,[20] it is occasionally apparently reanalyzed like the verb (→ II) as a transitive/active with a direct object (cf. "attending to something" with *yt* in the Palestinian Targum of Ex. 20:8, perhaps under the influence of the analogous construction with *šmr* in Dt. 5:12).[21]

Gzella

19. *DJPA*, 172b; *DJBA*, 400.
20. *LexSyr*, 190.
21. Klein, 1.267; 2.74.

זיו *zyw* /zīw/

I. Origin, Forms, and Occurrences. II. Meaning in Daniel and Qumran. III. Meanings in Later Occurrences.

I. Origin, Forms, and Occurrences. The noun *zīw* "brilliance" is borrowed from Akkadian,[1] where *zīmu*, more often in the plural than in the singular, denotes the "appearance, face (or facial features)" of gods, demons, humans, animals, and objects.[2] More precisely, like most of the Akkadian words and names in Aramaic, it derives from Babylonian, as the pronunciation of *m* between vowels as *w* typical there in the first millennium B.C.E. indicates.[3] The word is masculine (Dnl. 2:31; 4Q541 24 2:4) and distributed throughout Aramaic. It appears first in the books of Daniel and Enoch, both with roots in Babylonian. One derivative is *zīwān* "lustrous."[4] In addition to *zīw* (Samaritan with *b* for *w*),[5] Jewish Aramaic languages also attest a feminine *zīwā*,[6] from which Babylonian targumic,[7] Babylonian talmudic,[8] and Galilean[9] *zīwtān* (or: *zīwṯān*) "noble, leading, proud" derives; *zīw* and *zīwtān*/*zīwṯān* survive in rabbinic Hebrew. The Hebrew

S. A. Kaufman, *The Akkadian Influences on Aramaic*. *AS* 19 (1974).

1. Kaufman, 113.
2. *AHw*, III, 1528f., *CAD*, XXI, 121f.
3. Kaufman, 143.
4. Only Syriac: *LexSyr*, 195a, *ThesSyrSup*, 109.
5. R. Macuch, *Grammatik des samaritanischen Aramäisch* (Berlin, 1982), 35; *DSA*, 229a.
6. Targum II of Est. 1:7 var.
7. Zech. 10:3 incorrectly vocalized with *ē* instead of *ī*.
8. *DJBA*, 407b.
9. *DJPA*, 175a.

name of the spring month (1 K. 6:1,37) is hardly "the month of splendid blooms," as the Babylonian Targum translates the name.[10]

II. Meaning in Daniel and Qumran. To the extent that one can say anything given the very fragmentary 4Q texts, the singular *zīw* denotes the shine of the human visage: 4Q531 8:4 Book of Giants G 425;[11] 4Q536 1 1:4 Noah's Birth E 6:4; 4Q541 24 2:4 Second Testament of Levi L 5:4; the brilliance of the divine visage: 4Q212 1 5:18 (1 En. 93,12); a person's majesty: 11Q10 34:6 (Job 40:10) emended (Hebrew *hōḏ*); the king's majesty: Dnl. 4:33; the shine of a statue: Dnl. 2:31. The plural denotes a person's sanguine complexion, which pales in view of a threatening divine message: Dnl. 5:6,9,10 (writing on the wall); 7:28 + 4Q112 14:9 (a dream).

III. Meanings in Later Occurrences. From post-Christian times, the additional meanings "appearance" (Galilean)[12] and "best" (Hebrew)[13] are also attested for the singular.

Beyer

10. Kaufman, 113 n. 409.
11. L. T. Stuckenbruck, *The Book of Giants from Qumran. TSAJ* 63 (1997), 154.
12. *DJPA*, 175a.
13. *WTM*, I, 527a.

זכו *zkw* /zakū/; זכי *zky* /zakkāy/; זכי *zkī*

I. General Use. II. Forensic Use.

I. General Use. The feminine noun *zkw* /zakū/ "innocence," better attested in the determined state /zakūtā/, serves in the Targums as a translation of the Heb. *ṣ^eḏāqā*, e.g., in Targum Onqelos of Gen. 15:6; Dt. 6:25; 33:21. It derives from the verbal root *zkī* "to be clean, innocent, free," in contrast to *dkī* " to be (ritually) clean," in the D-stem "to cleanse." Neo-Babylonian also attests the verb *dkī* "to weed."[1] It translates Hebrew *ṭhr*, e.g., in Lev 12:7; 16:30. Contrariwise, the root *zkī*, independent of context, can have more of a ritual, ethical, legal, or monetary connotation. The noun is quite widespread

ATTM, 554, 569; 2, 390; A. F. L. Beeston et al., *Sabaic Dictionary* (Louvain-la-Neuve, 1982); K. Beyer, *Die aramäischen Inschriften aus Assur, Hatra und dem übrigen Ostmesopotamien* (Göttingen, 1998); *DJBA*, 337 and 413; *DNSI*, 320f.; S. A. Kaufman, *The Akkadian Influences on Aramaic. AS* 19 (1974); A. Negoită and H. Ringgren, "זָכָה *zākhāh*," *TDOT*, IV, 62-64.

1. *AHw*, I, 166f.

in Mishnaic Hebrew where it retains the ending /-t/ even in the absolute state (*zᵉkūṯ*). As a loanword in South Arabian, which otherwise has access only to a root *ḏky* "to send,"[2] related to Akkadian *dekû*,[3] *zkt* in *zkt rḥmnn* denotes more God's "integrity" than his "grace."[4]

If the emendation of l. 1 of the Palmyrene bilingual *CIS* II 3971[5] *ʿl ḥ[ywh] wz[kwth]* "for his life and his deliverance," is correct, it would mean "deliverance" there (σωτηρία in the Greek parallel version). In 11Q10 the verb *zkī* occurs in 26:7 (Job 35:7; emended to [*zky*] *t*) and 40:4 (Job 40:8; *tzkʾ*), where it translates Hebrew *ṣāḏaqtā* and *tiṣdāq*, respectively. In contrast, in the same text the adjective *zky* renders the verb *ʾhl* (causative stem) "to appear" in 9:8 (Job 25:5) and the adjective *ṣaddīq* in 20:4 (Job 32:1). Furthermore, an imperative of the Dt-stem *ʾzdky* occurs in T. Levi 34:22[6] in an allusion to priestly ritual purity: "Now, keep yourself clean in your body from any uncleanness of any man."

The use of the verb *zkī* and of the adjective /zakkāy/ in l. 10 of the incantation from Uruk seems to denote moral equity and possibly legal acquittal: "I was cleansed [*za-ke-et*] and I am clean [*za-ka-a-a*]." The same connotation occurs in *tizkūn* "you will be cleansed" in Targum Jonathan of Jer. 25:29.

The narrative framework of Aḥiqar employs the adjective *zky* substantially: "I am Aḥiqar, who saved you from killing an innocent [*mn qṭl zky*]."[7] As an epithet of king Sanatruq of Hatra, *zkyʾ*[8] is usually attributed the meaning "victorious,"[9] but "upright" may be the more appropriate translation.

II. Forensic Use. The sole biblical instance of *zāḵū* appears in Dnl. 6:23, where this noun functions as the subject of the verb *hištᵉḵaḥat* "was found." The meaning of the verb implies a preceding investigation, as the expression *daq wᵉʾaškaḥ* "he investigated and found [causative stem]" in the Babylonian Talmud suggests.[10] Consequently, *zāḵū* seems to have a forensic connotation here, the more so since God appears in his character as judge before whom the case is tried, while reference to the person of the speaker, Daniel, is made by means of the preposition *l-* "to my benefit." The role of the plaintiff fell to the king who must take action against Daniel because of his own command, yet Daniel was ultimately acquitted in the divine court procedure. His guilt could not be proven: "before him, innocence was found to my benefit."

The clearest and chronologically closest parallels to this forensic use of the noun occur in Mishnaic Hebrew, especially in Tananitic law according to *mSanh.* 4, where *zᵉkūṯ* appears frequently. According to *mSanh.* 4:1, e.g., "capital cases (*dīnē nᵉpāšōṯ*) begin (with arguments) for innocence (*pōṯᵉḥīn li-zᵉkūṯ*)"; "in capital cases, they decide

2. Beeston et al., 39.
3. *AHw*, I, 166f.; *CAD*, IV, 123-28.
4. Contra Beeston et al., 170.
5. *PAT* 0317.
6. *ALD* 6.5.
7. *TADAE* C1.1,46.
8. H79.1; 194.2; 203.3; 229a.2.
9. Beyer, 174.
10. *ʾAbod. Zar.* 10a.

with (the majority) vote for innocence (*mᵉṭīn ʿal pī ʾeḥāḏ li-zᵉḵūt*)"; "in capital cases all may plead for innocence (*hakkol mᵉlammᵉḏīn zᵉḵūṯ*)." In these contexts, *zᵉḵūṯ* is often translated "acquittal."

Lipiński

זמן *zmn* /zemān/; זמן *zmn*

I. Etymology. II. Imperial Aramaic. III. Biblical Aramaic and *šāʿā*. IV. Biblical Hebrew. V. Qumran and the Aramaic-Hebrew Documents from the Dead Sea. VI. Denominal Verb (Aram./Heb.).

I. Etymology. Since the fifth/fourth centuries B.C.E., *zmn* "(a specific) time" has been attested in Achaemenid Imperial Aramaic, Biblical Aramaic, and numerous later dialects, and, in the dissimilated form *zbn*, in Palmyrene and sometimes in Nabatean,[1] Samaritan, Syriac, Mandaic, etc.[2] As an Aramaic loanword, *zmn* was conveyed to Hebrew (*zᵉmān*), Arabic (*zama/ān*), and Ethiopic (*zaman*).[3] The origin of the loanword in Aramaic is disputed.[4] As a rule, a derivation from Akkadian *simānu* "(the right) moment, time."[5] The consonant shift /s/ > /z/ is problematic, however.[6] A derivation from Old Persian *ǰamāna-* "time, hour"[7] merits mention as an alternative. An argument for this etymology is the fact that the oldest Aramaic specimens do not appear in the pre-Achaemenid documents from the Syro-Mesopotamian region, but in Aramaic texts from the Persian period.

II. Imperial Aramaic. Egyptian papyrus fragments from the fifth through the fourth centuries B.C.E. preserve only four certain instances of Imperial Aramaic. They involve

---

S. A. Kaufman, *The Akkadian Influences on Aramaic. AS* 19 (1974); E. Jenni, "עֵת *ʿēt* time," *TLOT*, 951-61; E. Lipiński, "Araméen d'empire," in P. Swiggers et al., eds., *Le langage dans l'antiquité* (Louvain, 1990), 94-133; J. Naveh and S. Shaked, *Aramaic Documents from Ancient Bactria (Fourth Century B.C.E.)* (London, 2012); R. Ružiča, *Konsonantische Dissimilation in den semitischen Sprachen* (Leipzig, 1909); P. A. Verhoef, "Die aanduiding van tyd in die boek Daniël," In die Skriflig 28 (1994) 223-33; M. Wagner, *Die lexikalischen und grammatikalischen Aramaismen im alttestamentlichen Hebräisch. BZAW* 96 (1966).

1. *DNSI*, 305, 332.
2. Ružiča, 92f.
3. Wagner, 49.
4. Cf. *KBL*³, 1701f.
5. Kaufman, 92 (bib.); cf. *CAD*, XV, 268-71.
6. Lipiński, 109; contra e.g., *BLA* §33h.
7. So Lipiński, 109, et al.

general indications of time in fragmentary contexts: *bzk zmn*[ʾ] "at this time";[8] *bzmn*[ʾ] "at the time [. . .]";[9] [. . .] *mn zm*[*n* . . .] "since the tim[e . . .]."[10] In the context of a judicial document, *ʿd zmnʾ* "to the established time" denotes a juristic deadline.[11] With the meaning "agreed time," the noun appears an additional three times in the Aramaic letters from Bactria.[12]

III. Biblical Aramaic and *šāʿā*. Biblical Aramaic also employs *zᵉmān* for relative measurements of time. The often-attested *beh-zimnā* (*kᵉdī*) "at the moment (when)" (Dnl. 3:7,8; 4:33; Ezr. 5:3) is employed as a synonym of the expression *bᵉʿiddānā dī* (Dnl. 3:5,15) formed with *ʿiddān* "time." The emphasis lies on the simultaneity of two events regardless of their duration.

Short durations of time, in contrast, find expression in phrases formed with *šāʿā* "moment"; *bah-šaʿaṯā* "immediately" is frequently attested (Dnl. 3:6,15; 4:30; 5:5), with the addition of *kᵉšāʿā* in Dnl. 4:16. The expression *br šʿt-* "momentarily," later attested in Syriac, first occurs at Qumran.[13] A donation document from Naḥal Ḥever (120 C.E.) uses *šʿh* for a time of day in regard to water rights.[14]

Duration of time in regard to *zᵉmān*, in contrast, is conceived as a period up to a specific moment (Dnl. 7:22; cf. Dnl. 2:16 the deadline set by the king). In Dnl. 7:12, the determination of the duration of life occurs in an apocalyptic context. For a hendiadys comparable with *zᵉmān wᵉʿiddān*, cf. Dnl. 2:21, which, in hymnic participial style, praises the power of God to change times and deadlines (cf. Acts 1:7 and 1Thess. 5:1). The eschatological ruler described in Dnl. 7:25 strives for the same characteristic of divine power. No distinction between the festival times of the cultic calendar and the underlying "times" as cosmic orders is perceptible.[15] The term finds use in the sense of fixed prayer times in Dnl. 6:11,14.[16]

IV. Biblical Hebrew. The usage of the term as an Aramaic loanword in Biblical Hebrew also manifests reference to the festival calendar. Thus, the days of the Purim festival should be conducted annually at their established time (Est. 9:27 [sg.]; 9:31 [pl.]). At the same time, one encounters the concept of the "fixed/auspicious time" in a wisdom context (Eccl. 3:1). The subsequent list of noncultic examples (3:2-8), however, consistently employs the more common *ʿēṯ* instead of the synonym *zᵉmān*. Regarding the indication of a fixed terminus (the duration of a journey), cf. Neh. 2:6.

---

8. Segal Pap. 18.6.
9. Segal Pap. 80.4; perhaps also a proper noun, see ibid.
10. *TADAE* D5.31,1.
11. *TADAE* B8.9,4.
12. *TADAE* A2:3,4 and A4:2, Naveh and Shaked.
13. *DJD*, XXXI (2001), 404, on the Syriac see *ThesSyr*, 4252f.
14. 5/6Ḥev 7:12,47; 7:7,38; 7:43f.
15. O. Plöger, *Das Buch Daniel. KAT* 18 (1965), 105; J. C. H. Lebram, "König Antiochus im Buch Daniel," *VT* 25 (1975) 745.
16. Contra *KBL*³, 1702, which traditionally suggests following LXX τρίς "three times."

V. Qumran and the Aramaic-Hebrew Documents from the Dead Sea. The writings from Qumran exhibit a few differences from older material. Relative indications of time with no specific connotation are attested here, too: *zm*[*nyn*(?) *dy*] "as soon as" (4Q213 4:8) and *bzmn' dn'* "in this moment" (4Q541 10:3). As a rule, however, it involves a time with significant content, as in the dying words of Tobit, *kl' yt'bd lzm*[*nyhwn*(?)] "everything will happen in its time" (4Q198 1:5 [Tob. 14:4])[17] or in an apocalyptic context: *'d ywm dy ytdynn w'd zmn ywm qṣ'* "until the day on which they [the souls of the dead] are judged and until the moment of the Last Day" (4Q206 2:2 [1 En. 22:3]). The Targum of Job also diverges from MT ("Who channeled a ditch for the flood?") by introducing the element of the specific time in the first divine speech: *mn šwy' lmṭr' zmn* "Who establishes a time for the rain?" (11Q10 31:3 [Job 38:25]). Although largely destroyed, 1Q21 3:2 (T. Levi) offers a list of various times reminiscent of Eccl. 3:1-8: [*zmnyn*] *t'ml wzmnyn tn*[*wḥ*] "[times, in which] you labor, and times, in which you rest," cf. further *zmn mwl*[*dh*] "time of birth" (4Q535 2:1). In 11Q10 23:8 (Job 33:29)[18] and probably in 4Q156 2:3 (translation of Lev. 16:19), one finds *zmn* as a numeral adverb with no connotation of a "fixed" time.

The Aramaic and Hebrew contracts and documents from the Dead Sea (first-second centuries C.E.) employ *zmn* to specifically determine relevant points and deadlines, as in the frequent formula *wbzmn dy tmrwn ly 'ḥlp lk šṭrh dnh* "and at the point when you tell me, I will renew/revise this document."[19] In a slight variation, the freedom to select the time can also be indicated by (*b*)*kwl zmn dy tmr ly* "at any time when you tell me";[20] further *bkl zmn dy tṣb'* "at the moment that she wants."[21] Periods appear as deadlines *'d zmn dy* "until the point that"[22] or as a *terminus a quo*: *mn zmn ywmh dnh 'd š*[*nt*] *'rb'* "from this day until the fourth year."[23]

VI. Denominal Verb (Aram./Heb.). Biblical Hebrew attests the denominative verb *zmn* (ithpael) only in Dnl. 2:9 in the meaning "to make an appointment."[24] Compare 1QapGen 21:25 *kwl 'ln 'zdmnw kḥd' lqrb* "they all agreed as one to fight," further 4Q546 15 2:4]*hwh mzmnnh*[(reading/meaning uncertain). In Biblical Hebrew one also encounters a pual participle in the expressions *lᵉ'ittīm mᵉzummānīm* (Ezr. 10:14; Neh. 10:35) and *bᵉ'ittīm mᵉzummānōṯ* "at fixed times" (Neh. 13:31), which are apparently synonymous with *zᵉmān*.

Schwiderski

---

17. Cf. τοῖς καιροῖς αὐτῶν in Tob. 14:4 LXX Sinaiticus.
18. See *DSSStE*, 1192f.
19. XḤev/Ṣe 8:7; Mur 19:10,23; 27:5; regarding the uncertain meaning of *ḥlp* see *DJD*, XXVII (2001), 16.
20. Ṣdeir 2:5 (*DJD*, XXXVIII [2000] 127f.); Mur 21:19; 34Se 2:4; 5/6Hev 10:16; XHev/Se 9:10; cf. Hebr. *bkl zmn št*[*wm*]*r ly* "to pay at the time that you tell me" XḤev/Ṣe 49:8.
21. 5/6Ḥev 17:41.
22. 5/6Ḥev 10:14,16.
23. 5/6Ḥev 42:6.
24. On the form, see *BLA* §111k.

זמר *zmr*; זמר *zmr* /zamār/; זמר *zmr* /zammār/

I. Etymology. II. Verbal Noun "Music." III. Professional Designation "Musician."

I. Etymology. Like its cognate in East (Akk.) and Central Semitic (Ugar., Heb., Arab., OSA), the verbal root *zmr* "to make music" refers primarily to the singing of the human voice generally, the origin of all music and all language, and from there to instrumental music. The latter then came more clearly (but not exclusively) into the foreground in the specific use of the two deverbal nouns /zamār/ "music" and /zammār/ "musician," as attested in the various Aramaic languages beginning with Biblical Aramaic. In the individual Semitic languages, both the G-stem and the D-stem (which predominates in Hebrew) of the verbal root are productive. In Aramaic, attestations of the verb, in both stems, first occur in the literatures of West and East Aramaic in late antiquity,[1] Jewish Babylonian,[2] Syriac,[3] and Mandaic.[4] It can be employed intransitively or transitively with *zmr* "song" as a direct object and with an adverbial modifier.[5]

A relationship to the adjective /zamūr/ "blue" (often said of eyes) is not perceptible; the homonymous root *zmr* "to prune" may have other origins.

II. Verbal Noun "Music." All four of the older examples of the verbal noun *zmār* (from /zamār/) concentrate in the formulaically repeated construct relation *kol zᵉnē zmārā* "all kinds of music" Dnl. 3:5,7,10,15 and refer cumulatively to the sound of various instruments that sound at the presentation of a statue of King Nebuchadnezzar and that are meant to occasion all who hear it to prostrate themselves. Explicitly mentioned in the form of a list of wind and string instruments are: "horn" (*qarnā*), "flutes, pipes" (*mašrōqīṯā*), "zither" (*qīṯārōs* [vocalized with *K*], a Greek loanword, κίθαρις), "sambuca" (*śabbᵉḵā*, corresponding to σαμβύκη),[6] "harps" (*psantērīn*, from ψαλτήριον), and perhaps "double flutes, bagpipes" (*sūmpōnyā*, from συμφωνία, the usage of which for a specific

C. Barth, "זמר *zmr*," *TDOT*, IV, 91-98; K. Beyer, *Die aramäischen Inschriften aus Assur, Hatra und dem übrigen Ostmesopotamien* (Göttingen, 1998); M. A. Daise, "*zmr*," *ThWQ*, I, 855-57; P. Grelot, "L'orchestre de Daniel III 5, 7, 10, 15," *VT* 29 (1979) 23-38; H. Gressmann, *Musik und Musikinstrumente im Alten Testament. RVV* II/1 (1903); S. Kammerer, "Vorderasien B: Syrien und Palästina" *Die Musik in Geschichte und Gegenwart* (Kassel, ²1998), 9:1790-816; A. D. Kilmer, "Musik. A. I. In Mesopotamien," *RlA*, VIII (1993-1997), 463-82; T. C. Mitchell, "The Music of the Old Testament Reconsidered," *PEQ* 124 (1992) 124-43, esp. 134-40; J. A. Montgomery, *The Book of Daniel. ICC* (1927).

1. *DJPA*, 179a.
2. *DJBA*, 417a.
3. *LexSyr*, 199f.
4. *MdD*, 169b.
5. Cf. the instances in *DJPA*, 179a and *MdD*, 169b.
6. Cf. Gressmann, 26-28.

instrument in Greek is not entirely clear, however).[7] With the specific meaning "song," *zmr* is only attested in isolation and later, however.[8]

III. Professional Designation "Musician." The *nomen professionis zammār* "musician" occurs once in Ezr. 7:24 (in the plural) in a list along with other temple personnel exempted from taxation. It remains unclear, however, whether it refers to instrumental musicians or singers.[9] This last meaning continues to be attested later, e.g., in Jewish Palestinian.[10] As masculine (*zmr*)[11] and feminine[12] professional designations, "musician" is also known in the inscriptions from Hatra. As temple personnel, as in Ezr. 7:24, *zmrt'* "(female) musician" also appears there along with *qynt'* "(female) slave singer" (/qēntā/, det.) in a legal inscription according to which flight from temple service was punishable with death.[13]

Gzella

7. Regarding the terminology and factual background, cf. Grelot and Mitchell (older literature also in Montgomery, 202f.); for a broader panorama, including archaeological and iconographic witnesses, see Kammerer (with extensive bib.).
8. Cf. *DJPA*, 179a for Jewish Palestinian and *DJBA*, 417a for Jewish Babylonian.
9. Regarding the highly developed musical performance in Mesopotamian temples and the corresponding complex terminology, cf. Kilmer, 467-69.
10. *DJPA*, 179a.
11. H219,2.
12. Fem. sg. *zmrt* in H342.4,9; pl. in H202t.
13. H342.5,9.

זעק *z'q*; זעקה *z'qh* /za'aqā/

I. Etymology. II. Older Aramaic Usage. III. Biblical Aramaic. IV. Qumran and Targum.

I. Etymology. The root *z'q* occurs in (North) Arabic, in the Canaanite of the Amarna texts,[1] and often in Biblical Aramaic, where it alternates with the root *ṣ'q* in a similar meaning.

J. A. Fitzmyer, *The Aramaic Inscriptions of Sefire. BietOr* 19A (²1995); R. Fuller, "*z'q*," *ThWQ*, I, 863-65; G. F. Hasel, "זָעַק *zā'aq*," *TDOT*, IV, 112-22; J. T. Milik, *The Books of Enoch* (Oxford, 1976); A. F. Rainey, *El Amarna Tablets 359-79. AOAT* 8 (1970); M. H. Silverman, "Aramean Name-Types in the Elephantine Documents," *JAOS* 89 (1969) 691-709.

1. EA 366.24, niphal pf.

II. Older Aramaic Usage. The verbal noun *z‘qh* "outcry" may be attested once in Old Aramaic.[2] The context there has been destroyed, however, and the reading is therefore uncertain. The verb *z‘q* in the peal "to call, cry (out)" occurs once in the Aramaic documents from Egypt.[3] The alternative root *ṣ‘q* also appears in texts from this epoch,[4] which is occasionally attributed to Canaanite influence, however.[5]

III. Biblical Aramaic. The root *z‘q* appears in the entire Biblical Aramaic corpus only once (Dnl. 6:21), also as a verb in the peal, expressing King Darius's cry of lament to Daniel (introduced as the object by *l-*) on the morning after Daniel had been thrown into the lions' den at the instigation of the malevolent royal officials.

IV. Qumran and Targum. In the Aramaic texts from Qumran, the verbal noun *z‘qh* appears in the meaning cited above.[6] The verb *z‘q* in the peal is also attested.[7] In conjunction with a person as a direct object[8] or introduced by the preposition *l-*,[9] the cry is addressed to someone; thus, the verb has the nuance "to call to." The root *z‘q* is also attested in the haphel[10] and then has the specialized meaning "to call for help"; in such cases, the preposition *mn* can indicate the basis of the need.[11] Finally, Targum Onqelos and Jonathan (e.g., of 1 S. 5:10) also attest the verb *z‘q* in the peal in its basic meaning "to call, cry (out)"; in these texts, however, it typically denotes the cry of the children of Israel to their God (introduced as a prepositional object with *qdm*) in times of distress (e.g., Ex. 14:10).

Kuty

---

2. Sefire IA = *KAI* 222 A 29-30.
3. *TADAE* C1.2,1.
4. E.g., *TADAE* C3.3,6; possibly also in Sefire IIA = *KAI* 223 A 8-9.
5. Cf. Silverman, 701.
6. 11Q10 33:6 (Job 39:25) *z‘qt ʼštdwr* "war cry" (*DJD*, XXIII [1998], 158).
7. 11Q10 30:5 (Job 38:7), of the cry of the angels (*DJD* XXIII [1998], 149).
8. 4Q530 7 2:6 (*DJD*, XXXI [2001], 38).
9. 4Q204 1 6 (1 En. 14:8; Milik, 194); as in Dnl. 6:21 above.
10. 4Q206 (En[e]) 1 12 (1 En. 22:5; Milik, 229); the mangled instance in 11Q10 17:5 (Job 30:28; *DJD*, XXIII [1998], 120) is unclear.
11. 11Q10 26:3 (Job 35:9; *DJD*, XXIII [1998], 137).

זרע *zr‘*; זרע *zr‘* /zar‘/

I. Etymology. II. Old Aramaic Inscriptions. III. Imperial Aramaic Documents. IV. Biblical Aramaic. V. Aramaic Texts from the Dead Sea.

I. Etymology. Originally associated with the meanings "seed, sowing" and "to sow," the Aramaic root *zrʿ* traces back to the primitive Semitic **z/δrʿ*.[1] This root is common Semitic and appears in various forms in ancient and modern Semitic languages, e.g., in Akkadian, Ugaritic, Phoenician, Amorite, (North) Arabic, OSA, and Ethiopic (Geʿez, Tigrinya, Amharic).

II. Old Aramaic Inscriptions. Old Aramaic inscriptions often attest the noun *zrʿ* in the figurative meaning "descendant, posterity,"[2] a common development of the meaning "human seed," which, in turn, represents an expansion of the basic meaning "seed, sowing." The noun seems to be attested in the same sense in Sam'alian,[3] but the context of the entire passage is unclear. The verb *zrʿ* in the peal appears in Old Aramaic in its basic meaning "to sow," whether with what is sown as a direct object[4] or without.[5] It also occurs, however, in a nonagricultural context in the general meaning "to scatter."[6]

III. Imperial Aramaic Documents. The Imperial Aramaic documents from Egypt exhibit a comparable picture. Noun and verb (peal) *zrʿ* appear in their respective basic meanings "seed, sowing"[7] and "to sow."[8] The verb *zrʿ* also found use outside agricultural contexts.[9] Likewise, the noun *zrʿ* occurs in the figurative sense "posterity,"[10] and apparently also in the general meaning "family."[11] The noun is now also attested in a list with goods to be distributed from the late Achaemenid government of Bactria.[12]

C. Brockelmann, *Grundriß der vergleichenden Grammatik der semitischen Sprachen*, vol. 1 (Berlin, 1908); F. C. Fensham, "Salt as Curse in the Old Testament and the Ancient Near East," *BA* 25 (1962) 48-50; J. A. Fitzmyer, *The Aramaic Inscriptions of Sefire*. *BietOr* 19A (²1995); S. A. Kaufman, "Reflections on the Assyrian-Aramaic Bilingual from Tell Fakhariyeh," *Maarav* 3/2 (1982) 137-75; J. T. Milik, *The Books of Enoch* (Oxford, 1976); T. Muraoka, "The Tell-Fekherye Bilingual Inscription and Early Aramaic," *Abr-Nahrain* 22 (1983-84) 79-117; J. Naveh and S. Shaked, *Aramaic Documents from Ancient Bactria (Fourth Century B.C.E.)* (London, 2012); H. D. Preuss, "זָרַע *zāraʿ*," *TDOT*, IV, 143-62; M. A. Sweeney, "*zrʿ*," *ThWQ*, I, 878-83.

1. Brockelmann, 128f.
2. E.g., Tell Fekheriye (*KAI* 309.8); Nērab 1 (*KAI* 225.11).
3. *KAI* 214.20.
4. Tell Fekheriye 19 in the context of agricultural curses, cf. Dt. 28:38-42.
5. Tell Fekheriye 18f.
6. E.g., Sefire IA = *KAI* 222 A 36, with what is scattered, here salt, as a direct object, and what is scattered upon, here the daughters (daughter cities) of Arpad, as a prepositional object with *b-* as an indicator of place; on the curse context, cf. Fensham.
7. E.g., *TADAE* D7.3,2; also C3.11, 4.11.
8. E.g., *TADAE* B1.1,4, with the place sown as the direct object and what is sown as the object of the instrumental preposition *b-*.
9. E.g., *TADAE* D.23.1Va,13, with a dual accusative for the thing and the place strewn; the context is similar to that in Sefire IA 36 above.
10. E.g., *TADAE* A5.1,6; B2.7,8; Aḥiqar C1.1,180.
11. *TADAE* C2.1 col. I, l. 3.
12. C4,46 according to Naveh and Shaked: *ʿl zrʿ* "for seed."

IV. Biblical Aramaic. The root *zrʿ* is attested only once in the Biblical Aramaic corpus (Dnl. 2:43), namely in the context of Daniel's interpretation of King Nebuchadnezzar's dream (Dnl. 2:36-45). As a noun in the construct state, *zrʿ* there is part of the genitive phrase *zrʿ ʾnšʾ* "the seed of men," which refers to the human race as a whole (→ *ʾnš*, II.1).

V. Aramaic Texts from the Dead Sea. As do earlier Aramaic sources, the Aramaic texts from the Dead Sea also attest the noun *zrʿ* in the basic meaning "seed, sowing" (4Q211 1 i 2 [1 En. 82:20]; context destroyed);[13] it also stands as the second member of the genitive phrase *byt zrʿ* with the meaning "ground that needs to be sown" (XḤev/Ṣe 50:2).[14] Finally, in these texts, the noun *zrʿ* also has the figurative meanings "family" and "posterity" (e.g., 1Q10 21:13, etc.);[15] in this sense, it also appears in the fixed phrase *zrʿ dq*[*šṭ*] "seed of the truth" (4Q213a 2,7).[16]

Kuty

13. Milik, *Enoch*, 296.
14. *DJD*, XXVII (1997), 127.
15. *ATTM*, 2, 391.
16. *DJD*, XXII (1996), 29.

חבל *ḥbl*; חבל *ḥbl* /ḥabāl/; חבולה *ḥbwlh* /ḥabūlā/

I. Etymology, Grammatical Constructions, and Lexical Field. II. General Use of the Verb. III. Noun "Annihilation." IV. Noun "Crime."

I. Etymology, Grammatical Constructions, and Lexical Field. The Semitic languages document several homonymous *ḥbl* roots, which arose, in part, however, only through the coincidence of the originally distinct phonemes /ḫ/ ([x], pronounced like *ch* in "ach!") and /ḥ/ ([ħ], pronounced between an *h* and *ch*). Of them, the verb *ḥbl* "to perish, annihilate" (from an older *ḫbl*, as Arabic *ḫabala* "to confound, hinder," indicates) is especially productive in Aramaic and appears regularly there in the D-stem. It is related neither to the verb *ḥbl* "to be/become pregnant" (here the /ḥ/ is original, cf. the synonymous Arabic *ḥabila*),[1] whose nominal derivative *ḥblyn* /ḥebalīn/ "birth pangs" is attested twice in older Aramaic in 11Q10 32:1,3 (Job 39:1,3), nor with the common Semitic primary noun *ḥbl* /ḥabl/ "cord."[2]

U. Dahmen, "*ḥbl* III," *ThWQ*, I, 886-89; J. Gamberoni, "חָבַל *chābhal*," *TDOT*, IV, 185-88.

1. See further H.-J. Fabry, "חָבַל *chābhal*," *TDOT*, IV, 172-79.
2. *TADAE* A4.2,10; 11Q10 27:2 (Job 36:8) and 35:4 (Job 40:25); cf. further Fabry, 172-79.

As a (highly) transitive verb, *ḥbl* "to annihilate" appears with the effected living being (Dnl. 6:23), object (Dnl. 4:20; Ezr. 6:12), or abstraction (often in a *figura etymologica* with the verbal noun /ḥabāl/)[3] as object; the Dt-stem serves as a passive "to be annihilated" (Dnl. 2:44; 6:27; 7:14). A partially affected (thus, not fully destroyed) object can be introduced with the preposition *b-*; the meaning, then, is "to cause damage to."[4] Later, Jewish Babylonian also attests the G-stem in the meaning "to become sick."[5]

The verb denotes generally an extensive destruction, in reference to living beings, as the object of killing. Visions literature, as present in the book of Daniel and in Aramaic texts from Qumran, in particular, knows a wide range of synonyms for verbs of destruction which supplement *ḥbl* with broader, more concrete terms: in addition to → *dqq* "to crush," → *ḥrb* "to lay waste" (originally, mostly of cities), and → *tbr* "to break," also the comparably rare *gdd* "to cut down" (of trees: Dnl. 4:11,20), *dūš* "to trample,"[6] synonymous with *rps* (Dnl. 7:7), and finally *r*ʿʿ "to shatter" (Dnl. 2:40).

The two clearly semantically differentiated verbal nouns *ḥbl* /ḥabāl/ "destruction, damage," and the very rare *ḥbwlh* /ḥabūlā/ "crime" also belong to the root.

II. General Use of the Verb. As a verb, *ḥbl* is first identifiable in Imperial Aramaic. There it appears in a negated statement in the letter from the Jewish community in Elephantine requesting the reconstruction of the destroyed temple meant to make clear that the temple suffered no damage even during Cambyses's conquest of Egypt (so that its subsequent destruction by the Egyptian priests was naturally all the more egregious). In a similar context in Ezr. 6:12, it refers to the Jerusalem temple, upon whose destruction the Persian king placed a penalty. In contrast, the narrative framework of Aḥiqar[7] employs it for the damage that a high official inflicts on the land or that a person suffers as the result of a conspiracy. The nuance of the participle *mḥbl* with persons in *TADAE* A4.5,2 is unclear, however: it could involve physical injury or damage to reputation.[8]

The Aramaic book of Daniel employs the verb *ḥbl* several times as part of a hymnic predication of the kingdom of God, which no one can destroy (2:44, 6:27 and 7:14, all passives), but also negated literally for the harm from which Daniel is protected (6:23; on the noun *ḥbl* in 6:24 → III), and affirmatively for the destruction of the tree of life in the vision of Dnl. 4 (4:20, here in parallel with the graphic *gdd* "to cut down"). Figuratively for damage to the reputation (*šm*, literally "name), it is used once then in Levi's last testament;[9] regarding the *figura etymologica* in reference to the giant's destruction of the earth, → III. In the few additional occurrences from Qumran, insufficient context has been preserved. The feminine participle *kl mḥblh* "every despoiler" in a later Palestinian incantation also designates feminine demons.[10]

---

3. E.g., 4Q203 8:11; 4Q532 2:9.
4. So *bzyt'* in 1QapGen 13:16 for an olive tree first damaged by winds and only subsequently shattered.
5. *DJBA*, 426f.
6. 4Q246 1 2:3.
7. *TADAE* C1.1,36,44.
8. See *DNSI*, 344f. for a discussion.
9. 4Q213a 3-4:5.
10. *ATTM.E*, 265, l. 6; sixth or seventh centuries C.E.

III. Noun "Annihilation." Further, the verbal noun *ḥbl* /ḥabāl/ "destruction, damage" is also regularly attested since Imperial Aramaic. Presumably, it first appears, if the reading is correct, in a private letter on papyrus from Saqqara (*ḥbl ʿl ḥblʾ zy ln* "damage in addition to our damage"; paleographic difficulties render the context unclear, however).[11] In Biblical Aramaic, it denotes in the concrete sense in negated statements the injury from which the righteous, such as Daniel and his friends, are preserved by divine protection even in otherwise mortal threats such as the oven (Dnl. 3:25) and the lions' den (Dnl. 6:24). In each case, it is accompanied with *b-* "to" and with a partially affected object with the verb (→ I), i.e., not a hair on their heads was touched. It is also employed figuratively once in Ezr. 4:22 for the harm that could come to the king through the carelessness of his subordinate officials (→ *zhr* III).

Thereafter, the noun appears in the Aramaic from Qumran as an internal object of the verb and, in this construction, denotes (emphatically) the complete or (declaratively) definitive destruction of the earth by the giants with their supernatural power.[12] If Beyer's reading of 1QapGen 5:11[13] is correct, an identical usage occurs there, but the passage is very uncertain paleographically.[14]

In Aramaic memorial epigraphy, *ḥbl* serves as a cry of woe "Ah!" at the beginning or end of Palmyrene, Old Syriac, and Jewish Palestinian grave inscriptions.[15]

IV. Noun "Crime." The abstract noun *ḥbwlh* /ḥabūlā/ "crime," on the contrary, is very rare. It occurs once in older material in a negated statement along with → *zkw* (II) "innocence" in reference to Daniel's integrity demonstrated in the divine judgment of the lions' den. Later, it also occurs only in isolation, as in Jewish Palestinian.[16]

Gzella

11. No. 69b:2 in J. B. Segal, *Aramaic Texts from North Saqqara* (London, 1983), 93 n. 4.
12. 4Q203 8:11; 4Q532 2:9, there with degemination in the spelling of the second root consonant in the verb: *ḥnblw* for /ḥabbelū/.
13. *ATTM*, 2, 90.
14. See D. A. Machiela, *The Dead Sea Genesis Apocryphon. STDJ* 79 (2009), 41.
15. Cf. *DNSI*, 345 for instances.
16. *DJPA*, 184a.

חבר *ḥbr*; חבר *ḥbr* /ḥaber/; חבר *ḥbr* /ḥabr/

I. Etymology and General Usage. II. Noun "Companion, Other." III. Noun "Incantation."

I. Etymology and General Usage. Aramaic *ḥbr* "to tie" probably arose from the older **ḫbr*.[1] The verbal root appears less often than do some of its related nouns, but chiefly in the D-stem, which may indicate a denominal derivation. The verb is first directly attested in the ithpael at Qumran with the reflexive meaning "to consort with (*l*-)," namely in the context of the union of the giants with human women[2] and of association with evildoers.[3] It also occurs in postexilic Hebrew as an Aramaism ("to join oneself": 2 Ch. 20:35; Dnl. 11:23). The aphel often serves in Palmyrene as a legal term, to cede "a place to someone" in the cession texts that regulate the circumstances of the possession of graves.[4] Later, the verb is also used in the peal for "to gather" and in the ithpeel for "to congregate."[5]

The noun *ḥbr* /ḥaber/ "companion, other" (later /ḥabar/)[6] occurs in Aramaic more often than the verb in the Christian period, sometimes also related derivatives such as *ḥbwrh* /ḥabūrā/ "member of a group" (so in a Palestinian synagogue inscription for members of the congregation).[7] A special meaning appeared in *ḥbr* /ḥabr/ "incantation" as a magical term (→ III). Additional derivatives occur in later Aramaic languages.[8]

II. Noun "Companion, Other." According to the damaged and therefore unclear passage in an Old Aramaic Sefire inscription (*ḥb*[*wr*]*w*),[9] the noun *ḥbr* /ḥaber/ "companion" (or the related feminine) is attested in Imperial Aramaic at the latest. There, it often occurs with the suffix "his"[10] and continues to be frequent in this sense in Biblical Aramaic, e.g., in reference to Daniel and his companions (Dnl. 2:13,17f.). In addition, however, it can be employed quite generally for "other," as in Dnl. 7:20 in reference to the apocalyptic chimera and its horns, in the incantation text from Uruk for other demons,[11] and often at Qumran for equally ranked members of a group such as servants at court,[12] allies,[13] and

---

H. Cazelles, "חָבַר *chābhar*," *TDOT*, IV, 193-97; M. A. Daise, "*ḥbr*," *ThWQ*, I, 892-95; M. O'Connor, "Northwest Semitic Designations for Elective Social Affairs," *JANES* 18 (1986) 67-80, esp. 72-80.

1. For the etymology, see Cazelles, 193f.
2. 4Q202 4:9 (1 En. 10:11).
3. 11Q10 24:1 (Job 34:8).
4. So, e.g., *PAT* 0027.1; 0028.1; 0029.1; 0044.1; 0046.1; 0550.2; 0551.2,6; 0567.2; 0570 [the Greek counterpart in the parallel version reads: κοινωὸν προσλαβεῖν]; 1135.2; 1657.2.
5. *DJPA*, 186a; *DJBA*, 428.
6. *ATTM*, 107; → II.
7. ggBS 1:1 in *ATTM*, 377.
8. Cf. for East Aramaic *DJBA*, 429f.
9. In *KAI* 222 A 4, read as a place name by J. Fitzmyer, *The Aramaic Inscriptions of Sefire. BietOr* 19/A (²1995), 64f., however.
10. *TADAE* C3. 29,11f.; D7.56,2.
11. *ATTM*, 2, 26, l. 16.
12. 1QapGen 20:8.
13. 1QapGen 21:26,28; 22:17.

the Watchers or Giants in the book of Enoch and the book of Giants,[14] similarly in various legal texts from the Dead Sea.[15]

The root *ḥbr* also appears regularly thereafter specifically for members (often with the complement *bny*, → *br*) of a certain association. In Nabatean, it appears in relation to a cultic community[16] and together with the names of private individuals who belong to various professional groups, in the memorial inscriptions from Hatra.[17] Later, the technical meaning "chamber" is common in Jewish texts: one who belongs to the Pharisee community.[18]

In its general meaning, therefore, *ḥbr* overlaps with the usage of the term → *knh* "colleague" widespread in the official style of letters and contracts and possibly standard Aramaic, on the one hand, and of the adjective → *'ḥr* "other" or substantives such as → *'ḥ* "brother"[19] and → *gbr*,[20] on the other. Thus, it can also be employed as a reciprocal pronoun "one another," for which there is no proper form in Semitic, similar to *rēaʿ* in Hebrew: *'nth lḥbrth* "a woman (hugs) another."[21]

III. Noun "Incantation." The relationship of the noun *ḥbr* /ḥabr/ (post-Imperial Aramaic with anaptyxis /ḥabar/) "incantation" to the root "to tie," perhaps via the nuance "magical ties," is entirely unclear. It occurs at Qumran for the magic taught by the leader of the fallen angels;[22] in an unclear context, it occurs further in the Testament of Amram.[23] In addition, later Aramaic languages have instances of the related *nomen professionis* /ḥabbār/ "conjurer," et al. on magic bowls and in the Babylonian Talmud.[24]

Nebe/Gzella

---

14. 4Q201 1 4:21 (1 En. 9: 7); 4Q203 8:5; 4Q202 1 4:9; 4Q530 2 2+6-12:1,5f.

15. Cf. e.g., *ḥbry* "my colleague" in a Nabatean signature on a Greek contract, nV 15:38 in *ATTM*, 2, 229f.; for additional instances see *ATTM*, 2, 391.

16. As in a memorial inscription from Petra, *RÉS* 1423, text also in U. Hackl, H. Jenni, and C. Schneider, *Quellen zur Geschichte der Nabatäer*. *NTOA* 51 (2003), 253; for similar contexts, cf. ibid. 402f. and 404; on cultic community among the Nabateans in general, see J. F. Healey, *The Religion of the Nabataeans* (Leiden 2001), 147ff.,165-69.

17. Singular in H212.4, otherwise plural: H207.2; 209.3; 213.2; 283.2; 407.

18. See generally R. Meyer, "Φαρισαίος," *TDNT*, IX, 11-35; instances in *DJPA*, 185f. and *DJBA*, 428f.; so already on a grave inscription from Zoar, 431 C.E., for the daughter of a *ḥbr*: *ATTM*, 2, 304, l. 2.

19. Employed as a parallel in T. Levi 1c and 90:7 according to HS A = xL 21:21 and 44:7 in *ATTM*.

20. Cf. the instructions for behavior toward others in a late synagogue inscription from En-Gedi, yyEN 3:2,3,4 in *ATTM*, 364.

21. 11Q10 36:2f. (Job 41:9), MT: "one will cling to the other."

22. 4Q201 1 4:1 (1 En. 8:3).

23. 4Q547 5:5,6.

24. Cf. *DJPA*, 186a; *DJBA*, 429b; *LexSyr*, 212.

חדוה *ḥdwh* /ḥedwā/; חדי *ḥdī*

I. Etymology. II. Imperial Aramaic. 1. *ḥdī*. 2. *ḥdwh*. III. Biblical Aramaic *ḥædwā*. IV. Qumran. 1. *ḥdī*. 2. *ḥdwh*.

I. Etymology. Akkadian attests the root **ḫdū* well with *ḫadû(m)* "to rejoice" and many derivatives since the Old Akkadian period,[1] although its existence in Ugaritic is disputed.[2] Aramaic attests a noun and a verb beginning with Imperial Aramaic; it appears in Hebrew as an Aramaic loanword.[3]

II. Imperial Aramaic.

1. ḥdī. Imperial Aramaic attests *ḥdī* "to rejoice, to be happy" (peal) and "to make glad" (pael) almost exclusively in papyrus letters from Egypt dating to the fifth through the fourth centuries B.C.E. Expressions of feeling are typical of the genre and appear frequently in formulaic phrases: *šlmk šm't šgy' ḥdyt* "I have heard of your well-being and I have rejoiced greatly over it";[4] *ḥdh wšryr hwy bkl 'dn* "Be joyous and strong at all times."[5] The expression in *TADAE* A5.3,2 continues to be syntactically problematic: *ḥy' ḥdh wšryr' mr'y yhwy ytyr*[. . .] "[. . .] the living, happy, and the strong may my lord be more [. . .]."[6] Often *ḥdī* also serves to express satisfaction or dissatisfaction: *wyhb ly ksp sttrn 12 wḥdh mnh* [*'nh*] "then he gave me 12 staters of silver, and [I] am satisfied with that";[7] *w'nh l*['] *ḥdyt* "I was dissatisfied, however."[8] The satisfaction of the sender, a third party, or even of the gods can also appear as the foundation guiding behavior in instructions: *kn 'b*[*dw*] *kzy ly tḥdwn* "Behave such that you make me glad";[9] *kn 'bd kzy l'lhy' wl'ršm*

G. J. Brooke, "4QTestament of Levi^d(?) and the Messianic Servant High Priest," in M. C. De Boer, ed., *From Jesus to John. FS M. de Jonge*. JSNTSup 84 (1993), 83-100; E. Eshel and A. Kloner, "An Aramaic Ostracon of an Edomite Marriage Contract from Maresha, Dated 176 B.C.E.," *IEJ* 46 (1996) 1-22; H. Gzella, "*ḥdh*," *ThWQ*, I, 898-901; Y. Muffs, *Studies in the Aramaic Legal Papyri from Elephantine*. *HO* I/66 (2003); J. Naveh and S. Shaked, *Aramaic Documents from Ancient Bactria (Fourth Century B.C.E.)* (London, 2012); D. Schwiderski, *Handbuch des nordwestsemitischen Briefformulars*. *BZAW* 295 (2000); M. Wagner, *Die lexikalischen und grammatikalischen Aramaismen im alttestamentlichen Hebräisch*. *BZAW* 96 (1966); J. Zimmermann, *Messianische Texte aus Qumran*. *WUNT* 104 (1998).

1. *AHw*, I, 307f., *CAD*, VI, 25-27.
2. *DUL*^{3}, 351f.
3. Wagner, 51f.
4. *TADAE* A3.5,2, Schwiderski, 124.
5. *TADAE* A4.7/4.8,3; Schwiderski, 140; cf. A5.1,4.
6. Schwiderski, 140f; in a smooth translation, *TADAE* A S. 86: "May my lord be living, happy, and strong exceedingly."
7. *TADAE* A4.2,12.
8. *TADAE* A6.16,4.
9. *TADAE* A6.14,3f.

tḥd[y] Behave such that you please the gods and Aršama!"[10] A sole instance in wisdom occurs in the sayings of Aḥiqar: *bšgy' bnn lbbk 'l yḥdh wbz'ryhm* [. . .] "Let your heart not rejoice over a large number of children, and over a small number of them [. . .]."[11]

2. ḥdwh. The noun *ḥdwh* first appears in epigraphy in post-Achaemenid times in a marriage certificate from Maresha (176 B.C.E.): *qwsrm br qwsyd hw bḥdwt lbbh* [. . .] "PN, in the joy of his heart."[12] This expression involves a technical term for the voluntary nature of the act borrowed from Akkadian (< *ina ḫūd/ḫadê libbīšu* "in the joy of his heart = freely,"[13] which can be identified on into Seleucid times.[14]

III. Biblical Aramaic *ḥæḏwā.* Biblical Aramaic attests only the noun *ḥæḏwā* in Ezr. 6:16, where it is synonymous with Hebrew *śimḥā* in Ezr. 3:12f.; 6:22, etc.[15] Cf. two instances in Biblical Hebrew, where *ḥæḏwā* is also cultically motivated and denotes the "gladness in his place" (1 Ch. 16:27) and the "joy of Yahweh" himself (Neh. 8:10); correspondingly, in Ps. 21:7, Yahweh produces joy (*ḥdī pi*) through his presence.

IV. Qumran.

1. ḥdī. The causes of joy are, in part, theological in nature, but do not give evidence of a thematic focus: Noah rejoices "over the words of the Lord of heaven" (1QapGen 7:7) and 4Q541 24 2:6 (T. Levi) announces the coming salvation. A psalm of praise in the Aramaic book of Tobit calls upon Jerusalem to rejoice over the righteous (4Q196 18:2 [Tob.13:13]).[16]

Remarkable is the use of the term to express the effervescent vital power of the divine creatures in 11Q10: *wḥpr bbq' wyrwṭ wyḥd' // wbḥyl ynpq l'npy ḥrb* "and it (i.e., the steed) pawed at the valley floor and ran and rejoiced // and with power it went out against the sword" (33:2 [Job 39:21]).[17] The theme of joy in battle also appears in 11Q10 33:6f. (Job 39:25): *wlnqšt zyn wz'qt 'štdwr yḥdh* "and it rejoices over the clangor of weapons and the battle cry."[18]

2. ḥdwh. The noun is attested in the spellings *ḥdwh* and *ḥdw'.* In Aramaic Tobit, the term appears as a wish for a blessing in an intercessory prayer and thus is directly parallel to the greeting formulaic in Imperial Aramaic letters mentioned above: *lrḥmy*]*n wlḥdwh*["[end her life in merc]y and in joy [. . .]" (4Q197 5:1, emended based on Tobit

---

10. *TADAE* A6.16,1f., similarly in letters from Achaemenid officials from Bactria: B3.7 and 5.8 in Naveh and Shaked; cf. in Akk. *CAD*, VI, 27 s.v. *ḫadû* 5 (D-stem).
11. *TADAE* C1.1,90.
12. l. 2, Eshel and Kloner, 3f.
13. See *CAD*, VI, 25,223f.; extensively Muffs, 128-41.
14. Eshel and Kloner, 7.
15. G. Vanoni, "שָׂמַח *śāmaḥ*," *TDOT*, XIV, 142.
16. The Heb. version (4Q200 7 1:1) confirms the synonymity of Hebrew *śmḥ* and Aram. *ḥdī.*
17. MT of this passage leaves open the assignment of *b^e^ḵō^a^ḥ* to *yāśīś* "it rejoices over (its) power" or *yēṣē'* "it goes out with power."
18. On the relationship between the Aram. text and MT, see *DJD*, XXIII (1998), 160.

8:17 LXX).[19] A comparable motif appears in 4Q542 1 1:3f. (T.Qahat): *wyʿbd lkwn ḥdwʾ wšmḥʾ lbnykwn bdry qwšwṭʾ lʿlmyn* "and he (i.e., God) will prepare joy for you and happiness for your sons in the generations of truth forever." The expression "houses of joy" *bty ḥdwʾ* in 11Q18 18:6 involves an area of the temple with an unknown function.[20] Profane contexts include omitted joy at the marriage feast (4Q545 1a 1:7) or the joy of the giants over the curse of the princes (4Q530 2 2+6-12,3).

The context of 4Q541 24 2:5 (ApocrLevi) is unclear, *wtqym lʾbwkh šm ḥdwʾ* "and you will 'establish a name of joy' for your father."[21] A descendant thereby receives the postmortem call to remember the deceased father (cf. Dt. 25:7; Ruth 4:5,10). The precise designation "name of joy" is otherwise unattested in Aramaic (cf. Jer. 33:9). An overlapping of the word fields "joy" and "divine name" also occurs elsewhere in the OT (Ps. 5:12; 9:3; 33:21; 89:17; 105:3; 1 Ch. 16:10; cf. also Lk. 10:20). In 4Q541 24 2:5, *ḥdwʾ* is thus to be understood, on one hand, as the joy of a third party over the name of the father, represented and produced by the deeds of the son, but on the other, also as the reason for joy for the one named. A fragment of the Testament of Qahat attests a relationship between the good conduct of the descendants and the "good name" that results for the ancestry. It seems to employ *šm ṭb* and *šm ḥdwʾ* largely as synonyms (4Q542 1 1:10-12).[22]

Schwiderski

19. On *lrḥmyn* and *ḥdī* in Imperial Aramaic epistolary formulas, cf. *TADAE* A4.7/8,2-4 and Schwiderski, 137f.

20. *DJD*, XXIII (1998), 334; cf. *byt ḥdyʾ ʿlyʾ* in Hatra 107.5 and *DNSI*, 349, but see Gzella, 900.

21. See Zimmermann, 248f.

22. Cf. Nērab 2 (*KAI* 226.2f.).

חוי *ḥwī*

I. Etymology. II. Old and Imperial Aramaic. III. Biblical Aramaic. IV. Qumran.

J. A. Fitzmyer, *Tobit. CEJL* (2003); H. Gzella, "Deir ʿAllā," in G. Khan, ed., *Encyclopedia of Hebrew Language and Linguistics* (Leiden, 2013), 1:691-93; idem, "*ḥwh* I," *ThWQ*, I, 908-12; E. Jenni, *Die hebräischen Präpositionen*, vol. 1: *Die Präposition Beth* (Stuttgart, 1992); P. Joüon, "Les verbes 'voir' en araméen: *ḥzh, ḥmh, ḥwh*," *Or* 2 (1933) 117-19; I. Kottsieper, *Die Sprache der Aḥiqarsprüche. BZAW* 194 (1990); J. T. Milik, *The Books of Enoch* (Oxford, 1976); T. Muraoka and B. Porten, *A Grammar of Egyptian Aramaic. HO* I/32 ([2]2003); D. Schwiderski, *Handbuch des nordwestsemitischen Briefformulars. BZAW* 295 (2000); M. Wagner, *Die lexikalischen und grammatikalischen Aramaismen im alttestamentlichen Hebräisch. BZAW* 96 (1966).

I. Etymology. The verb *ḥwī* "to communicate, show" can be first identified in the inscription from Deir ʿAllā;[1] thereafter, Imperial Aramaic (haphel/pael) and the later Aramaic languages attest it quite frequently. The Hebrew verb *ḥwī* (piel "make known, proclaim") is apparently not an Aramaism, but its origin is disputed.[2]

II. Old and Imperial Aramaic. Older Aramaic attests *ḥwī* "to communicate, show" with no perceptible difference in meaning in the pael and haphel.[3] The oldest specimen identified so far from the ninth/eighth century B.C.E. designates an act of prophetic communication by the seer Balaam: *wyʾmr lhm šbw ʾḥwkm mh* "Then he said to them: Sit down, I will tell you what. . . ."[4] The Aramaic letters from Egypt offer various instances that refer to everyday life, so e.g., the showing of a boot,[5] a command to report,[6] or the conveyance of a command: *ʾp šlḥt lh lmḥwh ṭʿmʾ lhwšʿ* "I also sent him (news), to show (or communicate) the instruction to Hosea."[7] The connection of the sender with the recipient comes to expression in the so-called farewell formula of Imperial Aramaic epistolary salutations: *brktk l-*[divine name] *zy yḥwny ʾpyk bšlm* "I bless you by [divine name], who may show me 'your countenance' safe and sound"[8] and *šlm bytk wbnyk ʿd ʾlhyʾ yḥwwnn*[*y ʾpyk bšlm*] "Peace to your house and your sons until the gods show m[e your countenance safe and sound]!"[9] The "showing" of an opponent by the deity, in contrast, is to be understood as an expression of divine assistance and of the associated triumph over the enemy: *wmṣlyn lyhw mrʾ šmyʾ zy hḥwyn bwydrng zk* "And we prayed to Yahu, the Lord of heaven, who showed us this Widranga."[10] Parallels appear e.g., in Ps. 59:11 ("God let me look [triumphantly] on my enemies") and in the Moabite Mēšaʿ stele (*ky hrʾny bkl šnʾy* "for he let me look [triumphantly] on all my enemies").[11]

Two individual instances of *ḥwī* occur in the sayings of the wise man Aḥiqar: Thus, the sun god Šamaš favors it "if someone hears a word, but does not announce it" (*wyšmʿ mlh wlʾ yhḥwh*).[12] *TADAE* C1.1,207 refers to the senselessness of showing "a Bedouin the sea and [a] Sidonian [the paths in the steppe] for their works are differ[ent]" ([*ʾl th*]*ḥwy lʿrby ymʾ w*[*l*]*ṣydny* [*ʾrḥtʾ zy mdbrʾ*] *ky* ʿ[*b*]*ydthm pryš*[*n hny*]).[13] Additional Imperial Aramaic instances cannot be taken into consideration because of their fragmentary contexts.[14]

1. Regarding the disputed linguistic classification, see Gzella, 692 (bib.).
2. Kottsieper, 171, 201: from Egyptian *ḥw* "to report"; Wagner, 53: from Arabic *waḥā*.
3. Muraoka and Porten §49d.
4. Deir ʿAllā (*KAI* 312) I:4f.; regarding the various editions, cf. Gzella, 691.
5. *TADAE* A6.2,7f.
6. *ʾntm hḥwwhy* "You, inform him!" *TADAE* A6.11,5.
7. *TADAE* D7.24,16f.
8. Schwiderski, 126-128; e.g., *TADAE* A2.1,2; 2.6,1f. [Ptaḥ]; 3.3,3 [Yahu?]; cf. also A2.4,1f. the synonymous *yḥzny* instead of *yḥwny*.
9. *TADAE* A4.4,9; Schwiderski, 166.
10. *TADAE* A4.7,15f.; the second copy A4.8,15 offers the synonymous *ḥwynʾ* pael instead of *hḥwyn* haphel.
11. *KAI* 181.4.
12. *TADAE* C1.1, 188.
13. Text according to Kottsieper, 14.23, col. 16.1.
14. *TADAE* A6.2,5; B8.3,5; 8.5,a.1; 8.12,5; D7.14,8; 7.15,12; Segal 118,1.

III. Biblical Aramaic. Biblical Aramaic attests the verb only in the narratives in Daniel, where it denotes the communication of a dream interpretation (Dnl. 2:4; also 2:24 [pael]; 2:6f.,9,16 [haphel]; → II). The king demands that his divination priests also report the content of the dream itself (Dnl. 2:6; similarly 2:11 [pael]; 2:10,27 [haphel]). They decline by referring to the fact that this kind of soothsaying is reserved for the gods (Dnl. 2:11). In Dnl. 5, instead of dreams, ominous letters on the wall are to be interpreted (Dnl. 5:7; further 7:12,15 [haphel]). In Dnl. 3:32 *ḥwī* (haphel) designates King Nebuchadnezzar's proclamation of praise for God's deeds.

IV. Qumran. The Aramaic texts from Qumran attest the verb well. Often, the general meaning "to communicate" appears with no special nuance (1QapGen 2:19,21; 5:9; 22:3; 4Q196 2:1; 4Q209 26:7; 4Q530 2 2+6-12:1; 4Q545 4:14). As a rule, however, the theme is not the conveyance of mundane information, but the significant revelation of something otherwise hidden: *wk'n lk 'nh* [*m*]*ḥwh brz* [. . .] "and I now disclose to you the secret of [. . .]" (1QapGen 5:20, similarly 5:21 and 14:19); *wṭmrt rz' dn blbby wlkwl 'nwš l' 'ḥwyth* "Then I hid this secret in my heart and revealed it to no one" (6:12); [']*ḥwh lkh rz 'wbdh* "I will disclose to you the secret of his doings" (4Q545 4:16). In parallel with *ḥwī* (haphel) one finds → *ḥzī* (haphel) "to show": *yd' 'nh brzy* [*mry' dy*] *qdyšyn 'ḥwywny w'ḥzywny* "I know the secrets [of the Lord, the] Holy Ones have told and shown me" (4Q204 5 2:26 [1 En. 106,19]).[15] A communication can be either true (*bqwšṭ*) or false (*bkdbyn*): *w'nh bqwšṭ kwl' 'ḥwynk* "and I will disclose everything to you truthfully" (1QapGen 2:10); [*bqwšṭ*] *tḥwynny wl' bkdbyn hd'* [. . .] "tell me this (matter) [truthfully] and not with lies [. . .]" (2:6; cf. further 2:5,7 and 15:20). As in the older corpora of texts, *ḥwī* also denotes the communication of dream interpretations: *w'mr lh dy yḥw'* [*l*]*kh p*[*š*]*r ḥlmy'* "And tell him that he should disclose the interpretation of the dreams to you" (4Q530 2 2+6-12:23; cf. also 2 2+6-12:13). The superscription of 4Q543 introduces the book as a "copy of the visions of Amram" (*pršgn ktb mly ḥzwt 'mrm*), namely "[everything that] he told ['*ḥwy*] his sons and what he commanded [*pqd*] them on the [day of his death]" (4Q543 1a-c:1f.; cf. 4Q209 26:6).[16] As in Biblical Aramaic, the verb also denotes the proclamation of praise for God's deeds, to which a Jewish soothsayer prompts the Babylonian King Nabonidus in 4Q242: *hḥwy wktb lm'bd yqr wr*[*bw*] *lšm* '[*lh' 'ly*'] "Announce and write in order to show the name of the h[ighest God] honor and majesty" (4Q242 1-3:5; cf. Dnl. 3:32 and, for a similar confession, 4Q196 17 2:4 [Tob. 13:8]).

The Job Targum employs *ḥwī* to translate the Hebrew counterpart *ḥwī* (piel) or the synonymous *ngd* (hiphil) "to communicate, report" (11Q10 21:9 for MT Job 32:17; 27:3 for MT Job 36:9; 30:2 for MT Job 38:4). Regarding the passive of the causative stem, see Gzella, "*ḥwh* I," 909.

Schwiderski

15. Text according to Milik, 209f.; *ATTM*, 250f. emends alternatively *brzy*[*' dy*].
16. *DJD*, XXXVI (2000), 163f.

חור *ḥwr*

I. The Root *ḥwr* and Its Derivatives. II. The Verb Pael "To Cleanse." III. The Substantive "White" and the Adjective "White." IV. The Gentilic Adjective "White."

I. The Root *ḥwr* and Its Derivatives. The Aramaic and Arabic root *ḥwr* "white" underlies the Aramaic verb peal "to be white, pale" with the pael "to whiten, bleach, cleanse" (Jewish Aramaic, Syriac), "to demonstrate" (Jewish Babylonian), the aphel "to shame" (Jewish Babylonian, Syriac), and the noun /ḥewwār/,[1] at first a substantive "white," later an adjective "white" (in middle Aramaic also spelled *ḥwwr*, *ḥywr*) alongside the old *ḥwry* /ḥewwārāy/ "white" from the old substantive /ḥewwār/ "white" with the gentilic affix /-āy/.

II. The Verb Pael "To Cleanse." In the Nabatean rental contract Yadin, Documents II 6, 12[2] (119 C.E.), the denominated pael participle masculine singular absolute *mḥwr* /maḥawwar/[3] "removing from the woods" appears with a direct object (a plot of land).

III. The Substantive "White" and the Adjective "White." The noun /ḥewwār/ as a substantive signifies "something white": according to 5Q15 1 1:6,[4] the masculine singular absolute *ḥwr* after the construct *'bn* (fem., therefore, not an adjective!) "stone of white (material)" is the plaster on the new (heavenly) Jerusalem and, according to 2Q24 8:[3],[5] the material of the walls of its temple; so also in Dnl. 7:9 "Its wall was white"; masculine singular determinative *ḥwr'*: Palmyrene "the white building stone," Syriac "the white of the eye, of the egg." The older texts always employ it as an adjective "white" in the meaning "unplanted" as in an ostracon from Idumea (fourth century B.C.E.),[6] masculine singular determinative *ḥwr'* and eight times in Nabatean private documents from southern Judea Yadin, Documents II, 1-36,42 (93-132 C.E.)[7] feminine singular absolute *ḥwrh*, feminine determinative *ḥwrt'*.

I. Eph'al and J. Naveh, *Aramaic Ostraca of the Fourth Century BC from Idumaea* (Jerusalem, 1996); J. Naveh and S. Shaked, *Aramaic Documents from Ancient Bactria (Fourth Century B.C.E.)* (London, 2012); Y. Yadin et al., eds., *The Documents from the Bar Kokhba Period in the Cave of Letters II: Hebrew, Aramaic and Nabatean-Aramaic Papyri* (Jerusalem, 2002).

1. The nominal form for Aramaic color designations *quttāl* with the Aramaic dissimilation /-uww-/ > /-eww-/: *BLA* §52n.
2. *ATTM*, 2:216f.: nV 6.
3. *ATTM*, 107f.,464.
4. *ATTM*, 217: J 2:6. *DSSStE*, 1138f., seems to read this as an adjective: "white stone."
5. *ATTM*, 221: J 5:24. Note that *DSSStE*, 218-21, does interpret this as an adjective: "the{ir} walls of white stone."
6. Eph'al and Naveh 189.4.
7. *ATTM*, 2: 204-241,393: nV 1-36.

IV. The Gentilic Adjective "White." *ḥwry* /ḥewwārāy/ "white" serves as the gentilic adjective of /ḥewwār/ "something white": *TADAE* A6.9,3 (fifth century B.C.E.) masculine singular absolute *ḥwry*, of flour, as also often in Naveh and Shaked C1; Birth of Noah 4Q561 1:2[8] feminine plural absolute *ḥwryn* "(both) white (and black eyes like those of the Islamic Houris)"; synagogues from Rehov near Beth Shean (circa 600 C.E.)[9] feminine singular determinative *ḥywrth* "unplanted"; rare in Galilean-targumic.

Beyer

8. *ATTM*, 2, 163: E 3:2. *DSSStE*, 1116f., here reads "hi[s] eyes (will be) between pale and dark."
9. ggBS 3:6 *ATTM*, 378.

חזי *ḥzī*; חזו *ḥzw* /ḥazū/; חזי *ḥzy* /ḥazī/; מחזה *mḥzh* /maḥzǣ/; חזו *ḥzw* /ḥezū/; חזון *ḥzwn* /ḥezwān/; חזיון *ḥzywn* /ḥezyōn/; מחזי *mḥzy* /maḥzī/; חזה *ḥzh* /ḥazǣ/; רו *rw* /rēw/

I. Etymology, Lexical Field, and Grammatical Constructions. II. Verb "to See." 1. In the General Sense. 2. As a Core Term of Vision Literature. III. Noun "Vision, Appearance." IV. Noun "Dream Vision." V. Noun "Mirror." VI. Adjective "Customary, Necessary."

I. Etymology, Lexical Field, and Grammatical Constructions. Among the known Semitic languages, the verbal root *ḥzī* "to see" is productive only in Aramaic and constitutes, therefore, one of its lexical peculiarities. Aramaic influence or poetic archaism best explains the Hebrew instances that occur in poetic and prophetic texts. West Aramaic employs the synomymous form *ḥmī*,[1] which may have arisen secondarily from *ḥwī* with the meaning "to communicate, show" in the double and causative stems.[2] In contrast, Hebrew employs for "to see" the root *r'ī*, which appears in Aramaic as the noun */re'w/ "appearance" (→ III).

The ground stem of the verb meaning "to see" usually occurs with the thing seen as the direct object, but sometimes also with an object clause introduced by *dy* "that."

L. DiTommaso, "*ḥzh*," *ThWQ*, I, 928-34; J. A. Fitzmyer, *The Aramaic Inscriptions of Sefire. BietOr* 19A (²1995); H. Gzella, "Deir 'Allā," in G. Khan, ed., *Encyclopedia of Hebrew Language and Linguistics* (Leiden, 2013), 1:691-93; idem, "Presentatives," in Khan, *Encyclopedia of Hebrew Language and Linguistics*, 3:220-24; A. Jepson, "חָזָה *chāzāh*," *TDOT*, IV, 280-90; P. Joüon, "Les verbes 'voir' en araméen: *ḥzh*, *ḥmh*, *ḥwh*," *Or* 2 (1933) 117-19; H. Lozachmeur, *La collection Clermont-Ganneau: Ostraca, épigraphes sur jarre, étiquettes de bois*, 2 vols. (Paris, 2006); D. Vetter, "חזה *ḥzh* to see," *TLOT*, 400-403.

1. Isolated instances of *ḥzī* there come from other dialects: *DJPA*, 194; *ATTM*, 2, 394.
2. Joüon; cf. H. Gzella, "*ḥwh* I," *ThWQ*, I, 909.

Intransitively, *ḥzī* can be employed in the sense of "to direct the view" and be supplemented with prepositional expressions with *l-* "toward" or *ʿd* "upon" and, occasionally, with further adverbial complements such as "in a dream." In addition to the general sense, this verb belongs among the core terms of vision literature as extant in the book of Daniel and various Aramaic texts from Qumran. Figuratively, it can denote "to regard, to determine" or "to experience, to witness." Further, the imperative of the masculine singular *ḥzī* "look!" functions as a presentative marker.

The Gt-stem serves for the passive "to be seen" or the middle "to appear" (the latter often with an indirect object following *l-* "to someone"). The rare causative stem with the meaning "to show (someone something)" is usually constructed with a dual object, occasionally also with a direct and indirect object following *l-*, and overlaps with the much more frequent verb → *ḥwī* "to communicate, show," which is similarly constructed.[3] Less frequent is the usage with *ʿl* for "to be concerned with" (→ II.1). The corresponding inner-passive "to be shown" occurs only sporadically. Additionally, in Old Aramaic instances of the D-stem with the same meaning as the G-stem also occur.[4]

The many nominal derivatives of this root can also be divided into general terms and those with specifically revelation-theology connotations: the former include the feminine /ḥazū/ "sight, visibility" and the rare /ḥazī/ "sign" as well as the masculine /maḥzǣ/ "appearance"; the latter include the masculine /ḥezū/ "dream vision, appearance" and, less frequent, /ḥezwān/ "manifestation" and /ḥezyōn/ "dream revelation." In addition, the feminine substantive /maḥzī/ "mirror" and the frequent adjective /ḥazǣ/ "usual, necessary" are also attested. The noun /maḥōz/ "harbor, fortified place," probably an Akkadian loanword, is unrelated, however.[5]

II. Verb "to See."

1. In the General Sense. In the general meaning "to see," *ḥzī* has been widespread in both the active and nonactive usages since Old Aramaic. A state treaty from Sefire calls upon the gods as witnesses to open their eyes and look at the agreement;[6] according to a curse formula in the same inscription, may no green appear in the withering land of the oath-breaker.[7] A somewhat later Old Aramaic grave inscription from Nērab employs the verb in the deceased's retrospective on the day of his death, on which, at the end of his life, he was able (in his imagination?) to see sons in the fourth generation.[8]

Moreover, many instances from everyday discourse occur in the pre-Imperial Aramaic sayings of Aḥiqar with their colorfully mixed impressions from daily life: quite generally,[9]

---

3. Cf. the variation *yḥzny*/*yḥwny* in the farewell formula in the Hermopolis Papyri or the parallelism *ʾḥwywny wʾḥzywny* "they have told and shown me" in 4Q204 5 ii 26 (1 En. 106,19); → *ḥwī* II and H. Gzella, "*ḥwh* I," 908f.

4. *KAI* 222 A 13 (Sefire), perhaps also 226.5 (Nērab); cf. Fitzmyer, 77f. and *DNSI*, 358.

5. See *ATTM*, 2, 429f.

6. *KAI* 222 A 13; probably in the subsequently unproductive D-stem.

7. L. 28; Gt-stem.

8. *KAI* 226,5; although debate continues whether *mḥzh* represents a D-stem ptcp. "seeing" or a contracted spelling of *mh ḥzh* "what I see" with a G-stem ptcp.

9. *TADAE* C1.1, 173.189.204.

figuratively for "to experience" (ll. 80,85), as an adverbial phrase (*špyr mlk lmḥzh* "the king is nice to look at," l. 92), and the participle of the t-stem passive [*l'*] *mtḥzh* "not to see = invisible" (l. 90, said of death). The private letters from Hermopolis are similar: in the farewell formula, the causative stem *yḥzny 'pyk* "may he show me your countenance"[10] may represent the synonymous form with *yḥwny*;[11] with the preposition *'l*, the verb denotes "to be concerned about."[12] In a few other passages, the context is fragmentary.

Texts in the Imperial Aramaic literary tradition contain further nuances and constructions, but largely continue the older usage. Here, *ḥzī* occurs with the nuance "to regard"[13] or "to witness" (Ezr. 4:14) and with *b* "to look down on,"[14] absolutely also "to be able to see" (Dnl. 5:23, employed in the negative as an attribute of incorporeal idol deities, → *dhb* III) and with an object clause following *dy* "to determine that" (Dnl. 2:8; 3:27). Especially in private letters, as well documented in the Clermont-Ganneau ostraca from Elephantine, the imperative *ḥzy* often functions as a lexicalized presentative marker,[15] apparently as a synonym of other deictic particles such as *h'*.[16]

The post-Achaemenid literary languages also correspond essentially to these findings. Because of the many visions in the often apocalyptically stamped texts from Qumran, the verb occurs there mostly in a divine revelation (→ II.2); they also attest the general usage, however.[17] A few usages in later offshoots of Imperial Aramaic have no direct precursors and some may stand under the influence of other languages: thus *znh lmḥzh* "in view of which" in an Aśoka inscription from Kandahar[18] and the Gt-stem in the sense of "to be decided, decreed" in the tax scale form Palmyra[19] on the model of δεδόχθαι and ἔδ[ο]ξεν in the parallel version.

2. *As a Core Term of Vision Literature.* Yet, *ḥzī* already served in Old Aramaic as a term for divination, as in the participle "seer"[20] and similarly in the superscription of the Deir 'Allā wall inscription.[21] An ostracon from Elephantine[22] employs it for a dream, as does a Hatrene inscription that traces the construction of a temple to the previous vision in a dream.[23]

Most of the older instances are allotted to the symbolic dreams in Daniel (2:26,31,34,41, 43,45; 4:2,6,7,10,15,17,20; 7:2,4,6f.,9,11,13,21). The addition of presentatives (*w'lw*: 2:31; 4:7; *w'rw*: 7:6f.,13; followed by a substantive, a nominal clause or a verbal clause) relates

10. *TADAE* A2.2,2; 2.3,2; 2.4,2; 2.5,2.

11. *TADAE* A2.1,2; 2.6,2; so also in Imperial Aramaic: A3.3,3; 4.4, 9; D7.16,12f.

12. *TADAE* A2.3,11; 2.7,3; as in Imperial Aramaic: A3.5,6; 4.3,5.

13. As in the petitionary letter *TADAE* A4.7,23f., with *b'ly ṭbtk* "people who merit your good will" as object.

14. *TADAE* A4.7, 17, par. 4.8,16.

15. Gzella, "Presentatives."

16. So, in any case, in nos. 35cv2; 36cc1; 106cc4; 228cc2.cv1; 280cc2; for other possible instances cf. Lozachmeur, 541 s.v.

17. 1QapGen 20:9; 4Q424 3:3.

18. *KAI* 279.4.

19. *PAT* 0259 1.7; 2.114,123,129.

20. *KAI* 202 A 12, parallel to *'ddn.*

21. I,1; *r'ī* in l. 5 represents Canaanite influence; Gzella, "Deir 'Allā."

22. *TADAE* D7.17, Imperial Aramaic.

23. *TADAE* S1.6; without context also in H1039.8.

it explicitly to sense perception; in this regard, *ʿd* (*dy*) "as though at once" (2:34; 7:4,9,11) with the perfect expresses the surprise within the vision portrayed as a process by means of the periphrastic construction (→ *hwī*). The Aramaic visions from Qumran follow the same style.[24] The causative stem "to show" often appears in the seer's tour through the new Jerusalem.[25]

III. Noun "Vision, Appearance." Nominal derivatives occur only rarely. They primarily denote seeing, as such: feminine *ḥzw* /ḥazū/ "appearance" (Dnl. 4:8,17, of the world tree) or "sight,"[26] and perhaps *ḥzy* /ḥazī/ "sign,"[27] further the masculine *mḥzh* /maḥzǣ/ "appearance"[28] and the synonymous *rw* /rēw/.[29]

IV. Noun "Dream Vision." Of the nouns describing a dream vision, *ḥzw* /ḥezū/ is by far the most frequent. Since gender agreement demonstrates it to be a masculine, the ending /-ū/ must belong to the root and be differentiated from the abstract ending /-ūt/ in /ḥazū/ "vision."[30] The vision depictions in the book of Daniel and the Aramaic texts from Qumran, where it appears regularly, attest it. Only relatively rarely is it employed for "looks" (this, too, however, is usually within visions): Dnl. 7:20; 1QapGen 5:7; 4Q205 2 2:29 (1 En. 89:30); 4Q209 26:5 (1 En. 78:17); 4Q529 1:5; 4Q544 1:13f. (the parallelism between the description of Belial in l. 13 and of Michael in l. 14 demonstrates that *ḥzw* alone has no negative connotation).

Otherwise, this noun is employed both in the singular and in the plural for visions in a dream, as additions such as "(during) the night" (Dnl. 2:19; 7:2,7,13; 1QapGen 21:8), "of the/my dream" (Dnl. 4:6; 4Q544 1:10; → *ḥlm*), or "on the bed" (Dnl. 2:28; 4:7,10; 7:1) make clear. If the older reading in the dream ostracon from Elephanine is correct in l. 5 *ḥz*[*w*],[31] it would be predetermined there; contrast, however, *TADAE* D7.17 and *KAI*[5] 270 A: *tḥzy yḥmlyh* "May Yaḥmolia be concerned with."

In this regard, *ḥzw* in the plural designates the individual appearances in usually longer sequences in enigmatic images (Dnl. 2:28; 4:2,6,7,10; 7:1,7,13,15)[32] that join to constitute the entire dream.[33] In contrast, the singular occurs in reference to individual appearances of God with concrete communications.[34] Because of the lack of context for

24. E.g., 1QapGen 19:14; t-stem "to appear": 21:8; 22:27.
25. E.g., 5Q15 1 2:6.
26. 4Q213a 2:16, here together with /ḥezū/ for dream vision, and 4Q530 1 1:7; in the superscription of 4Q543, however, specifically *mly ḥzwt* "words of a vision," if the reading is correct.
27. *ʾbn ḥzyth* "his marked stone = cornerstone" in the difficult text of 11Q10 30:4 (Job 38:6).
28. 1QapGen 20:5; 4Q531 22:10.
29. From /reʾw/ and formally assimilated to /ḥezū/, *ATTM* 692; Dnl. 2:31; 3:25.
30. Consequently, it must have been an original *qitl*-noun */ḥizw/, cf. *ATTM*, 576.
31. *DNSI*, 357.
32. As does the absolute state *ḥzwyn* in 1QapGen 6:11,14 according to *ATTM* 2, 92, where, however, other editors read the singular *ḥzywn*; cf. D. A. Machiela, *The Dead Sea Genesis Apocryphon*. *STDJ* 79 (2009), 44f.
33. Employed in parallel with *ḥlm* in Dnl. 2:28; 4:2; 7:1; 4Q544 1:10.
34. Dnl. 2:19; 7:2; 1QapGen 21:8; 22:7; 4Q204 1 6:8.13 (1 En. 13:10; 14:4); 4Q246 1 1:3 is atypical since the context suggests a vision of history in the lost portion for which Dnl. has the plural.

other instances from Qumran, it remains unclear whether this termological distinction persists there, too. A later amulet employs the plural for "nightmares."[35]

Additional forms first occur in texts from Qumran. The rare *ḥzwn* /ḥezwān/ "appearance" may derive secondarily from /ḥezū/. In a difficult expression in 1QapGen 6:4, it describes Noah as an ideal image of uprightness and wisdom (*bḥzwn qwšṭ' wḥkmt'*; → *ḥrṣ* III). In contrast, the formally unusual noun *ḥzywn* /ḥezyōn/[36] stands specifically for a dream revelation, in both of the preserved passages together with a form of the verb *ḥzī*.[37] For 1QapGen 6:11,14, see n. 32 above.

V. Noun "Mirror." The feminine *mḥzy* /maḥzī/ "mirror"[38] is to be distinguished by form and meaning from the masculine noun *mḥzh* /maḥzǣ/ "sight, looks. The dowry lists in Imperial Aramaic marriage contracts mention mirrors of differing values.[39]

VI. Adjective "Customary, Necessary." Finally, the substantivized passive participle of the G-stem /ḥazǣ/ regularly serves beginning in the post-Achaemenid period as an adjective "usual, necessary" with *l-* "for" or "about," often in the combinations *dy ḥzh* "what is usual" or *kdy ḥzh* "according to what is usual." Instances of the general sense occur only in isolation: first Dnl. 3:19, of the oven that Nebuchadnezzar has heated to seven times hotter than usual; in 4Q534 1 1:6, according to *ATTM*, 2, 163 also with *lm'th* "to go" as a complement in reference to a path that only the angels are worthy to travel; according to other editions, however, a noun "visions" appears here.[40]

The expression *kdy ḥzh* (sometimes also spelled *ḥz'*) appears very frequently, however, in the legal diction of the contracts from the Dead Sea. There, it denotes usual agreements or the typical market value of real estate.[41] Meanwhile, the corresponding instances of *dy ḥzh* "what is necessary" in priestly regulations concerning washing and sacrifice in the Levi Document[42] have juridical connotations.

Gzella

35. ooXX 13:3 in *ATTM.E*, 266.

36. From */ḥuzyān/, *ATTM*, 576.

37. 4Q204 1 6:6 (1 En. 13:8) for a dream vision of Enoch; 4Q213a 2:15 for Levi's journey to heaven.

38. In *TADAE* B2.6,11 probably erroneously construed as a masculine; although the spelling with *y* here also points to the absolute state of a *maqlīt* form, which is regularly feminine in Semitic.

39. *TADAE* B2.6,11; 3.3,5; 3.8,13; in the first and third cases, made of bronze and more valuable; the second mentions a mirror with no indication of its composition.

40. *ATTM*, 577 assigns the instance to *ḥzy* "sign."

41. M 19:11,25; 21:20; XḤev/Ṣe 8:5,7; 9:5,11; 21:5; 50:6,7; nV 1:5,31; 2:4,7,28; 3:8,31; 6:13; 7:8,13,40,49; cf. *ATTM*, 2, 394.

42. Preserved in the Geniza manuscripts Bodl. c and d: *ALD* 21.7; 23.14; 25a.20; 29.12; 31.19, in addition, corr. following the Greek in l. 20.

חטא/חטי *ḥṭʾ/ḥṭī*; חטא *ḥṭʾ* /ḥeṭē/; חטי *ḥṭy* /ḥaṭāy/; זיד *zīd*; חוב *ḥūb*; חוב(ה) *ḥwb(h)* /ḥōb(ā)/; חיב *ḥyb* /ḥayyāb/; טעי *ṭʿī*; טעיה *ṭʿyh* /ṭāʿiyā/; טעו *ṭʿw* /ṭaʿū/; עויה *ʿwyh* /ʿawāyā/; עול *ʿwl* /ʿōl/

I. Etymology, Lexical Field, and Grammatical Constructions. II. Verb "to Sin." III. Noun "Sin." IV. "Guilt" and Its Derivatives. V. "To Err" and Its Derivatives.

I. Etymology, Lexical Field, and Grammatical Constructions. The verb *ḥṭī* "to sin" and its nominal derivatives /ḥeṭē/ and /ḥaṭāy/ "sin" serve as generic terms in the terminologically differentiated—but, because of the genres of texts common there, in older Aramaic only partially developed—lexical field of "sin." It arose from the older *ḥṭʾ* (< *ḫṭʾ*), which is also productive in Hebrew, when, already in Old Aramaic, verbs with /ʾ/ as the final radical after the loss of the glottal stop at the end of a syllable fused with the class of roots ending in vowels.[1] The typical G-stem "to sin" is intransitive and optionally supplemented with an addition following *ʿl* or *qdm* "to, toward," although Ezr. 6:17 also contains an instance of the infinitive of the D-stem "to atone" with a prepositional phrase following *ʿl* "for, to the benefit of."

Moreover, a few additional terms refer to specific forms of sin. In the sole older instance (Dnl. 5:20), the verb *zīd* in the causative-stem denotes the arrogance of King Nebuchadnezzar at the peak of his fame (*rūmeh tiqpaṯ lahᵃzāḏā* "his spirit became obdurate to the point of impudence," parallel to *rīm liḇᵉḇeh* "his heart became presumptuous"), which led to his fall.[2] Later Jewish Palestinian[3] and East Aramaic[4] also attest nominal derivatives with the broader meaning "bad," "wickedness."

In contrast, the root *ḥūb* "to owe," unattested in Biblical Aramaic, with its derivatives /ḥōb(ā)/ "debt" and /ḥayyāb/ "guilty" (→ IV) apparently have roots in legal terminology, where it is already attested in Imperial Aramaic, but was also employed later in the ethical sense of "sin" and sometimes alongside forms of the root *ḥṭī*. Further, a few Aramaic texts from Qumran employ the verb *ṭʿī* "to err" with the related feminine abstract /ṭaʿū/ for idol worship with an ethico-religious nuance (→ V).

Finally, /ʿawāyā/ "sin,"[5] which occurs in parallelism (Dnl. 4:24), and /ʿōl/ "wrong,

---

J. Dušek, *Les manuscrits araméens du Wadi Daliyeh et la Samarie vers 450-332 av. J.-C. CHANE* 30 (2007); R. Fuller and B. Schlenke, "*ḥṭʾ*," *ThWQ* I 943-50; R. Knierim, "חטא *ḥṭʾ* to miss," *TLOT*, 406-11; K. Koch, "חָטָא *chāṭāʾ*," *TDOT*, IV 309-19; J. Maier, "Jüdisches Grundempfinden von Sünde und Erlösung in frühjüdischer Zeit," in H. Frankemölle, ed., *Sünde und Erlösung im Neuen Testament. QD* 161 (1996), 53-75; J. Naveh and S. Shaked, *Aramaic Documents from Ancient Bactria (Fourth Century B.C.E.)* (London, 2012).

1. *ATTM*, 104.
2. On this topic → *gʾī*.
3. *DJPA*, 175a.
4. *DJBA*, 406b, which employed the term primarily in reference to demons.
5. Probably from a Semitic root **ġwī* "to sin."

crime,"[6] attested beginning at Qumran, cannot be clearly distinguished semantically from the noun /ḥaṭāy/. Besides *zīd*, all of these terms appear in the Aramaic texts from Qumran.

II. Verb "to Sin." Aramaic first attests the verb *ḥṭī* "to sin" in Ezr. 6:17. This infinitive of the D-stem in the meaning "in order to atone" denotes the offering of sacrifices[7] on the occasion of the rededication of the Jerusalem temple[8] as atonement for (*ʿl*) all of Israel. Later Jewish Palestinian, meanwhile, employs the D-stem for "to lead someone into sin," like the causative stem;[9] in East Aramaic, the G-stem can be employed for "to cause damage" with *b-* "to (someone)."[10]

Subsequently, the G-stem appears often in the Aramaic texts from Qumran. These texts sometimes paraphrase the concept of sinning as a transgression against God's commandments, and sometimes highlight the effects of sinning across generations. In a court narrative set at Xerxes's court, the verb occurs in the prayer of probably the main character, the Jew Bagasrau, to God:[11] *bḥwby ʾbhty dy ḥṭw qdmyk* "the sins of my fathers, who sinned against you"; the intention is *probably* that God knows these sins, but the precise relation to the preceding verb *ydʿ* in l. 1 is unclear because of a lacuna in the text. For personal guilt, in contrast, it surfaces in Tobit's admonition to his son Tobias to remember all the days of his life "not to sin" (*mḥṭʾ*)[12] and *not* to deviate from God's commandment.[13] The supposed, but partially emended instance of a t-stem in the expression *hmsh dy* [*ʾt*] *ḥṭy ʿlyh* "the wrong brought upon you [i.e., the earth]" in a description of the violence in the *preflood* generations[14] is paleographically controversial, and with no exact parallels for a t-stem of this verb,[15] semantically unlikely; Beyer reads instead *hmsh dqṭylyʾ* "wrong done to those killed."[16] Other passages are very fragmentary or depend on emendation.[17] Nonetheless, the root also seems to occur, as a verb or a noun, in the Book of Giants.[18]

The two known Palmyrene instances modulate between juridical and religious connotations: according to a grave inscription, anyone who sells an *ʿrb* ("security"?) commits a sin against himself/herself (*ʿl npšh ḥṭʾ*);[19] further, the verb appears in the rules for a symposium.[20]

---

6. From **ʿūl* "to deviate"; → III.
7. → *qrb.*
8. → *ḥnkh.*
9. *DJPA*, 196a.
10. *DJBA*, 449.
11. 4Q550 5+5a:2.
12. ἁμαρτεῖν in the Greek.
13. 4Q196 9:2 (Tob. 4:5).
14. 4Q201 1 4:8 (1 En. 9:1).
15. The Syriac passive (*LexSyr*, 227b) is not directly comparable.
16. *ATTM*, 237.
17. Thus, 4Q204 5 2:18 preserves only the ending so that this supposed instance plays no role in an analysis.
18. 4Q531 20:3; 35:2, both without context.
19. Probably a participle of the G-stem; *PAT* 0097.8-10.
20. *PAT* 0991.18.

III. Noun "Sin." Attestations of the derived noun *ḥṭ'* /ḥeṭē/ "sin" in the sense of concrete transgression begin with the pre-Achaemenid worldly wisdom of Aḥiqar and already have religious connotations in the oldest instance. There, it is described as *ḥṭ' mn 'lhn* "sin against (the) gods" if someone attacks another who is more just (*ṣdyk mnk*).[21] In the Imperial Aramaic narrative framework of Aḥiqar, *ḥṭ'* stands for the sin of a subject before (*qdm*) the king (certainly perceived as near the gods), which, however, another can "take away."[22]

These two aspects of *ḥṭ'* grounded in the older Aramaic evidence, the influence of sin on relationship with God and the fact that it can be forgiven, are further developed in later theological literature, especially in the Aramaic texts from Qumran. Tobit's song of praise[23] emphasizes that, while God punishes sin, he has mercy on his people dispersed among the nations. Similarly, in Nabonidus's prayer, *ḥṭ'* denotes his sins forgiven through the mediation of a Jewish soothsayer.[24]

The word *ḥṭ'* can also be employed in parallelism with *ḥwb* "debt" (→ IV): 4Q534 1 2+2:16 with an unclear relationship and 4Q537 6:1 probably in the context of a divine punishment, Isaac's speech concerning priestly purity in the Levi document alongside *ṭwm'h* "impurity."[25] Finally, *ḥṭ'* serves in 11Q10 (11QtgJob) for two different Hebrew lexemes: in 18:4 (Job 31:11) for *'wn*, in 22:3 (Job 33:9) and 24:1 (Job 34:6) for *pš'* 38:2f. (Job 42:10) does not correspond to MT, but to LXX.[26]

The alternative nominal form *ḥṭy* /ḥaṭāy/ is also employed with the same meaning as *ḥṭ'* /ḥeṭē/. It occurs in Dnl. 4:24 in parallel with the quite obviously semantic equivalent plural of *'wyh* /'awāyā/ "to offend" for the sins of Nebuchadnezzar, which he can erase, however, through righteousness and benevolence. The two terms also appear in the same context in 11Q10 26:1,2 (Job 35:6,8),[27] in 24:1 (Job 34:7) as a glossing supplement for *ḥṭy'* alone in MT (probably a sg. in the determined state).

Palmyrene uses *ḥṭy* for "punishment": in *PAT* 0991.13 with *ḥwb* (→ IV) for owing a penalty; similarly in a fragment of a religious law in *PAT* 1981.6, although in an unclear context.

Syriac theological literature knows a variety of additional nominal formations for the verbal concept and the *nomen agentis* "sinner."[28]

The noun *'wl* /'ōl/ "wrong, crime" cannot be clearly distinguished semantically from *ḥṭ'* and *ḥṭy*, on the one hand, and from *'wyh*, on the other. It probably derives from an older

---

21. *TADAE* C1.1,128; uncertain, in contrast, is the emendation at the beginning of l. 141, which preserves only the ending.

22. Causative stem of → *'dī*; *TADAE* C1.1,50.

23. 4Q196 17 1:15 (Tob. 13:5), the context can be reconstructed with the help of parallel versions.

24. 4Q242 1-3:4. The precise syntactical relationship between *ḥṭ'y* "my sin" and the subsequent verb → *šbq* "he ceased" is not entirely clear, however; cf. H. Gzella, "*šbq*," *ThWQ* III, 834-35.

25. *ALD*, 14,9f.

26. *DJD*, XXIII (1998), 171.

27. *'wyh* in l. 1, simultaneously, the only certain instance from Qumran, for Hebrew *pš'*, *ḥṭy* then for *rš'*.

28. *LexSyr*, 227.

Semitic verbal root *'ūl* "to diverge" and occurs in a few texts from Qumran, usually in apocalyptic passages and for a general state of sinfulness[29] that exceeds the forgiveable guilt of the individual designated by forms of the root *ḥṭī*: 4Q204 1 5:3 (1 En. 10:16) for the wrong[30] that the Watchers and their children have caused since primeval times, but that will be eradicated with their judgment; similarly in 4Q537 1+2+3:2 in parallelism with *šqr* "lie" for the unrighteousness in the ruined world;[31] and in 11Q10 22:4 (Job 33:10) in the plural for the Hebrew *tnw'wt* "avoidance." In contrast, *'wl* in 1QapGen 6:1 may refer to the primary noun /'ūl/ "embryo," which is unrelated to the verbal root *'ūl*.[32] Admittedly, the preserved context permits both possibilities.

IV. "Guilt" and Its Derivatives. In contrast to the ethical term *ḥṭī*, the root *ḥūb* "to owe" was originally a legal term. As such, it is attested beginning with Imperial Aramaic, but at Qumran also overlaps with the semantic spectrum of *ḥṭī*.

Private contracts employ the verb with the price as the direct and the creditor as the indirect object[33] or with the addition "and I will give you,"[34] synonymous with the adjective in the nominal clause (see below); similarly in contracts from the Dead Sea,[35] where the ithpael(?) participle also denotes "liable,"[36] and Palmyra.[37] It occurs in the pael probably in the meaning "to obligate" in a court transcript from Saqqara[38] and for "to condemn" in 11Q10 21:5 (Job 32:13, for *ndp*) and 34:4 (40:8, for *rš'*).

Of the noun *ḥwb* /ḥōb/ "obligation," the masculine is first attested,[39] at Qumran also for "debt";[40] after Qumran also the synonymous feminine.[41]

The adjective *ḥyb* /ḥayyāb/ "culpable, obligated" is also attested since the Achaemenid period as a technical legal and administrative term; it can be more specifically defined by an infinitive or another noun.[42] The letters from the Bactrian provincial archive use it of a subordinate official obligated to execute the orders of his superior,[43] and for subjects who owe taxes.[44] In a marriage contract from Elephantine[45] and

---

29. Cf. Maier regarding the "demonization of the world and history."
30. In the Greek text: ἀδικία.
31. So also in the expansion *šbyly 'wlh* "paths of wrong" in 1 En. 91:19 according to *ATTM*, 246.
32. *ATTM*, 2, 92. Regarding this word, cf. *GesB*, 1447 with bibliography; contra J. Fitzmyer, *The Genesis Apocryphon. BietOr* 18/B (^{3}2004), 145: "iniquity."
33. *TADAE* B3.6,14; 4.4,15f.
34. *TADAE* B3.5,14f.; 3.11,10f.13f.; 3.12,29f.; 3.13,6.
35. nV 2:15 and 3:44 in *ATTM*, 2.
36. *ATTM*, 2, nV 4:14.
37. *PAT* 0991.13; → III; 2760.2.
38. *TADAE* B8.6,10; reading and context uncertain.
39. *TADAE* B1.1,15.19; 4.7,5; Dušek, 1,10.
40. 4Q534 1 2+2:16; 4Q537 6:1, both alongside *ḥṭ'*; 4Q550 5+5a:2.
41. 4Q213 4:3; 4Q534 7:3: *ḥwbt lmtt* "death penalty"; 4Q536 2 2:12; nV 18:70: a specific sum.
42. *mks*: "taxable"; see below. *qṭlh*: "subject to the death penalty," xyRH l. 3, *ATTM*, 361.
43. Naveh and Shaked A6:4,7,8.
44. A1:2,11,12, in this case, camel drivers.
45. *TADAE* B3.8,42.

the Samaria papyri,[46] it denotes the obligation of a signatory under private law, as it does probably also in a fragment of a private document form the Dead Sea.[47] The Palmyrene tax table uses it for "taxable," a continuation of Imperial Aramaic legal terminology.[48]

At Qumran, the adjective was then used in the ethico-religious meaning "sinful" and in relation to the last judgment, for example in the Testament of Qahat of the "guilt of all sinners in eternity" (*ḥwbt kwl ḥyby ʿlmyn*), which the just will witness[49] in the last judgment.[50] A few instances are fragmentary; *wlʾ thwh ḥy[b* "and you will not be liable" in 4Q541 6:2 (Levi Apocryphon) may be said of the priest in the end time; 1 En. 10:14 is similar according to *ATTM*, 238.

This root also serves as a term for sin even later,[51] but the juridical nuance is well-attested primarily in Jewish Babylonian.[52]

V. "To Err" and Its Derivatives. Palmyrene Aramaic preserved the original meaning of the verbal root *ṭʿī* "to err," probably a by-form of the older **ṭʿū*.[53] In the tax table there,[54] it denotes the writing mistakes of a tax collector with the related abstract /ṭaʿū/ as an internal object. Comparable may be *lṭʿʾ ʿlyhwn* "he will forget her" in the curse formula of a puzzling post-Achaemenid building inscription form Assur.[55]

The Aramaic from Qumran employs the root for deviating[56] from the right path and walking *bʾrḥt ṭʿw* "on paths of error,"[57] the feminine G-stem particle for the idolatrous small livestock in Enoch's animal vision,[58] and similarly, the abstract for idols.[59]

Later, Jewish Babylonian attests the root well, also in the causative stem "to lead astray."[60]

Gzella

46. Dušek no. 1.9; 2.7; 6.9.

47. XḤev/Ṣe 23:7.

48. *PAT* 0259 i.4, followed here by *mksʾ* "with reference to taxes"; and in 2.108,113,119,146; in ll. 108,133 *mks lʾ* "not taxable" precedes, in ll. 199f. the amount of the tax *dnr* "one denar" follows and in l. 146 *mksʾ* precedes.

49. → *ḥzī*.

50. 4Q542 1 2:6.

51. *DJPA*, 189.

52. *DJBA*, 433f.

53. So Hebrew *ṭʿī*, the Aramaic form in the causative-stem also appears as a loanword in Ezk. 13:10.

54. *PAT* 0259 ii.99f.

55. A11b.3.

56. 4Q245 2:3; 4Q541 9 1:7.

57. 4Q537 5:2.

58. 4Q204 4:7f. (1 En. 89:35).

59. 4Q244 12:2.

60. *DJBA*, 509f.

חיי *ḥyī*; חי *ḥy* /ḥayy/; חיין *ḥyyn* /ḥayyīn/; חיוה *ḥywh* /ḥaywā/

I. Lexical Field and Constructions. II. Verb "to Live." III. Adjective "Alive." 1. General Usage. 2. Religious Usage. IV. Noun "Life." 1. Temporal Usage. 2. As a Quality. V. Noun "Animal."

I. Lexical Field and Constructions. The West Semitic languages[1] employ the root *ḥyī* primarily to denote creaturely life as the state of a breathing, moving body in opposition to the dead; in reference to God, it numbers among God's essential characteristics. In order to avoid forms with only one root consonant, the middle radical appears here as the glide /y/, not, as with the "hollow roots," as /ī/. Old and Imperial Aramaic conjugate the verb on the pattern of III *ī* roots; other dialects conjugate it, at least in the imperfect of the G- and causative-stems, as a *mediae geminatae*.

In the G-stem, *ḥyī* "to be or remain alive" is intransitive and usually stative, but can be supplemented with temporal or circumstantial phrase following *b-* or *l-*.[2] It sometimes occurs with the ingressive nuance "to recover, revive."[3] The subject is usually a person, rarely another living being; once in the meaning "to recover" also with *ḥrry'* "the ulcers" as subject.[4] For the present moment that denotes the current status of life, the adjective appears in a nominal clause.[5] The transitive causative-stem "to keep (someone) alive, to allow to live" takes a direct object.

More often than the verb, one encounters the adjective /ḥayy/ "alive,"[6] also substantivized, and the noun /ḥayyīn/ "life" as a *plurale tantum*;[7] it is utilized mostly for the lifetime or state of being. Further, the root also has the derived feminine /ḥaywā/ (later /ḥēwā/), either a collective for "animals" or for the individual "animal" in contrast to a human being. Various personal names already attested in the first millennium B.C.E., e.g.,

---

M. M. Bravmann, "North-Semitic *ḥajjīm/n* "Life" in the Light of Arabic," *Mus* 83 (1970) 551-57; K. Deller, "Zum *ana balāṭ*-Formular einiger assyrischer Votivinschriften," *OrAnt* 22 (1983) 13-24; K. Dijkstra, *Life and Loyalty: A Study in the Socio-Religious Culture of Syria and Mesopotamia in the Graeco-Roman Period Based on Epigraphical Evidence. RGRW 128* (1995); I. Eph'al and J. Naveh, *Aramaic Ostraca of the Fourth Century BC from Idumaea* (Jerusalem, 1996); G. Gerleman, "חיה *ḥyh* to live," *TLOT*, 411-17; H. Gzella, "Das Aramäische in den römischen Ostprovinzen: Sprachsituationen in Arabien, Syrien, und Mesopotamien zur Kaiserzeit," *BiOr* 63 (2006) 15-39; A. Lemaire, *Nouvelles inscriptions araméennes d'Idumée*, 2 vols. (Paris, 1996-2002); P. Riede, "Nochmal: Was ist 'Leben' im Alten Testament?" *ZAW* 119 (2007) 416-20; H. Ringgren, "חָיָה *chāyāh*," *TDOT*, IV, 324-44; A. Schofield, "*ḥyh*," *ThWQ*, I, 951-57 (Heb. only).

1. Akkadian employs instead the verb *balāṭu*.
2. E.g., *b/l'lm* "eternity"; in 1QapGen 19:20 *bṭlyky* "under your protection."
3. E.g., 1QapGen 20:22f.
4. 4Q197 4 1:15 (Tob. 6:9).
5. *TADAE* A2.5,9; → III.
6. Since the first half of the third century B.C.E. /ḥay/, *ATTM*, 120-22.
7. Perhaps derived from the plural of the adjective, cf. Bravmann.

Ḥayyay, Ḥayyā or Ḥayyān(ā), contain the term "life."[8] Contrary to an old folk etymology, however, the name Eve[9] should probably not be associated with *ḥyī* "to live," but with the primary noun /ḥewā/ "(female) serpent."[10]

II. Verb "to Live." The verb *ḥyī* first occurs unquestionably in the Old Aramaic of the seventh century B.C.E., namely in a decree from Syria with somewhat uncertain contents,[11] according to which those who do not hand over tax delinquents (or spies?) *l' yḥywn* "will not remain alive."[12] Imperial Aramaic offers additional instances. The G-stem for "to live" appears in a contract from Elephantine in reference to sustenance (*kl md'm zy yḥyh 'yš* "everything on which one can live").[13] It becomes clear here that *ḥyī* does not refer solely to purely vegetative existence, but to a life that satisfies certain minimal requirements. In the framework narrative of Aḥiqar, the causative stem "to keep alive" also appears[14] and contrasts directly there with → *qṭl* "to kill" (l. 51). Since Aḥiqar himself had allowed someone to live, he will also live.[15]

The court tales in the Aramaic book of Daniel regularly employ the imperative *malkā lᵉʿālᵉmīn ḥᵃyī* "O King, live forever!" as a wish in the address of subordinate officials to their lord (Dnl. 2:4; 3:9; 5:10; 6:7,22). This formulation with the addition of *ʿālᵉmīn* is unusual and diverges from the cry of obeisance "Long live the king!" (1 S. 10:24, etc.),[16] but is also associated with Achaemenid court ceremony in Neh. 2:3. Further, on Nebuchadnezzar's example, Dnl. 5:19 illustrates the king's power over life and death with the juxtaposition of the causative-stem of *ḥyī* "to let live" and *qṭl* "to kill" much as in the narrative framework of Aḥiqar (see above) and later, as part of the attribution *dy 'ḥyy wšyzb ʿmh* "to keep alive and delivered his people" in the Nabatean royal typology.[17]

Corresponding to the older usage, *ḥyī* also appears at Qumran for the survival of life-threatening situations, as in Abraham's dream vision of the threat of his destruction and deliverance (*w'ḥh bṭlyky wtplṭ npšy bdylyky* "and I will live through your protection and my life will be saved by you").[18] In 1 En. 5:1,[19] the participle *ḥy'* "living" and the complement *l(kwl) ʿlm* "for all eternity" denote eternal life as an attribute of God to which all of nature owes its persistence. Since, however, "life" is understood as healthy, vital life, the verb can also denote recovery from a life-threatening illness, including those

8. Cf. the commentary on *KAI* 24.1.

9. According to Gen 3:20, there the LXX renders ζωή "life."

10. *ATTM*, 574; for the discussion see A. S. Kapelrud, "חַוָּה *chavvāh*," *TDOT*, IV, 257-60.

11. *KAI* 317.8; V. Hug, *Altaramäische Grammatik der Texte des 7. und 6. Jh.s v.Chr. HSAO* 4 (1993), 4,15.

12. In the older Tell Fekheriye inscription, in contrast, *ḥyy* (*KAI* 309.7) may be the noun; → IV.2.

13. *TADAE* B4. 1,3.

14. *TADAE* C1.1,51.54.

15. Cf. l. 55.

16. Cf. H. Ringgren, 328.

17. Thus regularly in the date formula of Nabatean private contracts from the Dead Sea: *ATTM*, 2, nV 1:1,12; 2:1,5,18; 3:1,21,27.

18. 1QapGen 19:20.

19. 4Q201 1 2:11 and 4Q204 1 1:30; in the second fragment, *ḥy'* has apparently been transposed.

caused by supernatural forces: in 1QapGen 20:22,23 of the harsh distress that God sends the Pharaoh; in 4Q197 4 1:15 (Tob. 6:9) with *ḥrry'* "the ulcers" as subject, that heal by rubbing with fish bile (the immediately preceding context deals with a demon attack). Further, in an expansion of this nuance in the astronomical book of Enoch, the causative stem refers to the wind that heals (*rpī*) and revives the earth.[20]

In contrast, a few Palmyrene grave inscriptions employ *ḥyī* for the purely chronological lifespan.[21] This usage may reflect the influence of the noun in the same sense (→ IV.1). Finally, in Christian usage, the verb can refer to the resurrection of the dead, cf. *ḥyy b'lm* "Become alive again in eternity!" in a Christian-Palestinian grave inscription from the sixth century C.E.[22]

III. Adjective "Alive."

1. General Usage. Old Aramaic already employs the adjective *ḥy* /ḥay(y)/ "living" in the plural substantivized for "the living": according to the curse formula from a grave inscription form Nērab, the gods are to eradicate (*nsḥ*) "the place and the name from among the living" (*mn ḥyn*) of anyone who should remove the memorial and the sarcophagus.[23] Subsequently, this usage became even more frequent: in military diction, the Imperial Aramaic translation of the Behistun Inscription distinguishes formally between killing (*qṭl*) enemies and taking prisoners (*'ḥd*) alive (*ḥyn*).[24] More generally, (*kl*) *ḥyy'* "(all of) the living" can represent humanity as a whole.[25] Only rarely does it refer explicitly to animals.[26]

The regularly attested juxtaposition of life and death involving the verb appears in a private letter from Hermopolis in which the writer accuses the addressee of not inquiring after his well-being after a life-threatening snakebite: *hn ḥy 'nh whn mt 'nh* "whether I am alive or dead."[27] Furthermore, like the verb (→ II), the adjective can be used for "healthy."[28] The combination *myn ḥyn* means "flowing water."[29] Contrariwise, the figurative use as an attribute of *'dn* "contract" in a Sefire stele[30] is uncertain; according to this interpretation, nothing should be stricken from the agreements because they involve "living contracts," but the text *ḥy[n* has been emended.

---

20. 4Q210 1 2:2 (1 En. 76:4).
21. Cf. *PAT* 0716.5; 1830.4.
22. ccSA 21,2f. in *ATTM*, 404.
23. *KAI* 225.10.
24. *TADAE* C2.1 col V 5.11.17.23.34.43f., in each case with specific numbers.
25. Dnl. 2:30; 4:14; 4Q534 1 1:8.9; in 4Q530 2 2+6-12:19 once also in parallel with *bśr'*, → *bśr* IV.4; probably also in the fragments 4Q543 18:3 and 4Q580 1 1:14.
26. Thus probably in the ostracon fragment 58ccl; see H. Lozachmeur, *La collection Clermont-Ganneau*, vol. 1 (Paris, 2006), 227.
27. *TADAE* A2.5,9.
28. 4Q196 18:14 (Tob. 14:2).
29. 11Q18 10 1:1.
30. *KAI* 222 B 41; cf. J. A. Fitzmyer, *The Aramaic Inscriptions of Sefire*. *BietOr* 19/A (^{2}1995), 115.

2. Religious Usage. In religious speech, the predicate "living" pertains to God. This situation appears either in the weakened affirmational formula *ḥylyhh* "As Yaho lives!" in the near-colloquial tone of a private letter from Elephantine[31] or in the full theological sense in Biblical Aramaic, especially in hymnic predication. There, God is named by a substantivized *ḥy ʿlmʾ* "he, who lives eternally," in parallelism with *ʿlyʾ* "the eternal" (Dnl. 4:31); at the same time, the *ʾlhʾ ḥyʾ* "living God" (Dnl. 6:21,27) demonstrates himself to be *qym lʿlmyn* "enduring in eternity" (6:27) and efficacious as the reliable protector of his servants in danger of their lives (as in the lions' den). Whoever reveres him shares in his life. This combination occurs even later in apotropaic Palestinian-Aramaic amulets.[32]

IV. Noun "Life." The noun *ḥyn* /ḥayyīn/, identical with the plural of *ḥy*, denotes the abstract concept of "living." It is used alongside general expressions[33] for the lifespan or the state of being alive.

1. Temporal Usage. As a temporal time, it occurs beginning with Imperial Aramaic either with the preposition *b-* "in the lifetime of," as often in contracts,[34] but also elsewhere;[35] with *ʾryk*/*ʾrkh* "long/length" for a long,[36] yet temporally limited life (Dnl. 7:12, for the disempowered but not yet destroyed apocalyptic being); or with *kl ywmy* (alternative: *šny*) *ḥyy* "all the days (years) of my life" as an expression of totality.[37]

2. As a Quality. Old and Imperial Aramaic already attest the qualitative nuance of *ḥyn* as "well-being." It corresponds to the shading "to be vital/healthy" of the verb and the adjective (see above). With → *šlm*, *ḥyn* appears in epistolary formulas as the object of *šlḥ* "to send";[38] the combination *ʿl* (rarely *l-*) *ḥyy* "for the life of" is extremely frequent, however, in numerous inscriptions; an analogue appears in reference to the sacrifices in the new Jerusalem temple (Ezr. 6:10). This formula, probably Mesopotamian in origin,[39] occurs in Old Aramaic,[40] in Imperial Aramaic,[41] and then very often in Palmyrene, Old Syriac and Hatrene, less often in Nabatean.[42] Greek and Latin imitate it with ὑπὲρ

31. *TADAE* D7. 16,3.7; *ḥy ʾlhʾ* for *ḥy ʾl* in 11Q10 10:8 (Job 27:2); in contrast, with the name of a person in a first century B.C.E. grave inscription from Jerusalem, I 1,4 in *ATTM*, 329.
32. Cf. yyOX 1,5, *ATTM*, 367; ggAR 1,4, *ATTM.E*, 250.
33. 4Q196 14 1:6 (Tob. 6:15); 4Q197 2:1 (Tob. 4:21).
34. *TADAE* B2.3,3.8; 3.6, 4; 3.10,2; 3.11,13.13; nV 7:24,27 in *ATTM*, 2, 219; sometimes in parallelism with *bmwty* "at my death" for a grant beyond death; in the date of the Nabatean contract nV 2:1 with the preposition *ʿl*, *ATTM*, 2, 208.
35. 4Q196 6:5 (Tob. 3:10); *PAT* 0468.6.
36. *TADAE* A4.7,3, as a wish in the letter to a superior.
37. *ATTM*, nV 7:15,52; 4Q537 1+2+3:4.
38. *TADAE* A2.4,5; 2.7,1; D7.21,2.
39. Deller.
40. *KAI* 309.7.
41. *KAI* 229.4.
42. *DNSI*, 365-367; Gzella.

σωτηρίας[43] /ὑγιείας[44] or *pro salute*.[45] The biblical concept of the *spr ḥyn* "book of life"[46] also appears in late inscriptions.[47]

V. Noun "Animal." The feminine noun *ḥywh* /ḥaywā/ (/ḥēwā/) "animals, animal" first occurs with certainty in Imperial Aramaic. In ostraca from Idumea,[48] which apparently contain notes concerning the receipt of fees, the plural as a generic term encompasses the corresponding quantities of various animals such as goats, lambs, and ewes.

As a collective singular "animal" for nonhuman living beings, in contrast, *ḥywh* occurs very frequently in the book of Daniel, often in the combination *ḥywt br'* "the animals of the field": either explicitly as part of the all-encompassing dominion of the king (Dnl. 2:38) or in Nebuchadnezzar's dream for the wild animals that find protection and dwelling outside human civilization in the shadow of the tree of life as an image for the king (4:9,18,20,22,29). Daniel 4:13 juxtaposes "animal heart" and "human heart";[49] the exchange of the animal heart for a human heart symbolizes the king's devolution to animality during his cleansing penance at the end of which he attained recognition of God. Meanwhile, in the singular or plural, it denotes the chimera of the vision in Dnl. 7[50] as specific animals (pl. in Dnl. 7:3,7,12,17; sg. in 7:5,6,7,11,19,23). The repeated use of this word emphasizes their nonhumanity and monstrosity.

The Aramaic texts from Qumran utilize the word both as a generic term in distinction from human beings and together with human beings for all living beings: the determined state in the plural "the animals" as an expression of totality[51] and the combination, known from Daniel, *ḥywt br'* "the animals of the field" as a collective singular;[52] if the reading *ḥ[yw]t 'r'[h* in 4Q201 1 3:20 (1 En. 7:5) is correct, "animals of the earth" would probably be a synonym. In 4Q542 2:7, *b'nwš' wbḥy[wt* "the people and animals" may appear in explicit parallelism according to the emendation in *ATTM*, 2, 117; other editors read a form of the noun or adjective here, however. The context is entirely obscure, but the juxtaposition of human beings and animals suits the otherwise known usage nonetheless, while the association of "human beings" and "life" seems rather unusual.

Gzella

43. *PAT* 0247.
44. *PAT* 0344.
45. Dijkstra, 245-86.
46. Ringgren, 340f.
47. ggJR 1.5, *ATTM*, 388.
48. Eph'al and Naveh, 36, no. 46, l. 3; Lemaire, II, 129, l. 2.
49. → *lbb*.
50. → *gp* II.
51. 1QapGen 6:26, perhaps in connection with the destruction of creation by the giants.
52. 1QapGen 13:8, in a dream vision of Noah with obscure content; similarly probably also in an apocalyptic context in 6Q14 1:6.

חיל *ḥyl* /ḥayl/; חיל *ḥyl*

I. Lexical Field and Grammatical Constructions. II. In General Usage, "Power." III. In Military Usage, "Troop, Army." IV. Denominal Verb "to Strengthen."

I. Lexical Field and Grammatical Constructions. Like the findings in other Semitic languages, the masculine primary noun /ḥayl/ (later /ḥēl/) in Aramaic also initially denotes generally "power," namely male power. As an *abstractum pro concreto*, however, it often refers to "army" (perhaps including other forms of organized forces apart from a military band), in Elephantine also to a "garrison," which divides, in turn, into various smaller units (/dagl/). Later, in rabbinic discussion in West Aramaic texts, the nuance "argument, significance" also sometimes occurs.[1]

In addition, the noun /ḥayl/ also finds usage with *b-* as an adverbial modifier "powerful," as often in the book of Daniel (3:4; 4:11; 5:7), and sometimes in a genitive combination with the preceding noun in the construct state for the attribute "strong." In this usage, it differs from the semantic spectrum of the typical Aramaic verbal root → *tqp* "to be strong" and its related adjective /taqqīp/. In contrast, the analogous expression with *b-* and the noun /toqp/ tends to have a more instrumental connotation in the sense of "by force" (Dnl. 4:27) or "with violence,"[2] but /ḥayl/ can also have this connotation (cf. Ezr. 4:23). In contrast to /ḥayl/, which apparently emphasizes primarily physical power, /toqp/ and /taqqīp/ also occur, at least at Qumran, regularly for divine beings, natural forces, and official royal authority.[3]

The verb *ḥyl* "to strengthen" in the D-stem, at first still quite rare, derives from the noun.

II. In General Usage, "Power." Older Aramaic attests the likely original usage of *ḥyl* /ḥayl/ for "power" only rather rarely. A wisdom saying of Aḥiqar,[4] destroyed at the beginning of the line, employs the word in parallelism with the admonition not to become arrogant; it is unclear, however, whether it has the nuance "wealth" common in Biblical Hebrew.[5] Biblical Aramaic frequently employs *bḥyl* adverbially: in Daniel with the verb → *qrī* for "to cry loudly" in a royal or divine command proclaimed ceremoniously by a herald (Dnl. 3:4),[6] an angel (4:11) or, in a moment of extreme ex-

---

H. Eising, "חַיִל *chayil*," *TDOT*, IV, 348-55; B. Gregory, "*ḥyl*," *ThWQ*, I, 957-60; J. Naveh and S. Shaked, *Aramaic Documents from Ancient Bactria (Fourth Century B.C.E.)* (London, 2012); B. Porten, *Archives from Elephantine* (Berkeley, 1968).

1. *DJPA*, 199.
2. 1QapGen 20:14.
3. See the discussion of individual passages in H. Gzella, "*tqp*," *ThWQ*, III, 1158-62.
4. *TADAE* C1.1,137.
5. So *DNSI*, 370 and the translation in *TADAE*; on the Heb., cf. H. Eising, 352f.; 11Q10 4:6 has → *nksyn* in this sense.
6. Regarding the incorrect pointing as a Heb. pausal form, see *BLA* §23d.

citement, by the king himself (5:7); also once in Ezr. 4:23 in the combination *bᵉʾæḏrāʿ wᵉḥāyil* "with compulsion and force."[7] A similar combination occurs later as *btqwp ḥyl drʿy* "with the power of the strength of my arm" in the Book of Giants;[8] *tqwp* also appears alongside *ḥyl* in 4Q553 8 2:2,[9] but in an obscure context. The word itself has neither positive nor negative connotations: in 11Q10 16:8 (Job 30:18) *ḥyl* translates Hebrew *kḥ* with the nuance of a violent grip; in 33:3 (Job 39:21) in reference to the power of a horse that goes joyously into battle.

III. In Military Usage, "Troop, Army." Contrariwise, *ḥyl* /ḥayl/ is regularly attested with the meaning "army" since the Old Aramaic period. These cases often involve an explicit military context. The noun occurs first for the military assistance promised in the Sefire state treaties,[10] then in the letter of a prince from Palestine to the pharaoh with a request for auxiliary forces.[11] The bulk of Achaemenid occurrences appear in the war reports in the Behistun Inscription,[12] where this word appears with particular frequency.

In this regard, *ḥyl* can apparently designate a broad spectrum of military units of various sizes. In the Imperial Aramaic framework of Aḥiqar it even seems to refer to the total executive authority of the Assyrian king—and not just the army in the more restricted sense—that depends on the counsel of the high official Aḥiqar.[13]

Commercial texts from Elephantine employ it, however, in lists of grain allotments to certain garrisons[14] and as a collective singular for the individuals subsequently listed by name as members of the Jewish at Elephantine—both men and women—in the record of a collection for the temple of Yaho (*znh šmht ḥylʾ yhwdyʾ* "these are the names of the Jewish garrison"),[15] in the address of a letter,[16] or generally.[17] Consequently, *rb ḥyl* here means "garrison commander,"[18] in Palmyrene "military leader, commander," and corresponding to the Greek στρατηλάτης.[19] According to the Aramaic texts from Achaemenid Egypt, the *prtrk* "commander-in-chief"[20] was superior to the *rb ḥyl*.[21]

Apparently, then, *ḥyl* can denote both the soldiers of the garrison and their families in the texts from Elephantine and, therefore, includes the women in the list

7. Lit. "with arm and power" (→ *yd* II.3); also erroneously pointed as a pausal form.
8. 4Q531 22:3.
9. Vision of the four trees, reading following *ATTM*, 2, 145.
10. *KAI* 222 B 31f.
11. *TADAE* A1.1, 7.
12. *TADAE* C2.1.
13. *TADAE* C1.1,55.61; for references to other interpretations, see *DNSI*, 370.
14. *TADAE* C3.14,32.38; probably also in a fragmentary context in 3.5,7.
15. *TADAE* C3.15,1.
16. *TADAE* A4.1,1.10; 4.2,1.
17. *TADAE* 4.5,7.20.
18. *TADAE* A4.7,7; 3.1,5, second letter; 4.3,3; D17.1,2.
19. *PAT* 0293.2.
20. From Old Persian *frataraka*.
21. Cf. *TADAE* A4.7,5-8.

TADAE C3.15. The noun *dgl* /dagl/ "army division" (literally "standard"), however, designates the units constituting the subdivisions of a garrison and to which the respective families also belong.[22] More information concerning the terminology and the sociohistorical background appears in Porten,[23] but the military practices of the Achaemenid period and the specific military tasks of the garrison at Elephantine in particular (probably, primarily guarding the commercial route between Egypt and Nubia) remain little known.

Nevertheless, disregarding the many instances in a clearly military context, it is not certain whether *ḥyl* can also refer to hierarchically structured units other than the army or some other armed band.[24] This could be the case nonetheless in a few Imperial Aramaic letters of satraps from Egypt and Bactria that order the deployment of a *ḥyl* for civil purposes[25] or confirm the command authority of one official over another and that the *ḥyl* falls under his command[26] to guard the satrap's property.[27] The contexts of a few additional instances[28] remain unclear.

In Biblical Aramaic, *ḥyl* stands once for the royal army (Dnl. 3:20), *ḥyl šmy'*; once for the mythical image of the host of heaven under God's command (Dnl. 4:32); this probably originally referred to the stars (cf. Jgs. 5:20) and later to the angels. In 11Q10 15:3 (Job 29:25) *ḥyl* translates Hebrew *gdwd* "host, band, troop." A few other instances from Qumran are fragmentary and uncertain.

IV. Denominal Verb "to Strengthen." The denominal verb *ḥyl* "to strengthen" in the D-stem occurs in older Aramaic at the most in 1QapGen 8:28 according to *ATTM*, 2, 93 (*ḥylt* "I strengthened"), but the reading of these few letters with no more precise context remains controversial.[29] Undoubted examples only occur later in West[30] and East Aramaic,[31] including the corresponding t-stem for the middle "to grow stronger" and the passive "to be strengthened." Here, too, however, it occurs only rarely. In addition, Jewish Babylonian knows a related adjective *ḥyl* "strong."[32]

Gzella

---

22. Occurrences and literature in *DNSI*, 240f.
23. Pp. 28-61.
24. Such as the Egyptian *'m ḥyl' 'ḥrnn* "and other troops," which destroyed the temple at Elephantine: *TADAE* A4.7,8; in fact, they came *'m tlyhm* "with their weapons" (l. 8), but are not all described explicitly as soldiers.
25. A2,5.6 in Naveh and Shaked, but the exact context is unclear.
26. *lyd*, literally, "in the hand," → *yd*.
27. *TADAE* A6.8,1f.
28. E.g., *TADAE* C1.2,4.
29. Cf. D. A. Machiela, *The Dead Sea Genesis Apocryphon. STDJ* 79 (2009), 50, who thinks that he recognizes *'zlt* "I went" instead (l. 35).
30. *DJPA*, 198b.
31. *DJBA*, 455a; *LexSyr*, 230; *MdD*, 119.
32. *DJBA*, 455a.

חכם *ḥkm*; חכים *ḥkym* /ḥakkīm/; חכמה *ḥkmh* /ḥokmā/; ערם *ʿrm*; ערמן *ʿrmn* /ʿormān/; ערימו *ʿrymw* /ʿarīmū/; סכל *skl* /sakal/

I. Lexical Field and Grammatical Constructions. II. Verb "to Know." III. Adjective "Wise." 1. As an Attribute. 2. Substantivized "Expert." IV. Noun "Wisdom." V. Root "to Be Wise" and Derivatives. VI. Noun "Fool."

I. Lexical Field and Grammatical Constructions. Originally, the West Semitic root *ḥkm* meant "to know," but older Aramaic did not use it as a verb, replacing it in this function with → *ydʿ* "to know." The D-stem with the meaning "to teach" occurs, however, in isolation in Imperial Aramaic,[1] then the G-stem "to know, recognize" with the corresponding t-stem for the passive "to be recognized" in Aramaic literary languages from late antiquity.[2] Especially West Aramaic, probably under biblical influence, also attests the meaning "to have an intimate relationship with someone"; East Aramaic has the causative stem "to make/become wise."

Frequent already since Imperial Aramaic at the latest, however, is the adjective /ḥakkīm/ "expert, wise." Often employed as a substantive, it regularly denotes someone with access to rare specialized knowledge in a specific field, e.g., in manticism and dream interpretation. The feminine noun /ḥokmā/ also referred first to wisdom based on prudence and experience, but transcended this usage in the Aramaic of the book of Daniel and the texts from Qumran when employed theologically of the wisdom God grants to human beings. In Qumran, it overlaps semantically with the less frequent derivatives of the root *ʿrm* "to be clever." The antonym consists of the masculine /sakal/ "fool, sinner."

II. Verb "to Know." In Imperial Aramaic, the D-stem of *ḥkm* with the meaning "to teach (someone something)" in the framing narrative of Aḥiqar is constructed with a simple or a dual object.[3] Because of its relation to the firm attribute of Aḥiqar as "wise" (→ III) and the noteworthy frequency of the noun "wisdom" (→ IV), this rare verb could serve to underscore the function of this root in this text virtually as a leitmotif. Normally, meanwhile, the D-stem of → *ʾlp*, constructed in the same fashion, stands for "to teach" in Aramaic.[4] In contrast, the form of the D-stem *ḥkmnh* "he teaches us" in 11Q10 26:7

T. Elgvin, "*ḥkm*," *ThWQ*, I, 964-72; H. Gzella, *A Cultural History of Aramaic: From the Beginnings to the Advent of Islam. HO* 111 (2015); K. Koch, *Daniel 1–4. BK* XXII/1 (2005), 153-55; H.-P. Müller and M. Krause, "חָכַם *chākham*," *TDOT*, IV, 364-85; M. Sæbø, "חכם *ḥkm* to Be Wise," *TLOT*, 418-24; M. Weigl, *Die aramäischen Achikar-Sprüche aus Elephantine und die alttestamentliche Weisheitsliteratur. BZAW* 399 (2010).

1. → *ʾlp* in this sense is substantially more frequent in the older Aramaic languages.
2. *DJPA*, 200f.; *DJBA*, 460a; *LexSyr*, 230.
3. *TADAE* C1.1,1, where *l-* marks the animate and definite personal object; in ll. 9 and 10 with a personal pronominal suffix, but in a mangled context.
4. See also H. Gzella, "*ʾlp*," *ThWQ*, I, 195-97.

(Job 35:11) presumably imitates the same word in the Hebrew text, which in this passage also has the rare D-stem for this root.

III. Adjective "Wise."

1. As an Attribute. The adjective *ḥkym* /ḥakkīm/ "wise" functions both attributively and substantivally, "wise one, expert." In the first function, it is a regular epithet of the *spr ḥkym* "wise scribe" Aḥiqar, a high official (→ *y'ṭ* "councilor") at the Assyrian court in the novelistic depiction of his fall as the result of slander and his subsequent rehabilitation.[5] The Imperial Aramaic novel was combined with pre-Imperial Aramaic wisdom sayings, animal fables, and other manifestations of accumulated life experience and then attributed to the main character, Aḥiqar. In the course of time, the material entered the cultural memory of the ancient Near East. To be sure, it does not describe the precise character of Aḥiqar's wisdom, but he quite likely embodies the ideal of a cultured court official—something like a mandarin—as the Aramaic-speaking scribes with careers in imperial administration in Assyrian and Babylonian times imagined it.[6] It would have included literary education, advanced administration, statecraft, and perhaps a certain spiritual or personal demeanor.

An inscription from Arebsun in Cappadocia in the Imperial Aramaic tradition, but from the post-Achaemenid period, employs *ḥkym* together with *špyr* "beautiful" in praise of a woman, much like the substantive in 1QapGen 20:7 (→ IV): *'nt 'ḥty śgy' ḥkym wšpyr' 'nt mn 'lhn* "you, my sister, are very wise and more beautiful than goddesses."[7]

2. Substantivized "Expert." Otherwise, the substantival usage dominates. The Deir 'Allā wall inscription (circa 800 B.C.E.) already attests it.[8] This inscription presumably preserves a piece of Canaanite religious literature in Aramaic phonology and morphology.[9] Because of a large lacuna in the preceding text, the context is not entirely clear, but it may involve an example of the reversal of natural conditions, illustrated by different examples in which one who has no right to do so (thus, presumably a fool) derides the wise (*lḥkmn yqḥk*). An additional possibly pre-Imperial Aramaic instance appears in one of the sayings of Aḥiqar in the context of an oral speech,[10] but the fragmentaty context permits no conclusions as to whether *ḥkym* in *ḥkym mmll* is an adjective or a substantive.

The court tales of the book of Daniel frequently employ a substantivized *ḥkym* "wise one" in the plural to designate the experts of the Babylonian king (Dnl. 2:12,13,14,18,21,24,27,48; 4:3,15; 5:7,8,15). The repeated parallelism with various other, more specific (although no longer precisely differentiated as in their original usage) professional designations indicates that they all involve experts in the realm of dream inter-

5. *TADAE* C1.1,1.12.28.35.42.

6. See Gzella, 150-53.

7. *KAI* 264.5; the incongruence of the masculine adjective *ḥkym* and the feminine substantive here and in other Aramaic inscriptions from Asia Minor may have arisen through the substrate influence of the vernacular; cf. Gzella, 197.

8. *KAI* 312.11.

9. This is at least the sole linguistically and historically satisfying explanation, see Gzella, 87-91.

10. *TADAE* C1.1,114.

pretation and prognostication, for which *ḥkymyn* functions here as the umbrella term (Dnl. 2:27; 4:3f.; 5:7,15; as apparently does *kśdyn* "Chaldeans" at the conclusion of a comparable list in 2:2 in reference to native specialists): *ʾšpyn* "incantation priests," *ḥrṭmyn* "oracle priests,"[11] and *gzryn* "extispicy priests."[12] Thus, the professional specialized knowledge of the "wise one" in a substantivized function differs from the comprehensive educational ideal, for which stands—at least in Aḥiqar's case—the adjective "wise." In Daniel, however, *ḥkym* has a much more narrowly circumscribed meaning than its Hebrew counterpart *ḥkm*, which also includes scribes and officials (cf. Jer. 18:18; Est. 1:13).

Indeed, the literary portrayal in Dnl. 2–5 emphasizes the tense relationship that Daniel and his friends have with this group. On the one hand, they enjoyed the same education (Dnl. 1:4), were included among the *šʾr ḥkymy bbl* "rest of the wise men in Babylon" (Dnl. 2:18), and, at first, were supposed to be killed together with them (2:12-14). On the other hand, the juxtaposition of the completely overwhelmed members of the guild with the Jewish exiles successful on their home territory as recipients of divine revelation in Dnl. 2 and 5 emphasizes the different scope of limited worldly expertise and unlimited divine wisdom (2:27). Divine secrets, and thus the world and history as they truly are, open themselves only to those who serve the true God. At the same time, they do not constitute a contrast to natural, scientific knowledge, for even the wise have their wisdom ultimately from God. Thus, Daniel's hymn of thanksgiving in Dnl. 2:21 can parallel *ḥkmtʾ* "the wisdom" (→ IV) and *lḥkymyn* "to the wise" as direct and indirect objects of *yhb* "he gives" with *mndʿʾ* "perception" and *ydʿy bynh* "to those who perceive insight."[13] Ultimately, although not from the inner circle of Babylonian specialists, Daniel became their *sgn* "chief" (Dnl. 2:48; 5:11).

Contrariwise, *ḥkym* occurs only rarely in the preserved Aramaic texts from Qumran. The use as an umbrella term for experts at the Egyptian royal court in 1QapGen 20:19f., also under the influence of *ʾsyn* "physicians," who could not heal the pharaoh, corresponds to the evidence in the book of Daniel (see above). In the Testament of Amram, the wise and the fool also constitute ethical opposites.[14] Unclear are the contexts of *ḥ]kmt ʾnš wkwl ḥkym[yn* "wisdom of men and (of) all the wise"[15] and of a few other fragmentary passages, some[16] in apocalyptic passages. A possible emended instance as an attribute of the scribe Enoch[17] is paleographically dubious; *ATTM*, 246 reads *b]pwm* "in the mouth" instead of *[wḥ]kym* at the beginning of the line.

Later rabbinic texts regularly employ *ḥkym* for "scholar."[18]

IV. Noun "Wisdom." At first, the noun *ḥkmh* /ḥokmā/ can denote wisdom rooted in experience generally,[19] but the three fragmentary instances in the sayings of Aḥiqar permit no

11. → *ʾšp*; Koch, 143f.
12. → *gzr*.
13. → *ydʿ*.
14. 4Q548 1 2-2:12; → VI.
15. 4Q536 2 1+3:5, in the speech to a fallen angel.
16. Such as 4Q541 2 2:6.
17. 4Q212 1 2:23 (1 En. 92:1).
18. *DJPA*, 200; *DJBA*, 459.
19. Political in *KAI* 215.11.

greater precision.[20] In the narrative framework, Aḥiqar remarks that he trained his adoptive son as his successor and has communicated to him his wisdom and counsel (*ḥkmty wʿṭ[ty*).[21]

The court tales of the Aramaic book of Daniel, however, employ *ḥkmh* exclusively for the divinely inspired wisdom of Daniel (Dnl. 2:20,21,23,30; 5:11,14). It allows him to perceive the secrets of the course of the world and to surpass the *ḥkymyn*, the king's specialists (→ III). Ezra 7:25 combines the secular nuance with the religious since Ezra's installation of judges[22] should take place "according to the wisdom of his God" (*kḥkmt ʾlhk*).

This also establishes the foundation for the use of the word in the Aramaic texts from Qumran. The ethical connotation appears in the phrase *bḥzwn qwšṭʾ wḥkmtʾ* "in an appearance of uprightness and wisdom,"[23] as a component aspect of perfection in Sarah's song of praise[24] and as a characteristic of the priestly Messiah in 4Q541 9 1:2. Almost half of the instances appear in the Levi document, however: very often in the petition to God for wisdom,[25] then also in the concluding hymn to wisdom as the core of the divine commandments;[26] it will reveal all mysteries.[27] 11Q10 employs the same word for the Hebrew *bynh*[28] and *mzmh*.[29] In a significantly emended building inscription from Hatra, *ḥkmh* can also designate the wisdom of the builder.[30]

V. Root "to Be Wise" and Derivatives. Beginning in post-Achaemenid Aramaic, forms of the rarer root *ʿrm* "to be clever," also known from Hebrew, appear along with *ḥkm*. In 4Q534 1 1.6, it parallels the verb *ydʿ* "to know" in reference to Noah's wisdom and in the same context as the related feminine noun *ʿrmn* /ʿormōn/[31] "prudence" and *mlk* /melk/ "counsel" (so also in Dnl. 4:24) in the subsequent line. Additionally, at least 11Q10 13:1 (Job 28:20) attests the synonymous feminine abstract form *ʿrymw* /ʿarīmū/ for Hebrew *bynh* "insight." The few instances have positive connotations, but a clear semantic distinction from *ḥkm*—perhaps as natural common sense in contrast to expert knowledge[32]—cannot be determined on this limited foundation.

In later East Aramaic, the verb often has negative connotations of "to feign/feint."[33]

VI. Noun "Fool." The opposite of the wise one is the fool, designated in Aramaic by the masculine noun *skl* /sakal/. The derived verbal root *skl* in the t-stem (proba-

---

20. *TADAE* C1. 1,105.146.189; the last two emphasize the fact that one can also lose *ḥkmh*.
21. *TADAE* C1.1,19; → *yʿṭ*.
22. → *dyn* II.2.
23. 1QapGen 6:4, → *ḥzī* IV; similarly, 19:15.
24. 1QapGen 20:7; → II.
25. *ALD* 3,6; cf. 4Q543 2a-b:2.
26. *ALD* 13; cf. *DSSStE*, 56f.
27. 4Q534 1 1:8; cf. the eschatological opening of the "books of wisdom" in 4Q541 7:4.
28. 11Q10 30:2; 33:7.
29. 11Q10 37:4.
30. H272.2.
31. From an older /ʿormān/ via sporadic attenuation of a long vowel, see *ATTM*, 664.
32. Which suits the context of 4Q534 1 1.6 well.
33. *DJBA*, 882a, D-stem and Dt-stem; cf. *DJPA*, 419f. for the adjective and noun in West Aramaic.

bly the Dt-stem) means "to behave foolishly";[34] it first occurs in a pre-Achaemenid saying of Aḥiqar: *ʾl tstkl* "Do not act like a fool!"[35] Later, it also occurs in the G- and causative-stems.[36]

Post-Achaemenid Aramaic first definitively attests the noun "fool."[37] It also occurs with this original nuance in 4Q157 1 2:7 (Job 5:2), but, in the course of time, like the entire semantic field of foolishness in biblical wisdom literature, it took on the meaning "sinner." Thus, the Testament of Amram can employ the dualistic juxtaposition of *skl wrš*[*yʿ* "fool and evildoer" on the one hand, and [*ḥky*]*m wqšyṭ* "wise and true" on the other;[38] a similar situation also pertains in the speech to a fallen angel in 4Q536 2 2:11. With the same nuance, the hermit author of a Christian Palestinian letter to his abbot can employ it as a humble self-designation (eighth century C.E.).[39]

Gzella

34. Presumably not related to the homonymous root *skl* "to consider, deliberate," definitively attested only later, which corresponds to the Hebrew *śkl*.

35. *TADAE* C1.1,147. According to the likeliest interpretation reflecting the noun and later instances of the verb, other suggestions in *DNSI*, 785.

36. *DJPA*, 377b and *DJBA*, 810b, respectively.

37. The supposed instance in the Deir ʿAllā wall inscription should more likely be read *wkl*, cf. *KAI* 312.14.

38. 4Q548 1 2-2:12.

39. ccMI 1:2, *ATTM*, 403.

חלם *ḥlm*; חלם II *ḥlm*; חלם *ḥlm* /ḥelm/; הרהר *hrhr* /harhūr/

I. Etymology, Lexical Field, and Grammatical Constructions. II. Verb "to Dream." III. Noun "Dream." 1. Generally. 2. Dream Revelation. IV. Noun "Dream Images."

I. Etymology, Lexical Field, and Grammatical Constructions. From the West Semitic root *ḥlm* "to dream," the noun /ḥelm/ "dream"[1] is clearly significantly more productive in Aramaic than the verb. It appears regularly in the G-stem employed either absolutely or in a *figura etymologica* with the singular or plural of /ḥelm/ as an object.

J. Bergman, G. J. Botterweck, and M. Ottosson, "חָלַם *chālam*," *TDOT*, IV, 421-32; L. DiTommaso, "*ḥlm*," *ThWQ*, I, 988-93; F. Flannery-Dailey, *Jewish Dreams in the Hellenistic and Roman Eras*. *JSJSup* 90 (2004); J. M. Husser, *Dreams and Dream Narratives in the Biblical World* (Sheffield, 1999).

1. A *qiṭl* form in contrast to the Hebrew *ḥᵃlōm* "to dream" and the Arabic *ḥulm*.

There is no known etymological relationship with the homonymous verbal root *ḥlm* "to become powerful."[2] It is attested in Aramaic beginning at Qumran, namely in the Gt-stem meaning "to pluck up courage"[3] and in the causative stem for "to heal."[4] According to *ATTM*, 2, 93, 1QapGen 7:20 contains an additional specimen, but the supposed ʾ at the beginning of the word is paleographically uncertain so that it could also be a form of *ḥlm* "to dream."[5] It also has a Hebrew and an Arabic cognate with the same meaning.

The substantive /ḥelm/ "dream" can be employed both in a general sense for a "day-dream" arising from the subconscious or for a dream revelation produced externally, either directly or indirectly. For ancient dream interpretation, the two basic types constituted different categories.[6] It may be largely synonymous with the rare noun /harhūr/ "dream image," that belongs to the root *hrr* "to become agitated."

II. Verb "to Dream." Apart from a collection of mostly emended possibilities without immediate contexts in a significantly damaged Imperial Aramaic papyrus from Saqqara,[7] post-Achaemenid Aramaic first attests the verb *ḥlm* "to dream" with certainty. It occurs only rarely, however, even at Qumran, although many texts there deal with dreams and revelations. The two instances in 1QapGen 19:14,18 introduce the report of Abraham's symbolic dream (→ III.2) of the date palm and the cedar that warns him of the threat and, simultaneously, points to his deliverance by Sarah since he purports to be her brother and is spared for her sake. In both places, the verb *ḥlm* takes the noun from the same root in the absolute state of the singular as an internal object, "I dreamed a dream," as is also the case in a third of the instances in Hebrew.[8] If the dreams of several individuals are to be described, the internal object of the verb appears in the plural, as in the likewise symbolic dreams of the two giants Hahya and Uhya in a passage in the Book of Giants.[9]

Normally, however, the noun *ḥlm* appears with the verb *ḥzī* "to see"[10] because the visual element often stands in the foreground in a dream. The difference between the two verbs is that *ḥlm ḥlm* "to have a dream" emphasizes the fact of the dream itself, while, at least in the vision literature, *ḥzī ḥlm* or *bḥlm* "to see a dream/in a dream" is used for the specific content of what is dreamed.[11]

---

2. The naïve psychological speculation in *KBL*³, 307 regarding an explanation involving a common root via the phrase "to have erotic dreams" is nonsense since people dream long before puberty.

3. 1QapGen 22:5, of Abraham after weeping over Lot's capture and finally regaining courage.

4. 4Q242 4:1, an internal passive for Nabonidus's recovery from a year-long affliction with the help of a Jewish soothsayer.

5. See D.A. Machiela, *The Dead Sea Genesis Apocryphon. STDJ* 79 (2009), 48.

6. Cf. Sir 34:3 for a clear devaluing of fantasies that come from the dreamer himself or herself.

7. J. B. Segal, *Aramaic Texts from North Saqqara* (London, 1983), no. 68 ii,3; cf. the note on p. 92.

8. Cf. M. Ottosson, 427.

9. 4Q530 2 2+6-12:3.

10. → *ḥzī* II.2.

11. Although it remains unclear whether that also pertains in *TADAE* D7.17,1; → III.1.

Other instances are uncertain: 1QapGen 7:20 lacks context (→ I for a different interpretation); in 4Q242 4:1 *'ḥlmt* is more likely the third-person singular of the causative-stem of the homonymous root *ḥlm* "he healed" than the first-person "I dreamed" because the near context in the subsequent lines deal with the healing of the speaker, but nowhere does the text mention a dream. In light of the difference between *ḥlm ḥlm* and *ḥzī* (*b*) *ḥlm* established above, at least in 4Q204 1 6:10 (1 En. 14:1) one can with some certainty reconstruct the verb *ḥlmt* after *bḥlm' dy 'nh* "in the dream which I [dreamt]."[12]

In later Aramaic, the verb also appears occasionally.[13] The usage is unaltered.

III. Noun "Dream."

1. Generally. Because of the representative or documentary character of the mostly Old and Imperial Aramaic texts, personal subject matter such as dreams appear only as exceptions. Thus, virtually all the older instances of the noun *ḥlm* /ḥelm/ fall to the vision literature of the book of Daniel and to the Aramaic texts from Qumran (→ III.2). The sole undoubted exception consists of the report of a dream in an Imperial Aramaic private letter on an ostracon from Elephantine,[14] precisely where such a personal communication can be expected in the textual genre in use. The writer mentions a dream that he saw (*ḥlm ḥzyt*, ll. 1f.), and that, since, he has suffered a fever (ll. 2-7). Nonetheless, it is doubtful whether the author communicates the content of the dream itself, since l. 5 does not speak of an "appearance," but of the wish that someone would care.[15] It also remains unclear whether the reverse side with the request to purchase certain goods in order to free the family from economic difficulties represents an interpretation of the dream mentioned on the obverse,[16] or an independent communication.

In addition, a figurative use of the term "dream" as an image of the past, also known in many other languages (e.g., Ps. 73:20; Job 20:8), may already appear in the curse formulas of an Old Aramaic state treaty from Sefire.[17] If one reads in this line *kmlkt ḥl mlkt ḥlm*, the kingdom of the prince who breaks the treaty should become "like a kingdom of sand, a dream kingdom" with the subsequent relative clause *zy ymlk 'šr* "that Assyria governs."[18] Other editors, however, place the *m* at the end of the following word so that the text involves either an intentional or unintentional duplication of *mlkt ḥl* "kingdom of sand" and a temporal subordinate clause *mzy ymlk 'šr* "as long as Assyria governs" follows.[19] The second explanation corresponds better with older Aramaic usage since it constructs the verb *mlk* "to rule over" with a prepositional expression following *b-* or *'l* and not intransitively. Because the demarcation of the words is also controversial, the metaphorical use of "dream" for something futile in Old and Imperial Aramaic cannot be considered certain.

12. *DSSStE*, 414f., does not include *ḥlmt* in the text edition, but clearly assumed it, for it reconstructs "[dreamt]" in the translation.
13. *DJPA*, 203b; *DJBA*, 465a; *LexSyr*, 234.
14. *TADAE* D7.17 = *KAI* 270 A.
15. About the author's illness; → *ḥzī* IV.
16. So the commentary in *KAI*, S. 323f., with a very imaginative interpretation.
17. Sefire I = *KAI* 222 A 25.
18. So *KAI*; cf. the commentary there, 248.
19. See J. A. Fitzmyer, *The Aramaic Inscriptions of Sefire*. *BietOr* 19/A (^{2}1995), 83f.

2. Dream Revelation. Dreams as divine revelation frequently occur in the theological literature of the Hellenistic period, especially in the book of Daniel, in 1QapGen, and in texts from the Enoch tradition. They can be differentiated: first, as specific words of God issued directly to the sleeper who understands them, concern him personally, and call him to action; second, in fantastic scenes that the dreamer follows as spectator and auditor and that prove, with the aid of a decrypting interpretation,[20] to be insights into the secrets of the world and of history concealed to normal view. As the living world surrounding the person and preceding humankind in the creation of the environment, trees and animals stamp the symbolism of these stories.

The visions of the theology of history and their interpretations in the Aramaic book of Daniel combine wisdom and apocalyptic motifs. The capacity for interpreting dreams is generally regarded as an expression of extraordinary intellectual gifts and is mentioned in one breath with answering difficult questions and solving puzzles (cf. Dnl. 5:12). Furthermore, in two of the three dream accounts in Dnl. 2, 4, and 7, the interpretation develops a linear view of history according to which the sequence of various empires inevitably moves toward its goal.[21] In political and religious oppression, this knowledge gives comfort that even the most frightful force is finite and that the kingdom of God constitutes the conclusion of all dominion.

King Nebuchadnezzar's night vision of the colossus made of different metals on clay feet and its destruction by a boulder is described with particular frequency as a *ḥlm* "dream" (Dnl. 2:4,5,6,7,9,26,28,36,45). Only Daniel, graced with God-given wisdom,[22] can disclose to the king that this dream represents the four empires and their end with the advent of the kingdom of God.[23] Nebuchadnezzar's vision of the world tree, which is then cut down at the root, also transpires explicitly in a dream (Dnl. 4:2-6,15f.). Daniel interprets it, too, although as a personal prophecy of exile and penitence; it is fulfilled when, instead of dealing with his sins, the king indulged in his own majesty. In the end, however, he came to acknowledge God and returned purified. With regard to the third vision, it is only briefly mentioned at the beginning that it was a dream (Dnl. 7:1): here, Daniel himself sees the course of world history in the form of increasingly dehumanized chimeras,[24] the last of which is destroyed and the dominion over all creation falls to an anthropomorphic figure. All three accounts emphasize the disturbing effect of the vision on the dreamer (Dnl. 2:1,3; 4:2; 7:28) or even the interpreter (4:16); sometimes *ḥlm* also parallels *ḥzwy r'š* "visions of the head" (Dnl. 2:28; 7:1). Apparently, the plural here denotes the individual visions that constitute the dream.[25] Presentative markers such as *'lw* or *'rw* sometimes introduce and thereby enliven the depiction itself (Dnl. 4:7; 7:2; much as in Heb., cf. Gen. 28:12).

Night visions with personal warning and general revelations of history also occur side-by-side in the various documents from Qumran. In 1QapGen, Abraham's dream

20. → *pšr*.
21. → *mlk* IV.
22. → *ḥkm* III.2.
23. → *dhb* II.
24. → *gp*.
25. → *ḥzī* IV.

of the cedar that is supposed to be felled but is spared through the intercession of the date palm growing from the same root[26] symbolizes the threat that awaits him in Egypt, but also his deliverance through Sarah; the motif of fear appears here, too.[27] Conversely, the pharaoh, the source of the threat, learns in the dream that Abraham can heal him from his God-sent illness through prayer and the laying on of hands and responds by allowing him to go with Sarah.[28] The subject of 14:9ff. is the interpretation of Noah's dream of a cedar on a mountain peak that represents Noah himself and from which a shoot[29] comes forth. Another, although highly fragmentary, vision of Noah in 13:8-11 deals with an olive tree in the midst of mighty winds in the context of stars, various metals, and water, and thus may refer to the flood; the preserved text does not employ the term *ḥlm*, however. The reading of 1QapGen 15:19 is controversial.[30]

Elsewhere, the world order with its inevitable, imminent last judgment becomes evident to the seer in a dream. Enoch's journey to heaven occurs in a dream,[31] as does the animal vision[32] that symbolically presents him with the history of the world from Adam and Eve to Judas Maccabaeus in the form of various animals. Moreover, the Book of Giants reports the dreams of the giants, including a burning orchard as a reference to their punishment.[33] Other dreams of the giants Uhya and Gilgamesh receive mention,[34] although their contents remain unclear.[35] In his testament, Amram describes the legal dispute of the good and the evil angels over him as *ḥzwy ḥzwh dy ḥlm'* "sight from a dream vision"[36] and opens to the viewer an insight into the metaphorical powers that determine human fate.[37] According to 11Q10 22:9 (Job 33:15), God warns people of their sins in dreams (cf. Dnl. 4).

From Hatra, there are also instances of the function of the *ḥlm* /ḥallām/ "dream interpreter," who unlocks the divine instructions for building projects[38] and the penalty for robbing the temple.[39]

Later diction corresponds to these findings.[40]

---

26. 1QapGen 19:14-19.
27. 1QapGen 19:18.
28. 1QapGen 20:22.
29. → *ḥlp* IV.
30. Cf. *ATTM*, 2, 98.
31. 4Q204 1 6:10 (1 En. 14:1).
32. 4Q206 4 2:1 (1 En. 89:7), one should probably reconstruct *bḥl*]*my* "in my dream."
33. 4Q530 2 2+6-12:3-23; the vision and its interpretation here are apparently the subjects of two different dreams.
34. 4Q531 22:9,12.
35. Regarding their placement in the context, cf. L. T. Stuckenbruck, *The Book of Giants from Qumran. TSAJ* 63 (1997), 167.
36. 4Q544 1:10.
37. See H. Gzella, *"dyn," ThWQ*, I, 675f.
38. H106b.4; cf. S1.6.
39. H281.11.
40. *DJPA*, 203b; *DJBA*, 455f.; *LexSyr*, 234; *MdD*, 144.

IV. Noun "Dream Images." In the sole older usage (Dnl. 4:2), the noun *hrhr* /harhūr/ "dream image," whose gender is uncertain, may be largely synonymous with *ḥlm* /ḥelm/ "dream" and stands in parallel with it. It presumably belongs to the root *hrr* "to be exercised," in the D-stem—if it is not a distinct four-radical root *hrhr* "to brood, to have sinful thoughts."[41] Since it appears in Dnl. 4:2 in the plural, it could relate to the individual images or scenes that constitute the entire dream. In late West and East Aramaic, it also occurs with the meaning "thought"[42] or "illusion."[43]

Gzella

41. Cf. *ATTM*, 564; *DJPA*, 167f.; *DJBA*, 390.
42. *DJPA*, 167; *DJBA*, 390.
43. *LexSyr*, 183a.

חלף *ḥlp*; חלף *ḥlp* /ḥalp/; חלפה *ḥlph* /ḥelpā/

I. Etymology. II. Old and Imperial Aramaic. III. Biblical Aramaic. IV. Qumran.

I. Etymology. Hebrew, Phoenician, Moabite, and Ethiopic still attest the Aramaic root *ḥlp* "to pass, to change," as do Arabic and OSA still in the original form *ḫlp*, and Akkadian as an Aramaic loanword.[1] Furthermore, it occurs as the element /ḥalp/ (later /ḥelp/) "substitute" in male and female personal names,[2] the former often abbreviated Ḥalpay.[3]

II. Old and Imperial Aramaic. In Old and Imperial Aramaic, the verb *ḥlp* in the peal can mean "to succeed, replace" in the political[4] or military sense,[5] but can also mean "to

J. Dušek, *Les manuscrits araméens du Wadi Daliyeh et la Samarie vers 450-332 av. J.-C. CHANE* 30 (2007); J. A. Fitzmyer, *The Aramaic Inscriptions of Sefire. BietOr* 19A (^{2}1995); idem, *The Genesis Apocryphon of Qumran Cave 1 (1Q20). BietOr* 18B (^{3}2004); A. Lemaire, *Nouvelles tablettes araméennes. HEO* 34.1 (2001); H. Lozachmeur, *La collection Clermont-Ganneau: Ostraca, épigraphes sur jarre, étiquettes de bois*, 2 vols. (Paris, 2006); J. T. Milik, *The Books of Enoch*. (Oxford, 1976); J. Naveh and S. Shaked, *Aramaic Documents from Ancient Bactria (Fourth Century B.C.E.)* (London, 2012); S. Tengström and H.-J. Fabry, "חָלַף chālaph," *TDOT*, IV, 432-35.

1. *AHw*, I, 313.
2. In Greek sometimes emulated with ἀντί, e.g., *PAT* 0377 from Palmyra.
3. Cf. Αλφαιος in Mk. 2:14 and elsewhere.
4. Sefire inscription *KAI* 224.22, ptcp. act. m. sg. with 3ms suffix, if it is not the noun "successor"; the Aḥiqar novella *TADAE* C1.1,18, impf. 3ms, with an object introduced by *l*-.
5. Bar-Puneš Story C1.2,5 impf. 3ms, object with *l*-.

exchange (wares)," as in the invoice C3.27,4.[6] The term in the haphel frequently attested in the commercial[7] also has the latter meaning.

In addition to the verb, Imperial Aramaic also attests a noun *ḥlp* "substitute, service or goods in return," mostly in commercial documents of various origins,[8] almost always in the construct state with a subsequent noun.[9] In prepositional usage "instead of"[10] the word is frequent and is not genre-specific.

III. Biblical Aramaic. In Biblical Aramaic, *ḥlp* appears only as an impf. 3mp in the peal in the expression *šiḇʿā ʿiddānīn yaḥlᵉpūn ʿalōhī* "seven years will pass by for him," which recurs in Nebuchadnezzar's depiction of his dream of the tree in Dnl. 4:13,20,22,29. The form from Dnl. 4:13 is preserved fragmentarily in 4Q115 (4QDan^{d}) 3–7 13. Occurrences from Qumran with a human subject demonstrate the fact that the meaning "to pass by" is independent and need not derive, e.g., from "to change (seasons of the year)."

IV. Qumran. In Qumran, one finds both verb forms and nouns of the root *ḥlp*. As in Biblical Aramaic, the verb in the peal[11] has the meaning "to pass, to cross through" with the region passed as the direct object[12] appended. In addition to humans[13] and angels,[14] subjects include animals.[15] The aphel "to lead past, to cause to cross through" is attested twice in the pf. pass. 1cs *ʾḥlpt* in the second of Enoch's dream journeys[16] with the objects *[ʿl]ʾ mn y[mʾ] śmwqʾ* "[abo]ve the Red Se[a]"[17] and *lyd prds qšṭ[ʾ]* "along the garden of [the] truth."[18] Furthermore, the technical meaning of the pael "renew/exchange (a document)" in the formula *wbzmn dy tmrwn ly ʾḥlp lk šṭrh dnh* "and at the moment which you tell me, I will renew this document for you" regularly employed in various documents of sale and civil status[19] ties in with the Imperial Aramaic use of the verb.

---

6. Pf. 1cp with the volume of commerce as the direct object.

7. *TADAE* D7.16,5 and Lozachmeur, 152cc5 with the object of exchange as a direct object, the purchaser introduced with *l-*; *TADAE* B8.10,7, the exchange partner indicated with *ʿm*; Lozachmeur, 218cc1, probably with *b-* "toward."

8. Lemaire, 1.12, probably from the Khabur region; *TADAE* B2.4,10, Lozachmeur, 33cc5, and others, from Elephantine.

9. On an instance with uncertain meaning in the determined state in *WDSP* 7.14, cf. Dušek, 208.

10. *TADAE* C3.25,7; B3,3;4,2 and perhaps D2,2 in Naveh and Shaked, also, according to Dušek, 243 and 319 *WDSP* 10.3 and 16.6, but the context has been destroyed and would also suit a nominal use; constructed with a plural suffix: *ḥlpwhy TADAE* A6.4,3; C1.1,21.

11. As is clearly demonstrated by the infinitive form *lmḥlp*[in 4Q558 39 3.

12. 1QapGen 19:12,13; a determined object also with *l-*, 4Q530 (4QEnGiants^{b}) 7 2:5.

13. 1QapGen 19:13.

14. 4Q530 7 2:5.

15. 1QapGen 13:8.

16. 1 En. 32:2f.

17. 4Q206 (4QEn^{e}) 1 26:19.

18. 4Q206 1 26:21.

19. E.g., in XḤev/Ṣe 8,7; the Heb. version of the document, frs. e-k 10, exhibits the same terminology.

The nominal forms of the root from Qumran cannot always be defined with certainty. *ḥlphwn* in 11Q18 15 3 either exhibits a prepositional use[20] or is to be interpreted as a noun with a 3mp suffix "their substitute." In the fragmentary 4Q534 1 2:17, *ḥlp qllh* "in place of a curse" is probably prepositional. The usage of *tḥwt* in the meaning "in place of, instead of" in 11Q10 20:1 rises out of the underlying Hebrew of Job 31:40. Qumran first attests the feminine noun **ḥlph* "shoot, sprout" in Aramaic. In a dream vision of Noah, in which he appears as a cedar, three shoots, his sons, grow out of him. The noun, attested as *ḥlpt'* in the sg. determined state[21] and pl.,[22] relates to the Imperial Aramaic meaning of *ḥlp* "to succeed" (peal).[23]

Stadel

20. "Instead of them," but then in contrast to Imperial Aramaic usage with singular suffixes.
21. 1QapGen 14:11,14,15.
22. 1 QapGen 14:10.
23. Fitzmyer, 167.

חלק *ḥlq*; חלק *ḥlq* /ḥelq/; מחלקה *mḥlqh* /maḥloqā/

I. Etymology and Grammatical Constructions. II. Verb "to Allocate." III. Noun "Portion." IV. Noun "Division."

I. Etymology and Grammatical Constructions. Aramaic and Hebrew attest the root *ḥlq* "to allocate"[1] and its nominal derivatives well. No relationship has been demonstrated, however, to the root *ḥlq* (with the old /ḥ/), which is very productive in Hebrew ("to be smooth") and Arabic ("to shear"). If, at any rate, *ḥlq* "to allocate" corresponds to Arabic *ḫlq*, they represent two originally distinct lexemes whose similarity results from the secondary coincidence of */ḥ/ and */ḫ/. Similarly, no association with the verb *ḫlq* "to collapse" attested in Ugaritic can be confirmed.

As a verb, *ḥlq* functions as a transitive in the ground stem with that which is to be allocated—often land—as a direct object with possible prepositional modification fol-

J. Bremer, "*ḥlq* II," *ThWQ*, I, 996-98; J. A. Fitzmyer, *The Genesis Apocryphon of Qumran Cave 1 (1Q20). BietOr* 18B (^{3}2004); I. Eph'al and J. Naveh, *Aramaic Ostraca of the Fourth Century BC from Idumaea* (Jerusalem, 1996); A. Lemaire, *Nouvelles inscriptions araméennes d'Idumée*, 2 vols. (Paris, 1996-2002); J. Naveh and S. Shaked, *Aramaic Documents from Ancient Bactria (Fourth Century B.C.E.)* (London, 2012); H. H. Schmid, "חלק *ḥlq* to divide," *TLOT*, 431-33; M. Tsevat, "חָלַק *chālaq* II," *TDOT*, IV, 447-51.

1. Possibly related to the Arabic *ḫlq* "to form."

lowing *l-* "to someone" and *b-* or *l-* "as." In this regard, it connotes a legal allocation by an appropriate authority, while the similarly constructed → *plg* refers instead to the act of distribution itself with no direct claim to the binding nature of the act. In combination with a subsequent → *yhb* "to give," however, *plg* clearly overlaps with *ḥlq*.[2]

The masculine noun /ḥelq/ "portion," belongs to *ḥlq*; in purely consonantal spellings, this noun cannot be distinguished from the corresponding diminutive /ḥolāq/, which is apparently largely employed synonymously; further related is the rare feminine /maḥloqā/ "section."

Contrariwise, the noun /ḫalīqā/ "rule," also feminine, in the legal terminology of the Nabatean contracts from the Dead Sea may not have inner-Aramaic origins, but be borrowed from Arabic. There, together with the preposition *k-* "according to" and in the construct state with a subsequent noun, it denotes a proceeding that is procedurally correct or corresponding to prevailing practice.[3] If it is Arabic in origins, it is due to a native Nabatean legal tradition.

II. Verb "to Allocate." As a verb, *ḥlq* occurs quite rarely in Aramaic. Nonetheless, two instances in a list of the allocation of food rations for the journey of a Persian official through Bactria are certain (fourth century B.C.E.).[4] An equally late Achaemenid-period Aramaic ostracon from Idumea also attests it, apparently in relation to the allocation of an object characterized as *slmy'*.[5] In contrast, the reading and interpretation of *ḥlqn* in the treaty fragment *TADAE* B4.3,15 (with a destroyed context) is entirely uncertain.

In the texts from Qumran, the connotation "to allocate (according to the law)" in reference to goods, people, and abstract concepts, a connotation inherent in the noun, also comes clearly to light: it refers to the land that Noah allocated to Japhet and his sons (indirect object following *l-*) *b'db* "he apportioned in a lot" as an "eternal inheritance."[6] According to Beyer,[7] two additional, although partially emended and dubious instances of the verb appear in 1QapGen 17:7,8 in the same context. Other editors read a form of the noun (→ III) in the first case and decline to offer a suggestion in the second.[8] Furthermore, a passive participle of the verb stands in 4Q197 4 2:17 (Tob. 6:18) for the woman allocated to Tobias as a spouse according to divine counsel since eternity. Similarly, 4Q204 1 6:12 (1 En. 14:3) uses the verb with the spiritual gifts that God gave human beings at their creation.[9]

Finally, Beyer interprets two instances of *ḥlyqh* in Nabatean treaties from the Dead Sea[10] as a passive participle "the allocated" in an adverbial function following *rbī* "accretion (around)." According to the spelling, however, they cannot be distinguished by form from the Arabic /ḫalīqā/ "rule" (→ I); otherwise, however, this usually appears elsewhere with the preposition *k-*.

2. So in the allocation of the earth among Noah's sons, cf. 1QapGen 17:15f. with 12:16.
3. See in *ATTM*, 2, nV 1:38; 2:13,36; 3:40 (partially emended); 6:10; 7:24,65.
4. Naveh and Shaked C1,34.46.
5. Eph'al and Naveh, 66, no. 135, there translated "the ladders(?)."
6. 1QapGen 16:12; translation following *DSSStE*, 36f.
7. *ATTM*, 2, 100.
8. Cf. D. A. Machiela, *The Dead Sea Genesis Apocryphon. STDJ* 79 (2009), 67f.
9. For a similar creation theology context, cf. also 11Q10 26:5 (Job 35:10).
10. nV 1:17 in *ATTM*, 2, 205 and nV 42:34 on p. 247.

III. Noun "Portion." The assured attestation of the noun *ḥlq* /ḥelq/ and its by-form /ḥolāq/ "portion" begins with Imperial Aramaic. In contrast, a probably nominal form *ḥlq* in the context of death in the wall inscription from Deir ʿAllā that links Aramaic with Canaanite[11] could also, perhaps more likely, trace back to the root *ḫlq* "to perish" attested in Ugaritic.[12] Contracts and letters from Egypt employ *ḥlq* for rented farm land,[13] legally distributed slaves from common property,[14] for the portion of a house left to the wife as an inheritance[15] and a rented barge;[16] the purpose of a severely damaged ostracon is unclear.[17] Several commercial texts on ostraca from Idumea[18] offer additional specimens, apparently for parcels of land and sometimes probably in the same sense as *ʾšl*, literally "measuring line," then figuratively "demarcated land."

In Biblical Aramaic, *ḥlq b-* "a portion of" as an expansion of the usage for a distributed piece of land denotes the territorial rule over an entire region (Ezr. 4:16) as in the picturesque speech about Nebuchadnezzar's dream in which grass appears that the king shares with (*ʿm*) the animals as food (Dnl. 4:12,20, perhaps with conscious irony).

The six instances from Qumran all occur in 1QapGen and appear in the form of the diminutive *ḥwlq* /ḥolāq/, since a vowel letter indicates the short /o/ here, too. This indication is unusual in Imperial Aramaic so that it remains inexplicable whether the Qumran instance involves the form /ḥelq/ or already the form /ḥolāq/. Four of these instances concern the distribution of the earth among the sons of Shem and Japhet,[19] the other two concern a portion of Abraham's booty that he returns to the king of Sodom.[20]

In Nabatean land sale contracts, *ḥlq* appears as part of a formulaic expression alongside other terms for authorization,[21] sometimes also apart from this formula.[22]

Finally, an Aśoka inscription contains the abstract *ḥlqwtʾ* probably in the meaning "lot, fate,"[23] as could easily arise from "portion"; the Greek parallel is παρὰ τὰ πρότερον "as was formerly customary," however.

Later, /ḥelq/ for "fate"[24] and /ḥolāq/ for "portion"[25] are clearly differentiated semantically. The pre-Qumran instances, however, cannot be assigned to one of the two forms with certainty.

---

11. II,11.
12. Cf. *DNSI*, 379.
13. *TADAE* B1.1,11.
14. *TADAE* B2.11,3.5.7.9.10.12.14; l. 3 employs *plg* "to divide" as a verb, in the continuation associated with → *mṭī* "to attain," here "to come to."
15. *TADAE* B3.5,9.11.19.
16. *TADAE* A3.10,2f.
17. *TADAE* D1.17,7.10.12.
18. E.g., Ephʿal and Naveh, 86, nos. 189,1; 193,1; Lemaire, II, 133-38, 141-44, 147.
19. 1QapGen 17:10,11,15,19; possibly also 17:7 and 8. Yet → II regarding the paleographical difficulties.
20. 1QapGen 22:23f.
21. nV 2:5,25; 3:6,28; cf. *ATTM*, 2.
22. nV 2:13; 3:15,41; nV 6:7f.,12, a rental contract; V 81:3, contract for the sale of a home.
23. *KAI* 279.7.
24. *DJBA*, 456b; *LexSyr*, 237; *MdD*, 145.
25. *DJPA*, 191; *DJBA*, 439.

IV. Noun "Division." The feminine noun *mḥlqh* /maḥloqā/ "division" in Ezr. 6:18 and its subsequent reception[26] also belong to the same root. There, it designates the divisions of the Levites in parallel with the *plgn* "classes"[27] of the priests, who, arranged according to the Mosaic law (athough no specific instruction for this occurs in the Pentateuch), are summoned for ministry in the Jerusalem temple. The lexeme *mḥlqh* is generally regarded, however, as a Hebrew loanword,[28] since its counterpart *maḥ*ᵃ*loqæṯ* occurs frequently there—in contrast to Aramaic.

Gzella

26. *DJPA*, 300b.
27. → *plg.*
28. *BLA*, §51v'''; *ATTM*, 581.

חמה *ḥmh* /ḥemā/; בנס *bns*; קצף *qṣp*; רגז *rgz*

I. Etymology. II. Older Aramaic Usage. III. Biblical Aramaic. IV. Aramaic Texts from the Dead Sea.

I. Etymology. The substantive *ḥmh* /ḥemā/ is associated with the root *yḥm*[1] and has the basic meaning "heat." This or a meaning derived from it appears, not only in *wḥm*/*yḥm*, but also in the roots *ḥmū*/*ḥmī* and *ḥmm*, as they appear in Aramaic[2] and other Semitic languages.[3] This circumstance suggests a common origin in an ultimately two-consonantal root **ḥm*.

In Aramaic, the roots *qṣp* and *rgz* are explicitily linked to the lexical field for "wrath." Hebrew also attests both as verbs with the meaning "to rage" and "to be agitated; to

J. Barth, *Die Nominalbildung in den semitischen Sprachen* (Leipzig, ²1894); P.-E. Dion, *La langue de Ya'udi: Description et classement de l'ancien parler de Zencirli dans le cadre des langues sémitiques du nord-ouest* (Waterloo, 1974); C. A. Evans, "*ḥmh*," *ThWQ*, I, 1000-1002; J. A. Fitzmyer, *The Genesis Apocryphon of Qumran Cave 1 (1Q20)*. *BietOr* 18B (³2004); P. Kahle, "Textkritische und lexikalische Bemerkungen zum Samaritanischen Pentateuchtargum" (diss., Halle, 1898); J. M. Lindenberger, *The Aramaic Proverbs of Ahiqar* (Baltimore, 1983); J. T. Milik, *The Books of Enoch* (Oxford, 1976); G. Sauer, "חֵמָה *ḥēmâ* excitement," *TLOT*, 435f.; K.-D. Schunk, "חֵמָה *chēmāh*," *TDOT*, IV, 462-66; M. Sokoloff, review of *KBL*³, *DSD* 7 (2000) 74-109; R. C. Steiner, "Meaninglessness, Meaningfulness, and Super-Meaningfulness in Scripture," *JQR* 82 (1992) 431-49.

1. From an older **wḥm*; cf. Barth, §62e.
2. Cf. *ḥmm* "hot, fevery" in *KAI* 270 A 4.
3. Hebrew, Ugaritic, Akkadian, North Arabic, and Classical Ethiopic; cf. K.-M. Beyse, "חמם *ḥmm*," *TDOT*, IV, 473-77.

become disturbed, moved." Furthermore, the root *rgz* appears in Phoenician (including Punic) and possibly also in Arabic; in contrast, the root *qṣp* appears in Old Canaanite and may be related to Akkadian *kṣp*. Finally, the presumed root *bns* is not attested outside Aramaic[4] and seems to be of entirely non-Semitic origins. In the past, it was considered a Greek loanword,[5] but is now generally regarded as a combination of the preposition *b*- with the substantive *ns* "agitation" and, thus, not as an independent verbal root.[6]

II. Older Aramaic Usage. The two substantives *rgz* and *ḥm'* appear once each in Sam'alian.[7] Both seem to have the meaning "wrath" and are employed adverbially in a prepositional phrase introduced by *b*- "in wrath."[8] Furthermore, the Aramaic incantation text in cuneiform from Uruak contains several instances of the root *rgz*. Of them, three present the substantive *rgz* /rogz/ "anger," apparently in the plural, indeed, as a *nomen rectum* either in the determined state[9] or with a 3ms pronominal suffix.[10] Four additional instances[11] are participles of the verb *rgz*: two in the G-stem and two in the Dt-stem. Although *rgz* in the G-stem may express the basic meaning of the root "to be angry," the precise nuance of the Dt-stem is uncertain since it cannot otherwise be identified for the Aramaic verb. Some assume an ingressive meaning "to become wrathful,"[12] but this assumption remains controversial. Finally, the Aramaic texts from Egypt also contain an instance of the substantive *ḥmh* with a first-person singular pronominal suffix, i.e., *ḥmty* "my wrath,"[13] and of the substantive *kṣp* (for *qṣp*) with a 3ms pronominal suffix, *kṣph* "his wrath" in reference to the king.[14]

III. Biblical Aramaic. The substantive *ḥmh* occurs twice in the book of Daniel, once in the spelling *ḥmh* (Dnl. 3:13: *brgz wḥmh* "in rage and anger") and once as *ḥm'* (3:19: *nbwkdnṣr htmly ḥm'* "Nebuchadnezzar was filled with rage"). Similarly, the substantive *rgz* also appears once in Daniel, indeed in parallel with *ḥmh* (Dnl. 3:13, cited above), and the substantive *qṣp* once in Ezra (7:23: *lmh lhw' qṣp ʿl mlkwt mlk' wbnwhy* "so that [God's] wrath may not come upon the realm of the king and his sons"). In every case, it appears in the absolute state; in Ezr. 7:23, the preposition *ʿl* introduces the object of the wrath (*qṣp*).

In verbal usage, the root *rgz* appears once in the perfect of the causative stem with the meaning "to enrage" (Ezr. 5:12: *hrgzw 'bhtn' l'lh šmy'* "our fathers enraged the God of heaven"). The expression *mlk' bns wqṣp sgy'* "the king become very engraged and angry" in Dnl. 2:12 contains, in addition to *qṣp*, a form *bns*. Based on the parallelism,

4. Kahle, 53.
5. Kahle.
6. Steiner, 432-35; similarly *ATTM*, 2, 362.
7. *KAI* 214.23 and 33; regarding the final glottal stop and the form of the root *ḥm'*, cf. Dion, 60.
8. On the interpretation of *rgz* as an infinitive, see Dion, 273.
9. *ATTM*, 2, 26f., l. 20,24.
10. *ATTM*, 2, 26f., l. 30.
11. *ATTM*, 2, 26f., l. 19,23.
12. So *DNSI*, 1059.
13. Sayings of Aḥiqar, *TADAE* C1.1,140; for another reading, cf. Lindenberger, 138.
14. The framework narrative of Aḥiqar, *TADAE* C1.1,85.

both were interpreted in the past as perfect forms in the G-stem, but the unusual form of the root *bns* and the lack of a convincing etymology awaken doubt in such an analysis. If the form *bns* does indeed represent a combination of the preposition *b*- and the substantive *ns* (→ I), the subsequent *qṣp* in the same sentence is probably more likely a substantive than a verb.

Normally, the three substantives *ḥmh*/*ḥm'*, *rgz*, and *qṣp*, as well as the debated form *bns* and *qṣp*, are translated "anger" or "to be angry," sometimes also with a suitable synonym (e.g., "rage" and "fury," "to be/become wrathful/enraged," "to be angry," "to be furious"). In this regard, the use of the substantive *ḥmh* "heat" for "anger" quite likely arises from a metonymy in which the glow of the anger (i.e., the effect) was transferred to the anger itself (i.e., the cause; → IV). The usage of the root *rgz* in a closely related language like Hebrew may also suggest that *rgz* originally denoted feelings of unrest and agitation. Such speculation, however, finds no concrete moorings in the contexts in which the related verbs and nouns appear in Aramaic. Furthermore, it seems insignificant whether it involves human or divine anger: in Dnl. 2:12, the form *qṣp*[15] denotes the king's anger, yet in Ezr. 7:23 the substantive *qṣp* refers to God's wrath.[16] In the same fashion, the substantive *rgz* in Dnl. 3:13 refers to the king's rage, and in contrast, the verb *rgz* in the causative stem has God as object in Ezr. 5:12 (introduced by the preposition *l*-). Moreover, the use of the expressions treated here in hendiadys in some passages (Dnl. 2:12; 3:13) underscores their largely synonymous meaning.

IV. Aramaic Texts from the Dead Sea. The Aramaic texts from the Dead Sea attest the root *rgz* very well, both as a verb ("to rage") and as a noun ("rage"). In verbal usage, it appears in the G-stem; the object of the wrath can be additionally indicated with the preposition *'l*.[17] The substantive *rgz* is also employed in a variety of contexts. It occurs in the absolute state,[18] in the construct state[19] and with suffixes.[20] Particularly interesting is 11Q10 34:7 (Job 40:11): (*h'dy n'*) *ḥmt rgzk* "(cast aside) the heat of your wrath,"[21] where the substantive *ḥmh* serves as the *nomen regens* of a construct phrase in which *rgzk* serves as the *nomen rectum*. This circumstance underscores the suggestion made above that one can already identify the use of *ḥmh* "heat, glow" for "anger" in the early phases of the Aramaic language.

Kuty

15. Whether as a verb or a substantive, see above.

16. While the framework of Aḥiqar employs the same substantive of the king, see above regarding *TADAE* C1.1,85.

17. 4Q204 (4QEn[c]) 4:4 (1 En. 89:33): *wmr' 'n' rgz* "and the lord of the sheep became angry," Milik, 204; 1QapGen 2:25 *'l trgz 'ly* "do not be angry with me!," *ATTM*, 169, Fitzmyer, 138.

18. 11Q10 18:3 (Job 31:11): [*d*]*n' rgz* "this is (reason for) anger," *DJD*, XXIII (1998), 121.

19. 4Q204 1 6:5 (1 En. 13:8): *ḥzywn drgwz 'w*[*kḥh*] "a vision of the wrath of punish[ment]," Milik, 193.

20. E.g., 11Q10 2:1 (Job 19:11): [*wtq*]*p 'ly rgzh* "[and] his wrath [grew stron]g against me," *DJD*, XXIII (1998), 91.

21. *DJD*, XXIII (1998), 161.

חמר *ḥmr* /ḥamr/; גפן *gpn* /gapn/; כרם *krm* /karm/; ענב *ʿnb* /ʿenab/

I. Etymology, Lexical Field, and Meaning. II. Old and Imperial Aramaic. III. Biblical Aramaic. IV. Qumran.

I. Etymology, Lexical Field, and Meaning. In Aramaic, the masculine noun /ḥamr/ (arisen from an older */ẖamr/) appears as the general term for "wine" and corresponds to the umbrella term /yayn/ common in Hebrew and Ugaritic (perhaps an Indo-European loanword). It is not related to /ḥemār/ "ass" with an original initial /ḥ/.

The synonymity in the preserved Aramaic material seems, at first, less differentiated than in Hebrew; later, however, /ḥamr/ became more precise through a variety of supplements.[1] Other terms from the broader sphere of viticulture constitute independent lexemes: /karm/ "vineyard" is already attested quite early,[2] later, especially in West Aramaic, /ʿenab/ "grape"[3] and /gapn/ "grapevine" also appeared.[4]

II. Old and Imperial Aramaic. Wine was ubiquitous in the daily life of Syria-Palestine as a food since the Bronze Age. As a drink offering, it was already known in pre-Imperial Aramaic proverbial wisdom.[5] Beginning with Imperial Aramaic, it appears as a common import/export good in commercial texts[6] and in the distribution of foodstuffs.[7] Since, however, the enjoyment of wine is also an expression of zest for life, abstinence counted as a sign of sorrow-related fasting.[8]

M. Broshi, "Wine in Ancient Palestine," in idem, ed., *Bread, Wine, Walls, and Scrolls* (London, 2001), 144-72; M. Delcor, "De l'origine de quelques termes relatifs au vin en hébreu biblique et dans les langues voisines," in idem, *Études bibliques et orientales de religions comparées* (Leiden, 1979), 346-56; W. Dommershausen, "יַיִן *yayin*," *TDOT*, VI, 59-64; M. Dubach, *Trunkenheit im Alten Testament. BWANT* 184 (2009); R. Frankel, *Wine and Oil Production in Antiquity in Israel and Other Mediterranean Countries* (Sheffield 1999); M. Kepper, "*yyn*," *ThWQ*, II, 136-39; J. Naveh and S. Shaked, *Aramaic Documents from Ancient Bactria (Fourth Century* B.C.E.*)* (London, 2012).

1. Cf. *DJPA*, 207a; *DJBA*, 470f.

2. From Zincirli: *KAI* 214.7 [Sam'alian] and probably ll. 4 and 9 of the Kuttamuwa inscription (see D. G. Pardee, "A New Aramaic Inscription from Zincirli," *BASOR* 356 [2009] 51-71); Imperial Aramaic: *TADAE* C1.1,40; *TADAE* B8.4,6; in addition, commercial texts from Idumea; Qumran: 1QapGen 12:13; 22:14.

3. *DJPA*, 412a.

4. 11Q18 14 ii 1; *DJPA*, 134b.

5. *TADAE* C1.1,187f.; perhaps also l. 208, if the term here does not mean "ass."

6. Very often, e.g., in *TADAE* C3.7 and later in the numerous Parthian Nisa ostraca; cf. *DNSI*, 383f.

7. From Egypt: *TADAE* A6.9,3, here alongside *škr* /šekar/ "beer"; from Bactria: Naveh and Shaked C1,30.39.41.43.45.52; 3,40; 5,4.

8. So in the letter of the Judean community at Elephantine concerning the destruction of their temple, *TADAE* A4.7,21 par. 4.8,20.

III. Biblical Aramaic. Ezra mentions wine, a common accompaniment to sacrifice, twice in reference to the regular deliveries to the Jerusalem temple established by command of the Persian king (Ezr. 6:9; 7:22), in both passages together with grain,[9] oil,[10] and salt,[11] in 6:9 also with sacrificial animals. In contrast, the story of Belshazzar's banquet takes up the extravagant feast (Dnl. 5:1,2,4,23; cf. 1 S. 25:36). In arrogance, the drunken king allows himself to be carried away and desecrate the cultic implements of the Jerusalem temple, which seals his demise.[12]

IV. Qumran. The Aramaic texts from Qumran exhibit a similar distribution: Wine appears once in sacrificial regulations (4Q214 2:9; 11Q18 29:4), second as an intoxicant in the vision of Noah's viticulture (1QapGen 12:13f.), and, last, probably as part of a feast (19:27; the precise context is unclear).[13]

Gzella

9. → *ḥnṭh.*
10. → *mšḥ.*
11. → *mlḥ.*
12. The association of cup and punishment is also common in the picturesque speech of the prophets: Jer. 49:12; Ezk. 23.31; Hab. 2:16; Lam. 4:21.
13. Regarding the reception of the term, cf. A. Lehnardt, ed., *Wein und Judentum* (Berlin, 2014).

חנטה *ḥnṭh* /ḥeṭṭā/

I. Form and General Meaning. II. Instances.

I. Form and General Meaning. In Imperial Aramaic orthography, as also underlies the Biblical Aramaic consonantal text, the feminine /ḥeṭṭā/ "wheat" appears as *ḥnṭh* after the degemination of the long consonants.[1] Presumably, this is a purely orthographic phenomenon with no counterpart in pronunciation.[2] The word serves mostly as a collective term for grains of wheat and only as an exception for the plant itself.[3] Commercial texts often employ the abbreviation *ḥ*.[4] The umbrella term is *ʿbwr* "grain."

I. Eph'al and J. Naveh, *Aramaic Ostraca of the Fourth Century BC from Idumaea* (Jerusalem, 1996); H. Gzella, *A Cultural History of Aramaic. HO* 111 (2015).

1. In Sam'alian *ḥṭh*: *KAI* 215.6.9, here along with *śʿr* "barley," as often in Heb., cf. *GesB*[18], 340.
2. Gzella, 170f.
3. 11Q10 20:1 (Job 31:40).
4. Eph'al and Naveh, 11.

II. Instances. As an object in daily life, *ḥnṭh* "wheat" appears in the proverbial wisdom of Aḥiqar[5] and in Imperial Aramaic commercial texts.[6] The two Biblical Aramaic instances (Ezr. 6:9; 7:22) mention wheat alongside wine[7] as sacrificial material for the Jerusalem temple.

Gzella

5. *TADAE* C1.1,129, along with *dgn* "grain."
6. *TADAE* C3.28, 75.77.80f.82.84.99.101.104.110; furthermore, in numerous ostraca.
7. → *ḥmr* III.

חנכה *ḥnkh* /ḥanokā/

I. Etymology. II. General Use "Dedication." III. Specific Use for the Hanukkah Festival.

I. Etymology. The feminine noun *ḥnkh* /ḥanok(k)ā/ "dedication" may be a Hebrew loanword in Aramaic[1] and, therefore, first occurs in Biblical Aramaic; the lengthening of the consonants at the end with the addition of the ending to retain the short vowel in the pointing *ḥᵃnukkā* is secondary,[2] but difficult to date. The word is usually linked to the primary noun */ḥink-/ "palate" (as in Hebrew and Aramaic) or */ḥanak-/ (following the Arabic). The precise semantic development remains controversial, but a relationship with the mouth washing and dedication ritual of ancient eastern statues of deities[3] is nonetheless conceivable. The noun appears regularly in the construct state with the object to be dedicated as the next word. In contrast, the verbal root *ḥnk* "to dedicate"[4] known in Hebrew is very rare in Aramaic.[5]

II. General Use "Dedication." Biblical Aramaic employs *ḥnkh* once for the dedication of an idol image (Dnl. 3:2f.), which is depicted in the immediate context, however, not as a distinct ritual, but as veneration through proskynesis to the sound of various instruments (→ *zmr*). Otherwise, the noun can also designate the dedication of the Jerusalem temple by means of a sacrifice (Ezr. 6:16f.). *Megillat Ta'anit*, which lists various

A. Berlejung, *Die Theologie der Bilder*. *OBO* 162 (1998); W. Dommershausen, "חָנַךְ *ḥānak*," *TDOT*, V, 19-21.

1. Cf. *ATTM*, 582.
2. *BLe*, §219f.
3. Cf. Berlejung, 178-283.
4. Cf. *GesB*[18], 372.
5. E.g., *PAT* 1347.4.

memorial days predominantly from the period of the Maccabean wars,[6] employs the term for the day of the dedication of the city walls of Jerusalem (ll. 3.13) and of the altar by Judas Maccabeus exactly three years after its desecration by a pagan sacrifice offered by Antiochus IV on the twenty-fifth of Chislev 167 B.C.E. (l. 23).

III. Specific Use for the Hanukkah Festival. In this latter sense, finally, *ḥnkh* in the determined state also became the fixed term explicitly for the Feast of Hannukah,[7] which was popularly called the "Festival of Lights," probably in reference to the rekindled altar fire.[8] The model of the eight-day cleansing of the temple under King Hezekiah (2 Ch. 29:17) may explain the eight-day duration, beginning with the twenty-fifth of Chislev. The nuance of the determined state in Palmyrene[9] remains unclear.

Gzella

6. Text in *ATTM*, 354-58.
7. *DJPA*, 208f. and *DJBA*, 473a; Beyer, *ATTM*, 357, accordingly assumes a determined form already for l. 21 of *Megillat Ta'anit*.
8. τὰ φῶτα in Josephus, *Ant.* XII,7,7.
9. *PAT* 2099.

חנן *ḥnn*; חן *ḥn* /ḥenn/; תחנונין *tḥnwnyn* /taḥnūnīn/

I. Etymology, Lexical Field, and Meaning. II. General Use. III. Religious Use. IV. Noun "Favor."

I. Etymology, Lexical Field, and Meaning. The common Semitic verbal root *ḥnn* is also productive in the languages of Syro-Palestine and well known in Ugaritic, Hebrew, and Aramaic. Aramaic attests it less often than Hebrew, but constructs it similarly. As an expression of care, it overlaps with the rather widespread verb → *rḥm*. In the G-stem, it means "to have mercy" and can be supplemented with the person who receives mercy as a direct object. In addition, it occurs in the Dt-stem with the meaning "to plead for mercy," optionally supplemented with the person of the addressee following the preposition *l*- or, with reference to God, *qdm*, with a prepositional expression involving *ʿl* "for." The verb usually appears in religious diction where it refers to prayer to God.

Substantivized, the passive participle of the ground stem /ḥanīn/ "one who found mercy (before God)" often appears in masculine personal names. This form could be expanded with the affix of tenderness /-ā/ or /-ayy/. In Israelite names, the divine name

R. P. Bonfiglio, "*ḥnn*," *ThWQ*, I, 1022-25; D. N. Freedman, J. Lundblom, and H.-J. Fabry, "חָנַן *ḥānan*," *TDOT*, V, 22-36; H. J. Stoebe, "חָנַן *ḥnn* to be gracious," *TLOT*, 439-47.

appears as a theophoric element after the perfect /ḥanan/ "he has shown mercy," as in Ḥananiah (e.g., Dnl. 1:6; 2:17). The corresponding short form is Ḥanan; tenderness forms are also constructed with /ḥon-/, however. In addition, these various names formed with *ḥnn* can all be shortened to Ḥanna.[1]

Further related to the divine predication in names is the modifier *ḥnn* "gracious"[2] along with the otherwise more frequent *rḥmn* "merciful" and the *ṭyr* "forgiving" borrowed from Akkadian[3] in a Palmyrene dedicatory inscription for a god.[4] The masculine noun /ḥenn/ (later /ḥen/) "favor" and the plural /taḥnūnīn/ "to request, plead" belong to the same root.

II. General Use. Aramaic only rarely attests the verbal root with the general meaning "to have mercy" in the sense of human care for one in need. Possible instances in Old Aramaic are dubious: the emendation of]*ynw ʿmmʾ* in *TADAE* C1.1,189 (a proverb of Aḥiqar) as a supposed passive perfect with the meaning "the people were gifted"[5] is extremely speculative and incredible; an alleged additional instance with no context in *KAI* 223 A 13 (Sefire) remains paleographically ungrounded.[6]

Contrariwise, the general usage in the interhuman realm is yet evident in Dnl. 4:24, although the religious dimension still stands in the background: Daniel futilely admonishes King Nebuchadnezzar after his warning dream to do penance through good works for his pride and thereby to avoid expulsion from human society as a divine punishment; here the infinitive *miḥan*[7] "to have mercy (for the poor)" parallels *ṣdqh* "to do justice."[8]

III. Religious Use. Meanwhile, the remaining instances from Biblical Aramaic and the texts from Qumran exhibit *ḥnn* as a term of personal piety. Consequently, the verb occurs there in the Dt-stem "to plead for mercy" in the context of petitionary prayers and regularly in parallel with → *bʿī* "to petition." The earliest known instance is the general depiction of Daniel's daily prayer (Dnl. 6:12; the preceding verse speaks of praise). Daniel's opponents denounce him to the king and he is thrown into the lions' den precisely because of this religious practice; he survived, however, thanks to God's assistance. In Qumran, then, usages of the verb *ḥnn* for concrete petitions to God on behalf of (*ʿl*) specific persons close to the supplicant also appear, namely Abraham's petition for his wife Sarah[9] and Levi's prayer for his deathly ill son Merari;[10] furthermore, once for the petition of the Watchers for mercy in judgment.[11] Finally, 11Q10 35:6 (Job 40:27) translates an

1. For onomastic specimens, including transcriptions in cuneiform and Greek texts, see *ATTM*, 583; *ATTM*, 2, 399.
2. Probably identical with the adjective later attested as /ḥannān/, *DJPA*, 209a.
3. Attested primarily in Palmyrene: *DNSI*, 1212.
4. *PAT* 0430.2.
5. I. Kottsieper, *Die Sprache der Aḥiqarsprüche*. *BZAW* 194 (1990), 12,19.
6. Cf. *DNSI*, 389.
7. From an older /maḥḥan/, *ATTM*, 582.
8. → *ṣdq*.
9. 1QapGen 20:12.
10. 4Q204 1 6:18.
11. 4Q204 1 6:16 (1 En. 14:7).

adynaton formulated as poetry in Hebrew into prose. With the purely rhetorical question whether the leviathan would plead for mercy before Job, God points his dialogue partner to the insurmountable difference between the two of them.

IV. Noun "Favor." The noun *ḥn* /ḥenn/ "favor, popularity" is attested beginning with Old Aramaic. It can refer to the divine benevolence in favor of a king[12] or to the popularity of an honorable, reliable person.[13] In contrast, the expression "to find grace" in 1QapGen 6:23 is probably modeled on the very frequent Hebrew counterpart (said here of Noah, cf. Gen 6:8). In a Nabatean contract, *mn ḥn* means "voluntarily."[14] The plural *tḥnwnyn* /taḥnūnīn/ "petition, plea"[15] belongs semantically to the Dt-stem.

Gzella

12. *KAI* 217.8.
13. *TADAE* C1.1,132.
14. nV 2:4,23; *ATTM*, 2, 208f.
15. 4Q204 1 6:1,3 (1 En. 13:6).

חסן *ḥsn*; חסן *ḥsn* /ḥosn/; חסין *ḥsyn* /ḥassīn/

I. Lexical Field and Grammatical Constructions. II. Usage of the Verb "to Take into Possession, to Possess." III. Usage of the Noun "Strength." IV. Usage of the Adjective "Strong."

I. Lexical Field and Grammatical Constructions. Forms of the root *ḥsn* typify Aramaic in contrast to the other Semitic languages; Hebrew employs instead the verb *ḥzq*. The isolated instances of *ḥsn* there (verb: Isa. 23:18; noun: Isa. 33:6; Jer. 20:5; Ezk. 22:25; Prov. 15:6; 27:24; adj.: Ps. 89:9) may be borrowed from Aramaic. The meaning of the ground stem of *ḥsn* "to be strong" that developed persisted in the noun /ḥosn/ "strength"[1] and in the adjective /ḥassīn/ "strong." The verb itself, however, occurs in the first instance in the causative stem for "to take possession of, to possess" with a direct

J. Dušek, *Les manuscrits araméens du Wadi Daliyeh et la Samarie vers 450-332 av. J.-C. CHANE* 30 (2007); I. Kottsieper, "Zum aramäischen Text der 'Trilingue' von Xanthos und ihrem historischen Hintergrund," in *Ex Syria et Mesopotamia Lux. FS M. Dietrich. AOAT* 281 (2002), 209-43; H. Lozachmeur, *La collection Clermont-Ganneau: Ostraca, épigraphes sur jarre, étiquettes de bois*, 2 vols. (Paris, 2006); J. Naveh and S. Shaked, *Aramaic Documents from Ancient Bactria (Fourth Century B.C.E.)* (London, 2012); J. B. Segal, *Aramaic Texts from North Saqqara* (London, 1983).

1. As a *qutl*-form, presumably a masc., but the gender cannot be unequivocally determined.

object, later, especially also "to bequeath,"[2] from which in turn, then, the feminine noun /ʾaḥsānā/ "inheritance" (literally: "property") derived;[3] it rarely appears in the D-stem.

II. Usage of the Verb "to Take into Possession, to Possess." In Imperial Aramaic, the causative-stem of *ḥsn* "to hold/take in possession" serves as a technical term in private law for authorized possession, mostly in the sense of a long-term lease[4] or ingressively for the assumption of an inheritance in testaments.[5] In the listing of the involved parties at the beginning of legal texts, the substantivized participle *mhḥsn* can also represent "long-term lease holders."[6] Especially in the sale contracts from Samaria, the verb regularly stands in a formulaic expression for taking possession of slaves,[7] money,[8] or houses.[9] Thus, it is also employed for property in a border inscription from Asia Minor[10] and in contracts from the Dead Sea.[11] It refers, thus, to an enduring possession, while the D-stem of → *qbl* denotes the receipt of the purchase price. A few instances of a perhaps more general meaning "to have/hold" from Bactria[12] and Saqqara[13] are fragmentary. If the reading *ḥsn bytk* "take possession of your house" in a Clermont-Ganneau letter ostracon is correct,[14] it would attest the verb in everyday language. The meaning of *ktb zy mhḥsn* "a document that authorizes"(?)[15] in the Xanthos triglot[16] has not yet been fully explained.

Imperial Aramaic may already attest the expression for "to bequeath, to give possession of," common later in Jewish Palestinian and Jewish Babylonian, once in Imperial Aramaic in *TADAE* B7.3,6, but the interpretation of the passage is uncertain because of the destroyed preceding context. Thus, it could also involve the otherwise typical meaning "to take into possession."[17] "To inherit" is *yrt*.

The use of the causative stem of *ḥsn* for legally valid, permanent ownership in Imperial Aramaic legal terminology also constitutes the background for its usage in the

---

2. *DJPA*, 46b, in Jewish Palestinian apparently synchronously reanalyzed as a quadri-radical root; *DJBA*, 475b.

3. *DJPA*, 46b; *DJBA*, 104f.

4. *TADAE* A6.11,2.3.5, here, it was confirmed by the satraps of Egypt; similarly, A6.2,3 and apparently also A5.2,2 and 5.5,9; in B8.10,5 in a common lease, more precisely specified by the unclear, probably Iranian term *hmkrygrb*.

5. *TADAE* B2.3,26; similarly 2.9,7, 5.2,4, 2.9,11 and in the court transcript B8.8,10.

6. *TADAE* B2.3,2; B3.12,5; B7.2,2; D2.12,4; likewise, probably in A4.10,6 and perhaps in a few fragmentary court transcripts: B8.1,16; 8.2,1; 8.7,5.7.

7. *WDSP* 3.4; similarly *TADAE* B2.11,14.

8. *WDSP* 2.8; cf. Dušek, 146.

9. *WDSP* 15.8; the context of 7.9 is unclear.

10. *KAI* 278.3, of cities as the property of the goddess Kubaba.

11. V 36:1; nV 1:44; 7:14,18,19,23,51,58,60; for the possession of documents in nV 2:16,41 and 43:23.

12. A7:1 and 10a:8 in Naveh and Shaked.

13. Segal 75.1; 151.2; 169.1; 199.1.

14. Lozachmeur, 170cc6f.

15. Kottsieper, 217-19.

16. *KAI* 319.19.

17. Cf. *DNSI*, 392.

vision of the end time in Dnl. 7:18, briefly summarized in 7:22. There, the kingdom of God dawns after the destruction of the demonic powers, the "holy ones" (*qdyšyn*) will receive (*qbl*) the kingdom (*mlkwt'*), and they will possess it for eternity (*yḥsnwn mlkwt' 'd 'lm'*). In the same sense, Beyer[18] also emends a form of *ḥsn* in reference to the assumption of an earthly kingdom in 4Q196 2:4 (Tob. 1:21), while others read the verb *mlk* "to be king," however.[19]

Furthermore, in the Aramaic texts from Qumran, the plural passive participle[20] and the infinitive[21] can denote "possession, property." The t-stem of the causative for "to desist from (*mn*)" appears only in an unidiomatic inscription of Emperor Aśoka[22] and is sometimes subsumed under a homonymous root.[23]

III. Usage of the Noun "Strength." The Aramaic *nomen actionis ḥsn* /ḥosn/ "strength" may have originally been a *qutl*-form,[24] but appears in the Tiberian pointing of Biblical Aramaic as a *qitl*.[25] In Old Aramaic—if the same form—it occurs once in the plural for fortifications,[26] and perhaps also in Imperial Aramaic for "supply storage."[27] Otherwise, it stands abstractly in the adverbial expression *kḥsn* "with force" for breaking into someone's home,[28] absolutely in Biblical Aramaic for the God-given power of the king (Dnl. 2:37; 4:27),[29] and in Qumran in a series of synonyms from the lexical field of "power" for the violent strength of the giants.[30]

IV. Usage of the Adjective "Strong." The adjective *ḥsyn* /ḥassīn/ "strong" appears in isolation. The wisdom sayings of Aḥiqar employ it for various sensory perceptions like the intensely bitter taste of medlar (*'nz'rrt'*)[31] and for an ass neighing loudly (*ḥmr n'r*; here in the comparison: *mh ḥsyn hw mn* "what is stronger [= louder?] than. . .");[32] it refers, additionally, to a fortified city with water in its midst (*qr*[y]*h ḥsynh zy my*[*n*] *bg*[*wh*]*'yty*) as an image for a man who has both a handsome form and a good heart.[33] In Imperial Aramaic, it appears once for strong cedar wood for boat-building in contrast to other varieties of wood;[34] in the letters of high officials from Egypt and Bactria, it appears

18. *ATTM*, 2, 174.
19. *DSSStE*, 384; J. Fitzmyer, *Tobit. CEJL* (2003), 121.
20. 4Q536 1 2:10.
21. 4Q542 1 1:5.
22. *KAI* 279.4f.; the Greek parallel version has πέπαυνται.
23. *DNSI*, 392f.
24. *ATTM*, 583.
25. *BLA*, §183j'.
26. *KAI* 202 B 8; cf. P. Marrassini, "פתח 'aprire' etc.," *Quaderni di Semitistica* 1 (1971) 93f.
27. *TADAE* A4.5,11; the reading is disputed.
28. *TADAE* B7.2,5.8.9; 8.4,4.
29. Both along with → *tqp* "strength" and → *yqr* "honor," in 4:27 also → *hdr* "majesty."
30. 4Q531 22:3; → *gbr* V.
31. *TADAE* C1.1,89.
32. *TADAE* C1.1,174.
33. *TADAE* C1.1,95.
34. *TADAE* A6.2,13.

more often as an adverb "strictly" in context with the regulation of subordinates[35] or of a precise exercise of the power of office over personnel.[36] The agreement in the diction of various corpora indicates a fixed term in Achaemenid executive style.

In Qumran, *ḥsyn* is employed attributively with → *dyn* for "strong law"; an additional instance[37] remains unclear in relation to its context.

Gzella

35. *TADAE* A6.8,3; 6.10,9.
36. A6.10,1.4.6; from Saqqara Segal 26.7; from Bactria Naveh and Shaked A5.2.
37. 4Q243 16:3.

חסף *ḥsp* /ḥasap/

I. Etymology and Meaning. II. Usage.

I. Etymology and Meaning. The noun *ḥsp* /ḥasap/ "clay," initially quite rare outside Dnl. 2, stems from Akkadian;[1] its original gender (masc.?) remains unknown. Later, however, it appears more frequently, especially in the meaning "shard,"[2] while *bzq*,[3] already attested earlier, could mean "shard" or "pebble." Within Aramaic, through the addition of the ending /-āy/, *ḥsp* formed the gentilic adjective *ḥspy* /ḥasapāy/ "(of) clay."[4]

II. Usage. In the vision of the "Colossus with clay feet,"[5] *ḥsp* /ḥasap/ functions as the leitmotif (Dnl. 2:33,34,35,41,42,43,45) and also occurs in a series of various metals in the prayer of Nabonidus related to the motif.[6] According to the evidence of the Clermont-Ganneau Ostraca, it already belonged to the Imperial Aramaic lexicon.[7]

Gzella

S. A. Kaufman, *The Akkadian Influences on Aramaic. AS* 19 (1974); H. Lozachmeur, *La collection Clermont-Ganneau: Ostraca, épigraphes sur jarre, étiquettes de bois*, 2 vols. (Paris, 2006).

1. Kaufman, 54: *ḫaṣbu*.
2. *DJPA*, 211a: masc.; *DJBA*, 476: fem.; *LexSyr*, 251; *MdD*, 125.
3. *TADAE* C1.1,205.
4. First attested in 1QapGen 13:9, perhaps under the influence of Dnl. 2:31-45 or a common tradition.
5. → *dhb*.
6. 4Q242 1-3:8.
7. Lozachmeur 103cv1; 276cv2, where it is the only legible word, perhaps meaning "ostracon"; cf. Lozachmeur, 410 n. 578—then it would be the earliest instance of the meaning "shard."

חסר ḥsr; חסיר ḥsyr /ḥassīr/; חסרן ḥsrn /ḥosrān/

I. Lexical Field and Grammatical Constructions. II. Use of the Verb "to Have a Lack." III. Use of the Adjective "Little." IV. Use of the Noun "Lack."

I. Lexical Field and Grammatical Constructions. From the common Semitic root *ḥsr* "to have a lack," which occurs in Aramaic in the G-, D- ("to diminish, remove, damage"), and causative-stems, Biblical Aramaic attests only the adjective *ḥsyr* /ḥassīr/ "little." The texts from the Dead Sea and later, however, also attest the masculine noun *ḥsrn* /ḥosrān/ "lack."

II. Use of the Verb "to Have a Lack." As a verb in the G-stem with the meaning "to lack," *ḥsr* first appears in Imperial Aramaic where it functions as a transitive in relation to objects and persons: of a well that *myn l' ḥsrh* "has no lack of water,"[1] and of a delivery of goods that the recipient already had, however.[2] According to Lozachmeur's reading of 33cv1, it can also denote the impersonal "it is wanting," although this is not entirely certain from a paleographical perspective.

In the Levi Apocryphon from Qumran, it appears three times in sequence in a fragmentary context with a person as subject and → *nksyn* "property" as object.[3] In contrast, the causative-stem, also attested later at Qumran in the sense of "to lose,"[4] seems to have a specific and, perhaps, technical, astronomical nuance. The astronomical book of Enoch employs it for the shorter lunar month since the moon "lacks the leadership of the sun" (*mḥsr mn dbr šmš'*),[5] that is, it falls behind the course of the sun.[6] Judging from the spelling, a D-stem participle would be possible, but later Aramaic attests it for *ḥsr* only with the meaning "to diminish, damage,"[7] which is not suitable here. The stem of the verb in a Palmyrene honorary inscription in the sense of "to pay (from one's own resources)" remains unclear.[8]

III. Use of the Adjective "Little." Older Aramaic sometimes employs the adjective *ḥsyr* /ḥassīr/ "little" in measurements. In the sense of "too light" it belongs to the scale

---

H.-J. Fabry, "חָסֵר *ḥāsēr*," *TDOT*, V, 80-90; H. Lozachmeur, *La collection Clermont-Ganneau: Ostraca, épigraphes sur jarre, étiquettes de bois*, 2 vols. (Paris, 2006); F. Zanella, "*ḥsr*," *ThWQ*, I, 1036-41.

1. *TADAE* A4.5,7.
2. *TADAE* A6.16,4; preceding context destroyed.
3. 4Q540 1:1,2,3.
4. *LexSyr*, 249a.
5. 4Q209 26:3 (1 En. 79:5).
6. → *dbr* V.1.
7. *DJPA*, 211; *DJBA*, 476f., passive "to suffer damages"; *LexSyr*, 248b.
8. *PAT* 1415.2.

metaphor in the "Menetekel" of Dnl. 5:27,[9] after which Belshazzar cannot stand before God and, consequently, perishes. Legal texts from the Dead Sea employ the expression *hn ḥsyr ʾw ytyr* "either less or more" in reference to tracts of land whose size is not guaranteed, and an Old Syriac covenant from Dura Europos has *ytyr ʾw ḥsyr* with a number for "approximately,"[10] and the Palmyrene tax tables have a similar expression in the information concerning the tax on slaves who earn less than the normative sum of a denar.[11] The few instances from Qumran are fragmentary.

In the cuneiform incantation text from Uruk, the feminine form stands as a substantive for "something insufficient" that should be made whole.[12]

IV. Use of the Noun "Lack." Two possible Imperial Aramaic instances of the noun *ḥsrn* /ḥosrān/ "lack" have the nuance "(financial) loss,"[13] similar to the use for "devaluation" in a divorce letter from the Dead Sea.[14] It also refers to the loss of property in the Levi Apocryphon.[15] In 11Q10 29:4 (Job 37:13), however, the relation to the Hebrew text is unclear.

Gzella

9. → *mnī.*
10. Citations in *ATTM*, 2, 400.
11. *PAT* 0259 ii.127.
12. *ATTM*, 2, 26f., ll. 15 and 40.
13. *TADAE* A4.3,9f.
14. M 19,8 in *ATTM*, 308.
15. 4Q540 1:2. In the same context as the verb, → II.

חרב *ḥrb*; חרבן *ḥrbn* /ḥorbān/

I. Etymology. II. Sam'alian. III. Biblical Aramaic. IV. Qumran. V. Later Jewish Aramaic.

I. Etymology. Hebrew and Akkadian also attest the Aramaic root *ḥrb* "to be (laid) waste," originally *ḫrb* as is still the case in Arabic and Ugaritic. The consonant shift **ḫ > ḥ*[1] led in Aramaic to the coincidence with the common Semitic root *ḥrb* "sword, war," which also caused semantic approximation.

O. Kaiser, "*ḥereḇ*," *TDOT*, V, 155-65; P. M. Noorlander, "Sam'alian in Its Northwest Semitic Setting," *Or* 81 (2012) 202-38; S. Paganini, "*ḥrb* I," *ThWQ*, I, 1060f.

1. Circa 200 B.C.E., *ATTM*, 102.

II. Sam'alian. The sole instance of the root in Old Aramaic[2] appears in the Sam'alian memorial inscription of Barrakib for his father Panamuwa in the form of an adjective f.pl. abs. (or a pass. part. f.pl. abs. in the peal). The "desolated cities" (*qyrt ḥrbt*) contrast here with the "inhabited cities" (*qyrt yšbt*).[3]

III. Biblical Aramaic. The Biblical Aramaic instance of the root also refers to a city. In their complaint to the Persian King Artaxerxes against the reconstruction of Jerusalem by Jewish returnees, Elamites settled in Samaria and other Transeuphratenes refer to the fact that this city had been destroyed earlier because of its unruliness (*qiryᵉṯā ḏāḵ hoḥorᵉḇaṯ*, Ezr. 4:15). The verb *ḥrb* appears in the haphel pf. 3fs pass. and, thus, has the meaning "to be destroyed, desolated."

IV. Qumran. The root also appears in the aphel in the fragmentary 4QpsDan^{b} 12:3 *wl'ḥrb' 'r'hwn mnhwn* "in order to depopulate their land of them," where the verb (in the inf. const.) is constructed with a direct object and a prepositional object with *mn.* In the likewise fragmentary 4Q534 1 2:13, two imperfect forms of the root can be understood either as aphel "to lay waste, destroy" or as peal "to be desolated/destroyed." According to an additional imperfect form of the verb in the aphel from the letter 5/6Ḥ50 10 of Simon bar Kosiba from the period of the second Jewish rebellion, the root can denote the destruction of trees (object appended with *yt*) by cattle and is, thus, not restricted to the context of war or divine destruction. Alongside the verb, Qumran also attests a masculine noun *ḥrbn* "destruction," paired in 4Q531 (4QEnGiants^{c}) 18:2 with *'bdn* "demise." Further, a masc. noun *ḥrb* exists. Its meaning cannot be defined more precisely than as "destruction" or "sword," although the instances in the eschatological vision of the Son of God text[4] as well as the striking combination *bḥrb wbqrb* "through destruction/sword and war" permit both interpretations. The ambivalence may have been intentional.[5]

V. Later Jewish Aramaic. The noun *ḥrbn* serves in the phrase *šnt X lḥrbn byt mqdšh* "year X after the destruction of the temple" to date Aramaic Jewish gravestones from the fifth and sixth centuries C.E. from Zoar south of the Dead Sea.[6]

Stadel

2. In the broadest sense, cf. Noorlander.
3. *KAI* 215.4.
4. 4Q246 2:4.6.
5. → I regarding contamination of the root.
6. *ATTM*, yyZO; cf. H. Gzella, review of E. Meyers and P. Flesher, *Aramaic in Postbiblical Judaism and Early Christianity*, *BiOr* 67 (2010) 564f.

חרץ *ḥrṣ* /ḥarṣ/

I. Etymology. II. Biblical Aramaic. III. Qumran.

I. Etymology. The Biblical Aramaic word *ḥrṣ* "loin, hip," as in most Aramaic dialects, although Syriac *ḥaṣṣā*, Mandean *halṣa*/*haṣa*, and *ḥlṣ* in Qumran Aramaic and Tg. Neof., has counterparts in Hebrew *ḥlṣ*, Akkadian *ilṣu* and *ḫanṣātu*, Arabic *ḫaṣr* and in Modern South Arabian Soqotri *mónḥeṣ*.[1] Thus, a Proto-Semitic form *ḫlṣ* seems likely; its /l/ became /r/ under the influence of the sibilant /ṣ/.

II. Biblical Aramaic. The noun */ḥaraṣ/, as in Hebrew consistently construed as a plural (or dual), occurs only once: in Dnl. 5:6, where, after the appearance of the flaming writing on the wall, the deposition of Belshazzar was made apparent, among others, by the words *qiṭ*ᵉ*rē ḥar*ᵉ*ṣeh mištārayin* "his hip joints become loose" (**ḥ*ᵃ*raṣ* with a 3ms suffix). This expression formulates a counterimage to the tightly bound loins that represent power and strength in Hebrew and Qumran Aramaic.[2] The word appears in 4QDan^{a} 9:16 as *ḥlṣ*.[3]

III. Qumran. The Aramaic manuscripts from Qumran manifest the word "loin" in the forms *ḥlṣ*[4] and *ḥṣ*.[5] 11Q10 30:1 (Job 38:3) and 34:2f. (Job 40:7), the introductory verses of the first and second of God's speeches to Job, adopt the words *'sr n' kgbr ḥlṣyk* "gird your hips like a man"[6] almost literally from the Hebrew text.[7] The same linguistic picture also occurs in a metaphorical transformation in 1QapGen 6:4, where Noah boasts of his honesty and wisdom with the words *wḥṣy 'srt bḥzwn qwšṭ' wḥkmt'* "and I gird my loins with the appearance of truth and wisdom."[8] The phraseology alludes to Isa. 11:5.[9]

Stadel

M. J. Bernstein, "From the Watchers to the Flood," in E. G. Chazon et al., eds., *Reworking the Bible. STDJ* 58 (2005), 39-63; V. Hamp, "חֲלָצַיִם *ch*ᵃ*lātsayim*," *TDOT*, IV, 441-44; W. Leslau, *Lexique Soqoṭri (sudarabique moderne) avec comparaisons et explications étymologiques* (Paris, 1938); C. Stadel, *Hebraismen in den aramäischen Texten vom Toten Meer* (Heidelberg, 2008).

1. Leslau, 264.
2. Hamp, 443.
3. The meaning of *ḥlṣ* in Imperial Aramaic—sometimes interpreted "belt"—is, however, uncertain; cf. H. Gzella, review of E. Meyers and P. Flesher, *Aramaic in Postbiblical Judaism and Early Christianity*, *BiOr* 70 (2013), 471f.
4. Probably not a Hebrew loanword, Stadel, 116.
5. Cf. Syriac *ḥaṣṣā*.
6. Pl. with 2ms suffix.
7. In Hebrew *'zr* denotes "to gird."
8. Pl. of the form *ḥṣ* with a 1cs suffix.
9. Bernstein, 52.

חשב ḥšb; חשבן ḥšbn /ḥošbān/

I. Lexical Field and Grammatical Constructions. II. Use of the Verb "to Think, to Deem." III. Use of the Noun "Reckoning." 1. Calendrical. 2. Commercial.

I. Lexical Field and Grammatical Constructions. The common Semitic verbal root *ḥšb* appears in Aramaic in the G-stem with the typical meaning "to think, to deem" with a nominal phrase as object, sometimes supplemented with a prepositional expression following *k-* "as," or an object clause following *dy* "that." In juridical diction, it can have the nuance "to recognize." The Gt-stem expresses the passive "to be regarded," facultative with *k-* "as," or, more specifically, "to be credited" with an indirect object following *l-*.

Other Semitic languages, such as Hebrew, in particular, also utilize *ḥšb* regularly with the meaning "to think, plan."[1] This phenomenon also appears in Aramaic, however, in the first instance in the derived masculine noun *ḥšbn* /ḥošbān/ "reckoning, account, measurement,"[2] that can constitute a genitive relationship in the construct state with a following noun. In calculatory contexts (as in the chronologies or in relation to monetary sums), however, the verb *ḥšb* can also be employed for "to calculate" and sometimes takes /ḥošbān/ as an internal object. Later, /ḥašābā/ "plan" and its derivative *ḥšb* in the D-stem "to plan" appear.[3]

II. Use of the Verb "to Think, to Deem." Old and Imperial Amaraic material from the time before the book of Daniel and the texts from the Dead Sea preserve only a few instances of the verb *ḥšb*. Moreover, these instances stem from texts dating roughly to the eighth century B.C.E. whose Aramaic identity has been judged variously in the past. The Deir ʿAllā wall inscription with a prophetic announcement of judgment is, at its grammatical core, clearly and demonstrably Aramaic in phonology and morphology, but contains a few scattered Canaanite words and is composed in a narrative style comparable to Classical Hebrew, presumably as the result of a translation from a Canaanite religious text.[4] It also contains the first "prophetic" combination of the puzzling expression *ḥšb ḥšb*

K. Beyer, *Die aramäischen Inschriften aus Assur, Hatra und dem übrigen Ostmesopotamien* (Göttingen, 1998); E. Blum, "Die Kombination I der Wandinschrift vom Tell Deir ʿAlla," in I. Kottsieper, R. Schmitt, and J. Wöhrle, eds., *Berührungspunkte: Studien zur Sozial- und Religionsgeschichte Israels und seiner Umwelt. AOAT* 350 (2008), 573-601; H. Gzella, *A Cultural History of Aramaic. HO* 111 (2015); idem, "Deir ʿAllā," in G. Khan, ed., *Encyclopedia of Hebrew Language and Linguistics* (Leiden, 2013), 1:691-93; P. M. Noorlander, "Sam'alian in Its Northwest Semitic Setting," *Or* 81 (2012) 202-38; W. Schottroff, "חשב *ḥšb* to think," *TLOT*, 479-82; K. Seybold, "חָשַׁב *ḥāšab*," *TDOT*, V, 228-45; F. Zanella, "*ḥšb*," *ThWQ*, I, 1082-92.

1. → *ʿšt*.

2. After the shortening of the long vowel, at the latest at Qumran, sometimes also attested as /ḥošbōn/ and borrowed in Heb. as the dissimilated form /ḥešbōn/, cf. *ATTM*, 137.

3. *DJPA*, 216b; *DJBA*, 486; *LexSyr*, 260.

4. Gzella, "Deir ʿAllā"; idem, *History*, 87-91.

wḥšb,[5] but the exact forms and the respective meanings cannot be deduced either from the spelling or the context—perhaps the failure of the human intellect in a disjointed world. Consequently, they may even offer quite consciously a "wisdom-learned play for connoisseurs (to whom modern readers no longer belong)"[6] and are thus comparable to the "Menetekel" in Dnl. 5:27,[7] where, admittedly however, the text itself offers the solution.

In contrast, the N-stem participle *nḥšb* "recognized," which is foreign to Aramaic, in the Sam'alian memorial inscription *KAI* 215.10 constitutes a Canaanism or a lexicalized fossil.[8]

One first steps onto certain footing with Dnl. 4:32. Here, the passage participle *kᵉlā ḥᵃšīḇīn* "they were considered nothing"[9] appears with "all the inhabitants of the earth" in the converted king's hymnic description of God emphasizing the difference between God and human.

In 1QapGen *ḥšb* occurs once at the beginning of an apocalyptic scene (*ḥšbt blby* "I thought in my heart")[10] and at the end of a dream vision of Noah for contemplation in view of a divine revelation.[11] Further, together with the noun *ḥšbn* (→ III), 1QapGen 6:9 employs *ḥšb* for "to make a calculation" in reference to years. In a likewise calculatory context, the Gt-stem appears once as a passive with the same noun in the sense of "to be reckoned to."[12] Two instances from 4Q530 and one from 11Q10[13] are fragmentary.

A Nabatean loan agreement contains additional instances of the verb with the juridical meaning "to acknowledge" with a direct object.[14]

The Palmyrene tax scale also employs *ḥšb* in the Gt-stem with the passive meaning "to be reckoned," similar to the active form in 1QapGen 6:9 and the passive in 4Q530 2 1+3:4, here, however, not for an overarching chronology in years, but for the calculation of the stars listed in denari.[15] With the noun *ḥšbn* as object, it is also used in Hatra to mean "to make a calculation" (→ III).

III. Use of the Noun "Reckoning." In contrast to the verb, the noun *ḥšbn* /ḥošbān/ with its by-form *ḥšbwn* /ḥošbōn/ regularly has the specific mathematical meaning "calculation," indeed, usually in the chronological or commercial sense.

---

5. *KAI* 312.12.
6. Blum, 591 n. 86; for older, but all unsupportable and therefore unsatisfying suggestions, cf. *DNSI*, 410.
7. → *mnī*.
8. Cf. Noorlander; Gzella, *History*,.75.
9. *ATTM*, 615.
10. 1QapGen 2:1.
11. 1QapGen 6:16; as a consequence of paleographical difficulties, the construction with the subsequent nominal object or object clause following *dy* is the subject of debate; for a discussion see D. A. Machiela, *The Dead Sea Genesis Apocryphon. STDJ* 79 (2009), 45.
12. 4Q530 2 1+3:4.
13. 11Q10 2:1 (Job 19:11).
14. Of the contract conditions generally, and specifically of houses as payment: nV 42:3,23,24,26,32 in *ATTM*, 2, 244f.
15. *PAT* 0259 ii.103.

1. Calendrical. The former predominates, naturally, in calendrical passages, as regularly occur in the Aramaic texts from Qumran: in 1QapGen 6:9 for Noah's retrospective on the periods of his long life and in 4Q530 2 1+3:4 for a *ḥšbn šny'* "calculation of the years" in a corrupt context,[16] and in the astronomical book of Enoch for the calculation of the phases of the moon.[17]

It is unclear whether the three suffixed instances in 4Q534 1 1:9.10.11 "her/his *ḥšbn*"[18] concerning "God's chosen ones" announced in a prophecy has the meaning "plans" not attested here but otherwise common in Hebrew texts[19] or must be interpreted in accordance with the older Aramaic diction as "calculations."[20] In any case, this second interpretation also corresponds better to the divinatory context, since the birth of this figure had been predicted.[21] An additional pair of instances are fragmentary.[22]

2. Commercial. In contrast, Imperial Aramaic commercial texts already attest the accounting or financial nuance, as in the expression *ḥšbn 'bwr'* "accounting of the grain" at the beginning of a list with quantities of wheat distributed to five individual women[23] and in an ostracon from Idumea.[24] Post-Imperial Aramaic tradition continues this usage, which is strongly influenced, however, by Achaemenid administrative terminology: *lḥšbn* "as a sum" in the Nabatean summary of a Greek loan note,[25] "quantity" at the end of the dowry in an Egyptian marriage contract from late antiquity (418 C.E.),[26] *'l ḥšbn* "with reference to" in an Old Syriac sales contract,[27] "calculation" in a Palmyrene tax table,[28] and "accounting" in H49:3 from Hatra.[29]

Gzella

---

16. Both with the verb *ḥšb*, → II.
17. 4Q209 25:3 (1 En. 78:10); 26:7 (1 En. 79:1).
18. Unsuffixed, but in a fragmentary context, also in l. 13.
19. So e.g., *DSSStE*, 1071.
20. Beyer in *ATTM*, 2, 163.
21. Cf. *yswpw* "they are fulfilled" in l. 9 and *DJD*, XXXI (2001), 134.
22. 4Q209 27:3; 4Q204 1 12:24 (1 En. 35:1); 4Q346a 1; 4Q547 3:4.
23. *TADAE* C3.28,79.
24. A. Lemaire, *Nouvelles inscriptions araméennes d'Idumée* (Paris, 2002), 2:99.
25. nV 17:41 in *ATTM*, 2, 231f.
26. yyZZ 36:19, *ATTM.E* 244-247.
27. P1,13, H. J. W. Drijvers and J. F. Healey, *The Old Syriac Inscriptions of Edessa and Osrhoene. HO* 42 (1999), 232-36.
28. *PAT* 0259 ii.115; l. 75,87 are fragmentary.
29. Beyer, 41, interpreted in *DNSI*, 411 as a *nomen professionis* "bookkeeper."

חשח *ḥšḥ*; חשחו *ḥšḥw* /ḥāšeḥū/

I. Etymology and Grammatical Constructions. II. Use of the Verb "to Need." III. Use of the Noun "Need."

I. Etymology and Grammatical Constructions. Since very few roots with identical first and third radicals exist in Semitic (an exception being the number */ṯalāṯ-/ "three"), scholars usually explain *ḥšḥ* "to need" as an Akkadian loanword.[1] Nevertheless, controversy persists over whether the verb *ḫašāḫu* per se was borrowed or is merely the stative.[2] It is relatively rare and apparently limited to the standard register of the Imperial Aramaic literary tradition and its offshoots from Biblical Aramaic and later to Syriac. In the G-stem it can function as a transitive main verb, "to need" with a direct object or as a deontic modal verb "to have reason to" with the corresponding main verb in the infinitive. Otherwise, the genuinely Aramaic verb → *bʿī* "to want, seek, request" is employed for "to need," and, in addition to the imperative and the shortened imperfect, adjectives or participles employed adjectivally such as /ḥazǣ/ "typical, necessary"[3] for various deontic-modal shadings.

The feminine noun *ḥšḥw* /ḥāšeḥū/ "need," spelled beginning ca. 200 B.C.E. /ḥāšaḥū/[4] also belongs to the same root. Like the verb, Biblical Aramaic first attests it.

II. Use of the Verb "to Need." The sole Old Aramaic instance of *ḥšḥ* as a main verb presumably appears in the memorandum in Ezr. 6 giving permission to rebuild the Jerusalem temple.[5] There, as an impersonal, indefinite generic term *mh ḥšḥn* "whatever one needs" (Ezr. 6:9) it introduces a list of the various goods that would be necessary for temple service according to the information supplied by the priests: bulls, goats, and lambs as burnt offerings, in addition to wheat, salt, wine, and oil. This interpretation, however, requires reading an active masculine participle **mā ḥāšᵉḥīn*[6] instead of the Masoretic pointing *mā ḥašḥān*, which presupposes a plural of an otherwise unattested feminine noun */ḥašḥā/ "need, necessary thing."[7] This interpretation finds support in the consontantal text of Dnl. 3:16 (see below) and later

---

H. Gzella, *Tempus, Aspekt und Modalität im Reichsaramäischen. VOK* 48 (2004); S. A. Kaufman, *The Akkadian Influences on Aramaic. AS* 19 (1974); Y. Yadin et al., eds., *The Documents from the Bar Kokhba Period in the Cave of Letters II* (Jerusalem, 2002).

1. Kaufman, 54; such roots are no more frequent in Akkadian, however.
2. *LexLingAram*, 67; *GesB*[18], 1495.
3. → *ḥzī* VI; regarding the general background and marking of deontic modality in Aramaic, see the extensive treatment in Gzella, 271-74.
4. *ATTM*, 107.
5. → *dkr* III.
6. With *ATTM*, 586 and the apparatus of *BHS*.
7. So, e.g., *BLA*, §51s′ and *GesB*[18], 1495.

usage.[8] A summary, but similarly formulated expression in Ezr. 7:20 employs instead the noun *ḥšḥw* (→ III).

As a modal verb, in contrast, *ḥšḥ* serves in Dnl. 3:16 in the reply of the Jews who refused to venerate the statue of Nebuchadnezzar to the king's question concerning which god could deliver them from the oven: *l' ḥšḥyn 'nḥnh 'l dnh ptgm lhtbwtk* "We need not give you an answer." Here, too, the vocalization as *ḥašḥīn* is dubious, presumably because the pointers no longer recognized the verb as such; moreover, on the Syriac model, one would expect an active participle **ḥāšeḥīn.*[9]

Finally, it occurs in a Nabatean legal text concerning the security of the dowry as a finite verb in the imperfect of the G-stem *whn yḥšḥ 'l* "and if it is necessary for."[10] Because the verbal *ḥšḥ* is thereby also indubitably demonstrated already in pre-Christian Aramaic, *ḥšḥ(y)n* in Ezr. 6:9 and Dnl. 3:16 involve masculine plural active participles and not independent nouns.

The few late instances of an Št-stem in Christo-Palestinian Aramaic[11] may reveal the influence of Syriac.

III. Use of the Noun "Need." The abstract noun *ḥšḥw* /ḥāšeḥū/ "necessity" is also very rare in older Aramaic. In Ezr. 7:20, in the copy of the edict that King Artaxerxes gave the scribe Ezra, it denotes in the expression *š'r ḥšḥwt byt 'lhk* the "rest of the needs for the temple of your God" at the end of a list of specific goods including sacrificial animals and implements necessary for the operation of the temple.

In the only preserved donation document from the Dead Sea by which a rich man transfers his entire fortune to his wife but reserves the usufruct of it to himself until his death, the same noun denotes the "necessity," that is, the livelihood, of the grantor.[12] The internal section of this double document (l. 16) employs the expression *lprnws npšy* "for my personal maintenance"[13] which is more precise than the general *lḥšḥwt npšy* "for my personal need" of the outer document.[14]

Syriac knows a few additional nominal forms with the meaning "need, use";[15] in contrast to other varieties of Aramaic, the root *ḥšḥ* also remained productive there.

Gzella

---

8. Such as Syriac *ḥāšaḥ* "having need, appropriate," cf. *LexSyr*, 261f.

9. *BLA*, §58q; *ATTM*, 586.

10. Pap. Yadin 1 = nV 1:39 in *ATTM*, 2, 205-8; regarding the construction cf. also Yadin et al., 197f.

11. *LSP*, 71.

12. Pap. Yadin 7 = nV 7:54 in *ATTM*, 2, 217-23.

13. Often interpreted as a Greek loanword form πρόνοος, but it may be more likely Semitic: *prs* "to separate"; see *ATTM*, 2, 464.

14. Cf. Yadin, 100f.

15. See *LexSyr*, 262a.

חשך *ḥšk*; חשוך *ḥšwk* /ḥašōk/; חשיך *ḥšyk* /ḥaššīk/

I. Lexical Field and Forms. II. Verb "to Be Dark." III. Noun "Darkness." IV. Adjective "Dark."

I. Lexical Field and Forms. Forms of the root *ḥšk* "to be/become dark" occur in Canaanite and Aramaic, but, as in Hebrew, the verb and adjective are significantly more rare than the related substantive. At least in the theological literature of the texts from Qumran, they clearly have the connotation of distance from God. For darkness in the purely astronomical sense, the verb *qbl* in the G-stem "to grow dark,"[1] usually as a fixed expression in the astronomical book of Enoch,[2] and the related noun /qabl/ "darkness" in 11Q10 8:6 (Job 24:15)[3] are usually employed instead.

The masculine noun /ḥašōk/, as it appears in the vocalization of Biblical Aramaic, occurs in Hebrew and sometimes also in Syriac[4] as the *qutl*-form /ḥošk/. The unusual vocalization can best be explained with *ATTM*, 586[5] as a formal assimilation to its semantic opposite *nhwr* (→ *nhr*) /nahōr/ "light."[6] There are comparable examples of such a development in many languages.[7] In contrast, an older alternative suggestion that it is an original *qatāl*-noun borrowed from Canaanite with the vowel change typical there[8] fails on the exact distribution of the nominal forms, since in Canaanite /ḥošk/ itself was common.

Finally, the concentration of the adjective /ḥaššīk/ in older Aramaic falls in the Testament of Amram, where it functions virtually as a leitmotif.

II. Verb "to Be Dark." The two or three older instances of the verbs *ḥšk* all occur in the Aramaic texts from Qumran, although the context is fragmentary in each case. In a passage from Levi's last testament, which can be emended with reference to T. Levi 14:3f., *tḥškwn*, presumably in the G-stem "(if) you grow dark," refers to the addressees

H. Drawnel, *The Aramaic Astronomical Book (4Q208–4Q211) from Qumran* (Oxford, 2011); H. Gzella, "Deir 'Allā," in G. Khan, ed., *Encyclopedia of Hebrew Language and Linguistics* (Leiden, 2013), 1:691-93; P. Heger, "Another Look at Dualism in Qumran Writings," in G. Xeravits, ed., *Dualism in Qumran. LSTS* 76 (2010), 39-101; G. Ibba, "*ḥwšk*," *ThWQ*, I, 925-28; H. Lutzmann, L. T. Geraty, H. Ringgren, and L. Mitchel, "חָשַׁךְ *ḥāšak*," *TDOT*, V, 245-59; J. T. Milik, *The Books of Enoch* (Oxford, 1976).

1. Probably not related to the homonymous root → *qbl* "to accept."
2. 4Q208 1:3; 17:5; 24 1:1; 24 2:2; 4Q209 7 3:3.6; 9:1,3.
3. See more extensively H. Gzella, "*qbl* VIII," *ThWQ*, III, 452-53; and Drawnel, 249f.
4. *LexSyr*, 262b.
5. Similarly, I. Kottsieper, *Die Sprache der Ahiqarsprüche. BZAW* 194 (1990), 114.
6. For which the—naturally only sporadic—reduction of the original */ā/ to /ō/ takes place more easily because of the subsequent /r/, cf. *ATTM*, 137.
7. Cf. J. Barth, "Formangleichung bei begrifflichen Korrespondenzen," in *Orientalische Studien Theodor Nöldeke zum siebzigsten Geburtstag. FS T. Nöldeke* (Gießen, 1906), 787-96.
8. Probably first proposed by *BLA*, §51g''.

in a warning against corruption; they are compared figuratively to the sun, moon, and stars since they illuminate Israel just as the heavenly bodies illuminate the earth.[9] An astronomical context is also present in 4Q212 1 4:25 (1 En. 91:16), where Beyer[10] reconstructs the participle *ḥ[šk]yn* "they grow dark." The first letter is unclear, however; others read *ṣ[hr]yn* "they arise."[11] 11Q10 A 11:2 has a t-stem form; Jewish Babylonian Aramaic attests the Dt-stem "to become dark."[12] In addition, later Jewish Palestinian attests the D-stem for "to do something in the evening" and the causative stem for "to darken,"[13] similarly also in Syriac,[14] and in Jewish Babylonian with the reversed meaning.[15]

III. Noun "Darkness." The more common noun *ḥš(w)k* /ḥašōk/ "darkness" appears in its earliest occurrence, the wall inscription from Deir ʿAllā (ca. 800 B.C.E.),[16] in a mythical image: according to the judgment preaching of the seer Balaam, the gods command the sun (goddess) to block the watergates of heaven with clouds so that darkness (*ḥšk*) reigns instead of clear day.[17]

Otherwise, *ḥšwk* is predominately used metaphorically and functions, then, as the exact opposite either of knowledge, as in the older material, or of right behavior, as in Qumran. The literal meaning occurs, however, in a pre-Imperial Aramaic wisdom saying of Aḥiqar, but already appears here in a figurative comparison of a man who is so foolish that he chops wood in the dark and, therefore, is comparable to an intruder caught in the act.[18] In Daniel's praise of God's wisdom, a determined *ḥšwkʾ* "the darkness" (Dnl. 2:22, the sole Biblical Aramaic instance of this root), denotes explicitly, then, the realm that remains distant to human knowledge; God, the revealer of the profound and the hidden,[19] also knows what is there, but exists himself in the light (*nhwrʾ*) and is, thus, the opposite of that darkness (cf. 1 Jn. 1:5).

The Aramaic texts from Qumran often link the word with ethical categories such as crime and lying.[20] According to Noah's praise of honesty, the "path of lies" (*ntyb šqr*) leads directly to "eternal darkness" (*ḥšwk ʿlmʾ*);[21] although in a fragmentary context, it probably functions similarly in Enoch's admonition in 4Q212 1 3:16 (1 En. 92:5). This opposition of light and darkness also has apocalyptic dimensions, however; according to the Levi Apocryphon,[22] in the end time, when the sun of God will shine over the darkness

9. 4Q213 4:1.
10. *ATTM*, 248.
11. Milik, 266; *DSSStE*, 444f.
12. *DJBA*, 488a.
13. *DJPA*, 217b.
14. *LexSyr*, 262.
15. *DJBA*, 488a.
16. For the classification, see Gzella.
17. → *ngh*; see Dnl. 6:20; I,6f. = *KAI* 312.6f. The context of the second instance in l. 7 is uncertain on grounds of paleographical difficulties.
18. *TADAE* C1.1,173.
19. → *glī* [I] II.
20. Which have a wisdom connotation here, however; → *ḥkm*.
21. 1QapGen 6:3; on the metaphor of the path of life; → *hlk*.
22. 4Q541 9 1:4.

(*ʿl ḥšwkʾ*), darkness will disappear from the earth (*yʿdh ḥšwkʾ* [*m*]*n ʾrʿ*). The noun appears here in synonymous parallelism with the subsequent *ʿrplʾ* "dark clouds." The divine light and knowledge probably also stand in the background when Enoch reports that during his heavenly journey he was led along to paradise, *ʿl*[*ʾ*] *mn ḥšwkʾ rḥ*[*y*]*q mnh* "above the darkness, very far from it."[23] The Testament of Amram takes the dualism further and employs *ḥšwk* "darkness" and *nhwr* "light" like the Hebrew texts 1QS and 1QM,[24] as a leitmotif in the juxtaposition of the respective "sons":[25] the evildoers lead the path to downfall in darkness,[26] the truthful to light. In this respect, every person is subject by predestination to an evil and a good angel,[27] who has authority over darkness or light, respectively. The context of the light-darkness contrast in the Testament of Qahat[28] can no longer be determined. 11Q10 10:1 (Job 26:10) may correspond to the Hebrew *ʾwr ʿm ḥwšk*, but the reading is disputed.

In addition, Syriac knows a few other nominal forms from the same lexical field.[29] A feminine counterpart "darkness" for night is only attested with certainty later;[30] supposed older instances such as Dnl. 2:22, meanwhile, are masculine determinate forms and are due to lexicographers' errors.

IV. Adjective "Dark." All six or seven occurrences of the adjective *ḥšjk* /ḥaššīk/ "darkness" in older Aramaic appear together with the noun in the Testament of Amram from Qumran. There, the opposition of light and darkness constitutes the central leitmotif (→ III). The figurative wisdom and ethical meaning appear in the fact that *ḥšyk* applies here not only to the clothing of the evil angel (*ḥšyk ḥšwk*),[31] but also to its activity (*ʿbdh*)[32] and of the foolish and evil sons of the darkness, while the wise and truthful sons of the light are "radiant" (*nhyryn*),[33] and thus share in the divine brilliance.[34] Other instances are known only from later stages of the language.[35]

Gzella

23. 4Q206 1 26:21 (1 En. 32:2).
24. Cf. Heger.
25. 4Q548 1 2-2:10,11,13.
26. 4Q580 1 1:12.
27. 4Q543 5-9:5 par. 4Q544 1:13; 2:14f.; cf. H. Gzella, "*nwr*," *ThWQ*, II, 923.
28. 4Q542 2:11f.
29. *LexSyr*, 262.
30. *DJPA*, 217b, but perhaps already in *PAT* 0065.3 with the emendation *bḥšktʾ* "in the night" instead of *bḥškkʾ*.
31. 4Q543 5-9:5 par. 4Q544 1:13 and 4Q547 1-2 3:13.
32. 4Q544 2:14; modified further at the beginning of the same line, but with unclear reference.
33. 4Q548 1 2-2:10,12.
34. H. Gzella, "*nwr*," *ThWQ*, II, 924.
35. *LexSyr*, 262.

חשל ḥšl

I. Lexical Field and Semantic Spectrum. II. Usage.

I. Lexical Field and Semantic Spectrum. According to the evidence of the Akkadian *ḫašālu*, the Aramaic verb *ḥšl* traces back to an original **ḫšl*. It is attested in the transitive G-stem[1] and has in the various Aramaic languages, alongside the concrete meaning "to shatter," the meanings "to hammer, smith, prepare" in later East Aramaic,[2] then in Syriac and Mandean also the figurative sense "to contrive."[3] Since such an expansion of usage is semantically plausible,[4] it is not necessary to assume two homonymous roots.[5] In East Aramaic, nominal forms /ḥāšlā/[6] and /ḥāšōlā/ "smith, metalworker"[7] occur along with the passive participle "shattered, prepared." The nuance "to pay tax," whose origin is still unclear, is apparently a peculiarity of Imperial Aramaic administrative diction.

II. Usage. The first instance of the verb *ḥšl*, in a letter from the Achaemenid provincial administration of Egypt,[8] simultaneously reflects an idiomatic usage otherwise unknown in Aramaic: together with the Akkadian loanword *hlk* /helk/ "tax"[9] as object, it denotes "to pay tax" twice there. It is difficult to decide whether a root other than the known *ḥšl* "to shatter" is present here or an idiomatic use from a no longer comprehensible literal usage.[10] Two further occurrences in the Clermont-Ganneau ostraca may attest this same usage, but are not entirely certain.[11]

Contrariwise, *ḥšl* appears in the quite ordinary sense once in Dnl. 2:40 in the interpretation of the fourth, iron kingdom in Nebuchadnezzar's dream. Like iron, which "crushes and shatters" (*mhdq wḥšl*) everything, the last kingdom will "crush and smash" (*tdq wtrʿ*) everything. The verb thus functions like *rʿʿ* "to smash" as a rare synonym of the

---

G. R. Driver, *Aramaic Documents of the Fifth Century B.C.E.*, abridged and revised ed. (Oxford, 1965); S. A. Kaufman, *The Akkadian Influences on Aramaic. AS* 19 (1974); H. Lozachmeur, *La collection Clermont-Ganneau: Ostraca, épigraphes sur jarre, étiquettes de bois*, 2 vols. (Paris, 2006).

1. Syriac also attested the D- and causative-stems in isolation: *LexSyr*, 263a.
2. *DJBA*, 488b.
3. *LexSyr*, 263 and *MdD*, 154.
4. Cf. e.g., the German "Pläne schmieden" ("to make plans").
5. As in *DJBA*, 488.
6. *DJBA*, 487f.
7. *LexSyr*, 263a.
8. *TADAE* A6.11,6, concerning the renewal of a long-term lease.
9. → *hlk* IV.
10. Cf. Driver, 70f. with Kaufman, 54f. for a correction of the interpretation of Driver's interpretation of the Akkadian material.
11. Lozachmeur, 156cc8 and 200cv3.

otherwise more frequent → *dqq* "to crush" and thus contributes to the remarkably rich concretization of the lexical field "to destroy" in the book of Daniel.[12]

In addition, the usage in the sense "to devise, plan" productive in later East Aramaic (→ I) occurs once already in 4Q538 1-2:1 for Joseph's plans for (*ʿl*) his brothers to test their intentions.

Gzella

12. → *ḥbl.*

חתם *ḥtm*; חתם *ḥtm* /ḥātam/

I. Etymology and Grammatical Constructions. II. Verb "to Seal." III. Noun "Seal."

I. Etymology and Grammatical Constructions. Since the verb *ḥtm* "to seal, to close" and the related masculine noun /ḥātam/ "seal" are only dispersed in West Semitic, while the Akkadian employs the verb *kanāku* and the noun *kunukku*, it is often considered an Egyptian loan, like some other terms from scribal culture.[1] Then the original form would have been **ḫtm*. The verb is utilized as a transitive in the G-stem or the D-stem in the same meaning, although clearly attested only later[2] and can be supplemented with various prepositional expressions such as *b-* "with," *ʿl* "on," or *mn* "to protect from." Likewise, the causative stem "to cause to seal" also appears later.[3]

II. Verb "to Seal." Aramaic seals and bullae (clumps of clay with which the tied papyrus document is sealed) became widespread with the rapidly increasing use of Aramaic and also of more flexible writing materials such as papyrus and leather in the bilingual administration of the Neo-Assyrian Empire; about one hundred seals are known from the seventh century

J. Dušek, *Les manuscrits araméens du Wadi Daliyeh et la Samarie vers 450-332 av. J.-C. CHANE* 30 (2007); H. Gzella, *A Cultural History of Aramaic. HO* 111 (2015); H. Lozachmeur, *La collection Clermont-Ganneau: Ostraca, épigraphes sur jarre, étiquettes de bois*, 2 vols. (Paris, 2006); A. R. Millard, "Assyria, Aramaeans, and Aramaic," in *Homeland and Exile. FS B. Oded. SVT* 130 (2008), 203-14; B. Otzen, "חָתַם *ḥāṯam*," *TDOT*, V, 263-69; D. Schwiderski, *Die alt- und reichsaramäischen Inschriften*, vol. I: *Konkordanz. FSBP* 4 (2008); S. Thomas, "*ḥtm*," *ThWQ*, I, 1093-96.

1. B. Otzen, 264; cf. T. O. Lambdin, "Egyptian Loan Words in the Old Testament," *JAOS* 73 (1953) 145-55, yet cf. H. Gzella, review of C. Frevel, *Medien im antiken Palästina. BiOr* 65 (2008), 481.
2. *DJPA*, 218 and *DJBA*, 489f.; this can be easily explained if it derives from the noun.
3. *DJBA*, 490; see further → *ʿzqh*.

B.C.E.[4] Later, too, seals evidence the use of lost organic carriers of text.[5] The end of Imperial Aramaic contracts from Samaria mention witnesses who affix their seals.[6] Building on this practice, the verb *ḥtm* can also be employed for the sealing of containers with food,[7] of rooms,[8] and further of buildings, as in the story of Daniel in the lions' den in Dnl. 6:18.[9]

In Qumran, the verb is certainly attested in 4Q550 1:5 for a scroll sealed with the royal seal ring (→ III) and fragmentarily in 4Q196 15:1 (Tob. 7:13), where, given the evidence of the parallel version, it likewise involves a scroll.[10] Thus, both instances correspond to the use of the verb in older administrative practice. Furthermore, Beyer[11] reads in 1QapGen 6:18 a D-stem participle *mḥtm* "sealed," while most other editors prefer *mstm* "concealed"(?);[12] the context, however, is significantly corrupt and the form, therefore, very difficult to resolve. Legal texts from the Dead Sea employ the verb in an expansion of the original meaning for "to sign"[13] like the otherwise customary → *ktb*.

In contrast to Biblical Hebrew and the Hebrew texts from Qumran, the figurative use of the verb, for instance, in relation to secret revelations (Dnl. 9:24; 12:4,9) from older Aramaic is not yet known. It also occurs, however, in later Jewish amulets.[14]

III. Noun "Seal." The noun *ḥtm* /ḥātam/ "seal" appears regularly at the beginning of sealed clay tablets with commercial documents from the Neo-Assyrian period, namely in the construct state in connection with the subsequent names of the owner, and on stamp seals,[15] in Imperial Aramaic, also on an ostracon concerning a jug.[16] Just as in Biblical Hebrew narrative prose,[17] in an Aramaic novella from Qumran set at the court of the Persian king, the seal serves as an official expression of royal authority[18] in reference to a scroll. Later amulets know the noun, however, with the nuance of secret knowledge[19] already attested for the verb in Hebrew (→ II).

Gzella

4. Millard, 208.
5. Cf. e.g., for Asia Minor, Gzella, 195f.
6. *WDSP* 1.12 and 10.10 in Dušek; concerning the formula, see there p. 129.
7. *TADAE* D7.44,6; 7,57,9; numerous instances now also in the Clermont-Ganneau ostraca, cf. Lozachmeur, 541 s.v.
8. *TADAE* A4.1,8.
9. Later also in Mt. 27:66 of Jesus's grave as an "antitype."
10. In this case, with a marriage document; see J. Fitzmyer, *Tobit. CEJL* (2003), 234-36.
11. *ATTM*, 2, 92.
12. D. A. Machiela, *The Dead Sea Genesis Apocryphon. STDJ* 79 (2009), 45. *DSSStE*, 32f., conflates the readings, rendering *mstm* in the text edition but translating "sealed."
13. V 45, 14, *ATTM*, 320f. and 2, 261; both cases involve the internal pages of the document.
14. Cf. ooXX 10,6 in *ATTM*.E 264 in reference to a person with *mn* "to protect from."
15. Citations in Schwiderski, 336f.; regarding the function of such clay tables and the Aramaic addenda, cf. Gzella, 125-39.
16. Lozachmeur, 246cc3, with the verb.
17. See B. Otzen, 267f.
18. 4Q550 1:5, along with the pass. ptcp.
19. yyXX 16:2 in *ATTM.E*, 239.

טור *ṭwr* /ṭūr/; כף *kp* /kēp/

I. Etymology and Lexical Field. II. Noun "Mountain." III. Noun "Rock, Cliff."

I. Etymology and Lexical Field. Aramaic /ṭūr/ "mountain" derives from the Semitic primary noun */θ̣ūr-/ and, like its cognates including Hebrew *ṣūr* "rock, cliff," is a masculine.[1] It is typically utilized as a geographic term or in a toponym for a specific mountain, rarely as a collective for a mountain range,[2] and in Imperial Aramaic sporadically for "uncultivated field."

The use as a metaphor for God common in Hebrew occurs in Aramaic as an element in personal names such as Turiel "God is mountain"[3] and also echoes in the symbolism of Nebuchadnezzar's dream (→ II), but seems in the preserved material otherwise no further distinctive.

In contrast, → *'bn* designates individual stones or stone as building material (cf. Dnl. 2:35 for an individual stone that becomes a mountain in the vision), while /kēp/ (→ III) denotes a natural outcropping of stone. It probably arose from */kāp-/ through sporadic reduction ("imāla").[4]

II. Noun "Mountain." Aramaic attests *ṭwr* /ṭūr/ since the Achaemenid period. The typical meaning "mountain" as a geographical term appears in the narrative framework of Aḥiqar in the designation of the place, *byn ṭwry'*[*'l*]*h tryn* "between these two mountains," at which a eunuch was killed instead of Aḥiqar,[5] and in a partially emended instance in the Behistun Inscription as a toponym ([*bpr*]*g'* [*ṭw*]*r'* [*bprs* "near Perga, the mountain in Persia");[6] further, an inscription with a brief prayer to a Horus statue in Egypt mentions *'lh ṭwr'* "the god of this mountain."[7]

In contrast, the meaning "highland" in the sense of "uncultivated field," as it sometimes appears in Imperial Aramaic commercial texts,[8] seems very specialized. Conse-

I. Eph'al and J. Naveh, *Aramaic Ostraca of the Fourth Century BC from Idumaea* (Jerusalem, 1996); H.-J. Fabry, "צוּר *ṣûr*," *TDOT*, XII, 311-21; J. A. Fitzmyer, "Aramaic Kepha' and Peter's Name in the New Testament," in *Text and Interpretation. FS M. Black* (Cambridge, 1979), 121-32; idem, "The Meaning of the Aramaic Noun *kyp'/kp'* in the First Century and Its Significance for the Interpretation of Gospel Passages," in "*Il Verbo di Dio è vivo.*" *FS A. Vanhoye*. *AnBib* 165 (2007), 35-43; K. Koch, *Daniel 1–4*. *BK* XXII/1 (2005); A. S. van der Woude, "צוּר *ṣûr* rock," *TLOT*, 1067-71.

1. For the much later secondary by-form /ṭawr/ in West Aramaic, see *ATTM*, 2, 61.
2. 1QapGen 12:8.
3. In 1 En. 6:7 the name of a fallen angel, in later magical texts such as ooXX 10,5 in *ATTM.E*, 264 the name of a guardian angel.
4. *ATTM*, 138.
5. *TADAE* C1.1, 62.
6. *TADAE* C2.1,46.
7. *TADAE* D22.51,3.
8. For an ostracon from Idumea, see Eph'al and Naveh, 190,4.5.

quently, the corresponding uses in Syriac Gospel manuscripts not yet conformed to the later norm (after the fifth century C.E.) can now be attributed to the impact of Imperial Aramaic.[9]

Nebuchadnezzar's dream vision of the "colossus on clay feet" employs *ṭwr* for a surprising image: a stone (*'bn*), which separates from a mountain (*ṭwr*) apart from human intervention (Dnl. 2:34 with a supplement in 45), crushes the statue as a symbol of the sequence of world empires.[10] As an image of divine dominion, it then became itself "a great mountain and filled the entire world" (2:35: *hwt lṭwr rb wmlt kl 'r'*).[11] The use of the noun *ṣūr* "rock, cliff" as a metaphor for God probably stands in the background here.[12]

Most instances in the Aramaic texts from Qumran appear in 1QapGen, which indeed exhibits a significant interest in geography. Here *ṭwr* regularly serves as a general geographical term "mountain, mountains" alongside seas, deserts, etc.[13] or as a specific toponym with a subsequent place name.[14] "Highland" seems the more likely referent in 21:7 since it employs the *b-* preposition,[15] while one would expect *'l* for "on a mountain"; 12:8 has the singular after the preceding plural for "mountains." Mountains also appear frequently in the visionary descriptions of the landscape of Enoch's heavenly journey,[16] further in an apocalyptic vision[17] and, emended following T. Levi 2:5f.,[18] in a dream vision for the mountain peak from which one can enter heaven. A few instances are fragmentary;[19] *ṭwry[n]* in 11Q10 32:7 (Job 39:8) corresponds to *hrym* "mountains."

III. Noun "Rock, Cliff." The masculine *kp* /kēp/ denotes a natural rock outcropping: in Enoch's allegorical animal vision, Sinai;[20] in 11Q10 32:1; 33:9 (Job 39:1,28) it corresponds to *sl'*. It was also in use as a masculaine name and was understood in early Christianity as a nickname of Peter (Jn. 1:42, etc.) in keeping with its meaning (Mt. 16:18) as a firm building ground.[21]

Gzella

9. Lk. 12:28 in Sinaiticus and Curetonianus for the Greek ἀγρός; the Peshitta has *ḥaqlā*.
10. → *dqq*.
11. Koch, 186f. adduces a few very speculative mythological parallels to the growing mountain; they are not necessary, however, for understanding the passage.
12. Cf. Koch, 188; yet, see below on depictions of the afterworld.
13. 1QapGen 7:1; 11:9,16; 14:9 in the dream image of the cedar on the mountain peak (*'l r'yš ṭwry'*); according to Beyer, *ATTM*, 2, 93, also 7:18, but the reading of the few letters is uncertain.
14. 1QapGen 10:12 and 12:8: "the mountains of Ararat," so also 4Q196 2:4 (Tob. 1:21); 12:13: "the mountain of Lubar"; 17:10 and 21:16: "the mountain of Taurus/the Bull"; 19:8: "the holy mountain"; 21:29: "the mountains of Gebal."
15. Correctly *ATTM*, 588.
16. 4Q205 1 12:6.8 (1 En. 26:6); 4Q204 1 12:27.30 par. 4Q206 1 16:17.19 (1 En. 31:2; 32:1); 4Q204 1 12:27 (1 En. 32:1); 4Q209 23:10 par. 4Q210 1 2:20 (1 En. 77:4).
17. 4Q529 1:3.
18. *ATTM*, 194.
19. E.g., Mt. Sinai in 4Q556 1:2.
20. 4Q204 4:3 and 4Q206 4 3:19 (1 En. 89:29,32).
21. Fitzmyer.

טיב *ṭīb* and יטב *yṭb*; טאב *ṭʾb*; טב *ṭb* /ṭāb/; טבו *ṭbw* /ṭābū/; טוב *ṭwb* /ṭūb/

I. Lexical Field, Forms, and Grammatical Constructions. II. Verb. 1. In the G-stem "to Be Satisfied, Pleased." 2. In the Causative-stem "to Satisfy." III. Adjective "Good." 1. Generally. 2. Substantivized. 3. Various Idiomatic Expressions. IV. Noun "Good Deed."

I. Lexical Field, Forms, and Grammatical Constructions. In Aramaic as in Hebrew, the etymologically "hollow root" *ṭīb* "to be satisfied, pleased" is limited in the G-stem to forms of the perfect and, at the same time, forms the imperfect with the secondary by-form *yṭb*. The latter, furthermore, is employed for the entire causative-stem "to satisfy, to improve," which presumably provided the analogy for the formation of the corresponding imperfect of the G-stem.[1] As evidenced already by older spellings such as *yyṭb* for *yēṭaḇ* in the consonantal text of Ezr. 7:18 or *tyṭb* for /tayṭab/ in *KAI* 309.15, it was conjugated like regular roots and not like other I-yodh verbs (particularly those with a thematic /i/ vowel) with the omission of the initial /y/ in the imperfect.[2] The body of specimens, although limited, points clearly to a supplementary relationship between the two root forms. In addition, at least Biblical Aramaic knows a further alternative *ṭʾb* "to go well" (Dnl. 6:24) on the model of its semantic opposite → *bʾš* "to be bad."[3]

The G-stem of the verb is intransitive, mostly stative, and can be supplemented by prepositional expressions following *b-* "with," and *l-* or *ʿl* "to please someone/go well for someone"; it overlaps with the semantic spectrum of the root → *rʿī* "to have pleasure." The causative-stem "to satisfy, improve, do well" occurs with a direct object and, depending on nuance, with various prepositional supplements with *b-* or *ʿl* "with reference to" and *l-* or *ʿm* "to someone." Further, the verb occurs as predicate in theophoric personal names ("[may] the god [do]/does good").[4]

The ubiquitous adjective /ṭāb/ "good" as a designation of the unobjectionable quality of things or abstractions and of the ethical virtue of people also belongs to the same root. It appears with widely varied overtones and in idiomatic usages, sometimes also substantivized in the masculine or feminine as "good fortune, goodness." Further attested is the significantly more rare feminine abstract noun /ṭābū/ "excellence, benefit," and in the macarism "blessed is/are," the noun /ṭūb/.

H.-J. Fabry, "*ṭwb*," *ThWQ*, II, 11-19; I. Höver-Johag, "טוֹב *ṭôḇ*," *TDOT*, V, 296-317; Y. Muffs, *Studies in the Aramaic Legal Papyri from Elephantine*. *HO* 66 (2003); T. Muraoka and B. Porten, *A Grammar of Egyptian Aramaic*. *HO* 32 (^{2}2003); J. Naveh and S. Shaked, *Aramaic Documents from Ancient Bactria (Fourth Century* B.C.E.*)* (London, 2012); J. B. Segal, *Aramaic Texts from North Saqqara* (London, 1983); H. J. Stoebe, "טוֹב *ṭôb* good," *TLOT*, 486-95.

1. Cf. *BLH*, §55j.
2. *ATTM*, 482.
3. *BLA*, §45g; cf. the exact parallel with Dnl. 6:15.
4. Cf. /lōṭeḇ/ in names from Hatra H175, H1041c,1.

II. Verb.

1. In the G-stem "to Be Satisfied, Pleased." The first occurrence of the verb in the G-stem appears as an imperfect of *yṭb* in the oldest Aramaic inscription where it refers to the benefactor's wish that "the word of his mound may please gods and human beings" (*'mrt pmh 'l 'lhn w'l 'nšn tyṭb*).[5] Imperial Aramaic has it as a perfect of *ṭīb* presumably for Aḥiqar's advice that pleased the others,[6] otherwise often together with a suffixed → *lbb* "heart" as the subject of an expression of satisfaction or negated for "to have concern."[7]

The latter formulation together with *b-* "with" or *bgw* "so that" (→ *gw*) is very common in the juridical diction of contracts for a satisfied legal claim.[8] Akkadian and Demotic legal texts have parallels.[9] Ezr. 7:18 employs the imperfect in an impersonal construction for *mh dy 'lyk yyṭb* "as it pleases you." The one Biblical Aramaic instance of the perfect (Dnl. 6:24) employs the allomorph *ṭ'b*, but in a meaning and construction similar to *ṭīb*, namely "to go well" with *'l*, in order to express the king's satisfaction with the fact that Daniel survived the lions' den.

2. In the Causative-stem "to Satisfy." Sam'alian[10] and the Old Aramaic from Sam'al[11] attest the causative-stem as a "perfect" *hyṭb* "he improved." It appears in every case with *byt 'bh/'by* "the house of his/my father" as object and with the comparative expression following *mn* "in comparison to" and is part of a report of royal deeds. The contracts from Elephantine and Saqqara, in contrast, employ the verb with a suffixed *lbb* as object for the causative counterpart of the G-stem in an analogous usage, thus "to satisfy someone's heart" for "to satisfy someone's legal claim" (→ II.1), with *b-* or *'l* "with reference to" for the object.[12] Here, however, the form *hwṭb* with /w/ instead of /y/ appears.

In later Aramaic languages beginning with Qumran, forms of the verb appear only rarely, while the adjective remains highly productive and various nominal forms occur, in addition.

III. Adjective "Good."

1. Generally. The adjective *ṭb* /ṭāb/ "good" is also attested since Old Aramaic times. Its specific nuance depends on the meaning of the word that it modifies. Many shades already appear in the wisdom sayings of Aḥiqar with its cross section of everyday life;

---

5. *KAI* 309.15.

6. Following *'l*; *TADAE* C1.1,67, with the subject apparently in the lost section of the preceding line.

7. *TADAE* A3.3,2.

8. *TADAE* B2.6,15; 2.8,5; 2.9,9, mentioned here as the result of the verb in the causative stem in l. 8; 3.4,6; 3.8,[5]; 3.12,6.14.26; 4.4,9; 5.2,7; 5.5, 7; D2.13,2; rarely spelled defectively *ṭb*, but because of the parallel with *ṭyb* in the same text, probably perfect and not an adjective: *TADAE* B2.6,5; 3.2,4; cf. Muraoka and Porten, 130 n. 604.

9. See the extensive treatment by Muffs.

10. *KAI* 215.9.

11. *KAI* 216.12.

12. *TADAE* B2.2,11f.; 2.9,8, with the corresponding G-stem in the subsequent lines; 5.6,2f.; D1.15,3; Segal, 8.2.

they also already establish the most frequent of the later usages. In relation to people, *ṭb* regularly refers to moral goodness in contrast to immoral character (*lḥh*)[13] and is also used in this fashion of the *lbb* "heart,"[14] but also refers to good friends (*rʿyn ṭbn*)[15] or a good ruler.[16] Abstractions such as a prayer to a gracious god God[17] or good advice[18] are "good" in the sense of "advantageous," and a "good" countenance indicates a well-disposed person.[19] It expresses the unobjectionable quality of things: of sharp sensory organs like eyes,[20] of a vessel that closes well,[21] of pure gold,[22] of a proper meal,[23] of pleasant-smelling trees,[24] of full-weight coins,[25] of valuable grain,[26] of functioning incantations,[27] and, generally, of "whatever is good"[28] or "advantageous."[29]

In official Imperial Aramaic texts, the formulaic expression *hn ʿl . . . ṭb* "if it . . . pleases" predominates and usually appears in the formal register of official letters to higher ranking officials; the preposition *ʿl* usually appears with a pronominal suffix or with the noun *mrʾ* "lord."[30] The same expression also occurs in Ezr. 5:17 (with *ʿal malkā* "to the king" for Darius), in a passage in the style of an official letter, and became widespread via Aramaic in postexilic Hebrew (Neh. 2:5,7).[31] Another satrap's letter from Bactria contains the formulation *lʾ ṭb ʿbdt* "you have not acted well" in the criticism of an official by his superior.[32] Alone, *ṭb* can also serve to express agreement "good!"[33] An additional pair of possible instances from the Imperial Aramaic corpus[34] lack context.

Usages of the adjective from Qumran are mostly fragmentary. Apart from a few everyday expressions, *rwḥ ṭbh* "good spirit" occurs along with *lbb dkʾ* "pure heart" in Qahat's

---

13. *TADAE* C1.1,99.100.
14. *TADAE* C1.1,95.
15. *TADAE* C1.1,161.
16. *KAI* 224.22.
17. *KAI* 309.5.
18. *TADAE* C1.1,42.57.
19. *TADAE* C1.1,14.
20. *TADAE* C1.1,157.
21. *TADAE* C1.1,93; → *mʾn*.
22. Dnl. 2:32; 11Q18 10 1:2; 11:4; → *dhb*.
23. 4Q196 2:11 (Tob. 2:1).
24. 4Q204 1 12:24 (1 En. 30:2); 4Q206 1 26:18 (1 En. 32:1).
25. M 20:5, *ATTM*, 309; V 88,2, *ATTM*, 2, 260.
26. V 58:3.
27. E.g., ooKA 2:1, *ATTM*, 398; yyMA 4:1, *ATTM.E*, 237; in each case beginning with "an effective amulet."
28. *KAI* 224.3; *TADAE* C1.1,101.
29. *TADAE* C1.1,181.
30. Elephantine: *TADAE* A4.7,22 par. 4.8,22; A4.5,19.21; correspondence of the satraps of Aršama: A6.3,5; A6.7,8; A6.13,2; letters from the archive of the Bactrian administration: Naveh and Shaked, A1.9; B5.5.
31. *ATTM*, 2, 404.
32. Naveh and Shaked, A6.5; → *nṣḥ* II.
33. *TADAE* A3.10,6.
34. Like the Clermont-Ganneau ostraca.

admonition to hold fast to the transmitted law in a clearly ethical context,[35] and *gbrʾ ṭbʾ* for a certain "good man" in the story at the Achaemenid court.[36] Otherwise, Qumran texts express moral goodness with the opposition of light/darkness[37] or truth/lies.[38] Finally, in Palmyrene inscriptions, *ṭb* also functions as a predicate of male and female deities, sometimes along with *rḥmn* "merciful."[39]

2. Substantivized. Already in Old and Imperial Aramaic, the substantivized masculine or feminine adjective *ṭb* denotes quite generally "something good"[40] or in the masculine determinative *ṭbʾ* "the good": in contrast to *lḥyʾ* "the evil" of contract partners who share success and failure,[41] but also of goods that a deity bestows on people,[42] or that one person does for another;[43] proverbially in T. Levi: *dzrʿ ṭb ṭb mʿl* "whoever sows good, harvests good."[44] Specifically, the masculine can be employed for good fortune (*bṭb*),[45] the feminine for goodness in education[46] or good intentions for someone,[47] in official diction also for "benefit, assistance" of a superior[48] or in Old Aramaic for the loyalty of a vassal,[49] the feminine in the plural for "property, goods."[50] The last two nuances overlap with those of the abstract noun *ṭbw* /ṭābū/ (→ IV). In 11Q10 27:5 (Job 36:11), it translates Hebrew *ṭwb*, in 16:4 (Job 30:15) it paraphrases the rare word *ndybh* "nobility, dignity," in accordance with the tendency of the text to employ more prosaic and common Aramaic terms for unusual Hebrew lexemes.

3. Various Idiomatic Expressions. Of the idiomatic expressions with *ṭb*, older Aramaic exhibits especially the expression *dkyr lṭb/bṭb* "be remembered in a good way" (in contrast to *lbyš* "in a bad way") in the memorial epigraphy of Hellenistic and Roman times.[51] In addition, *šm ṭb* "a good name" is a circumlocution for fame,[52] *ywm ṭb* for "holiday."[53]

35. 4Q542 1 1:10.
36. 4Q550 5+5a:3,4; probably dittography, see *ATTM*, 2, 151.
37. → *ḥšk* III.
38. → *qšṭ*.
39. *PAT* 0301.7; 0318.3; 0367.1; 1912.2; 2751.3.
40. *TADAE* C1.1,163; fem. in l. 171.
41. *TADAE* B1.1,5f.
42. 1QapGen 21:3 with the verb *ʿbd* "to do," in Palmyra with *ʿnī* "to answer": *PAT* 0399.7.
43. *TADAE* D7.1,8, also with *ʿbd*.
44. 4Q213 1 1:8.
45. 4Q196 18:14 (Tob. 14:2).
46. *TADAE* C1.1,9.
47. *TADAE* C1.1,24.
48. On *bʿly ṭbtk* "entitled to your beneficence" in Imperial Aramaic → *bʿl* II.3.
49. *KAI* 222 C 4.19 and 223 B 2; cf. J. A. Fitzmyer, *The Aramaic Inscriptions of Sefire*. *BietOr* 19/A (^{2}1995), 116f. Similarly, *TADAE* A1.1,8, context partially destroyed, but on the whole in little doubt.
50. 1QapGen 21:3, alongside → *nksyn* "property holder"; 22:11; and apparently also 4Q537 5:1, although the context has not been preserved.
51. → *dkr* II.
52. 4Q542 1 1:10; 4Q550 2:2.
53. In the *Megillat Taʿanit*, a festival calendar: xyMT 21.25, *ATTM*, 357.

IV. Noun "Good Deed." The rare feminine abstract *ṭbw* /ṭābū/ appears in 1QapGen 19:19 in the plural for "beneficences" and, thus, overlaps with the substantival use of the adjective (→ III.2); further, a second century C.E. grave inscription from Armazi in Georgia employs it in praise of a prematurely deceased woman. There, *ṭbw* in the Aramaic expression *l' dm' yhwh mn ṭbwt* "no one was like [her] in excellence" corresponds to τὸ κάλλος "beauty" in the Greek version.[54] This aesthetic nuance, however, is foreign to the original use of the root *ṭīb* in Semitic.

Furthermore, the noun *ṭwb* /ṭūb/ "blessed is," in the plural "blessed are," literally "property," serves as an exclamation of blessing.[55] It may already occur in Sefire,[56] but in any case in Qumran[57] and then later.[58]

Gzella

54. *KAI* 276.11.
55. So perhaps in 4Q539 5:3.
56. *KAI* 222 B 6; cf. Fitzmyer, 101.
57. 4Q196 18:3 (Tob. 13:15), Greek μακάριοι; fragmentary 4Q536 2 2:10.
58. Cf. *ATTM*, 2, 404.

טל *ṭl* /ṭall/

I. Lexical Field and Meaning. II. Usage.

I. Lexical Field and Meaning. The masculine noun /ṭall/ (> /ṭal/) "dew" is common to the West Semitic languages and denotes a meteorological phenomenon in Aramaic. Mythological connotations, such as shine through in Ugaritic and Hebrew,[1] persist manifestly only in the translation of the personifying usage in Job 38:28 in 11Q10 31:6.

II. Usage. After a possible instance of a metaphorical usage for speech or the word in a corrupt context in the difficult second combination of the Deir ʿAllā wall inscription,[2] *ṭl* /ṭall/ occurs primarily in the dream of Nebuchadnezzar's dehumanization in Dnl. 4. There it appears in the repeated formula *ṭl šmy'* "dew of heaven" with the verb *ṣbʿ* "to dampen" (Dnl. 4:12,20,22,30; 5:21). Its function is not entirely clear; presumably, it underscores

B. Kern-Ulmer, "Consistency and Change in Rabbinic Literature as Reflected in the Terms Rain and Dew," *JSJ* 26 (1995) 55-75; B. Otzen, "טַל *ṭal*," *TDOT*, V, 323-30.

1. B. Otzen, 327-29.
2. II:36.

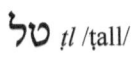

the fact that the king was stripped of all civilization as punishment for his arrogance and was remitted to nature for only basic provision.

Texts in the Enoch tradition from Qumran[3] associate dew and rain (*mṭr*) with the life-giving and destructive winds.[4] These usages offer a prelude to its later usage as a symbol of life.

Gzella

3. 4Q204 1 13:26 (1 En. 36:1); 4Q210 1 2:8 (1 En. 76:8).
4. The same combination, with lacunae, also in 1Q24 5:4 and 4Q203 11 2:2.

טלל *ṭll* /ṭelāl/ and טל *ṭl* /ṭell/, /ṭoll/; טלל *ṭll*; טלול *ṭlwl* /ṭalūl/; מטלל *mṭll* /maṭlal/

I. Lexical Field and Forms. II. Noun "Shadow." III. Nouns for "Roof." IV. Verb "to Shade," "to Find Shade."

I. Lexical Field and Forms. With the two masculine nouns /ṭelāl/[1] and /ṭoll/[2] for "shadow," Aramaic reproduces an older variation in Semitic. Meanwhile, the form /ṭoll/ is a shared peculiarity of East Aramaic[3] and, with the combination /men ṭoll/ "out of the shadow of," developed the new preposition /meṭṭoll/ "because of." Related are the verb verb *ṭll* and the masculines /ṭalūl/ and /maṭlal/ "roof." The connotation "protection" governs the lexical field.

II. Noun "Shadow." Imperial Aramaic frequently manifests the noun *ṭll* "shadow" in the combination *bṭll* for divine protection[4] and as *bṭlh* with a cataphoric suffix for Ahura Mazda in the Behistun Inscription;[5] it appears literally in the texts from the Dead Sea in descriptions of real estate[6] and in 4Q201 1 2:7 (1 En. 4:1) as protection from the sun.

H. Gzella, "*ṣl*," *ThWQ*, III, 415-18; J. Naveh and S. Shaked, *Aramaic Documents from Ancient Bactria (Fourth Century* B.C.E.*)* (London, 2012); H. Niehr, "צַלְמָוֶת *ṣalmāweṯ*," *TDOT*, XII, 396-99; E. Schwab, "צֵל *ṣēl*," *TDOT*, XII, 372-82.

1. Also Arabic and Ethiopic.
2. From the older */θ̣ill/, like the Akk. and the Heb. *ṣēl*.
3. *ATTM*, 98.590.
4. *TADAE* A4.3,5; C2.1 cols. I-III 2.4; an analogue in 1QapGen 19:16.
5. *TADAE* C2.1,10.16.26.42.55.
6. *ATTM*, 2, 404.

III. Nouns for "Roof." Of the two noun forms with the meaning "roof," *mṭll* /maṭlal/ appears in an Imperial Aramaic letter[7] and *ṭlwl* /ṭalūl/ in the description of the heavenly Jerusalem.[8] No distinction can be deduced from these few instances.

IV. Verb "To Shade," "To Find Shade." The verb *ṭll*, often attested in the Imperial Aramaic tradition, typically appears in the D-stem "to roof." It occurs in a satrap's letter from Bactria with *bytn* "houses" as object,[9] and in a Palmyrene inscription[10] with *'drwn* "dining hall(?)." The causative-stem means "to rest in the shade, to give shade" and functions in Nebuchadnezzar's dream as an image of protection for the animals under the world-tree (Dnl. 4:9).

Gzella

7. *TADAE* A4.7,11 par. 4.8,10.
8. 4Q554a 1 2:13.
9. Naveh and Shaked, A6.3. An inf. "in order to roof" and a subsequent pass. ptcp. "are (still not yet) roofed," in variation with the pass. ptcp. of the G-stem that may be lexicalized as an adj. in ll. 7, 9.
10. *PAT* 3917.4.

טעם *ṭʿm*; טעם *ṭʿm* /ṭaʿm/

I. Etymology and Distribution. II. Old and Imperial Aramaic. III. Biblical Aramaic. IV. Qumran, Jewish Aramaic. V. Miscellanea.

I. Etymology and Distribution. The verbal root *ṭʿm* is probably common Semitic since it is attested in all branches,[1] although East Semitic and, to a degree, West Semitic[2] and Neo-South Semitic no longer preserve the original ʿ. It is questionable whether the basic meaning of the root was originally a stative verb, "something has

J. Dušek, *Les manuscrits araméens du Wadi Daliyeh et la Samarie vers 450-332 av. J.-C. CHANE* 30 (2007); S. A. Kaufman, *The Akkadian Influences on Aramaic. AS* 19 (1974); H. Lozachmeur, *La collection Clermont-Ganneau: Ostraca, épigraphes sur jarre, étiquettes de bois*, 2 vols. (Paris, 2006); J. Naveh and S. Shaked, *Aramaic Documents from Ancient Bactria (Fourth Century B.C.E.)* (London, 2012); J. L. Palache, *Semantic Notes on the Hebrew Lexicon* (Leiden, 1959); J. B. Segal, *Aramaic Texts from North Saqqara* (London, 1983); J. Schüpphaus, "טָעַם *ṭāʿam*," *TDOT*, V, 345-47; A. Tal, *A Dictionary of Samaritan Aramaic*, 2 vols. (Leiden, 2000).

1. Citations in J. Schüpphaus, 345.
2. As in the Mandean *ṭam*.

taste, is tasty."[3] Judging from the evidence, it involves an action verb, "to taste, eat, enjoy, have a taste for," specifically of foods and drinks, but then also applied to other objects whether perceptible to the senses or not[4] and extended to further sensory perception "to test, to appreciate, to get a sense of, to understand, to pay attention";[5] then for "to perceive, to be concerned about something, to want, to obey"[6] to "to proclaim his will, to report, to command"[7] and quite neutrally "matter, affair, something, with respect to."[8]

Often, the last two meanings are not unequivocally distinguishable; finally, the noun in the Jewish Aramaic realm also means "taste," and thence "unit of meaning, expression, accent." In relation to the *qatl*-noun, the verbal root is probably primary, although, in individual languages, it may be denominal again as, perhaps, in Akkadian[9] and Samaritan-Aramaic.[10]

II. Old and Imperial Aramaic. In numbers, the verb *ṭʻm* is not as frequent as the noun: perfect "I have tasted the mistletoe and the taste was strong";[11] imperfect "so may/will it taste";[12] and with suffix ("(the friend?) of the wine is the one who savors it";[13] possible (or pael/aphel?) "for him, it is better then if he would savor [it]";[14] aphel perfect "he determined, decided about the boundary stone."[15]

The basic meaning of the noun *ṭʻm* "taste" may only be preserved in the emended *w[ṭʻm]* "and the taste."[16] Since the sentence structure has not been preserved, the meaning of *ṭʻmk* "your pleasure/your statement of intent" in *TADAE* A3.5,7 par. *šlmk* "your well-being" is uncertain; Imperial Aramaic does not attest the meaning "mind."

As early as the seventh century B.C.E. *ṭʻm* almost exclusively meant "command" or "matter." The former may be a loan translation from the Akkadian *ṭêmu*.[17] It occurs with

3. Sometimes in South Semitic.

4. West and South Semitic.

5. West Semitic: Hebrew e.g., "value" Sir. 10:28; Aramaic e.g., Mandean "content"; Akk. has the noun *ṭêmu* "understanding, plan, will"; cf. Latin *sapio* "to taste, perceive, to be sensible" and *sapiens* "wise," Palache, 36.

6. Akkadian (verb); Aramaic.

7. Noun: Akkadian *ṭêmu* "decision, report, command," corresponding to Aramaic and influenced by it in Jon. 3:7; in Aramaic either an Akkadian loanword or an independent semantic development of "mouth" to "command."

8. Imperial Aramaic, perhaps an Akkadian loanword (Kaufman, 109) or an independent semantic development like → *ṣbī* "to want" to *ṣabū* "issue, matter, something."

9. *AHw*, III, 1387: G- or N-stem.

10. Tal, 319: D-stem.

11. Wisdom saying of Aḥiqar, *TADAE* C1.1,89.

12. *KAI* 233.8; or aphel "determine, command" with F. M. Fales, *Aramaic Epigraphs on Clay Tablets of the Neo-Assyrian Period. SS* 2 (1986), No. 58?

13. *TADAE* C1.1,208.

14. *TADAE* C1.1,180f., par. "he does not eat."

15. Legal documents, Fales, 58.5: "agreeing with decisions" or, in accord with l. 2, "their boundary stone," following the Akkadian.

16. *TADAE* C1.1,89; see above.

17. Kaufman, 119.

the verb *ḥwī* in *TADAE* A4.4,9, although usually as the object of the verb *śīm* "to give a command": perfect *TADAE* C3.8IIIB,30; IV,7; Segal, 14.5; the passive (*kzy*) *śym ṭʿm* "(as) a command is given";[18] imperfect "the penalty that I gave them as a command";[19] imperative *TADAE* A6.3,7; A6.5,3; t-stem "may a command be issued (from you)";[20] in the construct for a genitive relationship "a command concerning the rate";[21] determinative "the command/decision."[22] With the G-stem participle/perfect *ydʿ ṭʿmʾ znh* "(name) knows this commandment" appears regularly at the end of the letters of the satraps from Aršama,[23] if not already a truncation for "these matters presented in the letter" (see below), sometimes also with *ḥwī* "to communicate."[24] The administrative letters from Bactria also conform to this usage.[25] A possible instance of the suffixed form *ṭʿmy* "my command" appears in *TADAE* D7.15,11, but the context is unclear. Regarding *bʿl ṭʿm* → *bʿl* II.3.

The second meaning of the word in the Imperial Aramaic texts is the flattened "matter, issue, something, concerning." This meaning may also involve an Akkadian loan translation.[26] It is often not entirely clear which of the two loan translations is at hand: absolute for domestic affairs;[27] in the construct with a subsequent personal name "concerning that [slave] N.";[28] in the determinative, "a proceeding concerning this matter," in a legal record;[29] negatively.[30] Often, the precise nuance of the fragmentary instances in the Clermont-Ganneau ostraca[31] cannot be determined.

III. Biblical Aramaic. Biblical Aramaic attests the verb in the pael (or aphel?) "to give to eat" with a direct object and *l-* "to someone" in Nebuchadnezzar's dream (Dnl. 4:22,29: "[herbage] will be given (you) [like the cow] to eat");[32] it also appears with suffix and a dual object (Dnl. 5:21).[33]

The variation of the nouns *ṭᵉʿēm* (Ezr. 6:14) and *ṭaʿam* (Ezr. 6:14; 7:23) may be an artificial Masoretic distinction ("human" versus "divine command"), or *ṭaʿam* is a He-

18. *TADAE* A6.2,22.23.25 (signature) and C3.8IIIB,7.
19. *TADAE* A6.3,6f.
20. *TADAE* A6.7,8 and Segal 15,3.
21. *TADAE* A6.1,2.
22. *TADAE* D7.48,8f.
23. *TADAE* A6.8,4; 6.9,5; 6.10,10; 6.11,6; 6.12[,3]; 6.13,5.
24. *TADAE* D7.24,16f.
25. Naveh and Shaked, A1,5.12; 3,4; 4,6; 5,1.2.3; 6,3.7.10.11; 7,2.
26. Kaufman, 109.
27. *TADAE* A2.3,12.
28. Dušek, *WDSP* 4.7.
29. *TADAE* B8.9[,2][.6].
30. *TADAE* A4.7,30 par. 4.8,29, here, however, "this commandment" may be expressly intended; see above.
31. Citations in Lozachmeur, 541.
32. In the execution of the threat in 4:30, the synonymous *ʾkl* appears with the impf. as the narrative tense; see H. Gzella, *Tempus, Aspekt und Modalität im Reichsaramäischen. VOK* 48 (2004), 137; with a slightly different wording and reordered in 4:12,20.
33. See Gzella, 138.

braism.[34] The basic meaning "to savor, enjoy" is still present in Dnl. 5:2 ("during the wine-tasting"); otherwise, the following nuances are attested: "mind" (Dnl. 2:14, cf. LXX); "caution, attention, obedience" (*ʿl* in reference to a person/matter: Dnl. 3:12; 6:14); "command" (*mn* "on the basis of": Ezr. 6:14; 7:23; with the pf. of the verb *śīm*: Dnl. 3:10; Ezr. 5:3,9,13; 6:1,3,12; impersonally in the passive: Dnl. 3:29; Ezr. 4:21; 6:11; 7:13), in a construction with a direct object and *l-* "to" (Ezr. 7:21), *mn qdmy* "from me" instead of *mny* (Dnl. 6:27), *lmʾ dy* instead of *dy* (Ezr. 6:8), with *l-* and infinitive "in order to" (Dnl. 4:3; Ezr. 4:21; 5:17) and with *w-* and a perfect (Ezr. 4:19); "report" (Dnl. 6:3), perhaps flattened like Imperial Aramaic "affair" (Ezr. 5:5; see above). Regarding *bʿl ṭʿm* → *bʿl* II.4.

IV. Qumran, Jewish Aramaic. Qumran does not attest the verb and attests the noun only rarely and fragmentarily, although in agreement with Imperial Aramaic usage (→ II): "understanding" or "report" in *bṭʿm rzy* "through insight into/communication of secret(s)," 4Q536 2 1:9; "command" (here, too, with *śīm)* 4Q545 2:2; construct "regulation [of God. . .]"(?) 4Q212 1 5:15 (1 En. 93:11).

In Jewish Palestinian and Jewish Babylonian, the verb in the G-stem means "to taste, to eat," both literally and figuratively, in the aphel "to cause to taste," the noun "taste" and "insight, reason, justification, sense, accent," in magical texts also "mind" as in Biblical Hebrew and Biblical Aramaic, furthermore, the *qatil*-adjective "tasty, sweet."[35]

V. Miscellanea. Nabatean employs the noun in accordance with the Imperial Aramaic meaning "will, regulation, decision" in the formula *mn ʿl ṭʿmʾ* in filiations of sons through adoption,[36] in the Palmyrene tax schedule as a feminine plural for "foodstuff."[37] In Syriac, the lexical field "taste" predominates.[38]

Nebe

34. *BLA*, §228f′, cf. *BLH*, §456k′ and Jon. 3:7.
35. Citations in *DJPA*, 228 and *DJBA*, 510f., respectively.
36. Citations in *DNSI*, 427.
37. *PAT* 0259 ii.109; the Greek parallel version has βρωτῶν in this sense in iv.187.
38. *LexSyr*, 283.

יד *yd* /yad/; **כף** *kp* /kapp/; **אצבע** *ʾṣbʿ* /ʾeṣbaʿ/; **דרע** *drʿ* /derāʿ/

I. Lexical Field and Grammatical Constructions. II. Anatomical. 1. Hand. 2. Finger. 3. Arm. III. Figuratively for the Power of God. IV. Combinations with *b-*, *l-*, *mn* and *ʿl*.

I. Lexical Field and Grammatical Constructions. With the feminine primary noun /yad/, the Semitic languages denote the hand, including the palm and back of the hand (/kapp/ > /kap/), the fingers (singular /ʾeṣbaʿ/) and the lower arm.[1] These other basic anatomical terms are also common Semitic.[2] In a more literal usage, the plural usually denotes several hands or the dual, a pair of hands; in idiomatic expressions, on the other hand, the singular is also usual in reference to the (one) hand of several persons.[3] Figuratively, in Biblical Aramaic and in the Aramaic texts from Qumran, the hand often represents the power of God. In addition, in conjunction with the prepositions *b-*, *l-*, *mn* and *ʿl* it forms various new and consistently frequent expressions denoting spatial, logical, or hierarchical relationships.

II. Anatomical.

1. Hand. Other than in fixed, lexicalized prepositional expressions (→ IV), "hand" occurs in the literal meaning as a body part only relatively rarely. Imperial Aramaic legal texts sometimes mention a slave *šnyt*(*h*) *bydh ymyn* "branded on the right hand" with the name of the owner in Aramaic script.[4] The song in praise of Sarah in 1QapGen describes the beauty of her hands, once distinguishing *yd* from *drʿ* "arm." On the other hand, it also functions as the term encompassing *kp* "palm" and *ʾṣbʿt ydyhʾ* "the fingers of her hands."[5] A Hebrew omen text confirms for Qumran, too, long, slender fingers as the timeless ideal of beauty.[6] In isolated instances, meanwhile, *yd* contrasts the lower arm explicitly with the description *ʾṣbʿth kpy* "the fingers of the hands."[7] In 4Q530 7 2:4, too, *wprḥ bydwhy knš*[*r* apparently signifies "and with his arms he [a giant] flew like a vulture,"[8] because the interpretation "hands" produces no sense here.

Together with certain verbs, *yd* is employed for various typical gestures: with → *nśī ʾl*/*l-* "to raise the hand in prayer";[9] later with the causative stem of → *rīm* "to raise for an oath";[10] with *smk* "to lay the hand on (to heal),"[11] in the cult 4Q156 2:5 (Lev. 16:21);

J. Bergman, W. von Soden, and P. Ackroyd, "יָד *yād*," *TDOT*, V, 393-426; H.-J. Fabry, "*yd*," *ThWQ*, II, 54-69; M. Jursa, "Nochmals: aramäische Buchstabennamen in akkadischer Transliteration," in *Von Sumer bis Homer. FS M. Schretter. AOAT* 325 (2005), 399-405; G.-W. Nebe, "Das Lied von Sarais Schönheit in 1Q20 = Genesis-Apokryphon XX, 2-8 und die Anfänge der aramäischen Poesie," in *Der Christliche Orient und seine Umwelt. FS J. Tubach* (Wiesbaden, 2007), 59-86; A. S. van der Woude, "יָד *yād* hand," *TLOT*, 497-502.

1. For the arm as a whole, Semitic languages have /derāʿ/, arisen from an older */δerāʿ/.
2. On the relationship of the other extremities to one another, → II.1.
3. *ATTM*, 2, 407.
4. *TADAE* B2.11,5.6; 3.6,3; regarding the backgrounds, see Jursa.
5. 1QapGen 20:4f.; on the text and its interpretation, see Nebe.
6. 4Q186 2 1:4f.
7. 4Q213a 1:9, in a gesture of prayer.
8. So correctly *ATTM*, 265.
9. *KAI* 202 A 11; in Samʾalian also *KAI* 214.29.
10. 1QapGen 22:21; cf. Dt. 32:40, Dnl. 12:7, Isa. 62:8; see J. Lust, "For I Lift Up My Hand to Heaven and Swear: Deut 32:40," in *Studies in Deuteronomy. FS C. J. Labuschagne*, ed. F. García Martínez et al. *SVT* 53 (Leiden, 1994), 155-64.
11. 1QapGen 20:22,29; not yet attested in the Bible; cf. D. Flusser, "Healing through the Laying-on of Hands in a Dead Sea Scroll," *IEJ* 7 (1957) 107f.

further, in accordance with biblical diction, *mlī yd* "to fill someone's hand" in the sense of "to install as priest."[12] As a sign of horror, *śīm yd ʿl* "to place the hand on (the mouth)" is translated from the Hebrew in 11Q10 4:4 (Job 21:5).

Such expressions have sometimes then, in turn, taken on a figurative meaning. Already since Old Aramaic, → *šlḥ yd* (*b*-) "to stretch out the hand (toward)" is attested in the sense "to offend (someone)" with the nuance of an unpermitted transgression[13] or, even more remotely faded from the original meaning, with *l*- and the infinitive "to dare to" (Ezr. 6:12). Further, → *mḥī byd* "to smite on the hand" stands for "to ward off, hinder someone" (for God's omnipotence, Dnl. 4:32; elsewhere *klī*), while, in contrast, with *yd* as object for "to guarantee" as a legal expression borrowed from Akkadian;[14] with → *mṭī* "to obtain" *kzy tmṭh ydky* in *TADAE* 2.6,5f. colloquially(?) for "(buy) whatever you can obtain in hand," figuratively in A2.4,4 "as well as I can."[15] Other passages remain unclear as a consequence of the lack of context.[16]

In combination with forms of the root → *ktb*, *yd* emphasizes that one has written with one's own hand: verbally, *ydyhm ktbt wqymt qdmy* "their hands have written (it) and confirmed before me";[17] nominally, *ktb yd ḥnwk* "document from Enoch's (own) hand"[18] and in witness lists at the end of contracts *ktb bydh* "he signed it with his own hand"[19] or more often *ktb ydh* "his autographed signature."[20] Such expressions may stand in the background of the fiery writing of Dnl. 5 (→ III).

Instead of *yd*, *kp* /kapp/ is used for the palm, and *kp rgl* for the sole of the foot,[21] in juxtaposition with the sole of the foot, *kp yd*.[22] Imperial Aramaic legal diction also knows the meaning "blow"[23] and figuratively *bkp ḥdh* "in one blow,"[24] and further *bkpy* "written by,"[25] for which the legal texts from the Dead Sea have *ktb bydh* or *ktb ydh* (see above). Proverbially, *ksī kpn* "to cover the hands" apparently signifies "to be inactive."[26] On the relationship between *kp* and *yd* according to 1QapGen 20:4f. and 4Q213a 1:9 see above. 11Q10 14:3 (Job 29:9) has the Hebrew counterpart freely translated "work of the

---

12. 4Q562 1:2; cf. *GesB*[18], s.v. *ml'*, piel 1a.

13. *KAI* 222 B 25.27.34 and 223 B 6, the covenant formula in a treaty of state.

14. Often in Assyrian commercial texts from the Neo-Assyrian period; cf. A. Lemaire, *Nouvelles tablettes araméennes*. *HEO* 34.1 (2001), 21.

15. Cf. *TADAE* A4.3,9.

16. E.g., *TADAE* C1.1,155, where it cannot be determined with certainty whether *ydy* "my hands" is the subject or the object; *KAI* 202 B 14 is similarly difficult.

17. *KAI* 233.9; with disagreement of the singular verb with the preceding plural or dual subject?

18. 4Q203 8:4.

19. nV 3:53 in *ATTM*, 2.

20. nV 1:56ff; 2:47f.; 3:51,54; 9:24; cf. *PAT* 1624.3.

21. 4Q561 1 1:9.

22. As in a court record to distinguish blows on the palms from those on the soles of the foot; *TADAE* B8.4,5; 8.6,10.

23. *TADAE* B3.8,24.28.

24. For a complete payment instead of installments: *TADAE* B2.6,28.

25. *TADAE* B2.7,17; 4.3,21.

26. *TADAE* C1.1,87.

hands" in 23:5 (Job 33:26). Later Aramaic languages employ *kp* exclusively for "scale pan"[27] and "scoop."[28]

The noun *ps* /pass/ serves in Dnl. 5:5,24 as a very rare synonym for "hand"—or perhaps only for the back of the hand in contrast to *kp*.[29] A possible extrabiblical instance in *TADAE* D7.37,7 is dubious because *kp* could also stand here. For the measure of capacity, "handful," Aramaic has /ḥopn/, for the measure of length, "hand's breadth" (⅙ ell), /pošk/.[30]

2. *Finger.* The likewise feminine noun *ʾṣbʿ* /ʾeṣbaʿ/ "finger" is sometimes employed in the same context as *yd* "hand,"[31] in relation to feet, it means "toe" (Dnl. 2:41f.).[32] The masculine by-form *ṣbʿ* /ṣebaʿ/[33] is employed as a measure of length "finger's breadth."[34]

3. *Arm.* As does *ʾṣbʿ*/*ṣbʿ*, so *drʿ* /derāʿ/ "arm" has a (feminine) by-form *ʾdrʿ* with a prosthetic glottal stop; Ezr. 4:23 employs it along with → *ḥyl* figuratively for "force" and it also appears later. In contrast, *drʿ* literally denotes only the upper arm (Dnl. 2:32, mentioned here together with the chest);[35] *TADAE* D7.9,4f. mention *drʿ* as the place for marking slaves, for which Imperial Aramaic contracts usually employ *yd*.[36] The word *drʿ* along with → *ḥyl* and other lexemes can also denote physical power.[37] With "an arm like God," 11Q10 34:5 translates the Hebrew cognate *zrwʿ* from Job 40:9 literally.

III. Figuratively for the Power of God. Especially in the biblical Psalms and the Hebrew texts from Qumran, the hand of God serves regularly as an image of God's power. At first sight, Daniel's account of the hand that wrote on the wall in fiery letters during Belshazzar's feast the oracle of judgment with the demise of the evil-doing king recalls this metaphor; the enigmatic message remained initially incomprehensible and required Daniel's interpretation (Dnl. 5:5,24).[38] The fact that while, on one hand, it speaks of the human form of the hand (*dy yd ʾnš*), on the other, it mentions only fingers[39] and a hand/back of the hand[40] without the person they belong to highlights the eerie character

27. *DJPA*, 266b.
28. *DJBA*, 594a.
29. In Dnl. 5:24, *psʾ dy ydʾ* specifies it as belonging to the hand and, thus, perhaps only a part of it.
30. *DNSI*, 395, 946.
31. On 1QapGen 20:5 and 4Q213a 1:9 → II.1; on Dnl. 5:5 → III; further 4Q156 1,7 (Lev 16:14).
32. It is sometimes stricken, however, because it does not appear in the vision itself (2:33); cf. K. Koch, *Daniel 1–4*. *BK* XXII/1 (2005), 102.
33. *TADAE* A6.2,16.18.19, etc.; cf. *DNSI*, 958.
34. 2.2 cm (about 1 in.), cf. *ATTM*, 520.
35. On 1QapGen 20:4, → II.1.
36. → II.1; → *ktb*.
37. 4Q531 22:3.
38. For the content → *mnī*.
39. *ʾṣbʿn*, → II.2.
40. *ps*, → II.1.

of this phenomenon. Since *yd* appears here together with the verb *ktb* "to write," the nuance "to write with one's own hand" known from the contracts could stand in the background and allude to the fact that it involves an immediate and, at the same time, binding announcement directly from God, which will inevitably come to pass (→ II.1). At the same time, the image of the court scribe may shine through, whereby even for those who do not understand the words it becomes clear that here an irreversible verdict has been issued. Thus, the reorientation of Imperial Aramaic administrative terminology evokes a court context.

Individual formulations with *yd* in the Armaic texts at Qumran approximate biblical prayer diction, most clearly in a passage from 1QapGen: when the pharaoh had taken Abraham's wife for himself, Abraham asked God, *ʾḥzy ydk rbtʾ bh* "show him your great hand."[41] Many other instances are fragmentary, however.

IV. Combinations with *b-*, *l-*, *mn* and *ʿl*. By far the most common usage of *yd* consists of its use with suffixes or a noun in construct state in lexicalized prepositional expressions with *b-* "in the power/possession of, by means of," *l-* "beside, at," *mn* "from the power of," *ʿl* "under the leadership, for the attention of." They can only be illustrated here with a few examples. An extensive overview, arranged by preposition, appears in *DNSI*, 435-38;[42] for Qumran see *ATTM*, 593 and 2, 406f.

Especially widespread is the combination *byd* "in the power of," which became fused in Ugaritic, the Old Canaanite of the Amarna correspondence and in Phoenician into an independent, new preposition, *bd* /bād-/ or /bōd/.[43] In Aramaic, it is used alongside the rare literal usage[44] either for the mediation of something by someone[45] or, if it refers to the subject, for "personal, by one's own hand";[46] further for posession,[47] authority (so for the binding interpretation of the law in Ezr. 7:14,25) or actual power.[48] Together with a subsequent infinitive, it also occasionally functions as an auxiliary/modal for "to be able,"[49] as does the verb → *ykl* otherwise.

---

41. 1QapGen 20:14f.

42. D. Schwiderski, *Die alt- und reichsaramäischen Inschriften. FSBP* 4 (2008), 1:346-51, offers more instances, primarily for the numerous commercial texts, although they are classified purely according to the spelling of *yd* in the respective expression and not according to usage.

43. See H. Gzella, "Linguistic Variation in the Ugaritic Letters and Some Implications Thereof," in W. H. van Soldt, ed., *Society and Administration in Ancient Ugarit. PIHANS* 114 (2010), 58-70, here 60 n. 13.

44. 1QapGen 15:10.

45. In *KAI* 202 A 12 by seers.

46. Often with verbs of bringing: *TADAE* A3.8,13; A6.16,2; B2.6,6f.25.28; B3.3,8.10.16.

47. *TADAE* A2.2,5; in contracts in a formulaic expression with legal documents: *TADAE* B2.3,18.22; B3.1,12.14.19.20.

48. Often of kings or God over individuals or entire peoples; locative "in the power" *KAI* 224.5.10.13; Dnl. 5:23; 7:25; terminative "in the power" *KAI* 224.2; Dnl. 2:38; Ezr. 5:12; 1QapGen 22:17; 4Q246 1 2:8.

49. *TADAE* C1.1,170f.; sayings of Aḥiqar.

In contrast, *lyd* is usually employed locally for the position "beside, at"[50] or for the direction "along toward."[51] The function of *lyd* with a subsequent official title is very specific, however, in administrative texts from Persepolis,[52] perhaps meaning "at the disposal of"[53] and in commercial ostraca from Idumea;[54] normally, however, *l* has this function (see below).

The combination *mn yd* sometimes serves as the ablative counterpart of *byd* meaning "from the power of" (Dnl. 3:15,17;[55] 6:28),[56] sometimes with *lqḥ* "to take"[57] although redundant for a simple *mn*,[58] similarly in an idiomatic expression, "to take revenge against," literally "from the hands of my enemies,"[59] later also "personally from."[60] If the reading is actually correct, *mn l*[*yd*] "from the coast" in 1QapGen 21:16 would be unusual.

In administrative diction, *ʿl yd*(*y*) designates the relationship "for the attention of"[61] or "under the direction of."[62]

The dual *ydyn* "mutually" with no preposition appears rarely and apparently functions adverbially.[63]

In later Aramaic, one also encounters other combinations or nuances, namely *yd* "influence, control" and *myd* from *mn yd* "promptly.[64]

Gzella

50. E.g., in the place descriptions in 1QapGen 14:15; 17:7 or those of the heavenly Jerusalem: 11Q18 6:2; 11:2; 13:8.

51. As in Abraham's migrations, 1QapGen 21:15,16,17.

52. Cf. the discussion in *DNSI*, 436f.

53. As a troop in an Aršama letter, *TADAE* A6.8,1.

54. I. Eph'al and J. Naveh, *Aramaic Ostraca of the Fourth Century BC from Idumaea* (Jerusalem, 1996), no. 2,2.

55. On the form, cf. *BLA*, §5d.

56. Of lions which naturally have no hands and thus figurative; the meaning "paw" is only clearly attested later: *DJBA*, 523b.

57. → *nśʾ*.

58. *KAI* 309.17f.; 224,2.

59. *KAI* 224.11.

60. nV 7:18f.,23,58, *ATTM*, 2, 218f.

61. *TADAE* B4.4,3, with → *yhb* "to give"; Eph'al and Naveh, no. 56:3; receipt V 37:4 in *ATTM*, 2, 241.

62. More often in Idumean ostraca, e.g., Eph'al and Naveh, no. 37.2; nV 1:38 in *ATTM*, 2, 205f.; 4Q531 1:4.

63. *TADAE* B2.6,8; B3.8,8.

64. *DJPA*, 314; *DJBA*, 523f.; also borrowed in Hebrew.

ידי ydī

I. Lexical Field and Grammatical Constructions. II. Juridical Usage "to Acknowledge." III. Religious Usage "to Praise, Thank."

I. Lexical Field and Grammatical Constructions. Instances of a verbal root *ydī*[1] "to acknowledge, praise" occurs in Aramaic and also in Hebrew and Arabic. The verb appears, as in Hebrew, mostly in the causative stem where it retains its original initial radical /w/. A possible relationship with the presumed homonymous root *ydī* "to throw (out)"[2] that appears rarely in Hebrew and Ugarit is in dispute.

The superordinant meaning "to publicly communicate" became differentiated into two semantic realms in Aramaic: on the one hand, the realm of the law and administration, where the verb functions to mean "to confirm" in the discourse of the Imperial Aramaic documentary tradition, later and Jewish Palestinian and Jewish Babylonian, further, it means "to acquiesce, agree";[3] on the other hand, in the diction of personal piety, *ydī* means "to praise, thank."

This second usage is very productive in Biblical Hebrew and the hymnic-liturgical Hebrew texts from Qumran that are often oriented toward the Bible. In contrast, the verb does not appear with particular frequency in Aramaic itself and overlaps semantically with the more typical Aramaic → *šbḥ* and other verbs of praise also attested in other Semitic languages, namely → *brk*, → *hdr* III, *hll* in the D-stem,[4] und → *rīm* in the L-stem.

In the two usages, *ydī* is constructed very similarly: "to acknowledge" transitive[5] or with the preposition *b-*,[6] alternatively with an object clause following *dy* "that"[7] and in some cases with an indirect object following *l-* "to someone"[8] or later also *l-* with an infinitive;[9] "to praise" transitive, with the nuance "to thank," however, with an indirect object following *l-* (Dnl. 2:23) or *qdm* (Dnl. 6:11); the reason for the praise can, further, be cited in a nominal phrase following *ʿl*[10] or in a verbal phrase following *dy* "that, because" (Dnl. 2:23). The t-stem of the causative stem serves as a middle-passive.[11]

J. Dušek, *Les manuscrits araméens du Wadi Daliyeh et la Samarie vers 450-332 av. J.-C. CHANE* 30 (2007); G. Mayer, J. Bergman, and W. von Soden, "ידה *ydh*," *TDOT*, V, 427-43; E. Schuller, "*ydh* II," *ThWQ*, II, 69-77; C. Westermann, "ידה *ydh* hi. to praise," *TLOT*, 502-8.

1. From an older **wdī*, with the common NW Semitic shift from an initial /w-/ to /y-/.
2. Judging from Arabic and Ethiopic also from **wdī*.
3. *DJPA*, 235a; *DJBA*, 524f.
4. Rather rare in Aramaic, cf. 1QapGen 21:2 and C. Stadel, *Hebraismen in den aramäischen Texten vom Toten Meer* (Heidelberg, 2008), 23.
5. *TADAE* D1.17, 10.
6. "To admit to," in reference to guilt; nV 4:14; 18:70; *ATTM*, 2.
7. nV 17,40.
8. nV 20:41.
9. Cf. *ATTM*, 2, 387.
10. 1QapGen 21:3.
11. Cf. M. Sokoloff, review of *Die aramäischen Texte vom Totem Meer samt den Inscriptionen*

II. Juridical Usage "to Acknowledge." At the moment, one cannot say with certainty when the evidence for *ydī* as a juridical term "to confirm, acknowledge" begins. In the past, the two forms *whwdt*[12] and *whdt*[13] in the late Achaemenid private contracts from Samaria, although in a largely destroyed context, were interpreted in terms of the later use as plene and defective spellings of the perfect first person singular "I (hereby) acknowledge"; the subsequent *dyn'*, which is a certain reading in the first case and likely in the second, would then serve as a direct object "the verdict."[14] According to the new edition by Dušek, however, both cases involve the Iranian personal name Vahudāta and the professional designation "judge"[15] in the determined state.[16] This interpretation gains probability from the fact that both passages seem to be part of a witness list and that Persepolis tablets also attest the name Vahudāta.[17] Thus, the first certain instance would be a fragmentatry Egyptian letter ostracon from the third century B.C.E.,[18] where here *zy twdh* probably means "that you will confirm" and relates to a delivery of goods mentioned in the preceding, but unpreserved, context. The recipient is introduced by *l-*.

The Nabatean contracts from the Dead Sea, then, which continue the Imperial Aramaic legal tradition, contain reliable examples: a pledge has the participle *mwd'* along with the participle of the Dt-stem(?) of *ḥūb*[19] as a performative "hereby I acknowledge and adhere" with a subsequent *b-* "for";[20] the alternative spelling *mdy* with a subsequent *bḥwbt ksp dnryn* "the debt of x silver denari" in the confirmation of a Greek marital contract is similar.[21] It appears in a similar function in the orthographic variant *mwdy* with an object clause following *dy* "that" in the summary of a Greek certificate of indebtedness,[22] so also *md'* in the obligation referring to a Greek certificate of inheritance with an object clause and the recipient of the certificate after *l-*.[23]

Further, in the same construction, it serves in a Palmyrene inscription establishing

---

aus Palästina, dem Testament Levis aus der Kairoer Genisa, der Fastenrolle und den alten talmudischen Zitaten... Ergänzungsband by K. Beyer, *DSD* 2 (1995) 223.

12. *WDSP* 2.10; l. 11 in the old enumeration.

13. *WDSP* 3.10.

14. *DNSI*, 439; *ATTM*, 2, 387.

15. → *dyn*.

16. 147-49 and 168f.

17. Cf. J. Tavernier, *Iranica in the Achaemenid Period (ca. 550-330 B.C.E.): Lexicon of Old Iranian Proper Names and Loanwords Attested in Non-Iranian Texts. OLA* 158 (2007), 342; and, in agreement, E. Lipiński, review of Jan Dušek, *Les Manuscrits Araméens du Wadi Daliyeh et la Samarie vers 450–332 av. J.-C. Palamedes* 3 (2008) 229.

18. *TADAE* D1.17, 10.

19. *mtḥyb*, → *ḥṭī* IV.

20. nV 4,14 in *ATTM*, 2, 215; for the participle in performative usage, cf. H. Gzella, "The Use of the Participle in the Hebrew Bar Kosiba Letters in the Light of Aramaic," *DSD* 14 (2007) 93f.

21. nV 18:70; *ATTM*, 2, 232f.

22. Which translates it ὡμολογήσατο; nV 17:40 in *ATTM*, 2, 231f.

23. nV 20:41.

burial rights[24] and in the three Old Syriac private contracts from Dura-Europos.[25] In the t-stem, it means "to have recorded."[26]

The legal expression *ydī* with *b-* "to acknowledge (publicly)" may also underlie the general usage, attested later, for "to confess (publicly) to someone." Finally, this expression occurs as an Aramaism in the Greek form ὁμολογεῖν ἐν in the sayings of Jesus in the New Testament, precisely where Aramaic influences are most expected: Mt. 10:32 and Lk. 12:8.[27]

III. Religious Usage "to Praise, Thank." As an expression of personal piety, *ydī* in the meaning "to thank, to praise" is first evident twice in Biblical Aramaic, and then in the Aramaic texts from Qumran. The instances in both places are easily overlooked, but analogous usages in Palmyrene inscriptions demonstrate that they do not represent an imitation of the very productive use of the verb in Hebrew, but a nuance that is also original in Aramaic.

In Daniel's song of thanksgiving to God as the grantor of wisdom,[28] the participle *mᵉhōḏē* stands alongside *mᵉšabbaḥ*, largely a synonym in hymnic contexts (Dnl. 2:23).[29] In the depiction of Daniel's daily prayer, the morphological variant *mōḏē*[30] follows the participle *mᵉṣallē* "prayer" (*ṣlī*; 6:11). In the immediate context of this second passage, the two terms constitute secondary actions or concretizations of the superordinant *bārēḵ ʿal-birḵōhī* "he fell to his knee,"[31] which precedes immediately, and are directed explicitly *qᵒḏām ʾᵉlāheh* "to his God." Thus, *ydī* designates a specific form of prayer, even if the semantic boundaries between *šbḥ* "to laud, praise" and *ṣlī* "to pray" become blurred, especially in parallelism.

Abraham's hymn in 1QapGen 21:3 also employs *ydī* along with *brk* and *hll* in the preceding verse, here, however, specifically in the meaning "to thank for" (*ʿl*) his flocks and other goods; a few passages from Tobit's song of praise[32] are similar. An additional, for the most part destroyed, form in 4Q1546 2:6 (Lev. 16:21)[33] is paleographically difficult. The noun *twdh* "sacrifice of thanksgiving" in the vision of the heavenly Jerusalem[34] is a Hebrew loanword (generally from the realm of religion) in the Aramaic from Qumran.

Palmyrene dedicatory inscriptions also employ the verb to express thanks (with an optional *l-*) to a deity.[35] Greek parallel versions have forms of εὔχομαι or εὐχαριστέω.

Gzella

24. *PAT* 1791.3.

25. H. J. W. Drijvers and J. F. Healey, *The Old Syriac Inscriptions of Edessa and Osrhoene*. *HO* 42 (1999), P1,7.20; P2,ii.vii.7.12.20.25f, with a perfect in l. vii.12.26; P3,6.22.

26. M 18:2, *ATTM*, 306f.

27. See *ATTM*, 565 and K. Beyer, "Woran erkennt man, daß ein griechischer Text aus dem Hebräischen oder Aramäischen übersetzt ist?" *Studia Semitica necnon Iranica. FS R. Macuch* (Wiesbaden, 1989), 30, with additional bib.

28. → *ḥkm* III.2.

29. → *šbḥ*.

30. *BLA*, §49i.

31. → *brk*.

32. 4Q196 17 2:3.9 (Tob. 13:6,10); 4Q196 18:15 par. 4Q198 1:1 (Tob. 14:2).

33. In Heb, hithpiel "to confess."

34. 11Q18 16 2+17 1:1.

35. *PAT* 0376.3; 0377.1; 0412.3; 1467; 1923.2; 2631.1.

ידע *yd*ʿ; מנדע *mnd*ʿ /maddaʿ/

I. Etymology and Lexical Field. II. Old and Imperial Aramaic. 1. Ground-stem. 2. Causative-stem. 3. Noun. III. Biblical Aramaic. 1. Ground-stem. 2. Causative-stem. 3. Construction with Object Clause. 4. Noun. 5. Translation in the Greek Versions. IV. Qumran. 1. For Various Degrees of Knowledge. 2. Noun. 3. Participle.

I. Etymology and Lexical Field. Like other verbs of knowing ("to remember," "to discover," "to experience"), the verb *yd*ʿ "to know" takes a nominal object (a noun or a pronominal suffix) or an object clause following *dy* "that." In the causative use, the verb takes two objects, the one knowing and the content of the knowledge, in one of two possible constructions. In the passive, the object can become the grammatical subject. The process of knowing usually begins with perception and deepens to understanding. The spectrum of meaning of the verb "to know" mirrors this psychological circumstance. On the common Semitic etymology, see J. Bergman, 449f.

In the known Aramaic corpus, the root *yd*ʿ occurs in the peal, (h)aphel, (h)ophal and ithpeel. The haphel of *yd*ʿ[1] is largely synonymous with the haphel and pael of → *ḥwī* "to make known, to instruct, show" and with → *glī* I "to reveal."[2] The noun *md*ʿ /maddaʿ/ "knowledge," in the Imperial Aramaic spelling *mnd*ʿ,[3] shares a semantic field with /ḥokmā/ (Dnl. 2:20,21,23,30; 5:11,14; Ezr. 7:25)[4] and /śokltānū/ "insight" (Dnl. 5:11,12,14).[5]

II. Old and Imperial Aramaic. Old Aramaic attests the root *yd*ʿ only as a verb. It occurs in the curse formula of a treaty of state:[6] *zy l' yd*ʿ "who does not understand," i.e., who ignores the grave consequences of an attempt to erase the words of the inscription.

1. Ground-stem. The root is better known from Imperial Aramaic, thanks particularly to the documentary texts from Egypt. As a verb, it occurs twenty-four times: mostly in the peal, three times in the haphel and once in the ithpeel. The general meaning of the peal of *yd*ʿ is "to know" in its entire breadth, from simple knowledge of facts as in *l' yd*ʿ*n* ʾ*nḥnw*

J. Bergman and G. J. Botterweck, "יָדַע *yādaʿ*," *TDOT*, V, 448-81; H.-J. Fabry, "*yd*ʿ," *ThWQ*, II, 79-93; H. Gzella, *A Cultural History of Aramaic. HO* 111 (2015); J. Naveh and S. Shaked, *Aramaic Documents from Ancient Bactria (Fourth Century* B.C.E.*)* (London, 2012); W. Schottroff, "ידע *yd*ʿ to perceive, know," *TLOT*, 508-21.

1. Treated here like a *I-*w* verb.

2. For the interplay of these three synonymous verbs in Dnl. 2 with → *rz* "secret" as the common object, cf. A. Gianto, "Notes from a Reading of Dnl. 2," in *Sôfer Mahîr. FS Schenker. SVT* 110 (2006), 59-68.

3. Also in Biblical Aramaic; for a discussion, see Gzella, 170f.

4. → *ḥkm* IV.

5. → *śkl*. See also P. Makiello, "Daniel as Mediator of Divine Knowledge in the Book of Daniel," *JJS* 60 (2009) 18-31, for Daniel's growing experience with this kind of knowledge.

6. Sefire II = *KAI* 223 C 8.

mnynh "we do not know its number"[7] to the forms of more profound knowledge such as "to have insight," as in the Wisdom sayings of Aḥiqar: *npšy l' td' 'rḥ'* "my soul does not know the way."[8] The object of knowledge can also be introduced with the preposition *b-*, which creates a stronger emphasis on the pertinent information e.g., *bznh zy 'byd ln kl' 'ršm l' yd'* "Aršama knew nothing at all about what was done to us."[9] In some cases, the verb takes an object clause, e.g., *td' zy* "You should understand that. . .";[10] in the Adon letter *TADAE* A1.1.6[11] "for the Lord of Kings, the Pharaoh, knows that [your] servant [*yd' ky 'bd(k)*]. . .." The formulaic expression "X knows [*yd'*] this command" serves in official correspondence to verify the relevant document.[12]

The periphrastic construction with the passive participle *ydy'* "known" and the auxiliary verb → *hwī* "to be" appears in *TADAE* A6.8,3 *yd[y]' yhwh lk* "it should be known to you."[13] This is presumably a loan translation of the Old Persian **avaθāitaiy azdā biyā*[14] and closely approximates the meaning of the ithpeel; it appears only once in the texts from Egypt: *yty[d']* "it will be made known (to our lord in agreement with what we say)."[15]

2. *Causative-stem.* The basic meaning of the haphel of *yd'* is "to cause to be that (someone) knows (something)." It can also mean "to instruct," as in "with respect to gold, we have sent a report and given instructions [*hwd'n*]."[16] In several other passages, contrariwise, the verb is employed simply for "to explain," e.g., *TADAE* A3.10,7 "Explain (*hwd'*) that to X."; see further *TADAE* C2.1,66 (Behistun) "Explain [*hwd'*] how it would be done!" The haphel participle *mhwd'* occurs twice in the Bactrian documents.[17]

3. *Noun.* In Imperial Aramaic, the noun *mnd'* appears in the expression *kmnd'* "as is known (literally: according to knowledge)" in the narrative framework of Aḥiqar.[18]

This noun is to be distinguished, however, from the indefinite pronoun *mnd'm* "something" that traces back to */man yada' mā/ "who knows what"[19] and not to the noun

7. *TADAE* D11.26,2.

8. *TADAE* C1.1,122; see also l. 164: "There are many stars in heaven whose names one does not know [*l' yd' 'yš*], so, too, one knows nothing about people [*l' yd' 'yš*]."

9. *TADAE* A4.7. 30 (par. 4.8,29).

10. *TADAE* A2.5,2 (Hermopolis).

11. *KAI* 266.6.

12. For instances → *ṭ'm* II.

13. See further *TADAE* A6.10,8 and the Aramaic letters from Bactria, Naveh and Shaked, A6,8; B3,4.

14. E. Benveniste, "Éléments perses en araméen d'Egypte," *Journal Asiatique* 242 (1954) 305; more on this construction in Gzella, 173, with bib.

15. *TADAE* A4.5,10.

16. *TADAE* A4.7,29.

17. Naveh and Shaked A1,3; A6,4.

18. *TADAE* C1.1.53; compare this usage with the Nabatean *bmnd'* "with the knowledge of" in the summary of a certificate of debt from the year 128 C.E. from the archive of Babata at the Dead Sea, nV 17:40 in *ATTM*, 2, 231f.

19. See I. Kottsieper, *Die Sprache der Aḥiqarsprüche*. *BZAW* 194 (1990), 51-54, and now also *ATTM*, 2, 408.

mnd' together with the interrogative /mā/ "something known."[20] The form appears in the known Imperial Aramaic texts from Egypt more than twenty times and once in Bactrian documents;[21] five additional instances have *md'm* with the assimilation of the /n/.[22]

III. Biblical Aramaic.

1. Ground-stem. Biblical Aramaic attests the verb forty-seven times, of them twenty-two times in the peal and twenty-five times in the haphel. With a direct object, the peal of *yd'* means simply, "to know." Thus, the nature of the object characterizes the specific form of the knowledge. All instances of the peal pertain to the realm of religion: Dnl. 2:22 refers to the knowledge of what lies in the darkness,[23] i.e., the secrets that only God can reveal. Dnl. 2:21 deals with an insight (*bīnā*) and 2:30 an unexpressed thought. The knowledge mentioned in Dnl. 5:22 concerns the previously mentioned kingdom of God over any human kingdom. In Ezr. 7:25 the participle refers to "those who know (the laws of your God)," to people who follow the Mosaic instructions,[24] and conversely, "those who do not know" to those who do not do it. In Dnl. 5:23 the plural participle refers to idol images that are not in a position to understand and appears in parallel with the affirmation that, in addition, they can neither see nor hear. This suggests that, in relation to higher beings, perception, both optical and acoustical, is inseparably linked to knowledge. There is no example here, however, of *yd'* with a person as object, as employed in Qumran (→ IV) in the idiomatic expression "to be intimately familiar with," "to associate intimately with."

2. Causative-stem. The basic meaning of the haphel of *yd'* is, as elsewhere, "to explain something (direct object) to someone (*l*- or a direct object), to communicate, to announce, to give an instruction." Thus, in Dnl. 5:8 Daniel explains the writing on the wall and its interpretation to Belschazzar (cf. also Dnl. 5:15,16,17). In similar fashion, in Dnl. 4:3,4,15 he communicates to Nebuchadnezzar the interpretation of his dream vision of a tree. In Dnl. 2:5,9,25,26,30, Daniel tells the king his dream and/or the related interpretation; according to Dnl. 2:45 God revealed the future to the king (see further Dnl. 2:28,29). Daniel 2:23 contains a confession of Daniel that God granted him the knowledge for which he and his companions had prayed. Daniel 7:16 reports how a divine being explained the vision of the heavenly judgment to Daniel. Finally, Ezr. 7:25 employs the haphel for the instruction of the Mosaic law so that those who share this knowledge become believers (that is, "those knowing the laws of God," a peal participle in the same verse; → III.1).

In contrast to these examples, the haphel infinitive in Ezr. 5:10 and the participle in Ezr. 4:16 are not employed in a religious context. They deal only with reporting something to the king. The verb also has no religious connotation in Dnl. 2:15; Arioch simply

20. So still *ATTM*, 594f.
21. Naveh and Shaked B2,2.
22. For an index and a brief discussion, see Gzella, 149.
23. → *ḥšk* III.
24. → *dt* II.

communicates to Daniel the king's decision to execute the wise men; the same applies to Daniel's transmittal of this report to his companions in Dnl. 2:17.

3. Construction with Object Clause. Although still rare in earlier stages of the Aramaic language, the use of the verb *yd‘* with a successive object clause introduced by *dy* is comparably frequent in Biblical Aramaic (fifteen times with the peal, twice with the haphel). This phenomenon reflects a semantic development from "to know something" to knowledge of the content of a statement. In Dnl. 4:14,22,23,29 and 5:21 the meaning corresponds more closely to "understand that. . .." All of these examples occur in a religious context. Contrariwise, there are no religious connotations in Dnl. 2:8,9; 4:6; 6:16 "know that"; Dnl. 6:11 and Ezr. 4:15 "experience/determine that." The construction *yᵉḏīa‘ lᵆhæwē lᵉ- . . . dī* "be it. . .known that. . ." in Ezr. 4:12,13; 5:8 and Dnl. 3:18 also belongs to official, not to religious diction. Furthermore, there are two instances of the haphel participle in the plural with a *dy*-clause, also not in religious discourse: *mᵉhōḏᵉ‘īn ᵓᵃnaḥnā lᵉmalkā dī* "we (the people from beyond-the-river) inform the king that (the Jews continue building the wall)" in Ezr. 4:16; according to Ezr. 7:24 Artaxerxes then wrote the treasurer of beyond-the-river: *lᵉḵom mᵉhōḏᵉ‘īn dī* "putting you in knowledge that (no form of tribute may be required of Jewish cultic personnel)."

4. Noun. The noun *manda‘* (vocalization of the Imperial Aramaic spelling) occurs in Biblical Aramaic only in the book of Daniel; all four instances have some religious connotation. The word is employed for the intellectual capacity of recognition, not primarily for knowledge itself: Nebuchadnezzar's restored intellectual capacity in Dnl. 4:31,33 and Daniel's ability to obtain profound knowledge in 2:21 (in parallel with *ḥoḵmᵉṯā* "the knowledge"). In Dnl. 5:12 it appears beside *rūaḥ yattīr*, thus an extraordinary spirit in Daniel, and *śoḵlᵉṯānū*, referring here to his gift of obtaining insight and interpreting dreams.

5. Translation in the Greek Versions. Theodotion usually translates the verb *yd‘* in the peal with γινώσκειν, but in Dnl. 2:8,21 (ptcp., also in Ezr. 7:25) with forms of ἰδεῖν and in Dnl. 3:18 (also in 4:12,13; 5:8) with γνωστὸς εἶναι. For the haphel he uses γνωρίζειν (also in Ezr. 4:14,16; 5:10; 7:24,25), but δηλοῦν in Dnl. 4:15 and ἀναγγέλλειν in Dnl. 2:9,25,26.

The unrevised original translation ("Old Greek") generally exhibits a more nuanced diction; for the peal of *yd‘* it employes γινώσκειν in Dnl. 2:9,22 and 4:17 (4:14 in the MT); ἰδεῖν in Dnl. 2:8; ἐπιγινώσκειν in Dnl. 6:11; εἶναι in Dnl. 3:18 in combination with φανερός, in Dnl. 2:30 with ἐν γνώσει and in Dnl. 2:21 with ἐν ἐπιστήμῃ. The rendition of *yd‘* in the haphel also varies there: δηλοῦν in Dnl. 2:5,23,25,26,28,29,30 (in 2:5 in combination with ἀπαγγέλλειν, as also in 2:9) and 7:16; σημαίνειν in Dnl. 2:15,23,30,45 (in 2:30 in combination with δηλοῦν); ὑποδεικνύναι in Dnl. 2:17; ἀπαγγέλλειν in Dnl. 2:5 (in combination with δηλοῦν, also in 2:9) and 5:8. Further, it translates *manda‘* in Dnl. 2:21 with σύνεσις; Theodotion has φρόνησις, but in passages for which no original version of the text exists, he wrote φρένες, as in Dnl. 4:34 (MT 4:31) and 4:36 (Aramaic 4:33), or σύνεσις, as in Dnl. 5:12.

IV. Qumran.

1. For Various Degrees of Knowledge. The texts from Qumran attest the verb *yd'* well. If one does not include instances in the fragments of the book of Daniel, there are at least seventy-three passages with the peal and four with the (h)aphel. The latter occurs in 4Q542 1 1:1 (God's intention to communicate his great name to Qahat's children); 4Q548 1 2-2:9,15 (Amram's wish to announce to his descendants the true path of the sons of light); 4Q202 1 4:8 (1 En. 10:11; God commands the angel Michael to communicate to Semiasa and his companions the fact that their children are consecrated to destruction); the passive in 1QapGen 6:11 means quite generally "to be informed."

As also in other stages of the Aramaic language, the individual usages of the peal all relate to various degrees of knowledge. This knowledge can consist simply of the knowledge of circumstances, such as Abraham's dream, which Sarah absolutely wants to know (1QapGen 19:18), or of the usual knowledge of a king by his subjects (4Q550 1:7). It refers to a deeper form of knowledge, however, in 1QapGen 2:20,22, where Enoch is said to know past and future things. He communicates his knowledge with his sons, so that they, too, as portrayed in the book of Enoch, have knowledge of what will happen (4Q212 1 2:19 [1 En. 91:18]). According to 4Q212 1 3:22 (1 En. 93:2), Enoch knows everything.[25]

Other forms of insight could only be obtained by much experience, such as Noah, according to 1QapGen 6:16, understands human behavior after long reflection, or as Zofar, according to 11Q10 3:5 (Job 20:4), asks whether Job does not know based on his long life experience that both joy and sorrow endure for only a short time. Job responds in 11Q10 5:7 (Job 21:27), that he knows Zofar's thoughts and plans. The nuance of *yd'* in these passages can be compared with the knowledge that obtains, through testing and searching what, according to the Levi Apocryphon, the law may require (4Q541 24 2:4).[26]

According to the wisdom hymn in T. Levi, the knowledge of wisdom is like a valuable possession (4Q213 1 1:20); 4Q213 4:8 calls for discovering the meaning of the eclipses of the sun and the moon. According to 4Q204 5 2:26 (1 En. 106:19) Enoch knows the divine secrets that the Watchers had revealed to him. The fragment of the birth of Noah 4Q534 1 1:4,5,6,8 (2×) reports of the chosen one, Noah, who knew nothing in his youth (l. 4) up to the moment when he became acquainted with "the three books" (l. 5) and later (l. 6) obtained the wisdom and knowledge to penetrate the higher spheres and ultimately to know all the secrets of humankind and the other animals (l. 7f.).[27]

According to 1QapGen 20:15 Abraham wishes that people would recognize God who is lord over all the kings of the earth. 11Q10 7A:3 (Job 23:3) relates how Job expressed his unfilled wish to know how one finds God and, then, two lines later, God's response (Job 23:5). A human person as object of the knowledge also appears in 4Q196 2:1 (Tob. 1:19) and 4Q196 14 2:10 par. 4Q197 4 3:6:7 (Tob. 7:4). These passages refer to a personal

25. For the broader theme complex, cf. the essays in Boccaccini, ed., *Enoch and Qumran Origins* (Grand Rapids, 2003).

26. With *dyn'* as subject according to the reading in *ATTM*, 2, 112; cf. H. Gzella, "*dyn*," *ThWQ*, I, 677 (top left) on the paleographic difficulties and other interpretations of this controversial passage.

27. On the "three books" and the chosen one, see M. Popović, *Reading the Human Body: Physiognomics and Astrology in the Dead Sea Scrolls and Hellenistic Early Roman Period Judaism. STDJ* 67 (2007), 281-85, esp. 281 n. 17.

acquaintance with God or another human being. The usage of the verb "to know" in the intimate sense of "to lie with" belongs to the same nuance.[28]

Some objects of knowledge are inaccessible even to a wise man like Job; consequently, 11Q10 28:4 (Job 36:26) emphasizes that the number of God's years is unknown. As 11Q10 29:6 (Job 37:6) confirms, what God has intended by his mighty works exceeds the human capacity for knowledge. In a similar sense, 11Q10 30:2 (Job 38:4) implies that only through the possession of wisdom could one claim to have been present at the creation and to know its extent. According to 11Q10 32:2 (Job 39:2) special knowledge can be described as the knowledge of the moment when mountain goats and does give birth and are in labor. In all these passages, the meaning corresponds to the Hebrew original. The same is also true of a specialized use of the verb "to know" with the preposition *l-* and the infinitive meaning "to be able, to be capable"[29] in 11Q10 29:7 (Job 37:16); it says that God understands how to clothe his clouds with power; cf. 11Q10 29:9 (Job 37:18): God understands how to inflate the dark clouds. Furthermore, T. Levi emphasizes that God knows thoughts and only he alone (4Q213a 1:11); 4Q203 9:3 *kwl rzy' y[d' 'nth]* "[you kno]w all secrets" presumably also refers to God.

The construction of *yd'* with a *dy*-clause is attested in 11Q10 37:3 (Job 42:2): Job knows that God can do everything; see likewise 4Q538 1-2:4; 4Q196 2:1 (Tob. 1:19); 6:9 (Tob. 3:14); 4Q197 3:5 (Tob. 5:14); 4 2:4f. (Tob. 6:13). Everywhere here the knowledge refers to the content of the *dy*-clause. The expression with the passive participle, *ydy' lhwh lkwn dy* "let it be known to you that. . ." (→ II.1), already attested in Imperial Aramaic, occurs in 4Q203,8,6 and 4Q550 1:7.

2. Noun. The noun *m(n)d'* appears at Qumran about twelve times. It essentially denotes the capacity for knowledge, not the knowledge itself. In the birth of Noah, spelled phonetically *md'*, it serves as a root-related object of the verb *yd'*. The same construction occurs in 11Q10 29:8 (Job 37:16), where God is said to "know knowledge," i.e., God has disposal over the capacity to know things hidden to normal human beings. One passage in the Testament of Amram (4Q548 1 2-2:11) refers to the ability of the sons of light to know the true path, which distinguishes them from the sons of darkness. The combination of knowledge and light also occurs in the related fragment 4Q580 3:2 *mnd' śgy'* "extensive capacity for knowledge." Further, the passage 4Q212 1 4:13 (1 En. 93:10) concerning the "(sevenfold wisdom) and knowledge" that will be given to the elect reflects this nuance. In T. Levi (4Q213a 1:14) the parallelism of *mnd'* and wisdom is even clearer; it, too, involves the capacity for knowledge. If the emendation is correct, this pair also occurs in 4Q531 2+3:10. Furthermore, there are two isolated instances: *ḥsyr mnd'* "lack of knowledge" (probably in reference to the giants) in 4Q581 1:2 and *mnd'* (presumably in reference to God's capacity for knowledge) in 4Q581 3:4. According to 11Q10 10:3 (Job 26:12), God killed the sea monster *bmnd'h* "with his (capacity for) knowledge."

---

28. See 1QapGen 20:17, which emphasizs that the pharaoh *l' yd'h'* "did not know her," i.e., he had no intimate relations with Sarah, although she remained with him.

29. For which, otherwise, the modal verb → *ykl* functions.

3. *Participle.* The substantival use of the participle of *yd'* in the sense of "acquaintance" is a Hebrew loan translation and appears in 11Q10 2:3 (Job 19:13, *yd'y* "my acquaintances") and in 38:5 (Job 42:11, *yd'why* "his acquaintances"). Otherwise, the participle of this verb in Aramaic means "knowing, knowledgeable."[30]

Gianto

30. → III.1 on Ezr. 7:25 and Dnl. 5:23.

יהב *yhb*

I. Lexical Field, Forms, and Grammatical Constructions. II. Literally. III. Theologically. IV. Idiomatic Expressions.

I. Lexical Field, Forms, and Grammatical Constructions. In the earlier stages of the Aramaic language, just as in Sam'alian, the verbal root *yhb* "to give"[1] related to the synonymous → *ntn* in complementary fashion. The latter regularly served for imperfect and infinitive, although in the earliest Old Aramaic, probably because of earlier dialectical variation, occasionally imperfects of *yhb* still occur. Thus, a negated form *lthb* "you do not give" appears in a Sefire state treaty,[2] although other imperfects of *yhd* or of *ntn* are not attested in this partial corpus and additional possible examples in the other Old Aramaic texts may be perfects (→ II), so the distribution remains unclear. Nouns with the meaning "gift," especially /mattanā/, also derive from *ntn*. Parallel expressions in the same context suggest that the choice of root results from purely morphological, not syntactical or semantic grounds.[3] Post-Imperial Aramaic languages manifest both the imperfect and infinitive of *yhb*, however.

The verb is employed in the G-stem and as a transitive; the recipient can be introduced as an indirect object following *l-* or *byd*.[4] Sometimes, other prepositional expansions also occur such as, e.g., with *mn* "from" (Ezr. 6:4,8). The passive diathesis "to be given" with the dropped inner passive—first with the imperfect, then, at the end of the first millennium, entirely—was assumed by the Gt-stem. It, too, appears in phrases governed by *l-* (Ezr. 6:8,9) or, less often, *byd* (Dnl. 2:38; 7:25) "to someone." Additional supplements such as *b-* "toward" or a final clause with an infinitive[5] may also be added.

H. Gzella, *Tempus, Aspekt und Modalität im Reichsaramäischen. VOK* 48 (2004); idem, "*yhb*," *ThWQ*, II, 94-97.

1. From **whb*, as in Arabic, but in the form with /y-/, typically Aramaic.
2. *KAI* 222 B 38.
3. Cf. the participle of *yhb* in 1QapGen 21:10 with the imperfect of *ntn* in 21:12 or the perfect of *yhb* in 22:25 with the infinitive of *ntn* in 22:24.
4. → *yd* IV.
5. *TADAE* A3.10,4f.

According to the nature of the abstract object and the context, *yhb* can assume, besides the literal sense "to give," various figurative nuances such as "to hand over," "to lay down," "to disperse," etc. The imperative /hab/ occurs sometimes in Hebrew, but need not be explained as an Aramaism, but can also represent a lexicalized remnant of root no longer productive at least in Judean.[6]

II. Literally. Old Aramaic attests the blanket verb *yhb* rather rarely, but already in a variety of usages. The Tell Fekheriye inscription, which constitutes the beginning of the Aramaic literary tradition, employs *yhb* with an implicit object to refer to the consecration of the related statue to Hadad, following *knn* "to erect";[7] a clause in a Sefire state treaty mentions in a destroyed context the presentation of food (*lḥm*);[8] and according to an officer's letter on an ostracon, also in a fragmentary context, the king had given the writer a group of persons as servants.[9] In a wisdom saying of Aḥiqar, the giving of the heart seems to represent "to trust someone."[10] Sam'alian[11] and the Deir ʿAllā wall inscription,[12] whose assignment to Aramaic is disputed, seem to employ this otherwise characteristic Aramaic verb in a comparable manner.

In addition, the late Old Aramaic private letters from Hermopolis contain further examples of the general meaning "to give" with various goods or monetary sums.[13] The usage in Neo-Assyrian legal documents for a sum of money already preludes the very extensively documented usage in Imperial Aramaic contracts.[14]

Alongside the general usage in letters,[15] Imperial Aramaic supplies several instances of the perfect, mostly in the first-person singular, in the formulas of sale and transfer of wealth in the very numerous contracts from Elephantine, Saqqara, and Samaria.[16] It remains unclear here, however, whether forms like *yhbt* are performatives ("I hereby give") or relate to a preceding payment.[17] The imperative *hb* also appears in official instructions to distribute food rations to personnel in the service of the administration[18] and is thus a term in the characteristic Achaemenid supply system.[19] With the noun *šḥd* "bribery" as

6. On the Hebrew texts from Qumran cf. Gzella, "*yhb*," 95.

7. *KAI* 309.10.

8. On the form → I.

9. *KAI* 233.7, if *yhb* here, as consistently in later Old Aramaic, is a perfect.

10. *TADAE* C1.1,105; → *lbb*.

11. *KAI* 214.12, of the gifts of the god.

12. I,7 = *KAI* 312.7, in the context of a solar eclipse.

13. E.g., *TADAE* A2.2,16; 2.4,9, here with *b-* "toward"; 2.6, 3.7.

14. For citations, see A. Lemaire, *Nouvelles tablettes araméennes*. *HEO* 34.1 (2001), 154, s.v. *yhb*, whose interpretation as an imperfect and translation with "il donnera" is hardly credible.

15. E.g., *TADAE* A4.2,12f.; with persons in A6.15,3; many additional examples from everyday communication in the ostraca of the Clermont-Ganneau collection, see H. Lozachmeur, *La collection Clermont-Ganneau* (Paris, 2006), 1:541.

16. E.g., *TADAE* B2.1,3; 2.3,3.13.20; the passages are listed in D. Schwiderski, *Die alt- und reichsaramäischen Inschriften I* (New York, 2008), 354-57.

17. Cf. Gzella, *Tempus*, 208 on this contract perfect.

18. Sg. *TADAE* A6.12,1; 6.15,4.7.10, here with *htb* "repay!" → *tūb*; pl. A6.9,2.4.5.

19. See H. Gzella, *A Cultural History of Aramaic*. *HO* 111 (2015), 182-84.

object,[20] *yhb* is synonymous with the verb *šḥd* "to bribe."[21] Furthermore, *yhb* occurs in reference to land that a god receives at the establishment of a cult.[22]

Imperial Aramaic also frequently attests the t-stem passive for "to be given."[23] It overlaps with the passive participle of the G-stem *yhyb* "is given" frequent in some commercial texts, although it emphasizes more the result than the process.[24]

The various general and technical administrative usages of the verb *yhb* survive in the post-Imperial Aramaic literary tradition. While in the book of Daniel it functions primarily as a key term in a theology of power (→ III), the Gt-stem in Ezra, as in the Imperial Aramaic documentary texts, appears regularly as a passive with the nuance "to be paid" (Ezr. 6:4,8), also of taxes (4:20), or "to be delivered" (6:9; 7:19). Something similar applies to 1QapGen, which employs *yhb*[25] also for "to make a gift,"[26] "to pay tribute,"[27] and for "to put in prison"[28] or "to marry";[29] it refers, further, to the distribution of land,[30] God's gifts to humans[31] and the demonstration of honor.[32] Additionally, the verb can assume the nuance "to hand over" and stand with the inheritance of the fathers (the religio-cultural traditions) as object which, according to the Testament of Qahat, is to be left to subsequent generations.[33] In legal texts from the Dead Sea *yhb* refers to donations,[34] in building inscriptions from Hatra[35] to endowments, similarly in Palmyrene honorary inscriptions.[36]

For the passive at Qumran, the internal passive of the perfect[37] still competes with the original middle-passive Gt-stem of the imperfect;[38] the former drops away in post-Christian Aramaic, however.[39]

---

20. *TADAE* A4.2,4.
21. *KAI* 224.28.
22. *KAI* 319.11f.
23. *TADAE* A3.3,5; 6.2,18.21.24; C3.12,1.
24. Cf. e.g., *TADAE* C3.14,32.34.41; 3.19,8; exactly the same usage is now attested in a list from Bactria, J. Naveh and S. Shaked, *Aramaic Documents from Ancient Bactria (Fourth Century B.C.E.)* (London, 2012), no. C1:46.
25. In enduring or repeated circumstances in a periphrastic construction with → *hwī* II; cf. Gzella, *Tempus*, 244-64.
26. 1QapGen 19:24; 20:29,31.
27. 1QapGen 21:27; 22:17.
28. 1QapGen 22:19,25.
29. 1QapGen 6:8.
30. 1QapGen 17:15f.; 21:10; → *ḥlq*.
31. 1QapGen 21:3; cf. Dnl. 2:21 and 4Q204 1 6:11 (1 En. 14:2).
32. 4Q213 1 1:17.
33. 4Q542 1 1:5; 1 2:11.
34. Regularly in nV 7; *ATTM*, 2, 218f.
35. E.g., H192,2.
36. E.g., *PAT* 0305.3.
37. 2Q24 4:15,16,17 par. 11Q18 20:6, a vision of the heavenly Jerusalem; 4Q245 1 1:4.
38. 4Q212 1 4:13,15f. (1 En. 93:10 and 91:12).
39. *ATTM*, 152.

III. Theologically. In the book of Daniel, the active and, especially, the passive of *yhb*[40] appears with notable frequency in relation to God's behavior. Power and powerlessness are the central motifs here that run through the various court tales like a red thread.[41] It is God who grants kings their power and honor (Dnl. 2:37f.; 5:18f.),[42] so that they can pass them on (Dnl. 2:48; 5:17), and he gives the wise their insight (Dnl. 2:21,23). God causes Nebuchadnezzar, whose dream in Dnl. 4 announces the king's period of penitence for his own arrogance, to be given the heart of an animal as a sign of rejection from society and the loss of human intellect (4:13, in the t-stem);[43] conversely, God grants the first animal in the vision in Dnl. 7, which symbolizes the most human of the various empires, human posture and a human heart (7:4). Thus, ultimately God commands the secular empires: he commands that Belshazzar's kingdom be divided (5:18), and even the animals in the vision in Dnl. 7 are given their power, have it taken, and finally given to the holy ones (Dnl. 7:6,12,14,22,27, internal passive). Thus, in the passive, *yhb* can also mean "to be delivered, handed over" (inner passive: 7:11; t-stem: 7:25),[44] in the active "to give over, to deliver" (Dnl. 3:28: one's own body, → *gšm*; Ezr. 5:12: God gives whoever enrages him into the hand of an enemy king).[45] In this regard, it denotes either a temporal test, which even the pious are not spared; or the ultimate destruction of the power hostile to God.

IV. Idiomatic Expressions. Since *yhb* is often used together with other verbs and with quite varied concrete and abstract objects, its meaning could expand with time and, in individual cases, overlap the semantic spectrum of the root → *śīm* "to put, place, lay." With the object *'uššayyā*[46] it means "to lay the foundation" in Ezra (5:16).[47] The usage in reference to scattering salt and flour may be related to this general nuance.[48] Later, *yhb* is also attested in the meaning "to effect"[49] and, depending on the object, in additional idiomatic expressions in West and East Aramaic.[50]

Gzella

---

40. Whether as an internal passive or as the Gt-stem.

41. H. Gzella, *Cosmic Battle and Political Conflict. BietOr* 47 (2003), 7-9; cf. also K. Koch, *Daniel 1–4. BK* XXII/1 (2005), 433-42.

42. Cf. *PAT* 1666.6f.

43. → *lbb*.

44. Similarly 4Q212 1 4:17 (1 En. 91:12).

45. Cf. 4Q213 1 1:11.

46. From Akk. *uššu* "foundation," → *'š*.

47. *yḥṭ* in 4:12 with the same word as object is often emended to a form of *yhb*, see *BLA*, §46e′ and *ATTM*, 574; alternatively, it may involve a by-form *yḥṭ* in the D-stem from the root *ḥūṭ* "to mend, repair": *LexLingAram*, 75.

48. 1QapGen 10:17; described here with the periphrastic construction as under way, which points to a more general meaning, since, after all, "to give" is a punctual verb; cf. generally Gzella, *Tempus*, 244-64.

49. E.g., yyEN 3,2 in *ATTM*, 364: *mn dyhyb plgw* "anyone who sows discord," a synagogue inscription from the fifth century C.E.

50. Cf. *DJPA*, 235f. and *DJBA*, 526-28.

יהוד *yhwd* /yahūd/; יהודי *yhwdy* /yahūdāy/

I. Derivation from /yahūdā/ "Judea." II. Ethnic Designation "Judean, Jew." III. Toponym "Judea."

I. Derivation from /yahūdā/ "Judea." Via its common Aramaic gentilic adjective (before whose affix /-āy/ the endings fall away), *yhwdy* /yahūdāy/, *yhwdy* (Heb. /yahūdī/) "Judaic, Jewish; Judean, Jew," the abbreviated official Imperial Aramaic provincial name *yhwd*, in cuneiform *Ia-a-ḫu-du* and *Ia-ku-du*[1] /yahūd/ "Judea" derive from the old Hebrew geographical, tribal, and state name *yhwdh* /yahūdā/ "Judea, Judah"[2] with an unknown etymology.[3]

II. Ethnic Designation "Judean, Jew." In the sixth century B.C.E. Babylonian cuneiform attests the term *yhwdy* /yahūdāy/ as *ia-a-ḫu-da-a-a*[4] and the fifth century B.C.E. Egyptian,[5] Biblical Aramaic and Dead Sea alphabetic script as *ywdy*, etc. The change in meaning from "Judean" (geographic) to "Jew" (religious) took place in the third to second centuries B.C.E.[6] "Jew" is then the self-designation over against non-Jews, "Israelite" over against Jews.[7]

III. Toponym "Judea." The official Aramaic name of the province of Judea with the capital city Jerusalem is *yhwd*, seldom *yhd*, Yahūd. It appears on Imperial Aramaic coins, seals, and jar handles (sixth to fourth century B.C.E.),[8] the petition of the Jewish community of Elephantine to the Persian governor of Judea (407 B.C.E.),[9] in Biblical Aramaic texts (Ezr. 5:1,8; 7:14; fourth century B.C.E.); Dnl. 2:25; 5:13; 6:14 (second century B.C.E.), and in the Syriac.

Beyer

C. Brockelmann, *Grundriß der vergleichenden Grammatik der semitischen Sprachen*, vol. 1 (Berlin, 1908); G. J. Brooke, "*yhwdh*," *ThWQ*, II, 97-101; B. Porten and J. A. Lund, *Aramaic Documents from Egypt: A Key-Word-in-Context Concordance* (Winona Lake, IN, 2002); D. R. Schwartz, "'Judaean' or 'Jew'? How Should We Translate ιουδαῖος in Josephus?" in J. Frey, D. R. Schwartz, and S. Gripentrog, eds., *Jewish Identity in the Greco-Roman World. AGJU* 71 (2007), 3-27; D. Schwiderski, *Die alt- und reichsaramäischen Inschriften*, vol. 1: *Konkordanz* (Berlin, 2008); J. Teixidor, *Bulletin d'épigraphie sémitique* (Paris, 1986); P. J. Tomson, "The Names Israel and Jew in Ancient Judaism and in the New Testament," *Biydragen* 47 (1986) 120-40,266-89; H.-J. Zobel, "יְהוּדָה *yehûḏâ*," *TDOT*, V, 482-99.

1. *ATTM*, 596.
2. Between Philistia and the Dead Sea; Zobel.
3. Brockelmann, 398 n. 1.
4. *ATTM*, 595.
5. *TADAE* B2.2,3, etc.
6. *ATTM*, 595; 2, 34.408.
7. Tomson.
8. Teixidor, 325.66 and 400.69; Schwiderski, 359b.
9. *TADAE* A4.7,1; 4.8,18 with Porten and Lund, 430.

יום *ywm* /yawm/

I. Lexical Field, Forms, and Constructions. II. As a Temporal Term. 1. Defined. 2. Undefined. III. Special Days.

I. Lexical Field, Forms, and Constructions. The common Semitic masculine noun /yawm/, in Aramaic and Hebrew in the course of time monophthongized as /yōm/,[1] initially denotes generally the day in the calendrical sense, i.e., the period from morning to the next morning[2] as day and night, but probably also originally daylight in contrast to the night. The word appears regularly in indications of time for a specific day, counted from a reference point; with demonstrative pronouns *ywm' znh*/*dnh* "this day" for the present,[3] in the distributive expressions *ywm bywm* or *ywm lywm* for intervals such as "daily"; with various other attributes or in the construct state for fixed memorial days or for the day of the last judgment toward which all of world history moves. The plural refers to a longer period (for which there is no independent word), usually as in the English "his days" to a lifetime; this chronological concept can also overlap functionally with *ḥyyn* "life" employed in indications of time as a vital status.[4] Its usage remains largely constant in Armaic diction.

The likewise masculine substantive *ymm* /yamām/ is also known since the astrological texts like the book of Enoch, however, specifically for the day in contrast to the night.[5] The ending suggests that it probably arose from an adverb "by day," yet it was reanalyzed as a noun and can, thus, appear in the determined state and after prepositions.[6]

II. As a Temporal Term.

1. Defined. The preserved material employs *ywm* predominantly as a unit of time; thus, the calendrical use for a period of 24 hours is substantially more frequent than the astronomical for the day in contrast to the night.[7] Date information, as found in documents in the Achaemenid period and from the Hellenistic-Roman period also in grave inscrip-

---

G. Brin, "*ywm*," *ThWQ*, II, 110-17; S. P. Brock, "Some Notes on Dating Formulae in Middle Aramaic Inscriptions and in Early Syriac Manuscripts," in *Intertestamental Essays. FS J. T. Milik* (Kraków, 1992), 253-64; E. Jenni, "יוֹם *yôm* day," *TLOT*, 526-39; B. Porten, "The Calendar of Aramaic Texts from Achaemenid and Ptolemaic Egypt," in S. Shaked and A. Netzer, eds., *Irano-Judaica II* (Jerusalem, 1990), 13-32; W. von Soden, J. Bergman, and M. Sæbø, "יוֹם *yôm*," *TDOT*, VI, 7-32; S. Stern, *Calendar and Community* (Oxford, 2001).

1. *ATTM*, 116-20.
2. *ATTM*, 2, 408,427.
3. "Today"; less often a previously named day: 1QapGen 21:5, for which the remote deixis *hw* serves otherwise.
4. → *ḥyī* IV.
5. → *lylh*.
6. Cf. *bymm'* "In days" in 4Q209 26:5 (1 En. 78:17).
7. The latter, however, underlies the presumably formulaic summons of day and night as witnesses to a state treaty from Sefire: *KAI* 222 A 12; cf. W. L. Moran, "Some Remarks on the Song of Moses," *Bibl* 43 (1962) 319 n. 5.

tions,[8] regularly use the expression *bywm* or an adverbial *ywm* in the construct state with a subsequent cardinal number or numeral.[9] In order to add precision, the reference figure can also appear with a preposition, thus, usually *l-* or *b-* with the name of the month[10] or *bšbh* "in the week," sometimes with another point of reference.[11]

Thus, the cardinal numbers in the absolute or determined state designate the days of the week in this construction: *ywm ḥd* (*bšbh*) "on Sunday,"[12] *ywm tryn* "on Monday,"[13] etc.;[14] yet, *ʿrwbt šbtʾ* "preparation day"[15] denotes "Friday." If *ḥd* or the sign "1" does not function as a numeral, however, but as a demonstrative pronoun to express the identity of "the same," *bywm ḥd* means "on the same day."[16] As an anchor point for relative indications of time, it functions in contracts that are, then, immediately in effect: *ywmʾ znh/dnh* "this day = today,"[17] with *mn* "beginning today" and *ʿd ʿlm* "forever."[18]

The enumeration according to an event, in contrast, is denoted by *bywm* in the construct state with a subsequent substantive[19] or infinitive[20] "on the day of/at the time of" or with an object clause after *zy/dy* "on the day when";[21] in reference to periods, the prepositions *mn ywm* "since the days"[22] or *ʿd ywm* "until the day"[23] in the plural with a number also for "within" (cf. *ʿd ywmyn tltyn* "up to thirty days" in Dnl. 6:8,13); in relation to an unlimited period, *ʿd ʿlm* or *lʿlm* "forever,"[24] in legal texts more often *mḥr ʾw ywm ʾḥrn* "tomorrow or on a later day = ever."[25] In this regard, *lqṣt ywmyh* "toward the end of days" (Dnl. 2:28) refers to a specific term, *bʾḥryt ywmyʾ* "at the end of days" (Dnl. 2:28) to the end of time altogether. The *b-* ubiquitous in such datings may denote a precise time; in contrast, *l-* may denote an approximate expectation (→ II.2).[26]

Distributive expressions such as "daily" are formed with *ywm bywm* (Ezr. 6:9), *ywm lywm*[27] or (*b*)*kl ywm* "on that day,"[28] also with numbers as in [*kw*]*l ywm šbyʿy* "every seven

8. Cf. Brock.
9. Later, as alternatives, also the number in the absolute state or a numeral with a subsequent *ywmyn*.
10. E.g., Ezr. 6:15; in Elephantine sometimes also following Egyptian enumeration.
11. E.g., 1QapGen 12:14 for a specific festival.
12. nV 3:25; 7:43 in *ATTM* 2.
13. nV 7:43.
14. For a complete list of examples, although from various periods, see *ATTM*, 2, 409.
15. *ATTM*, 2, 486.
16. *TADAE* B2.6,28 and 3.8,24.28, here parallel with *bkp ḥdh* "in one blow," → *yd* II.1.
17. *TADAE* D7.1,6f.; 7.2,2; 7.3,4; 7.8,10; 7.20,9 etc.
18. E.g., *TADAE* B2.3,9; 2.6,4; 2.8,7, etc.
19. *KAI* 223 B 12; *TADAE* A4.8,12.
20. 1QapGen 22:30.
21. *KAI* 222 B 31 and C 20; *TADAE* A3.3,2f.; 1QapGen 22:28; V 41:6; nV 42:21 in *ATTM*, 2.
22. nV 3:34; 43:14; 7:18,21,27,59,64; seldom with *ywmʾ* in the determined state.
23. *TADAE* B4.2,3.10; nV 7:63.
24. See above; → *ʿlm*.
25. *TADAE* B2.1,6.8; 2.3,18.20.26; 2.4,8.13; 2.6,17.22.26; 3.3,7.9.10.12.13; 3.8,21; 5.1,4.
26. Hebrew can demonstrate this difference more clearly: E. Jenni, *Die hebräischen Präpositionen 3: Lamed* (Stuttgart, 2000), 273.
27. *TADAE* A6.9,3.
28. *TADAE* A4.2,2, with *zy;* repeated *bkl ywm wywm* in 4Q210 1 3:4 (1 En. 78:6), perhaps emphatically for "every single day."

days."[29] The day divides into /šaparpar/ "daybreak" (Dnl. 6:20) or /ṣapr/ "morning,"[30] / ṭehr/ "midday" (only attested later) and /ramš/ "evening."[31] The nouns → *zmn* and → *ʿdn* represent "point of time."

2. Undefined. Thus, while the plural *ywmyn* coupled with a number denotes a specific number of days, in the construct state with a subsequent noun or suffixed, it has denoted, already since Old Aramaic, the lifespan, in reference to kings, also for a regnal period.[32] Hereby one can form the description *bywmy* "in the lifetime/reign of,"[33] less often in relation to a certain circumstance (*bywmy ršʿ* "in the time of iniquity").[34]

As an absolute, *ywmyn* can also indicate an undefined, as a rule, longer period as with *lywmn ʾḥrnn* "later times" (→ II.1),[35] in elegant style *bywmy šmyn* "as long as the heavens exist"[36] or *ywmt ʿlmʾ* "for a long time" (Ezr. 4:15,19). The more infrequent feminine ending of the noun in the plural[37] also designates unlimited time.[38] In a similar sense, *ywmyn* in Dnl. 7:9,13,22 denotes an *ʿtyq ywmyn* "ancient of days," thus "aged," who sits in judgment above the kingdoms of the world and transfers dominion to an anthropomorphic figure.[39]

III. Special Days. Special days such as festival and memorial days could be defined more precisely through adjectives or in the construct state with a subsequent noun: in the *Megillat Taʿanit ywm ḥnwk(t)h* the day of the consecration of the altar[40] or *ywm ṭb* "a good day" generally for a holiday.[41] The apocalyptic texts from Qumran contain various names for judgment day: *rbʾ* "the great day,"[42] *ywm dynʾ* "the day of Judgment"[43] or *ywm qṣ(ʾ)* "the day of the end (of the world)."[44] In contrast, the noun *šbh* /šabbā/ "week" is used for the Sabbath.[45]

Gzella

---

29. 11Q18 20:1.
30. *ATTM*, 2, 264.
31. *ATTM*, 2, 263; sometimes also /pānǣ/.
32. Cf. *KAI* 309.7, where *ywmwh* "his days" parallels *šnwh* "his years" in l. 8 and corresponds to *ḥywh* "his life" in l. 14; *KAI* 226.3; Dnl. 2:44 and 5:11; 1QapGen 3:3; 6:2,9; 14:12: *kwl ywmwhy* "his life long."
33. E.g., 4Q196 2:9 (Tob. 2:1); 4Q541 9 1:7.
34. 4Q536 2 2:11; contrariwise, *b-* with the singular *ywm* marks a specific moment; → II.1; *l-* with the plural an approximate time; see below.
35. *TADAE* C1.1,49.52; probably with *l-* to indicate the approximate time instead of the more precise *b-*.
36. *KAI* 266.3; cf. Dt. 11:21; Ps. 89:30.
37. *BLA*, §53j.
38. Cf. A17a,5; 32j,5 and H23,4 for Hatra and its surroundings.
39. Cf. J. J. Collins, *Daniel. Herm* (1993), 304-10.
40. xyMT 23, *ATTM*, 357; → *ḥnkh* II.
41. xyMT 21.25.
42. 4Q202 1 4:11 (1 En. 10:12).
43. 4Q205 1 11:1 (1 En. 22:13).
44. 1Q24 7:1; 4Q206 1 22:2 (1 En. 22,4).
45. *ATTM*, 699.

יכל *ykl*; כהל *khl*; כבשׁ *kbš*

I. Lexical Field and Grammatical Constructions. II. Use as a Modal Verb "Could." III. As a Main Verb "to Be Victorious."

I. Lexical Field and Grammatical Constructions. The root *ykl* serves mostly as an auxiliary verb of capability modality "could."[1] It overlaps with the synonymous *khl* although no complementary distribution overall is clearly perceptible; there may have originally been a distinction in register since only *ykl* appears in the less formal speech of the private letters while the old royal inscriptions contain instances only of *khl*. At the same time, an etymological relationship is entirely possible.[2] In Imperial Aramaic private contracts, *ykl* and *khl* appear alongside one another, although *ykl* is limited here to the imperfect, while *khl*, which appears approximately twice as frequently, also appears as a participle.

Both verbs appear in the G-stem[3] and are constructed similarly, usually with *l*- and the infinitive of the corresponding full verb. In older Aramaic, the full verb in the same form is regularly joined asyndetically instead.[4] In addition, *ykl* sometimes appears with an object clause "that. . .." In contrast to *khl*, *ykl* is attested sporadically as itself an intransitive main verb when it means "to defeat (someone)" (→ III). In addition, other constructions can occasionally denote the modality of capacity, e.g., a nominal clause with *byd* "it is in the hand of" together with an infinitive[5] or the verb "to know" with an infinitive.[6]

II. Use as a Modal Verb "Could." The explicit marking of the modality of capacity is not obligatory in Aramaic or in its Central-Semitic sister languages since "to be able" is also part of the wide functional sprectrum of the long imperfect. This usage covers the related realm (apparently with a common cognitive foundation) of present-future, process or imperfect aspect, as well as epistemic modality, while individual nuances assume their specific form only in context.[7] Thus, the long imperfect and constructions

---

H. Gzella, *Tempus, Aspekt und Modalität im Reichsaramäischen. VOK* 48 (2004); T. Muraoka and B. Porten, *A Grammar of Egyptian Aramaic. HO* 32 (²2003); B. Schlenke, "*ykl*," *ThWQ*, II, 145-49; J. A. Soggin, H. Ringgren, and H.-J. Fabry, "יָכֹל *yākōl*," *TDOT*, VI, 71-75.

1. Gzella, 274.
2. T. Muraoka and Porten, 25.
3. *ywkl* in Dnl. 2:10 may stand under Heb. influence, although one should probably read *ykl* with other MSS, to be pointed as a participle or an imperfect, cf. *BLA*, §45k.
4. E.g., *TADAE* A2.3,5; 2.5,5; see Muraoka and Porten, 255f.
5. *TADAE* C1.1,170f.; → *yd* IV.
6. 11Q10 29:7 (Job 37:16); → *yd*ʿ IV.1.
7. Cf. Gzella, 304f.; with typological and theoretical support, idem, "Some General Remarks on Interactions between Aspect, Modality, and Evidentiality in Biblical Hebrew," *FO* 49 (2012) 225-32.

with *ykl* appear alongside one another, cf. *l' yklyn lhškḥh* "they could not find" in Dnl. 6:5 with *l' nhškḥ* "we will not/could not find" in 6:6.[8]

There are already very early Old Aramaic instances of the root *khl;*[9] *ykl* begins with the Hermopolis papyri at the threshold of Imperial Aramaic.[10] In the legal diction of the contracts from Elephantine, both often occur negated for "to not have the right to," either in the sense of a legal disclaimer or of a prohibition.[11] Admittedly, the two occur in the same text only as an exception.[12] Furthermore, *khl* denotes "to be unable" as a result of advanced age and diminished physical strength.[13]

In contrast, *ykl* is more frequent in Biblical Aramaic. It serves to refer to intellectual capacity to interpret a dream or another secret (Dnl. 2:10,27,47; 4:15; 5:16), and to God's ability to deliver his servants (Dnl. 3:17,29; 6:21) or to humble the proud (4:34). The three instances of *khl* all stand in the participle with *l-* and an infinitive but correspond semantically to the use of *ykl* and interchange with it in the same context (Dnl. 2:26; 4:15; 5:8; all in reference to the explanation of secrets). The evidence from Qumran is similar.[14] Some usages project into the realm of permissive or voluntative modality;[15] *khl* is not definitely attested here.

A conjectural secondary derivation of *ykl*, evident in the meaning "to be able" only in Hebrew and Aramaic, from the imperfect of *khl*, which is much more widespread in Semitic, with a loss of the /h/,[16] is very unlikely and does not account for the use of *ykl* as a full verb "to overcome." Meanwhile, a better explanation for *ykl* "to be able" is the obvious semantic dilution of a full verb to a modal verb.[17] In Biblical Aramaic, *khl* and *ykl* are already interchangeable;[18] in the Aramaic literary languages of late antiquity, *khl* has disappeared, while *ykl*, perhaps strengthened by its continued use as a highly transitive full verb with a clearly demarcated semantics,[19] also continued in use as a modal verb.

III. As a Main Verb "to Be Victorious." The use of *ykl* to mean "to be victorious" is very rare. It occurs in Daniel with a direct object and a pejorative connotation in the vi-

---

8. Gzella, 221.

9. Clearly *KAI* 223 B 6 from the Sefire state treaties; also in a pre-Imperial Aramaic wisdom saying of Aḥiqar: "without strict discipline, one cannot sate a child" *TADAE* C1.1,176; → *nṣl.*

10. *TADAE* A2.3,5; 2.5,5.

11. See the passages in D. Schwiderski, *Die alt- und reichsaramäischen Inschriften. FSBP* 1 (Berlin, 2008), 369,385f.

12. So *khl* in *TADAE* B3.11,9 and *ykl* in l. 15.

13. *TADAE* C1.1,17.

14. 1QapGen 20:19f. for the failure of experts, l. 17 for the incapacity of the pharaoh to approach Sarah; 4Q212 1 5:15,16,20,22 (1 En. 93:11-14) for "to be unable to recognize"; 4Q204 4:2 (1 En. 89:31) for "to be unable to see."

15. Cf. 1QapGen 20:22 for "not to feel in the position to"; 4Q197 4 2:4 (Tob. 6:13) for "to be unable to refuse."

16. So J. Huehnergard and S. M. Olyan, "The Etymology of Hebrew and Aramaic *ykl* 'to Be Able,'" *JSS* 58 (2013) 13-19.

17. Cf., e.g., German "überwältigen" and "bewältigen."

18. Cf. *lā yāḵᵉlīn* "they could not" in Dnl. 4:15 with *lā ḵāhᵃlīn* in 5:8.

19. Cf. *DJPA*, 240; *DJBA*, 534.

sion of the animals from the sea in reference to the horn that battles against the holy ones and overpowers them (Dnl. 7:21) and, furthermore, as a free translation of the Hebrew text in 11Q10 35:3 (Job 40:24). Otherwise, the transitive verb *kbš* in the G- or D-stem is employed for "to defeat, subjugate"; it occurs once in the sense of "to make subservient" in an Imperial Aramaic treaty;[20] two further passages in the pre-Imperial Aramaic wisdom sayings of Aḥiqar are not entirely clear in terms of their contexts.[21]

Gzella

20. *TADAE* B3.9,5.
21. *TADAE* C1.1,152.187.

ים *ym* /yamm/; תהום *thwm* /tehōm/

I. Lexical Field and Meaning. II. General Use. III. In Toponyms. IV. Mythical Reminiscences.

I. Lexical Field and Meaning. Although the masculine *ym* /yamm/[1] "sea" is a common Northwest Semitic primary noun, it is only directly attested in Aramaic beginning with texts from the Achaemenid period. The Arameans of Syria were at home on the dry land, while the sea was the domain of the Phoenicians; this may also have contributed to the fact that *ym* plays no role in Old Aramaic inscriptions. It is employed for bodies of water that surround dry land,[2] or in toponyms for individual marginal seas bounded by peninsulas.[3] It appears with particular frequency in the geographic passages in 1QapGen from Qumran. According to old biblical mythology, however, all seas arise from a "primal flood" in the depths designated as *thwm* /tehōm/; Aramaic attests this (loan) word beginning with the texts from Qumran (→ IV).

II. General Use. In general, the sea is distinguished from the earth (i.e., from the inhabitable dry land) and the mountains as an additional part of the earth.[4] The same view underlies two wisdom sayings of Aḥiqar transmitted on an Imperial Aramaic papyrus:

K. Coblentz Bautch, "*ym*," *ThWQ*, II, 153-58; J. A. Fitzmyer, *The Genesis Apocryphon of Qumran Cave 1 (1Q20)*. *BietOr* 18B (^{3}2004); D. A. Machiela, *The Dead Sea Genesis Apocryphon. STDJ* 79 (2009); H. Ringgren, "יָם *yām*," *TDOT*, VI, 87-98; C. Westermann, "תְּהוֹם *tᵉhôm* flood," *TLOT*, 1410-14.

1. From the second century B.C.E. /yam/, *ATTM*, 120-22.
2. In contrast to interior bodies of water such as rivers → *nhr.*
3. Such as the Red Sea, above all.
4. Cf. 1QapGen 7:1; 4Q203 8:13, however, juxtaposes sea and wilderness.

Land animals such as lions are not in the sea,[5] and nations can also be divided—to cite a later formulation by Carl Schmitt—into "Landtreter" ("landlubbers") like Arabs and "Seeschäumer" ("sea-frothers") like the Sidonians.[6] Similarly, the Bar-Puneš novella mentions the sea, but the context is unknown because of its extremely fragmentary condition.[7]

A few instances occur, then, in the import and export lists in *TADAE* C3.7 in the expression *lym'* "to the sea" denoting goods for export.[8] In contrast, in a papyrus from Saqqara one reads *bby ym'* "the gates of the Nile."[9]

Most instances from the post-Imperial Aramaic literary tradition occur in 1QapGen, which expands and adds precision to the biblical text of Noah's allotment of the land and the promise to Abraham through geographical excurses.[10] This deepened knowledge may stand under the influence of Hellenistic geographers and the world maps produced subsequently.[11] Accordingly, toponyms formed with *ym* also appear here (→ III). Otherwise, *ym* occurs only rarely. According to the Vision of the Four Trees, *tqpy ym'* "the powers of the sea"[12] belong to the realm of the dominion of the second tree; this expression probably refers to the forces of nature.[13]

III. In Toponyms. The use of *ym* in toponyms occurs often in Qumran, especially in 1QapGen, and has parallels in Hebrew.[14] In the first line, *ym' rb'* "the great sea" may refer to the Mediterranean,[15] *ym' śmwq'* to the Red Sea,[16] *ym swp* to the Sea of Reeds,[17] *ym' mlḥ' rb'* to "the great salt sea,"[18] which generally denotes the Dead Sea in Hebrew, but could refer here to the Mediterranean in context[19] or perhaps the Atlantic.[20]

IV. Mythical Reminiscences. Aramaic exhibits a mythical meaning as in the Ugaritic epic and the related archaic Hebrew poetry,[21] although at most still in apocalyptic landscapes as in Dnl. 7:2f. (cf. Rev. 21:1). It describes how the fantastic chimeras, which symbolize all the sequential worldly empires to the dawn of the kingdom of God, arise

5. *TADAE* C1.1,165.
6. Phoenicians; *TADAE* C1.1,207.
7. *TADAE* C1.2,4.
8. References in *TADAE* C, xxxvi.
9. J. B. Segal, *Aramaic Texts from North Saqqara* (London, 1983), no. 26.13, cf. *DNSI*, 469.
10. 1QapGen16:11,17; 17:7; 21:15-18.
11. Cf. Machiela, 85-104.
12. 4Q552 2 2:10.
13. *ym' rb'* in 4Q540 1:3 remains unclear, however.
14. Ringgren, 91f.
15. 1QapGen 16:11,17; 21:11.
16. 1QapGen 17:7f.; 21:17f., see Fitzmyer, 225f.; 4Q206 1 26:20 (1 En. 32:2).
17. 1QapGen 21:18, distinguished here from the Red Sea; cf. Fitzmyer, 226.
18. 1QapGen 16:17; 21:16f.
19. Fitzmyer, 225.
20. As suggested by *ATTM*, 2, 410, although with a question mark.
21. See Ringgren, 92-94; J. Day, *God's Conflict with the Dragon and the Sea* (Cambridge, 1985).

out of "the great sea" (*ym' rb'*), elsewhere probably a term for the Mediterranean (→ III); the contours remain imprecise—presumably intentionally.

In the topic of God's power over the sea, too, *ym* may still have its old connotation as a chaos power, as apparently especially *ym' rb'* in 4Q541 7:3; the two other passages in 11Q10 10:3 (Job 26:10) and 30:6 (Job 38:8), however, are adopted directly from the Hebrew. In the second, the Hebrew loanword *thwm* /tehōm/ "primal sea"[22] is a plus in comparison to the MT. It occurs at Qumran further in 4Q246 2:9 and 4Q542 1 1:7, both in the plural "abysses," then also in later Aramaic languages.[23]

Gzella

22. With the typical Canaanite and, thus, non-Aramaic vowel shift from /ā/ to /ō/.
23. C. Stadel, *Hebraismen in den aramäischen Texten vom Toten Meer* (Heidelberg, 2008), 58.

ימא/ימי *ym'/ymī*; מומה *mwmh* /mawmǣ/

I. Etymology. II. Semantics. 1. Sam'alian. 2. Old Aramaic. 3. Imperial Aramaic. 4. Qumran.

I. Etymology. Aramaic *ymī* "to swear"[1] relates etymologically to Akkadian *tamû* II *wamā'um* "to swear."[2] Aramaic *mwmh* /mawmǣ/ (> /mōmǣ/) "oath, vow" and Akkadian *mamītu* "oath, contract" stand in the same relationship.[3]

II. Semantics.

1. Sam'alian. A Sam'alian instance of *mwmt* "oath, spell" may be present on the Hadad statue of King Panamuwa I (reigned ca. 790-750 B.C.E.), where he prohibits his successor from vengeance or punishment on the members of the royal house.[4]

A. Lemaire, "Le serment en ouest-sémitique, hébreu et araméen, au ler millénaire av. J.-C.," *Droit et Culture* 15 (1988) 115-29; E. Lipiński, *The Aramaeans. OLA* 100 (2000), 557-97; idem, *Studies in Aramaic Inscriptions and Onomastics. OLA* 1 (1975), esp. 41f.,150-53; Y. Muffs, *Studies in the Aramaic Legal Papyri from Elephantine. HO* 66 (2003); B. Porten, "An Aramaic Oath Contract: A New Interpretation (Cowley 45)." *RB* 90 (1983) 563-75; idem and H. Z. Szubin, "Litigants in the Elephantine Contracts," *Maarav* 4 (1987) 45-67; K. van der Toorn, "Herem-Bethel and Elephantine Oath Procedure," *ZAW* 98 (1986) 282-85; A. Verger, "L'amministrazione della giustizia nei papiri aramaici di Elefantina," *AANLR* ser. 8.19 (1964) 75-94, esp. 90-94; A. Vincent, *La religion des Judéo-Araméens d'Eléphantine* (Paris, 1937), esp. 520-41.

1. From an older **wm'*; on the disappearance of the syllable-ending /'/ cf. *ATTM*, 104-6.
2. *AHw*, III, 1317f.,1459.
3. *AHw*, II, 599f.; *CAD*, X, 189-95.
4. *KAI* 214.26; cf. P.-É. Dion, *La Langue de Ya'udi* (Waterloo, ON, 1974), 402f; on the rela-

2. *Old Aramaic.* Old Aramaic examples of *ym'/ymī* occur first in Sefire if one reads: *kh bqryt' ym'n whn lhn šq[rn bkl z]nh* "Thus have we sworn in the city and, if (it does) not (happen) so, [we] have forswor[n in all t]his."[5] Of course, *bqryt' ym'n* could also involve a place name.[6]

A late seventh century B.C.E. orthostat from the Euphrates region attests the expression *ymh pmh* in the haphel "have his mouth swear" in the sense of "to commit perjury" for the first and, so far, only time.[7]

3. *Imperial Aramaic.* One of the oldest Imperial Aramaic instances occurs in the Daskyleion inscription.[8] The text of the burial stele requires those who pass by to cast no shadow (on the grave) and underscores the demand with the formulation: *hwmytk bl wnbw* "I adjure thee by Bēl and Nabu."[9]

In Elephantine and Saqqara *ymī* and *mwmh* appear primarily in legal documents. A few instances of the oath are collected in *TADAE* B7.1-4. M. L. Folmer investigates the syntax of the oath clauses.[10]

The following fixed formulations merit emphasis: *yhb mwm' nprt* "to give another in court,"[11] *ṭ'n mwm'h* "to impose an oath,"[12] *bšm mwm'h dky* "in the name of/in reference to this oath,"[13] *šwb mn mwmh* "to turn away from an oath"[14] and *mwm'h zy* PN *ym' l* PN *b* DN "oath, that PN swore to PN by GN."[15] The once attested at Saqqara[16] *ymī* in the haphel means either "to adjure" as in the Daskyleion inscription (→ II.1) or "to administer an oath."[17]

Realms in which people swear or make oaths include declaration of real estate ownership,[18] declarations of property ownership,[19] accusations of theft,[20] physical injury,[21] and

---

tionship to Aramaic in general, see also P. M. Noorlander, "Sam'alian in Its Northwest Semitic Setting," *Or* 81 (2012) 202-38.

5. Sefire I = *KAI* 222 B 36f.; Lipiński, *SAIO* I, 41.

6. Cf. J. A. Fitzmyer, *The Aramaic Inscriptions of Sefire. BietOr* 19A (²1995), 51.

7. Cf. F. M. Fales, "An Aramaic Tablet from Tell Shioukh Fawqani (Syria)," *Sem* 46 (1996) 80-121, esp. 90.98f.

8. *KAI* 318.2f.

9. Lipiński, *SAIO* I, 151; cf. for an explanation of the verb form of *ymī* in the haphel F. M. Cross, "An Aramaic Inscription from Daskyleion," *BASOR* 184 (1966) 9 n. 19; *DNSI*, 460.

10. *The Aramaic Language in the Achaemenid Period. OLA* 68 (1995), 293f. n. 149, 544f.,565f. Cf. also ibid., 104,111f. regarding the orthography of *mwmh* with partial elision of the etymological /'/.

11. *TADAE* B8.9,5 from Saqqara; but cf. also J. B. Segal, *Aramaic Texts from North Saqqara* (London, 1983), 14f.

12. *TADAE* B2.2,6; 2.3,24; 2.8,4-5; 7.1,4(emend.).

13. *TADAE* B2.8, 9.

14. *TADAE* B7.1,5(emend.).

15. *TADAE* B7.3,1-3.

16. Segal, no. 27.2.

17. Cf. Segal, 44.

18. *TADAE* B2.2; cf. B2.3,24f.

19. *TADAE* B2.8; 7.3.

20. *TADAE* B7.1; 7.2; Segal, no. 17.

21. *TADAE* B7.2.

slave ownership.[22] The oaths taken by gods: Thus the Judeans in Elephantine swear by Yahu,[23] by the temple property, the temple, and Anatyahu.[24] Comparable is the appeal (*mqr'*) to a god in the sense of an oath-worthy achievement. Thus, a Judean calls (*qr'*) on Ḥerembethel in order to substantiate his innocence.[25] If, however, a Jewish woman marries an Egyptian, she gives him an oath by Egyptian gods. This is the case with Mibṭaḥyah, who, after her marriage to the Egyptian Pia', swears by the goddess Satet, the Paredra of Chnum, and the highest goddess of Elephantine.[26] In a legal dispute between a Persian and a Judean, the Judean swears by Yahu.[27]

Palmyra produces two specimens of *ymī* and one for the substantive *mwmh*. Line 11 of the statute of a *mrzḥ*-association[28] mentions *mwm' b'drwn'* "the oath in the banquet hall"[29] and continues with *wmn dy ym'* [*l*]*ḥmn yḥwb ḥṭy'* "and the one who having made an oath does not keep it (?) will be liable to a fine . . . ."[30] This interpretation is disputed, however, since *ym'* [*l*]*ḥmn* can also be understood as "to swear [by?] the shrine."[31] A fragmentary (legal?) text says: *ymh byjrḥbw*[*l*] "he has sworn by Yarḥibol."[32]

4. Qumran. In Palestine, Biblical Aramaic does not attest *ymī*/*mwmh*, but a few Aramaic texts from Qumran do. The astronomical book of Enoch parallels *nm'* [*bmwm'*] "we will swear [with an oath]" and *ḥrm* "to unite" (1 En. 6:4).[33] 1QapGen 2:14 mentions an oath by the great Holy One, the King of Heaven (cf. also 20:30). In 4Q560 2:5f., *ymī* haphel appears in the sense of "to adjure" as a technical term for exorcism.[34]

The legal documents from Naḥal Ḥever nV 2:10 [emend.],32;[35] 3:11,35;[36] 4:15,[37] and 7:18,21,23,27,59,64[emend.][38] attest *mwmh* "oath" frequently.

Niehr

22. *TADAE* B8.9.
23. *TADAE* B2.2,4.6.11; 7.1, 4f.
24. *TADAE* B7.3,1-3.
25. *TADAE* B7.2,6-8.
26. *TADAE* B2.8,4-6.
27. *TADAE* B2.2,4-6.11.
28. *PAT* 0991.
29. J. Teixidor, "Deux documents syriaques du IIIe siècle J.-C., provenant du moyen Euphrate," *CRAI* (1981) 307.
30. Ibid.
31. *PAT* S. 370 s.v. *ymy*; on *ḥmn* as "chapel, baldachin, etc." in the Palmyrene inscriptions, cf. P. Xella, *Baal Hammon. CSF* 32 (1991), 204-17.
32. *PAT* 2775.9.
33. *ATTM*, 234f.
34. *DSSStE* 1116f., with *rwḥ* "a spirit" as object.
35. *ATTM*, 2, 208f.
36. *ATTM*, 2, 212f.
37. *ATTM*, 2, 215.
38. *ATTM*, 2, 218f.

יעט *y't*; עטה *'th* /'eṭā/; יעט *y't* /yā'eṭ/

I. Etymology. II. Earlier Aramaic Usage. III. Biblical Aramaic. IV. Aramaic Texts from the Dead Sea.

I. Etymology. The Aramaic root *y'ṭ* (from **y'θ*) has the basic meaning "to advise"; cognates occur in Canaanite,[1] in the Deir 'Allā text,[2] in North Arabic,[3] and presumably also in classical Ethiopic[4] and in Modern South Arabian.[5]

The feminine substantive *'ṭh* /'eṭā/ "advice" belongs to the same root.[6] This is also the meaning of the noun *'ṣh* in the Deir 'Allā wall inscription,[7] where shortly thereafter in the same line, *'ūṣ* "to ask for advice, to be advised," the by-form of the verb configured as a hollow root, may appear.[8] This suggests that Aramaic *y'ṭ* and its Semitic cognates, including the by-form *'ūṣ* originally trace back to a biradical root **'θ̣*. In Jewish Palestinian and Jewish Babylonian Aramaic, the root also appears, as in Hebrew, as *y'ṣ*.[9]

II. Earlier Aramaic Usage. In the Aramaic texts from Egypt, the verbal root *y'ṭ* appears at least once as a substantival participle of the G-stem "advisor, counselor" in the expression *y'ṭ 'twr* "advisor of Assyria" as a title of the wise Aḥiqar.[10] In relation to the central figure Aḥiqar, the same text also contains various forms of the noun *'ṭh* "advice," e.g., in the absolute state *'ṭh ṭbh* "good advice,"[11] in the determined state *b'l 'ṭt' ṭbt'* "lord of good counsel" (i.e., "good advisor"),[12] with a pronominal

E. Blum, "'Verstehst du dich nicht auf die Schreibkunst. . . ?': Ein weisheitlicher Dialog über Vergänglichkeit und Verantwortung; Kombination II der Wandinschrift vom Tell Deir 'Alla," in *Was ist der Mensch, dass du seiner gedenkst? (Psalm 8,5): Aspekte einer theologischen Anthropologie. FS Janowski* (Neukirchen, 2008), 33-53; W. R. Garr, *Dialect Geography of Syria-Palestine, 1000-586 B.C.E.* (Philadelphia, 1985); H. Gzella, "Deir 'Allā," in G. Khan, ed., *Encyclopedia of Hebrew Language and Linguistics* (Leiden, 2013), 1:691-93; J. A. Hackett, *The Balaam Text from Deir 'Allā. HSM* 31 (1984); T. M. Johnstone, *Ḥarsūsi Lexicon* (London, 1977); C. Kumpmann, "*y'ṣ*," *ThWQ*, II, 191-99 (only Heb.); W. Leslau, *Comparative Dictionary of Ge'ez* (Wiesbaden, 1987); L. Ruppert, "יָעַץ *yā'aṣ*," *TDOT*, VI, 156-85; H.-P. Stähli, "יעץ *y'ṣ* to advise," *TLOT*, 556-59.

1. Hebrew *y'ṣ*, perhaps also Punic.
2. noun *'ṣh;* see below; for the linguistic classification, cf. Gzella.
3. *w'ẓ*.
4. *m'd* "to advise, warn, admonish"; according to Leslau, 325 from **w'd.*
5. E.g., Soqotri *ma'ad* "to intend," cf. Johnstone, 87.
6. Corresponding to the Heb. *'ēṣā*.
7. II,9; the spelling *ṣ* for /θ̣/ instead of the later *ṭ* conforms to Old Aramaic conventions.
8. So Hackett, 64, contra Garr, 133f.; cf. also Blum, 37 n. 17 on the form and 44f. on the wisdom context.
9. *DJPA*, 243a; *DJBA*, 539b.
10. *TADAE* C1.1,12.
11. *TADAE* C1.1,57.
12. *TADAE* C1.1,42; → *b'l* II.3.

suffix *ʿṭty* "my advice,"[13] and in the combination *ʿl ʿṭth wmlwhy* "based on his advice and his words."[14]

III. Biblical Aramaic. This usage of the root *yʿṭ* continues in Biblical Aramaic. Here, too, the suffixed participle of the G-stem *yāʿeṭ* appears twice in the meaning "advisor" (Ezr. 7:14: *šbʿt yʿṭwhy* "his seven advisors"; Ezr. 7:15: *mlkʾ wyʿṭwhy* "the king and his advisors"); likewise, the substantive *ʿēṭā* occurs once as a direct object in the idiomatic expression *htyb ʿṭʾ wṭʿm* "he answered with counsel and understanding" (i.e., "with sagacity and intelligence," Dnl. 2:14).[15] Furthermore, Biblical Aramaic knows a strictly verbal use of the root *yʿṭ* in the (h)ithpaal with the meaning "to deliberate" (Dnl. 6:8: *ʾtyʿṭw* "they deliberated with one another").

IV. Aramaic Texts from the Dead Sea. Two of the usages known from Biblical Aramaic also occur in the Aramaic texts from the Dead Sea. The noun *ʿṭh* "advice" occurs at least once,[16] and also possibly once the verb in the (h)ithpaal "to deliberate,"[17] but the passage is controversial because of paleographical difficulties and the destroyed context.[18]

Kuty

13. *TADAE* C1.1,53.
14. *TADAE* C1.1,60; → *mlk* VI also serves to mean "advice."
15. → *ṭʿm* III.
16. Const., in 11Q10 7:4 (Job 22:18): *ʿṭt rš[yʿyn* "the advice of the evi[ldoer" as a literal translation of the corresponding Heb. expression, see *DJD*, XXIII (1998), 99.
17. 11Q10 5:8 (Job 21:27), *DJD*, XXIII (1998), 96.
18. See the discussion in *DJD*, XXIII (1998), 98.

יצב *yṣb*; יציב *yṣyb* /yaṣṣīb/; יצבה *yṣbh* /yaṣbā/

I. Etymology, Overview. II. Imperial Aramaic. III. Biblical Aramaic. IV. Qumran.

I. Etymology, Overview. The not very often attested Aramaic root *yṣb* traces back to the Semitic root *wṣb*, which, outside of Hebrew,[1] occurs with certainty only in Ar-

J. A. Fitzmyer, *The Genesis Apocryphon of Qumran Cave 1 (1Q20). BietOr* 18B ([3]2004); T. Nöldeke, *Neue Beiträge zur semitischen Sprachwissenschaft* (Straßburg, 1910); J. Reindl, "נצב/יצב *nṣb/yṣb*," *TDOT*, IX, 519-29; A. Tal, *A Dictionary of Samaritan Aramaic*, 2 vols. (Leiden, 2000).

1. Hithpael "to situate oneself"; Reindl, 519-29.

abic.[2] Ugaritic forms are assigned variously.[3] Its relationship to the much more richly attested—also in Aramaic—common Semitic root → *nṣb* "to establish,"[4] which exhibits in Hebrew in the formation of suppletive stem forms, is not (no longer) clear in Aramaic. At the beginning of the tradition (*nṣb* in the ninth, *yṣb* in the fifth century B.C.E.), the roots—as far as the few instances permit an assured conclusion—in Aramaic are distinct semantically. This is also evident in 1 En. 93:2 (→ IV), where forms of both roots stand in a genitive connection.

By far the most frequent form in pre- and post-Qumranic Aramaic is the adjective /yaṣṣīb/ "valid, certain." In the later Targums, it appears regularly in the meaning "firm, rooted" for Hebrew *'ēzīrā* "native." In addition, forms of the D-stem occur and, at Qumran, the feminine substantive *yṣbh* "certainty" (4×).

The G-stem seems unattested. The form occasionally cited in dictionaries[5] traces back to J. Levy[6] and rests on an emendation. The root is even rarer in the East of the Aramaic linguistic area than in the West; while Samaritan attests it comparably well and in many forms,[7] the adjective occurs in the Babylonian Talmud only a few times,[8] perhaps under the influence of Biblical Aramaic; the root does not occur at all in Syriac and Mandean.

The descriptive function of the D-stem in relation to the adjective as a declarative ("to consider certain") suggests that it is to be understood as denominal; an additional indication of this is the absence of the G-stem. For the adjective, the later attested meaning "firm" may be primary in relation to the earlier attested, primarily colloquial "certain, reliable." The meaning of the G-stem "to be firm," attested only in Arabic, supports this approach.

II. Imperial Aramaic. Forms of the root occur pre-Qumran and outside the OT only twice in fifth-century Egyptian contracts. In the same meaning "valid, authentic, true" and as the component of formulas, an endorsement of authenticity, the passive participle of the D-stem /mayaṣṣab/ appears once[9] and once the adjective /yaṣṣīb/[10] as a designation for → *spr* "document" and antonymous to → *kdb* "lie": *spr' znh zy 'nh 'bdt lky hw myṣb* "this document that made for you is valid,"[11] and *zy yhnpq kdb hw znh spr' zy 'nh 'nny ktbt lky hw yṣb* "That which has been published is a lie; this document that I 'NNY, have written for you is valid."[12]

2. *waṣaba, yaṣibu* "to be firm, steady, rooted," Lane 2944f.
3. *DUL*³, 971 and *DNSI*, 465 with additional literature.
4. Nöldeke, 183.
5. *KBL*³, with perfect vocalization.
6. *WTM*, 256.
7. Tal, 354f.
8. *DJBA*, 540.
9. *TADAE* B3.10,22; emended by E. Y. Kutscher, "New Aramaic Texts," *JAOS* 74 (1954) 237.
10. *TADAE* B3.11,17.
11. *TADAE* B3.10,21f.
12. *TADAE* B3.11,16f.

III. Biblical Aramaic. In Biblical Aramaic, the root *yṣb* appears six times in the book of Daniel, once as a pael infinitive (7:19), five times as the adjective; in almost all cases it expresses the reliability or certainty of knowledge: A daydream is "reliable" (2:45, *yaṣṣīḇ* paralleling *mᵉhēman* "trustworthy"). With no substantive to modify, the adjective in 7:16 stands in the meaning "reliable (knowledge)" or even "certainty."[13] In the pael infinitive it renders: "Then I desired certainty [*lᵉyaṣṣāḇā*] concerning the fourth animal" (7:19). The adjective stands as an adverbial following *min* in relation to → *yd*ʿ "to know": "I know reliably" (2:8). The adjective stands entirely isolated in the exclamation "certainly!" (3:24). The form is probably a feminine absolute[14] in a predicative use. With a somewhat different nuance and linked to the juristic background of the two Imperial Aramaic instances is 6:13; here, a word is "valid" in the sense of "irrefutable."

IV. Qumran. The texts from Qumran attest the root five times (so far). The adjective occurs once in 4Q112/115 (Dnl. 3:24) with no divergence from the MT. In contrast, a substantive *yṣbh* (spelled *yṣbʾ*) "certainty" occurs four times. Its interpretation is not entirely simple. Since it occurs twice as feminine determinative, it should probably be distinguished from the infinitive pael with the same spelling and meaning attested in Biblical Aramaic.[15] In 1QapGen 2:20 it stands after *b-* related adverbially to *yd*ʿ "to know": *wkwlʾ mnh byṣbʾ yndʿ* "in order to learn everything from him reliably"; in parallel and probably related to the same event[16] 2:22 reads: *lmndʿ mnh kwlʾ bqwšṭʾ* "in order to learn everything from him in truth." The remaining instances are brief passages between lacunae: 4Q548 1 2-2:9 (Amram),[17] again with a form of *yd*ʿ: *yṣbtʾ ʾnh mwdʿ* "that . . . I proclaim the certainty to you"; 4Q212 1 3:20 (1 En. 93:2) *mn nṣbt yṣbtʾ* "from the establishment of the certainty"; 4Q530 2 2+6-12:24 (Book of Giants)[18] *byṣbtʾ hn ʾyty* "reliable, if . . . is."

Hug

13. *ʿal* over; Peshitta: *ʿal šrērē* "according to truth."
14. So also *ATTM.E.* 358.
15. *ATTM*, 599 suggests *qatl*; cf. however, the determined form of the inf. in Ezr. 5:9.
16. Fitzmyer, 53.
17. *ATTM*, 213. *DSSStE*, 1094f., treats *yṣbtʾ* here as an adjective complementing *ʾrḥ*]ʾ, "the desirable [way]."
18. *ATTM*, 2, 158.

יקר *yqr* /yaqār/; יקיר *yqyr* /yaqqīr/

I. Form and Etymology. 1. Common Semitic. 2. Common Aramaic. II. Biblical Aramaic Usage. III. Qumran.

I. Form and Etymology.

1. Common Semitic. The Aramaic lexeme /yaqār/ "honor"[1] belongs to the common Semitic **wqr* with the basic meanings "(to be) rare, heavy, valuable, honorable."[2] It is attested in the Akkad *(w)aqāru(m)* "to be rare, valuable," Š-conjugation "to honor, respect," etc.; Old Hebrew *yāqar* "to be hard, precious, regarded" and *yāqār* "rare, precious, noble"; and the Arabic *waqura* "to be worthy, serious," II. conjugation "to honor, respect" and *waqārun* "gravity, dignity, dignified demeanor." The uncertain Ugaritic word *qrt* "honor (?)" may also belong here.[3] Additionally, the Semitic of the Arabian peninsula and in Ethopia attests a homonymous root *wqr* with the basic meaning "to cleave, dig, incise," to which belong Arabic *waqara* "to shatter, cleave" and *waqrun* "cavity," Yemenite Arabic *waqqar* "to carve, chisel,"[4] OSA *wqr* "a document carved in stone," or Old Ethiopic *wäqärä* "to dig out, incise, carve" and *moqär(t)* "drill, chisel."

The lexeme *yᵉqār* also occurs as an indisputable Aramaism in Old Hebrew, e.g., Jer. 20:5, Ezk. 22:25, Ps. 49:13,21 or Est. 6:6,7,9,11.[5] As Pahlavi *ykl'* it has also wandered into Middle Iranian.[6]

2. Common Aramaic. The lexeme, which exhibits the common Northwest Semitic vowel shift *#*w*- > #*y*-,[7] occurs in nearly all varieties of Aramaic. Qumran attests *yqr*,[8] Palmyrene *yqr*,[9] Babylonian-Talmudic *yq(')r'* [yᵉ*qārā*],[10] and Jewish Palestinian *yqr* and *'yqr*.[11] The latter form, which exhibits #(')*ī*- for a nonvocalic /y/ and consequently also the (in some cases optional) orthography with an initial *aleph*,[12] occurs in Chris-

---

P. Behnstedt, *Die nordjemenitischen Dialekte: Teil 2; Glossar* (Wiesbaden, 2006); D. Cohen et al., eds., *Dictionnaire des racines sémitiques, ou attestées dans les langues sémitiques*, II/7 (Louvain, 1997); R. Macuch, *Grammatik des samaritanischen Aramäisch* (Berlin, 1982); C. Müller-Kessler, *Grammatik des Christlich-Palästinisch-Aramäischen* (Hildesheim, 1991); T. Nöldeke, *Compendious Syriac Grammar*, trans. James A. Crichton (Winona Lake, IN, 2001); K. Radner, *Die Macht des Namens. SANTAG* 8 (2005); H. Ritter, *Ṭūrōyo: Die Volkssprache der syrischen Christen des Ṭūr ʿAbdîn. B: Wörterbuch* (Wiesbaden, 1979); B. Schlenke, "*yqr*," *ThWQ*, II, 252-56; M. Wagner, *Die lexikalischen und grammatikalischen Aramaismen im alttestamentlichen Hebräisch. BZAW* 96 (1966); S. Wagner, "יָקַר *yāqar*," *TDOT*, VI, 279-87; H. Younansardaroud, *Der neu-ostaramäische Dialekt von Särdä:rïd* (Wiesbaden, 2001).

1. Vocalized **yᵉqār* in Biblical Aramaic; on the formation of the noun, see *BLA*, §187.
2. Regarding the root generally, see Cohen et al., 610ff.; for the semantic shift from "heavy" to "honorable"; cf. ibid., 611f. concerning the examples of old Hebrew *kāḇōḏ* "heaviness, honor" or Latin *gravis* "heavy, noble, honorable."
3. See *DUL*³, 702f.
4. Behnstedt, 1311.
5. *GesB*¹⁸, 489; Wagner, 62f.
6. *KBL*³, 1721.
7. *BLA*, §28.
8. *ATTM*, 599f.; 2, 411f.
9. *DNSI*, 467.
10. *DJBA*, 541.
11. *DJPA*, 54.
12. For the Syriac, cf. Nöldeke, 27.

tian Palestinian *ʾyqr* [*īqar*], determined state *ʾyqrʾ*,[13] Samaritan *ʾyqr* [*īqar*], determined state *ʾyqrʾ* [*īqāra*],[14] Syriac *īqārā*,[15] and Mandean *eqara*.[16] The form *lqr* "in honor of" attested at Palmyra and Hatra, which exhibits a phonetic spelling instead of the expected **lyqr*,[17] also belongs here. In modern Aramaic, Turic has *iqoro*[18] and modern NE Aramaic *īqāra*.[19]

II. Biblical Aramaic Usage. In the Biblical Aramaic text, **yᵉqār* occurs seven times, exclusively in Daniel. It only appears in connection with the monoconsonantal particles *wᵉ*- "and" and *lᵉ*- "to, for": **Ca-ya#* > **Ci-y#* = *C-ī#*.[20] Thus, the two forms *wīqār(ā)* (5× in Dnl. 2:6,37; 5:18,20; 7:14) and *līqār* (2× in Dnl. 4:27,33) are attested. The MT manifests the vocalization with *patach wᵉlīqar* once in Dnl. 4:33, for which the apparatus restores the reading with *qamets* following a fragment of the Cairo Geniza.

"Honor" consists in the attribution of personal integrity and, therefore, expresses a qualitative degree.[21] Consequently, the term denotes a relational parameter. In the OT, it usually involves a person's property and stands in close relationship to the person's position in society. "Honor" finds expression in the possession of knowledge, wealth, high status, or wisdom. In this regard, a higher authority grants a person "honor."

This becomes clear from Biblical Aramaic examples. Usually, God exercises this authority,[22] as in Dnl. 2:37: "You, O King, are the King of Kings, to whom the God of Heaven has given kingdom, power, and honor," similarly 5:18; otherwise, Dnl. 7:14 should be mentioned here: "and to him was given dominion, honor, and kingdom," even if this verse does not explicitly name the acting divine authority. Elsewhere, the king grants "honor," cf. Dnl. 2:6: "if you. . . , you will receive from me gifts, rewards, and much honor. Therefore, proclaim to me the dream and its interpretation!" "Honor" cannot only be granted a person, but also denied.[23] Dnl. 5:20 treats the loss of "honor" thematically: "when his heart was lifted up and he behaved arrogantly, he was deposed from his royal throne and (his) honor was taken from him." Here, too, as in 7:14, the divine agent goes unnamed. According to the witness of LXX, Peshitta, and Vulgate, one should read *wīqāreh* with a possessive clitic instead of the definite article in this verse. It becomes clear that in all these passages the term **yᵉqār* denotes the majesty, reputation, and the extraordinary statuses of a person, understood as the gift of a superior authority of divine or (less frequently) royal nature.

---

13. Müller-Kessler, 52,89.
14. Macuch, 249.
15. *LexSyr*, 307.
16. *MdD*, 356.
17. *DNSI*, 467.
18. Ritter, 253.
19. Younansardaroud, 152.
20. So *BLA*, §§37,258,263; the development **Ca-ya#* (vowel elision in an open syllable) > **C-y#* = *C-ī#* with a nonvocalic /y/ = (i:).
21. Cf. generally *TRE*, IX, 362f. and *RGG*⁴, II, 1103ff., among others.
22. → *yhb* III.
23. See *TRE*, IX, 363.

The term **y^{e}qār* usually appears in these passages with parallel lexemes that belong either to the lexical fields "gift, reward" or, more often, "power, dominion": In Dnl. 2:6 **y^{e}qār* stands alongside the lexemes *matt^{e}nā* and *n^{e}ḇizbāh*, both of which mean "gift, reward."[24] In the other verses, **y^{e}qār* parallels lexemes from the sphere of authority such as *ḥisnā* "power"[25] and *toqpā* "strength" (Dnl. 2:37),[26] *malḵūṯā* "kingdom,"[27] *r^{e}ḇūṯā* "magnitude,"[28] *haḏrā* "majesty" (Dnl. 5:18),[29] *šolṭān* "dominion,"[30] and, again, *malḵū* "kingdom" (Dnl. 7:14). In these cases, the actions are indicated by the verbs → *qbl* "to receive" (Dnl. 2:6) and especially → *yhb* "to give" (Dnl. 2:37; 5:18; 7:14). The causative of the root → *'dī* "to take away" expresses the denial of "honor" in Dnl. 5:20.

The two other verses in Daniel depict an action in favor of a person, indeed, for someone's glorification, *līqār* "in honor of." They involve expressions that denote the speaker's own honor so that the speaker acts to his own benefit. In Dnl. 4:27 the person acted for his own honor: "the great Babel that I built as a royal residence with the force of my might and to the honor of my majesty [*biṯqap̄ ḥisnī w^{e}līqār haḏrī*]." The royal architect who glorified himself in his structures (*bnī l-* "to build for") and thereby acquired lasting fame, is a well-known concept in the ancient Near East.[31] Finally, in Dnl. 4:33 the action with the king as object takes place to honor his royal status: "to honor [*w^{e}līqār*] my kingdom, my majesty, and my glory [*haḏrī w^{e}zīwī*] returned to me" (cf. Dnl. 4:27; 5:18).

The expression *līqār* appears often in older Aramaic,[32] cf., for example, Palmyrene [. . .] *bdyl kwt 'bdw lh ṣlm' dnh lyqrh* [. . .] "therefore, this was erected to honor him"[33] or Hatra *lqr tgry'* "in honor of the merchants."[34]

The LXX usually translates **y^{e}qār* in the book of Daniel with τιμή (Dnl. 2:6,37; 4:27,33; 5:18,20; 7:14) and δόξα (Dnl. 2:37; 4:33; 5:18; 7:14), sometimes the two lexemes even appear together, as in Dnl. 2:37 or 5:18. In Dnl. 2:37 Theodotion offers the additional ἔντιμον. Finally, in Dnl. 2:6 the *Vorlage* is resolved verbally as δοξασθήσεσθε. The Peshitta consistently employs the cognate lexeme *īqārā*. The Vulgate offers the substantives *honor* (Dnl. 2:6; 4:33; 7:14) and *gloria* (Dnl. 2:37; 4:27; 5:18,20).

III. Qumran. Qumran manifests several instances of *yqr*, which comport with and supplement the depiction to this point. The expression *lyqr* occurs, here, too, e.g., in the wisdom hymn of T. Levi [. . .] *'m*[*rt*]*kdy ylydt ly lyqr ylydt ly lkbwd lyśr'l* "[I] thou[ght:] 'As she has given birth to me to (my) honour, (thus) has she given birth to me to the glory of Israel.'"[35] In

24. On the etymologically unclear *n^{e}ḇizbāh* see *KBL*^{3}, 1742f.
25. → *ḥsn* III.
26. → *tqp*.
27. → *mlk*.
28. → *rb*.
29. → *hdr*.
30. → *šlṭ*.
31. Cf. Radner, 96ff.
32. Regarding Qumran → III.
33. *PAT* 0263.6.
34. *DNSI*, 468.
35. *DSSStE*, 54f. Similarly *ALD* 71, *ATTM*, 203; cf. *ALD* 90, preserved in 4Q213 1 1:12, *DSSStE*, 446.

another passage, in contrast, this combination depends on the verb *hwī*: [. . . *wthwh ḥwkmt' ʿmkwn*]*lyqr ʿlm* "[. . . and wisdom will be with you] for eternal honour."[36] In addition, the expression *byqr* "in honor" occurs as in the verse *hn yšmʿwn wyʿbdwn yšlmwn bṭb ywmyhwn wšnyhwn byqr wʿdnyn* "if they hear and behave (accordingly), their days will end in good and their years in honor and joy" (11QtgJob 27:6 [Job 36:11]). Additional instances appear in 4Q198 1:11 (Tob. 14:5) and 4Q213 2:16 = *ALD* 100 (T. Levi).[37] It is clear at Qumran, especially in T. Levi, that the possession of wisdom bestows "honor," cf. *dy 'lp ḥkmh yqr* [*hw' lh*] "he who teaches wisdom will be honoured [by it]"[38] or *ʿwtr rb dy yqr hy' ḥwkmth* "a great richness of glory is wisdom."[39] A seat of honor is granted the proclaimer of wisdom; this metaphor demonstrates his superior social status: [*wʿl krsy dy yqr lh mwtby*]*n lmšmʿ mly ḥkmth* "[And they shall seat him upon a throne of glory,] to listen to the words of his wisdom."[40]

An additional instance of the seat of honor stems from Enoch where it refers to a possession of God: [*kwrs*]*'* *yqrk* {*l*}^{lkl} *dr dry' dy mn ʿlm*['] "the [throne] of your glory / for all / the generations which exist since eternity" (4Q202 1 3:15 [1 En. 9:4]).[41] If one discards bad characteristics, he can clothe himself with honor: *hʿdy n' gwh wrm rwḥ wzyw whdr wyqr tlbš* "set aside pride and arrogance, then you can put on glory, majesty, and honor" (11QtgJob 34:6 [Job 40:10]). As in this passage, → *hdr* often appears alongside *yqr* at Qumran,[42] cf. further *kwl . . . rʿlyn mn qwdm hdr yqrkh* "all . . . tremble before the grandeur of your majesty" (Book of Giants). Other passages issue the demand to accord God honor: *wktb lmʿbd yqr wrbw lšm 'lh'* "he wrote (for me) to bestow upon the name of God honor and majesty" (Nabonidus's Prayer, 4Q242 1–3:5).

Aside from *hdr*, which has already been mentioned, Qumran attests terms such as *ʿdnyn* "joy," → *zyw* "glory," and *rbw* "grandeur" (→ *rb* VI) parallel with *yqr*. As in Daniel, Qumran attests the connection with the verb → *yhb*, as well as, e.g., → *lbš*, → *ʿbd* or the causative of *ytb* (cf. instances cited above).

Waltisberg

36. 4Q213 1 1:10, *DSSStE*, 446f.
37. *DSSStE*, 446f.
38. 4Q213 1 1:10-11, *DSSStE*, 446f.
39. CT. Levi ar f:16, *DSSStE*, 57f.
40. *DSSStE*, 446f.
41. *DSSStE*, 406f.
42. See also *ATTM*, 600.

יתב *ytb*; מותב *mwtb* /mawtab/; תותב *twtb* /tawtab/

I. Etymology. II. Old Aramaic Inscriptions. III. Imperial Aramaic Documents from Egypt. IV. Biblical Aramaic. V. Aramaic Texts from the Dead Sea.

I. Etymology. The Aramaic root *ytb* is common Semitic and traces back to Proto-Semitic *(*w*)*θb*; it has cognates in Akkadian *wšb*, Ugaritic *yṯb*, Canaanite (Hebrew, Phoenician-Punic, and Moabite) *yšb*, OSA *wṯb*, Old Ethiopic, and various Modern South Arabian languages *wsb*.[1] Its primary meaning is "to sit," but in the individual Semitic languages it has developed a number of secondary meanings such as "to remain," "to settle, stay, dwell" (a meaning almost as widespread as the primary "to sit"), and "to marry, to take a spouse."

II. Old Aramaic Inscriptions. The oldest Aramaic literary witnesses already attest the root *ytb*. There, it appears in the spelling *yšb*, as in Western Syria, or in the Tell Fekheriye inscription as *ysb*. These different spellings involve Old Aramaic orthography and most likely reflect various possibilities for representing the etymological phoneme */θ/ in writing, when it was still an independent sound and not yet fused with */t/ to /t/.[2]

Thus, the verb occurs often in the G-stem in the Aramaic from Sefire and in Sam'alian[3] with the primary meaning "to sit" (*yšbt ʿl mšb ʾby* "I have set myself on the throne of my father")[4] and the secondary meanings "to remain" (*šbw lthtk*[*m*] "Stay where you are!")[5] and "to abide, dwell" (*whn ly*[*šb*]*n bʾrqk* "and if they do not [dwell] in your land").[6]

This root also appears in a similar sense in the participle of the G-stem *ysb* "inhabitant" in the Tell Fekheriye inscription (*ysb skn* "inhabitants of Sikan").[7] The inscriptions from Zincirli also contain *mšb*, a *nomen loci* derived from the same root with the meaning "seat, throne."[8] Finally, the verb is also used in the haphel with the causative variants of the various nuances of the G-stem, e.g., "to put, cause to sit, establish" (*hwšbny mrʾ*[*y . . .*] *ʾby* "my Lord place me [on the throne][of my father")[9] or "to cause to dwell" (*whwšbt bh ʾlhy* "and I had my gods dwell therein").[10]

M. J. Chan, "*yšb*," *ThWQ*, II, 302-9; J. A. Fitzmyer, *The Aramaic Inscriptions of Sefire. BietOr* 19A (^{2}1995); M. Görg, "יָשַׁב *yāšab*," *TDOT*, VI, 420-38; H. Gzella, "Language and Script," in H. Niehr, ed., *The Aramaeans in Ancient Syria. HO* 106 (2014), 71-107; S. A. Kaufman, "Reflections on the Assyrian-Aramaic Bilingual from Tell Fakhariyeh," *Maarav* 3/2 (1982) 137-75; W. Leslau, *Comparative Dictionary of Geʿez* (Wiesbaden, 1987); J. T. Milik, *The Books of Enoch* (Oxford, 1976); T. Muraoka, "The Tell Fekherye Bilingual Inscription and Early Aramaic," *Abr-Nahrain* 22 (1983-84) 79-117; P. M. Noorlander, "Sam'alian in Its Northwest Semitic Setting," *Or* 81 (2012) 202-38.

1. Cf. Leslau, 619.
2. *ATTM*, 100ff.; Gzella, 80.
3. Regarding its relationship to Aramaic, cf. Noorlander.
4. *KAI* 214.8.
5. *KAI* 224.7.
6. *KAI* 224.6.
7. *KAI* 309.16.
8. Literally, "place where one sits," cf. *KAI* 214.8, cited above.
9. *KAI* 215.19f.
10. *KAI* 214.19.

III. Imperial Aramaic Documents from Egypt. The Aramaic documents from Egypt continue to employ these meanings. Thus, one finds the G-stem of the verb *ytb*[11] in the senses of "to sit" (*'rtḥšḥš mlk' ytb bkrs'h* "King Artaxerxes sat on his throne)[12] and "to abide, live, dwell" (*wtb bgw 'm 'nttk* "and dwell therein together with your wife";[13] *prsy ytb bprs* "a Persian who dwells in Persia").[14] There may also be an instance of the causative stem of *ytb* with the meaning "to put, place" (*ttb 'l mwzn' wtntn* [. . .] *ksp šqln* 7 . . . "she should place on the scale and give [. . .] silver, 7 shekels . . .").[15] Finally, the texts from Egypt also contain the word *twtb*, a substantive derived from the same root, which means "inhabitant, renter" (as in a wisdom saying of Aḥiqar: *wl' 'yty zy qlyl mn twtb* "and there is nothing as simple as a renter").[16]

IV. Biblical Aramaic. Biblical Aramaic employs the root *ytb* as a verb in the G- and causative-stems with the meanings cited. It occurs, then, for "to sit, to take a seat" (Dnl. 7:9: *w'tyq ywmyn ytb* "and the Ancient of Days sat"; 7:26: *wdyn' ytb* "and the court [= the judges] sat") and for "to dwell" (Ezr. 4:17: *wš'r knwthwn dy ytbyn bšmryn* "and the rest of their colleagues who dwell in Samaria"). Accordingly, *hwtb* is employed once with the causative nuance "to settle, colonize" (Ezr. 4:10: *dy . . . hwtb hmw bqryh dy šmryn* "whom he permitted to dwell in the city of Samaria").

V. Aramaic Texts from the Dead Sea. The Aramaic texts from the Dead Sea also continue the older usages. Again, *ytb* appears in the G-stem with the primary meaning "to sit" (4Q204 1 6 [1 En. 13:9]: *wkwlhwn knyšyn kḥdh wytbyn w'*[*blyn*] "and were all assembled and sat and cried"; 11Q10 27:1 [Job 36:7]: *mlkyn ytby* [*sic!*] *'l krsyhwn* "kings sat on their throne")[17] and the secondary meanings "to remain, settle, dwell" (1QapGen 21:5-7: *w'zl wytb lh bbq't yrdn'* [. . .] *wytb bh w'nh hwyt ytb bṭwr' dy byt 'l* "and he went away and settled in the Jordan Valley [. . . and he bought himself a house in Sodom] and inhabited it; but I remained in the mountains of Bethel"). Finally, this text may also contain the substantive *mwtb*; like *mšb* in Sam'alian (→ II), it is a *nomen loci* derived from *ytb* meaning "dwelling place."[18]

Kuty

---

11. Now spelled with *t*; → II.
12. *TADAE* B2.2,2.
13. *TADAE* B2.4,6.
14. Behistun, C2.1,36.
15. *TADAE* B3.8,26.
16. TADAE C.1.1,160.
17. Cf. *DJD*, XXIII (1998), 140.
18. Literally "place where one abides"; as in 4Q212 1 5:19 (1 En. 93:12): *lmtb lmw*[*tbh*] "to return back to [his] dwelling place" according to Beyer, *ATTM*, 249; for another reading, however, see Milik, 270.

כדב *kdb*; כדב(ה) *kdb(h)* /kadab(ā)/; כדב *kdb* /kaddāb/

I. Lexical Field and Grammatical Constructions. II. Usage of the Verb "to Lie." III. Usage of the Noun "Lie."

I. Lexical Field and Grammatical Constructions. Aramaic *kdb* belongs to the Semitic root **kδb* "to speak untruth" and appears, like its Hebrew cognate *kzb*,[1] in the D-stem. Thus, it serves as a *verbum dicendi*[2] along with other verbs or nouns of speech and can be supplemented with *l*-; it then has the nuance "to tell a lie/to slander."

The masculine substantive /kadab/ with its feminine counterpart /kadabā/ appears more frequently than the verb. Both mean "lie" with no discernible semantic distinction, although /kadab/ is also interpreted as an adjective.[3] In addition, Syriac knows a noun in the form /kaddāb/ "liar" similar to *nomina professionis* and bearers of characteristic features,[4] thus, someone who has made lying second nature. Specimens in older Aramaic are possible, but cannot be identified with certainty. Similarly, additional feminine abstracts based on /kaddāb-/ are known from Syriac, also with the meaning "lie."[5] A synonym is *šqr*.

II. Usage of the Verb "to Lie." As a finite verb, *kdb* occurs in Aramaic even less often than the nominal forms, which are themselves not frequent. A wisdom saying of Aḥiqar employs the participle *mkdb* "lying" in relation to a dishonest person who deserves death.[6] This basic concept in ethical praxis, which underlies the sayings employed, perhaps, in the education of royal officials, extends the admonition of Darius at the end of the Behistun inscription as the foundation of a royal program. The immediate context of the two imperfects *zy ykdb* "who lies" is fragmentary,[7] but apparently depicts the alternative outline of the concept of rule presented here. Otherwise, the verb seems uncommon and rare; the emended form in 11Q10 19:2 (Job 31:28) represents Hebrew *kḥš* in the same meaning.

III. Usage of the Noun "Lie." The masculine noun *kdb* /kadab/ "lie" first occurs in the same contexts as the verb (→ II).[8] In legal discourse, it denotes a counterfeit.[9] The

---

B. W. Breed, "*kzb*," *ThWQ*, II, 380-83; E. Jenni, *Das hebräische Piʿel* (Zurich, 1968); M. A. Klopfenstein, "כזב *kzb* to lie," *TLOT*, 606-10; R. Mosis, "כזב *kzb*," *TDOT*, VII, 104-21.

1. Also its synonym *kḥš*.
2. The G-stem, rarely demonstrated in Heb., and not at all in Aram., may mean "to be deceitful," cf. Jenni, 171.
3. *LexLingAram*, 79; *GesB*[18], 1503.
4. *LexSyr*, 318a.
5. Ibid.
6. *TADAE* C1.1,134.
7. *TADAE* C2.1,64f.
8. *TADAE* C1.1,133; 2.1,65.
9. *TADAE* B2.3,17; 3.11,16, explicitly in contrast to → *yṣb* II "valid"; nV 2:13,36; 3:39 in *ATTM*, 2.

texts from Qumran often employ it adverbially in the expression *wlʾ bkdbyn* "and without lies" paralleling *bqwšṭ* "according to the truth."[10] Since *kdb* obviously functions as a substantive here, the feminine form *kdbh* may also be a substantive and not an adjective. It denotes individual lies[11] and in apposition to *mlh* "word" parallel to *šḥyth* a "deceitful, false answer" (Dnl. 2:9).[12] It may be that *kdb* in *TADAE* C1.1,133 represents an instance of /kaddāb/ "liar," but it remains uncertain.

Gzella

10. 1QapGen 2:6f.; 3:13; 4Q204 5 2:30 (1 En. 107:2); emended forms of *kdb* appear in 4Q533 4:2; 4Q541 8:2; and 4Q541 9 1:6; also in the context of speech.
11. Thus, probably suffixed in *TADAE* C1.1,133.
12. On the construction, cf. *BLA*, §94e.

כהן *khn* /kāhen/; כהנו *khnw* /kāhenū/; לוי *lwy* /lewāy/; כמר *kmr* /komr/

I. Lexical Field and Forms. II. (Jewish) Priest. 1. Imperial and Biblical Aramaic Texts. 2. Qumran. III. Levite.

I. Lexical Field and Forms. By form, the masculine noun /kāhen/ "priest" in Aramaic and its Hebrew counterpart is an active participle of the G-stem. Instances in Ugaritic and Phoenician-Punic point at least to a common Northwest Semitic origin, but the etymology remains unclear. The known Aramaic material consistently employs *khn* explicitly for a priest of Israel's God in the Imperial Aramaic correspondence of the Jewish community at Elephantine, in Biblical Aramaic, in the scrolls from Qumran, and in later Jewish Palestinian and Jewish Babylonian both in Israel and in the diaspora. In addition to Samaritan,[1] Christian Aramaic languages such as Syriac follow this model for priests of the Triune God. It serves as a professional designation of title together with the name.

M. Brutti, *The Development of the High Priesthood During the Pre-Hasmonaean Period. JSJSup* 108 (2006); W. Dommershausen, "כֹּהֵן *kōhēn*," *TDOT*, VII, 60-75; H.-J. Fabry, "*kwhn*," *ThWQ*, II, 335-50; M. Leuchter and J. M. Hutton, eds., *Levites and Priests in History and Tradition. AIL* 9 (2011); D. Rooke, *Zadok's Heirs* (Oxford, 2000); H. Samuel, *Von Priestern zum Patriarchen. Levi und die Leviten im Alten Testament. BZAW* 448 (2014); J. VanderKam, *From Joshua to Caiaphas* (Minneapolis, 2004).

1. Cf. the synagogue inscriptions ssNA 1,10 and ssSY 1:6 from the eleventh century C.E. in *ATTM*, 401f.

Such a priest is also terminologically clearly distinguished from a "heathen" priest (that is, a priest of a cult centered on the veneration of idol images) by the use of the noun *kmr* /komr/ (later > /komar/), which can be more precisely specified in the construct state with the subsequent name of a god. Since *kmr* and its feminine counterpart occur regularly in non-Jewish realms such as the cults of Nērab,[2] Xanthos,[3] Tēma,[4] Hatra,[5] and Palmyra[6] as self-designations, it seems likely that it was otherwise the normal Aramaic word for "priest" since the Old Aramaic period.

Likewise, in light of its Northwest Semitic etymology, *khn* may also be an original Aramaic word, and thus not adopted from the Hebrew: Nabatean employs it alongside *kmr*[7] and the Deir ʿAllā inscription apparently already has the feminine.[8] A possible earlier semantic distinction from *kmr* can no longer be determined. Under Mesopotamian influence, then, the term *ʾpkl* also entered Aramaic as an additional designation for a (non-Jewish) priest.[9]

Consequently, an addition such as *zy yhw ʾlhʾ* "of the God Yaho"[10] or *khn lʾl ʿlywn* "priest of the supreme God"[11] is actually redundant; *khn*, however, is similarly modified by place names after *zy b-* "who is/are in."[12] In contrast, *khnʾ rbʾ* designates "the high priest"[13] in distinction from the ordinary priests.

Further related to the professional designation /kāhen/ are the feminine abstract noun /kāhenū/ "priesthood, priestly office," regularly employed in T. Levi,[14] and the very rare denominal verb *khn* in the D-stem "to be/become priest"; it also occurs in T. Levi and as an infinitive in the very fragmentary priestly prophecy 4Q562 1:2. Distinct from the priest in an unclear manner is the /lewāy/ "Levite." Aramaic attests this term, as a gentilic adjective based on the personal name Levi, as evidenced by the ending, since the book of Ezra.

II. (Jewish) Priest.

1. Imperial and Biblical Aramaic Texts. The first Imperial Aramaic specimens from the correspondence of the Jewish community at Elephantine already attest the use of *khn*

2. *KAI* 225.1; 226.1.
3. *KAI* 319.9.14.22.
4. *KAI* 228 B 2.
5. For the occurrences in various memorial inscriptions, see K. Beyer, *Die aramäischen Inschriften aus Assur, Hatra und dem übrigen Ostmesopotamien* (Göttingen, 1998), 177.
6. *PAT* 0314.1; 2017; 2743.5.
7. See *DNSI*, 491f. and cf. J. F. Healey, *The Religion of the Nabataeans. RGRW* 136 (2001), 103f.
8. *KAI* 312.11.
9. *DNSI*, 95f.
10. *TADAE* A4.3,1.
11. 1QapGen 22:15; borrowed from Gen 14:18, which already related this designation to the God of Israel.
12. *TADAE* A4.7,1: Elephantine; l. 2: Jerusalem, likewise Ezr. 6:9.
13. So already *TADAE* A4.7, 18.
14. Also in 4Q542 1 1:13, Testament of Qahat.

specifically for priests of the God of Israel.[15] There, the title *khn' rb'* also appears for the highest-ranking priest; the others (*knwth khny'* "his colleagues, the priests")[16] deposed him.[17] The same text also distinguishes the priests of Israel's God designated by *khn* from the Egyptian priests (*kmr*, l. 5). The function stands in the foreground throughout this literature, as in the book of Ezra in reference to the priests of the Jerusalem temple (6:9,16,18; 7:13,16,24) or Ezra himself (7:12,21). At the same time, Ezra knows a more complex hierarchy than the distinction between high priest and ordinary priests at Elephantine; rather, Ezra distinguishes priests and Levites from one another (→ III) and from the other cultic personnel (7:24)[18] and both, furthermore, arranged in various "divisions" (6:18).[19]

2. *Qumran.* Qumran supplements the cultic dimension of the priesthood, which dominated in the older texts, with an ontological one. Thus, the status of the priest in the cult roots in a fixed order of creation mirrored in this cult. The vision of the heavenly Jerusalem describes the sacrifice of bread and incense by large groups of priests around the high priest (2Q24 4:13-15; 11Q18 20:3f.,6). The Testament of Amram permits an even deeper look into the heavenly hierarchy. According to it, a priest ranks above the angels (4Q547 9:6, cf. Heb 1:4).[20] Furthermore, the fragmentary priestly prophecy 4Q562 3:4 parallels *khny'* "the priests" with *šby'* "the elders." 1QapGen 22:15 adopts from Gen 14:18 the tradition of the enigmatic Canaanite priest-king Melchizedek.[21] Furthermore, *khn* appears regularly in T. Levi,[22] just as does the abstract *khnw* "priesthood";[23] only faint traces of the passages have been preserved at Qumran, however.[24]

III. Levite. In older Aramaic, only Ezra speaks of the Levites. It consistently mentions them alongside the priests (6:16,18; 7:13), once also together with other temple personnel (7:24). Like the priests, the Levites are organized in classes (6:18), although nothing more is known about that phenomenon. A very piecemeal fragment of the heavenly Jerusalem mentions Levites in the context of sacrifices.[25]

Gzella

15. *TADAE* A4.7,1.18; in the prescript to a letter also A4.3,1.12 and as a title in a commercial document *TADAE* C3.28,85.113f.

16. → *knh*.

17. *TADAE* A4.7,18; cf. l. 1.

18. Consisting of singers, gate guards, temple servants, and other personnel.

19. → *ḥlq* IV.

20. Fragments of the same text also contain the expression *khn qdyš* "holy priest" 4Q545 4:16 and *khn ʿlmyn* "eternal priest" l. 19.

21. See J. Fitzmyer, *The Genesis Apocryphon. BietOr* 18/B (³2004), 248f.

22. *ALD* 9; 13; 17; 79; 99.

23. *ALD* 3; 9; 13; 15; 19; 67.

24. Regarding the backgrounds, cf. U. Dahmen, "*lwy*," *ThWQ*, II, 496f.; "*mlky ṣdq*," 698.

25. 11Q18 30:2.

כלל *kll*; כל *kl* /koll/; שיציא *šyṣy'*

I. Etymology. II. *kll*. III. *šyṣy'*. IV. *kl*. 1. As a Substantive. 2. As a Determinative. 3. The Phrase *kl qbl*.

I. Etymology. Various Semitic languages[1] attest the root *kll* with the meaning "to complete" in various stems. They are attributed to a root complex that contains, in addition to *kll*, also *kūl*, *klī*, and *kl'* (whose deriviates have very divergent meanings in the individual Semitic languages) and may trace to a biradical root **kl*.[2] In Biblical Aramaic, *kll* appears as *škll*, a causative formation with the prefix /š-/, which can generally be attributed to Akkadian influence, but does not unequivocally represent a lexical borrowing of this specific verb.[3]

The word, which serves as a determinative/qualifier "whole, every, all" in most if not all the Semitic languages, most likely traces, however, to the substantive */kull/ "entire(ty), totality," which ultimately also derives from the root *kll*. If such a relationship actually exists, the root in question would be one of the most prominent among all common Semitic roots.

Finally, the verb *šyṣy'* "to complete" in Biblical Aramaic is not Aramaic in origin since the causative prefix /š-/ that it shares with *škll* is not native to Aramaic[4] and the foundational root *yṣ'*, if indeed (as is generally assumed) originating from a Proto-Semitic root **wś'*, the grapheme ' (Old Aramaic *q*), should be written as the second consonant of the root. Therefore, *šyṣy'* is often considered an Akkadian loan, although Kaufman[5] pleads on semantic grounds rather for an origin in another Northwest Semitic language which had, on the one hand, a productive causative stem with /š-/, but, on the other, attests the shift /ṣ́/ > /ṣ/ as, e.g., Ugaritic.

II. *kll*. The root *kll* appears once in the Aramaic documentary texts from Egypt as a verb in the pael perfect "to complete."[6] As noted above, it occurs in Biblical Aramaic as a causative stem with /š-/; all instances come from Ezra: five times in the causative stem

---

G. J. Botterweck, *Der Triliterismus im Semitischen* (Bonn, 1952); J. A. Fitzmyer, "The Syntax of *kl*, *kl'* in the Aramaic Texts from Egypt and in Biblical Aramaic," *Bib* 38 (1957) 170-84; S. A. Kaufman, *The Akkadian Influences on Aramaic*. *AS* 19 (1974); W. Leslau, *Comparative Dictionary of Ge'ez* (Wiesbaden, 1987); H. Ringgren, "כֹּל *kōl*," *TDOT*, VII, 135-43; G. Sauer, "כֹּל *kōl* totality," *TLOT*, 614-16; M. Sokoloff, review of *KBL*³, *DSD* 7 (2000) 74-109; C. Stadel, "*kwl*," *ThWQ*, II, 367-72; idem, "Syntagmen mit nachgestelltem *kl* im Alt-, Reichs- und Mittelaramäisch," *JSS* 56 (2011) 37-70.

1. Akkadian, Ugaritic, Hebrew, Old South Arabian.
2. Cf., e.g., Botterweck, 36ff., who pursues this approach to an extreme degree.
3. Kaufman, 104.
4. Cf. ibid., 123f.
5. Ibid., 104f.
6. *TADAE* D23.1.13,2.

(Ezr. 4:12 Q; 5:3,9,11,14) with the meaning "to complete" and twice in the related passive (Ezr. 4:13,16), usually translated "to be completed." All cases, thus with active and passive diathesis, refer to the completion of a construction project: the city walls of Jerusalem (4:12,13,16) or the Jerusalem temple whether mentioned explicitly (5:11) or implied by the construction material *'šrn* "wooden members" (5:3,9); in 6:14 the verb *škll* admittedly has no direct object, but the context leaves no doubt that it, too, refers to the temple.

III. *šyṣy'.* The earliest stages of the Aramaic language apparently do not yet attest the verb *šyṣy'*, and it occurs only once in Biblical Aramaic (Ezr. 6:15). There it also relates to the completion of the temple with no perceptible difference from *škll* in the preceding context (→ II). Since, however, an active verb in the singular hardly suits the context, some interpret the form as an intransitive "was finished"[7] or emended to a plural *šyṣyw* "they completed."[8] Qumran further attests the verb *šyṣy(')* and its passive counterpart with the same meaning.[9] The use of *šyṣy(')* in *l'* [*š*]*yṣy mhwy* [*l'*]*št'yh* "Mahaway was not at the [e]nd of his [ac]count"[10] deserves special attention since an infinitive supplements it. This circumstance evidences its usage as an egressive verb ("to cease to do something"), a natural expansion of the basic meaning. Targums Onqelos and Jonathan also continue these two usages "to complete something" (e.g., at Gen. 2:2) and "to cease doing something" (e.g., Ex. 31:18), but add another: in conjunction with a living entity as direct object, *šyṣy(')* also develops the specific nuance "to kill, destroy" (e.g., 2 S. 22:38; literally: "prepare an end for someone").

IV. *kl.* Aramaic texts from all periods richly document the substantive *k*(*w*)*l* "entirety, totality" and its manifold pronominal and adjectival usages. For reasons of space, its use in Biblical Aramaic stands in the foreground here.

1. As a Substantive. In the use of *kl* as a substantive, which mirrors its actual origins, the word is formally determined either (a) in the determined state (then, depending on context, it is usually rendered "all, every"), e.g., Dnl. 2:40 *wḥšl kl'* "shattering everything"; 4:18 *wmzwn kl' bh* "and there was food for all on it"; 4:25 *kl' mṭ' 'l nbwkdnṣr* "all (this) came upon King Nebuchadnezzar";[11] or (b) with a suffixed pronoun, e.g., Dnl. 2:38 *whšlṭk bklhwn* "he made you ruler over all of them."

2. As a Determinative. In contrast to these usages as a substantive, the chief use of *kl* in Biblical Aramaic is as a determinative. Then it appears in the construct state, but its precise nuance and function depend on the nature of the subsequent word: (a) with a determined element in the singular (a singular noun in the determined state or with a suffix, a demonstrative pronoun, or a name), the original meaning still breaks through: Dnl. 2:35 *kl 'r'* "the whole earth"; 5:22 *kl dnh* "all this" ("the whole of this"); Ezr. 6:17 *kl yśr'l* "all

7. *GesB*[18], 1539.
8. So e.g., *LexLingAram*, 165; *KBL*[3], 1130.
9. E.g., 11Q18 15:2 (*DJD*, XXIII [1998], 329); 4Q545 1a 1:7 (*DJD*, XXXI [2001], 334).
10. 1Q23 29:5 (*DJD*, XXVI [1998], 78).
11. Yet, the form *kl'* has also been understood as an adverb, cf. the discussion in Fitzmyer, 178ff.

Israel." (b) The original meaning "entirety, totality" also becomes manifest when a determined element in the plural follows (a plural noun in the determined state or suffixed, a demonstrative pronoun in the plural): Ezr. 7:21 *kl gzbry'* "all treasurers" ("the totality of the treasurers"); Dnl. 2:40 *kl 'lyn* "all these." (c) Followed by an indetermined noun in the singular (i.e., in the absolute state) or by the particle *dy*, in contrast, *kl* expresses the meaning "every, each": Dnl. 3:29 *kl ʿm 'mh wlšn* "every people, nation, and language (group)." In such cases, its function approximates that of a pure indefinite adjective or pronoun (e.g., Ezr. 6:11 *kl 'nš dy yhšn'* "whoever transgresses . . ."). If *dy* follows *kl*, the context alone suggests the nature of the referent, whether animate (as in Dnl. 6:8 *kl dy ybʿh bʿw* "whoever makes a request," semantically equivalent to *kl 'nš dy* in Ezr. 6:11) or not (as in Ezr. 7:21 *kl dy yš'lnkwn ʿzr'* "whatever Ezra requires of you"; Dnl. 2:38 *wbkl dy d'ryn* [*Q*: *dyryn*] *bny 'nš'* "and wherever [literally; in what] people dwell. . ."). This indefinite character becomes particularly clear when joined by a negation, for then the noun following *kl* is negated and not the whole clause (e.g., Dnl. 2:10 *kl mlk . . . mlh kdnh l' š'l lkl ḥrṭm* "no king . . . has every required such a thing from a magus").

3. *The Phrase* kl qbl. Finally, the ubiquitous phrase *kl qbl*, which is always followed in Biblical Armaic either by the demonstrative pronoun *dnh* or the subordinating conjunction, does not contain, despite its appearance, the word *kl* but is a combination of the preposition *k-* with *lqbl*. The latter expression consists of the preposition *l-* and the noun *qbl*; it denotes the adverbial modifier "before, opposite," which also underlies the Biblical Aramaic usage: *k-lqbl dnh* "therefore, on which grounds" ("in view of which") and *k-lqbl dy* "because, insofar as, although" ("in view of the fact").

Kuty

כנה *knh* /kenā/

I. Etymology, Lexical Field, and Forms. II. Old and Imperial Aramaic Usage. III. Biblical Aramaic Usage.

I. Etymology, Lexical Field, and Forms. In the past, the Aramaic noun *knh* /kenā/ "colleague" was interpreted as an Akkadian load word from *kinattu*.[1] Yet, its apparent

J. Dušek, *Les manuscrits araméens du Wadi Daliyeh et la Samarie vers 450-332 av. J.-C. CHANE* 30 (2007); S. A. Kaufman, *The Akkadian Influences on Aramaic. AS* 19 (1974); I. Kottsieper, *Die Sprache der Aḥiqarsprüche. BZAW* 194 (1990); T. Muraoka and B. Porten, *A Grammar of Egyptian Aramaic. HO* 32 (^{2}2003).

1. So e.g., Kaufman, 64 and still Muraoka and Porten, 67 n. 326.

original meaning "subordinate" and the consistent masculine plural ending in the older texts have awakened doubts and suggested, instead, a genuine Aramaic root that, conversely, became widespread at the beginning of the first millennium B.C.E. in Akkadian.[2] The absolute state is not attested since the word appears suffixed in the singular or plural (as a rule with the third person suffix), but the nominal form can be deduced from the plural and may, therefore, conform to the *qilāt* type.

Despite the *qilāt* form of the Aramaic *knh* with /-ā/ in the singular and the related plural *knwt* /kenawāt/, which is essentially feminine in morphology, the substantive is treated as a masculine. As a designation of equally ranked members of a professional group such as priests and administrative officials, in a broader sense also for persons with the same social status, *knh* overlaps with the semantic spectrum of → *ḥbr* "comrade." The latter, however, also denotes those who share the same fate or members of a cultic community, and may, thus, have less specific connotations. Consequently, *knh* often seems to be a term in official style for members of a possible (but not necessarily) elite group which is, however, largely egalitarian in terms of internal status (like "fellow" in the British university system).

The distribution also suggests that *knh* belongs to the formal register since instances appear primarily in Imperial Aramaic documentary texts and in the book of Ezra, which is indebted to this diction. It cannot be identified at Qumran and also occurs later only rarely, perhaps under the influence of Biblical Aramaic or directly as a terminological remnant of the Imperial Aramaic administrative tradition.[3]

II. Old and Imperial Aramaic Usage. The first two instances of *knh* appear in the pre-Imperial Aramaic wisdom sayings of Aḥiqar. Here, in contrast to Imperial Aramaic, the meaning is still quite general:[4] the word refers to another person (*ʾyš mh blbb knth* "one [does not know?] what is in the heart of his neighbor")[5] or, as it seems, more precisely, one who does the same work.[6] In this regard, it could represent a general meaning, an authentic archaism, or an intentional antiquated coloring. In contrast, two other instances in the Imperial Aramaic narrative framework[7] for the companions of Nabumiskun, who should be appointed as the executioner of Aḥiqar, but who saves him, already appear to be closer to the usage of Achaemenid administrative language because it refers to persons from the same environment at court.

In Imperial Aramaic correspondence, *knh* occurs regularly then in the combination PN *wknwth* "PN and his colleagues"; often in the designation of the recipient, but sometimes also in the main text; in contrast to *ʾḥ*, however, it does not serve as a self-designation in the courtly third person. The respective personal name designates the highest-ranking member of the group by status or formal authority.

---

2. For the discussion see recently Kottsieper, 243f. with n. 23; also adopted by *ATTM*, 2, 418.
3. Cf. *DJBA*, 590 for Jewish Babylonian and *LexSyr*, 334 for Syriac.
4. Like, elsewhere → *ʾḥ*.
5. *TADAE* C1.1,99.
6. *TADAE* C1.1,185.
7. *TADAE* C1.1,56.67.

Documents from the archive of the Achaemenid administration of Egypt employ the word, on the one hand, for high officials whose function is then further specified by the addition of the precise professional designation,[8] on the other hand, however, apparently also for craftsmen[9] and slaves.[10] By no means does the fact that *knh* describes persons of various social ranks rule it out from belonging to the register of high diction. Letters from the archive of the Judean community in Elephantine employ the same expression for priests of the God of Israel, whether of their own community or of Jerusalem.[11]

Furthermore, in legal texts from Elephantine and Saqqara, *knh* refers to judges[12] and once, as *nšy knwth* "the wives of his peers" in a probably formulaic expression referring to the expected marital duties.[13] The latter nuance, for the same status, could also be on hand in a papyrus fragment from Samaria[14] and in the Xanthos stele for an equally ranked god.[15]

III. Biblical Aramaic Usage. In dependence on the Imperial Aramaic usage, *knh* also occurs frequently in the plural "his/her companions" in Ezra (4:9,17,23; 5:3,6; 6:6,13; once more as a Aramaic loan in the Heb. text of Ezr. 4:7). All passages refer to Achaemenid administrative officials whose precise function is further defined in the subsequent text with the appropriate title.

Gzella

8. *TADAE* A6.1,1.5f.: heralds and scribes; 6.11,1.7, 6.12,1.4 and 6.13,1.6, in each case for the same persons: bookkeepers.
9. *TADAE* A6.2,8.
10. *TADAE* A6.3,7; 6.7,7.
11. *TADAE* A4.7,1.4.18.22; cf. also 4.1,1.
12. *TADAE* B2.2,6; 8.4,2.
13. *TADAE* B3.8,38; cf. H. L. Ginsberg, "The Brooklyn Museum Aramaic Papyri," *JAOS* 74 (1954) 159.
14. *WDSP* 5,7; cf. Dušek, 187f.
15. *KAI* 319.8.23.

כנשׁ *knš*

I. Etymology. II. Old and Imperial Aramaic. III. Biblical Aramaic. IV. Qumran.

H.-J. Fabry, "*kns*," *ThWQ*, II, 402-4; J. C. Greenfield, "Three Related Roots: KMS, KNS and KNŠ," in *Studies in Hebrew and Jewish Languages. FS Morag* (Jerusalem, 1996), 33-39.

I. Etymology. According to Greenfield, the root *knš* has a relationship with the Akkadian verb *kms* "to gather," to the Hebrew root *kms* (biblical) with the same meaning, and *kns* (late Biblical and Mishnaic).

II. Old and Imperial Aramaic. Old Aramaic does not attest *knš*. It occurs in isolation in Imperial Aramaic in the Gt- and Dt-stems, namely in the Behistun inscription in relation to the gathering of enemy troups (*mrdy'*): *']tknšw;*[1] *'tknš[w;*[2] *'tknšw;*[3] and *wytknšwn.*[4] Neo-Assyrian and Neo-Babylonian borrowed the verb from Aramaic. It appears in the D-stem "to gather in (people or harvests)" and as a noun *kiništu* (*kinaštu, kinaltu, kinartu*) "priesthood, religious personnel."[5] In all later Aramaic languages, it is frequent in the G- and D-stems and the respective t-stems and means "to gather." A secondary meaning "to sweep" occurs in Jewish Babylonian, Mandean, and Syriac, as do other derived nuances in Syriac. Also widespread are the nominal forms *be kᵉneštā* "synagogue" in Jewish Babylonian and *knuštā* "congregation, synagogue" in Syriac.

III. Biblical Aramaic. The verb occurs once in Biblical Aramaic as a G-stem infinitive in Dnl. 3:2 *ūnḇūḵaḏnæṣṣar malkā šᵉlaḥ lᵉmiḵnaš* "and King Nebuchadnezzar sent to assemble (= called in)" as a participle of the Dt-stem *miṯkannᵉšīn* in Dnl. 3:3,27 for the convened officials.

IV. Qumran. The G-stem infinitive *lmknš* "to assemble" appears in Qumran in a biblical fragment of Dnl. 3:2 (4Q112 7:8; → III). The nonbiblical texts have a passive participle of the G-stem *wkwlhwn knyšyn kḥdh* "and they were all gathered together" (4Q204 1 vi 6 [1 En. 13:9]), and imperfect of the G- or D-stem *ynš[* (4Q562 2:2), a perfect of the Gt- or D-stem *'tknšn' kḥd'* "we were assembled together" (1QapGen 12:16), the t-stem imperfect *ytknšwn qry'y[n* "the chosen should be assembled" (4Q243 24:2), and *wyt-knšwn kl 'nš qrt'* "and all the men of the city will assemble (around the house)" (4Q551 4).

Fassberg

1. *TADAE* C2.1, 8.
2. *TADAE* C2.1,11.
3. *TADAE* C2.1,15,20,22.
4. *TADAE* C1.2,25.
5. *CDA*, 145,158.

כרסא *krs'* /korse'/

I. Etymology. II. Furniture and Symbol. III. Throne Visions.

I. Etymology. The Aramaic word for "chair," *krs'* /korse'/ (> /korsē/)[1] arose through dissimilation[2] from an original /kussi'u/, a form attested in Old Akkadian and Old Assyrian. One may assume that this word was also in use in Syria, although it has not yet surfaced in the lexical texts from Ebla. In any case, Ugaritic *ks'u* was most likely pronounced in the same way, as the vocative *ks'i* /kussi'/[3] indicates. The word /kussi'u/ must be borrowed from Sumerian égu–zí (with the determinative É for structures), while the typical Sumerian form GIŠ.GU.ZA[4] is a logogram that depicts a net (GU)[5] on four (ZA) wooden (GIŠ) legs. It follows from this that Sumerian had no native word for "chair" and that égu–zí must be a loanword adopted along with the furnishing. Hurritic *kešḫi/kišḫi*, spelled alphabetically *gšḫ/kšḫ* (in Semitic once *ksh*), is not borrowed from the Akkadian because the gentilic suffix *-ḫi* would otherwise be unsuitable. It must, therefore, trace back to a substrate word, perhaps from the proto-Hurritic or Transcaucasian. The spelling *kś'u*, which surfaces in isolation in Ugaritic,[6] still seems to betray a special, non-Semitic pronunciation of the geminated /s/, which, in turn, explains its dissimilation in Aramaic. The extraordinary spelling *khs'y* in a Sefire state treaty[7] confirms this interpretation and reflects an early stage of dissimilation with the widespread consonantal shift /s/ > /h/ before the more common breakthrough of the assimilated orthography *krs'*. Consequently, there is no reason to reckon an error to the stonecutter.

II. Furniture and Symbol. Thus, *krs'* /korse'/ originally denoted a seat without back or arms as the descriptive Sumerian logogram GIŠ.GU.ZA (→ I) explicitly indicates and the Hurritic logogram GIŠ.ŠÚ.A-*ḫi* at least implies, for GIŠ.ŠÚ.A in Akkadian represents *littu* "stool."[8] Yet, the oldest instance of *krs'* in the Tell Fekheriye

---

H.-J. Fabry, "כִּסֵּא *kissē'*," *TDOT*, VI, 232-59; I. J. Gelb, *Glossary of Old Akkadian. MAD* 3 (1957), esp. 152; E. Gubel, *Phoenician Furniture. Studia Phoenicia* VII (Louvain, 1985); S. A. Kaufman, *The Akkadian Influences on Aramaic. AS* 19 (1974), 28f.; H. Kienle, *Der Gott auf dem Flügelrad* (Wiesbaden, 1975); H. S. Kvanvig, "Throne Visions and Monsters," *ZAW* 117 (2005) 249-72; E. Laroche, "Glossaire de la langue hourrite," *RHA* 34-35 (1978-1979) esp. 143f.; S. Lieberman, *The Sumerian Loanwords in Old-Babylonian Akkadian. HSS* 22 (1977), esp. 268f., §247; 285f., §278; E. Lipiński, "Dissimilation of Gemination," in *Loquentes linguis. FS Pennacchietti* (Wiesbaden, 2006), 437-46; idem, "Emprunts suméro-akkadiens en hébreu biblique," *ZAH* 1 (1988) 61-75, esp. 67; L. Mildenberg, "Yehud: A Preliminary Study of the Provincial Coinage of Judea," in *Greek Numismatics and Archaeology. FS Thompson* (Wetteren, 1979), 183-96, pls. 21f., esp. 183-86, pl. 21,1; J. T. Milik, *The Books of Enoch* (Oxford, 1976); L. Stuckenbruck, "The Throne-Theophany of the Book of Giants," in *The Scrolls and the Scriptures. JSPSup* 26 (1997), 211-20; N. Tilford, "*ks'*," *ThWQ*, II, 415-17.

1. In 4Q246 i 1 in the determined state spelled *krsy'*.
2. *rs* from *ss*: Lipiński, "Dissimilation," 440f.,443.
3. *KTU* 1.161,13.
4. Copied once as *kuza'u*, *CAD*, VIII, 613b.
5. Cf. *CAD*, XIII, 286a.
6. *KTU* 1.53,7.
7. *KAI* 224.17.
8. *AHw*, II, 557.

inscription[9] already evidences that "armchair" was not only an attribute of status and dignity, but also served as a symbol of dominion. This circumstance finds further confirmation in the inscription from Bukan from the late eighth century B.C.E., for the curse formula against any king who should desecrate the stele contains the expression "May Hadad and Ḫaldi topple his throne [*krs'h*]."[10] The reference to *krs'* in a stele inscription of Barrakkab, the king of Sam'al,[11] apparently has the same symbolic meaning, and an additional stele of the same king shows him sitting on his throne,[12] the armrests of which culminate in steer heads, with his feet on a stool.[13] Furthermore, statues, reliefs, and seals contain royal chairs with backs and carved legs or chairs supported by figures in the form of caryatids or winged sphinxes.[14] Some of them were decorated with ivory carvings, as the inscription *'p krs'* "front of throne" on the back of a piece of ivory in the form of a stag from Arslan Taş indicates.[15]

The royal throne as a symbol of power and dominion also occurs in Dnl. 5:20, *TADAE* B2.2,2 and 4Q246 1:1. In T. Levi 44:14 and the sayings of Aḥiqar,[16] this image refers to the wise.[17] In contrast, an inscription from Tēma, circa 400 B.C.E.,[18] refers to the divine throne. The same is true for 1 En. 9:[4]; 14:18-20; 18:8; 4Q530 2 2:17f.; and Dnl. 7:9f., which betray the influence of older Enoch traditions, the Book of the Watchers (1 En. 14:18-20) and the Book of Giants.[19]

III. Throne Visions. The throne visions offer a few difficulties. 1 En. 14:18-20 and Rev. 4:2f. mention one throne, while 4Q530 2 2:17 and Dnl. 7:9 have the plural. The expression "the court took its place" (*dīnā y^eṯiḇ*)[20] may explain the plural in Dnl. 7:9, but 4Q530 2 2:18 lacks such a formulation. According to Rev 4:4, the twenty-four seats surrounding the divine throne were reserved for "elders, attired in white clothes and golden crowns on their heads." The rabbinic tradition proceeds from two thrones, but offers varying explanations. According to *b.Sanh.* 38b, one of the thrones was reserved for David. R. Akiba shares this interpretation in *b.Ḥag.* 14a, but his contemporary R. Jose the Galilean, upbraids him with this exegesis: it involves rather "one throne for righteousness and one for grace." Rev. 5:5 seems to agree with *b.Sanh.* 38b, since at the judgment, the shoot of David is supposed to open the book with the verdicts.

---

9. *KAI* 309.13.
10. *KAI* 320.11f.
11. *KAI* 216.7.
12. *KAI* 218.
13. *ANEP*, 460.
14. Gubel.
15. *NESE* II, 40f., pl. IV,7.
16. *TADAE* C1.1,133.
17. → *ḥkm*.
18. K. Beyer and A. Livingstone, "Die neuesten aramäischen Inschriften aus Taima," *ZDMG* 137 (1987) 286, l. 5.
19. 4Q530: Stuckenbruck, Kvanvig.
20. → *ytb*.

The form of the divine throne apparently remained enigmatic, but one must distinguish between God's battle chariot, whose view in later texts such as 4Q530 and Dnl. 7 was stimulated by Ezk. 1, and the actual throne as in 1 En. 14:18-20 and Rev. 4:2-8, whose author "knew the book of Enoch first hand, presumably in its Greek translation."[21]

The chariot-throne had "wheels of flaming fire" (Dnl. 7:9), while a "wheel like a shining sun" surrounded the throne in 1 En. 14:18, in the wording of the Greek version: καὶ τροχός ὡς ἡλίου λάμποντος. This wheel should not be associated with the reverse of a Judean drachma from the fourth century B.C.E. with a bearded male figure sitting on a winged wheel,[22] for the depiction there does not fit the general image of the throne. One can explain 1 En. 14:18 against the reminiscence in Rev. 4:2f., according to which there was ἶρις κυκλόθεν τοῦ θρόνου "a rainbow surrounding the throne." 1 En. 14:18 refers to the light surrounding the throne like the *melammu*-aura that surrounds Assyrian gods in glyptics.[23] It was certainly called *glgl* "wheel,"[24] like the solar disk (*glgl hšmš*) in CD 10:15. In the Old Ethiopic version, the subsequent expression "and the mountains of cherubim" is due to a misunderstanding of the Greek ορος, which can only mean ὅρος "boundary stone, stele," perhaps for *y*ᵉ*ḏā* "front foot (of a four-footed entity)." Its connection with χερουβίν indicates that the author alludes to a sphinx throne or a seat with animal-shaped sides.[25] The cherubim do not appear in Dnl. 7:9, but resurface in Rev. 4:6-8 again. An additional characteristic of the divine throne according to 1 En. 14:18 is that it was ὡς ὕ(δωρ) κρυστάλλινον "like frozen w(ater)," in the Old Ethiopic text "like crystal." The image appears again in Rev 4:6, but the author thought of the floor before the throne "which looked like a glass sea, like crystal." The author of 1 En. apparently took inspiration from the many seals and scarabs in green jasper that portray a god seated on a throne.[26]

Lipiński

21. Milik, 199f.
22. *ANEP*, 226.
23. G. Furlani, "L'aureola delle divinità assire," *ANLR*, 6. Ser., 7 (1931) 223-37.
24. → *gll* I.
25. Gubel.
26. Cf. Gubel.

כתב *ktb*; כתב *ktb* /ketāb/; כתבה *ktbh* /katobā/; רשם *ršm*

I. Lexical Field and Grammatical Constructions. II. General Use of the Verb. III. Juridical Use of the Verb. IV. Noun "Document." V. Noun "Symbol; Marriage Contract." VI. Root *ršm*.

I. Lexical Field and Grammatical Constructions. Both as a verb and a noun, the root *ktb* "to write" belongs to the common West Semitic lexicon. In Aramaic, the verb appears in the G-stem in agreement with the other Semitic languages; "to write" can also be understood in the broader sense as "to dictate." Further, it serves in official documents for contractual agreements and for "to sign" (→ III). The D-stem seems to be employed for the branding of slaves (→ II), but was probably restricted to this use. Other forms like the Gt-stem "to be written"[1] and the causative-stem "to have written"[2] are only attested with certainty and regularity in individual Aramaic literary languages.

The verb is usually construed as a transitive with what is written as the object, rarely with an object clause following *dy* "that" and an infinitive following *l-*. Various adverbial modifiers are marked by the prepositions *b-* or *bgw* "in, on" (Ezr. 5:7; 6:2), *l-* "to" (Ezr. 4:8) and *ʿl* "on" (Dnl. 5:5) or "in reference to" (Ezr. 4:8; 1QapGen 15:20).

Further, older Aramaic already attests the masculine */kitāb/[3] "writing," originally an inscription or a document, that is also a scroll (→ IV). Since the Aramaic contracts from the Dead Sea, one also encounters the juridical term /katobā/ "marriage contract" (→ V). With the growing prominence of scribal culture, additional nominal forms like the *nomen professionis* /kātōb/ "scribe"[4] or other meanings for */kitāb/, e.g., "manuscript, orthography" appear.

In contrast to *ktb*, which can refer to anything written, the noun /sepr/ (→ *spr*) specifically denotes an official document or book, and the professional designation /sāpir/[5] a scribe who also has administrative duties, thus a secretary and later a scholar. As a verb, *spr* is not productive in Aramaic, however. Finally, /magallā/ denotes the scroll (Ezr. 6:2) as the physical form of a book.[6] Additional specialized terms serve for various textual media such as tablets (*lwḥ* /lūḥ/)[7] and for various types of documents such as, above all, *ʾgrh* /ʾeggarā/ "letter" (Ezr. 4:8,11; 5:6).[8]

Notably, the book of Daniel frequently employs the verb *ršm* (probably originally "to inscribe"; → VI), unusual in Old and Imperial Aramaic, for signing of royal edicts in Dnl. 5 and especially 6. One also encounters the masculine noun /rošm/ "symbol" from the same root.

II. General Use of the Verb. Old Aramaic still attests the verb *ktb* rarely. The Sefire state treaties use it for the agreements recorded on steles[9] and prefigure, thus, the regular usage in Imperial Aramaic legal texts. Two additional instances in royal inscriptions,

---

H. M. Cotton, "'Diplomatics' or External Aspects of the Legal Documents from the Judaean Desert: Prolegomena," in C. Hezser, ed., *Rabbinic Law in Its Roman and Near Eastern Context. TSAJ* 97 (2003), 49-61; H. Haag, "כָּתַב *kātab̲*," *TDOT*, VII, 371-82; C. Metzenthin, "*ktb*," *ThWQ*, II, 455-60; A. R. Millard, "Words for Writing in Aramaic," in *Hamlet on a Hill. FS Muraoka. OLA* 118 (2003), 349-55; L. H. Schiffman, "Witnesses and Signatures in the Hebrew and Aramaic Documents from the Bar Kokhba Caves," in *Semitic Papyrology in Context. FS Levine. CHANE* 14 (2003), 165-86.

1. Cf. *DJPA*, 271f.; *DJBA*, 607f.; so also *PAT* 0259 i.5.
2. *LexSyr*, 352a; a possibly earlier example in *TADAE* D23.1.13,1 is unclear because of the fragmentary context.
3. In Aramaic perhaps /katāb/?
4. *PAT* 2743.7; *DJPA*, 272a.
5. Later mutated to /sāpar/.
6. → *gll*.
7. *ATTM*, 617.
8. Cf. Millard.
9. *KAI* 222 C 2 and to be emended with relative certainty in l. 1.

which also relate to the respective content of the stele, are emended to a great degree.[10] In the epistolary ostracon from Asshur, *ktb* along with → *yd* apparently serves once to refer to a personally signed confirmation (admission of guilt?) by prisoners,[11] and once in reference to a property symbol tattoed on the lower arm, as was common for slaves.[12]

Imperial Aramaic provides dozens of instances. In private letters, it involves the writing of confirmations of loans[13] or the letter itself,[14] in contracts the pertinent or another legal document between the parties to the contract,[15] in graffiti to the inscription.[16]

It is also used of the tattooing of slaves,[17] in this case, however, probably in the D-stem as corresponding forms of the participle and the infinitive suggest;[18] elsewhere, the verb *šnt* fulfills this function.[19] Occasionally, a noun derived from the same root *ktb* appears as the direct object (→ V). Many other passages in private letters on ostraca are fragmentary. Most specimens in Imperial Aramaic and in the post-Achaemenid administrative tradition, however, occur in the signature of contracts or other documents (→ III).

Biblical Aramaic employs the G-stem of *ktb* following Imperial Aramaic conventions for official letters to the Persian king (Ezr. 4:8; 5:10), and the passive participle *ktyb* "is written" for the content of a document (Ezr. 5:7; 6:2). In the court tales of Daniel, the verb also refers to a royal missive (Dnl. 6:26) and for the writing on the wall (5:5; → III).

The texts from Qumran refer with *ktb* to prophecies concerning the future[20] including heavenly writings.[21] In these cases, it sometimes explicitly involves the recording of visions in a dream, whereby the apocalyptic texts ultimately establish their own literary character.[22] Furthermore, it denotes the writing of the Jewish soothsayer who healed King Nabonidus from his illness.[23] In contrast, the history at the court of Darius and Xerxes takes up the topic of the old royal edict.[24]

III. Juridical Use of the Verb. With the numerous Imperial Aramaic private contracts from the Achaemenid period and the post-Achaemenid continuation of this legal

10. *KAI* 202 B 14; 320.10.
11. *KAI* 233.9.
12. → *yd* II.1; *KAI* 233.12.
13. *TADAE* A3.8,4; so already in the few older letters from Hermopolis: A2.6,5; similarly with the passive: 6.1,3.
14. *TADAE* A3.3,13.
15. Here with the nuance "to have prepared," since these documents were produced by professional scribes: *TADAE* B2.4,4.14; 2.7,9.12; 3.11,16, etc.
16. *TADAE* D22.47,3; 22.50,1; 22.51,1.9; this continues in the memorial inscriptions from Hatra and its environs, always in the first-person perfect *ktbt* "I have written": A11a,4; 21,4; 27h; H24a,b; passive *ktyb* "is written" in H235,3.
17. *TADAE* D7.9,4; see above.
18. *TADAE* D7.9,7,10.
19. Cf. *DNSI*, 1178.
20. 4Q529 1:6; 4Q536 2 2:12; so probably also 1QapGen 15:20 and 4Q533 3:3, both fragmentary.
21. 4Q204 5 2:27 (1 En. 107:1).
22. 4Q547 9:8; 4Q204 1 6:19 (1 En. 14:7); emended in 4Q212 1 ii 22 (1 En. 92:1).
23. 4Q242 1-3:5.
24. 4Q550 1:6, *ktyb* as in Ezr. 6:2; see above.

tradition, some instances of more specialized usages of *ktb* "to write" appear. In legally binding documents of various kinds, one regularly finds the name of the scribe at the end in a formulaic expression: in contracts,[25] official letters,[26] or receipts,[27] in certificates of indebtedness, also at the beginning.[28]

Furthermore, the passive participle *ktyb* in the singular and the plural refers in legal texts to specific, contractually established agreements,[29] in loans to the pertinent sum and the interest,[30] or in the sale of real estate to the more precise description of the size of the pertinent house.[31] This practice continues in the post-Achaemenid legal tradition.[32]

In the course of time, *ktb*, sometimes together with *kp* or → *yd* "hand" after the preposition *b-* "with," became a fixed expression for "to sign." This expression occurs in isolation already in Imperial Aramaic documents from Egypt,[33] but only became common practice in the Aramaic legal texts from the Dead Sea from Roman times. Here, the parties to the contract sign (with the addition *ʿl npšh* "obligated, on own's one responsibility") and the witnesses, either themselves or through an authorized person.[34] The autograph signature can be indicated by *(b)ydh* "(with) his hand" in relation to the verb and nouns (→ IV).[35]

Presumably, these technical juridical and administrative connotations of the combination of *ktb* "to write" with *yd* "hand" also stand in the background of the material writing of the invisible hand on (*ʿl*) the wall in Dnl. 5:5.[36] Thereby, both the authenticity of the message of judgment and its verdict character are accentuated. The positive counterpart is the "book of life," in which God writes the names of the righteous.[37]

IV. Noun "Document." Since Imperial Aramaic times, the masculine noun */kitāb/[38] is attested for "document" in the broader sense. Since the documentary texts from the Achaemenid period employ as a rule the more precise term *spr* /sepr/ "document" with an additional description of the pertinent document, it initially appears only rarely. Already in the Xanthos triglot, in the expression *ktb zy mhḥsn*[39] it denotes an official document, apparently a "certificate of authorization" by the Achaemenid provincial administration

25. Also on the back and together with the name of the client, e.g., *TADAE* B1.1,17.19; 2.1,15.20; 2.2,16.22.

26. *TADAE* A6.2,23; in a passive construction, in contrast, in A3.8,14; 3.9,8.

27. *TADAE* D8.13,3.

28. *TADAE* D2.27,1; 5.38,1.

29. Often with the addition of *mnʿl, mn lʿl* or *ʿlʾ* "above," later also *ltḥt* "below."

30. E.g., *TADAE* B3.13,7.8.10.12; 3.1, 8.

31. So, e.g., in *TADAE* B2.10,8; 3.10,12.

32. E.g., V 50:10, nV 20:42; 1:36; 7:25,49; 15:37f.; 17:42; 18:69,71; 22:34, all in *ATTM* 2; additionally, ibid., 422; furthermore, in the Palmyrene tax table: *PAT* 0259 i.4, cf. 8f.; ii.68,87,89, emended 142.

33. In reference to witnesses who sign with their own hand, in *TADAE* B2.7,17f. and 4.3,21: *ktb* PN *bkpy npšh*.

34. Cotton; Schiffman.

35. Cf., e.g., nV 3:51-54 in *ATTM*, 2, 213.

36. → *yd* III.

37. Haag, 380; cf. also ggJR 1,5 in *ATTM*, 388, sixth or seventh century C.E.

38. In Aramaic perhaps /katāb/?

39. *KAI* 319.19.

for the establishment of a new cult.[40] The broader usage, however, is still evident in Biblical Aramaic: there it represents "regulation" (Ezr. 6:18: *kktb spr mšh* "according to the regulation of the book of Moses") and, negated, either in expansion of this usage or in the sense of "without written authorization," adverbial for supplies "without restriction" (7:22: *l' ktb*). In Daniel, in contrast, it is also employed for the writing on the wall, thus for "written" in general (Dnl. 5:7f.,15-17,24f.), as well as for the royal prohibition (6:9-11), there, however, also diverging from Achaemenid diction, in association with *ršm* (→ VI).

The texts from the post-Achaemenid literary tradition reflect an even broader spectrum of nuances. At Qumran, *ktb* occurs in novelistic texts with an Imperial Aramaic complexion, also for a legal document, or in fact[41] some other official document[42] much as in contracts;[43] it is more frequent, however, in apocalyptic contexts for heavenly books of revelation[44] or the recording of words of revelation for the future.[45] Such passages recall the topic of "the book of fate" widespread in antiquity and the ancient orient (cf. Ps. 139:16f.) and which found broad reception in the literature of the early church.[46]

The meaning "manuscript" appears in contracts[47] and in the combination *ṭ'wn dy ktb* "scribal error" in the Palmyrene tax table.[48] In Hatra, *ktb* refers to memorial inscriptions by private individuals.[49]

V. Noun "Symbol; Marriage Contract." Imperial Aramaic employs the feminine *ktbh* /katobā/, if in fact the same formation is involved, first for "marking"[50] or "symbol, (informal) inscription,"[51] similar to its Hebrew counterpart in Lev 19:28. In such usages, however, it cannot be clearly differentiated semantically from /rošm/ (→ VI). Since the legal texts from the Dead Sea, it is also known as a technical juridical term for "marriage contract."[52] With this meaning, it became a fixed component of rabbinic legal terminology.[53]

---

40. → *ḥsn* II.

41. 4Q197 5:10 (Tob. 9:2).

42. 4Q550 7+7a:5.

43. nV 9:6 and 42:31 in *ATTM*, 2, 225 and 244-47.

44. 4Q529 1:1, apparently synonymous with *spr* in l. 6; 11Q18 19:5f.; presumably so also in a fragmentary context 4Q541 2 1:6.

45. 4Q536 2 i2:12 and 4Q204 1 4:19 (1 En. 14:7), both together with the verb; → II; judging from the context, also probably in 1QapGen 5:29, where, however, according to *ATTM*, 2, 91 the verb *ktb* appears

46. Much material on this subject is collected in L. Koep, *Das himmlische Buch in Antike und Christentum. Theophaneia* 8 (Bonn, 1952); cf. 25f. on Enoch.

47. V 37:10 and nV 1-3:9 in *ATTM*, 2; cf. *PAT* 1624.3 and → III.

48. *PAT* 0259 ii.99f.; → *ḥṭī* V.

49. H53.2; 101.2; 235.3; 1015.8.

50. Namely of a slave: *TADAE* D7.9,4, together with the verb; → II.

51. In a graffito: *TADAE* D22.47,3.

52. M 21:10,13 in *ATTM*, 310f.; nV 10:16 in *ATTM*, 2, 226-228; Imperial Aramaic still has → *spr 'ntw*.

53. *DJPA*, 272b; *DJBA*, 609.

VI. Root *ršm*. A remarkable characteristic of the book of Daniel is its use of the verb *ršm* for "to write" (Dnl. 6:9,10,11,13,14 of the signing of a royal prohibition; 5:24f. for the writing on the wall). Literally, it may mean "to inscribe," as in the sole Old or Imperial Aramaic example;[54] in Qumran, together with the noun /rošm/ "symbol," it refers to an exact copy.[55] In Imperial Aramaic, this word refers to the tattooing of slaves in a papyrus from Samaria.[56]

Gzella

54. *KAI* 223 C 1-3, Sefire.
55. 4Q530 2 2+6-12,19.
56. *WDSP* 2:1; J. Dušek, *Les manuscrits araméens du Wadi Daliyeh et la Samarie vers 450-332 av. J.-C.* (Leiden, 2007), 134f.

כתל *ktl* /kotl/; אגר *ʾgr* /ʾeggār/

I. Etymology and Lexical Field. II. Usage.

I. Etymology and Lexical Field. Aramaic designates the internal or external wall of a house with the masculine noun /kotl/. It is etymologically related to Akkadian *kutlu*, although as evidenced by its distribution in the Aramaic of Palestine (→ II)[1] and the simultaneous absence in Old and Imperial Aramaic as well as later East Aramaic, probably not borrowed from Akkadian.[2] It entered postexilic Hebrew from Aramaic, however.[3]

Imperial Aramaic employs instead the masculine /ʾeggār/,[4] which, in contrast, is very much an Akkadian loanword,[5] as does East Aramaic which demonstrates it beginning with the cuneiform incantation from Uruk (ll. 1,8), and it remained especially productive in the meaning "roof."[6] As the external or internal wall of a house, /kotl/ differs seman-

H. Gzella, "Deir ʿAllā," in G. Khan, ed., *Encyclopedia of Hebrew Language and Linguistics* (Leiden, 2013), 1:691-93; S. A. Kaufman, *The Akkadian Influences on Aramaic. AS* 19 (1974); M. Wagner, *Die lexikalischen und grammatikalischen Aramaismen im alttestamentlichen Hebräisch. BZAW* 96 (1966).

1. *DJPA*, 255a.
2. Cf. Kaufman, 65.
3. Biblical only in Cant. 2:9, later also in the Mishnah, cf. Wagner, 69, with additional bib.
4. *DNSI*, 12.
5. Kaufman, 57.
6. *DJBA*, 110.

tically from the city wall, /šūr/.[7] This distinction is evident in texts that employ both lexemes (cf. Ezr. 5:8 with 4:12,13,16).

II. Usage. The first instances of *ktl* "wall" occur in Biblical Aramaic. In Ezr. 5:8, it denotes the walls of the Jerusalem temple, which incorporated wood.[8] In contrast, it refers in Dnl. 5:5 to the whitewashed wall of the royal palace on which a hand began to write during Belshazzar's sacrilegious banquet. As the inscription from Deir ʿAllā in the form of a scroll demonstrates (it, too, contains a prophecy of destruction), plaster was a medium for writing as early as 800 B.C.E., at least in exceptional cases. In the vision of the new Jerusalem from Qumran, *kwtl* (spelled *plene*) is a frequent architectural term.[9] T. Levi employs the word for the sides of an altar.[10] It appears in the same meaning repeatedly in Palmyrene, too, sometimes explicitly for the sides of a brick.[11]

Gzella

7. → *šwr.*
8. For the historical background of the construction technique, cf. H. C. Thomson, "A Row of Cedar Beams," *PEQ* 92 (1960) 57-63.
9. 2Q24 3:4; 8:3; 4Q554 2 3:16; 4Q554a 1 2:9; 11Q18 11:2; 17 2:4.
10. 4Q214b 2-6:8.
11. *PAT* 0166.1; 1624.11; 1919.4.

לבב *lbb* /lebab/ and לב *lb* /lebb/

I. Form and Etymology. II. As the Center of Thought and Emotion. III. For the Insides. IV. Idiomatic Expressions.

I. Form and Etymology. Both of the synonymous masculines /lebb/ and /lebab/ "heart" are productive in Aramaic. The second clearly predominates in Old and Imperial Aramaic, but is usually regarded a secondary form,[1] perhaps arisen through the analogous back-formation of a bisyllabic plural foundation of an old common Semitic */libb-/ with an /a/-expansion.[2] In contrast to Hebrew, the plural of /lebab/ in Aramaic is also masculine in form. Meanwhile, post-Imperial Aramaic literary languages attest a suppletive

H.-J. Fabry, "לֵב *lēḇ*," *TDOT*, VII, 399-437; idem, "*lbb*," *ThWQ*, II, 466-76; F. Stolz, "לֵב *lēb* heart," *TLOT*, 638-42; M. Weigl, *Die aramäischen Achikar-Sprüche aus Elephantine und die alttestamentliche Weisheitsliteratur. BZAW* 399 (2010).

1. Cf. *BLe*, §61v‴.
2. J. Fox, *Semitic Noun Patterns. HSS* 52 (Winona Lake, IN, 2003), 215f.

distribution of /lebb/, which appears beginning with the book of Daniel and Aramaic texts from Qumran, as the basis for the singular and /lebab/ for the plural.[3]

The older Aramaic texts employ the noun almost exclusively for the "heart" as the center of inner experience, because there was no independent term like "conscience" or "awareness."[4] It includes thinking and planning as much as feeling and wishing and appears regularly in this function in adverbial expressions, often after the preposition *b-* "in." The anatomical use for the organ or the general use for the "insides," contrariwise, is rare.[5] Furthermore, in a few idiomatic expressions, the "heart" designates the emotional state of the entire person, as in the sense of arrogance or, as often in a formulaic expression of Achaemenid legal diction, of satisfaction. Consequently, it can also stand as the subject of verbs of feeling like → *ḥdī* "to rejoice"[6] and as the direct object of transitive verbs like *yhb* "to give"[7] or *ṭīb*, in the causative stem "to satisfy" (→ IV). In these cases, the "heart" denotes the entire person.

II. As the Center of Thought and Emotion. Old Aramaic already well attests *lbb* for a person's thinking and feeling, encompassing both concrete thoughts or plans and a general disposition. The state treaties from Sefire employ the expression *wtʿšt blbb[k* "and you think in [your] heart"[8] in parallel with *hn tʾmr bnbšk* "if you say in your mind" apparently in relation to the loyal behavior of a covenant partner[9] and, on the other hand, *hn tsq ʿl lbbk* "if it comes over your heart" together with *wtśʾ ʿl śptyk* "and it rises to your lips" for the first conceived and then announced plan of a treaty partner or his descendants to murder the other or his descendant.[10]

Widely varied nuances also occur in the Old Aramaic wisdom sayings of Aḥiqar: in the admonition to discretion *hwqr lbb* "make the heart heavy"[11] may mean "guard your sanity,"[12] that is "do not be frivolous," while the undiscerning gossip—if the reading is correct—is described as *gbr lʾ lb[b]* "man with no heart," that is foolish.[13] In contrast, a royal command should be executed *bḥmr* (or *bḥmd*) *lbbʾ* "with the fervor (or joy) of the heart," that is with great emotional agreement and not indolently.[14] Even the disproportionate joy over many sons (because they are no merit, any more than childlessness is a personal failure) roots in the heart as the seat of emotions (l. 90).[15] In juxtaposition

3. *DJPA*, 275; *DJBA*, 623f.; *LexSyr*, 354; *MdD*, 234.

4. Cf. H. Gzella, *Lebenszeit und Ewigkeit. BBB* 134 (Berlin, 2002), 100 n. 269, 119 and 122f.

5. → *gw* was generally available for the second.

6. As in the wisdom saying of Aḥiqar *TADAE* C1.1,90; probably also in l. 65 of the framing narrative but the verb is not preserved there.

7. *TADAE* C1.1,105; Dnl. 4:13 and 7:4.

8. → *ʿšt*.

9. *KAI* 223 B 5, although the immediately following context is destroyed.

10. *KAI* 224,14f.

11. *TADAE* C1.1,82.

12. Cf. Prov. 4:23 and Weigl, 88-91.

13. Ibid.

14. L. 88; cf. Weigl, 151f.

15. For the context in the history of tradition, see Weigl, 160-67.

with *špyr mddh* "beautiful form," *lbbh ṭb* "his heart is good" describes quite generally the "inner worth";[16] *mh blbb* "what is in the heart (of another)" represents the unspoken thoughts and perceptions.[17] In a partially destroyed context, *llb]bk* "for your heart" could also supplement the expression "may the word of the king be a cure."[18] If a causative stem of the root → *śgī* "to multiply" is present in *'l thśg' lbb'* (l. 137), the expression "do not let the heart become immoderate" would be a warning against arrogance, perhaps in relation to wealth.[19] Other instances preserve idiomatic formulations (→ IV).

In the documentary texts of the Achaemenid period, *lbb* occurs mostly together with forms of the root *ṭīb* "to be good" as part of a fixed formula in Imperial Aramaic contracts, also sporadically again in a few coined combinations (→ IV). In this regard, "heart" as subject generally designates the person as such in a certain emotional attitude.

The rational-emotional dual meaning of *lb*(*b*) well attested since old Aramaic reappears further in the various Biblical Aramaic instances (all from the book of Daniel); no grammatical or semantic difference between *lb* and *lbb* can be determined. The *r'ywny lbbk* "thoughts of my heart" (Dnl. 2:30) refer to God's communication to the king in the form of a dream vision that the king cannot immediately understand, but only with the help of the inspired interpreter Daniel. Daniel's affirmation at the end of the animal vision of the empires that he will keep this word (*mlh*) in his heart (*blby*; Dnl. 7:28)[20] recalls the admonitions in the Sayings of Aḥiqar, probably addressed primarily to scribes and officials, to handle confidential communications discreetly.[21] The emotional aspect appears in the combination of *lbb* as the subject of *rīm* "to arise" in relation to the arrogance of the proud King Nebuchadnezzar (Dnl. 5:20)[22] and as a synonym with the negated causative-stem of *špl* "to be lowly" for his son Belshazzar (5:22). Furthermore, the image of the exchange of a human for an animal heart appears three times in visions: King Nebuchadnezzar reduced to an animal state as penance will be given[23] an animal heart, that is, not only his lifestyle, but his entire thinking and feeling will be reduced to that of an animal (Dnl. 4:13).[24] Conversely, in the animal vision of the four empires, the first leonine creature, which symbolizes a still relatively humane dominion, receives in addition to an upright, and thus human stance, also a human heart (Dnl. 7:4).

At Qumran, too, *lbb* and *lb* appear alongside one another as in Daniel, but at the same time, with the spectrum of meaning known from older Aramaic. Here, too, reflection takes place in the heart,[25] and secrets are kept in it.[26] Similarly, the expression "the heart

---

16. l. 95, this, too, is proverbial; cf. Weigl, 199-203.

17. L. 99; apparently something quite similar in an Imperial Aramaic ostracon in H. Lozachmeur, *La collection Clermont-Ganneau*, vol. 1 (Paris, 2006), no. 255cv6.

18. L. 84; cf. Weigl, 111 n. 159.

19. See Weigl, 318f. on the problem and cf. the comment below on Dnl. 5:20.

20. → *nṭr*.

21. *TADAE* C1.1,82 (see above); perhaps also l. 93; → III.

22. See above on *TADAE* C1.1,137.

23. → *yhb*.

24. With → *šwī* "to be like" in contrast in 5:21.

25. 1QapGen 2:1, → *ḥšb*; cf. 4Q538 1-2:2.

26. 1QapGen 6:12.

changes" can denote a change of mood.[27] Further, the heart is the seat of conviction so that *bkl lb* "with the whole heart" refers to an upright disposition or behavior;[28] it probably has a similar connotation with the preposition *l*,[29] but the precise reading and interpretation of the pertinent passages are in dispute.[30] Similar expressions appear in the ethical admonitions of the last testaments: *l' blbb wlbb* "not with a divided heart"[31] or *blbb dk'* "with a pure heart."[32] In most of the passages from 11Q10, *lbb*/*lb* corresponds to the Hebrew *lb*: 18:2 (Job 31:9), 19:1 (Job 31:27), 27:7 (Job 36:13), and 36:9 (Job 41:16); in 3:3 (Job 20:2), on the other hand, it represents the difficult *hapax legomenon ś'py* "my thoughts."[33] Additional instances are fragmentary[34] or emended.

III. For the Insides. In contrast, *lbb* denotes the heart as an organ, or the "insides" in a general sense, only rarely. The first may indeed be the case in Tobit, because it contrasts the heart of a fish with the liver and the gall bladder,[35] and further in the phrase *št lbb* "heart fever" beside other terms for misbehavior and illnesses in an adjuration.[36] The sole possible older specimen for "insides" is a saying of Aḥiqar: *m'n ṭb ks*[*y*] *mlh blbbh* "a good (= sound) container[37] conceals what is inside it."[38] Indeed, this saying could involve a metaphor for the action of a silent person who handles a confidential word[39] with the necessary discretion, which other passages discuss by employing *lbb*.[40] In later Aramaic languages, other instances of "insides" or "stomach" appear occasionally.[41]

IV. Idiomatic Expressions. Finally, *lbb* is a component in idiomatic expressions. A few of them already surface in the Wisdom Sayings of Aḥiqar; because of a lack of pertinent parallels, their precise nuance requires deduction, however. As the object of → *yhb* "to give," it parallels the lifting[42] of the eyes and may denote confidence bestowed.[43] Contrariwise, *šbq ʿl lbb* seems to mean "to leave (someone) to his own will,"[44] which the fragmentary context describes as worse than corporal punishment. Achaemenid private

---

27. 1QapGen 2:2,11; with → *šnī* in the Dt-stem for a middle "to be different."
28. 4Q196 17 2:1 (Tob. 13:6) in parallel with *npš*, → *nšm*.
29. 4Q196 17 2:4 (Tob. 13:6b).
30. Cf. *ATTM*, 2, 184 with *DSSStE*, 386.
31. 4Q542 1 1:9.
32. 4Q542 1 1:10.
33. *GesB*[18], 1294.
34. 4Q541 6:5; 4Q543 18:2.
35. 4Q197 4 1:12 (Tob. 6:7); probably also in a fragmentary context in 4Q196 14 1:11 (Tob. 6:17).
36. 4Q560 1 1:4; so also presumably *lbb* in l. 1, but the context is corrupt.
37. → *m'n*.
38. *TADAE* C1.1,93; regarding the perfect in a gnomic statement, cf. H. Gzella, *Tempus, Aspekt und Modalität im Reichsaramäischen*. *VOK* 48 (2004), 275.
39. Also *mlh*.
40. *TADAE* C1.1,82.
41. Cf. *DJBA*, 616b, 624a; *LexSyr*, 354.
42. → *nṭl*.
43. *TADAE* C1.1,105.
44. *TADAE* C1.1,117.

letters offer additional combinations: as the subject of *dbq l-* "to cling to" for "to like,"[45] negated in reference to an article of clothing that the writer does not like, and *ʿlyk lbby šdyq* "for your sake my heart is torn"[46] with an unclear meaning, perhaps as an expression of solidarity in remembrance. Equally unclear is the connotation of *mnpq lbb* "to let one's heart go out" in a Clermont-Ganneau ostracon.[47] The word appears very frequently in Imperial Aramaic legal texts together with forms of the root → *ṭīb* "to be good"[48] as a standing formula for a satisfied legal claim, either as the subject of the G-stem "to be satisfied" or as the direct object of the causative-stem "to satisfy."[49]

Later, *lb* with prepositions is also used for "by heart" as in English.[50] Regarding *mn tḥt lbbk*[51] → *nṣl* II.

Gzella

45. *TADAE* A2.1,5.
46. *TADAE* A3.6,3.
47. Lozachmeur, no. 41cv4.
48. For instances, s.v. II.1. and II.2.
49. Cf. R. Westbrook, "The Phrase 'His Heart Is Satisfied' in the Ancient Near Eastern Legal Sources," *JAOS* 111 (1991) 219-24.
50. Jewish Babylonian *ʿl*: *DJBA*, 624b; Syriac *mn*: *LexSyr*, 354.
51. *TADAE* B3.3,13.

לבש *lbš*; לבוש *lbwš* /labūš/; לבש *lbš* /lebāš/

I. Lexical Field and Grammatical Constructions. II. G-Stem "to Put On." III. Causative-stem "to Clothe." IV. Nouns. 1. "Clothing." 2. "Robe."

I. Lexical Field and Grammatical Constructions. Aramaic *lbš* "to put something on, to wear" corresponds to a common Semitic verbal root employed in the G-stem simply as a transitive with the pertinent garment as a direct object; the causative-stem "to clothe" is regularly a double transitive with the person and the garment. The masculines /labūš/ "robe, clothes" and /lebāš/ "(a single) garment" belong to the same root. Later vocalizations such as the Syriac[1] prove /lebāš/ to be an independent lexeme. This lexeme, and not a defective variant of *lbwš*, e.g., may hide behind the *lbš* already evident in Old

C. Bender, *Die Sprache der Textilien. BWANT* 177 (2008); J. Gamberoni, "לָבֵשׁ *lāḇēš*," *TDOT*, IV, 471-83; M. Görg, "*lbš*," *ThWQ*, II, 480-82 (Heb.); H. Gzella, "Nudity and Clothing in the Lexicon of the Hebrew Bible," forthcoming in C. Berner et al., eds., *Handbook to Nudity and Clothing in the Hebrew Bible* (London, 2019); E. Jenni, "לבש *lbš* to clothe oneself," *TLOT*, 642-44.

1. *LexSyr*, 358a.

Aramaic. The Achaemenid period attests both substantives well; the Aramaic of Daniel and the texts from Qumran, however, attest only /labūš/.

II. G-Stem "to Put On." The verb first appears in the G-stem participle, namely in the expression *śqqn lbšn* "wearing mourning clothes" in the Imperial Aramaic petition of the Judean community at Elephantine.[2] It is not clear, however, whether *lbš* represents a defectively spelled passive participle /labīš/ "clothed" employed as a verbal adjective with the garment as the adverbial modifier[3] or the active participle /lābeš/ "wearing."[4] The first construction occurs unequivocally, however, in the cuneiform incantation text from Uruk.[5]

Finite forms appear in Dnl. 5:7,16 in King Belshazzar's promise that the one who could interpret to him the writing on the wall would *ʾrgwnʾ ylbš* "wear purple." In 11Q18 14 2:5 (new Jerusalem) and 4Q537 12:1 from Qumran, the verb appears in relation to priestly clothing. The two figurative expressions in 11Q10 14:9 and 34:6 (Job 29:14 and 40:10) correspond to the Hebrew text.

III. Causative-stem "to Clothe." The causative-stem usually denotes "to clothe someone with something." Yet, the (probably passive) participle *mlbš* appears in an Imperial Aramaic private letter from Hermopolis in the sense of "to wear."[6] In Dnl. 5:29, it appears, as would be expected, as the causative counterpart of the G-stem in 5:7,16 (→ II): Belshazzar fulfills his promise to clothe Daniel with purple.[7] 11Q10 29:7 (Job 37:16) reflects the Hebrew text once again.

IV. Nouns. Two different nouns for "garment" are available in *lbwš* /labūš/ and *lbš* /lebāš/. When a distinction is discernible, they are semantically differentiated. Sometimes, a genitive expression following *zy/dy* "of" can designate the material.

1. "Clothing." Regularly, /labūš/ functions as a collective term for "clothing," as already in Imperial Aramaic contracts.[8] The plural in Dnl. 3:21 at the end of a list of specific articles of clothing—robes and hats—of the condemned, meant to be thrown into the oven fully outfitted, could also represent clothing as such in summary fashion (the plural may then be employed distributively because the described applies to each of the condemned); it could also refer to the other individual garments.[9] Furthermore, in light

2. *TADAE* A4.7, 15 par. 4.8,14 and 4.7,20.
3. So *ATTM*, 616.
4. K. Beyer, "Der Wandel des Aramäischen veranschaulicht durch Transkriptionen alter aramäischer Texte," in *In the Shadow of Bezalel. FS B. Porten. CHANE* 60 (2013), 13-28, here the transcription on p. 18.
5. *ATTM*, 2, 26, ll. 20,24.
6. *TADAE* A2.1,6; see *DNSI*, 565.
7. *l-* here introduces the animate definite direct object, while the inanimate clothing is not separately marked as an object.
8. *TADAE* B2.8,4 and 3.13,11, in each beside other terms for grains and precious metals; the precise nuance in *TADAE* D11.19,1 is unclear.
9. Cf. K. Koch, *Daniel 1–4. BK* XXII/1 (2005), 253, for both opinions in the history of research.

of these usages, the singular *lbwš* in reference to the Ancient of Days in Dnl. 7:9 could also describe all of his snow-white clothing and not just the outer garment.

The texts from Qumran contain additional instances of the collective singular usage: in 1QapGen 20:31, in reference to pharaoh's gifts, *lbwš śgy dy bwṣ* "much clothing of linen" stands beside (silver and) gold; in the court narrative, *lbwš mlkwt'* denotes the "royal clothing."[10] In 11Q10 *lbwš* translates its Hebrew counterpart[11] or *bgd*.[12] Other instances are ambivalent because of a lacking[13] or at least emended context.[14]

2. "Robe." Meanwhile, /lebāš/, already attested earlier although it occurs only rarely in post-Imperial Aramaic, denotes a single garment. The lists of dowry items in marriage contracts where it often appears with a number sign or word demonstrate this.[15] In order to define it more precisely, the material can also be named following *zy* or a construct state.[16] The plural relates to several individual pieces.[17] Thus, private letters also employ *lbš*[18] already in Old Aramaic.[19]

Gzella

10. 4Q550 1:2.
11. 11Q10 16:8 (Job 30:18) and, somewhat emended, 30:7 (Job 38:9).
12. 11Q10 29:7 (Job 37:16).
13. 4Q531 12:2.
14. 4Q543 5-9:5, of the colorful garment of the evil angel in the Testament of Amram; 4Q544 1:13.
15. *TADAE* B2.6,7.10; 3.3,4; 3.8,6.8; D4.4,4; 4.22,3.
16. *TADAE* A2.4,8; B2.9,5.
17. *TADAE* B3.8,13; nV 1:24 in *ATTM*, 2, 205f.
18. *TADAE* A2.4,8; 3.3,9, with *ktwn* "undergarment"; D7.21,4.
19. *KAI* 226,7, for a burial garment; *TADAE* C1.1,107.

לחם *lḥm* /laḥm/

I. Etymology and Basic Meaning. II. Old and Imperial Aramaic. III. Biblical Aramaic. IV. Qumran.

W. Dommershausen, "לֶחֶם *leḥem*," *TDOT*, VII, 521-29; G. Krotkoff, "*Laḥm* 'Fleisch' und *leḥem* 'Brot,'" *WZKM* 62 (1969) 76-82; H. Lozachmeur, *La collection Clermont-Ganneau: Ostraca, épigraphes sur jarre, étiquettes de bois*, 2 vols. (Paris, 2006); S. Paganini, "*lḥm*," *ThWQ*, II, 510-14; J. Stetkevych, "Sacrifice and Redemption in Early Islamic Poetry: al-Ḥuṭay'ah's 'Wretched Hunter,'" *JAL* 31 (2000) 89-120, esp. 115f.; S. P. Stetkevych, "Pre-Islamic Panegyric and the Poetics of Redemption: Mufaddalīyah 199 of 'Alqamah," in idem, ed., *Reorientations: Arabic and Persian Poetry* (Bloomington, IN, 1994), 1-57, esp. 38; P. Swiggers, "The Meaning of the Root *lḥm* 'Food' in the Semitic Languages," *UF* 13 (1981) 307f.; E. Ullendorff, "The Contribution of South Semitic to Hebrew Lexicography," *VT* 6 (1956) 190-98, esp. 192.

I. Etymology and Basic Meaning. The common Semitic masculine noun *lḥm* designates an essential food[1] in each of the various individual languages: "meat" in Arabic, "cow" in classical Ethiopic, "bread" in Hebrew, "fish" in Modern South Arabian Soqotri. According to Swiggers, nomads eat primarily meat, sedentary populations bread, etc. Krotkoff has suggested that the basic meaning of the noun in Hebrew and Arabic may be "that which coheres,"[2] whereas S. Stetkevych traces the semantic distinction in these two languages to the cultural shift from agrarian (hence Hebrew "grain") to Bedouin (Arabic "meat"). Verbs of the root *lḥm* mean either "to fight"[3] or denominally "to eat, taste."

II. Old and Imperial Aramaic. Forms of the noun *lḥm* are frequent in all Aramaic languages and have the primary meaning "bread" or "loaf of bread" or the secondary "food." It already occurs in the Old Aramaic state treaties from Sefire[4] and the Tell Fekheriye inscription,[5] then in the Aḥiqar papyrus.[6] It further appears regularly in Imperial Aramaic private letters on ostraca where grain and bread belong to the most often mentioned goods of daily life.[7]

III. Biblical Aramaic. In Biblical Aramaic, *l^eḥæm* occurs only in Dnl. 5:1: *bēlšaṣṣar malkā ʿ^a*b*ad l^eḥæm ra*b* l^era*b*r^e*b*ānōhī ʾ^alap̄* "Belshazzar prepared a grand meal for his thousand nobles." The context makes it clear that a feast is involved. This meaning does not occur otherwise in Aramaic.

IV. Qumran. Finally, *lḥm* "bread, food" appears about fifteen times in various Aramaic texts from Qumran: 1Q68 3:1, 2Q24 4:5,8f.,14f. and 11Q18 8:3 (both new Jerusalem, in the description of the priestly ritual involving the showbread), 4Q530 1 1:6 (Book of Giants), 4Q541 12:4 (Levi Apocryphon), 4Q563 and 11Q10 6:7 (Job 22:7), 15:9 (Job 30:4), and 38:6 (Job 42:11). Many instances are, however, fragmentary.

Fassberg

1. Ullendorff.
2. From a root *lḥm* "to link, unite."
3. From "to band together"; Aramaic, however, used the verb → *qrb*, originally "to draw near."
4. *KAI* 222 A 24; B 38f.; 224, 5.7.
5. *KAI* 309,17f.22, as sacrificial material and as "bread" in the comparison of a curse formula.
6. Both the narrative framework and the sayings: *TADAE* C1.1,33.124.181.
7. Cf. *TADAE* D1.11,2; 7.1,13; 7.8,13; 7.10,3; 7.19,5; 7.44,5.8; in the Clermont-Ganneau ostraca *nwn* "fish," *qṭy* "cucumber," and *gbn* "cheese" also appear as widespread foods; cf. H. Gzella, review of Lozachmeur, *BiOr* 70 (2013) 467.

לחן *lḥn* /laḥen/; לחנה *lḥnh* /laḥenā/

I. Etymology and Usage. II. Masculine "Temple Worker." III. Feminine "Court Lady."

I. Etymology and Usage. Like many other terms from the cultic realm, the noun /laḥen/ "temple worker" is also an Akkadian loanword in Aramaic and appears first in post-Imperial administrative texts; its original form was *laḫḫinu*.[1] The feminine counterpart *laḫḫinatu*, Aramaic /laḥenā/, however, denotes a lady at court.[2] Other, often very speculative etymologies[3] have not been able to gain acceptance and may be considered refuted.

II. Masculine "Temple Worker." Almost all the older Aramaic specimens of the masculine *lḥn* /laḥen/ "temple worker" appear in an archive with contract texts from Elephantine[4] as the professional designation of a certain *ʿnnyh br ʿzryh*, as evidenced by the theophoric element *-yh* a Judean, in order to clearly identify him as a party to the contract. The same applies to the usage with other names in a share certificate[5] and on a grave marker from Saqqara.[6] The meaning here may conform entirely to that of the Akkadian word since the addition *lḥn zy yhh ʾlhʾ* "temple worker of the God Yahu" in the legal texts of *ʿnnyh*[7] points to a cultic context. Yet, because there is no indication of the precise function of a *lḥn*,[8] it cannot be demonstrated with certainty. In any case, Aramaic used → *khn* for "priest."

The feminine form *lḥnh*, however, seems to denote in this same (partial) corpus the wife of the *lḥn* mentioned in the same contract in contrast to the Akkadian and the Aramaic Daniel in the one preserved instance (→ III).[9]

III. Feminine "Court Lady." The feminine form *lḥnh* /laḥenā/ likewise traces to an Akkadian lexeme and is, thus, not formed secondarily from the Aramaic masculine. The first certain occurrence in a contract text from Elephantine,[10] however, may not have the original Akkadian and later Aramaic meaning "court lady," since there was no court

---

S. A. Kaufman, *The Akkadian Influences on Aramaic. AS* 19 (1974); B. Porten, *Archives from Elephantine* (Berkeley, 1968).

1. Kaufman, 66.
2. B. Landsberger, "Akkadisch-hebräische Wortgleichungen," in *Hebräische: Wortforschung. FS W. Baumgartner. SVT* 16 (1967), 198-204.
3. Cf. the overview in *DNSI*, 573.
4. *TADAE* B3.2,2; 3.3,2; 3.4,3.25; 3.5,2.23; 3.7,2; 3.10, 2.23.27; 3.11,1.9.17; 3.12,1.10.33.
5. *TADAE* C3.13,45. 48, an *ʿzryh* and perhaps the father of *ʿnnyh*.
6. *TADAE* D21.2,1, probably not for a Judean.
7. E.g., *TADAE* B3.3,2; 3.5,2; sometimes with *l-* instead of *zy*.
8. Probably that of an administrator, see Porten, 200f.
9. *TADAE* B3.12,2.
10. *TADAE* B3.12,2.

in Elephantine. As an exception, this instance may refer to the wife of the *lḥn* "temple worker";[11] one can think of the "Madame Professor" or "Madame Director" of earlier times and perhaps of the *nby'h* "prophetess" in Isa. 8:3.[12] In any case, this *lḥnh* also bore the title *zy yhw 'lh'* "of the God Yahu."

In contrast, the *lḥnth* at Belshazzar's dinner in Dnl. 5:2f.,23[13] seems to be "court ladies" or even "(female) administrators of the court," who, with the *rbrbn* "nobles" and *šgln* "consorts" previously mentioned in the same context, drank from the golden temple vessels. The later meaning "concubine, secondary wife" in the Targum Onqelos as a rendering of the Hebrew *plgš* (e.g., Gen 22:24; 25:6; etc.) is due, in all likelihood, to the parallel of *lḥnh* with *šgl* in Dnl. 5 and has no point of contact with the original, but already forgotten at the time, meaning in Aramaic and Akkadian.[14] Then, however, the conjectural emendation of the unknown word *dḥwn* in Dnl. 6:19 for something that the fasting king had brought to him for the night, customarily translated "tray with food",[15] to *lḥnn* "companion for the night"[16] is highly dubious.

There is probably no relationship between *lḥnh* and the *lḥnt* in a proverb of Aḥiqar[17] where it accompanies *'lym* "servant, slave." Instead, it may involve the preposition *l-* and a non-Semitic word *ḥnt* "maid, slave."[18]

Gzella

---

11. → II and *DNSI*, 573, with additional bibliography.
12. Bibliography in *GesB*[18], 774.
13. In each case in the suffixed plural and in a formulaic expression.
14. Landsberger, 204; likewise Kaufman, 66 n. 176.
15. Cf., e.g., *LexLingAram*, 37; *ATTM*, 548.
16. E.g., the apparatus of *BHS*, additional information in *GesB*[18], 1482.
17. *TADAE* C1.1,178.
18. See I. Kottsieper, *Die Sprache der Aḥiqarsprüche*. *BZAW* 194 (1990), 244f., who assumes an Egyptian loanword; additional bibliographical references in *DNSI*, 390.

לילה *lylh* /laylǣ/

I. Form and Pronunciation. II. Inflection, Occurrences, Gender. III. Usages.

R. P. Bonfiglio, "*lylh*," *ThWQ*, II, 514-20; H. Drawnel, *The Aramaic Astronomical Book (4Q208-4Q211) from Qumran* (Oxford, 2011); M. Sokoloff, *A Dictionary of Judean Aramaic* (Ramat Gan, 2003); A. Stiglmair, "לַיִל/לַיְלָה *layil/laylâ*," *TDOT*, VII, 533-42; K. L. Tallqvist, *Assyrian Personal Names* (Helsingfors, 1914); Y. Yadin et al., eds., *The Documents from the Bar Kokhba Period in the Cave of Letters II: Hebrew, Aramaic and Nabatean-Aramaic Papyri* (Jerusalem, 2002).

I. Form and Pronunciation. The Aramaic /laylǣ/ "night,"[1] later /lēlǣ/, is a quadriliteral primary noun of the noun form *qatlī*, whose /-ay-/ in the open first syllable was already monophthongized to /-ē-/ around 100 B.C.E., at least in Judean, Samarian, and Palmyrene Aramaic[2] and whose fourth radical /-ī/ beginning with instances before endings, entirely disappeared in Hebrew producing the common three radicals. The ending /-ay/ in at least Syriac *laylay* "at night" and elsewhere is secondary.[3]

II. Inflection, Occurrences, Gender. The absolute and construct states of the singular are spelled *lylh* (from the eighth century B.C.E.) and *lylʾ* (from the second century B.C.E.) for /laylǣ/ > /lēlǣ/; the determined state mostly *lylyʾ*, rarely *lylyh*, for /layliyā/ > /lēliyā/. The absolute state of the plural appears as *lylwn* /laylawān/ > /laylāwān/ > /lēlāwān/ (Babylonian-Targumic, East Syriac) and *lylwwn* (Galilean-Targumic).

Attested are (readings according to *ATTM*): absolute of the singular *lylh*: Sefire (eighth century B.C.E.);[4] Aḥiqar;[5] Enoch 4Q208;[6] *lylʾ*: 11Q10 22:9 (Job 33:15);[7] construct state of the singular *lylh*: 1QapGen 19:14[8] "on the night of my entry into Egypt"; *lylʾ*: new/heavenly Jerusalem 11Q18[9] "in the night of [. . .]"; Enoch 4Q208f.[10] and Yadin 7,[11] 6.12.47 "in the fifth night," etc.; determined state of the singular *lylyʾ*: Dnl. 2:19; 5:30; 7:2,7,13; 1QapGen 10:2,3; 19:17,21; 20:11,12,15,16; 21:8; 22:8f., etc.; *lylyh*: Enoch 4Q208f. (1 En.) is rare. The gender is masculine as in Hebrew.

III. Usages. Along with *nešep̄* "the cool of dawn and dusk" attested in Babylonian-Talmudic, *lylh* means "the dark of night." In Roman reckoning it divides into three and later four night watches and twelve hours. The astronomical book of Enoch 4Q208f. (1 En. 73) describes the lunar phases throughout all the days and nights of a month wherein the brilliance of the front of the moon at night corresponds to the darkness of the back in the day. As 1 En. 82:26[12] and Tob. 6:13(×2),16, where "in this night" means "in the coming night," demonstrate, the night normally belongs to the preceding day as in Egypt and already in Gen 1.[13] Accordingly, in the deed of gift Yadin 7,[14] ll. 12,47

1. The vocalic letter *h* denotes, as usual, an accented final /-ǣ/ from /-ī/; according to *APN* 119b.292b spelled in cuneiform circa 675 B.C.E. *la-a-a-li-e*.

2. *ATTM*, 116-20.

3. *ATTM*, 151.618; cf. H. Gzella, review of E. Gaß, *Die Moabiter: Geschichte und Kultur eines ostjordanischen Volkes im 1. Jahrtausend v.Chr. BiOr* 68 (2011) 164 (top).

4. *KAI* 222 A 12.

5. *TADAE* C1.1[,80]?

6. *ATTM*, 251-53; 2, 427: H 73 instead of the determined state before *dn* "these."

7. *ATTM*, 291.

8. *DSSStE*, 38f.

9. *ATTM*, 2, 129,134: J 7,9.

10. *DSSStE*, 430-39: 4Q208,4Q209 1-2.

11. Yadin, 73-108; *ATTM*, 2, 217-223: nV 7; 120 C.E.

12. *ATTM*, 258.

13. → *ywm*; the reverse is true, however, in the cultic order.

14. Yadin, 73-108; nV 7.

"the fourth night in the week" (= Wednesday/Thursday) follows[15] "the fourth day of the week" (= Wednesday).

Most frequently, the night appears as the time of a dream ("night vision"):[16] Dnl. 2:19; 7:2,7,13; 1QapGen 19:14,17,21; 21:8; Book of Giants 4Q530,[17] ll. 6,16; 11Q10 22:9 (Job 33:15); then of assault and killing: Dnl. 5:30; 1QapGen 20:16; 22:8f.; otherwise of coitus: 1QapGen 20:15; of birth: of Noah 4Q535,[18] 2; of sleep: ibid. 4; of crying: 1QapGen 20:11,12; of prayer: 1QapGen 20:12; of counsel: Tob. 6:13. In Sefire (eighth century B.C.E.),[19] day and night (in this sequence!) alongside all the gods, heaven, earth, sea, and wellsprings belong to the guarantors of a treaty of state.

Beyer

15. Contra Sokoloff, 60b.
16. → *ḥlm*.
17. *DSSStE*, 1062-65.
18. *DSSStE*, 1072f.
19. *KAI* 222 A 12.

לשן *lšn* /leššān/

I. Form and Etymology. II. Old and Imperial Aramaic. III. Biblical Aramaic. IV. Qumran.

I. Form and Etymology. The Aramaic noun /leššān/ "tongue" has cognates both in East (Eblaite and Akkadian) and in Old and modern West Semitic. Egyptian *nś*, Coptic *las*, and Berber *ils*, all with the same meaning "tongue," suggest a common biradical Afro-Asian root **ls*. In Semitic, the /-n/ belongs to an early derivation with the affix */-ān/, which is also preserved in other words such as Aramaic /šolṭān/ "dominion" or /benyān/ "building." Aramaic also preserves the original masculine gender. In contrast, various other languages, especially Hebrew *lāšōn* and Arabic *lisān* construe the word as a feminine when it refers to the tongue as part of the body. The Aramaic form with the otherwise sporadic lengthening of /š/ to /šš/ is secondary based on the evidence of comparative linguistics,[1] but already unequivocally attested in the cuneiform incantation text from Uruk.[2]

In many languages, the word for "tongue" can also mean "language." The same is true for words like "mouth" and "lips," as in Hebrew. Furthermore, in Biblical Aramaic,

R. P. Bonfiglio, "*lšn*," *ThWQ*, II, 539-45; H. Gzella, *A Cultural History of Aramaic*. *HO* 111 (2015); B. Kedar-Kopfstein, "לָשׁוֹן *lāšôn*," *TDOT*, VIII, 23-33.

1. Cf. C. Brockelmann, *Syrische Grammatik* (Leipzig, [10]1965), 41 n. 1.
2. On the forms see *ATTM*, 619.

/leššān/ can denote a (language) group (→ III). In many languages, the names of peoples depend on the name of the respective language, and vice versa. Finally, the flexibility, form, and color of the tongue underlie the figurative expression "tongues of fire" in various languages.

II. Old and Imperial Aramaic. Authentic Old Aramaic attests *lšn* only twice, both in figurative usages. A treaty text from Sefire prescribes in the event of a dispute over succession to the throne: *ltšlḥ lšn* "you should not send your tongue," i.e., "you should not become involved."[3] This expression corresponds to the Akkadian *lišāna wu''uru* "to send a tongue" in precisely the same sense. The figurative use of "tongue" for slander or discord also appears in Sam'alian:[4] *ḥrb wlšn* "sword and tongue" (i.e., slander),"[5] perhaps also in the Deir ʿAllā inscription,[6] although the literal meaning cannot be ruled out here.[7] For a similar usage in Hebrew, see Ps. 15:3; 50:19; 140:12 and in Ugaritic KTU 1.5 II 3, where *lšn* (parallel with *špt* "lips") could refer to Mot's boastful speech against the stars.

The Aramaic of the proverbs of Aḥiqar on a papyrus from the Achaemenid period knows examples of the literal and possibly also the figurative meanings. The first occurs in *TADAE* C1.1,156 *wynsḥ lšn* "and (El) will rip out the tongue of. . . ." Because of the uncertain context, *rkyk lšn* in *TADAE* C1.1,89 is ambivalent; it can mean "soft is the speech of . . ." or " soft is the tongue of. . . ." The reconstruction as *rkyk lšn m*[*lk* depends on *rkyk mmll mlk* "soft is the speech of the king" in *TADAE* C1.1,84 and, therefore, presupposes the figurative use.

The five instances from the cuneiform Uruk incantation text[8] refer to the tongue as a body part in the context of an exorcism.

III. Biblical Aramaic. All seven instances of the Biblical Aramaic *liššān* appear in the book of Daniel. They all refer to a group of people. In Dnl. 3:29 the singular appears in relation to *ʿam ʾummā wᵉliššān* "nation, tribe, or language," everywhere else, in contrast the plural, although in the very analogous expression *ʿamᵉmayyā ʾumayyā wᵉliššānayyā* "nations, tribes, or tongues" (3:4,7,31; 5:19; 6:26; 7:14). A few nations in the Persian Empire were designated by the ethnic term *ʿam*,[9] others with the tribal *ʾummā*, and the rest based on a technical administrative classification by language. This terminology reflects the official recognition of different languages under Achaemenid dominion, as also demonstrated in the three versions of the royal inscription from Behistun and their Aramaic translation from the west of the empire.[10]

---

3. *KAI* 224,17f., also in l. 21.

4. On its relationship to Old Aramaic, see P. M. Noorlander, "Sam'alian in Its Northwest Semitic Setting," *Or* 81 (2012) 202-38; Gzella, 72-77.

5. *KAI* 214,9.

6. II,17; on the classification, cf. Gzella, 87-91.

7. Cf. *DNSI*, 584.

8. *ATTM*, 2, 26f., l. 3.5.8.21.25; perhaps from the third century B.C.E., although an early representative of the East Aramaic and not the Imperial Persian tradition; see Gzella, 269f., which also treats the problem of dating.

9. → *ʿm*.

10. See the extensive treatment by Gzella, 178-85.

In Dnl. 3:4,7 the expression occurs in an edict to all the subjects of the king with the object of obligating them,[11] under threat of severe penalties, to venerate a statue of a god erected by Nebuchadnezzar. Daniel 3:29 represents a similar context in which the same formulation in the singular (see above) is part of the royal prohibition against blaspheming the God of Shadrach, Meshach, and Abednego; Daniel cites this prohibition to Belshazzar in 5:19 and it has another echo in the edict of King Darius in Dnl. 6:26. The same expression occurs further in Dnl. 3:31 in a letter to all the subjects of the king concerning his mental illness. Finally, Dnl. 7:14 employs the word in Daniel's vision of the heavenly court where the one "like a son of man"[12] approaches the "Ancient of Days" on the clouds of heaven in order to obtain the dominion, glory, and power so that all nations, tribes, and languages serve him. Both Theodotion and the unrevised old translation (Old Greek) employ γλῶσσα here.

IV. Qumran. The word *lšn* occurs twelve times in the Aramaic texts from Qumran. All seven of the certain occurrences in 1QapGen mean "gulf," a figurative usage not previously exhibited in Aramaic: 17:11 *lšn' dn* "(in the north of the enclosure) of this gulf (located at the point of the three sections in the south)," and similarly in 16:9; 17:13,17(×2),18; 21:18. This figuratively topographical usage is also known from Hebrew, e.g., Isa. 11:15 ("The Lord will dry up the tongue of the sea of Egypt"). The word appears twice in 11Q10, once in the literal meaning: *bḥbl tḥrz lšnh* "Can you drag his (i.e., Leviathan's) tongue on a cord?" (35:4 [Job 40:25]); once in the figurative: *blšny 'šh* "with tongues of fire" (36:5 [Job 41:11]), perhaps a convenient rendering of the incomprehensible Hebrew *hapax legomenon kīḏōḏē 'ēš*, traditionally translated "sparks of fire."[13] The expression *lšnyn dy nwr* "tongues of fire" also appears in the dream of the giants in the Book of Giants 4Q530 2 2+6-12:9; the same formulation should presumably be emended in 4Q204 1 6:22 (1 En. 14:9) and 4Q206 1 21:3.

Gianto

11. → *dhb* III.
12. → *'nš*.
13. Cf. *GesB*[18], 541.

מאן *m'n* /ma'ān/

I. Etymology and Form. II. Old and Imperial Aramaic: "Vessels." III. Biblical Aramaic: "Cultic Vessels." IV. Qumran: "Heavenly Body."

J. L. Kelso, *The Ceramic Vocabulary of the Old Testament. BASORSup* 5/6 (1948).

I. Etymology and Form. Although the etymology of the Aramaic masculine noun /ma'ān/ "vessel, object" is unknown, a connection with Akkadian *unūtu* or *enūtu* "apparatus"[1] and with Arabic *'inā* "vessel" seems likely; then, the /m-/ would be a prefix in Aramaic.[2] The pattern is also unclear, but one can best think of a *maqāl*-form[3] because a nominal form */ma'n/[4] would contradict the Aramaic laws of phonetics.[5]

The oldest Aramaic texts already attested the word and, as a comprehensive term corresponding to Hebrew *k^e lī*,[6] it first designates a "vessel" of any type, of whatever size, composition, and value, either as a useful object in daily life or in an explicitly cultic context. Specific terms denote particular kinds, terms such as /boqq/, /gerāb/ or /kadd/ "jug," /dūd/ and /qedr/ "pot," /'aggān/ "cup," /komār/ "cooking vessel,"[7] and still more.[8]

Later, /ma'ān/ is also used with the quite general meaning "object," frequently for clothing for which older Aramaic had /labūš/,[9] and for tools or other equipment.[10] The material or purpose can be added to the construct state or following *zy*/*dy*. The second, broader sense apparently also underlies the specific astronomical "heavenly body" in the book of Enoch from Qumran (→ IV).

II. Old and Imperial Aramaic: "Vessels." The earliest specimen of *m'n* already appears in the oldest Aramaic literary evidence, the inscription from Tell Fekheriye.[11] As later in Dnl. 5:2f. (→ III) it denotes cultic vessels, as the addition *zy bt hdd mr'y* "(vessels) of the temple of my lord Hadad" clearly emphasizes. The reader of the inscription is warned against removing the name of the donor from it. In a somewhat later Old Aramaic grave inscription from Nērab, it also refers to a particularly valuable vessel and grave goods[12] in silver or copper.[13] The statement that there are no valuable objects whatsoever with the corpse intends to keep away robbers and recurs in similar form in Phoenician[14] and Hebrew[15] grave inscriptions. In contrast, *m'n* appears in a proverb of Aḥiqar in reference to a common utensil and emphasizes the function, not the material

---

1. *AHw*, III, 1422f.

2. *ATTM*, 620 hesitantly suggests a reconstructed root *'*ūn* "to be strong, powerful"; *LexSyr*, 373a and *LexLingAram*, 96 in contrast *'*nī*.

3. *ATTM*, 620.

4. *BLA*, §51r'''; *LexLingAram*, 96.

5. At the end of a syllable, /a'/ naturally becomes /ē/, *ATTM*, 138. On the pointing *mān* in Daniel and Ezr. → III.

6. See K.-M. Beyse, "כְּלִי *k^e lî*," *TDOT*, VII, 169-75; cf. Kelso, 22, §49.

7. 1QapGen 12:15.

8. In the Clermont-Ganneau ostraca from Elephantine now perhaps also *krz* and *qlyt*, cf. H. Gzella, review of Lozachmeur, *BiOr* 70 (2013), 471 (regarding nos. 58 and 97).

9. → *lbš* IV.1.

10. See *DJPA*, 288b for Jewish Palestinian, *DJBA*, 637f. for Jewish Babylonian, and *LexSyr*, 373a for Syriac.

11. *KAI* 309,16f., corresponding to *unūtu* in l. 27 of the Akkadian version.

12. *KAI* 226.6.

13. *KAI* 226.7.

14. *KAI* 13.4.

15. *KAI* 191.1.

or sacral value: *m'n ṭb ks[y] mlh blbbh* "a good (=sound) vessel conceals what is in it," while a broken one allows the contents to leak.[16] This proverb may involve a figurative comparison with a silent person.[17]

The Imperial Aramaic instances stem for the most part from private contracts. "Vessels" or "implement"—apparently the difference in these cases was no longer legally relevant—appear there often in property lists, regularly including specification of the material (copper or iron or various types of wood): possessions[18] left as collateral,[19] and the dowry of a woman.[20] Along with clothing, such household objects constitute the contents of a household and thus the private property, sometimes supplemented with crops, slaves, and the house proper. Egyptian wine was also transported in *m'nn* "vessels."[21] Other instances in a letter and in lists and ostraca appear with insufficient contexts.[22]

This usage continues in the post-Achaemenid Imperial Aramaic legal tradition. A Nabatean contract from the Dead Sea still mentions *lbšyn wm'ny nḥšt* "articles of clothing[23] and vessels of bronze"[24] as collateral for a dowry, a Nabatean certificate of donation mentions *wm'ny by* "furnishings,"[25] and an ostracon with an Aramaic marriage contract from Edom (second century B.C.E.) mentions in the inventory of the dowry *lbwš wmn'y*[(scribal error for *m'ny*[) "clothing"[26] and household objects."[27]

III. Biblical Aramic "Cultic Vessels." All Biblical Aramaic occurrences of the word from Ezra and Daniel are plural and refer to temple vessels, not to everyday utensils. The addition "of gold and silver" (*zy zhb' wksp'* or in a construct relationship, → *dhb*) specifically emphasizes the extraordinary value. Here, the consonantal text *m'n* is vocalized *mān*; presumably, with the loss of the short, unaccented /a/ in an open syllable,[28] which the pointing presupposes, the glottal stop was also elided, because /'/ in a doubled consonant beginning a syllable cannot be pronounced without a vowel and nothing in this case calls for conformity.

In the account of Belshazzar's banquet in the book of Daniel (5:2f.), *m'n* appears twice. In his sacrilegious arrogance, the drunk king desecrates the sacred implements brought to Babylon by his father Nebuchadnezzar after the conquest of Jerusalem when

16. *TADAE* C1.1,93.
17. → *lbb* III, with additional bibliography.
18. → *nksyn.*
19. *TADAE* B2.9,5; similarly in an extensive list of pawnable goods B3.13, 11 and a court record B8.6,6; → *mḥī* III.
20. *TADAE* B3.8,13, emended in l. 15; here as the summary of a list of various vessels and a mirror, all with their corresponding value.
21. *TADAE* C3.12,9.
22. *TADAE* A3.9,5; C3.8 II 6; 3.13,10; D2.18,3; 7.24,7.
23. → *lbš* IV.2.
24. nV 1:24 in *ATTM*, 2, 205f.
25. nV 7:4,16 in *ATTM*, 2, 218f.
26. → *lbš* IV.1.
27. E. Eshel and A. Kloner, "An Aramaic Ostracon of an Edomite Marriage Contract from Maresha, Dated 176 B.C.E.," *IEJ* 46 (1996) 1-22, esp. 16.
28. *ATTM*, 128-36.

he and his court drink wine[29] from them and thereby pay homage to the idol images (Dnl. 5:4).

Four additional instances occur in Ezra. According to Ezr. 5:14f., King Cyrus directed that the "golden and silver vessels of the house of God" once stolen by Nebuchadnezzar be returned and then that the temple be rebuilt on its old site. The fact that the transfer of the cultic implements receives first mention and precedes the actual temple construction underscores their extreme significance. At the same time, their return serves as a sign of the continuity between the First and Second Temples.[30] The appended "memorandum," which officially decrees[31] the reconstruction of the temple, repeats the edict (Ezr. 6:5). Finally, Artaxerxes's letter to Ezra communicates the commission to transfer these vessels entrusted to him to God in Jerusalem (Ezr. 7:19).

IV. Qumran: "Heavenly Body." Of the few instances of *m'n* from Qumran, only fragment 4Q209 23:7 of the astronomical book of Enoch (1 En. 77:3) is noteworthy because it employs the word in the phrase *m'ny šmy'* for "heavenly body."[32] This elsewhere unknown semantic development presupposes the usage, unequivocally attested only later, of *m'n* for "object" quite generally and without direct reference to the household.[33] The same word appears further in 4Q558 58:2, but this small fragment preserves no context so that the meaning there remains unclear.

Gzella

29. → *ḥmr.*

30. So correctly, H. G. M. Williamson, *Ezra, Nehemiah. WBC* (1985), 16f.,79.

31. → *dkr* III.

32. According to *ATTM*, 248 *m'ny* is also to be supplied in 1 En. 91:16 in the lacuna before *šmy'*.

33. H. Drawnel, *The Aramaic Astronomical Book (4Q208-4Q211) from Qumran* (Oxford, 2011), 363, is apparently unfamiliar with this meaning and thinks that the heavenly bodies were described as "vessels" because they contained light; this is hardly correct.

מגר *mgr*

I. Etymology and Lexical Field. II. Usage.

I. Etymology and Lexical Field. The very rare verb *mgr* occurs in the older Aramaic languages of the Imperial Aramaic tradition in the transitive D-stem "to cast down,

F. L. Benz, *Personal Names in the Phoenician and Punic Inscriptions. StPohl 8* (1972); M. Wagner, *Die lexikalischen und grammatikalischen Aramaismen im alttestamentlichen Hebräisch. BZAW* 96 (1966), esp. 71.

overturn, demolish" and takes the affected item as direct object. Syriac, in contrast, attests the G-stem with the meaning "to fall,"[1] which may be primary in relation to the transitive D-stem.[2] The only certain specimen in Biblical Hebrew in Ps. 89:45, also a D-stem "to topple, cast down," may be borrowed from the Aramaic.[3] If, however, the Punic personal name *mgrb'l* also contains this root, which is by no means certain,[4] it may involve a common Northwest Semitic verb and the Hebrew instance, consequently, can be reckoned with equal right as a poetic or dialectal archaism.

With the meaning "to tear down," *mgr* in the D-stem belongs to the verbs of destruction.[5] Of the three preserved passages in older Aramaic, it refers twice to (sacred) buildings. In contrast, *gdd* "to cut down" is used of trees (Dnl. 4:11,20), while terms such as → *ḥbl* "to annihilate" or → *ḥrb* "to desolate" stand for a general destruction and others such as → *dqq* "to crush," → *tbr* "to shatter," or *r*'' "to smash" (Dnl. 2:40) for a quite specific form of destruction.

II. Usage. The petition of the Judean community from Elephantine to the Achaemenid administration concerning the reconstruction of the local temple first attests *mgr*: Cambyses is supposed to have destroyed the sanctuaries of the Egyptian gods when he conquered Egypt, but not the temple of God,[6] so that its destruction by the Egyptian priests was without precedent. The "memorandum" concerning the reconstruction of the Jerusalem temple in Ezra[7] employs the verb in the concluding curse: God will tear down (*mgr*) any king and people who should destroy (*ḥbl*) this sanctuary in the future (Ezr. 6:12). A verb otherwise employed in relation to structural engineering here in reference to persons may indicate the *contrapasso* through which the penalty is accommodated to the sin, but *mgr* also appears with a royal throne in Ps. 89:45. Similarly, 4Q196 18:1 (Tob. 13:12) employs it in the curse on all who destroy the holy city (cf. Bar. 4:31).

Gzella

1. *LexSyr*, 374a.
2. So *ATTM*, 620.
3. Wagner, 71; a possible G-stem in Ezk. 21:17 is text-critically controversial; cf. *GesB*[18], 629.
4. See Benz, 339f., with additional bibliography.
5. → *ḥbl*.
6. *TADAE* A4.7,14.
7. → *dkr* III.

מדי *mdy* /māday/; מדי *mdy* /mādāy/; פרס *prs* /pārs/; פרסי *prsy* /pārsāy/

I. Etymology and Meaning. II. Media. III. Persia. IV. In the Wordplay of "Menetekel."

I. Etymology and Meaning. As a consequence of the complicated acculturation process in the Iranian highlands between the Neo-Assyrian epoch and the formation of the Achaemenid Empires, the original meaning of the toponym /māday/ "Media" and of the related ethnic designation /mādāy/ "Median, Mede" remains largely unclear. Presumably, the Medes were one of the various Iranian tribes with an unknown social organization, who were originally at home in the Zagros mountains in northwest Iran and, in the course of an ethnogenesis between the eighth and sixth centuries B.C.E., merged with the non-Indo-Iranian Elamites into a new population.[1] Thereby, Media was incorporated into the empire,[2] although the precise administrative arrangement in the Achaemenid period is not clear.

In similar fashion, already during the same period, certain groups also formed in *Pārsa*, Aramaic /pārs/, the heart of the later Achaemenid Empire and the modern province of Fārs in south-central Iran, called "Persians,"[3] although it is not possible to speak confidently about their ethnic relationships.[4] In the book of Daniel, both terms are often employed as a doubled name "Medes and Persians." The "menetekel" of Dnl. 5 also alludes with the use of the Semitic root *prs* "to divide" to the Iranian name /pārs/.

II. Media. Aramaic first attests the geographical name *mdy* /māday/ "Media" in the Behistun inscription. It employs the name for the pertinent region in relation to Darius's military campaigns.[5] It appears then in Ezr. 6:2 as a Persian province (*mdynh*),[6] the location of the city Ekbatana. Daniel regularly employs the dual term *mdy wprs*, once for the empire that Babylon conquered (Dnl. 5:28; → III), and again, ethno-culturally for the "law of the Medes and Persians [literally: Media and Persia]" in the sense of an unalterable law sanctified by the tradition (Dnl. 6:9,13,16).[7] The terminological distinction between the two names was, thus, unclear in extra-Achaemenid sources.[8] For disputed reasons, the designation "Medes" for the Persians also appears often in classical Greek literature,[9] probably as a vague reminiscence.

P. Briant, *From Cyrus to Alexander: A History of the Persian Empire* (Winona Lake, IN, 2002); W. F. M. Henkelman, "The Achaemenid Heartland," in D. T. Potts, ed., *A Companion to the Archaeology of the Ancient Near East* (Oxford, 2012), 931-62; idem, "Persians, Medes and Elamites: Acculturation in the Neo-Elamite Period," in G. B. Lanfranchi et al., eds., *Continuity of Empire(?): Assyria, Media, Persia. HANE/M* 5 (2003), 181-231; C. Tuplin, "Persians as Medes," in H. Sancisi-Weerdenburg et al., eds., *Continuity and Change. AH* 8 (1994), 235-56.

1. See Henkelman, "Persians," esp. 88f.
2. Cf. Briant, 757-61.
3. In Aramaic, then designated by the gentilic adjective /pārsāy/ "Persian."
4. Regarding the geography and archeology, see the extensive treatment by Henkelman, "Heartland."
5. *TADAE* C2.1 Col I 4.7; 25.39f.
6. → *dyn* II.
7. → *dt*.
8. In *TADAE* C2. 1,40 *prs wmd[y* refers to two different troop contingents that stand in a syndetic relationship here only accidentally.
9. See Tuplin.

The five specimens from Qumran are all employed in the geographical sense: as a son of Japheth and mythical eponym of the region in the context of the post-flood division of the land;[10] as a region, the location of the city Ekbatana, the destination of the journey of Tobias, and home of his future wife;[11] and in an addition to the translation of Isa. 14:31f.[12]

The adjective *mdy* /mādāy/, which is identical in consonantal spelling, occurs in Imperial Aramaic in a private contract from Elephantine as the designation of the origin of one of the witnesses,[13] in Biblical Aramaic as an epithet of the Persian King Darius (Dnl. 6:1),[14] and at Qumran only in a fragment with no context.[15]

III. Persia. The term *prs* /pārs/ "Persia" was also employed geographically and ethnically. It is attested in Aramaic beginning with Achaemenid Imperial Aramaic. Official documents like the Behistun inscription employ it for the region of Persis[16] or the imperial administration.[17] It consistently occurs in Daniel as *pāras* together with *mdy* (Dnl. 5:28; 6:9, 13,16; → II), in Ezra in both passages for Persian kings (Ezr. 4:24; 6:14).[18] The vision of the four trees at Qumran utilizes it in an allegory for the Persian Empire,[19] the addition to the Aramaic version of Isa. 14:31f., apparently in a geographic description for the region (→ II).[20]

The adjective *prsy* /pārsāy/ "Persian" also occurs in isolation: often in the Behistun inscription,[21] once in Daniel (Dnl. 6:29, in reference to the king) for persons, and probably also once for *ṣl prsyn* "Persian leather (sandals)."[22]

IV. In the Wordplay of "Menetekel." In Dnl. 5:25,28, the verb *prs* "to divide" alludes to *prs* /pārs/ "Persia," into which the doomed Babylon was to be incorporated.[23]

Gzella

10. 1QapGen 12:12 and 17:17, although without definition.
11. 4Q197 4 1:11.15 (Tob. 6:6,10).
12. 4Q550f 4; cf. *ATTM*, 2, 171.
13. *TADAE* B3.6,17.
14. In contrast, Ezra has *prsy*; → III.
15. 4Q562 8:3.
16. *TADAE* C2.1,36.38.40.50.
17. As in the expression *mtqlt prs* "Persian weight" in a letter of Aršama, *TADAE* A6.2,21.
18. Although imprecisely *mdy* "Median" in Dnl. 6:1; → II.
19. 4Q552 2 2:6.
20. 4Q550f 4.
21. *TADAE* C2.1,19.36.39.77 and partially emended in 31.76.77.
22. *TADAE* B3.8,20.
23. → *mnī*.

מות *mwt* /mūt/; מית *myt* /mīt/; מות *mwt* /mawt/; מותן *mwtn* /mawtān/

I. Lexical Field and Grammatical Constructions. II. G-stem "to Die." III. D-stem "to Kill." IV. Adjective "Dead." V. Noun "Dead." VI. Noun "Plague."

I. Lexical Field and Grammatical Constructions. All branches of the Semitic languages know forms of the verbal root *mūt* "to die." The G-stem is intransitive. The periphrastic construction with the auxiliary verb "to be"[1] and the participle can describe the process "to be dying," however. In contrast, the rarer causative-stem "to kill" is construed as a transitive with a direct object and overlaps semantically with → *qṭl* and the causative-stem of →*'bd* in the meaning "to destroy." The texts do not transmit a definition of death. If, however, one regards life[2] as the effect of the breath of life[3] and the autonomous movement it enables,[4] death would enter with its exhaustion; modern criteria such as growth, respiration, and the capacity to reproduce result, in contrast, only with an expansion of the term "life" to include all organic structures.

Probably also because of the limited proportion of literary texts, synonyms for "to die" in older Aramaic material are less developed than in Hebrew.[5] Nonetheless, the standard register of the old royal inscriptions and the later narrative prose preserve euphemisms, which suggest themselves especially in relation to an often taboo subject such as death. As in many other languages, Aramaic can designate passing with *'zl*/*hlk* "to go";[6] *pṭr* "to remove (one's self)" is rare.[7] The form of *škb* "to lie down" in 11Q10 24:9 (Job 34:15) corresponds to the Hebrew *yšwb* (as the consequence of a misreading?). The G-stem of *'bd* "to perish" often denotes the demise of evildoers.

Furthermore, various nominal forms belong to the root: the adjective /mīt/ "dead," the two masculine substantives /mawt/ (later /mōt/) "dead," and /mawtān/ (> /mōtān/) "plague" formed from it through the addition of the affix /-ān/.

II. G-stem "to Die." The earliest instances of the verb *mūt* "to die" occur in the Old Aramaic state treaties from Sefire. *KAI* 224.16 employs the expression *bkl mh zy ymwt br*

G. Gerleman, "מות *mût* to die," *TLOT*, 660-64; H. Gzella, *Tempus, Aspekt und Modalität im Reichsaramäischen. VOK* 48 (2004); D. Hamidović, "*mwt*," *ThWQ*, II, 618-26; H. Ringgren, K.-J. Illman, and H.-J. Fabry, "מות *mût*," *TDOT*, VIII, 185-209.

1. → *hwī* II.
2. → *ḥyī*.
3. → *nšm*.
4. Because of which flowing water was considered "living": 11Q18 10 1:1.
5. Cf. K.-J. Illman, 206ff.
6. E.g., in the Old Aramaic Tell Dan inscription *KAI* 310,3, here with *l*[, presumably to be emended "to [his fathers"; further in 1QapGen 22:33, together with *mūt*.
7. 4Q549 2:6, clarified here by the addition of *lbyt 'lmh* "to his grave."

'nš "in whatever fashion someone dies" in a clause against coups d'état;[8] in *KAI* 223 C 10, the verb is conjectured after the adverbial modifier *blḥṣ 'lb y*[*mwt* "[he should die] in severe depression" in the clause against destroying the inscription. In contrast, the expression *l'wyn wmwt* in *KAI* 222 B 30 has not yet been sufficiently interpreted. In the Syriac Nērab grave inscription, the verb refers to the individuals interred there.[9] Furthermore, it occurs in two Aḥiqar proverbs, once of the demise of the enemies[10] and again in reference to corporal punishment in childrearing, which, presumably in contrast to laissez-faire,[11] does not lead to death (l. 177). A pre-Imperial Aramaic private letter from Hermopolis uses the periphrastic construction "to be dying" after a life-threatening snakebite.

Almost all of the Imperial Aramaic instances of the verb occur in the protasis of a formulation in legal texts which regulate the payment of a debt in the case of the death of the debtor by his children, warrantor, or another form of legal successor.[12] A couple of other passages[13] are fragmentary. A Nabatean certificate of debt employs it in a verification.[14]

At Qumran, the expectation of the last judgment[15] clearly stands in the foreground in contrast with the individual ("first") death. Besides the already biblical motif of the fear of dying childless,[16] the report of the death of a figure in narratives,[17] and translated passages,[18] only a few fragmentary instances occur in legal contexts[19] or prophecies.[20] A couple of other passages are very fragmentary.

III. D-stem "to Kill." The causative-stem of *mūt* with the meaning "to kill" occurs in older Aramaic instead of the more common verb → *qṭl* only in a Sefire inscription and always in the infinitive.[21] All instances stand in clauses concerning an assassination or a coup d'état. Often, the same form is restored in a lacunae in *KAI* 223 B 8. Meanwhile, it is unclear whether *mmtyn* in 11Q10 27:8 (Job 36:14) involves a causative participle ("killing") or a substantivized G-stem infinitive ("manners of death").[22]

---

8. Following the causative stem for "to murder" in l. 15; → III; on the spelling with the vowel letter in the middle of the word, still rare in Sefire, see Gzella, 322 n. 60.

9. Perfect in the speech placed in the mouth of the deceased in *KAI* 226,4, presumably the third-person perfect in 225,2.

10. *TADAE* C1.1,110.

11. → *lbb* IV, but the expression is difficult.

12. *TADAE* B2.1,8; 2.6,17.20; 3.1,14; 3.3,11.12; 3.5,17. 18; 3.7,18; 3.8,28.34; 3.13,8; also possibly in the fragmentary court record 8.10,2; regarding the construction, see Gzella, 234-36.

13. E.g., *TADAE* D1.12,6.

14. nV 42:19f. in *ATTM*, 2, 244-46.

15. According to Rev. 2:11, etc., the "second death."

16. 1QapGen 22:33, of Abraham, following Gen 15:2.

17. Tobit in 4Q196 18:12 (Tob. 14:2).

18. 4Q156 1:5 (Lev. 16:13); 4Q157 1 2:6 (Job 4:21) and 11Q10 5:5 and 24:9 (Job 21:25 and 34:15).

19. 4Q531 23:3, alongside the passive of *qṭl*; 4Q532 2:8, along with *'bd*; both from the Book of Giants.

20. 4Q536 2 2:11.

21. *KAI* 224.11,11,15,15,16.

22. Cf. *DJD*, XXIII (1998), 142; *ATTM*, 621.

IV. Adjective "Dead." The adjective *myt* (sometimes spelled defectively *mt*) /mīt/ "dead" appears relatively rarely. It is attested beginning with Old Aramaic and can refer to a person (on the context, → II)[23] or to an animal.[24] According to 4Q206 1 22:4 (1 En. 22:5) [*br*] *ʾnš mt* "a dead person" brings a charge at the last judgment. Because of its fragmentary context, one can also interpret an additional possible instance *mtyn* in 4Q545 1a-b 2:15[25] as the cardinal "two hundred."[26] Otherwise, the masculine lexeme *pgr* /pagr/ is employed for "corpse" as a physical object.[27]

V. Noun "Dead." In relation to the noun /mawt/ (later /mōt/) "death," the time or the manner can be primary. The former pertains also to the curse formula in an Old Aramaic grave inscription,[28] the latter to the numerous Imperial Aramaic instances in contracts to regulate legal succession.[29] A proverb of Aḥiqar also employs death as a metaphor for power[30] and Ezr. 7:26 for the death penalty, the sole example of forms of this root in Biblical Aramaic.

Instances from Qumran occur alongside the time of death of the patriarch Amram[31] in an apocalyptic context.[32]

VI. Noun "Plague." The noun *mwtn* /mawtān/ (later /mōtān/) "plague" appears twice in Old Aramaic in the curse formula: first in *KAI* 309.23, in association with the god of plagues Nergal [*k*]*l mh mwtnʾ* "every plague (there ever was") and then in 320.2.[33] In 4Q544 1:13 (the Testament of Amram), the description of the evil angel is sometimes emended to *dḥ*[*y*]*l* [*kmw*]*tn* "as frightful as a plague."[34] The word first reappears with certainty in later Aramaic.[35]

Gzella

---

23. *TADAE* A2.5,9.
24. *TADAE* C1.1,209.
25. "The dead [people]" according to, e.g., *DSSStE*, 1091.
26. So *ATTM*, 2, 119, R 2,2.
27. *KAI* 222 B 30; 223 B 11; *TADAE* C1.1,63; so also even later.
28. *KAI* 225,10: "with a bad death."
29. *TADAE* B2.3,3.8; 3.5,18.21; 3.6,4.12.14; 3.10,16.18; 3.1,11.13; with the prepositions *b*- "at," *ʿd* "until," or *ʾḥr* "after."
30. *TADAE* C1.1,90.
31. 4Q545 1a 1:2 3.
32. 4Q530 2 2+6-12:1, dream of the giants; 4Q548 1 2-2:4, of the death of evildoers alongside *ʾbdn* "destruction," which should probably be supplied and which, like the verb → *ʾbd* appears especially in reference to the demise of sinners
33. As an unexpected determined state following *kl*, possibly as the substrate effect of a non-Semitic language; on the formulation itself, cf. Gzella, 257f.
34. *ATTM*, 212; *DSSStE*, 1088.
35. Cf. *DJPA*, 297; *DJBA*, 651b; *LexSyr*, 378; *MdD*, 263.

מחא/מחי *mḥʾ/mḥī*

I. Etymology, Phonetic Development. II. "Hitting, to Strike, to Hammer." III. As a Gesture of Oath-taking.

I. Etymology, Phonetic Development. Aramaic *mḥʾ* is a phonetic variant of the root *mḫś*[1] that arose through the shift from */ṣ́/ to /ġ/, rendered in Old Aramaic orthography with the letter *q*, and the subsequent dissimilation of the fricative pharyngeal /ḫ/, spelled with *ḥ*, and the fricative velar /ġ/. The phonetic similarity of the two phonemes also sometimes manifests itself in cuneiform transcriptions of the Aramaic phoneme, which was reproduced alphabetically with *q* which corresponded to the older Semitic /ṣ́/ (/ḍ/) either with *q* or *ḫ*, as in *Ra-qi-a-nu* or *Ra-ḫi-a-nu*,[2] Hebrew *Rṣy(ʾ)n*. A simplification of the pronunciation produced the dissimilation that reduced the articulation of the sound indicated by *q* to a glottal. The incompatibility rules concerning incompatible root letters does not apply here since the phonetic similarity was not original but resulted from the typical Aramaic shift from */ṣ́/ (*/ḍ/) to /ġ/ (*q*). Thus, this development differs from the shift from /q/ to /ʾ/ in some modern Semitic languages.[3] The noun *mḥʾh* in *TADAE* C1.1,178 demonstrates that /ʾ/ is the third radical.

The later loss of the syllable-closing /ʾ/ (*mḥʾ* > *m*ᵉ*ḥā*)[4] led to the transfer of the root *mḥʾ* to the class of III-*ī* verbs and thus to the spelling *mḥy* or *mḥh* in later Jewish Palestinian[5] and Jewish Babylonian.[6] The shift is already apparent in Ezr. 6:9 (*mḥy*), Num 34:1 (*mḥh*), 4Q531 19:4 (4QGiantsᶜ) (*ntmḥh*), 1QapGen 2:1 (*mtmḥyn*); 21:28,[30] (*mḥw*); 21:28; 22:4 (*mḥyn*). Yet, *mḥq* "to eradicate, to wipe out," that appears in Jewish Palestinian[7] and Jewish Babylonian,[8] seems to be a scribal continuation of the nondis-

---

L. Alonso Schökel, "מָחָה *maḥâ*," *TDOT*, VIII, 227-31; H. Gzella, "*mḥh*," ThWQ, II, 638-41; E. Lipiński, "Gage et cautionnement chez les Sémites du Nord-Ouest," in J. Zablocka and S. Zawadzki, eds., *Šulmu IV: Everyday Life in Ancient Near East* (Poznań, 1993), 213-22; idem, "Old Aramaic Contracts of Guarantee," in *Written on Clay and Stone. FS K. Szarzyńska* (Warsaw, 1998), 39-44; idem, *Studies in Aramaic Inscriptions and Onomastics I. OLA* 1 (1975), esp. 19-21; idem, *Studies in Aramaic Inscriptions and Onomastics, III. OLA* 230 (2010), esp. 75-7; K. Radner, *Ein neuassyrisches Privatarchiv der Tempelgoldschmiede von Assur. StAT* 1 (1999), esp. 134-36; idem, *Die neuassyrischen Privatrechtsurkunden als Quelle für Mensch und Umwelt. SAAS* 6 (1997), esp. 361-7; M. Wagner, *Die lexikalischen und grammatikalischen Aramaismen im alttestamentlichen Hebräisch. BZAW* 96 (1996), esp. 74.

1. Formerly transcribed *mḫḍ*.
2. *PNA* 1028.
3. E. Lipiński, *Semitic Languages. OLA* 80 (²2001), §10.10; 18.8.
4. Cf. *ATTM*, 104-6.
5. *DJPA*, 299,300a.
6. *DJBA*, 655f.
7. *DJPA*, 301.
8. *DJBA*, 657.

similated old Aramaic root *mḥq*, which may have arisen from the specific meaning "to erase an inscription by hammering." A form of the Old Aramaic root *mḥq* in the original meaning "to strike" occurs in the Song of Deborah (Jgs. 5:26),[9] dissimilated *mḥʾ* in Isa. 55:12, Ezk. 25:6 and Ps. 98:8. The development *mḥʾ* > *m^{e}ḥā* led to confusion, perhaps already in *TADAE* C3.11,5.

II. "Hitting, to Strike, to Hammer." The first instance of the dissimilated from *mḥʾ* dates to the early eighth century B.C.E.,[10] some 250 years after the use of *mḥq* in Jgs. 5:26. Yet, in this inscription, *mḥʾ* does not mean, "to strike," but refers to the erection of a ramp or a siege wall that one stamps or tramps on the floor. The expression *mḥʾ mṣr ʿl* constitutes a parallel to the Akkadian *aram-ma kabāsu* or *šukbusu eli.*[11] The basic meaning "to strike" occurs in a Sefire stele from the middle of the eighth century B.C.E.[12] and in the Bukan inscription from the late eighth century. At the end of the curses against the king who desecrates the stele stands, "May the whole curse of this stele strike him."[13] The same meaning "to strike" also appears in Dnl. 2:34,35; 5:19 (ptcp.) and regularly in texts from Qumran, at least where sufficient context has been preserved.[14] The hithpeel in Ezr. 6:11 has the corresponding passive meaning: since *z^{e}qīp̄* in this context has the nuance "to stake" like *ana iṣē zaqāpu* in Akkadian,[15] the passage must be translated "a beam should be torn from his house and he should be impaled on it." A more figurative sense "to meet, encounter" appears in Nu. 34:11, while the plural *mḥy* of the derived noun in Ezk. 26:9 means "shocks."

III. As a Gesture of Oath-taking. Aramaic contracts from the seventh century B.C.E. employ *mḥʾ yd* in reference to someone "vouching, acting as guarantor" for a debtor.[16] That is an abbreviation for a more extensive formula that appears in various Neo-Assyrian clay tablets from the same period and reads in full: *qātāte ša* N_1 (debtor) N_2 (guarantor) *isse* (TA*) *qātāte* N_3 (creditor) *ittaḫaṣ*(*a*), literally "the guarantor smote the hand of the debtor with the hand of the creditor."[17] The form *ittaḫaṣ* is a perfect of *maḫāṣu* with assimilation *mt* > *tt*. The formula appears to describe a symbolic act, not just a handshake, and expresses the fact that the guarantor vouches for the debtor with the creditor. The fulfillment of the obligation was guaranteed primarily

9. H. Gzella, *A Cultural History of Aramaic. HO* 111 (2015), 99-101.
10. *KAI* 202 A 15f.
11. *SAIO* I, 20.
12. *KAI* 222 A 42.
13. *KAI* 320.13.
14. The individual passages listed in H. Gzella, "*mḥh,*" *ThWQ*, II, 639f., mostly in references to military conflicts.
15. *AHw*, III, 1512a, G4; *CAD*, XXI, 53 §4'd.
16. O. 3658:5; 3670:3; 3646:4f. (Lipiński, *SAIO* III); A. Lemaire, *Nouvelles tablettes araméennes* (Geneva, 2001), no. 1:12 (incorrect reading in T. Kwasman, "Two Aramaic Legal Documents," *BSOAS* 63 [2000] 275); W. Röllig, *Die aramäischen Texte aus Tall Šēḫ Ḥamad / Dūr-Katlimmu / Magdalu. BATSH* 17/*Texte* 5 (2014), D54,8f.; 60,5 (not recognized in this *editio princeps*).
17. See Radner.

by the assets of the debtor, including his family members, and only supplementarily could another person vouch that the debtor would meet his obligation to the creditor. Aramaic employs the singular *yd*, however, instead of the Akkadian plural *qātāte*, as in the analogous Hebrew formula *tāqaʿ lᵉyaḏ* (Job 17:3) or *tāqaʿ kāp̄* (Prov. 6:1; 17:18; 22:26; Nah. 3:19; cf. Prov. 11:15). It remains uncertain, therefore, whether the complete expression in Aramaic agreed exactly with the Neo-Assyrian. The expression *mḥ' yd b*-N_3 in D 54:8f.; 60:5 (see above) demonstrates, in any case, that "the guarantor struck his hand with the creditor." The parallel in Dnl. 4:32 also shows that the "hand" of the creditor was introduced by *b*- "with," which confirms the reading of the Neo-Assyrian sign TA* as *isse* "with."

The Greek translators (4:35) did not understand the expression *mḥ' byd* in Dnl. 4:32.[18] Literally, it clearly means, "There is no one who can vouch to him (for the heavenly host and the inhabitants of earth) or who can say, 'What did you do?'" A precisely parallel, abbreviated formula occurs in a Neo-Assyrian legal text from circa 633 B.C.E. There one reads at best, ᵐ*Aḫi-imme* ⌜*isse* ⌝ *qātāti ša-rēši* (⌜TA*⌝! ŠU.2.MEŠ LÚ*.SAG!) *ittaḫaṣa* "Ahimme (guarantor) vouched to the eunuchs (creditors)" for the debtor, not "the guarantor smote the witnesses" as the editor translates.[19] This parallel may demonstrate that the hymn in Dnl. 4:31b-32 was borrowed from a much older text. The abbreviation *mḥ' yd* already seems to occur as *ma-ḫa-ṣí i-da* in a bilingual word list from Ebla,[20] although entirely without context, while *māḥā ḵāp̄* in Isa. 55:12; Ps. 98:8 and *māḥā yāḏ* in Ezk. 25:6 means simply "to applaud."

A further abbreviation of the formula appears in Jewish Aramaic texts, namely the first century B.C.E. grave inscription of Jason from Jerusalem[21] and in tractates of the Talmud, especially in *B. Bat.* 38a-b and 39b. These texts employ the verb without *yd* in the sense of "to secure" and the verbal noun *mḥ'h* (derived from the D-stem) occurs in *B. Bat.* in the meaning "security." The Jason inscription, l. 4, reads, *ḥny br ywsh mḥ*⌜'⌝ *qwn' hyk ylyn šlm*,[22] "Honi, son of Yose, has secured this property, so that he may find rest. Peace!" There is still room for the right arm of the cursive ' after the *ḥ* of *mḥ'*; the letter is no longer visible, however.[23] According to *B. Bat.* the security of the property against unpermitted occupation must occur in the presence of two witnesses in order to be able to realize the claim to uninterrupted possession even without written evidence.

Lipiński

18. Often translated "to ward off, hinder," → *yd*.

19. V. Donbaz and S. Parpola, *Neo-Assyrian Legal Texts in Istanbul. StAt* 2 (2001), no. 176 [A 1937], 5f.

20. *MEE* 4, no. 0411.

21. Although interpreted by *ATTM*, 2, 265f. as a homonym *mḥī* "to weave."

22. Cf. É. Puech, "Inscriptions Funéraires Palestiniennes: Tombeau de Jason et Ossuaires," *RB* 90 (1983) 482,488f.; contrast *ATTM*, 328 and 2, 266.

23. Regarding *qwn'* see *ATTM*, 684.

מטא/מטי *mṭʾ/mṭī*

I. Etymology and Grammatical Constructions. II. "To Attain, Reach, Arrive." 1. Old Aramaic. 2. Imperial Aramaic. 3. Biblical Aramaic. 4. Qumran. III. "To Enter" and Various Legal Expressions.

I. Etymology and Grammatical Constructions. In Aramaic, the verbal root *mṭʾ*, in the G-stem an intransitive "to arrive" or transitive "to attain (something)," was transferred, after the disappearance of the glottal stop at the end of the syllable, into the class of verbs ending with a vowel already during the Old Aramaic period,[1] and, at the same time, inflected as *mṭī*, although the ʾ continued to be retained as a historical spelling even in the Imperial Aramaic literary tradition. An etymological connection with Hebrew *mṣʾ* "to find" and various other Semitic cognates, would suggest a ground form **mθ̣ʾ*, although some individual languages such as Ugaritic (*mġy*) also manifest unexpected counterparts. Persons, things, and abstract temporal concepts serve as subjects of the verb, the latter two in the sense of "to enter." Legal discourse knows additional specialized expression with the nuance "to come to" (→ III).

For the G-stem "to arrive, attain," the object of the motion can be constructed as a direct object or with a prepositional expression following *l-* "to" for places (e.g., Dnl. 4:8,17,19; 6:25) or *ʿl* "to" (Dnl. 4:21,25) or *ʿd* (Dnl. 7:13, probably in the terminal sense of "as far as") for persons.

Primarily post-Christian Aramaic languages know an additional transitive causative-[2] or, like the Syriac, D-stem[3] with the meaning "to bring, deliver" with what is brought as a direct object and the recipient following *l-*. An Imperial Aramaic ostracon from Idumea already attests this stem.[4] Otherwise, the causative-stem of → *ʾtī* "to come" is employed for "to bring."[5]

II. "To Attain, Reach, Arrive."

1. Old Aramaic. The first instances of *mṭī* "to attain, enter" are known from later Old Aramaic. In Adon's letter to the pharaoh with the request for military support,[6] if the reading is correct, *mṭʾw* "they attained" stands asyndetically after *ʾtw* "they came" with

I. Ephʿal and J. Naveh, *Aramaic Ostraca of the Fourth Century BC from Idumaea* (Jerusalem, 1996); G. Gerleman, "מצא *mṣʾ* to find," *TLOT*, 682-84; H. Gzella, *Tempus, Aspekt und Modalität im Reichsaramäischen. VOK* 48 (2004); C. Kumpmann, "*mṣʾ*," *ThWQ*, II, 740-46 (Heb.); J. Naveh and S. Shaked, *Aramaic Documents from Ancient Bactria (Fourth Century B.C.E.)* (London, 2012); S. Wagner, "מָצָא *māṣāʾ*," *TDOT*, VIII, 465-83.

1. *ATTM*, 104-6.

2. *DJBA*, 660; according to *DJPA*, 302b, however, the possible examples in Jewish Palestinian are dubious.

3. *LexSyr*, 381f.

4. Ephʿal and Naveh, no. 26.

5. Apparently synonymous with the causative-stem of *mṭī* in another Idumean ostracon, see Ephʿal and Naveh, no. 25.

6. *TADAE* A1.1,4 = *KAI* 266.4.

the Babylonian army as the subject and the place name Aphek as the direct object. In the private correspondence from Hermopolis, the verb occurs in reference to a garment that the addressee had previously sent as the subject and a suffix as the pronominal object[7] and figuratively in the expression *kdy mṭ'h ydy* "as far as my hand reaches" for "as well as I can."[8]

2. Imperial Aramaic. Imperial Aramaic private letters also employ the verb for the arrival of objects such as letters, in particular,[9] and further for persons[10] and in one case, for a boat.[11] A very fragmentary official letter from Bactria seems also to contain an example with goods as the subject,[12] but the context has been lost. Letters on ostraca also contain a few fragmentary passages.[13] With place names, a direct object and *l-* are apparently employed without distinction; with persons, *'l* often appears.[14] Occasionally, *mṭī* serves as a modal verb "to be far enough" with the main verb after *l-*, as in *mṭ't lmgz* "(the sheep) is far enough to be shorn."[15]

Remarkable, finally, is the repeated use of the infinitive *lmmṭh* for "on arrival" in the Aramaic version of the Behistun inscription.[16] Syntactically, it probably involves an adverbial infinitive, as is also attested in isolation in Aramaic;[17] the expression as such seems too restricted to this text, however. The Babylonian version has *ana kašādu.*[18]

3. Biblical Aramaic. All Biblical Aramaic passages with the *mṭī* stem are from the book of Daniel, most of them Nebuchadnezzar's account of the world tree dream. This tree, which symbolizes the king, grew powerful until its height reached heaven (*wrwmh ymṭ' lšmy'*, Dnl. 4:8, repeated practically verbatim in 17 and then as part of the interpretation in 19). Since, in terms of type of action, *mṭī* is essentially a punctiliar verb, the imperfect *ymṭ'* in 4:8,17 may describe a subordinate secondary act that occurs in the course of the growth designated with the perfect.[19] The perfect also occurs in this function in 4:19.

Further, *mṭī* appears twice in the figurative sense of "to arrive" for "to happen to" in Dnl. 4:21,25, in each case for the misfortune that King Nebuchadnezzar—following the

7. *TADAE* A2.1,4; in l. 6 with another object.

8. A2.4,4, similarly in 2.6,5f. for "whatever you can"; → *yd* II.1.

9. *TADAE* A3.5,2, subject deduced from the context; 3.8,7; 3.9,2; 4.2,15.

10. *TADAE* A3.10,8; 4.3,3; 6.9,5.

11. TADAE A3.9,7.

12. Naveh and Shaked, B2,2.

13. *TADAE* D7.45,3; 7.54,6.

14. A personal pronoun is linked either to *'l* or as an object suffix to the verb.

15. *TADAE* D7.8,3; cf. also J. C. Greenfield, "Le Bain des Brebis," *Or* 29 (1960) 99f.

16. *TADAE* C2.1,20.25; in the second case with the toponym → *mdy* "Media"; the orthographic variant *lmm*]*ṭ'* with the subsequent preposition *b-* may be supplied in l. 41.

17. In addition to the frequent *l'mr* "as follows," cf. also *lḥzdh* "presumptuously" in Dnl. 5:20 and Gzella, 294.

18. In keeping with classical usage, however, one would probably expect, instead, *ina*.

19. On this, see the extensive treatment in Gzella, 137-42.

preposition *ʿl* to indicate the person—meets as a consequence of the divine punishment for his arrogance.[20]

The two other instances from Daniel have a terminal nuance and denote the end of a movement: in 6:25 with "ground" as a spatial term following *l-* to depict how the lions overpowered Daniel's accusers even before they had reached the floor of the den; and in 7:13 with the person of the Ancient of Days following *ʿd*, until the "son of man" arrives in the judicial scene.

4. Qumran. In contrast, the Aramaic texts from Qumran contain only a very few instances of the verb because the description of the journey 1QapGen, where one would most expect it, unusually employs the root *dbq*[21] for "to attain." Only the Book of Giants exhibits *mṭī*: in Enoch's letter perhaps for the account of the evil conduct of the giants that reaches the archangel Raphael (4Q203 8:12),[22] and in a fragmentary context in 4Q537 8:1.

Furthermore, in several Nabatean private documents from the Dead Sea, *mṭī* appears with the payment that the seller obtains as subject.[23]

III. "To Enter" and Various Legal Expressions. Imperial Aramaic contracts employ the verb *mṭī* further as part of various idiomatic and possibly register-specific expressions: in reference to the establishment of deadlines for "to arrive,"[24] but also for the obligation to make a statement[25] or to take an oath,[26] and finally for a portion of something that comes to a party to a contract.[27]

The use for the arrival of the time, here for the transfer of worldwide dominion, recurs in the vision of the last judgment in Dnl. 7:22. It is not clear, however, whether this passage takes up a decidedly juridical formulation. A Nabatean treaty from the Dead Sea knows, in addition, the usage with *zmnʾ* "the (agreed) time"[28] as the object meaning "to meet a deadline."[29] With the nuance "to come to, to be entitled to," *mṭī* then once in a Palymrene grave inscription.[30]

Gzella

20. Otherwise, Aramaic also employs the rare verb *pgʿ* for "to meet, encounter," cf. *TADAE* C1.1,166.

21. Literally "to cling to"; → *dbq* III.

22. The subject stands in the preceding lacuna, but cf. the reconstruction in *ATTM*, 261, G 4:12.

23. nV 3:32 and partially emended also in 2:8,30 and in 43:12; with no context preserved in 9:5; all in *ATTM* 2.

24. *TADAE* B3.1,7; cf. 4.6,8.

25. *TADAE* B7.2,7.

26. *TADAE* B2.8,5; regarding the unusual ptcp. in a preterite tense in this passage, see Gzella, 131.

27. *TADAE* B2.11,3.5.7.9.10.12 and 5.1,4; further, generally, → *ḥlq* III.

28. → *zmn* V.

29. nV 1:16 in *ATTM*, 2, 205f.

30. *PAT* 0583.1, with *l-*.

מלאך *ml'k* /mal'ak/

I. Etymology. II. Semantics. 1. Old Aramaic. 2. Biblical Aramaic. 3. Qumran. III. LXX. IV. Aspects from the Perspective of the History of Religion. 1. Divine Messengers. 2. Protective Angels. 3. As an Element of DN and PN.

I. Etymology. Of the West Semitic languages, Ugaritic,[1] Phoenician,[2] Aramaic,[3] and Hebrew[4] attest the root *l'k* with its derivatives. The substantive *ml'k* is a nominal derivative of the verbal root *l'k* "to commission, send" on the *maqtal* pattern with the meaning "emissary, representative, messenger."[5]

II. Semantics. The masculine noun *ml'k* essentially denotes a representative, emissary, or messenger in a communication that is only possible by overcoming diatopic and diachronic linguistic hindrances. The institution of messenger, which in addition to oral messages also produces texts,[6] serves this purpose. The necessity of spanning diatopic and diachronic hindrances to communication exists between gods and between gods and human beings. Consequently, *ml'k* appears in most occurrences as the object of → *šlḥ*. Instances of the use of *ml'k* as a messenger between gods and as a divine messenger to human beings involve a divine being, for which the translation "angel" has become standard.

1. Old Aramaic. The oldest Aramaic *ml'k*-specimen appears in the mid-eighth century B.C.E. steles from Sefire. This treaty deals with the safeguarding of the unhindered

R. Comte du Mesnil du Buisson, *Les tessères et les monnaies de Palmyre* (Paris, 1962), esp. 259-84; J.-L. Cunchillos, "*La'ika, mal'āk* et *melā'kāh* en sémitique nord-occidental," *RSF* 10 (1982) 153-60; M. J. Davidson, *Angels at Qumran. JSPSup* 11 (1992); R. Ficker, "מַלְאָךְ *mal'āk* messenger," *TLOT*, 666-72; D. N. Freedman and B. E. Willoughby, "מְלָאכָה *m^elā'kâ*," *TDOT*, VIII, 308-25; L. K. Handy, *Among the Host of Heaven* (Winona Lake, IN, 1994), esp. 149-67; K. Koch, *Das Buch Daniel. EdF* 144 (1980), esp. 205-10; idem, *Daniel 1–4. BK* XXII/1 (2005), 302-5; idem, "Monotheismus und Angelologie," in W. Dietrich and M. A. Klopfenstein, eds., *Ein Gott allein? OBO* 139 (1994), 565-81; S. A. Meier, "Angel I," *DDD*², 45-50; idem, *The Messenger in the Ancient Semitic World. HSM* 45 (1988); F. Reiterer et al., eds., *Angels: The Concept of Celestial Beings—Origins, Development and Reception. DCLY* (2007); J. Teixidor, *The Pantheon of Palmyra. EPRO* 79 (1979), 34-52; C. Wassen, "*ml'k*," *ThWQ*, II, 675-81.

1. *DUL*³, 482f.,540.
2. *DNSI*, 629.
3. *DNSI*, 629.
4. *GesB*¹⁸, 678f.
5. *ATTM*, 616; 2, 425.
6. Cf. K. Ehlich, "Text und sprachliches Handeln," in A. Assmann, J. Assmann, and C. Hardmeier, eds., *Schrift und Gedächtnis. Archäologie der literarischen Kommunikation* 1 (Munich, 1983), 24-43.

communication between the king of *Ktk* and other kings.[7] Furthermore, the feminine substantive *ml'kh* "message" occurs in the Asshur letter (ca. 650 B.C.E.).[8]

2. Biblical Aramaic. The Aramaic Daniel narratives offer two references to *ml'km*, to be understood as divine messengers or angels. During the incineration of the three youths in the oven (Dnl. 3:19-30), Nebuchadnezzar sees in the oven a fourth youth who resembles a son of God (*bar ʾᵉlāhīn*, Dnl. 3:25). After the oven is opened, Nebuchadnezzar confesses that the fourth person must have been a "messenger" (*mal'ak̲*) God sent to deliver the three youths (Dnl. 3:28).

Daniel, imprisoned in the lions' den, explains his deliverance with the statement: "My God send his messenger [*ʾᵉlāhī šᵉlaḥ malʾᵃk̲eh*]" (Dnl. 6:23). This statement represents a revision of the account that inserts the messenger based on Dnl. 3:25,28.[9]

3. Qumran. The Aramaic texts from Qumran offer additional instances of the use of *ml'k* as "angel,"[10] although most of such contexts are corrupt so that the text can hardly be interpreted. Especially interesting is the Testament of Amram (4Q543-548),[11] in which Aaron is supposed to call the angels (4Q545 1 1:8f.) and is, himself, called the "angel of God" (4Q543 3:1). Regarding the angel's discretionary authority of human fate there, see H. Gzella, "*šlṭ* III," *ThWQ*, III, 949-54.

III. LXX. The LXX names God as Daniel's savior in Dnl. 6:23 and translates *mal'ak̲* in Dnl. 3:28 (LXX: 3:49) with ἄγγελος.

IV. Aspects from the Perspective of the History of Religion.

1. Divine Messengers. The concept of divine messengers designated as *ml'km* appears in Northwest Semitic religions already in late Bronze Age Ugarit, where they occupy the lowest rank in the hierarchy of the divine world.[12] This reference to the Late Bronze Age history of religion is important to the extent that, in reference to Old Testament/Jewish angelology, scholars repeatedly assert origins in the postexilic period. In so doing, they completely overlook the age of the messenger concept. Furthermore, they do not consider that a Jewish monotheistic concept of religion eliminates the ranks of gods lying between the highest God and the "angels" so that only the "angels" remain.

2. Protective Angels. An expansion of the angel concept of the Aramaic narratives in Daniel as deliverers of individual human beings fallen into distress (Dnl. 3:25,28;

---

7. *KAI* 224.8; cf. J. A. Fitzmyer, *The Aramaic Inscriptions of Sefire. BietOr* 19/A (^{2}1995), 136,150.

8. *KAI* 233,19 = V. Hug, *Altaramäische Grammatik der Texte des 7. und 6. Jh.s v.Chr. HSAO* 4 (1993), 21; cf. *DNSI*, 630.

9. So E. Haag, *Die Errettung Daniels aus der Löwengrube. SBS* 110 (1983), 42,46; R. Albertz, *Der Gott des Daniel. SBS* 131 (1988), 144-47; B. Schlenke, *Gottes Reich und Königs Macht. HBS* 76 (2013), 308 n. 84.

10. *ATTM*, 616; 2, 425.

11. Cf. *DSSStE*, 1084-95.

12. Handy, 149-63.

6:23) involves two aspects. The Hebrew parts of the book of Daniel manifest a concept of national angels who, as heavenly protective powers, minister to individual peoples (Dnl. 10:13,20; 12:1).[13] The Aramaic texts from Qumran know the concept of an individual protective angel,[14] as the Tobit narrative, too (Tob. 3:16f.;[15] 5-12). Regarding the protective angel → *'yr*.

3. As an Element of DN and PN. In the pantheon from Palmyra, *ml'k* occurs as an element of divine names. In addition to the triad of the gods of Ba'al-šamin, the god Malakbel belongs alongside the god Aglibol. The latter seems to be a hypostasis of the chief god of Palmyra, Bel, who thus maintains a connection with the triad of Ba'alšamin. Regarding the cult of Malakbel in Palmyra and Dura Europos, cf. L. Dirven, *The Palmyrenes of Dura Europos. RGRW* 138 (1999), 157-89, and T. Kaizer, *The Religious Life of Palmyra* (Stuttgart, 2002), 124-43. As a personal name formed with *ml'k*, one encounters *mlkbl* in Palmyra.[16]

Niehr

13. Cf. K. Koch, *Buch Daniel*, 207-10.
14. Cf. Wassen, 677f.
15. Qumran does not preserve this passage.
16. Cf. *PNPI* 32.95.

מלח *mlḥ* /melḥ/; מלח *mlḥ*

I. Etymology and Form. II. General Meaning. III. As an Offering. IV. Denominal Verb "to Salt."

I. Etymology and Form. All Semitic languages have a common primary noun, mostly in the *qitl* pattern, for "salt"; in Aramaic, it appears as /melḥ/, after the rejection of the doubled consonant at the end of the word as /melaḥ/.[1] It also appears in virtually all the known Aramaic forms of speech and is usually construed as a masculine, in East Aramaic, however, also as a feminine.[2]

K. J. Cathcart, "The Curses in Old Aramaic Inscriptions," in *Targumic and Cognate Studies. FS McNamara. JSOTSup* 230 (1996), 140-52; H. Eising, "מֶלַח *melaḥ*," *TDOT*, VIII, 331-33; D. T. Potts, "On Salt and Salt Gathering in Ancient Mesopotamia," *JESHO* 27 (1984) 225-71; A. Ravasco, "*mlḥ*," *ThWQ*, II, 684-86.

1. *ATTM*, 112-15.
2. *DJBA*, 667; *LexSyr*, 390; *MdD*, 266a.

As food, a sacrificial supplement, and probably also as a preservative, salt was ubiquitous. In addition, it occurs, as in Hebrew,[3] in geographical terms: once for *ym' mlḥ' rb'* "the great Salt Sea"[4] and otherwise as a component in place names that were presumably associated with salt production.[5] The verb *mlḥ* "to salt" is related to the noun (→ IV).

II. General Meaning. The first instances of the noun *mlḥ* /melḥ/ appear already in Old Aramaic. In the curse formula (already coined in Neo-Assyrian sources) of a state treaty from Sefire, it serves as in texts in the Hebrew Bible to express infertility;[6] the god Hadad should punish anyone who breaks the covenant by spreading salt on his country.[7] A similar formulation appears in the inscription from Bukan (→ IV).[8] In a saying of Aḥiqar, *mlḥ* appears proverbially along with *ḥl* "sand."[9]

In Imperial Aramaic, "salt" refers, in contrast, to trade goods and occurs almost exclusively in letters on ostraca. They refer to the transport,[10] the acquisition in relation to the boats from Elephantine,[11] or the use as an addition to flour.[12] Fine salt[13] is distinguished from coarse.[14] It also appears in relation to fish.[15] A later ostracon[16] mentions a "salt tax" (*ksp mlḥ'*); furthermore, the Palmyrene tax tables also mention such a tax.[17]

III. As an Offering. The Hebrew Bible also knows salt as a sacrificial supplement (Lev. 2:13; Ezk. 43:24). Aramaic attests it in this function beginning with Ezr. 6:9 and 7:22. There, it appears with grain, wine, and oil in a bill of lading to be sent regularly to the newly constructed Jerusalem temple on the promise of the Persian king and from his means.[18] Unlike the other goods, it is subject to no limitation.[19] The sole instance from Qumran appears in the same sense in the depiction of Noah's sacrifice.[20]

---

3. A. Ravasco, 685.
4. 1QapGen 16:17; 21:16f.; → *ym* III.
5. E.g., in a synagogue inscription from late antiquity, ggBS 3:18 in *ATTM*, 378-82, and a building inscription from the environs of Hatra, S1, 9; cf. the very common "hall" in German.
6. See Cathcart, 150.
7. *KAI* 222 A 36; → *zrʿ* II and cf. Jgs. 9:45.
8. *KAI* 320.9.
9. *TADAE* C1.1,159; → *nśī*.
10. *TADAE* D7.2,2; 7.7,2; 7.35,5; H. Lozachmeur, *La collection Clermont-Ganneau*, vol. 1 (Paris, 2006), no. 128cv2.5.
11. *TADAE* D7.2,4f.
12. *TADAE* D7.2,7.
13. *mlḥ* → *dqq*.
14. *ḥṣp*, *TADAE* D7.7,3.
15. *TADAE* D7.35,5.
16. *TADAE* D8.13,3.
17. *PAT* 0259 ii.64,69,72,130,134; cf. *DNSI*, 632 and regarding the problem "tax on salt" or "tax (paid) in salt," see 625.
18. → *ḥšḥ* II.
19. → *ktb* IV.
20. 1QapGen 10:17.

IV. Denominal Verb "to Salt." The verb *mlḥ* "to salt" may derive from the noun. Later, it is regularly attested in the G-stem,[21] but the D-stem, to be expected of a denominal root, is presumably attested once in the Old Aramaic inscription from Bukan. It threatens a king who destroys the stele, *ʾrqh thwy mmlḥ*[*h*] "may his land be salted";[22] alternatively, it may be the case of a feminine noun "salt-land."[23] The verb appears with the noun as an internal object in *mᵉlaḥ hēḵᵉlā mᵉlaḥnā,* literally "we have salted the salt of the palace," probably a demonstration of loyalty (Ezr. 4:14).[24] It occurs twice at Qumran in a sacrificial context: in reference to the temple cult in 11Q18 13:2 (new Jerusalem) and as a passive participle "salted members" in 4Q214b 2-6:9 (Levi document).

Gzella

21. *DJPA*, 309a; *DJBA*, 677b; *LexSyr*, 390b.
22. *KAI* 320.9.
23. Cf. Syriac *mālaḥṯā, LexSyr*, 390b.
24. → *hykl* II.3.

מלא/מלי *ml'/mlī*; מלה *mlh* /malǣ/

I. Etymology, Lexical Field, and Grammatical Constructions. II. G-stem "to Fill, to Be Full." 1. Intransitive. 2. Transitive. III. Causative-stem "to Fill." IV. Adjective "Full."

I. Etymology, Lexical Field and Grammatical Constructions. Since the disappearance of the glottal stop at the end of a syllable in Old Aramaic,[1] the original verbal root **ml'* "to be, become full," which has cognates in all chief branches of the Semitic languages, was conjugated as *mlī* on the model of verbs III-*ī*. The Gp-stem is ambitransitive (or "deficient") and can have either the stative-intransitive nuance "to be full" or the dynamic-transitive "to fill in, fulfill." In the first case, the verb appears, according to the evidence of later vocalizations, with the thematic vowel /ī/, in the second with /ā/.[2] In the intransitive construction that with which something is filled can be added as an adverbial supplement; the dynamic meaning, in contrast, occurs with a simple ("to fulfill something") or dual ("to fill something with something") direct object and is employed later figuratively for "to fulfill" in relation to temporal concepts or for "to complete."

M. Delcor, "מלא *ml'* to be full, fill," *TLOT*, 664-66; A. L. A. Hogeterp, "*ml'*," *ThWQ*, II, 669-74; L. A. Snijders and H.-J. Fabry, "מָלֵא *mālē'*," *TDOT*, VIII, 297-308.

1. *ATTM*, 104-6.
2. *ATTM*, 623.

Accordingly, the Gt-stem has the middle meaning "to fill" or "to become complete." Meanwhile, the D-stem is employed factitively "to fill something," but cannot always be identified in consonantal spellings. In addition, the form *tšml'* "to complete" in an Imperial Aramaic papyrus document from Saqqara[3] could also represent a lexicalized causative with the prefix /ša-/ adapted from the Babylonian; the passage is not entirely paleographically definite, however. Such a causative-stem with /ša-/ and various nouns derived from it with the meaning "completion" occur later in Syriac, in any case.[4]

The passive participle of the G-stem /malǣ/ serves as an adjective "full" and sporadically appears as substantivized with the meaning "abundance." Later Aramaic languages know additional nominal forms with the same nuance.[5]

II. G-stem "to Fill, to Be Full." The G-stem of the root *ml'* > *mlī* "to be full" or "to fill" is attested in both the spatial-concrete and the abstract senses beginning with later Old Aramaic. In the consonantal and mostly defective spelling, however, the difference in the thematic vowel (→ I) between the stative and the dynamic meanings remains obscure.

1. Intransitive. A saying of Aḥiqar concerning clever budgeting constitutes the beginning of the attestation of the verb; already at that time the rapid retirement of debts was recommended and the repayment[6] of a loan equated with the *mml' by* "filling up (or filling, infinitive of the G-stem) a house."[7] No negative connotation is evident;[8] instead, it may involve the multiplication of wealth.[9]

While the verb here can be understood intransitively or transitively, in Old and Imperial Aramaic letter style it surely means "to be full" in reference to a person and with the adverbial modifier *lbh* "anger."[10]

Often, the Gt-stem serves in the legal diction of the private documents as a term for "to be completely paid-off."[11]

2. Transitive. The transitive use of the G-stem in Aramaic can probably first be demonstrated in the fragmentary Imperial Aramaic Bar-Puneš novella[12] and where it is attested with a dual object *l' yml' bṭnhm lḥm* "he will not fill your bellies with bread."[13] The ex-

3. J. B. Segal, *Aramaic Texts from North Saqqara* (London, 1983), no. 52b, l. 8.
4. Cf. *LexSyr*, 389f.
5. See *LexSyr*, 388f.
6. → *šlm*.
7. *TADAE* C1.1,131.
8. *Pace* M. Weigl, *Die aramäische Achikar-Sprüche aus Elephantine und die alttestamentliche Weisheitsliteratur*. *BZAW* 399 (2010), 288-96.
9. For the same image, cf. Job 22:18; additional literature in *DNSI*, 627.
10. Suffixed *lbty* "of anger against me" in *TADAE* A2.3,6; the same expression unsuffixed in 3.3,10; further in reference to the present with the pass. ptcp. "full" used adjectivally (→ IV) in *KAI* 233.19f. and *TADAE* A4.2,11; with the perfect of → *hwī* for the past in 3.5,4.
11. *TADAE* B3.1,11.17, here with *bksp* "with money," in 4:4,17 and 4:6,17 in a partially destroyed context and with no preserved modifier.
12. In Sam'alian, meanwhile, already in *KAI* 215.4, where it involves the filling of prisons.
13. *TADAE* C1.2,18.

pression *ml'h s'r[n* in a fragmentary letter ostracon may also be transitive,[14] but the context has not been preserved. Further, the verb may occur once in another letter ostracon with *npš*[15] as object in the sense "to feed,"[16] but the reading is disputed.[17]

The two instances in Biblical Aramaic integrate into this spectrum of usage. Dnl. 2:35 uses the verb with a simple object in relation to Nebuchadnezzar's dream for the stone that has become a mountain,[18] which fills the whole earth (*mlt kl 'r'*, here *mᵉlāṯ* with /ā/-perfect). In Dnl. 3:19, the t-stem and an adverbial addition denote the middle or reflexive nuance "to fill with" (*nbwkdnṣr htmly ḥm'* "Nebuchadnezzar was filled with wrath") in contrast to the perfect (of course with /ī/) of the G-stem in the somewhat different Imperial Aramaic formulations (→ II.1). A possible, but probably only minimal semantic difference from this construction remains imperceptible; meanwhile, perhaps the intransitive nuance was less productive.

The Aramaic texts from Qumran contain a few mostly fragmentary instances. In any case, the Gt-stem appears in apocalyptic contexts for "to fill up" of the earth filled with injustice.[19] Furthermore, Beyer[20] reconstructs 1 En. 10:17 *yt[mlwn*, which would produce the first instance of "to fill up" in relation to a temporal term ("all the days of your youth and your old age"). The exact form in 11Q10 7A:5 (Job 23:4) is unclear and, therefore, could be a D-stem as in Hebrew (→ III). Finally, the meaning of H30.10 from Hatra is also unclear.[21]

Later Aramaic knows an entire series of additional nuances.[22]

III. Causative-stem "to Fill." In consonantal spellings, the factitive D-stem "to fill" with a direct object can only be identified for certain forms. In the light of the Akkadian parallels from *KAI* 309.22, examples include the two instances in an Old Aramaic curse formula, which, in consequence of the expansion of Aramaic, appear in similar wordings in ninth- and eighth-century texts widely dispersed geographically: the inscription from Tell Fekheriye[23] and the Bukan stele.[24] The curse should cause the greatest effort to produce the least result, as expressed, for example, with the picture of a hundred or seven women, respectively, baking bread in an oven but, nonetheless, being unable to fill it.[25] In any case, the transitive G-stem can also appear for "to fill" (→ II.2).

---

14. *TADAE* D7.12,4.
15. → *nšm* III.2.
16. *TADAE* D7.19,6.
17. Cf. R. Degen, *Die aramäischen Ostraka in der Papyrus-Sammlung der Österreichischen Nationalbibliothek. NESE* 3 (1978), 37.
18. → *ṭwr*.
19. 4Q201 1 4:8 (1 En. 9:1); similarly, probably, in 4Q243 25,3 and with no further context in the prophetic history 4Q558 37 2:4 and perhaps in 1QapGen 11:16 according to the reading in *ATTM*, 2, 95f.
20. *ATTM*, 238. Cf. *DSSStE*, 414f., which reconstructs *yt[mlywn*, translating "all the days of [your youth] and of your old age will be [completed] in peace."
21. There paralleling *nsk* "to pour out."
22. *DJBA*, 678f.; *LexSyr*, 388f.
23. *KAI* 309.22.
24. *KAI* 320.7.
25. *'l yml'nh* in *KAI* 309.22; *'l yml'why* in 320.7.

In a priestly prophecy from Qumran the expression "to fill the hand," presumably adopted from Hebrew, means "to install as priest."[26] Since, in Hebrew, this involves the D-stem,[27] one assumes the same for the Aramaic passage. In later Jewish Palestinian, as already in Imperial Aramaic, the D-stem resists confident identification because of the lack of unequivocal forms[28] and may, therefore, have only been productive in the east of the linguistic region.

IV. Adjective "Full." Older Aramaic attests the adjective *mlh* /malǣ/ quite rarely. In a nominal clause in reference to the present, it can represent the perfect of the verb employed as an intransitive, as in the expression *mlh lbh* "full of anger" (→ II.1), and marked with the perfect of → *hwī* clearly in reference to the past.[29] In Qumran, it refers to the earth in the context of the fullness of creation: 1QapGen 11:12; 4Q204 1 12:28 par. 4Q206 1 26:14 (1 En. 31:2); and perhaps 4Q553a 10:1. It is only attested later in a substantival use following a possible *ml'h* "full worth."[30]

Gzella

26. 4Q562 1:2.
27. Cf. *GesB*[18], 677.
28. *KAI* 233.19,20; *TADAE* A4.2, 11; *DJPA*, 309f.
29. *TADAE* A3.5,4.
30. *TADAE* B1.1,9.

מלך *mlk* /malk/; מלכה *mlkh* /malkā/; מלכו *mlkw* /malkū/; מלך *mlk*; מלך *mlk* /melk/

I. Etymology, Forms, and Lexical Field. II. Noun "King." 1. The Iron Age Syrian Principalities. 2. The Empires of the First Millennium. 3. The Local Kingdoms of the Hellenistic and Roman Periods. III. As a Divine Title. IV. Abstract "Kingship." V. Verb "to Rule." VI. Verb "to Advise" and Noun "Advice."

H. Gzella, *A Cultural History of Aramaic. HO* 111 (2015); T. L. Holm, *Of Courtiers and Kings. EANEC* 1 (2013), 260 n. 321 (on *mlkh* in Dnl. 5:10); M. Leuenberger, "*mlk*," *ThWQ*, II, 689-96; H. Ringgren, K. Seybold, and H.-J. Fabry, "מֶלֶךְ *melek*," *TDOT*, VIII, 346-75; J. A. Soggin, "מֶלֶךְ *melek* king," *TLOT*, 672-80; W. H. van Soldt, "The Vocalization of the Word *mlk*, 'King', in Late Bronze Age Syllabic Texts from Syria and Palestine," in *Hamlet on a Hill. FS Muraoka. OLA* 118 (2003), 449-71; M. Wagner, *Die lexikalischen und grammatikalischen Aramaismen im alttestamentlichen Hebräisch. BZAW* 96 (1966); C. Zimmermann, *Die Namen des Vaters* (Leiden, 2007), esp. 271ff.

I. Etymology, Forms, and Lexical Field. In Aramaic, the noun /malk/ "king" served as the usual term for those who held institutionalized and generally dynastic sole dominion since the beginning of the literary tradition, regardless of the extent of the region governed. The root *mlk* that underlies this noun and various other forms is common Semitic, but the semantic field "royal dominion" that dominates in West Semitic may represent a concretization of an older overarching meaning "to advise, decide."[1] It remained in use in Akkadian, which usually employs the noun *šarru* for "king," but also still occurs sporadically later in Aramaic.

The *qatl* form /malk/[2] for this word was apparently widespread primarily in northern and central Syria. In contrast, the *qitl* form /milk/ dominated in the southern and northwestern linguistic realms given the evidence of Phoenician and Ammonite names preserved in transcriptions.[3] It is unknown why the *qatl* form (preserved in the base form before suffixes, such as *malkī*) as in Aramaic prevailed in Hebrew rather than the expected Canaanite form, and whether it entered the later vocalization as an Aramaism.[4] If one considers the *qatil* form /malik/ original, which East Semitic also knew and Arabic still preserves, then both Aramaic /malk/ and Canaanite /milk/ would have developed from it secondarily.[5]

In addition to the masculine noun, the feminine counterpart /malkā/ "queen" also appears occasionally, although, in the absence of further information, debate continues as to whether in individual cases such as Dnl. 5:10 it refers to the (chief-)wife of the king or to his mother. Furthermore, Aramaic employs the feminine abstract /malkū/[6] frequently in the absolute or in combinations. Aramaic employs all of these nouns for divine beings and their dominion, too.

The related verb *mlk* "to be or become king, to rule" occurs mostly in the G-stem, in older Aramaic also in the transitive causative-stem "to make king" (with a deity as subject). It is noticeably less common than the nouns, since → *šlṭ* usually denotes "to rule" and can be supplemented with a prepositional expression following *b-* or *ʿl* "over."

As a fixed term for the head of an at least rudimentarily centralized state structure, /malk/ and its nearest derivatives have no exact synonyms and can, in certain cases, appear with the honorific → *mrʾ* "lord." Other terms such as *rbn* "great one"[7] or → *rʾš* "chief, leader," sporadically also → *ngd* III "prince" denote status or relative position, not a specific office associated with sovereign power. They may have served as a title for tribal princes of individual, smaller regions whose spheres of influence lay at the periphery of the royal capitals of Syria-Palestine and flourished within their own clans in the shadow of the central power.

Finally, the same root *mlk* occurs in isolation in Aramaic in the semantic field of "advice." This could also be the meaning of the originally masculine *qitl* noun /milk/

1. So, e.g., *ATTM*, 624; according to *GesB*[18], 685, however, two homonymous roots are more likely.
2. In Aramaic since the fifth century B.C.E. /maląk/, *ATTM*, 112-15.
3. For the distribution, cf. van Soldt.
4. K. Beyer, *Althebräische Grammatik* (Göttingen, 1969), 48.
5. Ibid.; *ATTM*, 624; van Soldt, 470.
6. From */malkūt/, whose /-t/ has disappeared in Aramaic in the abs.: *ATTM*, 97.
7. → *rb*.

(Aramaic /melk/), while Canaanite /milk/ "king" arose from */malik/ (see above). The related verbal root *mlk* "to advise, decide, discuss" also occurs only in isolation. Usually, Aramaic employs forms of the verbal root → *yʿṭ* "to advise" instead.

Nouns of various forms of the root *mlk* appear very often already since the earliest period as theophoric elements in West Semitic personal names. They may involve more a divine title than the name of a specific god,[8] although /milk/ "advice" also occurs.[9] Masculine names with /malk-/ at the beginning could all be abbreviated /Malkā/. They were common over a long period, as Μάλχος in Jn. 18:10 demonstrates, for example.

II. Noun "King." In the changing social and political conditions of Syria-Palestine from the Aramaic principalities of the Iron Age via the ancient Near Eastern empires of the Assyrians, Babylonians, and Persians, to the Hellenistic dominion and the Romans with their vassal kings in the eastern provinces, the same term *mlk* /malk/ "king" was used for forms of monarchial dominion in widely varied institutional and social contexts and over regions with highly varied territorial extent. As a title, *mlkʾ* in the determined state usually follows the name, but sporadically precedes it (Dnl. 2:28,46; 4:15; 5:9,11; 6:10).

1. The Iron Age Syrian Principalities. Initially, *mlk* served as the self-designation of Syro-Palestinian princes who, in the course of the political, economic, and cultural revolutions of the early Iron Age, seized their chances and rose to the top of a ruling dynasty. These principalities consolidated in steps after 1000 B.C.E. to more strongly centralized minor states equipped with a capital city and palace and with a society increasingly based on the division of labor, at least at the center. This development included the establishment of an official cult of a patron god of the ruling dynasty, to whom it owed its kingdom (→ IV), and the standardization of a local written language for administration and representation.[10]

The Aramaic inscriptions from the tenth through the eighth centuries B.C.E. originated primarily through royal commissions, as indicated by the self-introduction at the beginning.[11] They recall the prince's military campaigns,[12] construction activity,[13] alliances,[14] and piety.[15] In them, "king" refers to equal-ranking, sole rulers of minor regions who, because they shared a disposition, continually competed for influence and prestige, the motivation for the military reports[16] and the concern that memory of them might be erased.[17] Texts from Sam'al in the north[18] and the Transjordan in the south[19] follow the same rhetoric.

---

8. Cf. H.-P. Müller, *DDD*², 538-42, for an overview of the material and bibliography.
9. Van Soldt.
10. Cf. Gzella, 56-63.
11. *KAI* 309.1; 201.1f.; 202 A 1.
12. *KAI* 202; 310.
13. *KAI* 202.
14. *KAI* 222-224.
15. *KAI* 309; 201.
16. *KAI* 202 A 4ff.
17. *KAI* 202 B 18ff.; 320.
18. *KAI* 214-215.
19. *KAI* 181.

Therefore, the term *mlk* is ubiquitously frequent. In contrast, even high-ranking offices refer to themselves as → *ʿbd* "servants" in relation to the king.[20]

2. *The Empires of the First Millennium.* With the ascent of the three successive ancient Near Eastern empires, first the Assyrian, which fully incorporated the originally independent Aramaic city states of Syria until circa the mid-eighth century B.C.E., then the Babylonians and the Persians, each of which linked to its predecessor, the implications of the title "king" changes. Henceforth, it referred primarily to the emperor, such as that of Assyria (*mlk ʾšwr*), to whom the Syro-Palestinian vassals related as an → *ʿbd* "servant" to his → *mrʾ* "lord" and now proudly emphasize their loyalty.[21] A Philistine prince could also address the pharaoh as "lord of kings."[22] Thus, they employed the same diction as the Assyrian functionaries who spoke of *mrʾy mlkʾ* "my lord the king."[23] Within their own spheres of influence, however, these minor kings continued to act as sovereign rulers. Consequently, the prince of Gosan, already under Assyrian influence in the ninth century B.C.E., called himself *mlk* "king" in the Aramaic version of a bilingual inscription to Hadad,[24] but in the Akkadian *šakin* "governor." Other Assyrian vassals also emphasized later that their fathers had been kings.[25] In addition, Aramaic attests the concept of the "royal weight" as an authoritative unit of measure[26] beginning with this time.

Aramaic sources document the Neo-Babylonian period poorly.[27] In contrast, the Achaemenid kingdom left a clear deposit. Most Imperial Aramaic instances contain *mlkʾ* as a title of the Achaemenid ruler in the typical date formulas at the beginning of private documents[28] and official correspondence,[29] and even after Alexander the Great this dating system persisted in Bactria.[30] Here, the superlative title *mlk mlkyʾ* "king of kings," whose origins are not entirely clear (Babylonian or Persian?), was also common. The formulation *bʾbny mlkʾ* "according to the royal weight(-stone)" for an authoritative measurement is also common in legal texts,[31] just as is, occasionally, the attribute "of the king" in the description of official facilities like *šwq* "(king's) street,"[32] *ʾwṣr* "storehouse"[33] or *dyn* "judge."[34]

20. Cf. the Kuttamuwa inscription: D. G. Pardee, "A New Aramaic Inscription from Zincirli," *BASOR* 356 (2007) 51-71, l. 1.

21. E.g., *KAI* 216.3; 217.3f.

22. *KAI* 266.1.

23. *KAI* 233.8,17.

24. *KAI* 309.

25. *KAI* 216.

26. → *mnī* IV.

27. On the issue of the rise of Aramaic generally, cf. Gzella, 124-50; the Assyrian period already speaks of a *mlk bbl* "king of Babel," *KAI* 233,4.

28. *TADAE* B.

29. *TADAE* A4.

30. J. Naveh and S. Shaked, *Aramaic Documents from Ancient Bactria (Fourth Century B.C.E.)* (London, 2012), no. C4,1f.

31. For instances → *ʾbn*; rarer, as in *TADAE* B2.11,11 or 3.9,8, *bmtqlt* "according to the weight of."

32. *TADAE* B3.4,8, etc.

33. *TADAE* B3.4,9, etc.

34. *TADAE* B5.1,3; → *dīn*.

The literature paints a complex image of empire. In the pre-Achaemenid proverbs of Aḥiqar, which probably originated in the circle of court officials,[35] the king is the undisputed authority[36] and embodiment of majesty.[37] The framework narrative by the same name that relates the fall and rehabilitation of the high official depicts the king as merciful and with integrity.

In contrast, the book of Daniel accentuates both the opportunities and the danger that service at court offers for Jewish exiles. Nebuchadnezzar in Dnl. 2–4 like Darius in Dnl. 6 appears as aware of their power, but legitimate and benevolent,[38] yet simultaneously the victim of intrigues at court, who attain awareness of the true God, whose kingdom surpasses any on earth. Belshazzar in Dnl. 5, meanwhile, is a decadent evildoer who hastens his deserved fate. The central theme is the tension between the finite earthly and the eternal divine kingdoms (→ III).

Ezra also emphasizes the merits of the Achaemenid kings for Jewish religion and culture. As in Daniel, *mlk'* functions here as a pervasive title.

The feminine form *mlkh* /malkā/ in Dnl. 5:10 denotes the "queen" (or "queen mother"); in any case, the king's spouse was original designated by → *šgl*.[39]

3. The Local Kingdoms of the Hellenistic and Roman Periods. After the collapse of Hellenistic dominion, local kingdoms with dynastic legitimacy and their own cultural self-identification arose again in Arabia, Syria, and Palestine.[40] Their rulers renewed the title *mlk* and hearkened back, in part, to older royal traditions,[41] but, with the expansion of Rome, became vassals of the Caesar.[42] The inscriptions erected in great number at this time as representations, or expressions of individual *memoria* or personal piety, employ the title *mlk* sometimes in the dedicatory formula "for the life of the king";[43] in addition, the dating formula also appears, often, e.g., in the Nabatean contracts from the Dead Sea.[44] In a monolingual Aramaic inscription, Queen (*mlkt'*)[45] Zenobia of Palmyra even employed the title *mlk mlk'* "king of kings."[46] Once again, subordinates called the king → *mr'* "lord."

Narrative Aramaic texts from Qumran designate the mythical kings of the patriarchal era with *mlk*, as in the accounts of Abraham's wanderings in 1QapGen 20–22; a court

35. Cf. Gzella, 150-53.

36. *TADAE* C1.1, 84-88.

37. *TADAE* C1.1, 92.

38. Regarding the "charismata of the king," cf. K. Koch, *Daniel 1–4. BK* XXII/1 (2005), 190-97.

39. See B. Landsberger, "Akkadisch-hebräische Wortgleichungen," in *Hebräische: Wortforschung. FS W. Baumgartner. SVT* 16 (1967), 198-204.

40. Gzella, 212-80.

41. Cf. briefly H. Gzella, "Die Palmyrener in der griechisch-römischen Welt," *KLIO* 87 (2005) 451.

42. On this and the graphic representation of the underlying self-consciousness, although articulated variously locally, cf. A. Kropp, *Images and Monuments of Near Eastern Dynasts, 100 BC-AD 100* (Oxford, 2013).

43. → *ḥyī* IV.1.

44. Instances in *ATTM*, 2, 431.

45. *PAT* 0317.6.

46. *PAT* 0292.1; the Greek counterpart in 0317 is destroyed.

narrative set among the Achaemenids,[47] the Persian kings; and the introduction of Tobit, in accord with its literary setting, the Assyrian kings.[48] Nabonidus's prayer,[49] the vision of the four trees,[50] and the son of God text[51] are similarly associated with court narratives, but orient the sequence of worldly empires[52] to the kingdom of God. Otherwise, *mlk* functions as a title of God.

III. As a Divine Title. Since divine dominion represented the prototype of any human kingdom and the gods granted royalty,[53] *mlk* like → *mr'* "lord" also served as a widespread divine title. It may have gained added impetus with the experience of universal dominion through the ancient Near Eastern empires (→ II.2)—instead of the earlier dominions that were strictly limited in territory. Thus, the Old Aramaic title *'lh* (*mr'*) *šmyn*/*šmy'* "God (Lord) of heaven"[54] became "King of heaven."

With the expression in his hymn (Dnl. 4:34), King Nebuchadnezzar, having regained his senses, designated God, whose power transcends any human dominion and assigns it its due place;[55] a private letter from Hermopolis already attests a *mlkt šmyn* in Aramaic.[56] The title *mr' mlkn* "lord of kings" in Nebuchadnezzar's confession in Dnl. 2:47 applies a term previously utilized for earthly emperors (→ II.1)[57] to God. Yet, the kingdom of God expected at the end of time does not compete with the worldly powers, temporally limited and with determined courses. Instead, it constitutes the consummation, surpassing them (→ IV).

The Aramaic texts from Qumran also take up this terminology in hymnic style, although God's royal power appears with much greater prominence in the songs of praise composed in Hebrew and inspired by the style of the Psalms.[58] The title *mlk šmy'* as in Dnl. 4:34 occurs, however, in 1QapGen 2:14[59] and in 4Q196 17 2:6, as emended following the Greek text of Tob. 13:7; contrarily, in 1QapGen 10:10 and probably to be emended in 2:4 *mlk kwl 'lmy'* "king of all eternity" (21:2: *mrh 'lmu'*). In these formulas, then, *mlk* and *mr'* are generally interchangeable. 4Q196 18:5 (Tob. 13:15) has *mlk' rb'* "the great king." In the phrase *whw' mlk 'l kl rḥš* "and he (= God) is king over every crawling being" in 11Q10 37:2 (Job 41:26), *mlk* is adopted from the Hebrew. Moreover, it continues to be ultimately uncertain precisely which of the very fragmentary instances refer to God and which to earthly kings; both may occur.

---

47. 4Q550.
48. 4Q196 2:6-9 (Tob. 1:21f.).
49. 4Q242 1-3:1.
50. 4Q552 1:8.
51. 4Q246 1 1:2.
52. 4Q246 1 1:6 preserves *mlk 'twr* "king of Asshur."
53. → V on the causative-stem of the verb *mlk*.
54. →*'lh* II.2-3.
55. Cf. Koch, 214-23 and 438-42.
56. *TADAE* A2.1,1.
57. In *KAI* 266 for the pharaoh; Koch, 237f.
58. See Leuenberger, 689-96.
59. Otherwise more frequently with "lord": 11:13,15; 12:17; 22:16,21, there also with *w'r°* "and of the earth."

IV. Abstract "Kingship." The feminine abstract noun /malkū/ can also designate either a human or a divine dominion. In the first sense, it often refers to power as such or the form of the dominion (Dnl. 7:24; in 6:5 in the sense of "administration"). This is also the meaning in the oldest known specimen, a curse formula from Sefire that threatens the treaty-breaker that his kingdom should become *kmlkt ḥl* "like a kingdom of sand."[60] This nuance also underlies compound expressions involving the insignia of kingship: *byt* (Dnl. 4:27) or *hykl* (4:26; for God: 4Q212 1 4:18) "royal palace, residence" and *krs'* "throne." In some cases, however, *mlkw* also means the regnal period in dates[61] or the territory reigned (also attested in Biblical Aramaic: Dnl. 4:15; 5:11; 6:2,4,8; Ezr. 7:13,23).

Since God is also designated a king (→ III), the term *mlkw* also denotes his dominion already in older Aramaic. This may already be true of the beginning of the proverbs of Aḥiqar,[62] where the context is preserved only imperfectly, however. In the court tales of the book of Daniel, the relationship between human and divine (thus eternal: Dnl. 3:33; 4:31; 7:14,27) dominion becomes the central theme; consequently, the word *mlkw* appears very often in Dnl. 2–7.

The *mlkwt 'n(w)š'* "human kingship" is subordinate to the divine (repeated formulaically in Dnl. 4:14,22,29; 5:21); the kingdom of God, which dawns at the end of time, completes and surpasses all preceding worldly kingdoms (Dnl. 7:14,27). Thus, the experience of religious oppression became bearable, because even the greatest evil is finite. The investiture of an enigmatic anthropomorphic figure (in the modern era often identified with the people of God, but in any case a symbol of their triumph),[63] who, in addition to the kingdom also receives → *yqr* "honor" and *šlṭn* "control,"[64] symbolizes the beginning of the kingdom of God in the vision of Dnl. 7.

Alongside the human[65] and the divine kingdom,[66] the texts from Qumran also employ the *mlkwt khnwt'* "royal priesthood,"[67] which was enhanced in value with the loss of political power.

Under Aramaic influence, /malkūt/ increasingly replaced the formerly more common synonym /mamlakā/ in Hebrew (which retained the /-t/ of the absolute state) in exilic and postexilic times. Consequently, it serves as a criterion for dating biblical texts.[68]

---

60. *KAI* 222 A 25; for the reading, see J. A. Fitzmyer, *The Aramaic Inscriptions of Sefire. BietOr* 19/A (^{2}1995), 83f.

61. So more often in Biblical Aramaic: Dnl. 5:26; 6:29; Ezr. 4:24; 6:15; further in a private contract from Samaria, Dušek, no. 1, l. 1.

62. *TADAE* C1.1,79.

63. Cf. J. J. Collins, *Daniel. Herm* (1993), 304-10.

64. → *šlṭ*.

65. Employed temporally: 4Q553 6 1:4; politically: 4Q246 1 2:2; 4Q550; eschatologically for the foreign nations: 4Q554 3 3:15,21; and further in a few fragments of 4Q243.

66. In praise: 4Q203 9:6, similarly probably 4Q213 1-2 2:16; in a vision: 4Q246 1 2:5.

67. 1Q21 1:2; → *khn*.

68. Wagner, 130f.

Some dispute whether the rare *mlk* in the meaning "kingdom" in Old Aramaic[69] represents an expansion of /malk/ (cf. Dnl. 7:17) or some other nominal form (perhaps /molk/).[70]

V. Verb "to Rule." The verb *mlk* "to be, become king; to rule" with a person or a realm as subject is also already multiply attested in Old Aramaic, and thereafter only rarely. The G-stem is intransitive and can take as a supplement a prepositional expression indicating the region governed. A treaty of state from Sefire contains at least one clear example of this construction with the proposition *b-* (*mlky' zy ymlkn b'rpd* "the kings who rule in Arpad");[71] it could denote, however, either the seat of dominion itself (cf. Josh. 13:21) or the region ruled. It is employed absolutely in *KAI* 222 A 25,[72] while 222 B 6 probably contains the noun, not the verb.[73] In Sam'alian, *mlk* appears with the preposition *'l* "over."[74] Thereafter, the verb apparently first reappears at Qumran. It is certainly a verb in 4Q246 1 2:2 (imperfect) with *'l* "over" and without any complement in 4Q196 2:4 (Tob. 1:21) and 4Q550 1,7; all refer to rulers of earthly empires.

The transitive causative-stem "to install as king" also occurs in two Old Aramaic royal inscriptions, indeed with the respective patron deity as subject, since those who commissioned the inscriptions traced their dominion to divine favor: once in the Zakkur inscription,[75] and second in the Tell Dan stele.[76] Judging from context, Sam'alian seems in *mlkh* to have an unusual D-stem in Aramaic with the same meaning "he made him king."[77] In addition, in Syriac, the causative stem represents "to rule."[78]

VI. Verb "to Advise" and Noun "Advice." With the meaning "to advise, decide, promise," the root *mlk* is identifiable, probably beginning with Imperial Aramaic. In the sense of "to promise (someone) something," transitive with a direct object and an indirect object following *l-*, it seems to appear in a letter from the Aršama archives,[79] said here of persons, as also later often in Syriac.[80] Aramaic may have lent it to Hebrew, where it occurs as a middle N-stem form "to take counsel with one's self."[81] Otherwise, the verb appears with this meaning only in the post-Christian, Aramaic literary languages.[82] Its frequency there demonstrates that it remained productive in Aramaic.

69. *KAI* 222 B 6; 310.6.
70. Cf. Fitzmyer, 101.
71. *KAI* 222 B 22.
72. → *ḥlm* III.1.
73. → IV and → *ṭīb* IV.
74. *KAI* 214.20f., in a fragmentary context also l. 24.
75. *KAI* 202 A 3 and afterward partially emended in l. 13.
76. *KAI* 310.4.
77. *KAI* 215.7.
78. *LexSyr*, 392.
79. *TADAE* A6.15,4.
80. *LexSyr*, 391b.
81. Wagner, 77; *GesB*[18], 685.
82. *DJPA*, 310; *DJBA*, 680; *LexSyr*, 391f.; *MdD*, 273.

The masculine noun /melk/ "advice, decision"[83] first appears in Aramaic after the difficult passage in Deir ʿAllā II:9 with certainty in Dnl. 4:24 for Daniel's warning to Nebuchadnezzar that he should do penance for his sins with good works in order to avoid the punishment threatened in the dream. The texts from Qumran preserve a few additional specimens. The passage in Enoch concerning the fall of the angels employs it for their decision to wed human women.[84] In contrast, it has a positive connotation in the prophecy of the birth of Noah as a designation for the wisdom of God's chosen.[85] Syriac knows several other nominal forms and verbal stems of *mlk* "to advise."[86] The noun also survived in Aramaic, while Canaanite replaced it with the homonymous secondary by-form /milk/ from /malik/ "king."

Gzella

83. Syriac later /molk-/; *LexSyr*, 392a.

84. 4Q201 1 3:2 par. 4Q202 1 2:7 (1 En. 6:4); similarly probably in 4Q531 26:1 from the Book of Giants.

85. 4Q534 1 1:7, beside *ʿrmwm[h* "his wisdom."

86. *LexSyr*, 392.

מלל *mll*; מלה *mlh* /mellā/; ממלל *mmll* /mamlal/; אמר *ʾmr*; לאמר *lʾmr* /lēmar/; דברה *dbrh* /dabarā/

I. Root and Lexical Field. II. Old and Imperial Aramaic. III. Biblical Aramaic. 1. Daniel. 2. In the Greek Translations. IV. Qumran. V. "To Speak," Particle Introducing Speech, and Related Terms.

I. Root and Lexical Field. The root *mll* is typical of Aramaic. The related feminine noun /mellā/ "word, thing"[1] constitutes the origin of the denominal verb *mll* in the

J. Bergman, H. Lutzmann, and W. H. Schmidt, "דָּבַר *dābhar*," *TDOT*, IV, 84-125; J. A. Fitzmyer, *The Aramaic Inscriptions of Sefire*. *BietOr* 19A (²1995); G. Gerleman, "דָּבָר *dābār* word," *TLOT*, 325-32; H. Gzella, "*dbr*," *ThWQ*, II, 700-706; H. Lozachmeur, *La collection Clermont-Ganneau: Ostraca, épigraphes sur jarre, étiquettes de bois*, 2 vols. (Paris, 2006); C. Metzenthin, "*ʾmr*," *ThWQ*, I, 223-27; J. Naveh and S. Shaked, *Aramaic Documents from Ancient Bactria (Fourth Century* B.C.E.*)* (London, 2012); H. H. Schmid, "אמר *ʾmr* to say," *TLOT*, 159-62; S. Wagner, "אָמַר *ʾāmar*," *TDOT*, I, 328-45.

1. In plural with a masculine ending /mellīn/.

D-stem with the meaning "to pronounce words, to speak." In the sense of "word" (but not "thing"), the noun /mellā/ also appears in Hebrew.[2] The verb *mll* (D-stem) "to speak, announce" also occurs in Hebrew in a few passages (Gen. 21:7; Ps. 106:2; Job 8:2 and 33:3; presumably also in 1 Ch. 24:4,26). In Imperial Aramaic, however, the Persian loanword → *ptgm*[3] "edict" began to appear as a synonym for /mellā/ in the sense of "word."

Despite the phonetic similarity, Hebrew *mll* in the G-stem "to give a sign (by flicking the fingers)" in Prov. 6:13 is not related to *mll* "to speak."[4] Arabic *malla* "dictate" and *ʾimlā* "dictation" cannot be considered true cognates of the Aramaic verb either.[5]

II. Old and Imperial Aramaic. Early Old Aramaic preserves four instances of the noun *mlh* "word," all in the Sefire treaties of state.[6] It occurs in *KAI* 222 B 8 in reference to the words on the inscription: *wʾl tštq ḥdh mn mly sprʾ zn*[*h*] "And not one of the words in this inscription shall keep silent."[7] Furthermore, it appears in *KAI* 224.2 in the expression *mln lḥyt* "slanderous [lit.: evil] words," repeated as *mlyʾ* "the words" in the same line. The meaning "thing" may appear, at most, in the reconstruction of *KAI* 222 B 41,[8] if this conjecture is correct.

The verb *mll* is attested in context with the libelous words in *KAI* 224.2 (see above); the preceding lines contain the partially reconstructed expression *wy*[*ml*]*l ʿly* "and speaks against me" in the sense of an incantation against someone.

In the Imperial Aramaic corpus, a total of over forty unequivocal instances of *mlh* occur; of them, more than twenty-eight have the meaning "word," the rest "thing, matter, object."[9] An originally pre-Imperial Aramaic proverb of Aḥiqar attests the noun *mmll* /mamlal/: *rkyk mmll mlk* "soft is the speech of the king."[10] Although Aramaic literary languages of late antiquity employ it often, this is the sole example from older Aramaic. The form *mmll* in another proverb of Aḥiqar,[11] in contrast, is a participle of the verb: *ḥkym mmll ky* "a wise man speaks, because."[12]

The verb *mll* appears with certainty ten times, always in the meaning "to speak." Three of them are employed without prepositions,[13] the other seven with "about" *l* followed by

---

2. A total of thirty-eight times, of which thirty-four in Job alone, otherwise only in 2 S. 23:2; Ps. 19:5 and 139:4; Prov. 23:9.

3. Vocalized in Tiberian *piṯgām*.

4. Contra *GesB*[18], 668.

5. For similar only apparent agreements, see A. R. Millard, "Cognates Can Be Deceptive: Some Aramaic Distinctives," in M. J. Geller, J. C. Greenfield, and S. Weitzman, eds., *Studia Aramaica: New Sources and New Approaches* (Oxford, 1995), 145-49.

6. It may be possible to reconstruct two others, cf. Fitzmyer on I (= *KAI* 222) B 25f. and 41.

7. See similarly *KAI* 222 C 17.18.

8. Fitzmyer, 114.

9. Including a few new examples from the Clermont-Ganneau ostraca, see the references in Lozachmeur, 543 s.v.

10. *TADAE* C1.1,84, → *lšn* II.

11. *TADAE* C1.1,114.

12. On the context → *ḥkm* III.2.

13. *TADAE* B8.8,4.8.9.

the person.[14] If the context yields a negative connotation, the expression can also mean, "to speak against someone,"[15] hardly "to speak to someone," however.[16]

III. Biblical Aramaic.

1. Daniel. Biblical Aramaic knows five instances of the verb *mll*, all in Daniel. In 6:22 it refers to Daniel's speech to Darius, the other four stand in relation to the arrogant speech of the "little horn" to the Most High in 7:8,11,20,25, as the last verse makes clear. This entire passage alludes to the rise of Antiochus IV Epiphanes and his claim to power, especially, however, to his assault on Jewish religious practice. It constituted a crime directly against the Most High, which required immediate punishment, as the vision and its interpretation in 7:1-28 both emphasize.

The noun *millā* (as vocalized there) occurs twenty-four times, once again exclusively in Daniel. It designates a "word" or a "pronouncement" and has a broad spectrum of meaning: the oral edict of the king in 2:5,8 and 6:13; the words of the Chaldeans, whom the king regards as devious and deceitful, in 2:9; a command in 3:22,28; Nebuchadnezzar's praise for his own deeds in Babylon in 4:28; God's judgment on him in 4:30; the discussion between Belshazzar and his nobles in 5:10; the words of the "small horn" against the Most High in 7:11,25. It may well also involve written words like the judgment saying on the wall in 5:15,26.[17] In 7:1, *rēš millīn* designates the beginning of a vision report whose conclusion 7:8 depicts with *millᵉṯā* "the word."

The use of *millā* in the sense of "thing" is also attested. Thus, it refers in 2:10[2×],11,23 to King Nebuchadnezzar's repeated challenge to the Chaldeans to report his dream to him; in 2:15,17 to the command to execute the wise men who have proven incapable of satisfying the demands of the king; and in 6:15 to the accusations against Daniel who continued to pray to his God and, thus, transgressed the command of King Darius. The plural *millayyā* "the things" refers in 7:16 to the overall view of the heavenly court as one of the divine beings portrayed it to the visionary. Here, then, the word refers to a supernatural reality accessible only with divine assistance.

2. In the Greek Translations. Finer nuances in meaning and usage both of *mll* and of *mlh* can be determined with the aid of the original (unrevised) Greek translation (Old Greek [OG]) in comparison with Theodotion's rendition (Th). Essentially, both versions employ the Greek λαλεῖν for the verb *mll*. In 7:8, however, based on the context, OG has, for *mᵉmallil raḇrᵉḇān* "saying great things," ἐποίει πόλεμον πρὸς τοὺς ἁγίους "there was war against the holy ones." In contrast, the rendering in Th, as would be expected, is literal λαλοῦν μεγάλα "saying great things."

Greek generally rendered the noun *millā* in the meaning "word" with ῥῆμα or λόγος. In a few passages, the translation is idiomatic, however. Thus, OG has instead for *millā* in the Aramaic text of Dnl. 3:22,28 πρόσταγμα (3:22) and προσταγή (3:95 OG), both of

14. *TADAE* B8.5,6.11.14; 8.6,4.8; D2.34,2; 5.56,2.
15. Porten and Yardeni render it neutrally, however in *TADAE*.
16. *Pace ATTM*, 625; but cf. *ATTM*, 2, 432: "against."
17. → *mnī*.

which mean "command, directive," in contrast to the literal counterpart ῥῆμα in Th. In 5:26, OG has σύγκριμα τῆς γραφῆς "the interpretation of the writing," which is indeed the meaning of *pšr mlt'* in this context, again in contrast to the more literal counterpart σύγκριμα τοῦ ῥήματος "the interpretation of the word" in Th. When *millā* refers to "thing, matter," Th also tends toward a literal rendering with ῥῆμα or λόγος. Here, too, OG mirrors, instead, the specific sense in context. Meanwhile, in 2:10 it has ὃ ἑώρακε "what (the king) saw" for *millaṯ malkā* "the word of the king" and τοιοῦτο πρᾶγμα "such a matter" for *millā kiḏnā* "a word like this." Similarly, πρόσταγμα "command, directive" appears in 2:15. In all these passages, as elsewhere, Th has a literal translation. Nonetheless, his ὅραμα "vision" in 2:23 is more precise than ταῦτα "these (things)" in OG.

IV. Qumran. The Aramaic texts from Qumran have thirty-eight instances of the noun *mlh*. Of them, only four are singular. Clear are *mlh [b'y]š'* "an [ev]il word" in 4Q550 7+7a:2 and *m' 'ṭr ml' nš[m']* "what whisper of a word could we hear?" in 11Q10 10:5 (Job 26:14). The fragmentary context of 4Q531 40:2 and 4Q546 20:1 prohibits a conclusion concerning the exact nuance. The other thirty-four instances are plural; of them, a few refer to individual words, others to their context, i.e., the speech. In some usages, the speech intended is part of a divine revelation: the word of the Lord of Heaven to Noah in 1QapGen 7:7; the words of the holy ones in 4Q212 1 5:16 (1 En. 93:11); those of the Watchers in 4Q201 1 1:3 (1 En. 1:2); or of Rafael in 4Q197 4 2:19 (Tob. 6:18).

The expression *mly ḥkmth* "words of wisdom" in 4Q213 1 1:19 (T. Levi) refers to wise statements, much as "words of the commandments" in 4Q232 1-3:1 intend the commandment itself, or "words of the vision" in 4Q543 1a-c:1 (in the superscription of the Testament of Amram), the vision itself and "words of truth" in 4Q204 1 6:8 (1 En. 13:10) the accurate report of the subsequent vision, cf. further "the book of the words of truth" in 4Q204 1 6:9 (1 En. 14:1). In a text "(the book of the) words of Enoch" (1QapGen 19:25) or "words of Noah" (1QapGen 5:29) refer simultaneously to the deeds of these famed patriarchs and their memorable statements. The other passages preserved from Qumran for which sufficient context has been preserved employ the noun in an entirely literal sense, i.e., for words spoken by humans.

The verb *mll* occurs in the Aramaic from Qumran forty-five times and essentially has the meaning "to speak." Nine instances appear in 1QapGen, seven with the preposition *'m* "to speak with someone" (2:7,8,13,18; 5:25; 6:14; 11:15), one without preposition (*mmlyn* "they spoke" in 20:8), and perhaps one other in an unclear context (*mllt* "I spoke" in 7:10). Of the eleven specimens in 11Q10, eight are employed absolutely: 10:10; 14:3; 21:8; 22:7,8; 23:9; 37:5,6; two again with the preposition *'m*: 35:5,6; and one with the preposition *qdm*: 7A,4, also with the meaning "to speak with someone"; cf. 4Q204 1 6:7. Several texts utilize *mll* with *'l* in the sense of "to speak about something": 4Q541 2 1:7 *[wm]llt 'lwhy b'wḥydw'n* "I spoke about him in riddles"; in certain contexts, the combination takes on the nuance "to speak against someone" as in 4Q541 9 1:6 and 4Q196 17 2:7 (Tob. 13:8).[18] The precise nuance of the verb in the other passages can no longer be deduced because of their fragmentary contexts, even when the reading of the verb itself is clear.

18. Regarding the use of the various prepositions with this verb and the official character of *qdm* here, cf. also H. Gzella, "*dbr*," 701.

V. "To Speak," Particle Introducing Speech, and Related Terms. The verb *mll* "to speak" stands in close relation to the act of expression itself and should be clearly distinguished from *'mr* "to say," which is oriented toward the content of the speech. Since *mll* primarily designates the process of speaking, then, the actual content must be introduced independently by a preposition such as *l* "concerning." In the case of *'mr*, it is not necessary, although with it the content must be indicated. With *mll,* it can be omitted. The usage of *mll* is generally limited to human or divine subjects, which is not true of *'mr*. The difference between these two verbs corresponds to that between *dbr* (piel) and *'mr* in Hebrew.[19]

The form *l'mr*, grammatically the preposition *l*- with the infinitive of the G-stem of *'mr*, regularly introduces speech, often after a verb of speech, just like Hebrew *lēmōr*. Imperial Aramaic attests it at least sixty-five times, sixty-three of which are in various documentary texts from Egypt, the remaining two in the letter ostracon from Asshur.[20] Remarkably, such an infinitive of the G-stem without the prefix /m-/ is atypical in Imperial Aramaic since at this time the prefixed form was already widespread.[21] Presumably, the speech introduction *l'mr* itself is a fixed form that Imperial Aramaic adopted from an older phase of the language[22] or the result of a process of grammaticalization based on the literal meaning "to say." Since, however, along with the Imperial Aramaic instances from Egypt in the Achaemenid period, *l'mr* also occurs in exactly the same function in the pre-Achaemenid letter ostracon from Asshur written in Babylon, this process cannot be traced to contact with a specific language.[23]

Furthermore, one should note that the form of the typical infinitive of this root was, as expected, *lm'mr*[24] or, in phonetic spelling, *lmmr*[25] since late Old Aramaic. The Aramaic documents from Bactria also attest the first variant twice.[26] In Biblical Aramaic, even the particle for introducing speech has the form of the typical infinitive of the G-stem, like *l^emēmar* in Ezr. 5:11, a form that also occurs in the Targums and presumably corresponds to Hebrew *lēmōr*.

In the Aramaic of Daniel, *'mr* follows the perfect of the verb → *'nī* "to answer"[27] in the participle and functions in these passages as an introduction of speech: 2:7,10; 3:9,16; 5:10; 6:14. In twenty-three passages in Daniel, *'nī* also takes the form of the participle,

19. See W. H. Schmidt, "*dbr* III"; the many instances from Old and Imperial Aramaic are cataloged in D. Schwiderski, *Die alt- und reichsaramäischen Inschriften,* vol. I: *Konkordanz*. *FSBP* 1 (2008), 52-57.

20. *KAI* 233.

21. In the Old Aramaic of western and central Syria, the infinitive without /m-/ was still in use, although only prefixed forms appear in the Tell Fekheriye Inscription: *lm'rk* in *KAI* 309,7.14; *lmld* and *lmšm'* in l. 9; and *lmlqḥ* in l. 10; see H. Gzella, *A Cultural History of Aramaic*. *HO* 111 (2015), 43,65,74,116f.,163.

22. Gzella, 143.

23. Cf. also H. Gzella, review of N. Pat-El, *Studies in the Historical Syntax of Aramaic*, *Hugoye* 17 (2014) 147f.

24. *TADAE* C1.1, 163; D7.39,10.

25. *TADAE* A4.9,2.

26. Naveh and Shaked, A1,5 and B1,4.

27. With no preceding speech, often in the meaning "to begin."

e.g., in 2:5. This is doubtless a consequence of the expanding use of the participle as a historical present;[28] such is precisely the case now in the letter of a Bactrian official.[29] Yet, if *'mr* occurs with the more specific sense "to command," it does not appear as a participle to express the historical present.

The G-stem infinitive *m'mr* is also employed as a masculine "statement, command," as in *w^e^mēmar qaddīšīn* "the command of the Holy Ones" (Dnl. 4:14) and *k^e^mēmar kāh^a^nayyā d̲ī b̲īrūš^e^lœm* "on the promise of the priests who are in Jerusalem" (Ezr. 6:9). Furthermore, the same usage also underlies a few texts from Qumran where one also finds the nuance "statement" or "speech."[30]

The Persian loanword *pit̲gām* serves in Biblical Aramaic generally as a synonym of *millā*, but it can also take on specific, technical administrative nuances such as "decision, verdict" in Dnl. 4:14.[31] "Edict"[32] in Ezr. 6:11 or simply "word"[33] in Ezr. 4:17; further "report"[34] in Ezr. 5:7,11. In Dnl. 3:16 the word appears in the combination *'al d^e^nā pit̲gām* "concerning this matter" in reference to Nebuchadnezzar's threatening instruction for the three young men in v. 15 not to resist the veneration of his god. Theodotion translates *pit̲gām* in Dnl. 3:16 simply with ῥῆμα "word," although in Dnl. 4:14[35] with the here synonymous λόγος. In 3:16, the original Greek translation hits the sense with ἐπιταγή "instruction" more precisely than "matter," as many modern translations; it is absent, meanwhile, in the corresponding section of 4:14.

The noun /dabarā/[36] "matter" occurs only in the compound conjunction *'al dib̲rat̲ dī* to express purpose, "so that" (Dnl. 2:30)[37] and the synonymous *'ad̲ dib̲rat̲ dī* (Dnl. 4:14).[38] It occurs at Qumran in 11Q10 34:4 (Job 40:8) and as a compound preposition in 1:7 (Job 18:4) *h'l db[rtk. . .]* "is it for your sake?" These are the only specimens from Qumran; both render Hebrew *lm'n*.

Gianto

---

28. See H. Gzella, *Tempus, Aspekt und Modalität im Reichsaramäischen. VOK* 48 (2004), 131-36, and idem, "Erscheinungsformen des historischen Präsens im Aramäischen," *Or* 74 (2005) 399-408, esp. 406-8.

29. Naveh and Shaked, A4,2; cf. H. Gzella, review of J. Naveh and S. Shaked, *Aramaic Documents from Ancient Bactria (Fourth Century B.C.E.) from the Khalili Collecitons*, *BiOr* 71 (2014) 821.

30. *ATTM*, 515; 2, 349.

31. In parallel with *š^e^'ēlt̲ā* "the legal affair."

32. Something decided; *t̩'m*.

33. As an answer to a letter.

34. In a letter.

35. 4:17 for him.

36. Tiberian *dib̲rā*.

37. Cf. *'l dbr zn* in an Aramaic letter from Bactria, Naveh and Shaked, A1,8, and generally → *dbr* V.1.

38. Probably resulting from the assimilation of *'al* with the subsequent *d*, see *BLA*, §260z.

מנדה *mndh* /maddā/

I. Etymology, Form, and Lexical Field. II. Imperial Aramaic. III. Biblical Aramaic. IV. Qumran.

I. Etymology, Form, and Lexical Field. The feminine /maddā/ "tribute" was borrowed from the Akkadian *maddattu*/*mandattu* from *nadānu* "to give."[1] Aramaic attests it beginning with the Achaemenid period. There it appears in Imperial Aramaic orthography as *mndh* with degemination of the long /dd/, which was original and probably preserved in pronunciation;[2] in addition, the phonetic spellings *mdh* and *md'* are attested later. The one Hebrew occurrence of *middā* in Neh. 5:4 with the same meaning may be due to Aramaic influence.[3]

Together with /helk/ and /belō/,[4] this word belongs among the most common terms for "tax" and "(interest) income" in Achaemenid administrative terminology. The finer semantic differences are difficult to determine, however. Among the later Aramaic languages, Syriac still attests it.[5]

II. Imperial Aramaic. The occurrences of *mndh* concentrate in letters from the Achaemenid administration,[6] contracts[7] and commercial documents.[8] These findings demonstrate that the word is an official term. The precise meaning in the context of private law[9] remains unclear.

III. Biblical Aramaic. In Biblical Aramaic, *middā*[10] occurs four times in Ezra. According to 6:8, where the phonetic spelling *mdt* of the construct state appears, it is part

---

H. Gzella, *A Cultural History of Aramaic. HO* 111 (2015); S. A. Kaufman, *The Akkadian Influences on Aramaic. AS* 19 (1974); H. Klinkott, "Steuern, Zölle und Tribute im Achaimenidenreich," in idem, S. Kubisch, and R. Müller-Wollermann, eds., *Geschenke und Steuern, Zölle und Tribute. CHANE* 29 (2007), 263-90; J. Naveh and S. Shaked, *Aramaic Documents from Ancient Bactria (Fourth Century* B.C.E.*)* (London, 2012); Y. Yadin et al., eds., *The Documents from the Bar Kokhba Period in the Cave of Letters II* (Jerusalem, 2002).

1. Kaufman, 67.
2. Gzella, 170f.
3. Skeptically, V. Mankowski, *Akkadian Loanwords in Biblical Hebrew. HSM* 47 (Winona Lake, IN, 2000), 84, but without convincing grounds, since orthography and late vocalization have no probative value.
4. → *hlk* IV.
5. *LexSyr*, 374f.
6. *TADAE* A6. 13,3.4 and 6.14,2.3.5, about the income of the estates of the Egyptian satraps; Naveh and Shaked, A8,2 about those of the king.
7. *TADAE* B3.6,7, probably about interest or rates; fragmentary 8.5,3 and 8.11,2.3.
8. *TADAE* C3.5,7, about a payment to "the troop" → *ḥyl*; very frequent in bills of lading C3.7.
9. *DNSI*, 656.
10. In the Tiberian vocalization.

of the royal income[11] of the region "beyond the river," from which the costs for the construction of the Jerusalem temple were to be raised. In the other three passages 4:13,20 and 7:24, it serves, in the traditional spelling *mndh*, along with the subsequent *blw* and *hlk* as a fixed cumulative expression for all the taxes of an entire province.

IV. Qumran. 1QapGen 21:26,27 employs *md'* and the suffixed *mdthwn* (both in phonetic spellings) for the tribute that the four emperors laid upon the five minor kings. In the first passage, it functions as the object of the verb *šwī* "to place upon," and in the second in the same function with → *yhb* "to give."

If the emendation *mn]dyn* in a Nabatean rental contract from the Dead Sea is correct,[12] the noun was also used later in the sense of "rate," but this reconstruction is uncertain.[13]

Gzella

11. *nksy mlk'*; → *nksyn*.
12. So nV 36:7 in *ATTM*, 2, 240f.
13. E.g., Yadin, 146 differs.

מנחה *mnḥh* /manaḥā/; עלה *'lh* /'alā/; נסך *nsk*; נסך *nsk* /nesk/; נחוח *nḥwḥ* /nīḥōḥ/

I. Etymology and Origin. II. Semantics. 1. Imperial Aramaic. 2. Biblical Aramaic. 3. Qumran. III. Lexical Field. 1. *'lh*. 2. Verb *nsk*, Noun *nsk*. 3. *nḥwḥ*. IV. LXX.

I. Etymology and Origin. With regard to the etymology of Hebrew *minḥā*[1] and its cognates, the starting point is a primary noun "delivery, contribution, tribute, gift." The

G. A. Anderson, *Sacrifices and Offerings in Ancient Israel. HSM* 41 (1987), esp. 27-34,57-75; C. Dohmen, "נָסַךְ *nāsak*," TDOT, IX, 455-60; H.-J. Fabry and M. Weinfeld, "מִנְחָה *minḥâ*," *TDOT*, VIII, 407-27; S. Germany, "*nsk*," *ThWQ*, II, 991-93; D. Kellerman, "עֹלָה/עוֹלָה *'ōlâ/'ôlâ*," *TDOT*, XI, 96-113; K. Koch, "נִיחוֹחַ *nîḥôaḥ*," *TDOT*, IX, 412-15; B. A. Mastin, "Daniel 2,46 and the Hellenistic World," *ZAW* 85 (1973) 80-93; A. Marx, *Les offrandes végétales dans l'Ancien Testament. SVT* 57 (1994); R. Rendtorff, *Leviticus. BK* III (2004), esp. 66-69,86-90; idem, *Studien zur Geschichte des Opfers im Alten Israel. WMANT* 24 (1967), esp. 42-50,53-59,61,74-118,169-98,235-39; A. Rohrmoser, *Götter, Tempel und Kulte der Judäo-Aramäer von Elephantine. AOAT* 396 (2014), 198-211,214-18; I. Willi-Plein, *Opfer und Kult im alttestamentlichen Israel. SBS* 153 (1993), esp. 79-90; F. Zanella, "*mnḥh*," *ThWQ*, II, 712-18.

1. From an older */manaḥā/, *ATTM*, 627f.

specimens in Ugaritic[2] and Phoenician[3] demonstrate this circumstance. As a sacrificial term, *mnḥh* appears in Phoenician in the temple tariffs of Kition[4] and Carthage[5] and in Mactar.[6] In Aramaic, *mnḥh* can only be found in Elephantine, Biblical Aramaic, and Qumran.[7] This distribution speaks for a borrowing from Hebrew.[8] In the respective contexts, *mnḥh* appears as a *terminus technicus* for a vegetable sacrifice and no longer in the general sense of "delivery," etc.

II. Semantics.

1. Imperial Aramaic. The texts *TADAE* A4.7 to 4.10 related to the destruction and reconstruction of the Yahu temple at Elephantine permit a few glimpses into the sacrificial praxis involving *mnḥh.*

Since the destruction of the temple, the offering of *mnḥh wlbw*[*n*]*h w'lwh* "food offerings, incense, and burnt sacrifice" was halted.[9] Thus, the whole agricultural operation succumbed. The sought-after reconstruction of the temple would reactivate it: *mḥt'* [*sic!*] *wlbwnt' w'lwt' yqrbwn 'l mdbḥ' zy yhw 'lh'* "one should bring the food offering and the incense and the burnt sacrifice to the altar of Yahu, the god."[10]

The response letter of the governors of Jerusalem and Samaria permitted the reconstruction of the Yahu temple in the same passages and then added:[11] *wmnḥt' wlbwnt' yqrbwn 'l mdbḥ' zk* "and one should present the food offering and the incense on this altar." In comparison to the petition, *TADAE* A4.7 par. 4.8 the lack of the *'lh* "burnt offering" since *TADAE* A4.9 permits only vegetable sacrifice and incense. Now, this lack of *'lh* is no accident, but intentional on the part of the governors of Jerusalem and Samaria. This finds confirmation in another letter from the head of the temple community from Elephantine to Jerusalem which mentions explicitly that no sheep, oxen, and goat sacrifices will be offered as *mqlw* "burnt offering, instead only incense and food offerings.[12] The grounds for this decision are probably complicated. Thus, one can suspect a review of the hegemonial efforts of the Second Temple in Jerusalem. In this case, one thinks of the Chnum priest of the island,[13] who, as a worshiper of the goat god Chnum, probably took offense at the offering of sheep, ox, and goat sacrifices in the vicinity of the Chnum temple. Moreover, real estate disputes between the Judeo-Arameans and the Egyptians may also have been involved.[14]

---

2. *KTU* 3.10,1; 4.91,1; cf. *DUL*³, 555.
3. *KAI* 43.13.
4. *KAI* 43.13.
5. *KAI* 60.14; 74.10.
6. *KAI* 145.13; cf. *DNSI*, 659.
7. Where it is also once spelled phonetically *mnḥ'*: 1QapGen 21:20.
8. Cf. C. Stadel, *Hebraismen in den aramäischen Texten vom Toten Meer* (Heidelberg, 2008), 26.
9. *TADAE* A4.7,21 par. 4.8,21.
10. *TADAE* A4.7,25f.; cf. 4.8,24f.
11. → *dbḥ* V.1; *TADAE* A4.9,9f.
12. TADAE A4.10,10f.
13. *TADAE* A4.7,4-6 par. 4.8,4-6.
14. Cf. Rohrmoser, 153-290.

2. *Biblical Aramaic.* Biblical Aramaic evidences two instances of *minḥā*. The edict of Artaxerxes instructs Ezra to buy steers, goats, and lambs from the royal treasury "and your food and drink offerings" (*ūminḥāṯhōn wᵉniskēhōn*) and to present them on the altar of the temple (Ezr. 7:17). This statement demonstrates that the animal sacrifices include certain food offerings and libations. King Nebuchadnezzar issued the command "to offer . . . food offerings and incense" (*minḥā wᵉnīḥōḥīn . . . lᵉnassāḵā*: Dnl. 2:46) to Daniel, who had recounted and interpreted the king's dream, as though he were a god.

3. *Qumran.* The Aramaic texts from Qumran attribute to Abraham an offering of burnt and food offerings (*'l' wmnḥ'*) in Bethel and in Elone-Mamre, there followed by a meal (1QapGen 21:2,20); cf. also Noah's sacrifice in the same text (1QapGen 10:16). The term *qrbn mnḥt*[*h*] "food offering" in T. Levi 33:18f.h is textually difficult. Cf. Hebrew *qorban minḥā* in Lev. 2:1,4,13 in the same meaning.

III. Lexical Field.

1. ʿlh. The feminine *'lh* /ʿalā/ "burnt sacrifice" is, like *mnḥh* "food offering," adopted from the Hebrew and first attested at Elephantine.[15] According to *TADAE* A4.10, 10f., the synonym *mqlw* "burnt sacrifice" can replace it.[16] On the instances from Qumran, cf. T. Levi 35:6[17] and 1QapGen 21:2,20 where *'l'* sometimes parallels *mnḥh*/*mnḥ'*.

2. *Verb* nsk, *Noun* nsk. The verb *ntk* may be attested in Sam'alian as "to pour out"[18] and *nsk* certainly is in Aramaic, initially as "to pour out";[19] cf. also *nsk* in the inscriptions from Hatra.[20] As a *terminus technicus* for libation, it occurs in a text from Elephantine, according to which Jedaniah, the priest and leader of the community, received pitchers for libations.[21] In Biblical Aramaic, the verb *nsk* is employed with *minḥā* and *nīḥōḥīn* in the general sense of "to offer" (Dnl. 2:46). The masculine substantive *nᵉsaḵ*[22] means "libation" (Ezr. 7:17).[23] 11Q10 36:8 and 37:8 (Job 41:15 and 42:6) preserve the noncultic meaning "to pour out."[24] In addition, the formulation *ḥmr nsk* "to libate wine"[25] in CT. Levi Bodleian d:13.[26]

---

15. *TADAE* A4.7,21.25f. par. 4.8,21.24f.
16. Cf. S. A. Kaufman, *The Akkadian Influences on Aramaic*. *AS* 19 (1974), 70.
17. Partially reconstructed; cf. *ATTM*, 198.
18. Of wrath; *KAI* 214,23; the reading and interpretation are disputed, however, cf. *DNSI*, 205 s.v. *btk*.
19. Of rain; *KAI* 222 A 26f.
20. Cf. K. Beyer, *Die aramäischen Inschriften aus Assur, Hatra und dem übrigen Ostmesopotamien* (Göttingen, 1998), 36 no. H30:11.
21. *TADAE* C3.13,7.
22. From an older /nesk/.
23. *LexLingAram*, 113.
24. *ATTM*, 297f.
25. → *ḥmr*.
26. *DSSStE*, 52f.

3. nḥwḥ. *nḥwḥ* /nīḥōḥ/ is a Hebrew loanword in Biblical Aramaic; it derives from the root *nūḥ* "to come to rest."[27] It is employed as a *plurale tantum* in the meaning "(incense) offering" as an object of the verb *nsk* with *minḥā* as a parallel term (Dnl. 2:46) or as an object of *qrb* in the haphel (Ezr. 6:10).[28] The indication of purpose *lryḥ nyḥḥ* in context with the presentation of offerings (T. Levi 36:16) corresponds to the OT formulation.[29]

IV. LXX. The LXX translates *minḥā* with θυσία and *ʿᵃlā* with ὁλοκαύτωμα, *nᵉsaḵ* with σπονδή and *nīḥōḥ* with εὐωδία.[30]

Niehr

---

27. *KBL*[3], 1745a,1746b; on the form, see also *ATTM*, 634.
28. *LexLingAram*, 112.
29. Cf. Koch; Rendtorff, 66-69.
30. Cf. ὀσμὴ εὐωδίας in T. Levi 36:16.

מני *mnī*; מנין *mnyn* /menyān/; מנה *mnh* /manā/; מנה *mnh* /manǣ/; פרס *prs*

I. Etymology, Forms, and Lexical Field. II. Verb. 1. "To Count" (peal). 2. "To Determine" (pael). III. Nouns. 1. "Number." 2. "Portion." IV. "Mene." V. The Menetekel in Dnl. 5.

I. Etymology, Forms, and Lexical Field. Aramaic *mnī* "to count" traces to a common Semitic verbal root **mnū*, of which Akkadian, Ugaritic, Hebrew, Arabic, Old South Arabian, and Ethiopic have preserved cognates.

In the less frequent G-stem "to count," the verb is construed as an intransitive with that counted as the object and has points of contact semantically with the specific meaning "to calculate" of the verb → *ḥšb* in calculatory contexts. Meanwhile, it is employed like the G-stem of the Hebrew *spr*.[1] The more frequent D-stem of *mnī* "to determine, appoint"

H. Bauer, "Menetekel," in *Festgabe der Numismatischen Gesellschaft zu Halle zum 4. Dtsch. Münzforschertag vom 30. Sept. bis 3. Okt. 1925* (Halle, 1925), 27-30; J. Conrad, "מָנָה *mānâ*," *TDOT*, VIII, 396-401; F. M. Fales, "Assyro-Aramaica: The Assyrian Lion-Weights," in *Immigration and Emigration within the Ancient Near East. FS E. Lipiński. OLA* 65 (1995), 33-55; S. A. Kaufman, *The Akkadian Influences on Aramaic. AS* 19 (1974); J. Naveh and S. Shaked, *Aramaic Documents from Ancient Bactria (Fourth Century* B.C.E.*)* (London, 2012); M. A. Powell, "Weights and Measures," *ABD*, VI, 897-908; J. B. Segal, *Aramaic Texts from North Saqqara* (London, 1983); R. Telöken and B. Schlenke, "*mnh*," *ThWQ*, II, 709-12.

1. This root is productive in Aram. only in the form of the nouns → *spr* "document" and "scribe."

takes the person as the direct object and, in addition, often various adverbial modifiers to define the task or responsibility, either following *b-* "in,"[2] *ʿl* "over" (Dnl. 2:49; 3:12), or *ʿm* "together with,"[3] and occasionally also an additional verb in the infinitive following *l-* indicating the purpose "in order to"[4] or in an object clause following *dy* "so that."[5] Further, *mnī* in the D-stem functions like the causative-stems of → *qūm* and → *tqn* "to appoint." The corresponding t-stems denote the respective passive diatheses, thus "to be counted, calculated" for the G-stem and "to be appointed" for the D-stem; Imperial Aramaic also attests an internal passive in this sense, apparently with the same meaning for the perfect.[6]

Two nominal formations attested at the latest in Imperial Aramaic derive from *mnī* "to count": a masculine *mnyn* /menyān/ "number, quantity"[7] and a less common feminine *mnh* /manā/ "portion." As an authentic Aramaic word, the latter differs from the Akkadian loanword /manǣ/ "mene," which is identical in a consonantal text although it is masculine, denoting a weight. The multivalence of the consonantal text, which leads to confusion between the nouns *mnh* "mene" (twice), → *tql* "sheqel" and *prs* "demi-mine," on the one hand, and between the passive participles "counted," "weighed," and "divided,"[8] on the other, constitutes the core of the episode of the "menetekel" in Dnl. 5.

II. Verb.

1. "To Count" (peal). An Imperial Aramaic letter from Elephantine first attests the G-stem *mnī* "to count" in Aramaic. It refers there to the number of days until a festival.[9] Afterward, it occurs often in the Aramaic texts from the Dead Sea. The verb stands twice in the promise of innumerable descendants for Abraham,[10] first in the active in the comparison with the dust and then in the Gt-passive for the descendants themselves, and for the counting of the cattle in his possession after returning from Egypt (22:29). It always has a direct object. Two additional passages are either reconstructed or extremely fragmentary. In contrast, a Nabatean certificate of debt from the Dead Sea employs *mnī* intransitively in the sense of "to calculate."[11] The t-passive "to be counted" occurs outside 1QapGen 21:13 (with the nuance "to be numerable") in a fragment of the Book of Giants, yet without context.[12] With the nuance "to be calculated, register," it occurs in two difference private documents from the same period.[13] Thus, all the instances that preserve sufficient contexts have a clearly bookkeeping connotation.

2. *TADAE* A4.5,9.
3. *TADAE* C1.1,37; 1QapGen 20:32.
4. *TADAE* C1.1,37; Dnl. 2:24.
5. 1QapGen 20:32.
6. For the generalities, see *ATTM*, 152.
7. From an original /munyān/, cf. *BLA*, §51z''' and *ATTM*, 628.
8. Of *prs*, attested later in Aramaic also as a verb.
9. *TADAE* A4.1,3.
10. 1QapGen 21:13.
11. nV 42,9 in *ATTM*, 2, 244-247; in l. 24f. transitively.
12. 4Q530 2 i+3:3.
13. nV 2:14,38 in *ATTM*, 2, 208-11 and nV 3:42 in *ATTM*, 2, 212-15, two sales contracts for the same palm orchard.

2. *"To Determine" (pael).* The verb *mnī* also appears in Imperial Aramaic in the D-stem "to determine, name, appoint." It apparently belongs to administrative terminology and regularly refers in the literature of the Achaemenid period to the appointment of persons (construed as a direct object) in certain offices or with certain tasks (with a corresponding adverbial modifier) by superiors. With that nuance, it occurs both in literary texts like the narrative frame of Aḥiqar[14] and in official letters,[15] presumably also in two papyrus fragments from Saqqara.[16] Imperial Aramaic still employs the internal passive for the passive diathesis "to be appointed."[17]

Biblical Aramaic continues precisely this official diction. The verb occurs in Ezr. 7:25 in reference to the installation of judges by Ezra[18] and in the court narratives of Daniel for entrusting someone with individual tasks[19] and with structural offices.[20]

Pertinent examples of this also appear later in the texts from Qumran: 1QapGen 20:32 employs the verb to refer to the escort assigned to accompany Abraham. Here, however, the verb also appears in theological contexts for God's administration, i.e., of the flood that God determined in 1QapGen 10:1,[21] and in 11Q10 30:9 (Job 38:12) in a rhetorical question whether Job was the one who established the times of day. In the isolated instance of the t-imperfect *ytmnwn* in 11Q18 26:2 (new Jerusalem), the preposition *ʿl* "over" indicates a Dt-stem "to be installed," which replaced the internal passive, first in the imperfect, and later also in the perfect. The context remains unknown, however.

III. Nouns.

1. "Number." The masculine *mnyn* /menyān/ related to the verb *mnī* "to count" is the typical Aramaic word for "number, quantity." The thing counted in the plural can follow the construct state. A possible Old Aramaic instance from Sefire is incomprehensible in context and paleographically suspect;[22] one first treads on sure ground with the Imperial Aramaic private contracts from Elephantine. There, it occurs in the expression *bmnyn* with a subsequent sum meaning "according to the number of" in reference to gold[23] or "in an agreed amount" in reference to goods like grain[24] or wood,[25] but also absolutely,[26]

14. *TADAE* C1.1,37.
15. *TADAE* A4.5,9.
16. Segal 15.2 and presumably 26.7; regarding the second passage, cf. Segal, 43 n. 16.
17. Ptcp. in *TADAE* A6.7,5 and Naveh and Shaked, A4,5, and the pf. now also in Naveh and Shaked, A1,7.
18. → *dīn* II.2.
19. Such as the execution of the wise by a royal official according to Dnl. 2:24.
20. Namely, the high functions in the domestic and external service of the state, which, according to Dnl. 2:49 and 3:12, Daniel and his friends received.
21. Reading with *ATTM,* 2, 93f.; the photographic evidence confirms Beyer's *mny,* cf. D. A. Machiela, *The Dead Sea Genesis Apocryphon. STDJ* 79 (2009), 51; the broad sense results from the context.
22. *KAI* 222 B 23; see J. A. Fitzmyer, *The Aramaic Inscriptions of Sefire. BietOr* 19/A (^{2}1995), 107.
23. *TADAE* B3.12,14; 4.5,3.
24. *TADAE* B4.3,13 par. 4.4,14.
25. Often in the harbor register *TADAE* C3.7.
26. *TADAE* B8.4,5; the reading is not entirely assured; D11.26, 3.

also Naveh and Shaked, C7,8 in the determined state. With the preposition *l-* "according to the number,"[27] it appears in Ezr. 6:17. Qumran employs it in terms for time: 11Q10 5:3 (reconstructed) and 28:4 (Job 21:21 and 36:26)[28] and, similarly, *ʿl mnyn* "after the era"[29] in the date formula in Nabatean contracts.[30] A few other passages from Qumran have been preserved with no context.

2. "Portion." The feminine *mnh* /manā/ "portion" also occurs primarily in juridical and administrative contexts. An instance in a pre-Imperial Aramaic proverb of Aḥiqar,[31] two in Imperial Aramaic letters,[32] and one referring to the portion of a house in an ostracon[33] are unclear in terms of context. Furthermore, it occurs frequently in a private document from Elephantine concerning the exchange of shares of an inheritance[34] and for portions of oil in the harbor register from Elephantine.[35] It seems to function similarly in legal texts from the Dead Sea[36] and in Palmyrene inscriptions concerning the allocation of graves.[37] The few possible instances from Qumran are all uncertain.[38] No difference in meaning to the more frequent noun → *ḥlq* (III) is perceptible in view of the state of evidence.

IV. "Mene." The Akkadian loanword *mnh* /manǣ/ represents the unit of weight "mene."[39] Apparently adopted in the Neo-Assyrian period, as *mnh mlk* on a few lion weights from Nimrud, it denotes a royal standard.[40] Its growing use in commerce is evident in Neo-Assyrian commercial texts and Imperial Aramaic sales contracts from Samaria, which document its distribution from the Achaemenid epoch also in Palestine where the shekel[41] had previously dominated.[42] The mene was still in use in Roman times both in the Dead Sea region in the west[43] and in Hatra in the east,[44]

27. Here, twelve goats offered for an atoning sacrifice for the tribes of Israel at the dedication of the temple.
28. Both for the Heb. *mspr*.
29. ἐπαρχία, from March 22, 106 C.E.
30. nV 7:1; 8:2; 9:2 in *ATTM* 2.
31. *TADAE* C1.1, 144.
32. *TADAE* A4.2,12 and 6.1,2.
33. *TADAE* D5.8,1.
34. *TADAE* B5.1,3.4.6.7.
35. → *mšḥ*; for bibliography, see *DNSI*, 657.
36. M 23:2 in *ATTM*, 312 and V 41:7 in *ATTM*, 2, 242f.
37. E.g., *PAT* 1791.4,7.
38. At best 1QapGen 10:17 following *ATTM*, 2, 94, cf. Machiela, 53; but here too with no further context.
39. Kaufman, 69.
40. Fales; → *mlk*.
41. → *tql*.
42. Instances in D. Schwiderski, *Die alt- und reichsaramäischen Inschriften*, vol. I: *Konkordanz*. *FSBP* 1 (2008), 530f.
43. M 32:2 in *ATTM*, 316, defined here as 100 *zwz* "sous" (of 3.4g each).
44. H241:4; 243:2; 244:2.

although with noble metals mostly as a unit of money rather than as a weight. Standards varied with the time, but the Persian mene is assumed to have been 500g, the Roman 340g.[45]

V. The Menetekel in Dnl. 5. The judgment message that appeared on the wall during the sacrilegious feast (Dnl. 5:25-28) remains initially incomprehensible while unvocalized because the words *mn' tql wprsyn* seem to denote the customary units of weight, "mene," "shekel," and "demi-mene".[46] The divinely gifted Daniel recognizes, however, that the intention is the rather infrequent passive participles "counted," "weighed," and "divided"[47] with the king as subject.[48] Because the judgment[49] is, indeed, sealed, this knowledge no longer benefits the king.

Gzella

45. Cf. Powell, 905-8.
46. /pars/, Kaufman, 80.
47. Simultaneously an allusion to the Persians, → *mdy*.
48. → *pšr*, Bauer.
49. → *yd* III.

מרא *mr'* /mārǣ/; מראה *mr'h* /māre'ā/

I. Etymology. II. Semantics. 1. In Sam'alian. 2. Old Aramaic. 3. Imperial Aramaic. 4. Biblical Aramaic. 5. Qumran. III. LXX. IV. Perspectives from the History of Religions. 1. As a Divine Title. 2. As a Divine Name. 3. As a Component in Personal Names. 4. Fundamentals.

B. Aggoula, "Remarques sur les inscriptions hatréennes III," *Syr* 52 (1975) 181-206, esp. 196f; W. W. Graf Baudissin, *Kyrios als Gottesname im Judentum und seine Stelle in der Religionsgeschichte III* (Giessen, 1929), 57-61; K. Dijkstra, *Life and Loyalty. RGRW* 128 (1995), 171-244; P.-E. Dion, *Les Araméens à l'âge du fer: Histoire politique et structures sociales. ÉtB* NS 34 (1997), 242-47,259-64; H. Gzella, *A Cultural History of Aramaic. HO* 111 (2015); J. F. Healey, *The Religion of the Nabataeans. RGRW* 136 (2001); M. Heltzer, "An Old Aramean Seal-Impression and Some Problems of the History of the Kingdom of Damascus," in M. Sokoloff, ed., *Arameans, Aramaic and the Aramaic Literary Tradition* (Ramat Gan, 1983), 9-13; E. Lipiński, *Studies in Aramaic Inscriptions and Onomastics II*. OLA 57 (1994), 193-201; J. Naveh and S. Shaked, *Aramaic Documents from Ancient Bactria (Fourth Century B.C.E.)* (London, 2012); H. Niehr, *Ba'alšamem. OLA* 123 (2003); B. Porten, *Archives from Elephantine* (Berkeley, 1968), 45-53; H. H. Rowley, *The Aramaic of the Old Testament* (Oxford, 1929), 111-15; B. Schlenke, "*mr'*," *ThWQ*, II, 782-86; J. Tubach, *Im Schatten des Sonnengottes* (Wiesbaden, 1986), esp. 255-458.

I. Etymology. The old derivation of the noun *mr'* /mārǣ/[1] from the root *r'ī* "to see" in the sense of "looks, good-looking"[2] is as untenable as is recourse to *mr'* "well-fed,"[3] since in Akkadian one must distinguish between *māru* "son"[4] and *marû* "fatted, fat."[5] A root related to Aramaic *mr'* "lord" is Akkadian *māru/mer'u* "son,"[6] although one should note the semantic difference between the Akkadian and the Northwest Semitic. The oldest Northwest Semitic instance is the Ugaritic /mur'u/ "commander" (?).[7] Based on old spellings,[8] the feminine was originally pronounced /māre'ā/.[9]

II. Semantics.

1. In Sam'alian. The Aramaic inscriptions from Sam'al employ *mr'* on the political and the theological levels. Thus, a loan translation of Assyro-Babylonian titles designates Tiglath-pileser "lord of the four regions of the world" (*mr' rb'y 'rq'*).[10] Similarly, he is the "overlord" (*mr'*) of King Bar-Rakkab.[11] From the perspective of Bar-Rakkab, this corresponds to the self-designation "servant."[12] The ideological coherence of this vassal relationship ensues in the framework of the Near Eastern patronage system concentrated in the → *ṣdq* concept.[13] King Bar-Rakkab also applies this system on the theological level to the gods Rakkab'el[14] and Ba'alḥarran[15] likewise as *mr'*, i.e., as his overlord. This use of *mr'* as "overlord" simultaneously establishes the semantic difference with *b'l* as "possessor, owner."[16]

2. Old Aramaic. The oldest specimen of *mr'* in Old Aramaic occurs in the stele inscription from Tell Fekheriye from the mid-ninth century B.C.E.[17] The weather god Hadad is the "overlord" (*mr'*) of King/Governor Hadadyisi' (l. 6,17). Thereby, the same

---

1. Probably from */māre'/.
2. So H. Bauer, "Das Originalwort für 'Witwe' im Semitischen," *ZDMG* 67 (1913) 343.
3. *ATTM*, 629.
4. *AHw*, II, 615f.; *CAD*, X, 308-16.
5. *AHw*, II, 616f.; *CAD*, X, 306-8.
6. *AHw*, II, 615f.; *CAD*, X, 308-16.
7. J. Huehnergard, *Ugaritic Vocabulary in Syllabic Transcription. HSS* 32 (^{2}2008), 148f.; W. H. van Soldt, *Studies in the Akkadian of Ugarit. AOAT* 40 (1991), 390 n. 19; J. Sanmartín, "Zur Schreibpraxis der ugaritischen Siegelschneider," *UF* 27 (1995), 460f.; *DUL*^{3}, 563f.; regarding later instances, cf. *DJBA*, 707-9; *ThesSyr*, 2204-8; *MdD*, 251.
8. So *KAI* 309.18.
9. Later /mārā/.
10. *KAI* 216,3f.; 217,1f. (partially reconstructed).
11. *KAI* 216,6.9; 217,3f.
12. *KAI* 216,3; 217,1.
13. Cf. H. Niehr, "The Constitutive Principles for Establishing Justice and Order in Northwest Semitic Societies with Special Reference to Ancient Israel and Judah," *ZABR* 3 (1997) 111-29, esp. 116-18.
14. *KAI* 216.5.
15. *KAI* 218.
16. → *b'l* II.
17. *KAI* 309.

loyalty relationship binds Hadad and Hadadyisiʿ as the one binding King Bar-Rakkab and Rakkab'el or Baʿalḥarran in Sam'al. Furthermore, Hadad bore the title "overlord" (*mr*ʾ) of the Khabur (region), since the Khabur region is subject to the god Haddad of Sikan (l. 16). Likewise, Hadadyisiʿ addresses Šuwala, the Paredra of Hadad, as "my lady" (*mr'ty*, 18).

The stele inscription of King Bar-Hadad from Bit Agusi in northern Syria (ninth/eighth century B.C.E.) mentions the god Melqart as the king's lord.[18] An inscription on a horse medallion from Samos (end of the ninth century B.C.E.) attributes the title *mr'n* to King Hazael of Damascus.[19] This title of Hazael's also appears on an ivory inscription from Arslan Tash.[20] A seal from Khorsabad may attest the title *mr srsy srgn* "chief of the eunuchs of Sargon."[21]

The Adon papyrus addressed to Pharaoh Necho II by a Philistine vassal from Ekron ca. 604/603 B.C.E. designates the Pharaoh as "lord of kings (*mr*ʾ *mlkn*).[22] The vassal designates himself *ʿbd* (ll. 1,6,8). As in Sam'al, here, too, *mr*ʾ and *ʿbd* are clearly correlated terms denoting a vassal relationship. The so-called Asshur Letter from c. 650 B.C.E. also exhibits the title *mr'y* in address to the king.[23]

On the political and religious levels, the connotation of *mr*ʾ as "overlord" in contrast to → *bʿl* as "lord, owner" is clear. A contamination of the two meanings appears on a seventh-century stele inscription form Lebanon with the construct phrase *mr*ʾ *byt*ʾ "lord of the house," which could refer to the overlord or the owner.[24] Because of the fragmentary state of the text, the instance on a docket from Dūr-Kat-limmu/Magdalu (Tall Šēḫ Ḥamad) remains unclear.[25]

3. *Imperial Aramaic.* In contracts from Elephantine, *mr*ʾ denotes a leadership position, sometimes alongside the judge,[26] alongside the → *sgn*,[27] and alongside both *sgn*

18. *KAI* 201.3f.

19. *KAI* 311; I. Ephʿal and J. Naveh, "Hazael's Booty Inscriptions," *IEJ* 39 (1989), 192-200; F. Bron and A. Lemaire, "Les inscriptions araméennes de Hazaël," *RA* 83 (1989) 35-44; H. Kyrieleis and W. Röllig, "Die aramäische Inschrift für Haza'el und ihr Duplikat," *MDAIA* 103 (1988) 62-75.

20. *KAI* 232; cf. also E. Puech, "L'ivoire inscrit d'Arslan-Tash et les rois des Dames." *RB* 88 (1981) 544-62.

21. M. Sprengling, "An Aramaic Seal Impression from Khorsabad," *AJSL* 49 (1932) 53-55; E. Lipiński, *SAIO* I, 66; yet, according to S. A. Kaufman, "On Vowel Reduction in Aramaic," *JAOS* 104 (1984) 94, it is part of the name: . . .-[*l*]*mr srs* [*z*]*y srgn*.

22. *KAI* 266.1,6; regarding the backgrounds, see Gzella, 139-41.

23. *KAI* 233,6[*mry*].7(emend.)8.17; V. Hug, *Altaramäische Gramatik der Texte des 7. und 6. Jh.s v.Chr. HSAO* 4 (1993), 20f.; Gzella, 142-44.

24. *KAI* 317.5; A. Caquot, "Une inscription araméenne d'époque assyrienne," *FS Dupont-Sommer* (Paris, 1971), 9-16; Hug, 14f.; Lipiński, SAIO I, 77-82; I. Kottsieper, "Der Mann aus Babylonien—Steuerhinterzieher, Flüchtling, Immigrant oder Agent? Zu einem aramäischen Dekret aus neuassyrischer Zeit," *Or* 69 (2000) 369f.

25. Cf. W. Röllig, *Die aramäischen Texte aus Tall Šēḫ Ḥamad / Dūr-Katlimmu / Magdalu. BATSH* 17/5 (2014), 46f., no. 13.5.

26. *TADAE* B3.2,6; → *dīn* II.1.

27. *TADAE* B3.10, 19; 3.11,13; 5.4,2(partially emend.).5.

and judge.[28] Examples in the lists *TADAE* B8.2,5 and 8.5,14 are unclear because of the fragmentary preservation of the papyri. The contexts of the Elephantine correspondence reveal that the title *mr'* designates high officials. Bearers of the title mentioned by name are Aršama, the satrap of Egypt,[29] and Bagohi, the Persian governor of Judah.[30] In the letter addressed to Bagohi,[31] Yedaniah and the priests from Elephantine describe themselves as *'bdn* of Bagohi,[32] wherein the correlated terms for the vassal relationship known from the Old Aramaic epoch reappear. Comparable is also *TADAE* A4.10,4.7.13, which attests the same relationship. Further comparable is a fragmentary private letter[33] that addresses the superior as *mr'ty* "my lady" and *mr'y* "my lord." The private letter Herm. 2 reveals a similar situation. In it, a son addresses his father as *mr'y* "my lord" and designates himself as *'bd.*[34] Regarding *mr'* as "owner," cf. *TADAE* A4.4,8. The letters from Bactria also employ *mr'y* in address to superiors.[35]

On the theological level, the god Yahu is designated *mr' šmy'* "lord of heaven."[36] The designation represents a literal translation of the originally Phoenician DN Ba'alšamem. The title "God of heaven"[37] substantially parallels Yahu's designation as "lord of heaven."[38]

The Aḥiqar novella with the proverb collection found at Elephantine also knows the correlation of *'bd* and *mr'*.[39] The reconstruction of *mr'* in I. Kottsieper[40] and M. Weigl[41] is dubious.[42]

The Palmyrene inscriptions exhibit *mr'* in reference to the Caesar: *qsr mrn* "Caesar, our lord."[43] Comparable is the title *mrh* "lady" in reference to Zenobia,[44] who also carries the title *mlkt'* "the queen" in this inscription (l. 2).[45] In *PAT* 1442.6f., a freed slave also remembers the sons of his lord.[46] In addition, the title *mr'gr'* "leader of the Agora" is also attested.[47]

---

28. *TADAE* B3.12,28; 4.6,14(partially emend.).
29. *TADAE* A4.5,2.
30. *TADAE* A4.7,1.2.18.23; par. 4.8,1(emend.).17.22.
31. *TADAE* A4.7.
32. *TADAE* 4.7,1.4.22; cf. 4.8.1.3.21.
33. *TADAE* A3.7.
34. *TADAE* A2.4,1, cf. l. 14.
35. Naveh and Shaked, 280, s.v.
36. *TADAE* A4.7,15; par. 4.8,14.
37. *TADAE* A4.7,15; par. 4.8,14.
38. → *šmyn*; Niehr, 191-95.
39. *TADAE* C1.1,72f.(emend.).191.197(partially emend.). 198.
40. *Die Sprache der Aḥiqarsprüche. BZAW* 194 (1990), 12 col. X,1.
41. *Die aramäischen Achikar-Sprüche aus Elephantine und die alttestamentliche Weisheitsliteratur. BZAW* 399 (2010), 73f.
42. Cf. *TADAE* C1.1,79. On the orthography of *mr'* with elision of the etymological glottal stop in the Elephatine texts, cf. M. L. Folmer, *The Aramaic Language in the Achaemenid Period. OLA* 68 (1995), 104-16.
43. *PAT* 0284.3.
44. *PAT* 0293.4.
45. Regarding the continuity of Aramaic royal ideology; cf. Niehr, 177f.; Gzella, "Palmyrener," 451.
46. Cf. Dijkstra, 143 with n. 72; 147,150.
47. *PAT* 0574.2.

Hatrian inscriptions relate *mr'* sometimes to the king; one also finds other, unspecific occurrences.[48]

Among the Nabateans, one title of the god Dušara was "the god of our lord" (*mrn*), which expressed the close relationship between Dušara and the king of the Nabateans.[49] Another title for Dušara, *mr byt*, "the lord of the temple" characterizes him either as the chief god of the temple at Petra or as lord of the dynasty.[50] Then, Dušara was designated *mry ʿlm'* ("lord of the world").[51] In the Nabatean inscriptions from Mada'in Salih, *mr* occurs as a title of the Nabatean king,[52] and in contracts.[53]

4. Biblical Aramaic. In accordance with Old and Imperial Aramaic diction, Biblical Aramaic also employs the title *mārē* for kings and Yahweh. King Nebuchadnezzar is the *mārē malḵīn*, the "Lord of kings" (Dnl. 2:47),[54] a reappearance of the titulature for the pharaoh from the Adon papyrus.[55] Daniel addresses Nebuchadnezzar as *mār'ī* "my lord" (Dnl. 4:16,21).

In one passage in the book of Daniel, Yahweh bears the title *mārē šᵉmayyā* (Dnl. 5:23). Again, it represents the literal translation of the Phoenician DN Baʿalšamem, as already attested at Elephantine and in the Amherst Papyrus 63 I. The parallel formulations "God of heaven" and "King of heaven"[56] also appear in the book of Daniel.

5. Qumran. The Aramaic texts from Qumran attest an absolute *mr'* as a title of Yahweh only rarely; instead, various construct phrases dominate.[57] Thus *mry* "my Lord" (1QapGen 20:12,15),[58] *mr' ʿlm'* "Lord of the world" (Aram. En. 9:4, etc.; 4Q529 1:6f.,11f.),[59] *mrh ʿlmy'* "Lord of the Universe" (1QapGen 21:2),[60] *mrh rbwt'* "Lord of the Multitudes" (1QapGen 2:4),[61] *mrh kwl'* "Lord of all" (5:23), and *mrh šmy'* "Lord of heaven" or "Lord of the Heavens" (7:7; 12:17; 22:16,21, both of these passages also have *w'rʿ'* "and of the earth")[62] appear in address to Yahweh.

---

48. B. Aggoula, *Inventaire des inscriptions hatréennes*. *BAH* 139 (1991), 188, s.v. *mr'/mry*; and K. Beyer, *Die aramäischen Inschriften aus Assur, Hatra und dem übrigen Ostmesopotamien* (1998), s.v. 179f.; idem, "Die aramäischen Inschriften aus Assur, Hatra und dem übrigen Ostmesopotamien, Nachträge," *WO* 43 (2013) 59 s.v.

49. *CIS*, II, 201; 208; 209; 211; 350, etc.; Healey, 92f.

50. Healey, 92, 116.

51. Healey, 95,189.

52. J. F. Healey, *The Nabataean Tomb Inscriptions of Mada'in Salih*. *JSSSup* 1 (1993), 262, s.v.

53. *ATTM*, 2, 435.

54. → *mlk*.

55. *KAI* 266,1; → II.2 and K. Koch, *Daniel*. *BK* XX/1 (2005), 237f.

56. Niehr, 198-204.

57. Cf. H. Stegemann, "Religionsgeschichtliche Erwägungen zu den Gottesbezeichnungen in den Qumrantexten," in M. Delcor, ed., *Qumrân*. *BETL* 46 (1978), 212f.

58. *DSSStE*, 40-43.

59. 4Q202 3:14; *DSSStE*, 406f.

60. *DSSStE*, 42f.

61. *DSSStE*, 28f.

62. *DSSStE*, 32-35,48f. Cf. also T. Levi 34:6, which has *lm'ry šmy'* "of the Lord of Heaven"; *DSSStE*, 50f.

III. LXX. The LXX of the book of Daniel translates *mr'* with κύριος; Theodotion's translation of Dnl. 5:23 renders the title *mārē šᵉmayyā* (→ II.4) as κύριος Θεὸς τοῦ οὐρανοῦ.

IV. Perspectives from the History of Religions. In relation to the use of *mr'* for deities, one can identify a development that runs from the title "lord/lady" borne by various deities to the formation of a true DN. Analogously, one can refer to → *b'l(t)* in the Northwest Semitic religions, which employed it as a divine title and as a divine name.

1. As a Divine Title. In the religion of the Arameans of Syria, the title *mr'* indicates the lordship of a god over persons and regions. According to the stele inscription from Tell Fekheriye, Hadad of Sikan was the lord of the king/governor Hadadyisi',[63] his consort, Šu-wala, the ruler's lady (l. 18), and Hadad was, furthermore, the "lord of the Khabur (region)" (l. 16). Near Aleppo, King Bar-Hadad erected an image of the god Melqart as his lord.[64] In Sam'al the gods Rakkab'el and Ba'alḥaran were the lords of King Bar-Rakkab.[65]

This theology also appears in the documents of Elephantine that call Yahu "Lord of heaven."[66] Other divine titles formed with *mr'* occur in Palmyra. They designate Ba'lšamin as *mr' 'lm'* "lord of the world,"[67] the "anonymous god" as *mr' kl* "lord of all,"[68] and as *m[r]' nšmt'* "lord of living beings."[69] Furthermore, a *mrt byt'* "lady of the temple" also occurs[70] as an epithet of the goddess Allat.[71] It recalls the title for Dušara *mr' byt'* "lord of the temple" in Nabatean religion.

The transition from divine title to divine name manifests itself especially well in *mr'lh'* "lord of the gods," which appears first as an Akkadian epithet of the lunar god Sin from Harran (*šar/bēl ilāni*),[72] then as epithet for various deities, and finally, however, as an independent god in a pantheon.[73]

2. As a Divine Name. As a divine name, *mr'* appears in Papyrus Amherst 63 found in western Thebes.[74] Although the discussion concerning the deities that appear in this text

---

63. *KAI* 309.6.
64. *KAI* 201.3f.
65. *KAI* 216.5; 218
66. *TADAE* A4.7,15; par. 4.8,14.
67. *PAT* 0258.1; → *'lm* II.3.
68. *PAT* 0344.5.
69. *PAT* 0065.1.
70. *PAT* 0323 A 3; 0188.1; cf. *PAT* S. 387 s.v. *mrt byt'*; 1929.3,5(emend.).
71. J. Teixidor, *The Pantheon of Palmyra. EPRO* 79 (1979), 54; S. Krone, *Die altarabische Gottheit al-Lat. HOS* 23 (1992), 124f.
72. Cf. C. J. Gadd, "The Harran Inscriptions of Nabonidus," *AnSt* 8 (1958) 46f.,56f.
73. Overview and index in Tubach, 386-458; C. S. Lightfoot and J. F. Healey, "A Roman Veteran on the Tigris," *EpAn* 17 (1991) 5; S. Gündüz, *The Knowledge of Life. JSSSup* 3 (1994), 194,198-201.
74. Cf. the complete translation in R. C. Steiner, "The Aramaic Text in Demotic Script," *COS*, I, 1997, 309-27.

and their identities has not yet ended,[75] the reading of the DN *mr'* is disputed. The identity of the god *mr'* is questionable given proposals that it refers to both Bethel[76] and El.[77]

Gaza attests the veneration of a god Marna "our lord," a god that bears the epithets "lord of the rain" and "Zeus, source of fertility."[78]

With regard to divine name, the triad attested at Hatra, *mrn* "our lord," *mrtn* "our lady," and *brmrn* "son of our dominions" merit particular reference.[79] In this context, *mrn* and *brmrn* clearly stand in the foreground of overall religious life at Hatra. The goddess *mrtn* appears only rarely in the inscriptions. *Mrn* is the supreme god of Hatra; it was originally a solar deity, as is obvious in the fact that two inscriptions designate *brmrn* as the son of Šamaš. *Brmrn* manifests a lunar character and adopted the title *mr'lh'* "lord of the gods" from lunar god theology. In independent depictions, *brmrn* receives solar features and has the role of a cosmocrator.[80]

3. As a Component in Personal Names. In Nabatean PN, *mr'* appears in masculine and feminine forms as a theophoric element.[81] Gaza attests the PN *ʿbdmr'n,*[82] who appears in context with the god Marna mentioned above, and the PN *mrdgn* ("my lord is Dagan").[83] For additional PN formed with *mr'*, cf. E. Lipiński, *SAIO* I, 65f. and for PN Μαρα/ Μαρθα/ Μαρτα "lady" *ATTM*, 630 and 2, 435f. The derivation of the Ammonite PN *mr'l* is disputed.[84] Furthermore, the interpretation of a few PN containing *mr* from Dūr-Katlimmu/Magdalu (Tall Šēḫ Ḥamad) is uncertain because *mr* here can also mean "son."[85]

4. Fundamentals. The transition of *mr'* from a divine title to a divine name is a widely observable phenomenon in the religions of Syro-Palestine and Mesopotamia in the first millennium B.C.E.[86] Thus, already in the Late Bronze era, one can point to the designation of the weather god Haddu as *bʿl* at Ugarit and, in the first century B.C.E., to the Phoenician /'adōn/ and the GN Adonis. Likewise, in postexilic Judaism, the DN Yahweh was increasingly replaced with *'ᵃḏōnāy*, especially in spoken language.[87] Reference can also be made to contemporary Mesopotamia, where Marduk was increasingly addressed

75. → *'lh* V.2.

76. S. P. Vleeming and J. W. Wesselius, "Betel the Saviour," *JEOL* 28 (1983/84) 118.

77. I. Kottsieper, "Anmerkungen zu Pap. Amherst 63. Teil II-IV," *UF* 29 (1997), 411.

78. H. Grégoire and M. A. Kugener, *Marc le Diacre: vie de Porphyre, évêque de Gaza* (Paris, 1930), 19,23f.,35, 47-63.

79. → *'lh* V.5.

80. Tubach, 255-335.

81. Cf. F. al-Khraysheh, "Die Personennamen in den nabatäischen Inschriften des Corpus Inscriptionum Semiticarum" (diss., Marburg, 1986), 114f.

82. J. A. Fitzmyer and S. A. Kaufman, *An Aramaic Bibliography I* (Baltimore, 1992), 34 B.1.48.

83. Cf. R. Deutsch and M. Heltzer, *New Epigraphic Evidence from the Biblical Period* (Tel Aviv, 1995), 14f. no. 42/8.

84. Cf. W. E. Aufrecht, *A Corpus of Ammonite Inscriptions* (Lewiston, NY, 1989), 128-30, no. 49.

85. Cf. W. Röllig, 80.

86. Cf. Tubach, 276-86.

87. Cf. M. Rösel, *Adonaj: Warum Gott "Herr" genannt wird* (Tübingen, 2000).

with the designation *bēlu.* Under his influence, the supreme god of Palmyra was also called Bel so that his proper name is no longer known. K. Koch has rightly designated this tendency as denominalization and dominionization.[88]

Niehr

88. K. Koch, "Syrien–Kanaan," in E. Brunner-Traut, ed., *Die großen Religionen des Alten Orients und der Antike* (Stuttgart, 1992), 71-94, here 87.

מרד *mrd*; מרד *mrd* /marrād/; מרד *mrd* /merd/

I. Etymology. II. Imperial Aramaic Documents from Egypt. III. Biblical Aramaic. IV. Qumran.

I. Etymology. Besides Aramaic, Hebrew, Arabic, Ethiopic, and early northern Arabic Safaitic also attest the root *mrd*;[1] proper names of a (homonymous?) root *mrd* also occur in other early North and Old South Arabian languages.[2]

II. Imperial Aramaic Documents from Egypt. The noun *mrd* /marrād/ "rebel, insurgent,"[3] always in the determined state of the masculine plural *mrdy'*, regularly serves in the Aramaic version, from Elephantine, of the Behistun inscription of the Persian King Darius I to designate the enemies of his military campaigns, for example in the phrase *ḥ[yl]' zk mrdy'* "the h[os]t, the rebels."[4] Similarly, the word appears at the end of an official letter concerning a rebellion.[5] A verb *mrd* in the peal "to rebel, revolt" should be reconstructed in the Behistun inscription;[6] otherwise, three letters attest it, saying, "divisions of the Egyptian army rebelled" (*dgln zy mṣry' mrdw*, pf. 3 pl.),[7] or that "Egypt revolted" (*mṣryn mrdt*, pf. 3fs).[8]

A. Al-Jallad, *An Outline of the Grammar of the Safaitic Inscriptions. SSLL* 80 (2015); H. Grimme, *Texte und Untersuchungen zur ṣafatenisch-arabischen Religion. Studien zur Geschichte und Kultur des Altertums* 16,1 (New York, 1929); R. Knierim, "מרד *mrd* to rebel," *TLOT*, 684-86; D. M. Penney and M. O. Wise, "By the Power of Beelzebub: An Aramaic Incantation Formula from Qumran (4Q560)," *JBL* 113 (1994) 627-50; D. Schwiderski, *Handbuch des nordwestsemitischen Briefformulars. BZAW* 295 (2000); L. Schwienhorst, "מָרַד *māraḏ*," *TDOT*, IX, 1-5; F. Zanella, "*mrd*," *ThWQ*, II, 786-88.

1. Grimme, 91; Al-Jallad, 328.
2. Cf. *ANKS* 1 in Al-Jallad, 223.
3. On the noun pattern, see *ATTM*, 629.
4. *TADAE* C2.1,19, etc.; → *ḥyl*.
5. *TADAE* A5.5,13.
6. *TADAE* C2.1,39.
7. *TADAE* A4.5,1, similarly A6.10,1.
8. *TADAE* A6.7,6.

III. Biblical Aramaic. The three Biblical Aramaic instances of the root occur in the Artaxerxes correspondence in the book of Ezra. Elamite and other Trans-Euphratene migrants to Samaria grounded their complaint to the Persian king against the reconstruction of Jerusalem by Jewish returnees with the assertion that the Jews were refortifying "the rebellious and evil city" (*qiryᵉṯā mārāḏtā ūbīštā*, deter. of the fem. sg., Ezr. 4:12), which it had already been (cf. 2 K. 18:7, etc.). The adjective */mārād/ "rebellious, insurrectionist"[9] recurs in Ezr. 4:15 in the form *mārāḏā* (fem. sg. abs.). In his reply, Artaxerxes takes up the objection and utilizes the masculine noun *mᵉraḏ* "rebellion, insurrection" in the singular absolute: *ūmᵉraḏ wᵉʾæštaddūr miṯʿᵃḇæḏ bah* "rebellion and tumult are made in it (i.e., Jerusalem)" (Ezr. 4:19).

IV. Qumran. A form of the verb *mrd* in the peal perfect third-person masculine plural appears in 1QapGen 21:27,[10] which describes the rebellion of the five southern Canaanite kings against the Elamite Chedorlaomer; the passage paraphrases Gen 14:4 and probably adopts the verb form from the Hebrew prototype. Furthermore, one reads of *mrdwt yldn* "unruliness bearing/of midwives" in the fragmentary demon invocation 4Q560 1 1:2, which also apparently attests a feminine noun *mrdw* "unruliness, insubordination" in the singular construct.[11] This would be the sole instance in which the root *mrd* does not relate to the political sphere.

Stadel

9. Although, according to *ATTM*, 629, identical with the noun /marrād/.
10. The object of the rebellion appended with the preposition *b-*.
11. Cf., however, Penney and Wise, 635 for another understanding.

משח *mšḥ*; משח *mšḥ* /mešḥ/; משיח *mšyḥ* /mašīḥ/

I. Etymology, Forms, and Lexical Field. II. Verb "to Anoint." III. Noun "Oil." 1. In Everyday Life. 2. In the Cult. IV. Messiah.

I. Etymology, Forms, and Lexical Field. Traditionally, the common Semitic verbal root *mšḥ* I "to anoint" with its nominal derivatives is distinguished from its homonym

J. J. Collins, "*mšḥ*," *ThWQ*, II, 810-17; H. Gzella, "Verheißung: Die Zukunft angesichts Gottes," in H. Ausloos and B. Lemmelijn, eds., *Handbuch zur Septuaginta,* vol. 6: *Theologie* (Gütersloh, forthcoming); J. Naveh and S. Shaked, *Aramaic Documents from Ancient Bactria (Fourth Century B.C.E.)* (London, 2012); H. Ringgren, "שֶׁמֶן *šemen*," *TDOT*, XV, 249-53; A. E. Rüthy, "Die Pflanze und ihre Teile im biblisch-hebräischen Sprachgebrauch" (diss., Basel, 1942); K. Seybold, "מָשַׁח *māšaḥ*," *TDOT*, IX, 41-54; T. Waliszewski, *Elaion: Olive Oil Production in Roman and Byzantine Syria-Palestine* (Warsaw, 2014).

mšḥ II "to measure."[1] Since it is not entirely clear whether /ḥ/ in *mšḥ* II may not have arisen from an original /ḫ/, this view depends primarily on semantic grounds. Both roots continue to be productive in Aramaic.

As a verb in the G-stem, *mšḥ* "to anoint" has appeared since Old Aramaic and is construed in the preserved passages with the related noun as an adverbial modifier, "oil," then transitively "to anoint someone." The masculine noun /mešḥ/[2] "oil" appears beginning in the Achaemenid period and is attested very much more frequently as an object of daily life. It corresponds roughly to the Hebrew *šœmœn* in the meaning "oil."[3] The precise variety of the oil can be more exactly specified with a phrase such as *mšḥ zyt* "olive oil,"[4] *mšḥ bśm* "aromatic oil,"[5] and *mšḥ zrʿ ktn* "linseed oil,"[6] the purpose with *l-* as in *mšḥ lnwrʾ* "oil for fire."[7]

Early Judaism employed the Aramaic passive participle /mašīḥ/ "anointed one" as a fixed designation for the end-time redeemer figure and in the transcription of the determined state Μεσσιας "Messiah" (so already Jn. 1:41; 4:25)[8] and its Greek translation Χριστός as the Christ title.

II. Verb "to Anoint." The first instance of the verb *mšḥ* "to anoint" appears in a curse formula in one of the Sefire treaties of state.[9] The immediate context with a possible direct object is destroyed, but since the following lines apparently deal with the nursing of children, it is often assumed that the expression refers to the anointing of the mother's breast, possible to avoid abrasions.[10] A pair of occurrences in Imperial Aramaic in the petition of the Jewish community at Elephantine to the Achaemenid administration concerning the reconstruction of the local temple mentions forgoing salve along with abstinence[11] as gestures of fasting for mourning;[12] here the noun (→ III) serves as an adverbial modifier of the participle: *mšḥ lʾ mšḥyn* "(we will not) anoint (ourselves) with oil." The form *mšḥ* at the beginning of the likewise Imperial Aramaic Bar-Puneš novella[13] can no longer be determined because of the subsequent gap in the text; the verb *mšḥw* in B1,5 in Naveh and Shaked (transitive with an army as object) could belong to either root *mšḥ* I or II.

Thereafter, the verb first reappears in the Aramaic of late antiquity, although also in the Gt-stem for the passive "to be anointed."[14] It continues overall to be rare, however.

1. *ATTM*, 631; cf. *GesB*[18], 751 regarding *mišḥā* I "anointing" and *mišḥā* II "portion."
2. Later /mešaḥ/, cf. *ATTM*, 114.
3. Cf. Ringgren, 249-53.
4. *TADAE* A2.2,11, etc.
5. *TADAE* A2.2,12; A2.4,10f., etc.
6. *TADAE* C3.11,4.11.
7. Naveh and Shaked, C1,26.
8. The *e* instead of the etymological /a/ in this word reflects the furtive vowel that eased pronunciation after the loss of the unaccented short vowel in an open syllable in Aramaic, see *ATTM*, 115f.
9. *KAI* 222 A 21.
10. Cf. Hos 9:14 and K. Galling, "Miscellanea Archaeologica," *ZDPV* 83 (1967) 134f.
11. → *ḥmr* II.
12. *TADAE* A4.7,20 par. 4.8,20.
13. *TADAE* C1.2,1.
14. Cf. *DJBA*, 333b; 712b; *LexSyr*, 407; *MdD*, 279.

III. Noun "Oil."

1. In Everyday Life. Oil, in Syria-Palestine obtained mostly from olives (*zyt*) and in Mesopotamia and often Egypt from sesame, was employed, among other things, as cooking oil, as a household product for personal hygiene, or as a basis for cosmetic salves, for lamps, and in the cult. The term *mšḥ* /mešḥ/ "oil" occurs, consequently, mostly in relation to various realms of daily life, as they appear, since the private letters and documents of the Achaemenid period, in the literary documentation of Aramaic. In pre-Imperial Aramaic letters from Hermopolis, it occurs in instructions to deliver[15] or to barter[16] oil. An official letter from Elephantine mentions its use as salve (→ II); in lists of the woman's dowry, two marriage contracts of members of the same communities include *mšḥ bśm* "aromatic oil"[17] or *mšḥ zyt* "olive oil";[18] cf. also a later Nabatean document securing the dowry.[19] Then, the list of customs dues in the Elephantine harbor register very frequently mention oil as an export,[20] as do, further, a list of oil distributions,[21] and a few other isolated commercial texts.[22] A pair of occurrences on Egyptian ostraca are fragmentary. From Bactria, *mšḥ ḥwry* "white oil"[23] and *mšḥ lnwr'* "oil for fire" have recently become known (l. 26). Furthermore, the ostraca with commercial texts from Achaemenid Idumea contain a large number of instances of *mšḥ*.[24]

2. In the Cult. In contrast, the two Biblical Aramaic instances employ *mšḥ*, along with → *ḥnṭh* "wheat," → *mlḥ* "salt," and → *ḥmr* "wine,"[25] explicitly in relation to the royally authorized deliveries for the temple. This accords with ritual regulations.[26] A sacrificial context also underlies the few preserved passages from Qumran: 1QapGen 10:16 in relation to Noah's sacrifice of fine flour and oil and both 4Q555 1:2 and 11Q18 29:4 in the description of the temple cult in the heavenly Jerusalem.

IV. Messiah. The substantival passive participle /mašīḥ/ "anointed one, Messiah," which was then also understood as a name, is first attested in Aramaic in the post-Christian era.[27] Indeed, the hope for an end-time redeemer, which combines the old ritual royal anointing with the promise of an eternal dominion of the Davidic dynasty, took form soon

---

15. *TADAE* A2.2,11f.; 2.4,10f.
16. *TADAE* A2.1, 7.
17. *TADAE* B3.3,5; in B3.8,20 apparently *mšḥ m[b]śym* "infused oil" and in D3.16,8 *mš]ḥ bśym*, possible differences in meaning are imperceptible.
18. *TADAE* B3.8,20.
19. nV 1:26 in *ATTM*, 2, 205-7.
20. *TADAE* C3.7.
21. *TADAE* C3.29.
22. *TADAE* C3.11,4.11; 3.18,15.
23. Naveh and Shaked C 1,25.
24. Collected in D. Schwiderski, *Die alt- und reichsaramäischen Inschriften,* vol. I: *Konkordanz*. *FSBP* 1 (2008), 549f.
25. Generally in Ezr. 6:9; with a statement of the precise quantities in 7:22, which seem incredibly high, however; see H. G. M. Williamson, *Ezra, Nehemiah. WBC* (1985), 102f.
26. For the mixture of flour and olive oil, cf. Ex. 29:40 and for the necessity of salt, Lev. 2:13.
27. *DJPA*, 334a; *DJBA*, 713a; *LexSyr*, 407; *MdD*, 280.

after the second century B.C.E.,[28] although at Qumran, the term *mšyḥ* occurs only in the Hebrew documents.[29] The identification of the "son of God" in 4Q246[30] with the messiah is also pronouncedly controversial. In the foreground clearly stands the expectation of the kingdom of God.

Gzella

28. Gzella.
29. Cf. Collins, 810-17.
30. → *br* IV.

נביא *nby'* /nabī(')/; נבא *nb'*; נבואה *nbw'h* /nabū'ā/

I. Etymology, Forms, and Lexical Field. II. Biblical Aramaic. III. Qumran.

I. Etymology, Forms, and Lexical Field. Presumably, Aramaic adopted the masculine noun *nby'* /nabī/[1] "prophet" from the Hebrew; this assumption finds support, in any case, in the fact that it first appears in the Aramaic of the Jewish literary tradition in Palestine and consistently refers to the prophets of Israel: first in Ezra, then in a few fragments from Qumran. There, it always occurs in the traditional spelling *nby'* with the etymological ', while the pointing in Ezr. 5:1 indicates the pronunciation /nabī/ to be expected according to the laws of phonetics.[2]

The phenomenon of prophecy, that is of the communication of divine messages through persons specially gifted for the purpose, was, admittedly, already known in other cultures of Syria-Palestine at the beginning of the Iron Age. As a term for this, however, Aramaic employed the participle *ḥzh* /ḥāzǣ/ "seer,"[3] as already occurs in the Old Aramaic Zakkur stele[4] and the wall inscription in the form of a literary text from Deir

E. Blum, "Israels Prophetie im altorientalischen Kontext," in I. Cornelius and L. Jonker, eds., *"From Ebla to Stellenbosch." ADPV* 37 (2008) 81-115; H. Gzella, *A Cultural History of Aramaic. HO* 111 (2015); idem, "Deir 'Allā," in G. Khan, ed., *Encyclopedia of Hebrew Language and Linguistics* (Leiden, 2013), 1:691-93; J. Jeremias, "נָבִיא *nābî'* prophet," *TLOT*, 697-710; H.-P. Müller, "נָבִיא *nāḇî'*," *TDOT*, IX, 129-50; C. Stadel, *Hebraismen in den aramäischen Texten vom Toten Meer* (Heidelberg, 2008); J. Stökl, *Prophecy in the Ancient Near East. CHANE* 56 (2012); M. Weippert, *Götterwort en Menschenmund. FRLANT* 252 (2014); G. Xeravits, "*nby'*," *ThWQ*, II, 847-52.

1. From an older */nabī'/.
2. Since a glottal stop concluding a syllable disappeared at the end of the Old Aramaic period, *ATTM*, 104-6; cf. Stadel, 63.
3. → *ḥzī* II.2.
4. *KAI* 202 A 12, here for the soothsayer in the service of the king in a siege.

'Allā.[5] The latter indicates that judgment prophecy was also known in the Transjordan already ca. 800 B.C.E.[6] and that lines of tradition in common with Canaanite religious literature existed, which can be clearly demonstrated further from the linguistic evidence.[7] Meanwhile, the specific lexeme *nby'* first appears in Biblical Aramaic. In addition to the designation for a function /nabī/ "prophet," Biblical Aramaic also attests the verb *nb'*, probably derived from the noun, in the Dt-stem "to appear as a prophet" and the feminine abstract noun /nabū'ā/ "prophecy," presumably also borrowed from Hebrew.

In Syriac, the noun became widespread, probably under the influence of the Bible translations. In addition to the already known forms, it also attests an adjective "prophetic" and a D-stem of the verb "to predict."[8]

II. Biblical Aramaic. The noun first occurs in Ezra for specific Israelite prophets. In Ezr. 5:1 and 6:14, the singular in the determined state serves as a title, "the prophet," after the name of Haggai. In 5:1f. the plural "the prophets"[9] encompasses Haggai and Zechariah, who supported the construction of the temple.[10] Both passages, moreover, relate them explicitly to "the God of Israel" via the adverbial addition "in the name of" (5:1) and a genitive circumlocution with *dy* (5:2).

The verb *nb'* "to appear as prophet" also appears once in the Dt-stem (Ezr. 5:1), where the subject is the plural of the noun. Hebrew employs the verb in both the N-stem and the D-stem,[11] but since no N-stem exists in Aramaic, the evidence corresponds to grammatical expectations.

The feminine abstract *nbw'h* /nabū'ā/ "prophecy" in a genitive construction in Ezr. 6:14 designates the activity of the prophets Haggai and Zechariah.

III. Qumran. Qumran preserves three sure instances of the noun: the singular in the determined state in the priestly prophecy 4Q562 7:1 as the subject of the verb → *mll* "what the prophet said" and in the report of future history 4Q556 1:7, although neither has a broader context, and the plural in the phrase *nby'y [š]qr'* "the lying prophets"[12] at the beginning of a list of false prophets from Num., 1–2 K., and Jer. with their Hebrew titles (4Q339 1:1).[13]

Gzella

5. *KAI* 312.1.

6. See Blum's fundamental treatment.

7. See recently Gzella, *Cultural History*, 87-91, and idem, "Deir 'Allā."

8. *LexSyr*, 411b.

9. Regarding the form *nby'y'* see *BLA*, §57z.

10. → *s'd.*

11. On the principal difference in the type of action between these stems, cf. H. Gzella, "Voice in Classical Hebrew against Its Semitic Background," *Or* 78 (2009) 317f.

12. For similar expressions, cf. Isa. 9:14 and Jer 23:26; see Stadel, 66.

13. Regarding the relationship of the two languages in this text, cf. H. Gzella, review of K. Berthelot and D. Stökl Ben Ezra, *Aramaica Qumranica*, *BiOr* 69, 2012, 119f.

נגד *ngd*; נגד *ngd* /negd/; נגוד *ngwd* /nagōd/; נגידו *ngydw* /nagīdū/

I. The Root. II. Use of the Verb. III. Nouns.

I. The Root. The words *ngd* and *nqd* trace back to the same root with the meaning "to move (out), to set out." It occurs with a variety of specific nuances and underlies several nominal derivations.

II. Use of the Verb. The verb is well known in Hebrew,[1] and in Arabic, Ethiopic, and Libyco-Berber.[2] The intransitive meaning "to move out" occurs in several literary texts: 1QapGen 19:8,10 (Abraham's migrations); 22:4,7 (an army marching out); 4Q213a 2:11 (T. Levi); T. Levi 33:9; 4Q547 6:5; 4Q550 5+5a:2; or *m. 'Abot* 1:13. The peal active participle refers in Dnl. 7:10 to a "stream of flowing fire,"[3] that proceeds from the throne of the Ancient of Days.[4] The passive participle describes resultatively a boat "drawn onto the dry land."[5] The hitpaal imperfect likewise describes a boat that first must still be pulled ashore. One of the satrap's letters from Bactria seems to employ the verb with the previously unattested nuance "to bring in" in relation to a disproportionate tax.[6] A physiognomic omen text from Qumran describes a nose (*'p*) with the peal passive participle as "drawn,"[7] thus, probably, as "sharply cut."[8]

III. Nouns. The noun *ngd* denotes a royal dignitary ("emissary"): in a Sefire stele,[9] in the letter of prince Adon to the pharaoh,[10] and in the narrative frame of Aḥiqar.[11] Parallels in Job 29:10; 31:37 and Prov. 8:6[12] confirm this interpretation. The meaning "to report" of

---

K. Blumental and C. Kumpmann, "*ngd*," *ThWQ*, II, 864-68; F. García López, "נגד *ngd*," *TDOT*, IX, 174-86; E. Y. Kutscher, J. Naveh, and S. Shaked, "*Hktwbwt hr'mywt šl 'šwqh*," *Leshonenu* 34 (1970) 125-36, esp. 126; E. Lipiński, "'Leadership': The Roots *DBR* and *NGD* in Aramaic," in *"Und Mose schrieb dieses Lied auf." FS O. Loretz. AOAT* 250 (1998), 501-14, esp. 509-14; J. Naveh and S. Shaked, *Aramaic Documents from Ancient Bactria (Fourth Century* B.C.E.*)* (London, 2012); C. Westermann, "נגד *ngd* hi. to communicate," *TLOT*, 714-18.

1. García López, 174-86.
2. *nkd* "to go to the top."
3. → *nhr*.
4. → *krs'* III; *npq* II.2.
5. *TADAE* A6.2,8.
6. Naveh and Shaked, A1,2. 11.
7. 4Q561 1 1:2.
8. *ATTM*, 2, 163. *DSSStE*, 1116f., translates "long."
9. *KAI* 224.10.
10. *KAI* 266.8.
11. *TADAE* C1.1,10.
12. Texts that exhibit linguistic affinities with Aramaic in general: Lipiński, 510f.

the Hebrew denominal *higgīḏ* traces back to this nuance of the noun. The general usage to mean "emissary with flax" (*ngdy ktn*) or "emissary of the judges" (*ngdy dtbry'*) occurs in *TADAE* C3.11,12 and Segal 13.3. The noun *ngdwt'*[13] is an abstract "advance" derived from *ngd* "leader," employed as a counterpart to the Prakrit *anaraṃleho* "nonkilling."[14] Finally, there is the preposition *ngd*, vocalized *nægæḏ* in Biblical Aramaic (Dnl. 6:11), for a movement "in the direction of" something. Its function corresponds to the basic meaning of the verb.

Lipiński

---

13. Aśoka inscription *KAI* 273.3f. from Taxila; text damaged.

14. H. Humbach, *Die aramäische Inschrift von Taxila* (Mainz, 1969), esp. 9, perhaps in the sense of "to survive."

נגה *ngh* /nogh/

I. Etymology and Lexical Field. II. Usage.

I. Etymology and Lexical Field. The Aramaic masculine noun *ngh* /nogh/ "broad daylight" "dawn," later with syllable expansion /nogah/,[1] belongs to the verbal root *ngh* "to shine." Hebrew attests it frequently[2] in the G- ("to shine") and causative-stems ("to cause to shine, to illuminate"), but it also has cognates in other Semitic languages and appears in Aramaic first in late antiquity;[3] otherwise, Aramaic has → *nhr* for "to shine." The noun designates broad daylight, either generally as the opposite of darkness or specifically as dawn. It is also sometimes explicitly the time when divine assistance manifests itself. For "morning" as a chronological instead of a meteorological term, one employed /ṣapr/.[4]

H. Eising, "*nāgah*," *TDOT*, IX, 186f.; B. Janowski, *Rettungsgewißheit und Epiphanie des Heils*. *WMANT* 59 (1989); J. F. Quant "*ngh*," *ThWQ*, II, 868f. (only Heb.).

1. *ATTM*, 114.

2. *GesB*[18], 778.

3. *DJPA*, 340; *MdD*, 288.

4. Cf. a few older specimens in a first-century B.C.E. list of outgoing goods; text in *ATTM*, 2, 264.

II. Usage. In the judgment prophecy of wall inscriptions from Deir ʿAllā with the first instance from the Old Aramaic period,[5] *ngh* constitutes the opposite of → *ḥšk* "darkness." This does not coincide with the night as part of the normal course of the day, but is produced by active intervention of the gods as the reversal of the natural order.

Then, one occurrence appears in the depiction of King Darius's walk to the lions' den in Dnl. 6:20. The parallel with /šaparpar/ "daybreak"[6] makes it clear that it refers to dawn. After a night of fasting, the king sets out immediately to see about Daniel whom he had been required, although based on an accusation, to throw to the lions according to his own law. Daniel, however, had survived the night through the protection of an angel,[7] so that the old motif of God's help in the morning shines through here.[8]

The same motif complex may also be involved when, according to the vision of the Four Trees from Qumran, *nwgh'* "the light of day"[9] shines, probably on the interpreting angel (the end of the preceding line preserves only *dy ʿlwhy* "on him")[10] and thus reveals the true nature of the secular empires in divine clarity. Another possible instance is very fragmentary.[11]

Gzella

5. *KAI* 312.6f.
6. → *špr*.
7. → *ml'k* II.2.
8. See, generally, Janowski.
9. 4Q552 2 2:1.
10. See the reconstruction in *ATTM*, 2, 144.
11. 4Q580 1 2:15.

נדב *ndb*

I. Etymology, Distribution, and Lexical Field. II. Imperial Aramaic. III. Biblical Aramaic. IV. Later Jewish Aramaic Languages.

I. Etymology, Distribution, and Lexical Field. The verbal root *ndb* may be common Semitic; this assumption finds support especially in the occurrence of the element *ndb* as a verb or noun in Amorite, Ugaritic, Phoenician, Moabite, Ammonite, Idumean, Hebrew,

J. Conrad, "*ndb*," *TDOT*, IX, 219-26; D. Dimant, "*ndb*," *ThWQ*, II, 879-83; Y. Sabar, *A Jewish Neo-Aramaic Dictionary* (Wiesbaden, 2002); K. L. Tallqvist, *Assyrian Personal Names* (Helsingfors, 1914); idem, *Neubabylonisches Namenbuch* (Helsingfors, 1905); J. P. Weinberg, "The Word *ndb* in the Bible," in *Solving Riddles and Untying Knots. FS J. Greenfield* (Winona Lake, IN, 1995), 365-75.

Old South Arabian, and Arabic names.[1] In any case, all of the cuneiform instances refer to West Semitic personal names. At least in the Northwest Semitic personal names, this element *ndb* seems to have the meaning "to prove to be generous," which is not entirely clear for the others.

Apart from this issue, the basic meaning of the probably primary verbal root is not easy to deduce; in any case, it persists in the Akkadian *nadābu* "to call over" (?), Arabic *nadaba* "to lament, bemoan, delegate, commission" and *nadiba* "to scar over, heal,"[2] Sabean "to build, to work on" (IV. stem), and Biblical Hebrew *ndb* (G-stem) "to drive, push" (with "heart, spirit" as subject) and "to be willing, to give freely" (Dt-stem) primarily in the postexilic books of 1–2 Ch. and Ezr.[3] and, thus, perhaps under Aramaic influence. Hebrew also attests the feminine substantive /nadabā/ "free impulse, will" and the adjective /nadīb/ "willing, noble," which also functions as a substantivized feminine to mean "nobility, dignity."[4]

Based primarily on Hebrew and Akkadian, one may deduce a basic meaning "to drive, push," and, probably via the passive, the meaning "to be generous, ungrudging, genteel, noble" arises.[5]

In Aramaic, the G-stem of *ndb* appears in personal names,[6] and further, the verb otherwise appears in the G-, D-, and occasionally perhaps in the causative stem along with the noun /nadabā/. Biblical Aramaic, in contrast, employs the verb only in the Dt stem "to be willing, to give freely" either as a modal verb or, in the full sense, the infinitive in the construct state as a verbal noun with the specific meaning "grant" (Ezr. 7:16, cf. Heb. in 1:6). The extrabiblical Aramaic texts from the Dead Sea and non-Jewish Aramaic dialects attest the verb and the feminine noun /nadabā/ "grant" only sparsely,[7] in Jewish, meanwhile, down to the present.[8]

Synonyms include, in addition to → *qrb* in the D-stem "to offer" once, also the later attested *pšq* "to designate as a grant," → *bʿī* "to seek, request" and → *ṣbī* "to want," and *ndr* "to vow."

II. Imperial Aramaic. Imperial Aramaic attests the verb *ndb* once as a participle of the D-stem (or causative-stem?) in an Egyptian court record (fifth century B.C.E.): *mndb mnky b'lh mly'* "Mannuki vows with these words."[9] In a Sam'alian royal inscription (eighth century B.C.E.), the noun /nadab/ "delegation, commission" already appears much earlier.[10]

---

1. Representative specimens in *GesB*[18], 783, s.v. *nāḏāḇ*.
2. In the VIII Stem: "to delegate, entrust to, to devote oneself to, to comply willingly, to be ready."
3. *GesB*[18], 783.
4. *GesB*[18], 783f. Regarding Qumranic Hebrew, cf. Dimant, 879-83.
5. Much as with Hebrew *nūd*, the external movement "to fluctuate" applied to the inner passive "to demonstrate sympathy, to have compassion."
6. Cf. M. Maraqten, *Die semitischen Personennamen in den alt- und reichsaramäischen Inschriften aus Vorderasien. TStO* 5 (1988), 122f.,124f.,186.
7. Cf. regarding Mandean, *MdD*, 290.
8. See, e.g., Sabar, 230.
9. *TADAE* B8.7,3.
10. *KAI* 214.32f.; for the meaning, see *DNSI*, 716.

III. Biblical Aramaic. In Biblical Aramaic, one encounters only the verb; it is restricted to Artaxerxes's letter to the priest Ezra. While the verb *ndb* and the noun *ndbh* refer in the Hebrew parts of Ezra only to the donations for the Jerusalem temple, Aramaic also offers the more general meaning "to be willing." The verb in the full sense appears in the Dt-stem with *l-* "to donate for": *wlhyblh ksp wdhb dy mlk' wy'ṭwhy htndbw l'lh yśr'l dy byrwšlm mšknh* "and in order to deliver the silver and gold that the king and his council have donated for the God of Israel, whose dwelling is in Jerusalem" (Ezr. 7:15; constructed similarly in 7:16 with the participle for a circumstantial clause expressing simultaneity);[11] the participle also appears as a modal verb "to be willing" with *l-* and an infinitive: *dy kl mtndb bmlkwty mn 'mh yśr'l wkhnwhy wlwy' lmhk lyrwšlm* "to that, whoever in my empire of the people Israel and its priests and Levites is willing to move to Jerusalem" (Ezr. 7:13). The infinitive construct functions as a noun "donation" with a subsequent genitive: *'m htndbwt 'm' wkhny'* "together with the voluntary gifts of the people and the priests" (Ezr. 7:16).

IV. Later Jewish Aramaic Languages. The Targums employ the verb *ndb* in the G-stem "to drive" as in Biblical Hebrew, in the Gt-stem for "to donate," as sometimes also in Jewish Palestinian.[12] Jewish Babylonian employs the Dt-stem in this usage.[13] The Targums, Jewish Palestinian, and Samaritan also attest the noun /nadabā/ "donation."[14]

Nebe

11. Cf. *BLA*, §339n.
12. *DJPA*, 341b.
13. See *DJBA*, 730b.
14. Cf. *DJPA*, 349a; *ATTM*, 633.

נדד *ndd*; נוד *nūd*; ערק *'rq*

I. Etymology, Grammatical Constructions, and Lexical Field. II. Biblical Aramaic and Qumran. III. *'rq* "to Flee."

I. Etymology, Grammatical Constructions, and Lexical Field. As with other verbal roots with a long second radical (*mediae geminatae*), *ndd* "to flee" along with semantically related verbs, such as, especially, the Hebrew *ndī* "to cast out" (D-stem) and *nūd* "to move back and forth," trace back to an originally biradical base.

W. Gross, "נָדַד *nāḏaḏ*," *TDOT*, IX, 227-31; E. Jenni, "'Fliehen' im akkadischen und hebräischen Sprachgebrauch," *Or* 47 (1978) 351-59; C. Stadel, *"ndd," ThWQ*, II, 883-84.

For Aramaic, the lexicographical tradition usually assesses *ndd* "to flee" (such as the "perfect" *naddaṯ* "it fled" in Dnl. 6:19) and the apparently synonymous *nūd* (such as the short imperfect *t^enuḏ* "it should flee" in Dnl. 4:11) as distinct lexemes.[1] *ATTM*,[2] however, proceeds, following Dnl. 4:11 and the long imperfect *tnwd* "will flee" (of sleep) in a Geniza manuscript of T. Levi 33:6, from a common, even later—although with another nuance—well-attested root *nūd*. The perfect in Dnl. 6:19 must have originally been pronounced /nādat/ and the transmitted pointing as *naddaṯ* would have been secondarily conformed to the pattern of the verb *ndd* which is much more frequent in Hebrew. Conversely, *LexLingAram*[3] hesitantly contemplates including the form in 4:11 under *ndd* and revocalizing it *tinnoḏ*. Of the two forms, Biblical Aramaic first attests the root once in the G-stem. A prepositional expression following *mn* "from" (Dnl. 4:11) or *ʿl* "to the detriment of" (6:19) can modify it.

In East Aramaic in post-Christian times, *nūd* with the meaning "to move, to wobble," in the causative-stem "to shake" with the corresponding t-passive, is productive;[4] *ndd*, to the contrary, remains marginal in Aramaic. In Aramaic, the typical verb for "to flee" in all eras was *ʿrq* (→ III). Meanwhile, Aramaic employs the G-stem of *plṭ*[5] for a successful flight from danger, that is, for "to escape."[6]

II. Biblical Aramaic and Qumran. In Biblical Aramaic, *nūd* appears in the literal sense in Nebuchadnezzar's dream of the world tree. Because of the divine command announced with a mighty voice to fell the proud tree, the animals that have previously found protection in its shadow and branches[7] should also flee. Here, the verb, like the Hebrew *ndd*, has the connotation of a panicked flight effected by divine intervention (cf. Jer. 49:5), and is accordingly constructed with the ablative preposition *mn* "from . . . away," but with no indication of direction.

Thereafter, the form in Dnl. 6:19, linked with *ndd* in the traditional vocalization and appearing in a figurative expression with the preposition *ʿl* "from it = in its shade," designates the flight of sleep (*šnh* /šenā/), for which Hebrew also knows parallels (Gen. 31:40; Est. 6:1). After Daniel had fallen victim to court intrigue because of his religion, King Darius, himself, who had unknowingly approved the fatal law, could no longer help his protégé and consigned him to the lions' den. In the night, he went to bed hungry, could not sleep, and set out[8] immediately at daybreak to see about Daniel, who, protected by God, had survived.[9] The topos of the sleepless king symbolizes here, as in Est. 6:1, the burden of power.

The same image occurs in Qumran in a passage in the Book of Giants as the effect of a disturbing dream of the giants, thus awakening in terror and not, as the context of

1. E.g., *LexLingAram*, 110; cf. regarding *ndd BLA*, §48d and *GesB*[18], 1514.
2. *ATTM*, 634 and 2, 438.
3. *LexLingAram*, 110.
4. *DJBA*, 734f.; *LexSyr*, 418; *MdD*, 293.
5. → *nṣl*.
6. Regarding the lexical field in the older Semitic languages in general, see Jenni.
7. Collective singular *ḥwytʾ*, → *ḥyī* V.
8. → *ngh*.
9. → *nṣl*.

Dnl. 6:19 implies, for sleep difficulties.[10] In general, people in premodern times rarely slept throughout the night so that, because of the many interruptions, they experienced dreams[11] as particularly disturbing and realistic.

In contrast, Aramaic has the verb *ʿīr*[12] in the Gt-stem, sometimes modified with the addition of *mn šnh* "from sleep," for "to awaken" in nonfigurative expressions.[13]

III. *ʿrq* "to Flee." The typical Aramaic verb for "to flee," however, is *ʿrq* in the G-stem. It arose from an original **ṣ́rq* and is, therefore, still spelled *qrq* in Old and Imperial Aramaic.[14] In the Old Aramaic state treaties from Sefire, it refers to political refugees,[15] and often in the somewhat later letter ostracon from Asshur.[16] Imperial Aramaic manifests it thereafter in the translation of the Behistun inscription for fleeing troops[17] and in a letter from the chancellery of the satrap Aršama in reference to a slave who fled after a theft[18] and who should be punished; it appears further in a fragmentary context in Segal nos. 26.6 und 86a.6 from Saqqara.

These nuances known from older Aramaic reappear at Qumran, where the verb occurs in the form *ʿrq* following the meanwhile introduced dissimilation of the Aramaic reflex of */ṣ́/ to /ʿ/: in 1QapGen 21:32[19] and 22:9 for the flight after a battle, in 20:21 again for flight because of political circumstances.[20] In 11Q10 10:4 (Job 26:13), finally, it translates the Hebrew *brḥ* in reference to a fleeing serpent.

The verb *ʿrq* remained very much in use in Aramaic even later, which also attests it in the D-stem "to drive out."[21]

Gzella

---

10. 4Q530 2 2+ 6-12:4; probably also to be reconstructed in 4Q531 22, 10.
11. → *ḥlm*.
12. → *ʿyr*.
13. Cf. e.g., 1QapGen 19:17.
14. Cf. *ATTM*, 2, 460.
15. *KAI* 224.4,19f., presumably also to be read in 222 B 45; in the participle substantivized "refugee."
16. *KAI* 233.9,13,16,17f.
17. *TADAE* C2.1,60.
18. *TADAE* A6.3, 5.
19. Corresponding to Heb. *nûs* in Gen 14:10.
20. In 4Q196 14 1:12 (Tob. 6:16) it is presumably to be supplied following the other versions in reference to the flight of an expelled demon.
21. See *DJPA*, 420f.; *DJBA*, 883; *LexSyr*, 550; *MdD*, 38.

נדן *ndn* /nedān/

I. Etymology and Form. II. Usage.

I. Etymology and Form. The meaning of the noun *ndn* /nedān/ "covering" is disputed. Following W. B. Henning,[1] Wagner,[2] Vogt,[3] Beyer,[4] and *GesB*[18 5] assume an Iranian loanword from */nidāniya/ "depot, storehouse."[6] The pointing in Dnl. 7:15 as *nidnǣ* is dubious; consequently, *LexLingAram*[7] suggests *nᵉḏānah*, but the text is often considered corrupt (→ II). The word occurs with certainty mediated by Aramaic[8] in 1 Ch. 21:27 with *ḥrb* for "scabbard" ("[in] its scabbard") and with the vocalization *nᵉḏānāh* expected given an Iranian etymology.

II. Usage. Both of the possible instances preserved in Aramaic are figurative. In Dnl. 7:15, the difficult expression *bgwʾ ndnh* as an adverbial supplement following *ʾtkryt rwḥy* "my spirit was grieved"[9] refers to the effect of the vision on the four chimeras. If one points *nᵉḏānah* (→ I), it would mean "in its covering," and thus "in me." Likely, however, is the conjecture *bgyn dnh* "for this reason."[10] Admittedly, one could refer to the metaphorical usage in 1QapGen 2,10 *wnšmty lgw ndnhʾ* "and my breath in its covering" (in a vigorous conversation),[11] but it could, in turn, reflect the influence of Dnl. 7:15 (not preserved at Qumran) with the misunderstanding of *bgwʾ ndnh*.

Gzella

W. Hinz, *Altiranisches Sprachgut der Nebenüberlieferungen. GOF.I* 3 (1975); J. Tavernier, *Iranica in the Achaemenid Period (ca. 550-330 B.C.). OLA* 158 (2007); M. Wagner, *Die lexikalischen und grammatikalischen Aramaismen im alttestamentlichen Hebräisch. BZAW* 96 (1966).

1. Cited in Hinz, 175.
2. Wagner, 81.
3. *LexLingAram*, 110.
4. *ATTM*, 633.
5. *GesB*[18], 786.
6. Cf. also Tavernier, 439, §4.4.8.15, who does not refer to Aramaic, however.
7. *LexLingAram*, 110.
8. → *nštwn* III.
9. From *krī*.
10. → *gw*; so also *GesB*[18], 1514.
11. → *nšm*.

נהר *nhr* /nahar/

I. Etymology and Meaning. II. General Usage. III. Place Names. 1. For Individual Bodies of Water. 2. "Beyond the River" and "Mesopotamia." IV. Figuratively in Visions.

I. Etymology and Meaning. In the Semitic languages, the most common words for "river" or "canal" trace back to the common primary noun /nahar/, including Aramaic where, as elsewhere, it is a masculine. The word is also associated with the names of certain streams.[1] As an absolute, it refers, as in Hebrew, to the most important river in a region; thus, the expression *'br nhr'* "(the land) beyond the river (= west of the Euphrates)" refers in Achaemenid administrative terminology to the entire region of Syria-Palestine, and *byn nhryn* "between the rivers" survives in the Greek geographical designation Mesopotamia. In visions, /nahar/ is rarely also employed in a figurative manner.

As a term for a large, usually natural, river, /nahar/ differs from the also masculine substantive /yabal/ "brook"[2] and /naḥl/ "brook, creek valley,"[3] both of which are first attested in the post-Imperial Aramaic period. In contrast, the feminine /'amm/ can designate an artificial canal.[4]

II. General Usage. In the general sense, one encounters *nhr* "river" sporadically in texts from the Old and Imperial Aramaic periods. The first instances occur in the introductory hymn to Hadad in the Tell Fekheriye inscription as part of the divine epithet *gwgl nhr klm* "Master of the waters of all streams."[5] Since the third-person plural suffix *-m* in *klm* apparently refers to the singular *nhr*, *nhr* is considered either a collective noun "waters" or as an internal plural "rivers" minus the later regular ending through ablaut.[6] Otherwise, *nhr* behaves like a normal masculine, so that both explanations have so far been valid only for this one passage. A dedicatory gift harness from Hazael of Damascus also stems from the Old Aramaic period. It is dated *bšnt 'dh mr'n nhr* "in the year in which our lord Hazael crossed the river."[7]

Imperial Aramaic preserves four specimens in everyday texts from Elephantine.[8] The episode of Darius's crossing of the Tigris, still current in later reception, reported in the Behistun inscription (§17),[9] is not preserved in the fragmentary Aramaic papyrus version.

I. Eph'al and J. Naveh, "Hazael's Booty Inscriptions," *IEJ* 39 (1989) 192-200; J. J. Finkelstein, "Mesopotamia," *JNES* 21 (1962) 73-92; J. A. Fitzmyer, *The Genesis Apocryphon of Qumran Cave 1 (1Q20). BietOr* 18B (³2004); N. Hasemann and B. Schlenke, "*nhr*," *ThWQ*, II, 897-901; E. Lipiński, "Aramaic Broken Plurals in the Wider Semitic Context," in H. Gzella and M. L. Folmer, eds., *Aramaic in Its Historical and Linguistic Setting. VOK* 50 (2008), 27-40; H. Lozachmeur, *La collection Clermont-Ganneau: Ostraca, épigraphes sur jarre, étiquettes de bois*, 2 vols. (Paris, 2006); A. F. Rainey, "The Satrapy 'Beyond the River,'" *Australian Journal of Biblical Archaeology* 1 (1969) 51-78; L. A. Snijders, "נָהָר *nāhār*," *TDOT*, IX, 261-70.

1. Cf. *flumen Tiberis* in Latin or "the River Thames" in English.
2. From the root *ybl*, in the causative-stem "to bring."
3. From an old */naḫl/.
4. Cf. *ATTM*, 513 and 2, 348.
5. *KAI* 309.4.
6. Cf. Lipiński's discussion.
7. *KAI* 311; see Eph'al and Naveh.
8. *TADAE* C3.13,34, very fragmentary; D7.9,14; Lozachmeur, no. 140cv8 with *b-* "in" and 236cv3 with *tḥt* "under."
9. On the historical background, see recently especially R. Rollinger, *Alexander und die großen Ströme. Schwimmschläuche, Keleks und Pontonbrücken* (Wiesbaden, 2013).

III. Place Names.

1. For Individual Bodies of Water. Sometimes a subsequent *nhrʾ* in the determined state "the river" also expands specific river names. Especially numerous examples of this geographical information appear in the passages concerning the distribution of land and the migrations of Abraham in 1QapGen from Qumran, which are significantly more precise in comparison to Genesis: in 16:9,15f. and 17:16 for the *ṭynh* "Tina" or Tanais, that is the Don;[10] 19:11 for the *krmwnʾ* "Karmon" or, according to *ATTM*, 172, *nrmwnʾ* "Narmon";[11] 21:15,19 for the *g(y)ḥwn* "Gihon" (probably the Nile);[12] 21:17,28 for the *pwrt* "Euphrates"; and in 17:7 perhaps for the *ḥdql* "Tigris."[13] In the determined state, *nhrʾ* can also refer explicitly to a river previously mentioned by name.[14] The *nhr mṣryn* "River of Egypt"[15] is, of course, the Nile.

In everyday life, rivers also served as convenient unchanging points of orientation. In the description of the pertinent property, a Nabatean endowment contract from the Dead Sea once mentions *nhrʾ rbʾ* "the great river" as a boundary,[16] then the *nhrʾ dkrʾ* (ll. 9,42), which is translated either as a name "the river 'Ram'"[17] or as an attribute "the masculine (= wild) river."[18] Meanwhile, it remains unclear which river it intends.

2. "Beyond the River" and "Mesopotamia." At the latest in Achaemenid times, the official designations of the regions relative to the great rivers were common, as though they had always been natural borders. Since Syria-Palestine lies west of the Euphrates, the older geographical term *ʿbr nhrʾ* "Beyond the River" (i.e., as far as the Egyptian border) became the official name in the prevalent Semitic languages.[19] Ezra employs it regularly,[20] but so do postexilic Hebrew texts (Ezr. 8:36; Neh. 2:7,9).

Furthermore, since the fourth century B.C.E., the region of the two rivers north of Baghdad was called "Between (the) Rivers," in Greek "Mesopotamia."[21] In Aramaic, one encounters the corresponding expression *byn nhryn* in 1QapGen 21:24 as an explanatory gloss for "Goyim," here the dominion of Tidal, one of the four emperors.[22] It describes Aram more precisely in 17:9 as *ʾrʿʾ dy byn tryn nhryʾ* "the land between the two rivers."[23]

---

10. Fitzmyer, 171.
11. For a discussion, see ibid., 182.
12. Ibid., 225.
13. In the reading of ibid., 96, the passage is paleographically difficult, however, and *ATTM*, 2, 100 refrains entirely from attempting to decipher it.
14. So twice in 1QapGen 19:12.
15. 1QapGen 21:11.
16. nV 7:8,40 in *ATTM*, 2, 218-23.
17. → *dkr* /dakar/ I.
18. *ATTM*, 2, 220; hardly, however, "the river mentioned" from the verbal root → *dkr*, which would contradict spelling and pronunciation.
19. Rainey.
20. Thirteen times in 4:10-7:25.
21. See Finkelstein.
22. Cf. Fitzmyer, 232f.
23. Ibid., 174.

IV. Figuratively in Visions. Finally, figurative uses of *nhr* sometimes appear. In the court scene in Dnl. 7:10, a *nhr dy nwr* "stream of figure" proceeds from the divine throne;[24] subsequently, this element became a fixed feature of the divine throne. Furthermore, an end-time vision from the Book of Giants contains the comparison *knhryn rbrbyn* "like great streams,"[25] in a fragmentary content and possibly in reference to blood.[26]

Gzella

24. On the tradition history → *krs'* III.
25. 4Q531 7:6.
26. So the reconstruction in *ATTM*, 2, 158f., G 10:26.

נהר *nhr*; נהור *nhwr* /nahōr/; נהיר *nhyr* /nahhīr/

I. Etymology, Forms, and Distribution. II. Biblical Aramaic. III. Qumran.

I. Etymology, Forms, and Distribution. The common Semitic root *nhr* belongs to the semantic field "to be light, light." In addition, there is a related biradical root → *nwr* /nūr/, attested in Aramaic as a noun "fire" and as a verb in the causative-stem "to shine."[1] The root *nhr* is distinct from the primary noun → *nhr* /nahar/ "river."

The masculine noun *nhwr* /nahōr/ "light"[2] has been attested since the post-Achaemenid period. In addition to the texts from Qumran (→ III), it appears in the older Jewish Targums, e.g., *n^ehōrā* in Onqelos. It has parallels in the Biblical Hebrew *n^ehārā* (Job 3:4)[3] and Arabic *nahār* "daylight, daytime."[4] In West Aramaic[5] it appears as *nwhrh* /nohrā/. Similarly, *nhyr* /nahhīr/, an adjective "light," belonging to the same root appears in various forms of the Aramaic language. After Biblical Aramaic and the Aramaic of the texts from Qumran, it also occurs in the Jewish Targums, e.g., in the fragmentary Targum MS V Ex. 12:42. A feminine abstract noun *nhyrw* /nahhīrū/ based on the adjective also appears after Biblical Aramaic in Syriac and Samaritan.

H. Gzella, "*nhr*," *ThWQ*, II, 919-25; E. Y. Kutscher, *Studies in Galilean Aramaic*, trans. M. Sokoloff (Ramat Gan, 1976), esp. 23.

1. Regarding the relationship between roots II-*ī*/-*ū* and II-*h* in general, see A. Reuveni, *Leshonenu* 3, 1932, 257-64 (article in Hebrew); cf. *ATTM*, 413.
2. On the form, cf. *ATTM*, 634.
3. In contrast to *ḥošæḵ*, cf. *GesB*[18], 789f.
4. In Aramaic, in contrast→ *ngh*.
5. Jewish Palestinian and Neo-West Aramaic, see Kutscher.

II. Biblical Aramaic. Biblical Aramaic attests the noun *nᵉhōrā* "light" in the *Qere* of the consonantal text *nhyr' ʿmh šr'* "light dwells with him" (Dnl. 2:22). The *Ketib nhyr'* occurs in Biblical Aramaic only in this passage. Various Aramaic languages attest the word *nhyr* as an adjective "light, bright, clear" in the *qattīl* pattern, yet it can also be employed as a noun "light."[6] In addition, *nhyr* constitutes the foundation of the abstract noun *nahīrū* (from /nahhīrū/) "enlightenment" in Dnl. 5:11,14. There it appears in the same context as *śokḵlᵉṯānū* "insight"[7] and *ḥoḵmā* "wisdom."[8]

III. Qumran. In the Aramaic texts from the Dead Sea, the noun *nhwr* "light" appears frequently and is attested more than thirty times in the various manuscripts: 4Q204 (Enoch), 4Q208-210 (astronomical Book of Enoch), 4Q531 (Book of Giants), 4Q544 and 4Q548 (Testament of Amram), 4Q580, 4Q590 and 11Q10.[9] The adjective *nhyr* is attested three times in a nominal usage: *ytglwn nhyr*[*y'*] "[the] lights will become evident" in 4Q536 2 1+3:3 (Noah's Birth); *wtḥdh bnhyr ʿlm'* "you will rejoice in the light of the world" in 4Q541 24 2:6 (Levi Apocryphon); and *wynhr nhyrh ʿlykwn* "and may his light shine over you" in 4Q542 1 1:1 (Testament of Qahat). In contrast, it functions as an adjective in two other passages: [*'rw kl bny nhwr'*] *nhyryn lhwwn* "[See, all the children of the light] will become bright" in 4Q548 1 2-2:10 (Testament of Amram) and *wk*[*l ḥky*]*m wqšyṭ nhyr* "and a[ny wis]e and upright person is bright" in the following lines. An additional instance is too fragmentary for a precise determination:] *wnhyr lhn* ["and bright/a light for them"(?) in 4Q542 2:12 (Testament of Qahat). The abstract *nhyrwt'* "enlightenment" occurs only once in 4Q548 1 2-2:14 (Testament of Amram) in a fragmentary context.

The related verb *nhr* in the causative-stem "to illuminate" appears in the expression *wynhr nhyrh ʿlykwn* already cited above. In contrast, the causative-stem of the root *nūr*[10] occurs more than twenty times in the following manuscripts: 4Q209-210 (astronomical book of Enoch), 4Q541 (Levi Apocryphon), and 4Q545 (Testament of Amram).

Fassberg

6. As in Syriac and Samaritan-Aramaic.
7. → *śkl*.
8. → *ḥkm* IV.
9. Regarding the individual passages, see the extensive discussion by Gzella, 919-25.
10. → *nwr* V.

נור *nwr* /nūr/; נור *nūr*

I. Etymology, Forms, and Lexical Field. II. Imperial Aramaic. III. Biblical Aramaic. IV. Qumran. V. Verb "to Shine."

I. Etymology, Forms, and Lexical Field. In the Semitic languages, the primary noun /nūr/ originally meant "light," as in Akkadian and Arabic. Under the influence of the probably secondary verbal root → *nhr* "to be bright"[1] the meaning of the noun /nūr/ in Aramaic has been restricted since the beginning to "fire" and has, thus, been synonymous with the inherited /ʾeššā/.[2] In contrast, the old usage for "light" endured in the element /nūrī/ of personal names as an onomastic archaism on into post-Christian times. In Aramaic, the noun is sometimes masculine and sometimes feminine. A semantic distinction is not (any longer) perceptible. The Aramaic texts from Qumran also contain a causative-stem of the verb *nūr* "to shine" with stars as the subject, but the state of the evidence suggests that it derives from the noun.

The root *yqd* appears since Old Aramaic times as a semantically related verb "to burn"; furthermore, since Biblical Aramaic, the related feminine noun /yaqedā/ "blaze, flame,"[3] and at Qumran also *ʾzī* in the Gt-stem, *dlq* (also in Dnl. 7:9), and *ḥrr*.[4] Figurative speech—primarily in visions—associates the rapidly moving fire with the "stream,"[5] and the flame with the "tongue."[6]

II. Imperial Aramaic. Imperial Aramaic first attests the noun with certainty in the expression → *mšḥ lnwrʾ* "oil for (the) fire," and therefore presumably lamp oil, in a list with the distribution of goods from Achaemenid Bactria.[7] This represents the only instance known today from Old and Imperial Aramaic, while /ʾeššā/ "fire" already appears in texts from the eighth and seventh centuries B.C.E.[8] An additional possible example of *nwr* in a corrupt context on an ostracon from Elephantine[9] is entirely hypothetical since the reading and interpretation of the passage remain controversial.

III. Biblical Aramaic. In Biblical Aramaic *nwr* /nūr/ "fire" only appears in the book of Daniel in the story of the fiery furnace (Dnl. 3:6-26) into which Daniel's friends were cast as royal punishment for their worship of God. Its very frequent usage in this passage identifies it as a leitmotif. The agreement with the participle *yqdthʾ* in the expression *ʾtwn nwrʾ yqdtʾ* "the flaming furnace" attests the feminine gender of the noun here, while it behaves as a masculine in 3:27. The repetition of the term "fire," which was additionally heated seven times hotter than usual (Dnl. 3:19) and killed even the executioner's assistants (3:22), emphasizes the inescapable situation against which the divine deliverance,

---

H. Drawnel, *The Aramaic Astronomical Book (4Q208-4Q211) from Qumran* (Oxford, 2011); H. Gzella, "*nwr*," *ThWQ*, II, 919-25; K. Koch, *Daniel 1–4. BK* XXII/1 (2005); J. Naveh and S. Shaked, *Aramaic Documents from Ancient Bactria (Fourth Century B.C.E.)* (London, 2012).

1. In contrast, the primary noun /nahar/ designates the "river."
2. → *ʾšʾ*.
3. → *ʾšʾ*.
4. Citations in Gzella, 920.
5. → *nhr* /nahar/.
6. → *lšn*.
7. Naveh and Shaked, C1.26.
8. → *ʾšʾ* III.1.
9. H. Lozachmeur, *La collection Clermont-Ganneau*, vol. 1 (Paris, 2006), no. 46cv5.

also accentuated as a leitmotif (3:15,17,28f.), stands out even more pronouncedly. Koch[10] mentions widespread parallel motifs for execution by immolation and for trial by fire.

In the throne vision in Dnl 7, too, fire in the form of flames (7:9) and of a stream (7:10) symbolizes superhuman power, here, admittedly in the context of divine majesty.

IV. Qumran. The Aramaic texts from Qumran employ *nwr* /nūr/ for the burnt offering (1QapGen 10:14; 11Q18 1:3), as a symbol of judgment (1QapGen 15:10), and generally in apocalyptic contexts (4Q206 1 21:3 and 4Q205 1 11:5 [1 En. 21:3 and 24:1]; 4Q530 2 2+6-12:9f.), further in relation to stars (4Q541 9 1:3f. for the eternal sons of God), and in the comparison with a wondrous child (1QapGen 5:13). Here, too, the dual nature of fire on one side, as destructive, and on the other as a cleansing and illuminating force is in evidence. Moreover, a few passages are fragmentary.[11]

V. Verb "to Shine." Additionally, the Aramaic texts from Qumran contain numerous instances of the verb *nūr* in the causative-stem meaning "to shine."[12] As a frequent astronomical term, it dominates in the description of the course of the moon in 4Q208-209 (1 En. 73),[13] indeed as a gnomic perfect for conditions valid across time. It can also be reflected in metaphor, as when the Levi Apocryphon announces that, in the end time, God's eternal sons will shine over the darkness (i.e., sin; 4Q541 9 1:3f.; → IV).[14]

Gzella

---

10. Koch, 269-71.
11. For a more extensive treatment, see H. Gzella, 921f.
12. So correctly *ATTM*, 635; in contrast, Drawnel, 248, is hardly credible when he traces the verb to *nhr* with the loss of the radical /-h-/. It would otherwise naturally be retained (→ *nhr* III).
13. On this generally, cf. Drawnel.
14. More in Gzella, 922.

נזק *nzq*; נזק *nzq* /nezq/

I. Lexical Field and Grammatical Constructions. II. Use of the Verb. 1. "To Suffer Affliction" (peal). 2. "To Damage" (aphel). III. Use of the Noun "Damage."

I. Lexical Field and Grammatical Constructions. Various Semitic languages attest a verbal root *nzq*, although it has different nuances of meaning in each. Aramaic employs

---

H. L. Ginsberg, "Lexicographical Notes," in *Hebräische Wortforschung. FS W. Baumgartner. SVT* 16 (1967), 71-82, esp. 81; Y. Yadin et al., eds., *The Documents from the Bar Kokhba Period in the Cave of Letters II* (Jerusalem, 2002).

it in the G-stem intransitively to mean "to suffer inconvenience, damage," in the causative-stem transitively to mean "to harm (someone), to cause difficulties (for someone)." Biblical Aramaic first attests the verb with certainty; there it always refers to the king. Further, the masculine noun /nezq/ "damage" belongs to the root. It can be found at the very earliest in several private documents from the Dead Sea, and, presumably, once as an Aramaic loanword, however, already in Biblical Hebrew (Est. 7:4) in the sense of "harassment (of the king)" (→ II.1).

II. Use of the Verb.

1. "To Suffer Affliction" (peal). A supposed Imperial Aramaic instance of the verb *nzq* or perhaps of the noun in a letter from Elephantine[1] is uncertain given the context and could mean "to forfeit" or "lose."[2] The G-stem of *nzq* surely occurs as a participle in Dnl. 6:3: King Darius places Daniel and two other trusted men over the 120 satraps of the empire as the supreme officers to whom the provincial governors must henceforth give account so that the king *l' lhw' nzq*. This is usually translated under the influence of the better-attested causative-stem as "should suffer no harm" (thus, dominion should be exercised to the satisfaction of the king). The context, however, also permits an interpretation in light of the Hebrew verb in Est. 7:4: the supervisors of the governors should assume the work of the king so that he "might not be bothered" by it.[3] No such "supervisory council" in Achaemenid provincial administration can be identified, but in the background may stand the very high degree of control that obligated even satraps of large regions to make regular visits with the king, which the late Achaemenid letters from Bactria now demonstrate in documentary primary sources.[4]

The corresponding t-stem meaning, "to suffer harm" in 4Q205 1 12:1 (1 En. 22:13) may function synonymously with the G-stem in Dnl. 6:3; it refers to the inconvenience suffered at the last judgment. Later, Jewish Palestinian also employs the G-stem actively for "to injure,"[5] which 4Q205 1 11:1 probably already announces because the passage implies a transitive G-stem.

2. "To Damage" (aphel). The causative-stem "to damage" first occurs three times in Ezr. (4:13,15,22), in each case in reference to the city of Jerusalem. According to the opponents of its reconstruction, Jerusalem is known to be rebellious,[6] has, consequently, already damaged earlier kings (Ezr. 4:15), and will indubitably do so again by refusing to pay tribute after the completion of the construction of the wall (4:13,22). According to MT, the imperfect (4:13) has a direct object, the participle

1. *TADAE* A4.2,14.
2. Cf. *DNSI*, 724.
3. So Ginsberg, 81.
4. Cf. H. Gzella, review of J. Naveh and S. Shaked, *Aramaic Documents from Ancient Bactria (Fourth Century B.C.E.)*, *BiOr* 71 (2014) 820, and more extensively idem, "Local Administration: Bactria," in B. Jacobs and R. Rollinger, eds., *A Companion to the Achaemenid Persian Empire* (Oxford, forthcoming).
5. *DJPA*, 345b.
6. → *mrd.*

(4:15) and the infinitive construct (4:22) with the subsequent noun. The difficult context of 4:13, with the unclear word *ʾptm* "request" (?) at the beginning of the clause and the Hebraicized ending *mlkm* for the subject, has led, among other clarification attempts, to the conjecture *mlky mhnzq* "my king suffers inconvenience," but it does not seem convincing.[7]

In the prophecy of the birth of Noah from Qumran, the verb refers to the damage that the *rwḥyn* "spirits" (or "winds"?) would cause the elect.[8] In later magical texts, the substantivized participle *mzq* also sometimes describe demons as "damagers."[9]

A Nabatean alliance treaty from the Dead Sea apparently employs the participle *mzq* in relation to the damaging of items for sale,[10] but the preceding context is destroyed.[11] Jewish Babylonian knows the verb in the causative-stem also with the meaning "to injure" and the corresponding t-stem as a passive.[12]

III. Use of the Noun "Damage." The noun /nezq/ "damage" appears often in a contract clause in Aramaic private documents from the Dead Sea. It obligates a seller to forgo any *ḥrr wtgr wnzg* "objection, litigation, or tort,"[13] or removes the seller's obligation in relation to damages and other matters.[14] In certificates of divorce, the noun refers to damages, along with devaluations and other losses, to the wife's property to be recompensed by the husband.[15]

Gzella

7. So also H. G. M. Williamson, *Ezra, Nehemiah. WBC* (1985), 56.
8. 4Q534 1 1:7.
9. E.g., in yyMA 2:8 found in *ATTM.E*, 235f.
10. Here with *b-* instead of a direct object, perhaps for partial impact?
11. nV 6:13 in *ATTM*, 2, 216f.; cf. Yadin, 266.
12. *DJBA*, 740.
13. V 48:9 in *ATTM*, 2, 251f.
14. nV 2:13,36 in *ATTM*, 2, 208-11 par. 3:39 in *ATTM*, 2, 212-15; contra Yadin, 201-31 and 233-44, however.
15. M 19:9,22 in *ATTM*, 308.

נחת *nḥt*

I. Etymology, Lexical Field, and Grammatical Constructions. II. General Use of the G-stem "to Descend." III. General Use of the Causative-stem "to Bring Down, Deposit." IV. Theological Use.

C. Kumpmann, "*nḥt*," *ThWQ*, II, 946-48; H. Lozachmeur, *La collection Clermont-Ganneau: Ostraca, épigraphes sur jarre, étiquettes de bois*, 2 vols. (Paris, 2006).

I. Etymology, Lexical Field, and Grammatical Constructions. The verb *nḥt* "to descend" is, like its semantic counterpart → *slq* "to ascend" and the analogous pair of verbs of direction → *npq* "to exit," → *ʿll* "to enter," typically Aramaic, but has a Northwest Semitic cognate in Ugaritic *nḥt* "to bring down."[1] A handful of instances in Hebrew, which otherwise employs the root *yrd* in this meaning, are, therefore, often attributed to Aramaic influence;[2] some of the pertinent passages are in dispute textually and morphologically, however. Consequently, it may very well be that the examples in poetic texts may be archaisms in poetic diction. Thus, Aramaic presumably expanded significantly a related, but originally much more restricted spectrum of usage of a verb inherited from an older phase of the language.

Aramaic attests the root beginning with Imperial Aramaic in the intransitive G-stem "to descend" (both of persons and of inanimate things such as tears or water) and from Old Aramaic in the transitive causative-stem. Both were productive.[3] Prepositional modifiers define the direction of movement more precisely: in the G-stem for the starting point *mn* (e.g., Dnl. 4:10,20), for the destination *l*-[4] or, more specifically, *ʿl* "to";[5] in the causative-stem directionally *l*- or *ʿl* "toward, to" or locatively *b*- "in" (at least in Ezr. 5:15 and 6:1,5 explicitly for "to deposit"), additionally, the seldom ablative *mn* "from." The internal passive (Dnl. 5:20) indicates, as one would expect, "to be brought down," here in the sense of "to be toppled."

Both stems often refer to meteorological phenomena such as rain, in theological context, furthermore, to the descent of divine beings to the earth (→ IV). For "to go" with no direct reference to direction, meanwhile, Aramaic has → *hlk*/*ʾzl* and for "to come" →*ʾtī*. For an (unguided) vertical movement from top to bottom, Aramaic employs → *npl* "to fall" and the less frequent → *ntr*.

II. General Use of the G-stem "to Descend." Imperial Aramaic documentary texts employ the G-stem of *nḥt* as an everyday verb. In a private letter from Elephantine concerning a loan and house sale, it appears in the demand that the addressee come to Memphis;[6] furthermore, this letter has the causative-stem in the same context (l. 13; → III). An additional private latter on an ostracon[7] is similar.

A contract concerning the usufruct of a house describes the use of a *drg* /darg/ "stairway" with *nḥt* in parallelism with its antonym *slq*,[8] just as does a last testament.[9] In

1. At least in the poetic register, see the analysis in *DUL*³, 620.

2. See *GesB*¹⁸, 808 with bibliography; in contrast, I. Kottsieper, *Die Sprache der Ahiqarsprüche*. *BZAW* 194 (1990), 217 is skeptical (s.v.).

3. Regarding the supposed D-stem, → III.

4. With place names apparently freely alternated with the "accusative of direction" without preposition, cf. *TADAE* A3.8,7 and 11.

5. 4Q209 23:10 (1 En. 77:4).

6. Thus, following the Nile, in the direction of the coast; *TADAE* A3.8, 7.8.13 imperative *ḥt*, l. 11 perfect or participle in a conditional clause, l. 8 alongside *ʾzl ʿl* "go to."

7. Lozachmeur, no. 82cv2.

8. *TADAE* B3.7,10.13.

9. *TADAE* B3.10,15.

contrast, the verb appears in the fragmentary Bar-Puneš novella for the descent into the underworld.[10] A few other passages, however, preserve no context.[11]

In Biblical Aramaic the G-stem occurs only twice in Nebuchadnezzar's dream in reference to the descent of the messenger angel (→ IV), then at Qumran in a range of different contexts: for Noah's descent from Mt. Ararat and ark landing;[12] for Abraham's tears[13] while praying to God;[14] for Tobias's descent to the river;[15] for the drainage of the receding waters in the flood according to Enoch's animal vision;[16] for the descent into the underworld;[17] and for the falling of snow[18] on mountains.

Palmyrene honorific inscriptions employ the verb frequently in relation to caravan traders as donors.[19] The citizens so honored had apparently rendered outstanding service by transporting wares without incident.[20]

III. General Use of the Causative-stem "to Bring Down, Deposit." With regard to the two instances of *nḥt* in the pre-Imperial Aramaic proverbs of Aḥiqar, it is uncertain whether *mnḥtwthm* or *mnḥtwth*, respectively,[21] is a suffixed infinitive of the otherwise entirely unused D-stem[22] or of the typical causative-stem for /maḥḥātūtohūn/ or /maḥḥātūtahā/, respectively, "to bring her down."[23] The second solution corresponds precisely with Aramaic usage and, consequently, clearly merits preference. The verb here stands, in any case, for a footstep as an example that not even one everyday act stands under human control (instead, as one may supply, fate of the divine will determines all).

Private letters from the Achaemenid period employ *nḥt* in the causative-stem "to bring down" for the delivery of goods from Hermopolis[24] and from Elephantine;[25] a similar situation pertains in a few other documents.[26]

---

10. *TADAE* C1.2,6.
11. *TADAE* C3.16,1; D1.1,5; Segal, nos. 62.1 and 124.3.
12. 1QapGen 12:8.
13. *dm'y*, with a 1 sg. suff.
14. 1QapGen 20:12.
15. 4Q197 4 1:6 (Tob. 6:2).
16. 4Q206 4 2:3 (1 En. 89:8).
17. 11Q10 1:2 (Job 17:16).
18. *tlg*, 4Q209 23:10 (1 En. 77:4).
19. *PAT* 0279.4, the Greek parallel version has κατελθόντες; 1411.3; 1419.3.
20. Bibliography on the cultural backgrounds in H. Gzella, "Das Aramäische in den römischen Ostprovinzen," *BiOr* 63 (2006) 22-31.
21. *TADAE* C1.1,170f.
22. So I. Kottsieper, *Die Sprache der Ahiqarsprüche*. *BZAW* 194 (1990), 217, s.v.
23. *ATTM*, 150; the *n* would then be attributed to a "degeminating" Achaemenid spelling of the Imperial Aramaic papyrus that transmits these sayings.
24. As in *TADAE* A2.5,6; an infinitive in the final clause "in order to bring" following *'th* "he comes."
25. *TADAE* A3.8,13; → II for the G-stem in the same text.
26. *TADAE* C3.28,119; B8.12,3; D1.13,5; presumably also Lozachmeur, no. 140cv9 (with *mn*).

Three of the four Biblical Aramaic occurrences appear in Ezra; two of them (Ezr. 5:15 and 6:5) stand in relation to the return of the stolen temple implements,[27] which are supposed to be deposited (*nḥt b-*) in the Jerusalem temple after its reconstruction. Both instances are in the context of *hlk*/*'zl* as verbs of motion. The likely passive participle[28] in Ezr. 6:1 refers to old documents deposited in the archives[29] of the empire, including the edict of King Cyrus for the reconstruction of the temple. The internal passive "to be brought down" occurs once in Dnl. 5:20, which recalls that Nebuchadnezzar's kingdom[30] was toppled from the throne,[31] here paralleling the causative stem of → *ʿdī*.

The usage in the Aramaic texts from Qumran conforms with known linguistic usage. In 1QapGen 12:14 *nḥt* refers to the wine that Noah brought down, in 4Q211 1 1:2 to *mṭr* "rain," the subject is unclear, however.[32] This second sense "to cause to rain" also underlies two of the three passages from 11Q10, where, in accordance with the unifying translation technique of this text, it represents various Hebrew verbs: in 31:3 (Job 38:26) for *mṭr* and in 28:5 (Job 36:37f.) for *nzl*. In 16:9 (Job 30:19), it translates the causative-stem of *yrd* "to throw."

IV. Theological Use. In the G- and causative-stems, *nḥt* also denotes the contact between the divine and the human spheres. The causative-stem already appears in the oldest Aramaic inscription in the hymnic beginning in the form of the participle *mhnḥt ʿsr* "who brings down plenty" as a title of the god Hadad.[33] As the weather god, he is responsible for rain and, thus, for fertility in general.

In Biblical Aramaic, the G-stem of the verb appears in Nebuchadnezzar's dream of the world tree in reference to the angel[34] who descends from heaven in order to fell the tree (Dnl. 4:10,20).[35] The felling of the tree symbolizes the derangement as penance for the proud king. Similarly, Enoch's animal vision depicts the descent of God as "Lord of small cattle."[36]

Gzella

27. → *m'n*.
28. So *BLA*, §216q.
29. → *gnz* II.
30. → *mlk* IV.
31. *mn* → *krs'*.
32. *ATTM*, 258 suggests "the clouds."
33. *KAI* 309.2; the /n/ is not assimilated, probably because of the subsequent /ḥ/.
34. → *ʿyr*.
35. In contrast, in 4:28, → *npl* "to fall" refers to a voice from heaven.
36. 4Q206 4 2:21 (1 En. 89:16); 4Q530 2 2+6-12:16 and 4Q530 7 2:11 (Book of Giants) are similar.

נטל *nṭl*

I. Etymology, Lexical Field, and Grammatical Constructions. II. Usage in Older Aramaic. III. Qumran.

I. Etymology, Lexical Field, and Grammatical Constructions. Aramaic *nṭl*, in the G-stem "to lift, raise high," may be related to the very rare Hebrew *nṭl*, in the G-stem intransitively "to weigh," transitively "to lay before, to lay on," and in the D-stem "to raise up."[1] Concerning the nuance, "to lift the eyes" (as in Dnl 4:31), it may be possible to establish a relationship to the Akkadian *naṭālu* "to look."[2] In terms of semantics, it is ingressive, describing a momentary event. In contrast, the Aramaic verbal root → *nśī* (literally, to raise high, to take away) or → *sbl* in the G-stem serves to mean a terminative "carrying," often with a durative or iterative nuance; in reference to loads, Aramaic is more likely to employ *ṭʿn* "to carry, to load."[3]

Aramaic constructs the verb transitively with the thing elevated as a direct object and occasionally with an adverbial modifier following the preposition *l-* "to" or *ʿl* "toward, against" (directionally) or *mn* "from" (ablatively). Relatively often, it denotes the elevation of the eyes as a gesture of trustful attention. The internal passive[4] appears once in the sense of "to be upright."

II. Usage in Older Aramaic. The oldest known instance of the root *nṭl* appears in a proverb of Aḥiqar. Here, *ʿyny zy nṭlt ʿlyk* "my eyes that I raised to you" parallels *wlbby zy yhbt lk* "and my heart that I gave to you."[5] While the context of the passage remains unclear, broader usage (see below) suggests that it involves an expression of confidence. The reading of the only proposed Imperial Aramaic instance[6] is uncertain.

The verb also refers to the lifting of the eyes in Dnl. 4:31. Here it introduces Nebuchadnezzar's hymnic confession in which, cleansed by penance, he acknowledges God, looks up to heaven[7] and thereupon regains possession of his mental powers. The other Biblical Aramaic instance, Dnl. 7:4, employs the internal passive in the sense of "to be set upright" in the vision of the four chimera representing the sequential empires; the first, which in the form of a winged lion symbolizes a comparably mild dominion, is robbed

---

E. Jenni, *Das hebräische Piʿel: Syntaktisch-semasiologische Untersuchung einer Verbalform im Alten Testament* (Zurich, 1968).

1. Cf. Jenni, 191.
2. *AHw*, II, 766f.
3. → *nśī* VI.
4. Replaced later by the Gt-stem.
5. *TADAE* C1.1,105; → *lbb* IV.
6. H. Lozachmeur, *La collection Clermont-Ganneau*, vol. 1 (Paris, 2006), no. 136cv2.
7. *ʿyny lšmyʾ nṭlt*; probably as a sign of the acknowledgment of God's power and simultaneously a petition for mercy as in Ps. 123:1f.

of its wings and set upon its feet, thus in an anthropomorphic posture, and receives a human heart as a sign of human thoughts and feelings.[8]

III. Qumran. The Aramaic texts from Qumran attest the verb with significantly greater frequency. 4Q196 6,8 (Tob. 3:12) and 4Q213a 1:8 (T. Levi without a direct object, however) employ it for the lifting of the eyes already known in older Aramaic, both as in Dnl. 4:31 in the context of a prayer; 11Q10 35:3 employs it similarly, probably as the result of a misunderstanding of the Hebrew text of Job 40:24; 4Q543 5-9:4 apparently utilizes it ingressively with *ʿyny* "my eyes" for looking up; 2Q24 4:5 (new Jerusalem) uses it in relation to elevating bread in a priestly ritual;[9] and 2Q26 1:3 employs it of the raising of a table from (*mn*) the water. According to Beyer's reading,[10] 1QapGen 6:3 contains an example of the suffixed infinitive *mṭly* in the meaning "to go," but other editors suggest instead *msly* "paths of."[11]

Gzella

8. → *lbb* II.
9. → *lḥm* IV.
10. *ATTM*, 2, 91f.
11. See the discussion in D. A. Machiela, *The Dead Sea Genesis Apocryphon. STDJ* 79 (2009), 43.

נטר *nṭr*; מנטרה *mnṭrh* /maṭṭarā/

I. Etymology, Lexical Field, and Grammatical Constructions. II. Verb "to Keep." 1. Old and Imperial Aramaic. 2. Biblical Aramaic and Qumran. III. Noun "Watch."

I. Etymology, Lexical Field, and Grammatical Constructions. Resulting from various correspondences of consonants and secondary phonetic developments in individual languages, the common Semitic verbal root **nθ̣r* "to guard, keep" appears in various forms in Northwest Semitic: Hebrew, as expected, *nṣr*; Ugaritic, however, *nġr* with the not yet sufficiently explained /ġ/ for */θ̣/; and in Old Aramaic. There, however, the *ṣ* is only purely graphical for the interdental */θ̣/ apparently still preserved

H.-J. Fabry, "*nṭr* II," *ThWQ*, II, 960-63; J. A. Fitzmyer, *The Aramaic Inscriptions of Sefire. BietOr* 19A (²1995); H. Gzella, *A Cultural History of Aramaic. HO* 111 (2015); H. Lozachmeur, *La collection Clermont-Ganneau: Ostraca, épigraphes sur jarre, étiquettes de bois*, 2 vols. (Paris, 2006); H. Madl, "נָטַר *nāṭar*," *TDOT*, IX, 402-6; J. Naveh and S. Shaked, *Aramaic Documents from Ancient Bactria (Fourth Century* B.C.E.*)* (London, 2012); G. Sauer, "נצר *nṣr* to guard," *TLOT*, 762f.; S. Wagner, "נָצַר *nāṣar*," *TDOT*, IX, 541-49.

as an independent phoneme which did not have its own grapheme in the Phoenician alphabet of twenty-two letters. The spelling with *ṣ* is still attested until approximately 600 B.C.E.;[1] after the fusion of the interdentals with the dentals in Aramaic toward the end of the Old Aramaic period and the shift from */θ̣/ to /ṭ/, the initially historical orthography assimilated to the new pronunciation with some delay so that this verb appears afterward as *nṭr*.[2]

The verb usually occurs in the G-stem transitively with the concrete or abstract object of the thing kept in a literal or figurative sense "to keep, to protect, to preserve." At the latest, the post-Christian Aramaic languages also attest the essentially synonymous D-stem, presumably, indeed, already in *KAI* 225,12f. (→ II). An adverbial modifier *b*- "in" or *mn* "from" can sometimes be added. At least Old Aramaic still manifests a difference between the internal passive "to be protected" and the middle Gt-stem "to be careful" (→ II).[3]

The less frequent feminine substantive /maṭṭarā/, in Imperial Aramaic spelling *mnṭrh*, derives from the verbal root *nṭr*; the likewise feminine form *nṭrh* may also appear once (→ III).

The few occurrences of forms of the root *nṭr* in Biblical Hebrew (verb in Cant. 1:6; 8:11f., noun *maṭṭārā* "watch" in Jer. 32:2,8,12; 33:1; 37:21; 38:6,13,28; 39:14f.; Neh. 3:25; 12:39) are (probably postexilic) Aramaisms and should be distinguished from the homonymous root *nṭr* II "to be angry" on semantic grounds.[4]

II. Verb "to Keep."

1. Old and Imperial Aramaic. Old Aramaic *nṣr*[5] first appears three times in a state treaty from Sefire (8th cent. B.C.E.) and can be semantically associated there with the imprecisely differentiated realms of law and religion. In the preamble, which places the alliance of the pertinent princes and their successors under divine protection, the gods appear as the subject of the verb *yṣrn* "they will keep"[6] with the treaties (*'dy'*) as object. Presumably, this usage emulates the Akkadian expression *ade naṣāru*.[7] Meanwhile, the significantly damaged blessing formula employs the deontic-modal short imperfect *yṣrw* "let them keep," always with the gods as subject, but presumably in the apotropaic sense with the addition of *mn ywmh wmn byth* "from his day and from his house."[8] In the immediately following curse formula, *lnṣr*[9] "whoever does not observe" refers to those

1. *KAI* 266.8.

2. Gzella, 113f.

3. Regarding *KAI* 225.12f. and *TADAE* C1.1, 96; cf. generally, H. Gzella, "Voice in Classical Hebrew against Its Semitic Background," *Or* 78 (2009) 292-325.

4. Cf. *GesB*[18], 813 with bib.

5. For the spelling, → I.

6. *KAI* 222 B 8; the long imperfect here denotes the present-future or epistemic modality, cf. Gzella, 32f.,176.

7. Cf. Fitzmyer, 102 and Pss. 25:10; 119:2.

8. *KAI* 222 C 15; the object is not preserved, but see Fitzmyer, 118 for the construction with the privative *mn*.

9. With a prefixed negative, Gzella, 68.

who break or subsequently alter the treaty. The object here is *mly spr' zy bnṣb' znh* "the words of the document on this stele."[10]

In contrast, the two forms *tnṣr* "you keep" and the passive *ynṣr* "it will be kept" in a somewhat later Old Aramaic grave inscription from Nērab[11] may be attributed to the synonymous and later clearly attested D-stem, since a degeminizing spelling of the imperfect of the G-stem first appears in Achaemenid times.[12] In the concluding curse formula, they refer to the inscription and the sarcophagus in the sense of the deed-consequence relationship: whoever protects them, that is, leaves them intact, will himself stand under divine protection.

The originally pre-Imperial Aramaic proverbs of Aḥiqar, but transmitted in an Achaemenid text and thus in Imperial Aramaic spelling, employs the verb twice to mean "in order to keep" in the sense of the responsible handling of goods placed under someone's care,[13] once figuratively for *ṭr pmk* "watch your mouth!" in the admonition to discretion (→ III).[14] The same text uses the Gt-stem once with a middle nuance "to be careful."[15] As in *TADAE* C1.1,191 the author of the letter of Adon, a Syro-Palestinian prince who asks the pharaoh for military assistance,[16] emphasizes as an expression of loyalty that he has kept the goods of his lord.[17]

Imperial Aramaic attests the verb, now consistently spelled *nṭr*, in a letter of the Egyptian satrap Aršama. It appears there as an admonition, as before, to guard the property and the staff of the governor during unrest among the population.[18] A few instances in the papyri from Saqqara also refer to the guarding of goods and persons,[19] as does, further, a satrap's letter from Bactria in reference to the guarding of royal camels.[20]

The passive participle (?) *n]ṭyr* "preserved" may occur in a private letter on one of the Clermont-Ganneau ostraca;[21] an additional possible instance of *nṭ[r*[22] is fragmentary.

2. Biblical Aramaic and Qumran. In Biblical Aramaic, *nṭr* occurs once in Dnl. 7:28 where it refers to the preservation of a vision and its divine interpretation in the heart as the seat of innermost perception.[23] Of the otherwise manageable instances of the verb in

10. *KAI* 222 C 17; also similar to a corresponding Akkakian formulation, cf. Fitzmyer, 118.
11. *KAI* 225,12f.
12. For a discussion, see Gzella, 146 n. 464, with additional bib.
13. *TADAE* C1.1,191 of water and fragmentary in l. 208.
14. *TADAE* C1.1,82, along with the noun.
15. *TADAE* C1.1,96, alongside the Gt-stem of *šmr*; otherwise → *zhr* denotes "pay attention."
16. Regarding the context, cf. Gzella, 139-41.
17. *TADAE* A1.1,8 = *KAI* 266.8.
18. *TADAE* A6.10,2.4.6; together with the adjective *ḥsyn* "strict" employed as an adverb → *ḥsn* IV.
19. Segal, 26.5,7, in l. 7 also with *ḥsyn*; of goods in 2.1; fragmentary thus not entirely certain but still possibly also in 37.5, 77b.2 and 131.2,3.
20. Naveh and Shaked, A1.3.
21. Lozachmeur, no. 33cv3, here, if the reading and interpretation are correct, of a *nwn* "fish" left over *l-* "for" someone's wife.
22. Lozachmeur, no. 40cc4.
23. → *lbb* II; cf. Lk. 2:19 of the angel's message to Mary.

the Aramaic texts from Qumran, the majority are fragmentary and lacking in sufficient context. It can be identified with sufficient certainty, however, at least in reference to the enduring preservation of Noah's vision (4Q534 7:4) and of the religio-cultural heritage of the fathers in the admonition of a last testament (4Q542 1 1:11).

III. Noun "Watch." The feminine verbal noun *mṭrh* /maṭṭarā/ "watch" or "to be guarded"—the nuance in the two older examples is not clear—first appears in a proverb of Aḥiqar in the Achaemenid spelling *mnṭrh*:[24] one should watch one's mouth (→ II.1) *mn kl mnṭrh* "more than any watch/than everything to be guarded"[25] and further in a letter from Elephantine either for "post" or "to be guarded."[26] Hebrew also exhibits it as an Aramaic loanword *maṭṭārā* "watch" (→ I) and it occurs thereafter in Qumran spelled phonetically as *mṭrh* in a fragment of the Testament of Amram.[27]

Another nominal of the form *nṭrh*[28] may occur in a fragment from Saqqara,[29] but, due to the lack of context, it remains rather uncertain.

Gzella

24. Cf. Gzella, 170f.
25. *TADAE* C1.1, 82.
26. *TADAE* A4.5, 1.
27. 4Q543 4:3, probably in the sense of "custody."
28. Feminine *nomen professionis* /naṭṭārā/?
29. Segal, 33b.1.

נכסין *nksyn* /nekasīn/

I. Etymology, Lexical Field, and Meaning. II. Imperial Aramaic. III. Biblical Aramaic. IV. Qumran.

I. Etymology, Lexical Field, and Meaning. The masculine noun /nekasīn/ "possession," attested only in the plural, is apparently an Akkadian loanword, adopted, in turn, from the Sumerian. The inner-Akkadian semantic development from an original "reckoning" also seems likely so that it became part of the Aramaic lexicon only in the Neo-Babylonian era.[1] There, it was integrated into the noun system as a plural on the pattern of the etymological nouns *qital*.

K. Göransson, "*nksyn*," *ThWQ*, II, 975-78; S. A. Kaufman, *The Akkadian Influences on Aramaic*. *AS* 19 (1974).

1. Kaufman, 77.

While it first appears in Imperial Aramaic documentary texts, it thence entered the post-Achaemenid literary tradition and continued in use even later.[2] From Aramaic, it migrated further into Hebrew (Josh. 22:8; Eccl. 5:18; 6:2; 2 Ch. 1:11f.; and on into the Mishnah). A relationship with the verb *nks* "to slaughter" and the related noun /neksā/, attested only later in Aramaic,[3] has yet to be demonstrated.

Usage overlaps with that of the noun *qnyn* (→ II)[4] and with the substantivized feminine plural of the adjective *ṭb* "goods," which can parallel /nekasīn/.[5] It is generally employed for moveable valuables, while *ksp* /kasp/ serves to refer to "money"—literally "silver (cf. Ezr. 7:15-18,22). The noun shares a semantic field with the verb *ḥsn*, in the causative-stem "to hold/take in possession," a fixed term in Imperial Aramaic administrative diction for a legally valid possession,[6] and with *qnī* "to acquire."

II. Imperial Aramaic. Numerous instances of *nksyn* "possession" occur in the Imperial Aramaic letters and private documents from Elephantine. Legal texts that contain the establishment of someone's possession[7] distinguish fundamentally between *nksyn* and *ksp* "silver, money."[8] No distinction from *qnyn*, which is often mentioned along with *nksyn*,[9] is clear. It also refers once to the exchange of a house for *nksyn*.[10] Primarily, it denotes the mobile property of private persons, which can also be bequeathed, together with the umbrella term *nksyn*, and can then be further specified as articles of clothing, household implements, grain, and still more.[11]

Private letters from the same period and region employ *nksyn* in a similar sense, say for stolen property resulting from a break-in or otherwise alienated,[12] or property that one can obtain and lose,[13] once even explicitly for "furniture,"[14] and similarly in contrast to *ksp*.[15] In this regard, it can also involve very expansive property-owners such as the Egyptian satrap.[16] In the narrative framework of Aḥiqar, it denotes the goods that one receives from someone of higher rank, including even the king.[17] A couple of other examples on ostraca are too fragmentary for further definition,[18] as is one on a papyrus from Saqqara.[19]

---

2. Cf. *DJPA*, 351; *LexSyr*, 429.
3. Occurences in *ATTM*, 637.
4. From the verbal root *qnī* "to buy" and frequently alongside *nksyn*.
5. 1QapGen 21:3, → *ṭīb* III.2.
6. → *ḥsn* II.
7. E.g., regularly in marriage contracts in reference to the dowry.
8. *TADAE* B2.6, 14; 3.3,6; 4.6,4; 6.4,7.
9. *TADAE* B2.6,21f.30.35; 3.8,27.29f.31(emend.).35.
10. *TADAE* B2.7,4.6; 2.8,4.
11. *TADAE* B2.8,4. 6.8; 2.9,5.8.12.15; → *m'n* II.
12. *lqḥ*; *TADAE* A4.4,8; cf. 6.3,5, 6.15,9 und B7.2,5.9.
13. *TADAE* A4.7,16.
14. *TADAE* A4.3,9.
15. *TADAE* A4.5,4; 4.8,5.
16. *TADAE* A6.10,1.3.6.8, here along with *grd* "staff, household personnel."
17. *TADAE* C1.1,66.74.
18. *TADAE* D1.11,3; 1.17,6; 3.45,2.
19. Segal, 50.10.

The Aramaic private contracts from the Dead Sea essentially correspond to Imperial Aramaic usage: *nksyn* designates distrainable property[20] or property being acquired,[21] is differentiated from a house,[22] and is once even mentioned along with *m'ny by* "household implements,"[23] but not as an umbrella term.

III. Biblical Aramaic. In Ezra, *nksyn*,[24] at least at first glance, refers twice to "estate" in the broader sense to include "wealth" in the broader sense. If this actually represents an expansion of the original use for "mobile property," this semantic development can be compared with Latin *pecunia* "money" from *pecus* "cattle."[25]

In any case, the expression *nksy mlk'* (Ezr. 6:8) with a partitive *mn* designates the royal income from the tribute[26] that the province of Syria-Palestine produces, which is supposed to finance the reconstruction of the Jerusalem temple. An accounting nuance "royal property/wealth/means" instead of "money" is also possible.

Likewise, modern translations sometimes understand *'nš nksyn* (Ezr. 7:26) as "fine";[27] the plural *'nšn* alone means "penalty" in a Nabatean contract from the Dead Sea.[28] This sanction constitutes the third in a catalogue of four possible penalties in increasing severity, after death and expulsion from the community, but before imprisonment, for the transgression of divine and royal law. Here, too, however, it is not certain whether *nksyn* explicitly refers to monetary wealth or not, more likely to a more extensive seizure of valuables altogether.[29] Broader Imperial Aramaic usage (→ II) suggests the latter.

IV. Qumran. Of the relevant specimens from Qumran, a majority appear in 1QapGen, where *nksyn* specifically denotes the flocks of Abraham and Lot (20:33f., along with gold and silver; 21:3,5f.; 22:1,3,11,31f., in l. 31 along with *'tr* "wealth"), but also the property of a population (21:33, of Sodom) or other kings (22:17,19,22,24). The usage for cattle is typical of this text and emphasizes as a leitmotif Abraham's wealth in cattle, which constitutes the foundation of a nomad's wealth. In 4Q540 1:1,2,3, the noun is associated with → *ḥsr* "lack." It functions figuratively in 4Q212 1 4:17 (1 En. 91:13) for the possession of the truth. In 11Q10 4:6 (Job 21:7), it translates *ḥyl* with the nuance "wealth," which cannot be clearly demonstrated from its Aramaic cognate.[30]

---

20. *ATTM*, 2, nV 1:19.
21. *ATTM*, 2, V 93:7.
22. *ATTM*, 2, nV 10:10.15; V 36:9.
23. *ATTM*, 2, nV 7:16. 54f.
24. Vocalized in Tiberian as *niḵsīn*.
25. In general, cf. Göransson, 978.
26. → *mndh* III.
27. Cf. *GesB*[18], 1515.
28. nV 1:24 in *ATTM*, 2, 205-7.
29. So *LexLingAram*, 112: *multatione bonorum*.
30. → *ḥyl*.

The juxtaposition of "house" and "property" in 4Q550 2:6, a court narrative set among the Persian kings, depends on Imperial Aramaic legal terminology; a further instance in 11Q18 23 2:3 (new Jerusalem) is corrupt.

Gzella

נמר *nmr* /nemr/

I. Pronunciation and Meaning. II. Older Aramaic Occurrences. III. The Leopard in Old Aramaic Literature and in the New Testament.

I. Pronunciation and Meaning. The substantive /namer/, from which Arabic *namira* "to be spotted" probably derives because of the characteristic coat markings, is a common Semitic primary noun of the *qatil* pattern.[1] In Aramaic, as in Akkadian,[2] the *qitl* form dominates on the evidence of later vocalization, which became /nemar/ after the separation of the final doubled consonant by an auxiliary vowel.[3] Of the large Asiatic cats (*Felidae*) in question, leopard or panther (*Panthera pardus*; English employs the terms as near-synonyms) and tiger (*Panthera tigris*), it must refer to leopards based on figurative representations from Egypt and Mesopotamia,[4] descriptions (Jer. 13:23), and the range of distribution.

II. Older Aramaic Occurrences. In texts from the Old Aramaic period, the leopard first appears in the masculine singular absolute *nmr* in the first combination of the wall inscription from Deir ʿAllā (ca. 800 B.C.E.).[5] It unites an Aramaic grammatical core with

---

E. Blum, "Die Kombination I der Wandinschrift vom Tell Deir ʿAlla," in I. Kottsieper, R. Schmitt, J. Wöhrle, eds., *Berührungspunkte: Studien zur Sozial- und Religions-geschichte Israels und seiner Umwelt. AOAT* 350 (2008), 573-601; H. Gzella, "Deir ʿAllā," in G. Khan, ed., *Encyclopedia of Hebrew Language and Linguistics* (Leiden, 2013), 1:691-93; S. Heydasch-Lehmann and A. Weckwerth, "Panther (Leopard)," *RAC* XXVI, 899-916; O. Keel and U. Staub, *Hellenismus und Judentum: Vier Studien zu Daniel 7. OBO* 178 (2001); M. J. Mulder, "נָמֵר *nāmēr*," *TDOT*, IX, 432-37; N. Nys and J. Bretschneider, "Research on the Iconography of the Leopard," *UF* 39 (2008) 555–616.

1. Arabic attests it in the pattern as both a masculine and a feminine; Hebrew and Ethiopic attest it as well.
2. *AHw*, II, 790.
3. *ATTM*, 114.
4. *ANEP*, nos. 52,297; 678.
5. *KAI* 312.15.

Canaanite stylistic characteristics, individual words, and probably literary traditions.[6] The immediate context has been lost; the broader context depicts the upheaval of natural conditions even in the animal world in a judgment prophecy.[7]

Additional, genuinely Aramaic instances of the masculine noun occur in the pre-Imperial Aramaic proverbs of Aḥiqar (ca. seventh century B.C.E.)[8] and in Dnl. 7:6 (164 B.C.E.); the feminine *nmrh* appears in an Old Aramaic state treaty from Sefire (eighth century B.C.E.).[9] In a synagogue inscription from late antiquity, *nymryn* "leopards" also stands as a place name (circa 600 C.E.)[10] like Nimrim in Isa. 15:6.

III. The Leopard in Old Aramaic Literature and in the New Testament. In the ancient Near East, the leopard was holy especially to goddesses.[11] A Sefire inscription[12] threatens in the event of a breach of contract a *nmrh* "leopardess" together with a *dbh{h}* /dobbā/ "female bear" sent by the gods.[13]

The proverbs of Aḥiqar[14] recount animal fables about a voracious leopard and a defenseless goat.[15] In the first instance, it involves the fact that an apparently generous gesture can conceal evil intention: according to ll. 166f., the leopard offers to cover the naked goat with his pelt (and apparently means thereby that it will eat the goat); the goat knows, however, that the leopard is only interested in his prey and offers to leave the skin to him.

In Dnl. 7, a leopard[16] with four wings and four heads serves as an image of the penultimate empire before the last judgment,[17] probably the Persian Empire with its four kings (Dnl. 11:2). This monster from Dnl. 7:6 together with its predecessors, the lion and the bear, inspired the author of the New Testament Rev. 12:18–13:2 (ca. 90 C.E.) to depict a mixture of panther, bear, and lion as an image of the Roman Empire. Regarding more history of motifs in Judaism and in the church fathers including the reception of Dnl 7:26, see the recent contribution by Heydasch-Lehmann and Weckwerth, 910-14.

Beyer

---

6. See Gzella.

7. See Blum.

8. *TADAE* C1.1,210 in the abs. and l. 166f. in the deter.

9. *KAI* 222 A 31.

10. ggBS 3:17 in *ATTM*, 381.

11. Regarding Greco-Roman antiquity, especially in the Hellenistic period, cf. further Heydasch-Lehmann and Weckwerth, 903f.

12. *KAI* 222 A 31.

13. For the reading and interpretation of the passage, see J. A. Fitzmyer, *Aramaic Inscriptions of Sefire*. *BietOr* 19/A (^{2}1995), 88.

14. *TADAE* C1.1,166f. and, in a corrupt context, 210.

15. → *'z*.

16. In the Greek translations πάρδαλις.

17. → *gp* II.

נפל *npl*; נפילין *npylyn* /napīlīn/; מפלה *mplh* /mappalā/

I. Lexical Field, Forms, and Grammatical Constructions. II. General Use. 1. Old and Biblical Aramaic. 2. Qumran. III. Idiomatic Usage. 1. For Prostration. 2. Various Other Expressions. IV. Noun "Giant." V. Noun "Fall."

I. Lexical Field, Forms, and Grammatical Constructions. As in Hebrew, the verbal root *npl* "to fall" also has in other Semitic languages (in addition to the other Canaanite languages, especially in Akkadian and Arabic) a broad spectrum of meaning, which only becomes concrete in specific nuances by context and through certain prepositional modifiers. To fall generally means minimal guidance by the subject ("minimal agency"); consequently, the verb appears as one might expect in the G-stem in intransitive constructions. Often, adverbial determinations of the place or direction following *b-*,[1] *l-*,[2] or *lgw'* "in" (Dnl. 3:23), *ʿl* "on" (in reference to prostration, Dnl. 2:46), *qdm* "before" or *mn* "from" are added. Thus, in addition to the general usage meaning "to fall from a certain height to the ground," it also serves in various idiomatic and figurative expressions, quite frequently in the preserved material in reference to (voluntary) prostration as a gesture of obeisance.

Meanwhile, → *nḥt* "to go away" usually denotes a voluntary and controlled movement (thus a higher degree of "agency"). Furthermore, *npl* has points of semantic contact with the less common *ntr* "to fall away/out." Contact with the ground itself finds expression through → *mṭī* "to arrive, reach";[3] → *rmī* serves for "to throw." The causative-stem with the meaning "to cast down" occurs beyond doubt only later.[4] Syriac also has the D-stem with the t-passive.[5]

Qumran, like its Hebrew prototype, employs the noun /napīl/ "fallen one" in the plural as a fixed term for "giants" (→ IV). Furthermore, the feminine verbal noun /mappalā/ "fall, demise" also belongs to the root (→ V).

II. General Use.

1. Old and Biblical Aramaic. The common meaning "to fall (involuntarily)" of the verb *npl* occurs regularly in Aramaic. Later Old Aramaic first attests it in the proverbs

---

K. Atkinson, "*npl*," *ThWQ*, II, 996-1000; S. P. Brock, "A Palestinian Targum Feature in Syriac," *JJS* 46 (1995) 271-82; K. Koch, *Daniel 1–4*. *BK* XXII/1 (2005); H. Seebass, "נָפַל *nāpal*," *TDOT*, IX, 488-97; L. T. Stuckenbruck, "The 'Angels' and 'Giants' of Genesis 6,1-4 in Second and Third Century B.C.E. Jewish Interpretation," *DSD* 7 (2000) 354-77; idem, *The Book of Giants from Qumran*. *TSAJ* 63 (1997).

1. *TADAE* C1.1,121.
2. Dnl. 3:5,7,10,15; 4Q198 2:4 (Tob. 14:10).
3. Cf. Dnl. 6:25 and → *mṭī* II.3.
4. *DJPA*, 356; *DJBA*, 762f.; *LexSyr*, 436f.; the supposed example in 4Q531 12,2 is partially reconstructed and uncertain.
5. *LexSyr*, 437.

of Aḥiqar, always with an *ss* /sās/ "moth" as subject.[6] Admittedly, the context of both passages remains largely incomprehensible because of lacunae in the text, but *bbyt nḥš' nplt ss'* "the moth fell (or gnomically: "falls"?) in the house of bronze (/noḥāšā/; alternatively: in the house of the soothsayer, /naḥḥāšā/)" in l. 121 could also mean "to descend on" in the sense of higher agency.

The nonactive and involuntary character of the pertinent action in Dnl. 3:23 becomes clear, however: the fall of the young men into the burning oven (*lgw' 'twn nwr'*)[7] parallels the throwing action of the assistant executioners in 3:21.[8] It is difficult to determine whether this constitutes a conscious play on words with the remarkably frequent use in Dnl. 3 in the sense of "to cast down" in prostration before the statue of a god (→ III), which the young men had refused to do, but it remains entirely possible.

Daniel 4:28 can also be assigned to the common usage; here it refers to something noncorporeal, namely a voice that falls *mn šmy'* "from heaven" and announces to the arrogant King Nebuchadnezzar the end of his dominion. Furthermore, it appears in Dnl. 7:20, which describes how in a vision the horns of an apocalyptic animal fall down *mn qdm* "before" another horn.

2. Qumran. Corresponding examples also occur at Qumran: 1QapGen 21:33 (the king of Sodom falls into asphalt pits); according to *ATTM*, 2, 98f. also in 1QapGen 14:12, but with no broader context.[9] It occurs figuratively of the fall into (*l-*) the trap (*pḥ*) of death in an intertextual allusion to the fate of Aḥiqar in 4Q198 2:4 (Tob. 14:10; reconstructed following the other versions), just as in the proverb "whoever digs a grave for another falls into it himself."[10]

III. Idiomatic Usage.

1. For Prostration. Specifically for prostration, *npl* finds usage in the sense of "to fall down," but also as a conscious movement guided by the subject. Daniel first attests this usage. There, in various facets, it alludes to court ceremony.[11] According to Dnl. 2:46, in a reversal of the customary circumstances, Nebuchadnezzar fell down "on his face" (*'l 'npwhy*) before Daniel and paid homage to him because he recognized in Daniel divine wisdom. In the story of the young men in the fiery furnace in Dnl. 3, the verb functions as a leitmotif: by royal decree, one should pray to a golden statue,[12] which is repeated throughout the chapter in litanylike fashion (Dnl. 3:5,6,7,10,11,15),[13] and the worshipers of the true God, who refuse this idol worship, should be thrown into the fiery furnace.[14]

6. *TADAE* C1.1,119.121.
7. → *gw* II.
8. → *rmī*, with the identical adverbial modifier *lgw' 'twn nwr'*.
9. For the paleographical difficulties and other suggestions, cf. D. A. Machiela, *The Dead Sea Genesis Apocryphon. STDJ* 79 (2009), 60.
10. Cf. J. Fitzmyer, *Tobit. CEJL* (2003), 334.
11. Cf. Koch, 235 and 288f.
12. Here also in combination with *sgd*.
13. → *dhb* III.
14. → II on the possible word play with *npl* "to fall" in 3:23.

The Aramaic texts from Qumran employ the verb in the same sense. The modifier *ʿl ʾnp* "on the face" known from Dnl. 2:46 reappears in 4Q531 14:3 (Book of Giants).[15] The "son of God" text has the preposition *qdm* "before" in 4Q246 1 1:1 which it may have adopted from Achaemenid formal style.[16] The verb appears at the beginning of the report of a dream interpretation before a king at which the seer falls down[17] before the throne.

2. *Various Other Expressions.* In addition, various figurative nuances of *npl* are attested; they result in natural fashion from the literal meaning and also have parallels in Hebrew,[18] which offers many more instances than the older Aramaic, or to the use of the verb "to fall" in other languages. It is first attested in the sense "to fall to, to come to" in Ezr. 7:20 with *l-* and the infinitive of another verb. It occurs there as part of King Artaxerxes's commission for Ezra to rebuild the temple and refers to the need to procure what is necessary and which should be covered from royal means.

The meaning "to fall to (*l-*) someone" occurs at Qumran in the land distribution in 1QapGen.[19] Related is the nuance "to happen" in 4Q580 1 2:13.[20] Further, it appears figuratively either for the "decline" of errors or the "toppling" of idols (*ṭʿwʾn*) in 4Q541 1 2:2 (Levi Apocryphon)[21] and in 11Q10 27:6 (Job 36:12) for "to perish" with the modifier *bḥrbʾ* "by the sword."[22]

Depending on the reading and interpretation of the subject in 4Q550 2:4, *npl ʿl* has either the connotation "to fall upon" with *ʾwmh* /ʾommā/ "people"[23] as agent[24] or "to overcome" with *ʾwmh* /ʾēmā/ "horror."[25]

Some other passages have been preserved without context or are significantly reconstructed. Because of the lacking context, a Palmyrene instance[26] is also unclear. Later phases of the language attest various other literal or figurative nuances.[27]

IV. Noun "Giant." Biblical Hebrew already prefigured Qumran's usage of the original adjective *npylyn* /napīlīn/ as a plural substantive "fallen ones" for "giants," which it very likely adopted from Hebrew into Aramaic.[28] In the Pentateuch, this term occurs once

15. Similarly perhaps also in 4Q204 1 6:27 (1 En. 14:14), which preserves only the verb, however.
16. *ATTM*, 679f.; cf. Brock.
17. → *krsʾ*; regarding the controversial interpretation of the text overall → *br* IV.
18. Cf. Seebass, 488-97.
19. 1QapGen 17:7 and probably in l. 10 in a corrupt context.
20. With *ʿbd* "to do," the broader context is unclear.
21. → *ḥṭī* V.
22. Freely translated for the idiomatic Hebrew *bšlḥ ʿbr*, presumably "to get into the weapon"; cf. *GesB*[18], 1362.
23. → *ʿm*.
24. So *ATTM*, 2, 150, U 2,4: "the people of . . . fell upon them."
25. So, e.g., the translation in *DSSStE*, 1099, which does not, however, suit the reading *ʾwmh* there.
26. *PAT* 1584.7.
27. See *DJPA*, 356; *DJBA*, 761-63; *LexSyr*, 436f.; *MdD*, 303.
28. See C. Stadel, *Hebraismen in den aramäischen Texten vom Toten Meer* (Heidelberg, 2008), 12f., with additional literature.

in reference to the mythical original population of Canaan (Num. 13:33 with emphasis on their gigantic size), and otherwise for the illegitimate descendants of subordinate deities ("angels") with human women (Gen. 6:4). Already beginning with the LXX (γίγαντες) and the Vulgate (*gigantes*), the word is often rendered "giants," although the precise etymology in Hebrew is controversial:[29] there is either a relationship with *npl* "to fall" involving the "fall of the angels" or with "to be born in an unnatural manner" as with the Hebrew noun *nēp̄æl* "untimely birth."[30]

The Book of Giants, which originally belonged to the Enoch tradition, especially, depicts the fate of these figures, based on Gen 6:1-7, in epic breadth;[31] the "fallen angels" and their descendants produced corruption on the earth, but the flood destroyed them as God's judgment. In principle, a distinction should be made between the common word /gabbār/ "giant" and the /napīlīn/ in the more narrow sense, but it is not clear the degree to which the two designations were understood as synonyms since, in fact, they also occur together in the combination *gbryn wnpylyn*.[32] In any case, /gabbārīn/, which also occurs later in the Targums, may be the native Aramaic word for "giant."

1QapGen also takes up the tradition from Gen 6.[33]

The determined singular *npyl'* /napīlā/ "giant" occurs once, however, in the phrase *syg npyl'* "fence[34] of Orion" for the constellation.[35] This apparently reveals the influence of the conceptual convergence of *npyl* and *gbr* in the giant tradition since Aramaic otherwise designates the constellation Orion with /gabbārā/ "the giant, hero."[36]

V. Noun "Fall." The verbal noun *mplh* /mappalā/ "fall, demise" occurs in older Aramaic only in 4Q531 26:2 (Book of Giants, no context) and 11Q10 5:1 (Job 21:20, for *kyd* "misfortune"). It continued in use later, however,[37] always in the figurative sense.

Gzella

29. Cf. *GesB*[18], 830 and Atkinson, 1000.
30. *GesB*[18], 832.
31. See the extensive treatment by Stuckenbruck.
32. 4Q531 5:2; → *gbr* IV; cf. *DSSStE*, 1066.
33. 2:1 of Lamech's doubt concerning the identity of the father of his child, employing *npylyn* along with *'yryn* "watchers" (→ *'yr*) and *qdyšyn* "holy ones" (→ *qdš*) and then of their destruction on the earth 6:19.
34. /siyāg/, from the verbal root *sūg*.
35. 11Q10 31:8 (Job 38:31), for Heb. *mškwt ksyl* "chains of Orion," literally "of the fool."
36. Cf. *LexSyr*, 103a.
37. See *DJPA*, 324a; *DJBA*, 697b; *LexSyr*, 437.

נפק *npq*; נפקה *npqh* /napaqā/; מפק *mpq* /mappaq/

I. Etymology, Lexical Field, and Grammatical Constructions. II. G-stem "to Go Out." 1. Old and Imperial Aramaic. 2. Biblical Aramaic. 3. Qumran and Hatra. III. Causative-stem "to Bring Out." IV. Nouns "Expenses" and "Entrance."

I. Etymology, Lexical Field, and Grammatical Constructions. Aramaic differs from the other Syro-Palestinian languages through its use of the root *npq*, in the G-stem "to go out," causative-stem "to bring out," although of unclear origins. The conceptual counterpart → *ʿll* "to go in" represents a lexical peculiarity, just as do the two other verbs of direction → *nḥt* "to climb up" and → *slq* "to climb down." In contrast, the common Semitic verb **wṣ́ʾ* "to go out," in Canaanite (such as Hebrew) and Ugaritic *yṣʾ*, is rare in Aramaic, where it occurs later in the form *yʿī*, and limited to the very special meaning "to sprout." Later, *npq* displaced it.

As a fixed element of the basic lexicon, *npq* appears throughout older Aramaic. It denotes not just the voluntary movement of animate objects, but also of natural phenomena such as stars,[1] lightning, and landscape elements, things like plants, fluid, smoke, and more, and also for abstract concepts such as words. It appears frequently in relation to descendants. The G-stem functions as a transitive modified with various adverbial modifiers following prepositions: usually *mn* "out of" for the starting point or origin, less often *b-* "through" or *l-* "after." In the ingressive meaning "to set out," *ʾzl*/*hlk* often follows as a second verb of motion. Like → *qūm* "to stand up" in a similar construction, the combination means "he left."[2]

The causative-stem "to bring out, to fetch from" is transitive, also often with the addition *mn* "out of" and sometimes with an indirect object "to someone" after *l-*.

Especially in the administrative language of the Imperial Aramaic tradition, one also encounters the feminine verbal noun /napaqā/ "cost." The infinitive of the G-stem /mappaq/ also appears as a masculine substantive "free exit."

II. G-stem "to Go Out."

1. Old and Imperial Aramaic. The broad spectrum of meaning of *npq* is already evident at the beginning of the literary tradition. The oldest Aramaic inscriptions attest the verb twice. It occurs once as part of a curse formula in a state treaty from Sefire: the land of the rebellious king is to decay *wʾl ypq ḥṣr* "and sprout no grass," so that no green

---

H. Drawnel, *The Aramaic Astronomical Book (4Q208-4Q211) from Qumran* (Oxford, 2011); H. Gzella, *Tempus, Aspekt und Modalität im Reichsaramäischen. VOK* 48 (2004); T. Hansberger and C. Kumpmann, "*npq*," *ThWQ*, II, 1001-7; E. Jenni, "יצא *yṣʾ* to go out," *TLOT*, 561-66; J. Naveh and S. Shaked, *Aramaic Documents from Ancient Bactria (Fourth Century B.C.E.)* (London, 2012); H. D. Preuss, "יָצָא *yāṣāʾ*," *TDOT*, VI, 225-50.

1. So frequently in the astronomical Book of Enoch.
2. Gzella, 146f.

appears.[3] The Tell Dan inscription, in contrast, employs it in the report of a campaign of the one who commissioned the inscription, presumably King Hazael of Damascus, against the kings of Israel and Judah: his divine protector Hadad went before him (*wyhk hdd qdmy*) and he joined in the battle (*[w]'pq mn. . .*).[4] The role of the preposition *mn* is not entirely clear because of the corrupt following section, but the verb here probably has the ingressive nuance "to set out."

Three specimens in the somewhat later proverbs of Aḥiqar attest the figurative use with abstract subjects: "the evil"[5] *mn 'lhn l' npqt* "does not proceed from the gods," but from an evil person,[6] just as good[7] can also proceed from the mouth (*mn pm*) of a person.[8]

In the documentary texts of the Achaemenid period, the common literal meaning "to go away" dominates in the letters, often with *mn* "from" and a subsequent place name in relation to persons;[9] it functions analogously in official diction.[10]

Private documents employ *npq* literally in contracts concerning real estate for the regulation of access rights;[11] marriage contracts employ the phrase *npq mn* for the wife leaving the husband.[12] In a commercial text from Bactria, it refers further to the delivery of sheep;[13] otherwise, the causative-stem appears in commercial contexts (→ III).

2. Biblical Aramaic. In Biblical Aramaic, the G-stem *npq* occurs only in Daniel. It refers literally to the young men who exit the fiery furnace (Dnl. 3:26; a command with subsequent execution), and in the vision of the divine throne in reference to the stream of fire that proceeds from it (7:10).[14] It is employed with an abstract term[15] for the "issuance," that is, the public proclamation of a royal command (2:13f.).[16]

Finally, in the episode of the writing on the wall at Belshazzar's banquet, it denotes the appearance of the fingers of a hand from nowhere to announce to the king his doom in encrypted form (Dnl. 5:5).[17] Here, *npq* connotes "to appear." MT transmits a hybrid

3. *KAI* 222 A 28.

4. *KAI* 310.5; on the function and implications of the imperfect often misunderstood in older scholarship, see the discussion in H. Gzella, *A Cultural History of Aramaic*. *HO* 111 (2015), 79-87.

5. *lḥyt'*, → *b'š* II.

6. *TADAE* C1.1,135; cf. l. 139.

7. *ṭbh*, → *ṭīb* III.2.

8. *TADAE* C1.1,171.

9. *TADAE* A2.5,3; 3.3,3.6; D1.20,5; 7.8,9.12; 7.10,7.

10. In *TADAE* A4.7,5 par. 4.8,4 together with *'zl* in reference to the official travel of the satrap to the king; the Behistun inscription, *TADAE* C2.1,25, should quite probably be reconstructed to refer to the departure of Darius from Babylon.

11. *TADAE* B2.1,12.14; 3.7,14; 3.10,14; 3.11,3f.; 3.12,22, here together with the antonym → *'ll*, as also later in similar documents from the Dead Sea: see nV 7: 25,67 in *ATTM*, 2, 218-23; cf. further Segal, no. 26.3.

12. *TADAE* B2.4,9; 3.8,26.

13. Naveh and Shaked, C2.1.

14. Paralleling → *ngd* II.

15. As already in Aḥiqar, → II.1.

16. → *dt*; cf. ἐξῆλθεν δόγμα in Lk. 2:1.

17. → *yd* III.

spelling: the consonantal text *npqw* presupposes the Imperial Aramaic form /napaqū/, the third-person masculine perfect which also stands for the feminine; the vocalization is based on feminine /napaqā/, which Palestinian Aramaic distinguishes from the masculine.[18]

It cannot be said with certainty whether the use of *npq* here consciously alludes to the causative-stem of the same root in the depiction of the outrageous plundering of the temple implements (Dnl. 5:2f.; → III), which represents a reason for the punishment. In light of other Aramaic diction, the nuance "to appear" for *npq*, however, seems more unusual since *npq* otherwise usually denotes exiting a room or leaving a place and the Gt-stem → *ḥzī* represents "to appear."[19]

3. Qumran and Hatra. The numerous instances of *npq* in the Aramaic texts from Qumran contain other nuances that either continue the older diction or, like the astronomical and sometimes geographical contexts prominent here, attest new specific usages.

As narrative that unites episodes of quite varied content, 1QapGen reflects a relatively broad spectrum of usages of the verb some of which were already attested earlier: literally for "to set out" (11:11, with *hlk*; 21:31; 22:28,30), but also genealogically for "to be produced" (6:1; 14:10; 22:34). In addition, it also occurs here for "to proceed from [*mn*]" in reference to geographical entities such as peninsulas (21:18) or streams (possibly in 16:15) and other fluids (4Q204 1 12:26 [1 En. 31:1]); occasionally also for "to fall to" (16:14, probably after the corresponding Heb. formulation *yṣ' gwrl*, e.g., in Nu. 33:54 or Josh. 16:1), for which → *npl* serves otherwise.

Some of these and related nuances also occur in other fragments: in reference to persons (4Q537 14:1,3; in reference to God in 4Q201 1 1:5 [1 En. 1:3]); of water that flows out of a city and under[20] its walls (4Q537 12:3; similarly 4Q205 1 12:3; 4Q554 9:2); of streets in the sense of "to be directed toward" (4Q554 2 2:16.20 par. 5Q15 1 1:3f., new Jerusalem; so also probably of towers in 4Q554 3 2:22, where "to be directed toward," as *ATTM*, 2, 132 translates, better suits the semantics of the verb than "to protrude," etc.); and often of descendants (4Q530 2 2+6-12:8; 4Q531 46:3; 4Q535 3:2).

In addition, the book of Enoch attests the use of *npq* as a component of technical astronomical and meteorological diction (1 En. 73). There, the formulaic expression *npq mn tr'* "he (the moon) comes out of the gate" denotes the rise of a luminary (preserved completely in 4Q209 7 2:10, but often-repeated in 4Q208-209, sometimes in abbreviation and fragmentarily preserved).[21] The formulation indicates that one cannot think of the meaning "to appear" (as atypically in Dnl. 5:5, → II.2), but of the "emerging" as leaving a room, although the Gt-stem of *ḥzī* may have been used in such circumstances.[22] According to 4Q210 1 2:4f.7.9 (1 En. 76:4-7), the winds[23] exit out their respective gates in analogy to the stars.

18. Cf. Gzella, 125 n. 31.
19. E.g., generally in *KAI* 222 A 28; for God in 1QapGen 21:8; 22:27.
20. *mn tḥt*.
21. See Drawnel, 254,258.
22. Cf. Drawnel, 271, but both of the possible instances are fragmentary.
23. → *rwḥ*.

The rendition of passages in the book of Job dealing with creation theology in 11Q10 portrays the breadth of *npq*: 30:7 (Job 38:8) and 31:6 (Job 38:29) "to exit" of water and ice; 36:5,7 (Job 41:11-13) of fire and smoke; 33:3 (Job 39:21) "to set forth" of a warhorse. The Aramaic verb renders various Hebrew verbs according to context. Indeed, 4Q549 2:6 has *pṭr* "to go away" for "to die." A few other instances have survived without sufficient context or require significant reconstruction.

The meaning "to go out" for a divine commandment (→ II.2 on Dnl. 2:13f.) also occurs in an inscription from Hatra dealing with sacral law[24] in the literal usage in another legal regulation together with *ʿll* to mean "all those who enter and exit Hatra," thus to emphasize the universal validity of the prescription even for the occasional visitors of this regionally significant pilgrimage site.

III. Causative-stem "to Bring Out." In comparison with the G-stem, the usage of the causative-stem "to bring out, to retrieve"[25] is significantly more restricted. It first occurs twice in the proverbs of Aḥiqar, which originated in pre-Imperial Aramaic but were transmitted on an Imperial Aramaic papyrus, in both passages figuratively for speech: once in a martial metaphor,[26] then, in the comparison of a discreet heart to a sound vessel, while the broken allows the contents to leak.[27]

Private letters employ the verb for the delivery of wares[28] or money[29] and with a person as object for "to accompany, lead out."[30] The meaning of the proverb *klbyʾ hnpqw kblʾ mn rglwhy* "the dogs removed the bonds from the legs"[31] cited in the petition of the Jewish community from Elephantine concerning the reconstruction of their temple is not entirely clear.[32]

In contracts, the specifically legal nuance "to produce" of a document[33] dominates,[34] in marriage contracts, the sense "to take along" for the wife's dowry in the event of divorce.[35] The latter nuance also appears in the context of robbery,[36] but is neutral, in contrast, in an instruction letter from Bactria.[37] In an inscription from Tēma concerning the establishment of a new temple staff,[38] if the emendation *yhn[pq]* is correct,

---

24. H342.8.

25. Imperial Aramaic often in degeminating orthography with the assimilated /n/: *hnpq*, *ynpq*, etc.

26. *TADAE* C1.1,83.

27. *TADAE* C1.1,93; → *lbb* III.

28. *TADAE* A2.5,3; 3.9,5; D7.7,6.8; 7.14,3.

29. *TADAE* A6.13,3.5.

30. *TADAE* A2.6,4.

31. *TADAE* A4.7,16 par. 4.8,15.

32. See *DNSI*, 485 for bib.

33. → *spr*.

34. TADAE B2.3,15.17.27; 2.7,12; 3.10,21; 3.11,15f.; 3.12,29; so also later in a Nabatean contract from the Dead Sea: nV 42:22,24 in *ATTM*, 2, 244-47.

35. *TADAE* B2.6,25.28; 3.3, 8.10.

36. *TADAE* B7.2,5; later *gnb* is attested in the proper sense of "to steal."

37. A2,4.7 in Naveh and Shaked; the form *np[q]* in l. 9 is unclear.

38. *KAI* 228 A 21.

the verb means "to remove" and refers to a priest whose descendants are to perform cultic tasks forever.[39]

As a commercial term, *npq* appears regularly in the causative-stem in the harbor register *TADAE* C3.7 for the export *lym'* "by sea" of natron; perhaps a similar usage, although without context, may also appear in the Bar-Puneš novella[40] and like *npqh* (→ IV).

The four instances in Biblical Aramaic (Dnl. 5:2f.; Ezr. 5:14 and 6:5) all have the meaning "to dispose" and refer to the temple furnishing stolen in the conquest of Jerusalem.[41]

The evidence at Qumran corresponds to circumstances established in older Aramaic: in addition to ambiguous fragments, primarily "to lead out" in reference to persons,[42] "to retrieve" of foods,[43] or "to remove" of organs.[44] The translation of creation theology passages in the book of Job in 11Q10 employs the verb for the power of God over nature: 29:1 (Job 37:11); 31:2 (Job 38:23); 31:5 (Job 38:27, "to cause to sprout");[45] 32:3 (Job 39:4).

At Palmyra Imperial Aramaic commercial terminology continues.[46] In addition to "to export,"[47] *npq* also refers there to the expenditures of private benefactors (→ IV).[48]

IV. Nouns "Expenses" and "Entrance." The verbal noun *npqh* /napaqā/ (collective singular) "expenses" is a commercial term and appears primarily in Imperial Aramaic business documents.[49] The sense is usually "costs" as also in Ezr. 6:4,8 (for the construction of the temple), nV 1:40 and still in Palmyrene (→ III).[50] In addition, it denotes the "allocation" for officials.[51] Furthermore, post-Imperial Aramaic has the substantivized infinitive *mpq* "free exit,"[52] Palmyra also has *mpqn* "export."[53]

Gzella

39. Cf. nV 36:8 in *ATTM*, 2, 240f.
40. *TADAE* C1.2,22.
41. See above on the Imperial Aramaic examples of the nuance "to take along."
42. 1QapGen 20:32.
43. 1QapGen 22:14.
44. 4Q197 4 1:8 (Tob. 6:4).
45. Cf. 4Q211 1 1:3.
46. H. Gzella, "Die Palmyrener in der griechisch-römischen Welt," *KLIO* 87 (2005) 451f.
47. *PAT* 0259 ii.81,111.
48. *PAT* 1378.5, with the object *npqh.*
49. *TADAE* C3.12,6; 3.14,30.32; 3.17b, 5; 3.19,7.14; 3.27,29; D3.18,1; Segal, 36.4; 37.1; 38.14; 51.5; 56.3.
50. *PAT* 1378.5.
51. Naveh and Shaked, C4.35.
52. M 25:3, V 45:10 and 46:6 in *ATTM*; *PAT* 1791.6.
53. *PAT* 0259 ii.27,66.

נצב *nṣb*; נצבה *nṣbh* /neṣbā/

I. Etymology and Forms. II. Common Usage of the Root and Its Derivatives in Older and Later Aramaic. III. Noun and Adjective in Biblical Aramaic. IV. Qumran. 1. Noun. 2. Verb. 3. Adjective.

I. Etymology and Forms. The root *nṣb* alternates in the Semitic languages with → *yṣb*,[1] which led, in Hebrew, to a complementary relationship between the verbal forms of the N- and causative-stems of *nṣb* and of the nouns *n^eṣīḇ* and *maṣṣēḇā* (both in the meaning "column, stele"), on the one side, and the Dt-stem of *yṣb*, on the other. Verbal and nominal forms of the root *nṣb* essentially refer to planting or a firm graft. An additional semantic development led then from "firmly graft" to "make certain" and led in Aramaic to a differentiation in meaning.[2]

II. Common Usage of the Root and Its Derivatives in Older and Later Aramaic. The various Aramaic languages attest the root *nṣb* well. A derived noun *nṣb* "raised stone, stele" occurs in a few Old Aramaic inscriptions[3] and in Sam'alian.[4] Nabatean and other late forms of the language know further a plethora of various nouns from the semantic field of planting, e.g., Syriac *neṣbā* and *neṣbtā*[5] or Mandean *niṣ(u)bta, niṣibta*.[6] According to Kutscher, *nṣbt'* could also mean "the seed,"[7] because both in the Peshitta and in Targum Neofiti it renders Hebrew *zæraʿ* in Gen. 1:11f. The by-form of the root *yṣb* appears less often in Aramaic, but occurs once each as a participle of the D-stem and as an adjective /yaṣṣīb/ with the same meaning "valid" in Imperial Aramaic contracts from Elephantine;[8] the adjective also appears later in Targum Onqelos and in Jewish Palestinian,[9] and, finally, the verb in the Dt-stem and the adjectives *yṣyb* and *yṣwb* in Samaritan Aramaic.[10]

III. Noun and Adjective in Biblical Aramaic. The noun *nṣbh*, in the determined state *nṣbt'*, occurs once in Biblical Aramaic in relation to iron: *ûmin niṣb^eṯā ḏī p̄arz^elā* (Dnl.

U. Dahmen, "*yṣb*," *ThWQ*, II, 231-35; J. A. Fitzmyer, *The Genesis Apocryphon of Qumran Cave 1 (1Q20). BietOr* 18B ([3]2004); T. Nöldeke, *Neue Beiträge zur semitischen Sprachwissenschaft* (Straßburg, 1910); J. Reindl, "נצב/יצב *nṣb/yṣb*," *TDOT*, IX, 519-29; A. Tal, *A Dictionary of Samaritan Aramaic*, 2 vols., *HO 50* (2000); P. A. Tiller, "The 'Eternal Planting' in the Dead Sea Scrolls." *DSD* 4 (1997) 312-35.

1. Nöldeke, 183f.
2. → *yṣb* I.
3. *KAI* 201, 222.
4. *KAI* 214, 215.
5. *LexSyr*, 442.
6. *MdD*, 299.
7. See Fitzmyer, 133.
8. → *yṣb* II.
9. *DJPA*, 243.
10. Tal, 354f.

2:41), according to medieval Jewish commentators such as Rashi, Ibn Ezra, and others even today, often translated "and of the firmness of iron," because *niṣbᵉṯā* "strength, firmness" is associated with the meaning "to firmly implant" of the verb *nṣb*. This meaning also underlies the usage of the variant root *yṣb* in Biblical Aramaic: of the infinitive in Dnl. 7:19, of the adjective in Dnl. 2:45; 3:24; 6:13; 7:16, and in the adverbial expression *min yaṣṣīḇ* "surely" in 2:8.[11] Others, in contrast, translate Dnl. 2:41 "the iron generation"[12] in accordance with the otherwise quite common meaning of *nṣbh* "planting" (→ IV.1).[13]

IV. Qumran.

1. Noun. The Aramaic scrolls from the Dead Sea frequently attest the noun *nṣbh* "planting" with the meaning "planting": in addition to Dnl. 2:41 in 4Q112 3 2:5 (→ III), also *nṣbt qwšṭ* "planting of truth" in 1QapGen 14:13, 4Q204 1 5:4 (1 En. 10:16) and fragmentarily in 4Q537 13:1; further *wmnk nṣbt pr'y* "the planting of the fruit (= the child) is by you" in 1QapGen 2:15 and *mn nṣbt yṣbt'* "from the establishment of certainty"(?) in 4Q212 1 3:19f. (1 En. 93:2; → IV.3). One passage may evidence the meaning "firmness," often also assumed for Dnl. 2:41 (→ III): *nṣbtn' blyly'* "our firmness in the night" in 11Q10 26:5 (Job 35:10, for Hebrew *nōṯēn zᵉmīrōṯ ballāylā*).

2. Verb. The verb "to plant" is attested in the G-stem, the Gt- and D-stems: figuratively *lqwšṭ nṣybt* "I was planted for uprightness (i.e., predestined for righteousness)" in 1QapGen 6:1; literally *wnṣbt krm rb* "I planted a large vine" in 1QapGen 12:13; *wkwlh ttnṣ[b* "and all of it will be plant[ed" in 4Q204 1 5:7 (1 En. 10:18), and *ttnṣb bh* "will be planted in it" in 4Q204 1 5:8 (1 En. 10:19), both for the new creation at the end of time. Furthermore, there is an example of the verbal noun *mnṣb* of the G-stem, *mnṣbhwn*, in 11Q18 14 2:2 (new Jerusalem).

3. Adjective. Qumran attests only the adjective /yaṣṣīb/ "certain" of the root *yṣb*, namely in the adverbial expression *byṣb'*[14] in 1QapGen 2:20 and 4Q530 2 2+6-12:24.[15] Two additional instances may be either a feminine plural determined form of the adjective or an abstract noun:[16] *[y]ṣbt'* in 4Q548 1 2-2:9 (Testament of Amram) and *mn nṣbt yṣbt'* "from a planting of reliability (or: from certain/reliable things?)" in 4Q212 1 3:19f. (1 En. 93:2).

Fassberg

11. For more on this → *yṣb* III.
12. *ATTM*, 640; *GesB*[18], 1516; so already Ps.-Theod.: ἀπὸ τῆς ῥίζης τῆς σιδηρᾶς "from the iron root."
13. Further literature in K. Koch, *Daniel 1–4. BK* XXII/1 (2005), 102.
14. Cf. *min yaṣṣīḇ* in Biblical Aramaic, → III.
15. For a brief discussion → *yṣb* IV.
16. Like Biblical Aramaic *niṣbᵉṯā*, → III.

נצח *nṣḥ*

I. Forms and Grammatical Construction. II. Usage.

I. Forms and Grammatical Construction. The verbal root *nṣḥ* is presumably common Semitic, but has widely varied nuances of meaning in the individual languages. Of them, the use of the G-stem for "to triumph" attested in Aramaic since Qumran[1] may be primary and has parallels in later Hebrew and, apparently, in Phoenician.[2] It links well with the Dt-stem for "to distinguish one's self," already attested in Imperial Aramaic, which may be supplemented with *ʿl* "over against, more than" (Dnl. 6:4). The same is true for the nuance "to shine" of the G-stem later in East Aramaic.[3]

According to Beyer's reading and interpretation of 1QapGen 7:21,[4] this corrupt passage may include an instance of a D-stem "to make successful," but that is very uncertain for paleographical reasons.[5]

II. Usage. In Imperial Aramaic, *nṣḥ* in the Dt-stem "to excel" is limited to official texts.[6] The Behistun inscription uses it for the confidants of Darius who supported him during a rebellion.[7] In the correspondence of Achaemenid officials, the same form of the verb often appears in the admonition to distinguish oneself before one's superiors.[8] Thus, it belongs to the same rhetoric of motivation as *ḥdī*, in the D-stem "to please,"[9] and *ṭb ʿbd* "to do good"[10] in similar provincial administrative contexts from Egypt to Bactria. The servants of the state everywhere were thus admonished to give their best in matters of the king and the empire.

Against the background of Imperial Aramaic court and administrative diction attested in authentic sources, the corresponding usage of *nṣḥ* in the literature describing Daniel's extremely successful work in service of the king (Dnl. 6:4) gains contours—just as later Ignatius of Loyola in his spiritual exercises encourages the desire in following Christ, the true king, always to be outstanding (*insignes esse*).

G. W. Anderson, "נֶצַח *neṣaḥ*," *TDOT*, V 529-33; G. Gelardini, "*nṣḥ* I," *ThWQ*, II, 1017-19 (Heb. only).

1. 4Q545 1a-b 2:19.
2. Cf. *GesB*[18], 838f. and *DNSI*, 751f.
3. *LexSyr*, 443; the adjective *nṣyḥ* "illuminating"—of stars—in Jewish Babylonian is also related, *DJBA*, 771b.
4. *ATTM*, 2, 93f.
5. D. A. Machiela, *The Dead Sea Genesis Apocryphon*. *STDJ* 79 (2009), 48.
6. Segal, 82b.2 is unclear.
7. *TADAE* C2.1,75; presumably also to be emended for the action of the king in C2.1 Col III, l. 4.
8. *TADAE* A6.10,4f.; 6.14,3; 6.16,1.
9. → *ḥdwh* II.1.
10. → *ṭīb* III.1.

The G-stem "to triumph" occurs first at Qumran: certainly in 4Q545 la-b 2:19 (Testament of Amram), and according to *ATTM*, 2, 91f. also in 1QapGen 6:1, where, however, most read *nṣybt*.[11]

Gzella

11. → *nṣb* IV.2.

נצל *nṣl*; פלט *plṭ*

I. Etymology, Lexical Field, and Grammatical Constructions. II. Old and Imperial Aramaic. III. Biblical Aramaic and Qumran. IV. Verb *plṭ*. 1. G-stem "to Escape." 2. D-stem "to Deliver." 3. Nouns.

I. Etymology, Lexical Field, and Grammatical Constructions. Besides Hebrew, Ugaritic, and Arabic, the Ethiopian and Modern South Arabian Semitic languages also know the Semitic verbal root *nṣl*. In Aramaic, as predominantly in Hebrew, it regularly appears in the transitive causative-stem in the meaning "to snatch, deliver (someone)" with the person involved as a direct object. It first appears in sources from the Achaemenid period. The verb occurs in Imperial Aramaic mostly as a juridical term "to reclaim," but the older Aramaic of Aḥiqar already exhibits the common usage. In post-Achaemenid times, it became increasingly rare; its usage in Jewish Babylonian may trace to Hebrew influence.[1]

An original G-stem may have once meant "to separate, to cease." The middle nuance "to withdraw, escape," in contrast, is associated with the N-stem, as Ugaritic[2] and Hebrew[3] demonstrate. However, Aramaic does not have this stem; there the likewise common Semitic verb *plṭ* (→ IV) in the G-stem, which in turn occurs in Hebrew with certainty only in Ezk. 7:16,[4] serves for "to escape"; rarely → *ndd/nūd* "to flee" has this function.

U. Bergmann, "נצל *nṣl* hi. to rescue," *TLOT*, 760-62; U. Dahmen, "*nṣl*," *ThWQ*, II, 1019-23; J. C. Greenfield, "Aramaic HNṢL and Some Biblical Passages," in *Meqor Ḥajjim. FS G. Molin* (Graz, 1983), 115-19; F.-L. Hossfeld/B. Kalthoff, "נצל *nṣl*," *TDOT*, IX, 533-40; E. Jenni, *Das hebräische Pi'el* (Zurich, 1968); J. Naveh and S. Shaked, *Aramaic Documents from Ancient Bactria (Fourth Century B.C.E.)* (London, 2012).

1. Cf. *DJBA*, 771.
2. *DUL*³, 638.
3. *GesB*¹⁸, 840.
4. *GesB*¹⁸, 1054.

A nuance of the causative-stem of *nṣl* with modal shadings "to want to snatch/deliver, to seek to deliver" (sometimes with *mn* "from), primarily oriented toward the action or the purpose of the action and not on the result,[5] can also be observed in Aramaic primarily in association with a modal verb (→ II und III). It does not constitute, however, a marked contrast to the factitive as does *plṭ* in the D-stem "(actually/successfully) to deliver." Meanwhile, speaking technically, *nṣl* has no "actuality entailment"; one may compare, e.g., in Italian *i bambini potevano giocare* "the children had permission to play" (whether they actually did) in contrast to *i bambini hanno potuto giocare* "the children could play" (and actually played).[6]

Semantically, *nṣl* overlaps with → *šyzb* "to deliver" (also a verb in the causative-stem lexicalized in this form) adapted from Babylonian and occurs in parallel with it (Dnl. 6:15,28). In the usage for "to snatch, take away," it can stand as a synonym for → *nśī*; → *šbq* (rarely *pṭr*) denotes "to (set) loose."

II. Old and Imperial Aramaic. The first occurrence of *nṣl* "to snatch, deliver" in Aramaic is in a proverb of Aḥiqar, originally pre-Imperial Aramaic but transmitted as part of an Imperial Aramaic papyrus. In relation to education, it asserts that one should not spare his son the rod, otherwise one may not be able to deliver him (*l' tkhl thnṣlnh*[*y*]).[7] Here, the asyndetic linkage with the auxiliary verb *khl* "to be able,"[8] as is sometimes the case also in legal diction (see below), specifically emphasizes the modal nuance inherent in the verb "to seek to deliver" (→ I).

Otherwise, the verb occurs predominantly in private documents from the Achaemenid period where it serves as a juridical term for "to wrest away" in the sense of "to reclaim" with the object of the contract (field, house, dowry, etc.) as the explicit or implicit direct object.[9] Occasionally, a prepositional expression following *mn* "from" for the recipient of the claim appears.[10] With a person as object, it refers to the child of a slave woman whom the owner may reclaim only in case of her divorce.[11] It occurs here with a modifier *mn tḥt lbbk* "from under your heart = from your care."

In the formulaic expression *ṣbyt 'hnṣl*,[12] which denotes the reclamation that the contract party resists, *ṣbyt* "I will" may serve not as an independent main verb ("I would like it; I demand it back"), but, like *khl*/*ykl*, as a modal verb ("I would like to reclaim it"), which would correspond to the inner-causative nuance of *nṣl*. Together with → *ntn* in the

5. So convincingly Jenni, 258f. for the Heb.

6. Additional literature in H. Gzella, "Some Remarks on Interactions between Aspect, Modality, and Evidentiality in Biblical Hebrew," *Folia Orientalia* 49 (2012) 227.

7. *TADAE* C1.1,176.

8. → *ykl*.

9. *TADAE* B1.1,14, dated to 515 B.C.E.; here, also with the supplementary preceding '[*kl*] and object; B2.3,18, see below; 2.4,10; 3.5,20; 3.8,42; 6.4,8.

10. *TADAE* B3.7,15, twice, once with *'khl* in l. 14; 3.11,10.

11. *TADAE* B3.3, 13, again with a preceding *'kl* and *l-* as object marker before the personal name, as is common in Imperial Aramaic with definite and animate objects.

12. *TADAE* B3.7,15; 3.8, 41f.; 6.4,8.

purpose clause "in order to give," it has the sense of "to hand over."[13] In court records,[14] *hnṣl* denotes the proclaimed, but not necessarily successful, reclamation.

In contrast, the verb *nṣl* often has a pejorative nuance "to snatch away" in a late Achaemenid official letter from Bactria. In it, a high administrator—probably the satrap himself—reacts to the grievance of an inferior that another official had illegally "snatched" a steer and sheep from camel keepers in his service and that they must be returned.[15]

This nuance finds a counterpart in the use of the verb in the Xanthos triglot, which also dates to the middle or even the second half of the fourth century B.C.E. and confirms the institution of a cult by the Persian administration. It places the attempt to remove[16] something from the venerated god and his priests or other gods under divine punishment.[17] The Greek parallel version employs the verb μετακινήσειν,[18] but phrases it somewhat differently overall.

The evidence does not permit one to determine whether the contextual difference between the earlier contracts from Elephantine ("to reclaim") and the somewhat later texts from Bactria and Asia Minor ("to take away") reflects a semantic development between the fifth and the fourth centuries B.C.E. or simply depends on the differences in genre with the relevant linguistic register.

III. Biblical Aramaic und Qumran. Against this background in Imperial Aramaic diction, the nuance of the verb in Biblical Aramaic can also be determined more precisely. It occurs three times in the book of Daniel, always with the nuance "to deliver" and in the context of mortal danger, as the older proverb of Aḥiqar *TADAE* C1.1,176 already implies (→ II): once in the account of the young men in the fiery furnace (Dnl. 3:29) and twice in the story of Daniel in the lions' den (Dnl. 6:15, 28, in both passages in parallel with *šyzb*). God is twice the agent (Dnl. 3:29 and 6:28), always in a laudatory prayer of thanksgiving; once the king (6:15), who, without desiring it, became enmeshed in a court intrigue of those envious of his successful protégé Daniel who thereby became a victim of a law issued by the king himself against the exercise of other religions.

These passages also still glimmer with the original modal nuance of the causative-stem of *nṣl*. In each case, the emphasis lies on the action itself, which can lead to success but not necessarily. The combination of the infinitive with a finite form of the auxiliary verb *ykl* "to be able" in Dnl. 3:29 as in the older Aramaic instances (→ II) emphasizes the saving ability of God ("there is no other god who can save in this fashion"). The use of *nṣl* as a verbal complement after the Dt-stem of the auxiliary verb *šdr*[19] "to try" in Dnl. 6:15 characterizes the king's attempt yet to protect Daniel from the lions' den as a mere

13. *TADAE* B2.3,18f.; cf. Gen 31:9 and Greenfield.

14. *TADAE* B8.2 I 15; 8.6,5.

15. Naveh and Shaked A1,2.8.10; perhaps also to be reconstructed in l. 6, which would result, however, in the *plene*-spelling *hn*]*ṣyl* which is very unusual in Imperial Aramaic.

16. Impf. *KAI* 319.20, ptcp. in l. 26.

17. In l. 23 perhaps the corresponding pass. ptcp. for the evildoer: "he will be snatched away"; in l. 27 with the verb *bʿī* "to demand," as sometimes also refers to sanctions elsewhere, → *bʿī* II.

18. Ll. 30-33.

19. → *šlḥ*.

effort which ultimately did not lead to success, however. Dnl. 6:28 emphasizes through the resumption of the parallelism of *nṣl* and *šyzb* in 6:15 that only God himself can save from such danger, and no king, however powerful. The modal usage in Aramaic constitutes, then, no more a contrast to the factual than it does in Hebrew, for which reason *nṣl* can interchange there with resultative verbs of deliverance.[20]

In post-Achaemenid Aramaic, *nṣl* seems to disappear from usage and Qumran seems to attest it with certainty only twice. In 1QapGen 22:10,19, it occurs in an expansion of the corresponding formulation from Genesis in the meaning "to fetch back" in reference to Abraham's successful attempt to take back the stolen goods and captives from the enemies.

IV. Verb *plṭ*. Aramaic attests the root *plṭ*, in the G-stem "to escape" and in the D-stem "to deliver, set loose," both occasionally supplemented with *mn* "from," beginning at Qumran. It already appears once, however, in a Sam'alian royal inscription that says that the gods of the place "saved him [the father of the one who commissioned the inscription] from his destruction" (*plṭwh . . . mn šḥth*).[21] Thus, context suggests a D-stem. Additionally, the verb continues in usage in later Aramaic.[22]

1. G-stem "to Escape." The G-stem of *plṭ* stands in 1QapGen 19:20 with *npšy* "my life-force"[23] as the subject in the sense of "to survive" at the end of Abraham's interpretation of his dream that announces the threat of mortal danger: if Sarai will portray him as her brother, he may escape on her account. It serves similarly in 4Q204 5 2:24 (1 En. 106:18f.)[24] in the announcement that Noah will escape (the destruction of the flood), and similarly of the escape of the righteous in the judgment in 4Q204 1 5:5. In 1QapGen 22:2, it refers to Lot who escaped captivity (*mn šby'*) after a raid. The text of 4Q552 4:12 is fragmentary.

2. D-stem "to Deliver." The D-stem "to deliver" also occurs in 1QapGen, specifically in 12:17 for God's deliverance from the destruction (*mn 'bdn'*) of the flood, and probably also in an unclear context in 11:14. In 11Q10 4:9 and 32:2 (Job 21:10 and 39:3) it means, "to set free."

3. Nouns. The feminine *plṭh* /paleṭā/ "deliverance" is attested in 4Q530 1 1:3; for later forms, see *ATTM*, 668.

Gzella

20. Jenni, 258.

21. *KAI* 215,2f.; on the relationship of Sam'alian to Aramaic, see P. M. Noorlander, "Sam'alian in Its Northwest Semitic Setting," *Or* 81 (2012) 202-38.

22. See *DJPA*, 435; *DJBA*, 912b; *LexSyr*, 573; *MdD*, 374.

23. → *nšm*.

24. Reconstructed also in 4Q204 5 2:21.

נקה *nqh* /neqǣ/; נקי *nqī*; נקה *nqh* /naqǣ/

I. Etymology and Forms. II. Occurrences and Usage. III. Verb "to Be Clean," Adjective "Clean."

I. Etymology and Forms. The Aramaic noun *nqh* /neqǣ/ "sheep" (at least in Syriac a feminine) may involve an Akkadian loanword from *nīqu* "sheep offering."[1] In contrast with the traditional explanation in older Hebrew and Aramaic lexicography, this noun is distinct from the root *nqī* "to be clean," well known from Hebrew but also native to Aramaic.[2] One cannot rule out an original shared etymology for the two lexemes, but over time, they became clearly distinct in Aramaic. Aramaic otherwise typically employs *dkī* for "to be clean."

II. Occurrences and Usage. The meaning "sheep" for *nqh* /neqǣ/ is also indicated for older Aramaic by the word /neqiyā/ marked as a feminine in *nqyh wgzth* "a sheep and its wool" in a pre-Imperial Aramaic private letter from Hermopolis.[3] The apparently related form *nqwh* /neqwā/ occurs for a sheep offering[4] in the Imperial Aramaic Xanthos inscription[5] concerning the institution of a new cult.

In the light of these parallels, the expression *kʿmr nqʾ* in the description of the white robe[6] that the Ancient of Days wears in the vision of Dnl. 7:9 doubtlessly means "like wool."[7]

III. Verb "to Be Clean," Adjective "Clean." The verb *nqī*, in the D-stem "to cleanse," is also rare in Aramaic, but appears in an alliance treaty from the eve of the Imperial Aramaic tradition as a legal term "to free from foreign claims."[8] Later, the verbs *mrq* or *ṣpī* serve this function.

The adjective *nqʾ* /naqǣ/ "innocent"[9] occurs in older Aramaic only in 11Q10 22:3 (Job 33:9) where it renders the Hebrew *hapax legomenon ḥp*, probably under the influence of Hebrew *nqy*.[10]

Gzella

G. Geiger, "*nqh*," *ThWQ*, II, 1028-31; S. A. Kaufman, *The Akkadian Influences on Aramaic. AS* 19 (1974); C. van Leeuwen, "נקה *nqh* ni. to be innocent," *TLOT*, 763-67; M. Sokoloff, "*ʿămar nĕqēʾ*, 'Lamb's Wool' (Dnl. 7:9)," *JBL* 95 (1976) 277-79; C. Stadel, *Hebraismen in den aramäischen Texten vom Toten Meer* (Heidelberg, 2008); G. Warmuth, "נָקָה *nāqâ*," *TDOT*, IX, 553-63.

1. *ATTM*, 641 following Kaufman, 77.
2. → III and Sokoloff.
3. *TADAE* A2.2,8.
4. With the verb *zbḥ*; → *dbḥ*.
5. *KAI* 319.15.
6. → *ḥwr*.
7. Not "like pure wool," as, e.g., *LexLingAram*, 115 still has and the ancient Greek translations of the passage that had καθαρόν.
8. *TADAE* B1.1, 10f.
9. For which one otherwise used → *zkī* in Aramaic.
10. Stadel, 112f.

נשא/נשי *nś'/nśī*; נסב *nsb*; לקח *lqḥ*; טען *ṭ'n*; טעון *ṭ'wn* /ṭa'ūn/

I. Etymology, Forms, and Lexical Field. II. Old and Imperial Aramaic (Usually *nśī*). III. Biblical Aramaic (*nśī*). IV. Qumran and Later Aramaic (*nsb*). V. Verb *lqḥ* "to Take." VI. Verb *ṭ'n* "to Load" and Noun *ṭ'wn* "Load."

I. Etymology, Forms, and Lexical Field. Aramaic *nśī* "to take (away)" arose from the common Semitic verbal root **nś'* "to take up" and is employed mostly as in Hebrew "to lift, carry" in the G-stem and transitively. After the loss of the glottal stop ending the syllable still in the Old Aramaic period, it was transferred to the class of verbs ending in vowels,[1] but the ' for the original glottal stop was still long retained in a historical spelling here, too.

The verb *nśī* is common in this form in Old and Imperial Aramaic for "to lift up, take away," then generally "to take" and also occurs in three Biblical Aramaic passages, both in Ezra and in Daniel, where it appears everywhere with the meaning "to take (away)." It is usually employed literally with persons as subjects and concrete material objects, but can also stand with an inanimate subject such as the wind (Dnl. 2:35) or abstract objects (e.g., words). In contrast, it occurs at Qumran only very sparsely and was replaced there as in all other post-Imperial Aramaic literary languages by *nsb* "to take."

Its etymology is unclear. It may be that an association with Arabic *našiba*, as once suggested by Nöldeke and often repeated since,[2] should be abandoned.[3] The hypothesis that *nsb* may have arisen from *nśī b-*[4] already fails, on one point alone in that *nsb* already occurs in the proverbs of Aḥiqar in exactly this spelling,[5] but is distinct from *nśī* with which it once appears there in parallel. Since in the Aḥiqar papyrus, in accordance with Imperial Aramaic orthography, the reflections of the old */ś/ (spelled *ś*) and /s/ (spelled *s*) are always maintained in distinction from one another,[6] the assumption of a scribal error becomes superfluous. Moreover, there is no evidence of a frequent use of *nśī* with *b-*, which would have facilitated such an elision.

More likely, then, one may regard *nsb*, at least in the sense of "to take," as a rare and for Aramaic typical, yet independent lexeme that, in comparison to the typical *nśī* prob-

T. Elgvin and C. Kumpmann, "*lqḥ*," *ThWQ*, II, 532-37; D. N. Freedman, B. E. Willoughby, and H.-J. Fabry, "*nāśā'*," *TDOT*, X, 24-55; C. Kumpmann, "*nś'*," *ThWQ*, II, 1035-41 (Heb.); H. H. Schmid, "לקח *lqḥ* to take," *TLOT*, 648-51; H. Seebass, "לָקַח *lāqaḥ*," *TDOT*, VIII, 16-21; F. Stolz, "נשא, *nś'* to lift, bear," *TLOT*, 769-74.

1. III-*ī*; *ATTM*, 104-6.
2. Cf. *LexSyr*, 432.
3. So I. Kottsieper, *Die Sprache der Aḥiqarsprüche*. *BZAW* 194 (1990), 37, who suspects a relationship to Arabic *nasaba* "to stand in relation to someone," which, however, is not immediately illuminating for semantic reasons.
4. M. Sokoloff, *A Syriac Lexicon* (Winona Lake, IN, 2009), 923a.
5. *TADAE* C1.1,160.
6. Kottsieper, 36.

ably had a very specific, but no longer precisely determinable nuance. This conclusion finds further support in the fact that quite frequently in parallelism, the less common or precise word appears in the second member, entirely in analogy to the juxtaposition of *nśī* and *ṭʿn* "to load" in the proverb in the preceding lines that has a parallel structure (→ VI).

Then, one would assume an original meaning "to lift" or the like for *nsb* which first expanded in post-Imperial Aramaic perhaps under the influence of the increasing spelling *s* for the historical */ś/ which later fused with /s/ at least in pronunciation.[7] Finally, in the course of such a semantic extension, *nsb* ultimately replaced the old Semitic verb *nśī* in Aramaic,[8] but since then shared its meaning with *ṭʿn*. Presumably, this development began in the spoken dialects beneath the surface of the more conservative literary language.

Synonyms of the verbs for taking are well defined in Aramaic and well represented in literary and documentary texts. With the meaning "to take away" *nśī* has points of contact with → *nṣl* (causative-stem) "to snatch away"; explicitly for "to raise up," in addition to → *nṭl*,[9] the causative-stem of → *rīm* can also be employed. Originally in reference to cargo, *ṭʿn* denotes "to load" (→ VI). In contrast, *lqḥ* serves in older Aramaic for "to take" in general and as an antonym of → *yhb*/*ntn* "to give" (→ V), but was also later replaced with *nsb*. For "to receive," that is, when the act of giving proceeds from someone else, older Aramaic usually utilizes the verb → *qbl* in the D-stem.

Only very rarely is *nśī* used for this in the Dt-stem when it means "to arise" (Ezr. 4:19), sometimes with the supplement *ʿl* "against." Better attested in this function is the similarly constructed Lt-stem of *rīm*. For "to carry" → *sbl*.

II. Old and Imperial Aramaic (Usually *nśī*). The oldest Aramaic inscriptions employ *nśī* often with the nuance "to raise up," either literally for the lifting of the hands as a prayer gesture in the reports of royal acts[10] or figuratively for the "raising" of an intention *ʿl śpt* "to the lips" in parallel with *slq ʿl lbb* "to come over the heart" in a state treaty.[11] In contrast, it appears in *KAI* 222 B 39 apparently with the meaning "to carry away" with food (*lḥm*) as the object; an additional specimen in *KAI* 224.26 is fragmentary.

The somewhat later proverbs of Aḥiqar, with their richly picturesque mode of expression, also employ the verb in the sense of "to raise up," "to take," and "to carry away," each in a variety of shades: "to lift" in a comparison regarding a heavy or light burden (→ I);[12] "to take," here of loot;[13] and then "to carry away";[14] "to lift" of a foot;[15] "to carry"

7. *ATTM*, 102.
8. And also in later West and East Aramaic: *DJPA*, 353; *DJBA*, 756; *LexSyr*, 432; *MdD*, 302.
9. In older Aramaic primarily for the lifting of the eyes.
10. *KAI* 202 A 11, also in Sam'alian: *KAI* 214,29; → *yd* II.1.
11. *KAI* 224.14,15,16, the direct object is unexpressed; here for the plan to murder the treaty-partner or one of his descendants; → *lbb* II.
12. *TADAE* C1.1,159f., in the first case parallel with *ṭʿn* "to load," in the second with *nsb* "to lift up."
13. Impv. C1.1, 169, apparently an ingressive with the ethical dative following *l-*; cf. H. Gzella, *Tempus, Aspekt und Modalität im Reichsaramäischen. VOK* 48 (2004), 254.
14. Impf. in the same line, supplemented with *mn* "from."
15. *TADAE* C1.1,170f., in contrast to the causative-stem of → *nḥt* "to put down."

figuratively of shame and literally of a load;[16] also figuratively for something that God (in heaven) has lifted.[17]

In the Aramaic material from the Achaemenid period, *nśī* primarily has the meaning "to carry" and often appears in juridical texts and in relation to the transport of goods.[18] The same is true for ostraca with commercial documents[19] and a marriage contract from Idumea.[20] Furthermore, it refers to slaves bearing a brand at least once.[21]

With the Iranian loanword *dšn'* "the donation" as object, *nśī* also occurs once in the meaning "to accept."[22] The relevant text is a letter from the chancellery of the Egyptian satrap Aršama; in idiomatic Aramaic, one would normally expect the verb *qbl* (D-stem) for "to accept." It is unclear whether this specific formulation traces to the substrate influence of Iranian.

In post-Achaemenid Aramaic, *nśī* still appears in cuneiform incantation formula from Uruk for "to take" in a certain ritual act.[23] Linguistically, this text does not belong to the Imperial Aramaic literary tradition, however, but to the earliest witnesses to East Aramaic.[24] In later East Aramaic, as in Jewish Babylonian, Syriac, and Mandean, *nsb* replaced the verb (→ I).

III. Biblical Aramaic (*nśī*). Two of the three Biblical Aramaic instances of *nśī* are forms of the G-stem and conform closely to older Aramaic diction. In Ezr. 5:15, the imperative "take!" appears in the original command of Cyrus to take the temple vessels, set out on the path to Jerusalem,[25] and to deposit them there,[26] in order to initiate the reconstruction. On the other hand, Dnl. 2:35 employs it figuratively in the vision of the colossus on clay feet in reference to the wind that carried away remains of the once powerful statue now reduced to dust as a symbol of the four sequential empires.[27]

The Dt-stem in Ezr. 4:19, which is unusual for this verb, means "to rise up against [*'l*] someone" and has as its subject Jerusalem, which is supposed to have repeatedly rebelled[28] against ruling kings in the past. With a similar meaning and an identical construction, however, Dnl. 5:23 employs the Lt-stem of → *rīm* to refer to Belshazzar's sacrilege; there

---

16. *TADAE* C1.1,185 (2×); in a corrupt context possibly also in C1.1,193.
17. *TADAE* C1.1,79; in reference to wisdom, but with a missing subject.
18. *TADAE* B1.1,13f.; 3.8,19; 8.1,14; the context of 8.7,7 is unclear.
19. A. Lemaire, *Nouvelles inscriptions araméennes d'Idumée*, vol. 2 (Paris, 2002), no. 284, l. 5; probably also Arad ostracon no. 41, ibid., 226f., l. 1.
20. E. Eshel and A. Kloner, "An Aramaic Ostracon of an Edomite Marriage Contract from Maresha, Dated 176 B.C.E.," *IEJ* 46 (1996) 1-22, l. 11.
21. *TADAE* B8.9,1.
22. *TADAE* A6.4,4.
23. *ATTM*, 2, 26f., ll. 1.27.
24. H. Gzella, *A Cultural History of Aramaic. HO* 111 (2015), 269f.
25. *'zl.*
26. Causative-stem of *nḥt.*
27. → *dhb* II; → *dqq.*
28. Parallel with → *mrd.*

are parallels for this elsewhere in Aramaic. No semantic or stylistic distinction between these two expressions can be determined.

IV. Qumran and Later Aramaic (*nsb*). The Aramaic texts from Qumran reflect the disappearance of the root *nśī* from the lexicon after the disintegration of Imperial Aramaic as the originally most widespread Aramaic literary language. Qumran attests the verb with certainty only as *ynswn* "they will carry" in 11Q10 11:4 (Job 27:13), on the one hand, with the loss of the ' in keeping with pronunciation, but on the other, with degemination of the /n/ in contact position according to Imperial Aramaic orthography. In this text, it stands for Hebrew *lqḥ* with the nuance "to accept" and is supplemented by the preposition *mn*] *qdmhwy* "from him (i.e., God)" instead of the simple *mn* as is often the case in relation to God.[29] An additional possible specimen of the Dt stem already known from Ezr. 4:19 "to arise" (→ III) in 4Q203 7a:7[30] is fragmentary and the reading somewhat uncertain.

Otherwise, the verb *nsb* for "to take" appears at Qumran as in other Aramaic varieties from the same period and later. Narrative texts, in particular, attest it well. For "to raise" (of the countenance) in 1QapGen 5:12, it still stands quite close to older usage, but it now appears frequently for "to take,"[31] sometimes in ritual instructions,[32] and specifically for "to take someone [*l*-] as wife,"[33] as often later, as well.[34] The causative-stem, then, means, "to give in marriage."[35] Various others of the overall numerous instances are fragmentary.

In Palmyrene and at Hatra, *nsb* is now also used in contexts in which one formerly encountered *nśī* and *lqḥ* (→ V): *PAT* 1624.7 (→ II) and 2775.10 (→ III),[36] as well as H344.7 with the nuance "to take," H281.3,9 in the sense "to take away."[37] "To carry" is now *ṭʿn* (→ VI).

V. Verb *lqḥ* "to Take." Like **nś'* (Aramaic *nśī*), *lqḥ* "to take" is a common Semitic root. In contrast to *nśī*, *nsb*, and other verbs of carrying or removing (→ I), it does not primarily designate a physical exertion, but grasping an initiation. It is common in the G-stem in Old and Imperial Aramaic and conjugated, as in Hebrew, like a verb I-*n* with assimilation of the /l/ in contact position,[38] which is sometimes preserved in the spelling.[39]

---

29. → *qdm*.
30. *ATTM*, 263, G 7,7a. Cf. *DSSStE*, 410f., which translates "will be forgiven."
31. 1QapGen 13:9-11; 22:22; 4Q196 14 1:11f. (Tob. 6:17); 4Q537 1+2+3:3,5; 4Q545 1a-b 2:18 par. 4Q546 2:4.
32. 2Q24 4:9; 4Q156 1:5 (Lev. 16:14).
33. 1QapGen 6:7f.,10; 20:9,27,34; 4Q197 4 2:3.5 (Tob. 6:13).
34. Earlier, on the other hand, *lqḥ*.
35. 4Q545 1a 1:5.
36. Cf., in contrast, the first instance in *TADAE* C1.1, 169 and Ezr. 5:15.
37. Also in the second instance in *TADAE* C1.1.169 and in Dnl. 2:35; for a discussion of the passages, see *DNSI*, 734.
38. /yeqqaḥ/ "he takes," thus always /qaḥ/ "take!"
39. H. Gzella, "Language and Script," in H. Niehr, ed., *The Aramaeans in Ancient Syria. HO* 106 (2014), 71-107, esp. 82.

Old Aramaic evidence already reflects a broad spectrum of possible usages: in addition to the common usage,[40] the acceptance of words[41] and sacrificial offerings,[42] the seizure of land and property,[43] the capture of cities,[44] and the imprisonment of persons.[45]

Documentary texts from the Achaemenid periods also indicate a broad distribution as a blanket term. In letters, it often denotes "to take away,"[46] in contracts "to take possession"[47] or "to take as wife."[48] It occurs figuratively in an oath formula with "life" as an affirmation,[49] and in a grave context, to take "water before Osiris."[50] It also appears in commercial texts in the literal sense. The Gt-stem "to be taken"[51] overlaps with the internal passive, which was disappearing in post-Imperial Aramaic.[52]

Biblical Aramaic does not attest *lqḥ*, but the few specimens from Qumran indicate that it was disappearing in post-Imperial Aramaic and would ultimately be replaced by *nsb* (→ IV): the passive participle of light that would be "taken away" in astronomical jargon[53] and two fragmentary passages.[54] The Nabatean confirmation of a Greek marriage contract has the causative-stem "to give as wife."[55] The few Jewish Babylonian occurrences in legal contexts trace back to Hebrew influence.[56]

VI. Verb *ṭ'n* "to Load" and Noun *ṭ'wn* "Load." Finally, the verb *ṭ'n* in the G-stem denotes "to load." It is the Aramaic counterpart of the common Semitic root **θ̣'n*.[57] The nuance "to load up" presumably arose from "loading animals" and in relation to "to set out," for which Arabic and OSA employ the verb. It is transitive, takes a simple ("to carry something") or dual object ("to load someone/something with something), and forms a passive.

The term *ṭ'n* first appears already in the Old Aramaic sayings of Aḥiqar. In *TADAE* C1.1,159, it stands alongside *nśī* "to raise high" in reference to a heavy load,[58] which the parallel expression in the subsequent lines takes up again with *nśī* and *nsb* in reference

40. *TADAE* C1.1,108.
41. *KAI* 309.10; 224.2.
42. *KAI* 309.17.
43. *KAI* 222 B 27; *TADAE* C1.1,167, → *nmr*.
44. *KAI* 222 B 35.
45. *KAI* 222 A 42, internal passive.
46. *TADAE* A4.4,8; 4.7,12; probably also 5.2,4.6f.; 6.3,5; 6.15,6.7.9.10; 7.2,6.9; 8.4,4; generally "to take" in A2.4,9.
47. *TADAE* B1.1,9; 2.4,9.11; 2.9,6; 3.1,9.13.17 and 3.13,10, of securities.
48. *TADAE* B2.5,2; 3.8,36).
49. *TADAE* D7.16,4.
50. *TADAE* D20.5,3.
51. *TADAE* A2. 3,9; B2.3,17.
52. In *TADAE* C2.1 col. III l. 1 but quite specifically as a resultative.
53. 4Q209 6:9 (1 En. 73[c]).
54. 4Q531 24,2; 4Q547 9,10.
55. nV 18,68 in *ATTM*, 2, 232f.
56. Cf. *DJBA*, 632b.
57. Heb. *ṣ'n*; the Aram. form in Gen 45:17 is probably borrowed, cf. *GesB*[18], 426.
58. *ḥl* "sand" and → *mlḥ* "salt."

to a light load.[59] If the two verbs were chosen consciously to clarify *nśī*, as is common in parallelism, *ṭʿn* would have originally been associated with a major physical exertion like the English "to load up" and *nsb* with a lesser exertion such as "to raise up" (→ I). In l. 186, it appears with the noun *ṭʿwn* for loading a camel load (see below).

In Imperial Aramaic in a letter-contract with *b-* it literally denotes the loading of a boat[60] and in a contract figuratively for the imposition of an oath;[61] the corresponding passive also occurs once in the same sense.[62] The passive participle *ṭʿyn* "loaded," as in the Palmyrene tax tables,[63] is later understood in Aramaic as an active "bearing."[64]

If the meaning in Old and Imperial Aramaic was still quite specific, the verb occurs in later Aramaic languages with a broader semantic spectrum that also includes the usages "to carry, lift up" which were previously associated with *nśī*.[65] There, it is more closely associated with physical exertion than *nsb* (→ V), which has also assumed some of the meanings of *nśī*.

The masculine substantive *ṭʿwn* /ṭaʿūn/ "load" belongs to the same root. A proverb of Aḥiqar first attests it in the phrase *ṭʿwn gmlʾ* "camel load" as an internal object of the verb[66] and remains productive in Aramaic even in post-Christian times.[67]

Gzella

59. *tbn* "straw" and *prn* "clay."
60. *TADAE* A3.10,3.
61. *TADAE* B2.2,6.
62. *TADAE* B2.3,24.
63. *PAT* 0259 ii.118.
64. See T. Nöldeke, *Mandäische Grammatik* (Halle, 1875), 380; a few other verbs function similarly.
65. Cf. *DJPA*, 228f.; *DJBA*, 511; *LexSyr*, 283; *MdD*, 175.
66. *TADAE* C1.1,186.
67. Cf. *DJPA*, 227; *DJBA*, 508f.; *MdD*, 177; Syriac the feminine: *LexSyr*, 284.

נשם *nšm*; נשמה *nšmh* /našamā/; נשם *nšm* /našam/; נשב *nšb*; נפש *npš* /napš/

I. Etymology, Lexical Field, and Forms. II. Noun "Breath." 1. Breath of Life. 2. Breath of Air. 3. Verb "to Blow." III. "Soul." 1. In the Full Sense. 2. "Self." 3. "Tomb."

H. Bauer, "Wechsel von *p*, *m*, *b* mit *u* im Aramäischen und Arabischen," *ZS* 10 (1935) 11-13; R. P. Bonfiglio, "*npš*," *ThWQ*, II, 1007-17 (Heb.); J. A. Fitzmyer, *The Genesis Apocryphon of Qumran Cave 1 (1Q20)*. *BietOr* 18B (³2004); H. Gzella, *Lebenszeit und Ewigkeit*. *BBB* 134 (2002); K. Koch, "Der Güter gefährlichstes, die Sprache, dem Menschen gegeben . . . Überlegungen zu Gen 2,7," *BN* 48 (1988) 50-60; H. Lamberty-Zielinski, "נְשָׁמָה *nᵉšāmâ*," *TDOT*, X, 65-70; C. Schneider, "*nšmh*," *ThWQ*, II, 1050-52 (Heb.); H. Seebass, "נֶפֶשׁ *nepeš*," *TDOT*, IX, 497-519; L. Triebel, *Jenseitshoffnung in Wort und Stein*. *AGJU* (2004); C. Westermann, "נֶפֶשׁ *nepeš* soul," *TLOT*, 743-59.

I. Etymology, Lexical Field, and Forms. Aramaic first attests a verbal root *nšm* "to breathe" with certainty in post-Christian East Aramaic,[1] but it has a cognate in the Hebrew *nšm* "to blow" (Isa. 42:14) and in the Arabic *nasama* "to blow softly," and also underlies the feminine noun /našamā/ "breath of life" already attested in Biblical Aramaic and with the masculine variant /našam/ "breath of air" at Qumran.

It presumably constitutes a by-form of the root *nšp* "to blow" also known from various Semitic languages[2] and its variant *nšb*.[3] The interchange between the voiced bilabial /b/ and its unvoiced counterpart /p/ and the bilabial nasal /m/ is easily explained phonetically and appears sporadically elsewhere in Semitic.[4]

It is less clear whether this root bears a direct etymological relationship with the also common Semitic feminine primary noun /napš/ "self," but a metathesis of *šp* to *pš* would not be problematic from a phonetic perspective and a relationship would be semantically plausible. To be sure, Biblical Aramaic does not attest this substantive, but it is quite frequent in other Aramaic languages, either in the concrete full sense "breath of life, life force" or, mostly, diminished to "self" and also used in the place of an absent reflexive pronoun; sometimes it denotes a grave symbol (or the grave itself), which represents the postmortem presence of the deceased.

Old Aramaic spelled the word *nbš* instead of the otherwise common *npš*. It continues to be disputed, however, whether this is the result of a secondary shift from /p/ to /b/ in contact with /š/, as most assume,[5] a purely orthographic peculiarity with no differentiation in the pronunciation between /pš/ and /bš/ or, the most unlikely explanation, the reflection of an old by-form.

The lexical field of *nšm* with its corresponding variants and nominal derivations also includes → *rwḥ* "wind, spirit," which is sometimes employed in the same context.

II. Noun "Breath." "Breath" was perceived as the physical expression of the force that enables people to move autonomously and be active intellectually. It correlates, thereby, to being alive, per se. Since life was considered an essential characteristic of God, God is also the one who gives life and takes it. In the invisible and intangible yet directly perceptible breath of air, the mystery of life has the corresponding natural manifestation. Consequently, one also conceives of the animating creation of humankind as an "in-breathing" (Gen 2:7). Indeed, one could distinguish the human breath of life, as designated by *nšmh* in Hebrew, at least according to an Israelite conception, from the animal because in it the divine spirit subsists (the human is, thus, an individualized *rwḥ*) and thereby first enabled the human being to think and speak.[6]

---

1. *LexSyr*, 451; *MdD*, 307.
2. Hebrew in Ex. 15:10, further attested in Akk. as *našāpu* and in Arab. as *nasafa*; for the Aramaic, see *DJPA*, 361f.; *DJBA*, 779; Syriac has the D-stem "to polish": *LexSyr*, 451.
3. Regarding 1QapGen 13:16 → II; later instances in *DJPA*, 361; *DJBA*, 778a; *LexSyr*, 450.
4. Cf. the material in Bauer.
5. Cf., e.g., *ATTM*, 420.
6. So Koch; adopted by *ATTM*, 2, 444, where "thought, understanding" serves as a gloss for *nšmh*.

1. Breath of Life. The feminine *nšmh* /našamā/ "breath of life" occurs in Aramaic first in Dnl. 5:23 where it appears in the Tiberian vocalization as *nišmā*. Daniel declares to KingBelshazzar why God has condemned him to inevitable demise: at his feast, he desecrated the holy temple vessels from Jerusalem and paid homage to lifeless idols, but did not glorify[7] God, in whose power[8] are Belshazzar's life-breath and his fate.[9] The life-breath as a physical expression of the vital force is, thus, the gift of God, the source of all life[10] and who alone merits unlimited veneration for it. God, as the truly living, also contrasts with the purely material, lifeless idol images. This idol polemic acquires marked features in the postexilic period.[11]

In contrast, 1QapGen 2:10 from Qumran, with the difficult expression *nšmty lgw ndnh'* "my breath is in its covering," apparently emphasizes the primarily physical aspect of the intense breath in the body[12] during a heated conversation[13] between Lamech and his wife Bettenosh concerning who may have sired their son Noah. The formulation may imitate Dnl. 7:15 and has no parallels otherwise, but may depend on an already old misunderstanding of the text there, which may once have read differently.[14] Admittedly, the immediate context is fragmentary and permits no conclusions concerning the significance of the obvious relationship between *nšmh* and emotions.

An additional specimen may appear in 11Q10 24:8, where *nšm*]*th* "his life-breath" can be emended with relative certainty following the Hebrew text of Job 34:14. As in Dnl. 5:23, the word here denotes the God-given life force of a human being; if God withdraws it, the inanimate body decays to dust. In the preceding part of the sentence, not preserved in Aramaic, *nšmh* parallels *rwḥ* "spirit."[15] According to this passage, too, to be alive is not merely a vegetative process, but is linked indivisibly with thought and emotion, just as the concept of "life" itself transcends the purely biological.[16]

2. Breath of Air. While the feminine *nšmh* /našamā/ serves as a collective noun for the (human) breath as such, the related masculine *nšm* /našam/[17] can designate the individual breath of air. Such an arrangement of collective nouns into a genus and an individual element is common in Semitic languages.[18]

---

7. → *hdr*.
8. *bydh*, literally, "in his hand"; → *yd* IV.
9. *'rḥt*, literally "ways," i.e., the biography which is an attribute of the unfolding human life.
10. → *ḥyī* III.2.
11. → *dhb* III.
12. Cf. *bḥlṣ tqyp* "with strong emphasis" in 2:8.
13. So Fitzmyer, 131; otherwise, however, *ATTM*, 168: "my soul in its sheath."
14. For a discussion → *ndn*.
15. See below on *nšm* and *rwḥ* in 4Q534 1 1:10.
16. For corresponding instances from older Aramaic → *ḥyī*.
17. According to the evidence of comparative linguistics, a *qatal*-form, although later vocalized in Syriac as a *qitl*-form.
18. Examples in C. Brockelmann, *Grundriss der vergleichenden Grammatik der semitischen Sprachen*, vol. 1 (Berlin, 1908), 419f.,427.

The first instances of this also appear in the texts from Qumran, although all are fragmentary: in 4Q534 1 1:10 and 4Q541 1 2:3 the suffixed plural *nšmwhy* or *nšmyh*[*wn*] "his, their breaths," respectively; in 4Q534 1 1:10 in a construct relation with *rwḥ* "breath" in the context of the announcement of Noah's birth, but with no further context. Also preserved only as a fragment, 4Q541 1 2:3 (Levi apocryphon) employs the word with *kwl* "all." 11Q10 10:5 (Job 26:14) has *ʿṭr* "breath" for Hebrew *šmṣ*.

3. Verb "to Blow." The verb *nšb*, which is probably related to the root *nšm* (→ I), occurs as a participle with the meaning "to blow" in reference to strong[19] winds in 1QapGen 13:16. It appears there in the context of a vision. The "four winds of heaven" are a fixed element of apocalyptic visions such as, e.g., Dnl. 7:2.[20] The imperfect appears in 11Q10 31:2 (Job 38:24), also in reference to wind.

III. "Soul." Since the ancient translations of the Bible, the feminine substantive *npš* /napš/[21] has been traditionally and over-simplistically rendered "soul" (ψυχή). In fact, however, the anthropological concept underlying Hebrew, as well as other West Semitic usage, eludes a strict division of the person (admittedly never systematically defined as such) into corporeal and immaterial components.[22] Meanwhile, → *bśr* "flesh" can also denote a living being overall, and not just in relation to its materiality, while organs like the → *lbb* "heart" are closely associated with intellectual and emotional states. In essence, then, /napš/ denotes the body given vitality by the breath of life (→ II) in its totality, and, abstracted from this notion, the "self," and from the fifth century on a tomb as its symbol.

1. In the Full Sense. Since older Aramaic literature reflects only isolated facets of the theological lexicon, the full sense of *npš*/*nbš* in particular continues to be paradigmatic, and in most cases, the word denotes the "self" (→ III.2). Line 5 of the Kuttamuwa inscription, which stands linguistically between Sam'alian and Old Aramaic, seems, however, to constitute an exception. On this monument for a high official, one finds, together with a depiction of a funeral meal, the instruction that, in dedication, a sacrifice should be offered to a series of gods and *lnbšy zy bnṣb zn* "for my *nbš* in this stele."[23] The context does not indicate whether the sacrifice was to take place while the donor was still alive. If not, the *nbš* would have been the spirit of the deceased that remains present beyond death.

This concept has no parallels in Aramaic texts, however, and could, therefore, represent a peculiarity of the cult of the dead at Sam'al, which probably displayed Hittite features.[24]

---

19. *btqwp* "with power."
20. More in Fitzmyer, 165.
21. With the opening of the syllable later /napəš/; *ATTM*, 112-15.
22. Gzella, 96-111.
23. Cf. ll. 11-13, where *lnbšy* parallels *ly* "for me."
24. For literature on the history of religions and the text with translation, see G.-W. Nebe, "Eine neue Inschrift aus Zincirli auf der Stele des Kutamuwa und die hebräische Sprachwissenschaft," in J. Heil and D. Krochmalnik, eds., *Jüdische Studien als Disziplin—Die Disziplinen der Jüdischen Studien* (Heidelberg, 2010), 311-32, esp. 323f.; on the linguistic status, see especially P. M. Noorlander, "Sam'alian in Its Northwest Semitic Setting," *Or* 81 (2012) 202-38.

The Sam'alian inscription *KAI* 214.17f.,22 also mentions the *nbš* of the dead as a participant in a sacrificial meal.

Otherwise, the association of *npš* with the life force shines through only in isolated instances: when an inscription is dedicated to a god *lḥyy nbšh/npšh* "for the life of his (the donor's) *npš*,"[25] in an oath formula,[26] or when deliverance from mortal danger is described as the escape of the *npš*.[27] As in Hebrew, *kl npš* serves at Qumran for "every living being."[28] Here, it denotes all who are subject to judgment and are thus responsible, which explicitly presupposes belief in an individual afterlife.

2. *"Self."* In contrast, *npš* usually has the sense "self" already in Old Aramaic, explicitly so in the identification of a person with a wax figure in the rite accompanying a curse formula;[29] further, in the place of a pronoun[30] and as a collective term as in the English "souls" for "people."[31] Sometimes, the *npš* as the seat of emotion and thought comes to the foreground, either paralleling *lbb*[32] or alone.[33]

With *lqḥ*[34] and the preposition *l-*, *npš* often serves in Imperial Aramaic for "to acquire" with the connotation "to seize."[35] Legal diction also employs it as a circumlocution for "one's own,"[36] including one's own signature.[37] The formulation *ʿl npš* for "obligated to fulfill the contract" appears in private documents from the Dead Sea and Dura Europos.[38] Furthermore, in legal and commercial texts, *npš* denotes "individual."[39] The three passages in 11Q10 5:5 (Job 21:25: "mind"); 10:9 (Job 27:2: "me"); 36:6 (Job 41:13: "breath") all correspond to the Hebrew text and its nuances. A pair of additional instances from all periods is too fragmentary to be classified as a specific usage.

Syriac, especially, employed other nouns such as /qnōmā/ along with *npš* as reflexive circumlocutions, probably because the t-stems there were largely restricted to the passive.

3. *"Tomb."* At the latest since the fifth century B.C.E., *npš* designated a grave in Aramaic. This usage first appears at Tēma in northern Arabia where the word refers to

25. *KAI* 309.7; 229.4; → *ḥyī* IV.2.

26. *TADAE* D7.16,3.

27. 1QapGen 19:20, → *nṣl* IV.1; similarly perhaps 4Q545 6:3 par. 4Q547 3:3.

28. 4Q530 2 2+6-12:2; similarly, judging from the context, also 4Q206 1 22:1 (1 En. 22:3).

29. *KAI* 222 A 37.

30. *KAI* 222 B 39f.42; in l. 40 "person," probably similarly in 224.5f. and 217.7; *TADAE* C1.1,122; 4Q196 6:12 and 17 2:6 (Tob. 3:15; 13:7).

31. *TADAE* D7.19,6; 1QapGen 22:19, here adopted from Gen 14:21: *ATTM*, 640.

32. *KAI* 223 B 5; according to the versions, also in 4Q196 17 2:1 (Tob. 13:6).

33. In the admonition, not to allow the *npš* rest if one has accepted a loan in *TADAE* C1.1, 130, or for the wish to claim the return B3.7, 15; cf. later 1QapGen 19:23 for an emotion *bnpš*.

34. → *nśī* V.

35. *TADAE* A4.7,13; 6.15,6; perhaps also 4.5,18; B7.2,6.

36. *TADAE* B1.1,4.7.14; cf. later 4Q530 2 2+6-12:1: "our own death."

37. *TADAE* B2.7,18; 4.3,21; → *yd*.

38. Citations in *ATTM*, 640 and 2, 443.

39. J. Dušek, *Les manuscripts araméens du Wadi Daliyeh et la Samarie vers 450-332 av. J.-C.* *CHANE* 30 (2007), nos. 2.9; 5.12; 8.9; 9.12; *TADAE* C3.9, 5; 3.14,26.29.

memorial stones with a stylized death mask (with no mouth) and stands at the beginning of the text in the construct state with the subsequent name. In the Nabatean kingdom, it referred to pyramid-shaped gravestones and later made its way from Arabia via an unknown path to Syria, where such a use of *npš* is well known from Palmyra, and then spread farther to Judea.[40]

The basis of this semantic development is no longer perceptible. As a structural term, *npš* may trace back to the spirit of the dead whose presence at the grave one assumed like a (transitory?) after-glow, in a manner similar to the way the *nbš* according to the older Kuttamuwa inscription from northern Syria was in the stele (→ III.1); or the memory of the deceased itself evokes his person just as the workplaces or the home of a person can still give an immediate impression of his presence even after his death. It is not possible, however, to draw further conclusions concerning the nature of the presence of the one represented in this way and his relationship to the grave. It would be premature, consequently, to assume "bodiless souls" everywhere here since the same terms could refer to the mutating eschatological hopes.

Gzella

40. Triebel has a useful collection of materials; citations also in *DNSI*, 746, *ATTM*, 640, and 2, 443.

נשר *nšr* /nešr/

I. Form and Meaning. II. Occurrences.

I. Form and Meaning. The masculine substantive /našr/ is a Central Semitic primary noun of the most common noun form *qatl*.[1] In the third century B.C.E., it was revocalized in Aramaic as the *qitl*-form /nešr/.[2] The LXX (ἀετός) and the Vulgate (*aquila*), however, always translate it "eagle," but since it is bald (Mi. 1:16) and feeds on carrion (Job 39:29f.), only the vulture is suitable.

K. Beyer, *Die aramäischen Inschriften aus Assur, Hatra und dem übrigen Ostmesopotamien* (Göttingen, 1998); E. Blum, "Die Kombination I der Wandinschrift vom Tell Deir 'Alla," in I. Kottsieper, R. Schmitt, and J. Wöhrle, eds., *Berührungspunkte*. *AOAT* 350 (2008), 573-601; H. Gzella, "Deir 'Allā," in G. Khan, ed., *Encyclopedia of Hebrew Language and Linguistics* (2013), 1:691-93; T. Kronholm, "נֶשֶׁר *nešer*," *TDOT*, X, 77-85; W. von Soden, "*aqrabu* und *našru*," *AfO* 18 (1957/58) 393; G. Vittmann, "Semitisches Sprachgut im Demotischen," *WZKM* 86 (1996) 435-47, esp. 440.

1. In cuneiform according to *AHw*, II, 761b and von Soden *na-áš-ru*, also Arabic and Hebrew, adopted as a loanword in Demotic and Coptic.
2. *ATTM*, 116.

Apparently, in Palestine it involved the now almost extinct griffon vulture (*Gyps fulvus*), the largest bird with a wingspan reaching to three meters. In eastern Mesopotamian Hatra (first century B.C.E. to third century C.E.) *nšr* is clearly the eagle as a symbolic animal for the supreme god, the sun, based on figurative representations.[3] 11Q10 33:8f. (Job 39:27), in fact, distinguishes between *nšr'* "the vulture" and *'wz'* "the eagle." Yet, one cannot always rule out confusion of the two high-flying predatory birds.

II. Occurrences. The first instance of *nšr*, in the singular absolute, appears in the Deir 'Allā wall inscription I.8 (Gilead ca. 800 B.C.E.)[4] mocking the swallows in the image of an overturned world in the context of a judgment prophecy.[5]

In Biblical Aramaic, the word occurs in Dnl. 7:4 in the expression "a lion with the wings of a vulture [*wgpyn dy nšr lh*]" for a chimera[6] as an image of the Babylonian Empire; as a sign of the comparatively human character of this dominion, the wings were torn off the animal, it was placed in a human stance, and it was equipped with a human heart. The figurative comparison in Dnl. 4:30 has the plural absolute, however: Nebuchadnezzar was dehumanized during his time of contrition so that "his hair became as long as (the feathers) of eagles [*ś'rh knšryn rbh*] and his nails like a bird's talons."

Only a few instances have been preserved at Qumran: 4Q558[7] "a vulture"; Book of Giants 4Q530[8] "he flew with his hands like an eagle";[9] finally, the singular determined *nšr'* in 11Q10 33:8 (Job 39:27) "the vulture arose." The word occurs further in Nabatean[10] and in later East and West Aramaic.[11]

Beyer

3. Beyer, 149; → *mr'* IV.2.
4. *KAI* 312.8.
5. For the linguistic classification, see Gzella; for the substantive context, Blum.
6. → *gp*.
7. *ATTM*, 2, 127.
8. 4Q530 1 3:4; *DSSStE*, 1064f.
9. → *yd* II.1.
10. Cf. *DNSI*, 765.
11. *DJPA*, 362a; *DJBA*, 780a; *LexSyr*, 451; *MdD*, 300.

נשתון *nštwn* /neštāwan/

I. Etymology and Lexical Field. II. Imperial Aramaic Usage. III. Biblical Aramaic.

I. Etymology and Lexical Field. Borrowed from Iranian in the Achaemenid period, the masculine *ništwn* "official letter, decree" is also a specific term in Aramaic administrative diction. The pronunciation is usually reconstructed as /neštāwan/,[1] but the Tiberian pointing *ništᵉwān,* if it is reliable, would argue more for /neštawān/.[2]

The word apparently has a significantly more restricted spectrum of usage than the much more widespread Semitic noun → *ṭʿm* "order" and refers particularly to specific written instructions, sometimes explication as a reaction to a disturbance in the execution of an official directive (→ II). It also differs, however, from *dkrn* "record, memorandum"[3] and is used in Biblical Aramaic together with *ʾgrh* "letter" (Ezr. 4:18 par. 4:11; 5:5 par. 5:6).

II. Imperial Aramaic Usage. The few Imperial Aramaic instances of *ništwn* all stem from the context of Achaemenid provincial administration. Nonetheless, their occurrence in letters both from Egypt and from Bactria indicates the high degree of the standardization of Aramaic Imperial diction and its terminology. All known passages refer to concrete decisions in individual cases. It occurs once in a letter from officials of the satrap Aršama to their superior concerning an "allotment,"[4] together with *ktyb* "stands written," and, consequently, a document; the context, however, is fragmentary. Here *ništwn* seems to supplement the *ṭʿm* "order" mentioned in l. 2 (thus *ʾp* "also").

Two additional instances appear in somewhat later letters from the Bactrian satraps: first in the admonition of a higher official that the addressee, a subordinate provincial administrator, has acted contrary to an official directive (*mn šṭr ništwnʾ zyly*)[5] by exploiting camel keepers. Here, too,[6] the context makes it rather clear that it involves a document since *ništwnʾ zyly* "my instruction" seems to refer to an order designated in l.5 by → *ṭʿm* that had already been sent (*šlyḥ*) to the addressee demanding that he refrain from this behavior. This new decree responded to a complaint by another official.

The second instance from the Bactrian archive[7] also appears in the satrap's appeal to the same subordinate in reaction to a complaint; the addressee was not fulfilling his obligations in the organization of agricultural work and repairs of the satrap's estate and

---

J. Naveh and S. Shaked, *Aramaic Documents from Ancient Bactria (Fourth Century* B.C.E.*)* (London, 2012); J. Tavernier, *Iranica in the Achaemenid Period (ca. 550-330 B.C.). OLA* 158 (2007); M. Wagner, *Die lexikalischen und grammatikalischen Aramaismen im alttestamentlichen Hebräisch. BZAW* 96 (1966).

1. Cf. Tavernier, 409, §4.4.3.8, and *ATTM*, 642.

2. So also, with reference to the Iranian etymology, H. W. Bailey, "Iranian Studies," *BSOAS* 7 (1933-1935) 76, in the same sense Wagner, 85 and *GesB*[18], 858; for additional older Iranistic literature, see the references in *DNSI*, 766.

3. → *dkr* III.

4. *TADAE* A6.1,3.

5. Naveh and Shaked, A1,10.

6. *Pace* Naveh and Shaked, 75.

7. Naveh and Shaked, A6,6.

was, thus, acting *l'... lqbl nštwn' zyly* "not in accordance with my instruction."[8] Once again, the context suggests that an earlier order[9] had not been followed.

III. Biblical Aramaic. All three attestations of the term *ništ^e wān* in Ezra correspond to official Imperial Aramaic diction. It always involves an official document (→ II). Ezra 4:18 employs the word for the letter[10] that the opponents of the construction of the Jerusalem wall sent to Artaxerxes; it refers in 4:23 to the king's response that, in reaction to the complaint, had forbidden the rebuilding until further notice. It also serves as a term for a royal reaction to a missive in 5:5.[11]

From the Aramaic, Hebrew borrowed the term in the same pronunciation.[12] There are, however, no indications to be taken seriously or even approaching plausibility that Iranian loanwords came directly into Hebrew; moreover, such a thesis would contradict the known socio-linguistic evidence both with regard to the Aramaic language situation in Palestine and to the complete lack of any indication of a continued use of Persian in the western provinces. The word appears twice in the same meaning for written instruction in the Hebrew parts of Ezra (4:7 and 7:11).

Gzella

8. The expression *l' lqbl* "not according to" is apparently synonymous with *mn šṭr* in A1,10.
9. A1,3, there too, *ṭ'm*.
10. Designated with *'iggartā* in 4:11.
11. In 5:6 again explicitly called *'iggartā* "letter."
12. Wagner, 85.

נתן *ntn*; נתין *ntyn* /natīn/; מ(נ)תנ(ה) *m(n)tn(h)* /mattan(ā)/; נבזבה *nbzbh* /nabizbā/(?)

I. Etymology, Suppletive Relationship with *yhb*, and Lexical Field. II. Usage of the Verb. III. Noun "Temple Slave." IV. Noun "Gift."

I. Etymology, Suppletive Relationship with *yhb*, and Lexical Field. In Aramaic, the common Semitic (with the exceptions of Arabic and Ethio-Semitic) root *ntn* "to give" in the G-stem overlaps with the synonymous verb → *yhb*, which is, however, within

H.-J. Fabry, "*ntn*," *ThWQ*, II, 1054-61; H. Gzella, *A Cultural History of Aramaic*. *HO* 111 (2015); C. J. Labuschagne, "נתן *ntn* to give," *TLOT*, 774-91; E. Lipiński and H.-J. Fabry, "נָתַן *nāṯan*," *TDOT*, X, 90-108; F. Zanella, *The Lexical Field of the Substantives of "Gift" in Ancient Hebrew*. *SSN* 54 (2010).

Northwest Semitic, typically Aramaic. Otherwise, *ntn* appears in a number of variants: in addition to this form, dominant in the Judean and Transjordanian linguistic regions, it appears in Akkadian as *nadānu* and in Ugaritic and Phoenician, thus the languages distributed throughout northern Syria-Palestine, as *ytn*. Meanwhile, Aramaic *yhb* probably developed from an older **whb*, which still appears in Arabic and OSA with the meaning "to give."

The various semantic nuances of *ntn* and *yhb* for older Aramaic can no longer be determined. At the latest since the fifth century B.C.E., the two roots stand only in a suppletive relationship,[1] in which the forms that assimilate the initial /n/ are formed on the biradical basis *tn*, that is, the imperfect[2] and the infinitive. In contrast, the verb *yhb* serves for the other forms, i.e., perfect, participle, and the also biradical imperative (*hb*). The latter root, to be sure, at least occasionally forms an imperfect in Old Aramaic, although the precise distribution of forms remains unknown in consequence of the sparsity of instances.

The suppletive relationship of this pair may result from a semantic expansion of an originally very specific verb (say from "to make a gift" to "to give") similar to that still evident for the antonymous lexical field "to take" in post–Imperial Aramaic times. There, too, the frequent common Semitic verb → *nśī*, originally, "to lift up, to take," became marginalized and was ultimately replaced by the less common *nsb* with the likely old meaning "to lift up." In any case the sole certain example of an imperfect of *yhb* in the oldest Aramaic inscriptions[3] already has the general meaning "to give" and refers to the contractually established delivery of foodstuff.[4] It apparently occurs here in antithetical parallelism with a partially reconstructed form *t*]*ś'* of *nśī* "to take (away)" following a lacuna in the same line. Thus, the Aramaic evidence itself no longer permits one to deduce a possibly once more restricted older meaning of *yhb*. The instability of *ntn* as an independent paradigm could, however, involve the fact that roots with identical first and third radicals occur in Semitic only very sporadically.

In post-Christian East Aramaic the two secondary forms *ntl*[5] and *ntb*[6] appear. One may explain them as the contraction of the last radical with the prepositions *l-* "to someone" or *b-* "for," common in relation to this verb in particular,[7] as dissimilation to a related consonant,[8] or as assimilation to the /b/ of *yhb*, potentially also as an interaction of both causes.

The passive "to be given" of the Gt-stem of *ntn* occurs only very rarely. Normally, however, the Gt-stem of *yhb* serves this function in all forms, including the imperfect,[9] for which, contrariwise, *ntn* serves in the G-stem (see above).

---

1. Similar to → *hlk* and *'zl*.
2. Although in Imperial Aramaic orthography then secondarily degeminated again, thus, e.g., *yntn* "he gives" for /yatten/ > /yetten/; see Gzella, 170f.
3. *KAI* 222 B 38, a treaty of state from Sefire.
4. *lḥm*.
5. Syriac, *LexSyr*, 298f.
6. Jewish Babylonian, *DJBA*, 780b.
7. Cf. C. Brockelmann, *Syrische Grammatik* (Leipzig, [10]1965), 87.
8. The interchange of /l/ and /n/ is indeed likely phonetic and pervasive in the various East Aramaic languages for the preformative of the imperfect; see Gzella, 266f.
9. Cf. e.g., for unequivocal forms even in the consonantal text Ezr. 6:4; Dnl. 7:25.

The nouns in the lexical field of giving already attested in older Aramaic belong to *ntn*, not to *yhb*: the substantivized masculine passive participle /natīn/ "given" for a slave given to the temple (or the court?) or his descendants[10] and the verbal noun on the *maqtal* pattern /mattan/ with its feminine /mattanā/[11] "gift."

Additional nouns from the same lexical field include the rare Iranian loanword /dāšn/[12] and in personal names Aramaic /zabd/.[13] The substantive *nbzbh*,[14] of unknown origins, perhaps related to the likewise unclear *nbz* "receipt,"[15] parallels /mattanā/ for "gift" in the book of Daniel (→ IV).

In relation to individual forms of giving, the vocabulary becomes further refined in various terms for "sacrifice" and "to sacrifice,"[16] "donation,"[17] "tribute" and other forms of taxation,[18] and *šḥd* for "bribery."[19]

II. Usage of the Verb. The verb *ntn* appears beginning in the Old Aramaic period, both in Old Aramaic itself[20] and in Sam'alian. Only a few specimens survive from this earlier period, as a rule, in the imperfect. A few sixth century B.C.E. pre-Imperial Aramaic texts from Egypt attest a perfect, however: the private correspondence from Hermopolis[21] and a private contract dated to 515 B.C.E.[22] Both already stand under the influence of Achaemenid orthography, but, with the exception of a few morphological peculiarities, presumably belong to a form of Aramaic already widespread in Egypt in pre-Achaemenid times.[23] The Hermopolis correspondence also employs *yhb* apparently without distinction.[24] From the fifth century B.C.E., the root becomes prevalent in the whole linguistic region for the perfect (→ I),[25] so that the distribution even according to otherwise completely parallel formulations is only purely morphological, at the latest from this time forward.

Thus, *ntn* appears with the same shades of meaning and constructions as *yhb*, which are treated more extensively there: in the literal sense for concrete things or goods (including sums of money or tribute, Ezr. 4:13; 7:20), for abstractions such as time

10. Also common, however, as a personal name.
11. Spelled *mntnh* in Imperial Aramaic.
12. *TADAE* A6.4,3f.6, here a tract of land; cf. further *DNSI*, 262f.
13. *ATTM*, 566.
14. Vocalized *nᵉḇizbā* or *nᵉḇazbā* in Biblical Aramaic, *BLA*, §244l.
15. *TADAE* B4.2,6; cf. *DNSI*, 711f.
16. → *mnḥh*; → *qrb*.
17. → *ndb*.
18. → *mndh*.
19. *DNSI*, 1120.
20. *KAI* 320.12, figurative of the weather god Hadad raising his voice with *qlh* as object as an expression for thunder, rain, and thus fertility.
21. *TADAE* A2.2,5.
22. *TADAE* B1.1,2,11,12.
23. For the linguistic classification, see Gzella, 112-19, 148.
24. Cf. *TADAE* A2.2,14,16.
25. And for the impv. and ptcp.

(Dnl. 2:16), but also gifts of the gods, such as a long life[26] and, especially in the book of Daniel, god-given royal power (Dnl. 4:14,22,29).[27] Furthermore, it occurs, depending on the object, in a few idiomatic expressions.[28]

III. Noun "Temple Slave." An old cultic use of the verb *ntn* in the sense of "to consecrate, sacrifice" survives in the noun *ntyn* /natīn/ for a slave dedicated to a specific service. It has an exact counterpart in the Hebrew term *n*^{e}*ṯīnīm*, attested only in the plural.[29] The *qatīl*-form instead of the *qatūl*-form of the passive participle typical in Hebrew and its distribution in postexilic sources such as Ezra, Nehemiah, and 1 Chronicles indicates the Aramaic origin of this designation.

The sole older Aramaic instance other than personal names, Ezr. 7:24, uses it to denote King Artaxerxes's provision of temple servants come from Babylon who, together with the other temple personnel were to be exempt from taxation. They were subordinate to the Levites and could have become part of the temple personnel through debt slavery, as prisoners of war, or by birth. The word appears as part of a list before *plḥy byt 'lh' dnh* "the servants of this house of God,"[30] which refers to an additional group[31] or, summarily, all those previously named.

If, indeed, the personal name Natīn, already frequent in Old Aramaic times, presupposes this specific meaning "temple servant" (and not just a general dedication of a child to a deity), the pertinent institution in the Aramaic linguistic realm may have already had substantially older roots. Since Babylon may have already become largely Aramaic-speaking in the sixth century B.C.E.,[32] the Aramaic term for this group of persons would also have been adopted.

IV. Noun "Gift." The masculine verbal noun *mtn* /mattan/ first appears in Aramaic in a list on a third century B.C.E. ostracon in the formulation *lmtn'* "as a gift," in each case after a personal name.[33] It may involve a list of gifts for a land purchase.[34]

Furthermore, since Biblical Aramaic, the related feminine *mtnh* or *mntnh* /mattanā/ appears. In Daniel, it occurs three times for the king's gift as a reward for interpreting a dream (Dnl. 2:6,48) or the writing on the wall (5:17), always in the plural and spelled phonetically *mtnn*. In two of these passages, it parallels the otherwise unknown noun *n*^{e}*ḇizbā* (Dnl. 2:6 and 5:17).[35]

In addition, in context, the discussion concerns either special honors (2:6) or a very high position in state service (2:48; 5:16f.). These extraordinarily elevated distinctions

---

26. *TADAE* A4.7,3.

27. → *mlk.*

28. An overview of the Old and Imperial Aramaic instances appears in D. Schwiderski, *Die alt- und reichsaramäischen Inschriften I. FSBP* 2 (2008), 583-86.

29. Cf. Lipiński, 105-7.

30. → *plḥ.*

31. Following the parallels in Ezr. 2:55, the sons of Solomon's slaves.

32. Gzella, 134-39.

33. *TADAE* D8.3,5,7,11f.,16.

34. P. Grelot, *Documents araméens d'Égypte* (Paris, 1972), 103.

35. Literature on the putative etymology in K. Koch, *Daniel 1-4. BK* XXII/1 (2005), 90.

correspond to the difficulty and significance of the tasks performed. Even the king's experts failed in them, but the exile Daniel knew how to solve them with bravado thanks to his gift of divine wisdom—after all, it involved the explanation of world history. Notably, he accepted only the gifts of the positively described King Nebuchadnezzar (2:48) and rejected those of the arrogant evildoer, Belshazzar, condemned by God to destruction (5:17).

In the sole instance of the word in the Aramaic texts from Qumran[36] *mntn*[*n*] also designates royal gifts, in this case of the pharaoh to Abraham who had healed the pharaoh of a God-sent illness. Here, as in Dnl. 2:48, it is linked with the verb *yhb* "to give,"[37] while *qbl* "to receive" appears in Dnl. 5:17. In Nabatean contracts from the Dead Sea, the word designates gifts in the legal sense.[38]

Gzella

36. 1QapGen 20:30.
37. *DSSStE*, 42f.
38. nV 3:43 and often in nV 7; *ATTM*, 2.

נתר *ntr*

I. Etymology and Lexical Field. II. Imperial Aramaic. III. Biblical Aramaic. IV. Qumran.

I. Etymology and Lexical Field. Along with the typical verb for "to fall," → *npl*, Aramaic also knows the less common root *ntr*. It also has a common Semitic origin and, considering Akkadian *našāru* and Arabic *naṯara*, developed from an original **nθr*. The meaning of the G-stem ("to fall away, out of/away from)" is only discernible in older Aramaic, since the verb appears there only in the C-stem "to set free, to liberate," but it can be identified very well later.[1] As "to fall out," it appears regularly there in relation to hair or leaves and is, therefore, more specific than *npl* "to fall."

Normally, scholars assume some relationship to *ntr* "to jump" as in the Hebrew G- and D-stems. In reference to a lamb jumping off in 4Q206 4 2:20 (1 En. 89:16), it may, however, if the reading and emendation *nt*[*r* based on the Ethiopian parallel version is correct, be borrowed from the Hebrew.[2] Ugaritic *ntr* with the same meaning[3] and perhaps

P. Maiberger, "נָתַר *nāṯar*," *TDOT*, X, 119-22.

1. *DJPA*, 363; *DJBA*, 781b; *LexSyr*, 452f.; *MdD*, 308.
2. Cf. C. Stadel, *Hebraismen in den aramäischen Texten vom Toten Meer* (Heidelberg, 2008), 89.
3. Differently now *DUL*³, 643 (but compare *DUL*², 652).

Arabic *natala* in the specific sense of "to jump forth" argue instead for a homonymous root.[4] It is unclear whether there is an etymological relationship to /netr/ "natron."[5]

II. Imperial Aramaic. In Imperial Aramaic, *ntr* in the C-stem serves in legal texts to mean "to take away again"[6] or "to set free."[7] For the former, however, one more frequently finds → *nṣl* "to snatch away, to reclaim," for the second → *šbq*. The reading and interpretation of *ntyrh*[8] are uncertain; R. Degen[9] reads the imperative *ktyrh* "wait on it!"

III. Biblical Aramaic. The sole Biblical Aramaic instance of *ntr* is the C-stem in Dnl. 4:11, where it denotes the shedding of the leaves of a tree and parallels → *bdr*, in the D-stem "to scatter." In a dream vision, the tree symbolizes King Nebuchadnezzar; the denuding and felling on an angel's comment represents the penance of exile.

IV. Qumran. In the same sense as in Dnl. 4:11, the verb also appears in 1QapGen 13:17 from Qumran (→ III), also together with *bdr.* Here, the subject is a wind that denudes a tree in a vision.

Gzella

4. P. Maiberger, 120f.; *GesB*[18], 865.
5. Attested in Segal, 24.9.
6. *TADAE* B2.6,35, with *mn* "from someone."
7. *TADAE* B8.3,6; probably also in Segal, 142.3.
8. So *TADAE* D7.56,11, identified as a fem. adj. or pass. G-stem ptcp. and translated "available."
9. *NESE* 3 (1978), 54f.

סבל *sbl*; סבול *sbwl* /sabūl/; סמך *smk*

I. Etymology, Lexical Field, and Meaning. II. G-stem "to Carry." III. D-stem "to Support." 1. Old and Imperial Aramaic. 2. Ezra 6:3. IV. Noun "Support."

I. Etymology, Lexical Field, and Meaning. Aramaic *sbl*, in the transitive G-stem "to carry," has a homonymous Hebrew cognate; Arabic *zabala* and Akkadian *zabālu* with an identical meaning may involve a possible secondary by-form.[1] The root has been attested since the pre-Imperial Aramaic proverbs of Aḥiqar. More often, especially in Imperial Aramaic, the D-stem "to support" appears, usually as a return service and, in legal texts, also

D. Kellerman, "סָבַל *sāḇal*," *TDOT*, X, 139-44.

1. Whose nominal derivate *zabbilu* "basket" Aramaic, in turn, borrowed as *zbyl*; see *LexSyr*, 187a,201a.

in the sense of "to provide support, to care for"; in Biblical Aramaic, in contrast, it denotes literally "to support" in reference to a foundation (Ezr. 6:3).[2] The related t-stem denotes the corresponding passive and occurs once in Imperial Aramaic. In view of the generally good Imperial Aramaic evidence concerning the D-stem of *sbl*, the older hypothesis of a causative stem involving an /s/-prefix of *wabālu* borrowed from the Assyrian[3] has fallen into disfavor.

For the meaning "to carry," the G-stem of → *nśī* is otherwise employed more often elsewhere.[4] The G-stem of *smk* sometimes serves for "to support" and also as a construction term in *TADAE* B3.10:14, and later in 1QapGen 20:22,29 for the laying-on-hands as part of a healing.[5]

The infrequent masculine noun /sabūl/ "support" occurs in the sense of "support" and sometimes in accord with the meaning of the D-stem.

II. G-stem "to Carry." The G-stem of *sbl* "to carry" is rare in comparison to → *nśī*, but probably occurs in a fragmentary animal fable in the proverbs of Aḥiqar.[6] The context and the parallel with the subsequent *nśī* indicate the G-stem; the D-stem "to support" occurs in l. 203 of the same text (→ III). Thereafter, the G-stem of *sbl* may also occur in two partially destroyed fragments from Qumran.[7] In addition, Beyer[8] reads the imperative *sb]wl* "take!" in 4Q197 5:6 (Tob. 8:21), although only the *l* can be read with any certainty; in contrast, the reconstruction *'wb]yl*[9] does not conform well with otherwise known older Aramaic diction where *ybl* in the C-stem means "to bring"[10] and not "to take," as would be expected given the context and the other versions; consequently, Beyer may have drawn the correct conclusion. A Nabatean private document from the Dead Sea also has *sbl* once,[11] although its immediate context is fragmentary.

Some attribute the t-stem form *ystblwn* in the Imperial Aramaic Aḥiqar narrative framework[12] to the G-stem and understand it as "to be carried,"[13] but, given the clear D-stem in the preceding lines in the same context, the form more likely belongs to it and means "to be supported" (→ III).

III. D-stem "to Support."

1. Old and Imperial Aramaic. The pre-Achaemenid period already attests *sbl* in the D-stem "to support." It probably first appears in a fragmentary animal fable of

2. → III regarding this not entirely unequivocal passage.

3. So *BLA*, §92k; still considered by *GesB*[18], 1517, with additional older literature.

4. Later *nsb*.

5. Thereafter, especially in the NT frequently with the verb ἐπιτίθημι; cf. J. A. Fitzmyer, *The Genesis Apocryphon of Qumran Cave 1 (1Q20)*. *BietOr* 18/B ([3]2004), 213.

6. *TADAE* C1.1,185.

7. 4Q530 18:2; 4Q539 2-3:6.

8. *ATTM*, 2, 182.

9. So J. A. Fitzmyer, *Tobit*. *CEJL* (2003), 251.

10. Cf. the specimens in *DNSI*, 431-33 and *ATTM*, 592.

11. nV 42:33 in *ATTM*, 2, 244-47.

12. *TADAE* C1.1,73.

13. So *ATTM*, 643.

Aḥiqar[14] and later certainly in a private letter from Hermopolis.[15] The first form is morphologically ambiguous, but the preserved context is usually understood such that only the meaning "to provide" suits it, because it seems to mean a return service: the untameable wild ass[16] refuses to allow someone to ride it[17] in return for feed (→ IV).[18]

Imperial Aramaic also manifests the verb *sbl* regularly with persons as objects for a provision of support. In the court context of the Aḥiqar narrative framework, it refers to the provision that the high official Aḥiqar, fallen into disgrace, receives from his deliverer.[19] In contrast, it appears in a more general usage in the Aramaic Behistun inscription in reference to the support that Darius received from other princes.[20] In a private document from Elephantine, it denotes the provision and care that a slave and her daughter guarantee their owner and after his death his son in exchange for freedom on the passing of their owner.[21] The phrase "as a son or a daughter supports his or her own father" (*zy ysbl br wbrh l'bwhy* in l. 11, abbreviated somewhat in l. 12f.) qualifies the provision more precisely. Similarly, a testament employs it of a house that the testator, who needs care, leaves to his daughter in exchange for her caregiving.[22] An additional specimen on an ostracon from Elephantine is quite fragmentary.[23]

2. Ezra 6:3. The participle *mswblyn* as a construction term "to stabilize" in reference to a foundation[24] in the instructions concerning the construction of the temple in Ezr. 6:3 differs from this otherwise well-attested Imperial Aramaic figurative usage, "to support." The difficult form has given rise to a variety of explanations, but, in light of the other Imperial Aramaic usages, one should likely assume, in contrast to the pointing *mᵉsōḇᵉlīn*,[25] a passive participle of the D-stem /masobbalīn/ "stabilized."[26] Thus, the word serves most likely to characterize the foundation.[27] The expression probably means, then: "be built . . . and its foundation stabilized."

---

14. *TADAE* C1.1,203.
15. *TADAE* A2.3,5.
16. → *'rd.*
17. So, along with *TADAE* (s.v.), the translation in I. Kottsieper, *Die Sprache der Ahiqarsprüche. BZAW* 194 (1990), 23, above.
18. Noun *sbwl.*
19. *TADAE* C1.1,48,72,73f.; so probably also the corresponding t-passive in l. 73, although the immediate context is unclear.
20. *TADAE* C2.1,78.
21. *TADAE* B3.6,11-13.
22. *TADAE* B3.10,17.
23. *TADAE* D1.12,4.
24. → *'š.*
25. Which presupposes an L-stem for strong verbs not otherwise demonstrable in Aramaic.
26. Cf. *ATTM*, 643 and H. Gzella, *Tempus, Aspekt und Modalität im Reichsaramäischen. VOK* 48 (2004), 178f.; it would then, admittedly, involve an unusual *plene* spelling of the short /o/.
27. And probably not as a predicative "is bearing/should be retained" as the Vulgate with *ut ponant*, *LexLingAram* 117 with *conserventur*, and H. G. M. Williamson, *Ezra, Nehemiah. WBC* (1985), 68,71 suppose, because a modal ptcp. would be unusual in Imperial Aramaic, Gzella, 178 n. 189.

IV. Noun "Support." The noun *sbwl* /sabūl/ "support" first occurs in an animal fable in Aḥiqar in context with the D-stem of the verb and with the nuance "support" as a return service (→ III.1).[28] This shading results, however, from the possibly conjectural interpretation of the fragmentary passage. An Imperial Aramaic private document also employs the same word for support involving a monetary loan, which the context does not describe further, however.[29]

Gzella

28. *TADAE* C1.1,204.
29. *TADAE* B5.5,4.

סגד *sgd*; סגיד *sgyd* /saggīd/; סגדה *sgdh* /segdā/; סגדו *sgdw* /segdū/; מסגד *msgd* /masgad/

I. Verb. II. Derived Nouns. 1. For Worship of a God. 2. As a Priestly Title. 3. For a Place of Worship.

I. Verb. The juxtaposition of the verbs *npl wsgd* in Dnl. 2:46; 3:5,6,7,10,11,15 and *plḥ wsgd* in Dnl. 3:12,14,18,28 permits one to determine definitively the meaning of *sgd*. On the one hand, it is more than "to bow, fall down," which is expressed with → *npl*, and, on the other, more than "to serve," which is the basic meaning of → *plḥ*. Because of the gradation in the use of these verbs, *sgd* must represent "to demonstrate honor, to pay homage, to worship, to give divine honor." Humans can receive such a form of honor.

According to 4Q538 1-2:3f., Joseph's brothers in Egypt "bowed before Joseph and showed him honor," *wqdm ywsp* [*nplw wlh*] *sgdw* (cf. Gen. 43:28). The narrative framework of Aḥiqar has instead of *npl* the verb *ghn*: *ghnt wsgdt lm 'ḥyqr qdm 'srḥ*[*'d*]*n* [*mlk*]

R. P. Dougherty, *The* shirkûtu *of Babylonian Deities. YOSR* 5/II (1923), esp. 28-32; I. Eph'al and J. Naveh, *Aramaic Ostraca of the Fourth Century BC from Idumaea* (Jerusalem, 1996), esp. no. 188.3; M. Gawlikowski, "Une coupe magique araméenne," *Sem* 38 (1990) 137-43, tables XXIV-XXV, l. 2; P. Gignoux, *Glossaire des inscriptions pehlevies et parthes. CIISup* 1 (1972), esp. 33; J. T. Milik, "Les papyrus araméens d'Hermoupolis et les cultes syro-phéniciens en Égypte perse," *Bib* 48 (1967) 546-622, table I, esp. 578-80; J. A. Montgomery, *Aramaic Incantation Texts from Nippur* (Philadelphia, 1913), esp. 207f., no. 25.4; W. W. Müller, "Ergebnisse der Deutschen Jemen-Expedition 1970," *AfO* 24 (1973) 150-61, esp. 153-55; É. Puech, "Le dieu Turmasgada à Césarée Maritime," *RB* 89 (1982) 210-21; V. Scheil, "La libération judicaire d'un fils donné en gage sous Nériglissar en 558 av. J.-C.," *RA* 12 (1915) 1-13.

ʾtwr, "I fell down and showed true honor, I Aḥiqar, to Asarhaddon, the King of Assyria."[1] Contrarily, the use of *sgd* in Dnl. 3 implies the veneration due the golden statue of a pagan deity. In Dnl. 2:46, *npl wsgd* refers to Daniel, to whom Nebuchadnezzar paid homage. The text's reference to the *minḥā* offered to Daniel[2] suggests the enduring cultic significance of the act so described. Aquila and Symmachus surmised this correctly and accordingly replaced *minḥā* with δῶρα "gifts" in their translations because the customary translation of the word with θυσία "sacrifice" would have implied that Daniel had been venerated as a god. Nevertheless, Daniel appears in Dnl. 2:47 indeed as the representative of his God. Precisely this must also be the case in 4Q246 1 2:7, which says in reference to the eschatological king: *wkl mdyntʾ lh ysgdwn* "and all provinces will show him honor."[3] It states the reason immediatlely: *ʾl rbʾ bʿylh hwʾ* "the great God stands with him," which recalls the "great God" of Dnl. 2:45 (cf. Ezr. 5:8).

II. Derived Nouns.

1. For Worship of a God. Frahang XIX.13 and the Pahlavi inscriptions utilize the heterogram SGDH in the religious sense "to worship" and in the profane sense "to honor." The word *sgdh* "(idol) veneration" occurs in Targum Neofiti 1 of Gen. 11:4,[4] while the Fragmentary Targum has *byt sgdw*.[5] Targum Onqelos of Num. 31:10 mentions a *bēt siḡdaṯᵉhōn*, but translates *ʾæḇæn siḡdā* "the stone of worship" at Lev. 26:1,[6] thus, apparently a cult monolith. Apparently, there were two nouns with the nuance "(idol) worship," i.e., *siḡdā* and *siḡdū*.

2. As a Priestly Title. A Neo-Babylonian legal document dated to 558 B.C.E.[7] deals with a special case of a pledge for a loan: an oblate (*širku*) gave his son for ten years, practically in a kind of slavery, to a *sa-gi-it-tum* or *sa-git-tú*, a female cult employee, whose precise function has not yet been defined. After four years, the original creditor died and another assumed her official position and her rights. Her title, admittedly Aramaic,[8] must be analyzed as *saggīd* + *tu*, as the masculine form of the same noun, attested much later in the name of an angel *sgydʾl* "worshiper of God," indicates. It appears in the inscription on a magic bowl found on the island of Biḡān[9] and was pronounced /saggīdu/, as the dissimilation in another specimen, *sngy(d)ʾl*, indicates.[10] The feminine counterpart must, therefore, have been *saggīd-tu* > *saggittu*. So far, there are no other indications concerning the cultic function it denotes.

---

1. *TADAE* C1.1,13.
2. → *mnḥh*.
3. For the discussion concerning this text → *br* IV.
4. *DJPA*, 367a.
5. *DJPA*, 94b.
6. A. Sperber, *The Bible in Aramaic* (Leiden, 1959), 1:212.
7. Scheil, Dougherty.
8. *AHw*, II, 1003a; *CAD*, XV, 25.
9. Gawlikowski.
10. Here with loss of the *d*; Montgomery.

3. For a Place of Worship. "The place of worship" is called /masgadā/. The oldest instance of this word occurs in a Jewish oath formula from Elephantine: *bḥ[yy mlk]' bmsgd' wbʿnt yhw*,[11] "by the li[fe of the king], by the place of worship, and by the service of Yaho!" This text is easily reconstructed with the help of the oath formula of the Aramaic clay tablet AO 25.341, l. 12f., *ḥyy mlk'*,[12] while Palmyrene,[13] *wnt dy bl* "the service of Bēl,"[14] and Jewish Palestinian, *ʿnt' dṣlwt'* "fixed prayer time"[15] attest the meaning of *ʿnt*, "prayer time, service." Admittedly, the oath formula employs the noun *msgd'* instead of *mqdš'*,[16] perhaps because the Yaho temple in Elephantine was already destroyed at this time. In any case, *msgd'* here is not a divine name, contrary to Milik's understanding. This last development is first attested in Roman times, namely by the theonym Ṭūr-Masgadā, "Mount of the Worship Place," found at Caesarea Palestinae.[17] The plural *msgdy'* appears on an ostracon from Maqqeda in Idumea, dated to the fourth century B.C.E. It introduces the quantity of seed for the sowing of various fields, one apparently called "the terrace field of the worship place," *rpyd msgdy' s 16*.[18] The noun *rpyd* derives from the Semitic root *rpd* and compares to the Sabean *rfd* "retaining wall, support," thence the translation "terrace field."[19] Another ostracon from the same region mentions local sanctuaries,[20] one of them "the house of Yaho" (*byt yhw*). Arabic adopts *masǧid* "mosque" from Aramaic, but apparently through the mediation of South Arabian *ms1gd-n*, with s_1 instead of the older s_3, which points to the coincidence of these two phenomena.[21]

Lipiński

11. *TADAE* B7.3,3, although with other emendations of the lacunae.
12. P. Bordreuil, "Une tablette araméenne inédite de 635 av. J.C.," *Sem* 23 (1973) 96-102.
13. J. T. Milik, *Dédicaces faites par des dieux* (Paris, 1972), 145, 283-85; M. Gawlikowski, "Liturges et custodes sur quelques inscriptions palmyréniennes," *Sem* 23 (1973) 118f.
14. *PAT* 2043.3f.
15. *DJPA*, 412.
16. The customary word for "temple."
17. Puech.
18. Eph'al and Naveh, no. 188:3, p. 84, which reads *msgry'*, however.
19. Cf. E. Lipiński, review of A. Lemaire, *Nouvelles inscriptions araméennes d'Idumée*, *BiOr* 61 (2004) 192.
20. A. Lemaire, *Nouvelles inscriptions araméennes d'Idumée*, vol. 2 (Paris, 2002), no. 283; cf. Lipiński, review of A. Lemaire, *Nouvelles inscriptions araméennes d'Idumée*, *BiOr* 61 (2004) 193.
21. Müller.

סגן *sgn* /sagan/

I. Etymology and Meaning. II. Imperial Aramaic. III. Biblical Aramaic. IV. Qumran.

I. Etymology and Meaning. Aramaic borrowed the official title *sgn* /sagan/ from Akkadian in Neo-Assyrian times. In Akkadian, the word, originally pronounced *šaknu*,[1] initially denoted a governor or prefect, in general. It migrated from Aramaic further into Hebrew[2] and probably referred to various administrative offices. In the course of time, it could also simply refer to a "leader." For the root → *škn*.

II. Imperial Aramaic. The precise function of a *sgn* in Achaemenid times is disputed and is variously identified with that of a *frataraka*[3] "under-satrap (of a certain district)" or of a *rb ḥyl'* "commandant."[4] The variety is because this title appears in different contexts and, apparently, in no fixed sequence with various other designations.[5] As a legal authority to whom one could register a complaint,[6] the *sgn* appears with the honorific → *mr'* II.3 "lord" or the professional designation *dyn* "judge"[7] in a formulaic expression in the various private documents from Elephantine,[8] and further as a title in contracts from Samaria[9] and in a severely corrupt context in Saqqara.[10] The relationship does not permit one to conclude, however, whether it involves a specific office or the meaning was already so diluted that *sgn* could refer to quite different offices.[11] In addition to legal documents from provincial administration, more than 160 brief inscriptions on stone objects such as mortars and pestles from the royal treasury in Persepolis regularly attest the term, in any case.[12] It occurs there in the stereotypical opening *lyd*, possibly "at the disposal of,"[13] together with the personal name and *sgn* as title. Here, it seems to involve a low-ranking administrative official. Finally, *sgn* can also simply designate the leader of a hierarchically organized group in a broader sense, such as the *sgn ngry'* "leader of the carpenters" in a letter from Elephantine.[14]

R. A. Bowman, *Aramaic Ritual Texts from Persepolis. OIP* 91 (1970); E. Lipiński, "*Skn* et *sgn* dans le sémitique occidental du nord," *UF* 5 (1973) 191-207; J. Wiesehöfer, "*PRTRK, RB ḤYL', SGN* und *MR'*," in H. Sancisi-Weerdenburg and A. Kuhrt, eds., *Asia Minor and Egypt. AH* 6 (1991), 305-9.

1. Mediation through Assyrian also explains the shift from /š/ to /s/, see Lipiński, 195.
2. *GesB*[18], 873.
3. Aram. *prtrk*.
4. → *ḥyl*.
5. For the discussion see Wiesehöfer, who supposes that in the contracts from Elephantine, *sgn* means the *rb ḥyl'* and is subordinate to the *prtrk*.
6. → *qbl*.
7. → *dīn*.
8. *TADAE* B2.3:13; 3.1:13,18; 3.10:19; 3.11:13; 3.12:28; 4.6:14; 5.4:2,5.
9. *WDSP*, 8.12 and 11r.13.
10. Segal, no. 102a.3.
11. So T. Petit, "L'évolution sémantique des termes Hébreux et Araméens PHH et SGN et Accadiens PAHATU et SAKNU," *JBL* 107 (1988) 58f.
12. Bowman, esp. 25-28; regarding the function, cf. J. Naveh and S. Shaked, "Ritual Texts or Treasury Documents," *Or* 42 (1973) 445-57.
13. → *yd* IV.
14. *TADAE* A6.2,9,21.

III. Biblical Aramaic. While *sgn* refers to officials in the Achaemenid provincial administration in Nehemiah and the Hebrew portions of Ezra, the word appears in Biblical Aramaic only in the court narratives of Daniel. There, it occurs mostly in a very generic sense in a list of various official titles describing the entire upper leadership of the empire and its provinces (Dnl. 3:2,3,27; 6:8), once also for Daniel's function as the leader of Babylon's sages (Dnl. 2:48). Both the official and the general usage bear the marks of Imperial Aramaic diction (→ II).

IV. Qumran. At Qumran, the word occurs only once in 11Q10 14:4 (Job 29:10) for the Hebrew *ngydym*, "princes, leaders," also a title with a very broad spectrum of use.[15]

Gzella

15. Cf. *GesB*[18], 779.

סוף *sūp*; סוף *swp* /sawp/; סיפין *sypyn* /sayāpīn/; בטל *bṭl*

I. Etymology and Lexical Field. II. G-stem "to Stop." III. C-stem "to End, Destroy." IV. Noun "End" (Usually Temporal). V. Noun "Ending" (Spatial).

I. Etymology and Lexical Field. A verbal root *sūp* in the G-stem "to cease, disappear" occurs in Aramaic and quite infrequently in Hebrew—mostly prophetic—texts; Arabic employs it in stem IV for "to collapse, lose."[1] It probably has a by-form in *spī* with the ambitransitive G-stem "to carry off (transitive), to perish (intransitive)" in Hebrew[2] and in later Aramaic languages. The precise nuance of *sūp* depends on the character of the subject; it generally means that something passes and ceases to exist, similar to → *'bd* and Hebrew *klī*.[3] As might be expected, the C-stem means "to end, destroy."

In contrast, the verb *bṭl*, in the G-stem "to stop," in the D-stem "to shut down," refers to the end of an activity; Ezra employs it often in relation to the work on the re-

H.-D. Neef, "*swp*," *ThWQ*, II, 1084-86 (Heb.); M. Sæbø, "סוֹף *sôp*," *TDOT*, X, 188-90; M. Wagner, *Die lexikalischen und grammatikalischen Aramaismen im alttestamentlichen Hebräisch. BZAW* 96 (1966); idem, "קֵץ *qēṣ* end," *TLOT*, 1153-56.

1. See T. Nöldeke, review of E. Kautzsch, *Die Aramaismen im Alten Testament*, *ZDMG* 57 (1903) 419.

2. Also in the medio-passive N-stem and in the C-stem; cf. H. Ringgren, "סָפָה *sāpâ*," *TDOT*, X, 303-5.

3. Aramaic employs this term only very sporadically for "to cease": C. Stadel, *Hebraismen in den aramäischen Texten vom Toten Meer* (Heidelberg, 2008), 87f.

construction of the temple,[4] according to *ATTM*, 2, 93 also in 1QapGen 10:1 for the end of the flood, although, because of unclear, fragmentary letters, the reading is disputed.[5] It occurs in most branches of the Semitic languages, although with different meanings, and migrated into Hebrew.[6]

In addition, the root *sūp* includes the common Aramaic masculine *qatl* noun with the ground form /sawp/, later /sōp/, "end," and the rare plural *qatāl* form /sayāpīn/ for "ending" in a spatial sense. Meanwhile, the noun /sōp/ appears only rarely in Hebrew and first in late texts such as Eccl. 3:11; 7:2; 12:13 or 2 Ch. 20:16, so that it is usually regarded an Aramaic loanword.[7]

II. G-stem "to Stop." The first clear instances of the verb *sūp* appear in Biblical Aramaic.[8] Daniel 4:30 attests the G-stem with the otherwise very rare nuance "to be fulfilled, to fulfill" in reference to a word[9] together with the supplement *ʿl* "to someone."

The typical meaning "to cease, disappear" first occurs at Qumran, most often in context with the evil[10] that ends with the dawn of the kingdom of God.[11] In such passages at Qumran, *ʾbd* appears otherwise. The verb also refers to plans that come to naught,[12] and to water after the flood.[13] In 11Q10 20:2 (Job 31:40), it translates the Hebrew *tmm* for the end of a speech. A few additional instances in fragmentary passages[14] cannot be determined more precisely because of the lack of context.

III. C-stem "to End, Destroy." The causative, transitive meaning "to end, destroy" can be explained naturally in relation to the G-stem. Its spectrum of usage is, therefore, similar. Daniel 2:44, the earliest instance, employs the verb in the interpretation of Nebuchadezzar's dream of the colossus with clay feet with the kingdom of God that crushes[15] and destroys all earthly kingdoms as the subject.[16] It appears in the same sense in the "son of God" text from Qumran for the eradication of violence[17] from (*mn*) the earth in

---

4. The G-stem twice in 4:24, the D-stem in 4:21,23; 5:4; 6:8.

5. Cf. D. A. Machiela, *The Dead Sea Genesis Apocryphon. STDJ* 79 (2009), 53.

6. Wagner, 34.

7. Ibid., 87.

8. The reconstruction of the supposed imperative *s]p* in the proverb of Aḥiqar *TADAE* C1.1,88 following I. Kottsieper, *Die Sprache der Ahiqarsprüche. BZAW* 194 (1990), 20 is entirely uncertain and, with the conjectural meaning "to stop"—here in reference to the word of a king—does not conform to the usage of the verb known otherwise; it may be that one should read *ʾ]p* "also" with *TADAE* and consider supplying a finite verb.

9. *mlh.*

10. *ršʿ.*

11. 4Q204 5 2:28 (1 En. 107:1), in parallel with *klī*; 4Q245 2:2 and perhaps 4Q532 2:8, although neither has context.

12. 4Q534 1 1:9.

13. 4Q206 4 2:3 (1 En. 89:8), after *nḥt* "to sink."

14. Including Noah's dream in 1QapGen 13:12.

15. → *dqq.*

16. The Tiberian pointing with a lengthened penultima is not Aram., cf. *BLA*, §148c.

17. → *ḥrb.*

the end time.[18] The immediate context of 1QapGen 13:11 is unclear; it appears directly in context with the G-stem as the result: "destroyed . . . died away" (→ II). In 11Q10 18:9 (Job 31:16), the verb represents the Hebrew *klī* in the D-stem "to cause to swelter," in 21:2, the conclusion of a speech (Job 32:11).[19]

IV. Noun "End" (Usually Temporal). Like the verb, the masculine noun *swp* /sawp/ > /sōp/ "end" first appears in Biblical Aramaic. With the otherwise rare spatial meaning, it refers in Dnl. 4:8,19 to the "end of all the earth" (*lswp kl 'r'*), up to which the mighty world tree in Nebuchadnezzar's second dream could be seen; otherwise, the plural /sayāpīn/ known from Qumran functions in this sense (→ V). The word can also denote the end of an account (Dnl. 7:28),[20] at Qumran, furthermore, the end of a dream[21] or of honor.[22]

More often, the word has a temporal meaning. In the phrase *'d swp'* "forever," it also refers to the eternal dominion of God already in Daniel (6:27) and the enduring destruction of worldly power (7:26).[23]

The texts from Qumran employ it as *lswp* "at the end of" = "after" in the construct state with a subsequent temporal expression for the terminus of a specific time span.[24] Absolutely for "at the end" = "finally," one finds *'m swp*[25] or *bswp*.[26] Additionally, *swp* can also represent "death, destruction" in apocalyptic contexts.[27] A similar combination of *swp* and *'bdn* appears in 4Q580 1 1:12. In 11Q10, *l' swp* "without end" translates the Hebrew *l' ḥqr* "unfathomable";[28] probably under the influence of this passage, *swp* was added in 21:2 (Job 32:11) to the verb *ḥqr* "to fathom" also employed in the Hebrew text. In 1:5 (Job 18:2), it represents the unclear Hebrew *qnṣ*,[29] which the translator apparently understood as a variant of *qṣ* "end" with a degeminated spelling[30] so that the Aramaic rendition reads "to make an end of words."

V. Noun "Ending" (Spatial). In a few texts from Qumran, in reference specifically to the "ends of the earth," one encounters the plural *sypyn* /sayāpīn/, mostly in the construct

18. 4Q246 1 2:6; probably a C-stem in agreement with *ATTM*, 2, 446; contra *ATTM*, 645, however.

19. Although with no direct counterpart in MT and perhaps inspired by 20:2 (Job 31:40).

20. According to *BLA*, §353f. and *LexLingAram*, 118 as an antonym of → *r'š* in 7:1, but this interpretation as a double gloss is not compelling.

21. 4Q530 2 2+ 6-12:12,20.

22. 4Q213 1-2 2:17.

23. Here almost with the nuance "completely."

24. 1QapGen 19:23; 20:18; yet undetermined in 4Q212 1 4:26 (1 En. 91:17).

25. 4Q212 1 4:17 (1 En. 91:13).

26. 4Q554 3 3:16.

27. 4Q212 1 2:21 (1 En. 91:19), after the verb *'bd* "to expire" as an adverbial modifier *lswp* "to a pernicious end" with a subsequent *'bdn*, the form of which, however, is not entirely clear because of the paleographically difficult final letter before the lacuna. *DSSStE*, 442f., reads *lswp 'bdn'* "utter destruction."

28. 11Q10 25:1 and 28:4 (Job 34:24 and 36:26).

29. Cf. *GesB*[18], 1177.

30. *ATTM*, 89-95.

state with *'r'*[31] and sometimes *sy'py* with ' written as a vowel letter for /ā/.[32] In addition to 4Q558 34:1 and 4Q568:1, the word can presumably be reconstructed in 11Q10 10:1 (Job 26:10) where it would represent the Hebrew *tklyt* as the boundary between light and darkness, i.e., the point to which light can advance. In contrast, the reconstruction in 4Q204 1 13:25, where only the first letter can be read, seems much less certain.

Gzella

31. → IV for *swp* in the same sense in Daniel.
32. Other examples in *ATTM*, 2, 315f.

סלק *slq*

I. Verbal Root and Etymology. 1. Common Semitic. 2. Common Aramaic. II. Biblical Aramaic Usage. III. Qumran. 1. G-stem. 2. Causative-stem "to Sacrifice."

I. Verbal Root and Etymology.

1. Common Semitic. Among the Semitic languages, Aramaic almost exclusively attests the verbal root *slq* (with Semitic *s_3), which denotes upward motion in its most general sense and thus has the basic meanings "to climb up, to go up." While Neo-Babylonian *salāqu*/*selēqu*[1] and Hebrew *'æssaq* (Ps. 139:8)[2] indubitably involve borrowings from Aramaic, Arabic *tasallaqa* "to climb up, to scale a wall," should it be genuinely Arabic,[3] demonstrates the root as at least common Central Semitic. The basic meanings of the Arabic root *slq* in the I. stem, however, are "to throw down, bribe, to remove, to cook,"[4]

C. Brockelmann, *Syrische Grammatik* (Leipzig, ¹⁰1965); G. Dalman, *Grammatik des jüdisch-palästinischen Aramäisch* (Leipzig, ²1905); R. Degen, *Altaramäische Grammatik der Inschriften des 10.–8. Jh. v. Chr. AKM* 38,8 (1969); K. Göransson, "*slq*," *ThWQ*, II, 1099-1102; P. Haupt, "Elul und Adar," *ZDMG* 64 (1910) 703-14; P. Heger, "*Qṭr*: *nsq*/*slq*? A Study of Two Different Verbs Used by Onkelos to Translate the Term *qṭr* of the Masoretic Text," *ZAW* 107 (1995) 466-81; C. Müller-Kessler, *Grammatik des Christlich-Palästinisch-Aramäischen* (Hildesheim, 1991); T. Nöldeke, *Compendious Syriac Grammar* (trans. James A. Crichton; Winona Lake, IN, 2001); M. Wagner, *Die lexikalischen und grammatikalischen Aramaismen im alttestamentlichen Hebräisch. BZAW* 96 (1966).

1. *CAD*, XV, 93.
2. Wagner, 87.
3. So Nöldeke, review of E. Kautzsch, *Die Aramäismen im Alten Testament*, *ZDMG* 57 (1903) 419.
4. Cf. Lane, 1409ff.

which suggest a borrowing from the V. verbal stem from Aramaic.[5] The ithpaal that corresponds to the Arabic V. stem also occurs in Aramaic.[6] Consequently, it is entirely conceivable that the root *slq* in the meaning "to climb up" originally characterized Aramaic alone.

2. *Common Aramaic.* Since the earliest specimens, the contact position has exhibited mostly a progressive assimilation in the sequence */sl/ > /ss/, e.g., in the imperfect peal, Old Aramaic *ysq,*[7] and Syr. *nessaq.*[8] Exceptions may occur in Imperial Aramaic *mslq*[9] or in Jewish Babylonian *myslq.*[10] The assimilation resists explanation according to the laws of phonetics;[11] it may rather be an analogous formation after the antonym → *nḥt* "to climb down,"[12] whose first radical /n/ is subject to assimilation according to the laws of phonetics.[13] The haphel and the related t-stem also exhibit the same assimilation.[14] Instead of lengthened consonants, one also finds forms with geminate dissimilation /ss/ > /ns/,[15] e.g., haphel participle Qumran-Aramaic *mhnsq*[16] and Biblical Aramaic infinitive *l^ehansāqā* (Dnl. 6:24). Despite these and assimilated forms, the assumption of a root **nsq* is unjustified.[17]

The base vowel in the perfect peal, when transmitted or orthographically recognizable, is /i~e/,[18] in the imperfect /a/[19] or /u~o/,[20] perhaps even /i~e/ judging from the Jewish Babylonian secondary imperative *slyq.*[21] In the perfect, forms with a prosthetic *aleph* can also occur, such as Jewish Palestinian *ʾyslyq.*[22]

---

5. Cf. Haupt, 713; *LexSyr*, 477; *MdD*, 332; *GesB*[18], 891.

6. E.g., Syriac *estallaq*, *LexSyr*, 478.

7. Degen, 41 and recently also *KAI* 310.2; 317.1; regarding the expression *slq ʿl lbb* "to come over the heart" in *KAI* 224.14f. often attested among the few Old Aramaic instances → *lbb* II.

8. Nöldeke, 133.

9. Inf., *TADAE* B3.10,15; on *yslq* see *DNSI*, 788.

10. Inf.; *DJBA*, 812.

11. Contra, e.g., E. Lipiński, *Outline of a Comparative Semitic Grammar. OLA* 80 ([2]2001), 133,429ff.; cf. II-*l* roots treated according to the rules such as *šlm, dlq* or *šlṭ*.

12. Three of the handful of Imperial Aramaic specimens employ both verbs in parallel, → *nḥt* II.

13. E.g., impf. peal Syr. (Nöldeke, 115) *neḥḥoṯ;* A. Spitaler, cited in Degen, 41; likewise regarding the Syr. impv. *saq*, Brockelmann, 70.

14. *ATTM*, 646; Nöldeke, 133.

15. See generally *BLA*, §50; A. Spitaler, "Zur Frage der Geminatendissimilation im Semitischen," *IF* 61 (1954) 257-66; *ATTM*, 89ff.; M. L. Folmer, *Aramaic Language in the Achaemenid Period. OLA* 68, 84ff.

16. CT. Levi Bodleian d:4; *DSSStE*, 52.

17. See, e.g., Heger, 472.

18. Biblical Aramaic *s^eliqū*, Ezr. 4:12, Dnl. 2:29; Syr. *s^eleq*, *LexSyr*, 477; Mand. *sliq*, *MdD*, 332.

19. Syr.; Mand. *nisaq*, *MdD*, ibid.

20. Christian Palestinian *yswq*, Müller-Kessler, 55; Jewish Palestinian *tyswq*, Dalman, 293, see also *DJPA*, 379.

21. Alongside *sq*, *DJBA*, 812.

22. Alongside *slyq*, Dalman, 258.

In addition to the peal and the less frequent pael or ithpaal, the root appears chiefly in the causative haphel and its passive-reflexive counterparts.[23]

The root *slq* appears in its original form in all the older varieties of Aramaic and in modern dialects such as Neo-West-Aramaic and Ṭuroyo. In both the older and the modern varieties, variants of the root developed on the basis of the irregular forms. These variants include the perfect forms of the Samaritan *sq* formed on the analogy of II-*ū* or II=III[24] and Mandaic *saq*.[25] Most modern varieties construct I-*y*[26] or I-ʾ forms.[27] Occasionally, various roots coexist.

A series of nouns derive from the root *slq*, including Syriac *massaqṯā*[28] and Mandaic *masiqta*,[29] both "ascent," or Syriac *sullāqā*[30] with the same meaning.

II. Biblical Aramaic Usage. The verb is very rare in Old and Imperial Aramaic (→ I.2). In the Biblical Aramaic text, *slq* occurs eight times in seven verses, five times peal (four pfs., one ptcp.), twice in the haphel (pf., inf.), and one in the hophal (pf.). Only one of the passages appears in Ezra (4:12). Daniel 7:8 attests the peal perfect *silqaṯ*,[31] as does Dnl. 7:20; Ezr. 4:12 and Dnl. 2:29 attest *sᵉliqū*; and Dnl. 7:3 attests the participle *sālᵉqān*. The haphel perfect *hassiqū* occurs in Dnl. 3:22, and the infinitive *lᵉhansāqā* in Dnl. 6:24.[32] This verse also has the sole instance of the hophal perfect *hussaq*.

The Biblical Aramaic text manifests the basic meaning of *slq* in various ways. Ezra 4:12 designates the ascent to Palestine from the plain of Babylonia with *slq*: [. . .] *dī yᵉhūḏāyē dī sᵉliqū min lᵉwāṯāḵ ʿᵃlǣnā ʾᵃṯō līrūšlǣm* "that the Jews, who have come to us from near you, have arrived in Jerusalem."[33] In addition, Dnl. 7:3 employs the verb for ascent from the water, *wᵉʾarbaʿ ḥēwān raḇrᵉḇān sālᵉqān min yammā* "then four large animals arose from the sea."[34] Similarly, *slq* refers to the growth of horns from a head, Dnl. 7:8 *wᵃʾalū qǣrǣn ʾoḥºrī zᵉʿērā silqaṯ*[35] *bēnēhēn*[36] "and, look, another small horn grew up between them," and Dnl. 7:20 *wᵉʿal qarnayyā ʿᵃśar dī ḇᵉrēšah wᵉʾoḥºrī dī silqaṯ* "and (I wanted to learn) about the ten horns on his head and the other (horn) that had grown up." In a figurative meaning, *slq* serves in Dnl. 2:29 to describe the occurrence of thoughts, *ʾant malkā raʿyōnayiḵ*[37] *ʿal miškᵉḇāḵ sᵉliqū mā dī lǣhᵉwē ʾaḥᵃrē ḏᵉnā* "to you, O King, thoughts came on your bed concerning what will one day be."

23. Hophal, ittaphal; *ATTM*, 646; *DNSI*, 788ff.; *LexSyr*, 477ff.; *DJBA*, 812ff.
24. R. Macuch, *Grammatik des samaritanischen Aramäisch* (Berlin, 1982), 139.
25. T. Nöldeke, *Mandäische Grammatik* (Halle, 1875), 84.
26. Present *yasəq*.
27. Present *ʾasəq*.
28. *LexSyr*, 477.
29. *MdD*, 249.
30. *LexSyr*, 478.
31. MT *silqāṯ*, the apparatus restores the form with *pataḥ*.
32. With geminate dissimilation.
33. Cf. *KAI* 317.1.
34. → *ym* IV.
35. MT *silqāṯ*, see above.
36. MT *bēnēhōn*.
37. According to the apparatus of MT, *raʿyōnāḵ*.

The haphel indicates the cause of the upward motion, twice as an active, once in reference to prisoners in Dnl. 3:22, *gub̲rayyā ʾillek̲ dī hassiqū lᵉšad̲rak̲ mēšak̲ waʿᵃb̲ed̲ neg̲ō qaṭṭil himmōn šᵉb̲īb̲ā dī nūrā* "those men who brought up Shadrach, Meshach, and Abednego, the flames of the fire killed," and once with the command to Daniel to come out of the den in Dnl. 6:24, *ūlᵉd̲āniyyel ʾᵃmar lᵉhansāqā min gubbā* "and he commanded that Daniel be brought from the den." The latter passage appends a description of the execution of the instruction passively in the hophal, *wᵉhussaq dāniyyel min gubbā* "and Daniel was brought from the den."

Apart from the unformulated passage Dnl. 3:22, the LXX typically renders *slq* peal with ἀναβαίνω, the causative haphel in contrast with ἀναφέρω. The Peshitta employs the corresponding Syriac forms of *slq*, only Dnl. 3:22 exhibits, again, a sharply altered form. The Vulgate offers the verbs *ascendo* and *orior* for the peal, and, in contrast, *educo* for the haphel. Once again, Dnl. 3:22 diverges.

III. Qumran.

1. G-stem. The diction at Qumran essentially coincides with that of Ezra and Daniel. Here, too, *slq* functions primarily as a verb of upward motion, either geographically to climb up from a lower-lying region, e.g., from Egypt to Palestine, *wslqt mn m[ṣ]r[y]n* "and I arose from Egypt" (1QapGen 20:33), or from Sodom to Jerusalem, *wšmʿ mlk swdm dy ʾtyb ʾbrm kwl šbytʾ wkwl bztʾ wslq lʿwrʿh wʾth lšlm hyʾ yrwšlm* "(when) the king of Sodom heard that Abram had brought back all the captives and all the plunder, he went to him and came to Šalem—that is Jerusalem" (1QapGen 22:13).[38] The ascent of a cliff or a height is attested often, e.g., *wslq lrʾš kpʾ dn* "and (the lamb) climbed to the point of this rock" (4Q204 4:3 [1 En. 89:32]) or *wʾmr ly slq lk lrmt ḥṣwr* "and (God) said to me: Climb to the height of Ḥaṣor" (1QapGen 21:8).[39] Ascent to an upper story appears in 4Q196 6:2 (Tob. 3:10), the rise of a spiral stairway on a column in the heavenly Jerusalem (5Q15 1 2:4f.). The ascent of noise or orders can also be described with *slq*, e.g., *wq[lh] slq q[dm šmyh* "and [the] out[cry] went rig[ht up to the heaven" (4Q201 1 4:6 [1 En. 8:4])[40] or *wrḥ mqtwrty l[š]myʾ slq* "and the odor of my burnt offering rose up to [h]eaven" (1QapGen 10:17).[41] In a figurative sense, *slq* denotes the rise of mysteries, *lqdmyn [. . . s]lq rzʾ* "first [. . .] the mystery [ar]ose" (4Q536 2 1+3:12, Noah's birth).

2. Causative-stem "to Sacrifice." The most important aspect not represented in Ezra and Daniel, but frequent at Qumran in numerous instances, is the use of *slq* chiefly as a C-stem in relation to the offering of a sacrifice.[42] Here, *slq* designates the ascent of the altar as, e.g., in [. . .] *lhqrbh lkl dy slyq lmdb[ḥʾ]* "the woo[d] that is fitting to offer for all that goes up to [the] altar"[43] or *wʾsqh lmdbḥʾ kwlh* "and he brought (the bull) whole on

38. A similar description of a field maneuver in 21:28; see also 4Q545 la-b 2:11f., Testament of Amram.

39. Cf. also 4Q206 4 3:19 [1 En. 89:29] or 1QapGen 21:10.

40. *DSSStE*, 402f.

41. Cf. 4Q214b 2-6:4 and 4Q202 1 3:10 (1 En. 9:2).

42. See on Heb. *ʿlī* and derived nouns in D. Kellermann, "עֹלָה/עוֹלָה *ʿōlâ/ʿolâ*," *TDOT*, XI, 96ff.

43. CT. Levi Bodleian d:20-21 in *DSSStE*, 54f. = *ALD* 31:20.

the altar" (11Q18 13:4, heavenly Jerusalem).[44] On the other hand, it means "to sacrifice" directly, namely in the sense that something for the offering of a sacrifice[45] is brought onto the altar,[46] cf., e.g., *wbnyt tmn mdbḥ w'sqt 'lwhy 'l' wmnḥ' l'l 'lywn* "and I built God an altar there and sacrificed to God Most High a burnt and a grain offering" (1QapGen 21:20) or *wb'dyn hsq 'ynwn* "and then offer (the wood)."[47]

Waltisberg

44. Cf. also 4Q537 12:2, Jacob at Bethel.
45. → *qrb.*
46. See Heger, 478.
47. CT. Levi Bodleian c:11 in *DSSStE,* 52 = *ALD* 22:11; cf. also ALD 26:3.

סעד *s'd;* סעד *s'd* /sa'd/; עדר *'dr*

I. Etymology and Lexical Field. II. Imperial Aramaic. III. Biblical Aramaic. IV. Qumran (Including the Noun "Help").

I. Etymology and Lexical Field. The G-stem of the West Semitic verbal root *s'd* may have originally meant "to support, undergird" in the sense of "to steady," as Hebrew still sporadically attests (Isa. 9:6; Ps. 18:36; Prov. 20:28), while it appears in Aramaic in the G- (as in Ezr. 5:2) and D-stems for "to help" with a direct object. No clear semantic difference between the two stems emerges from the limited distribution of instances. Yet, the verb probably appears in the Behistun inscription in the G-stem, always for divine assistance (→ II),[1] while the unmistakable D-stem in Ezr. 5:2 (→ III) has more the nuance of moral support. The first meaning also underlies the rare usage of the verb in West Semitic personal names.[2] The root appears further in the masculine noun /sa'd/ "help" (→ IV).

Otherwise, for "to help," Aramaic also employed the Semitic verbal root *'δr,[3] spelled *'dr* in post-Old Aramaic, and the related noun /'eδr/ (> /'edr/ > /'edar/). The pre-Imperial Aramaic proverbs of Aḥiqar already attest the root and relate it to divine assistance.[4] The noun also appears in names.[5] In *KAI* 233.13, *'zrk* "your assistance" could represent

G. Warmuth, "סָעַד *sā'aḏ,*" *TDOT*, X, 287-91.

1. Similarly in Hebrew prayer diction: Pss. 20:3; 41:4; 94:18; 119:117.
2. Cf. *TADAE* C3.2,4 with R. Degen, *NESE* 2, 1974, 68.
3. In keeping with Old Aramaic orthography one would expect *'zr.*
4. *'drh* "his helper," *TADAE* C1.1:126.
5. Instances in *ATTM*, 653.

a participle of the verb or the noun. Concerning the few possible, although disputed, Imperial Aramaic instances, see *DNSI*, 830; Qumran manifests only two passages from 11Q10 (9:10 and 14:7 [Job 26:2 and 29:12]), both for the Hebrew cognate *'zr*. In addition, *sīʿ* appears later.[6] Meanwhile, *smk* appears in the literal sense "to support, to prop up."[7]

II. Imperial Aramaic. Aramaic evidences the verb *sʿd* since the Achaemenid period, although Sam'alian already manifests it.[8] All the Imperial Aramaic instances come from the Behistun inscription as a component in the formulaic phrase *'hwrmzd sʿdny* "Ahuramazda helped me" in King Darius's reports concerning successful military campaigns.[9] There, the clause following this expression is always "through the protection [*bṭlh*] of Ahuramazda"[10] with reference to the destroyed enemy.[11] Since it involves perfects, the consonantal spelling permits no distinction between the G- and the D-stems, but in light of later usage, the G-stem seems plausible.

III. Biblical Aramaic. This root appears in Biblical Aramaic only as a D-stem participle in Ezr. 5:2 where it refers to the prophets Haggai and Zechariah who supported Zerubbabel and Joshua in the construction of the temple. The preposition *ʿm* "with" suggests the subordinate role of the first two and 6:14 emphasizes prophetic activity so that one must speak here of "moral, rather than manual, support."[12] It remains unclear, however, whether this distinction rests on the choice of the D-stem rather than the more common G-stem.

IV. Qumran (Including the Noun "Help"). Forms of the root *sʿd* are also very rare at Qumran. *ATTM*, 2, 93 reads the D-stem infinitive *lsʿdwtny* "in order to help me" in 1QapGen 7:19.[13] In any case, the context is almost entirely destroyed.

The related noun *sʿd* "help" appears in 1QapGen 22:31 in a divine promise to Abraham alongside *tqp* "strength." Later Aramaic also attests both the noun and the verb,[14] but it could also assume the meaning "to eat, to nourish," which gives rise to *sʿwdt'* "meal."

Gzella

---

6. *ATTM*, 645; 2, 447.
7. *ATTM*, 647; cf. *DNSI*, 792.
8. *KAI* 214:15,21.
9. *TADAE* C2.1:10,12,16,26,32,42,55.
10. → *ṭll* II.
11. → *qṭl*.
12. H. G. M. Williamson, *Ezra, Nehemiah. WBC* (1985), 70; also *LexLingAram*, 119: *animum addebant*.
13. Accepted by D. A. Machiela, *The Dead Sea Genesis Apocryphon. STDJ* 79 (2009), 48, who, however, incorrectly fails to recognize a *n* before the *y* and, therefore, assumes a possessive rather than an objective suffix; judging from the photograph, the reading with *s* is better in any case than *lhʿdwtny* "to remove me" following J. A. Fitzmyer, *The Genesis Apocryphon of Qumran Cave 1 (1Q20)*. *BietOr* 18/B (²2004), 78, and others.
14. *DJPA*, 384f.; *DJBA*, 823.

ספר *spr* /sepr/; ספר *spr* /sāper/; אגרה *ʾgrh* /ʾeggarā/

I. Etymology and Lexical Field. II. Writing. 1. "Document." 2. "Book." 3. "Literacy." III. Professional Designation "Scribe, Secretary." IV. "Letter."

I. Etymology and Lexical Field. In Aramaic, the common Semitic verbal root *spr*, employed otherwise with various nuances in individual languages for different particular intellectual activities,[1] is only productive in nominal forms. Instead, a series of other lexemes produced the differentiation in the lexical field of the verb in Aramaic. Thus, the West Semitic root → *ktb* serves for "to write," → *mnī* for "to count," usually → *ḥšb* for "to reckon," and *šʿī* and sometimes *tnī* (properly, "to repeat") for "to recount."

The masculine /sepr/[2] "manuscript" may be a primary noun[3] and refers to a variety of documents independent of their material forms. It usually represents documents, but also inscriptions and letters, then also books. In such usages, it overlaps with more specific terms such as → *nṣb* "stele," *ʾgrh* or *ʾgrt* "letter" (→ IV), and *mglh* "scroll."[4] It can sporadically denote literacy, itself, however, similar to Latin *litterae*.

In contrast, the professional designation /sāper/[5] "scribe," by form a G-stem active participle, in distinction from /sepr/ "document," is probably secondary.[6] Depending on the area of responsibililty, it denotes officials of various ranks, from a secretary to a high official of state. In the diglot administrations of the Neo-Assyrian and Neo-Babylonian empires, *sēpiru*[7] distinguishes a scribe of texts in alphabetic script and probably also in the Aramaic language from a cuneiform scribe (*ṭupšarru*).[8] Later, it also meant "scholar."

II. Writing. Aramaic documents from Syria-Palestine originated from the, at least incipient, structures of state and the associated administrations after circa 1000 B.C.E. The increasing use of the alphabetic script in the public realm for representation and bookkeeping required professionally trained chancellery officials and established forms for reports of royal activity and state treaties, as preserved in the oldest inscriptions, as well as for letters,

---

J. Conrad, "סָפַר *sāpar*," *TDOT*, X, 308-18; C. Dohmen, F.-L. Hossfeld, and E. Reuter, "סֵפֶר *sēper*," *TDOT*, X, 326-41; H. Gzella, *A Cultural History of Aramaic. HO* 111 (2015); J. Kühlewein, "סֵפֶר *sēper* book," *TLOT*, 806-13; D. A. Machiela, "*spr*," *ThWQ*, II, 1105-11; A. R. Millard, "Words for Writing in Aramaic," in *Hamlet on a Hill. FS T. Muraoka. OLA* 118 (2003), 349-55; H. Niehr, "סֹפֵר *sōpēr*," *TDOT*, X, 318-26.

1. Hebrew "to count, recount"; Ugaritic also "to write, to reckon"; Akkadian "to send, to write"; Ethiopic "to measure," as also occasionally in Hebrew.
2. Later /separ/, *ATTM*, 114.
3. Or an early borrowing, cf. *ATTM*, 647.
4. → *gll*.
5. Revocalized /sāpar/ circa 200 B.C.E., *ATTM*, 108.
6. *ATTM*, 648 considers an adoption of the Assyrian *šāpiru*.
7. Or *sepīru*, the grammatical form is unclear.
8. Gzella, 138; presumably, *sēpiru* traces back to /sāper/ with a shift from /ā/ to /ē/.

memoranda, receipts, lists, and documents in private law.[9] Admittedly, this second group clearly appears only beginning with the Neo-Assyrian period with its extensive bilingual administrative apparatus, but may have had precursors already in the chancelleries of the independent Aramaic city-states; oral traditions and sayings were also written down for nondocumentary purposes (for training?).[10] Thus, *spr* /sepr/ refers both to (mostly) official and to literary texts, and overlaps with /kitāb/ "something written."[11]

1. "Document." Depending on the nature of the preserved literature, the majority of the Old and Imperial Aramaic instances of /sepr/ refer to state or private legal documents. In the Sefire steles, the word regularly denotes the vassal treaties recorded in the inscriptions there, either as a locative with *b-* "in" or in conjunction with *mly* in the construct state,[12] denoting both the wording,[13] and, in the plural (for the steles as wholes?), their physical form.[14]

In the Achaemenid period, the center of gravity of the textual corpus shifted to private contracts and letters. By far the majority of the instances of *spr* in this period stem from the various legal documents from Elephantine. It denotes a contract and, in the construct state with an additional term, can more precisely define the nature of a document in relation to the legal affair at its base, in the colophon the respective document itself: *spr ḥwb* "record of debt,"[15] *spr ʾgrʾ* "document concerning a wall,"[16] *spr by* "document concerning a house,"[17] *spr ksp* "document concerning money,"[18] *spr ʿbwr* "document concerning grain,"[19] *spr plgn* "partnership agreement,"[20] *spr mrḥq* "waiver declaration,"[21] and *spr ʾntw* "marriage contract."[22] As the direct object of transitive verbs, it also denotes various stages in a juridical process: → with *ktb* the drafting of a document,[23] with → *yhb* the delivery,[24] with the C-stem of → *npq* the production,[25] with *lqḥ*[26] the acceptance,[27] and finally with → *ʿbd dyn spr* the execution of a contractually established legal claim.[28]

9. Ibid., 57-63.
10. Ibid., 124-53; cf. 87-91.
11. → *ktb* IV.
12. → *mll* II.
13. *KAI* 222 B 8,28,33; C 17; 223 B 18; C 13; 224.4,14,17,23.
14. *KAI* 223 C 2,4,6,9.
15. *TADAE* B1.1:19, → *ḥṭī* IV; similarly probably also *spr ʾsrn* in B8.10:1.
16. *TADAE* B2.1:20, → *ktl*.
17. *TADAE* B2.3:35; 2.7:21; 3.4:25; 3.5:25; 3.10:27; 3.11:21; 3.12:35.
18. *TADAE* B3.1:23.
19. *TADAE* B3.13:15.
20. *TADAE* B2.11:14,17.
21. *TADAE* B2.2:22; 2.3:23,25; 2.8:14; 2.10:20.
22. *TADAE* B2.8:4; 3.3:17 (partially reconstructed); 3.8:45; 3.11:9f.; 3.12:18; 4.6:4f.
23. Very frequent, e.g., *TADAE* B2.1:15; 2.2:16; 2.4:14,16; impersonal pass., e.g., in 3.1:8; 3.7:9.
24. *TADAE* B2.3:25; 2.7:6.
25. *TADAE* B2.3:16f.,27.
26. → *nśī* V.
27. *TADAE* B2.3:17.
28. *TADAE* B2.6:31; 3.8:32.

In letters, contrariwise, *spr* also refers to the pertinent document and often serves as the object of the verb → *šlḥ* "to send,"[29] less often of the synonymous C-stem of **wšr*[30] or of the verb *ktb*.[31] Thus, it occurs mostly in private letters, while the more formal register of official correspondence, at least since the Achaemenid period, prefers *'grh*/*'grt* (→ IV).[32]

2. *"Book."* As a designation for a book, *spr* first becomes common with the development of local Aramaic literary traditions around the middle of the first millennium B.C.E., although the form of the Deir 'Allā inscription as recorded on a scroll (ca. 800 B.C.E.)[33] already prefigures this usage. The three Biblical Aramaic occurrences refer to three different books: *spr dkrny'* in Ezr. 4:15 to the Persian court chronicles or collected edicts,[34] *spr mšh* in 6:18 to the Mosaic law,[35] and the plural absolute *spryn* in the apocalyptic court scene of Dnl. 7:10 to books, not further defined, opened in the proceedings against the monsters, symbols of the secular empires.[36] At Qumran, as with the often synonymously employed → *ktb* IV, references to revelations[37] and the wisdom of the patriarchs[38] dominate. The documentary meaning, however, also appears occasionally.[39]

3. *"Literacy."* As in Hebrew, /sepr/ can additionally signify "literature" (cf. Dnl. 1:4) and "writing" (Isa. 29:12), e.g., as the subject of learning in 4Q213 1 1:9 and 1-2 2:8.[40] In conjunction with the verb → *yd'*, meanwhile, it means "to be able to read and write." Negated in post-Achaemenid legal texts, this expression denotes "to be illiterate."[41]

III. Professional Designation "Scribe, Secretary." The professional designation /sāper/ "scribe" first occurs as an addition to personal names in Neo-Assyrian administrative texts.[42] While it probably involves lower ranking administrative officials here, "scribe" is also a fixed title of the legendary, high-ranking counselor, Aḥiqar, who em-

---

29. *TADAE* A2.1:12; 2.2:17; 2.3:5,12; 2.4:13; 2.5:9; 2.7:4; 3.4:5; D7.21:6; 7.24:1.

30. *TADAE* A2.5:4,7.

31. *TADAE* A3.8:4.

32. Yet, *spr* in the pre-Imperial Aramaic letter of Adon A1.1:9 refers to an official document, see *DNSI*, 800f.

33. *KAI* 312.1; regarding its linguistic and cultural classification, see Gzella, 87-91.

34. → *dkr* III.

35. Probably not identical with the Pentateuch; see H. G. M. Williamson, *Ezra, Nehemiah. WBC* (1985), xxxvii-xxxix.

36. → *ptḥ* II.1.

37. 4Q204 1 6:9; 4Q213 1-2 2:12; 4Q529 1:6; 4Q530 2 2+6-12:18, cf. Dnl. 7:10; possibly also 4Q534 1 1:5.

38. 1QapGen 19:25; 4Q541 7:4.

39. 4Q550 1:4f.

40. = *ALD* 88.17 and 90.23; because of the parallelism with *mwsr* "discipline" and *ḥkmh* "wisdom" probably in the holistic sense "literacy" and not restricted to the alphabet.

41. *PAT* 1624.4; P1.22 and 2.26 in H. J. W. Drijvers and J. F. Healey, *The Old Syriac Inscriptions of Edessa and Osrhoene. HO* 42 (1999), 232-42.

42. D. Schwiderski, *Die alt- und reichsaramäischen Inschriften*, vol. I: *Konkordanz. FSBP* 4 (2008), 610f.

bodies the ideal of the clever and upright servant of state.[43] The Achaemenid provincial chancelleries of Egypt and Bactria also refer to scribes.[44] In the first case, official letters distinguish the scribe from another official, who *ydʿ ṭʿmʾ znh* "knows this commandment," in the second, the same person seems to have performed both functions.[45] Scribes were responsible not just for drafting letters and documents, however, but could also hear complaints concerning unpaid wages[46] and receive grain deliveries for the royal storehouse.[47] The records yield only sporadic insights into the highly specialized spectrum of duties of this very heterogenous profession, however. Common to the scribes of various ranks is an education meant to lead, in addition to literacy itself, to mastery of the current document forms and Aramaic literary diction, which was extremely standardized beginning in the Achaemenid period,[48] with its rhetorical possibilities. Higher officials, in particular, may also have enjoyed additional academic education since they created the literary works.[49]

In the book of Ezra, "scribes" in the sense of higher servants of state also include the opponents of the construction of the Jerusalem temple (Ezr. 4:8f.,17,23) as well as its protagonist, Ezra. He was simultaneously "priest"[50] and "expert" in the divine law (7:12,21),[51] expanding the function of the well-educated official to the religious realm—perhaps in the sense of the recording of cultic regulations.[52]

At Qumran, too, the title implies theological knowledge and serves as an attribute of Enoch who received insights into the secrets of the world and history in visions recorded in writing.[53] With the canonization of binding religious texts, which require interpretation and are inexhaustible, the "scribes" became the NT scholars (γραμματεύς).

IV. "Letter." The feminine *ʾgrh* /ʾeggarā/ and, without distinction until the Achaemenid period *ʾgrt* /ʾeggert/,[54] refers mostly to "letter" in official diction.[55] Nonetheless, in addenda to some Neo-Assyrian cuneiform texts it refers to "document,"[56] since the administrative terminology was not yet standardized.

Imperial Aramaic knows a variety of specific lexemes for a written edict from a high office: *dkrn*,[57] → *ṭʿm*, → *nštwn* and → *ptgm*.

Gzella

43. *TADAE* C1.1:1,11,18,35,42, → *ḥkm* III.1.
44. In *TADAE* A6.1:1,6 designated as *spry mdyntʾ* "scribes of the province."
45. For instances → *ṭʿm* II.
46. *TADAE* A3.3:5.
47. *TADAE* B4.4:12,14.
48. Gzella, 178-82.
49. Cf. ibid., 201-8.
50. → *khn*.
51. As also in the Hebrew sections: Niehr, 324f.
52. See K. Koch, "Ezra and the Origins of Judaism," *JSS* 19 (1974) 183 n. 5.
53. 4Q203 8:4; 4Q206 2:2; 4Q530 2 2+6-12:14; → *prš* IV.
54. From Akkadian *egirtu*.
55. *KAI* 233.4; *TADAE* A3.5:5; 4.3:10; 4.7:7 par. 4.8:6; 6.13:2; 6.15:4; more in Schwiderski, 11f.; corresponding to Ezr. 4:8,11; 5:6.
56. W. Röllig, *Die neuassyrischen Texte aus Tall Šēḫ Ḥamad. BATSH* 6/2 (2002), 23; cf. Gzella, 127.
57. → *dkr* III.

סרושׁי *srwšy* /srōšī/

I. Etymology and Form. II. Usage.

I. Etymology and Form. The feminine noun *srwšy* /srōšī/ "corporal punishment" derives from the Old Persian **sraušyatā*[1] and appears in Aramaic beginning with the Achaemenid period. The word was integrated into the noun system as an abstract form with /-īt/.[2] Since the etymology was not transparent, the initial /s/ could be incorrectly understood as an old */ś/ (already pronounced like /s/),[3] so that the word appears in Biblical Aramaic as *šᵉrōšī* (Ezr. 7:26).[4] Only the pointing differentiated graphically between *š* and *ś* and spelled, perhaps through assimilation, *š*.

II. Usage. In Imperial Aramaic, official documents from the provincial administration of Egypt[5] and Bactria[6] attest *srwšy* "punishment." In *TADAE* A6.3:6f., it accompanies the verb → *ʿbd* "to do, perform" and designates a punishment of slaves prescribed by edict.[7] In contrast, the Bactrian text is a list for the distribution of food (flour, wine, and oil) to administration workers. Here, as an *abstractum pro concreto*, the word evidently refers to the officials responsible for administering floggings.

Ezra 7:26 mentions punishment in a series of penalties for violations of the divine and the royal law in second place after execution, but before monetary fines and imprisonment. LXX understood the word correctly throughout and translated it with παιδεία, which also serves normally as the rendering of forms of the Hebrew root *ysr*.[8] Because of the misspelling *šršw*, the later history of interpretation sees here a form of *šrš* "to uproot" and understands the word as "rejection (from the community)."[9] In Aramaic, however, "to uproot" is only → *ʿqr*. Consequently, this can hardly have been the original meaning.

Gzella

J. Naveh and S. Shaked, *Aramaic Documents from Ancient Bactria (Fourth Century B.C.E.)* (London, 2012); J. Tavernier, *Iranica in the Achaemenid Period (ca. 550-330 B.C.). OLA* 158 (2007).

1. Tavernier, 448.
2. In Aram. with the absolute state /-ī/; Naveh and Shaked, 196.
3. *ATTM*, 648.
4. According to the *Qere*, because the consonantal text reads *šršw* as the result of an additional error.
5. *TADAE* A6.3:6f.
6. Naveh and Shaked, C3,41.
7. → *ṭʿm*.
8. H. Gzella, *Lebenszeit und Ewigkeit. BBB* 134 (2002), 326f.
9. Thus *exilium* in the Vulgate; see H. G. M. Williamson, *Ezra, Nehemiah. WBC* (1985), 97.

סרך *srk* /sārak/

I. Etymology and Lexical Field. II. Usage.

I. Etymology and Lexical Field. Generally, scholars trace the masculine *srk* /sārak/ to an Iranian origin.[1] In Aramaic, it first served as the title of a high official and later—if, in fact, the same lexeme—also as a designation of an established and juridically valid order.

II. Usage. First attested in Imperial Aramaic administrative texts from Persepolis, *srk* has the meaning "administrator, treasurer."[2] Unclear so far is its relation to *srkr* "leader, overseer"[3] in a Bactrian list of food to be distributed.[4] In the episode of Daniel in the lions' den, *srkyn* are very high officials to whom even the satraps (provincial governors), with whom they are regularly mentioned, must render account; thanks to the favor of King Darius, Daniel also numbers among them (Dnl. 6:3,4,5,7,8). No historical foundation for this hierarchy is perceptible.

In Aramaic texts from Qumran, in contrast, *srk* represents "order." With some certainty, one may emend *bs*[*rk* "accordingly" for the prescribed sacrificial practice.[5] The creation-theological interpretation of the courses of the stars[6] may constitute an additional instance, but the reading is dubious.[7] One encounters *srk* very often denoting "order, rule" in a few Hebrew documents, especially the Community Rule and the War Scroll.[8] In any case, it is uncertain whether exactly the same Imperial Aramaic official title or another form serves at Qumran for the abstract concept "order," especially since the word occurs in Jewish Babylonian as a *qitl*-noun /sirk/.[9]

Gzella

C. Hempel, "*srk*," *ThWQ*, II, 1111-17; W. Hinz, *Altiranisches Sprachgut der Nebenüberlieferungen. GOF* III/3 (1975); J. Naveh and S. Shaked, *Aramaic Documents from Ancient Bactria (Fourth Century* B.C.E.*)* (London, 2012); J. Tavernier, *Iranica in the Achaemenid Period (ca. 550-330 B.C.). OLA* 158 (2007).

1. **sāraka* "standing at the point"; so Hinz, 221, other suggestions in *GesB*[18], 1518.
2. *DNSI*, 803.
3. < **sārakāra*, Tavernier, 431.
4. Naveh and Shaked, C3,40.
5. 4Q214 2:10.
6. 4Q201 1 2:1 (1 En. 2:1).
7. E. M. Cook, *Dictionary of Qumran Aramaic* (Winona Lake, IN, 2015), s.v. *ʾrk*.
8. Hempel, 1111-17.
9. *DJBA*, 809a; see the extensive discussion in B. A. Levine, "Aramaic Texts from Persepolis," *JAOS* 92 (1972) 72-75.

סתר *str*; סתר *str* /setr/; מסתר *mstr* /mastar/; טמר *ṭmr*; צפן *ṣpn*

I. Etymology and Lexical Field. II. Use of the Verb "to Conceal." III. Use of the Noun "Hiding Place."

I. Etymology and Lexical Field. In Aramaic, the West Semitic verbal root *str* "to conceal" is less productive than in Hebrew. It appears in the factitive D-stem "to conceal something" and in the related t-passive "to be concealed"; later, the C-stem and the Gt-stem "to seclude oneself," synonymous with the D-stem, appear.[1] There is no etymological relation to the synchronous, homonymous root *str*,[2] in the G-stem "to destroy."[3] The masculines /setr/[4] and /mastar/, both meaning "hiding place," derive from *str* "to conceal."

The semantic nuance of this verb makes it difficult to distinguish it from its synonyms: on one hand *ṭmr* in the G- and C-stems;[5] on the other *ṣpn* in the G-stem "to be hidden"[6] and in the C-stem "to conceal."[7] Furthermore, it overlaps with *ksī*, in the G-stem "to conceal oneself" and in the D-stem "to cover."[8]

II. Use of the Verb "to Conceal." As a verb, *str* first appears in Biblical Aramaic as a substantival feminine passive participle *mstrt'* "the hidden" (Dnl. 2:22). It parallels *'myqt'* "the profound, unfathomable" in a wisdom praise of God who reveals the hidden.[9] The three certain instances from Qumran are translations: 4Q583 1:2[10] corresponds with *ḥsī* "to conceal oneself" from Isa. 14:32; 11Q10 13:2 and 25:5 (Job 28:21; 34:29) render the Hebrew cognate.[11] In contrast, 4Q531 11:1 and 4Q541 24 2:3 are so corrupt that the reading and context remain unclear.

M. Becker, "*str*," *ThWQ*, II, 1121-26; S. Wagner, "סָתַר *sāṯar*," *TDOT*, X, 362-72; G. Wehmeier, "סתר *str* hi. to hide," *TLOT*, 813-19.

1. *DJBA*, 834b.
2. Originally **śtr*.
3. *TADAE* C1.1:173; Ezr. 5:12; also later: *DJPA*, 390b; *DJBA*, 834f.; *LexSyr*, 503; *MdD*, 339.
4. > /setar/ with anaptyxis, *ATTM*, 114.
5. Attested beginning at Qumran, 1QapGen 6:12; 4Q209 6:9 (1 En. 73); 4Q213 1-2 2:6; 4Q213b 1:3; 4Q214b 8:2; 4Q553a 3 2:2; 11Q10 14:4 and 34:8 (Job 29:10 and 40:13); for both abstract and concrete concepts.
6. 4Q209 23:6 (1 En. 77:3), of heavenly bodies like *ṭmr* in 4Q209 6:9; middle as sometimes in Heb.; cf. H. Gzella, "Voice in Classical Hebrew against Its Semitic Background," *Or* 78 (2009) 295.
7. *TADAE* C1.1:49; C2.1:71f.; of persons and ideas.
8. *DNSI*, 532; *ATTM*, 608; 2:419.
9. → *glī* [I] II; *yd'* III.1.
10. Dt-stem.
11. In 13:2 in the Dt-stem for the Heb. N-stem.

III. Use of the Noun "Hiding Place." The noun *str* /setr/ appears in the proverbs of Aḥiqar,[12] *mstr* /mastar/ in 4Q201 1 2:7 (1 En. 4:1), both denoting "protection, cover."

Gzella

12. *TADAE* C1.1:111,183.

עבד *ʿbd*; עבד *ʿbd* /ʿabd/; עבידה *ʿbydh* /ʿabīdā/; עבד *ʿbd* /ʿobād/; מעבד *mʿbd* /maʿbād/; אמה *ʾmh* /ʾamā/

I. Lexical Field and Grammatical Constructions. II. Usage of the Verb. 1. "To Make." 2. "To Act, to Do." 3. Passive. III. Noun "Servant." IV. Noun "Work, Service." V. Noun "Act, Action." VI. Verbal Noun "Deed."

I. Lexical Field and Grammatical Constructions. Forms of the common West Semitic root *ʿbd* and its numerous nominal derivatives are very productive in Aramaic. In contrast to Hebrew, Ugaritic, and Arabic, here the verb does not mean "to serve," but either "to make" in the sense of "to produce" in terms of a concrete result or "to do, to demonstrate" with a view to the action itself. For this meaning, Hebrew usually employs the verb *ʿśī* and Phoenician and Arabic *pʿl* (rare in Hebrew), while Aramaic employs → *plḥ* and, at first only sporadically, *šmš* for "to serve."

ʿbd occurs in the G-stem with the related t-stem and in pre-Christian Aramaic with the internal passive for the nonactive diathesis "to be made" or "to be bestowed" (→ II.3). The exact nuance depends on the nature of the concrete or abstract object. Furthermore, various prepositional supplements appear with particular regularity for "to do," *l-* for the indirect object "to someone,"[1] *ʿl* "against, to the disadvantage of,"[2] *b-* "with/to someone,"[3] and *ʿm* also "to"[4] or "with,"[5] and *qdm* "to";[6] in the t-passive "to be bestowed" also *mn* "to someone"[7] or, rarely, of the agent.[8]

C. Hezser, *Jewish Slavery in Antiquity* (Oxford, 2005); J. Naveh and S. Shaked, *Aramaic Documents from Ancient Bactria (Fourth Century B.C.E.)* (London, 2012); H. Ringgren, U. Rüterswörden, and H. Simian-Yofre, "עָבַד *ʿāḇaḏ*," *TDOT*, X, 376-405; B. Schlenke, "*ʿbd*," *ThWQ*, III, 1–11; D. Schwiderski, *Die alt- und reichsaramäischen Inschriften*, vol. I: *Konkordanz*. *FSBP* 2 (2008); C. Westermann, "עֶבֶד *ʿebed* servant," *TLOT*, 819-32.

1. E.g., *KAI* 224.3; 1QapGen 19:20.
2. *KAI* 224.22.
3. Ezr. 7:10.
4. Ezr. 4:22; Dnl. 3:32; 1QapGen 21:3,24f.
5. Dnl. 7:21; 1QapGen 21:24f.
6. Dnl. 6:23.
7. Ezr. 7:26; 4Q206 1 22:3 (1 En. 22:4).
8. *TADAE* A4.5:9.

The related nouns represent the entire semantic spectrum of the root. The meaning of the verb "to serve," no longer productive in Aramaic, survives in /ʿabd/ (> /ʿabəd/) "servant";[9] either the substantival feminine passive participle /ʿabīdā/ "work, service," usually employed specifically, or the general masculine verbal noun /ʿobād/ "act, action" refers to the act; finally, the rare, also masculine verbal noun /maʿbād/ "deed" denotes the result of the action.

II. Usage of the Verb. The verb *ʿbd* belongs among the most frequent Aramaic roots, is already ubiquitous in older material, and occurs in very many general or register-specific shadings.[10] Nevertheless, a fundamental difference may be identified between usages that refer to a specific result ("to make, produce), and those in which the action stands in the foreground ("to do") and that must be translated with a variety of main verbs depending on the nature of the object. The use of "to do" as an auxiliary verb, as, e.g., in Modern Persian or Turkish, seems marked, especially beginning with Imperial Aramaic; its frequency even in comparison to other Semitic languages stands out. It remains unclear, however, whether it involves an independent Aramaic development, with at least an element of Iranian influence, or primarily a reduction of lexical complexity in the course of the far-reaching use of Aramaic as a contact language.

The participle serves as a *nomens agens* "creator" or "doer." Because of its dual nature, it also appears in a nominal usage in the construct state when it can be defined by a genitive relationship with the subsequent word. The diction in this regard remains constant over the centuries.

1. "To Make." The earliest Aramaic sources already attest *ʿbd* with a specific material object to denote a creative activity that leads to a tangible result. Already in the Tell Fekheriye inscription (ca. 850 B.C.E.), the verb denotes the production of a statue by its commissioner.[11]

In the Achaemenid period and later, the number of occurrences increases sharply. Here, alongside "to (have) produce(d),"[12] specialized usages also appear. In reference to divine subjects, the verb denotes "to create,"[13] in reference to wine "to produce."[14] With a dual direct object, the verb can denote "to turn something into something"[15] and, therefore, overlaps with the D-stem of → *šwī* and the G-stem of → *śīm*. The participle can also be employed substantivally for "producer of."[16]

---

9. Regarding the denominative *šʿbd* "to enslave," → III.

10. For occurrences, see Schwiderski, 618-23 with passages from the Bactrian satrap correspondence in Naveh and Shaked, 281; *DNSI*, 806-16; *ATTM*, 649f. and 2, 448f.

11. *KAI* 309.15, here as often later in the sense of "to have produced," cf. *Caesar pontem fecit*.

12. *TADAE* A6.12:2 and Dnl. 3:1,15, both of statues; *TADAE* D17.1:2; 20.1:2 and Naveh and Shaked, A4,3,6 of a building; *TADAE* A3.3:10 probably of a garment; *TADAE* B3.10:22 of a document; 4Q202 1 2:26 (1 En. 8:1) of swords.

13. Of heaven and earth: Jer. 10:11; 11Q10 24:7 (with no counterpart in Job 34:13) and 30:2 (Job 38:4); of human beings: 4Q204 1 6:12 (1 En. 14:3); 11Q10 26:4f. (Job 35:10).

14. 1QapGen 12:13, distinct from the C-stem of → *npq* III "to fetch."

15. *TADAE* B3.9:6f.,9.

16. *TADAE* C3.11:4,11, of oil; 4Q550 1:2, of garments.

2. *"To Act, to Do."* Further, the nuance *'bd* "to do, to effectuate" with an abstract object appears regularly since Old Aramaic: thus already often in the Sefire treaties of state "to act thusly [*kn*],"[17] "to do whatever is good,"[18] and "to commit a treaty infraction [*mrmh*]."[19]

From the fifth century B.C.E., everyday speech and then literary texts also attest the verb well so that the diction in the sources develops further. It occurs in the quite general sense "to do, act, proceed,"[20] "to do something for someone, to do something to someone,"[21] in official regulations for "to behave (thusly/in accordance with the agreement)."[22] Furthermore, numerous idiomatic expressions occur, as in administrative diction "to convey,"[23] "to adopt something (of goods) as one's own [*lnpšh*],"[24] "to perform" (e.g., of repairs or other tasks),"[25] "to issue (an instruction)"[26] or "to make an oath."[27] Similarly, in reference to events as object such as a sacrifice,[28] a rebellion (Ezr. 4:15), a temple dedication (Ezr. 6:16), a banquet (Dnl. 5:1),[29] or a battle[30] it can denote "to organize." Further, it means "to commit a crime" (Dnl. 6:23) and "to work a miracle" (Dnl. 3:32; 6:28). In the terminology of documents, *'bd dyn* "to hold a proceeding,"[31] with → *dt* also "to follow a law" (Ezr. 7:26), and officially with *zmn'* "to establish the time."[32] The numerous, although mostly fragmentary instances in Imperial Aramaic private correspondence on ostraca suggest that the verb was also widespread in colloquial speech.

Specific expressions with other abstract objects first appear at Qumran, but connect as a whole with the Imperial Aramaic evidence: "to make something sound,"[33] "to produce joy,"[34] "to show honor,"[35] "to exercise dominion,"[36] and "to pass time."[37] Otherwise,

17. *KAI* 222 C 20f.
18. *KAI* 224.3, → *ṭīb* III.1; cf. *KAI* 222 C 5 and 223 B 2, → *ṭīb* III.2.
19. *KAI* 224.22.
20. *TADAE* A3.5:6f.; 3.10:3; B3.8:33; so also Dnl. 4:32; 6:11; Ezr. 6:8; 7:18.
21. *TADAE* A2.3:4,7; 2.4:4; 4.3:8,10; 6.7:9, C1.1:50f. and D20.5:2: "bad"; A4.2:16: "a matter"; 4.2:5: "to behave like a thief"; B3.6:12; 1QapGen 21:3: "good"; cf. 21:26; 4Q550 5+5a:4.
22. *TADAE* A6.2:22; 6.8:3; 6.10:5; 6.16:2; Ezr. 4:22; 6:13; 4Q196 11:2 (Tob. 5:1); also in a request: *TADAE* A4.7:27.
23. *TADAE* A6.10:3,7; 6.15:7.
24. *TADAE* A4.7:13; 6.15:6; B7.2:6, following *lqḥ*.
25. *TADAE* A6.2:22, etc.; 6.7:9.
26. *TADAE* A6.3:8; 6.13:3f.; 6.14:3; Naveh and Shaked, A6,6,9.
27. *TADAE* B2.8:6.
28. *TADAE* A4.7:22.
29. Cf. 4Q545 1a 1:6.
30. *TADAE* C2.1:12,15,22,32, etc.; Dnl. 7:21; 1QapGen 21:24; 4Q246 1 2:8; 4Q531 22:4.
31. *TADAE* B2.6:31; 3.8:32,38; 6.4:6; 1QapGen 20:13; → *dīn* II.1.
32. As in the correspondence of Bactrian satraps: A4,2 in Naveh and Shaked, probably also to be reconstructed in A2,4.
33. 4Q246 1 2:6.
34. 4Q542 1 1:3.
35. 4Q242 1-3:5.
36. 4Q550 1:6f.
37. 1QapGen 22:28; cf. J. A. Fitzmyer, *The Genesis Apocryphon of Qumran Cave 1 (1Q20)*. *BietOr* 18/B (^{3}2004), 254, with NT parallels.

along with other terms for criminal behavior such as *ḥms* "wrong," one can also "do" a lie;[38] cf. "to do the truth" in Jn. 3:21 and 1 Jn. 1:6.[39]

3. Passive. Imperial Aramaic formed the actual passive of *ʿbd* internally through an ablaut.[40] Except for the participle, this internal passive disappears at the end of the first millennium B.C.E., first in the imperfect. Because of this development, the sometimes middle, sometimes reflexive Gt-stem was expanded with the passive diathesis.[41] To date, Old Aramaic has yielded no pertinent instances of *ʿbd*, but Imperial Aramaic and later attest the passive categories for a variety of the usages also attested in the active, mostly in the Gt-stem: "to be made into something" in Dnl. 2:5; 3:29 and Ezr. 6:11;[42] "to be performed" in Ezr. 5:8;[43] 6:12 or 7:21,23;[44] "to be instigated" in Ezr. 4:19 (rebellion, active in 4:15); "a proceeding will be held" in Ezr. 7:26;[45] sporadically even others, such as *TADAE* A6.8:4; 6.10:9; D1.32:15 with *ptgm* "word" for "to be admonished." Most of the Imperial Aramaic instances of the t-stem come from official letters, where passive expressions apparently already belong to the bureaucratic writing style of the period.

The passive participle points to the result "made, done,"[46] even in specialized usages,[47] and is often indistinguishable from the passive perfect third-person masculine singular; the t-stem participle emphasizes an action underway "being made, done."[48]

Idiomatically, the passive participle *ʿbyd* "made" in *ʾyk ʿbyd* can represent "how it is going, what is happening"[49] and together with *ʾtr* "place," "resident."[50]

III. Noun "Servant." In the noun *ʿbd* /ʿabd/ "servant," Aramaic preserves the meaning of the root "to serve" that disappears for the verb after the Old Aramaic period. As a term for legal or social status, *ʿbd* can mean "slave,"[51] with *ʾmh* /ʾamā/ "maid" as a feminine

38. *šqr*; 1QapGen 11:14; 11Q10 24:2 (Job 34:8); here, as in similar passages, a const. ptcp.; consequently, *ATTM*, 650 and 2, 449 interpret it substantivally as "doer of" and, together with comparable cases, list it as a separate lexeme.

39. According to *ATTM*, 2, 184 also 4Q196 17 2:4f. (Tob. 13:8); but the reading is controversial, contra J. A. Fitzmyer, *Tobit*. *CEJL* (2003), 310 (Tob 13:6).

40. See e.g., *ʿbyd* "it was done" in *TADAE* A4.7:15, probably a passive perfect.

41. Thus, e.g., *ytʿbd* "it will be done," *TADAE* A4.5:9; 4Q198 1:5 (Tob. 14:4); 4Q529 1:10.

42. Active in *TADAE* B3.9:6f.,9.

43. Work, active, e.g., in *TADAE* A6.2:22.

44. Commands, active, e.g., in *TADAE* A6.3:8.

45. Active, e.g., in *TADAE* B2.6:31.

46. E.g., *TADAE* A3.3:9 or A4.7:20; in a periphrastic phrase "to be built" in Naveh and Shaked, A5,2.

47. Thus, very often "is conveyed" in reference to taxes in the import and export list *TADAE* C3.7.

48. Cf. *TADAE* A4.9:11 *lqbl zy lqdmyn hwh mtʿbd* "to care to be done exactly as before" Naveh and Shaked, A5,1 "being built," the result appears then in l. 2 with the pass. ptcp., see above.

49. *TADAE* A3.3:6; 4Q552 1:9; cf. H. Gzella, *Tempus, Aspekt und Modalität im Reichsaramäischen*. *VOK* 48 (2004), 180,186; see also the discussion there of the difficult expression in C2.1:66.

50. *TADAE* B2.2:3; D2.12:3.

51. *KAI* 233.13, the king gave these persons [l. 7]; *TADAE* B2.11:4,5,17; 3.9:5,7,9.

counterpart,[52] and then is often mentioned together with the owner.[53] Consequences of bondage include beating and sale, as proverbs[54] and legal texts[55] demonstrate. As a designation for subordination, in contrast, *'bd* means "servant."[56] In this sense, which is sometimes indistinguishable from simple servants,[57] *'bd* can even refer to high-ranking persons[58] and, in reference to a vassal relationship, it functions as a counterpart for → *mr'* "lord" even in royal self-designations.[59] Formal style, such as in letters or at court, also knows it as a self-designation when relating to a person deserving respect.[60] As a parallel, religious speech employs the word for "servant of God."[61] Consequently, together with a theophoric element, it constitutes a frequent component of masculine names.[62] In 11Q10 2:5; 18:6; 35:7 (Job 19:16; 31:13; 40:28) it represents the homonymous Hebrew counterpart. The term → *'lym* can also act as a synonym.[63]

The verb *š'bd* "to enslave," first attested with certainty later in East Aramaic, derives from the noun with an analogous expansion of the *š*-causative borrowed from the Akkadian on a West Semitic root.[64] The suggestion by E. M. Cook[65] to reconstruct a corresponding form in 4Q246 1 I 8 *yšt]'bdwn* "they shall be subject to him" is highly questionable. Indeed, É. Puech's interpretation[66] as "to serve" must be incorrect since Aramaic never employs *'bd* in this manner. Instead, as long as only East Aramaic attests *š'bd*, one of the other possible emendations in the preceding lacunae is preferable, e.g., *y]'bdwn* "they [will d]o."[67]

IV. Noun "Work, Service." The verbal noun *'bydh* /'abīdā/ "work, service" is originally a feminine passive participle, but was probably no longer perceived as such, especially since it parallels the semantic spectrum of the noun /'abd/. It already appears beginning with the late Old Aramaic proverbs of Aḥiqar in the later widely employed usage as the object of the verb *'bd* "to perform a task,"[68] likewise l. 21, *TADAE* B2.4:10 and A6.7:9, presumably also in A4.1:5 (in reference to the prohibition against working

52. *TADAE* B3.1:10; 3.13:11; in property lists.
53. Cf. *TADAE* A6. 3:7; B8.7:5.
54. *TADAE* C1.1:178f.
55. Sales contracts from Samaria.
56. Often as a title in seal and other inscriptions on objects, see Schwiderski, 624.
57. Perhaps 1QapGen 22:6.
58. *KAI* 224.13.
59. *KAI* 216.3; 217.4; 266.1,6,8; → *mlk*.
60. Father: *TADAE* A2.1:13; 2.4:1; superior: A4.7:1,4,22; king: Dnl. 2:4,7; Ezr. 4:11.
61. Dnl. 3:26,28; 6:21; Ezr. 5:11; 4Q213a 2:8,10.
62. E.g., *'bd ngw* for an original *'bdnbw* "servant of Nabu" in Dnl. 2:49; 3:30; cf. *ATTM*, 650 and 2, 449.
63. Literally "boy."
64. *DJBA*, 1166f.; *LexSyr*, 506; *MdD*, 2; *ATTM*, 650.
65. *Dictionary of Qumran Aramaic* (Winona Lake, IN, 2015), s.v. *'bd*.
66. *DJD*, XXII (1996), 167.
67. *DSSStE*, 492f.
68. *TADAE* C1.1:127, in parallel with *kṣr kṣyr* "to harvest a crop"; l. 207 is fragmentary, but seems to refer to the different lifestyles of the Phoenicians and the Arabs.

on the festival; partially destroyed). With the marker of existence, *ʾyty ʿbydh l-* means "to have something to create."[69] In the construct state, it refers to "work on": Ezr. 4:24; 5:8 (with *ʿbd*); 6:7 "construction on"; Ezr. 6:18 "worship"; Dnl. 2:49; 3:12 to service in the royal administration, as in the court novella 4Q550 1:3; 2:7; 4:2. The supposed meaning "worker" is uncertain.[70]

V. Noun "Act, Action." Only post-Achaemenid Aramaic attests *ʿbd* /ʿobād/ "action," especially in the plene spelling *ʿwbd* at Qumran, where the word occurs regularly. There it mostly denotes, not an accomplishment, like *ʿbydh*, but, similar to → *ʾrḥ* II.2 the manner of action or the behavior.[71] It sometimes occurs together with a negative term such as *šqr* "lie,"[72] *ḥšyk* "dark,"[73] or *qšh* "gruesome"[74] for the misdeeds that reveal the corrupt character of a being, but also positively for action rooted in holiness and truth.[75] In addition, it can refer to the regular behavior of nature[76] and to the established sacrificial procedures.[77] In 11Q10, it once represents *mʿbd*, which was probably borrowed from Aramaic (25:2 [Job 34:25], → VI), otherwise the authentically Hebrew *pʿl*.[78] Finally, in building inscriptions, it denotes "construction."[79]

VI. Verbal Noun "Deed." Less common in older Aramaic is the verbal noun *mʿbd* /maʿbād/ "deed," which can be distinguished by context from the infinitive of the verb *mʿbd* /maʿbad/, which is identical in a consonantal spelling. It has no specific nuance: in Dnl. 4:34 the plural denotes God's majestic demonstrations of power; in 4Q201 1 4:5 (1 En. 8:3), the misdeeds that humans learned, to their undoing, from the fallen angels; and in 4Q542 1 1:2, God's creation in a genitive construction with → *mrʾ*.[80] Jason's epitaph,[81] if this interpretation is correct, seems to employ it for "construction," supporting the interpretation above of 4Q542 1 I 2 as "manufactured." The word then appears in East Aramaic with the very specific connotation "magical deed."[82]

Gzella

69. *TADAE* A6.15:9.

70. See *DNSI*, 820; even in 4Q544 1:2 par. 4Q545 1a-b 2:15, it may mean simply "work"; *WDSP* 10.5 and 12.6 are fragmentary.

71. 1QapGen 5:11,22; 6:11; 21:5; 4Q201 1 2:12 (1 En. 5:4); 4Q534 1 2+2: 15; 4Q536 2 2:13.

72. 4Q212 1 4:14 (1 En. 91:11).

73. 4Q544 2,14.

74. 4Q531 2+3:8.

75. 4Q213 1 1:6; 4Q545 4:16.

76. 4Q204 1 1:18,20 (1 En. 2:1f.); 4Q201 1 2:10 (1 En. 5:1).

77. 4Q214 2,10.

78. 11Q10 27:3; 28:1; 29:2 (Job 36:9,24; 37:12).

79. *ATTM*, 651.

80. So probably correctly *ATTM*, 2, 116; "lord of all works" according to *DSSStE*, 1083 would correspond to the otherwise common expression, but is less than convincing in this context.

81. *ATTM*, 329, l. 3.

82. *DJBA*, 693; *LexSyr*, 505; *MdD*, 238.

עבר ʿbr; עבר ʿbr /ʿebr/; מעבר mʿbr /maʿbar/; עבור ʿbwr /ʿebbūr/

I. Etymology and Lexical Field. II. Verb. 1. G-stem "to Cross." 2. Causative-stem "to Convey." III. Noun "Something Beyond." IV. Rare Noun Forms.

I. Etymology and Lexical Field. All branches of the Semitic languages know forms of the verbal root *ʿbr* "to pass through, over," including Aramaic and the other languages of Syria-Palestine. Beginning at Qumran, the verb is well attested, appears mostly in the transitive or intransitive G-stem, and with a living subject literally denotes the movement of "going through, passing over, passing by," and is, therefore, more specific than → *hlk*/*hūk* and *ʾzl* "to go." Less often, it appears figuratively for the transgression of commandments or for "to disappear."[1] In descriptions of places, it occurs with geographical terms for "to extend." Depending on the nuance, prepositional supplements may accompany it, such as *b-* "to pass by" or *l-* "to extend toward." Less common is the transitive C-stem "to bring over." Jewish Palestinian and Jewish Babylonian, however, attest the D-stem in this and a few other nuances,[2] while Syriac and others retain the C-stem.[3] All stems form a t-passive.

The most common nominal form of this root is the masculine /ʿebr/[4] "opposite side (i.e., of a river, etc.)." Since the Achaemenid period, it functioned generally as part of the place name *ʿbr nhrʾ* "beyond the river" for Syria-Palestine (→ III). Other, although substantially more rare, derivatives include the likewise masculine nouns /maʿbar/ "ford" and /ʿebbūr/ "intercalation" (with calendrical expressions), attested only later.

So far, no relationship has been established between the verbal root *ʿbr* and the masculine /ʿabūr/ "grain," well-attested beginning with Imperial Aramaic in legal and commercial texts.[5] It probably involves a word with a still unclear etymology and the original meaning "harvest."[6] Aramaic does not attest the homonymous Hebrew root *ʿbr* II "to be angry, to grumble"[7] with certainty (→ II.2).

II. Verb. As a verb, *ʿbr* in the G-stem "to cross over" may already appear in Imperial or even later Old Aramaic, but the similarity between *r* and *d* does not permit a confident

---

H.-J. Fabry, "*ʿbr* I," *ThWQ*, III, 11-17; H. F. Fuhs, "עָבַר *ʿaḇar*," *TDOT*, X, 408-25; H.-P. Stähli, "עבר *ʿbr* to pass by, pass over," *TLOT*, 832-35.

1. → *ʿdī*.
2. *DJPA*, 394b; *DJBA*, 840f.
3. *LexSyr*, 509a.
4. Later with anaptyxis /ʿebar/, see *ATTM*, 107,114.
5. See the instances in D. Schwiderski, *Die alt- und reichsaramäischen Inschriften*, vol. I: *Konkordanz*. *FSBP* 2 (2008), 628f., then also in 1QapGen 11:12, probably to be reconstructed in 19:10, and in later Aramaic languages: *DJPA*, 393a; *DJBA*, 840a; *LexSyr*, 509; *MdD*, 340.
6. Cf. S. A. Kaufman, *The Akkadian Influences on Aramaic*. *AS* 19 (1974), 47.
7. See K.-D. Schunck, "עֶבְרָה *ʿeḇrâ*," *TDOT*, X, 425-30.

distinction from *'bd* "to make, to do,"[8] especially not in the fragmentary context of the oldest possible instances.[9] The same is true for the difficult expression at the beginning of the unidiomatic Aśoka inscription *KAI* 279.1.[10] The verb first definitely appears in Aramaic texts from Qumran. The oldest absolutely certain instance of the C-stem "to bring over" also appears, after one disputed Old Aramaic instance, at Qumran.

1. G-stem "to Cross." Because of the broad spectrum of usage, the precise nuance of *'br* essentially depends on the context, but it always denotes a movement in a specific direction. For the terminative "to arrive, to reach," in contrast, Aramaic employs → *mṭī*, 1QapGen notably → *dbq*. In 4Q243 12:3, with persons as the subject, it refers to the crossing of the Jordan River, which follows the suffixed infinitive *m'brhwn* "its crossing" here as a direct object. Metaphorically, it serves in religio-ethical speech for the transgression of divine laws.[11] An additional form of *'br* may appear in 4Q201 1 2:1 (1 En. 2:1) in reference to the stars, which do not leave their fixed courses.[12]

The apocalyptic terminology of the book of Enoch employs the verb with heaven as a subject to mean "to disappear"[13] in an expansion of the literal meaning "to pass over," as it appears in 4Q213 1-2 2:18 negated in reference to an eternal kingdom or priesthood (the subject is lost in the lacuna in the preceding text) with *mn* "from." According to *ATTM*, 2, 97, it also occurs with a similar nuance at the end of 1QapGen 13:16 in reference to a wind.[14]

Contrariwise, with a geographical term like a boundary (*tḥwm*), *'br* denotes "to pass through"[15] or with a section of land (*ḥwlq*) "to extend toward (*l-*)."[16]

Other idiomatic usages, such as *'br 'l* "to come over someone" in 4Q545 la 1:4, are uncertain.[17] Similarly, Beyer reads a Gt-stem *yt'br* "it will run out" in 4Q198 1:5 (Tob. 14:4), while others prefer *yt'bd* "will happen."[18] Regarding 4Q343, → II.2.

2. Causative-stem "to Convey." Outside Aramaic proper, the C-stem of *'br* "to convey" already appears in Sam'alian in the eighth century B.C.E. where both the morphology and the context confirm it.[19] The earliest possible Old Aramaic specimen is *KAI* 224.17

8. Cf. *DNSI*, 822.

9. *TADAE* C1.1:98,182; D7.12:10; 7.19:3; 7.24:4,10; in addition, four other passages in the Clermont-Ganneau ostraca also come into question, see H. Lozachmeur, *La collection Clermont-Ganneau* (Paris, 2006), 1:543, s.v.

10. Donner and Röllig, however, read *'byd* "has been done" here.

11. 4Q204 5 2:18 (1 En. 106:13); it may be that 4Q201 1 2:13 (1 En. 5:4) should be emended *t'*]*brwn* "you transgress," but with *ATTM*, 233 better *t*]*mrwn* "you say."

12. Cf. *DSSStE*, 400. *ATTM*, 233 does not recognize any letters here.

13. 4Q212 1 4:23f. (1 En. 91: 16).

14. Beyer's reading contra Fitzmyer and others is correct, as confirmed by the photo; cf. D. A. Machiela, *The Dead Sea Genesis Apocryphon*. *STDJ* 79 (2009), 59.

15. 1QapGen 16:11,18.

16. 1QapGen 17:10,17.

17. See R 1:4 in *ATTM*, 2, 118. *DSSStE*, 1088f., does not read the word *'br* here.

18. For Beyer's reading see *ATTM*, 2, 185. For *yt'bd*, see for example *DSSStE*, 394f.

19. *KAI* 215.18, of a corpse; for the classification, cf. P. M. Noorlander, "Sam'alian in Its Northwest Semitic Setting," *Or* 81 (2012) 202-38.

from Sefire. In the context, *yʿbrnh* may very plausibly mean "and he removed him" (i.e., the successor to the throne from his position) and is grammatically possible as an early phonetic spelling without /-h-/.[20] To be sure, a form of *ʿbr* II "to be angry" merits consideration,[21] but this root is unusual later in Aramaic.

Furthermore, the form *yʿbr* with the added phrase *lydyk* in a letter in Nabatean script circa the birth of Christ[22] may be added and translated "and he will be transferred into your hands."[23] Contrarily, *ATTM*, 2, 450[24] assumes a G-stem with the meaning "to pass over (into someone's hands)" when, however, one would expect, in light of other Aramaic texts, *npl* with the nuance "to fall to."[25] Since almost nothing of the broader context survives and cannot be reconstructed from parallels, no decision can be made.

Meanwhile, only the internal passive of the C-stem in 4Q206 1 26:20 (1 En. 32:3) "to be brought over" can be considered assured for older Aramaic. It appears in the report of Enoch's heavenly journey.

III. Noun "Something Beyond." In Biblical Aramaic, the root occurs only in the form of the noun /ʿebr/ (> /ʿebar/) in the toponym *ʿbr nhrʾ* "Beyond the River" (Ezr. 4:10f.,16f.,20; 5:3,6; 6:6,8,13; 7:21,25). Since Achaemenid times, it was the official name of Syria-Palestine,[26] which the official style of the book of Ezra also employs. Furthermore, it appears on coins from Cilicia.[27] Later, the word appears in compound prepositions meaning "beyond."[28]

IV. Rare Noun Forms. Of the other nouns, *mʿbr* /maʿbar/ "ford"[29] may already occur in 1QapGen 11:9 according to *ATTM*, 2, 94, but the reading is disputed.[30] Gravestones from Zoar[31] contain additional instances of *ʿbwr* /ʿebbūr/ "leap year"[32] and Jewish Palestinian and Jewish Babylonian have the D-stem of the verb.[33] Later, West and East Aramaic literary diction attests further noun forms from the lexical field of crossing.[34]

Gzella

---

20. Cf. *yskr* "he will deliver" instead of *yhskr* in l. 3.
21. Bibliography in J. A. Fitzmyer, *The Aramaic Inscriptions of Sefire. BietOr* 19/A (^{2}1995), 155f.; cf. further *DNSI*, 821f.
22. 4Q343 7, actual site of origin unclear.
23. See A. Yardeni in *DJD*, XXVII (1997), 286-88.
24. Under nV 71:7.
25. → *npl* III.2.
26. As in Heb., imitated in Akk. as *eber nāri*; → *nhr* III.2.
27. *DNSI*, 823.
28. *DJPA*, 393f.
29. See *DJPA*, 321b.
30. See Machiela, 53.
31. 11:7 and 21:6 in *ATTM*, 2, 301-9.
32. I.e., of 13 months; *DJPA*, 402a.
33. *DJPA*, 394b; *DJBA*, 841.
34. *DJPA*, 393a; *DJBA*, 841f.; *LexSyr*, 508f.

עדי *ʿdī*; עדי *ʿdy* /ʿady/(?); עדינה *ʿdynh* /ʿedyānā/

I. Etymology and Lexical Field. II. G-stem "to Go Away." 1. Old and Imperial Aramaic. 2. Biblical Aramaic. 3. Qumran. III. Causative-stem "to Take Away." IV. Noun "Payout." V. Possible Noun "Pregnancy."

I. Etymology and Lexical Field. Aramaic *ʿdī*, in the G-stem "to go away," developed from an older, common West Semitic root **ʿdū* with cognates in Ugaritic, Arabic, Old South Arabian, and a few Ethiopian Semitic languages.[1] In contrast, the two Hebrew instances[2] are probably borrowed from Aramaic, but that cannot be demonstrated with certainty. Although plausible, there is no etymological relation to the homonymous root *ʿdī* II "to adorn (oneself)," well-known in Hebrew,[3] which is apparently not native to Aramaic.

Old Aramaic already attests the root *ʿdī* "to go away," which remains productive throughout older Aramaic. Its distribution in royal representation texts, official correspondence, private documents, and religious literature, indicates that it belongs to the register of literary language; at the same time, it has points of contact with the semantic spectrum of various colloquial verbs. The G-stem usually functions as a transitive for "to go away," negated, often to designate imperishability, and, with an abstract subject, to mean "to cease." Consequently, it overlaps with the use of *ʿbr* "to pass over" in the same sense,[4] with the frequent verb → *sūp*, and with *bṭl*. As a verb of motion, *ʿdī* takes the supplement *mn* "from" and expresses the additional nuance "to come, to arrive at (*b*-)" (→ II), which → *mṭī* usually expresses.[5] In a few Old and Imperial Aramaic instances, however, the verb seems to serve intransitively for "to pass over" and, thus, to correspond exactly to *ʿbr*.

Contrariwise, the transitive C-stem has the meaning "to take away, remove" and occurs with concrete or abstract objects. It seems more often to have specifically juridical or constitutional legal connotations. The preposition *mn* "from" may accompany it. With this nuance, the root denotes a verbal act of high transitivity and, thus, forms a t-passive of the C-stem "to be removed," as one might expect. Mostly, however, the very

---

F. M. Cross, "An Aramaic Inscription from Daskyleion," *BASOR* 184 (1966) 7-10; I. Ephʿal and J. Naveh, "Hazael's Booty Inscriptions," *IEJ* 39 (1989) 192-200; J. A. Fitzmyer, *The Genesis Apocryphon of Qumran Cave 1 (1Q20)*. *BietOr* 18B (^{3}2004); J. Naveh and S. Shaked, *Aramaic Documents from Ancient Bactria (Fourth Century B.C.E.)* (London, 2012).

1. Cf. *GesB*[18], 924 for references on etymology; more extensively treated in J. A. Thompson, "Expansions of the עד Root," *JSS* 10 (1965) 227-29, although only useful for its collection of materials.

2. G-stem "to step" in Job 28:8; C-stem "to remove" in Prov. 25:20.

3. See H. Madl, "עָדָה *ʿaḏâ*," *TDOT*, X, 462-68.

4. → *ʿbr* II.1; cf. also Hebrew *lʾ yʿbr* "will not perish" in Est. 1:19 and 8:8 with the Aramaic *lʾ yʿdh* in Dnl. 7:14.

5. In 1QapGen, however, → *dbq* instead.

general verb *lqḥ* "to take,"[6] and less often, → *nṣl* "to snatch away" or, in older phases of the language → *nśī* "to lift up, to take away" fulfilled this function. The very general verb usually denotes "to take away" in the everyday sense, however. Jewish Babylonian preserves the C-stem of *'dī* only as an archaism, however, and has otherwise given way to the D-stem "to remove," "to cast."[7]

The related masculine noun *'dy* "payout" also belongs to technical legal diction and occurs in some Nabatean private documents.[8] Because of the final /-w/, which preserves the original third radical of the root, on the other hand, the noun *'dw* /'adw/ "garnishment" in another Nabatean contract[9] cannot be originally Aramaic, but stems from the Arabic. It would then belong to a native Nabatean legal tradition.

Finally, the feminine *'dynh* /'edyānā/ "pregnancy" occurs very rarely—if at all. It seems to be interchangeable with its synonym *hrywn* /heryōn/[10] and belongs to the nuance "to be pregnant" of the D-stem of *'dī* in later Jewish Palestinian.[11] The two possible instances in older Aramaic are disputed, however (→ V).

Syriac knows numerous additional noun forms, most of which have the common nuance "strange, strangeness."[12]

II. G-stem "to Go Away."

1. Old and Imperial Aramaic. The meaning of the verb *'dī* "to go away" seems to be less specific so that it occurs with widely varied nuances. In the earliest instance, the text of an Old Aramaic dedication gift on a horse bridle, it refers transitively to "crossing over" with a river as direct object[13] and, therefore, quite in analogy with *'br*. Something similar pertains to an Imperial Aramaic grave inscription from Dascyleion,[14] which addresses passers-by on the street.[15] Three additional instances from the Imperial Aramaic documents of the Bactrian archive have instead the typical meaning "to go away from [*mn*]."[16]

2. Biblical Aramaic. The post-Imperial Aramaic material attests an even broader usage. In Dnl. 3:27, *'dī* referring to the smell of smoke denotes "to reach," the preposition *b-* presumably designates the goal "to,"[17] thus, "to adhere to," for which, based on typical Aramaic diction, one would expect *mṭī* or *dbq*.[18] Otherwise in the book of Daniel, *'dī* has

---

6. → *nśī* V.
7. *DJBA*, 845a.
8. *ATTM*, 2, 451 posits /'adi/ (/-i/ would then have arisen from the /-y/), /'edi/, and /'adāy/ as options.
9. nV 42:2f.,5,11,13-16,23f. in *ATTM*, 2, 244-247; further partially reconstructed in nV 4:18: *ATTM*, 2, 415f.
10. From an older */huryān/, to *hrī* "to be pregnant," cf. *ATTM*, 137,564.
11. *DJPA*, 397a.
12. *LexSyr*, 511f.
13. *KAI* 311, Eph'al and Naveh; → *nhr* II.
14. *KAI* 318:3f., Cross.
15. With → *'rḥ* as object.
16. Naveh and Shaked, A2,1; C1,3,51, the latter also with *'l* "to" in reference to a person.
17. With the young men who escaped unscathed from the fiery furnace.
18. *LexLingAram*, 123 entertains the conjecture *'d bhwn* "was [not] yet in them"; the alternative

the nuance "to decay" and refers to the dominion that earthly kings can lose,[19] but the people of God cannot (7:14). This usage relates to the corresponding use of the C-stem in statements concerning God's power to install and depose kings at will (→ III). The negated verb also appears in Dnl. 6:9,13 in a formulaic expression for an inalterable law.[20]

3. *Qumran.* At Qumran, alongside the literal meaning "to go away,"[21] the figurative meaning "to pass away, disappear" predominates, as in 4Q536 2 2:13,[22] 4Q542 1 2:8,[23] and 4Q541 9 1:4.[24] The form *ʿd'*, which *ATTM*, 2, 97 reads as the penultimate word in 1QapGen 13:12 paralleling *sp*[25] "he decayed and perished," has the same meaning. The fragments of the letters are unclear, however, and other editors have instead translated "the water" as the subject of the verb *sp*.[26] In 11Q10 3:7 (Job 20:5) *lʿbʿ tʿd'* "it perishes soon" rather freely translates the Hebrew expression *ʿdy rgʿ* "only a moment," singular in this specific combination, presumably primarily because of the graphic similarity of the verb.

The legal diction of the Nabatean contracts from the Dead Sea knows the verb with the nuance "to become invalid," as in Dnl. 6:9,13 (→ II.2), either in the formulaic expression at the conclusion of a document, *yʿd' dyn l' brš'* "a decision will be invalid without a creditor"[27] or in other formulations.[28]

Finally, *ʿdī mn* appears in the *Megillat Taʿanit* in the sense "to depart from" in reference to a religious law.[29]

III. Causative-stem "to Take Away." In comparison to the G-stem, the C-stem "to take away, remove" has a more closely defined meaning. The oldest instance from the proverbs of Aḥiqar employs the verb with an abstract object in the admonition not to remove wisdom;[30] the narrative framework employs it similarly in reference to the "removal" of sin (l. 50). In the official petition from the Elephantine community to the Persian government, it denotes the destruction of the temple;[31] in legal diction, the theft of property;[32] and in the Memphis harbor registry, the removal of a boat.[33]

---

suggestion by K. Koch, *Daniel 1-4. BK* XXII/1 (2005), 255, "did [not] go out from them," would be difficult to defend linguistically.

19. 4:28 with *mn* in the sense of "to depart from."
20. → *dt*; → II.3 for the legal diction.
21. 1QapGen 20:27, with *mn* "from" and the *dativus ethicus* expressing ingressive action; see H. Gzella, *Tempus, Aspekt und Modalität im Reichsaramäischen. VOK* 48 (2004), 254.
22. Negated in reference to a preserved vision account.
23. Of the demise of the evildoers, like the typical → *'bd*.
24. Of the darkness, that is the sin and evil, that disappears in the eschaton; → *ḥšk* III.
25. → *sūp*.
26. So Fitzmyer, 88 and Machiela, 58.
27. *ATTM*, 2, nV 2:15; 3:46; 4:18; 43:22.
28. *ATTM*, 2, nV 7:2,32, in reference to an irrevocable donation; 9:6.
29. L. 35, text in *ATTM*, 354-58; the juridical usage "to become invalid," also in l. 10.
30. *TADAE* C1.1:146.
31. *TADAE* A4.7:6 par. 4.8:6.
32. *TADAE* B2.6:35; 3.11:13.
33. *TADAE* C3.8IIIA:3.

The book of Daniel applies this official diction to the terminology of political theology; here the verb refers to the retraction of secular sovereignty (Dnl. 5:20, with *mn* "from"; 7:12,26) by God who has authority over the kings (2:21).[34] It serves for God's eradication of evildoers in 1QapGen 11:13,[35] in 19:21 for "to take away."[36] 11Q10 34:4,6f. (Job 40:8,10f.) employs it freely for *prr*, *ʿdī*, and *pūṣ*.

The t-passive occurs in *TADAE* A6.6:3, but without sufficient context. Meanwhile, some assume a possible t-stem of the G- or C-stem for the reading *ytʿdwn* in 4Q548 1 2-2:11.[37] The probable meaning "they (the sons of darkness) will be removed" argues for a t-causative stem. Yet, the two interior letters of the word are unclear and there is no immediate context that could supply clues as to the intent; Beyer[38] suggests *ytqrwn* "they will be called." No conclusion is possible.

IV. Noun "Payout." *ʿdy* "payout" occurs in a few Nabatean contracts from the Dead Sea,[39] mostly along with the Arabic loanword *ḥlṣ* "payment."[40]

V. Possible Noun "Pregnancy." Beyer[41] interprets the paleographically indisputable word *ʿdynh* in the episode of Lamech and Bettenosh[42] as a feminine noun /ʿedyānā/ "pregnancy," for which, however, the same passage has *hrywn*;[43] it has a parallel in later Palestinian Targums.[44] Otherwise, however, it is associated with the noun *ʿdn* "arrogance,"[45] which is otherwise unattested in this form, and translated "joy, delight" like the Hebrew *ʿdnh*.[46] This second option better suits the context, but postulates an otherwise unknown word, while the first conforms to the Palestinian-Aramaic usage of *ʿdī* but does not explain the alternation between *ʿdynh* and *hrywn* for "pregnancy." Thus, the arguments are uncertain.

Gzella

---

34. Alongside the antonym *qūm* in the C-stem "to install"; → *mlk* IV.
35. With → *ʾbd*.
36. Regarding 7:19 → *sʿd* IV.
37. E.g., *DSSStE*, 1094.
38. R 5:11 in *ATTM*, 2, 120.
39. nV 1:18,28,33; 2:12; 3:38; 43:18; all in *ATTM*, 2.
40. *ATTM*, 2, 397.
41. *ATTM*, 167.
42. 1QapGen 2:9,14.
43. 1QapGen 2:1,15; in contrast, the two other instances in 5:7 and 6:1 are dubious, according to *ATTM*, 2, 90f.; see Machiela, 40,43.
44. *ATTM*, 2, 451.
45. 1QapGen 11:12, also "Eden" in Heb.
46. Fitzmyer, 130; Machiela, 35f., in contrast, fluctuates and has "desire" in l. 9 and "pregnancy" in l. 14.

עדן *'dn* /'eddān/

I. Root and Lexical Field. II. Imperial Aramaic. III. Biblical Aramaic. IV. Qumran.

I. Root and Lexical Field. Research manifests an increasing consensus linking the masculine substantive /'eddān/ "fixed time" with the common Semitic root **w'd* "to determine."[1] Nouns related to this root designate a specific and limited time span. Nonetheless, /'eddān/ need not refer to the exact moment of a specific event. In Akkadian, *adānu* (*adannu*) denotes a limitation of time or a fixed date, just like Aramaic /'eddān/. In Ugaritic, *'dt* and *m'd* refer to an assembly of deities that occurs on special occasions such as Kirta's celebration of his wife in the presence of the gods in *KTU* 1.15 II 7.11. The Hebrew *mō'ēḏ* also generally means "fixed time" in reference to a ritual or a procedure; the word *'ēḏā* denotes the religious community itself. Here, the concept of "time" has close ties with "holy time," i.e., the experience of the holy in the course of time through religious festivals and the seasons of the year. It differs from the spatial dimension as it appears in temples, sanctuaries, and sites of prayer.

Such a semantic development, however, cannot be demonstrated for the Aramaic /'eddān/; this word consistently has a purely chronological meaning. Its synonym → *zmn* expresses the chronological nuance even more clearly. The two occur together in Dnl. 2:21 and 7:12 (→ III). The temporal adverb *k't* "now" in a Sefire stele[2] represents an additional temporal term.[3] The form *k'n* occurs in Imperial Aramaic also in *TADAE* A4.7:3; the parallel version in 4.8:3 has *k't*. Both introduce a new topic.

II. Imperial Aramaic. Old Aramaic does not attest /'eddān/. Imperial Aramaic employs the word in various prepositional expressions with adverbial functions,[4] the most frequent of them with more than twenty certain examples in *bkl 'dn* "at any time," i.e., "ever," further in *b'dn zy* "at the time when, immediately" and *mn 'dn'* "since that time." Other examples are *bzk 'dn'* "at that time";[5] *l'dn 'ḥrwn* "at a later time" (l. 49); *kzy 'dn* "as soon as it passes."[6]

G. Brin, *The Concept of Time in the Bible and the Dead Sea Scrolls. STDJ* 39 (2001); H.-J. Fabry, "*y'd*," *ThWQ*, II, 181-91; M. Görg, "יָעַד *yā'aḏ*," *TDOT*, VI, 135-44; E. Jenni, "עֵת *'ēt* time," *TLOT*, 951-61; T. Kronholm, "עֵת *'eṯ*," *TDOT*, XI, 434-51; J. Naveh and S. Shaked, *Aramaic Documents from Ancient Bactria (Fourth Century* B.C.E.*)* (London, 2012); G. Sauer, "יעד *y'd* to appoint," *TLOT*, 551-54.

1. Cf. *ATTM*, 653.
2. *KAI* 224.24.
3. Cf. *ke'æṯ* in Ezr. 4:17 and *ke'ænæṯ* in Ezr. 4:10,11; 7:12.
4. Cf. the overview in D. Schwiderski, *Die alt- und reichsaramäischen Inschriften*, vol. I: *Konkordanz. FSBP* 2 (2008), 634.
5. *TADAE* C1.1:70, Aḥiqar.
6. *TADAE* B2.11:13 and in a satrap's letter from Bactria, Naveh and Shaked A4,6.

III. Biblical Aramaic. All thirteen specimens of the word in Biblical Aramaic, vocalized *ʿiddān*, occur in Daniel. Two of them appear in the adverbial expression *bᵉʿiddānā dī* "immediately" (3:5,15). In two others, it stands as a noun in the true sense, as in 2:8 where it designates the time that the dream interpreters want to gain,[7] and in 2:9 with "as soon as the time changes" in reference to a situation in which there is no need to hurry. Seven passages employ the noun in the sense of "year," that is for a full cycle of months. Thus, the expression *šiḇʿā ʿiddānīn* in Dnl. 4:13,20,22,29 (LXX 4:16,23,25,32) denotes the seven years of Nebuchadnezzar's insanity. The same usage appears three times in the indication of the period in 7:25 *ʿaḏ ʿiddān wᵉʿiddānīn ūp̄ᵉlaḡ ʿiddān* "for one year and two years and a half year." Furthermore, the word appears twice together with *zᵉmān* for time in its natural course, thus for the seasons of the year: 2:21 *ʿiddānayyā wᵉzimnayyā* "times and periods";[8] 7:12 *zᵉman wᵉʿiddān* "for a period and a time," i.e., a limited span of time. The underlying concept of time is inseparable from the belief that God establishes the time of a specific event. Thus, *ʿiddān* and *zᵉmān* express this idea. Ecclesiastes 3:1 employs the two Hebrew terms *ʿēṯ* and *zᵉmān* for this same idea.

In the Greek translations of the book of Daniel, καιρός consistently represents *ʿiddān* with the nuance "fixed moment." If the noun refers to the year, after all, the original Greek version (Old Greek, OG) of 4:16 (4:13 MT; OG does not have it in 4:20,22,29) renders it passably with ἔτος "year," while Theodotion (Th) has καιρός. In 7:25, however, both OG and Th translate καιρός. The adverbial expressions, in turn, have various counterparts: *bᵉʿiddānā dī* in 3:5 appears as ᾗ ἂν ὥρᾳ "at whatever time" Th, but as ὅταν "when" in OG. In 3:15 Th writes ὡς ἂν "if, when," OG employs ἅμα "immediately."

IV. Qumran. At Qumran, the word appears nineteen times, frequently in the adverbial expression *ʿd ʿdn dy* "until the moment in which; until," e.g., in 2Q24 4:19; 4Q534 1 1:4; 4Q546 9:5; 4Q554 3 3:20. Qumran also attests its use as a noun in the sense of "fixed time," however: *ʿdn ršyʿyn* "the time of the evildoers" (4Q536 2 2:13), *bʿdn qṣ* "the time of the end" (4Q558 28:1), *dynyn bʿdnyhn* "judgments at their times" (4Q568 1:1), *ʿdn ʿ[qt]ʾ* "the fixed time of oppression" (11Q10 31:1 [Job 38: 23]), and *ʿdn mwldhyn* "the time of their (i.e., the mountain goats and hinds) bearing" (11Q10 32:2 [Job 39:2]). The other instances resist precise definition because of their poorly preserved contexts.

Gianto

7. In Nebuchadnezzar's words, "to buy."
8. Cf. Acts 1:7; 1 Th. 5:1.

עור *ʿwr* /ʿūr/; אדר *ʾdr* /ʾedder/

I. Etymology and Lexical Field. II. Noun "Chaff." III. Noun "Threshing Floor."

I. Etymology and Lexical Field. The substantive *ʿwr* /ʿūr/ "chaff" may involve an Aramaic primary noun;[1] Hebrew employs the word *mōṣ*.[2] It occurs in older Aramaic only in the vision of the colossus with clay feet in Dnl. 2:35, but Syriac also attests it thereafter[3] as a feminine that may be related to the Arabic *ʿuwwār* "dust."[4] The masculine noun *ʾdr* /ʾedder/ "threshing floor" belongs to the same semantic field,[5] originally a *qittil*-form subsequently revocalized as /ʾeddar/.[6] In Dnl. 2:35 it appears with /ʿūr/, but also appears elsewhere in isolation. In any case, the exact paradigm in the Tiberian vocalization of the plural cannot be deduced from the construct state (*ʾiddᵉrē*) attested only here.

II. Noun "Chaff." The context of the sole instance of *ʿwr* in older Aramaic is the comparison in a dream vision of the statue pulverized[7] with a stone to chaff on a threshing floor in the summer (*whww kʿwr mn ʾdry qyṭ*). The statue of various metals, but with feet of mixed iron and clay, symbolizes four empires with diminishing worth, the latter weak because of a lack of internal unity, and the stone the kingdom of God that constitutes the conclusion of history. This vision pictures the reversal of circumstances: a single stone[8] smatters the colossus and itself grows into a mountain that fills the earth,[9] while the gigantic statue collapses into dust. The wind, however, carries the dust away,[10] so that it cannot be found anywhere. Thereby, all memory of the central concerns of the earthly kings who glorify their deeds in inscriptions also vanishes.[11] The formulation of the comparison alludes to the summer as the time of harvest and judgment.[12] Consequently, secular and divine power prove to be incommensurable.

III. Noun "Threshing Floor." Besides Dnl. 2:35 (→ II), *ʾdr* "threshing floor" also appears in debt instruments of the Neo-Assyrian period in the translation of the Akkadian expression *ina adri* "on (a) threshing floor," which establishes where the lent grain

---

H. Ringgren, "מֹץ *mōṣ*," *TDOT*, VIII, 464-65.

1. Cf. *BLA*, §511.
2. *GesB*[18], 719.
3. *LexSyr*, 517f.
4. Ibid.
5. Heb. has instead *gorœn*, *GesB*[18], 229f.
6. *ATTM*, 107,505.
7. → *dqq*.
8. → *ʾbn*.
9. → *ṭwr*.
10. → *nśʾ*.
11. → *ṣlm* III.
12. Cf. Am. 8:1f. and J. Hausmann, "קַיִץ *qayiṣ*," *TDOT*, XIII, 24f.

should be returned.[13] The word occurs further in an early Achaemenid lease agreement (515 B.C.E.)[14] in relation to the transportation of grain by ass. It continues in dispute, however, whether the Babylonian name of the twelfth month, /ʾadar/ (Feburary/March), is etymologically related as the "month of threshing."[15]

Gzella

13. V. Hug, *Altaramäische Grammatik der Texte des 7. und 6. Jh. s v. Chr*. *HSAO* 4 (1993) 23,26.
14. *TADAE* B1.1:13.
15. So P. Haupt, "Elul und Adar," *ZDMG* 64 (1910) 706; *ATTM*, 505 assumes separate lexemes.

עז *ʿz* /ʿezz/; צפיר *ṣpyr* /ṣapīr/

I. Etymology, Overview. 1. Goat. 2. Male Goat. II. Imperial Aramaic. III. Biblical Aramaic. IV. Qumran.

I. Etymology, Overview.

1. Goat. The initial form of the Semitic designation for goat in general and the female goat in particular was apparently */ʿanz/. The form */ʿinz/[1] also comes into question, although not only *ʿanz* in Arabic, which retains an accented *-i-* after ʿ at least in nominal forms, but also Akkadian *enzu, ezzu*[2] with regular *e-* < **ʿa-*,[3] and the early Canaanite instances of *ḫazzum* and *ḫazzatum*[4]—*ḫ* is the cuneiform spelling of ʿ—speak more for an old *a*.

The word may have originally been a collective, as suggested by the Old Canaanite *nomen unitatis ḫazzatum* (see above) and the Old South Arabian *ʿnz* "goats."[5] Even Old Arabic, where *ʿanz* denotes the female goat, preserves remnants of the *nomina unitatis* in

I. Eph'al and J. Naveh, *Aramaic Ostraca of the Fourth Century BC from Idumaea* (Jerusalem, 1996); E. Kautzsch, *Die Aramaismen im Alten Testament* (Halle, 1902); T. Nöldeke, *Compendious Syriac Grammar*, trans. James A. Crichton (Winona Lake, IN, 2001); D. Schwiderski, *Die alt- und reichsaramäischen Inschriften*, vol. I: *Konkordanz*. *FSBP* 2 (2008); W. von Soden, *Grundriss der akkadischen Grammatik*. *AnOr* 33 ([3]1995); A. Tal, *A Dictionary of Samaritan Aramaic*, 2 vols. (Leiden, 2000); M. Wagner, *Die lexikalischen und grammatikalischen Aramaismen im alttestamentlichen Hebräisch*. *BZAW* 96 (1966); H.-J. Zobel, "עֵז *ʿēz*," *TDOT*, X, 577-83.

1. *KBL*[3], 1757a.
2. *AHw*, I, 221f. "1. female goat, 2. goat generally," *CAD*, IV, 180f.
3. Von Soden, *GaG*, §9.
4. *AHw*, I, 339.
5. *BGMR*, 17; Biella, 373.

a figurative use.[6] Akkadian forms the plural mostly as a feminine, Ugaritic,[7] like Hebrew and Aramaic, as a masculine.

In Aramaic neither the reference to the gender of the designated animal—although most instances refer to female animals—nor (as in Hebrew) the grammatical gender is fixed. The construction as a feminine occurs twice in the Aramaic of the Aḥiqar text (fifth century B.C.E.) and once as a masculine on a third-century ostracon from Egypt.[8] Even the genitive phrase *ṣᵉpīrē ʿizzīm* "male goats" (Ezr. 6:17) employs *ʿēz* generically.

The later Aramaic forms[9] of the pointed texts[10] consistently have *ʿizz* as the ground form, with an assimilated *n* and *i* before an accented ending, whether under the influence of the sibilant,[11] or because the singular absolute was formed anew from the other forms with an accented ending by omitting the ending. The Syriac construct *ʿnez* still exhibits the *n* radical.[12]

2. *Male Goat.* The Aramaic word for male goat, first attested in the OT and at Qumran, may have been pronounced /ṣapīr/ before the loss of the short vowel.[13] With the sole exception of Hebrew, where it has the same pronunciation, there are no assured counterparts in other Semitic languages. Consequently, and in view of the passages in which it occurs (Dnl. 8:5,8,21; Ezr. 8:35; 2 Ch. 29:21), it seems likely that Hebrew borrowed the word from Aramaic.[14] Later dialects[15] also have a feminine *ṣpyrh*[16] or *ṣpyrtʾ* for the female animal in addition to *ṣpyr* "ram." Syriac has in *ṣep̄rāyā*[17] another form of the same root with an ending formally equivalent to the nisba, as often happens with animal designations;[18] a counterpart to *ṣprytʾ* appears in an eleventh century Babylonian text;[19] Mandean lacks the word entirely.

The equally late[20] attested *tayš* "male goat"[21] is not clearly distinct semantically; *gadǣ* < **gady* denotes only the young male animal.

---

6. Lane, 2173.
7. ʿz, *DUL*³, 193.
8. *TADAE* D7.57; cf. *DNSI*, 875 ("subst. f. goat") with literature on the question concerning whether the word also denotes male goats.
9. Regarding Sam., cf. Tal, 630 "n.f.; female goat."
10. *WTM*, 207, Dalman, 309, *DJBA*, 852 "n.fem.," *DJPA*, 401 "n. goat" with no indication of gender.
11. *ATTM*, 116.
12. *LexSyr*, 535.
13. *BLA*, §188h, *ATTM*, 677.
14. Kautzsch, 75, Wagner, 248.
15. Dalman, 367, *DJPA*, 469, *DJBA*, 970 only feminine.
16. Sam. Tal, 742b.
17. With the feminine *ṣep̄rāytā*.
18. Nöldeke, 83 §137.
19. *DJBA*, 971.
20. First in 1Q23, ca. first century B.C.E., and Syriac.
21. Hebrew *tayiš*, Arabic *tays*.

II. Imperial Aramaic. Older Aramaic does not attest /ṣapīr/. Of the eight assured (with an additional four reconstructions) Imperial Aramaic instances of */ʿanz, ʿinz/ "goat," all still spelled with the nonassimilated *n*, only the most recent instance, a fourth century B.C.E. ostracon from Tell ʿIra in Israel,[22] may exhibit forms both with and without assimilation, although one is reconstructed and the other uncertain in reading and interpretation.

The assured specimens are singular forms, four times the absolute *ʿnz* and four times the determined *ʿnzʾ*.[23]

Absolute: *TADAE* A4.10,10: "and sheep, cattle, and goat will not be offered (literally, "made") as a whole-offering (*mqlw*), but incense and . . . -offering"; *TADAE* D7.1:10, a letter: "In the morning, I will go home, and they will give you a goat before I come to you"; ostracon *TADAE* D7.57:5, a letter (third century B.C.E., Egypt): "And now, I send you via the brother of *TM* (a name), the wife of *Mlkyh br ʿzgd* a goat [*ʿnz ḥd*]"; Idumea ostracon Ephʿal and Naveh 72f. (fourth century B.C.E., Palestine):[24] "the skin of a goat."

Determined: *TADAE* C1.1:166f. (proverbs of Aḥiqar) three times:[25] "the leopard met/touched the goat and she [*hy*] was freezing/naked [*ʿryh*], the leopard raised up and said to the goat, 'Come [*ʾty*]! . . .' The goat raised up and said to the leopard"; l. 209, a partially damaged context, but again feminine: "and the goat[s] raised up (*ʿnt*). . . ."[26]

III. Biblical Aramaic. There is only one (common) occurrence of both words, goat and male goat, in a sort of dually expressed plural[27] *ṣᵉpīrē ʿizzīm* "billy goats" in a sacrifice list (Ezr. 6:17): "And, to dedicate this house of God, they brought one hundred steers, two hundred rams, four hundred lambs, and, as a sin offering for all Israel, twelve male goats according to the number of the tribes of Israel."

IV. Qumran. Qumran offers no instance of *ʿz* "goat." There are two instances of *ṣpyr* "male goat" in 4Q156 2:5 and 2:6; the fragment translates Lev. 16:20f. and belongs to the oldest preserved Targum (ca. 150 B.C.E.). Twice, partially emended or difficult to read—both in a destroyed context—one finds *ṣpyrʾ ḥyʾ* "living male goat" for the Hebrew *ʾæṯ-haśśāʿīr hæḥāy*, "the living male goat" or *ʿal rōš haśśāʿīr haḥay* "(will place both of his hands) on the head of the living male goat."

Hug

---

22. Schwiderski, Ira:2(4),1.
23. All fifth through third centuries, mostly from Egypt, once from Palestine.
24. = Schwiderski, IdOstrEN:151.
25. Construed as a feminine.
26. Regarding the context → *nmr*.
27. Cf. *KBL*³, 1757a.

עזקה ʿzqh /ʿezqā/

I. Etymology and Lexical Field. II. Usage.

I. Etymology and Lexical Field. There is no agreement concerning the etymology of the feminine noun *ʿzqh* /ʿezqā/ "signet ring." It is not possible to establish that it was borrowed from Akkadian,[1] but a relationship with the Semitic root **ʿzq* "to break open, to dig" (perhaps via "to push in"?) may be possible, nonetheless.[2] The lexical field includes → *ḥtm* "to seal."

II. Usage. The signet ring is the paradigmatic mark of official authority. The milieu of the royal court also constitutes the origin of the themes of the oldest Aramaic literature.[3] The diction of Achaemenid administration was simultaneously the foundation of narrative prose that defined the form and motifs of novelistic stories that mirrored the tension in early diaspora Judaism between integration into world politics and its own cultural traditions.[4] Thus, the royal signet ring traces as a fixed element from the early narrative framework of Aḥiqar via the court narratives of Daniel to the diaspora novellas from Qumran.

The Achaemenid period first attests *ʿzqh*. Among the Imperial Aramaic documentary texts, it occurs twice in letters from Egypt, once in a fragmentarily preserved official writing of unknown contents[5] in the expression *bʿzqt* in the construct state with a subsequent personal name "with the signet (ring) of PN," and again as a plural *bʿzktyh* (scribal error) in a later ostracon with the shipping note for a sealed jug.[6]

The other specimens come from literature. In the account of the fate of the high Assyrian official Aḥiqar, *ṣbyt ʿzqth* "keeper of his (i.e., the king's) signets"[7] belongs among the main character's titles (ll. 3,60) and those of his designated successor (l. 19). The title denotes the high position in the imperial administration and the confidence that a royal signet-bearer enjoyed.

Daniel 6:18, then, deals with the function of the signet ring: the king seals with (*b-*) his own ring and that of his nobles the stone at the opening of the lions' den; the verb is → *ḥtm*. The intention is to rule out the possibility for Daniel to receive external aid,[8] which proves that his survival through the assistance of an angel was a miracle.

H. Gzella, *A Cultural History of Aramaic*. *HO* 111 (2015); S. A. Kaufman, *The Akkadian Influences on Aramaic*. *AS* 19 (1974).

1. See Kaufman, 61 n. 142.
2. Cf. *GesB*[18], 947.
3. See Gzella, 150-53.
4. Ibid., 201-8; 230-34.
5. *TADAE* A5.1:6.
6. *TADAE* D7.57:7.
7. *TADAE* C1.1:3,19,60, all three instances admittedly partially emended but hardly doubtful.
8. Cf. LXX.

The tradition of the court novella continues in texts from Qumran. 4Q196 2:7 (Tob. 1:22) explicitly establishes Tobit's relationship with Aḥiqar, whose title here is *rb 'zqn* "signet master," and situates the material via this reminiscence into the broader corpus of Aramaic literature. Another story that plays out among the Persian kings employs *'zqh*, again with the preposition *b-* modifying the verb *ḥtm*, to denote a scroll sealed sevenfold by Darius.[9]

A magical text from late antiquity employs *b'zqth dšlmh* "by the signet ring of Solomon"[10] in an apotropaic formula. The noun continues in use in later Aramaic literary languages.[11] The verb *'zq* "to seal"[12] instead of the old *ḥtm* presumably derives from the noun.

Gzella

9. 4Q550 1:5.
10. ggAR 1:2 in *ATTM.E*, 250.
11. *DJBA*, 853a; *LexSyr*, 519; *MdD*, 348,354.
12. *DJBA*, 850a.

עין *'yn* /'ayn/; נבע *nb'*; עור *'ūr*; שכן *škn* /šekn/; בבה *bbh* /bābā/

I. Forms and Lexical Field. II. As a Body Part of Human Beings. III. In Prepositional Phrases with *b-*, *k-*, *l-*.

I. Forms and Lexical Field. As the designation for a body part present in pairs, the common Semitic noun *'yn* /'ayn/ "eye" is feminine in gender. In Aramaic, where at the latest circa 200-150 B.C.E. it was consistently revocalized /'ēn/ with the monophthong,[1] it appears predominantly in the construct state or with suffixes. On into post-Christian times, the dual[2] with the meaning "eye" generally represented the plural but was mostly unrecognizable as such since, in the construct and thus also before suffixes, the dual and plural are identical in form. Consequently, the consonantal text of Dnl. 7:8,20 *'ynyn* still reflects the original dual /'aynayn/, but was vocalized in the pointing, which no longer recognized this old form, as a plural *'aynīn*.[3]

T. Hansberger, "*'yn*," *ThWQ*, III, 98–104; E. Jenni and D. Vetter, "עַיִן *'ayin* eye," *TLOT*, 874-80; F. J. Stendebach, "עַיִן *'ayin*," *TDOT*, XI, 28-44; M. Weigl, *Die aramäischen Achikar-Sprüche aus Elephantine und die alttestamentliche Weisheitsliteratur*. *BZAW* 399 (2010).

1. *ATTM*, 116-20.
2. Absolute *'ynyn*, *TADAE* C1.1:157,212,214.
3. So, correctly, *BLA*, §54e.

In contrast, the word when used for "spring" takes the feminine plural.[4] This second meaning is rare in Aramaic and occurs before Palmyrene[5] and the literary languages of late antiquity[6] only as part of sparsely transmitted place names such as En-Dina "Spring of Justice,"[7] there in the singular, however.[8] Instead of it, the texts from the Dead Sea attest two forms of the root *nbʿ* "to bubble" for "spring" following /maʿyān/,[9] /nebaʿ/,[10] and /mabbūʿ/,[11] which continue to occur later.[12]

In the typical sense of "eye," *ʿyn* regularly appears in set phrases. Besides the usage with certain verbs such as → *nṭl* "to lift" or → *ptḥ*[13] "to open," it appears with particular frequency in prepositional expressions with *b-* "in the judgment of" or *l-* "before the eyes of" (→ III).

The broader lexical field includes the verb → *ḥzī* "to see" and the noun /ʿawār/ "blindness"[14] with the corresponding adjective /ʿawīr/ "blind"[15] and with the verb *ʿūr* "to blind."[16] The eye has a /šekn/ "lid" and a /bābā/ "pupil" (→ II).

II. As a Body Part of Human Beings. Expressly for the body part—of humans and of gods—*ʿyn* "eye" appears in older Aramaic only in nondocumentary texts. The oldest instance occurs in a state treaty from Sefire in an appeal to the gods as watchful guarantors of the agreement established in the text: *pqḥ ʿynykm lḥzyh ʿdy* "open your eyes in order to regard the treaty of. . . ."[17] Thereafter, the pre-Achaemenid proverbs of Aḥiqar employ the term frequently in statements concerning behavior between people and its foundation in religious ethics. The admonition to discretion, since "their" (with no antecedent) eyes and ears are ubiquitous (*kzy bkl ʾtr ʿ[yny]hm w ʾdnyhm*),[18] suits—as the figure Daniel must also often experience—the life of the court official in which these sayings presumably have roots.[19] Eyes and ears[20] also appear in l. 157 in the very com-

4. *ATTM*, 447; cf. *PAT* 0259 ii.58: *ʿynn trtn* "two springs."
5. *PAT*, 395f.
6. *DJPA*, 404a; *DJBA*, 857a; *LexSyr*, 522; *MdD*, 15.
7. 1QapGen 21:30.
8. Regarding 16:17, → III.
9. *KAI* 222 A 12, as a numen.
10. nV 1:22; 2:6,26; 3:29; as an emendation in 43:8; all in a formulaic juridical expression for "source of money," *ATTM*, 2, 437.
11. 4Q531 4:1, without context; according to E. Puech, *DJD*, XXXI (2001), 188, the reading of 4Q537 24:1 is entirely uncertain.
12. *DJPA*, 289a; *DJBA*, 639a; *LexSyr*, 412.
13. Rarely *pqḥ*.
14. 4Q245 2:3, paralleling *ṭʿw* "error" (→ *ḥṭī* V) and metaphorically for error.
15. *TADAE* C1.1:212, presumably also in B8.11:5.
16. *KAI* 222 A 39, an inner passive of the C-stem; later employed in the D-stem.
17. *KAI* 222 A 13; cf. the parallel formulation in an appeal to God in 2 K. 6:20; 19:16; Isa. 37:17; Dnl. 9:18.
18. *TADAE* C1.1,81.
19. Cf. Weigl, 84-86 for similar admonitions from biblical wisdom literature.
20. "Good," therefore "sharp," → *ṭb* III.1.

mon parallelism,[21] but with no clear context. Raising the eyes[22] together with giving the heart[23] seems to denote the demonstration of benevolence and trust (l. 105) apparently also central in the same milieu.

Aḥiqar also states that *ʿyny ʾlhn ʿl ʾn[šʾ* "the eyes of the gods [rest] on human bings" (l. 172). Biblical diction also employs this formulation frequently,[24] although its precise significance in these passages remains unclear because, first, the end of the clause has been lost and, second, the relation to the context has not been explained: if one relates the statement as the conclusion of a chiastic contrast with the preceding text,[25] the gods' glance signifies good for human beings; if, contrariwise, one links it to the subsequent saying,[26] it could emphasize that no sin goes unnoticed. Two additional instances[27] do not preserve sufficient context.

Biblical Aramaic takes up such usages in older epigraphical material. The motif of the "eye of God"[28] appears in Ezr. 5:5 as an expression of the divine protection over[29] the elders of the Jews so that the construction of the temple could proceed undisturbed. In Dnl. 4:31, the raising of the eyes serves to express devotion to God.[30] With apocalyptic imagery, however, new usages also appear: in the vision of the animals as an image for the four empires, the "eyes like human eyes" of the "little horn" of the last being (Dnl. 7:8,20)[31] accentuate its particularly eerie nature with no counterpart whatsoever in the range of human experience.[32]

With the texts from Qumran, the known spectrum of usage expands yet again. Raising the eyes serves once here, as in Dnl 4:31, as a prayer gesture,[33] in another instance, ingressively for gazing.[34] Furthermore, eyes serve as a characteristic of the beauty of extraordinary people.[35] Similarly, they are considered the seat of sleep.[36] A priestly prophecy mentions a "pupil [*bbh*] of his eye,"[37] but without context. In Enoch's animal allegory, the opening (*ptḥ*) of the eyes[38] represents divine revelation. Finally, 11Q10 renders the

---

21. See Weigl, 375-80.
22. → *nṭl*.
23. → *lbb* IV.
24. See Weigl, 427-30 for parallels.
25. I. Kottsieper, *Die Sprache der Aḥiqarsprüche*. *BZAW* 194 (1990), 22; Weigl, 422-30.
26. *TADAE* C, p. 47.
27. Ll. 212, with *ʿwyr* "blind," and 214.
28. For biblical parallels, cf. Stendebach, 40-42.
29. *ʿl*, as in *TADAE* C1.1:172.
30. → *nṭl* II.
31. On the form, → I.
32. → *qrn*.
33. 4Q196 6:8 [Tob 3:12], even without direct object 4Q213a 1:8.
34. 4Q543 5-9:4 with *nṭl*; 1QapGen 21:9 with *šql*; 4Q204 1 6:4 (1 En. 13:8) does not preserve the verb, but *škny ʿyny* "my eyelids" serves as the object.
35. 1QapGen 20:3, in the song praising Sarah; similarly in 5:12 for lighting up of eyes like that of the sun in reference to the son of Lamech and Bettenosh; 4Q561 2 for Noah's black-and-white eyes.
36. *šnh*; 4Q530 2 2+6-12:4 and 4Q547 9:8.
37. 4Q562 7:2.
38. 4Q206 4 3:17 (1 En. 89:28).

Hebrew word in its varied usages, sometimes also attested in originally Aramaic texts: 5:1 (Job 21:20; seeing with one's own eyes); 14:5 (Job 29:11; parallelism of eye and ear); 35:3 (Job 40:24; hooks in the eyes in an adynaton); 36:4 (Job 41:10; the shining eyes of Leviathan); 37:7 (Job 42:5; the vision of God). A pair of additional instances are too fragmentary to permit the determination of the content.

Finally, magical texts from late antiquity employ *ʿyn byšh* or just *yn* for the "(evil) look,"[39] that unleashes its own demonic effect, but is rooted in the eye.

III. In Prepositional Phrases with *b-*, *k-*, *l-*. In conjunction with the three proclitic prepositions *b-*, *l-*, and *k-*, the full sense of *ʿyn* "eye" weakens into a designation for modal or local relationships. Old Aramaic already attests *bʿyny* "in the judgment of,"[40] then also at Qumran.[41] Imperial Aramaic also manifests *lʿyny* "in the presence of,"[42] as does 11Q10 4:7 (Job 21:8, literally as in the Heb. text). Finally, in 1QapGen 16:17 *kʿyn* certainly means "accordingly,"[43] just as is also true later.[44]

Gzella

39. Instances in *ATTM*, 2, 452.

40. *KAI* 224.3 with → *ʿbd ṭb* "to do what seems right to someone"; yet, it appears literally and instrumentally in 226.5 "with my [own] eyes."

41. 4Q542 1 1:6.

42. *TADAE* A3. 5,7; 6.2,22; fragmentarily D5.23:2.

43. As first recognized by *ATTM*, 2, 452, contrary to earlier editor's interpretation "spring," which is nonsensical in the context; cf. the extensive justification in H. Gzella, review of D. A. Machiela, *The Dead Sea Genesis Apocryphon*, *BiOr* 68 (2011) 378f.

44. See *DJBA*, 857.

עִיר *ʿyr* /ʿīr/

I. Etymology. II. Meaning. III. Biblical Aramaic. IV. Qumran.

I. Etymology. The root that underlies the noun *ʿyr* /ʿīr/ is the subject of broad discussion. Most[1] derive it from the common Semitic verbal root *ʿīr* "to be awake," which, for example, 1QapGen 19:17; 4Q213b 2; 4Q547 9:8 attest as a t-stem "to awaken." Alternative

J. A. Fitzmyer, *The Genesis Apocryphon of Qumran Cave 1 (1Q20)*. *BietOr* 18B (³2004); R. Murray, "The Origin of Aramaic *ʿîr*, Angel," *Or* 53 (1984) 303-17; F. Reiterer et al., eds., "Angels: The Concept of Celestial Beings," *DCLY* (2007); R. M. M. Tuschling, *Angels and Orthodoxy*. *STAC* 40 (2007), esp. 89-91.

1. E.g., *ATTM*, 655.

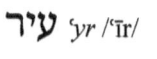

suggestions[2] assume, among others, a relationship with the Proto-Semitic **śīr*[3] or a purely inferred Aramaic and Hebrew root **ġīr*.[4]

II. Meaning. Because of the derivation from the root *ʿīr* (→ I), translators have long often rendered the noun /ʿīr/ "watcher" (i.e., someone who holds watch). Already, the Greek and Old Ethiopic versions of the book of Enoch render it mostly with "awake."[5] The same Greek word also appears in the translations of the book of Daniel by Aquila and Symmachus.[6] The noun appears in relation to the heavenly world and denotes an angelic being who serves as a messenger.[7] Aramaic first attests it beginning with the book of Daniel, but it also appears in the Hebrew apocryphal literature from Qumran: *nplw*] *ʿyry h*[*šmym* "the watchers of the [heavens fell],"[8] cf. *nplw ʿydy* (= *ʿyry*) *hšmym*[9] and *wgm ʿl hʿyrym* "and also against the watchers."[10]

III. Biblical Aramaic. In Biblical Aramaic, the noun *ʿīr* occurs three times, always together with the adjective *qaddīš* "holy":[11] *waʾᵃlū ʿīr wᵉqaddīš min šᵉmayyā nāḥiṯ* "and see, a holy watcher descended from heaven (Dnl. 4:10); *ʿīr wᵉqaddīš nāḥiṯ min šemayyā* (Dnl. 4:20); *biḡzēraṯ ʿīrīn piṯḡāmā umēmar qaddīšīn šᵉʾelṯā* "this decision was announced by the watchers; this statement was demanded by the holy ones" (Dnl. 4:14).[12]

IV. Qumran. The Aramaic texts from the Dead Sea attest the noun well. In addition to the occurrences of *ʿyryn* in *bgzrt*] *ʿyryn ptgmʾ wmʾmr qdyšyn šʾl*[*tʾ* in 4Q115 (= Dnl. 4:14; 4QDan[d]), it appears another sixteen times in nonbiblical manuscripts: 1QapGen (2:1,16; 6:13; 7:2), 4Q202 (1 4:6 [1 En. 10:9]), 4Q203 (7a:7; 7b 1:4; Book of Giants), 4Q204 (1 5:19 [1 En. 12:3]; 1 6:8 [13:10]), 4Q206 (1 22:5 [1 En. 22:6]), 4Q212 (1 3:21 [1 En. 93:2]), 4Q531 (partially emended in 1:1 and 36:1; Book of Giants), 4Q532 (2:7; Book of Giants), 4Q534 (1 2+2:15; Noah's birth), 4Q546 (22:1; Testament of Amram). The biblical dual expression *ʿīr wᵉqaddīš* occurs twice: *lʿyrʾ wqdyšʾ* in 4Q206 1 22:5 (1 En. 22:5) and *ʿyryn wqdšyn* in 4Q212 1 3:21 (1 En. 93:2). Particularly noteworthy is the formulation *mn ʿyryn hryʾtʾ wmn qdšyn zrʿ* "the conception was from the Watchers and the seed from the Holy Ones" (1QapGen 2:1, in reference to Noah).[13]

Fassberg

2. Cf. Murray.
3. Heb. *ṣīr* "messenger, emissary."
4. Cf. Arabic *ġyr* "to protect."
5. ἐγρήγορος and *təguh*; in 1 En. 22:6, in contrast, ἄγγελος.
6. The LXX has ἄγγελος, however.
7. → *mlʾk* "messenger."
8. 4Q266 2 2:18 (4QD[a]).
9. CD II 18.
10. 4Q227 2:4 (4QPs-Jub[c]?); regarding the "fallen angels" → *npl* IV.
11. → *qdš*.
12. → *ptgm*.
13. → *qdš*.

עלה *ʿlh* /ʿellā/

I. Etymology and Lexical Field. II. Usage.

I. Etymology and Lexical Field. The feminine noun *ʿlh* /ʿellā/ "grounds for an accusation" apparently belongs to a root **ʿll* "to act" also known from Hebrew[1] and Arabic and is therefore related neither to the Aramaic verb → *ʿll* "to enter" nor to the common Semitic root *ʿlī* "to go up."[2] The distribution of occurrences indicates that the word is a term in court proceedings and legal diction related semantically to *qbylh* /qabīlā/ "accusation."[3]

II. Usage. Aramaic first attests *ʿlh* in Dnl. 6:5f.: other court officials envied Daniel his outstanding success, but could find no grounds in his blameless execution of office to accuse him before the king and, therefore, charged him (successfully) because of his religious practice. The noun appears here with the verbs → *bʿī* "to seek" and → *škḥ* "to find," in 6:5 along with *šḥyth* "evil."

Further, formulaic expressions in a few private documents from the Dead Sea also exhibit the term.[4] Comparable is the use of αἰτία in Greek legal diction, as also reflected in Mt. 27:37 par. Mk. 15:26, Jn. 18:38 and 19:4:6, or Acts 23:28. Later, *ʿlh* appears explicitly in the sense of "pretense."[5] The same nuance underlies the translations of Dnl. 6:5f. in Pseudo-Theodotion[6] and the Vulgate.[7]

Gzella

1. Heb., "to do something to someone," see W. Roth and H.-J. Fabry, "עלל *ʿll*," *TDOT*, XI 139-47.
2. → *ʿly*.
3. → *qbl*.
4. M 27:3 in *ATTM*, 314f.; nV 7:27 in *ATTM*, 2, 217-23 in the construct *kl ʿlt mndʿm* "grounds for whatever accusation"; perhaps also in nV 3:43 in *ATTM*, 2, 211-15, but reading and interpretation are not clear.
5. *DJPA*, 404a; *LexSyr*, 524.
6. πρόφασις "pretense."
7. *occasio* "opportunity."

עלי *ʿly* /ʿellāy/; עליון *ʿlywn* /ʿelyōn/; עלי *ʿly* /ʿalī/; עליה *ʿlyh* /ʿelliyā/

I. Etymology. II. Designation for a Deity. 1. Biblical Aramaic. 2. Qumran. III. Profane Use. 1. Old and Imperial Aramaic. 2. Biblical Aramaic and Qumran.

I. Etymology. Akkadian, Canaanite, Arabic, and Old South Arabian also attest the root *ʿlī/ū* "to go up, to be above." Among Aramaic verb forms, the synonymous root → *slq* also finds usage. Hebrew, Ugaritic, Akkadian, Arabic, and Old South Arabian Sabean manifest a divine designation or predicate from the root *ʿlī*.

II. Designation for a Deity.

1. Biblical Aramaic. Besides "in the presence of El and ʿElyān" (*qdm ʾl wʿlyn*) concluding an Old Aramaic Sefire treaty[1] as Canaanite treaty gods, the root first appears in Biblical Aramaic as a divine designation in the form of the masculine singular adjective in the determined state *ʿillāʾā*[2] "the Most High," either alone (Dnl. 4:14 [4Q115 3-7:15],21, 22,29,31; 7:25) or in the phrase *ʾælāhā ʿillāʾā* "the Most High God" (Dnl. 3:26,32; 5:18 [4Q112 12:4],21 [4Q113 6:1]), although always uniformly within a literary unit. Nebuchadnezzar shifts to the designation *ʾælāhā ʿillāʾā* in Dnl. 3:26,32 after the pericope has otherwise employed only *ʾælāhā* "God," as soon as the miracle in the fiery furnace demonstrated to him the God's character (vv. 15,29). Standing alone, *ʿillāʾā* returns at a prominent place in Nebuchadnezzar's dream vision, and in its depiction, interpretation, and fulfillment (Dnl. 4:14,22,29), again in the phrase "(to know) that the Most High has power over the kingdom of human beings" (*dī šallīṭ ʿillāʾā bᵉ-malkūṯ ʾanāšā*).[3] Meanwhile, Daniel's reference to these events in this interpretation of the flaming writing in Dnl. 5:18,21[4] employs *ʾælāhā ʿillāʾā*.

In the expression *qaddīšē ʿælyōnīn* "Holy Ones of the Most High"[5] that recurs in the interpretation of Daniel's animal vision, the masculine plural noun in the absolute state, borrowed from the Hebrew, functions as a divine designation in the plural of majesty. In v. 25, the expression parallels *ʿillāʾā* "the Most High."

2. Qumran. At Qumran, three forms appear as divine designations: *ʿlyʾ* "the Most High" (m.sg. det., 1QapGen 6:9, 4Q550 7a:1, 4Q568 1:1; in 1QapGen 6:24; 10:18 without context), *ʿlywn* "Most High" (with certainty only in 4Q246 2:1; in 4Q543 22:2 without context; in 4Q536 3:8 a pl. abs.), and the borrowed Hebrew phrase *ʾl ʿlywn* "Highest God" (1QapGen 12:17; 20:12,16; 21:2,20; 22:15,16,21; 4Q552 6:10; and perhaps 4Q558 88:1). In the fragmentary narrative from the Persian court 4Q550 7a:1, *ʿlyʾ* appears in the expression *ʿlyʾ dy ʾntwn dḥlyn w[p]lḥyn hw šlyṭ b[kwl ʾr]*[6] "the Most High whom you fear

---

J. Goldingay, "'Holy Ones on High' in Daniel 7:18," *JBL* 107 (1988), 495-97; C. von Pilgrim, "Textzeugnis und archäologischer Befund," in *Stationen. FS R. Stadelmann* (Mainz, 1998), 485-97; C. Stadel, *Hebraismen in den aramäischen Texten vom Toten Meer* (Heidelberg, 2008); idem, "Hebrew Influences on the Language of the Aramaic Qumran Scrolls," *Meghillot* 8-9 (2010) 393-407; D. Talshir, "The Relativity of Geographic Terms," *JSS* 48 (2003) 259-85; G. Wehmeier, "עלה *ʿlh* to go up," *TLOT*, 883-96; H.-J. Zobel, "עֶלְיוֹן *ʿelyôn*," *TDOT*, XI, 121-39.

1. *KAI* 222 A 11.
2. *Ketib ʿlyʾ*.
3. → *mlk* IV.
4. → *yd* III; *mnī* V.
5. A kind of angel, → *qdš*; Dnl. 7:18,22,25,27 (4Q112 14:7; 4Q113 15:20).

and worship rules over the [whole ear]th," which echoes the phraseology of Dnl. 4:14, etc. (→ II.1). In 1QapGen 6:9, the noun lends validity to the existing, but disputed in the intertestamental period, marriage regulations by designating them as "eternal law [that] the Most High [gave] human beings" (*[dy yhb]h ʿlyʾ lbny ʾnšʾ*).

Only the apocalypse 4Q246 1 2:1 has *ʿlywn* "Most High" standing alone in the meaning "God"; the parallelism "he will be named son of God and people will call him son of the Most High" (*brh dy ʾl ytʾmr wbr ʿlywn yqrwnh*) depends, however, on the phrase *ʾl ʿlywn.*[6] In contrast, one should probably translate the masculine plural absolute form *ʿlywnyn* in the fragmentary 4Q536 3:8 "angel" following Biblical Aramaic terminology.

The Hebrew divine designation *ʾl ʿlywn* "Highest God" from the Melchizedek pericope (Gen. 14), beloved in the Hellenistic period, typifies the Abraham cycle in 1QapGen. The instances in col. 22 appear in the treatment of the biblical passage and have influenced the other usages. In addition to other divine designation, the phrase also appears once in the mouth of Noah, 1QapGen 12:17: "I blessed the Lord of Heaven, the Highest God, the great Holy One, who saved us from annihilation."

III. Profane Use.

1. Old and Imperial Aramaic. In the Old Aramaic Sefire inscription, the feminine noun *ʿly* "upper story, rooftop" occurs in the curse on the treaty breaker, of whose house the gods will "make its basement into its [r]ooftop";[7] on the other hand, the adj. *ʿly* defines the toponym "upper Aram,"[8] whose location is disputed. In the Imperial Aramaic Aršama correspondence,[9] the pair of feminine singular determined adjectives *ʿlytʾ wtḥtytʾ* elliptically designate "Upper and Lower (Egypt)." The same pair of adjectives[10] serves in contract texts from Elephantine[11] to indicate the north-south dimensions of property. Contrary to the use of *ʿlytʾ* as "Upper Egypt," the archaeological evidence suggests the meaning "northern" for *ʿly* here.[12]

2. Biblical Aramaic and Qumran. In Dnl. 6:11, the noun form *ʿillīṯeh*[13] "his rooftop"[14] denotes the room in which Daniel, despite the prohibitions of the Persian King Darius, prays toward Jerusalem three times daily. Sara, the daughter of Raguel, also withdrew in 4Q196 6:2 (Tob. 3:10) "to the rooftop of the house [of her father" (*lʿlyt byt [ʾbwh)*[15] to pray. In the poetic passage 1QapGen 20:7, in contrast, the courtiers praise Sarah's beauty to pharaoh with the words "she is the highest in her beauty, higher than them all" (*ʿlyʾ*

6. For the overall interpretation → *br* IV.
7. *KAI* 222 C 23f.; [ʿ]*lyth*, sg. with a 3ms suff., antonym *tḥty*.
8. *KAI* 222 A 6; *ʿly ʾrm*, ms cstr.
9. *TADAE* A6.4:3; A6.7:6.
10. Ms det. or with a 3s suff.
11. E.g., *TADAE* B2.3:4; B3.10:6.
12. Pilgrim.
13. On the form, cf. *ATTM*, 657.
14. Fs with 3ms suff.
15. Sg. cstr.

šprh' lʿl' mn kwlhn).[16] Additional instances of the feminine noun *ʿly*[17] and of the adjective,[18] without context, appear in descriptions of the architecture of the new Jerusalem.

Stadel

16. Fs det. adj. with a noun employed adverbially.
17. 11Q18 9:1; 21:3.
18. 11Q18 18:2.

עלים *ʿlym* /ʿolaym/

I. Etymology. II. Old Aramaic Inscriptions. III. Imperial Aramaic Documents. IV. Aramaic Texts from the Dead Sea.

I. Etymology. The Aramaic substantive *ʿlym* /ʿolaym/[1] "boy, youth" corresponds to the **qutayl* paradigm and belongs to the root *ʿlm*. The **qutayl* noun paradigm in Semitic languages typically signifies diminutives.[2] The root *ʿlm* traces to the Proto-Semitic **ġlm* and has cognates in Ugaritic, Arabic, Canaanite (both Hebrew and Phoenicio-Punic), Eblaite, and perhaps in Akkadian. Its basic meaning seems to be connected to the state of sexual maturity and the emotions that arise from it; the noun *ʿlym* refers mostly to a young (and especially in the case of its feminine counterpart *ʿlymh*, marriageable) human being in puberty.

II. Old Aramaic Inscriptions. Already the oldest Aramaic textual witnesses exhibit instances of the substantive *ʿlym*. It occurs once in the bilingual Tell Fekheriye inscription

C. Brockelmann, *Grundriss der vergleichenden Grammatik der semitischen Sprachen*, vol. 1 (Berlin, 1908); C. Dohmen, "עַלְמָה *ʿalmâ*," *TDOT*, XI, 154-63; I. Eph'al and J. Naveh, *Aramaic Ostraca of the Fourth Century BC from Idumaea* (Jerusalem, 1996), esp. no. 199.7; J. A. Fitzmyer, *The Genesis Apocryphon of Qumran Cave 1 (1Q20). BietOr* 18B (^{3}2004); J. Fox, *Semitic Noun Patterns. HSS* 52 (2003); H. Gzella, "Deir ʿAllā," in G. Khan, ed., *Encyclopedia of Hebrew Language and Linguistics* (Leiden, 2013), 1:691-93; J. A. Hackett, *The Balaam Text from Deir ʿAllā. HSM* 31 (1984); J. Hoftijzer and G. van der Kooij, *Aramaic Texts from Deir ʿAlla. DMOA* 19 (1976); T. Muraoka and B. Porten, *A Grammar of Egyptian Aramaic. HO* 32 (^{2}2003); J. Naveh and S. Shaked, *Aramaic Documents from Ancient Bactria (Fourth Century B.C.E.)* (London, 2012); W. von Soden, "Diminutiva nach der Form *qutail* > *qutīl* und vergleichbare vierkonsonantige Bildungen im Akkadischen," in *Semitic Studies in Honor of Wolf Leslau on the Occasion of His Eighty-Fifth Birthday. Fs. W. Leslau* (Wiesbaden, 1991), 2:1488-92.

1. > /ʿolēm/, *ATTM*, 116-20.
2. Brockelmann, §137; Fox, 229.

(*wmʾh nšwn lhynqn ʿlym wʾl yrwy* "and may one hundred women suckle a child and it still not have enough!")[3] and one at Sefire (*wšbʿ [mhy]nqn ymšḥ[n šdyhn w]yhynqn ʿlym wʾl yšbʿ* "and may seven [nur]ses salve [their breasts and] feed a child and may it still not be satisfied"),[4] both as part of curse formulas. In these passages, *ʿlym* refers to a not yet weaned infant, which suggests that Old Aramaic already employed it for (sometimes very) young people in general and, consequently, with no explicit relation to puberty.

Finally, a feminine form *ʿlymh* may appear in the Deir ʿAllā Inscription (II.4), perhaps in the meaning "virgin, marriageable maiden, young woman," but the context permits no certain conclusions.[5]

III. Imperial Aramaic Documents. From the Achaemenid period, four instances of the substantive *ʿlym* appear in the Imperial Aramaic texts from Egypt. There, in a majority of cases, it refers to a youth that belongs to a certain person or household, e.g., *TADAE* A4.3:8 *ḥwr ʿlym ḥnnyh* "Ḥor is the lad of Ḥananya"; C3.27:30 *ʿlymy bytʾ* "lads of the house(hold)"; A3.5:6 *ḥzy ʿl ʿlymyʾ wbyty* "concern yourself with the lads and my house(hold)." In a similar sense, a few documents from this period attest the feminine counterpart *ʿlymh* "maiden, maid," as in an ostracon from Idumea:[6] *hbw lh ḥdh mn ʿlymtʾ* "give him one of the maids"; the context makes it clear that the pertinent maid was subordinate to another person so that she could not act autonomously. Notably in this context, a possessive suffix can denote "my lad,"[7] but the letters of Aršama often employ the independent pronoun *zyl-*.[8] This indicates a possessive relationship between a person in authority and a subordinate in his service.[9] For the same reason, translators often render the substantives *ʿlym* and *ʿlymh* as "servant" or "slave." Nonetheless, it should be emphasized that the meaning "servant, slave" does not seem to belong to the semantics of the terms *ʿlym* and *ʿlymh* themselves,[10] but that only the context in which they appear establish this nuance. Thus, in B2.11:12f., *ʾyty tbʾ šmh ʾmhm zy ʿlymyʾ ʾlh* "there is a certain Taba, the mother of these lads" and in D7.9:6-8 *lʾ yškḥn ʿlymth mktbh ʿl šmh* "they do not want to find his maid marked with his name,"[11] the substantives *ʿlymyʾ* "the lads" and "*ʿlymth* "his maid" apparently refer to slaves. Yet, in B3.9:3 *ʿlym[ʾ zyl] k* "[you]r la[d]" appears in a document that expressly prohibits the pertinent person from ever falling into slavery,[12] which includes marking with a brand, but, instead, he should be treated like a son. In D23.1.2:13 *wʿlymʾ ʾzl ʿl ʿsrs*["and the lad went to ʿOsirs," too, although

---

3. *KAI* 309.21.

4. *KAI* 222 A 21f.; for the expression → *mšḥ* II.

5. Cf. Hoftijzer and van der Kooij, 221 and Hackett, 56; on the text overall and its relation to Aramaic, see Gzella.

6. Eph'al and Naveh, no. 199, l. 7.

7. As, e.g., in *TADAE* D23.1.9:7: *ʿlymy snḥrw* "my lad Snḥrw."

8. E.g., A6.4.2: *ʾḥḥpy ʿlymʾ zyly*, literally "ʾAḥḥapi, the servant of me"; likewise in a satrap's letter from Bactria, A6.1 in Naveh and Shaked.

9. Muraoka and Porten, 164, §40h; cf. M. L. Folmer, *The Aramaic Language in the Achaemenid Period. OLA* 68 (1995), 264ff.

10. Otherwise → *ʿbd* III.

11. = branded, → *ktb* II.

12. Indicated with the root → *ʿbd*.

the context is fragmentary, includes no indication that the youth involved belonged to anyone as property. In two lists from Bactria with the distribution of rations, *ʿlymn* appears with other servants.[13]

IV. Aramaic Texts from the Dead Sea. Biblical Aramaic does not attest the substantives *ʿlym* and *ʿlymh*, but the Aramaic texts from the Dead Sea do so well with the meanings known from the older material. Thus, *ʿlym* refers to a newborn (1QapGen 2:2: *wlby ʿly mštny ʿl ʿwlymʾ dnʾ* "and my mind changed in me because of this child," a reference to the child Noah, the son of the speaker Lamech; likewise 5:2,13 and 4Q204 5 2:23,30 [1 En. 106:18; 107:2]). Further, the masculine refers to a young man (e.g., 4Q196 13:2 [Tob. 6:7]: [*wbʾdyn š*]*ʾl ʿwlymʾ lml*[*ʾk*] "[then] the young man asked [the an]gel";[14] elsewhere in Tobit, this is the fixed expression for the central character: 4Q197 4 1:6f.,16 [Tob. 6:3,11]; 4Q197 4 3:5 [7:2]; cf. further 11Q10 14:2; 23:3 [Job 29:8; 33:25]). Meanwhile, the feminine *ʿlymh* denotes a young, marriageable woman (4Q197 4 2:3 [Tob. 6:13]: *wtmll bʿl*[*m*]*tʾ dʾ blylyʾ dn* "tonight you will talk about this [youn]g maiden").[15] With the same nuance, a feminine abstract noun *ʿlymw* "youth" also derives from *ʿlym* (4Q534 1 1:3f.: *bʿlymwth lhwh klṭyš* "in his youth, he will be like a sharp-witted person";[16] cf. 11Q10 23:3; 36:8 [Job 33:25; 41:14]). Finally, in the case of 1QapGen 22:23, *brʾ mn dy ʾklw kbr ʿwlymy dy ʿmy* "besides what my young men, who are with me, have already consumed," the broader context (i.e., the use of *ʿbd* in 22:6) indicates a reference to Abraham's slaves (→ III).[17]

Kuty

13. C3.21 and 4.18 in Naveh and Shaked, in the latter case alongside *ʾmht* "maids," → *ʿbd*.
14. Cf. *DJD*, XIX (1995), 18.
15. *DJD*, XIX (1995), 48.
16. *DJD*, XXXI (2001), 132.
17. → *ʿbd* III.

עלל *ʿll*; עלל *ʿll* /ʿalāl/; עללה *ʿllh* /ʿalalā/; מעל *mʿl* /maʿal/; מעלין *mʿlyn* /maʿʿālīn/

I. Etymology, Forms, Lexical Field, and Grammatical Constructions. II. Verb in the G-stem "to Enter." 1. Old and Imperial Aramaic. 2. Biblical Aramaic. 3. Qumran. III. Verb in the C-stem "to Lead In." 1. Imperial Aramaic. 2. Biblical Aramaic. 3. Qumran. IV. Nouns.

H. Drawnel, *The Aramaic Astronomical Book (4Q208-4Q211) from Qumran* (Oxford, 2011); I. Ephʿal and J. Naveh, *Aramaic Ostraca of the Fourth Century BC from Idumaea* (Jerusalem, 1996); H. Gzella, "*ʿll* II," *ThWQ*, III, 126-30; idem, *A Cultural History of Aramaic*. *HO* 111 (2015); J. Naveh and S. Shaked, *Aramaic Documents from Ancient Bactria (Fourth Century B.C.E.)* (London, 2012).

I. Etymology, Forms, Lexical Field, and Grammatical Constructions. In contrast to the other Northwest Semitic languages, Aramaic employs the verbal root *ʿll* for "to go into, to enter."[1] In turn, it corresponds etymologically to the old **ġll*.[2] With the antonym → *npq* "to go out," as with → *nḥt* "to descend" and → *slq* "to ascend," Aramaic crystallized a unique pair of very productive verbs of direction. Here, *ʿll* appears in the widespread G-stem "to enter"[3] and in the more specialized C-stem.

The fact that a few historical spellings survived for a long time in the post-Achaemenid literary tradition probably has to do with the extensive use of this verb. The graphically degeminizing spelling of the long /ʿʿ/ in forms with preformatives or prefixes according to an Achaemenid convention[4] as *-nʿ-*[5] and, beginning with Biblical Aramaic, the spelling of the plural participle with a doubled *l*,[6] that sometimes extended to the perfect of the third-person feminine singular, presumably by analogy,[7] are relatively frequent. These orthographic characteristics indicate that the Aramaic texts from the Bible and Qumran have deep roots in the Imperial Aramaic literary tradition.[8]

In the G-stem, prepositional expressions regularly indicate the direction of movement: *b-* "in"[9] or *l-*;[10] later also *bgw*[11] and *lgw*[12] "among";[13] *ʿl* "near" with persons;[14] in court style for persons sometimes *qdm* (Dnl. 4:5). Yet, as with other verbs of coming and going, the objective can also follow directly.[15] Furthemore, in a greeting formula, *bšlm* "safely" appears as an adverb of manner.[16]

The transitive C-stem is constructed similarly: *l-* "in"[17] or *lgw*,[18] of persons in court style *qdm* "before" (Dnl. 2:25; 4:3,5; 6:19; in each case of the king). In pre-Christian times, it also formed an internal passive "to be brought,"[19] which the t-stem later replaced (→ III).

1. Heb., on the other hand, employs part of the spectrum of **bāʾ* "to come," whose nuances differ in the various individual Semitic languages; Aram. does not attest it, instead → *ʾtī* serves for "to come."

2. Attested in Ugaritic, Arabic, and Ethiopic with various meanings and therefore common Semitic, Hebrew only in the L-stem in Job 16:15.

3. Sometimes in connection with other verbs of motion.

4. In which verbs with a long second radical lengthen the first vowel of the root, thus, e.g., /taʿʿol/ "you enter," /haʿʿel/ "he brought in"; *ATTM*, 148,484f.

5. *tʿnl*, *TADAE* B3.12:22; *hnʿl*, Dnl. 2:25; Gzella, 170f.

6. E.g., Dnl. 4:4: *ʿllyn* for /ʿāllīn/ "entering" from the older */ʿālelīn/; cf. 4Q197 4 2:8; 11Q18 15:3; 24:6; *ATTM*, 485.

7. Thus *ʿllt* "she entered" in Dnl. 5:10; *BLA*, §54y.

8. See, generally, Gzella, 205-8,230-34.

9. *KAI* 317.5; *TADAE* A4.7:9, etc.

10. Frequent first in the post-Achaemenid period, e.g., Dnl. 5:10; 6:11; 1QapGen 19:13f.; 20:6; 2Q24 4:3.

11. 1QapGen 14:16f.

12. 4Q197 4 1:15 (Tob. 6:10).

13. → *gw*.

14. *TADAE* B2.6:5,15; 3.8:5; 1QapGen 2:3.

15. *KAI* 222 A 6, → II.1; *TADAE* B3.12:22; D7.24:2; 4Q213 1-2 2:1.

16. 4Q197 4 3:4 par. 4Q196 14 2:7 (Tob. 7:1); 4Q550 6+6a-c:6.

17. 4Q197 4 3:4 (Tob. 7:1).

18. E.g., 4Q554 1 2:11.

19. Dnl. 5:13; 6:19; 4Q538 1-2:2.

Of verbal nouns, besides the substantival G-stem infinitive /maʿʿal/ "access," older Aramaic attests the masculine /ʿalāl/ "entrance," the feminine /ʿalalā/ "income," and the presumably masculine plural /maʿʿālīn/ "sinking" (of the sun).

II. Verb in the G-stem "to Enter." In the G-stem, *'ll* "to enter" is a generic verb that appears in widely varied categories of texts and linguistic registers beginning with Old Aramaic. Consequently, primarily the context more precisely defines its nuance—also including quite specific shades such as "to invade," "to break in," "to go in," and still more.

1. Old and Imperial Aramaic. Old Aramaic state and royal inscriptions employ the verb, on the one hand, for "to enter a house," either in reference to a private dwelling where someone finds lodging,[20] or with reference to the palace as *kl 'll byt mlk* perhaps to designate the entire palace complex[21] to which the validity of the state treaties from Sefire refer.[22] On the other hand, *'ll* with an enemy king as subject can denote "to invade" in the context of military conquests.[23]

(The meaning of *yn'l* in *TADAE* C1.1,205, which probably belongs to another root, is open to speculation; in any case, cf. *DNSI*, 737, s.v. *n'l*.)

In Imperial Aramaic documents from Elephantine, *'ll* with *b-* often serves for "to break in"[24] and in contracts for "to enter" of wares or money,[25] but it also regularly appears in the general sense.[26] Especially in the colloquial speech of the ostraca correspondence, it seems to have faded also to "to go, to come."[27] It appears once already in Old Aramaic for "to invade."[28]

The post-Achaemenid tradition of Imperial Aramaic knows additional contexts of usage: in a marriage contract on an ostracon from Idumea the man's entry into the house in relation to the marriage ceremony;[29] in Palmyrene grave inscriptions in the descriptions of direction "if you enter";[30] in Hatra to emphasize the validity of a law even for

---

20. *'l bbyth* in *KAI* 317.5f., in reference to a spy, tax evader, or some other enemy of state; literature in Gzella, 109 n. 302.

21. See *DNSI*, 857, with other suggestions.

22. *KAI* 222 A 6; for the grammatical analysis, see J. A. Fitzmyer, *Aramaic Inscriptions of Sefire. BietOr* 19/A (^{2}1995), 68f.: it apparently involves a ptcp. followed immediately by the goal of the movement.

23. *KAI* 222 B 35, together with *lqḥ* "to take" and similarly in the Tell Dan stele, *KAI* 310.3; concerning the imperfect *wy'l*, which can be either the full or the apocopated form, see the extensive discussion in Gzella, 80-87.

24. *TADAE* A4.4: 8; 4.7:9 par. 4.8:8; B7.2:4,8, → *ḥsn* III.

25. *TADAE* B2.6:5,15; 3.8:5.

26. *TADAE* A5.2:6; 6.7:7; B3.12:22, together with the antonym → *npq*.

27. *TADAE* D7.3:4; 7.5:12; 7.20:2; 7.24:2; 7.33:1.

28. *TADAE* A4.7:13, of the Persian conquest of Egypt.

29. E. Eshel and A. Kloner, "An Aramaic Ostracon of an Edomite Marriage Contract from Maresha, Dated 176 B.C.E.," *IEJ* 46 (1996) 1-22, l. 11.

30. E.g., *PAT* 0555.7; see M. O'Connor, "The Grammar of Finding Your Way in Palmyrene Aramaic," in *Fucus. FS A. Ehrman* (Amsterdam, 1988), 353-69.

"day guests";[31] and perhaps in H29.5f. in the prohibition against entering a sacred site wearing shoes (cf. Ex. 3:5).[32]

2. Biblical Aramaic. All instances of the verb in Biblical Aramaic come from the book of Daniel. There, *ʿll* refers mostly to the appearance of members of the court staff before superiors, either with a request or in response to a summons.[33] Such a nuance has no direct parallel in the older material. Meanwhile, if the queen appears before the court (5:10),[34] it may also mean simply "to enter (into a room)" as the preposition *l-* suggests. This is surely the case for Daniel's arrival in his own house (6:11, again with *l-*).

3. Qumran. At Qumran, one can easily observe the breadth of the use of *ʿll* in the narrative texts 1QapGen, Tobit, and the Persian court tale. Here, the verb appears mostly with an animate subject and *l-* for entrance into a building such as the royal palace (4Q550 6+6a-c:6f.), a private home (4Q197 4 3:4 par. 4Q196 14 2:7 [Tob. 7:1], a greeting formula; 1QapGen 20:6 of the bridal chorus), or the temple (2Q24 4:3; similarly probably also 11Q18 15:3,6; 16 2+17 1:4), and for entry into a country (1QapGen 19:13f.; 4Q197 4 1:15 [Tob. 6:10]; 4Q570 2:4) or a city (4Q197 4 3:1 [Tob. 7:1]). Together with *ʿl*, it denotes coming to a person (1QapGen 2:3; 4Q197 4 2:8 [Tob. 6:14]). In connection with *b-*, it appears with an inanimate subject to denote "to encroach on."[35] The wider context of the comparably frequent occurrences in the Book of Giants is unclear (4Q530 1 1:8 and perhaps 2 2+6-12:1; 4Q531 46:2; 4Q532 2:7). In 11Q10 6:3 and 36:2 (Job 22:4 and 42:8) it renders *bōʾ*.

A peculiarity of the astronomical book of Enoch is the formulaic use of *ʿll* for "to set" in reference to a heavenly body, mostly for the course of the moon (e.g., 4Q209 7 2:5 bis 7 3:6), sporadically for the sun (so surely in 4Q209 35:1), since, according to the underlying concept, when setting, heavenly bodies entered into (*l-*) a gate[36] on the western horizon (4Q209 3:7; 7 2:8; 7 3:6).[37] A few additional specimens have been transmitted without context or are in dispute paleographically.[38]

III. Verb in the C-stem "to Lead In." The meaning of the C-stem "to lead in" (of persons) or "to bring in" (of goods) is more specific than the G-stem and common be-

---

31. *wkwl dy ʿl[yl] wnpyq* "whoever goes in and out" in H336b.5, perhaps with an explicative *w-* to define the previously mentioned "Arabs" and in contrast to permanent inhabitants (l. 6).

32. Other interpretations in *DNSI*, 856.

33. Daniel before the king: 2:16; 4:5 (with *qdm*); Daniel before Arioch: 2:24 (with *ʿl*); the wise before the king: 4:4; 5:8.

34. On the form, → I.

35. 1QapGen 14:16f., of the motion of a treetop in Noah's dream of the olive tree; 4Q560 1 1:3 of evil in someone's body; 4Q213 1-2 2:1 in the figurative comparison of a castle.

36. → *trʿ*.

37. Cf. Drawnel, 249.

38. In addition to the specimens discussed here, they are treated in H. Gzella, "*ʿll* II," *ThWQ*, III, 127-29.

ginning with Imperial Aramaic documental texts. The D-stem with a similar spectrum of usage also appears later.[39]

1. Imperial Aramaic. Marriage contracts employ *ʿll* of the dowry that the wife brings to the husband (*l-*) "in her hand" (*bydh*)[40] and takes with her in the event of divorce.[41] It denotes "to deliver" in reference to bondservants[42] and goods,[43] "to bring in" in Idumean commercial ostraca,[44] "to deliver" (wine) in the Parthian Nisa Ostraca,[45] and "to import" in the Palmyrene tax tables.[46]

2. Biblical Aramaic. Biblical Aramaic employs the verb entirely in accord with the G-stem (→ II.2) for "to lead in" in the context of an audience with the king (with *qdm*: Dnl. 2:24f.; 4:3; 6:19; absolutely: 5:7) and in analogy with the internal passive (with *qdm*: 5:13; absolutely: 5,15).

3. Qumran. The texts from Qumran attest an additional use: "to make enter" (4Q197 4 3:4 [Tob. 7:1]),[47] also in reference to visionary journeys (4Q554 1 2:11; 1 3:15 par. 5Q15 1 1:18; 5Q15 1 2:6; 4Q204 1 6:21), and "to bring in" (4Q213 1 1:8, cf. Sir. 6:19f.); passive in 4Q538 1-2:2.

IV. Nouns. The related nouns appear significantly less often than the verb. In the vision of the heavenly Jerusalem from Qumran, the infinitive of the G-stem *mʿl* /maʿʿal/ functions as the noun "entrance" for the verbal action.[48] This usage is distinct from *ʿll* /ʿalāl/ "entrance" in 4Q554 1 3:19 par. 5Q15 1 2:2[49] and in 4Q554 1 3:17 in the expression *ʾsp ʿll* "entry foyer"[50] and the juridical "access" in contracts from the Dead Sea.[51]

The plural *mʿlyn* /maʿʿālīn/ in *mʿly šmšʾ* "sunset" (Dnl. 6:15)[52] is also subsumed under another paradigm because of the /ā/.[53] Otherwise, older Aramaic has *mʿrb* for "west, sunset."[54]

In addition, at least a few Nabatean contracts from the Dead Sea firmly attest the feminine *ʿllh* /ʿalalā/ "income."[55] Some assume the same meaning for *ʿll* in an Imperial

39. *DJBA*, 865f.
40. *TADAE* B2.6:6f.24,27; 3.3:4,8,10,16; 3.8:5,22.
41. → *npq* III.
42. *TADAE* A6. 10:7, with → *ʿbd* "to convey."
43. Naveh and Shaked, A6,4,8,10.
44. E.g., Ephʿal and Naveh, 34.1; 51.2; 75.1; 152.1.
45. *DNSI*, 856.
46. *PAT* 0259 ii.80,149; t-passive ii.56,119.
47. Following *DSSStE*, 392f. Cf. also 4Q550c 1:7, though the context there is fragmentary.
48. 4Q554 1 3:17 par. 5Q15 1 2:1, adverbially "when entering."
49. Perhaps a construction term, but without context.
50. *ATTM*, 519.
51. nV 7:50 (emend.); 42:6,12; V 47:4; 48:5,16; 81:5 in *ATTM* 2.
52. Later in other combinations "dusk": *DJBA*, 695a.
53. *BLA*, §57i. §195w''; *ATTM*, 658.
54. *ATTM*, 664.
55. nV 1:21,26; 6:5; 7:4,50; 22:31,34; all following *ATTM* 2.

Aramaic papyrus from Saqqara,[56] but it is uncertain because of its insufficient context.[57] For other nouns attested in Syriac, see *LexSyr*, 524f.

Gzella

56. Segal, no. 46.3,5
57. Literature in *DNSI*, 858, s.v. *'ll*$_3$.

עלם *'lm* /'ālam/

I. Etymology. II. Usage. 1. Sam'alian. 2. Old Aramaic and Deir 'Allā. 3. Imperial Aramaic. 4. Biblical Aramaic. 5. Aramaic Texts from the Dead Sea.

I. Etymology. For Northwest Semitic *'lm* /'ālam/, *DNSI*[1] offers a bandwidth from *'lm*$_1$ to *'lm*$_6$, of which, however, only *'lm*$_4$ is pertinent to Aramaic, although *'lm*$_6$ will also be treated here (→ II.1). The etymology of *'lm*, which continues as a subject of debate,[2] suggests that one begin only very generally with a concept of extremes that signifies distant times, either past or future, or both.[3] On this basis, one can assume a transposition of the concept of a temporal extreme to a local realm so that the extreme signified with *'lm* can also be the outer realm of the inhabited world, i.e., the underworld. Restricted to the resting place of the dead, *'lm* can also denote the grave.[4] Since *'lm* unites temporal and local extremes, it can also assume the meaning "world" at Palmyra and "epoch" in apocalyptic texts.

M. Albani, *Astronomie und Schöpfungsglaube. WMANT* 68 (1994), esp. 101-5,132-35; G. Dalman, *The Words of Jesus* (trans. D. M. Kay; Edinburgh, 1902), 162-79; M. L. Folmer, *The Aramaic Language in the Achaemenid Period. OLA* 68 (1995), 685-87,716f.,722,745; M. Gawlikowski, "La notion de tombeau en Syrie romaine," *Berytus* 21 (1972) 5-15; A. Hurvitz, "*Bjt-hqwdwt* and *bjt-'wlm*: Two Funerary Terms in Biblical Literature and Their Linguistic Background," *Maarav* 8 (1992) 59-68; E. Jenni, "עוֹלָם *'ôlām* eternity," *TLOT*, 852-62; P. Joüon, "Glanes palmyréniennes," *Syr* 19 (1938) 99-102; K. Koch, *Das Buch Daniel. EdF* 144 (1980), 149-54,214-16; idem, "Sabbatstruktur der Geschichte," *ZAW* 95 (1983) 403-30; J.-J. Lavoie, "Étude de l'expression *bjt-'wlm* dans Qo 12,5 à la lumière des textes du Proche-Orient ancien," *Où demeures-tu? (Jn 1,38): la maison depuis le monde biblique. FS G. Couturier* (Montreal, 1994), 213-26; H. Niehr, "Zur Semantik von nordwestsemitisch *'lm* als 'Unterwelt' und 'Grab,'" in *Ana šadî Labnāni lū allik. FS W. Röllig. AOAT* 247 (1997), 295-305; H. D. Preuss, "עוֹלָם *'olām*," *TDOT*, X, 530-45; C. Stadel, "'*wlm*," *ThWQ*, III, 61–68.

1. *DNSI*, 858-62.
2. Cf. Preuss, 531ff.
3. Cf. Jenni, 853.
4. Cf. Niehr, 301.

II. Usage. The oldest instances of *ʿlm* in the Northwest Semitic languages, especially in Ugaritic, exhibit a semantic distinction between *ʿlm* as "underworld"[5] and *ʿlm* as "long time." The latter occurs primarily in legal documents as a terminus *ʿd ʿlm*. This semantic distinction between *ʿlm* as "underworld" and "long time" survives into the first millennium in Phoenician, Hebrew, and Aramaic.[6]

1. Samʾalian. The inscription of King Panamuwa I, attributable to the eighth century B.C.E. and affixed to the statue of the god Hadad erected at the site of the king's future cult of the dead, reports: *ʾnk pnmw br qrl mlk yʾdy zy hqymt nṣb zn lhdd bʿlmy* "I am Panamuwa, son of QRL, King of Yādiya, who has erected this statue for Hadad *bʿlmy*."[7] Scholars have suggested that *bʿlmy* be understood as "for my eternity"[8] or as "in my youth."[9] Yet, justified reservations against both translations arise[10] suggesting that *ʿlm* be understood as "grave."[11] Such an understanding also suits well the royal cult of the dead at Sam'al discussed in *KAI* 214.[12] Thus, the meaning for *ʿlm* "underworld" known from Ugaritic is restricted and concretized. The same situation also manifests itself in the Phoenician inscription on the Aḥirom sarcophagus.[13] In contrast, *ʿlmt* "youth" in a Cilician grave inscription[14] involves the later clearly attested abstract formation of → *ʿlym* "lad."[15] Regarding the relationship of Sam'alian to Old Aramaic, see P. M. Noorlander, "Sam'alian in Its Northwest Semitic Setting: A Historical-Comparative Approach," *Or* 81 (2012) 202-38.

2. Old Aramaic and Deir ʿAllā. Old Aramaic attests the temporal term *ʿd ʿlm* "forever" with certainty in *KAI* 224.25; cf. perhaps [*mn*] *ʿlm* "since the beginning" in l. 24;[16] the reading in *KAI* 222 B 7 could be [*lʿl*]*mn* "forever."[17] Because of its fragmentary context,

---

5. Cf. E. Gaál, "Osiris-Amenophis III in Ugarit," *Recueil d'études dédiées à Vilmos Wessetzky à l'occasion de son 65e anniversaire. FS Wessetzky* (Budapest, 1974), 97-99; A. Cooper, "MLK 'Eternal King' or 'King of Eternity,'" *Love and Death in the Ancient Near East. FS M. Pope* (Guilford, CT, 1987), 1-7; D. Pardee, *Les textes para-mythologiques* (Paris, 1988), 89-91; Niehr, 295-97.

6. Niehr, 297-301.

7. *KAI* 214.1.

8. Donner and Röllig, s.v., 217.

9. E.g., H. Sader, *Les états araméens de Syrie* (Beirut, 1987), 163; *DNSI*, 862 s.v. $ʿlm_6$; B. Margalit, "K-R-T Studies," *UF* 27 (1995) 178.

10. J. Tropper, *Die Inschriften von Zincirli. ALASP* 6 (1993), 60f.

11. Tropper, 60f.; Niehr, 299.

12. Cf. H. Niehr, "Zum Totenkult der Könige von Sam'al im 9. und 8. Jh. v. Chr.," *SEL* 11 (1994) 57-73; idem, *The Aramaeans in Ancient Syria. HO* 106 (2014), 184-87; P.-E. Dion, *Les Araméens à l'âge du fer: Histoire politique et structures sociales. ÉtB* 34 (1997), 265-70.

13. *KAI* 1.1; Niehr, 297f.

14. A. Lemaire, *Epigraphica Anatolica* 23 (1994) 92, l. 4.

15. Ibid., 95.

16. For the reconstruction see J. A. Fitzmyer, *Aramaic Inscriptions of Sefîre. BietOr* 19/A ([2]1995), 160.

17. Ibid., 101.

the reference to *bt ʿlmn* in the inscription from Tell Deir ʿAllā remains unclear;[18] it may refer to the grave.[19]

3. Imperial Aramaic. The legal texts from Elephantine employ the formulation *mn ywmʾ znh wʿd ʿlm* (variants: *mn ywmʾ znh ʿd ʿlm*/*ʿd ʿlmn*) "from this day and forever more" to establish the beginning of the marriage in the marriage formula[20] and in other legal texts that relate to real estate, mobile property, and slaves.[21] Regarding the Ugaritic counterpart *ʿd ʿlm*, cf. *DUL*³, 155.

So far, the sole Nabatean instance of *b(y)t ʿlmʾ* appears on an inscription from the Negev.[22] In addition, legal texts have the time designation *lʿlm*,[23] which also appears in the grave inscriptions to emphasize the inviolability of the grave, the inalterability of ownership, or the eternal duration of the curse on the grave robbers.[24]

The Palmyrene inscriptions often manifest *b(y)t ʿlmʾ* as an umbrella term for "grave site." In this respect, it can refer, like *mʿrtʾ*, to a hypogeum and, like *qbrʾ*, to a grave tower.[25] In the Greco-Palmyrene diglots, (μνημεῖον) αἰώνιον or αἰώνιος τειμή represents *b(y)t ʿlmʾ* which introduces the aspect of eternity. For the Greco-Palmyrene diglots, it is necessary to consider that some of them may have been translated from Greek into Palmyrene and, consequently, in certain cases, a strong Greek influence may underlie the Palmyrene.[26]

Furthermore, *ʿlm* as "world" appears in the divine title "lord of the world." Thus, at Palmyra, one designated Baʿalšamin as *mrʾ ʿlmʾ* "lord of the world."[27] Additional instances of this title appear in an Arabic inscription from Mada'in Salih.[28]

The Hatrian inscriptions know only the time reference *lʿlm*/*ʿl ʿlm* "forever."[29]

---

18. II,6; cf. J. Hoftijzer and G. van der Kooij, *Aramaic Texts from Deir ʿAlla. DMOA* 19 (1976), 174,224 with n. 113; *DNSI*, 160.

19. Cf. E. Blum, *TUAT.NF* 8 (2015), 472.

20. *TADAE* B2.6:4; 3.3:4; 3.8:4; 6.1:3f. (partially emend.).

21. *TADAE* B2.3:9; 2.8:f.; 2.9:9f.; 2.11:7; 3.4:11; 3.5:4f.; 3.11:8; 3.12:22f.; 5.2:8 (emend.); 5.5:4,8 (emend.); 5.6:6 (partially emend.).

22. A. Negev, "A Nabatean Epitaph from Trans-Jordan," *IEJ* 21 (1971) 50-52.

23. Texts in *DNSI*, 859-62.

24. Cf. J. F. Healey, *The Nabataean Tomb Inscriptions of Mada'in Salih. JSSSup* 1 (Oxford, 1993), 263 s.v. *ʿlm*.

25. J. Cantineau, *Inventaire des inscriptions de Palmyre* (Paris, 1930-1936), IV 3.3; 5.2; 6b.1; 9a.1; 9b.1; 13.1; 14.1 (emend.); 21.1; 22.1; VII 4.1; 5.1; VIII 58.1; 74.1 (partially emend.).

26. Cf. H. J. W. Drijvers, "Greek and Aramaic in Palmyrene Inscriptions," in M. J. Geller, J. C. Greenfield, and M. Weitzman, eds., *Studia Aramaica. JSSSup* 4, 1995, 31-42; yet H. Gzella, "Die Palmyrener in der griechisch-römischen Welt," *KLIO* 87 (2005) 445-58, is critical of generalizing this hypothesis.

27. Citations in H. Niehr, *Baʿalšamem. OLA* 123 (2004), 106 n. 99; → *mrʾ* IV.

28. *JS* 17; cf. J. F. Healey and G. R. Smith, "Jaussen-Savignac 17: the Earliest Dated Arabic Document," *Atlal* 12 (1989) 77-84; Healey, *Nabataean Tomb Inscriptions*, 60; F. Briquel-Chatonnet, "La pénétration de la culture du Croissant fertile en Arabie," in H. Lozachmeur, ed., *Présence arabe dans le Croissant fertile avant l'Hégire* (Paris, 1995), 133-41, esp. 138f.

29. B. Aggoula, *Inventaire des inscriptions hatréennes. BAH* 139 (1991), 189 s.v. *lʿlm*; K. Beyer, *Die aramäischen Inschriften aus Assur, Hatra und dem übrigen Ostmesopotamien* (Göttingen,

4. Biblical Aramaic. Biblical Aramaic attests *'ālam* with eighteen occurences in the Aramaic book of Daniel. Semantically, the term does not always denote "eternity," but, with a view to the older ten-week apocalypse (1 En. 93:1-10; 91:11-17), "epoch."[30] This is likely in the praise of God's name *min 'ālᵉmā wᵉ'aḏ 'ālᵉmā* "from epoch to epoch" (Dnl. 2:20). The characterization of the dominion of the son of man as *šolṭān 'ālam*, which can be understood as "dominion for an epoch" (Dnl. 7:14; cf. 4:31),[31] also merits mention. The saints of the Most High receive and take possession of a kingdom *'aḏ 'ālᵉmā wᵉ'aḏ 'ālam 'ālᵉmayyā* "until the epoch and until the epoch of epochs" (Dnl. 7:18). The designation of the duration of the last kingdom as *lᵉ'ālᵉmayyā* (Dnl. 2:44) stands in contrast. The discussion of a *malkūṯ 'ālam* "eternal kingdom" (Dnl. 3:33; 7:27)[32] corresponds to this usage. The aspect of eternity occurs in the wish addressed to the king *malkā lᵉ'ālᵉmīn ḥᵉyī* "O King, live for eternity" (Dnl. 2:4; 3:9; 5:10; 6:7,22)[33] and in the characterization of God as *qayyām lᵉ'ālᵉmīn* "enduring for eternity" (Dnl. 6:27). Likewise, the last kingdom will not be destroyed *lᵉ'ālᵉmīn* (Dnl. 2:44).[34] The LXX renders *'ālam* with αἰών.

With reference to the distant past, Ezr. 4:15,19 has *min yōmāṯ 'ālᵉmā* "since ever and always."[35]

5. Aramaic Texts from the Dead Sea. Of the Aramaic texts from the Dead Sea, the astronomical book of Enoch (1 En. 72-82) and the ten-week apocalypse (1 En. 93:1-10; 91:11-17) are primarily relevant for this use of *'lm*. In them, *'lm* is the "epoch" that contains spatial and temporal structures, i.e., "the unity of space and time that arose from the will of the Creator . . . in which human life plays out"[36] or put otherwise, "the space-time of the creation, structured by the courses of the stars."[37] Chronologically, the *'lm* divides into ten epochs of 490 years each.

Otherwise, Qumran regularly also exhibits the typical temporal concept *l(kwl) 'lmyn* or *'d (kwl) 'lmyn* "forever" (e.g., *l-* 1QapGen 20:12f.; 21:10,12; *'d* 21:14; in 1QapGen with the Hebraizing ending *-m*, however) or *'lm(')* following a substantive in the construct state "eternal" (e.g., 1QapGen 6:2,8; 4Q246 1 2:5.9, like Dnl. 7:14,27, → II.4). Furthermore, the meanings "grave" and "world" occur in the Palestinian inscriptions.[38]

Niehr

1998), 182; idem, "Die aramäischen Inschriften aus Assur, Hatra und dem übrigen Ostmesopotamien (datiert 44 v. Chr. bis 238 n. Chr.) – Nachträge," *WO* 43 (2013) 60, s.v. *l'ālam*.

30. Koch, *Buch Daniel*, 214-6.
31. → *šlṭ*.
32. → *mlk* IV.
33. → *ḥyī* II.
34. See *LexLingAram*, 131.
35. *LexLingAram*, 131; A. H. J. Gunneweg, *Esra. KAT* XIX/1 (1985), 83.
36. Koch, "Sabbatstruktur," 427.
37. Albani, 103.
38. Citations in *ATTM*, 658f. and 2, 455f., respectively.

עלע *ʿlʿ* /ʿelaʿ/

I. Etymology, Form, and Lexical Field. II. Usage.

I. Etymology, Form, and Lexical Field. Aramaic *ʿlʿ* /ʿelaʿ/ "rib" apparently developed from an older Semitic */ṣ́ilaʿ/.[1] Despite the masculine plural ending, in agreement it behaves like a feminine.[2] At the same time, the spelling with ʿ already in the oldest preserved specimen,[3] a saying of Aḥiqar transmitted on a papyrus from Elephantine in Imperial Aramaic orthography, reflects the secondary consonantal shift from the original Aramaic reflex of */ṣ́/, represented in Old Aramaic with the letter *q* and probably pronounced like a voiced, fricative /q/,[4] to /ʿ/.[5] As with */ʿiṣ́/ "wood,"[6] the first /ʿ/ in this unstable transitional form dissimilates to /ʾ/ in post-Christian Aramaic languages.[7] They also have *dpn* /dapn/ for "side, ribs (collectively)."[8]

II. Usage. On the whole, the word is very rare in older Aramaic. A proverb of Aḥiqar uses it for something particularly hard in a paradoxical metaphor of "soft speech,"[9] perhaps a royal command,[10] which, however, is simultaneously so strong that it "can break the ribs of a dragon like death" (*wʿlʿy tnyn ytbr kmwtʾ*).[11]

The association of *ʿlʿ* with a monster of superhuman strength also shines through in Dnl. 7:5. There, the second of the four apocalyptic beasts, which can only be roughly compared to real animals[12] and symbolizes the ravaging power of secular empires, appears with "three ribs in its mouth" (*tlt ʿlʿyn bpmh*).[13] The reference is not necessarily anatomical, rather more likely a sign of incessant voracity (cf. Am. 3:12), especially since it still boldly consumes "much flesh."

H.-J. Fabry, "צֵלָע *ṣēlāʿ*," *TDOT*, XII, 400-405; H. Gzella, *A Cultural History of Aramaic*. *HO* 111 (2015); M. Weigl, *Die aramäischen Achikar-Sprüche aus Elephantine und die alttestamentliche Weisheitsliteratur*. *BZAW* 399 (2010).

1. At least central Semitic, with an unclear etymology beyond this.
2. Thus, *tlt ʿlʿyn* "three ribs" in Dnl. 7:5, → II.
3. *TADAE* C1.1, 90.
4. Gzella, 24.
5. Now first attested in the middle of the seventh century B.C.E., see Gzella, 114.
6. *ATTM*, 519f.; → ʿʿ.
7. *ATTM*, 659; *DJPA*, 60a; *LexSyr*, 22a.
8. *ATTM*, 557.
9. *rkyk* → *lšn*.
10. Depending on the emendation of the lacuna at the end of l. 89.
11. *TADAE* C1.1:90; for parallels—in the broadest sense—cf. Weigl, 121-27, esp. Prov. 25:15 and Sir. 28:17f.
12. → *dmī* II.
13. LXX and Theodotion: τριὰ πλευρά, Pseudo-Theodotion: τρεῖς πλευραί.

Later, the noun also appears as *ʾlʿ*[14] in the geometrical or architectural sense of "side, flank."[15]

Gzella

14. On this form, → I.
15. See *LexSyr*, 22a.

עם *ʿm* /ʿamm/; אמה *ʾmh* /ʾommā/; ארם *ʾrm* /ʾaram/

I. Etymology, Forms, and Lexical Field. II. Ethnic Term. III. Religious Use. IV. "Tribe." V. "Aram."

I. Etymology, Forms, and Lexical Field. Aramaic *ʿm* /ʿamm/ "people"[1] preserves a common West Semitic primary noun and is, as in the other languages, masculine in gender. It may be identical with the word otherwise employed for "paternal uncle; tribes-fellow," which Aramaic attests, however, only as an element of old personal names.[2]

The oldest Aramaic spelled the plural with a simple *m* as in the determined state *ʿmyʾ* "the nations,"[3] later with a doubled consonant as in *ʿmmyʾ* for the bisyllabic basis /ʿamam-/ (only historically in Dnl. 3:4, etc.). There is controversy concerning whether *ʿmmʾ* in two sayings of Aḥiqar[4] represents the same word or belongs to another lexeme of the *qatal* paradigm, "totality," otherwise not evident in Aramaic.[5]

In the course of its usage in biblical and postbiblical Jewish literature, the meaning of /ʿamm/ as an older designation for a population that falls under a specific territorial government acquires a primarily religious connotation in the sense of "people of God." In accordance with Biblical Hebrew's use, it also appears in later Jewish texts for "pagans" or "common folk" (*plebs*). The Old Aramaic instances reflect the first meaning; Imperial Aramaic does not attest the word.

H.-J. Fabry, "*ʿm*," *ThWQ*, III, 134-45; H. Gzella, *A Cultural History of Aramaic. HO* 111 (2015); A. R. Hulst, "עַם/גּוֹי *ʿam/gôy* people," *TLOT*, 896-919; E. Lipínski, "עַם *ʿam*," *TDOT*, XI, 163-77; K. Weingart, *Stämmevolk—Staatsvolk—Gottesvolk? FAT* II 68 (2014).

1. After the abbreviation of doubled ending consonants between 200 and 150 B.C.E. /ʿam/, cf. *ATTM*, 120-22.
2. See M. Maraqten, *Die semitischen Personennamen in den alt- und reichsaramäischen Inschriften aus Vorderasien. TStO* 5 (1988), 57; *ATTM*, 2, 51.
3. *KAI* 224.10.
4. *TADAE* C1.1: 89,189.
5. Cf. the discussion in Gzella, 152f., with bib.

In Aramaic, the feminine *ʾmh* /ʾommā/ "tribe" serves as a broader ethnic term. In the older phases of the language, only Ezra and Daniel attest it, but with Ugaritic /ʾummatu/,[6] Arabic *ʾumma*, Hebrew *ʾummā* (Gen. 25:16; Num. 25:15; Ps. 117:1) and perhaps Akkadian *ummānu* and *ummatu*,[7] it has a clear Semitic etymology, although a relation to */ʾimm-/ "mother" is only speculation.[8] The context of its usage in Ugaritic and Hebrew (in Num. 25:15 glossed with *bēṯ-ʾāḇ*) suggests that, at least in Northwest Semitic, the genealogical nuance "clan, extended family" stands in the foreground. Yet, this word already serves in Biblical Aramaic quite generally for "nation."

Further, the book of Daniel also employs alongside /ʿamm/ and /ʾommā/ in the same formulaic expression the language (/leššān/, "tongue) to denote a nation.[9] This is unparalleled, however, in the older Aramaic sources.

Even the place name *ʾrm* "Aram" with the related adjective *ʾrmy* /ʾaramāy/ "Aramaic, Aramean" is not fixed on an ethnic meaning.

II. Ethnic Term. Although *ʿm* /ʿamm/ originally meant a people in reference to relataionship traced genealogically to a mythical clan-founder, this specific nuance "clan" is already no longer perceptible in the oldest preserved Aramaic sources. At the latest, after the economic, political, and demographic revolutions in Syria-Palestine between the Late Bronze and the Early Iron Ages, "ethnicity" could not be limited to an agnatic community. Instead, after the demise of city lifestyles—and in the case of the Arameans of Syria perhaps also the demise of the Hittite Empire—population groups reconstituted. With the rise of state structures after 1000 B.C.E., clan-associations still in existence with traditional family structures probably interacted further with charismatically and dynastically legitimized, territorially defined, and religio-culturally undergirded forms of monarchy, served by palace and temple as their political, economic, and cultural centers.[10] Thus, one cannot reconstruct a common Aramaic "people" with clearly identifiable material culture, customs, national tradition, and unified language, but only individual local phenomena. Already the earliest Aramaic written witnesses attest a multiplicity of dialects,[11] and the sources of the period employ the name "Aram" only geographically (→ V).

Therefore, *ʿm* appears in the Old Aramaic Sefire state treaties, which contain all the oldest instances, for "nation" as the population of a region subject to a political prince, who will share the penalty of his treaty violation.[12] The supplement *zy bydy* "that is my power"[13] makes explicit the definition in the sense of a common state authority.[14] One text[15] associates

6. *DUL*³, 72.
7. *AHw*, III, 1413f.
8. So *GesB*¹⁸, 71 and *ATTM*, 513, both with doubts.
9. → *lšn* III.
10. Cf. Gzella, 56-63; → *mlk* II.1.
11. Gzella, 63-77.
12. *KAI* 222 A 29f.; B 5; 223 B 3; C 16; all from Arpad.
13. *KAI* 224:5 par. 13, yet pl. in l. 10, → I.
14. → *yd* IV.
15. *KAI* 222 B 11.

ʿm with a local sanctuary and, thus, emphasizes, along with the juridical and social aspects, the religio-cultic aspect of the organization of the inhabitants of a specific region, but the key word (*ʾšrthm*) is unclear. "People of my nation" *bny ʿmy* denotes membership in such an internally structured and externally delimited group,[16] cf. *ʿmh* "his nation" at Deir ʿAllā.[17]

With the incorporation of the once independent Aramaic principalities into the Neo-Assyrian Empire around the middle of the eighth century B.C.E., the term *ʿm* disappears from the documentary material and, on into Roman times, appears only in literary texts. The Aramaic-speaking inhabitants of Syria were now part of the multiethnic state and remained so under Babylonian, Achaemenid, Greek, and Roman rule. Indubitable specimens of the word first reappear in Biblical Aramaic. It is unclear whether *ʿmmʾ* in *TADAE* C1.1:89,189 involves the plural "nations" or another word "totality" (→ I);[18] in l. 98 this contrasts this lexeme with the individual; the context of l. 189 is unclear. The *ʿm* in l. 109 could be the preposition "with."[19]

In the court tales of Daniel, almost all instances appear in the formula *ʿamᵉmayyā ʾumayyā wᵉliššānayyā* "nations, tribes, or languages" (Dnl. 3:4,7,31; 5:19; 6:26), in Dnl. 3:29 instead the synonymous singular *ʿam ʾummā wᵉliššān*. This formula emphasizes the universal validity of royal edicts and announcements in the empire, but with reference to the pagan state religion and, after the king's conversion, to the worship of the true God. The administrative recognition of several official languages in the Achaemenid Empire may have influenced the division into language groups.[20] One cannot say with certainty, however, whether *ʿam* differed, e.g., as an ethnic category from *ʾummā* as a social category, especially since the latter, like *ʿam*, denotes entire national groups in Ezr. 4:10 (→ IV). Ezra 6:12 simply employs the word *ʿam* for the same, all-encompassing target group of a royal mandate—here the protection of the Jerusalem temple from destruction.

Then, Dnl. 7:14 transfers the same expression from the political to the religious realm in the vision of the investiture of the "son of man" by promising the people of God (→ III) eternal dominion after their oppression by the sequence of secular powers.

Finally, among the Nabateans, the old meaning returns in the royal epithet *rḥm ʿmh* "who loves his people"[21] and *dy ʾḥyy wšyzb ʿmh* "who kept his people alive and delivered them" in the dating formula of Nabatean treaties from the Dead Sea.[22]

III. Religious Use. In Israel, the veneration of an official god of the kingdom and the dynasty, as other Syro-Palestinian minor states also knew, developed into an all-encompassing relationship far beyond political relations and the well-being of the ruling house. Thus, the social organization understood as a relationship was expanded into the "people of God," who have entered into a covenant with the divine ruler of all who transcend any historical or

16. *KAI* 224.21; → *br*.
17. *KAI* 312.4; Gzella, 87-91.
18. Further I. Kottsieper, *Die Sprache der Aḥiqarsprüche*. *BZAW* 194 (1990), §190.
19. Kottsieper, 224.
20. → *lšn* III.
21. In inscriptions, see the citations in *DNSI*, 865; corresponds to the Hellenistic title φιλόπατρις, cf. Gzella, 243.
22. nV 1:12,47; 2:1f.,5,18; 3:21,27; all in *ATTM* 2.

national limitation, who experience unity from this bond, grounded ethically through exclusive worship and solidarity among human beings, and who expect eschatological restoration after the experience of exile and foreign domination. Scholars often associate the beginning of this process with the fall of the Northern Kingdom to the Assyrians in 722 B.C.E.[23] Thus, Israel's Aramaic literature from the postexilic period also reproduces the nuance of *ʿm* as "people of God." It is tied to God over generations so that the exile can be perceived as a penalty for the sins of the fathers (Ezr. 5:12), it stands in a close relationship with its priests regardless of the dwelling place of individuals (Ezr. 7:13,16),[24] and the divine law guides it (Ezr. 7:25).[25] In the apocalyptic expectation, the people of God, whatever its precise definition may be, will triumph at the end of times as the "people of the saints of the Most High"[26] over all powers (Dnl. 7:27; 2:44).

This understanding also determines the use of *ʿm* at Qumran, where it appears mostly in apocalyptic passages. The opposition of the people of God and the nations in 4Q246 1 2:3f.,8 closely resembles Daniel; cf. 4Q243 16:3; 24:3f., and the passages concerning the eschatological battle with the "nations," the representatives of the evil, clearly exaggerated historical enemies of Israel.[27] The "people" will be purified[28] and is simultaneously the medium of enlightenment,[29] but its wisdom will also be shared with the other nations.[30] In contrast, 4Q213a 3-4:6 is proverbial: individual purity ennobles the entire nation. 11Q10 employs *ʿm* for *gwy*[31] and *ʾdm*.[32] Additional instances are very fragmentary.[33] In Jewish Palestinian, it represents uneducated people in contrast to the literate[34] or the pagans;[35] more in *DJPA*, 410.[36]

IV. "Tribe." Biblical Aramaic first attests the rare synonym /ʾommā/ "tribe" as *ʾummā*. Outside Ezr. 4:10, where it uniquely represents "nations," it occurs only in Daniel, consistently in an expression of totality to denote the royal authority valid equally for all (→ III). The singular appears only in Dnl. 3:29; the plural in Dnl. 3:4 and Ezr. 4:10 is vocalized in accordance with the etymology with *ʾmm* /ʾummayyā/, otherwise, probably secondarily *ʾumayyā*. *ATTM*, 2, 150 reads the same word in 4Q550 2:4,[37] for other suggestions → *npl* III.2.

23. Cf. e.g., R. G. Kratz, "Israel als Staat und als Volk," *ZThK* 97 (2000) 1-17.
24. → *khn*.
25. → *dt*.
26. → *qdš* IV.2.
27. 4Q554 3 3:21f. and 4Q550f 2; likewise, probably the fragments 4Q537 15:1; 4Q556 3:3; 4Q556a 5 1:2.
28. 4Q541 9 1:3.7.
29. 4Q548 1 2-2:14; → *nhr* III.
30. 4Q534 1 1:8; → *ḥkm* IV.
31. 11Q10 25:5 (Job 34:29).
32. 11Q10 28:6 (Job 36:28).
33. E.g., 1QapGen 15:18; 4Q543 15:1; 16:2.
34. xyRE, *ATTM*, 361.
35. xyMT 33 in *ATTM*, 358; yyEN 3:3,5 ibid. 364.
36. Cf. *DJBA*, 869b; *LexSyr*, 529.
37. *ATTM*, 2, U 2:4. *DSSStE*, 1098f., translates the same word "dread" in this instance.

V. "Aram." The Old Aramaic texts consistently employ the name *ʾrm* "Aram" as a territorial designation for Syria (thus, roughly, the Syrian wilderness as far as the Euphrates) or parts of it, although the broader distinction between *kl ʾrm* "all of Aram" and *kl ʿly ʾrm wtḥth* "all of upper and lower Aram" in the description of the region in which the state treaties of Sefire are valid[38] remains unclear. Thus, it could refer to various Aramaic states[39] and serves in biblical texts to designate the kingdom of Aram-Damascus.[40] The genealogical association of the name with Arama, Shem's son, in 1QapGen 12:11; 17:9 depends on the tradition of the division of the land after the flood. The definition of the name "Syria" in Greco-Roman sources varies similarly.[41]

Imperial Aramaic private documents from Elephantine first attest the adjective *ʾrmy* /ʾaramāy/ "Aramaic, Aramean." An "Aramaic people" as an ethnic entity cannot be identified, however (→ II), although this concept is widespread as a retrojection in the identity formation of modern Aramaic-speaking minorities. The term interchanges with *yhwdy* "Judean,"[42] even in reference to the same person, at Elephantine, too.[43] Meanwhile, the genealogical relationships of the partriarchs with the Arameans (Gen. 25:20; 28:5; 31:24; Dt. 26:5) have no known historical foundation, but probably serve to underscore the understanding of their own foreignness in Canaan according to the national theological historiography.[44] In later Jewish Palestinian and Jewish Babylonian *ʾrmy* means "non-Jew, Gentile,"[45] as also in Syriac translations of the Bible.[46]

The adverb *ʾrmyt* /ʾaramāyt/ "in the Aramaic language" derives from the adjective.[47] It appears in Biblical Aramaic in Dnl 2:4a introducing the Aramaic portion, rendered in Greek as Συριστί (see above), but also denotes Aramaic as the administrative language (2 K. 18:26; Ezr. 4:7).

In fact, based on certain phonetic, morphological, and sometimes also lexical characteristics, Aramaic can be plausibly differentiated from the other Semitic languages, specifically those of Syria-Palestine.[48] In the course of its long history, however, various population groups in the Near East employed it as a colloquial, administrative, or literary language.[49] Consequently, there was no uniform ancient designation of the language and

---

38. *KAI* 222 A 5f., cf. 222 B 3f.; see J. A. Fitzmyer, *The Aramaic Inscriptions of Sefire. BietOr* 19/A (^{2}1995), 65,67f.

39. *KAI* 201.3; 202 A 4.

40. See recently H. Sader, "History," in H. Niehr, ed., *The Aramaeans in Ancient Syria. HO* 106 (2014), 11-36, esp. 15f.

41. Cf. T. Nöldeke, "Ἀσσύριος, Σύριος, Σύρος," *Hermes* 5 (1871) 443-68.

42. → *yhwd.*

43. Cf. *TADAE* B2.1:2 with 2.2:3.

44. Cf. A. Berlejung, "Nachbarn, Verwandte, Feinde und Gefährten," in eadem and M. P. Streck, eds., *Arameans, Chaldeans, and Arabs in Babylonia and Palestine in the First Millennium B.C. LAOS* 3 (2013), 57-86.

45. *DJPA*, 76a; *DJBA*, 169a.

46. *LexSyr*, 50a.

47. *TADAE* B2.11:4,6, of the tattooing of slaves, probably in reference to alphabetic script; → *ktb* II.

48. Gzella, 16-22.

49. Ibid., passim and, in summary, 383-87.

inhabitants of Syria.[50] In the modern Semitistic sense, "Syriac" means the Aramaic language of Edessa that became the theological and liturgical lingua franca of a great portion of the Christian orient with the expansion of Christianity.[51] Thus, Syriac is Aramaic, but Aramaic is more than Syriac.

Gzella

50. Cf. T. Nöldeke, "Die Namen der aramäischen Nation und Sprache," *ZDMG* 25 (1871) 113-31.
51. See Gzella, 256-61 and 366-79.

עמק *'mq*; עמק *'mq* /'omq/; עמיק *'myq* /'ammīq/

I. Etymology and Lexical Field. II. Verb "to Be Deep," "to Deepen" (C-stem). III. Noun "Depth." IV. Adjective "Deep."

I. Etymology and Lexical Field. In Aramaic, the root *'mq* "to be deep" functions as it does in Hebrew and other Northwest Semitic languages. The stative G-stem (Hebrew only in Ps. 92:6, figuratively) is still rare in the better-attested later literary languages;[1] older Aramaic has only one instance of the C-stem "to deepen," for which Jewish Palestinian and Jewish Babylonian have the D-stem.[2] The nominal forms have a literal or figurative meaning: the masculine *'mq* /'omq/[3] "depth" also designates the "valley," and the adjective *'myq* /'ammīq/ "deep," formed in Aramaic on the *qattīl* pattern, denotes "profound, concealed."

II. Verb "to Be Deep," "to Deepen" (C-stem). The verb first appears as a C-stem "to dig deeply" in a construction report in the Old Aramaic royal inscription of Zakkur[4] with a grave (*ḥrṣ*) as object. In contracts from the Dead Sea, it also occurs as a construction term along with *ḥpr* "to dig."[5]

III. Noun "Depth." The first instances of the noun *'mq* /'omq/ appear at Qumran. In 1QapGen 21:25,32 and 22:13f., it represents *ēmæq* in Gen. 14:3,17, both of a certain

K.-M. Beyse, "עֵמֶק *'ēmeq*," *TDOT*, XI, 202-8; A. E. Meyer and T. Hansberger, "'*mwq*," *ThWQ*, III, 153–57.

1. *LexSyr*, 531a.
2. *DJPA*, 411b: "to insert deeply"; *DJBA*, 870b.
3. Later expanded to /'omoq/, see *ATTM*, 112-15.
4. *KAI* 202 A 10.
5. V 47:7 and 81:6; *ATTM*, 2, 250,256-58.

valley with this name, likewise in 4Q537 24:2. The contract V 47:4[6] has it in a property description in contrast to *rwm* "height."

IV. Adjective "Deep." The adjective *'myq* /'ammīq/ "deep" as a substantival plural in Dnl. 2:22 denotes "secrets" (fem.), similarly in 4Q541 3:3 with *bīn*[7] *b-* "to pay attention to," thus clearly as a wisdom term.

Gzella

6. *ATTM*, 2, 250.
7. T-long stem.

עני I *'nī*

I. Etymology, Lexical Field, and Grammatical Constructions. II. Generally "to Commence, to Answer." III. Religiously "to Answer Prayers."

I. Etymology, Lexical Field, and Grammatical Constructions. Forms of the Semitic verb **'nī* I "to answer" can be quite clearly distinguished semantically from the homonymous root **'nī* II "to be humble, poor."[1] At least the second, based on Moabite,[2] Arabic, and Old South Arabian, may trace to an original **'nū*.[3] Aramaic also attests both, but so far they cannot be subsumed plausibly under a common root. If, as is customary in Hebrew lexicography, one assigns the particle *lm'n* "thereby"[4] and the masculine noun /'enyān/ "matter"[5] to a further homonymous verb **'nī* III "to make an effort, to be busy,"[6] one can also assume the same for Aramaic.

Aramaic usually employs *'nī* I together with a subsequent *'mr* "to say"[7] which either represents a reaction to something previously said in the sense of "to answer" or,

H. Gzella, "Erscheinungsformen des historischen Präsens im Aramäischen," *Or* 74 (2005) 399-408; idem, *Tempus, Aspekt und Modalität im Reichsaramäischen. VOK* 48 (2004); C. Kumpmann, "*'nh* I," *ThQW*, III, 162–66; C. J. Labuschagne, "ענה *'nh* I to answer," *TLOT*, 926-30; F. J. Stendebach, "עָנָה *'ānâ* I," *TDOT*, XI, 215-30.

1. → *'nī* II.
2. *KAI* 181.6; cf. H. Gzella, review of E. Gass, *Die Moabiter*, *BiOr* 68 (2011) 162.
3. According to *ATTM*, 661, *'nī* I, also.
4. Old Aramaic *KAI* 309.14; 226.2.
5. E.g., 4Q550 1:5.
6. *ATTM*, 662 with 2:458; *GesB*[18], 713,992.
7. → *mll* V.

if it does not introduce a response, serves to express an ingressive action, "to begin, to chime in." Naturally, it occurs in this usage normally only in narrative texts and is attested in this function since the late Old Aramaic sayings of Aḥiqar. Employed absolutely with a divine subject, *ʿnī* can also function in religious language with the nuance "to answer prayer." It is less common, but early Old Aramaic already attests it.

In addition, the C-stem of → *tūb* can signify "to answer" and, in official diction, the noun → *ptgm*[8] denotes "answer." Meanwhile, → *šmʿ* "to hear" mostly indicates "to answer prayer" and the C-stem of *ṣūt* absolutely or in a construction with a direct object occasionally does so.[9]

Older Aramaic employs "to answer" intransitively, sometimes supplemented with an indirect object following *l-* "someone" or, in court style, the person following *qdm* "before." Later, it also appears as a double transitive "someone something."[10]

The form with *ʿnī* in relation to *ʾmr* in introductions to speech merits particular attention. Old and Imperial Aramaic employ both verbs in the perfect, as the morphologically unequivocal forms of the third-person plural *ʿnw wʾmrw* in the still Old Aramaic sayings of Aḥiqar[11] and of the first-person singular in the Imperial Aramaic framework narrative *ʿnyt wʾmrt* (l. 45) indicate. In contrast, the third-person masculine singular in Daniel in the same combination is vocalized as a participle (Dnl. 2:15,26; 3:24; 5:13; 6:21),[12] as is *ʾmr* alone in the meaning "to say" (Dnl. 4:4; 6:7,13,16; Ezr. 5:3).[13] Verbs introducing direct speech often appear in present forms and, thus, anticipate the temporal reference of the speech itself.[14] With regard to *ʿnī . . . ʾmr*, however, the form of *ʾmr* may have initially been reduced to the participle as the result of a "reduction of markedness,"[15] as the spelling *ʿnw wʾmryn* in the consonantal text with the third-person plural perfect of *ʿnī* and the participle of *ʾmr* indicates (Dnl. 2:7,10; 3:9, etc.).[16]

II. Generally "to Lift, to Answer." In combination with *ʾmr* in narrative texts, *ʿnī* serves to introduce speech "he began and said," in relation to a preceding speech also "he answered and said." It appears first in the fables of Aḥiqar used of talking animals[17]

---

8. As the object of *tūb* or → *šlḥ* "to send," also in the sense of "to answer," as in Ezr. 4:17.

9. 1QapGen 14:9, with *šmʿ*, and for various Heb. lexemes respectively in 11Q10 23:9 (Job 33:31); 26:9 (Job 35:13); 29:5 (Job 37:14).

10. According to *ATTM*, 2, 124 already *ʿnwk* "they answer you" in 4Q543 18:1 (R 8:3), although this is without context and otherwise read *ʿnyk*.

11. *TADAE* C1.1,169.

12. The fem. in 5:10 is vocalized differently.

13. But not in the meaning "to command": Dnl. 2:12,46; 3:13,20; 4:23; 5:2,29; 6:17,24f.

14. Gzella, *Tempus*, 95 with n. 125.

15. Gzella, "Erscheinungsformen," 74; similar to the German or English common omission of the subject pronoun in such cases: "he began and said" instead of "he began and he said."

16. Otherwise only in 3:24, where *ʿnw* is often conjectured, however, cf. *BLA*, §295u and *BHS*.

17. L. 102.

or plants,[18] likewise in the framework narrative[19] and in the Bar-Puneš story.[20] It structures the course of the text, while in documentary genres such as contracts, a simple *ʾmr* introduces quotations.[21]

Daniel follows the same usage, employing third-person singular verbs as participles for the historical present in the transition to direct speech (2:15,26; 3:24; 5:13; 6:21), but preserving the old construction with the feminine singular (5:10) and the transitional form masculine plural perfect as a participle (2:7,10; 3:9, etc.; → I). In a pair of passages from Qumran, which preserve sufficient contexts, two or three parallels appear with the third-person masculine singular that could be either the perfect or the participle,[22] and further a few examples from 11Q10 as literal renderings of the same construction in Hebrew.[23] Only fragments without context preserve perfects of *ʿnī* in other persons.[24] Introducing speech, *ʾmr* transmitted alone apparently stands in the perfect.[25]

III. Religiously "to Answer Prayers." The use of *ʿnī* in religious diction for "to answer prayer" as in Hebrew (cf., e.g., 1 S. 7:9; Isa. 30:19) is uncommon. A comparison, in the broadest sense, occurs in the Old Aramaic inscription of Zakkur,[26] where *wyʿnny* "and he [i.e., the dynastic god Baʿalšamin] answered me" denotes a reaction to the raising of the hands in prayer.[27] Meanwhile, the use of the imperfect as a past, otherwise atypical in Old Aramaic, suggests that here, too, *ʿnī* was primarily understood as a verb of speech "to answer," i.e., like the participle in Daniel (→ I), it denotes the historical present.[28]

Otherwise, *ʿnī* first denotes "to answer (a prayer)" again in the prayer language of Palmyrene dedicatory inscriptions.[29] In a dialogue with God consisting of speech and response, such as 11Q10 34:2 (Job 40:6), meanwhile, it also means "to answer" with a divine subject (→ II).

Gzella

18. *TADAE* C1.1:94,102 (*ʿnh* emend.),166,169; 194,209 are heavily emended and uncertain.
19. Ll. 14 (*ʾmr* emend.),45; *ʿnh* should probably be reconstructed in ll. 54,59.
20. *TADAE* C1.2:2 (*ʾmr* partially emend.).
21. *TADAE* B3.1:2; 5.5:1.
22. 4Q550 6+6-c:8; in addition, the reading or emendation in 4Q530 2 2+6-12:15 and 4Q546 4:1 is quite certain.
23. 11Q10 7A:1; 34:2; 37:3 (Job 19:16; 40:6; 42:1); in 9:3 (Job 25:1) a possible *ʾmr* is not preserved.
24. 4Q203 7b 1:3; 4Q541 12:2; 4Q543 18:1; 32:1.
25. Cf. *ʾmrw* in 4Q201 1 3:1; 1 4:9 (1 En. 6:4; 9:2).
26. *KAI* 202 A 11.
27. → *yd* II.1.
28. And, therefore, is morphologically a long imperfect; see the discussion in H. Gzella, *A Cultural History of Aramaic. HO* 111 (2015), 84f.; the interpretation sometimes represented earlier as a narrative short imperfect is unsubstantiated.
29. *PAT* 0393.4; 0413.3; 1911.8; fragmentarily 0065.4; etc., cf. *PAT*, 398, s.v.

עני II ʿnī; ענה ʿnh /ʿanǣ/; ענוה ʿnwh /ʿanwā/; עתר ʿtr /ʿotr/

I. Etymology and Lexical Field. II. Usage of the Adjective "Poor, Poor (Person)." III. Antonym "Wealth."

I. Etymology and Lexical Field. Unlike Hebrew, Aramaic rarely attests the root *ʿnī II "to be humble, poor"[1] and, when it does, it is primarily as the adjective *ʿnh* /ʿanǣ/ "humble, poor." Probably under the influence of Hebrew, the D-stem "to humble," however, appears in Jewish Palestinian[2] and in Jewish Babylonian.[3] Presumably, the Dt-stem in Syriac has the same basis because the examples in *LexSyr*[4] all originate from the respective biblical passages translated from the Hebrew.

A proverb of Aḥiqar attests the feminine *ʿnwh* /ʿanwā/ "poverty"[5] and describes it as the most bitter of all; the abstract /ʿanw/utānū/ and related forms for the virtue of humility appear in later literary languages.[6]

Semantically, it is difficult to differentiate *ʿnī* II from forms of the root → *špl* "to be humble," which is more productive in Aramaic. Later, the root *dwī* denotes "to be woeful"[7] and *mskn*, borrowed from the Akkadian and reanalyzed as a quadriradical, denotes "poor."[8] The noun *ʿtr* /ʿotr/ > /ʿotar/ "wealth"[9] serves as an antonym. The verb *ġθr > *ʿtr* "to be/become rich" with additional derivatives is attested later.[10]

II. Usage of the Adjective "Poor, Poor (Person)." The first instance of *ʿnh* /ʿanǣ/ occurs at the beginning of the self-presentation *ʾš ʿnh ʾnh* in the Old Aramaic royal inscription of Zakkur.[11] Since the formulation "a humble man am I" poorly suits the self-conscious tone of texts in this genre, the meaning of the word is debatable.[12] It most likely indicates Zakkur's nonroyal parentage as a *homo novus* or his pious relationship with the dynastic god Baʿalšamin and, in either case, would be self-praise.

Daniel 4:24 employs the plural *ʿnyn* substantivally for "poor, woeful" by which Nebuchadnezzar seeks pity after Daniel's warning in order to avoid the penalty for his sinful

E. S. Gerstenberger, "עָנָה *ʿānâ* II," *TDOT*, XI, 230-52; D. Markl, "*ʿnh* II," *ThWQ*, III, 166–72; R. Martin-Achard, "ענה *ʿnh* II to be destitute," *TLOT*, 931-37.

1. For the distinction between the various homonyms, → *ʿnī* I.
2. yE 80:3 in *ATTM*, 347 and in the superscription of *Megillat Taʿanit*, *ATTM*, 355; *DJPA*, 412.
3. *DJBA*, 872a.
4. *LexSyr*, 534b.
5. *TADAE* C1.1,89.
6. *DJPA*, 412; *DJBA*, 857b; *LexSyr*, 535a.
7. *DJPA*, 140b; *DJBA*, 317b; *LexSyr*, 143; *MdD*, 103.
8. *DJPA*, 320; *DJBA*, 691a; *LexSyr*, 475; *MdD*, 276.
9. < */ġoθr/, *ATTM*, 100-103,112-15.
10. *DJPA*, 422f.; *DJBA*, 885; *LexSyr*, 554; *MdD*, 43; dubious, in contrast, *TADAE* B2.4:5.
11. *KAI* 202 A 2.
12. *DNSI*, 874.

arrogance. Relatedly, care for the poor belongs to the royal ideal.[13] The word also appears as a substantive at Qumran, in three of four instances in passages translated from the Hebrew and rendering the Hebrew cognate: 4Q583 1:2 (Isa. 14:32), 11Q10 14:6; 25:4 (Job 29:12; 34:28). Finally, 4Q569 1-2:8 "remember the poor"[14] lacks context.

III. Antonym "Wealth." The noun /ʿotr/ appears immediately at the beginning of the Aramaic textual tradition in the Tell Fekheriye inscription designating the abundance that the weather god Hadad brings to the earth.[15] In accord with the orthographic tradition of Gosan, it is spelled *ʿsr* there.[16] In a proverb of Aḥiqar, it appears along with the substantival adjective *ʿtyr* /ʿattīr/ "rich," which occurs only here in Old Aramaic; the rich should not become haughty and say: *bʿtry hdyr ʾnh* "in my wealth I am glorious."[17] In 1QapGen 22:22,31f. *ʿtr* refers to Abraham's God-given possessions.[18]

Gzella

13. See K. Koch, *Daniel 1-4. BK* XXII/1 (2005), 428.
14. → *dkr*.
15. *KAI* 309:2; → *nḥt* IV.
16. H. Gzella, "Language and Script," in H. Niehr, ed., *The Aramaeans in Ancient Syria. HO* 106 (2014), 71-107, esp. 72,79-81.
17. *TADAE* C1.1:206; → *hdr*, cf. Jer. 9:22.
18. → *nksyn*.

ענן *ʿnn* /ʿanān/; ערפל *ʿrpl* /ʿarapel/; מטר *mṭr* /maṭar/; תלג *tlg* /talg/

I. Etymology and Lexical Field. II. Noun "Cloud." III. Noun "Rain." IV. Noun "Snow."

I. Etymology and Lexical Field. Aramaic, like Hebrew and Arabic, designates the "cloud" generally with the masculine *ʿnn* /ʿanān/. Yet, Aramaic seems not to use the noun collectively so that the word appears mostly in the plural.

Along with the feminine *ʿrpl* /ʿarapel/ "dark cloud," the same lexical field also encompasses the masculine terms → *ṭl* /ṭall/ "dew," *mṭr* /maṭar/ "rain," and *tlg* /talg/[1] "snow." In addition, they all belong to the common Semitic lexicon; Hebrew also has a more fully

D. N. Freedman, B. E. Willoughby, and H.-J. Fabry, "עָנָן *ʿanān*," *TDOT*, XI, 253-57; E. Jenni, "עָנָן *ʿānān* cloud," *TLOT*, 937-39; A. R. Meyer, "ʿ*nn*," *ThWQ*, III, 173–77. M. J. Mulder, "עֲרָפֶל *ʿărāpel*," *TDOT*, XI, 371-75; H.-J. Zobel, "מָטָר *māṭār*," *TDOT*, VIII, 250-65.

1. From */θalg/, later expanded to /taləg/.

developed set of synonyms for "cloud," "mist," etc.[2] The older Aramaic written sources preserve meteorological vocabulary primarily in the depictions of nature and passages dealing with the theology of creation in 11Q10.

II. Noun "Cloud." The first occurrence of *ʿnn* is in the vision of the investiture of the "son of man."[3] After the collapse of all secular kingdoms, he appears *ʿm ʿnny šmyʾ* "with the clouds of heaven" before the throne of the Ancient of Days and receives from him eternal power (Dnl. 7:13). In contrast to the monsters, which symbolize the empires in the preceding course of the vision and arise from the depths of the sea (7:2f.), long an image of chaos,[4] the "son of man" comes from the bright heights, which the reference to heaven in the formulation[5] specifically emphasizes. The LXX accentuates the convenient relationship with the old Canaanite myth of Baal as the rider of the clouds,[6] as in the Ugaritic epic, more through the translation ἐπί "on" instead of "with." It continues as a matter of debate, however, whether this rendering presupposes an original text with, e.g., the preposition *ʿl*.[7] Familiarity with this myth, at any rate, cannot be excluded.

At Qumran, the word appears quite frequently because of the numerous instances in 11Q10 rendering both the Hebrew cognate *ʿnn* and related terms such as *ʿb* "rain cloud," *nṭp* or *ʾgl* "drops," *ḥzyz* "thundercloud," and *sʿrh* "storm wind."[8] Thus, the range of Hebrew synonyms was reduced, indeed in conformity with the translation style of 11Q10.

Elsewhere, *ʿnn* occurs only sporadically at Qumran, but always in the context of creation theology: in 1QapGen 12:1 of the rainbow in the clouds as a sign of God's post-flood covenant (following Gen. 9:13), as the donor of the winter rain in Enoch's speech concerning the constancy of nature,[9] in the translation of the sacrifice regulation from Lev. 16:13 in 4Q156 1:4 of the incense cloud, and, in an unclear context, in a demon incantation.[10] In 4Q157 1 1:2 (Job 3:5) *ʿnnʾ* would normally be considered a spelling of the determined state;[11] in a nonstandard orthography, however, it could also denote the feminine *nomen unitatis ʿnnh* "(individual) cloud" borrowed from Hebrew and otherwise foreign to Aramaic, especially since the (poetic) original has an indetermined form "a cloud."

The more specific synonym *ʿrpl* /ʿarapel/ "rain cloud, dark cloud" appears in 11Q10 29:8 and 30:7 (Job 37:18; 38:9) for its Hebrew cognate, but may not be a loanword based on the broader Semitic etymology. In 4Q541 9 1:5, an apocalyptic passage, alongside *ḥšwk* "darkness,"[12] it appears in the determined state figuratively denoting the metaphysical

---

2. E. Jenni, 938.
3. → *ʾnš* III.
4. → *ym* IV.
5. → *šmyn*.
6. J. J. Collins, *Daniel. Herm* (1993), 286-94.
7. See H. Gzella, *Cosmic Battle and Political Conflict. BietOr* 47 (2003), 128.
8. 11Q10 3:8 (Job 20:6; *ʿb*); 16:4 (30:15; *ʿb*); 28:5 (36:27; *nṭp*); 29:1,2,6f. (37:11 [*ʿb*],15 [*ʿnn*],16 [*ʿb*]); 30:7 (38:9; *ʿnn*); 31:3,6 (38:25 [*ḥzyz*],28 [*ʾgl*]); 34:2 (40:6; *sʿrh*).
9. 4Q201 1 2:4 (cf. 1 En. 2:3).
10. 4Q560 1 2:7.
11. *ATTM*, 662.
12. L. 4; → *ḥšk* III.

darkness of the sin and uncertainty that the "eternal sun of God" will illuminate in the eschaton.

III. Noun "Rain." The noun *mṭr* /maṭar/ "rain" appears in Aramaic beginning with the texts from Qumran. In 11Q10, it occurs in the same contexts as *ʿnn* "cloud": 28:5 (Job 36: 27); 31:3,5 (38:25,28; → II). In 31:3 (Job 38:25), it represents the Hebrew *šṭp*, elsewhere the cognate *mṭr*. The synonyms in the lexical field "rain" are also less developed than in Hebrew.[13] Furthermore, 4Q204 1 13:26 (1 En. 36:1) employs it along with → *ṭl* "dew"; as does 4Q211 1 1:2 (1 En. 82:22), indeed with "clouds" as the subject[14] and the C-stem of *nḥt* "to bring down" as the verb,[15] cf. 1Q24 5:4 and 4Q201 1 2:4. It is also part of the angel name Matarel "rain of God" in 4Q201 1 3:9 par. 4Q204 1 2:27 (1 En. 6:7). *ATTM*, 2, 93 emends following Gen. 8:2 at the end of 1QapGen 10:1 *m*[*ṭr*ʾ "the rain."

IV. Noun "Snow." "Snow," *tlg*, appears in comparison to the white clothing of the Ancient of Days in Dnl. 7:9[16] along with → *nqh* "wool," in Enoch's dream of the punishment of the angels in reference to a house with a foundation of snow, contrary to human experience, hot and cold simultaneously,[17] and for snow-covered mountains in reference to the cardinal directions.[18] Outside the mountains, snow was very rare[19] and represents purity or threat (cf. Prov. 31:21).

Gzella

13. See Zobel, 250-65.
14. Following the emendation in *DSSStE*, 440.
15. → *nḥt* III.
16. → *ḥwr*; *lbš* IV.1.
17. 4Q204 1 6:24,26; 1 7:2 (1 En. 14:10,13,20).
18. 4Q209 23:10 (1 En. 77:4).
19. G. Dalman, *Work and Customs in Palestine*, vol. 1, trans. N. Abdulhadi-Sukhtian (Ramallah: Dar Al Nasher, 2013), 239-42.

עצב ʿṣb; עציב ʿṣyb /ʿaṣīb/; אבל ʾbl; בכי bkī; כרי krī

I. Etymology and Lexical Field. II. Usage.

I. Etymology and Lexical Field. The verbal root *ʿṣb* "to be sorrowful" appears only very rarely in Aramaic, but it has a West Semitic etymology and appears in the Gt-stem

A. Baumann, "אָבַל *ʾābhal*," *TDOT*, I, 44-48; V. Hamp, "בָּכָה *bakhāh*," *TDOT*, II, 116-20; C. Meyers, "עָצַב *ʿāṣāḇ*," *TDOT*, XI, 278-80.

indicating the medium in reference to psychic circumstances. The adjective *ʿṣyb* /ʿaṣīb/ "sorrowful" derives from it. The nuance of *ʿṣb* hardly differs from that of *krī* (also in the Gt-stem). The parallelism of *krī* with → *bhl* in the sole older Aramaic instance (Dnl. 7:15), however, suggests a state of terror (after a disturbing vision), while *ʿṣb* and *ʿṣyb* find usage in the context of care and sorrow. Thus, they approach the semantic spectrum of the root *ʾbl* "to mourn." For the verb, see 4Q531 17:3[1] and 4Q541 24 2:2,[2] for the noun /ʾebl/ > /ʾebəl/ "grief" 6Q14 2:3,[3] and perhaps, 1QapGen 6:11 according to *ATTM*, 2, 92.[4] The verb *bkī* in the G-stem denotes crying/wailing as a physical symptom of mourning,[5] optionally supplemented with *ʿl* "over,"[6] later in the D-stem "to beweep someone."[7] "To worry" can also be indicated by *yṣp*.[8]

II. Usage. The verb *ʿṣb* appears in older Aramaic only in 1QapGen 20:12. It serves as an infinitive *bʾtʿṣbʾ* to modify the verb *ʾmr* "to say" in Abraham's petition abounding in concern for Sarah. The adjective *ʿṣyb* occurs with a very similar nuance in Dnl. 6:21 as an attribute of → *ql* in *bql ʿṣyb* "with an anxious/sorrowful voice." Thus, after a sleepless night, King Darius inquires after the well-being of Daniel, who, through a court intrigue involving his envious opponents, had been thrown into the lions' den because of his piety, but survived with God's help.

Gzella

1. G-stem.
2. Gt-stem.
3. With *bky* "crying."
4. D. A. Machiela, *The Dead Sea Genesis Apocryphon. STDJ* 79 (2009), 11 criticizes this position.
5. 1QapGen 19:21; 20:10f.,16; 22:5; 4Q197 4 1:4; 4 3:8 (Tob. 5:23; 7:6); 4Q203 4:6; there are other smaller fragments with no contexts.
6. 1QapGen 22:5.
7. So perhaps already in 4Q543 17:2, cf. *ATTM*, 2, 361.
8. *ATTM*, 2, 411.

עקר *ʿqr*; עקר *ʿqr* /ʿeqqār/

I. Etymology and Lexical Field. II. Usage of the Verb "to Eradicate." III. Noun "Root Stock."

I. Etymology and Lexical Field. Aramaic *ʿqr* "to eradicate" in the G-stem and the related t-passive has a Hebrew cognate; Akkadian *uqquru* "disabled"[1] and Arabic

H.-J. Fabry, "עָקַר *ʿāqar*," *TDOT*, XI, 320-23.

1. *AHw*, III, 1427.

ʿaqara "to wound" (if not borrowed) may argue for a common Semitic etymology. The same root underlies the masculine *ʿqr* /ʿeqqār/ "rootstock, stem," but the question of priority is like that of the hen and the egg. The root[2] emanates from the stem.[3] The two terms often appear in the same context. In Nabatean private documents from the Dead Sea, one also finds *ʿqrn* (/ʿeqqārān/?) "groundstock, base amount" as a commercial term.[4]

II. Usage of the Verb "to Eradicate." As a verb, *ʿqr* first appears[5] in Dnl. 7:8 in the vision of the horns of the fourth animal to depict how three of them were ripped out before (*mn qdm*) the fourth, worst horn. Interpreters usually relate it to Antiochus Epiphanes, three of whose dynastic predecessors were eradicated.[6] In Abraham's dream of the cedar and the palm, it also expresses enduring destruction,[7] and similarly in 4Q212 1 4:14 (1 En. 91:11) the end of evildoers. No context has been preserved for 11Q10 12:6 (Job 28:9). In nV 43:10[8] it means "to clear."

III. Noun "Root Stock." Old Aramaic already attests *ʿqr* "rootstock." Use as a botanical metaphor for "descendants" seems obvious, but its very frequent occurrence in the Sefire treaties of state[9] is a typical characteristic of the style of these texts.

Nebuchadnezzar's dream vision of the world tree employs it in a different sense: on divine command, the tree should be cut down to the rootstock (root and branch) and the trunk remaining in the grass[10] placed in fetters (Dnl. 4:12,20). According to Daniel's interpretation, this announces the proud king's penance in exile, but Nebuchadnezzar will not be ultimately destroyed so that the way back to dominion remains open via the acknowledgement of the superior power of the true God (4:23). Meanwhile, even in banishment, basic provisions, symbolized by dew[11] and herbs[12] as nourishment, keep him alive. The sole instance from Qumran, 4Q530 2 2+6-12:8 (Book of Giants), also stems from a dream vision of an orchard, just as trees, in general, dominate the imagery of the visions. It deals with roots that sprout their stem.

Gzella

---

2. → *šrš*.
3. Cf. 4Q530 2 2+6-12:8, with the verb → *npq*.
4. nV 1:15,17 and 4:14,16 in *ATTM*, 2, 205-7,215f.
5. In the Gt-stem.
6. J. A. Montgomery, *The Book of Daniel*. *ICC* (1927), 292f.
7. 1QapGen 19:15, with → *qṣṣ* "to fell."
8. *ATTM*, 2, 247f.; pass. ptcp.
9. *KAI* 222 A 3,15,25,41; 222 B 2,25,32; 223 B 6; 223 C 15; 224.1,3,11,12,13,15f.,21f.,25.
10. *dtʾ*, → *ʿśb* III.
11. → *ṭl*.
12. → *ʿśb*.

ערד *'rd* /'arād/

I. Form and Denotation. II. Individual and Allegorical Meanings.

I. Form and Denotation. *'rd*, cuneiform *ḫarādu*,[1] in Aramaic originally /'arād/, pointed *'ᵃrād*, is the exclusively Aramaic designation for *Equus hemionus*[2] "onager" (not domesticated) in the North and *Equus africanus* "African wild donkey"[3] in Africa and Arabia, along with /ḥemār/[4] masculine, /ḥemārā/ and /'atān/ feminine; the sayings of Aḥiqar from the seventh century B.C.E. first attest the word in Aramaic. As *ḥᵃmōr* masculine and *'āṯōn* feminine, it also constitutes the normal Hebrew expressions. The temperament, speed, frugality, and endurance of the animal, which symbolized the unfettered and wild in the Near East, fascinated the poets and sages. Today, it is extinct in the Semitic-speaking Near East.

II. Individual and Allegorical Meanings. The word *'rd* denotes the genus or the stallion and is masculine in gender: 11Q10 32:4 (Job 39:5).[5] In 1 Ch. 8:15 and perhaps[6] in *TADAE* B8.4:15 (431 B.C.E.), it is a masculine name. Hebraized as *'rwd*, it already appears in Job 39:5,[7] always in rabbinic Hebrew, thence also occasionally in Babylonian Targumic and in Galilean Targumic under the influence of the Babylonian, in Babylonian Talmudic,[8] in the graffito *TADAE* D22.29:3 (493 B.C.E.), and also as a name in rabbinic Hebrew.

The earliest instances describe the onager as untamable,[9] an inhabitant of the hostile wilderness, in which the king who has become like an animal abides.[10] In the animal vision from Enoch 85-90 4Q201-212,[11] an allegory of world history, Ishmael appears (following Gen. 16:12) as the father of many onagers, the Arabs (following Gen. 37:25-

T. Bauer, *Altarabische Dichtkunst* (Wiesbaden, 1992); G. Denzau and H. Denzau, *Wildesel* (Stuttgart, 1999); A. Sima, *Tiere, Pflanzen, Steine und Metalle in den altsüdarabischen Inschriften. VOK* 46 (2000); M. Wagner, *Die lexikalischen und grammatikalischen Aramaismen im alttestamentlichen Hebräisch. BZAW* 96 (1966); H.-J. Zobel, "פֶּרֶא *pere'*," *TDOT*, XII, 72-76.

1. *AHw*, I, 322b.
2. In Syria-Palestine the sub-group *Equus hemionus hemippus*.
3. From the fourth millennium B.C.E. domesticated as *Equus asinus*.
4. *qitāl* noun paradigm.
5. *DSSStE*, 1196f.
6. In the reading there is *'dr*, which remains uncertain because of the similarity between *d* and *r*.
7. Wagner, 93, no. 224.
8. *DJBA*, 881a.
9. Sg. det. *'rd'* in Aḥiqar, *TADAE* C1.1: 203f., seventh century B.C.E. (for the context → *sbl* III.1). Cf. Job 39:5-8, esp. v. 5, which is preserved in 11Q10 32:4 (*DSSStE*, 1196f.). Here *'rd'* is the translation of the Hebrew *'rwd*, while Aramaic *pr'h* translates Hebrew *pr'* "wild ass," in the same verse, with the two equids in *parallelismus membrorum*.
10. Pl. det. Dnl. 5:21, for which the parallel 4:12,20 has "wild animals."
11. *DSSStE*, 398-445.

28) that overtake the lamb, Joseph.[12] As the designation for the mare, *ʿr(w)d* receives the feminine ending.[13]

Beyer

12. Pl. abs. and det. in 4Q205 2 1:25,28 (2×): 1 En. 89:11,13.
13. Babylonian Targum and Syriac.

ערר *ʿrr*; ער *ʿr* /ʿarr/; ערר *ʿrr* /ʿarār/

I. Etymology and Lexical Field. II. Verb "to Object." III. Noun "Opponent." IV. Noun "Objection."

I. Etymology and Lexical Field. Forms of the root *ʿrr* "to feud with," arisen from an older common Semitic **ṣ́rr*,[1] occur in Aramaic mostly in legal diction. The verb is unusual; Biblical Aramaic attests the masculine *ʿr* /ʿarr/ (ca. 200-150 B.C.E.)[2] "opponent" and, at the latest in private documents from the Dead Sea, the likewise masculine *ʿrr* /ʿarār/ "objection." Unrelated is *ʿrr* "to strip."[3]

II. Verb "to Object." Jewish Palestinian first attests the verb with certainty. It serves as a legal term "to object."[4] The supposed instance for "to incite" with *dyn* as object in *TADAE* B2.3:27[5] should probably be read with *TADAE ʿbdy* "sue."[6]

III. Noun "Opponent." The noun *ʿr* /ʿarr/ "opponent" occurs in older Aramaic only in Dnl. 4:16 where it is suffixed as *ʿryk* along with *śnʾyk* "your enemies"[7] in the disturbed Daniel's unfulfilled wish, probably spoken out of loyalty,[8] that Nebuchadnezzar's disas-

E. Jenni, "צרר *ṣrr* to show hostility toward," *TLOT*, 1098f.; H. Ringgren, "צַר *ṣar*," *TDOT*, XII, 464-68; F. Zanella, "*ṣrr* II," *ThWQ*, III, 444–46.

1. Hence Heb. *ṣrr*.
2. Abbreviated to /ʿar/, *ATTM*, 120-22.
3. *KAI* 222 A 41, pass.; see J. A. Fitzmyer, *The Aramaic Inscriptions of Sefire*. *BietOr* 19/A ([2]1995), 97f.
4. *DJPA*, 421a.
5. *ATTM*, 665 and *DNSI*, 889f.
6. Fem. sg. impv. *ʿbd* for "to sue someone," → *ʿbd* II.2 and *dīn* II.1; and consequently deleted in *ATTM*, 2, 460.
7. → *śnī*.
8. Cf. K. Koch, *Daniel 1-4*. *BK* XXII/1 (2005), 423f.

trous dream about his banishment and the related interpretation would befall the king's enemies.

IV. Noun "Objection." A possible early instance of *ʿrr* "objection" in a saying of Aḥiqar is uncertain.[9] It occurs for certain, however, in Aramaic contracts from the Dead Sea in waiver declarations.[10]

Gzella

9. *TADAE* C1.1:103, where one can also read *ʿdr* "help."
10. V 48:9 and 81:7; in a slight variation in V 2:6 and 3:29; Heb., but under the heavy influence of Aram. legal terminology, hV 39:27; 40:10; all in *ATTM* 2.

עשׂב *ʿśb* /ʿeśb/; דתא *dtʾ* /datæ/

I. Etymology, Lexical Field, and Forms. II. Usage of the Noun "Herb, Herbage." III. Noun "Grass."

I. Etymology, Lexical Field, and Forms. The Aramaic masculine collective substantive *ʿśb* /ʿeśb/[1] "herb, herbage" corresponds to a, probably common Semitic, primary noun. It denotes the greens that God's creation gave humanity as nourishment. The same lexical field includes *ʿśb* and the likewise masculine noun *dtʾ* /datæ/ "(fresh) grass," which arose, after the lost of the glottal stop in the final syllable[2] and the fusion of the interdentals and the dentals[3] around the ninth century B.C.E., from an old */daθʾ/, with a retained /ʾ/ in a historical spelling. The Akkadian *dašʾu* and Syriac *taḏā* (with metathesis) indicate a *qatl*-form, but the word appears in Biblical Aramaic pointing, in Hebrew, and sometimes in Syriac as a *qitl*-noun.[4] The two terms often appear together, and *ʿśb* also with *yrq* (/yarūq/?) "greenery."

II. Usage of the Noun "Herb, Herbage." Daniel 4 first attests *ʿśb*[5] in an angel's repeated formulaic command to expel Nebuchadnezzar from human society as a punishment for his arrogance so that he is wet with the dew of heaven[6] and shares herbs as

P. Maiberger, "עֵשֶׂב *ʿēśeḇ*," *TDOT*, XI, 383-86; H. Ringgren, "דֶּשֶׁא *deshe'*," *TDOT*, III, 307-9.

1. Later lengthened by an auxiliary vowel, see *ATTM*, 112-15.
2. *ATTM*, 104-6.
3. *ATTM*, 100.
4. *ATTM*, 558.
5. Det. *ʿiśbā*.
6. → *ṭl*.

nourishment with the animals; first in the dream of the world tree (4:12), then in Daniel's interpretation (4:22), and finally as a genuine, immediately executed command (4:29f.; taken up again in 5:21), as the object of the verbs → *ṭʿm* III. and *ʾkl*.[7] It refers to the fact that the king will be stripped of his majesty, but will nevertheless be kept alive through basic provisions. Analogously, Qumran employs *ʿśb* for the nourishing abundance of creation in the postdiluvian world.[8] Furthermore, it appears in the Palmyrene tax tables.[9]

III. Noun "Grass." In older Aramaic, *dtʾ* "grass" occurs three times in the same context as *ʿśb*: in Dnl. 4:12,20[10] for the grass of the field where the rootstock of the felled royal tree should be left, in 1QapGen 11:12 in the description of the nourishing earth, and similarly in 11Q10 31:5 (Job 38:27).

Gzella

7. The impf. of a contemporaneous action; H. Gzella, *Tempus, Aspekt und Modalität im Reichsaramäischen. VOK* 48 (2004), 136-41.
8. Together with *dtʾ* "grass" in 1QapGen 11:12 and *yrq* "greenery" in l. 17; likewise as a sign of fertility in 4Q211 1 1:3 (1 En. 82:22) and 4Q531 2+3:5.
9. *PAT* 0259 ii.123: hay?
10. Det. *diṯʾā*.

עשת ʿšt

I. Lexical Field and Grammatical Constructions. II. G-Stem "to Plan." III. Middle-Passive "to Be Understood."

I. Lexical Field and Grammatical Constructions. The verb *ʿšt* "to plan, think," which occurs in the G-stem in reference to a specific intention and in the related t-stem with a middle nuance for a favorable attitude, appears to involve a peculiarity of the Aramaic lexicon. The sole Hebrew instance Jon. 1:6 "to think of someone" may have been borrowed from the Aramaic, likewise the derived nouns *ʿštw* "idea" (Job 12:5) and *ʿštnt* "thought, plan" (Ps. 146:4).[1] It also appears in Old Aramaic, but otherwise has no known semantic cognates and seems, as evidenced by its distribution in literary or official

H. L. Ginsberg, "Lexicographical Notes," *Hebräische Wortforschung. FS W. Baumgartner. SVT* 16 (1967), 71-82; J. Naveh and S. Shaked, *Aramaic Documents from Ancient Bactria (Fourth Century* B.C.E.*)* (London, 2012).

1. see *GesB*[18], 1027.

texts, to be associated with the register of standard speech. For “to remember” in general, Aramaic has → *dkr*, and for “to consider, acknowledge, calculate” → *ḥšb*.

Besides the indirect object following *l-*, *ʿl* for “against” or “about,” *b-* “with”, or adverbial expressions can supplement the verb.

II. G-Stem “to Plan.” The first instance of *ʿšt* in the G-stem consists of the provision in a Sefire treaty of state against attacking a loyal treaty partner.[2] The “thinking in the heart” (*ʿšt blbb*)[3] along with *ʾmr bnbš* refers to unexpressed contemplations. In the framework narrative of Aḥiqar, *ʿšt* refers once to the harm that Aḥiqar's nephew has in mind against (*ʿl*) him,[4] and again to a plan (*ʿbd lqbl zy ʾnt ʿšt* “do what you have in mind,” l. 68). Imperial Aramaic will employ *ʿšt l-. . . bḥyy* in the sense “to think of [the envisaged heir] in life.”[5] Corresponding precisely to this usage, *ʿšyt* in Dnl. 6:4 denotes the king's intention to (*l-*) promote Daniel because of his accomplishments. Interpreters usually take the form to be a passive participle “to be intent on,”[6] which now finds support from *hww ʿšytyn l-* “they planned to” in 4Q532 2:6 (although with no further context). It consistently refers to specific, executable intentions.

III. Middle-Passive “to Be Understood.” The Gt-stem expresses more of a generally favorable attitude toward (*l-*) someone and functions as a wish for well-being in formal letters to authorities.[7] The occurrence in 4Q206 3 1:5 has no context.

Gzella

2. *KAI* 223 B 5.
3. → *lbb* II.
4. *TADAE* C1.1,25.
5. *TADAE* B3.6:3; 3.10:2.
6. T. Nöldeke, *GGA* (1884) 1019; *BLA*, §90k; *LexLingAram*, 136; *GesB*[18], 1523; contra *ATTM*, 666: pf. with a short vowel in a rare *plene*-spelling.
7. *TADAE* A4.7:23 par. 4.8:22, with *l-* and infinitive; D6.8f:1; Naveh and Shaked, A1,9; B5,5; *KAI* 319.6: “it pleased.”

עתיק *ʿtyq* /ʿattīq/

I. Etymology and Lexical Field. II. General Use. III. The Ancient of Days in Dnl. 7.

I. Etymology and Lexical Field. The Aramaic adjective *ʿtyq* /ʿattīq/ “old” belongs to the common Semitic root *ʿtq* “to depart, to advance,” which first occurs as a verb “to

J. Naveh and S. Shaked, *Aramaic Documents from Ancient Bactria (Fourth Century* B.C.E.*)* (London, 2012); H. Schmoldt, “עתק *ʿtq*,” *TDOT*, XI, 456-58.

age" in Aramaic in post-Christian literary languages.[1] In the Imperial Aramaic written tradition, the word consistently refers to objects from earlier times that do not age as people do. Thus, the "Ancient of Days" on his divine throne in Dnl.7 denotes an age beyond the typical human lifespan. Instead of this term, the noun → *śb* /śāb/ or the adjective → *rb* /rabb/ serves as "old person," *qšyš* /qaššīš/ also serves as the honorific "senior, elder."[2] The specific age of a person finds expression through /bar šanīn/ with a number ". . . years old."[3]

II. General Use. Imperial Aramaic usages of the adjective *'tyq*[4] generally describe things of undetermined age. In the formulaic certification of validity in legal texts such as endowments, which specifically establish their validity for all coming generations, the word means an "old one," that is an earlier document that can no more invalidate the present document than a new one (*ḥdt*) can.[5] A satrap's letter from Bactria employs it of old houses,[6] the harbor register from Elephantine[7] employs it often in the unexplained expression *lq 'tyq*,[8] and a letter ostracon for *qmr' 'ty[q'* "the old wool."[9] In a Palmyrene honorary inscription it depicts old wine[10] and in another[11] "old" (παλαιά) gold denari, probably according to an old weight.

III. The Ancient of Days in Dnl. 7. Thus, *'attīq yōmīn* "an Ancient of Days" (Dnl. 7:9; 7:13,22 in the determined state *'attīq yōmayyā*) in reference to the divine figure before whose throne the "son of man"[12] receives eternal dominion at the end of time does not mean an old person, but a transcendent figure lost in reverie that has existed since primeval times.[13]

Gzella

1. *DJPA*, 422b, D-stem; *LexSyr*, 553f., G-, D-, and C-stems.
2. Often attested at Hatra: K. Beyer, *Die aramäischen Inschriften aus Assur, Hatra und dem übrigen Ostmesopotamien* (Göttingen, 1998), 184, and idem, "Die aramäischen Inschriften aus Assur, Hatra und dem übrigen Ostmesopotamien (datiert 44 v. Chr. bis 238 n. Chr.) – Nachträge," *WO* 43 (2013) 60.
3. → *br*; *šnh*.
4. Rarely spelled defectively *'tq*.
5. *TADAE* B2.3:16; 2.7:12; 3.10:22; 3.11:15; 3.12:29 (cf. 2.7:6).
6. Naveh and Shaked A6,2.
7. *TADAE* C3.7.
8. For the citations, see *TADAE* D, S. xlviii, translated as "old rudder."
9. *TADAE* D7.23:3.
10. → *ḥmr*, *PAT* 2743.4.
11. *PAT* 0294.4.
12. → *'nš* III.
13. → *ywm* II.2.

פחה *pḥh* /pāḥā/

I. Etymology, Forms, and Lexical Field. II. Old and Imperial Aramaic. III. Biblical Aramaic.

I. Etymology, Forms, and Lexical Field. Aramaic *pḥh* /pāḥā/ "governor" is borrowed from Assyrian *pāḫatu*[1] and as *pæḥā*, as it also is in Biblical Aramaic pointing, made its way further into Hebrew. It behaves as a masculine, but in form has assimilated to the feminine of the *qālāt* type and therefore forms the plural with the extension /-awā-/[2] as in the determined state /pāḥawātā/. It was employed in the Achaemenid period as a naturalized official title, although not always for the same rank.[3]

II. Old and Imperial Aramaic. The letter of the Canaanite prince Adon to the pharaoh from the end of the seventh century B.C.E.[4] first attests *pḥh* "governor," but the context remains unclear. In the Achaemenid period, it denotes a provincial governor, subordinate to the satrap, who, for his part, functions as the chair of the district administration for which, in turn, the term *pqyd*[5] serves. The salutation of the petition from the Elephantine community concerning the construction of the temple addresses Bagohi as "governor of Yehud"[6] and calls Sanballat "governor of Samaria" (l. 29). The governor of Bactria appears in the Behistun inscription;[7] a letter from its chancellery attests a *pḥh* of Bactria subordinate to the satrap in late Achaemenid times.[8] The reference to the governor of Samaria in private documents[9] may mean that they required authorization from the provincial prefecture.

Meanwhile, *pḥw'*, as in *TADAE* A3.3,4[10] and, if the reading is correct, a few stamp seals, probably refers to a low-ranking official and is, then, probably not identical with *pḥh* "governor."[11]

J. Dušek, *Les manuscrits araméens du Wadi Daliyeh et la Samarie vers 450-332 av. J.-C. CHANE* 30 (2007); S. A. Kaufman, *The Akkadian Influences on Aramaic. AS* 19 (1974); J. Naveh and S. Shaked, *Aramaic Documents from Ancient Bactria (Fourth Century B.C.E.)* (London, 2012); H. G. M. Williamson, "The Governors of Judah under the Persians," *TynB* 39 (1988) 59-82.

1. Kaufman, 82 with *ATTM*, 2, 461.
2. *ATTM*, 455.
3. → *sgn*.
4. *TADAE* A1.1,9.
5. See *DNSI*, 933.
6. *TADAE* A4.7:1; the title is removed in the second version, cf. A4.8:1.
7. *TADAE* C2.1:31, the context can be reconstructed following the parallel versions.
8. Naveh and Shaked, A2,8.
9. *WDSP* 7.17; 8.10.
10. Pl., in context a complaint about wages.
11. See E. Lipiński, review of Jan Dušek, *Les Manuscrits Araméens du Wadi*, *Palamedes* 3 (2008) 231, yet cf. Williamson.

III. Biblical Aramaic. The usage in Biblical Aramaic is imprecise and refers sometimes to the satraps of Syria-Palestine, itself (Ezr. 5:3,6; 6:6f.,13), to the governor of Yehud (5:14), and in the court tales of Daniel generally to high officials along with other titles with no precise differentiation (Dnl. 3:2f.,27; 6:8).

Gzella

פלג *plg*; פלג *plg* /palg/; פלגן *plgn* /palogān/; פלגן *plgn* /polgān/

I. Etymology, Lexical Field, and Grammatical Constructions. II. Verb "to Divide." III. Noun "Half." IV. Noun "Departments." V. Noun "Apportionment."

I. Etymology, Lexical Field, and Grammatical Constructions. The verbal root *plg*, which is at least West Semitic and possibly even older, occurs in individual languages with various nuances, of which Aramaic "to share, divide" becomes distinct from Arabic "to split." The Achaemenid period first attests it as a verb normally construed as a transitive with that which is to be divided as a direct object. Yet, because of the lack in the consonantal texts of unequivocal forms such as the participle, it cannot be determined whether the later differentiation between the G-stem "to share" and the D-stem "to divide"[1] was already common in pre-Christian times.

Additional supplements can be indicated individually by prepositional expressions following *l-* for the indirect object and *ʿl* "under," later also *byn*, or *ʿm* "with." In pre-Christian times the internal passive denoted the result "to be shared/apportioned,"[2] the passive Gt-stem, the action "to be divided."[3] In post-Christian times, this usage displaced the internal passive in Aramaic.

Among the nominal forms, the masculine *qatl*-form /palg/ "half"[4] is the most common and clearly differs in Hebrew from the corresponding *qatl*-noun *pælæḡ* "ditch, water course."[5] On occasion, the plural of the *qutal*-form /palogān/ "departments" appears;[6] in

---

H. Gzella, "*plg*," *ThWQ*, III, 287-92; J. Naveh and S. Shaked, *Aramaic Documents from Ancient Bactria (Fourth Century B.C.E.)* (London, 2012); K.-D. Schunck, "פָּלַג *pālag*," *TDOT* XI, 546-48; D. Schwiderski, *Die alt- und reichsaramäischen Inschriften*, vol. I: *Konkordanz*. *FSBP* 2 (2008).

1. See instances in *DJPA*, 434; *DJBA*, 909.
2. Pf. in 1QapGen 2:21; pass. ptcp. in a periphrastic construction (→ *hwī* II) for the future in Dnl. 2:41.
3. 2Q24 4:10 par. 11Q18 20:3.
4. Later /paləg/, *ATTM*, 112-15; Syriac *qitl*.
5. Hebrew has *ḥ^aṣī* for "half."
6. In Tiberian pointing with a secondary gemination of the /g/ like the Heb. counterpart in 2 Ch. 35:5.

the Aramaic contracts from the Dead Sea (legal diction?), the feminine abstract /palgū/ serves for "half," and later for "conflict."[7] The masculine /polgān/ "apportionment" known in contracts from the Achaemenid period denotes the verbal action.

The verb *plg* usually denotes dividing as such while → *ḥlq* serves for allocation by a responsible authority. In certain contexts, however, *plg* also appears interchangeably with *yhb*.[8]

II. Verb "to Divide." The attestation of the verb *plg* begins with an Aramaic treaty from the year 515 B.C.E. There, it occurs in relation to a common land lease to denote the sharing of the seeds with (*ʿm*) the contract partner in the eighth year of the lease[9] and the mutual (*kḥdh*) sharing of "good and bad," that is, of success and failure (l. 6). It functions similarly in a document more than a hundred years later concerning the allocation of slaves from common property (*kḥdh*) among (*ʿl*) the pertinent parties.[10] These contracts were called *plgn* (→ V).

In Biblical Aramaic, the verb occurs as a passive participle (→ I) in the interpretation of the vision of the colossus as a symbol of the empires,[11] its clay feet symbolizing the last "divided, split" kingdom.[12]

At Qumran, *plg* occurs in the context of the postdiluvian land apportionment,[13] for the lot (*ʿdb*) assigned to Enoch with the angels,[14] and in relation to the division of the bread in the offering.[15] In 11Q10, *plg* translates the Hebrew *ḥlq*[16] and *ḥṣī*.[17] For a discussion of passages lacking context and in dispute, see Gzella.

III. Noun "Half." The noun *plg* "half," as a number also "one-half," appears very often in the indications of quantity in Imperial Aramaic legal and commercial texts.[18] It appears as a temporal term *p̄ᵉlag̱ ʿiddān* "half a year" in Dnl. 7:25.[19] Almost all the instances from Qumran appear in the phrase *šbyʿ plg* "a fourteenth" in a formulaic expression for the calculation of the course of the moon in 4Q208-209 (1 En. 73), similarly *bplg šbyʿyn* "in fourteenths" in 4Q210 1 3:6 (1 En. 78:7). Others appear in measurements in the precise description of the new Jerusalem.[20] No difference from *plgw* (→ I) is perceptible and the relationship to *plg* at Persepolis[21] is unclear.

---

7. *ATTM*, 668 and 2, 462; *DJPA*, 434; *DJBA*, 911.
8. Cf. 1QapGen 17:15f. with 12:16.
9. *TADAE* B1.1:4.
10. *TADAE* B2.11:3,13; concerning additional terms → *ḥlq* III.
11. → *dhb* II.
12. Examples for the meaning "composite, heterogenous" are absent from the relevant stages of Aramaic.
13. 1QapGen 17:15f. and probably 3:17.
14. 1QapGen 2:21.
15. 2Q24 4:10 par. 11Q18 20:3.
16. 11Q10 11:8 (Job 27:17).
17. 11Q10 35:9 (Job 40:30).
18. Cf. Schwiderski, 682-84, including a few older texts from the Assyrian period; *DNSI*, 912f.; the Bactrian distribution lists should be added: Naveh and Shaked, C1,34f.; 3,39.
19. → *ʿdn* III.
20. 4Q554a 1:12; 5Q15 1 1:11; 11Q18 6:3.
21. *DNSI*, 913.

IV. Noun "Departments." In Ezra, the root *plg* appears as a plural of the noun /palogān/ "priestly department" (Ezr. 6:18) paralleling the plural of /maḥloqā/ in reference to the Levites[22] in the arrangement of temple service. In the sacrificial ritual of the new Jerusalem from Qumran, the word returns as a construct *plwgt ptry* "table groups."[23]

V. Noun "Apportionment." The noun *plgn* /polgān/ occurs in Achaemenid era legal texts in the meaning "apportionment" as a contractual matter,[24] thus in the same text as the verb in reference to the action (→ II).

Gzella

22. → *ḥlq* IV.
23. 11Q18 20:3a.
24. *TADAE* B1.1:3; 2.11:14,17.

פלח *plḥ*; פלחן *plḥn* /polḥān/

I. Etymology and Lexical Field. II. General Use "to Serve." III. Religious Use. IV. Noun "Service."

I. Etymology and Lexical Field. Of the various nuances of the root *plḥ* attested in several Semitic languages, Aramaic settled on "to work, to serve" in the G-stem in contrast to the related meanings "to plow" and "to divide" for the G- (Ps. 141:7, the text is uncertain) and D-stems (2 K. 4:39; Job 16:13; 39:3; Prov. 7:23) in Hebrew. Via "to handle" one can establish a relationship to "to work" and further to "to serve," "to revere." Meanwhile, many consider Arabic *falaḥa* "to plow, to farm" an Aramaic loanword.[25]

Imperial Aramaic first attests *plḥ* as a verb, although initially only rarely. It can take a direct object with the person as a pronominal suffix or following the object marker[26] or an adverbial expression with *b*- "in, at." Already in the Achaemenid period, it appears both in the profane sense "to serve (a superior)," for either noble or humble work, and also in the religious sense "to revere (God)." The second nuance always appears in Bib-

K. Beyer, *Die aramäischen Inschriften aus Assur, Hatra und dem übrigen Ostmesopotamien* (Göttingen, 1998).

25. Wehr[5], 979.
26. In the Imperial Aramaic tradition *l*-.

lical Aramaic and often at Qumran. Older Aramaic attests it in the meaning "to work, to handle" only once (→ II),[27] but later more frequently.[28]

The masculine noun *plḥn* /polḥān/ "service" already occurs once in Ezr. 7:19 for "worship," in Jewish Palestinan as a *qitlān*-form.[29]

In the usage for "to serve," *plḥ* overlaps with → *šmš*; the nuance "to revere" finds expression in → *sgd* or → *dḥl* meaning "to fear (God)." As a noun for "work, worship," Aramaic knows the feminine /ʿabīdā/;[30] "servant" is normally /ʿabd/[31] or infrequently /ʿolaym/.[32] The meaning "to toil" belongs to the root *ʿml* in the G-stem with the related masculine noun /ʿamal/ "toil," sometimes also "work."[33]

II. General Use "to Serve." In general usage, *plḥ* first represents "to serve" regardless of the nature of the service itself. It can refer equally to the service of a very high official *bbb hyklʾ* "in the palace gate," that is, at court[34] and to the work of a slave and her daughter who are contractually bound to serve their owner and his son until his death and who will be rewarded with freedom at his death in the disposition of his will.[35] The service itself can be more precisely defined with the verb → *sbl* "to support" (*zy ysbl br wbrh lʾbwhy* "as a son or daughter supports his/her own father"), but even here includes the meaning "to attend to, to look after, to take care of." The few nonreligious examples of *plḥ* from Qumran have the connotation "to work": once in the phrase *plḥ bʾrʿ* "to work the earth (literally: to work in the earth)" of Noah's agricultural activity,[36] and otherwise in the translation of the rhetorical adynaton in Job 39:9 "Will the wild ox want to be your servant [*ʿbdk*]?" in 11Q10 32:8, which, as the following lines make clear, also refers to work with the plow.

Furthermore, in a memorial inscription from Hatra,[37] the probably substantival participle of *plḥ* can represent "servant" or[38] "soldier." In any case, the supplementary *dmlkʾ* "of the king" indicates a nonreligious usage. In fact, the meaning "soldier" explicitly arises from the analogous usage in reference to a legionnaire (*dblgywnʾ*) in a Palmyrene honorary inscription.[39]

---

27. 1QapGen 12:13.

28. See *DJPA*, 435a; *DJBA*, 912a, there also in the D-stem "to bribe"; *LexSyr*, 572; *MdD*, 374 and 366 with the by-form *phl* involving metathesis (in addition to the merger of /ḥ/ and /h/ in Mandean).

29. *DJPA*, 435a.

30. → *ʿbd* IV.

31. → *ʿbd* III.

32. → *ʿlym*.

33. Cf. *DNSI*, 870f.; *ATTM*, 660; 2, 457.

34. *TADAE* C1.1:17, Aḥiqar framework narrative.

35. *TADAE* B3.6:11.

36. 1QapGen 12:13; following *wyḥl nḥ ʾyš hʾdmh* "Noah began to be a farmer" in Gen. 9:20.

37. H1031a.2.

38. So Beyer, 112.

39. *PAT* 0290.4f.; στρατιώτης λεγ[in l. 6f. of the Greek version.

III. Religious Use. Since Aramaic also designates God as "lord"[40] beginning in the earliest sources, a religious use of the verb *plḥ* to mean "to serve God" is obvious. This service finds expression primarily in cultic worship and personal piety, while *plḥ* has the nuance here of "to revere, to worship." Thus, it occurs in Imperial Aramiac in a grave inscription from Egypt in the wish that the deceased may serve Osiris in the afterlife: *hwy plḥh*, thus an imperative with a verbal participle "be serving" or, more likely, with a substantival participle "be a servant/worshiper."[41] In any case, the participle functions substantivally in the construct. In the phrase *plḥ 'lh'* "worshiper of the gods" it occurs in memorial inscriptions from Hatra.[42]

Biblical Aramaic employs *plḥ* exclusively with a religious connotation: in Dnl. 3:12,14,18,28 for idol worship that Daniel and his companions avoid, in 6:17,21[43] for the worship of the true God, and, finally, in 7:14,27 for the defining relationship of the whole world—all nations and especially all powers[44]—with God at the dawn of his eschatological kingdom. Ezra 7:24 employs the participle *plḥy byt 'lh'* in a more restricted, probably summary, sense for the other cultic personnel in addition to various functions previously mentioned explicitly.[45]

The few pertinent instances from Qumran reflect the same semantic spectrum: in 4Q550 7+7a:1, *plḥ* denotes the worship among the Jews; in a vision of Noah in 1QapGen 15:18, in contrast, perhaps pagan idol worship (although in a very fragmentary context). The two small fragments 4Q570 16:4 (C-stem?) and 17:2 are preserved with insufficient contexts.

IV. Noun "Service." In keeping with the use of the verb in Ezra, the noun *plḥn* /polḥān/ there also denotes "worship" (7:19) with explicit reference to the temple liturgy in Jerusalem and the sacral vessels.[46] Likewise, the feminine abstract /pālḥū/ in a memorial inscription from Hatra apparently designates temple worship.[47] Additionally, the G-stem participle is a *nomen agentis* "servant/worker" and "worshiper" (→ II and III).[48] Syriac also knows the *nomen professionis* /pallāḥ/ "farmer," just as in Arabic.

Gzella

40. → *mr'*.
41. Cf. H. Gzella, *Tempus, Aspekt und Modalität im Reichsaramäischen. VOK* 48 (2004), 266 n. 63.
42. H21.2; 412a.5.
43. In the second case, the ptcp. with → *'bd* III.
44. → *'m*; *šlṭ*.
45. → *khn* II.1.
46. → *m'n* III.
47. H409c.5.
48. Cf. *DJPA*, 434b; *LexSyr*, 572.

פם *pm* /pomm/

I. Etymology and Lexical Field. II. As a Body Part. 1. Human. 2. Animal. III. Figurative Usage. IV. In Prepositional Expressions with *k*-, *l*-, and *ʿl*.

I. Etymology and Lexical Field. In Aramaic, /pomm/ "mouth" appears initially as a /qull/ form, as the spelling *pu-um-mi-e* in the cuneiform Uruk text and the pointing in Biblical Aramaic indicate, in West Aramaic secondarily as a /qill/ form.[1] Around 200 B.C.E. or shortly thereafter, the final long /-mm/ was shortened to /-m/.[2] In contrast to the paired body parts like /śapā/ "lip" and the similar /šenn/ > /šen/ "tooth" (Dnl. 7:5,7,19),[3] but very much like /leššān/ "tongue,"[4] it is a masculine. Aramaic shares the ending /-m(m)/ with Arabic. The latter, however, has the vowel ending /-ū,-ī,-ā/, depending on the case, in the construct state and especially with suffixes, like Ugaritic and, finally, also Hebrew *pǣ*, which probably arose from the accented final /-ī/ of the genitive.[5] The historical relationship between the two old forms remains a matter of dispute.[6] The oldest Aramaic written sources attest the noun. In addition to the literal use for the body part, the "mouth" of humans and the "mouth" of animals (e.g., Dnl. 6:23; 7:5) are not differentiated, but have different connotations; /pomm/ can also stand figuratively for "opening" (Dnl. 6:18) reflecting its form or for "speech" reflecting the prominent function as an organ of speech even in the literal use as a body part. This second usage underlies the usage, attested frequently especially in Imperial Aramaic documentary texts, in various, somewhat interchangeable prepositional phrases[7] and in the less frequent adverbial combination (*k*)*pm ḥd* "in agreement with."[8]

II. As a Body Part.

1. Human. All the earliest Aramaic instances attest the use of *pm* /pomm/ "mouth" as a human body part directly related to speech through which the inner attitude becomes perceptible. The Tell Fekheriye inscription already employs the word twice as part of the

---

H.-J. Fabry, "*ph*," *ThWQ*, III, 263–72 (Heb.); F. García López, "פֶּה *peh*," *TDOT*, XI, 490-503; C. J. Labuschagne, "פֶּה *peh* mouth," *TLOT*, 976-79; T. Nöldeke, *Neue Beiträge zur semitischen Sprachwissenschaft* (Strassburg, 1910).

1. *ATTM*, 669.
2. *ATTM*, 120-22.
3. Dual "rows of teeth."
4. And perhaps */ḥenk/ > /ḥekk/ > /ḥek/ "gums."
5. Like the demonstrative *zǣ* "this" < */ðī/ preserved in the Aramaic genitive/relative marker since it was not perceived as an ending.
6. Cf. the survey in Nöldeke, 171-78; J. Barth, "Vergleichende Studien," *ZDMG* 41 (1887) 633-35, assumes a phonetic development.
7. *kpm* "according to the instructions of" or "pursuant to," *lpm* "pursuant to," and *ʿl pm* "at the direction of."
8. Heb., e.g., in 1 K. 22:13 par. 2 Ch. 18:12; Josh. 9:2.

expressions *ʾmrt pmh* "the word of his mouth"[9] in the wish that Hadad accept the word of the donor[10] and that his speech please both gods and human beings (l. 14).

In contrast, the self-testimony of the deceased priest in a somewhat younger grave inscription from Nērab employs the formulation *bywm mtt pmy lʾtʾḥz mn mln* "on the day of my death, my mouth was not closed to words"[11] as confirmation that the one who commissioned the inscription was clear-minded to his last breath, for the intellectual powers of a person are evidenced in one's capacity to speak.

In Aḥiqar's admonitions, *pm* in conjunction with *šmr* "to guard" and *nṭr* "to watch over" serves to recommend discrete treatment of words and thus to depict the ideal of the circumspect and reliable court official: the eyes and ears of other people lurk everywhere, so one should guard one's mouth,[12] for the word[13] is like a bird.[14] It should only be free advisedly, but is then a powerful stratagem (*ʿzyz ʾrb*, l. 83). Thus, it is true of behavior generally that the gods will punish (ll. 171-72) people whose mouths issue evil (*lḥyh tnpq m[n]pmhm*).[15] The interpretation of l. 162 is controversial because of paleographical difficulties,[16] but here it may involve the consequences of (boastful?) speech for one's own fate, similar to the deed-consequences relationship in l. 156: May El contort (*ʾpk*) the mouth of the one who contorts words. Two further instances appear in a fragmentary context in ll. 114,155.

Against this background, the usage of *pm* in the book of Daniel, which contains the only Biblical Aramaic occurrences of the word, attains clearer contours: Nebuchadnezzar still had his boast, under the influence of the mighty Babylon, his city, in his mouth (*bpm*), when, with this folly committed despite a divine warning, he spoke about his majesty and was sent into banishment as a penance on a command from heaven (Dnl. 4:28). Likewise, the "mouth" of the small horn in Dnl. 7:8,20, which represents the peak of power at enmity with God, is not simply an anthropomorphic element that emphasizes the interpretation in relation to Antiochus Epiphanes, but an expression of folly and arrogance. Thus, both passages expressly state *pm mmll rbrbn* "a mouth that boastfully." In both cases, naïve or arrogant speech has roots in a moral breach that the practical ethics of the sayings of Aḥiqar illuminates in various facets. The same applies to Enoch's address to the evildoers from whose mouth comes *rbrbn wqšyn* "grand and hard things."[17]

9. Poetically in Heb.: Dt. 32:1; Ps. 19:15; 54:4.

10. *KAI* 309.10.

11. *KAI* 226.4.

12. TADAE C1.1:81 with the Gt-stem of *šmr* "to be on guard" and in l. 82 with *nṭr* and *pm* as object, regarding the context → *ʿyn* II; the precise expression in l. 81 is unclear because the preceding word can be read either as *lwt* or *lhn*, which does not seem to make a great difference in substance, however.

13. *mlh*, → *mll*.

14. → *ṣpr*.

15. For parallels to this central theme of wisdom in the history of traditions, see M. Weigl, *Die aramäische Achikar-Sprüche aus Elephantine und die alttestamentliche Weisheitsliteratur. BZAW* 399 (2010), 82-110.

16. Cf. the various translations in *TADAE* C, p. 46, and I. Kottsieper, *Die Sprache der Ahiqarsprüche. BZAW* 194 (1990), 21, regarding XII,4.

17. 4Q201 1 2:13 (1 En. 5:4), *bywm* emend. to *bpwm*.

2. *Animal.* In reference to animals, in contrast, *pm* regularly occurs pejoratively for destructive voracity. According to a curse formula in the Old Aramaic treaties of state from Sefire, the gods are to send *mn kl mh 'kl* "everything that consumes" into the land of the prince who violates the treaty[18] so that it suffers[19] from the mouth (*pm*) of serpent (*ḥwh*), scorpion (*'qrb*), bear (*dbhh*),[20] and leopardess (*nmrh*).[21] In an apparently similar, although very fragmentary, context, another passage mentions the devastating impact of the mouth of the lion[22] and again of the leopard.[23]

These connotations already established in older Aramaic literature left a deposit in Biblical Aramaic: first, after his escape from the lions' den, Daniel says that an angel closed (*sgr*) the lion's mouth and thereby saved him from its voracity; then, in Dnl. 7:5, in the description of the second apocalyptic animal, traditionally regarded as bear-like, which has *tlt 'l'yn bpmh* "three ribs in its mouth," and thus, presumably, consumes incessantly.[24] The fire-spewing "mouth"—here probably better "throat"—in the description of Leviathan according to 11Q10 36:4,7 (Job 41:11,13, for *pæ̂*) also belongs to the topos of the destructive monster.

III. Figurative Usage. Older Aramaic only manifests isolated cases of figurative usages of *pm*. Aside from the obvious use for "opening" in the lions' den in Dnl. 6:18,[25] as a dual *pm*[*yn*], it may describe the "blades" of a knife (*skyn*) in a saying of Aḥiqar (→ II.1).[26] Also likely, although not entirely without doubt, is the meaning "edge, seam" in the description of a dress as *pšk 1 lpm 1* "one handwidth per side" and *ṣb'n 2 lpm 1* "two fingerwidths per side" in the dowry lists in marriage contracts from Elephantine.[27]

The metaphorical use of the word also continues to be rare at Qumran. In the address to a fool,[28] *pm* "mouth" serves metonymically for "speech"[29] in *skl' dy pmk yrmnkh* "you, fool, whose mouth will throw you." Similarly, *bkl pmkwn* "with your whole mouth" appears in the summons to praise in 4Q196 17 2:2 (Tob 13:7) for the feeling expressed with the voice;[30] cf. the modifier *bp*]*m* "(I was) in the mouth (of a widow in prayer)" in 11Q10 14:8 (Job 29:13).

---

18. *KAI* 222 A 30.
19. *KAI* 222 A 31, the verb probably stood at the end of l. 30 and is lost.
20. → *db*.
21. → *nmr*.
22. → *'ryh*.
23. *KAI* 223 A 9.
24. → *'l'*.
25. As often in Heb. and even later; → *gb*.
26. *TADAE* C1.1,84, admittedly, however, in a close relationship with speech.
27. *TADAE* B3.8:8,10 and 6.1:8; D3.16:2; *DNSI*, 917; cf. the interpretation of Hebrew *pē'ā* "side" and its cognates as a feminine of the word for "mouth" sometimes suggested; discussed by A. Angerstorfer, "פֵּאָה pē'â," *TDOT*, XI, 461, for example.
28. 4Q536 2 2:11; correctly translated in *ATTM*, 2, 165 [E 7:11], contra, e.g., *DSSStE*, 1075 "the folly of your mouth" since, otherwise, *skl* always refers to the person, not the characteristic: *ATTM*, 646; 2, 447.
29. Otherwise *mlh*, as in *mly pmn'* "the words of our mouths" in 4Q557 1:4; → *mll*.
30. Parallel to *lb* and *npš* in l. 1 (Tob. 13:6), → *lbb* II.

IV. In Prepositional Expressions with *k*-, *l*-, and *ʿl*. Contrariwise, the construct state of *pm* in combination with the prepositions *k*- or *ʿl* "on the instruction of" and *l*- "accordingly,"[31] is very frequent in Imperial Aramaic legal diction. Numerous examples of *kpm* and *ʿl pm* appear at the end of private documents in the specification of the scribe and his employer,[32] sporadically, however, also for a hearing in a court record.[33]

The same formulation found in Elephantine, with *ʿl*, appears in the Nabatean summary of a Greek sales contract from the Dead Sea.[34] Another Nabatean contract employs *kpm rʾš* to express a numerical proportion.[35] Finally, *kpm ḥd*[36] or adverbial *pm ḥd*[37] denotes "(as though) from one mouth," i.e., "in agreement."

Gzella

31. As in Heb., see García López, 493.
32. *kpm*: *TADAE* B2.1:15; 2.2:17; 2.3:28; 2.4:16; 2.7:17; 2.8:12; 2.9:16; 2.10:17; 2.11:15; 3.1:21; 3.2:10; 3.4:23; 3.5:22; 3.6:16; 3.8:43; 3.9:9; 3.10:23; 3.11:17; 3.12:33; 3.13:12; 5.5:11; 6.4:9; a rare (older?) variant *ʿl pm*: B1.1:18; 4.2:16; 4.4:18.
33. *TADAE* B8.10:6, *kpm*.
34. nV 22:34 in *ATTM*, 2, 236f.; in Greek διά.
35. nV 42:9, *ATTM*, 2, 244-47.
36. *TADAE* B3.12:11,33.
37. 1QapGen 20:8.

פרק *prq*

I. Etymology and Lexical Field. II. Old Aramaic. III. Biblical Aramaic. IV. Qumran.

I. Etymology and Lexical Field. Of the various nuances of the common Semitic verbal root *prq* in individual languages in the semantic field "to separate,"[1] Aramaic stabilized with the connotation "to release, liberate" in the G-stem, while the verb in Hebrew generally refers to "to tear off, tear loose, tear up" in the G- and D-stems and in the passive Dt-stem.[2] It can hardly be determined beyond doubt whether the rare, poetic use in Hebrew for "to liberate" (Ps. 7:3; 136:24; Lam. 5:8) reflects Aramaic influence.[3]

The few instances in older Aramaic occur in religious literature or private documents, and, therefore, have an ethical or legal connotation. Later, the verb in the G-, causative-,

F. Reiterer, "פָּרַק *pāraq*," *TDOT*, XII, 111-14; *M. Wagner, Die lexikalischen und grammatikalischen Aramaismen im alttestamentlichen Hebräisch. BZAW* 96 (1966).

1. → *prš*.
2. *GesB*[18], 865.
3. So Wagner, 95.

and D-stem with the related t-passives, and the nominal derivative /porqān/ "liberation, deliverance"[4] are very frequent.

Otherwise, Aramaic also employs the G-stem of *pṣī* for "to liberate."[5] The C-stem of → *nṣl* or → *šyzb* denotes "to snatch away, deliver"; rarely *plṭ* in the D-stem serves for "to set free."[6]

II. Old Aramaic. In the first possible instance of *prq*, a provision in an Old Aramaic treaty of state from Sefire, the meaning is not yet identical with the one known later. Here, the verb seems to stand in a formulation, preserved fragmentarily, that apparently prohibits those who live near a well from "severing" it,[7] but with no object, or from laying a hand on the water supply (*wlmšlḥ yd bmy by*[*r'*]).[8] This would nonetheless suit the older Semitic meaning "to separate" (i.e., to interrupt the flow of water?) or perhaps "to break up" (in the sense of "to destroy"?),[9] that could then have still survived in this eighth century B.C.E. passage.[10] Since this is the sole occurrence of the verb in all of Aramaic before Daniel, one can only posit very vague suppositions concerning a possible shift in meaning.

III. Biblical Aramaic. The next instance, Dnl. 4:24, is a few centuries later and may already reflect the typical usage, "to release":[11] Daniel warns King Nebuchadnezzar in the interpretation of his dream "to redeem" his own sins,[12] namely his arrogance, through good works (*bṣdqh*),[13] that is "to make amends," in order to avoid his fall as a threatened penalty.

The usage of *pqr* "to liberate" well known from later Aramaic languages with the one to be liberated as object in no way speaks against this interpretation. Rather, the verb in Dnl. 4:24 has a precise parallel in its juridical usage for the "redemption" of one's distraint document (*šṭr*) from (*mn*) the creditor by paying the debt, as a Nabatean private contract from the Dead Sea offers.[14] Since the usage of *prq* for "to tear" in Aramaic is not sufficiently demonstrated because of the controversial interpretation of *KAI* 222 B 34 (→ II) and would, in any case, lead to the difficult image of "tearing sins," and, on the other

4. *DJPA*, 450f. 427; *DJBA*, 937f.; *LexSyr*, 605; *MdD*, 380.

5. Attested beginning at Qumran: 1QapGen 22:11; 4Q547 9:2; 11Q10 16:1 and 23:1 (Job 30:13 and 33:24); in contrast, Heb. has "to unblock the mouth," as in 11Q10 11:5 (without counterpart in Job 27:14).

6. → *nṣl* IV.2.

7. *l*]*prq*, probably a G-stem inf. as a complement to the preceding, partially reconstructed *lyk*[*hl* from *khl* "to be able"; → *ykl*.

8. *KAI* 222 B 34.

9. Suggested by J. A. Fitzmyer, *Aramaic Inscriptions of Sefîre. BietOr* 19/A (1995), 112.

10. For the discussion, cf. the literature in *DNSI*, 943.

11. Contra F. Reiterer, 111, who reckons with Hebrew influence, and K. Koch, *Daniel 1-4. BK* XXII/1 (2005), 385, who assumes two homonymous roots *prq* and assigns this passage to the first "to break," as in Hebrew; the common basic meaning "to separate" makes such a division into two etymological lexemes unnecessary, however.

12. *ḥṭyk*, → *ḥṭī* III.

13. → *ṣdq*.

14. nV 42:23 in *ATTM*, 2, 244-47.

hand, a comparable formulation exists in legal diction, which is also related in substance, one can best attribute Dnl. 4:24 to the verb's typical spectrum of usage in Aramaic. LXX, Theodotion,[15] and the Vulgate[16] have also understood the passage in this way, although all place the accent in their respective formulations of divine grace, not on works.[17]

IV. Qumran. Most of the very few possible cases in which *prq* occurs at Qumran are for the most part emended or paleographically disputable. The passive participle]*pryqn* in 4Q541 24 2:3 could mean "amendable" in the sense of Dnl. 4:24 (→ III),[18] but the context permits no firm conclusions. The later typical meaning "to deliver" appears in 11Q10 27:9 (Job 36:15) for the Hebrew *ḥlṣ* I in the D-stem "to save" and, if the prevalent emendation is correct, in 23:6 (Job 33:28) for *pdī* "to redeem." A private document from the Dead Sea also employs it thusly in reference to the wife in the event of her imprisonment.[19]

The emendation *mp*]*rq*[*n* "from deliverance" in 4Q157 1 2:9 (Job 5:4) offered by *ATTM*, 284 transmits the first instance of the masculine noun *prqn* /porqān/, but is quite uncertain. Thus, the oldest assured occurrence may be a passage in the *Megillat Ta'anit* (67-70 B.C.E.).[20]

Gzella

15. 4:27: λύτρωσαι.
16. *Redime*.
17. Koch, 430.
18. So *ATTM*, 2, 112.
19. nV 10:10 in *ATTM*, 2, 226-8; regarding nV 42:23, → III.2.
20. xyMT 33 in *ATTM*, 358.

פרש *prš*; פרש *prš* /parāš/

I. Etymology and Lexical Field. II. Verb in the G-stem "to Separate, to Differ, to Interpret." III. Verb in the D-stem "to Separate, to Divide." IV. Noun "Interpretation."

I. Etymology and Lexical Field. Outside Aramaic, Hebrew still sporadically attests the verb *prš* "to separate (oneself), to differ" in this form. Some, however, also assume a relationship to the root *prs* "to cut, cut off, decide,"[1] more widespread in Semitic languages,

M. Becker, "*prš*," *ThWQ*, III, 345–49.

1. So *GesB*[18], 1084.

whose counterpart in Aramaic (Dnl. 5:28, although in paronomasia)[2] and Hebrew[3] must also be *prs* according to the laws of phonetics. Late Old Aramaic attests *prš* beginning with the sayings of Aḥiqar. Mostly, it occurs transitively in the G-stem for "to separate," sometimes intransitively for "to separate oneself." In both cases, it can take a supplementary prepositional expression following *mn* "from." In addition, the nuance "to explain, explicate" easily arises from "to separate," optionally expanded by an indirect object with *l*-. The substantival passive participle with the Aramaic form /parīs/[4] "separated" underlies the name Φαρισαῖοι "Pharisees" (literally: "those set apart") first attested in the New Testament. In the intransitive usage, the G-stem overlaps its t-passive meaning "to separate oneself."

In the two older instances, the D-stem seems to have a more specific, but debated, meaning; they employ it as a technical term of Achaemenid administrative diction, usually understood in the sense of "word for word."[5] Post-Christian Aramaic attests it as "to separate" generally, even the C-stem and the corresponding t-passive.[6] In consonantal spelling, the D-stem and the G-stem are often indistinguishable, however.

This root also includes, furthermore, the masculine noun *prš* /parāš/ "interpretation," attested beginning with the texts from Qumran. Contrariwise, no plausible relationship exists with the homonymous primary noun /paraš/ "horse," whose derivative /parrāš/ "cavalry soldier" already occurs in Old Aramaic.[7]

II. Verb in the G-stem "to Separate, to Differ, to Interpret." The body of occurrences of *prš* in older Aramaic reflects the beginning of evidence for the broad semantic spectrum of the verb. The passive participle *pryš* occurs in the sense of "separate, different from one another" in a saying of Aḥiqar referring to the different lifestyles[8] of the Arabs and the Phoenician Sidonians.[9] It seems, alternatively, to represent "separated" in reference to persons in the Imperial Aramaic letter *TADAE* A4.5:10, but the subsequent context is missing, as it is in D5.58:2. An additional letter ostracon from Elephantine employs the verb instead for "to explain" with *mlh* "word, matter"[10] as the direct and *ly* "to me" as the indirect object.[11]

Qumran continues the same diction. There, *prš* appears in the meaning "to part from (*mn lw't*)" in the sense of "to go away"[12] and thus similar to → *npq*, as well as in reference to a plant that has separated from its implantation (*mnṣbhwn*);[13] the passive participle in architectural descriptions probably means "detached," but with insufficient context,[14]

2. Cf. *ATTM*, 2, 464 on *prns*.
3. *GesB*[18], 1079.
4. The corresponding form in Hebrew must be /parūs/.
5. See the discussion → III.
6. *DJPA*, 451f.; *DJBA*, 939f.; *LexSyr*, 607f.; *MdD*, 381.
7. *KAI* 202 B 2.
8. *'bydh*; → *'bd* IV.
9. *TADAE* C1.1:207.
10. → *mll*.
11. *TADAE* D7.24:15.
12. 1QapGen 14:12; 21:5,7.
13. → *nṣb* IV.2; 11Q18 14 2:1.
14. 11Q18 12 i 2f.; 33:3.

apparently similar to *bpryš*[15] in 4Q552 1 1+2:10, although it, too, is fragmentary and in a difficult context. It serves as an astronomical term for the separation of days in 4Q209 28:4 (1 En. 82:11). Against the background of these usages, and, especially of the G-stem passive participle, one definitely may also analyze the nuance "to separate, to differ" in 11Q10 26:6 (Job 35:11)[16] as the G-stem,[17] although, given later evidence, a D-stem cannot be excluded either.[18] The t-passive of the G- or D-stem for "to separate oneself" in 11Q10 36:3 (Job 41:9)[19] appears in an intransitive construction like the G-stem.

III. Verb in the D-stem "to Separate, to Divide." Clear instances of the D-stem are rare in older material, restricted to the Imperial Aramaic bureaucratic register, and seem to have the optional nuance "to set apart." The probable passive participle *mprš* occurs in *TADAE* A6.1:3 in relation to the list of a "share"[20] for administration, followed by the two distributive expressions *zn zn* [*y*]*rḥ kyrḥ* "(listed individually) by kind, month by month."[21]

Beginning here, one can comprehend more clearly the much-discussed expression concerning the reading[22] of a letter[23] before the king *mprš* in Ezr. 4:18 (similarly, probably also in Neh 8:8). The customary interpretation as "clearly, distinctly" makes little sense in context, since one must presume it, and H. H. Schaeder's suggestion, "in translation,"[24] is purely hypothetical, lacking linguistic foundation. The semantics of *prš* overall and *mprš* in *TADAE* A6.1:3 argue for the interpretation "piece by piece," thus "literally" and unabridged.[25]

IV. Noun "Interpretation." Related to the meaning of the verb "to explain," as *TADAE* D7.24:15 attests in Imperial Aramaic (→ II), is the noun *prš* /parāš/ "interpretation." In 4Q209 23:2 (1 En. 76:14) it refers to Enoch's explanation of the twelve wind gates; in the Book of Giants, it is part of Enoch's epithet *spr prš'* "the scribe"[26] of interpretation,"[27] i.e., probably "who can interpret."[28]

Gzella

---

15. *ATTM*, 2, 465 cautiously glosses it with "alone."

16. The translator seems to have derived the phonetically spelled *mlpnw* "who teaches us," from *'lp*, from the less frequent *plī* "to set apart."

17. So *ATTM*, 672.

18. So M. Sokoloff, *The Targum to Job from Qumran Cave XI* (Ramat Gan, 1974), 137.

19. Corresponding to Heb. *prd* in the Dt-stem.

20. → *mnī* III.2.

21. Other, less likely, suggestions in *DNSI*, 944.

22. → *qrī*.

23. → *nštwn* III.

24. See *GesB*[18] 1525.

25. *LexLingAram*, 140; *ATTM*, 672; 2, 465; H. G. M. Williamson, *Ezra, Nehemiah*. *WBC* (1985), 56, with bib.

26. → *spr* III.

27. 4Q203 8:4; 4Q530 2 ii+6-12:14.

28. So *ATTM*, 648; the translation "the distinguished scribe," e.g., in *DSSStE*, 411, does not coincide with the use of the noun otherwise and is also less convincing syntactically; better would be "the scribe of distinction" (ibid., 1063); → *pšr* IV.

פרשגן *pršgn* /parešagn/

I. Etymology and Lexical Field. II. Usage.

I. Etymology and Lexical Field. Aramaic *pršgn* /parešagn/ "copy" is borrowed from the Old Persian **patičagniš*,[1] whose original /t/ survives in the Hebrew *paṯšæḡæn* (Est. 3:14; 4:8; 8:13).[2] Even this may have been transmitted through Aramaic,[3] but since, to date, there are no examples from Achaemenid Imperial Aramaic, one cannot verify whether the two forms already appeared alongside one another there. As *pršgn* it also occurs in the Peshitta of the Old Testament, but, in comparison to *peḥmā*, it is otherwise very rare in Syriac.[4]

II. Usage. The word first appears in Biblical Aramaic pointed *paršæḡæn* (Ezr. 4:11,23; 5:6).[5] It always refers to the copy of an official letter (*'grh*:[6] 4:11 and 5:6; → *nštwn*: 4:23 and 7:11) to the king concerning the construction of the temple. The archival storage of letters from the correspondence of Aršama and now of the Bactrian satraps is well known. At Qumran, it twice represents the copy of a document: once a tablet (*lwḥ*)[7] and again in the superscription of a book (*ktb*).[8]

Gzella

J. Tavernier, *Iranica in the Achaemenid Period (ca. 550-330 B.C.). OLA* 158 (2007); M. Wagner, *Die lexikalischen und grammatikalischen Aramaismen im alttestamentlichen Hebräisch. BZAW* 96 (1966).

1. Tavernier, 410, §4.4.3.12.
2. See *GesB*[18], 1094.
3. Wagner, 97; direct borrowing from Persian into Heb. is very unlikely.
4. L. Van Rompay, "Some Preliminary Remarks on the Origins of Classical Syriac as a Standard Language," in G. Goldenberg and S. Raz, eds., *Semitic and Cushitic Studies* (Wiesbaden, 1994), 77.
5. In the Heb. section in 7:11.
6. → *spr* IV.
7. 4Q203 8:3.
8. 4Q543 1a-c:1 par. 4Q545 1a 1:1, Testament of Amram, in this sense apparently employed as a synonym of *spr*, → *ktb* IV.

פשר *pšr*

I. Etymology, Occurrences, External Influences, and Ancient Translations. II. Aramaic Texts from Egypt and Murabba'at. III. Daniel. IV. Book of Giants.

I. Etymology, Occurrences, External Influences, and Ancient Translations. Aramaic texts from Egypt[1] and Murabbaʿat, the book of Daniel, the Book of Giants, and many later forms of Aramaic attest the Aramaic root *pšr*. Its etymology and meaning are linked to the Akkadian verb *pašāru*,[2] Biblical Hebrew *pāṯar* and *pittārōn* (Gen. 40-41), postexilic *pāšar*,[3] and *pēšær*.[4] The widespread assumption[5] of an original Semitic root **pθr* "to resolve" is difficult, however: forms of *ptr* in Gen. 40–41, which do not conform to the laws of phonetics, must trace back to Aramaic influence and, conversely, the Aramaic *pšr* in Daniel and the Book of Giants to a late Babylonian or Hebrew borrowing. Instances of the root *pšr* in Imperial Aramaic texts from Egypt (→ II) with meanings that one could associate with *pašāru* point to an original Semitic root **pšr* preserved in Akkadian, Aramaic, and Hebrew. Meanwhile, Arabic may have borrowed *fassara* "to explain" and the related verbal noun (*masdar*) *tafsīr* from Syriac or another Aramaic language.[6]

In Gen. 40–41, *ptr* may involve an originally Egyptian loanword,[7] although semantically it overlaps for the most part with the technical meaning of *pšr* in reference to dreams.[8] Regardless of the two different roots, they merit treatment as synonyms based on their meaning. Thus, for example Targum Onqelos (but not Neofiti) and the Peshitta translate the Hebrew *ptr* with *pšr*.

The basic meaning of **pšr* "to solve," "to set free" can be derived from the Akkadian, but was also apparently known to the LXX translator of Eccl. 8:1, who rendered *pēšær dāḇār* with λύσιν ῥήματος. Akkadian also attests many derived meanings, e.g., "to release someone from an obligation" or "to pay." Postexilic Hebrew and Aramaic utilize the root mostly in reference to the interpretation of dreams (in Aramaic texts) and prophecies (in the texts from Qumran). Daniel LXX generally translates the noun *pēšær* with κρίσις or σύγκρισις and thereby employs Greek terms for the explanation of dreams.

The precise semantic and historical relationship between the technical use of these terms in Akkadian, Aramaic, and Hebrew is unclear and in dispute, however. While the

---

G. J. Brooke, "Pesher and Midrash in Qumran Literature: Issues for Lexicography," *RevQ* 24 (2009) 79-95; H.-J. Fabry and U. Dahmen, "*pešer*," *TDOT*, XII, 152-58; U. Gabbay, "Akkadian Commentaries from Ancient Mesopotamia and Their Relation to Early Hebrew Exegesis," *DSD* 19 (2012) 267-312; M. Görg, "Josef, ein Magier oder Seher?" *BN* 103 (2000) 5-8; A. Lange, "*pšr*," *ThWQ*, III, 352-59; H. Lozachmeur, *La collection Clermont-Ganneau: Ostraca, épigraphes sur jarre, étiquettes de bois*, 2 vols. (Paris, 2006); M. Nissinen, "Pesharim as Divination," in K. De Troyer and A. Lange, eds., *Prophecy after the Prophets? CBET* 52 (2009), 43-60.

1. Both the verb *pšr* and the noun *pšrn*.
2. *CAD*, XII, 236-45.
3. Only attested with certainty as a verb in 1QpHab 2:8, but also in rabbinic Heb.
4. Eccl. 8:1; CD 4:14 and texts from Qumran.
5. With the exception recently of Görg and *GesB*[18], 1088.
6. A. Rippin, "Tafsīr," in *Encyclopedia of Islam*[2] (Leiden, 1999), X, 83-88.
7. So Görg.
8. CD 13:8 employs the Hebrew noun *ptr* in *bprtyh* differently than *pēšær* (yet see 4Q267 9 4:5 *bp*]*tryhm* and 4Q298 3-4 2:9).

use of *pēšær*[9] in Daniel points to familiarity with the Akkadian noun *pišru*, it remains uncertain whether Aramaic mediated the specific usage in Hebrew texts from Qumran or whether some may trace directly to Babylonian. In any case, one cannot simply proceed from the presupposition of a shared cultural background for the two terms. In particular, one cannot say with certainty whether the meaning of the verb *pšr* in Daniel and the texts from Qumran relates to a nuance of the Akkadian verb *pašāru*, or, as seems more plausible, derives from the noun *pišru*.

II. Aramaic Texts from Egypt and Murabbaʿat. In a few Aramaic ostraca from Egypt, instructions to come or to send something precede the concluding expression *wlʾ pšrn*, translated in *TADAE* as "without fail."[10] This formulation may emphasize that the commission must be executed as stated ("without error") or with attention to the time ("without tarrying"). It could also, however, have a juridical connotation and indicate that the addressee cannot evade an obligation placed on him.

The verb *pšr* could have the same meaning and the same tone as the noun. Two lines after *wlʾ pšrn TADAE* D7.20:4 repeats: *ʾl tpšr lmʾth mḥr* "do not delay coming in the morning": in D7.27:14 (last ll.) may read: *ʾp ʾl tpšr* "tarry no longer"; in Lozachmeur, 146cc4 one may presumably better read *wlʾ*]*tpšry lm*["do not delay to" as]*twšry lm*[(the same text ends with *wlʾ pšrn*). Furthermore, *TADAE* deciphers the verb in the literary text D23.1.5a:12 as *whn ltpšr* "and if you will not tarry." In *TADAE* C3.13:50 (earlier *AP* 63:14), the haphel form *hpšr*[11] may mean "to pay," as in later Aramaic.[12] The *aleph* in the reading *wʾpšr* in the certificate of debt Mur 18:6[13] is difficult to read, but a form of *pšr* is likely nonetheless, which would then refer to a repayment. Only this latter text has a religious meaning at the same time: the signatory obligates himself to repay his debts completely, even in a year of remission (cf. l. 7).

III. Daniel. Scholarship compares the meaning and usage of the verb *pšr* and of the noun *pēšær* in the book of Daniel with those of Akkadian *pašāru* and *pišru*. The verb occurs only in Dnl. 5:12, which, in the Masoretic pointing, describes Daniel as *m^e^p̄aššar ḥelmīn* (usually translated "interpreter of dreams"), and in Dnl. 5:16, which states that he is in the situation *pišrīn l^e^mip̄šar* ("to give interpretations"). The syntax suggests, however, that the two pael participles *m^e^p̄aššar ḥelmīn* and *m^e^šārē qiṭrīn* ("untier of knots")[14] in 5:12 should be read as the peal infinitives *mip̄šar* and *mišrē*. The two expressions in 5:12 and 5:16, *mip̄šar ḥelmīn* and *mip̄šar pišrīn*, could refer to the same activity, but

9. < /pišr/.

10. Cf. *TADAE* D7.20:2; D7.37:10 (in the last line of the ostracon); Lozachmeur, 146cv6 (last ll.); 217:4 (last ll.; here *pšrn* should be read instead of the editor's *pšry* and a preceding *wlʾ* should be supplied); X7cv2.

11. Paleographically better than the reading *hwšr* preferred by TADAE.

12. Cf. also *CAD*, XII, s.v. "pašāru" 6: "to sell, release in view of a payment."

13. So *DJD*, II (1961), 101-3 and *ATTM*, 307; A. Yardeni, *Textbook of Aramaic, Hebrew and Nabataean Documentary Texts from the Judaean Desert* (Jerusalem, 2000), I, 15, refrains from attempting to decipher the passage.

14. → *qtr*.

specify two different aspects of it: Daniel is capable of solving dream puzzles by giving their interpretations.[15] The variation may have a literary function, for Daniel is known for interpreting dreams, but now he is required to explicate the meaning of the writing on the wall.

Because of the Babylonian context of this story, some have suggested that the rare Akkadian combination of *pašāru/puššuru* with *šuttu* ("dream") in the sense of "to recount dreams" or "to interpret"[16] may be relevant for understanding it.[17] In any case, the predominant meaning of this expression in Akkadian is "to resolve" or "to dispose" of a dream, i.e., to get rid of its unpleasant consequences by magical or ritual procedures, and not to give a report or interpretation.[18] The first meaning may still stand in the background of Dnl. 5, because the king indeed summons Daniel in order to alleviate his horror and the "untying of knots" may allude to the breaking of incantations. In the context of the narrative itself, however, and with a view to the parallel expression in 5:12 *'aḥ^a wāyaṯ ^'a ḥīḏān* ("to explain a riddle")[19] a verbal interpretation is more likely involved here.

The connection between *pēšær* in the book of Daniel (thirty times in the singular) and Akkadian *pišru* is closer. Here *pēšær* refers directly to dreams,[20] (written) words, or matters (*k^e ṯāḇā ḏ^e nā upīšrēh,* → *ktb*; *p^e šar mill^e ṯā*; *p^e šar millayyā,* → *mll*) to be expounded, published, or recounted. In doing so, *pēšær* functions mostly as the object of the verbs → *ḥwī*,[21] → *yd'*[22] or *'mr*.[23] Twice the expressions *ḏ^e nā pīšrā* (4:21) and *ḏ^e nā p^e šar mill^e ṯā* (5:26) explicitly introduce the verbal explication of the *pēšær*.

Meanwhile, Akkadian does not employ *pišru* in reference to dreams, but chiefly in the letters of Neo-Assyrian scholars to the king concerning astronomical observations and their significance. The typical scheme consists of the description of an astronomical observation, followed by *piširšu* ("its interpretation") or *anniu piširšu* ("this is its interpretation"), and finally a citation from the omen literature that deciphers the significance of the respective phenomenon for future events. Meanwhile, the citation itself is cryptic and requires further clarification, which is also called *pišru*. In form, the description of a dream or a document with *ḏ^e nā pīšrā* or *ḏ^e nā p^e šar mill^e ṯā* (see above) followed by the decoding of the inherent meaning—instead of applied interpretation—with a view to the future suits the milieu of Babylonian scholarship in which Daniel's court tales play out. These agreements suggest that, in Daniel too, *pēšær* denotes more the "sense" inherent in the dream itself than the verbal act of interpretation that then deciphers this sense.

---

15. → *ḥlm*.
16. *CAD*, XII, 241f.
17. The sole example of *pašāru piširšu*, BAM 574 iv.39, appears in a fragmentary context in a medicinal incantation.
18. A. Zgoll, *Traum und Welterleben im antiken Mesopotamien. AOAT* 333 (2006), 383-96.
19. → *'ḥyḏh*.
20. See the expressions *p^e šar ḥelmā* and *ḥelmā upīšrēh*, → *ḥlm*.
21. Both pael and haphel.
22. Haphel.
23. Peal, → *mll*.

Dnl. 2 describes "dream" and "meaning" together as *rāz* ("secret")[24] that God reveals. Since the "meaning" comes from God, it is *mᵉhēman* ("reliable," 2:45)[25] and *gᵉzērat ʿillāyā* ("a decision of the Most High," 4:21).[26] A comparison with Babylonian texts also unearths the distinctions that give information concerning Daniel's theological position. The usage of *pēšær* in reference to dreams, visions, and descriptions, but not to astronomical phenomena, corresponds to a belief that God reveals the future through dreams and writings (Dnl. 2:28f.). The fact that the "meaning" itself is also the subject of revelation and is not accessible through technical literature challenges the utility of mantic scholarship.

IV. Book of Giants. The Aramaic fragments of the Book of Giants from Qumran describe two dreams of the giants Hahya and Uhya with apocalyptic content. Hahya is summoned to recount his dream to Enoch, the "scribe with the power of judgment" (*spr prš'*),[27] *wypšr ln' ḥlm'* ("so that he can give us the interpretation of the dream").[28] Mahawai is sent to Enoch so that Enoch can report to him *p[š]r ḥlmyj'* ("the interpretation of the dreams").[29] Mahawai tells Enoch that they want to learn *pšrhwn* ("their meaning").[30] Although the figure of Enoch bears elements of Mesopotamian kings (Enmeduranki, Ziusudra) and sages who are associated with the mantic arts, they have no direct relation to the dream interpretation. There may be a relationship between Enoch's status as scribe of *prš'* and his capacity to exposit the meaning of dreams. The juxtaposition of the two expressions in 4Q530 2 2:14 may reflect such a general connection between dream interpretation and the scribal arts. Nonetheless, it is doubtful whether the epithet *spr prš'* itself also includes semantically the gift of dream interpretation. Like the Greek κρίνω, the verb → *prš* "to separate, to differentiate" has a broad spectrum of meaning indeed that also extends to a good faculty of judgment and the capacity to explain some things. It remains unclear, however, whether *prš*, as is the case for κρίνω, finds express usage for dream interpretation. In 4Q203 8:13, the reading *wpšr ṣbwt[' d'* ("and the interpretation of this matter")[31] could be understood as a variant of *pᵉšar millᵉṯā* (→ III) and thus allude to the preceding description of a destruction. Otherwise, with a view to the reference to "loosening bonds" in the subsequent lines, *wpšr* may be a verb or noun with the basic meaning "to loosen."[32]

Tigchelaar

24. → *rz.*
25. → *'mn.*
26. → *gzr* VI.
27. → *prš* IV.
28. 4Q530 2 2:14.
29. 4Q530 2 2:30.
30. 4Q530 7 2:10; yet one should not read *pš[r'* in l. 7.
31. *DJD*, XXXVI (2000), 28.
32. Possibly followed by *ṣbw d[y*; → *ṣbī.*

פתגם *ptgm* /pategām/

I. Etymology and Lexical Field. II. General Usage "Report, Answer." 1. Imperial Aramaic. 2. Biblical Aramaic. 3. Qumran. III. Theologically for "Divine Judgment."

I. Etymology and Lexical Field. The Aramaic masculine noun *ptgm* /pategām/ "communication, decree," which spread from Aramaic into Hebrew and is vocalized in the Tiberian system in both cases as *piṯgām*, traces to Old Persian **pati-gāma*.[1] Thus, Imperial Aramaic texts first attest it, although, as evidenced by its use in private letters on ostraca, it soon became part of the broader lexicon of the written language. As the object of → *šlḥ* and the C-stem of → *tūb*, it denotes "to answer"[2] or "to report." Religious diction applies the old meaning "royal edict" to a divine judgment. For "edict" in the stricter sense, → *ṭ'm* and → *nštwn* are available.

II. General Usage "Report, Answer."

1. Imperial Aramaic. Among the Imperial Aramaic instances of *ptgm* one first finds those in official documents. In two letters from the provincial chancellery, the expression *gst ptgm* represents "punishment" threatened against a low-ranking official for defective execution of a command.[3] In Naveh and Shaked, A1,4 from Bactria, however, it functions for "decision."[4] A court record utilizes it in the diminished sense of "word."[5] Thus, in private letters it can also serve with *šlḥ* for "report, answer."[6]

2. Biblical Aramaic. In Biblical Aramaic, too, *šlḥ ptgm(')* denotes reports and written responses to (*'l*) the king and high officials (Ezr. 4:17; 5:7),[7] once, additionally, an edict (Ezr. 6:11, with → *šnī* "to transgress"). The usage for an oral answer (Dnl. 3:16) is even more anemic and general.

3. Qumran. The expression *tūb* (in the haphel) *ptgm* for "to answer," already idiomatic in Biblical Aramaic, also occurs three times in 11Q10 from Qumran (9:2; 30:1; 34:3 [Job 24:25; 38:3; 40:7]; without object 37:5,7 [Job 40:5; 42:4]). This formulation frequently represents a diluted translation of the Hebrew *hwdy'ny* "teach me!" (30:1; 34:3; 37:7)

H. Gzella, "*ptgm*," *ThWQ*, III, 359-61; J. Naveh and S. Shaked, *Aramaic Documents from Ancient Bactria (Fourth Century B.C.E.)* (London, 2012); J. Tavernier, *Iranica in the Achaemenid Period (ca. 550-330 B.C.). OLA* 158 (2007).

1. Tavernier, 410.
2. For which otherwise → *'nī* I serves.
3. *TADAE* A6.8:3; 6.10:9; in each case the subject of the t-stem of → *'bd* "to be done."
4. With the passive of *'mr* "to be pronounced."
5. *TADAE* B8.8:2f. and perhaps 5, also with *'mr*.
6. *TADAE* D1.32:15; 7.39:8; perhaps 1.28:5.
7. Probably synonymous with *tūb* (haphel) in 5:11.

in God's speech, in 37:5 *ʿnī*. In contrast, the nuance "matter," in the plural "events,"[8] stands under the influence of Hebrew *dbr*,[9] as may also *ptgm ṭb* "a good word" for "a good matter" in 11Q10 29:4 (Job 37:13), but the relation to the Hebrew text *lḥsd* "for a blessing" is indirect.[10] A few additional passages are fragmentary (4Q546 13:4; 4Q533 3:3; 4Q556a 5 i 7).

III. Theologically for "Divine Judgment." Probably beginning from the use of *ptgm* for a royal edict as in Ezr. 6:11, religious diction applied the word to a divine pronouncement of judgment.[11] The first attestation of this usage refers to the expulsion of Nebuchadnezzar decreed by a heavenly council (Dnl. 4:14).[12] The juridical connotations of this usage become particularly clear in conjunction with *biḡzērat̲* "by decision."[13] A parallel use appears in the development of the same theme in the "Prayer of Nabonidus" 4Q242 1-3:2, where *bptgm ʾlhʾ* "according to God's edict" also refers to the dehumanization of the king as a penalty.

Gzella

8. As in 1QapGen 22:27 following Gen. 15:1, also in the Targums of this passage.
9. See *ATTM*, 672.
10. See Gzella, *ThWQ*, III, 360.
11. Cf. H. S. Gehman, "Notes on the Persian Words in the Book of Esther," *JBL* 43 (1924) 325f.
12. → *ʿyr; qdš*.
13. → *gzr* VI.

פתח *pth*

I. Etymology and Lexical Field. II. Usage of the Verb. 1. Generally. 2. Figuratively. III. Passive Participle "Open."

I. Etymology and Lexical Field. All of the chief Semitic languages know forms of the root *pth*, the basic meaning of which "to open" also gave rise to secondary uses such as "to conquer, to judge" in Arabic[1] and Old South Arabian,[2] and "to release, to judge" in classical Ethiopic.[3] The verb occurs in Aramaic initially only mostly in the transitive

R. Bartelmus, "פָּתַח *pāṯaḥ*," *TDOT*, XII, 173-91; H.-J. Fabry, "*pth*," *ThQW*, III, 365–71. H. Gzella, *Tempus, Aspekt und Modalität im Reichsaramäischen. VOK* 48 (2004).

1. Wehr[5], 939.
2. Biella, 417.
3. *LexLingAeth*, 1364f.

G-stem with an internal passive (Dnl. 7:10); in post-Christian times, the Gt-stem overtook these functions.[4]

In addition to concrete objects such as a door, a chamber, a grave, etc., *pth̩* also takes abstract objects and appears with various figurative nuances. Intransitively, furthermore, in the participle as a construction term "opening," it can denote a door. The Dt-stem finds sporadic usage as "to become seeing," which results from the usage for "to open the eyes."[5] Old Aramaic times already attest figurative usages.

In addition, the passive participle of the G-stem *ptyḥ* /patīḥ/ "opened" functions as an adjective "open" (→ III); furthermore, two home sale contracts from the Dead Sea also contain two old specimens of the masculine noun *mptḥ* /mapteḥ/ (> /maptaḥ/) "key" in relation to the transfer.[6] In isolated instances, /pomm/ "mouth"[7] denotes "opening"; either *sgr* or *skr* serves as an antonym "to close,"[8] in reference to a door, also *'ḥd* (→ II.1).

II. Usage of the Verb.

1. Generally. An Imperial Aramaic private document from Egypt first attests the general usage of *ptḥ* "to open" with material objects. This building permit grants one party to the contract the right to open a gate or a gateway (*'nt šlyṭ lmptḥ tr'*).[9] The participle *ptḥ* /pāteḥ/ "opening" in reference to a door (*dš*) appears in a description as the antonym of *'ḥd* /'āḥed/, literally "stopping," here probably in the sense "closing."[10] The precise meaning is unclear. The usage in a commercial text[11] is also unclear.

Biblical Aramaic has only one instance of the fientic usage "to open" in the court scene of Dnl. 7:10, which depicts how the heavenly judgment on the secular powers took place and *spryn ptyḥw* "books were opened."[12] The text does not characterize their contents, but in context, one can best think of heavenly books of revelation or of the "book of life"[13] that lists the course of the world or the deeds of every individual, respectively.

Paralleling the internal passive of the perfect in Dnl. 7:10, which first disappears from Aramaic in the imperfect and around the time of Christ's birth also in the perfect,[14] the Levi apocryphon in an apocalyptic scene employs the imperfect of the Gt-stem for the

4. Cf. Dnl. 7:10 with 4Q541 7:4.

5. For this, Hebrew has mostly *pqḥ*, see *GesB*[18], 1072f.

6. V 47:4 in *ATTM*, 2, 249f.; with → *tr'* "gate"; 81:4 on pp. 256-58; with the plural of *dš* for "leaves of a door."

7. → *pm* III.

8. *ATTM*, 644,646.

9. *TADAE* B2.1:14; conversely, the negated infinitive *l' lmptḥ* later in Jewish Palestinian ossuary inscriptions denotes "not to open," i.e., "one may not open," instances in *ATTM*, 673 and *DNSI*, 949.

10. *TADAE* B3.10:13.

11. *TADAE* C3.28:48.

12. → *spr* II.2.

13. → *ḥyī* IV.

14. *ATTM*, 152.

opening of the *spry ḥkm[tʾ* "books of wisdom."[15] The opening of books in the agentless passive, which echoes official style, also occurs elsewhere at Qumran in the story at the Achaemenid court in reference to a scroll[16] and in the Book of Giants, as in Dnl. 7:10 for books in a court scene,[17] both in the internal passive of the perfect.

A few other texts from Qumran contain additional uses of the verb in the concrete sense: the active in 1QapGen 12:15 for a vessel (*kmr*) and the internal passive of the perfect in 4Q206 4 1:17 (1 En. 89:3) for the subterranean reservoir of water in the flood in Enoch's animal allegory (*ḥdr* "chamber").[18] Otherwise, only a couple of debated and emended instances in fragmentary contexts remain.[19]

Furthermore, grave inscriptions also employ *pṯḥ* regularly in the prohibition against opening the pertinent grave, e.g., in addition to Jewish ossuaries,[20] in Nabatean[21] and in Palmyrene.[22] Such formulas follow an old West Semitic tradition[23] and intend to hinder the grave, as the last connection to the living, from being taken from the deceased.

2. *Figuratively.* Isolated uses of *pṯḥ* with nonmaterial objects already in Old Aramaic point to a broader, sometimes figurative usage. In a treaty of state from Sefire, it occurs as an intransitive with → *ʾrḥ* "way" as subject in the agreement to give a messenger[24] of the treaty partner free passage.[25] One can explain the feminine participle *pṯḥh* "is opened" most naturally as a passive (→ III);[26] in this case, it would appear in a deontic-modal nominal clause,[27] for which one would otherwise expect the short imperfect of *hwī*.[28]

Thereafter, later Old Aramaic attests the verb frequently in the sayings of Aḥiqar. Two instances appear in the context of the admonition to cautious handling of speech with →

15. 4Q541 7:4; → *ḥkm* IV.

16. 4Q550 1:6; *mglh*, → *gll*.

17. 4Q530 2 2+6-12:18; one can plausibly supply *sp*]*ryn* here as the preceding subject.

18. Borrowed from the Heb., cf. *ATTM*, 573.

19. 4Q530 2 2+ 6-12:4; 4Q546 14:3; according to *ATTM*, 2, 144 (there F 1:11) also 4Q552 1 1:11, where, however, other editors, such as *DSSStE*, 1102 read only *ḥd*.

20. *ATTM*, 673, see above; sometimes with the prepositional expression introduced with *ʿl* "concerning."

21. E.g., H11.3 and 13.1 as cited in J. F. Healey, *The Nabataean Tomb Inscriptions of Madaʾin Salih*. *JSSSup* 1 (1993), 131,144, both in the t-stem, the first of which unexpectedly, however, appears in an active construction, and thus is probably either a scribal error or a benefactive "for one's self."

22. *PAT* 0574.6; 1240.2; for the report of an actual opening, cf. 0208.2,5.

23. Regarding the Phoenician, e.g., *KAI* 1.2; 13.4; 14.4; for Hebrew, *KAI* 191 B 2f.

24. → *mlʾk*.

25. *KAI* 224.8f.

26. So, among others, J. A. Fitzmyer, *Aramaic Inscriptions of Sefire*. *BietOr* 19/A (^{2}1995), 151.

27. Cf. R. Degen, *Altaramäische Grammatik der Inschriften des 10.–8. Jh. v. Chr.* *AKM* 38,8 (1969), 118, penultimate l.

28. Gzella, 271-74; → *hwī* II.

pm "mouth" as the object,[29] and a possible additional instance with the heart (l. 98), but the reading of a form of *ptḥ* there is not entirely assured.

Jewish, and later especially Christian, Aramaic literature employs *ptḥ* with the eyes[30] and ears, too. In Enoch's allegorical vision of the history of the world in the form of animals, it denotes the reception of the divine revelation at Sinai,[31] here in the t-passive "their eyes were opened." Further, Mk. 7:34 transmits a reflexive or middle form of the Gt-stem in Jesus's saying "Ephphatha" as a pronouncement of healing for a deaf and dumb person: based on the pronunciation, εφφαθα is an imperative */ʾetpataḥ/[32] "open" transcribed as *ʾeppaṯaḥ* and glossed in the Greek as διανοίχθητι. These usages and the abbreviation of "to open the mouth" meaning "to begin to speak"[33] are also common later,[34] in Jewish Babylonian more often for "to begin."[35] Beyer[36] already finds an example of the last nuance in *ptḥw qrbʾ* "they opened = began the battle."[37]

III. Passive Participle "Open." The passive participle *ptyḥ* "opened = open" can function adjectivally. In Imperial Aramaic, it refers only to windows (*kwh*) and doors (→ II.1) in an architectural sense "opened in the direction of."[38] It occurs with this nuance in descriptions of real estate in private documents[39] and analogously in Dnl. 6:11[40] LXX (6:10), although translated differently in Theodotion and the Vulgate "he opened the window," which makes objective sense (since windows can be closed with wooden shutters), but is linguistically difficult. It appears in the same meaning in the descriptions of a gate "opened into (the court)" in the vision of the heavenly Jerusalem[41] and in sales contracts for homes from the Dead Sea ("has an entrance").[42] Meanwhile, it seems to mean "open gates" in 4Q204 1 13:23 (1 En. 35:1).

Gzella

---

29. *TADAE* C1.1:114,162.
30. → *ʿyn*.
31. 4Q206 4 3:17 (1 En. 89:28).
32. < */ʾetpateḥ/, see *ATTM*, 130.
33. For which older Aramaic utilized → *ʿnī* I.
34. *DJPA*, 454f.; *LexSyr*, 616f.
35. *DJBA*, 946f.
36. *ATTM*, 182.
37. 1QapGen 21:31; so also D. A. Machiela, *The Dead Sea Genesis Apocryphon. STDJ* 79 (2009), 80.
38. *l-*; then *lgw*, *lgh*; in Dnl. 6:11 *ngd*.
39. *TADAE* B2.10:6; 3.12:21.
40. See the more extensive treatment in Gzella, 174-77c6; → *ṣlī* II.
41. 5Q15 1 2:2; fragmentarily in l. 14.
42. V 45:4, *ATTM*, 320f.; V 81:2, *ATTM*, 256-58.

צבי *ṣbī*; צבו *ṣbw* /ṣabū/; צבין *ṣbyn* /ṣebyān/

I. Etymology, Overview. II. Imperial Aramaic. 1. Verb. 2. Noun. III. Biblical Aramaic. IV. Qumran.

I. Etymology, Overview. *Ṣbī* "to want, to seek" is a verb with a III-*ī* root from an original III-*ū* (Arabic), attested only in the G-stem with an *i*-perfect (*ṣabī*),[1] and with a verbal abstract *ṣbyn* /ṣebyān/ "pleasing" based on the *qutlān* pattern[2] first attested at Qumran, and which appears later in West Aramaic as *ṣbywn* /ṣiḇyōn/. Otherwise, a noun in the *qalūt* pattern[3] meaning "concern, matter" appears in the earliest specimens from the fifth century B.C.E., but in later times can also mean "will,"[4] for which, however, the peal infinitive is still available (Dnl. 4:32). Regarding the development of meaning from "will, desire" to "concern, matter," compare Hebrew *ḥēp̄æṣ* "pleasure, interest, intention, concern"[5] and Arab. *šay'* "matter" from *šā'a* "to will/want."

Ugaritic and Phoenician do not attest the root; Hebrew does not have it as a verb, but the noun *ṣ^eḇī* "ornament, finery" probably belongs here. Akkadian has the cognates *ṣabū i/ī*[6] "to wish" and *ṣibūtu* "wish, intention, want,"[7] and Arabic has *ṣabā yaṣbū* "to seek, to strive."[8] Old South Arabian and Ethiopic lack the root. The post-Imperial Aramaic literary languages, Nabatean and Palmyrene,[9] and the later dialects[10] well attest the forms mentioned for the most part. Old Aramaic, Imperial Aramaic, Biblical Aramaic, and Qumran attest *ṣbī* "to want"; Imperial Aramaic and Biblical Aramaic (once) attest *ṣbw* "matter, concern"; Qumran first has *ṣbyn* "pleasure" (only once).

H. Madl, "צְבִי *ṣ^eḇî*," *TDOT*, XII, 232-38; J. Naveh and S. Shaked, *Aramaic Documents from Ancient Bactria (Fourth Century B.C.E.)* (London, 2012); D. Schwiderski, *Die alt- und reichsaramäischen Inschriften*, vol. I: *Konkordanz. FSBP* 2 (2008); A. Tal, *A Dictionary of Samaritan Aramaic*, 2 vols. (Leiden, 2000).

1. *ATTM*, 491,673.
2. *ATTM*, 2, 322; Syr. *ṣeḇyānā*, *LexSyr*, 619.
3. *ATTM*, 444,674; the /ū/ is the vocalized third radical before the fem. ending /-t/.
4. Syriac *ṣḇūṯā*, *LexSyr*, *loc. cit.*, "1. voluntas, 2. negotium, res, 3. res concreta"; Jewish East Aramaic *ṣbwt'*, *DJBA*, 950 n.f. "will, thing, affairs"; Mandean *ṣbu*, *MdD*, 388ff. "a) will, desire, b) business, affair, thing."
5. *GesB*[18], 380f.
6. *AHw*, II, 1073 dubiously "*ṣbī* ?"
7. *AHw*, II, 1099, *CAD*, XVI, 167-71.
8. Lane, 1649.
9. *DNSI*, s.v. *ṣbh*.
10. Dalman, 357: *ṣb'*, *ṣbh* "to want, wish," 358: *ṣbwt' ṣ^ebūṯā* "will"; *loc. cit. ṣbywn ṣiḇyōn* "will, desire"; Jewish West Aramaic *DJPA*, 457: *ṣby* "to want, desire," *ṣbw* n.f. "thing, object"; Jewish East Aramaic *DJBA*, 950: *ṣby* "to want, desire"; *ṣbyyn'* (*sic*) "will, free will"; Mandean *MdD*, *loc. cit.*: *ṣba* I "to want"; *ṣubiana* I "will, wish; desire, purpose"; Samaritan Tal, 719.

II. Imperial Aramaic.

1. Verb. In six of the rather old graffiti from Ḥamā (ninth through eighth centuries),[11] the very brief texts consist of the form *ṣbh* which follow a (not always legible) personal name; the interpretation is very uncertain.[12] Apart from these, there are nineteen instances from Egypt, mostly from the fifth century, and one from Bactria; fifteen times it appears in the perfect, twice in the imperfect, three times as a participle in various constructions, employed absolutely, with an asyndetic imperfect, with an accusative, or with *zy* "that." In the latest instance (from the third or second century)[13] the participles appear with *l-* and an infinitive.

a) With no object or dependent verb, in a relative clause (or with a relative pronoun as object): *TADAE* B2.6:25,28f. (contract) perfect third-person feminine singular *ṣbyt* /ṣabíyat/, twice in the same formulation: "and she goes (wherever) she wants to."[14] *TADAE* B2.7:16 second-person feminine singular imperfect *tṣbyn* /tiṣbǣn/: "it is yours forever, and to whomever you want (to give it), give it!" With an object, it also appears in the conditional clause with a vetitive in the apodosis *TADAE* D7.17:8 (ostracon fifth century Egypt) second-person feminine singular perfect *ṣbty* /ṣabītī/: "if you want, do not sell it!"

b) With an asyndetic imperfect: TADAE A3.10:3 (Papyrus, fifth or fourth century) perfect /ṣabī/ (or, depending upon the separation and interpretation of the *zy*, with accusative): *wzy ṣby yʿbd lh* "(sees. . .) what he would like to do in respect to that" (or, less likely, "what he would like may he do"). *TADAE* B3.7:15 (contract) with subject/verb disagreement[15] *npšy ṣbyt ʾhnṣl mnky* "I myself [*npšy*] will take her away from you again." *TADAE* translates as two clauses: "I want her; I will take her away from you," one should probably understand it as does *TADAE* B3.8:41f. and B6.4:7 with *ṣbyt* first-person singular perfect /kaʿan ṣabīt ʾaṣṣel hu-mū/: "I gave these goods to PN. Now, I will take them back."[16] The much attested formulation "you are justified in giving" lacks the complement for /ṣabī/:[17] *TADAE* B2.11:7,12 (contract), twice the second-person masculine singular perfect /ṣabītā/: *ʾnt . . . šlyṭ . . . lmn zy ṣby tntn* "you, PN (masc.), are justified . . . (regarding this slave) . . . (to give him) to whom(ever) you want to give (him)." *TADAE* B3.4:12,14,15,16, four times like the above, but with an infinitive: *ʾnt . . . šlyṭ . . . lmn zy/dy ṣbyt lmntn* "you, PN (masc.), are justified, . . . (regarding this house) . . . to whom(ever) you want (to give it)."

c) With a direct object: *TADAE* A2.4:7 (Hermopolis, sixth through fifth centuries) second-person masculine singular imperfect *zy* (object) with *tṣbh* "And now: everything that you want (to send), send me!" Similarly, perhaps Naveh and Shaked, B3,4 (letter from Bactria) participle *ṣbh*: *hn lk ṣbh* "if he longs for you,"[18] yet there is no context.[19]

11. AAB 13 B 1.5 HamGr.8,11,12,14,20,26, four of them also in *KAI* 205-208.
12. Cf. the discussion on *KAI* 205.
13. *TADAE* D7.56.
14. Similarly, but emended, in *TADAE* B3.8:24.
15. /ṣabíyat/ is a 3s pf. because of the *npš*, in contrast /ʾaṣṣel/ (*nṣl* haphel) is 1s.
16. → *nṣl* II.
17. Impf. or inf.
18. Or pass ptcp., which would otherwise be spelled *ṣby*, however, "if it is wished by you"?
19. Cf. Naveh and Shaked, 150.

d) With *zy* "that" (uncertain): *TADAE* C1.1:149 (a saying of Aḥiqar) participle *ṣbh* /ṣābǣ/ (the reading of *h* is uncertain): "if you wish, my son, that you are . . ." (the remaining broken off).

e) With *l-* and infinitive: *TADAE* D7.56:7 (third or sceond century) participle plural absolute *ṣbyn* /ṣābēn/ with *l-* and infinitive: "if they do not want to come, they should send a letter."

f) Without context: *TADAE* D1.20:9 (letter) *ṣbyt* first- or second-person masculine singular (lacking the beginning and end of the line) ". . .] what I/you want therein [. . . ." Similarly, perhaps also Lozachmeur, no. 251cc1 and cv2,[20] but the pertinent words here also stand between lacunae and are difficult to read.

2. Noun. Of the seven instances of the noun *ṣbw* in Imperial Aramaic texts,[21] only four offer sufficient context to permit one to say something about the meaning: In *TADAE* A4.3:6 the absolute *ṣbw* stands apparently as a strengthening parallel to *mlh* "word, matter":[22] *ḥzw ʿlyhm ṣbw wmlh* "see to it, what(ever) the concern and matter is (that [PN] wants from you)"; but the meaning "wish" may come into question here, as presumably in Naveh and Shaked, B1,5: *bṣbwtʾ zy*[23] *npšy* "on my own wish." *TADAE* A6.8:2 has the construct *ṣbwt* twice in the same line in the general meaning: ". . . do not obey me in the matter of my lord [*bṣbwt mrʾy*] that I share with you" and "With regard to the concern of my house [*ṣbwt bytʾ zyly*], that (PN) will tell you, . . . obey him and do (it)."

In *TADAE* B8.11:3 (court record) the determined *ṣbwtʾ* stands without context, apparently at the end of the clause; in *TADAE* A5.1:3 (letter from Saqqara), one cannot be sure of the reading *bṣbw zy*: "with the matter that you ha[ve]"; and in *TADAE* D7.19:8 the suffixed form *ṣbwty* with a somewhat uncertain final letter stands between lacunae.

Furthermore, in two Imperial Aramaic ostraca from Egypt in the Clermont-Ganneau collection, it is difficult to distinguish paleographically between the noun and the verb, if, indeed, a form of *ṣbī* is present at all.[24]

III. Biblical Aramaic. Biblical Aramaic attests the verb ten times in seven passages: Dnl. 4:14,22,29,32; 5:19,21; 7:19. The forms include one perfect, four imperfects, one suffixed infinitive, and four active participles. Dnl. 7:19 has the first-person singular perfect with *l-* and an infinitive: *ʾᵃḏayin ṣᵉḇīṯ lᵉyaṣṣāḇā ʿal ḥēwṯā rᵉḇīʿāyᵉṯā* "Then I desired assurance concerning the fourth animal";[25] 4:14,22,29 have the third-person masculine singular imperfect in relative clauses, three times in the same expression: *ulᵉman-dī yiṣbē yittᵉninnah* "and gives it (the kingdom), to whomever he wants"; similarly 5:21: *ulᵉman-dī yiṣbē yᵉhāqēm ʿᵃlaya*[26] "and installs thereupon whomever he wants"; in 4:32 peal infin-

20. H. Lozachmeur, *La collection Clermont-Ganneau*, vol. 1 (Paris, 2006).

21. Six of which from fifth century Egypt, one from Bactria.

22. → *mll.*

23. These two letters are added above the line and difficult to read.

24. See Lozachmeur (→ II.1), no. 187cv4 and 236cv1; both specimens in very fragmentary contexts.

25. → *yṣb* III.

26. *BLA*, §49e′.

itive with a third-person masculine singular possessive suffix: *ūkᵉmiṣbᵉyeh ʿāḇēḏ bᵉḥēl šᵉmayyā* "and, in accordance with his will, he proceeded with the host of heaven. . ."; in 5:19: four times following *hᵃwā* in the active participle after *dī* "whom(ever)" as the object clause of a main verb in the participle also following *hᵃwā*: *dī-hᵃwā ṣāḇē hᵃwā qāṭēl* . . . "He killed whom he wanted to [he let live whom he wished, he elevated whom he wished, and he humbled whom he wished]."[27]

The noun *ṣᵉḇū* occurs only once in Biblical Aramaic in the expression *l'* . . . *ṣbw* "nothing" in Dnl. 6:18: *dī lā-ṯišnē ṣᵉḇū bᵉḏānīʾēl* "(the king sealed it. . .,) so that nothing would change with Daniel."[28]

IV. Qumran. The few instances of the verb[29] stand in poorly preserved surroundings; the construction without object in a relative clause and the construction with *l-* and the infinitive reappear: 4Q204 4:6 (first century B.C.E., Book of Enoch) participle plural absolute with *l-* and infinitive in a damaged context: *l*[*' hww*] *ṣbyn lm*[*t*]*b* "did not want to return"; 4Q213 1 1:17 (second century B.C.E.; T. Levi 44:11),[30] with the supplied *l-* and infinitive based on the parallel text from the Cairo Geniza:[31] *bdy kl' ṣbyn* [*lm'lp* "for all desire [. . . to learn . . .]"; 4Q550 5+5a:6 (document of Darius, first century B.C.E.),[32] participle singular masculine absolute with the relative *zy* and an imperative in the apodosis: *mh dy 'nth ṣ*[*b*]*' pqdny* "However, what you wish command it of me!"; 4Q550 7+7a:1[33] imperfect: *kwl dy yṣb' qryb* "All that he wants is near." The imperfects *tṣb'* in 4Q203 10:3 and *yṣbh* in 4Q346a 2 stand without context.

There are three instances of *ṣbw* "matter, concern": 4Q203 9:4 (Book of Giants, first century B.C.E.)[34] *l'* with *ṣbw* "nothing" as in Dnl. 6:18 (→ III), surrounded by lacunae: *wkwl ṣbw l' tqptkh* "nothing has conquered you"; 11Q10 5:2 (Job 21:21): [*h*]*ṣbw l'lh' bbyth* [. . .] "[Is/lies] there something for God for his house [after his death . . .]?" In 4Q203 8:13 *ṣbw* appears before a lacuna after a hardly legible word.[35]

Qumran attests the noun *ṣbyn* /ṣebyān/ "pleasure" only once, 11Q10 15:6 (Job 30:2; first century B.C.E.): *l' hw' ly ṣbyn* "[In . . .], I had no pleasure."

The same construction is also attested elsewhere, cf. Syriac *LexSyr*, 619 *ṣeḇyānā* "1. gratia, 2. voluntas, 3. voluptas" and with *hwā l-* "placuit." *ATTM*, 2, 467 (s.v. "Wille") lists later West Aramaic instances of the word.

Hug

27. Regarding the construction, cf. H. Gzella, *Tempus, Aspekt und Modalität im Reichsaramäischen. VOK* 48 (2004), 166.

28. Regarding the context of the passage → *ʿzqh* II.

29. *DSSConc* 911 has six, s.v. *ṣbh*.

30. *DSSStE*, 446f.

31. *ATTM*, 191.

32. 4Q550c 1:6 in *DSSStE*, 1098f.

33. 4Q550c 3:1 in *DSSStE*, 1100f.

34. *DSSStE*, 410f.

35. For a discussion of the passage → *pšr* IV.

צדק *ṣdq*; צדק *ṣdq* /ṣedq/; צדקה *ṣdqh* /ṣadaqā/; צדיק *ṣdyq* /ṣaddīq/

I. Etymology, Forms, and Lexical Field. II. Verb "to Be in the Right." III. Noun "Righteousness." IV. Adjective "Righteous."

I. Etymology, Forms, and Lexical Field. Forms of the root *ṣdq* "to be righteous" are common to the West Semitic languages and occur in Aramaic as a verb and in nominal forms. Besides the verb in the intransitive G-stem "to be in the right" and in the D-stem "to declare righteous," the masculine substantive /ṣedq/[1] and the feminine /ṣadaqā/ "righteous conduct, action" are productive, in addition to the adjective /ṣaddīq/ "righteous," often employed substantivally for "righteous person." East Aramaic dissimilates the first vowel of the root, so that the form there is *zdq*.[2]

In accordance with the character of the transmitted sources, the older Old Aramaic instances of the word-group *ṣdq* relate to the realm of royal ideology, the later Old Aramaic of the proverbial wisdom of Aḥiqar to that of practical ethics, and that of the Jewish Aramaic literature of the book of Daniel and the texts from Qumran to religiously based intrahuman solidarity. This distribution of usages depends first on the state of the evidence; because of the very heterogenous material and the relatively restricted attestation in pre-Christian times, no semantic development can be identified. The various nuances have in common a direct relation to a fixed order which enables the conduct of the business of state, the law, necessary for stable communal life, and defines behavior in daily interaction. This order requires renewed internal consent and external actualization. Hebrew scripture develops it theologically.

Consequently, near synonyms first arise, after rudiments in the sayings of Aḥiqar, in the religious literature of Qumran.[3] Instead of the juridical and ethical term *ṣdq*, Qumran prefers the wisdom terms → *qšṭ* "truth," and *b'yš* "bad," *lḥh* "evil," *ršʿ* "crime,"[4] *ḥms* "injustice,"[5] and *šqr* "lie"[6] appear as antonyms. For "justice" in the sense of case law, like Hebrew *mišpāṭ*, Aramaic employs instead forms of the root → *dīn*. In contrast, *ṣdq* denotes the higher principle of order that also underlies case law.

K. Koch, "צדק *ṣdq* to be communally faithful, beneficial," *TLOT*, 1046-62; H. Ringgren and B. Johnson, "צָדַק *ṣāḏaq*," *TDOT*, XII, 239-64; M. Weigl, *Die aramäischen Achikar-Sprüche aus Elephantine und die alttestamentliche Weisheitsliteratur*. *BZAW* 399 (2010); F. Zanella, "*ṣdq*," *ThWQ*, III, 383-93 (Heb.).

1. From the fifth century B.C.E. /ṣedəq/, see *ATTM*, 112-15.
2. Cf. *ATTM*, 98; *MdD*, 162.
3. Esp. in 1 En., cf. *ATTM*, 226.
4. Regarding all → *b'š*.
5. *ATTM*, 581; 2, 398.
6. *ATTM*, 718; 2, 499.

II. Verb "to Be in the Right." As a verb "to be in the right," *ṣdq* finds significantly less usage in Aramaic than its nominal derivatives. The oldest known instance of the G-stem appears in a saying of Aḥiqar, apparently as an expression of misfortune as a consequence of character assassination: *'m mn 'ṣdq* "with whom can I be in the right?"[7] A parallel formulation in the following lines has the declarative-factitive D-stem *mn 'pw ṣdqny* "who, then, has declared me righteous?" with a pronominal object.[8] In the first case, it appears in context with *lḥyty* "my calamity," in the second with *ḥms* "act of violence."[9] Thus, this text understands agreeing with another's righteousness as part of a good reputation.

Three Imperial Aramaic examples come from Elephantine legal texts and employ the G-stem explicitly in the technical juridical sense of "to obtain justice before a court."[10] In each case, the verb is part of a formula confirming that the possessor of the pertinent document has a valid legal claim that cannot be denied him by another party in a legal proceeding.

The meaning of the partially reconstructed verb *ṣ[dq]w* in an Imperial Aramaic stele from North Arabian Tēma[11] is controversial, however. This inscription documents the installation of the priest of a deity venerated at the site and guarantees its temple a certain quantity of date palms annually. Thus, it employs Imperial Aramaic as the language of religious law.[12] If one accepts the proposed emendation, *ṣdq* can readily be identified, from purely morphological and semantic perspectives, as a declarative-factitive D-stem "to declare righteous" with "the gods of Tēma" as the subject.[13] The subsequent preposition *l-* with the name of the priest may then indicate the direct object (especially if animate) with a transitive verb, common in Imperial Aramaic.

Alternatively, however, *ṣdq* could also be a form of the noun *ṣdqt'* in the feminine determinative in l. 15 of the same text (→ III). Since the further course of the text defines it as an annual delivery of date palms and apparently means "gift," some associate it with Arabic *ṣadaqat* and attribute this nuance to the verb, too, in the sense of "to contribute," strange in Aramaic, but very common in Arabic;[14] in this case, *l-* following the verb indicates the indirect object. Because of the fragmentary state, a final decision would be superfluous, but an Arabic substrate influence seems entirely possible.

---

7. *TADAE* C1.1:139.
8. *TADAE* C1.1:140; the function of the perfect is unclear and could be gnomic, if it is not, in fact, an imperfect [*y*]*ṣdqny*.
9. For content parallels, cf. Weigl, 328-39.
10. *TADAE* B2.3:22; 3.1:19; 3.11:15.
11. *KAI* 228 A 11.
12. Cf. H. Gzella, *A Cultural History of Aramaic*. *HO* 111 (2015), 193-95.
13. So, e.g., Donner and Röllig, *KAI*, p. 280.
14. So G. A. Cooke, *A Text-Book of North-Semitic Inscriptions* (Oxford, 1903), 197 and the translation "made grants to" on p. 196; recently repeated by P. Stein, *Babylonien und seine Nachbarn in neu- und spätbabylonischer Zeit*. *AOAT* 369 (2014), 219-45, esp. 228-31, with an extensive bibliography and Old South Arabian parallels, although his interpretation as a pure land grant document falls short.

The only certain specimen from Qumran, 11Q10 9:7 (Job 25:4), employs *ṣdq* in the G-stem exactly like the Hebrew text for "to be righteous" in the context of a rhetorical question concerning how a person could be righteous before God. Following the Hebrew, an additional form should be supplied in 26:1 (Job 35:7),[15] but only a barely legible]*t* appears after a lacuna.

III. Noun "Righteousness." The nouns *ṣdq* /ṣedq/ and *ṣdqh* /ṣadaqā/ find usage more often and in a broader spectrum than the verb. No semantic difference is perceptible since both denote "to act righteously," but one can nonetheless conceive of a, at least original, relationship between general "rectitude" and the specific "(individual) righteous deed."[16] After the Old Aramaic period, however, *ṣdqh* apparently largely displaced *ṣdq* /ṣedq/ (see below).

The Old Aramaic royal inscriptions utilize *ṣdq* in the sense of the political loyalty of a vassal king to his suzerain, as developed upon the incorporation of the minor principalities of Syria into the Neo-Assyrian Empire as a component of the politico-religious order.[17] All the preserved occurrences come from Sam'al and trace the royal dignity of the vassal back to his own loyalty[18] and that of his father;[19] similarly in an inscription written in Sam'alian, the Aramaic of Syria soon replaced the local language.[20] The attributive form *ṣdq* "righteous, loyal"[21] may be an active G-stem participle /ṣādeq/, not[22] (as one would expect here) a defectively spelled adjective (→ IV). Names also have /ṣedq/.[23]

In a Palmyrene inscription, which reflects the old West Semitic royal typology, this usage recurs almost one thousand years later in the description of Queen Zenobia as *zdqt'*.[24] The Greek parallel version has εὐσεβής "god-fearing," apparently, therefore, it does not represent a translation of the Greek, but recourse to substantially older native forms of expression.[25]

Otherwise in older Aramaic, the noun *ṣdq* appears with certainty only as a technical legal term "justification" in a few Nabatean private documents from the Dead Sea.[26] According to *ATTM*, 2, 94, the word may also appear in the general sense in 1QapGen

15. So *ATTM*, 292 on Y 35:7.

16. Then *ṣdqh*, the feminine form, would function as *nomen unitatis*, as often occurs in Semitic languages.

17. → *mlk* II.2.

18. With *b*- "through."

19. *KAI* 216.4f.; 219.4 (fragmentary).

20. *KAI* 215.19; see P. M. Noorlander, "Sam'alian in Its Northwest Semitic Setting," *Or* 81 (2012) 202-38.

21. *KAI* 217.5; significantly reconstructed in l. 3.

22. So, e.g., *DNSI*, 963.

23. *ATTM*, 674.

24. *PAT* 0293.1; here of the East Aramaic form of the root, → I.

25. Cf. H. Gzella, "Die Palmyrener in der griechisch-römischen Welt," *KLIO* 87 (2005) 445-58, esp. 451.

26. In each case formulaically alongside *ršw* "power of disposition" in nV 2:5,25; 3:6,28; 43:8; all in *ATTM* 2.

11:14 as part of the expression *'bd ṣdq'* "doer of righteousness" (of Noah). This would indeed allude to the preceding antonym *'bd ḥms'* "doer of unrighteousness" in the same line, but would presuppose an unusual word for the Aramaic of the time. Moreover, the fragments of letters cannot be recognized clearly so that other editors prefer here *gbr<'> ṣdyq'* "(the) righteous man."[27] In any case, the adjective *ṣdyq* (→ IV) better suits the diction of the Imperial Aramaic tradition.

Similarly, *ATTM*, 674 reckons the spelling *ṣdqh* in T. Levi following the Cairo Geniza[28] to be a determinate of *ṣdq* "the righteous," but an indetermined form of *ṣdqh* "righteousness" seems significantly more likely for this reading. *ATTM*, 2, 107 now reads the determined *ṣdqt'* "the righteousness" from *ṣdqh* with the much older textual witness 4Q213 1 1:7 from Qumran, which may also be correct. Consequently, one can conclude that *ṣdq* as a noun found only very limited usage as a legal term after Old Aramaic. The Syriac occurrences[29] also have such specific juridical connotations.

The typical word beginning in the seventh century B.C.E. was *ṣdqh* /ṣadaqā/. It first occurs in late Old Aramaic in a grave inscription from Syrian Nērab[30] where it refers to the piety of the deceased priest who emphasizes that, through his righteousness (*bṣdqty*) before (*qdm*) his god, he maintained a good name and a long life. The overarching, divinely sanctioned, principle of order in which *ṣdq(h)* is rooted expresses itself, then, in a direct deed-consequence relationship. Already in this earliest instance, it denotes "right action" collectively and in general.

In an expansion of this usage, *ṣdqh* can denote, in individual cases—at least in the context of Israelite religion—the merit itself that someone has before (*qdm*) God through a good act. Entirely in the sense of the primacy of rectitude, the Judean priests of Elephantine in their petition concerning the reconstruction of the local temple call to the attention of the Persian administrator of Judea the fact that he would gain more merit through his agreement than through any kind of sacrifice.[31]

A very fragmentary passage from the Bar-Puneš story depicts, in colors that recall[32] the Iron Age era of classical literature, a future brutalization of morals after the demise of *ṣdqh*.[33]

(Meanwhile, the use of *ṣdqh* for "gift" in an Imperial Aramaic stele from northern Arabia,[34] is influenced by the Arabic vernacular of the region and does not represent the meaning of the Aramaic word.[35] The same apparently applies to *bṣdqt* "through the donation/bequest of" in a Nabatean inscription concerning the usage rights of a grave.[36]

27. Furthermore, D. A. Machiela, *The Dead Sea Genesis Apocryphon. STDJ* 79 (2009), 54, thinks that he recognizes a *y* in the photograph.

28. *ALD* 85:12 = xL 43:12: *ATTM*, 205. So also *DSSStE*, 56f.

29. Cf. *LexSyr*, 189a.

30. *KAI* 226.2.

31. *TADAE* A4.7:27.

32. → *dhb* II.

33. *TADAE* C1.2:21f.

34. *KAI* 228 A 15.

35. See the discussion above II.

36. H34:8 in J. F. Healey, *The Nabataean Tomb Inscriptions of Mada'in Salih. JSSSup* 1 (1993), 219.

The Nabateans employed Arabic both as the language of daily life and religion and for administrative purposes.)[37]

The religious implications of right action known already from the few Old and Imperial Aramaic instances continue in the next occurrence chronologically, Dnl. 4:24. In his interpretation of Nebuchadnezzar's dream vision of the world tree, Daniel admonished the king "to redeem"[38] his sins (that is, his arrogance, as 4:27f. indicates) "through right action."[39] The parallel expression in the same verse specifies this action as "having mercy on the poor."[40] At the same time, *ṣdqh* here cannot be limited to the later meaning "alms."

This meaning is first perceptible in the translation of 4Q198 1:1 (Tob. 14:2) with ἐλεημοσύνας and in post-Christian Aramaic.[41] One cannot say when this shift in meaning occurred. At Qumran, at any rate, *ṣdqh* still refers generally to "right action," also as part of the religio-cultural heritage of the fathers.[42] 11Q10 26:3 (Job 35:8) renders the Hebrew cognate "sons of right action" for the sons of light. 4Q548 1 2-2:7 is largely reconstructed. Regarding 4Q213 1 1:7, see above.

IV. Adjective "Righteous." The adjective *ṣdyq* /ṣaddīq/ "righteous" first occurs in the sayings of Aḥiqar. It is employed mostly as a substantive "righteous one" and denotes an ethical quality that binds humans with gods[43] and places them under the protection of the gods,[44] but also secures the assistance of other humans.[45]

With a legal meaning "justified to own," it describes a person in two Imperial Aramaic documents from Elephantine.[46] Otherwise, the apparently general term *šlyṭ* "entitled to dispose of"[47] serves this function.

Only a few instances appear at Qumran, too. Besides the predication of Noah following Gen. 6:9[48] and presumably of Abraham in a prediluvian conversation between two angels,[49] it occurs in apocalyptic contexts denoting the righteous in the eschaton,[50] and can otherwise only be reconstructed in fragmentary contexts.[51]

With the juridical connotation "just heir," *ṣdyq* occurs in a Nabatean contract from

37. See Gzella, *Cultural History*, 238-49.

38. → *prq* III, with an extensive discussion of the passage.

39. *bṣdqh*, as in *KAI* 226.2.

40. *mḥn ʿnyn*, → *ḥnn* II and *ʿnī* [II] II.

41. Cf. F. Rosenthal, "Sedaka, Charity," *HUCA* 23 (1950-1951) 411-30, and *DJPA*, 458b.

42. 4Q542 1 1:8:12, along with → *qšṭ* "truth," *yšyrw* "uprightness," *tmymw* "perfection," *dkw* "purity," → *qdš* "holiness" and *khnw* "priesthood."

43. *TADAE* C1.1:109: someone is established → *qūm* (haphel) by El *bṣdyq* "as a righteous one."

44. *TADAE* C1.1:126,128; cf. Weigl, 274-81,285f.

45. *TADAE* C1.1:103; here one should probably read *ʿdr* "help," not *ʿrr* "objection" as part of a legal metaphor, → *ʿrr* IV.

46. *TADAE* B5.6:8; 7.3:6.

47. → *šlṭ*.

48. 1QapGen 11:14, → III for a discussion; with no direct context probably also in 15:23.

49. 4Q529 1:16.

50. 4Q537 1+2+3:1; 4Q556a 1 1:6.

51. 4Q531 22:1; 4Q541 24 2:3.

the Dead Sea.[52] Otherwise, under Arabic influence, *ʾṣdq* /ʾaṣdaq/, demonstrably Arabic by form, fulfils this function,[53] similarly in Nabatean grave entitlement inscriptions.[54]

Rare forms, spelled defectively as *ṣdq*, in attributive usages such as the Old Aramaic in *KAI* 217.5 and the Palmyrene in *PAT* 0293.1[55] are more likely G-stem participles (→ III). In any case, Syriac *zādeq*[56] supports this interpretation.

Later Aramaic languages attest additional nominal forms.[57]

Gzella

52. nV 42:1 in *ATTM*, 2, 244-47.
53. In 42:20f. apparently synonymous with *ṣdyq*; further nV 7:21-23 in *ATTM*, 2, 217-23.
54. Instances in Healey, 264, s.v. *ṣdq*.
55. East Aramaic *zdq* in the det. of the fem. sg.
56. *LexSyr*, 189a.
57. Cf. *DJPA*, 458b for /ṣaddīqū/ as an abstract based on the adj.; *DJBA*, 952b for the new adj. /ṣadqān/; further *LexSyr*, 189.

צלח *ṣlḥ*

I. Etymology and Lexical Field. II. Usage.

I. Etymology and Lexical Field. Aramaic *ṣlḥ*, in the C-stem either a transitive "to advance, make successful" or an intransitive "to have success," can be traced to a common Central Semitic, and perhaps even to a common West Semitic, root.[1]

Traditionally, *ṣlḥ* "to divide" in the D-stem[2] is differentiated as a homonymous root,[3] but the hypothesis of a common etymology from "to intrude" via "to permeate" to "to succeed" also has adherents.[4]

II. Usage. The first appearance of *ṣlḥ* "to be/make successful" is in Biblical Aramaic. Dnl. 3:30 utilizes it for the king's advancement of Daniel and his friends after God had saved them from the fiery furnace;[5] Dnl. 6:29 employs it intransitively for Daniel's un-

P. J. Harland, "*ṣlḥ*," *ThWQ*, III, 420-22; J. Hausmann, "צָלַח *ṣālaḥ*," *TDOT*, XII, 382-85; M. Sæbø, "צלח *ṣlḥ* to succeed," *TLOT*, 1077-80.

1. If Ethiopic and Modern South Arabian forms have been inherited; see *GesB*[18], 1118.
2. *TADAE* C1.1:173 (for the context → *ḥšk* III); 4Q214b 2-6:1; both of wood.
3. So also *ATTM*, 2, 468.
4. See Hausmann, 382f.
5. With *l*- as an object marker, as is also typical in Imperial Aramaic.

interrupted success under Darius and Cyrus. Both passages emphasize how the worship of God in a foreign land links with a successful life in the service of the empire. In Ezr. 5:8 and 6:14, it represents the good progress in the construction of the temple, according to 6:14 thanks to the assistance of the prophets.[6] The meaning, "to thrive" or "to divide," in 1QapGen 6:17, in a fragmentary context, is unclear.

Gzella

6. → *nby'*.

צלי *ṣlī*; **צלו** *ṣlw* /ṣalō/; **תצלו** *tṣlw* /taṣlū/

I. Etymology, Lexical Field, and Grammatical Constructions. II. Verb "to Pray." III. Noun "Prayer."

I. Etymology, Lexical Field, and Grammatical Constructions. Among the various branches of Semitic languages, the most likely direct relation to the Aramaic verb *ṣlī* "to pray" is with the Akkadian root *ṣullû* "to appeal to, to plead."[1] It arose from an old **ṣlū*, as the nominal form /taṣlū/ indicates (see below). The broader body of evidence could support the hypothesis of an Akkadian loanword.[2] On the one hand, Ugaritic *ṣlī* "to appeal to, to adjure"[3] may have been taken independently from Akkadian, especially since it occurs in the context of a magical adjuration of the clouds[4] and Akkadian was widespread as the language of ritual. On the other hand, the verb is sometimes considered an Aramaic loanword in Arabic,[5] whence it could have migrated further into Ethiopic. None of this is certain, however. Hebrew employs *pll*.

In older Aramaic, *ṣlī* appears in the D-stem, predominantly as an intransitive, but it can also take a root-related noun as internal object (→ III). Prepositional modifiers expressing various adverbial relationships are introduced by *l-* "to" (in Ezr. 6:10 "for" instead) or in formal language in the Imperial Aramaic tradition by *qdm* "before," in addition to *'l*

U. Ehrlich, *The Nonverbal Language of Prayer*. *TSAJ* 105 (2004); E. S. Gerstenberger and H.-J. Fabry, "פלל *pll*," *TDOT*, XI, 567-78; H.-P. Stähli, "פלל *pll* hitp. to pray," *TLOT*, 991-94; S. C. Reif, *Judaism and Hebrew Prayer* (Cambridge, 1993); C. Stadel, "*ṣlh*," *ThWQ*, III, 419-20.

1. *AHw*, III, 1110.
2. So already H. Zimmern, *Akkadische Fremdwörter als Beweis für babylonischen Kultureinfluss* (Leipzig, 1917), 65; recently adopted by *DJBA*, 965; *ATTM*, 2, 468.
3. *DUL*^{3}, 772f.
4. *KTU* 1.19 I 39.
5. Zimmern, 65; *GesB*^{18}, 1527.

"for." As a designation for mostly private, but also public prayers, it remained common in both Jewish Palestinian[6] and Jewish Babylonian,[7] as well as in Syriac[8] and other Aramaic languages on into the modern era.

In East Aramaic, the meaning "to bow, to turn" is also productive.[9] It is either associated with the same root[10] or, less likely in view of the body of evidence, considered a homonymous verb.[11] Older evidence does not manifest it.

Furthermore, the root *ṣlī* also includes the feminine abstract noun *ṣlw* /ṣalō/ "prayer," a *qalāt* form;[12] the Tell Fekheriye inscription has instead the *taqlūt*-noun *tṣlw* /taṣlū/, later no longer still in use, apparently with the same meaning (→ III).

The verb *ṣlī* designates prayer as an expressly personal devotion to a deity in conversation quite generally; various verbs with more concrete meanings and their nominal derivatives specify the nature of the prayer itself: → *bʿī* "to request" or → *ḥnn* "to plead for mercy" (sometimes in parallelism) for the petition, → *brk* and → *ydī* "to thank, praise," as well as → *šbḥ* "to sing praise" for praise. Actions accompanying prayer include kneeling (Dnl. 6:11),[13] raising the hands[14] and the eyes,[15] in certain situations also crying.[16] The communicative act of prayer is distinguished terminologically from cultic veneration and obeisance,[17] which arise from the acknowledgment of divine power and find visible expression in the gesture of prostration,[18] and from the offering of sacrifices.[19]

II. Verb "to Pray." While the contexts of the veneration of Mesopotamian and Egyptian gods also attest the roots → *sgd* "to do obeisance" and → *plḥ* "to serve, to venerate" and the noun *tṣlw* occurs in reference to a prayer addressed to the Syrian god Hadad, all the older instances of the verb *ṣlī* including the earliest Imperial Aramaic appear in the environment of Israelite-Judean religion.[20] In the preserved material, the petition of the Judean community at Elephantine concerning the reconstruction of the temple of Yaho, destroyed at the instigation of Egyptian priests, constitutes the first attestation. The authors emphasize to the Persian governor of Judea that, since the plundering and destruction of the cultic center, the community, including women and children, have worn mourning clothes (*śqqn lbšn hwyn*), fasted (*ṣymyn*),[21] and prayed to Yaho, the Lord of

---

6. *DJPA*, 465f.
7. *DJBA*, 965.
8. *LexSyr*, 628f.
9. *LexSyr*, 628; Jewish Babylonian in the C-stem: *DJBA*, 964f.
10. *LexSyr*, 628; *ATTM*, 676.
11. *DJBA*, 964.
12. Regarding the reduction */ā/ > /ō/, esp. with /l/, cf. *ATTM*, 137.
13. → *brk* V.
14. → *nśī*.
15. → *nṭl*.
16. 1QapGen 20:12.
17. → *sgd, plḥ*.
18. → *npl*.
19. → *mnḥh*, with additional lexemes; → *qrb*.
20. Even if, as in 4Q242 1-3:7, they refer to idol worship in the literary context of a Jewish text.
21. From *ṣūm*.

heaven (*mṣlyn lyhw mr' šmy'*).[22] The subsequent lines describe more precisely the content and objective of the prayer: Yaho should let them "look down on"[23] the evildoers. In return, they assure the governor, in gratitude for the permission to rebuild, that they will offer sacrifices (l. 25) on the altar of Yaho in his name (*bšmk*, l. 26) and will all pray for him (*'lyk*, l. 26).[24]

Conversely, according to Ezr. 6, the royal memorandum that authorizes the reconstruction of the Jerusalem temple takes up precisely this reciprocal relationship between the privilege of religious practice, on the one hand, and, on the other, vicarious sacrifice[25] and prayer for (*l-*) the well-being[26] of the ruler and his sons by the community favored in this manner (Ezr. 6:10).

By mentioning sacrifice first and prayer second in the same context of a communal cultic act here, as in the letter from Elephantine, the personal relationship with God and individual prayer, revitalized with the loss of the Jerusalem temple and the exile, receive a clear up-valuation. For life in the diaspora, such as the court tales in Daniel also depict literarily,[27] unconditional loyality to the true God and intimate conversation with him are the load-bearing columns of ever-endangered religio-cultural identity.

They also serve as such in the prayer scene in Dnl. 6 in the context of the story of the lions' den. The envy of Daniel, extremely successful in the imperial administration, incites an intrigue against him, which cannot find any objection[28] with his faultless execution of office, however, and brings the king, otherwise well-disposed toward him, unwittingly to place Jewish worship under the death penalty; in the context of the story, Daniel's religion was known, then, and not a private matter. Daniel's enemies packaged the actual objective as an apparently objective prohibition against addressing a petition to any god or human being other than the king (Dnl. 6:4). The account then describes how Daniel, after learning of the king signing the prohibition, withdrew to the upper story (*'lyh*) of his house, that is, the most intimate place available to him, but with the windows open in the direction of the old, now spiritual, cultic center Jerusalem[29] and thus linked with the overarching context of his religion. Thus, he prayed, imbedded in the framework of form and tradition, three times a day according to this custom (6:11). Here, the text links the act of praying, denoted by the participle *mṣl'*, with the gesture of kneeling,[30] and first specifies it with the parallel form *mwd'*[31] as "praise," and in the subsequent verse, through the parallelism of → *b'ī* and → *ḥnn*, as a petition (6:12). Even if conceptual boundaries in juxtapotion can blur and nothing is known of the context in the history of liturgy, it is nonetheless likely that one should see in

22. *TADAE* A4.7:15.
23. → *hzī* (haphel) with *b-*.
24. Par. *TADAE* A4.8:25 (the subsequent context there is reconstructed).
25. Here *nyḥwḥyn* "incense," → *mnḥh* III.3.
26. Lit. *ḥyy* "the life," const., as already in earlier and then in later inscriptions; → *ḥyī* IV.2.
27. On which, cf. H. Gzella, *Cosmic Battle and Political Conflict*. *BietOr* 47 (2003), 75.
28. → *'lh*.
29. → *ptḥ* III.
30. → *brk* V.
31. from → *ydī*.

mwd' an introductory thanksgiving for God's already demonstrated beneficences and in *b''* as well as *mtḥnn* then the request before God (*qdm*), motivated by help in the past, for deliverance now.[32]

At Qumran, half of the instances of *ṣlī* appear in the story of Abraham at Pharaoh's court in 1QapGen. Here, as in Biblical Aramaic, prayers take place both in private and in public contexts. Abraham's petition to God that Pharaoh not assault his stolen wife Sarah,[33] shares with Dnl. 6:11f. the intimate framework (here at night), personal distress as the occasion, and the combination of *b'ī* and *ḥnn*. Likewise, it begins with praise of God.[34] In contrast, Abraham's petitionary prayer to God at the wish of Pharaoh, in his presence and for (*'l*) him and his house,[35] that the god-sent demon that had plagued him for years since Abraham's earlier petition disappear,[36] has models by form and content in Ezr. 6:10 and in *TADAE* A4.7:26 (see above). The laying on of hands to heal is new.[37]

The healing of a foreign ruler by a Jew is also the theme of the Prayer of Nabonidus, which deals with the topic of the expulsion and restitution of Nabonidus[38] as evidence of the superiority of the true God. Here, *ṣlī* occurs once in the superscription with *ṣlw* (→ III) as the direct object "the prayer that . . . prayed,"[39] then in the king's confession itself in reference to his futile prayer to idols (l. 7). The other instances are fragmentary.[40]

III. Noun "Prayer." Of the two related old nominal forms for "prayer," *tṣlw* /taṣlū/ is known so far only from the Tell Fekheriye inscription. There, it occurs once in the introductory hymnic description in a relative clause modifying Hadad, the merciful[41] god, "whose" prayer[42] is "good" (*ṭb*),[43] that is, effective.[44] In the subsequent dedication report, "the granting of his (i.e., the donor's) prayer [*lmšm' tṣlwth*] parallels "accepting the words of his mouth" (*lmlqḥ 'mrt pmh*)[45] as the purpose of the dedication of the pertinent statue and, thus, depicts it as an act of loyalty.[46]

Otherwise, Aramaic employs the noun *ṣlw* /ṣalō/, attested beginning at Qumran. It has survived in only a few instances: in 4Q213a 2:8 for Levi's petition,[47] in 4Q242 1-3:1 as the object of the verb (→ II), and in 11Q10 14:8 as a free translation "I became a prayer

32. Cf. 1QapGen 20:12, see below.
33. 1QapGen 20:12; not in Gen. 12 and 20.
34. *brk*; see above on *ydī* in Dnl. 6:11.
35. 1QapGen 20:21f.,23,28.
36. 1QapGen 20:16ff.
37. → *yd* II.1.
38. In Dnl. 4 Nebuchadnezzar.
39. 4Q242 1-3:1.
40. 4Q203 8:15, Enoch's penitential letter to the fallen angels from the Book of Giants with the call to prayer; 4Q243 1:3; 4Q533 3:1.
41. → *rḥm*.
42. Suffixed *tṣlwth*, for "the prayer to whom."
43. → *ṭīb*.
44. *KAI* 309.5.
45. *KAI* 309.9f.; → *pm* II.1.
46. → *ṣlm* II.
47. *ṣlt* preserving the /-t/ in the const.

in the mouth of" for "I cause the heart of . . . to rejoice [*ʾrnn*]" in Job 29:13. It belongs to the vocabulary of later varieties of Aramaic, however.[48]

Gzella

48. See *DJPA*, 464f.; *DJBA*, 964a; *LexSyr*, 628; *MdD*, 387.

צלם *ṣlm* /ṣalm/; נצב *nṣb* /naṣīb/; נצבה *nṣbh* /neṣbā/; צורה *ṣwrh* /ṣūrā/

I. Forms, Lexical Field, and Grammatical Constructions. II. Old and Imperial Aramaic. III. Biblical Aramaic and Qumran. IV. Northern Arabia, Syria, and Eastern Mesopotamia.

I. Forms, Lexical Field, and Grammatical Constructions. The Semitic languages employ the common primary noun *ṣlm* /ṣalm/ to denote the plastic representations of gods and humans widespread in the ancient Near East until the Byzantine era. In Aramaic, doubled consonants at the end of the word are attested since the earliest known texts, but from about the fifth century B.C.E. they were separated, in this case yielding /ṣaləm/.[1] The word is masculine in gender, but in the rapidly blooming memorial epigraphy of the Aramaic languages in the Hellenistic and Roman eras, its gender corresponds to the sex of the person depicted, thus, masculine *ṣlm* /ṣaləm/ for the statue of a man and feminine *ṣlmh* /ṣalmā/ for that of a woman. Since no relief depiction of women with *ṣlm*(*h*) in an Aramaic inscription from earlier times is known, it remains unclear when this development began. Only rarely does *ṣlm* serve figuratively for the facial expression of a living person (→ III).[2]

Because *ṣlm* explicitly designates a plastic representation, it also differs altogether semantically from *dmw* /damū/ "image, likeness,"[3] employed in a more abstract sense for directly perceptible agreements in form. In individual cases, in fact, the two terms

A. Berlejung, *Die Theologie der Bilder. OBO* 162 (1998); H. J. W. Drijvers and J. F. Healey, *The Old Syriac Inscriptions of Edessa and Osrhoene. HO* 42 (1999); H. Gzella, *A Cultural History of Aramaic. HO* 111 (2015); A. Kropp, *Images and Monuments of Near Eastern Dynasts, 100 BC-AD 100* (Oxford, 2013); J. Middlemas, *The Divine Image. FAT* II 74 (2014); H. Niehr, "Die Grabstelen zweier Priester des Mondgottes aus Neirab," in *Kulte, Priester, Rituale. FS Seidl* (St. Ottilien, 2010), 41-60; F. J. Stendebach, "צֶלֶם *ṣelem*," *TDOT*, XII, 386-96; H. Wildberger, "צֶלֶם *ṣelem* image," *TLOT*, 1080-85.

1. *ATTM*, 112-15.
2. Dnl. 3:19; 1QapGen 20:2.
3. → *dmī* III.

can appear together in reference to the same object,[4] but *dmw*, which is more rare in any case, occurs less frequently for a concrete object than do the comparative prepositional expressions, *bdmwt*, *kdwmt* and *ldmwt*[5] attested since Imperial Aramaic.

In contrast, the noun *nṣb* /naṣīb/[6] serves to denote a stele, an erected stone. In this sense, it can involve a statue with a pictorial depiction, as in the case of the two large Sam'alian royal statues,[7] but the image character, in contrast to *ṣlm*, is not inherent to the meaning of the term. Meanwhile, *nṣb* can denote columns and other generally stone objects,[8] as can the feminine *nṣbh* /neṣbā/.[9] Since the Achaemenid period, northern Arabian sources, and later also Syrian and Judean, evidence the rather specialized usage of *npš*[10] for a stone grave memorial with a stylized face, and sources from the Nabatean kingdom for a pyramidal grave marker.

In addition, the feminine *ṣwrh* /ṣūrā/ "image, form, figure," used to designate both paintings, and reliefs and sculptures, occurs later.[11] Furthermore, beginning in the Achaemenid period, the Iranian word *ptkr* appears.[12]

The noun *ṣlm*, as well as *ṣlmh*, generally appears as the object of a verb of establishment,[13] in West Semitic formulas for dedicatory and honorific inscriptions also in the identifying nominal clause with the subsequent name of the one depicted (→ IV).[14] The nouns *nṣb*/*nṣbh* behave analogously.[15]

II. Old and Imperial Aramaic. Only a handful of instances of *ṣlm* "statue" occur in all of the Old and Imperial Aramaic corpus. All occurrences relate to depictions of human beings. At the beginning of the textual tradition (ca. 850 B.C.E.) stand the bilingual Akkadian-Aramaic dedicatory inscriptions of the king (governor, according to the Akkadian version) of Gosan on a statue that represents the king himself[16] and that he "established"[17] for his own benefit before (*qdm*) Hadad, his local patron deity (l. 16). Simultaneously, the text mentions the dedication of temple vessels in the name of the

4. Cf. *dmw* in *KAI* 309.1,15 with *ṣlm* in ll. 12,16.

5. → *dmī* III.

6. Probably a pass. ptcp. of → *nṣb*.

7. Both called *nṣb* in the accompanying inscriptions: *KAI* 214.1,14f.; 215.1,20; also Kuttamuwa: D. G. Pardee, "A New Aramaic Inscription from Zinjirli," *BASOR* 356 (2009) 51-71.

8. E.g., *KAI* 201.1; 202 A 1; B 14,18f.

9. As in old Syriac inscriptions, see Drijvers and Healey, As36.3 and 37.4,9; further in Palmyrene: *PAT* 1546.3.

10. → *nšm* III.3.

11. Attested beginning with Qumran: 4Q212 1 5:22 (1 En. 93:13), for the form of the earth; 4Q531 19:4, with the Gt-stem of → *mḥī* "to be separated" *mn ṣwrtn'* "from our form," possibly of the punishment of the fallen angels; 4Q552 2 2:3, for a tree in an apocalyptic vision as the symbol of the Babylonian Empire, apparently linked with the Persian Empire; *ATTM*, 675; 2, 468.

12. *DNSI*, 952.

13. In *KAI* 309,16 → *śīm*, later the C-stem of → *qūm*.

14. So already *KAI* 309.12; 318.1.

15. E.g., *KAI* 201.1; 202 A 1 with *śīm*.

16. *KAI* 309.12.

17. → *śīm*.

king (ll. 16ff.).[18] This text apparently employs *ṣlm* and *dmw* interchangeably (→ I). The statue with an inscription serves as a demonstration of the prince's loyalty to his divine overlord, but, at the same time, also reflects the claim, inherent in the petition for well-being,[19] that the deity shares responsibility for the king's ruling house and people (*ʾnšwh*, "his people"). The Aramaic text says nothing about Gosan already being an Akkadian vassal at the time.

If the self-awareness of the originally independent Aramaic kings still echoes in the Gosan inscription,[20] in the course of the Neo-Assyrian period, the use of Aramaic inscriptions on graphic depictions expanded to other high-standing personalities from the environs of the king. After the Kuttamuwa Inscription from Samʾal, which employs the word *nṣb* (mid-eighth century B.C.E.; → I), two basalt steles with burial inscriptions for priests from Syrian Nērab are preserved (ca. 700 B.C.E.);[21] both utilize *ṣlm* in the identification of the graphic depiction of the deceased.[22] Additionally, *KAI* 225 places the statue, like the sarcophagus, under divine protection via a curse formula.

Burial or dedicatory inscriptions for individuals survive from the Achaemenid period from different parts of the empire, in fact, namely from Egypt,[23] Asia Minor,[24] and northern Arabia.[25] Yet, to date, only one inscription from Daskyleion in Asia Minor attests the designation *ṣlm*.[26] *KAI* 258.1,4 and 260 B 2.4, also from Asia Minor, have for "stele" the Persian loanwords *ptkr* (→ I) and *stwnh*.[27]

In Imperial Aramaic inscriptions from Tēma,[28] *ṣlm* also appears as the name of a local deity and as a theophoric element.

III. Biblical Aramaic and Qumran. Biblical Aramaic evidences *ṣlm* only in the book of Daniel. There it functions both in the story of the "colossus with clay feet" (Dnl. 2) and in the story of the young men in the fiery furnace (Dnl. 3) as a symbol of royal power, but in each case with different emphases. Daniel 2:31f.,34f. employs it of the gigantic (*śgyʾ*)[29] statue of different materials that King Nebuchadnezzar saw in the dream. According to Daniel's divinely inspired interpretation, it represents the sequence of different empires up to the dawn of the kingdom of God, in which the materials of descending value[30] rep-

18. → *mʾn* II.
19. *šlm*, ll. 8f.
20. → *mlk* II.1.
21. Niehr, cf. Gzella, 145f.
22. *KAI* 225.3,6,12; 226.2.
23. *KAI* 269.
24. *KAI* 258; 260; 262; cf. Gzella, 195-98.
25. E.g., *KAI* 229-30; see Gzella, 193-95.
26. *KAI* 318.1; see F. M. Cross, "An Aramaic Inscription from Daskyleion," *BASOR* 184 (1966) 7-10, but according to Cross, the text gives no evidence of a burial context and the interpretation of *npš* (l. 2) as "grave marker," which was otherwise restricted to northern Arabia in this period, instead of the typical "for one's self," is unfounded (→ *nšm* III.2 and III.3).
27. *DNSI*, 804.
28. E.g., *KAI* 228; 229.
29. → *śgī*.
30. → *dhb* II.

resent increasing decay culminating in the feet of mixed clay and iron. Thus, the statue is ultimately unstable and a stone, that then grew into a mountain[31] and represents divine power, destroyed it. The detailed anatomical description of head, breast, arms, torso, hips, legs, and feet (Dnl. 2:32f.) accentuates the form inspired by royal statues (→ II), which although inflated to gigantic proportions, remains, nonetheless, human. Meanwhile, the stone become a mountain breaks with all familiar conceptions.

While the royal symbolism in Dnl. 2 depicts the politico-theological statement that even the greatest human power faces the limits of divine sovereignty,[32] the story of Nebuchadnezzars's similarly large (sixty times six cubits) golden statue in Dnl. 3 foregrounds the relationship between divine and human authority. In the festal consecration ceremony (Dnl. 3:5-7),[33] all subjects of the empire should prostrate themselves[34] on a musical signal ("on command") and do obeisance to the image.[35] The Jewish officials who refused to venerate[36] the statue were vilified and cast into the fiery furnace, but God delivered them from it so that, ultimately even the king converted.

Although in context it does not explicitly involve a cultic image,[37] the Jews' refusal to venerate it bears elements of aniconic polemic, as became more vigorous under the influence of prophetic critique in the postexilic period.[38] Thus, the repetition of the term *ṣlm*, which normally refers to a copy for representation and not for worship, in Dnl. 3:1-3,5,7,10,12,14f.,18 consistently emphasizes that it involves only a human image, and thereby in context loads it with negative connotations. Only the invisible God deserves veneration (3:17, *plḥ*), consequently, homage is also denied the statue, too (3:18, *sgd*). Likewise, the affirmation that only God can deliver (3:17f.) characterizes idol polemic. The usage of *ṣlm* in 3:19 diverges from the typical usage once to refer to the king's facial expression.

The few instances from Qumran add nothing: 1QapGen 20:2 utilizes *ṣlm 'npyh'* "the form of your face" (in the song praising Sarah), as in Dnl. 3:19; the isolated fragment 4Q243 31:2 seems to belong to a text from the circle of the Daniel traditions.

IV. Northern Arabia, Syria, and Eastern Mesopotamia. Under the influence of Hellenistic culture, the production of plastic pictorial representations of private persons with Aramaic inscriptions underwent an explosive increase in northern Arabia, Palmyra, and Edessa in Syria, as well as in Hatra in East Mesopotamia in the Roman Imperial period.[39] The standardization of new, locally varied Aramaic chancellery languages coincided with a multiplicity of iconographic programs.[40] The introductory formula *ṣlm'* (*dnh*) *dy*, etc.,

31. → *ṭwr*.
32. → *'wr* II.
33. → *ḥnkh*.
34. → *npl*.
35. → *sgd*.
36. → *plḥ*.
37. Considered the material form of the transcendent deity; see Berlejung.
38. Cf. K. Koch, *Daniel 1–4*. *BK* XXII/1 (2005), 284-95.
39. Gzella, 238-76.
40. See Kropp.

"(This is the) statue of" in many inscriptions, revived the West Semitic formulary.[41] At Palmyra, it primarily served the public representation, at Hatra, personal piety.

Gzella

41. Cf. *DNSI*, 968f.; Drijvers and Healey, 273; K. Beyer, *Die aramäischen Inschriften aus Assur, Hatra und dem übrigen Ostmesopotamien* (Göttingen, 1998), 183; and idem, "Die aramäischen Inschriften aus Assur, Hatra und dem übrigen Ostmesopotamien (datiert 44 v. Chr. bis 238 n. Chr.) – Nachträge," *WO* 43 (2013) 60.

צפר *ṣpr* /ṣeppar/

I. Etymology, Overview. II. Old and Imperial Aramaic. III. Biblical Aramaic. IV. Qumran.

I. Etymology, Overview. In the possible Aramaic base form /ṣeppar/, the concluding /r/ produces the likely secondary /a/.[1] Almost all of the attested vocalized forms conform to this etymology,[2] even Mandaic *ṣipra*[3] and Jewish Palestinian *ṣypr* in a *plene* spelling;[4] Samaritan has by-forms.[5] Forms with /o/ may be archaic or influenced by Hebrew. In older Aramaic, one finds the spelling *ṣnpr* (sayings of Aḥiqar)[6] with a secondary *n* either as the result of the dissimilation of a geminate[7] or as an incorrect etymological indication of the long /p/.[8] The gender varies; in the oldest Aramaic instance, the word is feminine.

It is difficult to deduce a Semitic ground form. Hebrew *ṣippōr* and presumably also Phoenician *ṣpr*[9] may correspond to /ṣippur/, more original than /ṣippar/,[10] but Ugaritic

C. Brockelmann, *Grundriss der vergleichenden Grammatik der semitischen Sprachen*, vol. 1 (Berlin, 1908); W. Fischer, *Farb- und Formbezeichnungen in der Sprache der altarabischen Dichtung* (Wiesbaden, 1965); H. Gzella, "Deir 'Allā," in G. Khan, ed., *Encyclopedia of Hebrew Language and Linguistics* (Leiden, 2013), 1:691-93; J. A. Hackett, *The Balaam Text from Deir 'Allā. HSM* 31 (1984); I. Kottsieper, *Die Sprache der Aḥiqarsprüche. BZAW* 194 (1990); C. R. Krahmalkov, *Phoenician-Punic Dictionary. OLA* 90 (2000); E. Schwab, "צִפּוֹר *ṣippôr*," *TDOT*, XII, 443-49; A. Tal, *A Dictionary of Samaritan Aramaic*, 2 vols. (Leiden, 2000).

1. *ATTM*, 677; 2, 469; *KBL*³, 1770.
2. *LexSyr*, 635; *DJBA*, 692 besides *ṣippᵉrā* n.m. *ṣippartā*, but also *ṣipportā* n.f.
3. *MdD*, 394.
4. *DJPA*, 463 n.f., also 464 *ṣyprh* n.f.
5. Tal, 742 s.v. $ṣpr_2$ with: *ṣpwr*, *ṣpyr*, *ṣprh*, all fem.
6. *TADAE* C1.1:82, etc.
7. *ATTM*, 92.
8. Kottsieper, 54ff. with discussion; *ATTM*, 2, 469: "hyper-correct Imperial Aramaic."
9. Krahmalkov, 420: n.m. "fowl"; cf. *DNSI*, 973.
10. *ATTM*, 2, 469.

has two forms: in addition to *ṣpr*,[11] the more abundantly attested and not very similar *'ṣr*,[12] to which can be linked Akkadian *iṣṣuru*,[13] although with no indication of an old /ʿ/. The link for a common original form is Arabic *'uṣfūr* "sparrow; any passerine bird"[14] with both /p/ and /ʿ/. Kottsieper assumes[15] for the Akkadian and Ugaritic the assimilation of /p/ and derives the word from the verb "*ṣpr*, to twitter, to whistle," which is not very well attested, however,[16] and may, rather, belong to a root *ṣbr*.[17] The /ʿ/ is surely secondary.[18]

Despite the not entirely parallel development in the individual Semitic languages, one can say that /ṣippar/, whatever its oldest form may have been, designated an individual, small (song-)bird, in contrast to the collective /ʿawp/ "birds," in addition—as still in Aramaic—to designating a species, presumably the most common small bird, the sparrow.

II. Old and Imperial Aramaic. There are five instances in Old and Imperial Aramaic. The word first appears in the very early Bileam Text from Deir ʿAllā (ninth century B.C.E.) in a somewhat uncertain context in the spelling *ṣpr*; a lacuna begins after the *r*. The passage[19] presumably involves a list of bird species so that the meaning here should more likely be determined as "sparrow":[20] "swallow, . . .-bird (?), dove and house sparrow."[21]

The form spelled with *n* (→ I) occurs three times in the sayings of the Aḥiqar story (fifth century B.C.E.) in the singular absolute *ṣnpr* and constructed as a feminine: "guard your mouth and . . . make your heart hearvy for a word is (*hyj*) a bird";[22] twice in the plural determinate *ṣnpry'*.[23]

III. Biblical Aramaic. Biblical Aramaic has four instances, Dnl. 4:9,11,18,30, in the description of Nebuchadnezzar's dream vision. They are plurals, once absolute (4:30: "his hair grew as long as eagle feathers and his nails as bird talons" [*wᵉṭip̄rōhī ḵᵉṣippᵉrīn*]), once determined (4:11: "so that the animals lying under it run away and the birds flee from its branches" [*wᵉṣippᵉrayyā min-ʿanp̄ōhī*]), and twice the construct "the birds of heaven" (*ṣippᵉrē šᵉmayyā*; 4:9: "Tree . . . all the animals of the field found shade under it and the birds of the heaven sat on his branches" and 4:19: "Tree. . . , under which the animals of the field dwelt and on whose branches the birds of heaven sat, that is you, O King").

---

11. *DUL*³, 777f.
12. *DUL*³, 184 with further literature; both "bird."
13. *AHw*, I, 390 with reference to Ugaritic.
14. Lane, 2064.
15. Kottsieper, 57f.
16. Dalman, 367.
17. Akkadian *AHw*, III, 1065; Syriac *LexSyr*, 620; *ATTM*, 2, 469 *ṣpr* > *ṣbr*.
18. Cf. Brockelmann, 372f. and Fischer, 203 on animal names in the form *'uqtūl* from *'uqtūl* and on the identity of *'afʿal*, *'ifʿil*, and *'ufʿul* with *'ufʿūl* in Arabic.
19. Combination I, l. 9 = *KAI* 312.9 following E. Lipiński, *SAIO* II. *OLA* 57 (1994), 103-70.
20. Hackett, 133: "sparrow."
21. For the linguistic classification and more recent literature, cf. also Gzella.
22. *TADAE* C1.1:82; for the context → *pm* II.1.
23. *TADAE* C1.1: 186 and 198, both before a lacuna in a destroyed context.

IV. Qumran. The three Aramaic specimens from Qumran occur in the Targum of Job (11Q10 13:2; 26:6; 35:8; first century B.C.E.) and translate Job 28:21; 35:11; and 40:29. The plural construct *ṣpry* appears in 13:2 (Job 28:21): "[from] the birds of heaven they were hid[den]"; the plural determined *ṣpryʾ* in 26:6 (Job 35:11):[24] "God . . . who . . . made us wiser [than] the birds";[25] and the singular absolute *ṣpr* in 35:8 (Job 40:29): "will you laugh with him as with a bird."[26]

Hug

24. On the relationship with the Hebrew text → *prš* II.
25. Both times translating Hebrew *ʿôp̄ haššāmayim.*
26. Hebrew *ṣippōr.*

קבל *qbl*; קבל *qbl* /qobl/; קבילה *qbylh* /qabīlā/

I. Etymology, Lexical Field, and Constructions. II. G-stem "to Accuse." III. D-stem "to Receive." IV. Preposition "Before." V. Noun "Accusation."

I. Etymology, Lexical Field, and Constructions. Aramaic *qbl* belongs to a verbal root, common at least in West Semitic. The Aramaic G-stem "to accuse, raise an accusation," known from the earliest texts, contrasts with the D-stem "to receive, to accept" also known in other individual languages. Both remain largely constant throughout the history of the Aramaic language and some derive them from a common basic meaning "to confront someone,"[1] while others assume two homonymous roots.[2]

Although the verb also seems once to have been native in Canaanite for "to receive," as evidenced by its use in the Amarna Correspondence,[3] *lqḥ* with the originally less specific nuance "to take"[4] replaced it in Hebrew, Moabite, and Phoenician. Meanwhile, at least the sporadic instances in postexilic prose texts stand under Aramaic influence.

J. Dušek, *Les manuscrits araméens du Wadi Daliyeh et la Samarie vers 450-332 av. J.-C. CHANE* 30 (2007); I. Ephʿal and J. Naveh, *Aramaic Ostraca of the Fourth Century BC from Idumaea* (Jerusalem, 1996), esp. no. 199.6; G. Geiger and H. Gzella "*qbl*," *ThWQ*, III, 447-53; H. Gzella, *Tempus, Aspekt und Modalität im Reichsaramäischen. VOK* 48 (2004); J. Naveh and S. Shaked, *Aramaic Documents from Ancient Bactria (Fourth Century B.C.E.)* (London, 2012); F. Reiterer, "קבל *qbl*," *TDOT*, XII, 482-86.

1. So *LexSyr*, 640 and Reiterer, 482; *ATTM*, 677f. and 2, 470 also subsume both under the same verb.
2. *DJPA*, 472f.; *DJBA*, 979f.
3. *ti-qà-bi-lu* in EA 252.18.
4. Which also occurs in the earlier phases of the Aram. language → *nśī* V.

The older stages of the Aramaic languages differentiate between *qbl* in the D-stem for the passive reception of something and various other verbs for the active taking or removing; → *yhb*/*ntn* "to give" serve as antonyms. For a discussion of the lexical field → *nśʾ* I. For the meaning "to accuse," however, the G-stem of *qbl* is the typical verb. An Imperial Aramaic commercial ostracon from Idumea[5] also seems to attest a C-stem of *qbl* for "to pay," but this usage is unusual elsewhere.

The G-stem "to complain, to accuse" can be construed intransitively or with a direct object "before,"[6] frequently supplemented with a prepositional expression with *ʿl* "against," *l-* or *qdm* "before," and *ʿl* (*dbr*) or *mn* "because of" or an object clause following *dy* "about, that." Meanwhile, the D-stem is generally transitive with that received as a material or abstract object, in which case *mn* "from" may specify the giver. The corresponding t-stem serves as a passive.[7]

Prepositions in conjunction with /qobl/ (from the fifth century B.C.E.)[8] "before, in front of, corresponding to" are especially productive in Aramaic. It represents a *qutl*-noun from the same root and forms the basis of various conjunctions. Legal diction also knows the feminine /qabīlā/ "accusation."

Yet, to date, no relationship has been established with the homonymous root *qbl*, in the G-stem "to be dark," and the related noun /qabl/ "darkness." Aramaic first attests both in the texts from Qumran: the verb in a formulaic expression for the waning moon in the astronomical book of Enoch, the noun in 11Q10 8:6 (Job 24:15) for Hebrew *næšæp̄* "twilight."[9]

II. G-stem "to Accuse." The G-stem of *qbl* "to accuse" first appears in a curse formula in the Tell Fekheriye inscription, the oldest written Aramaic witness: should someone remove the name of the donor of the statue, then may the God Hadad be *qblh* "his accuser."[10]

Thereafter the verb occurs frequently in documentary texts beginning with the Achaemenid period. In letters, it appears with the general nuance "to complain,"[11] but mostly for a formal complaint either before a state authority[12] or to a superior in the official hierarchy.[13]

5. Eph'al and Naveh, no. 199.6.
6. E.g., *TADAE* A4.2:3.
7. nV 27:11 in *ATTM*, 2, 238f.
8. With anaptyxis /qobəl/ > /qobol/, *ATTM*, 112-15.
9. Cf. G. Geiger and H. Gzella, *qbl*, 452-53.
10. *KAI* 309.12, here a substantival ptcp.
11. *TADAE* A2.2:10, with *ʿl* "against."
12. *TADAE* A4.2:3, with the official title *ptyprsn* (pl.), possibly "investigative official," here as a direct object indicating the recipient of the complaint; in *TADAE* A3.3:4 with *l-* "before" and *ʿl* "about" in a complaint concerning the unpaid wages of an administrative employee, → *pḥh* II.
13. *TADAE* A6.3:1; 6.14:1f, also with *l-* "before" and *ʿl* "concerning"; Naveh and Shaked, A1,1,4,6,8, with *mn* "concerning" in l. 1.

In private documents, it has the specifically juridical sense of "to accuse."[14] Here, in a fixed formula, one waives a later accusation before a "prefect"[15] or "judge."[16] A court record[17] registers an actually executed complaint, but the context is fragmentary; a similar situation pertains in a Nabatean contract from the Dead Sea.[18]

Several texts from Qumran, mostly associated with the Enoch tradition, employ *qbl* in religious language for a complaint to God: Abraham in his prayer about the theft of his wife Sarah,[19] the spirits of the dead about their murders,[20] and the earth about the unnatural sexual behavior of the Watchers.[21] A few additional instances are fragmentary.[22] In 11Q10 8:2 (Job 24:12), *qbl* translates the Hebrew *šūʿ* "to call for help."

III. D-stem "to Receive." The first examples of the D-stem "to accept" occur in Imperial Aramaic private documents from Samaria,[23] all in the formula *lʾ mqbl ʾnh mn* "I have not received from." The grammatical analysis has always been controversial: either it involves a passive participle "having received," possibly in analogy to the Akkadian stative *maḫir* in the corresponding Neo-Babylonian formula,[24] but with an active meaning "possessing,"[25] or an active for the present indicating the conclusion of the contract.[26] In the second case, however, the perfect indicating coincidence would be more likely.[27] It also appears in the same meaning in contracts from the Dead Sea[28] and a Palmyrene grave warranty,[29] which also continues the Imperial Aramaic legal tradition.

In Biblical Aramaic, *qbl* once denotes the acceptance of gifts from the hand (*mn qdm*) of the king (Dnl. 2:6) and twice the assumption of rule (Dnl. 6:1; 7:18).[30]

---

14. *TADAE* B2.2:5,16, with *ʿl* "about" and *ʿl dbr* "because of," in l. 5 also *qdm* "before"; 2.3:13, 3.10:19, 3.11:12 and 3.12:28 with *ʿl* "about" and *l-* "before"; similarly probably in 4.6:14; 3.1:12,18 and 5.4:1 with *ʿl* "about" and *qdm* "before"; in 3.2:4,5f. with *ʿl* "about," in ll. 4,6 with *bgw* "in this matter" (→ *gw* II), and in l. 5 with the recipient as object.

15. → *sgn*.

16. → *dīn*.

17. *TADAE* B8.2:22.

18. nV 42:35 in *ATTM*, 2, 244-7: *qblt mlk wdyn* "I lodged a complaint before king and court."

19. 1QapGen 20:14, here with an object suffix "with you" together with an object clause following *dy* "because"; *qbltk* is a perfect for the coincidental "hereby"; cf. Gzella, 205-15.

20. 4Q206 1 22:4 (1 En. 22:5); 4Q530 1 1:4 (1 En. 9:10).

21. 4Q203 8:10.

22. 4Q201 1 4:11 par. 4Q202 1 3:11; 4Q530 2 2+6-12:3; 4Q531 34:1.

23. *WDSP*, 1.8; 2.2(emend.),6; 3.8.

24. Gzella, 131 n. 42.

25. *ATTM*, 2, 470.

26. Dušek, 136-39; cf. E. Lipiński, review of Jan Dušek, *Les Manuscrits Araméens du Wadi*, *Palamedes* 3 (2008) 228.

27. Cf. H. Gzella, review of J. Dušek, *Les manuscrits araméens du Wadi Daliyeh et la Samarie vers 450-332 av. J.-C. BiOr* 69 (2012), 607.

28. Cf. *ATTM*, 2, 470.

29. *PAT* 1791.3.

30. → *mlk* IV.

Texts from Qumran attest additional expressions and uses of the verb for the acceptance of instructions[31] and offices,[32] and in the context of sacrifices.[33] In 11Q10 it represents the Hebrew *lqḥ*.[34] The contexts of the fragments 4Q213 4:2 and 4Q586 a:2 remain unclear.

The meaning of *qbl*[35] in a marriage contract on an ostracon from Idumea[36] is debated.

The t-passive, very rare in older Aramaic, means "to be accepted" and initially appears only in bureaucratic style.[37] Jewish Palestinian then attests it somewhat more frequently.[38]

IV. Preposition "Before." Prepositional phrases based on the noun *qbl* "front side, in front of" (and accordingly with singular suffixes) appear beginning in the Achaemenid period and typify Aramaic. At the same time, *lqbl* frequently denotes "before" in the spatial sense[39] or "vis-à-vis,"[40] moreover, "accordingly" in the sense of manner,[41] "against,"[42] and "based on, because of."[43] In such expressions, it overlaps partially with → *qdm*.

Thus, with the nuance "accordingly" in conjunction with the demonstrative pronouns *znh*/*dnh* and/or the relative particle *zy*/*dy*, the typical basis of subordinating conjunctions in Aramaic, it can also constitute the introduction of (usually) causal clauses or expressions indicating a comparison: *lqbl dnh* "according to"[44] or "on the basis of" (Ezr. 4:16); *lqbl dy* "like,"[45] with a subsequent *'yk* "like" also Naveh and Shaked, A5,1, or "because";[46] *klqbl dnh* "therefore" (Dnl. 2:12,24; 3:7f.,22; 6:10; Ezr. 7:17) or *klqbl dy* "because" (Dnl. 2:8; 3:29; 4:15; 5:12; 6:4f.,23; Ezr. 4:14; 7:14), "since" (Dnl. 2:10,40f.,45; 6:11); in contrast, it is only rarely a concessive "although" (Dnl. 5:22). Such phrases can then be further expanded, like *lqbl dnh dy* "according to that which"[47] or *klqbl dnh mn dy* "for this reason, because" (Dnl. 3:22). Here, despite the spelling as a distinct word and the vocalization

---

31. 4Q550 1:3, with no explicit object.
32. 4Q550 2:7; possibly also 3:7.
33. 11Q18 16 2+17 1:2, although the object goes unnamed or has not been preserved.
34. 11Q10 7:8 (Job 22:22); 26:2 (Job 35:7); and probably 35:2 (Job 40:23), perhaps under the influence of the subsequent verses, see G. Geiger and H. Gzella, *qbl*, 452.
35. Perhaps "has accepted," cf. *DJBA*, 979f.?
36. E. Eshel and A. Kloner, "An Aramaic ostracon of an Edomite marriage contract from Maresha, dated 176 B.C.E.," *IEJ* 46 (1996) 1-22, l. 11, see the discussion there, p. 18.
37. nV 27:11 in *ATTM*, 2, 238f.; *PAT* 0259 ii.136.
38. Cf. *DJPA*, 473.
39. *TADAE* A6.2:7; Dnl. 2:31; 3:3; 5:1; 1QapGen 6:14; 14:9; 4Q204 4:2; 4Q205 1 12:1; 4Q550 5+5a:3; 11Q18 19:1.
40. Dnl. 5:5; 4Q554 1 3:18.
41. *TADAE* A6.9:4f.; 2.3:27; B8.7:2 and probably l. 9; 8.12:1; D1.17:7; *WDSP*, 2.9; 3.9; 10.9; Naveh and Shaked, A6,6; 4Q344 5.
42. In the sense of "for": *TADAE* B1.1:5; in the hostile sense: 1QapGen 21:32; 4Q201 1 3:20.
43. *TADAE* B5.5:3; Dnl. 5:10; 4Q201 1 4:5.
44. *TADAE* A4.5:10; *WDSP*, 1.11.
45. Esp. frequent: *TADAE* A4.3:9; 4.7:25 par. 4.8:24; 4.9:10; 6.11:6; 6.12:2; C1.1:52,68; D1.32:11; Naveh and Shaked, A6,5,8f.; Ezr. 6:13.
46. *TADAE* B3.10:17.
47. *TADAE* A6.2:23.

kol in the biblical text, *kl-* is not the quantifier "all," but is a combination, otherwise rare in Semitic languages, of the two mono-consonantal prepositions *k-* and *l-*.[48]

The frequent occurrence of these phrases in official Imperial Aramaic letters and private documents, indeed only comparably rare in private letters on ostraca, suggests that it originated in the linguistic register of Achaemenid administrative diction and, thence, spread in the literary language.

The participle *mqbl* "lying opposite" in an attributive function in the path descriptions of Palmyrene grave authorizations[49] apparently also belongs to the noun *qbl*. Some assign it to the C-stem, which is otherwise not well attested in Aramaic,[50] but it could be, and perhaps even more likely is, a D-stem as is often the case with denominal verbs.

V. Noun "Accusation." The feminine noun *qbylh* /qabīlā/ "accusation" belongs to the meaning of the G-stem (→ II) of *qbl*. It occurs in a few Imperial Aramaic official letters in reference to an official complaint.[51] Like the verb, it appears once in 11Q10 25:4 (Job 34:28) from Qumran for a complaint before God, where it translates the picturesque Hebrew *ṣʿqh* "cry (of complaint"), thus faded, but entirely in keeping with the original text. It appears with very similar nuances in the post-Christian era, e.g., in Jewish Palestinian,[52] in Jewish Babylonian,[53] and in Syriac.[54]

These later Aramaic languages also attest additional related nominal forms.[55]

Gzella

48. *BLA*, §69q'; → *kll* IV.3.
49. *PAT* 0039.1; 0527.7; 0551.6; 0555.8f.
50. E.g., *DNSI*, 980; so also already G. A. Cooke, *A Text-Book of North-Semitic Inscriptions* (Oxford, 1903), 310.
51. *TADAE* A6.15:5,11; 6.8:3.
52. *DJPA*, 472a.
53. *DJBA*, 978b.
54. *LexSyr*, 641.
55. Cf. *DJBA*, 980b for Jewish Babylonian and especially *LexSyr*, 641-43 for the numerous pertinent Syriac forms.

קדם *qdm*; קדם *qdm* /qodām/; קדמה *qdmh* /qadmā/; קדמי *qdmy* /qadmāy/; קדים *qdym* /qadīm/

I. Etymology. II. Preposition. 1. Old and Imperial Aramaic. 2.Biblical Aramaic and Qumran. III. Nouns. 1. Old and Imperial Aramaic. 2.Biblical Aramaic and Qumran.

I. Etymology. The root *qdm* "front, before, first" in both temporal and local meanings is common Semitic. The derived meaning "east"[1] arose in Ugaritic and Hebrew out of the tendency to orient oneself, with the Mediterranean at one's back, forward, toward the sunrise. In Qumran Aramaic, the noun with this meaning is probably a loanword.[2] As a verb, *qdm* in the G- and D-stems "to precede, to anticipate" and in the C-stem "to do first" first appears in the post-Christian era.[3]

II. Preposition.

1. Old and Imperial Aramaic. The preposition *qdm* "before," constructed with plural suffixes (e.g., Dnl. 7:13), mostly in a local,[4] although also in a temporal meaning,[5] is frequent. Theologically relevant are Old and Imperial Aramaic expressions for destiny "before God": at the erection of statues, thrones, or steles in a pagan context,[6] where, given the presence of the statue of a deity, "before" can be understood spatially; in relation to treaties concluded before treaty gods;[7] in the blessing formula *bryk* PN *qdm* GN *'lh'* "blessed be PN by the god DN" on Egyptian burial steles;[8] in the phrase "righteousness before God"[9] or "favor (*rḥmn*) before God."[10] The preposition here assures the quality of the characteristic mentioned, comparable with the Biblical Hebrew *bᵉʿēnē Yhwh*, Nu. 24:1 etc., *lip̄nē Yhwh*, 2 Ch. 31:20, etc.

2. Biblical Aramaic and Qumran. The pairing of mostly good characteristics with the modifier "before/with God," already known in Imperial Aramaic, also occurs in Biblical Aramaic and at Qumran. Thus, Daniel explains his deliverance from the lions' den in Dnl. 6:23 with "the fact that innocence was found in him [i.e., God]" (*dī qᵒḏāmōhī zāḵū hištᵉḵaḥaṯ lī*, 3ms suff.); the Tobit manuscript 4Q196 17 2:5 (Tob. 13:6) had "do the righ]t before hi[m" (*qw[šṭ' ʿbdw]qdmwh[y*, 3ms suffix); and the petitionary prayer from T. Levi

K. Beyer and A. Livingstone, "Die neuesten aramäischen Inschriften aus Taima," *ZDMG* 137 (1987) 285-96; I. Eph'al and J. Naveh, *Aramaic Ostraca of the Fourth Century BC from Idumaea* (Jerusalem, 1996); H.-J. Fabry, "*qdm*," *ThWQ*, III, 458-62; M. L. Klein, "The Preposition *qdm* ('Before')," *JTS* 30 (1979) 502-7; T. Kronholm, "קֶדֶם *qeḏem*," *TDOT*, XII, 505-11; D. Shepherd, "*MN QDM*: Deferential Treatment in Biblical Aramaic and the Qumran Targum of Job?," *VT* 50 (2000) 401-4; C. Stadel, *Hebraismen in den aramäischen Texten vom Toten Meer* (Heidelberg, 2008).

1. Aramaic *mdnḥ*.
2. Stadel, 93.
3. See *DJPA*, 475; *DJBA*, 984f.; *LexSyr*, 646-648; *MdD*, 405.
4. So also once **qdmh*, *TADAE* A2.2:15.
5. Cf. **qdmh* otherwise.
6. "To erect before": Old Aramaic *śm qdm*, *KAI* 309.1,15f., 202 B 13f. (→ *śīm*); Imperial Aramaic *hqm qdm*, *KAI* 258.1f., Beyer and Livingstone, 286 ll. 5f. (→ *qūm* IV).
7. *KAI* 222 A 7-11.
8. *TADAE* D20.3:1f., etc.; → *brk* II.
9. As a pagan affirmation, *KAI* 226.2 *bṣdqty qdmwh* "because of my righteousness before him," 3ms suff.; as a Jewish wish, *TADAE* A4.7,27 *ṣdqh yhwh lk qdm yhw* "may righteousness be to you before Yaho."
10. A Jewish letter *TADAE* A4.3:2f.

4Q213a 1:15f. says "to f]ind your grace before you [. . .] what is well and good with you" (*l'*]*škḥ' rḥmyk qdmyk* [. . .] *dšpyr wdṭb qdmyk*, 2ms suff.). The phrase "evil before my lord/master" (*b'yš qwdm rby*) appears in 4Q529 1:10.

In respectful speech, the preposition *qdm* can replace other prepositions (*mn qdm* replaces *mn*) if the object is God. This is a further development of Imperial Aramaic court diction in which *qdm* found usage in reference to the king or other high officials,[11] as was still the case in Dnl. 2:9,10; Ezr. 7:14, etc. This manner of speech in reference to a god first appears on an Imperial Aramaic pagan burial stele,[12] then in Biblical Aramaic and at Qumran, e.g., Dnl. 6:11, where Daniel in his upper story "prays and praises his God" (*meṣallē ūmōḏē qoḏām ʾælāheh*).[13] Abraham relates in 1QapGen 21:3 of his return to Bethel, "there I praised God" (*w'wdyt tmn qwdm 'lh'*). In the Book of Giants 4Q533 3:1 "children prayed (or pray!) before him" (] *ṣlw yldyn mn qdmwh* [)[14] and in 4Q557 1:7[15] "and mercy with G[od" (]*wrḥmyn mn qdm '*[*lh'*),[16] the pairing *mn qdm* appears instead of the expected *qdm*.[17]

III. Nouns.

1. Old and Imperial Aramaic. Old and Imperial Aramaic attest the morphologically feminine noun **qdmh*[18] "former time, former status," sometimes with suffixes,[19] sometimes with a preposition meaning "chronologically before" with a subsequent noun.[20] In Imperial Aramaic, the adjective *qdmy* "former, first" can function attributively[21] or substantivally.[22]

2. Biblical Aramaic and Qumran. In Biblical Aramaic and documents from the Judean wilderness, one finds the combination *min qaḏmaṯ dᵉnā* "before, previously,"[23] in comparison to Imperial Aramaic, expanded with *mn*. Otherwise, only 1QapGen 21:23 attests the noun **qdmh* "former time" (*qdmt ywmy' 'ln* "before these days").[24] The adjective */qadmāy/ "former, first" in substantival usage characterizes the first animal in Daniel's animal vision (Dnl. 7:4: *qaḏmāyᵉṯā* "the first")[25] and the previous kings in its

11. *TADAE* A4.2:9; C1.1:10, etc.
12. *KAI* 269.3.
13. Also Dnl. 2:18; 6:12; 4Q203 9:2; 11Q10 37:3 (Job 42:1).
14. Probably a defective 3ms suff.
15. If one should not supply a verb form as in the similar expression in Dnl. 2:18.
16. With a supralinear *mn*.
17. Cf. *PAT* 1680.3.
18. Always in the sg. const.
19. *TADAE* A2.3:9; A4.3:10; Sam'alian *KAI* 215.9 for its relationship to Aram., cf. P. M. Noorlander, "Sam'alian in Its Northwest Semitic Setting," *Or* 81 (2012) 202-38.
20. *TADAE* C1.1:2; A4.7:17: phrase *qdmt znh* "prior to that, previously."
21. *TADAE* A6.10:1,7f. *pqyd' qdmy'* "the previous official," in the masc. sg. deter. state.
22. Eph'al and Naveh, 187.3 *qdmyh* "his/her first (?)," masc. sg. with 3 sg. suff.; l. 4 has the antonym *'ḫry* "last."
23. Dnl. 6:11; Ezr. 5:11; contracts: M 19:17; V 46:4; V 50:6; all in *ATTM*.
24. Sg. const.; → *ywm* II.2.
25. Fem. sg. det.

interpretation (Dnl. 7:24: *qaḏmāyē* "the former ones"),[26] and in adjectival use "the first horns" (Dnl. 7:8: *qarnayyā qaḏmāyāṯā*)[27] of the fourth animal.

In Noah's dream vision 1QapGen 14:11, "the first shoot" (*ḥlpt' qdmyt'*)[28] grows on the stump of the great cedar, which symbolizes Noah.[29] The reference to "the first pilgrimage feast" (*rgl' qdmy'*),[30] probably Succoth, after the flood in 1QapGen 12:14 is also relevant.

Furthermore, the adjective typifies the astronomical book of Enoch;[31] the correct etymology (→ I) of the masculine noun *qdym* "east" appears in 4Q210 1 2:15:[32] "[One calls the east, east] because it is the first" ([*qryn lqdym' qdym*] *bdy hw' qdmy'*).[33] Otherwise, 4Q210 1 2:4,5,6 in the phrase "east wind" (*rwḥ qdym*)[34] and 4Q548 2 1:9, 4Q244 4:1, and 4Q580 1 1:9 attest this word.

For the adjective in Palmyrene, cf. *PAT* 0259 i.4 (*bzbny' qdmy'* "in earlier times")[35] and l. 9 (*nmws' qdmy'* "the former law")[36] and also in an architectural description;[37] it also functions adverbially *qdmy* "at first."[38]

Stadel

26. Masc. pl. det.; → *ḥyī*.
27. Fem. pl. det.; regarding the context → *qrn* II.
28. Fem. sg. det.; substantivized in ll. 16,17.
29. On this expression → *ḥlp* IV.
30. Masc. sg. det.
31. Masc. sg. det. 4Q209 7 3:2; 4Q210 1 2:4.7: *tr'' qdmy'*, "the first gate [of heaven; → *tr'*]"; 4Q211 1 2:5: *ywm' qdmy'* "the first day."
32. Par. 4Q209 23:3.
33. Masc. sg. det., the emended context is uncertain.
34. → *rwḥ*.
35. Greek πάλαι χρόνοις.
36. Greek πρώτου νόμου.
37. *PAT* 0040.1.
38. *PAT* 0042.8.

קדשׁ *qdš*; קדשׁ *qdš* /qodš/; קדישׁ *qdyš* /qaddīš/; מקדשׁ *mqdš* /maqdaš/

I. Etymology and Lexical Field. II. Usage of the Verb. III. Nouns. 1. "Holiness." 2. "Sanctuary." IV. Adjective "Holy." 1. As an Attributive. 2. Substantivized "Holy One" (God and Especially Angels).

H. Gzella, "Beobachtungen zur Angelologie der Sabbatopferlieder im Spiegel ihrer theologiegeschichtlichen Voraussetzungen," *ETL* 78 (2002) 468-81; G. Holtz, "*qdš*," *ThWQ*, III, 463-94; W. Kornfeld and H. Ringgren, "קדשׁ *qdš*," *TDOT*, XII, 521-45; H.-P. Müller, "קדשׁ *qdš* holy," *TLOT*, 1103-18.

I. Etymology and Lexical Field. All branches of the Semitic languages know the root *qdš* "to be/become holy" and related nominal forms to designate the fundamental religious experience of the holy. In this context, "holiness" means the transcendent perfection of God; therefore, persons (human or angelic), things, places, and times that have a direct connection with God and witness to God's presence are "holy." As a concept in the phenomenology of religion, *qdš* first appears regularly in Aramaic from the Jewish theological literature of the book of Daniel and the documents from Qumran, and, in the inscriptions witnessing to pagan personal piety, from the Roman Imperial period. Yet, even if the root does not seem to belong typically to the register of the old royal inscriptions, the documents from the provincial administration, and the practical ethics of the sayings of Aḥiqar, an accidental instance from later Old Aramaic[1] demonstrates that, already in the first half of the first millennium B.C.E., it belonged to the Aramaic lexicon.

In contrast to Hebrew, the verb *qdš* in Aramaic is not in use in the intransitive G-stem "to be/become holy" and appears primarily as a transitive in the factitive D-stem "to make holy, to declare holy" (with a view to the action itself) or in the C-stem "to make holy, to sanctify" (with emphasis on the result).[2] In addition, the root also forms the two masculine nouns /qodš/[3] "holiness" and /maqdaš/ "sanctuary" as well as the very frequent adjective /qaddīš/ "holy," which can also be employed substantivally for "holy one."

The concept of the holy has affinities with that of cultic and ethical purity,[4] as the parallelism of these lexemes in 4Q542 1 1:8.13 demonstrates (→ III.1 and IV.1), but goes beyond it. As an antonym, in relation to a phenomenology of religion approach, the root *ḥll* is first attested at Qumran, in the D-stem "to desecrate,"[5] whose usage here could stand partially under the influence of Hebrew, but need not itself be borrowed.[6] In relation to "holy" in the sociologically or theologically supported ecclesiological sense, the opposite is not "profane" but "heathen." It is denoted by, among others, *ʿm* /ʿamm/ "people"[7] and in post-Christian Jewish literature the adjective *ʾrmy* /ʾaramāy/, literally "Aramaic."[8]

No connection exists with the masculine Akkadian loanword /qodāš/ "earring"[9] that first appears in 11Q10 38:8 (Job 42:11) for Hebrew *næzæm*, but continued in usage later.

II. Usage of the Verb. As a verb, *qdš* first occurs in the D- and perhaps C-stems with the meaning "to sanctify," that is, for the transfer of the divine quality of holiness to a person or an object, at Qumran. Besides the translation of Lev. 16:19 in 4Q156 2:3, employing the D-stem of the Hebrew cognate in the instructions for the preparation of

---

1. *TADAE* C1.1:79, in the hymnic introduction to the collection of Aḥiqar's sayings.

2. For the general distinction, see E. Jenni, *Das hebräische Piʿel* (Zurich, 1968), 59-61.

3. Then /qodəš/ > /qodoš/, *ATTM*, 112-15.

4. Aram. *dkī* and *nqī* "to be pure," → *nqh* III.; *zkī* "to be innocent," → *zkw*.

5. 4Q213a 3-4:3, already weakened in reference to the desecration of the good reputation of a man and his family, apparently by disgraceful behavior.

6. Cf. C. Stadel, *Hebraismen in den aramäischen Texten vom Toten Meer* (Heidelberg, 2008), 44f.

7. → *ʿm* III.

8. → *ʿm* V.

9. See S. A. Kaufman, *The Akkadian Influences on Aramaic. AS* 19 (1974), 86.

the altar for the atonement ritual, the same form occurs in a fragmentary context, but presumably also in relation to the cult in 11Q18 32:7 (new Jerusalem). Furthermore, a fragment of the Book of Giants[10] lacking virtually any context may contain an instance of the C-stem with *qš]yṭyn* "truthful ones" as object, but the reading is not entirely clear because of a scribal error. As in Hebrew (→ I), then, the D-stem may denote a one-time ritual action and the C-stem an enduring result.

In Palmyrene, too, the D-stem denotes the consecration of persons[11] and objects,[12] the C-stem of things.[13] Here, no semantic distinction is perceptible.

In later stages of the Aramaic language, the D-stem is more frequent and also forms a corresponding t-passive "to be sanctified."[14] Jewish Palestinian and Jewish Babylonian have adopted a few very specific meanings from the Hebrew.

III. Nouns.

1. "Holiness." Similarly, the earliest instances of the noun *qdš*[15] /qodš/ are at Qumran. Initially, it denotes the abstract quality "holiness," as in a list of positive characteristics as the foundation of the upright and holy life.[16] It finds regular usage, however, in a genitive construction with a preceding noun in the construct state as an attributive "of holiness" and, thus, like the adjective "holy" (→ IV.1): with a place,[17] a city,[18] possibly words,[19] or a tithe.[20] 4Q580 2:3 and 11Q18 25:1 have survived without sufficient context. Two other possible instances in defective spellings and fragmentary contexts are dubious and could also be assigned to the adjective (→ IV.2).[21]

The precise meaning of the plural of *qdš* in a Palmyrene dedicatory inscription is debated.[22] A building inscription from Hatra has the singular with a subsequent genitive attributive "of the gods" once,[23] perhaps to indicate a holy precinct.

In later diction, the usage of the word for the quality itself as an attributive in a genitive relationship and metonymically for holiness (in the plural instruments or sacrifices) continued.[24]

---

10. 4Q531 17:1.

11. *PAT* 1372.2, in Greek ἱεράσαντα.

12. *PAT* 0095.3.

13. *PAT* 0514.1, in l. 2 of the Greek version ἀφιέρωσαν; similarly in 0570.

14. *DJPA*, 477a; *DJBA*, 987f.; *LexSyr*, 649f.; *MdD*, 405.

15. Or in a *plene* spelling *qwdš*.

16. 4Q542 1 1:13, paralleling *ṣdqh* "righteousness," *qšṭ* "truth," *yšyrw* "uprightness," *tmymw* "perfection," *dkw* "purity," and *khnw* "priesthood."

17. *byt* for "sanctuary" in 4Q156 2:4 (Lev. 16:20).

18. *qryh*, 4Q196 17 2:8 (Tob. 13:10); of Jerusalem.

19. *mlyn*, 4Q212 1 5:16 (1 En. 93:11); *DSSStE*, 445, to the contrary "of the holy one," the rest lost because of a lacuna.

20. *m'śr*, 4Q213a 3-4:8.

21. 4Q201 1 4:7 and 4Q531 22:6.

22. *PAT* 1347.5; perhaps "holy objects" as in Jewish Palestinian, yet cf. *DNSI*, 994 and *PAT*, p. 405 s.v. for various other interpretations.

23. H1017.2.

24. *DJPA*, 476f.; *DJBA*, 989b; *LexSyr*, 649; *MdD*, 406.

2. *"Sanctuary."* In contrast, *mqdš* /maqdaš/ "sanctuary," also attested beginning at Qumran, refers explicitly to the temple in Jerusalem.[25] Later, it appears in the same sense only rarely as an absolute, but mostly as part of the expression *byt mqdš'*, as in the dating formula "after the destruction of the temple" in the gravestones from Zoar,[26] and elsewhere in Jewish Palestinian,[27] in Jewish Babylonian,[28] and in Syriac.[29] The usage of the word may correspond to a perceptible tendency in postbiblical Judaism to restrict the status of holy place to Jerusalem and the temple mount;[30] yet, the adjective *qdyš* designating the cult building appears nonetheless in synagogue inscriptions (→ IV.2).

IV. Adjective "Holy." The adjective *qdyš* /qaddīš/ "holy," is the first form of this root to appear in Aramaic, and it remains the most frequent of all the forms. It characterizes mostly gods and angels, for whom holiness is an essential characteristic, as is already true in late Old Aramaic and in the book of Daniel; it rarely characterizes humans, and only occasionally places and objects that have a special relationship with the divine. In reference to persons, it often occurs substantivally in both the singular and the plural "holy one(s)." Additionally, later Aramaic attests an abstract noun "holiness" based on the adjective.[31]

1. *As an Attributive.* The prototypical usage of *qdyš* for gods as an attributive of the plural *'lhyn* first occurs in Daniel where it consistently appears in the mouths of pagans,[32] which finds a parallel in the expression *'[ḥy]' qdyš'* "the holy brothers" for two unnamed (apparently divine) beings in a Palmyrene dedicatory inscription.[33] Otherwise, it usually appears as a substantival denoting God or angelic beings (→ IV.2).

Sporadically it serves as an attributive of the name of God,[34] of angels (*ml'ky'*),[35] of a holy mountain,[36] of a height (*rym*),[37] of the temple,[38] or of a person like the priest[39] Aaron

---

25. 4Q554 2 2:18 par. 5Q15 1 1:4; 11Q18 9:6; also presumably 4Q540 1:5, but in a fragmentary context.

26. *ATTM*, 2, 301-9; → *ḥrb* V.

27. *DJPA*, 326.

28. *DJBA*, 215b,701b.

29. *LexSyr*, 649b.

30. On the pertinent passages in rabbinic literature, cf. E. Ben Eliyahu, "The Rabbinic Polemic against Sanctification of Sites," *JSJ* 40 (2009) 260-80.

31. See *LexSyr*, 649b.

32. In Dnl. 4:5f.,15 by Nebuchadnezzar before his conversion to the true God and in 5:11 by the sages of Belshazzar.

33. *PAT* 0347.3; 0348.2.

34. → *šm*; 4Q196 6:7 (Tob. 3:11), along with *yqyr* "weighty," → *yqr*.

35. 4Q553 2 2:1, although partially emend.

36. 1QapGen 19:8; in keeping with usage in Biblical Hebrew, probably Mt. Zion, as *ATTM*, 171 n. 2 suspects, yet see J.A. Fitzmyer, *The Genesis Apocryphon of Qumran Cave 1 (1Q20). BietOr* 18/B (^{3}2004), 180, with additional bib., for the hypothesis that it refers to Bethel.

37. 4Q531 18,1.

38. → *hykl*; 11Q18 19:3.

39. → *khn*.

and his descendants.[40] As a predicative, it appears along with *dkh* in the call "Be holy and pure!" in the Testament of Qahat.[41] A few other instances lack context.[42]

In Palestinian synagogue inscriptions from late antiquity, *qdyš* as an attributive of *qhlh* "community"[43] or *ḥbwrh* "confraternity"[44] designates the community of believers and, together with *'tr* "place," the synagogue itself.[45] Contrarily, one employs the noun *mqdš* "sanctuary" (→ III.2) for the sanctuary par excellence, the temple mount in Jerusalem. In the Christian realm, *qdyš* in conjunction with *'bht'* "the fathers" serves as a title of the church fathers.[46]

2. Substantivized "Holy One" (God and Especially Angels). As a substantive, *qdyš* in the singular of plural "holy one(s)" often refers to angels since they are members of the divine court and, thus, participate in God's holiness. Already in the oldest known instance, the designation *b'l qdšn* "Overlord of the holy ones"[47] for the supreme god, who can elevate something (wisdom?) to himself in heaven, it serves as a word for subordinate divine beings.

Like so many individual aspects of the history of Syro-Palestinian religion, a differentiated understanding of the role of angels and demons in piety, and of the hierarchy of the heavenly pantheon in the first half of the first millennium B.C.E. remains incomprehensible. In early Judaism, mediator figures then underwent a marked up-valuation with an increasing awareness of the transcendence and uniqueness of God, but were no longer understood as independent gods. In the theological literature of the postexilic period, old images like that of the heavenly council received a new interpretation influenced by wisdom and apocalyptic, which also left traces in the book of Daniel and in the texts from Qumran.[48] Thus, the conceptions became further differentiated and *qdyš* in a substantival use functioned alongside → *'yr* "watcher" and → *ml'k* "messenger" (less frequent in Aram.) as an extremely widespread term for "angel." Its usage accommodates the conviction that their participation in the divine perfection and their access to divine knowledge are the defining characteristics of the angels.

The suffix as in *qdyšwhy* "his holy ones"[49] or genitive constructions like *qdyšy šmyh* "the holy ones of heaven"[50] express their close connection with God. The rare intensified form *qdyšy qdyšy'* "the holy of holy ones,"[51] that is, "the extremely holy," also presumably refers to angels. Conversely, Qumran no longer describes God as the lord of all angelic

40. → *zr'*; 4Q545 4:16f.
41. 4Q542 1 1:8.
42. 4Q531 29:4; 47:2.
43. yySU 7 and ggJR 1:2; *ATTM*, 368,388.
44. ggBS 1:1; *ATTM*, 377.
45. ggHM 1:2; ggKH 1:1; *ATTM*, 386,388.
46. ccAD 1:7; *ATTM*, 402.
47. *TADAE* C1.1:79.
48. Cf. Gzella.
49. 4Q204 1 1:15 (1 En. 1:9).
50. 4Q201 1 4:10 (1 En. 9:1).
51. 11Q18 15:5.

powers with *bʿl qdšn* "Lord of the holy ones," as does *TADAE* C1.1:79 (see above), but with *qdyšʾ rbʾ* "the grand Holy One."[52]

The dual designation *ʿyr wqdyš* in the singular for one being[53] and in the plural *ʿyryn wqdyšyn* for a group[54] characterizes Daniel and the book of Enoch. The origin of this distinction remains obscure; synchronically, however, because of the parallelism and the usage in reference to one angel, it is no longer possible to distinguish between two different classes. Qumran employs only the word *ʿyr* for the fallen angels who, according to Gen. 6:4 begot descendants with human women, while reserving *qdyš* exclusively for the angels who remained true to God. Thus, the addition *qdyš*, which occupies second position in all certain instances of the combination,[55] disambiguates the whole expression and makes clear that it involves good angels. If *qdšyʾ* in 4Q531 22:6 is a defective spelling of the adjective[56] and does not represent the noun (→ III.1), the contrast would be explicit for, then, a fallen angel would say that his opponent dwells "among the holy ones" (*bʿly dyny*).

Angels designated as *qdyš(yn)* function as messengers of heavenly commands (Dnl. 4:10,20), decide the fate of humans (4:14, with echoes of the concept of the divine council), and bear eschatological secrets.[57] Lamech believed that they may have sired his son Noah.[58]

In contrast, the referent of the expression *qaddīšē ʿælyōnīn* "the holy ones of the Most High"[59] in the vision of the dawn of the eschatological kingdom of God in Dnl. 7:18,22,25,27[60] remains controversial. They obtain the eternal kingdom after their battle with the worldly powers. The background of the typical diction in Daniel and later at Qumran suggests interpreting it in relation to the angels, for that corresponds not only with the by far most frequent usage of the substantival adjective *qdyš* per se, but also with the various genitive or possessive constructions that connect it with God.[61] Then, the angels would be the heavenly protectors of the people of God and would fight for them against the powers of chaos hidden behind human empires.[62] In this context, it is difficult, however, to distinguish between the people of God itself[63] and its guardian angels; scholars often suggest a collective interpretation especially of the "son of man,"

52. 1QapGen 0:11; 2:14; 6:13,15; 7:7; 12:17; 4Q201 1 1:5 (1 En. 1:3); 4Q530 2 2+6-12:17; → *rb*.

53. Dnl. 4:10,20; 4Q206 1 22:5 (1 En. 22: 6), here of the archangel Raphael.

54. Dnl. 4:14 and 1QapGen 2:1, both in a parallelism; 4Q212 1 3:21 (1 En. 93:2); furthermore, *ʿyryn* should probably be supplied in 4Q201 1 1:3 (1 En. 1:2).

55. In 4Q534 1 2+2:17 the subsequent word is not clear, but probably not a form of *ʿyr*.

56. So *ATTM*, 262.

57. 4Q201 1 1:3 (1 En. 1:2); 4Q212 1 3:21 (1 En. 93:2); 4Q204 5 2:26 (1 En. 106:19).

58. 1QapGen 2:1.

59. → *ʿly* II.1.

60. Probably as an abbreviation, *qaddīšīn* appears twice in 7:21f.

61. See above for examples from Qumran; cf. J. J. Collins, *Daniel. Herm* (1993), 312-20.

62. See the extensive discussion by H. Gzella, *Cosmic Battle and Political Conflict. BietOr* 47 (2003), esp. 138-41.

63. So with Dnl. 8:24; J. A. Montgomery, *The Book of Daniel. ICC* (1927), 307, and often in older scholarship.

who receives dominion here, as the people.[64] The association is, thus, so close that the two entities, the people and its angels, fuse with one another and the precise relationship may be intentionally left in suspense. The abbreviated expression in 7:21f. further heightens the ambiguity.

Otherwise, in pre-Christian Aramaic, *qdyš* refers only in exceptional cases to humans, as perhaps in *qdyšyn mn ʿmʾ* "holy ones of the people,"[65] although the broader context is unknown; such references are also sporadic in Jewish Palestinian[66] and Jewish Babylonian,[67] and in Syriac for monks.[68]

A pair of other passages cannot be more precisely analyzed because of insufficient contexts, but a form of *qdyš* is clearly legible in each case: 4Q201 1 4:7 (1 En. 9:1);[69] 4Q203 8:5;[70] 4Q245 2:5; 4Q531 19:5; 4Q534 1 2+2:17; 4Q536 2 1+3:2.

Gzella

64. → *ʾnš* III.
65. 4Q213a 3-4:7.
66. As in *ʿm qdyšyn* "people of holy ones" in Targum Neofiti of Dt. 7:6 and 33:2; *DJPA*, 474b.
67. *DJBA*, 984a, alongside the frequent use for God and the angels already quite early.
68. *LexSyr*, 649b, also for angels.
69. According to *ATTM*, 237 a defectively spelled adj.
70. According to *ATTM*, 680, the third line from the end of G 4:5 may refer to Enoch, previously mentioned in the clause.

קום *qūm*; קים *qym*/qayām/; מקם *mqm* /maqām/; קומה *qwmh* /qawmā/; קים *qym* /qayyām/

I. Etymology, Lexical Field, and Constructions. II. G-stem "to Stand (Up)." 1. In the Full Sense. 2. Figuratively "to Rise," "to Remain." 3. As a Phase Verb. III. D-stem "to Decree." IV. C-stem "to Erect." V. Noun "Decree." VI. Noun "Status, Position." VII. Noun "Growth." VIII. Adjective "Steady."

I. Etymology, Lexical Field, and Constructions. In agreement with the other West Semitic languages, Aramaic employs the root *qūm* for "to stand." In the G-stem, the verb covers a broad spectrum of different usages. Both with a stative nuance "to stand" and with a dynamic "to stand up," it can denote literally an attitude or a movement, figuratively "to acquire, to appear," also with an abstract subject, or "to endure, to remain,"

S. Amsler, "קום *qûm* to stand up," *TLOT*, 1136-41; H.-J. Fabry, "*qwm*," *ThWQ*, III, 509-16; J. Gamberoni, "קום *qûm*," *TDOT*, XII, 589-612; H. Gzella, *Tempus, Aspekt und Modalität im Reichsaramäischen. VOK* 48 (2004).

and, diminished to a mere phase verb, for the ingressive action "to be about to" together with an additional full verb.

In contrast, the transitive D-stem[1] "to decree, to decide," at first still quite rare in pre-Christian Aramaic, and the more frequent, also transitive C-stem "to stand up, to erect" with a concrete or an abstract object, with persons as object also "to install, to appoint," have more specific meanings. Furthermore, both the D- and the C-stem manifest a corresponding t-passive "to be confirmed" or "to be reestablished," and the C-stem also has in pre-Christian Aramaic an inner passive "to be established" whose functions the related t-stem assumes in the post-Christian period.[2]

Depending on the precise usage, *qūm* overlaps with other verbs or contrasts with them as an antonym: the literal meaning "to stand" corresponds with → *ytb* "to sit, to settle"; for "to begin" → *srī* is also used in the D-stem and its counterpart "to end," etc. is the C-stem of → *sūp*. The nuance "to decide, to determine" finds expression through → *gzr*; further, → *śīm* "to set, to place,"[3] later *zqp*, serves for "to establish," with the counterparts → *mgr* "to topple" and → *ʿqr* "to eradicate," especially in reference to statues in Old Aramaic also a verb that appears as *yhns/thns*[4] and may be traceable to the C-stem of *nūs* or *nss*.[5] The D-stem of → *mnī* and the C-stem of → *tqn*, sometimes also of → *šlṭ* denote "to install, to appoint" with → *šbq* in the sense of "to dismiss" as antonym. In contrast, Aramaic attests the root *ʿmd* "to go up to, to stand," as in Hebrew, only in the noun *ʿmwd* /ʿammūd/ "pillar" (< /ʿamūd/)[6] and fuses the meaning of the verb with that of *qūm*.

Prepositional phrases can supplement the G-, D-, and C-stems depending on the nuance: in the G-stem "to stand up" *ʿm* "together with" with the nuance "to help" or *ʿl* "against" in the sense of "to accuse," in the D-stem "to conclude (a contract)" together with *ʿm* "with" and in the C-stem "to install" *l-* "as" or "to appoint" with *ʿl* "over."

Furthermore, the root underlies a variety of nominal forms, along with the masculine /qayām/ "decree, contract" and /maqām/ "status, position," the rare feminine /qawmā/[7] "growth, stature," and the rather frequent adjective /qayyām/ "steady." Later West Aramaic also attests the feminine /maqāmā/ "matter, thing."[8]

II. G-stem "to Stand (Up)." Earlier Old Aramaic already attests the G-stem of *qūm* "to stand" or "to stand up," which remains very productive as a verb in everyday speech in later phases of Aramaic. The precise nuance depends on the nature of the subject and the construction. In relation to persons, the full sense with an ingressive action "to stand up" (→ II.1) cannot always be clearly distinguished from the usage as an auxiliary verb

1. Which in contrast to Canaanite, still forms hollow roots other than → *rīm* on the pattern of verbs with three consonants, see *ATTM*, 488.

2. *ATTM*, 152.

3. → *nṣb* "to plant" is more specific.

4. *KAI* 202 B 20; 320.1; 225.6.

5. Cf. M. Sokoloff, "The Old Aramaic Inscription from Bukan," *IEJ* 49 (1999) 108; other suggestions in *DNSI*, 290.

6. *DNSI*, 869f.; *ATTM*, 660; 2, 456.

7. At the latest by the post-Imperial Aramaic period, /qōmā/.

8. *ATTM*, 682; *DJPA*, 327.

"to set about to, to prepare to." As in Hebrew, the imperative can also function simply as an interjection "up!" (→ II.3).

1. In the Full Sense. In the royal inscriptions of the Old Aramaic era, *qūm* occurs with a divine subject with the preposition *ʿm* "he arose with me" designating the help that the respective king received from his dynastic deity in disputes with others. The formulation in the Aramaic inscription of Zakkur[9] has parallels in Sam'alian;[10] similarly, later in an Imperial Aramaic private letter, it denotes "to stand by."[11]

In contrast, the sayings of Aḥiqar employ the verb in the context of court ethics for a subordinate before the king, once in the warning against rising before the countenance of the ruler,[12] and again in the assertion that only someone with whom (*ʿmh*) the god El is could stand before (*qdm*) the king, which can be interpreted either as "to serve" or "to survive" (l. 91).[13]

Imperial Aramaic marriage contracts employ *qūm* in the literal sense for "to stand up" as part of a formula by which a spouse initiates divorce by standing and declaring (publicly): "Hereby I reject. . . ."[14] With things as subject, the participle means "standing" and refers in architectural descriptions to walls[15] and perhaps doors (→ VIII).[16]

Biblical Aramaic also has in the narratives of the book of Daniel instances of both the stative usage "to stand"[17] and of the fientic "to stand up, to arise" (Dnl. 3:3,24; 6:20).[18]

Correspondingly, Qumran uses *qūm* for "to stand"[19] and for "to stand up";[20] similarly later, e.g., "Get up!" (to gods) in H74.1 from Hatra or "to stand" of a statue in *PAT* 2786.2.

2. Figuratively "to Rise," "to Remain." The stative and fientic usages also underlie various idiomatic expressions that are identifiable in growing numbers beginning with the Achaemenid period. In a few of the private letters with affinities to colloquial speech, *qūm* occurs for "to remain" in contrast to → *nḥt* "to come down,"[21] once with the unusual

9. *KAI* 202 A 3.14.

10. *KAI* 214.3; 215.2; see P. M. Noorlander, "Sam'alian in Its Northwest Semitic Setting," *Or* 81 (2012) 202-38 regarding the linguistic relationship.

11. *TADAE* D7.1:5; cf. 7.24:5.

12. *TADAE* C1.1:85.

13. For the discussion of the passage with biblical parallels, cf. M. Weigl, *Die aramäische Achikar-Sprüche aus Elephantine und die alttestamentliche Weisheitsliteratur*. *BZAW* 399 (2010), 174f.

14. *TADAE* B2.6, 22.26; 3.3:7,9; 3.8:21; cf. Gzella, 207.

15. *TADAE* B3.4:4.

16. *TADAE* A4.7:10.

17. Dnl. 2:31, of a statue; 7:10,16 of all those who stand before the heavenly throne in the last judgment.

18. Regarding the difficult imperfect for a past circumstance in the latter passage, see Gzella, 146f.

19. 1QapGen 6:14, of an angel; 4Q550 5+5a:5, of humans; 4Q206 4 1:19 (1 En. 89:4) of water; of a tree in 1QapGen 14:9 and 4Q552 2 2:2.

20. 4Q542 1 2:5.

21. *TADAE* A3.8:7,13.

qdmh[22] probably for "to stand in the way";[23] in conjunction with money and *byd* "in the hand,"[24] it functions as an auxiliary verb "to be, to be situated,"[25] in reference to a price and *ʿl* "to insist on."[26] With the meaning "to stand up" and the preposition *ʿl* "against" in the legal diction of contracts, it is a term for "to accuse."[27]

Biblical Aramaic manifests the meaning "to stand" for "to remain" with the eternal kingdom of God (Dnl. 2:44; along with the C-stem, → IV), "to stand up" in the sense of "to appear, to arise" for the sequence of transient human empires seen in visions (Dnl. 2:39 and 7:17,24).[28] The evidence at Qumran corresponds with both "to remain"[29] and "to arise, to appear,"[30] with *ʿl* also "to be responsible for."[31]

These nuances remained current, such as, e.g., "to have stability" in H272.3 from Hatra, *qūm ʿl* "to be responsible for"[32] or *qūm brš* "to stand at the point" for "to have leadership."[33]

3. As a Phase Verb. In the G-stem, however, *qūm* often serves merely to mark the ingressive action of the subsequent, mostly syndetically linked verb, and then, if it is not perceived as a mere filler,[34] has the meaning "to get to, to set about." It is attested in this usage beginning with the Achaemenid period,[35] it cannot always be distinguished from cases in which it has the nuance "to appear" (→ II.2).[36] This usage continues in Biblical Aramaic (Ezr. 5:2)[37] and later.[38] Thus, the corresponding imperative can also be used as a mere interjection "Go!"[39]

Conversely, post-Christian East Aramaic developed from the participle of *qūm* "standing" a prefixed morpheme /qā-/[40] to mark first the process then the present per se.[41]

---

22. → *qdm* II.1.
23. *TADAE* A2.2:15.
24. → *yd.*
25. *TADAE* A3.10:7; C3.15:123; cf. *DNSI*, 1000f.
26. *TADAE* A3.8:6.
27. *TADAE* B2.6:29; 3.6:7; 3.7:16; 3.8:30; 3.9:7; similarly probably also in 4.7:4; 6.3:9.
28. For the context → *mlk* IV.
29. 4Q542 1 2:4, in eternity.
30. 4Q246 1 2:4, of the people of God; 4Q339 1:1, of lying prophets; 4Q212 1 4:15 (1 En. 91:12), of a week.
31. 4Q550 4:2.
32. *PAT* 1358.7; H. J. W. Drijvers and J. F. Healey, *The Old Syriac Inscriptions of Edessa and Osrhoene. HO* 42 (1999), As5:14.
33. *PAT* 0261.2.
34. So *ATTM*, 681.
35. See *TADAE* B1.1:10; 3.4:20; 3.6:13; 3.9:6.
36. So perhaps *TADAE* C2.1:36, of the beginning of a speech.
37. Where, however, the D-stem of *šrī* indicates the ingressive nuance and *qūm* is consequently superfluous.
38. E.g., 1QapGen 22:5, cf. with inf. 20:20 and 4Q544 1:1; H1039.6 from Hatra; *PAT* 0312.5; and the frequent ἀναστάς in the same sense in NT Greek as in, e.g., Acts 5:17; 8:27; 9:11.
39. E.g., Dnl. 7:5; 1QapGen 21:13; 11Q10 29:5 (Job 37:14); cf. Gzella, 271.
40. From /qā'em/, later /q-/ and /k-/.
41. See H. Gzella, "Zu den Verlaufsfonnen für die Gegenwart im Aramäischen," *Or* 75 (2006) 184-88; idem, *A Cultural History of Aramaic. HO* 111 (2015), 340f.

III. D-stem "to Decree." In contrast to the broad spectrum of usage for the G-stem, the D-stem "to decree, to decide, to confirm" initially has juridical connotations and appears mostly in legal contexts. The first example, from the late Old Aramaic Asshur ostracon,[42] stands in a destroyed context, but may refer to a written guilty plea.[43] In Dnl. 6:8 it refers to a royal decree with *qym* "edit" (→ V) as object. Precisely the same formulation in 11Q10 35:6f. (Job 40:28) translates the Hebrew *krt bryt*.

Aramaic documents from the Dead Sea also employ the verb for "to confirm" with the subject of a contract as the object[44] or "to fulfill."[45] The t-passive seem to be used in the more general sense of "to be preserved, to remain,"[46] in *TADAE* D1.17:6 probably also corresponding to the active for "to be confirmed"; both remain productive.[47]

IV. C-stem "to Erect." The C-stem "to set up, to erect" is attested regularly with material objects, especially in relation to statues.[48] The verb already occurs several times in this usage in Sam'alian,[49] in Aramaic itself then since the Achaemenid era.[50] The report of the statue of King Nebuchadnezzar in Dnl. 3:1,2f.,5,7,12,14,18 follows the same usage, where the frequent leitmotif-like repetition of "that the king had erected" makes it emphatically clear that it involves a pure human product that deserves no veneration. This formulation also designates the donor of private dedicatory and honorific inscriptions in the memorial epigraphy of the Hellenistic-Roman epoch.[51] In such cases—sometimes in the same text—the more general verb → *ʿbd* (II.1) "to make" also occurs.[52]

With a person as object, the C-stem of *qūm* signifies figuratively "to establish, to install,"[53] regularly with the official nuance "to appoint"[54] and correspondingly of the dominion that God grants (Dnl. 2:21; 4:14; 5:21). With an abstract object, the verb rep-

42. *KAI* 233.9.

43. Cf. *KAI*, 285 on the passage.

44. nV 7:2,32 in *ATTM*, 2, 218-23, with *mtnh* "gift" as object, paralleling *yhb* "to give" and together with *bmlh qymh* "by a valid pronouncement."

45. So in V 46:12 in *ATTM*, 322f., with the purchase (*zbn*) as object; the precise nuance in V 48:8 and 81:6 in *ATTM*, 2, 251f.,256-58, with plots of land as the object, is not entirely clear and probably "to keep free of foreign claims," cf. *ATTM*, 2, 472.

46. 1QapGen 0:5, with a person; 4Q201 1 2:5 (1 En. 3:1) and 4Q211 1 1:6, with leaves.

47. See *DJPA*, 481b; *DJBA*, 998f.

48. → *ṣlm*.

49. *KAI* 214.1,14,28; 215.18.

50. *KAI* 258.1 from Asia Minor; it should surely be emended in K. Beyer and A. Livingstone, "Die neuesten aramaischen Inschriften aus Taima," *ZDMG* 137 (1987) 286, l. 2, for a throne ll. 5f., → *qdm* II.1, and probably also in *KAI* 228.9, both from northern Arabia.

51. From Palmyra, see *PAT* 0115.8; 0260.1; 0279.3; 0285.2; 0286.2; 0289.3; 0302.4; 1357.2; from Edessa Drijvers and Healey (→ II.2) As37.5; 61.2; for the many examples from Hatra, cf. K. Beyer, *Die aramäischen Inschriften aus Assur, Hatra und dem übrigen Ostmesopotamien* (Göttingen, 1998), 183, and idem, "Die aramäischen Inschriften aus Assur, Hatra und dem übrigen Ostmesopotamien (datiert 44 v. Chr. bis 238 n. Chr.) – Nachträge," *WO* 43 (2013) 60.

52. Cf. in addition to *KAI* 309.15, e.g., *PAT* 0276.1; 0277.1; 0302.2; H287.8.

53. *TADAE* C1.1:109, in religious speech, but in a fragmentary context.

54. *TADAE* C1.1:12,23,44; Dnl. 5:11; 6:2,4; in each case of service at court; in reference to priests, Ezr. 6:18; similarly of a wife in 4Q197 4 2:3.6 (Tob. 6:13).

resents "to establish (a kingdom)"[55] or "to issue (an edict)" (Dnl. 6:9,16). On a commercial ostracon from Idumea, it serves to mean "to confirm, to promise,"[56] in the private documents from Samaria with *'sr* as object "to enter into a contractual obligation," "to make a contract,"[57] a function the D-stem fulfills otherwise (→ III).

Regarding the singular formulation "to establish a joyous name" in the T. Levi from Qumran[58] → *ḥdwh* IV.2. In 11Q10 25:1 (Job 34:24), the verb translates the C-stem of *ʿmd*, in 30:4 (38:6) *yrī* "to cast," here "to lay the foundation stone."

The inner passive appears in Dnl. 7:4 in the fientic sense of "to become established," in 7:5 in the resultative sense of "to be established," the Ct-stem in 1QapGen 20:29 "to be reestablished" in reference to the healing of an illness produced by God.[59]

V. Noun "Decree." The noun *qym* /qayām/ in the context of private law denotes "obligation,"[60] in a royal edict, "decree" (Dnl. 6:8,16, in 6:8 as the object of *qūm* in the D-stem, → III), in religious speech "covenant."[61] Two fragments from Qumran[62] permit no precise conclusions. Syriac utilizes it for intellectual status, among others, and like the corresponding feminine, also for the resurrection from the dead.[63]

VI. Noun "Status, Position." Of the various other nominal forms of this root, the masculine *mqm* /maqām/ "stance, position" appears in older Aramaic only in texts from the Dead Sea. The Book of Giants seems to use it with the geographical meaning *rwm mqm* "height of the place,"[64] yet with no context; in T. Levi it refers to a lifestyle equated with *šqr wḥms* "lie and violence."[65] In a Nabatean confirmation, *bmqm* functions for "in the presence of."[66]

VII. Noun "Growth." The rare feminine *qwmh* /qawmā/ (> /qōmā/) "stature" first occurs in a fragmentary description of Noah from Qumran,[67] and later in West[68] and East Aramaic.[69] In addition, Syriac attests the masculine "stance, standing, resurrection," etc.[70]

---

55. *TADAE* C2.1 col. III 1; Dnl. 2:44.
56. I. Eph'al and J. Naveh, *Aramaic Ostraca of the Fourth Century BC from Idumaea* (Jerusalem, 1996), no. 199, l. 1.
57. *WDSP* 1.5,11; 3.9; also probably 8.5; 9.6; 15.17.
58. 4Q541 24 2:5.
59. Otherwise → *ḥyī* II.
60. Segal, 27.3; *TADAE* B5.6:10; nV 6:8 in *ATTM*, 2, 216f.
61. 11Q10 35:7 (Job 40:28) for *bryt*, similarly in Jewish Palestinian: *DJPA*, 490b.
62. 4Q243 40:3; 4Q584 1:4.
63. *LexSyr*, 653.
64. 4Q531 18:1.
65. 4Q541 9 1:7.
66. nV 15:38 in *ATTM*, 2, 229f.; according to p. 473, perhaps an Arabism.
67. 4Q561 1 2:8.
68. *DJPA*, 481b.
69. *LexSyr*, 653a.
70. *LexSyr*, 652f.

VIII. Adjective "Steady." Finally, the adjective *qym* /qayyām/ "enduring" also belongs to *qūm*. With *lʿlmyn* "forever,"[71] it serves in Dnl. 6:27 as a predicate of God,[72] in Dnl. 4:23 for Nebuchadnezzar's empire, which is fated to endure only if the king acknowledges God's superior power.[73]

In legal diction, in contrast, it connotes "valid, binding"[74] and corresponds to the spectrum of the verb in the D-stem (→ III). Similarly, in reference to sums of money, it represents "established, binding."[75]

According to K. Beyer,[76] *qym* in *TADAE* A4.7:10 involves the adjective for the nuance "indestructible" in reference to doors, but the form is generally understood elsewhere as a G-stem participle "standing" (→ II.1).

Gzella

71. → *ʿlm*.
72. Probably not yet weakened to "living, existing" as in Jewish Palestinian and Syriac; *DJPA*, 490a; *LexSyr*, 654.
73. → *mlk* IV; *ʿqr* III.
74. M 19:9; 20:6; 26:2; 28:10; following *ATTM*; nV 4:12; 7:2,24,29,65; 10:11; V 36:9; 37:7; 50:9; following *ATTM* 2.
75. *TADAE* B1.1:13; C3.11:6; → II.2 on the usage of the verb in A3.8A,6.
76. "Der Wandel des Aramäischen veranschaulicht durch Transkriptionen alter aramäischer Texte," in *In the Shadow of Bezalel. FS B. Porten*. *CHANE* 60 (2013), 13-28, here 18f.

קטל *qṭl*; קטל *qṭl* /qaṭl/

I. Etymology, Forms, Lexical Field, and Grammatical Constructions. II. G-stem "to Kill." III. D-stem "to Kill" (Plural). IV. Noun "Execution."

I. Etymology, Forms, Lexical Field, and Grammatical Constructions. Aramaic *qṭl* "to kill" may have arisen secondarily from an older **qtl*, which conforms to the Arabic, Old South Arabian, and Classical Ethiopic form of the root and survives in the earliest Aramaic inscriptions from Tell Dan[1] and Sefire.[2] In this case, *qṭl* results from an assimilation /t/ > /ṭ/ under the influence of the /q/.[3] Apart from sporadic, again dissimilated

C. Brockelmann, *Grundriss der vergleichenden Grammatik der semitischen Sprachen*, vol. 1 (Berlin, 1908); H.-F. Fuhs, "הָרַג *hāragh*," *TDOT*, III, 447-57; H. Gzella, "*qṭl*," *ThWQ*, III, 520-23.

1. *KAI* 310.6,8.
2. *KAI* 222 B 27; 223 B 9; 224.11,17f.,21.
3. Brockelmann, 154; → *qšṭ* I.

forms such as one instance of *kṭl* in later Old Aramaic,[4] this form of the root established itself in the Imperial Aramaic literary tradition, but appears in Mandean because of the dissimilation of two "emphatic" consonants regular there as *gṭl*.[5] The distribution of cognates indicates a common Central or West Semitic verb.[6] Meanwhile, despite its use as a typical paradigmatic verb in instruction since the grammar by J. A. Danz,[7] it is extremely rare in Hebrew (Ps. 139:19; Job 13:15; 24:24) in contrast to *hrg*, which also occurs at least in Sam'alian,[8] and is, consequently, often regarded as an Aramaic loanword.[9]

As a rule, *qṭl* occurs in the G-stem, but occasionally appears in the D-stem with a probably old plural nuance "to kill many," but otherwise exactly synonymous.[10] The verb itself does not specify the nature of the killing so that it overlaps the C-stem of → *mūt*, in the G-stem "to die," on the one hand, and also occurs in the same context as the C-stem of → *'bd* "to destroy," on the other.[11] The antonym is the D-stem of → *ḥyī* "to leave alive." Furthermore, the G- and D-stems each form their own t-passives "to be killed" and pre-Christian Aramaic also attests the inner passive of the G-stem. It has mostly a resultative nuance,[12] while the t-passive emphasizes the action.[13]

Mostly, a human or divine person appears as the subject; in accordance with the semantics of the verb, the object is animate and is often introduced by an object particle.[14] For atelic circumstances in relation to partially affected objects, *b-* "to kill among" also occurs.[15]

The masculine noun /qaṭl/[16] "execution" appears less often than the verb. Yet, both active and passive participles of the G-stem can function as substantives for "killer" (/qāṭel/) and "killed" (/qaṭīl/; → II).[17]

II. G-stem "to Kill." As a rule, in older Aramaic *qṭl*[18] denotes the killing of enemies in a battle or on the command of superiors. The first use naturally appears in reports of royal deeds like the old Aramaic Tell Dan stele[19] and then very often in the depictions of the military campaigns of King Darius in the Imperial Aramaic version of the Behistun

4. *KAI* 225.11.
5. *MdD*, 87f.
6. Depending on whether the Ethiopic and neo-South Arabic forms are original.
7. *BLe* 41 n. 2.
8. See Fuhs, 447.
9. Brockelmann, 154; *GesB*[18], 1530.
10. Cf. the parallelism in Dnl. 2:13, where the only difference consists in the number of the objects.
11. See *KAI* 225.11; cf. Dnl. 2:12,24 with 2:13f.
12. *TADAE* C1.1:72; Dnl. 5:30; 7:11; 1QapGen 20:10; 22:3.
13. *TADAE* C1.1:62; 4Q550 7+7a:2.
14. *l-* in the Imperial Aramaic tradition and later in East Aramaic.
15. 1QapGen 22:8f., here in combination with an imperfect depiction of the events underway, for a discussion → *hwī* II.
16. From the mid-fifth century B.C.E. /qatəl/, *ATTM*, 112-15.
17. Both probably in 4Q530 1 1:4 (1 En. 9:10), → *qbl* II.
18. And in Old Aramaic its older allomorph *qtl*.
19. *KAI* 310.6,8.

inscription,[20] often in contrast to captive survivors (*ʾḥd ḥyn*)[21] and sometimes also as a substantival passive participle "killed";[22] furthermore, in the context of the report concerning a rebellion,[23] but the context is incomplete. This usage continues in the reports about the raids of the King of Elam in 1QapGen.[24] The Old Aramaic treaties from Sefire employ the verb in agreements prohibiting a coup d'état; there, it refers to the treaty partner and his legal successor whose murder is explicitly forbidden.[25]

Instead, *qṭl* in the genre of court tales designates execution ordered or actually performed on royal command. The relative frequency of this usage gives an impression of perceptions of the shadow side of service at the center of power and the continuous danger of intrigues and caprice. This is true of the framework narratives of Aḥiqar,[26] and equally so for the book of Daniel (Dnl. 2:13; 5:19)[27] and the threat posed Abraham by pharaoh's sheriffs.[28] The context of *TADAE* C1.2:4,23, another court tale set in Egypt, is unclear.

In addition, in religious speech or in narratives, *qṭl* can also appear with divine or demonic beings as subjects. An Old Aramaic grave inscription from Nērab employs it in this sense in the curse against a potential grave robber.[29] It appears here in parallel with the immediately following C-stem of *ʾbd* with *zrʿk* "your descendants" as object. In contrast, it refers to an undeserved death in the story of the demon in Tobit, who murdered the seven fiancés of Tobias's future bride.[30]

In 4Q157 1 2:7 (Job 5:2), as one would expect, *qṭl* translates the Hebrew *hrg* as part of a proverbial expression, 11Q10 10:3 (Job 26:12), less picturesquely, an original *mḥṣ* "to shatter" with God as subject. Additional passages from Qumran do not preserve sufficient context.[31]

The passive forms often appear in Imperial Aramaic, in the book of Daniel, and at Qumran in the context of executions on royal orders; for the inner passive, cf. *TADAE* C1.1:71; Dnl. 5:30 and 4Q550 6+6a-c:7 and for the t-passive, which first assumes the functions of the imperfect of the inner passive and constitutes the only passive in post-Christian times, *TADAE* C1.1:62; Dnl. 2:13 and, to be reconstructed with relative certainty, 4Q550 7+7a:2.[32] The inner passive twice appears negated and is resultative in the sense

---

20. Fully preserved or to be reconstructed with confidence: *TADAE* C2.1:13,16,26,33,43,47,54,58,61f.,74.

21. → *ḥyī* III.1.

22. *TADAE* C2.1:49 and probably to be reconstructed in l. 61.

23. *TADAE* A5.5:3.

24. 1QapGen 22:4,8.

25. *KAI* 222 B 27; 223 B 9; 224.11,18,21.

26. *TADAE* C1.1:49,51f.,61.

27. Regarding the D-stem in the same context, below III.

28. 1QapGen 19:19,21; 20:9f.

29. *KAI* 225.11; the preceding *mwt lḥh* in l. 10 may be an adverbial modifier "may they kill you with a harsh death."

30. 4Q196 14 1:5 (Tob. 6:15); 4Q197 1:3 (Tob. 3:8).

31. 4Q531 7:4; 4Q569 1-2:7; see Gzella, 522-23.

32. Regarding the rather varied semantic nuances, → I.

of "to have survived."[33] The realm of Jewish religion and Jewish religious literature, however, already in pre-Christian times, attests a couple of instances of the inner passive of *qṭl* for the destruction of God's enemies.[34] The contexts of the inner passive in 4Q203 5:3; 4Q558 72:1; 103:1 and of the Gt-stem in 4Q531 23:3 from Qumran are unclear.

III. D-stem "to Kill" (Plural). While the G-stem of *qṭl* can refer to the killing of a few and, as evidenced by morphologically unequivocal forms such as the participles in 1QapGen 22:4,8, also to the killing of many,[35] the D-stem of *qṭl* in all of the certain cases, finds only plural usage: Dnl. 2:14 of the planned bloodbath among the sages of Babylon,[36] 3:22 of the darting flames of the superheated fiery furnace that lapped at the executioner's assistants (with a rare inanimate subject), and 4Q201 1 3:19 (1 En. 7:4) for the mass death at the destruction (*ḥbl*) of the earth. Jewish Palestinian attests the same distribution.[37]

IV. Noun "Execution." Older Aramaic attests the noun *qṭl* /qaṭl/ "killing" with certainty only in *TADAE* C1.1:46 for "execution," but it remained productive.[38]

Gzella

33. 1QapGen 20:10; 22:3.
34. *TADAE* A4.7:17 par. 4.8:16; Dnl. 7:11; both with resultative tones.
35. In contrast, the perfects in the Behistun inscription are ambivalent in the consonantal text, as is 1Q23 9+14+15:4.
36. Also the t-passive in 2:13; on the construction → *bʿī* I.
37. *DJPA*, 486f.
38. *DJBA*, 1007; *LexSyr*, 658; *MdD*, 89; for additional forms, see *DJPA*, 487a.

קטר *qṭr*; קטר *qṭr* /qeṭr/

I. Etymology. II. Old and Imperial Aramaic. III. Biblical Aramaic. IV. Qumran, etc. V. Later Aramaic.

I. Etymology. The etymology of Aramaic *qṭr* "to bind" is complicated. Akkadian *kaṣāru* "to knot, to connect, to gather,"[1] Ugaritic *qṣr* "ankle bone,"[2] Hebrew *qṣr* "to harvest" (Phoenician as a noun "harvest"),[3] and Arabic *qaṭara* in the II stem "to link camels

J. Conrad, "קטר *qṭr*," *TDOT*, XIII, 9-16; J. Naveh and S. Shaked, "A 'Knot' and a 'Break,'" *IEJ* 53 (2003) 111-18.

1. *AHw*, I, 456.
2. *DUL*³, 706.
3. *DNSI*, 1022.

to one another"[4] suggest tracing the Aramaic form to **qθ̣r*.[5] According to another suggestion, *qṭr* arose from **qθr* with assimilation of /θ/ to /q/,[6] which takes account of Hebrew *qšr* "to bind" and may be confirmed by the Aramaic *qṭr* as the counterpart of Hebrew *qšr* in Pap. Yadin 43:7 (→ IV). A possible Ugaritic *qšr* "to bind" and Jewish Palestinian *qyšwr* "ligation" do not contradict this etymology: the meaning of the first is uncertain[7] and the second may have been borrowed from Hebrew.[8] Sometimes, /q/ dissimilates to /k/,[9] in *qtr* "receipt,"[10] if the same word is involved, the assimilation */θ/ > /ṭ/ would be lacking.[11] According to Beyer,[12] around the ninth century B.C.E., old */θ/ and */θ̣/ shifted to /t/ and /ṭ/ in Aramaic. It is conceivable that the two roots **qθr* and **qθ̣r* intermingled in Old Aramaic times via */qt/ > /qṭ/ and */qṭ/ > /qt/; in Aramaic, *qṭr* prevailed.

The two roots **qθ̣r* and **qθr* display a broad spectrum of meaning: "to bind, to know," "to join together"; with regard to the noun, Aramaic /qeṭr/ (> /qeṭar/), "band, knot," "bundle," "association," "puzzle," "binding," "knotted document/obligatory," "penalty."

II. Old and Imperial Aramaic. Old and Imperial Aramaic yield no specimens other than the noun "knot" in the ban formula in the exorcism of Uruk.[13]

III. Biblical Aramaic. Biblical Aramaic attests the noun *qṭr* "knot, link" three times, always with → *šrī* "to loosen": twice in the list of Daniel's abilities as *mšrʾ qṭryn* "to solve difficult tasks" or "to loosen (magical) bonds" (5:12,16), along with the interpretation of dreams and puzzles,[14] and once in the phrase *qṭry ḥrṣh mštryn* "his hip-joints became powerless/shook" (5:6) in Belshazzar's reaction to the writing on the wall.[15]

IV. Qumran, etc. At Qumran, the G-stem of the verb appears twice in 11Q10 32:9; 35:8 (Job 39:10; 40:29), both for Hebrew *qšr* "to bind" and in a rhetorical question "can you bind?" The *qatl*- or *qitl*-noun *qtr*[16] appears in a rent receipt from the Dead Sea[17] for "receipt" (from "obligation" or "knotted document") with the predicate *yhwʾ qym* "will be valid,"[18] like *qšr* in Hebrew.[19] On knots and broken canes as receipts, see Naveh and Shaked.

---

4. Wehr^5, 690.
5. So *ATTM*, 683.
6. *BLA*, §33d.
7. *DUL*^{2}, 718 (no longer mentioned in *DUL*^{3}).
8. So *DJPA*, 492b; *GesB*^{18}, 1199.
9. *ATTM*, 103; 2:52; Mandean > /g/, *MdD*, 75,88f.
10. Pap. Yadin 43.7.
11. *ATTM*, 2, 478.
12. *ATTM*, 100.
13. *ATTM*, 2, 26f., ll. 1,27; → V for later magical bowls and amulets.
14. → *ʾḥydh*; *pšr*.
15. → *ḥrṣ* II.
16. Regarding the form → I.
17. Pap. Yadin 43.7, V 37.7 in *ATTM*, 2, 241f.
18. → *qūm* VIII.
19. *ATTM*, 2, 478.

V. Later Aramaic. Jewish Palestinian,[20] Jewish Babylonian,[21] Syriac,[22] and Mandean[23] attest the verb "to tie" and the noun "knot, association, band."[24] In magical texts, the noun can mean the knots, the bindings, the fetters (of a spell), the verb "to bind (through magic)," but also in the counterspell "to bind (the bound)"' *qṭr* stands as a synonym for → *'sr* and *ḥtm*. The loosening of knots is expressed mostly with → *šrī* "to loosen" or → *nśī* "to take" (→ II).[25]

Nebe

20. *DJPA*, 488f.
21. *DJBA*, 1008,1011f., the noun also in the meaning "penalty."
22. *LexSyr*, 661f.; also "puzzle."
23. *MdD*, 88f.
24. Cf. from Hatra H79.12f. for "force, power."
25. Cf. J. Naveh and S. Shaked, *Magic Spells and Formulae* (Jerusalem, 1993), B 19.6; 23.11; 26.12.

קל *ql* /qāl/

I. Etymology and Lexical Field. II. "Voice." III. "Sound."

I. Etymology and Lexical Field. With the masculine *ql* /qāl/ "voice, sound," Aramaic and other West Semitic languages designate either the sound that living beings produce[1] or other noises such as the sound of instruments. The etymological relationship to the overall rare Semitic verbal root *qūl* "to say, to speak," as often in Arabic, suggests an original usage for human or animal sounds. It does not, however, distinguish between articulated sounds, like speech or song, and others, or between the sometimes subjective difference between sonority and noise. For sounds perceived melismatically or rhythmically, such as song and music, the noun /zamār/[2] serves instead, for speech → *mll* and *'mr*, for a call or unarticulated cry /za'aqā/,[3] rarely the C-stem of *klī*,[4] for comprehensible calls or recitations the verb → *qrī*, for "to rejoice" *dūṣ*,[5] and for "to make noise" *hmī*.[6] The root *ybb* designates horn and trumpet

B. Kedar-Kopfstein, "קוֹל *qôl*," *TDOT*, XII, 576-88; C.J. Labuschagne, "קוֹל *qôl* voice," *TLOT*, 1132-36; D. Markl, "*qwl*," *ThWQ*, III, 505-9 (Heb.).

1. In older Aramaic, gods and humans; no instance of animals occurs.
2. → *zmr*.
3. → *z'q*.
4. 1QapGen 19:16.
5. *ATTM*, 2, 373; *DJPA*, 141b; *LexSyr*, 146a; also for leaping for joy.
6. 11Q10 32:6 (Job 39:7), inf.

blasts.[7] Old Aramaic already attests the noun with both nuances, "voice" and "sound, noise." It serves more often as the object of → *šmʿ* "to hear," sometimes as the subject of → *slq* "to arise" or → *npl* "to fall" (Dnl. 4:28) indicating the direction from which a sound comes; it also occurs in the adverbial expression *bql.*

II. "Voice." The earliest specimen of *ql* "voice" occurs in a curse formula from the Old Aramaic Bukan inscription:[8] in the land of the one upon whom the curse falls, the weather god Hadad should not raise his voice for seven years,[9] i.e., the absence of storms should cause drought. The voice of a god as a designation for "thunder" is obvious and was also widespread in the near cultural surroundings of Syria-Palestine; many instances are known from Ugaritic[10] as well as from Hebrew, one of which, Job 40:5, Aramaic preserved in translation in 11Q10 34:5.[11] As a term for articulated divine speech, it then occurs in reference to the bodiless voice of Dnl. 4:28 that announces the heavenly verdict to Nebuchadnezzar and the message to Noah in 1QapGen 6:15.[12]

In relation to human speech, *ql* may first occur in a saying of Aḥiqar for the "high" (*gbh*), i.e., in context, "august" or "powerful" voice of the king,[13] then in Dnl. 6:21 for the cry (*zʿq*) of the king *bql ʿṣyb* "with a sorrowful voice,"[14] as he inquired after Daniel. For a "noise, cry" that arose (*slq*) to heaven, it occurs in 4Q201 1 4:5 par. 4Q202 1 3:6 (1 En. 8:4) and 4Q201 1 4:9 (1 En. 9:2); similarly, but with no further contexts, in 4Q530 2 2+6-12:23 and 4Q531 14:3.[15] Entirely isolated are 4Q531 29:2 and 4Q561 1 2:1. 11Q10 14:4 (Job 29:10, syntax debated) renders the Hebrew cognate; 38:2 reflects a different vorlage than Job 42:9 MT.

III. "Sound." In addition, *ql* can designate various sounds made by inanimate things. It is attested in reference to millstones (*rḥyn*), which are to stand still because of a famine, in a curse formula,[16] otherwise often for the sound of instruments: in *KAI* 222 A 29 also in a curse in reference to the absence of the sound of the harp (*ql knr*) as a sign of diminishing joy in life in the land of the oath-breaker (cf. Ezk. 26:13; Rev. 18:22) and in Dnl. 3:5,7,10,15 in relation to the festive dedication of the statue of Nebuchadnezzar.[17] In Dnl. 7:11, it denotes the "sound of words." 11Q10 22:2 (Job 33:8; words) and 33:5 (Job 39:24) correspond to MT.

Gzella

---

7. *DJPA*, 233b; *DJBA*, 521b; *LexSyr*, 293; *MdD*, 188.
8. *KAI* 320.12; on the usage for "noise" in l. 8, → III.
9. → *ntn* II.
10. *DUL*³, 688f.
11. Here with the verb *rʿm* "to thunder."
12. With *šmʿ*.
13. *TADAE* C1.1:91; contra I. Kottsieper, *Die Sprache der Aḥiqarsprüche*. *BZAW* 194 (1990), 21: "as his emissary, he elevated him."
14. → *ʿṣb*.
15. Both with *šmʿ*.
16. *KAI* 320.8, → II on l. 12.
17. → *ḥnkh*.

קצץ *qṣṣ*; קצי *qṣī*; קצת *qṣt* /qaṣāt/; קצה *qṣh* /qaṣǣ/; קץ *qṣ* /qeṣṣ/

I. Etymology and Forms. II. Old and Imperial Aramaic. III. Biblical Aramaic. IV. Qumran, etc. V. Later.

I. Etymology and Forms. The verbal root occurs in some languages as *qṣṣ* "to cut off, to cut down"[1] and as *qṣī/ū* "to divide, to separate."[2] The feminine /qaṣāt/ "part" derives from the second form, which led, through the dissimilation of /q/ before /ṣ/, to the by-form *kṣt* in a few Imperial Aramaic documents.[3] Aramaic also forms the plural construct *qṣwy* in the Hebrew expression *qṣwy ʾrṣ* "the ends of the earth" (Isa. 26:15; Ps.48:11; 65:6) and the plural absolute and construct *qṣw*(*w*)*t* "the ends" (Ps. 65:9; Ex. 37:8; 39:4; with article Ex. 38:5), similarly at Qumran.[4]

It is unclear whether the expression (*mn*) *qṣt* means "(from a) part (of)" or "(something) from (a large number)," and whether one may assume a semantic spectrum from "part, piece" and "end, extreme" to "all, total."[5] Alternatively, one thinks of a semantic path from "end, extreme, margin" to "totality." For "end" in the spatial sense is the plural of *qṣh* /qaṣǣ/, "end of the world" is *qṣ* /qeṣṣ/ (> /qeṣ/); → *sūp*.

II. Old and Imperial Aramaic. The cuneiform incantation text from Uruk[6] employs *qṣt*/*kṣt* without preposition in the meaning "fragment." Otherwise, Imperial Aramaic uses the preposition *b*- or a preceding or following *mn*: *bkṣt* "in part/partially" or "in all" in Segal, no. 18.5[7] and *bkṣt šnt* 6 "that belongs to part of year 6" in the tax calculation *TADAE* C3.11:9; in contrast, *mn qṣt* "from/to (part)" appears in relation to wool to be sent in *TADAE* A2.2:7 (letter) and a claim to a portion of silver in B4.5:3 (certificate of debt) and 4.6:4 (marriage contract), without context in D4.15b+c:3 (*kṣt*); and, finally, *qṣt mn* "a (part of)" occurs in relation to a granary in *TADAE* A4.5:4f. (petition) and in reference to a private house in B3.10:3 (authorization: described in the subsequent text as a free-standing house with its dimensions and boundaries).

III. Biblical Aramaic. In Biblical Aramaic, the verb *qṣṣ* appears in the D-stem "to cut down" regarding the tree in Nebuchadnezzar's dream vision (Dnl. 4:11), the noun *qṣt* in the

---

H.-J. Fabry, "*qṣ*," *ThWQ*, III, 544-50; S. Talmon, "קֵץ *qēṣ*," *TDOT*, XIII, 78-86; W. Thiel, "קָצַץ *qāṣaṣ*," *TDOT*, XIII, 96-98; M. Wagner, "קֵץ *qēṣ* end," *TLOT*, 1153-56.

1. Along with Aramaic, also Akkadian, Ugaritic, Hebrew, and Arabic.
2. In Aramaic, only post-Christian, also Hebrew, Phoenician-Punic, and Arabic; for the respective cognates, see *GesB*[18], 1180,1183 and Thiel, 96.
3. Cf. *ATTM*, 103 and 2, 52.
4. 1QM 1:8.
5. Palmyrene also "elite," → V?
6. L. 17 par. 42 in *ATTM*, 2, 26; here *kṣt*, → I.
7. No context preserved and apparently at the end of a clause.

prepositional phrase *lqṣt* as a temporal term "at the end of" with months (Dnl. 4:26) and days (4:31). Furthermore, *mn qṣt* "a part of" appears in the interpretation of the mixed iron and clay feet of the statue in Dnl. 2 in "a part of the kingdom will be strong" alongside "a part of it [only the suffixed preposition *mnh*] will be weak" (2:42). Yet K. Koch[8] understands *mn qṣt* as "predominantly." Hebrew adopts the whole expression as *mqṣt*[9] "part, end" (Dnl. 1:2,5,15; Neh. 7:69) and can again provide it with the preposition *l-* "after" (Dnl. 1:18).

IV. Qumran, etc. Qumran attests the verb *qṣṣ* in 1QapGen 13:9,10,11 and 19:15f. in dream visions of trees, as in Dnl. 4 (→ III), and in the t-passive in 4Q558 37 2:3 (of holes, but with no further context). The form *qṣī* "to separate" appears in nV 6:12.[10]

The noun *qṣt*, apart from *kl qṣt* "every end/part" (4Q573 1:8), which has no context, appears only in the singular construct. In contrast, the plural construct *qṣw*[*t*] *ʾrʿ* in "the ends of the earth" (1QapGen 7:19;[11] 4Q201 1 1:7 [1 En. 1:5, partially emend.]) more likely derives from the noun *qṣh* /qaṣǣ/, as does the masculine plural construct *qṣwy* in 11Q10 13:5 (Job 28:24) and 4Q541 9 1:4.

Otherwise, along with *bqṣt* "in a part"[12] only *mn qṣt* "(from) a part of" occurs: 1QapGen 14:16f. (part of a tree) and without context in 1:10; 4Q537 12 2:2 (part of a sacrifice); 4Q541 9 2:6 (a part of sons); and in the Nabatean deed of gift nV 7:19,23,25,29,58,62,67[13] for parts of the pertinent gift.

The noun *qṣ* "end (of the world), last day" occurs often in Enoch: 4Q204 1 5:5 (1 En. 10:14); 4Q206 1 22:2 (1 En. 22:4); 4Q212 1 4:23 (1 En. 91:15); always together with *dynʾ rbʾ* "the great court";[14] without context in 4Q558 28:1 (fragments of prophetic histories).

V. Later. As an attributive in Palmyrene memorial inscriptions, the determined state of *qṣtʾ* probably means "part, division, elite": *PAT* 2730.4 and 2810.3, both with a preceding *brš* "at the head (of the division)" and a subsequent *bʾsṭrṭgwt* "under the command of."

Jewish Aramaic languages, as in Hebrew, often choose *mqṣt* instead of *mn qṣt*, Babylonian Talmudic always does so,[15] sometimes for "part" in contrast to *kwl* "all."[16] Regarding *qṣ* "end," *qṣī* "to cut into pieces," and *qṣṣ* "to cut off" in Jewish Palestinian, see *DJPA*, 500f.; regarding *qṣī* and *qṣṣ* in Jewish Babylonian, *DJBA*, 1033f.

The verb *qṣṣ* appears in Syriac meaning "to cut off" and *qṣī* "to break (bread)"; the noun *qeṣṣā* and the corresponding feminine mean "end," with and without the preposition *b-* (sometimes *mn*) also "in the end, because"; *qṣāṯā* denotes "chunk, portion."[17]

Nebe

8. Koch, *Daniel 1–4*. *BK* XXII/1 (2005), 102.
9. With assimilation of the /n/ of the preposition.
10. In *ATTM*, 2, 216.
11. In the reading of *ATTM*, 2, 93.
12. nV 42:11 in *ATTM*, 2, 244f.
13. According to *ATTM*, 2, 218f.
14. Cf. H. Gzella, *ThWQ*, I, 677.
15. *DJBA*, 1035.
16. → *kll*.
17. *LexSyr*, 686f.

קרא/קרי qr'/qrī

I. Etymology and Overview. II. Older Aramaic and Sam'alian. III. Biblical Aramaic. IV. Qumran.

I. Etymology and Overview. Four of the five major branches of the Semitic language group attest the common Semitic root *qr'* well, only the most southern branch constitutes an exception. Akkadian *qerû(m)*, Assyrian *qarā'u(m)*[1] means 1. "to call, to invite, to summon" and 2. "to lead away," often as a euphemism for "to withdraw (in death)."[2] In Ugaritic it also means "to call out, to invite, to send for (gods),"[3] in Phoenician primarily "to call, to call to" and "to read";[4] regarding Hebrew, cf. the extensive treatment in *TDOT*, XIII, 109-35. In Arabic usage, the semantic field of "reading" dominates with developments toward "to study"[5] on the one hand, and toward "to read aloud, to declaim, to recite" on the other; the proper meaning of *qur'ān* "Quran" is "recitation." In addition, older Arabic has the well-attested meaning "to gather, to draw together," which Lane[6] cites as the basic meaning in Arabic. If one considers the semantic development of German "lesen" and Latin *legere*, it may cast light on the basic meaning of the root in Semitic, as it often shines through in Arabic where influences of other Semitic languages can be excluded. For Old South Arabian, cf. the few passages and the rather varied approaches to its meaning in Biella[7] ("to summon/to send for") and *BGMR*[8] ("to command," with a question mark); some discuss the possibility of an St-stem (reflexive of the causative). The root does not appear at all in Ethiopic if one disregards later borrowings from the Arabic.

In Aramaic,[9] the basic meaning of the peal is "to speak aloud, to call," with further differentiation on the one hand toward "to summon, to invite; to invoke; to appoint," almost always in reference to persons or gods, and, on the other, in the direction of "to read, to read aloud, to recite," while one should certainly conceive of "reading" in ancient practice as reading aloud. The post-Imperial Aramaic literary languages[10] confirm this approach; some of the later dialects develop the spectrum of meaning even further,[11]

U. Dahmen, F.-L. Hossfeld, E.-M. Kindl, H. Lamberty-Zielinski, and G. Schauerte, "קָרָא *qārā'*," *TDOT*, XIII, 109-35; T. Hansberger, "*qr'* I," *ThWQ*, III, 550-56; C. J. Labuschagne, "קרא *qr'* to call," *TLOT*, 1158-64.

1. *AHw*, II, 918, *CAD*, XIII, 242f.
2. See esp. *CAD*, XIII, 243a.
3. *DUL*[3], 697f.
4. *DNSI*, 1025-28.
5. As in a few later Aramaic dialects and perhaps under their influence.
6. Lane, 2502.
7. J. Biella, *Dictionary of Old South Arabic. HSS* 25 (1981), 465.
8. *BGMR*, 106.
9. *DNSI*, 1025; *KBL*[3], 1775; *ATTM*, 687; 2, 476.
10. For Nabatean, Palmyrene, and Hatra, see *DNSI*, 1025ff. s.v. qr'_1.
11. Syriac *LexSyr*, 689f. including *commovit*; Jewish Babylonian *DJBA*, 1039-42 s.v. *qry*

in Mandaic as far as "to create";[12] regarding Samaritan, cf. Tal.[13] A technical juridical meaning becomes apparent in *TADAE* B7.2:7f.,10, where in the construction with *l* + a personal designation and *'l* + a divine name, the verb can even be translated "to swear to someone by god"—a development, perhaps, of the meaning "to declare aloud, i.e., publicly." In a few Aramaic dialects,[14] the verb also denotes animal sounds, especially the crowing of a rooster.

Only forms of the peal appear in early Aramaic, in the OT and at Qumran also the hithpaal. The final *aleph* had already disappeared very early on,[15] soon thereafter the root was understood as a III-*ī* and became interchangeable with the older root *qrī*. Already in the earliest instance from the periphery of Aramaic,[16] it is no longer written; its l. 13 has *qrny*.[17] The Imperial Aramaic texts no longer attest this root beginning in the fifth century B.C.E.,[18] but it is spelled historically long thereafter.

II. Older Aramaic and Sam'alian. There are nine certain instances of the root in Imperial Aramaic, with the exception of the Asshur ostracon (seventh century B.C.E.) all from fifth/fourth century Egypt. The verb only occurs in the peal, five times in the imperfect, once in the imperative, and once clearly in the perfect. The remaining two instances[19] manifest the form *qr'n* with no clear contexts so that the question arises as to whether they are first-person plural perfects or plural participles and the interpretation remains dubious. The first-person singular imperfect *'qr'* in *TADAE* D7.43:10[20] and the negated third-person singular imperfect *lyqr'* in the cave inscription D23.1.13:1[21] do not contribute to the more precise determination of the meaning because of destroyed contexts. The Sam'alian Hadad inscription mentioned above[22] has the verb in the third-person singular perfect (or imperfect) already mentioned with the first-person singular suffix in the meaning "to call, to summon" (+ accusative someone + *l* + inf.): "Hadad . . . called me to build." The remaining occurrences exhibit the following meanings:

(1) "to summon" (+ acc. someone): *KAI* 233.12, imperative *qr'*: "So, call them here and ask them" (direct speech follows).

(2) "to name" (+ *l* + acc. something): *TADAE* C1.1:165, third-person plural imperfect *yqr'wn*: "A lion (*'ryh*) is not in the sea, therefore one names a tidal wave (?) a lion (*lb'*)."

1# including "to know scripture"; Jewish Palestinian. *DJPA*, 504f. s.v. *qry* including "to learn scripture."

12. *MdD*, 414f. s.v. *qra* I including "call into being."

13. A. Tal, *A Dictionary of Samaritan Aramaic* (Leiden, 2000), 799.

14. Syriac *LexSyr*, 689f., Jewish.Palestinian *DJPA*, 504f.; on the Heb. see Hossfeldt and Kindl, 116 II.3.

15. According to *ATTM*, 481 around 800 B.C.E.

16. The Sam'alian Hadad inscription (*KAI* 214).

17. Or *yqrny*, if the first *y* does not belong to the preceding word.

18. *TADAE* B7.2.

19. *TADAE* D2.30:2 and Segal, 104.2.

20. *TADAE*: "I will call."

21. *TADAE*: "will not read."

22. *KAI* 214.13.

(3) "to declare, to swear" (+ *l* someone + *ʿl* by): *TADAE* B7.2 (obligation for a juristic declaration to repudiate an accusation), l. 7, first-person singular imperrfect *ʾrqʾ*: "I, *Mlkyh*, will swear to you by *Ḥrmbytʾl* (divine name) among 4 . . . (unclear title) as follows:" and l. 10, first-person singular perfect in the conditional clause *qryt*:[23] "And if I do not swear to you by these 4 . . ." (the remainder is missing).

(4) "to read" (+ acc. something): *TADAE* D22.51 (the reading is not entirely certain), third-person singular imperfect *yqrʾ*: "blessed be the one who reads this inscription."

III. Biblical Aramaic. The OT attests the root nine times, eight in the peal (including two passives), and once in the hithpaal. The usage divides—sometimes involving repetitions or in parallel construction—into the meaning "to call" and "to read" as follows: (1) "to call": Dnl. 3:4; 4:11; 5:7;[24] Dnl. 5:12;[25] (2) "to read": Dnl. 5:7f.,15f.,17;[26] Ezr. 4:18,23.[27]

IV. Qumran. Qumran attests the root well, *DSSConc* 919 alone has fifty-one entries (s.v. *qrh*), although many readings are uncertain, emended, or without context. The roughly forty remaining—forms of the peal and of the hithpaal—divide again into the basic meaning "to call, to name" on the one hand, and "to read" on the other (the following lists all constructions with the most importance occurrences):

(1) "to call" (+ presumably direct speech): 1QapGen 19:25 *qryt*: "and I called before them. . . ."

(2) "to call, to name" (+ acc. the name): 1QapGen 14:12 ithpaal third-person singular imperfect *ytqrh* "and in (the midst) of his descendants, your name will be called."

(3) "to name, to designate as" (either + two acc. or as above in *TADAE* C1.1:165 + *l* + acc., including once elliptically with only + acc.): (+ acc.): participle plural absolute masculine *qryn*: 4Q209 (astronomic text) 23:5 "and therefore one names (it) west." Entirely parallel to this usage are 4Q209 23:3 and 4Q210 1 2:15 "and one names the south, south"; (+ two acc.): *yqrwnh* /yeqrōnnéh/[28] third-person plural imperfect + third-person masculine singular suffix: 4Q246 1 2:1 "and they will call him son of the Most High." The corresponding passive appears in 4Q246 1 1:9 with ithpaal *ytqrʾ* paralleling *ytknh* (ithpaal *knī*) "to designate": "he will be called the great [king] and he will be designated by his name."

(4) "to summon, to invite" (+ *l* someone): third-person singular perfect *qrʾ*: 1QapGen 20:19f. "and he sent (a command) and had all the sages of Egypt summoned [. . .] and summoned me"; similarly 4Q545 1a 1:5,8,10; first-person singular perfect *qryt*: 1QapGen 12:16 "I summoned my sons and the sons of my sons"; 21:21 "And I sent (a message) and invited"; imperative *qry*: 4Q545 1a 1:9 "Summon me, my son, the. . . ." The substantival passive participle /qārī(ʾ)/ "summoned one" seems to appear in the plural construct *qryʾy*

23. Spelled like a III-*ī*.
24. Peal active, always the ptcp. *qārē* with *b^eḥayil* "aloud."
25. Hithpaal: *yiṯq^erē* "to be called."
26. Peal act., always impf.: *yiqrē*, *yiqrōn*, *ʾæqrē*, always + *k^eṯāḇā* "writing."
27. Peal pass.: *q^ærī*, always + *q^oḏām* "before."
28. *ATTM*, 497.

(subsequent word is illegible) in 4Q245:[29] "Thereafter, those of the nations who have been called will assemble."

(5) "to call to" (+ *bšm* a god): first-person singular perfect *qryt*: 1QapGen 21:2 "and there I called to the name of the Lord of eternity": 19:7 "and there I called to God. . . ."

(6) "to read, to read aloud" (+ acc. something): imperative *qry'*: 4Q537 1+2+3:3 (probably related to 1QapGen) "And now, take the tablets and read everything!"; (+ *b* in, from a writing) participle plural absolute masculine *qryn*: 4Q550 7+7a:5 "they will appear after *Bgsr*[*w*] (PN) reading (aloud) from this document"; (+ *l* someone) infinitive in 11Q18 19:5 "he began to read aloud to me from this document."

Hug

29. *ATTM*, 2, 140.

קרב *qrb*; קרב *qrb* /qarāb/; קרבן *qrbn* /qorbān/; קריב *qryb* /qarrīb/

I. Etymology, Lexical Field, and Constructions. II. G-stem "to Draw Near." III. D-stem "to Bring." IV. C-stem. V. Noun "Battle, War." VI. Noun "Sacrifice." VII. Adjective "Near."

I. Etymology, Lexical Field, and Constructions. The verbal and nominal forms of the root *qrb*, which differ in the individual languages, all have a common Semitic etymology. In Aramaic, very much as in Hebrew, the intransitive G-stem "to draw near, be near" appears along with a D- and C-stem "to bring here." Meanwhile, the contrast between immediate proximity expressed by the D-stem and relative proximity by the C-stem,[1] more clearly demonstrated in Hebrew, is less perceptible in Aramaic since "to present, to sacrifice" appears in otherwise identical contexts as the D-stem (Ezr. 7:17) and, as in Hebrew, the C-stem (Ezr. 6:10,17); the same is true of "to bring something before someone."[2] In the meaning "to bring," the verb overlaps with the C-stem of *ybl* and → *'tī*, in the meaning "to offer, to sacrifice" with that of → *slq* III.2, in the specific meaning "to sacrifice" with the G-stem of → *dbḥ* II.

Related to the verb are the adjective /qarrīb/ near" (substantivally "relative") and the

H.-J. Fabry, "קָרְבָּן *qorbān*," *TDOT*, XIII, 152-58; R. Gane and J. Milgrom, "קָרַב *qārab*," *TDOT*, XIII, 135-48; E. Jenni, *Das hebräische Pi'el* (Zurich, 1968); J. Kühlewein, "קרב *qrb* to approach," *TLOT*, 1164-69; C. Kumpmann, "*qrb*," *ThWQ*, III, 556-62 (Heb.); J. Naveh and S. Shaked, *Aramaic Documents from Ancient Bactria (Fourth Century* B.C.E.*)* (London, 2012).

1. Jenni, 75-77.
2. Cf. the D-stem in *TADAE* C1.1:50 with Dnl. 7:13; → III.

masculine noun /qorbān/ "sacrificial offering,"[3] which all have a corresponding counterpart in Hebrew. Typically Aramaic is the masculine /qarāb/ "battle," which exists in Hebrew only as a loanword.[4] Otherwise, for this concept, Hebrew employs *milḥāmā* from the root *lḥm* "to struggle, to fight," which is not productive in Aramaic outside of *KAI* 320.2; instead, *pgš* "to fight" and /pagš/ "battle" appear later.[5] In older Aramaic, → *ʿbd qrb* denotes "to fight" (→ V). "To be far" → *rḥq* serves as an antonym for *qrb* in its basic meaning "to be near."

As a verb of spatial relation, *qrb* gains added precision in usage through prepositional supplements: the intransitive G-stem "to draw near" with *l-* in reference to a place (e.g., Dnl. 3:26; 6:21) and *ʿl* in reference to a person,[6] less often with *b-* in the sense of "to touch";[7] the transitive D- and C-stems "to bring near, to sacrifice" with *l-* for the indirect object (e.g., Ezr. 6:10) and/or *ʿl* "on" (Ezr. 7: 17) for the place,[8] with the nuance "to bring before" *ʿl* "before,"[9] in courtly style also *qdm*.[10]

II. G-stem "to Draw Near." Late Old Aramaic first attests the verb *qrb* in the G-stem, regularly with the dynamic nuance "to draw near," while the adjective serves to denote the static "be near" (→ VII). Its usage together with another verb of motion such as *ʾzl*[11] in an animal fable of Aḥiqar[12] also makes this clear. Another saying juxtaposes *qrb ʿly* "Come (closer) to me!" with the antonym *r[ḥ]q mny* "Get away from me!"[13]

Furthermore, *qrb ʿly* also appears in the Imperial Aramaic narrative frame,[14] although the G-stem is otherwise rare in Imperial Aramaic: the fragment *TADAE* D5.41z:2 preserves no context and both reading and analysis of the likewise fragmentary instances in Segal, 12.2 and 67a.1[15] are unclear. It occurs with a general meaning in Naveh and Shaked, A7,1; B4,2.

Biblical Aramaic employs *qrb* twice absolutely with the nuance "to appear, to turn up."[16] In both passages, it introduces slander of the respective main figure(s) by their enemies at court. With a prepositional expression of direction, it functions instead to designate the location[17] or the person[18] whom the subject approaches.

---

3. For additional terms see → *mnḥh*.
4. M. Wagner, *Die lexikalischen und grammatikalischen Aramaismen im alttestamentlichen Hebräisch. BZAW* 96 (1966), 103.
5. *ATTM*, 667.
6. E.g., *TADAE* C1.1:193; Dnl. 7:16.
7. E.g., 1QapGen 20:17.
8. Both in 1QapGen 21:2.
9. *TADAE* C1.1:54.
10. In reference to persons of higher rank in *TADAE* C1.1:10,50; A6.3:6f.; in reference to God in Dnl. 7:13.
11. → *hlk* II.
12. *TADAE* C1.1:94, appended asyndetically.
13. *TADAE* C1.1:193.
14. *TADAE* C1.1:57, partially emend., but relatively certain.
15. Perhaps a D-stem "to sacrifice"?
16. Dnl. 3:8; 6:13, where, instead of *qrybw*, it is better to read the defective spelling *qrbw* with many MSS.
17. *l-* in Dnl. 3:26 and 6:13 the fiery furnace and the lions' den.
18. *ʿl* in 7:16 in the sense of "to turn to," with an interpreting angel in a vision.

In addition to the known usages, the texts from Qumran contain *qrb* absolutely to mean "to appear" at the beginning of a narrative unit,[19] perhaps as an imperative "Come (closer), approach!,"[20] with *ʿl* "to" in reference to persons,[21] and instances with the preposition *b-*. In this usage, *qrb* means "to touch," either neutrally in relation to objects[22] or in the intimate sense in relation to a person.[23] Further, one can with some certainty emend *q[rbw* in 4Q197 4 1:11 (Tob. 6:6) with *l-* and the place designation "to Media." The also rather certain reconstruction of the ethical dative *l]hwn* here indicates ingressive action "to arrive at";[24] thereby, the verb receives a telic nuance ("to attain"), regularly indicated by → *mṭī*, instead of the otherwise typical atelic nuance ("to approach").

III. D-stem "to Bring." The transitive D-stem of *qrb* occurs with the meaning "to bring near, to bring to a place" and persons or things as object; it regularly denotes "to offer, to sacrifice." This usage cannot be distinguished systematically from that of the C-stem (→ IV), especially since in consonantal spelling not all forms are unequivocal and, after the loss of the /-h-/ between vowels, the imperfect of the C-stem also appears as *yqrb* instead of the original *yhqrb*.[25] Yet, the D-stem alone also occurs in morphologically unmistakable specimens in the absolute sense, to bring "into the immediate (physical) proximity," as in relation to objects[26] and persons,[27] while both the D- and C-stems can denote "to bring into relative proximity, to carry or bring before someone of higher rank." The basic difference between absolute and relative proximity, as Jenni[28] has demonstrated for the stem difference of the Hebrew *qrb*, can also be assumed in principle for Aramaic.

Through the overall significant semantic agreement of the two stems, however, they converge in actual usage so that the scribe of *TADAE* A4.7:25 removed the *h* from the original *yhqrbwn* "they will offer" (C-stem) and *yqrbwn* can also be read as a D-stem, as in the parallel passages *nqrb* "we will sacrifice" in 4.8:25, *yqrbwn* in A4.9:9, and *yqrb* "he sacrificed" in A4.7:28 par. 4.8:28. It is unclear whether this involves only an orthographic (since the historical and the phonetic spellings of the C-stem coexist in Imperial Aramaic) or morphological alteration.

It involves the food, incense, and burnt offerings the Elephantine community promised the Persian governor of Judea in his name on the altar of Yaho as thanks for the requested support in the reconstruction of the local temple.[29] Together with

19. 1QapGen 22:18 also marked as a new section by a space at the beginning of the line.
20. 4Q550 7+7a:1; contra both *DSSStE*, 1100f. (4Q550 c 3:1), and *ATTM*, 2, 152 (U 6:1), which read the adjective *qryb*.
21. 4Q538 1-2:3, partially emend.
22. 4Q541 24 2:5; 4Q562 7:2.
23. 1QapGen 20:17, paralleling → *ydʿ* IV.1. with the same nuance.
24. Cf. H. Gzella, *Tempus, Aspekt und Modalität im Reichsaramäischen. VOK* 48 (2004), 254.
25. *ATTM*, 148.
26. So the pfs. in 4Q196 2:11 [Tob. 2:12]; nV 42:18, *ATTM*, 2, 244-47, and probably also the impfs. in ll. 2,23.
27. Naveh and Shaked, A4,2: allowing troops to approach.
28. Jenni, 75-77.
29. For the discussion → *mnḥh* II.1.

prayer,[30] sacrifice constitutes the foundation of religion; consequently, both are mentioned in the same breath. The verb appears in an analogous usage in Ezr. 7:17 for sacrifice on the altar in temple worship in Jerusalem reintroduced by royal edict and later in 1QapGen 21:2 for Abraham's sacrifice;[31] 4Q547 8:2 is similar. Along with the cultic context in relation to sacrifices in the temple, *qrb* can also represent personal offerings of private individuals as on a few Imperial Aramaic silver bowls from Egypt[32] and votive inscriptions from northern Arabia,[33] always in morphologically unequivocal perfect with *l-* and the deity. This usage continues in Nabatean,[34] Palmyrene,[35] and Hatrene[36] dedicatory inscriptions.

In reference to persons, the verb denotes "to bring before someone, to introduce to someone," before the king in a court context[37] and before God in religious speech;[38] in relation to objects, it signifies "to bring, to offer" and in the sense of immediate proximity.[39]

IV. C-stem. The C-stem of *qrb* seems to correspond largely with the D-stem.[40] Morphologically unquestionable forms occur in miniature inscriptions from the Neo-Assyrian period meaning "to offer,"[41] Imperial Aramaic in *TADAE* A6.3:6f. for "to bring before [*qdm*]" in reference to slaves brought before their masters for punishment, and in the uncorrected text from *TADAE* A4.7:25 for a sacrifice (→ III); similarly in Biblical Aramaic in Ezr. 6:10,17 for temple sacrifice and in Dnl. 7:13 for the "son of man," who is led before the time- and space-transcending "Ancient of Days"[42] for investiture in order to receive from him eternal dominion. Qumran offers no unequivocal specimens.[43] Overall, then, it involves only a relative proximity in which an unbridgeable distance persists; in contrast, the D-stem can indicate both relative and absolute proximity.

V. Noun "Battle, War." The noun *qrb* /qarāb/ first occurs in the Aramaic version of the Behistun inscription and, as the object of → *'bd*, means "to fight." It occurs repeatedly

30. → *ṣlī*.

31. D-stem *qrbt* according to *ATTM*, 178 and recently adopted by D. A. Machiela, *The Dead Sea Genesis Apocryphon. STDJ* 79 (2009), 79, while other editors read the C-stem *'qrbt* here.

32. *TADAE* D15.2:1; 15.3:1; 15.4:1.

33. *KAI* 229:1f.; K. Beyer and A. Livingstone, "Eine neue reichsaramaische Inschrift aus Taima," *ZDMG* 140 (1990) 1f., l. 1.

34. *DNSI*, 1028f.

35. *PAT* 0249; 0269.4; 0312.5; 0324.3; 1677.1; 1683; Greek ἀνέθηκεν; the possible C-stem in 1679.2 is dubious, cf. *PAT*, p. 407.

36. D4.2; H22; 222.1; 292.6; T1a.3.

37. *TADAE* C1.1:10,50 with *qdm*, l. 54 with *'l*.

38. 4Q213a 1:18, with God as subj. and the objective instead of the direction: *lmhw' lkh* [*'bd*] "in order to be [a servant] for you."

39. 4Q196 2:11 (Tob. 2:12), of food; nV 42:2,18,23; see above.

40. → III on the relationship of the two to one another and possible differences.

41. W. Röllig, "Alte und neue Elfenbeininschriften," *NESE* 2 (1974) 50f.

42. → *'tyq* III.

43. On 1QapGen 21:2 → III.

for the campaign reports of King Darius,[44] either absolutely, with a local designation following *b-* "near"[45] or *ʿm* "with = against."[46] Daniel 7:21 employs the same expression (in the abs.) for the battle of the growing small horn against (*ʿm*) the holy ones.[47] Both expressions also occur at Qumran, for military campaigns,[48] a war,[49] and the eschatological battle.[50] In 11Q10 31:1; 33:6 (Job 38:23; 39:25), it translates *mlḥmh.* 4Q537 14:3 and 4Q562 1:1[51] are fragmentary.

VI. Noun "Sacrifice." Assured old specimens for Aramaic *qrbn* /qorbān/ "offering (for God)" stem mostly from Jewish texts from Palestine.[52] It has Semitic parallels, however, and is common later in Syriac and Mandean,[53] as well as Hebrew. In Palestinian Aramaic, it designates any kind of sacrifice as a donation and cultic, as once in ossuary inscriptions,[54] in T. Levi[55] and Mk 7:11 and for others in the temple liturgy of the new Jerusalem[56] and the description of Aaron's sacrifice.[57] In Mt. 27:6 and Josephus,[58] it designates the temple treasury. Christian Palestinian also employed it.[59]

VII. Adjective "Near." Imperial Aramaic private documents from Elephantine first attest the adjective *qryb* /qarrīb/ "near" with certainty.[60] Substantivized there, it represents a "relative" in a list with decreasing claims to legal succession or degree of relationship after *ʾḥ wʾḥt* "brother and sister" and before the antonym *rḥ(y)q* /raḥḥīq/ "stranger" (or "distant relative"?), in individual cases supplemented before and sometimes after with *br wbrh* "son and daughter" and persons with no familial relationship such as business partners, etc.[61] Reduced to *rḥyq wqryb* "nonrelatives and relatives," the expression occurs

44. Preserved in *TADAE* C2.1:12f.,15,22,32f.,43,47,57, mostly in the abs. state, rarely the deter. state.
45. *TADAE* C2.1:15.
46. *TADAE* C2.1:32.
47. → *qrn.*
48. 1QapGen 21:24 (with *ʿbd ʿm*),25,31; 22:6.
49. 4Q545 1a-b 2:16:19 par. 4Q547 1-2 3:1; 4Q544 1:4.
50. 4Q202 1 4:6 (1 En. 10:9), with *ʾbdn*; 4Q246 1 2:8 (*ʿbd l-* "for"); 4Q531 22:4 for the war of the fallen angels against human beings.
51. With → *ḥrb.*
52. *qrbn* in the Old Aramaic inscriptions *KAI* 219.2 appears in a corrupt context; *qrbwn* in the Nabatean temple inscription could be another noun; on the text, see R. N. Jones, "A New Reading of the Petra Temple Inscription," *BASOR* 275 (1989) 41-46.
53. *LexSyr*, 692; *MdD*, 409.
54. yJE 19b and 21:2 in *ATTM*, 343f.
55. 4Q213a 3-4.8.
56. 2Q24 4:2; 11Q18 28:4.
57. 4Q547 5:1; 8:1; fragmentary.
58. *B.J.* 175; on the form κορβωνας cf. *ATTM*, 137.
59. Cf. ccSW 2:2 in *ATTM*, 405 in reference to a donated monk's cell.
60. Sometimes spelled defectively *qrb*, but demonstrably an adj. given the parallel with *qryb* in the same formulaic expression.
61. *TADAE* B2.1:9; 2.2:13; 2.7:10; 2.9:10f.; 3.2:9; 3.6:5; 5.1:5; 5.5:5; for the discussion of the precise meaning, see *DNSI*, 1031 s.v. qrb_9.

in Nabatean contracts from the Dead Sea.[62] Palmyrene grave certificates also employ *qryb* for "relative" in a juridical setting.[63]

It occurs at Qumran both in the relational[64] and in the spatial senses.[65] On 4Q550 7+7a:1 → II.

Gzella

62. nV 2:11,33; 3:36; 4:14; 7:23,60; 9:7; all according to *ATTM* 2.
63. *PAT* 0027.1; 0028.2.
64. 4Q197 4 1:18 (Tob. 6:12), with *l-* "with"; 4Q563 1:5, destroyed context.
65. 4Q196 6:11 (Tob. 3:15); 4Q210 1 2:6, of winds; 4Q541 2 1:8, *qryb lʿly* "near to me" in contrast to *rḥyq mny* "far from me."

קריה *qryh* /qaryā, qeryā/; קריה *qryh* /quryā/; קרי *qry* /qaray, qeray/; קרתה *qrth* /qartā/; קיר *qyr* /qīr/

I. Etymology, Lexemes. 1. *qryh*. 2. *qry*. 3. *qrtʾ/h*. 4. *qīr*. II. Usage. 1. Old Aramaic. 2. Texts from Egypt. 3. Texts from the Levant. 4. Heterograms.

I. Etymology, Lexemes. The nouns *qiryā/qiryᵉṯā*, *qartā*, *qᵉrē* and *qīr* mean "city, village" and trace to a common basis *qar*,[1] which, in turn, could be a substrate word in the Mediterranean region.[2]

1. qryh. Transcriptions in Greek and Latin texts—the LXX, Flavius Josephus, Eusebius, and Hieronymus—through the fifth century C.E. have the forms καριαθ-, καριωθ-, *cariath-* and *cariah*, that point to the first syllable *qar-*,[3] exactly as does Arabic *qarya(tᵘⁿ)*. In contrast, the vocalization *qiryā* appears only in the pointing of biblical and targumic

M. Avi-Yonah, *Gazetteer of Roman Palestine. Qedem* 5 (Jerusalem, 1976), esp. 47,74; R. Borger, *Beiträge zum Inschriftenwerk Assurbanipals* (Wiesbaden, 1996), esp. 61, A VII 108; A. Caquot, "Une inscription araméenne d'époque assyrienne," in *Hommages à André Dupont-Sommer. FS A. Dupont-Sommer* (Paris, 1971), 9-16, esp. l. 6; P. Gignoux, *Glossaire des inscriptions pehlevies et parthes. CIISup* 1 (1972), esp. 51,62; E. Lipiński, *Semitic Languages: Outline of a Comparative Grammar. OLA* 80 (²2001); J. Margain, "Les termes relatifs à la ville dans le Targoum samaritain (Ms. J)," *Sem* 43-44 (1995) 169-75; M. J. Mulder, "קִרְיָה *qiryâ*," *TDOT*, XIII, 164-67; J. Naveh, "The Aramaic Inscriptions on Boundary Stones in Armenia," *WO* 6 (1971) 41-46; idem, *ʿl psyps wʾbn* (Jerusalem, 1978), Index 151; S. Paganini and S. Jöris, "*qyr*," *ThWQ*, III, 531-33 (Heb.).

1. Mulder, 164f.
2. Lipiński, §67,19.
3. Avi-Yonah.

manuscripts. It must reflect a specific dialect, similar to the numerous cases of /i/ for /a/ reported with reference to the Old Arabic dialect of Najd. Syriac *qrīṯā* could trace back to */qarītā/, however. Only additional instances can contribute to an explanation of this interchange of /a/ and /i/. It is very old, however, because the Old Babylonian place name *Qí-ir-Da-ḫa-at*^ki^ also appears in the variant *Qar-Da-ḫa-at*^ki^.[4] The ending *-yōt* instead of *-yat-* represents a well-known pronunciation as, e.g., in *Byt-ʿnt* par. *Byt-ʿnwt* or *ʿštrt* par. *ʿštrwt* (1 S. 31:10), which has a parallel in Phoenician[5] and has nothing to do with the plural.

2. qry. *qry*/*qr*ʾ is the word that occurs with the meaning "village" in Targum Onqelos of Gen. 47:21,[6] in Targum Jonathan of Isa. 19:2,[7] and in the Peshitta of Gen. 47:21 (*Q*). Targum Neofiti 1 of Ex. 21:13 employs *qry šyzbh* in the sense of "place of refuge." The word seems to have survived as *qrayya*/*e* in Syriac and Lebanese Arabic dialects. The earliest occurrence of *qry* appears in Ezr. 4:10, where *bqryh dy šmryn* "in the villages of Samaria" intends the broken plural *quryā*. Syriac attests it well and it corresponds to the dialectic Arabic *qura*. The *-h* at the end of the word can either indicate the determined state, as in the Hermopolis papyri,[8] or represent a cataphoric suffix.[9] Syriac and Arabic employ *quryā*/*qura* as the plural of *qrīṯā* and *qarya*, respectively, but, formally, it arises from */qaray, qiray/ > *q^e^rē* with the *-ay* affix often used to form diminutives,[10] thus "small settlement." Palestinian Aramaic also attests the broken plural *quryā*, as the vowel letter *w*, e.g., in *qwryy* in Targum Pseudo-Jonathan of Gen. 24:60 and Num. 21:3 and in Christian Palestinian *qwry*[11] indicate. The word appears in the absolute state in the Aramaic inscription on boundary stones found in Armenia stemming from the first half of the second century B.C.E.[12] A typical characteristic of these inscriptions is the absence of the determined state, presumably under the influence of the scribe's mother tongue.[13] The determined state appears in the Palmyrene tax tables,[14] where *qry*ʾ corresponds to the Greek plural χωρία,[15] and possibly in 4Q244 8:4. In contrast, *qry*ʾ in *PAT* 2013 may be linked to the Syriac *qrāyā* "invitation." It is written as a tessera, yet, very surprisingly, it does not appear elsewhere there in great numbers although the tesserae themselves serve as invitations and "entry cards" for cultic meals. The word *qry* appears with a suffix as *qryhwn* in 11Q10 8:1 (Job 24:12).

---

4. E. Lipiński, *The Aramaeans. OLA* 100 (2000), 41 n. 99.
5. J. Friedrich and W. Röllig, *Phönizisch-punische Grammatik. AnOr* 55 (³1999), §228.
6. *Q*, cf. Sperber, I, 82
7. *Q*, cf. Sperber, III, 37.
8. Except for *TADAE* A2.7.
9. Lipiński, §51.20.
10. Lipiński, §29.42.
11. *LSP*, 183.
12. *qry*: Naveh.
13. Cf. H. Gzella, *A Cultural History of Aramaic. HO* 111 (2015), 196f.
14. *PAT* 0259 ii.112.
15. *PAT* 0259 ii.189f.

3. qrt'/h. In the seventh century B.C.E., the place name *Qarti-Ḫaldi*[16] first attests *Qart-*. The name denotes a city in the Mannaeen region southwest of Lake Urmia where the Bukan inscription[17] exhibits Aramaic influence. The word then appears in a papyrus from Saqqara from the fifth century B.C.E. as the qualifier of the Egyptian title *p3-sḫ-nsw* "the royal scribe":[18] *psḥns qrt'* "the royal city-scribe."[19] It is not necessary to assume Phoenician influence here, although it cannot be excluded either. The word may appear in place names in the place of πόλις, as in *Tigrano-kerta* (Armenia), built in the first century B.C.E., or *Natounissaro-kerta* (Gordyene), if it does not represent the Iranian *krta* "built." *Qart-* certainly appears in Jewish Aramaic synagogue inscriptions in Palestine,[20] in Targum Onqelos of Gen. 4:17, Targum Jonathan of Isa. 19:18, Targum Pseudo-Jonathan of Nu. 22:29 (*qartā rabbᵉṯā*), etc.

4. qīr. *qīr* means "city," not only in Moabite, but also in an Old Aramaic dialect as the determined state *Gi-ra-a* ᵘʳᵘ*A-za-ar-ìli* in Assurbanipal's reports of his campaigns against the Arabs indicate.[21] The spelling *Gi-ra-a* attests to the use of GI to express the voiced pronunciation of /q/, as in ᵏᵘʳ*Gi-di-ra-a-a*[22] for "Qedarites." Similar cases are known from various periods and portions of the Semitic language region.[23] The word *qīr* is also the basis of Jewish Aramaic *qirwā* "city, village." Yet, it should not be associated with Qīr, the area from which the Arameans came originally according to Am. 9:7. The correct reading there would be *qwr*,[24] possibly the equivalent of *ġūr* "mountain."

II. Usage.

1. Old Aramaic. The determined state *qryt'* in a treaty of state from Sefire indicates that it refers to a specific city, but the fragmentary context hinders its identification.[25] In contrast, the city (*qryh*) in *KAI* 224.12 is not specified. A decree from the seventh or sixth century B.C.E.[26] explicitly mentions the *ḥzn qryt'* "mayor of the place"[27] among those who were to be punished for failure to observe the pertinent edict, which explains the use of the determined state.

2. Texts from Egypt. Aramaic texts from Egypt often mention specific localities or villages, but they can only rarely be identified, e.g., Korobis[28] or Chastemehi.[29] A pair of

16. *SAA*, XI, 133, II, 17'.
17. *KAI* 320.
18. Segal, 75.
19. Segal, 52b.9.
20. Naveh, *'l psyps w'bn.*
21. Borger.
22. Nimrud Letter XIV:11.
23. Lipiński, §18.8 and *SAIO* I, 122f.
24. E. Lipiński, *Itineraria Phoenicia. OLA* 127 (2004), 52 n. 66.
25. *KAI* 222 B 36.
26. *KAI* 317.
27. Caquot.
28. *TADAE* B1.1:3,18: *qryh krb.*
29. *TADAE* D20.3:1: *ḥstmḥ qryt'.*

texts mention the "citizens of a city"[30] in a stereotypical formula,[31] one presumably refers to the "village elders" (*kšyš qryth*),[32] others mention *qryt'* in a letter or a story[33] and employ *qryh* sporadically in a proverb: *kqr[y]h ḥsynh* "like a fortified city,"[34] *[qryt] rš'yn* "[a city] of evildoers."[35] Most of the instances of *qryt'* appear in commercial texts, however.[36]

3. Texts from the Levant. The determined state *qryt'* occurs in the Samaria papyri from the Wadi Daliyeh,[37] in a letter to the Persian king (Ezr. 4:11-16), and in his response (4:17-22). In Ezr. 4, it always refers to Jerusalem (4:12,13,15,16,19,21). In contrast, the plural of *qᵉrē* "villages" appears in the narrative portion of Ezr. 4:1-10 (v 10; → I.2) and in the Aramaic of Qumran.[38] In the eschatological work about the new Jerusalem, *qryt'* naturally refers to the holy city,[39] but the preserved fragments never mention Jerusalem by name. It is also very likely the reference of the surname Ἰσκαριώθ (Lk. 6:16)[40] "city dweller"; *'īš* finds usage in Aramaic legal formulas[41] or as a title.[42] Following Gen. 10ff., 4Q529 1:9 refers to Babylon.[43]

In *krbyl w-kršy qryt'*,[44] the boundary stone of Bahadırlı probably employs the determined plural /qiryātā/, but the absolute plural /qᵉrē/ appears on boundary stones from Armenia: *ḥlq 'rq byn qry* "he divided the land between the villages";[45] → I.2 on the usage of the noun states. Both *qry* and *qryh* appear in 11Q10. 11Q10 8:1 (Job 24:12) alludes to the "villages" of the suffering (*qryhwn*), but 14:1; 32:6 (Job 29:7; 39:7) mention "city gates" and a "strong city" (*tq' qry'*).

The Palmyrene tax tables refer to goods that Palmyra leaves "to the villages" (*lqry'*) or brings in "from the villages" (*mn qry'*).[46] Palmyrene dedicatory inscriptions mention the "Gad (patron deity) of the city" (*gd' dy qryt'*),[47] i.e., Arak in one text, then the Gad of another city (*gdh dy qryt'*)[48] on the site of Chirbet Faruan, and the Gad of a third located near Chirbet Ramadan (*gd qryt'*).[49] A dedication "to the jinn of the city" (*lgny'*

30. *b'l qryh*, → *b'l* II.3.
31. *TADAE* B2.1:9; 2.7:10; 2.9:10f.; 6.3:7.
32. Segal, 22.1.
33. Segal, 68.7; 100.3.
34. *TADAE* C1.1:95.
35. *TADAE* C1.1:104.
36. *TADAE* C3.20:[1,]2,4f.; 3.21:[2,]3[,4f.]; C3.24[:1-3]; D3.44:3.
37. *WDSP* 14.1; 19.1.
38. 11Q10 14:1; 32:6 (Job 29:7; 39:7): *qry'*.
39. 5Q15 1:5f.; 4Q554 2 2:12,22f.; 3 1:17; as does *qryt qdš'* "the holy city" in 4Q196 17 2:8 (Tob. 13:10).
40. Cf. *ATTM*, 57.
41. *SAIO* I, 78.
42. *PAT* 1375.1; cf. *m. Yoma* 1:7.
43. See *ATTM*, 2, 165f.
44. *KAI* 278.1f.
45. Naveh, "Aramaic Inscriptions."
46. *PAT* 0259 ii.112.
47. *PAT* 1622.6.
48. *PAT* 1707.4.
49. *PAT* 1716.2f.

dy qryt')[50] also refers to Chirbet Faruan. In addition, "the citizens of the city" (*bny qryt'*)[51] or "the community of the city" (*dyr' dy qryt'*),[52] although not geographically identified in any of these cases, commend themselves to their jinn.

The mention of *qryh* in Pseudo-Daniel[53] appears in the context of the flood and Mount Lubar, where, according to Jub. 5:28; 7:1, the ark landed and in whose vicinity the three sons of Noah built a city (Jub. 7:14-17). Since Pseudo-Daniel summarizes the biblical story, the word *qryh* could represent the broken plural *quryā* in keeping with the context of Jub. 7:17: "These three cities are near Mount Lubar." Indeed, *quryā* refers otherwise to "villages," but this text may refer to the initial settlements of Noah's sons.

4. Heterograms. The heterogram QRYT' occurs in several ostraca from Nisa and in the Frahang-i Pahlavīk 2:8c, where it represents middle Iranian *rōtastāk* or *rōstāk* "district, province." In the Nisa inscriptions, QRYT' seems to denote localities in Mihrdātkirt; it was a *diz* (fortification) and seat of a *dizpat* (*dyzpty*), "fortification commander,"[54] and is always indicated by the heterogram BYRT' (→ *byrt*).

Lipiński

50. *PAT* 1704.1.
51. *PAT* 1746.1f.
52. *PAT* 2625.4f.
53. 4Q244 8:4.
54. M.-L. Chaumont, "Les ostraca de Nisa," *JA* 256 (1968) 20f.,28 n. 55.

קרן *qrn* /qarn/

I. Etymology. II. Of Animals. III. Instrument. IV. Altar.

I. Etymology. Aramaic *qrn* /qarn/[1] rests on a common Semitic primary noun for "horn." Since horns occur in pairs in most animals, the word behaves as a feminine. In addition to the literal sense, it refers to the wind instrument by the same name, to the horns on the corners of horned altars, then, figuratively, to "corner" in general, later also

U. Dahmen, "*qrn*," *ThWQ*, III, 567-70; H. Gzella, *Cosmic Battle and Political Conflict. BietOr* 47 (2003); B. Kedar-Kopfstein, "קֶרֶן *qeren*," *TDOT*, XIII, 167-74.

1. Secondarily expanded to /qarən/, *ATTM*, 112-15.

to the crescent moon, in financial contexts to "original capital,"[2] and finally in place names.[3] The dual is attested only in the absolute state (Dnl. 7:7).

II. Of Animals. All the older instances of the concrete meaning "horn (of animals)" occur in symbolic contexts. It first appears in the vision in Dnl. 7 of the four monsters as representatives of the empires. There it denotes the ten horns of the fourth, most terrible being that, in contrast to its predecessors, is not compared to any known animal (Dnl. 7:7; dual). Among them grows another, small, horn before which three of the others are "rooted out" (7:8).[4] The small horn superficially represents Antiochus IV, who desecrated the temple, the uprooted horns stand for three of his dynastic predecessors. It is described as having human eyes and a mouth that speaks insolently (7:8,20), which on the one hand further heightens its unnatural character, and on the other hand exploits the topos of boastful speech.[5] The historical allegory conceals a demonic power, however, that wages war (7:21) against the "holy ones,"[6] and will ultimately be destroyed (7:11). Dnl. 8:8-12 takes up the same theme again.[7] Also in a symbolic context, *qrn* refers to the ram that gores its enemies with its horns in Enoch's animal allegory for King Saul.[8] In contrast to Dnl. 7, *qrn* has positive connotations here.

III. Instrument. The narrative of the festal dedication of the statue of Nebuchadnezzar first employs *qrn* of a wind instrument in a formulaic expression including other instruments (Dnl. 3,5.7.10.15),[9] then 11Q10 33:5 (Job 39:25) representing Hebrew *šōp̄ār*; both instances have → *ql* "sound."

IV. Altar. The usage for "horns" of an altar[10] common in Hebrew occurs in the translation of Lev. 16:18 in 4Q156 2:2 and in the description of the temple cult in the new Jerusalem.[11] It cannot be clearly distinguished, however, from the general usage for "corners" (of a street, of a building, etc.) clearly attested later.[12]

Gzella

2. *DJPA*, 506b; *DJBA*, 1044f.; *LexSyr*, 697; *MdD*, 403.
3. 1QapGen 21:29.
4. → *ʿqr* II.
5. → *pm* II.1.
6. → *qdš* IV.2.
7. Gzella, 111-20,139-41.
8. 4Q205 2 3:27 (1 En. 89:43); *DSSStE*, 424f., reads *bqrnwhy* "with his horns." On the meaning → *dkr* /dakar/ III.
9. → *zmr* II.
10. In Aramaic *mdbḥ*, → *dbḥ* V.1.
11. 11Q18 22:1.
12. So *PAT* 0029.2; → I.

קשט *qšṭ* /qošṭ/

I. Root and Forms. II.1. Elephantine. 2. Aśoka. 3. Palmyra. III. Lexical. 1. Greek Translations. 2. Hebrew Translations. 3. Synonyms and Antonyms. IV. Semantics. 1. Speech. 2. Behavior. 3. Law. 4. Miscellanea.

I. Root and Forms. The root *qšṭ* is not common Semitic, but essentially Aramaic. Most consider Hebrew and Arabic (*qsṭ*) forms to be loanwords.[1] Since East Aramaic exhibits the general West Semitic incompatibility of two emphatic radicals,[2] variants appear there such as *kšṭ* and *qšt*.[3] The relationship with *qšt* "bow" and the verbal derivative "to shoot" is debatable. Indeed, Palestinian Aramaic and Syriac first attest Aramaic forms with this meaning and /ṭ/ instead of /t/, although *qošæṭ* "bow(-shooting)" in Ps. 60:6[4] already reflects a corresponding exchange. A second verbal root *qšṭ* covers the semantic range from "to prepare" to "to adorn." The third, *qšṭ* "to be (proven) correct," appears in only a few verbal forms that are generally spelled *qwšṭ* or *qšwṭ* and are associated with nouns translated "trust, uprightness." Some[5] assume a semantic development from "to shoot an arrow" (i.e., "to aim at") to "what is correct," "truth." Consequently, all[6] or the last two[7] are subsumed under one lexeme. In individual cases, the classification remains unclear.[8] Since the assumption of a development of meaning rests the semantic analysis on an etymological hypothesis, but Imperial and post-Imperial Aramaic attest only a few verb forms in contrast with the noun *qšṭ*[9] and the adjective *qšyṭ*, the meaning must be deduced from usage and the old translations.

M. M. Bravmann, *Verbs Derived from the Noun *qaš/st "Bow." Studies in Semitic Philology* (Leiden, 1977), 559-62; G. P. Carratelli and G. Garbini, *A Bilingual Graeco-Aramaic Edict by Aśoka* (Rome, 1964); A. Cody, "Notes on Proverbs 22,21 and 22,23b," *Bib* 61 (1980) 419-26; K. Koch, "History as a Battlefield of Two Antagonistic Powers in the Apocalypse of Weeks and in the Rule of the Community," in G. Boccaccini, ed., *Enoch and Qumran Origins* (Grand Rapids, 2005), 185-203; A. Lange, "'So I Girded My Loins in the Vision of Righteousness and Wisdom, in the Robe of Supplication' (1QapGen ar VI.4)," *AS* 8 (2010) 13-45; C. Stadel, "*qwšṭ*," *ThWQ*, III, 516-20; L. T. Stuckenbruck, *1 Enoch 91–108* (Berlin, 2007); M. Wagner, *Die lexikalischen und grammatikalischen Aramaismen im alttestamentlichen Hebräisch. BZAW* 96 (1966).

1. Yet cf. Bravmann.
2. E. Lipiński, *Semitic Languages. OLA* 80 (^{2}2001), §10.9.
3. Cf. T. Nöldeke, *Neue Beiträge zur semitischen Sprachwissenschaft* (Strassburg, 1910), 132f.
4. LXX τόξον.
5. E.g., Bravmann, Lange.
6. Bravmann.
7. *ATTM*, 687f.; *KBL*^{3}, 1776f.
8. So sometimes in Palmyrene, where *qšṭ* can be understood either as "adornment" or "right."
9. At Qumran often *qwšṭ*, in the abs. state also *qšwṭ* and once *qwšwṭ*.

II. *1. Elephantine.* Line 158 of the sayings of Aḥiqar reads *kšyṭ' wy'mrnh,*[10] apparently in a fragmentary code of behavior for scribes. Depending on the reconstruction, one can understand the adjective *kšyṭ'* as the object of *y'mrnh* ("they should speak the truth"),[11] of a preceding verb, or substantivally ("the truthful one").[12]

With no context, *hqšṭ* appears in an epistolary ostracon from Elephantine about barley;[13] the translation "to arrange" or "to prepare"[14] is obtained from later Aramaic.

2. Aśoka. The first Aramaic lines of the Aśoka diglot from Kandahar[15] announces: *šnn* 10 *ptytw 'byd zy mr'n prydrš mlk' qšyṭ' mhqšṭ*, something like the Greek δέκα ἐτῶν πληρη[. . .]ων βασιλεὺς Πιοδασσης εὐσέβειαν ἔδειξεν τοῖς ἀνθρώποις. Most understand *qšyṭ' mhqšṭ* as paronomasia, either as an affirmation "he promotes the truth" or as an attributive "the king, who. . . ."[16] The nuance remains unclear; if, as most assume, εὐσέβεια and *qšyṭ'* are imprecise[17] equivalents of the Indian concept of *dhamma*, they refer to proper behavior. Yet in the broader context of Aśoka's mission, *qšyṭ'* and *mhqšṭ* could literally mean the foundation of piety through the erection of stone edicts. Then *mhqšṭ* could belong with *qšṭ* "to prepare."[18]

3. Palmyra. Palmyrene-Aramaic inscriptions contain several forms spelled *qšṭ*, sometimes as variants of *qšt* "archer,"[19] but once the verb occurs in a rare curse against grave robbers: *wl' yqšṭ lmn dy yptḥyhy,*[20] usually understood as "may whoever opens this never be exonerated."[21] A noun *qšṭ* also occurs: in the tax table *'l mlḥ' qšṭ[' ']tḥzy ly dy b'tr dy dms thw' mtzbn'* "With respect to salt; it seems right to me that it should be sold in a public place."[22] The sense of the table is to record the still unwritten tax regulations. "It seems right to me" differs from *'tḥzy dy* "it is determined that" (l. 128) and *hyk dy nmws' mwḥ' pšqt* "as the law announced, so I have decided" (l. 128), thus, *qšṭ* may refer to (common) law. It is more difficult to explain *qšṭ* in some grave certificate texts. Following δίκαια in the Greek versions,[23] it seems likely that the suffixed *wqšṭ* as the conclusion of a list with right of usage[24] should be understood as "(legal/customary) right." In conjunction

---

10. On the form with /q/ > /k/, see I. Kottsieper, *Die Sprache der Ahiqarsprüche. BZAW* 194 (1990), 42,211.
11. H. Niehr, *Aramäischer Ahiqar. JSHRZ* 2.2 (2007), 49.
12. Kottsieper, 17; cf. *TADAE* C p. 44.
13. *TADAE* D1.20:8.
14. Impv. or pf.
15. *KAI* 279.
16. Garbini, 47; contra B. A. Levine, review of G. P. Caratelli and G. Garbini, *A Bilingual Graeco-Aramaic Edict by Aśoka, JAOS* 87 (1967) 186: "the truthful, the doer of the truth."
17. See, e.g., D. H. Sick, "When Socrates Met the Buddha," *JRAS* 17 (2007) 257-60.
18. Cf. Targum Onqelos on Am. 9:6.
19. E.g., *PAT* 0253, in Latin *sag[ittarius]*.
20. *PAT* 0574.5.
21. See *DNSI*, 1038.
22. *PAT* 0259 ii.130-132.
23. *PAT* 0565; 2786.5; 0057.1; in each the wording can be reconstructed.
24. Always with → *rḥq*.

with *tṣb(y)t* "decoration"[25] in the Aramaic text, an Aramaic reader can also understand the word as "adornment."

III. Lexical.

1. Greek Translations. Greek translations of Jewish Aramaic writings from the time of the Second Temple usually render *qšṭ* with ἀληθ- or δίκαιο-: Dnl. 2:47; Theodotion at 4:34;[26] the Greek text of T. Levi at 4Q213a 1:12[27] and 2:9,[28] in keeping with the meaning, has the adjective instead of the noun in the genitive 2:7;[29] also throughout in the books of Enoch where Greek and Aramaic texts are preserved,[30] there occurs a double translation or a later insertion[31] in 1 En. 10:16.[32] This rendering is not systematic, however; ἀληθ- appears repeatedly in the Greek book of Enoch where one would expect *qšṭ* in the lost Aramaic text.[33] In 1 En. 106:18 and 107:2, *bqšwṭ* is understood, contrary to the sense of the Aramaic, as an attribute of Noah's and translated with δικαίως.[34] The reconstruction of a verb in 4Q201 1 6:3 is paleographically dubious.

The Qumran fragments of Tobit also preserve remnants of *q(w)šṭ*, twice corresponding to δικαιοσύνη in 4Q196 17 2:3.5 (Tob. 13:7). Other passages are more difficult. The reading *q* in *bq[šṭ'*[35] is highly uncertain; with regard to 4Q196 17 2:9, a comparison with Tob. 13:9f. (Vaticanus) points more to *bny qw]šṭ'*[36] instead of Fitzmyer's *bqw]šṭ'*.[37] In 4Q197 4 2:2 *dyn qšṭ'* "a lawful right"[38] corresponds to δεδικαίωταί σοι in Tob. 6:13 (Sinaiticus), also with the same δίκαιο- word group. The adjective *qšyṭ* in 4Q197 4 3:9 presumably corresponds to καλός in Tob. 7:7; there is no reason to assume with Lange that it was translated with καλὸς καὶ ἀγαθός in the sense of Greek "beautiful goodness."[39] The nuance "straight" appears in *d]brny qšyṭ' lbyt r'w'l*,[40] corresponding to ἀπάγαγέ με εὐθεῖαν πρὸς Ραγουήλ (Tob. 7:1 Sin.).

2. Hebrew Translations. In 11Q10 7A:8 (Job 23:7), *rw qšṭ wdt[* corresponds more to LXX (ἀλήθεια γὰρ καὶ ἔλεγχος) than MT; the converse is true of *qšyṭh yplg* in 11:8 (Job

---

25. Greek: σὺν παντὶ κόσμῳ.
26. The equivalent is missing in the unrevised translation.
27. *ALD* 3:2.
28. *ALD* 3:17.
29. *ALD* 3:15.
30. Δικαιοσύνη/δικαίως for *qwšṭ* and δίκαιος for *qšyṭ*.
31. Τῆς δικαιοσύνης καὶ τῆς ἀληθείας.
32. Eth. *ṣedq* and *ret'*, both corresponding to *qšṭ*.
33. E.g., 1 En. 15:1; 104:9,13.
34. L. T. Stuckenbruck, "Revision of Aramaic-Greek and Greek-Aramaic Glossaries in The Books of Enoch," *JJS* 41 (1990) 16,34f.; Lange, 25-28.
35. 4Q197 3:5 (Tob. 5:14: τὴν ἀλήθειαν).
36. So also *ATTM*, 2, 184.
37. *DJD*, XXIX (1997), 26. *DSSStE*, 386f., reads *bqw]šṭ'*.
38. *DSSStE*, 390f.
39. → III.3 for *qšṭ* and *ṭb*. All the translations have "noble and good" here, but the medieval Aramaic text A5 following the manuscript Bodleian Heb. Ms. 2339 reads *br zk'y wqšyṭ*.
40. 4Q197 4 3:2.

27:17). In 24:7f. (Job 34:13) the rare verb *qšṭ* occurs in the D-stem for the Hebrew *śām* "he arranged" (→ II.2), but presumably evokes the meaning of the noun. In the same section, in fact, the translator employs the noun and verb *šqr* repeatedly (in Job 34:8,10,12,17) and, therefore, appends Job 34:12f. directly.

Additional sporadic agreements manifest themselves in fixed expressions: *blbb dk' wbrwḥ qšyṭh wṭbh* "with a pure heart and a right and good spirit" in 4Q542 1 1:10 corresponds to *lēḇ ṭāhōr* and *rūᵃḥ nāḵōn*[41] in Ps 51:12. *'rḥ(t) qšṭ(')*[42] corresponds to the Hebrew *drky 'mt/ṣdq.*[43] Aramaic *nṣbt q(w)šṭ(')* corresponds to Hebrew *mṭ't 'mt,*[44] *dyn qšṭ(')* ("judgment of *šṭ*") perhaps to the very frequent concept *mšpṭ ṣdq*. Spelled the same way, *dyn qšṭ['* ("judge of *qšṭ*") has a Hebrew parallel in *dyn h'mt.*[45]

In the Targums, too, *qšṭ* functions as the most common rendering of *'mt* and *ṣdq*, almost entirely so in the Pentateuch of Onqelos. In addition, *bqwšṭ'* often appears as a formula introducing speech. The adjective *qšyṭ* sometimes renders Hebrew forms of *'mn, yšr,* and *ṣdq*.

The translation equivalence of Aramaic *qšṭ* with Greek ἀληθ-/δίκαιο- and Hebrew *'mt/ṣdq* corresponds to ἀληθ- (sometimes δίκαιο-) for *'mt* and δίκαιο- for *ṣdq* in the LXX just as in Palmyrene (→ II.3). All of these terms, however, were fluid in the respective traditions and attained their semantic precision through their cotexts and contexts.

3. Synonyms and Antonyms. A near synonym is *yṣyb* "valid, true,"[46] cf. 1QapGen 2:20 with 2:22; Dnl. 2:8 with 2:47; 4Q212 1 3:19f. (1 En. 93:2) with 1QapGen 14:13 and 4Q204 1 5:4 (1 En. 10:16); perhaps the original of 1 En. 106:12 (ἀκρίβειαν . . . ἀλήθειαν). In reference to speech, *bqšṭ* "truly" appears three times with *(w)l' bkdbyn* "without lies."[47] The apocalypse of weeks[48] contrasts *qš(w)ṭ* with *ḥms* "violence" and *šqr* "lie, deceit";[49] regarding 11Q10 24 → III.2; similarly 1QapGen 6:3 with D. A. Machiela.[50] Cf. *ALD* 13:3[51] for *ṣdqt'*, 4Q542 1 1:9 for *yšyrwt'* and 1 1:12 for both together with *tmymwt'*. For *qšyṭ* and *ṭb* "good," see 4Q537 10 1 (reading uncertain) and 4Q542 1 1:10; on Tob. 7:7 → III.1, similarly probably also 1 En. 91:4; 92:4;[52] furthermore *dyn* (par. in Dnl. 4:34).

---

41. LXX: εὐθής, → III.1 on Tob. 7:1.
42. Three times in Enoch's apocalypse of weeks 4Q212; twice in *ALD*, 4Q213 4:5 and 4Q213a 1:12; with the reading *'rḥt* instead of *'wḥt* also in 1QapGen 6:3.
43. Cf. *šbyly 'mt* in 1QapGen 6:2.
44. 1QHª 16:11.
45. 11Q5 24:6.
46. → *yṣb*.
47. 1QapGen 2:6 (emend.); 2:7; 3:13; 4Q204 5 2:30 (1 En. 107:2).
48. 1 En. 93:1-10; 91:11-17, partly in 4Q212 1 3-4.
49. 4Q212 1 3:25; 4:14.
50. D. A. Machiela, *The Dead Sea Genesis Apocryphon. STDJ* 79 (2009), 43.
51. 4Q213 1 1:7.
52. Ethiopic *ṣedq* and *ḫirut*.

IV. Semantics.

1. Speech. *qšṭ* is often employed in relation to speech and the communication of knowledge, as in the conversation between Lamech and Bettenosh in 1QapGen 2,[53] similarly in 15:20. First Enoch 106f. also relates this story, parts of which are preserved in 4Q204.[54] Qahat's teaching[55] and speech (*mmr*)[56] are also associated with "uprightness";[57] cf. II.1. Furthermore, direct speech can be qualified as true by *mn qšṭ* (Dnl. 2:47)[58] as an introductory formula. In a few passages,[59] the context permits understanding *bqšṭ* as "direct," "frank," comparable to Greek εὐθύς (→ III.1). Elsewhere *qšṭ* does not refer to the manner of speech, but to its content as reliable, like Greek ἀλήθεια.

2. Behavior. A second semantic field concerns the use of *qšṭ* for behavior, sometimes directly and as the object of → *ʿbd* "to do,"[60] which leads to *ʿbdy qšṭʾ*.[61] Mostly, however, the behavior finds expression metaphorically as walking on paths of *qšṭ*, distinguished from evil paths.[62] The doctrine of two paths reflects the ethical dualism of two patterns of behavior and, accordingly, of two fates. In the ninth week of the apocalypse of weeks, after the destruction of evil, all human beings will view the *ʾrḥt qšṭ ʿlmʾ*,[63] in which *ʿlmʾ* "eternal" refers to the entire expression "path of truth." The path of wrong, in contrast, leads to darkness.[64] The Aramaic Levi Document does not know of a contrast between two paths, but the one path of *qšṭ* that one should not abandon,[65] cf. also *ALD* 2:4f., as well as 4Q213a 1:12[66] and *ALD* 3:9 for the plea for the right path. With the nuance "straight,"[67] *qšṭ* suits this image very well. Other combinations arise through its use with *ʾḥd bqwšṭʾ* "hold firm to *qwšṭ*" in 1QapGen 2:6 and 4Q542 1 1:9, in the second passage paralleling "to walk [*ʾzl*][68] in uprightness." The adjective *qšyṭ* usually designates the same idea of the good of right behavior and those who act in this manner. Three aspects can stand in the background: the image of the straight path, the association with reliability,[69] and the agreement between one's behavior and divine instruction.

---

53. With → *ḥwī* in 5:10 and → *mll* in 7:18, then → *ydʿ* in 20:22.
54. See *bqšwṭ* in 4Q204 5 2:22.30.
55. → *ʾlp.*
56. → *mll.*
57. 4Q542 1 2:1.
58. On *bqwšṭʾ* in Targum Onqelos → III.2.
59. 1QapGen 2:5,7,10,18.
60. 4Q202 1 4:26 (1 En. 93:17); cf. perhaps 4Q196 17 2:5 (Tob. 13:7).
61. 4Q580 1 1:11.
62. 1QapGen 6, 2f.; 4Q212 1 2:20 (1 En. 91:18-20); 1 5:25 (1 En. 94:1); Stuckenbruck, 165-68.
63. 4Q212 1 4:22 (1 En. 91:14).
64. 1QapGen 6:3.
65. 4Q213 4:5; → *šbq.*
66. *ALD* 3:4.
67. → III.1 on Tob. 7:1.
68. → *hlk.*
69. 4Q550 4:3.

3. *Law.* Associated with this diction is the juridical usage (→ II.3). Repeatedly, *qšṭ* characterizes the word → *dyn* "legal proceeding, legal decision": 4Q212 1 4:16 (1 En. 91:12); *ALD* 3:17,[70] here as in *ALD* 6:2 with reference to the laws and judgments of the Levites according to Dt. 33:10, just as Jub. 31:15. 4Q197 4 2:2 (Tob. 6:13 Sin.) probably refers to the legally valid decision in the case of Tobias and Sarah.[71] Daniel 4:34 is not just a hymn praising God, but "his deeds" refer to 4:31f. and the whole clause, thereby to Nebuchadnezzar's insight that everything God had done to him was right and appropriate. According to 4Q246 2:5f., an expression that recalls 1 En. 91:12 and Dnl. 4:34 refers to the eschatological kingdom of God's people: *wkl ʾrḥth bqšwṭ ydy*[*n*] *ʾrʿʾ bqšṭ* "and all his paths are *bqšwṭ* and he/it judges the earth *bqšṭ*." The whole lexical field is theologically loaded: God himself is just and guarantees a just verdict, both through the Levites and eschatologically through the upright, his people. Because of lacunae, however, it is unclear whether *dyn* in 4Q205 1 11:2 (1 En. 22:14) means "verdict" or "judge." Sometimes, *qšṭ* can represent *dyn qšṭ* in an ellipsis, such as (*spr*) *mly qwšṭʾ* in 4Q204 1 6:8f. (1 En. 13:10-14:1), which refers to God's verdict on the Watchers.

4. *Miscellanea.* Proceeding from Isa. 60:21; 61:11f., the metaphor of "planting" in context with *qšṭ* was widespread in early Jewish texts,[72] i.e., the planting of the righteous, the people Israel. In analogous expressions, *qwšṭʾ* can denote Israel and/or the eschatological upright ones, so also at the beginning of 1QapGen 6, which says that Noah was "planted for uprightness" (*lqwšṭ nṣybt*), i.e., should become the ancestor of the people of God. 1QapGen 6:4[73] may elaborate on Isa. 61:11 if one reads *b<ḥ>zwn qwšṭʾ* "with a belt of *qšṭ*."

In some texts, *qšṭ* appears as an abstract term, either absolutely or in contrast to "wrong." With this nuance in 1QapGen 6:4, the word refers to human "right behavior" or "uprightness" (see above). Yet other texts portray *qwšṭʾ* as an independent, supernatural, positive force equally associated with moral behavior, a higher power, and the historical role of God's upright people. According to the apocalypse of weeks, it belongs to the fundamental cosmic principles of history and manifests itself in various manners during its course, always in opposition to *šqrʾ* "the lie" and *ḥmsʾ* "the violence." Koch compares this contrast with the Iranian antithesis between *asha* and *drug*, traditionally translated "truth"[74] and "lie" or "deceit." Aspects of the concept of *asha* (sometimes also translated "order") and the development of a dualistic worldview may have enriched the semantics of the term *qwšṭʾ*. Historically, it is more likely, at any rate, that *qwšṭʾ* compares with *asha* than with the Egyptian *maat*. Yet the inclusion of this concept in early Jewish texts also led to new concepts such as the relationship to election: according to 4Q212 1 4:12 (1 En. 93:10) some are chosen (*ytbḥrwn*) to be *śhdy qšṭ* "witnesses of *qšṭ*"; among lacunae, 4Q580 1 1:10 also mentions *bḥyr lqšṭ*.

---

70. 4Q213a 2:9; κρίσιν ἀληθινῆν.
71. Corresponding to Nu. 36:8f.
72. For the occurrences of *nṣbt qwšṭʾ* → *nṣb* IV.1.
73. → *ḥrṣ*.
74. Already in Plutarch, *De Iside et Osiride* 47: ἓξ θεοὺς . . . τὸν δὲ δεύτερον ἀληθείας.

In individual cases, it sometimes remains unclear which of these aspects of the meaning of *qšṭ* stands in the foreground. The expression *dry qwšṭʾ* in 4Q542 1 1:4 means the clans of the Levites[75] and points to a relationship between *qwšṭʾ* and levitical rights. Yet, in 4Q543 1 2:8 it refers to the clans of the end time and suggests an eschatological manifestation of *qwšṭʾ*. 4Q204 5 2:28 (1 En. 107:1) seems to imply the same notion. In 4Q213a 2:7,[76] *zrʿ dq*[*šṭ* could describe the proper behavior of the descendants or the "rights" of the Levites. Presumably, *prds qšṭ*[ʾ[77] refers either to the original status of Adam and Eve in paradise or the future dwelling of the righteous dead, if not paradise itself, as part of the physical and temporal scope of *qwšṭʾ* in contrast to wrong. Other occurrences like 4Q565 1:5 are too fragmentary.

Tigchelaar

75. Cf. perhaps 4Q547 9:7.
76. *ALD* 3:15.
77. 4Q206 1 26:21 (1 En. 32:3).

ראש *rʾš* /rēš/

I. Etymology. II. Old and Imperial Aramaic. III. Biblical Aramaic. IV. Qumran.

I. Etymology. Derivatives of the masculine noun *rʾš* "chief, head" occur in all Semitic languages. Regarding the form of Aramaic /raʾš/ > /rēš/, see *ATTM*, 104,138.

II. Old and Imperial Aramaic. An Old Aramaic specimen occurs in the Sefire treaty text *KAI* 224.11 in the reference to the case that an enemy "demands my head, to kill me" (*ybʿh rʾšy lhmtty*); it implies the practice of beheading an enemy and presenting his head, as, e.g., in the OT in 1S. 17:51,57; 31:9.

Imperial Aramaic does not attest *rʾš* in the literal meaning. It stands *pars pro toto* in regulations of divorce. If one declares hatred for one's partner in marriage, then "hate-silver" falls "on his/her head" (*ksp śnʾh brʾšh*),[1] i.e., he must pay compensation for the

W. Beuken and U. Dahmen, "ראשׁ *rōʾš*," *TDOT*, XIII, 248-61; U. Dahmen, "*rʾš* I," *ThWQ*, III, 579-86; J. Dušek, *Les manuscrits araméens du Wadi Daliyeh et la Samarie vers 450-332 av. J.-C. CHANE* 30 (2007); J. A. Fitzmyer, *The Aramaic Inscriptions of Sefire*. *BietOr* 19A (²1995); idem, *The Genesis Apocryphon of Qumran Cave 1 (1Q20)*. *BietOr* 18B (³2004); D. Flusser, "Healing through the Laying-on of Hands in a Dead Sea Scroll," *IEJ* 7 (1957) 107f.; H.-P. Müller, "ראשׁ *rōʾš* head," *TLOT*, 1184-94; Y. Muffs, *Studies in the Aramaic Legal Papyri from Elephantine*. *HO* 66 (2003).

1. With 3m/fs suff., *TADAE* B2.6:23; B3.3:8,9; B3.8:22,25.

broken marriage.[2] In the figurative meaning "beginning,"[3] the noun occurs in indications of time, *r'š yrḥ'* "beginning of the month,"[4] *r'š mlkwt [d]ryhwš* "beginning of the reign (i.e., enthronement year) of [Da]rius" in the date of papyrus *WDSP* 1.1 from the Wadi Daliyeh in Samaria.[5] In another metaphorical use, *r'š* "head" serves in the Behistun inscription of Darius I to designate the leader of a group.[6] In addition, *r'š* is a *terminus technicus* for "capital" in contrast to *mrby*[7] "interest."[8]

III. Biblical Aramaic. Biblical Aramaic attests the noun fourteen times, mostly in the literal meaning, six of which occur in the phrase *ḥæzwē rēš* "face of the head."[9] Daniel 3:27 describes the men in the fiery furnace "the hair of whose head (*śᵉʿar rēšhōn*)[10] was not singed." The noun appears in descriptions in prominent positions in visions. Daniel depicts for Nebuchadnezzar his vision of a statue, *rēšeh dī ḏᵉhaḇ ṭāḇ* "his head was of fine gold" (Dnl. 2:32),[11] and interprets the head[12] in Dnl. 2:38 as the king. In the animal vision, the third animal, according to Dnl. 7:6, has four heads, *'arbᵉʿā rēšīn lᵉḥēwᵉṯā*,[13] the fourth, according to 7:20, has ten horns on its head,[14] and the Ancient One who sits in judgment in Dnl. 7:9, "the hair of his head (*śᵉʿar rēšeh*) was like pure wool."[15]

Metaphorically, the noun denotes leaders, as in Ezr. 5:10 *guḇrayyā ḏī ḇᵉrāšēhom* "the men at their heads,"[16] and the phrase in Dnl. 7:1 *rēš millīn* means *summa rerum*.[17]

IV. Qumran. In the Aramaic at Qumran, *r'š*[18] appears literally in the theologically significant 1QapGen 20:28f. (a treatment of Gen. 12). Pharaoh asks Abraham for healing and Abraham recounts: *wṣlyt ʿl [mr]dp' hw wsmkt ydy ʿl [r'y]šh* "thus, I prayed for this [torment]er and laid my hands on his [hea]d" and the plague was removed. Neither the OT nor rabbinic literature mentions the NT practice of healing by the laying-on of hands

---

2. → *śnī*.
3. In contrast to *swp* "end" (→ *sūp* IV).
4. *KAI* 319.15, cf. 11Q18 19 1:2, Heb. *rōš ḥoḏæš*, Nu. 10:10; 28:11.
5. Cf. Dušek, 118f.; perhaps a loan translation from the Akk. *rēš šarrūti*, Muffs, 192; similarly *TADAE* B2.2:1.
6. *TADAE* C2.1:52 *'yš ḥd br'šhw[m* "a man at the[ir] head," sg. with 3mp suff.; cf. Palmyrene *qūm brš* "to stand at the head, to have leadership" in *PAT* 0261.2; on Ezr. 5:10 → III.
7. → *rb*.
8. *TADAE* B3.1:6 [*rš'*]; B4.2:5; D1.17:5; *WDSP* 10.7; later → *qrn* also fulfills this function.
9. Always with suff., Dnl. 4:7,10; 7:15; → *ḥzī* IV; in 2:28; 4:2; 7:1 paired with *ḥēlæm* "dream"; → *ḥlm*.
10. Sg. with 3mp suff.; → *śʿr*.
11. On the context → *dhb* II; *ṣlm* III.
12. Sg. det.
13. Pl. abs.
14. Sg. with 3fs suff.; → *qrn* II.
15. → *ʿtyq* III; *nqh* II.
16. Pl. with 3mp suff., → II on *TADAE* C2.1:52.
17. → *sūp* IV.
18. Also spelled *r'yš*, *ryš* or *rš*.

(e.g., Mk. 5:23; Lk. 4:40).[19] In the sense of "head," *r'š* also appears in the poem praising Sarah's beauty 1QapGen 20:3: *km' rqyq lh ś'r r'yšh* "how soft is the hair of her head."[20]

In the sense of "leader,"[21] the noun appears in fragmentary contexts in 4Q566 1 4[22] and 4Q209 28:3, 4Q542 1 1:7;[23] 4Q213 2:10 has the phrase *r'šyn wšpṭyn* "leader and judge." 11Q18 19 1:2 *r'šy ḥ[dš'* "beginnings [of the month]"[24] and the unclear 4Q546 2:1 *b]šnt ryšy bršw[ty* "in the] year of my beginning, with my authori[ty" (→ II, *r'š mlkwt'*) retain the temporal meaning "beginning." A local meaning often occurs in genitive phrases, such as "point, peak" of a mountain, → *ṭwr*,[25] rocks, *kp*,[26] or tracts of lands, *ḥwlq*,[27] or as the "source" of a river, → *nhr* /nahar/.[28]

Stadel

19. → *yd* II.1.
20. *ś'r ršh* also as a characteristic in the physiognomic omen text 4Q561 7:4.
21. Imperial and Biblical Aramaic also have other expressions for this, → II on *TADAE* C2.1:52, Ezr. 5:10, similarly 11Q10 15:3 *br'š ḥylh* "at the head of his army" for Job 29:25 *baggᵉdûd*.
22. Sg. abs.
23. Pl. abs.
24. Pl. const. with a Heb. loanword, → II, *r'š yrḥ'*.
25. 1QapGen 14:9; 17:9.
26. 4Q204 4:3; 4Q206 4 3:19; → *ṭwr*.
27. 1QapGen 17:11; → *ḥlq* III.
28. 1QapGen 16:9; 17:8; 19:12 (2×).

רב *rb* /rabb/; רבן *rbn* /rabbān/; רבו *rbw* /rebbō/; רבי *rbī*; רבו *rbw* /rabū/; רבה *rbh* /rabǣ/

I. Etymology, Forms, and Lexical Field. II. Adjective "Large." 1. Literally. 2. Pejoratively. 3. "(Al)mighty" as a Title for God and Outstanding Persons. 4. Substantivally. III. Noun "Leader." IV. Number "Ten Thousand." V. Verb. 1. G-stem "to Grow." 2. D-stem "to Make Great." VI. Noun "Grandeur." VII. Noun "Officer."

I. Etymology, Forms, and Lexical Field. In the Semitic languages, the biconsonantal root *rb-* underlies the various terms for "large." West Semitic differentiated it into forms with a long /bb/ and those with a vocalic ending. The first form is productive in Aramaic chiefly as the adjective /rabb/ "large" with several literal and figurative nuances,[1] but it

H.-J. Fabry, E. Blum, and H. Ringgren, "רַב *raḇ*," *TDOT*, XIII, 272-98; H.-J. Fabry and M. Gomolka, "*rb* I," *ThWQ*, III, 592-604; T. Hartmann, "רַב *rab* many," *TLOT*, 1194-1201.

1. After the simplification of double consonant ending around 200-150 B.C.E. /rab/; cf. *ATTM*, 120-22.

also appears as a masculine noun /rabbān/ "great one" and as a feminine /rebbō/ "ten thousand" (or also "innumerably many"), while, in Aramaic, the root → *śgī*, characteristic there, assumed the meaning of the related Hebrew verb *rbb* "to be many." Consequently, the concepts of "large" and "numerous" are distinct in Aramaic. Aramaic attests *rbī*[2] as a verb, however, in the G-stem "to grow," in the D-stem "to make great." This can be linked through the common vocalic ending and the short /b/ with the various nominal formations, of which the feminine /rabū/ "grandeur, majesty"[3] and the masculine /rabǣ/ "great one"[4] occur in Old Aramaic, later also other forms. Along with the sporadic, regular /rabbīn/, Aramaic also forms the plural of the adjective "large," in both an attributive and a substantival function, very frequently with reduplication of the root: /rabrabīn/.

With the connotation "mighty," the forms of /rabb/ stand very near the semantic spectrum of → *šlṭ*, the substantive with the nuance "lord" also to → *mr'*. For "leader" in the general sense, → *sgn* and → *r'š* also occur. Old and Imperial Aramaic can already express "mighty" with forms of the root *kbr* "to be many" and the adjective /kabbīr/ "mighty,"[5] although they appear only sporadically. Finally, "to be long" is the meaning of a distinct Semitic root, *'rk*, with the related substantives and the adjective, all of which can have both spatial and temporal senses.[6]

II. Adjective "Large." With regard to the adjective *rb* /rabb/, one can distinguish roughly the literal sense "large,"[7] the pejorative nuance "arrogant," and from it, in turn, the specific nuance "mighty" (of God: "almighty") and, as a substantive, "leader, great one, noble," all with their own respective connotations.

1. Literally. In the literal sense "large," *rb* refers to things, living beings, and abstract concepts. It belongs to the everyday lexicon and is, consequently, very frequent. In documentary texts, it refers to houses,[8] gates,[9] rooms,[10] ships,[11] vessels;[12] furthermore, in reference to sheep;[13] in reference to persons, the meaning is unclear, perhaps, as later, "older";[14] also probably in a place name;[15] finally, many times it has an unknown referent.[16]

The Bible and Qumran manifest additional usages: for gifts (Dnl. 2:48), cities (4:27) and

2. From an older *rbū.
3. In the religious literature of the book of Daniel and the texts from Qumran.
4. In Imperial Aramaic.
5. See *DNSI*, 485f.
6. For instances, see *DNSI*, 108f.; *ATTM*, 522f.; 2, 355.
7. Of living beings also "old."
8. *TADAE* A3.8:6.
9. *TADAE* A4.8:9.
10. *TADAE* B3.5:3,6; 3.10:4,11; 3.11:6; 3.12:13,21.
11. *spynh*, often in the export list *TADAE* C3.7.
12. *TADAE* C3.28:108f.; D7.9:15; 7.46:2.
13. *TADAE* D7.8:3.
14. *TADAE* C3.9:3,6,9,12,14; D6.1:3; 8.6:7.
15. Segal, 103.2.
16. *TADAE* C3.13:49; 3.28:121; D7.5:3; 7.35:9; 7.45:5; Segal, 42b.5.

other locations such as wildernesses,[17] valleys[18] and seas,[19] Noah's vineyard,[20] persons in the sense of "older";[21] but also for immaterial concepts such as a royal banquet (Dnl. 5:1) and one of God's miraculous acts of deliverance (3:33), the innocence of the books of patriarchs,[22] and the last judgment.[23] Vision reports, in particular, employ *rb* "great" just like *śgy'* "many" to illustrate the gigantic proportions of the things seen: a statue (Dnl. 2:31) and mountain (2:35) in Nebuchadnezzar's dream, the sea (7:2) and the animals that it produces (7:3,17), with their attributes (7:7: teeth; 7:20: horns). Qumran is similar.[24] Size, then, characterizes the expenditure of royal representation, the might of God, the hidden forces of world history, and, perhaps under the influence of Hellenistic geographers, the extent of the earth and the heavenly world. For a complete list of occurrences, see *ATTM*, 689f.; 2, 478f.

2. *Pejoratively.* In conjunction with words (*mlyn*) and verbs of speech,[25] *rb* appears with the pejorative nuance "magniloquent, arrogant." This can be first identified in reference to the "small horn" of the vision in Dnl. 7.[26] This topos also appears later for the speech of the evildoer.[27] A derivative of this usage is the verb in the reduplicated-stem *rbrb* "to boast," which, according to *ATTM*, 2, 97 already appears in 1QapGen 13:14,[28] and certainly, later, however.[29]

3. *"(Al)mighty" as a Title for God and Outstanding Persons.* Since the earliest textual witness, *rb* is already a divine title[30] recognizing divine power. It can also refer to a king,[31] high official,[32] or high priest.[33]

4. *Substantivally.* In a substantival usage, the adjective can appear as a title, as later the noun *rbn* does. In Old Aramaic times, it designates in the plural the elite at the court

17. 1QapGen 21:12.
18. 1QapGen 22:4.
19. 1QapGen 16:11,17; 21:11,16.
20. 1QapGen 12:13.
21. 1QapGen 12:10, also Eve as the mother of humankind: 4Q206 1 27:10 (1 En. 32:6).
22. 4Q542 1 2:13.
23. 4Q206 1 22:3 (1 En. 22:4); 4Q212 1 4:23 (1 En. 91:15).
24. 1QapGen 14:9; 4Q204 1 6:28 (1 En. 14:15); 4Q204 1 7:2 (1 En. 14:20); 4Q205 2 2:29 (1 En. 89:30); 4Q530 2 2+6-12:8; 7 2:5; 4Q531 7:6; 4Q554 1 2:15.
25. → *mll.*
26. Dnl. 7:11 as an attribute of *mly'* "the words"; in abs. of the fem. pl. as the obj. of *mll* in 7:8,20; regarding the context → *qrn.*
27. 4Q204 1 1:17; 4Q201 1 2:13 (1 En. 1:9; 5:4); 11Q10 22:7 (Job 33:13).
28. Paleographically very unclear.
29. *DJPA*, 515b.
30. Old Aramaic: *KAI* 309.6; Imperial Aramaic: *TADAE* C3.12:26; D22.49:3; *KAI* 259.4; Qumran: 1QapGen 6:13,15; 7:7; 4Q196 18:5; 4Q202 1 3:14 (1 En. 9:4); 4Q204 1 6:11 (1 En. 14:2); 4Q246 1 1:9; 1 2:7; 4Q542 1 i 1:1; 11Q10 22:6 (Job 33:12); in the animal allegory: 4Q205 2 2:29 (1 En. 89:30).
31. *KAI* 216.10; 222 B 7; Dnl. 2:10; Ezr. 4:10; 5:11.
32. *TADAE* C1.1:60.
33. *TADAE* A4.7:18; 11Q18 14 2:5; → *khn.*

of the prince.[34] In the empires, it was used for "commander"[35] or in the construct in a compound expression for various functions such as in Elephantine especially the *rb ḥyl'*[36] and others,[37] which continued in later tradition.[38] Regarding the honorific "rabbi," cf. *ATTM*, 690; 2, 479.

III. Noun "Leader." Alongside the substantival *rb*, the derived noun *rbn* refers to "great one, leader." It occurs in *TADAE* B4.3:11, probably already an Imperial Aramaic text, but in a corrupt context, in the court tales of Daniel of those surrounding the king who accompany him at official functions (Dnl. 4:33; 6:18) and debaucheries (5:1f.,3,9f.,23), and similarly at Qumran,[39] even for the leader of the fallen angels;[40] moreover as an honorific like ραββουνι "master" (Mk. 10:51; Jn. 20:16).[41]

IV. Number "Ten Thousand." The number *rbw* /rebbō/ "ten thousand" appears in older Aramaic only in Dnl. 7:10 in the construct relation *rbw rbwn* "then thousand times ten thousand = one hundred million," a combination of the highest number word with multiplication as the highest mathematical operation that could be expressed in everyday language, in reference to the incomprehensible mass of human beings who stand before the throne of the Ancient of Days at the Last Judgment, much like T. S. Eliot's "I had not thought death had undone so many." The connection with *'lp 'lpym*[42] "a thousand times a thousand" in the same verse accords with the old stylistic technique of number parallelism.[43] Scholars usually attribute the form /rebbō/ instead of */rebbā/, to be expected for a *qillāt*-form, to Canaanite influence;[44] the plural *rebbᵉwān*[45] with */-āt/ is Aramaic. Even the Greek number words only go as high as μύριοι.

V. Verb.

1. G-stem "to Grow." In the G-stem, the verb *rbī* functions as an intransitive for "to grow" and appears with either a concrete or an abstract subject: figuratively of a small braggart[46] or of ascent to the court,[47] literally of the maturation of a human being (l. 18) and of the growth of a tree (Dnl. 4:8,17,19), of hair and fingernails, or along with *ṣmḥ* "to

34. → *mlk*; *KAI* 222 A 39.41; 223 A 7; B 3; C 15f.; so still 1QapGen 19:24; 4Q244 1-3:1; 11Q10 14:3 (Job 29:9).

35. *TADAE* C2.1 col. IV 4; 59; D22.25, 1; 22.27:1.

36. → *ḥyl*; other instances: *TADAE* A5.2:7; B2.9:5; 2.10:2,4; 3.9:3; 5.1:3.

37. See *TADAE* A5.5:7; B8.5a:8.

38. 4Q196 2:7 (Tob. 1:22): cupbearer; for Palmyra see H. Gzella, "Die Palmyrener in der griechisch-römischen Welt," *KLIO* 87 (2005) 450.

39. 4Q550 5+5a:3.

40. 4Q201 1 3:13 par. 4Q202 1 2:17; 4Q202 2:2 (1 En. 6:8; 7:1).

41. With a darkening of the /ā/ before /n/, *ATTM*, 137,144,690.

42. With the Hebrew pl. ending in MT.

43. Since numbers have no synonyms, the next-highest number word is employed instead.

44. *BLA*, §57e''''; *ATTM*, 691.

45. < /rebbawān/, cf. the *Q*.

46. *TADAE* C1.1:162.

47. L. 2; cf. the D-stem in Dnl. 2:48, → V.2.

sprout" and *rḥš* "to creep" for organic life in general.[48] In commercial contexts, it designates the growth of capital[49] through interest.[50] Finally, the contexts of *TADAE* A4.5:1,12; 1QapGen 15:19; 4Q545 7:1; 4Q561 3:4 and 6Q8 3:1 are unclear.

2. D-stem "to Make Great." The factitive D-stem "to make great" appears only rarely in older Aramaic. In *TADAE* C1.1:25 it denotes "to rear," as it also did later,[51] while 11Q10 32:3 (Job 39:4) employs the C-stem *qšš* for this purpose. Dnl. 2:48 utilizes the verb in connection to Daniel's promotion by the king, which is otherwise expressed by means of "to install in," however;[52] cf. the G-stem in *TADAE* C1.1:2 (→ V.1).

VI. Noun "Grandeur." Because of the vowel ending, the feminine *rbw* /rabū/ "size" belongs with the verb *rbī*, but occurs mostly in religious language and denotes royal or divine majesty. The first occurrences appear in Biblical Aramaic, where the grandeur of the world tree represents Nebuchadnezzar's kingdom (Dnl. 4:19,33), but the word also explicitly designates royal power (5:18f.) and the surpassing majesty of the kingdom of God (7:27). It also refers to the majesty of God at Qumran[53] or to the wisdom associated with God.[54] In 11Q10 9: 4; 16:4 (Job 25:2; 30:15) it translates *pḥd* and *ndybh*, respectively.

VII. Noun "Officer." A stylistic peculiarity of the narrative framework of Aḥiqar is the use of the noun *rbh* /rabǣ/,[55] which occurs otherwise only in fragmentary context in *WDSP* 7:7. Most associate it with the Akkadian *rabû* and translate it "officer."[56]

Gzella

48. 4Q210 1 2:3 (1 En. 76:4).

49. → *r'š*.

50. Neo-Assyrian: *AssU* 5:4; 6:3 and 8:4 in V. Hug, *Altaramäische Grammatik der Texte des 7. und 6. Jh.s v. Chr. HSAO* 4 (2003), 24f.; partially emended *THU* 1:7 and 26; A. Lemaire, *Nouvelles tablettes araméennes* (Geneva, 2001), nos. 12:4; 13:3; 15:3; 34*:4; Imperial Aramaic from Elephantine: *TADAE* B3. 1:4,6; 4.2:2,5,9; 4.7:2; contracts from the Dead Sea: nV 1:17; 42:9 in *ATTM* 2; sometimes supplemented with *b-* "with" for the interest or *'l* "in addition to."

51. *DJPA*, 514a; *DJBA*, 1056b; *LexSyr*, 707f.

52. Among others, with → *qūm* in the C-stem.

53. 1QapGen 2:4; 4Q196 17 2:4. 7; 18:15 (Tob. 13:8f.; 14:2); 4Q203 9:6; 4Q212 1 4:18 (1 En. 91:13); 4Q242 1-3:5.

54. 4Q213 1 1:12.

55. *TADAE* C1.1:33,38,41,54,56,58f.

56. Cf. *DNSI*, 1054.

רגל *rgl* /regl/; **שק** *šq* /šāq/; **ירך** *yrk* /yarek/; **מעין** *m'yn* /me'ayn/

I. Etymology and Lexical Field. II. General Usage. III. Figurative Usage.

I. Etymology and Lexical Field. The feminine primary noun *rgl* /regl/ "foot"[1] designates the foot of humans and animals including the lower leg in Aramaic just as in other Semitic languages. In analogy to the hand, *kp* /kapp/ serves to denote the sole of the foot, occasionally given added precision as *kp rgl* "sole of the foot,"[2] and *'ṣb'* the "toe" or the "finger" of the hand.[3] The upper leg, of animals the haunch,[4] is the *yrk* /yarek/,[5] as in Dnl. 2:32 or 4Q534 1 1:3. The Aramaic word for the whole leg, including the thigh and the lower leg, but distinct from the foot, is *šq* /šāq/,[6] for the knee, *brk* /berk/.[7] All three terms refer to paired body parts and are, consequently, like *rgl*, feminine in gender. Connected to the legs above are the "stomach," *m'yn* /me'ayn/ > /me'ēn/,[8] and the "loins, hips," designated with the plural of → *ḥrṣ*. "Lame" is *ḥgyr* /ḥagīr/,[9] from *ḥgr* "to hinder, to lame,"[10] and "shoe" (usually a "sandal") is *ś'n* /śe'n/ > /śēn/[11] or *mś'n* /maś'ān/.[12]

In addition to the literal use for the body part, *rgl* can also appear figuratively for "times" in multiplicative terms and, less often, for "table leg"; additional idiomatic expressions also occur (→ III). In contrast, the masculine plural *špwlyn* /šepōlīn/ denotes the foot of a mountain.[13]

II. General Usage. The first Aramaic instances of *rgl* "foot" occur in the wisdom maxims of Aḥiqar, which still belong linguistically to later Old Aramaic. Here, the lifting[14]

J. Brümmer, "*rgl*," *ThWQ*, III, 609-13; J. A. Fitzmyer, *The Genesis Apocryphon of Qumran Cave 1 (1Q20). BietOr* 18B (³2004); G.-W. Nebe, "Das Lied von Sarais Schönheit in 1Q20 = Genesis-Apokryphon XX, 2-8 und die Anfänge der aramäischen Poesie," in *Der Christliche Orient und seine Umwelt. FS J. Tubach* (Wiesbaden, 2007), 59-86; F.-J. Stendebach, "רֶגֶל *regel*," *TDOT*, XIII, 309-24.

1. From the middle of the first millennium B.C.E., altered to /regəl/ and later in West Aramaic mutated to a *qatl*-form, *ATTM*, 112-15,141 with n. 2.
2. 4Q561 1 1:9; → *yd* II.1.
3. → *yd* II.2.
4. 4Q214 2:6.
5. Arisen from an older */warek/.
6. Dnl. 2:33; 1QapGen 20:6; 4Q561 2:3.
7. → *brk* V.
8. Masc. pl.; Dnl. 2:32; 1QapGen 6:1 (par. to *kwr* /kūr/, here for "womb"); 4Q197 4 1:9 (Tob. 6:4).
9. 11Q10 14:10 (Job 29:15).
10. *ATTM*, 572.
11. *TADAE* C1.1:205, gender unclear.
12. 1QapGen 22:21, masc.; cf. Fitzmyer, 252.
13. Cf. 1QapGen 12:8 and for the form, *ATTM*, 2, 498.
14. → *nśī*.

and placing[15] of one's own feet represents an everyday accomplishment which is, nonetheless, not in the hand of a human being;[16] further, a fetter (*'rḥh*)[17] on the feet represents discipline through strict instruction;[18] *rgl* appears once in an unclear context.[19] The context of *TADAE* D3.27:1,3,4,5 is also fragmentary; on B8.4:5; 8.6:10 (blows to the sole of the feet as punishment) → *yd* II.1.

In Daniel and several times at Qumran, the word is part of always rather extensive descriptions of a person or, at least, a human-like body. In reference to the "colossus on clay" feet, *rgl* (Dnl. 2:33f.,41f.) together with *m'yn* "stomach" (2:32), *yrk* "thigh" (2:32), and *šq* "leg" (2:33) belong to an anatomically detailed vision, depicted from the head down, of a gigantic statue of various metals of diminishing value,[20] while accenting its human form. It symbolizes four sequential empires; the foot "partly of iron, partly of clay" (*minhēn dī parzœl ūminhēn dī ḥ^a^sap̄*, 2:33), attached to iron legs, stands for Hellenistic dominion.[21] Just as iron and clay do not mix, this rule is also "divided."[22]

Contrariwise, feet appear in the equally apocalyptic vision of the four animals in Dnl. 7 once in relation to the first being standing "on its feet like a human" and provided with a human heart, which symbolizes a human dominion (7:4), and again in reference to the fourth, most terrible monster that "tramples [*rps*] [everything] with its feet" (7:19).

Furthermore, Qumran offers two descriptions of the physiques of extraordinary people that mention their feet in the same context as thighs (*yrk*) and legs (*šq*): the song praising the all-outshining Sarah with her beautiful feet (*špyryn*)[23] and the ominous description of Noah, the elect of God, blessed both with outstanding intellectual gifts and an extraordinary external appearance.[24]

Furthermore, feet are mentioned in the account of Tobias at the river[25] and the regulations concerning priestly law.[26] 11Q10 also has *rgl* in the literal sense for the homonymous Hebrew cognate: 12:1 (the only word in the line, but also in the Heb. text); 14:10; 22:5 (Job 28:4; 29:15; 33:11). In a fragmentary context, it appears alongside "hands" in 4Q206 4 1:12 (1 En. 88:3).

III. Figurative Usage. Of the figurative uses of *rgl*, Imperial Aramaic already attests "times."[27] The usage "table leg" is known from Qumran.[28] Finally, the nuance of *rgl* "(pil-

15. → *nḥt* in the C-stem.
16. *TADAE* C1.1:170f.; on form and context → *nḥt* III.
17. For the discussion about this word, see the references in M. Weigl, *Die aramäische Achikar-Sprüche aus Elephantine und die alttestamentliche Weisheitsliteratur*. *BZAW* 399 (2010), 450.
18. *TADAE* C1.1:175.
19. *TADAE* C1.1:205; cf. *DNSI*, 737, s.v. *n'l*.
20. → *ṣlm* III.
21. → *dhb* II.
22. → *plg* II.
23. → *špr*; 1QapGen 20:5, see Fitzmyer, 195f. and esp. Nebe.
24. 4Q561 1 1:9f.
25. 4Q197 4 1:7 (Tob. 6:2).
26. 4Q214 2:2; cleansing the hands and feet of sacrificial blood.
27. In the plural with a preceding number: *TADAE* C2.1:11; Segal, 28b.4. *TADAE* A4.7:16 par. 4.8:15 is unclear (→ *npq*).
28. 11Q18 8:1; 13:1f.

grimage) festival" better attested later,[29] may also already be present in 1QapGen 12:14. In this improper use, agreement with *qdmy'*[30] "the first"[31] demonstrates it to be masculine.

Gzella

29. Cf. *DJPA*, 516a.
30. → *qdm* III.2.
31. So correctly read by *DSSStE*, 34f.; *ATTM.E*, 68; cf. Fitzmyer, 161f.

רגשׁ *rgš*

I. Etymology and Lexical Field. II. G-stem "to Be Angry." III. C-stem "to Pressure, to Oversee."

I. Etymology and Lexical Field. The rather infrequent Aramaic verbal root *rgš*, in the G-stem "to tremble," in the C-stem "to pressure" or "to oversee," presumably has a cognate in the Arabic *rağasa* "to thunder."[1] Hebrew examples[2] are borrowed from Aramaic,[3] especially since other Semitic languages of Syria-Palestine exhibit no connections. Yet, one cannot exclude the possibility that poetic diction preserves original archaisms. Moreover, one cannot determine the moment of a possible borrowing. Aramaic attests the word since the Achaemenid period and it remains productive in both West and East Aramaic. Along with the C-stem "to notice,"[4] East Aramaic also knows the G-stem "to quiver" (along with "to notice").[5]

II. G-stem "to Be Angry." The sole older instance of the G-stem appears in the narrative framework of Aḥiqar, probably in reference to the king's expected reaction to Nadin's intrigue against Aḥiqar, although between lacunae.[6] To be sure, the customary translation of the imperfect *yrgš* "to be angry"[7] suits the context,[8] but later evidence supports the general nuance "to tremble" (in anger or for some other reason).

T. Hansberger, "*rgš*," *ThWQ*, III, 614f.

1. *LexSyr*, 713a; *GesB*[18], 1534.
2. G-stem in Ps. 2:1; the *qitl*-noun /regš/ "unrest," first attested in late Aramaic, in Ps. 55:15 and its fem. counterpart in 64:3.
3. M. Wagner, *Die lexikalischen und grammatikalischen Aramaismen im alttestamentlichen Hebräisch. BZAW* 96 (1966), 105.
4. *DJPA*, 516b.
5. *DJBA*, 1059f.; *LexSyr*, 713; *MdD*, 425.
6. *TADAE* C1.1:29.
7. *ATTM*, 692; *DNSI*, 1061.
8. Thus, not a phonetic spelling of the C-stem with loss of the intervocalic /-h-/.

III. C-stem "to Pressure, to Oversee." Daniel 6 employs *rgš* three times in the C-stem, in each case supplemented with *'l* and the person involved. It occurs twice with the connotation "to pressure" of the influence that Daniel's enemies at court exert on the king to disable their successful competitor through intrigue (Dnl. 6:7,16), once in the context of their surveillance of Daniel (6:12). These differing contexts of usage led, since antiquity, to quite differing definitions.[9] The Hebrew occurrences point to a connotation "unrest," " uproar," and thus "to repair somewhere in agitation,[10] later Aramaic diction points to a basic meaning "to feel," which, in the sense of "to reconnoiter" includes not only the surveillance of Daniel according to 6:12,[11] but, with a something other than normal nuance, could also suit 6:7,16: then the court officials would be seeking to influence the king, not with impertinence but with subtle shrewdness. If one attempts, however, to link this with the meaning of the G-stem and the noun (→ I), all three instances of the C-stem can best be subsumed under the shading "to show unrest, to be active" as the causative counterpart of the G-stem "to be unrestful."[12] The verb stands in complete isolation in 1QapGen 4:1.

Gzella

9. J. A. Montgomery, *The Book of Daniel. ICC* (1927), 272f., and J. J. Collins, *Daniel. Herm* (1993), 265f.; the overview in D. Helms, *Konfliktfelder der Diaspora und die Löwengrube. BZAW* 446 (2014), 207 n. 20 has extensive information concerning the paths taken, true and false.

10. So *GesB*[18], 1534.

11. Cf. *ATTM*, 692: "to surveil, not allow out of sight."

12. So in principle also *ATTM*, 692.

רוח *rwḥ* /rūḥ/

I. Etymology. II. "Time to Breathe," "Space," "to Make Wide." III. "Breath." IV. "Breeze," "Wind." V. "Soul." VI. "Evil Spirit, Demon." VII. "Spirit of God."

I. Etymology. The ambiguous root *rūḥ* has a broad spectrum of different connotations, all of which have arisen from the quite general sense "breath," "to breathe." The spatial dimension leads to the meaning "to move out," "to expand." On one hand, physical experience gives rise to the nuances "breeze," "time to breathe," "breathing room," and thence the broader connotations "space," "to be/become broad," "respite,"

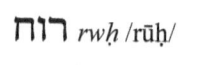

R. Albertz and C. Westermann, "רוּחַ *rûaḥ* spirit," *TLOT*, 1202-20; B. Becking, "A Divine Spirit Is in You," in A. S. van der Woude, ed., *The Book of Daniel in the Light of New Findings. BETL* 106 (1993), 515-19; D. Bloch, "The Prophet of the Spirit," *JETS* 32 (1989) 27-49; J. H. Charlesworth, "rest." On the other hand, the meaning "breath of life" leads to "soul," extends further to "spirit" and even "demon." All of these connotations, although quite different, occur in Aramaic. Admittedly, lexicographers link them to two roots *rūḥ* I and *rūḥ* II,[1] but an appropriate understanding of their cultural background requires the assumption of a single, monosyllabic root. The root is fundamentally a feminine, rarely a masculine in Syriac, while it is masculine or feminine in the astronomical book of Enoch and thus gender-indifferent.[2] The feminine gender applies not only to the grammatical category, but includes the concept, as the Syriac Ode of Solomon 19 demonstrates: "the Holy Spirit opens his/her womb" (l. 4).

II. "Time to Breathe," "Space," "to Make Wide." Several Palmyrene inscriptions employ the noun *rwḥ* in the sense of "time to breathe, pause to breathe." A dedicatory inscription[3] recalls the lack thereof during a long illness, while two others thank God who heard the prayer and granted a "time to breathe."[4] The same connotation may occur in the sayings of Aḥiqar,[5] but there *ywm rwḥ* more likely means "windy day."[6] A very beautifully prepared Palmyrene inscription, which documents an agreement determining the rights of use of graves in the hypogaeum of Malku, first employs the noun *rwḥ'* in the sense of "space, place,"[7] further the infinitive of the C-stem *mrḥ* (l. 9) and the imperfect of the C-stem (l. 11) with the connotation "to make wide."

"Les Odes de Solomon et les manuscrits de la Mer Morte," *RB* 77 (1970) 522-49, esp. 541-43; E. G. Dafni, "Rwḥ šqr und falsche Prophetie in I Reg 22," *ZAW* 112 (2000) 365-85, esp. 378-81; J. Ebach, "Ezechiels Auferstehungsvision (Ezk. 37)," *BiKi* 55 (2000) 120-24; E. Gass, "Genus und Semantik am Beispiel von 'theologischem' *rūḥ*," *BN* 109 (2001) 45-55; F. O. Hvidberg-Hansen, *The Palmyrene Inscriptions* (Copenhagen, 1998), esp. no. 131; A. Lange, H. Lichtenberger, and K. F. D. Römheld, eds., *Die Dämonen* (Tübingen, 2003); J. R. Levison, *Filled with the Spirit* (Grand Rapids, 2009); W. Ma, "The Spirit (*ruah*) of God in Isaiah," *AsJT* 3 (1989) 582-96; idem, *Until the Spirit Comes. JSOTSup* 271 (1999); J. T. Milik, *The Books of Enoch* (Oxford, 1976); idem, *Dédicaces faites par des dieux (Palmyre, Hatra, Tyr) et des thiases sémitiques à l'époque romaine. BAH* 92 (1972); J. Naveh, "A Nabatean Incantation Text," *IEJ* 29 (1979) 111-19, tablet 14; É. Puech, "L'Esprit Saint à Qumran," *SBFLA* 49 (1999) 283-98; H. Graf Reventlov, "Ein immer wieder aktuelles Thema," *TRev* 89 (1993) 454-58; H. Schüngel-Straumann, *Rûaḥ bewegt die Welt. SBS* 151 (1992); idem, "*Rûaḥ* und Gender-Frage am Beispiel der Visionen beim Propheten Ezechiel," in B. Becking and M. Dijkstra, eds., *On Reading Prophetic Texts. BibInt* 18 (1996), 201-16; A. E. Sekki, *The Meaning of* ruaḥ *at Qumran. SBLDS* 110 (1989); S. Tengström and H.-J. Fabry, "רוּחַ *rûaḥ*," *TDOT*, XIII, 365-402; E. J. C. Tigchelaar, "*rwḥ*," *ThWQ*, III, 618-32; W. von Soden, "Der Genuswechsel bei *rûaḥ* und das grammatische Geschlecht in den semitischen Sprachen," *ZAH* 5 (1992) 57-63; M. Witte, "Wie Simson in den Kanon kam," *ZAW* 112 (2000) 526-49, esp. 530f., 547.

1. See, e.g., *GesB*[18], 1224f.: *rūḥ* I "to be broad," *rūḥ* II "to breathe."
2. Milik, *Books of Enoch*, 287,290.
3. *PAT* 0404.5; cf. Milik, *Dédicaces faites par des dieux*, 181f.
4. *PAT* 0446.5; 1911.8.
5. *TADAE* C1.1:104.
6. So *TADAE* C, p. 38; I. Kottsieper, *Die Sprache der Ahiqarsprüche. BZAW* 194 (1990), 17.
7. *PAT* 1624.8; see Hvidberg-Hansen.

III. "Breath." The meaning "breath" appears in a messianic text from Qumran[8] in which the author interestingly mentions the puff of God's breath. A few modern translations of these passages do not take this into account because they understand *mwldh* there as "birth" or "birthday." Now *mwldh* is doubtlessly the passive participle of the C-stem /mōlad/ with the meaning "begotten." In other words, one must translate the clause *kdy bḥyr 'lh' hw' mwldh wrwḥ nšmwhy*: "because God chose him, begot him, and the puff of his breath."[9] The fragment alludes to Ps. 2:7 and is certainly messianic. It also makes clear how the word *rwḥ* could become "spirit of God," the Holy Spirit (→ VII). A synonymous expression with reference to human beings occurs in the treaties of state from Sefire, where *rwḥ 'pwh*[10] means the "breath" or the "snorting of his nose" in a hostile sense.[11] On the broader lexical field → *nšm*; on "smell" → *ryḥ*.

IV. "Breeze," "Wind." The use of *rwḥ* with the meaning "breeze, wind" appears in the sayings of Aḥiqar (→ II),[12] in 11Q10,[13] in the Targums, e.g., Targum Jonathan of Ezk. 1:3f. and Am. 1:14, and in Dnl. 2:35 and 7:2, which mention the "four winds of heaven." These winds also play a role in the astronomical book of Enoch (1 En. 76) and serve to designate the four cardinal directions.[14] In Dnl. 7:2 they presumably represent the Ptolemies, the Macedonians, Pergamon, and the Seleucids.

V. "Soul." In Dnl. 5:12,20; 7:15; 1QapGen 2:13,17; 11Q10 3:4; 34:6,8 (Job 20:3; 40:10,12) *rwḥ* means "soul." Yet "soul" should not be understood in analogy to the Platonic or Aristotelian use of ψυχή; instead, it involves an inner force from which proceed the human feelings, intentions, etc. Similarly, the word in this sense can denote the "soul" of a decedent.[15] This nuance already appears in a proto-Canaanite inscription from Wadi el-Ḥōl in Egypt.[16]

VI. "Evil Spirit, Demon." The meaning "demon" is rather well attested. It appears in 1QapGen 20:16,20,26,28,29 and in 11Q10 2:6 (Job 19:17) where *rwḥ hmkt l'ntty* must mean: "a spirit has possessed my wife." Additional more precise designations appear with the use for illness-demons, such as *rwḥ mkdš* [for *mktš*] "spirit of the plague"[17] or *rwḥ šḥlny'* "ulcer-causing spirit."[18] "Spirit of error," [*rwḥ*]*y ṭ'wt'*, may occur in 1Q21 31:1; the more general concept of an "evil spirit," *rwḥ b'yš'/h*, occurs in 1QapGen 20:16f. and 4Q538 1-2:4, "spirit

8. 4Q534 1 1:10.
9. E. Lipiński, "The Qumran Issue of the Cracow 'Studia Judaica,'" *Qumran Chronicle* 16 (2008) 67.
10. *KAI* 224.2.
11. For a discussion → *'np* II.1.
12. *TADAE* C1.1:104.
13. 11Q10 13:6; 16:4; 31:2; 36:2 (Job 28:25; 30:15; 38:24; 41:8).
14. 1QapGen 22:8; 11Q10 33:8 (Job 39:26).
15. 4Q206 1 22:3f. (1 En. 22:5f.).
16. E. Lipiński, "Émergence et diffusion des écritures alphabétiques," *Rocznik Orientalistyczny* 63/2 (2010) 71-126, esp. 92f.
17. 1QapGen 20:16.
18. 1QapGen 20:26.

of evil," *rwḥ b'yšt'*, in 1QapGen 20:28f.[19] A Nabatean incantation text, found about ten kilometers from Beersheba and dated to the period around 100 B.C.E., bans a spirit, apparently a kind of "cupid," that is supposed to be expelled by the smell of burned henna.[20] The first word on the photo clearly reads *'ġy*, a C-stem imperative of the Arabic verb *ġawā*: "Expel the spirit [*'aġiyy rūḥā*], O henna-smoke!" (l. 1), "Unbind, unbind a man, disenchant him from a woman!" (l. 8). The client of the incantation priest was presumably another woman, perhaps the wife of the man in question. The word *rwḥ'* later occurs often in Jewish, Syriac, and Mandean spells.[21] An Akkadian derivative *ruḫu*[22] designates a kind of "witchcraft" but should not be directly associated with the Aramaic connotation of *rwḥ* "(evil) spirit."

VII. "Spirit of God." *rûaḥ 'ᵉlāhīn qaddīšīn* in Dnl. 4:5,6,15; 5:11f. 14; 6,4 does not refer to a spiritual being, but to an inner power that God bestowed ("inspired") on Daniel for certain circumstances. Theodotion correctly translated the plural as a singular πνεῦμα Θεοῦ Ἁγίου because Aramaic could utilize the plural of majesty with the name "God,"[23] as do Hebrew, Phoenician, Assyrian, and Babylonian.[24] This connotation does not appear, however, in Galilean targumic texts of the book of Exodus which add the attributive "holy" to *rwḥh*,[25] nor in the Syriac Odes of Solomon 6:7; 11:2; 14:8; 19:2,4; 23:22 (first century C.E.). Some of these poetic pieces have a Jewish Christian background, like Ode 11:2 which attributes the circumcision of the heart to God's Holy Spirit.

Lipiński

19. See H. Gzella, *ThWQ*, I, 345.
20. Naveh.
21. Cf. *ATTM*, 693 and 2, 480f. for a few examples.
22. *CAD*, XIV, 408; *AHw*, II, 993b.
23. *TADAE* C1.1:126.
24. Cf. E. Lipiński, *Semitic Languages. OLA* 80 (²2001), §34.2; 50.24.
25. *ATTM*, 333, l. 1.[7s,8u]: *dqdšh*.

רז *rz* /rāz/

I. Etymology. II. Biblical Aramaic. III. Qumran and Synagogue Inscriptions. IV. East Aramaic and Magical Texts.

C. A. Ciancaglini, *Iranian Loanwords in Syriac* (Wiesbaden, 2008); J. A. Fitzmyer, *The Genesis Apocryphon of Qumran Cave 1 (1Q20). BietOr* 18B (³2004); W. Hinz, *Altiranisches Sprachgut der Nebenüberlieferungen. GÖF* III/3 (1975); A. Lange, "*rz*," *ThWQ*, III, 648-57; T. Nöldeke, *Compendious Syriac Grammar*, trans. James A. Crichton (Winona Lake, IN, 2001); A. Schoors, "The Language of the Qumran Sapiental Works," in C. Hempel, ed., *The Wisdom Texts from Qumran. BETL* 159 (2002), 61-95; S. Telegdi, "Essai sur la phonétique des emprunts iraniens en araméen talmudique," *JA* 226 (1935) 177-256.

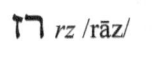

I. Etymology. The masculine noun *rz* /rāz/ is a Persian loanword, Old Persian */rāza-/,[1] Avestic /razah-/ "loneliness, remoteness,"[2] Middle and Neo-Persian *rāz* "secret," probably not yet borrowed in Achaemenid times, but only later, primarily in the Jewish realm, but also in Syriac and Mandean. The earliest instances are those from Biblical and Qumran Aramaic; it probably arrived in Hebrew via Aramaic, but not in Biblical Hebrew; the Hebrew Sirach and Qumran Hebrew are commonly considered the earliest instances (from ca. second century B.C.E.); it occurs twice in Sirach: in the general maxim concerning behavior in relation to a stranger Sir. 8:18[3] and in relation to an enemy Sir. 12:11 "do <not?> act toward him like someone who reveals something secret."[4] Rabbinical Hebrew then borrowed it from Jewish Aramaic (→ III). In Syriac, the form also appears in writing as *ʾrzʾ*, which points to a preposed vowel;[5] the pointing provides the corresponding *ʾ* with a *linea occultans*.[6] The Jewish amulet ooKA 3:3[7] has *bryz pryš* or *brwz prwš* "isolated secret/most secret secret" or "entirely in secret" with an ablaut or through assimilation to *prwš* (if the reading is correct).

II. Biblical Aramaic. Biblical Aramaic attests the noun in the singular and the plural.[8] It occurs only in the Aramaic Daniel and there only in the account of Nebuchadnezzar's first dream in Dnl. 2 and once in the account of the second in Dnl. 4. The word *rz* refers to dream contents and dream interpretation.[9] That concealed in the dream is a secret and God is the revealer of secrets. Only Daniel, gifted with it by God, has the knowledge and the capability to interpret dreams. Thus, *rz* is linked with → *ḥwī* "to announce" (2:27) and mostly with → *glī* I "to disclose, to reveal" (Dnl. 2:19,28,29,30,47). LXX has μυστήριον/μυστήρια (κρυπτά) for *rz(yn)*. In a concept synonymous with *rz*, and with *glī*, one finds *ʿmyqtʾ* "secrets"[10] and *mstrtʾ* "hidden things" (2:22).[11] The absolute state occurs in relation to Daniel's capacities for solving mysteries (4:6), the determined state for a specific mystery (i.e., the king's dream: 2:18f.,30,47), also as the object of a verb (2:27, *ḥwī*). The absolute plural occurs in reference to the description of God as revealer of secrets (2:28,47), as does the determined plural (2:29, as the object of *glī*). Regarding the lexical field of wisdom → *ḥkm* III.2; *ydʿ* III.2; *pšr* III.

III. Qumran and Synagogue Inscriptions. The word *rz* belongs among the central terms of Jewish apocalyptic times and literature. In the Aramaic from Qumran, it occurs

1. Hinz, 203.
2. Telegdi, 254f. no. 125.
3. LXX κρυπτόν.
4. Contra LXX.
5. Either already in the borrowed form or as an internal development in Syriac.
6. Nöldeke, 37 §51 and recently Ciancaglini, 252f.
7. *ATTM.E*, 260f.
8. As also, e.g., in Qumran Hebrew.
9. → *ḥlm*.
10. → *ʿmq*.
11. → *str*.

less than in Hebrew;[12] it is a term used primarily in the literary circles of Enoch, Noah, and the priests. Enoch, Noah, and Abraham have a special nearness to God's world and participate in heavenly knowledge. The Enoch traditions may reach back to Achaemenid times. Here *rz* concerns the question of who begot Noah, the projection of events in visions and dreams, knowledge of the heavenly books, and the revelations of the evil angels (Gen. 6). Sections of Enoch, preserved not in Aramaic, but Greek and Ethiopic, are also thematically related (such as 1 En. 9:6; 10:7; 16:3).

It occurs adverbially in the absolute state with *b-* "secretly" as a supplement of → *mll*[13] and in the construct state with a more precise identification of the pertinent mystery,[14] partly in an unclear context.[15] In the determined state, it refers to a previously mentioned mystery.[16] The plural in the absolute state appears in association with the disclosure of secrets by higher beings,[17] as does the construct state with additional definition[18] and the determined state.[19]

Similar uses appear in the Targums. Remarkably, the betrayal (*glī*) of secrets, i.e., perhaps an arcane discipline,[20] is a shameful act according to the synagogue inscription yyEN 3:4.[21]

IV. East Aramaic and Magical Texts. In Syriac (→ I), *rz* denotes "secret, mystery, symbol, sacrament," also in *brāz(ā)* "secret, mystical." It forms many derivates, including a verb, in the G-stem "to do secretly," and also appears in other stems.[22] In Mandean, it is a central profane and religious term for everything invisible, concealed,[23] also as an adverb *braz* "secretly, privately" and a denominal verb "to do secretly." Furthermore, *rz* "secret, secret magic" belongs to the terminology of magical texts, including Jewish ones.[24]

Nebe

---

12. See Lange, 651-57.

13. 1QapGen 5:25; so probably correctly *DSSStE*, 30 contra Fitzmyer, 75, cf. H. Gzella, *ThWQ*, II, 702.

14. 1QapGen 1:2, presumably of the corruption of humanity before the flood; 4Q545 4:16 "his deeds," as the object of → *ḥwī*.

15. 4Q546 12:4.

16. 1QapGen 5:21, with *ḥwī*; 6:12, with *ṭmr* "to conceal"; context is unclear in 1:3 and, as subject of → *slq* "to ascend," 4Q536 2 1:12.

17. The unfaithful angels who betray their secrets to corrupt humankind: 4Q201 1 4:4f. par. 4Q202 1 3:5 (1 En. 8:3); similarly Noah: 4Q536 2 1:8.

18. Noah knows the secrets of the living: 4Q534 1 1:8; the context is unclear in 4Q536 2 1:9.

19. "All mysteries" in Enoch's prayer concerning God: 4Q203 9:3; Enoch's explanation of his knowledge: 4Q204 5 2:26f. (1 En. 106:19), cf. 1 En. 103:2; 104:12.

20. M. Weinfeld, "*ḥswr šl qhylt ʿyn-gdy*," *Tarbiz* 51 (1981) 125-30 with VIII.

21. *ATTM*, 364.

22. *LexSyr*, 722f.

23. *MdD*, 420.

24. J. Naveh and S. Shaked, *Amulets and Magic Bowls* (Jerusalem, ²1987), no. A3:3 (ooKA 3:3, *ATTM.E*, 260f.); B1:3; B6:1f.; cf. *DJBA*, 1067f.

רחם *rḥm*; רחם *rḥm* /rāḥem/; רחים *rḥym* /raḥīm/; רחם *rḥm* /raḥm/; רחמה *rḥmh* /raḥmā/; רחמן *rḥmn* /raḥmān/; חבב *ḥbb*

I. Etymology, Lexical Field, and Constructions. II. Verb. 1. G-stem "to Love." 2. D-stem "to Have Mercy." III. Participles. 1. Active "Friend." 2. Passive "Beloved, Darling." IV. Noun. 1. Singular "Womb." 2. Plural "Mercy." 3. Adverb "Voluntarily." V. Noun "Love." VI. Adjective "Merciful."

I. Etymology, Lexical Field, and Constructions. Aramaic attests forms of the root *rḥm* "to love" since the earliest textual witnesses. They were already widespread as verbal or nominal derivations in the older phases of the language. Thus, the one occurrence of *rḥmyn* "mercy" in Dnl. 2:18 (→ IV.2) is not representative of the actual volume of usage. As a verb "to have mercy, feel compassion"[1] and noun with the apparently old double-meaning "womb, mercy," it occurs in all the chief branches of the Semitic languages. Meanwhile, the frequent usage in Aramaic for "to love, to like" reflects an indigenous semantic development;[2] Hebrew and Ugaritic[3] employ instead the no longer productive root *'hb*.

Otherwise, Aramaic expresses "to love" with the G-, D-, and C-stems of the root *ḥbb* with the corresponding t-passives, which is also very productive in Arabic, as an adjective *ḥbyb* /ḥabbīb/ "beloved" beginning at Qumran[4] and later as a verb[5] that largely replaced the G-stem *rḥm* in Jewish Babylonian. Both stems of *rḥm* continue in use in Jewish Palestinian[6] and in Syriac.[7] In addition to the substantival active and passive participles of the G-stem /rāḥem/ "friend" and /raḥīm/ "beloved," the masculine noun /raḥm/,[8] in the singular "womb," in the plural "mercy," with its feminine counterpart /raḥmā/ "love" and the adjective /raḥmān/ "merciful," Syriac also attests various other nominal forms;[9] the feminine abstract noun /raḥmū/ "love" is common East Semitic.[10] Furthermore, → *ḥnn*, attested with certainty as a verb beginning with the book of Daniel and Qumran, denotes "to have mercy," "to favor."

Resulting from its very broad spectrum of meaning especially in Aramaic, forms of the root *rḥm* there refer to quite different types of affection: the gracious attention of those

---

U. Dahmen and F. Zanella, "*rḥm*," *ThWQ*, III, 662-69; T. Kronholm, "רֶחֶם *reḥem*," *TDOT*, XIII, 454-59; H. Simian-Yofre and U. Dahmen, "רחם *rḥm*," *TDOT*, XIII, 437-54.

1. Like Heb. in the D-stem.
2. Therefore, the one instance of the G-stem "to love" in Ps 18:2, lacking in the parallel 2 S. 22, may be a later Aram. insertion; see E. Jenni, *Das hebräische Pi'el* (Zürich, 1968), 222f.
3. *DUL*³, 30.
4. 4Q204 1 6:16; 4Q539 2-3:2.
5. *DJPA*, 184; *DJBA*, 424f.; *LexSyr*, 208; *MdD*, 129.
6. *DJPA*, 521.
7. *LexSyr*, 723f.
8. Then > /raḥəm/; *ATTM*, 112-15.
9. *DJPA*, 521f. and, esp. *LexSyr*, 723-25.
10. *DJBA*, 1069a; *LexSyr*, 724b; *MdD*, 419.

of higher status such as God or kings; paternal love with the incomparable bond between mother and child as its pure form; the friendship based on fidelity and similar disposition; further the attraction, also with a sensual basis, oriented on the ideal of unity and community; and finally mere fondness. All of these nuances, with various interim stages, already occur in older Aramaic, although distributed across various lexical forms, periods, and genres.

The verb *rḥm* in the G-stem "to love" with its less often attested diminished shading "to like" or "to be grateful" is transitive and usually takes a person as object; the D-stem "to have mercy" can take the supplement *ʿl* "about."

II. Verb.

1. G-stem "to Love." In the G-stem, *rḥm* first appears in the later Old Aramaic of the sayings of Aḥiqar in conjunction with *npš* "self,"[11] but because of the lacunae in the lines, in an unclear context,[12] and then in the Imperial Aramaic framework narrative for the king's favor for his trusted advisor.[13]

The legal terminology of the Imperial Aramaic private contracts, in contrast, employs it in the perfect, weakened to mean "to wish, to want (to choose)" exactly like → *ṣbī* and apparently interchangeable with it for the generalizing expression of the free availability of a transferred property.[14]

In narrative texts from Qumran, the usage for love between husband and wife predominates, as well as for the illegitimate desire of pharaoh who fell in love with Abraham's wife Sarah after he heard a description of her beauty,[15] for the demon's possessive and destructive desire for Tobias's bride,[16] and for the authentic, seminal love of Tobias for this woman predestined for him whom he knew at first only from the angel's account but whose feelings agreed with the divine plan.[17] In the first and third cases (i.e., with humans as subject), the adverb *śgy(ʾ)* "very"[18] supplements it. The same passage from Tobit also employs the verb once for the father's love for his daughter.[19] Other examples are fragmentary.[20]

2. D-stem "to Have Mercy." Pre-Christian Aramaic attests with certainty the D-stem of *rḥm* "to have mercy" only once at Qumran, namely in 1QapGen 11:13 for God's mercy on (*ʿl*) the earth that eradicated evil in Noah's song of praise after the flood.

---

11. → *nšm* III.2.

12. *TADAE* C1.1:153.

13. Ll. 11,51; *ATTM*, 694 assumes for this passage the nuance "to be thankful" for an act of Aḥiqar, as with ἀγαπᾶν in Lk. 7:42,47, but neither passage designates it with the verb itself.

14. *TADAE* B2.3:10,19; 2.7:8; 2.10:9; 3.10:21; on the formulation see H. Gzella, *Tempus, Aspekt und Modalität im Reichsaramäischen. VOK* 48 (2004), 166 with nn. 146f.

15. 1QapGen 20:8.

16. 4Q196 14 1:4 (Tob. 6:15).

17. 4Q197 4 3:1 par. 4Q196 14 2:14 (Tob. 6:18); here along with an expression with *lb* "heart," but the verb ("to cling to?") is lost.

18. → *śgī*.

19. 4Q197 4 2:1 (Tob. 6:12).

20. 1Q21 57:2; 4Q569 1:6.

III. Participles.

1. Active "Friend." The active participle /rāḥem/ "friend" already occurs in early Old Aramaic. The earliest instance comes from a state treaty at Sefire and refers to an amiable king in the context of assuring free exchange of messengers between treaty partners.[21] Here, then, it has the connotation "ally."

The three instances in the somewhat later proverbs of Aḥiqar[22] are all more or less fragmentary, but seem to refer in maxims from community ethics to the social environment, not to close confidants; especially since l. 141 recommends not disclosing[23] something (perhaps secrets; the pertinent word at the beginning of the line is lost) to one's own "friends" and not allowing one's own name to be "light" to them, it must mean "others."

In contrast, the petitionary letter of the Jewish community from Elephantine to the Persian governor of Judea concerning the reconstruction of the Elephantine temple utilizes the expression *rḥmyk* "your friends" parallel to *bʿly ṭbtk* "beneficiaries of your goodness"[24] thus, not in an egalitarian fashion but for well-disposed subjects of state power.

Both nuances appear in the texts from the Dead Sea: absolutely *rḥmyʾ* "the friends" in Jason's grave inscription from Jerusalem[25] for the people who constructed a grave for a deceased private citizen; similarly somewhat later in Palmyra;[26] in Nabonidus's prayer from Qumran between lacunae *rḥmy* "my friends" probably of the closest circle around the king; in 1QapGen 21:21 Abraham's friends; and in 11Q10 38:5 (Job 42:11) *kl rḥmwhy* "all his friends" alongside *kl ʾḥwhy* "all his brothers" for the circle of Job's acquaintances. Meanwhile, language concerning "God's friends" in religious diction presupposes a difference of rank.[27]

Finally, under the influence of Hellenistic titles for rulers, the kings of the Aramaic-speaking states in the Roman east province also employ the epithet /rāḥem ʿammeh/ "loving his people," both in the Nabatean kingdom[28] and in Hatra (/rāḥem māteh/ "loving his country").[29] The model is probably φιλόπατρις or φιλόδημος;[30] on *rḥym* at Palmyra → III.2.

2. Passive "Beloved, Darling." If the active participle of *rḥm* designates an affection (of whatever degree) that proceeds from a self, the passive /raḥīm/ is used for "beloved, darling," and, thus, is oriented on the favorable attitude that proceeds from another. In most cases, it refers to someone favored by God, so already in the earliest instance in a saying of Aḥiqar of one who is *rḥym ʾlhn* "beloved by the gods,"[31] so that they supply

21. *KAI* 224.8.
22. *TADAE* C1.1:112,141,222.
23. → *glī* I.
24. *TADAE* A4.7:24 par. 4.8:23; → *bʿl* II.3.
25. I 1.2:3 in *ATTM*, 328f.
26. *PAT* 0285.4; 0286.5; 0306.6; 0407.7.
27. 4Q196 18:3; 19:2 (Tob. 13:14; 14:7); in the parallel versions: "who love God."
28. E.g., nV 2:2 in *ATTM*, 2, 208-11, dating formula in a treaty.
29. H1039.3.
30. Cf. H. Gzella, "Das Aramäisch in den römischen Ostprovinzen," *BiOr* 63 (2006) 20,37f.
31. *TADAE* C1.1:163.

him with something good to say. It appears with the same nuance in 1QapGen 2:20 of Enoch[32] and perhaps to be emended in 11Q10 27:1.[33]

Meanwhile, a few honorific inscriptions from Palmyra employ the attributive *rḥym* in combination with *mḥwzh* or *mdythwn* on the model of φιλόπατρις (→ III.1) for loyal citizens who have distinguished themselves as benefactors,[34] but may be a passive participle "beloved of his/her city" here since a plene spelling for a short /e/ as in /rāḥem/ would be very unusual in Palmyrene.[35] Thus, Aramaic appears as a means of expressing a self-conscious municipal middle class.[36]

In the address of a papyrus letter from Egypt in late antiquity, *rḥymy* "my beloved" stands beside *ḥbwby* "my darling" and also refers to esteem among people.

IV. Noun. The meaning of the *qatl*-noun *rḥm* /raḥm/ depends on the number, in the very rare singular "womb, lap," in the plural "mercy." Lexicalized in *brḥmn*, the latter can also denote "voluntarily."

1. Singular "Womb." In older Aramaic, *rḥm* "womb" occurs only in 11Q10 30:6 (Job 38:8) from Qumran as the literal rendering of *ræḥæm*, here metaphorically for the primal sea the source of all water in creation;[37] the literal meaning, very old judging by the etymology, first appears in post-Christian times.[38] Elsewhere, *bṭn* /baṭn/ (> /baṭən/) "stomach"[39] appears in the meaning "womb."

2. Plural "Mercy." The plural *rḥmyn* for the "mercy" of God or a high-ranking person occurs since Imperial Aramaic. It first appears in the official letter style in the address in the wish for favor for the addressee: *TADAE* A4.3:2[40] and 4.7:2 par. 4.8:2,[41] both with → *qdm*; apparently similarly, although fragmentary, in the wish for blessing in a graffito.[42]

Since Biblical Aramaic, religious speech attests the word expressly for God's mercy. In Dnl. 2:18 it appears in a request for deliverance from mortal danger. At Qumran this mercy appears in petitionary prayer in general,[43] as an attribute of God, who can

32. Who, according to the widespread tradition, kept company with God and knew his secrets; see the parallels in J. A. Fitzmyer, *The Genesis Apocryphon of Qumran Cave 1 (1Q20). BietOr* 18/B (^{3}2004), 135.
33. *DSSStE*, 1194f., arises from Job 36:7, yet with no parallel in MT.
34. *PAT* 0260.3; 1375.2; cf. Gzella, 27.
35. F. Rosenthal, "Die Sprache der Palmyrenischen Inschriften und ihre Stellung innerhalb des Aramäischen," *MVÄG* 41,1 (1936), 14.
36. N.J. Andrade, *Syrian Identity in the Greco-Roman World* (Cambridge, 2013), 187-204.
37. → *ym* IV.
38. *LexSyr*, 724a.
39. *TADAE* C1.1:216; 11Q10 31:6 (Job 38:29); "stomach": *TADAE* C1.2:18; figuratively "storeroom": A6.2:11; "birth, origin" (also of the father): C1.1:139.
40. Before God.
41. Before the king as the supreme lord of the addressed governor.
42. *TADAE* D22.51:4.
43. 4Q213a 1:15.

grant mercy (→ VI)[44] and also demonstrates it,[45] and as the mercy that continues to fail evildoers.[46]

3. Adverb "Voluntarily." Lexicalized as *brḥmn* "voluntarily, as a gift, gratis," the word appears regularly as an adverbial modifier of → *yhb* "to give" in Imperial Aramaic private documents.[47] In this usage, it seems to be synonymous with the somewhat less common expression *brḥmh* (→ V), which is based on the feminine singular.

V. Noun "Love." Originally, *rḥmh* /raḥmā/ may have been the feminine of /raḥm/ (→ IV),[48] but its meaning in older Aramaic is closer to the plural *rḥmyn*. The nuance "love" evident later[49] may first appear in a formula in a Nabatean marriage contract from the Dead Sea concerning the security of the dowry.[50] If one should, in fact, read *rḥmh* here, the word along with *šwptw* "partnership" refers to marital community.[51] The meaning is weakened to "voluntarily, as a gift" in the Imperial Aramaic legal flourish *brḥmh* or adverbial *rḥmt* with *yhb* "to give" in analogy to the more frequent *brḥmn* (→ IV.3).[52] It appears once in Palmyrene in the combination *mn rḥm'* to serve for "out of grace."[53]

VI. Adjective "Merciful." Finally, the adjective /raḥmān/ "merciful" functions as a predicate of God since the earliest Aramaic sources (→ IV.2) and was borrowed in Arabic. The introductory hymn of the Tell Fekheriye inscription (ca. 850 B.C.E.) employs it as an attribute of Hadad, who shares his plenty with the earth.[54] In the later sayings of Aḥiqar, it could appear substantivally as a title, "the merciful" for El in comparison to the king;[55] in the Imperial Aramaic framework narrative, however, it also denotes a gracious king (l. 53). It continues to appear regularly as a divine predicate at Palmyra.[56]

Gzella

44. 4Q529 1:12.

45. 11Q10 38:3, corresponds to Job 42:10, but without parallel there.

46. 4Q201 1 2:15 (1 En. 5:5). This is probably also the same sense as in the small fragment 4Q557 1:7 (with *mn qdm* "from"), for which see *DSSStE*, 1112f.

47. *TADAE* B2.10:11,14; 3.5:4,12; 3.8:41; 3.10:5,12,17; 3.11:9; 5.2:10 [fragmentary]; 5.5:3; 6.4:7.

48. So *ATTM*, 694.

49. *DJBA*, 1070b; cf. *LexSyr*, 724a.

50. nV 1:28 in *ATTM*, 2, 205-8.

51. So *ATTM*, 2, 207: "love"; contra Y. Yadin et al., *The Documents from the Bar Kokhba Period in the Cave of Letters II* (Jerusalem, 2002), 196, who read *rḥmm* and translate it "gift."

52. *TADAE* B2.4:7; B3.7:14; 3.12:23,26,31; for the old feminine ending /-t/ in adverbial expressions, cf. H. Gzella, "Imperial Aramaic," in S. Weninger, ed., *The Semitic Languages* (Berlin, 2011), 578.

53. *PAT* 0281.4, probably corresponding to εὐνοία in the Greek.

54. *KAI* 309.5.

55. *TADAE* C1.1:91; see I. Kottsieper, *Die Sprache der Aḥiqarsprüche*. *BZAW* 194 (1990), 231, s.v.

56. *PAT* 0368.3; 0379.2; 1430.6; 1558.9; 1571.1.

רחץ *rḥṣ*; רחצן *rḥṣn* /roḥṣān/

I. Etymology. II. Biblical Aramaic. III. Aramaic Texts from the Dead Sea. IV. Targums Onqelos and Jonathan.

I. Etymology. The Aramaic root *rḥṣ*[1] has cognates in Akkadian and Arabic. It is not related, however, to the Hebrew root *rḥṣ* "to wash," which other Semitic languages also attest, and, as evidenced by the correspondence of phonemes, arose from an original **rḥṣ́*. Consequently, it appears in Aramaic, where Imperial Aramaic attests it sporadically and then at Qumran, as *rḥʿ*.[2] Semantically, Aramaic *rḥṣ* relates to the realm of benevolence and confidence.

II. Biblical Aramaic. The root *rḥṣ* first appears in Aramaic in the Biblical Aramaic of Daniel as a perfect verb in the Gt-stem. It occurs here together with the preposition *ʿl* in the meaning "to trust, to depend on someone": *wšyzb lʿbdwhy dy htrḥṣw ʿlwhy* "and he delivered his servants, who place their confidence in him (God)" (Dnl. 3:28).

III. Aramaic Texts from the Dead Sea. In the Aramaic texts from the Dead Sea, *rḥṣ* also occurs as a verb in the Gt-stem with the nuance "to trust, to be confident." In 11Q10 32:10 (Job 39:11), [*h*]*ttrḥṣ b*[*h*] "Do y]ou trust hi[m]?"[3] the preposition *b-* introduces the object; in 11Q10 35:2 (Job 40:23), *ytrḥṣ dy yqblnh ʾgwgʾ* "he trusts that the fissure will receive him,"[4] in contrast, the conjunction *dy* "that" introduces an object clause following the verb.

Finally, the Aramaic texts from Qumran contain the masculine substantive *rḥṣn* /roḥṣān/ "security" derived from the same root: 11Q10 9:5 (Job 25:3) *hʾyty rḥṣn lḥš*[. . .] "Is there security for . . .?";[5] 27:1 (Job 36:7) [*wkl r*]*ḥymwhy lrḥṣn yrmwn* "[and all] his [fr]iends will be raised in security."[6] The meaning of the substantive may suggest a more profound semantic nuance for the root *rḥṣ*, namely the feeling of confidence that arises from the feeling of trust and security with something else.

IV. Targums Onqelos and Jonathan. Targums Onqelos and Jonathan continue the use of the substantive *rḥṣn* "security" and of the verb in the Gt-stem. As already in Dnl. 3:28, the verb takes the preposition *ʿl* (e.g., in 2 S. 22:31: *tqwp hwm lkl dmtrḥṣyn*

G. Dalman, *Grammatik des jüdisch-palästinischen Aramäisch* (Leipzig, ²1905); R. J. Kuty, *Studies in the Syntax of Targum Jonathan to Samuel. ANESSup* 30 (2010).

1. From an original **rḫṣ*.
2. *TADAE* D7.8:7,11; *ATTM*, 694; 2, 482.
3. For Hebrew *bṭḥ*; cf. *DJD*, XXIII (1998), 155.
4. *DJD*, XXIII (1998), 162; the reading of the word after *yqblnh* is disputed.
5. Cf. *DJD*, XXIII (1998), 104.
6. *DJD*, XXIII (1998), 140.

ʿl mymryh "He is power for all who place their confidence in him") or as in 11Q10 the preposition *b-* (e.g., 2 K. 18:5: *bmymrʾ dywy ʾlhʾ dyśrʾl* "he trusted the Memra of the Lord, the God of Israel"). The G-stem also expresses the same meaning "to trust," however; *rḥṣ* belongs to the group of verbs that could easily be employed as passive participles,[7] e.g., 2 S. 22:3: *rḥṣny dʿl mymryh ʾnʾ rḥyṣ bʿdn ʿqʾ* "my security that trusts his Memra in the time of distress." Finally, *rḥṣ* also forms a verb in the C-stem, "to give confidence," e.g., 2 K. 18:30: *wlʾ yrḥyṣ ytkwn ḥzqyh ʿl mymrʾ dywy* "and Hezekiah should not give you confidence in the Memra of the Lord. . .!" Cf. *DJPA,* 522a; *DJBA*, 1070f.

Kuty

7. Dalman, 283f.; Kuty, 167.

רחק *rḥq*; רחיק *rḥyq* /raḥḥīq/

I. Etymology, Lexical Field, and Constructions. II. G-stem "to Be Far." III. C-stem "to Remove." IV. Adjective "Far."

I. Etymology, Lexical Field, and Constructions. All branches of the Semitic languages know forms of the common root *rḥq* "to be far, to depart," although its productivity differs widely in the individual languages. It constitutes the opposite of → *qrb* "to be near." In older Aramaic, the intransitive G-stem occurs primarily as a fixed term in the Imperial Aramaic legal tradition for "to relinquish," modified with *mn* indicating the thing relinquished. The transitive C-stem "to remove, to take away" (with *mn* "from") is relatively rare; later in Aramaic, the D-stem "to remove, to banish" appears most, sometimes with a t-passive, sometimes also the C-stem.[1] Usually, the adjective /raḥḥīq/ "far" expresses the state of spatial distance,[2] the verbs → *ʿdī* or → *npq* express the process of going away, and *lqḥ*, → *nṣl* or → *nśī* denote "to remove, to take away." In reference to legal succession, /raḥḥīq/ can also mean "not related" in contrast to /qarrīb/ "related" (→ IV). It functions as a temporal future expression only quite rarely; otherwise Aramaic generally uses *ʾḥr*.[3]

J. Kühlewein, "רחק *rḥq* to be distant," *TLOT*, 1230-32; C. Kumpmann, "*rḥq*," *ThWQ*, III, 674-79; Y. Muffs, *Studies in the Aramaic Legal Papyri from Elephantine. HO* 66 (2003); L. Wächter, "רָחַק *rāḥaq*," *TDOT*, XIII, 468-73.

1. *DJPA*, 522b; *DJBA*, 1071; *LexSyr*, 725; Mandean *rhq*, *MdD*, 427.
2. Pointed *raḥīq* in Biblical Aramaic; cf. *ATTM*, 122; additional synonyms there, too.
3. → *ʾḥry*.

II. G-stem "to Be Far." The G-stem of *rḥq* appears literally for "to be far, to go away" once each in late old Aramaic,[4] in Imperial Aramaic[5] and at Qumran,[6] always with *mn* "from."

It appears more often, however, in Imperial Aramaic legal texts in the first-person perfect together with *mnk* or *mnh* "I/we have distanced myself/ourselves from you/him" as by far the most common expression for relinquishing a property or legal claim.[7] It regularly occurs there in conjunction with → *ṭīb lbby* to designate a previously satisfied need.[8]

This juridical terminology continues in the phraseology of the Palmyrene grave certification inscriptions, which were rooted in Imperial Aramaic legal traditions.[9] In exorcisms, the verb can also refer to a demon to be expelled.[10]

III. C-stem "to Remove." The C-stem of *rḥq* first occurs in Aramaic four times at Qumran. In the active voice, the verb appears in Levi's prayer in the petition that God remove everything evil from the supplicant,[11] and three other times, presumably in the passive voice:[12] twice in the context of the heavenly journey of Enoch who was taken in a dream into the very remote otherworldly landscape,[13] and once in a fragmentary context in 11Q10 2:3 (Job 19:13).

At least in the latter passage, the verb could also appear as an intransitive meaning "are gone away,"[14] as is sometimes true of the C-stem of *rḥq* in Hebrew (e.g., Gen. 44:4; Ex. 8:24; Josh. 8:4; etc.). For Enoch that is unlikely, however, because the other actions are also passive and, typical for the genre, the visions appear to the visionary only as a nonparticipating spectator,[15] similarly → *ḥlp* IV.

In the magical text ooXX 10:3, the participle "you are removed" stands as the result in accord with the G-stem (→ II).

IV. Adjective "Far." The root appears at Qumran as the adjective /raḥḥīq/ "far" in the spatial sense, mostly defined further by *mn* "from" in reference to distant locations, both earthly[16] and heavenly,[17] or for a relative distance.[18] Figuratively, it appears with →

4. *TADAE* C1.1:193, as an antonym along with *qrb*.
5. *TADAE* A3.10:8.
6. 4Q552 2 2:2 par. 4Q553 6 2:3.
7. *TADAE* B2.7: 7,16; 2.8:6; 2.10:4; 3.2:7; 3.4:11,13; 5.2:8; 5.5:4 (partially emend.).
8. Cf. Muffs, 25f.,48-50.
9. Cf. *PAT* p. 411 s.v. and *DNSI*, 1073f. for citations.
10. ooXX 10:2 in *ATTM.E*, 264.
11. 4Q213a 1:2.
12. So *ATTM*, 694.
13. 4Q204 1 12:23 (1 En. 30:1); 4Q206 1 26:20 (1 En. 32:2).
14. So T. Muraoka, *A Grammar of Qumran Aramaic*. *ANESSup* 30 (2011), 111,166.
15. Cf. esp. *'ḥzy't* "it was shown me" with that shown as the subject in 4Q204 1 12:27,30; 4Q206 1 27:1,21; 4Q204 1 13:27 (1 En. 31:2; 32:1,3; 34:1; 36:2), which, given the construction, must be a passive in analogy to the active with the interpreting angel as subject in the journey through the new Jerusalem; see 5Q15 1 2:6.
16. 4Q529 1:13.
17. 4Q206 1 26:19,21 (1 En. 32:2).
18. 4Q541 2 1:8, *rḥyq mny* "far from me" in contrast to *qryb l'ly* "near me."

hwī in Ezr. 6:6 for "Keep out!" as the king's comment to the opponents of the construction of the Jerusalem temple and temporally in "distant generations" in contrast to the present (*dr*)[19] in 4Q201 1 1:4 (1 En. 1:2). In 11Q10 28:3; 33 (Job 36:25; 39:25) with *mn*, it translates Hebrew *mērāḥōq* "from afar"; the context of *TADAE* A3.5:7 is fragmentary; 4Q571 2 is an isolated fragment.

Contrariwise, two nuances in Imperial Aramaic private documents are specifically juridical: first, corresponding to the verb in the G-stem (→ II) "relinquishing,"[20] and, second, for "not related" (or "not a near relative"?) in contrast to *qryb* "related."[21]

Gzella

19. → *dūr* III.1.
20. *TADAE* B2.2:15; 2.8:11; 2.9:15; 2.11:11; 3.6:5; cf. Muffs, 119.
21. For citations → *qrb* VII.

ריח *ryḥ* /rēḥ/; ריח *rīḥ*

I. Etymology. II. Noun "Smell." III. Verb "to Smell."

I. Etymology. Apparently, the noun *ryḥ* /rēḥ/ "smell" is related to /rūḥ/ "wind, spirit,"[1] yet the exact morphological relation is not entirely clear.[2] Like /rūḥ/, it can behave as a masculine or a feminine. The verb *rīḥ*, in the transitive C-stem "to smell," is a derivative. In older Aramaic, the noun occurs once in Daniel and several times at Qumran, the verb beginning at Qumran. Both still appear later,[3] in Mandean only the noun.[4] This distribution makes the assumption of a Hebrew loanword[5] rather unlikely.

II. Noun "Smell." The first occurrence of *ryḥ* "smell" is in Dnl. 3:27 in the phrase *ryḥ nwr* "smell of burning" in the hyperbole of the miracle story of the fiery furnace:[6] the

J. Screnock, "*ryḥ*," *ThWQ*, III, 683-85.

1. → *rwḥ*.
2. According to *BLA*, §51w′ and *ATTM*, 83 from */raweḥ/ > /rēḥ/; according to *LexSyr*, 727 a diminutive.
3. *DJPA*, 523; *DJBA*, 1075; *LexSyr*, 727.
4. *MdD*, 432f.
5. *BLA*, §51w′.
6. On the passage → *'dī* II.2.

power of the fire left behind not only no visible trace, but it could not even be smelled. At Qumran, it refers to the fragrance of incense offerings.[7]

III. Verb "to Smell." Judging from the parallel versions in 4Q196 14 1:12 (Tob. 6:18, partially emend.), the verb *rīḥ* "to smell" appears in a demon exorcism through the burning of fish entrails and figuratively in 11Q10 33:6 (Job 39:25) for "to smell battle."[8] The readings of 4Q531 16:3 and 11Q18 18:1 are uncertain.

Gzella

7. 1QapGen 10:17, with *mqṭwrt*; indeed, consistently in a fixed phrase with *nḥwḥ* "aroma of incense offering" (→ *mnḥh* III.3) or "pleasing fragrance" (*ATTM*, 2, 481) in 11Q18 13:7; 22:5; 29:6; 33:1; perhaps also in 4Q204 1 12:29 [1 En. 31:3], contra *DSSStE*, 418f. (*bš*]*m ryḥ* "fragrant [aro]ma").

8. → *qrb* V.

רים *rīm*; רם *rm* /rām/; רמה *rmh* /rāmā/; רום *rwm* /rūm/; מרום *mrwm* /marōm/

I. Etymology and Forms. II. G-stem "to Be High." III. C-stem "to Elevate." IV. L-stem "to Praise." V. Adjective "High," "Elevated." VI. Noun "Height."

I. Etymology and Forms. The Aramaic *rīm*, as a verb in the G-stem "to arise," apparently developed from a common Semitic **rūm* "to be high," whose */ū/ vowel survives in both of the derived masculine nouns /rūm/ "height" and /marōm/ "located high, highland." Personal names transmitted in cuneiform, however, indicate /ī/ as a thematic vowel in the imperfect of the G-stem, which suggests a secondary transfer in the II-*ī* root class in Aramaic.[1]

For "to arise" in the literal sense of "to stand up," however, Aramaic generally employs → *qūm* so that *rīm* often denotes either figuratively and/or ingressively "to elevate oneself, to become haughty" or "to laud," or causatively "to elevate, to make high." The meaning "to arise" is linked to the rare intransitive G-stem "to be/become high," "to elevate" with the transitive C-stem and its t-passive. The verb appears with the declarative-estimative nuance "to praise" in older Aramaic in an allomorph of the D-stem, which was apparently uncommon in this time, and for "to overdo" in the related t-stem.

U. Dahmen, "רום *rûm*," *TDOT*, XIII, 402-12; idem, "*rwm*," *ThWQ*, III, 632-40; H.-P. Stähli, "רום *rûm* to be high," *TLOT*, 1220-25.

1. So *ATTM*, 695.

Forms such as the participle /marōmem/ in Dnl. 4:34 and the t-imperfect in 5:23 involve an L-stem, apparently formed in Aramaic on the *pawlel* pattern[2] and therefore cannot, or at least not directly, correspond to the Arabic purpose stem *fāʿala* since, according to phonetic principles, Aramaic would have preserved its /ā/.[3] It can take prepositional modifiers (*l*-, *ʿl*, *ʿd*).

In addition to the substantives (see above), the root also forms the adjective /rām/ "high" in the literal or the figurative ("august") senses. In the spatial nuance "high," *rīm* overlaps the rare Aramaic root *gbh*,[4] → *gʾī* also often represents the connotation of arrogance. Also regularly employed figuratively, → *špl* "to be lowly" functions generally as an antonym, rarely does *mkk* do so.[5] For "poor, miserable" → *ʿnī* II.

II. G-stem "to Be High." The G-stem "to rise, to become high/arrogant" occurs only sporadically; the adjective usually denotes "to be high" (→ V). Besides a possible instance in an Aśoka inscription, unexplained in form and meaning,[6] it can first be identified with certainty as a perfect in Dnl. 5:20. It refers to Nebuchadnezzar's arrogance and has → *lbb* "heart, mind" as subject and parallels *rwḥh tqpt lhzdh* "his spirit gathered strength to behave arrogantly."[7] The perfect here probably designates an ingressive change of state which then provoked divine punishment; the cause that brought the vessel to overflow was, according to the parallel passage Dnl. 4:26-28, the king's sudden feeling of self-satisfaction.

The instance nearest in time[8] is also best understood in context as fientic-dynamic and not stative. In the dream of the olive tree and the cedar, Noah saw how the shoots from the cedar *rʾmʾ* "shot out" *ʿd rwmh* "up to its (the cedar's) heights." Thus, the meaning here is also "to become high" (consequently it is not an adjective), indeed in the literal sense. Similarly, 11Q10 27:1 (Job 36:7), the third instance from earlier times, has the finite verb form *ymwn* "they will arise"[9] in reference to the righteous.

III. C-stem "to Elevate." The C-stem "to make high" is somewhat better attested. It already occurs in Old Aramaic and refers to the erection of a wall in an account of royal deeds[10] and in a clause in a contract from Sefire[11] probably in reference to the prohibited instigation of refugees against an ally, possibly in the sense that, in arrogance, they

---

2. So T. Nöldeke, review of M. Hartmann, *Die Pluriliteralbildungen in den semitischen Sprachen. ZDMG* 30 (1876) 184; *BLA*, §46t; *ATTM*, 488,695.

3. On the Hebrew *poʿel* and *polel*, whose origins are disputed, see H. Gzella, "So-Called Poʿel Forms in Isaiah and Elsewhere," in *Isaiah in Context. FS A. van der Kooij. SVT* 138 (2010), 63-81.

4. *ATTM*, 540.

5. *ATTM*, 623.

6. *KAI* 279.3, in the event that *rʾm* here is truly an active participle of *rīm*,"*šty* [joy?] arises," in the Greek version πάντα εὐθηνεῖ; see *DNSI*, 1198f.

7. → *tqp*.

8. 1QapGen 14:10.

9. For Heb. *gbh* "to become high."

10. → *šwr*, *KAI* 202 A 10; here supplemented with *mn* "higher than."

11. *KAI* 224.5f.

renounce their loyalty to the former lord or that, raised from their old dependence, they become arrogant—which better suits the otherwise attested use of the C-stem.

Daniel 5:19 employs the verb with this second nuance for the absolute rule of Nebuchadnezzar, who elevates and humbles,[12] whereby he then became arrogant himself.[13] Here, the verb has affinities with the D-stem of *rbī* "to make great."[14]

The texts from Qumran also exhibit both literal and figurative uses. 1QapGen 22:20 uses the verb for raising the hands of another.[15] Otherwise, Aramaic uses for this first *nśī*, and sometimes *nsb*,[16] but the analogous form in Gen. 14:22 may have influenced the choice of words. 11Q10 33:9 (Job 39:27), "to build a nest on high," also employs it for the Hebrew *rīm*.

As a construction term for "to erect," it appears in a contract[17] along with *ʿmq* "to deepen."

The Ct-passive "to be elevated" first appears in 4Q547 9:6. In this passage, it means "to be elevated," in reference to a priest,[18] who stands above even the angels.[19]

IV. L-stem "to Praise." The specific figurative shading "to laud" belongs to the narrowly defined functional spectrum of the L-stem.[20] In the active, it functions as a rare synonym of other verbs of praise such as the general → *šbḥ* and the likewise specific → *hdr*[21] and appears, along with them, in the praise for God by the reinstalled King Nebuchadnezzar in Dnl. 4:34. The combination of *šbḥ* in first with *rīm* in second and *hdr* in third position may well be based in the fact that Nebuchadnezzar now acknowledges God's superior majesty and glory and thus sees his own dominion in an appropriate perspective.[22]

According to the parallel versions, one should reconstruct an additional form *wry[wmmw* in Tobit's call to praise,[23] according to *ATTM*, 2, 93 also at the end of 1QapGen 10:9, which, however, the few and unclear remnants of letters render unverifiable.

In the Lt-stem, the declarative-estimative nuance "to present as august" refers directly to the subject elevated, which then takes on the nuance "to boast, to arise." Such a form also probably appears in *TADAE* C1.1:138, where, with *ATTM*, 488,695 and others, one should presumably correct *ytrwm* to *yrwmm* since older Aramaic nowhere else attests forms of the D-stem on the pattern of trilateral verbs;[24] furthermore, one

---

12. C-stem of the antonym → *špl*.

13. In view of the synonyms available, the use of the same root in the G-stem in 5:20 is probably intentional; → II.

14. → *rb*.

15. → *yd*.

16. → *nśī*; as in reference to raising the head in 1QapGen 5:12.

17. V 47:8 in *ATTM*, 2, 249f.

18. → *khn*.

19. Cf. Heb. 1:4.

20. On the form, → I.

21. Both in the D-stem.

22. Cf. K. Koch, *Daniel 1–4*. *BK* XXII/1 (2005), 442f.

23. 4Q196 17 2:3 (Tob. 13:7).

24. Contra I. Kottsieper, *Die Sprache der Aḥiqarsprüche*. *BZAW* 194 (1990), 152-55, who denies that Aramaic has an L-stem and regards corresponding forms in Dnl. 4:34; 5:23 (see below) and

would expect /y/ in a strong form. This passage intends the boasting positively because it refers to the names (*bšm*)[25] of father and mother and thus fulfills the commandment to honor parents.

Contrariwise, it has a negative connotation in Dnl. 5:23 in the rationale for the divine judgment against Belshazzar: with the blasphemy "against the Lord of heaven [*ʿl mrʾ šmyʾ*]" he had "vaunted himself [*htrwmmt*]." In the light of the uses of the verb otherwise, this refers less to an act of rebellion on the king's part than to the gesture of sitting in God's place at his own feast and drinking wine from God's holy cultic vessels, i.e., of relating the fame reserved for God to himself. In 11Q10 27:3 (Job 36:9) *gbr* functions similarly.

V. Adjective "High," "Elevated." In Aramaic, the adjective *rm* /rām/ "high" replaced the corresponding forms of *gbh*, which is attested only in rudiments, although in light of its use in names[26] it was once apparently the more common root. In addition to the literal sense, it also found figurative use, more often positively for "august" in reference to human and divine beings, sporadically negatively for "arrogant." The earliest instances stem from the proverbial wisdom of Aḥiqar and employ the word for the status difference in the warning not to quarrel with a superior,[27] a maxim widespread in wisdom literature;[28] further in a fragmentary context, perhaps as the object of the C-stem of *špl* "to debase."[29]

To date, no certain Imperial and Biblical Aramaic instances are known, but at Qumran, the literal meaning "high" occurs several times in visions: for a cliff,[30] a mountain reaching to the heavens,[31] and with an unclear reference in relation to the new Jerusalem.[32] It appears figuratively for "arrogant" in 11Q10 34:6 (Job 40:10, for *gbh*) and 34:7f. (40:12, for *gʾh*), with the reduction of the synonyms available in Hebrew that characterizes this translation, it appears in 5:4 (21:22) as a substantive for "nobles,"[33] whom God judges. The substantival feminine occurs in the place name Ramat Hazor "Heights of Hazor,"[34] the first component of which l. 11 ("these heights. . .") alludes to. In contrast, in 14:10 /rūm/ is meant (→ VI). *ATTM*, 2, 90 interprets *rmwhy* at the beginning of 5:11 as "his high (angels)," but the fragmentary context also permits one to consider a form of → *rmī* "to throw." Beyer suspects the same word in 4Q534 1 1:6.[35]

---

later in West Aramaic as Hebraisms, which, however, because of their occurrence in Christian Palestinian and Samaritan, is very unlikely.

25. → *šm*.

26. *ATTM*, 540.

27. *TADAE* C1.1:142, paralleling *ḥṣyp* "tough" and *ʿzyz* "strong, superior" in l. 143.

28. M. Weigl, *Die aramäische Achikar-Sprüche aus Elephantine und die alttestamentliche Weisheitsliteratur*. *BZAW* 399 (2010), 350-58.

29. *TADAE* C1.1:150, although partially reconstructed, [*r*]*m*; cf. Weigl, 366f.

30. 4Q206 4 3:19 par. 4Q205 2 2:27 (1 En. 89:29), Sinai in Enoch animal allegory.

31. 4Q213a 2:17, Levi's dream.

32. 11Q18 11:1.

33. Heb. *rmym*.

34. 1QapGen 21:8,10.

35. → *ḥzī* VI.

VI. Noun "Height." Finally, *rwm* /rūm/ designates the abstract concept of "height": so in Dnl. 3:1 of a statue, in 4:7f.,17 of the world tree, and in Ezr. 6:3 of the temple to be newly built. Everywhere, the height is determined more precisely or exactly. Parallels occur in the two tree visions of 1QapGen 13:13; 14:10[36] and in the dimensionally precise description of the new Jerusalem.[37] Furthermore, the height of heaven is part of Enoch's secret knowledge.[38]

The rare noun *mrwm* /marōm/ "highly placed" should be emended in 11Q10 9:5 (Job 25:2) as [*bmrw*]*mh* following the Hebrew counterpart[39] and refers to heaven.

Gzella

רמי *rmī*

I. Etymology, Lexical Field, and Constructions. II. Literally "to Throw." III. Figuratively "to Place On."

I. Etymology, Lexical Field, and Constructions. To be sure, the verbal root *rmī* "to throw" has a common etymology as evidenced by its cognates in the major branches of the Semitic languages, including Akkadian and Classical Ethiopic, but among the languages of Syria-Palestine, it is only more productive in Aramaic.[40] In contrast, the few instances in Hebrew, which otherwise uses *ṭūl* and especially *yrī* I for "to shoot,"[41] belong to poetic diction (Ex. 15:1,21; with the nuance "to shoot" Jer. 4:29 and Ps. 78:9), and the meaning of the one possible occurrence in Ugaritic is uncertain.[42]

In Aramaic, this verb occurs in the transitive G-stem, sometimes supplemented with adverbial local designations following the prepositions *l-* "into" (directional), and less often *b-* (locative) or *ʿl* "on." Most usages fall under the literal use "to throw" of objects or persons, including "to set up" (Dnl. 7:9) or "to cast down." Occasionally, the word functions figuratively for "to place upon" (of a tax, Ezr. 7:24). Pre-Christian Aramaic expresses the passive through an ablaut (inner passive) or the Gt-stem. Initially, this replaced the inner passive of the imperfect and also spread, at the latest in the post-Christian era, to the perfect. Consequently, the distribution of forms in Biblical Aramaic depends on the conjugation.[43]

---

36. If one should actually read *rmh* in both cases, it is a defective spelling, but the first letter is illegible; *ATTM*, 2, 97 has *rwmh*. Regarding the context, → II.

37. 4Q554 2 2:17,19; 3 2:14,17; 4Q554a 1 2:5f.,12f.; 4Q555 2:2; 5Q15 1 1:13,19; 1 2:1,5,12,14; 11Q18 8:4; 11:3; 17 2:2.

38. 4Q212 1 5:23 (1 En. 93:14).

39. According to *ATTM*, 695 borrowed.

40. Which links it within Central Semitic with Arabic; cf. Wehr[5], 501f.

41. Less often *ydd* and *ydī*.

42. See *DUL*[3], 730.

43. Thus, the pf. of the inner pass. in Dnl. 3:21, but the t-stem of the impf. in a similar construction in 3:6,11,15.

Contrariwise, the relationship to the verb *rmī* "to deceive," attested in Hebrew and post-Christian Aramaic in the D-stem, is controversial. Because of its quite different meaning, lexicographers usually associate it with a homonynous root *rmī* II.[44]

Furthermore, post-Christian Aramaic has the verb *ṭlq* in the D-stem with a related t-passive[45] and, especially East Aramaic, the verb *šdī* in the G-stem[46] for "to throw." Besides possibly in a few Imperial Aramaic ostraca from Idumea,[47] this second verb also already occurs in later offshoots of the Imperial Aramaic written tradition, namely in Frahang and Palmyrene.[48]

II. Literally "to Throw." With the literal meaning "to throw," *rmī* first appears in the book of Daniel where, in most passages, it refers to the punishment of persons thrown into the fiery furnace[49] or the lions' den[50] because of their exercise of religion. In both stories, the issuance of a royal law[51] results, first, in the punishment,[52] then, in God's wondrous deliverance, and, finally, in the king's acknowledgement of the true God. In contrast, the verb in Dnl. 7:9[53] refers to the establishment of thrones in the divine judgment scene.

A series of additional nuances appears in texts from Qumran. In addition to the concrete meaning "to throw on the fire [*ʿl nwr'*]"[54] or "to throw into the abyss [*lbwr*]"[55] in a fragment in relation to the fall of the angels,[56] all mostly as in Daniel as a punishment, Qumran also employs the word several times for "to throw down."[57] In the address to a fool, into whose mouth it will be "thrown,"[58] either the first or the second nuance may be intended given the fragmentary context. With *ʿl*, *rmī* appears in Abraham's attack against the great kings in 1QapGen 22:8 and may mean intransitively "to lunge at"[59] or "to shoot."[60] For

44. Cf. M. Kartveit, "רמה *rmh*," *TDOT*, XIII, 500-504, esp. 500; so also *GesB*[18], 1245 and recently *ATTM*, 2, 483.

45. *DJPA*, 226a; *LexSyr*, 278.

46. *DJBA*, 1109-12; *LexSyr*, 757; *MdD*, 449; rare in West Aramaic, cf. *DJPA*, 538a.

47. I. Eph'al and J. Naveh, *Aramaic Ostraca of the Fourth Century BC from Idumaea* (Jerusalem, 1996), nos. 169, l. 1; 170, l. 1; 171, l. 2; always in conjunction with *tbn* "straw"; the meaning is not assured, however.

48. *DNSI*, 1111.

49. Act. Dnl. 3:20; inner pass. 3:21; t-pass. in the corresponding edict: 3:6,11,15.

50. Act. Dnl. 6:17,25; t-pass. again in the underlying law: 6:8,13.

51. With the forms of the verb *rmī* in pass.

52. Here with the act. verb.

53. Also an inner pass.

54. 1QapGen 15:12.

55. 4Q212 1 4:21 (1 En. 91:14).

56. 4Q206 4 1:12 (1 En. 88:3).

57. Of enemies: 4Q246 1 2:9; 11Q10 25:2 (Job 34:26), for picturesque *spq* "to smack"; of idol images: 4Q198 1:13 (Tob. 14:6).

58. 4Q536 2 2:11, with *b-* "in."

59. So *ATTM*, 183, et al.; cf. *DSSStE*, 46f. ("he fell upon them"); J. A. Fitzmyer, *The Genesis Apocryphon of Qumran Cave 1 (1Q20)*. *BietOr* 18/B (³2004), 243.

60. As in Hebrew → I; later, Aramaic also attests it (*DJPA*, 526a), but older Aramaic, besides *rkb* "to place upon" in *TADAE* C1.1:126, preserves no passage in which a word for "to shoot" appears.

1QapGen 6:13, where *ATTM*, 2, 92f. suggests *rm'* "he surprised," other editors suggest the adjective *rb'* "the great."[61] Regarding 5:11 → *rīm* V.

III. Figuratively "to Place On." Older Aramaic attests the meaning of *rmī* "to place on" only in Ezr. 7:24. There the verb appears with three different terms for taxes (*mndh, blw, hlk*)[62] as object and the preposition *ʿl* "on someone" in relation to the tax exemption of the temple personnel. It also appears later with the same nuance;[63] otherwise, older Aramaic has *śīm*[64] or *šwī* II.[65]

The reading and meaning of a supposed additional instance in the Xanthos inscription[66] are debatable since *dm'* "estate" may appear here instead of *rm'*.[67]

Gzella

61. So *DSSStE*, 32f.; cf. D. A. Machiela, *The Dead Sea Genesis Apocryphon*. *STDJ* 79 (2009), 45.
62. For a discussion → *hlk* IV.
63. *DJBA*, 1086b; *LexSyr*, 732b.
64. *KAI* 320.3, with a plague as a curse; → *śīm* III.2.
65. 1QapGen 21:26.
66. *KAI* 319.17f.
67. For bibliography, see *DNSI*, 1077f.

רעי *rʿī*; רעו *rʿw* /raʿū/; רעין *rʿyn* /reʿyān/

I. Etymology and Lexical Field. II. Verb "to Be Well Pleased." III. "Pleasure, Will." IV. "Idea, Wish."

I. Etymology and Lexical Field. In accordance with the principles of Aramaic phonetics, the root *rʿī* "to be well pleased" traces back to an older West Semitic **rṣ́ī* and is related to the Hebrew *rṣī*. The verb appears in Old Aramaic, which still preserved an equivalent of */ṣ́/, as *rqī*.[1] Since Biblical Aramaic, two related nouns appear, a feminine /raʿū/ "pleasure, will" and a masculine /reʿyān/[2] "idea," less often "wish." Both also occur as Aramaic loanwords in Qoheleth with the meaning "to strive" and apparently are interchangeable.[3] The semantic spectrum evident in forms of the root is close to that of → *bʿī* "to seek," → *ṭīb* "to be satisfied," → *ṣbī* "to wish, to want," and → *rḥm* "to

H. M. Barstad, "רָצָה *rāṣâ*," *TDOT*, XIII, 618-30; T. Elgvin, "*rṣh* I," *ThWQ*, III, 714-18 (Heb.); G. Gerleman, "רצה *rṣh* to be pleased with," *TLOT*, 1259-61.

1. *ATTM*, 99,101.
2. With a vowel shift to /reʿyōn/ and pointed in Tiberian as *raʿyōn*, see *ATTM*, 697.
3. The former in Eccl. 1:14; 2:11,17,26; 4:4,6; 6:9; the latter in 1:17; 2:22; 4:16.

love, to like, to find pleasing" with their various peculiarities according to context and linguistic register.

II. Verb "to Be Well Pleased." The earliest instances of the verb appear in a treaty of state from Sefire and, in context, mean "to appease, to pacify,"[4] although debate continues whether the G- or the D-stem is involved here.[5] As a legal term, sales contracts from Samaria also employ it for "to be united with one another [*ḥd mn ḥd*]," probably in the G-stem. It arises from a tradition other than Elephantine documents.[6] Two possible instances of "to accept graciously" at Qumran[7] are debatable paleographically.

III. "Pleasure, Will." The substantive *r'w* /ra'ū/ "pleasure, will" first occurs in Biblical Aramaic. Ezra 5:17 employs it for a royal decree parallel to the typical Imperial Aramaic expression *hn 'l . . . ṭb* "if it . . . pleases."[8] In 7:18 it accompanies *k-* "according to" of God's will. The second nuance predominates in the texts from Qumran. There, in addition to the adverbial usage *kr'wth* "according to his will," as in Ezr. 7:18, in the context of God's omnipotence[9] or a just doctrine[10] in the genitive with another noun in the construct state, the word denotes a sacrifice well-pleasing to God[11] or people who stand in God's favor.[12] The parallels with this and with *bny rṣwnw* in 1QH from Qumran indicate that, with ἄνθρωποι εὐδοκίας, the angels' message of peace at the birth of Jesus (Lk. 2:14) originally meant not people "of good will" (*bonae voluntatis*), but those—not just available through good intentions—well-pleasing to God. The old Syriac version of Sinaiticus has *'r'wt'* in this passage.[13]

The noun refers to the human will in religious documents at most perhaps in 1QapGen 2:23, but the preceding text is lost. It is common, however, in legal diction in the combination *mn r'wt* "from the free will of" with a suffix.[14]

IV. "Idea, Wish." The distribution of *r'yn* /re'yān/ is much more confined in older Aramaic. The book of Daniel utilizes it throughout in the sense of "idea," always in the context of disturbance or terror in view of a revelation concerning the relationship between divine and human power. In Nebuchadnezzar's night vision of the statue, it denotes the king's "growing"[15] concern in his bed (*'l mškb*, Dnl. 2:28)[16] regarding the future and

4. *KAI* 224.6,18f.
5. *DNSI*, 1083.
6. *WDSP* 2:3; fragmentary 3:4; 8:4; cf. J. Dušek, *Les manuscrits araméens du Wadi Daliyeh et la Samarie vers 450-332 av. J.-C. CHANE* 30 (2007), 139-42.
7. 1QapGen 2:20; 4Q213b 1:1.
8. → *ṭīb* III.1.
9. 4Q542 1 1:2f.
10. 4Q541 9 1:3; fragmentary in 2 1:5.
11. 2Q24 4:2, *qwrbn*; → *qrb*; like Heb. *rṣwn*.
12. 4Q545 4:18, *'nwš*; → *'nš*.
13. *ATTM*, 697.
14. M 19:2,3; 34:1; V 45:3 in *ATTM*; V 48:2,13; nV 7:2,26,61,69 in *ATTM*, 2; as an Aramaism also in the Greek text of V 17:3,20, cf. *ATTM*, 2, 484.
15. → *slq*.
16. → *škb* III.

the thoughts of his heart,[17] which, thanks to Daniel's interpretation, he can recognize himself (2:29). In Belshazzar's horrified reaction to the writing on the wall, it is the subject of the verb → *bhl* "to terrify" and accompanies the paling of the king (Dnl. 5:6,10). Also together with *bhl*, it occurs in reference to Daniel himself in his role as interpreter of Nebuchadnezzar's second dream concerning the world-tree (4:16), and, finally, in Daniel's own vision of the four apocalyptic monsters that leaves him disturbed (7:28). Everywhere, then, the cause is a puzzling and, as with Hieronymus Bosch, ambivalent/ fascinating insight into the invisible fundamental structures of the world.

The nuance "wish," in contrast, surely underlies the use in Qohelet (→ I). J. P. M. van der Ploeg and A. S. van der Woude[18] and *ATTM*, 289, however, also assign *rʿyn* in 11Q10 15:7 (Job 30:3) to this word: "green(ery) was a wish" with a subject *hwʾ* as copula. The alternative interpretation as a masculine plural participle of *rʿī* "to pasture" in a periphrastic construction with → *hwī*[19] is also possible, since the expected /hawō/ "they were" is spelled *hww* or *hwwʾ*[20] and rarely also *hwʾ*.[21] The picturesque expression in Hebrew "who gnaw away [*ʿrq*] the dry land" fundamentally permits both possibilities. The relationship of "idea" and "wish" is semantically easy since, e.g., in many languages "must" functions both epistemically ("it must be the case. . .") and deontically ("he must be present [is obligated]").

Gzella

17. → *lbb.*
18. J. P. M. van der Ploeg and A. S. van der Woude, *Le Targum de Job* (Leiden, 1971), 41.
19. M. Sokoloff, *The Targum to Job from Qumran Cave XI* (Ramat Gan, 1974), 124f.
20. *ATTM*, 560.
21. *ATTM*, 2, 383.

שׂב *śb* /śāb/; שׂיבה *śybh* /śaybā/

I. Etymology. II. Usage in Older Aramaic. III. Biblical Aramaic. IV. Aramaic Texts from the Dead Sea.

I. Etymology. The Aramaic root *śīb* "to be/become old," first attested as a verb in post-Christian times,[1] has cognates in Canaanite (especially in Hebrew), Ugaritic, Akkadian, North Arabic, Modern South Arabian, Classical Ethiopic, and in various modern

H.-J. Fabry, "שֵׂבָה *śêḇâ*," *TDOT*, XIV, 79-85; W. Leslau, *Comparative Dictionary of Geʿez* (Wiesbaden, 1987); J. T. Milik, *The Books of Enoch* (Oxford, 1976).

1. Under *sʾb* in *DJPA*, 364a; *DJBA*, 782a; *LexSyr*, 453; *MdD*, 308.

Semitic languages of Ethiopia.[2] It originally had the meaning "to have gray/white hair, to become gray/white-haired" and, consequently, often refers to various degrees of age and aging. After the merger of */ś/ with /s/ in the second half of the first millennium B.C.E.,[3] it also appeared in Aramaic as *sīb*. In addition, → *ʿlym* functioned as the antonym "youth," and *zʿyr* "small" as "young."[4]

II. Usage in Older Aramaic. In a few Imperial Aramaic documents from Egypt, one encounters the root *śīb* as the adjective[5] *śb* /śāb/ "old,"[6] as in *TADAE* B3.10:17: *lqbl zy sbltny wʾnh ymyn sb* "because she supported me,[7] when I was aged of days."[8]

Furthermore, the adjective *śb* occurs at least twice in the framework narrative of Aḥiqar, indeed in a substantival use "old man":[9] *ʾḥyqr zk śbʾ spr ḥkym* "that Aḥiqar, the old man, a wise scribe" and perhaps also (if not adjectival) in l. 17: *śb ʾnh lʾ ʾkhl lmplḥ bbb hyklʾ* "I am (an) old (man), I will not be able to serve in the gate of the palace."[10]

III. Biblical Aramaic. Biblical Aramaic also attests *śīb* several times as an adjective or participle in a substantival use, although here in the plural. All of the examples come from Ezra and do not denote "old (person)" generally, but the elders of the Jews specifically, e.g., Ezr. 5:5: *wʿyn ʾlhhm hwt ʿl śby yhwdyʾ* "but the eye of their God was on the elders of the Jews"; 5:9: *ʾdyn šʾlnʾ lśbyʾ ʾlk knmʾ ʾmrnʾ lhm* "then we asked those elders; thus we said to them: [. . .]." Ezr. 6:7f.,14 also employs it in the same function as a title.

IV. Aramaic Texts from the Dead Sea. Furthermore, the adjective/participle *śb* "old" appears in the Aramaic texts from the Dead Sea, e.g., in 2Q24 4:13 *śbyʾ dy bhwn* "the oldest among them."[11] In addition, its substantival use in the plural with the meaning "elders" appears frequently, e.g., 4Q562 2:4 *khnym wkl śbyʾ* "the priests and all the elders."[12] It may also constitute a component of the masculine name *brśbʾ*,[13] literally "son of the old (man)."

Finally, *śīb* constitutes an (abstract) feminine verbal noun *śybh* /śēbā/ (< /śaybā/) "(old) age," first identifiable in 4Q204 1 5:6 (1 En. 10:17): *wkwl ywmy* [. . . *w*]*śybtkwn bšlm yt*[*mlywn*] "and all the days of [. . . and] your old age will be [filled] with well-being/peace."[14]

Kuty

2. Leslau, 539.
3. *ATTM*, 102f.
4. *DNSI*, 337f.; *ATTM*, 570; 2, 391.
5. Or G-stem act. ptcp.
6. For the form, cf. *ATTM*, 83.
7. → *sbl* III.1.
8. Here linked with the substantive *ymyn* "days"; remarkable is the early spelling with *s* instead of *ś*, which *ATTM*, 706 regards as a spelling error.
9. *TADAE* C1.1:35.
10. → *plḥ* II.
11. *DJD*, III (1962), 86.
12. *DJD*, XXXVII (2009), 326.
13. *ATTM*, 706; transcribed Βαρσαβ(β)ας in Acts 1:23; 15:22.
14. Milik, 348.

> שְׂגֵי/שְׂגָא‎ *śg'/śgī*; שַׂגִּיא‎ *śgy' /*śaggī/; שְׂגָא‎ *śg' /*sogǣ/; מִשְׂגָּה‎ *mśgh /*maśgǣ/

I. Etymology, Forms, and Lexical Field. II. Verb in the G-stem "to Be Many." III. C-stem "to Multiply." IV. Noun "Quantity." V. Adjective. 1. "Many." 2. "Very."

I. Etymology, Forms, and Lexical Field. Through the use of forms of the root *śgī* "to be many," arisen from **śg',*[1] Aramaic differs from other Semitic languages; therefore, the occurrences in Hebrew (Ps. 73:12; 92:13; Job 8:7,11; 12:23; 36:24) are probably borrowings. Because of this development, the meaning of → *rb/rbī* in Aramaic is limited to "large" and "to grow." After the merger of */*ś/* with */s/*,[2] phonetic spellings with *s* appear. In addition to the verb, in the G-stem "to be many" and in the C-stem "to multiply," the root primarily forms the very frequent adjective /śaggī/ "many,"[3] also employed as an adverb "many." Modifiers following *k-* can indicate the quantity via a comparison with both stems.[4] Substantives with the meaning "quantity," masculine /śogǣ/ and feminine /maśgǣ/, are rare and appear first at Qumran; no difference in meaning is perceptible. Normally, Aramaic employs /menyān/ and /manā/ for "number, quantity."[5] The D- or C-stems of *ytr* also denote "to multiply," and *rbī* in the G-stem denotes "to grow." Antonyms of "many" are /ḥassīr/[6] and /zo'ayr/ "few."

II. Verb in the G-stem "to Be Many." Biblical Aramaic first attests the intransitive G-stem of *śgī* "to be many" three times, once in the challenge not to be lazy "so that no damage to the king multiply" (Ezr. 4:22)[7] and twice in Nebuchadnezzar's stereotypical greeting formula in Imperial Aramaic epistolary style, but not identified as such, *šlmkwn yśg'* "may your peace be much!" in his circular to the nations (Dnl. 3:31; 6:26). At Qumran, it refers to Abraham's property,[8] to the "years of the demise" of the evildoer,[9] and in 11Q10 11:7 (Job 27:16) to the Hebrew *kūn* in the C-stem "to prepare," which was probably understood here as "to pile up."

H. Gzella, "*śgh*," *ThWQ*, III, 744-47.

1. *ATTM*, 102-4.
2. *ATTM*, 102f.
3. < */*śaggī/, therefore often still spelled historically *śgy'*.
4. With the G-stem, e.g., 1QapGen 22:29 and 11Q10 11:7 (Job 27:16); with the C-stem 1QapGen 21:13 and 11Q10 4:6 (Job 21:7).
5. → *mnī* III.1 and III.2.
6. → *ḥsr*.
7. → *ḥbl* III.
8. 1QapGen 22:29,32; in l. 29 and 21:13 (→ III) together with a negated form of → *mnī* emphasizing innumerability.
9. 4Q201 1 2:15 (1 En. 5:5).

III. C-stem "to Multiply." Even rarer than the G-stem, the C-stem "to multiply" appears in older Aramaic; from pre-Christian times, the texts from Qumran preserve two certain instances: in God's promise of innumerable descendants to Abraham[10] and in 11Q10 4:6 (Job 21:7) for the increase of property rendering the Hebrew *gbr* "to grow."[11]

IV. Noun "Quantity." Qumran also attests the two nouns *śg'*[12] and *mśgh*[13] "quantity" in reference to things and abstractions. Instead of the noun in the construct state with the subsequent word "quantity of," as in 4Q541 9 1:5 and 1QapGen 13:14, the adjective "many" appears more frequently in an attributive function.[14]

V. Adjective. The most frequent manifestation of the root, the adjective *śgy'* /śaggī/ "many,"[15] already occurs, in contrast, beginning with later Old Aramaic. It can refer to collective or individual nouns, also substantivally to "many," and serve as an adverb "very."

1. "Many." Thus, in the sayings of Aḥiqar it already refers to sons,[16] thorns,[17] stars,[18] and once without context;[19] in the Imperial Aramaic framework narrative in reference to life[20] and days;[21] in the Behistun inscription to lies.[22] It occurs in letters in the context of financial loss,[23] of years,[24] and, without context, of goods,[25] in J. Naveh and S. Shaked, A4,3[26] of a locust plague, and B1,5 of a troop. Other instances are allotted to the opening greeting in the letter formula, in which the sender sends the addressee *šlm wšrrt śgy(')* "much well-being and health."[27]

In Biblical Aramaic, the word functions in the known sense "many" in reference to the "many years" that the temple stood in Jerusalem (Ezr. 5:11), to the gifts of the king (Dnl. 2:6,48), to the fruit of the tree in Nebuchadnezzar's dream (4:9,18), and to the command to the second animal in Daniel's vision to devour "much flesh" (7:5). In each case, here,

10. 1QapGen 21:13.
11. See further Gzella, *śg'* II.
12. 4Q204 4:5 (1 En. 89:33); 4Q541 9 1:5f.
13. 1QapGen 13:14 (*DSSStE*, 36f.).
14. Thus, the parallel expression "many words" in 4Q541 9 1:5f.
15. Also spelled phonetically *śgy* or *sgy*.
16. *TADAE* C1.1:90; paralleling *z'yr* "few."
17. *TADAE* C1.1:101.
18. *TADAE* C1.1:164.
19. *TADAE* C1.1:181.
20. *TADAE* C1.1:11, partially emend.
21. *TADAE* C1.1:50.
22. *TADAE* C2.1:65.
23. *TADAE* A4.3:10; → *ḥsr* IV.
24. *TADAE* A6.14:4.
25. *TADAE* A7.5:5.
26. J. Naveh and S. Shaked, *Aramaic Documents from Ancient Bactria* (London, 2012).
27. *TADAE* A3.8:1; 3.9:1; 6.3:1; 6.4:1; 6.7:1; 6.16:1; D1.12:1; also from Bactrian writings, see Naveh and Shaked, B1.1; 4.1.

it designates abundance and exorbitance, especially in visions. In reference to the height of the tree in 4:7, it appears exceptionally in the sense of a quantity (*rwmh śgy'* "its height was many, i.e., great"),[28] not a number. A meaning "high"[29] cannot be derived from this.[30]

The texts from Qumran also employ the adjective with concrete and abstract, with numerable and innumerable terms.[31] Accumulated, it stands for opulence, as in Noah's dream of the olive tree[32] and Abraham's wealth after his Egyptian sojourn.[33] The rendering of the Hebrew *rb* "many" with *śgy'* in 11Q10 demonstrates that Aramaic distinguishes it from *rb* "great."[34] The feminine also appears in the singular as *śgy'*.[35] Substantivally, *śgy'yn* denotes "multitude,"[36] but is clearly demarcated from *kl* with a suffix "all."[37] No Aramaic instance of *śg'yn* "multitude" instead of "all" is known.

2. *"Very."* As an adverb "very" in the masculine singular absolute, *śgy'* occurs beginning in Imperial Aramaic and characterizes emotional states,[38] characteristics,[39] and actions.[40] Biblical Aramaic also has it in reference to emotions, negative (Dnl. 2:12; 5:9; 6:15; 7:28) and positive (6:24), and in the difficult expression from Dnl. 2:31 presumably with the following adjective → *rb* "great,"[41] thus as an intensive.[42] In contrast, neither an adjectival usage for "great" (→ V.1) nor meaning "multiform"[43] conforms to otherwise known usage.

Various other instances of the adverb in the same usage occur at Qumran,[44] in addition, a restrictive use, *wl' śgy'* "not too much."[45]

Gzella

28. Consequently, *LexLingAram*, 159 glosses appropriately: *altitudo . . . erat multa numeris metienda.*

29. So *GesB*[18], 1536.

30. Regarding Dnl. 2:31 → V.2.

31. E.g., 1QapGen 22:32 (property); 20:7 (wisdom); 5:18 and 4Q531 19:2 (force); 4Q196 2:11f. (Tob. 2:2; food rations); 4Q201 1 4:7 (1 En. 9:1; blood); 4Q206 4 1:11 (1 En. 88:3; stars); and 4Q554 3:2 (gates).

32. 1QapGen 13:13-15; with noun and adverb.

33. 1QapGen 20:31-34.

34. 11Q10 26:1,3f. (Job 35:6,9 [2×]); 28:6 (Job 36:28); 32:10 (Job 39:11).

35. 1QapGen 12:9; 20:7.

36. 11Q10 26:4 (Job 35:9); 4Q545 1a-b 2:14, here with *mn* "of"; according to *ATTM*, 182 also 1QapGen 21:33.

37. → *kll* IV.

38. *TADAE* C1.1:29,51; probably also in l. 74; *TADAE* 6.16:4.

39. *KAI* 264.5: "very wise."

40. *TADAE* A3.5:1f.; 4.7:1; greeting formula.

41. *LexLingAram*, 159; *ATTM*, 703.

42. LXX rearranged the text.

43. K. Koch, *Daniel 1–4. BK* XXII/1 (2005), 97.

44. E.g., 1QapGen 2:11; 13:15; 20:8; 21:6; 4Q196 14 2:4 par. 4Q197 4 3:1 (Tob. 6:18); 4Q206 1 6:20 (1 En. 32:2); 4Q541 3,5; with *hwī* "to happen in great measure" 4Q534 1 1:9; in a nominal clause 1QapGen 22:32.

45. 4Q561 1 1:1.4.

שׂהד *śhd*; שׂהד *śhd* /śāhed/; שׂהדו *śhdw* /śāhedū/

I. Verb. II. Nouns. 1. "Witness." 2. "Testimony."

I. Verb. Aramaic and Arabic attest the root *śhd*. Its verbal forms in the G-stem exhibit a stative inflection and designate the state of "being a witness," but classical Arabic *šahāda* and Syriac *sahhed*[1] have the active meaning "to testify, to witness." The verb occurs in *TADAE* D1.17:6 (*wśhdw ʿl*) in the fragmentary context of a legal document presumably dated to the third century B.C.E. Furthermore, it appears often in Palmyrene honorary inscriptions in the spellings *śhd* or *shd*,[2] always with the active meaning "to witness" in reference to someone's positive characteristics and accomplishments. The subject can be a deity,[3] the Senate and the people,[4] or the members of a caravan. Otherwise, no verbal forms are preserved in older Aramaic; a couple of alleged instances on clay tables are due solely to false readings and erroneous grammatical determinations in modern secondary literature.

II. Nouns.

1. "Witness." The noun *śhd* "witness" presumably represents the active participle of the verb *śhd* /śāhed/. The plural *śhd* appears in relation to the deities invoked as witnesses of the treaties of state from Sefire.[5] This usage projects a common legal practice into the world of deities, since every agreement must name the persons who could testify to its conclusion and the corresponding stipulations, although not whether the document appropriately portrays past circumstance. Consequently, beginning ca. 700 B.C.E., Aramaic contracts on clay tablets or papyrus list the names of the pertinent witnesses preceded by *śhd* in the singular or the plural. Hundreds of examples have recently come to light from Assyria, northern Syria, Egypt, Samaria, and the Judean wilderness. The pertinent documents are in Old, Imperial, Jewish, or Nabatean Aramaic.[6]

In documents from the wilderness of Judah, *śhd* follows the names of the witnesses and is sometimes replaced with *ʿd* "witness."[7]

F. O. Hvidberg-Hansen, *The Palmyrene Inscriptions* (Copenhagen, 1998), esp. no. 131; A. Lemaire, *Nouvelles tablettes araméennes* (Geneva, 2001), esp. 155; D. Schwiderski, *Die alt- und reichsaramäischen Inschriften*, vol. I: *Konkordanz*. *FSBP* 2 (2008).

1. Pael, *LexSyr*, 462a.
2. Cf. *ATTM*, 102f.
3. *PAT* 0278.6; *PAT* 1415.2.
4. *PAT* 2769.5.
5. *KAI* 222 A 12.
6. For an overview, see *TADAE* B, pp. xlf.; Lemaire, 155; Schwiderski, 771-73; W. Röllig, *BATSH* 17/*Texte* 5, 2014, 270 [glossary]; *ATTM*, 703 and 2, 489; regarding the variation in formulation between singular and plural, cf. H. Gzella, *A Cultural History of Aramaic*. *HO* 111 (2015), 128 n. 393.
7. Cf. H. Simeon-Yofre and H. Ringgren, "עוד *ʿwd*," *TDOT*, X, 495-516; *ATTM*, 2, 450.

A couple of individual cases merit closer attention. In the Samaria papyri from Wadi Daliyeh, *śhd* can precede the witness list;[8] the formula *śhdy' zy yḥtmwm gṭ'* [*znh mhymnn hmw*] "The witnesses who will seal this document[9] are reliable"[10] can complete or replace it. In a few Nabatean papyri from Naḥal Ḥever, the names of the witnesses who sign the document follow the expression *śhd ktb ydh*, "Witness, the signature of his hand."[11] The analysis of this phrase as supposed haplography of **ktb bydh*[12] is incorrect as the use of *ktb yd* in the Palmyrene inscription on the grave of Malku[13] and in *m. Ketub.* ii:2f. indicates. Literary texts contain the combination *śhd ḥms*, "false witness" (sayings of Aḥiqar)[14] and *śhdy qšṭ* "truthful witnesses."[15] Furthermore, the word *śhd* occurs in Job 16:19,[16] spelled in a Transjordanian dialect related to Aramaic.

2. *"Testimony."* The feminine *śhdw*, "testimony" or "evidence," appears in Gen. 31:47,[17] in 4Q542 1 2:12, a fragment of the Testament of Qahat from the third or second century B.C.E., and in the Nabatean signature of Pap. Yadin 15:25 (*śhdt'*)[18] from the Babatha archive.

Lipiński

8. *WDSP* 11 recto, l. 12.
9. → *ḥtm.*
10. *WDSP* 10:14; cf. 1:12; 4:13.
11. Pap. Yadin 1, 55-65; 9:13; → *ktb* IV.
12. *DNSI*, 435,541f.
13. Hvidberg-Hansen = *PAT* 1624.3; cf. l. 13.
14. *TADAE* C1.1:140.
15. 4Q212 1 4:12 (1 En. 93:10); → *qšṭ.*
16. In parallel with *'d.*
17. In the place name *y^e^gar śāh^a^ḏūṯā* "stone heap of testimony."
18. Also published as nV 15:38 in *ATTM*, 2, 230, although according to p. 489 a fem. form of the ptcp.

שׂים *śīm*; שׂימה *śymh* /śīmā/

I. Etymology, Lexical Field, and Constructions. II. Literal Use "to Set, to Place, to Lay." III. Figurative Use. 1. "To Install." 2. Various Idiomatic Expressions. IV. Noun "Treasury, Treasure."

I. Etymology, Lexical Field, and Constructions. Forms of the verbal root *śīm* "to set, to place, to lay" appear in all the major branches of the Semitic languages, although

H.-J. Fabry, "*śym*," *ThWQ*, III, 757-62; G. Vanoni, "שִׂים *śîm*," *TDOT*, XIV, 89-112.

with varied productivity. Aramaic uses the verb, mostly as does Hebrew, in the transitive G-stem with a spectrum of meaning similar to the Latin verb *ponere*. Depending on the nature of the direct object, one can distinguish between a literal use with objects and a figurative use with abstract terms; the latter occurs with particular frequency in administrative terminology with → *ṭʿm* "order." With a dual direct object in reference to objects, it has the nuance "to make something into," in reference to persons "to install, to name as." The broad semantic field covered by this lexeme has points of contact with various other verbs. The roots → *ytb*, → *qūm*, and → *škb* typically express the intransitive circumstance "to sit, to stand, to lie," usually with persons as subject; the C-stem of *qūm*[1] often serves the meaning "to set up"; and it together with the D-stem of → *mnī* and the C-stem of → *tqn* or → *šlṭ* denote "to install." Sometimes, *šwī* II in the D-stem represents "to lay" and *šwī* I, likewise in the D-stem and not always clearly distinct from *šwī* II, signifies "to make into."[2]

In the usage meaning "to lay, to place," the verb sometimes takes adverbial modifiers following *b-* "in, to" or *ʿl* "on." The passive took form toward the end of the first millennium B.C.E. through ablaut (inner passive) or the Gt-stem and corresponds with the nuance of the active voice. Passive constructions often appear in administrative terminology. With the loss of the inner passive, first in the imperfect and then in the perfect, the Gt-stem assumed its functions. The inner passive has a resultative nuance and emphasizes the result "placed," the t-passive points to the action itself. The participle retains this distinction.[3]

In geographical descriptions, the passive participle /śīm/ can denote "located, situated"; the feminine form /śīmā/ serves quite rarely in a substantival use for "treasury, treasure" (like "deposit," literally "stored goods, put away things").

After the fusion of */ś/ and /s/, spellings with *s* appear sporadically already in older Aramaic.[4]

II. Literal Use "to Set, to Place." The earliest Aramaic already attests the verb *śīm* in the concrete sense of "to lay, to place, to set up" very well. It usually refers there to the erection of a statue,[5] but can also denote other construction activities[6] and the attachment of the name to something.[7] Such expressions, furthermore, can include → *ʿbd* (II.1) "to make" in the sense of "to (have) prepare(d)";[8] from Imperial Aramaic onward, → *qūm* in the C-stem more commonly serves for "to erect" statues and inscriptions. In addition, Old Aramaic already manifests figurative meanings (→ III.2); the context of

---

1. Later also *zqp*.
2. For the discussion → *šwī*.
3. E.g., compare the pass. ptcp. "is placed" in *TADAE* C1.1:79 or A4.3:10 with that of the Gt-stem "is installed" in Ezr. 5:8.
4. 11Q10 4:4 (Job 21:5).
5. → *ṣlm*; *KAI* 309.1,16; 201,1; 202 A 1; B 13; 222 A 7, the erection of an inscription with a treaty of state simultaneously seals the treaty: *KAI* 222 B 6.
6. *KAI* 202 A 9; perhaps also B 6, but the context has not been preserved.
7. *KAI* 309.11f.
8. Cf. *KAI* 309.15.

KAI 310.9 remains unclear. In later Old Aramaic, one finds the nuance "to lay down" of grave goods,[9] possibly also "to confine, to bind" of persons.[10]

In contrast, the large corpus of Imperial Aramaic exhibits significantly fewer instances of *śīm* in a literary meaning because the pertinent situations rarely find expression in the texts,[11] but there can be no doubt that this verb continued to be productive in the living language.

In the literal usage, passive forms also correspond to the use of the active, as with the participle of the inner passive "is placed"[12] and perhaps "are handed over";[13] the perfect in *TADAE* D7.10:2 is unclear, as is the t-passive "to be attached."[14] It appears more frequently, however, for "to be given" in reference to an order (→ III.1).

Biblical Aramaic knows two instances of the usage with concrete objects, both in the passive: the inner passive of the perfect of the stone placed on the opening (*ʿl pm*) of the lions' den (Dnl. 6:18), and the t-passive participle of wood to be installed in temple walls (Ezr. 5:8).[15]

In 11Q10 4:4 (Job 21:5), the sole relevant occurrence from Qumran, the verb renders literally the synonymous Hebrew cognate *śīm* for "to place one's hand on (*ʿl*) one's mouth."

III. Figurative Use.

1. "To Install." Of the usages with a nonmaterial object, the combination with → *ṭʿm* for "to give an order," attested since Imperial Aramaic, is most frequent by number of occurrences in all of older Aramaic. It belongs to the register of administrative diction and, consequently, appears primarily in official letters from the chancelleries of the satraps. Because of the written style employed there, it occurs in the passive[16] more often than in the active.[17] The letters from the archive of the Bactrian provincial administration follow exactly the same diction.[18] The preposition *l-* indicates the recipient of the order; *mn*, also in a passive construction, indicates the one giving the order, apparently due to Iranian influence.[19]

The same usage also occurs elsewhere in documents that employ the same administrative idiom[20] and regularly in Biblical Aramaic. There, one finds a rather frequent

9. *KAI* 226.7.

10. *KAI* 233.7, but in a fragmentary context.

11. Such as, exceptionally, "to add salt" in *TADAE* D7.2:7; only fragmentarily preserved are D4.1:4 and Segal, 26.15; 50.4.

12. *TADAE* C1.1:79, here figuratively of something that is raised to the god El in heaven.

13. *TADAE* B8.5b:2; destroyed context.

14. *TADAE* C1.1:175, perhaps of foot shackles; → *rgl* II.

15. For the historical background → *ktl*.

16. *TADAE* 6.1:2; 6.2:22f.,25; 6.7:8; 6.13:5 (*ṭʿm* left unexpressed, but clearly intended); presumably also A4.5:21.

17. *TADAE* A6.3:6f.; 6.5:3.

18. J. Naveh and S. Shaked, *Aramaic Documents from Ancient Bactria (Fourth Century B.C.E.)* (London, 2012), A1,5; 5,1f.; 6,2,7,9; in a probably elliptical formulation without *ṭʿm* further B3,3.

19. Cf. H. Gzella, *Tempus, Aspekt und Modalität im Reichsaramäischen. VOK* 48 (2004), 184-94.

20. Segal, 14.5; 15.3; *TADAE* C3.8IIIB:7.

usage of the passive (Ezr. 4:19; 5:17; 6:8,11; 7:13,21; Dnl. 3:29; 4:3; 6:27) approximating Achaemenid epistolary style, but the active also appears (Ezr. 4:21; 5:3,9,13; 6:1,3,12; Dnl. 3:10). The distribution between inner passive and Gt-stem corresponds to the overall situation in Imperial Aramaic: the former appears with the perfect or the participle, the second with the imperfect (Ezr. 4:21). This bureaucratic nuance differs from *śīm* with *ṭʿm* for "to focus attention" (→ III.2 [point f]).

2. *Various Idiomatic Expressions.* Additionally, since Old Aramaic times, *śīm* functions in a number of other idiomatic expressions in which, as a widely applicable, semantically loosely defined verb, it overlaps with various other more specific lexemes:

(a) With a plague as object (*mwtn*)[21] it appears in the curse formula of the Bukan inscription meaning "to place upon,"[22] for which, in relation to taxes or other payments, → *rmī* and less often *šwī* II[23] appear later.

(b) Additionally, with → *šm* as object, it can mean "to bestow a name,"[24] but the context always implies an award, thus constituting a distinction from → *qrī* for "to name."

(c) In reference to established terms, *śīm* can mean "to establish" as with sums of money[25] or of quantities.[26]

(d) In Imperial Aramaic epistolary style, the formulation "cause to share in grace" or "to give salvation" with *rḥmn*[27] or → *šlm* as object and a divine subject.[28] Here, there is a close relationship to the meaning of → *yhb* or *ntn* "to give."

(e) Further, an overlap with the lexical field "to give" exists with the expression "to put something (good words) in the mouth" in a wisdom saying of Aḥiqar[29] with "to treat oneself [*npš*] to rest [*šlyn*]."[30]

(f) Twice in Biblical Aramaic, *śīm* appears with *ṭʿm* for "to take note" (→ III.1).[31] Notably, in both passages, it is negated in relation to the religious exercise of the Jewish exiles, which their opponents portray as defiance of the king (Dnl. 3:12; 6:14). Here *ṭʿm* has the meaning "regard, attention, obedience."[32] Distantly related is the use with → *bl* as object "to focus attention" (Dnl. 6:15), which, however, in the one instance, has a positive

---

21. → *mūt* VI.

22. *KAI* 320.3.

23. 1QapGen 21:26.

24. *KAI* 226.3, here with *šm ṭb* "a good reputation" as a divine gift; Dnl. 5:12, of the royal official name of Daniel.

25. *TADAE* A4.3:10; nV 10:8 in *ATTM*, 226-28, here for support in a marriage contract, both as pass. ptcps.

26. 11Q10 30:3 (Job 38:5), in the act. reflecting the Heb. cognate.

27. → *rḥm*.

28. *TADAE* A4.7:2 par. 4.8:2, of the grace of the king; 6.16:5; D22.51:4; fragmentary *TADAE* A6.6,1; cf. D. Schwiderski, *Handbuch des nordwestsemitischen Briefformulars*. *BZAW* 295 (2000), 138f.

29. *TADAE* C1.1:163.

30. → *šlī* IV. L. 130; here negated: whoever has assumed debt will not come to rest until it is retired.

31. Distinct from the typical Imperial Aramaic meaning "to give an order."

32. → *ṭʿm* III.

connotation regarding the efforts of the king to deliver Daniel from a court intrigue.[33] Later Aramaic also attests the noun /hawn/ "mind, understanding" for "attention."[34]

(g) In a corrupt context, but reconstructable using the parallel versions, the Aramaic version of the Behistun inscription employs *śīm* for "to stake" as a penalty for rebels.[35] In Ezr. 6:11, *zqp* has this meaning.[36] This other verb appears more frequently later for "to erect,"[37] also with the meaning "to crucify."

(h) With a dual object, *śīm* means "to make something into" and Old Aramaic already attests it as such[38] in the corresponding passive "to be made into" in Dnl. 2:5. In this usage, it can hardly be distinguished from → *ʿbd* or *šwī* in the same construction. In reference to a person, it appears once in Biblical Aramaic for "to install" (Ezr. 5:14), as otherwise → *mnī*, *tqn*, or *šlṭ* do.

(i) The passive participle "placed, located" can stand for "placed" in geographical descriptions without implying an active verbal action.[39] A nominal clause can appear instead.[40]

IV. Noun "Treasury, Treasure." The substantival passive participle *śymh* /śīmā/ for "treasure (treasury)" may be first evident in an Imperial Aramaic inscription from North Arabian Tēma where in the phrase *śymt' zy mlk'* it probably means "the king's treasury," which is to support a local temple.[41] Figuratively for "treasure" in a picturesque comparison of wisdom, it then appears twice in T. Levi from Qumran.[42] Postbiblical Hebrew also adopted it with this meaning.[43] An Aramaic inscription in Greek transcription could use the word (σιμαθα) either for earthly or for heavenly treasures.[44] Examples also occur later, although in the phonetic spelling *symh*.[45]

Typically, however, official diction since Imperial Aramaic employs for treasure the Persian loanword */ganza/ and, correspondingly, for "treasury" *byt gnzy'*.[46]

Gzella

33. On the context → *nṣl* III.
34. *DJPA*, 161; *LexSyr*, 173.
35. *TADAE* C2.1:49.
36. The same root as in the Babylonian version of the Behistun inscription; regarding the context → *mḥī* II.
37. *DJPA*, 181; *DJBA*, 419; *LexSyr*, 204; *MdD*, 169.
38. *KAI* 222 C 19,23; perhaps also 310.9.
39. 1QapGen 22:10; 4Q552 2 2:4.
40. Cf. 1QapGen 21:8.
41. *DNSI*, 1129 criticized this interpretation, but at least the later diction may support it.
42. 4Q213 1 1:20, here with the attributive *ṭbh* "valuable"; 1-2 2:3, in context with *mṭmwr* "something concealed, a concealed treasure" (see *ATTM*, 591) in l. 1.
43. Sir. 41:14; 4Q200 2:9 (Tob. 4:9); 4Q504 7:9.
44. yWG 1:1 in *ATTM*, 353.
45. *DJPA*, 375a; *DJBA*, 805b; *LexSyr*, 470b.
46. → *gnz*.

שׂכל *śkl*; שׂכלתנו *śkltnw* /śokltānū/

I. Etymology and Lexical Field. II. Verb "to Pay Attention." III. Noun "Insight."

I. Etymology and Lexical Field. Older Aramaic attests *śkl* as a verb almost exclusively in the Dt-stem "to pay attention, to understand" and may be supplemented with a prepositional expression following *b-* "to." With this nuance, it may derive from the feminine abstract noun /śokltānū/ "insight,"[1] in which case the t-stem expresses middle voice with affixation of the subject. As in Hebrew, it constitutes a wisdom term. An active D-stem with the meaning "to proclaim" is attested, perhaps already in a Jewish Palestinian ossuary inscription for "to permit publicly,"[2] but the further Aramaic and Semitic etymology is uncertain. After the fusion of */ś/ with /s/, it is also spelled *skl.*

The root *śkl* is not related to the noun *skl* /sakal/ "fool, sinner,"[3] from which, then, the verb in the Dt-stem "to act foolishly" derives. Here, the initial sibilant traces back to an original /s/. Together with *šṭī* "to be foolish,"[4] *skl* forms the antonymous lexical field of *śkl*. In the meaning "to pay attention," *śkl* also has points of contact with *śīm* and *bl* "mind" for "to focus the mind on something,"[5] but, in the attested usage, it has more of a contemplative nuance and refers to the contemplation of concealed circumstances. For synonyms of the noun → *ydʿ*.

II. Verb "to Pay Attention." In originally Aramaic texts from pre-Christian times, the verb *śkl* in the Dt-stem "to pay attention" occurs only in Dnl. 7:8. This text describes how, in the symbolic display of world history in the form of apocalyptic animals, Daniel concentrated on the ten horns on the head of the fourth animal. This introduces the apex of the whole scene, the appearance of the arrogant small horn, its destruction, and the judgment of the world. Otherwise, the word, spelled *skl*, occurs frequently in 11Q10 representing various Hebrew lexemes: mostly *bīn*,[6] and once each *śkl*[7] and *skn*.[8]

III. Noun "Insight." The parallelism with *rwḥ*, *nhyrw*, *ḥkmh*,[9] and *mndʿ* in Dnl. 5:11f.,14 restricts the meaning of the noun *śkltnw* /śokltānū/ "insight" to Daniel's divinely inspired knowledge.

Gzella

M. Euteneuer, "*śkl*," *ThWQ*, III, 762-66; K. Koenen, "שָׂכַל *śāḵal*," *TDOT*, XIV, 112-28; M. Sæbø, "שׂכל *śkl* hi. to have insight," *TLOT*, 1269-72.

1. So *ATTM*, 708.
2. yJE 35:1 in *ATTM*, 346.
3. 4Q157 1 2:7 (Job 5:2); 4Q534 7:2 par. 4Q536 2 2:11; 4Q548 1 2-2:12.
4. *ATTM*, 705f.
5. → *śīm* III.2.
6. 11Q10 7A:6; 10:6; 29:5 (Job 23:5; 26:14; 37:14).
7. 11Q10 25:3 (Job 34:27).
8. 11Q10 7:7 (Job 22:21).
9. → *ḥkm* IV.

שנא/שני *śn'/śnī*; שנאה *śn'h* /śen'ā/; שנא *śn'* /śānē/ (< /śāne'/)

I. "To Hate, Hatred." II. "Enemy." III. In Divorce Law.

I. "To Hate, Hatred." Texts from the first millennium B.C.E. only rarely use the Aramaic verb *śn'*[1] and its derivatives in the simple meaning for the feeling of strong antipathy. Usually, they employ instead terms denoting hostile actions such as the attempt to kill,[2] to destroy, or to damage,[3] or the intention to initiate divorce proceedings. Yet, the emotional connotation may appear in a saying of Aḥiqar,[4] where the noun *śn'th* characterizes a liar more precisely and forms a contrast with *hymnwth* "his reliability":[5] *ḥn gbr hymnwth wśn'th kdbt śpwth* "The courtesy of a man (shows) his reliability, but the lies of his lips (announce) his ugliness."[6]

The affective nuance may also occur in the fragmentary and unclear context of a passage in the Deir 'Allā inscription: *hn tśn'n y'nš* "if you show hatred, he will be weak."[7]

II. "Enemy." The substantival active participle (peal) quite often expresses animosity. In the Sefire inscription, it occurs in political and military contexts,[8] so also in 1QapGen 22:17 and presumably in Dnl. 4:16.[9] In contrast, in *Megillat Ta'anit* it has more of a religious connotation[10] and, in a proverb of Aḥiqar, means personal

---

K. Abraham, "Echtscheiding volgens de Elefantine huwelijkscontracten" (diss., Louvain, 1985); U. Dahmen, "*śn'*," *ThWQ*, III, 781-84 (Heb.); M. A. Friedman, "Divorce upon the Wife's Demand as Reflected in Manuscripts from the Cairo Geniza," *Jewish Law Annual* 4 (1981) 103-26; E. Jenni, "שנא *śn'* to hate," *TLOT*, 1277-79; E. Lipiński, "Contrats de mariage judéo-araméens du Ve siècle av.n.è. La position juridique de l'épouse," *Biblical Annals* 4 (2014) 9-41, esp. 23-29; idem, "שָׂנֵא *śanē'*," *TDOT*, XIV, 164-74; idem, "The Wife's Right to Divorce in the Light of an Ancient Near Eastern Tradition," *Jewish Law Annual* 4 (1981) 9-27; C. Locher, *Die Ehre einer Frau in Israel. OBO* 70 (1986), esp. 296-99; H. Nutkowicz, "Concerning the Verb *ŚN'* in Judaeo-Aramaic Contracts from Elephantine," *JSS* 52 (2007) 211-25; D. Piattelli, "The Marriage Contract and Bill of Divorce in Ancient Hebrew Law," *Jewish Law Annual* 4 (1981) 66-78; A. M. Rabello, "Divorce of Jews in the Roman Empire," *Jewish Law Annual* 4 (1981) 79-102; Z. H. Szubin and B. Porten, "The Status of a Repudiated Spouse," *Israel Law Review* 35 (2001) 46-78.

1. Later > *śnī*.
2. → *qṭl*.
3. → *ḥbl*, with additional synonyms.
4. *TADAE* C1.1:132.
5. → *'mn* II.
6. → *kdb*.
7. II:10; cf. *SAIO* II, 147f.
8. *KAI* 222 B 26; 223 B 14; 224.12.
9. Alongside *'r*, → *'rr* III.
10. Cf. *śn'* in 4Q541 24 2:6, according to *DSSStE*, 1080f.; *ATTM*, 2, 497 a substantival ptcp. in the determined state "the enemy"; also in a fragmentary context in 4Q243 39:2 (*sn'*); 4Q543 15:3 (*śn'yn*).

animosity:[11] "My enemies should die, but not by the sword," apparently in order to avoid blood revenge.

III. In Divorce Law. In marriage contracts from Elephantine, the verb *śn'* expresses the intention to initiate divorce proceedings,[12] but does not designate the actual divorce. This is evident from the use of → *npq* in clauses like *hn . . . tśn'nk wtnpq mnk* "if . . . she hates you and goes away from you," wherein *npq* denotes the completion of the intended divorce, as later in rabbinic literature. The phrase *śn' l-* appears six times in private documents from Elephantine[13] and is replaced by *śn'* with a pronominal suffix twice.[14] The subject of the verb is either masculine or feminine, since the Elephantine papyri attest the right of the marital partner to dissolve the marriage even though marital duties have not been damaged by marital misconduct. These contracts correspond, then, to a legal practice also attested in a few other ancient Near Eastern documents.[15] In this context, the related noun *śn'h* refers directly to the reason for the divorce, the "hatred," yet it also further denotes the overall legal proceeding, as the expressions *dyn śn'h* "hatred law"[16] and *ksp śn'h* "hatred silver"[17] demonstrate. Even without further qualification, the noun *śn'h* refers to the entire proceeding.[18] The documents from the wilderness of Judah do not employ the verb *śn'* to indicate divorce proceedings.

Lipiński

11. *TADAE* C1.1:110; *ś'ny* here is a scribal error for *śn'y*.
12. See E. Lipiński, "שָׂנֵא *śanē'*," 168-72.
13. *TADAE* B2.6:23[,27]; B3.3:7,9; B3.8:21 (*śnyt*),24.
14. *TADAE* B2.4:8; B3.8:25.
15. See Lipiński.
16. *TADAE* B3.8:34.37,39; B6.4:2,6.
17. *TADAE* B2.6:23; B3.3:8 (*śn'*),9 (*śn'h*); B3.8:22,25.
18. *TADAE* B3.8:34,(37),39,40; B6.4:(2),4,6.

שׂער *ś'r* /śa'r/

I. Etymology, Form, and Lexical Field. II. Usage.

I. Etymology, Form, and Lexical Field. As in Arabic, the masculine Semitic primary noun *ś'r* "hair" appears in Aramaic as a *qatl*-form /śa'r/,[1] while in Hebrew the

G. J. Botterweck, "גִּלַּח *gillach*," *TDOT*, III, 5-20.

1. Later with anaptyxis /śa'ar/, *ATTM*, 112-15.

qiṭl-formation /śiʿr/ is productive. In contrast, the usage does not differ; Aramaic also employs it essentially as a collective term for body hair, although it mostly refers specifically to the hair of the head as its more notable manifestation.[2] For the purpose of more precise definition, it occurs in the construct with → *r'š* "of the head" or *dqn* /daqan/ (< */δaqan/) "of the beard."[3] Etymologically, it is generally associated with *śʿrh* /śaʿārā/ "barley," *śʿryn* /śaʿārīn/ "barley corns,"[4] which appeared because of its long awns to be a "hairy" grain.

II. Usage. "Hair" and its lexical field are much less prominent in the older Aramaic texts than in Hebrew.[5] The word *śʿr* appears in the everyday sense in the story of the three men in the fiery furnace, the hair of whose heads (*śʿr r'šhwn*) was not even singed (*ḥrk*)[6] despite the especially high heat, although hair and clothing catch fire easily (Dnl. 3:27), which emphasizes the wondrous character of the deliverance. Unkempt hair signified a lack of culture; consequently, the text says that Nebuchadnezzar's hair[7] became as long (*rbh*) as eagle feathers[8] during his period living as an animal. According to Dnl. 7:9, snow-white hair (again *śʿr r'šh*) as a sign of advanced age and exalted dignity characterizes the figure of the Ancient of Days, outside of time and space, in the vision of the judgment of the world.[9]

A couple of texts from Qumran employ hair as a characteristic of special people: once in the praise of Sarah's perfect beauty[10] and again in the ominous, but largely fragmentary description of Noah, which bestows superhuman features upon him.[11] His hair[12] is reddish (*śmqmq*),[13] which was still very rare among the native population and, as with David (*'dmwny*, "reddish, auburn"), constituted a mark of beauty (1 S. 16:12; 17:42).

Gzella

---

2. Regarding the feminine form, first clearly attested only later, → II.
3. 4Q561 4-6 2:4.
4. An Aramaic feminine plural, cf. *ATTM*, 717.
5. See Botterweck, 5-20.
6. Dt-stem pass.
7. Here without *r'š* and thus probably including the beard.
8. → *nšr* II.
9. → *ʿtyq* III; *nqh* II.
10. 1QapGen 20:3, the sole old instance of a woman's hair.
11. 4Q561 11:16; 2:4; 10:4; in addition to the "delicate" beard, → *dqq*; according to *ATTM*, 2, 498, *śʿrn* in 4Q561 1 1:16 is an adjective "hairy" (cf. *DJPA*, 572a), not the plural of an only later certainly attested fem. individual noun *śʿrh* "a single hair" (*DJPA*, 572a.; *DJBA*, 1189f.; *LexSyr*, 689).
12. *śʿrh* in the reading of *ATTM*, 2, 163, thus with a possessive suff. and not a fem.
13. 4Q534 1 1:2.

שאל š'l; שאלה š'lh /ša'elā/

I. Etymology, Lexical Field, and Constructions. II. General Meaning "to Ask, to Request." III. Idiomatic Expressions. 1. Salutation. 2. Passive. 3. Noun "Question."

I. Etymology, Lexical Field, and Constructions. In the older Aramaic languages, the common Semitic verbal root *š'l* "to ask, to request" appears only in the G-stem. Since a stated question per se implies the wish for an answer, the usage for "to request" arises from the general meaning for a verbal communication; thus, *š'l* can also find usage as a verb of speech and introduce direct address.[1] In contrast, → *bʿī* "to seek, to wish, to request" emphasizes the intention so that it can also function mostly, in contrast to *š'l*, as a modal verb "to want to, to be about to." With the general nuance, "to ask," *š'l* generally appears in narrative texts with passages of dialogue, in pre-Christian times chiefly in the framework narrative of Aḥiqar, then in Biblical Aramaic and in narrative texts from Qumran. The frequent usage of the verb in the introductory formula of Imperial Aramaic letters is related to the usage "to ask about someone's well-being" (→ III.1).

The passive, in pre-Christian Aramaic both in the form of the inner passive and of the Gt-stem, finds usage in the specific sense of "to be questioned," "to be called to account," and is part of Imperial Aramaic legal and administrative terminology. Other stems first appear in the post-Christian era, especially the C-stem for "to loan out, to lend."[2]

In the transitive G-stem, *š'l* occurs with an animate direct object "to ask someone," then in Imperial Aramaic often after the object particle *l*-, or with an inanimate object "to ask something." Both could appear alongside one another in the construction with a dual object "someone something" (e.g., Dnl. 2:10; Ezr. 5:10). The content of the question or request can also be specified through a prepositional expression with *ʿl* "with respect to."[3] Analogously, the verb with the meaning "to request" takes a dual (Ezr. 7:21) or simple object with the preposition *mn* "from."[4] If the emphasis does not lie on the verbal act itself (see above), a verb of speech such as *'mr*[5] can specify the content.[6] No difference in meaning is evident, since *š'l* appears both with and without *'mr* in otherwise identical connections.[7] Furthermore, the particle /ha-/ can introduce a question.[8]

H.-F. Fuhs, "שָׁאַל *šā'al*," *TDOT*, XIV, 249-64; G. Gerleman, "שאל *š'l* to ask, request," *TLOT*, 1282-84; M. Shemesh, "*š'l*," *ThWQ*, III, 799-802.

1. E.g., in 4Q196 13:2 (Tob. 6:7).
2. *DJPA*, 532f.; *DJBA*, 1098; *LexSyr*, 748.
3. *TADAE* A2.3,6; 5.2,9.
4. *TADAE* A6.15:3.
5. As a finite form or as an inf. functioning as a particle introducing speech, → *mll* V.
6. Ezr. 5:10f.; 4Q243 1:1.
7. Cf. 4Q196 13:2 (Tob. 6:7) with 4Q197 4 3:5 (Tob. 7:3).
8. *ATTM*, 558; 2, 382.

The feminine /šaʼelā/ functions as a verbal noun "question." In addition, nominal forms of the verb appear in names: in analogy to the Hebrew form /šaʼūl/ "Requested One," the passive participle /šaʼīl/ as in Σιλας (Acts 15)[9] and sometimes also another feminine noun of the *qatāl* pattern /šaʼālā/ as in Shealtiel "El is my question" in, e.g., Ezr. 5:2 and already attested in earlier cuneiform.[10]

II. General Meaning "to Ask, to Request." Since its earliest appearance in later Old Aramaic, *š'l* appears in varied contexts. The relationship between subject and addressee also differs in that, in addition to the purely informative "to ask," various nuances occur ranging from "to ask pleadingly" (when addressing a superior) and "to ask demandingly" (to inferiors). The Asshur ostracon also seems to relate to an official investigation,[11] which may have given rise to the use of the passive for "to be questioned" (→ III.2); it first appears generally for "to ask after" (*'l*) someone in a private letter from Hermopolis;[12] and then in an Imperial Aramaic administrative letter for "to request" in reference to an official request[13] and in a petition in relation to a legal authority *š'l 'l dnh* "to ask/request concerning."[14] Passages of dialogue in narrative texts employ it similarly for "to ask,"[15] in marital law also for "to ask for someone's hand."[16] It also appears frequently in letters on ostraca without sufficient context.

Biblical Aramaic employs *š'l* consistently in relation to information demanded by superiors: In Ezra of the opponents to the construction of the temple who want to see authorization from the Jewish elders and ask the name of the pertinent persons to notify (Ezr. 5:9f.),[17] and in Daniel of the king who wants to know his own dream and its interpretation from the sign interpreters (Dnl. 2:10f.,27). Ezra thus utilizes the verb in the context of an official hearing, in Daniel in the sense that the king's wish is an order.

Qumran also manifests *š'l* primarily in narrative contexts where the question so indicated usually addresses a bearer of superhuman knowledge, however, and aims at higher understanding, as with Tobias who asks the angel about the healing and exorcizing power of fish entrails,[18] Amram, who seeks an explanation from the two angels of the good and evil powers that determine the human fate,[19] or the visionary of the historical apocalypse of the four trees who wants to know from each of them what their name is (*mn šmk*), i.e., what (which empire) each symbolizes.[20] If the

9. Cf. *ATTM*, 131 and, for later examples, 699.
10. Cf. *ATTM*, 95.
11. *KAI* 233.12.
12. *TADAE* A2.3:6, cf. D7.13:4,6; without addition 7.33:4.
13. *TADAE* A6.15:3, for a certain number of Cilician following *mn* "of."
14. *TADAE* A5.2:9.
15. *TADAE* C1.1,77; furthermore in l. 11 perhaps 'to request," but the immediate context is lost.
16. *TADAE* B3.8:3; 6.1:3.
17. In 5:4 a simple *'mr* introduces a similar question with no verb.
18. 4Q196 13:2 (Tob. 6:7).
19. 4Q544 1:11; 3:1.
20. Obtained in two cases: 4Q552 1 2:5.8 par. 4Q553 3+2 2+4:4 and always introducing speech, in 4Q553 3+2 2+4:5 together with *'mr*; → I on the two constructions.

widely espoused emendation *wš'*]*lw* in 1QapGen 19:25 is accepted,[21] it also applies to pharaoh's question concerning Abraham's divine wisdom and probably also to the fragmentarily preserved question to Daniel in 4Q243 1:1. Beyer's emendation of the lacuna *d*[*y š'y*]*l* "what is asked" in Enoch's introduction to his vision report[22] conforms to this pattern as does Enoch's question to the interpreting angel in 1 En. 22:6.[23] Edna's question to Tobias and the angel concerning who they are[24] is admittedly neutral, but she does ask it in a similar context of a wondrous encounter. Thus, it regularly involves the communication of divine knowledge, either through an *angelus interpres* in a vision or through an otherwise gifted mediator of superhuman understanding. Further examples of this situation include the literally translated passages in the dialogue between Job and God in 11Q10 30:1 (Job 38:3) and 37:6 (42:4), and in an ironic reversal of roles in 34:3 (40:7). The infinitive in 11Q10 19:7 (Job 31:30) can presumably be emended by comparison to the MT, but the fragmentary context permits no certain conclusions. A few additional passages are likewise fragmentary or uncertain as to the reading.[25] The verb occurs once clearly in the sense of "to petition" in a contract text.[26]

III. Idiomatic Expressions.

1. Salutation. With → *šlm* "joy, well-being" as the object, *š'l* with a human subject means "to greet," in communication the greeting of a third party ("sends you greetings") in a letter[27] or in an account.[28] With a divine subject, it apparently has the nuance "to be concerned about" and is part of a frequent salutation in Imperial Aramaic letters, between equals[29] and to superiors.[30] It occurs in several variants and with various divine names; the version with only *šlm* is probably an abbreviation.[31] A few examples on ostraca are fragmentary.

2. Passive. For the passive, the perfect still employs the inner passive, but the Gt-stem replaces it in the imperfect.[32] It appears in the context of juridical procedures for "to be

---

21. Presumably correctly, *ATTM*, 173; cf. D. A. Machiela, *The Dead Sea Genesis Apocryphon. STDJ* 79 (2009), 73.

22. 1QapGen 5:9 following *ATTM*, 2, 90; Machiela's critique (41), without offering a counter-suggestion, does not pertain to the emendation *š'y*]*l* itself.

23. *ATTM*, 241.

24. 4Q197 4 3:5 (Tob. 7:3).

25. 4Q541 17:2; 4Q543 14:1; 25:3; 4Q546 4:3.

26. V 50:11 in *ATTM*, 2, 253f., in reference to an illiterate person who sought someone else to sign in her place; → *ktb* III.

27. *TADAE* A2.3:3; 2.6:2,7; D1.1:7.

28. 4Q197 4 3:3 (Tob. 7:1), in reference to an encounter; 4Q213 1 1:18, as homage.

29. *TADAE* A3.5:1; 3.6:1; 3.10:1; 4.4:1.

30. *TADAE* A3.7:1; 3.9:1; 4.2:2; 4.7:2 par. 4.8:2.

31. See D. Schwiderski, *Handbuch des nordwestsemitischen Briefformulars. BZAW* 295 (2000), 115-26.

32. Cf. the parallels *TADAE* A5.2:3 and 5.4:5.

questioned"[33] and in letters from superior officials as a threat "to be brought to account (for flawed fulfillment of a task)."[34]

3. Noun "Question." In older Aramaic, only Dnl. 4:14 attests the noun *š'lh* /ša'elā/ "question" with the juridical connotation "demand" of a divine verdict alongside *gzrh*[35] and → *ptgm*.

Gzella

33. *TADAE* In addition to A5.2:3 and 5.4:5 also B2.9:8; 7.1:3; 7.2:6; 8.7:2; 8.8:5, with the rare corresponding active in l. 8; 8.10:6; Segal, 7.5; 13.1.
34. *TADAE* A6.8:3; 6.15:8; 6.10:9; J. Naveh and S. Shaked, *Aramaic Documents from Ancient Bactria (Fourth Century* B.C.E.*)* (London, 2012), A1,3f.,10.
35. → *gzr* VI.

שאר *š'r*; שאר *š'r* /šo'ār/; שארי *š'ry* /šērī/

I. Etymology and Lexical Field. II. Verb "to Survive, Remain." III. Noun "Remnant."

I. Etymology and Lexical Field. The root *š'r* "to survive, remain" belongs to the common West Semitic lexicon. In accordance with its medial significance, it appears in Aramaic in the Gt-stem in analogy with the N-stem in Hebrew. More frequent are the nominal forms, masculine /šo'ār/ and feminine /šērī/,[1] both with the meaning "remnant" and, as in Hebrew, semantically not clearly distinguishable from one another. In any case, /šērī/ seems typical of Imperial Aramaic texts from the Achaemenid period, while /šo'ār/ knows a broader distribution.

II. Verb "to Survive, Remain." In usage as a verb in the Gt-stem, *š'r* first appears twice in Imperial Aramaic contracts for a sum already[2] or not yet[3] paid. In both passages, *'l* "at the expense of" supplements it.[4] A few instances of the G-stem perfect *š'r* "remain" also occur here,[5] others could be nouns (→ III). At Qumran, the Gt-stem occurs only in

R. E. Clements, "שְׁאָר *šā'ar*," *TDOT*, XIV, 272-86; P. B. Hartog, "*š'r*," *ThWQ*, III, 802-6; H. Wildberger, "שאר *š'r* to remain," *TLOT*, 1284-92.

1. From */se'rī/, cf. *ATTM*, 2, 486.
2. *TADAE* B3.12:6.
3. *TADAE* B4.2:9.
4. Cf. *DNSI*, 1098 for bib.
5. *TADAE* D7.8:16; 7.17:12, with *l'* "not"; perhaps also 7.47:2.

small fragments; every case seems to involve eschatological contexts,[6] perhaps under the influence of Hebrew prophecy.

III. Noun "Remnant." The noun *š'r* /šo'ār/ "remnant" often appears in Imperial Aramaic in commercial contexts in reference to goods,[7] in the Behistun inscription to troops.[8] In Biblical Aramaic it denotes "the remaining" in general.[9] The examples from Qumran all stem from formulaic expressions in the calculation of the course of the moon in 4Q208-209 (1 En. 73) for the "rest of the night" or "of its light." Further, two Nabatean treaties employ it of the rest of the goods or of a harvest.[10] In Palmyrene, it designates the remainder of persons[11] or part of a building.[12]

Similarly general is the use of *š'ry* /šērī/ in Imperial Aramaic,[13] but unlike *š'r* clearly recognizable as a noun even in the consonantal spelling.

Gzella

6. 4Q537 1+2+3:1, presumably of the holy remnant of the righteous, *ṣdyqy'*; 4Q556a 5 1:8; 4Q581 1-2:5.

7. *TADAE* C3.22:7; 3.28:2f.,4,17,44,55,69f.; Segal, 24.6; 38.20.

8. *TADAE* C2.1:40.

9. Persons: Dnl. 2:18; Ezr. 4:7,9f.,17; 6:16; the animals of the vision: Dnl. 7:7,12,19; goods: Ezr. 7:18,20.

10. nV 7:4 and 22:34 in *ATTM*, 2, 218-23,236f.

11. *PAT* 1063.4.

12. *PAT* 0047.2.

13. *TADAE* A4.7:11 par. 4.8:10; B3.8:23,26f.; 8.1:11.

שבח *šbḥ*; תשבחה *tšbḥh* /tašboḥā/

I. Etymology and Lexical Field. II. "To Praise." III. "Praise."

I. Etymology and Lexical Field. In contrast to the common Semitic root *hll* and to the common West Semitic → *ydī*, *šbḥ* "to praise" is, at least during the historical period, a characteristic of the Aramaic lexicon and came, thence, into Hebrew[1] and further into

E. Jenni, *Das hebräische Pi'el* (Zurich, 1968); C. Stadel, "*tšbwḥt*," *ThWQ*, III, 1164-68.

1. M. Wagner, *Die lexikalischen und grammatikalischen Aramaismen im alttestamentlichen Hebräisch. BZAW* 96 (1966), 111.

Arabic and Ethiopic.[2] If the once-attested Ugaritic personal name *ʾašbḥ*[3] is related, the verb may have an older Semitic etymology, however.

It appears in the transitive D-stem and, in religious literature, often refers to the praise of gods, including pagan deities (Dnl. 5:4,23). It is difficult to make a semantic distinction between it and → *brk*, → *hdr*, *hll* (rather rare in Aramaic), → *ydī*, and → *rīm* in the L-stem, with which if often stands in parallel, but *šbḥ* could be meant more neutrally and descriptive "to declare someone praiseworthy," while the other verbs imply more of personal knowledge or thanks for a demonstration of divine grace; accordingly, *šbḥ* also denotes praise for a human being (→ II). Related is the feminine substantive /tašboḥā/ "praise," which also appears together with nouns from the same root as the verb.

II. "To Praise." Evidence of *šbḥ* begins with Biblical Aramaic; the book of Daniel uses it five times: twice in the account of Belshazzar and his court praising the idols (Dnl. 5:4,23) and, each time in the first-person, once in the confession of Nebuchadnezzar who has reached knowledge of the true God (4:31,34), and in Daniel's song of thanksgiving for the knowledge that God has shared with him (2:23). Both of the latter two passages employ *šbḥ* as praise for God for an evident benevolence and appear together with semantically related terms, → *ydī* in 2:23, → *brk* and → *hdr* in 4:31, and → *rīm* with *hdr* in 4:34. It is therefore entirely possible that *šbḥ* had a more general meaning[4] that was given added precision through parallelism with more specific verbs of thankful confessions or acknowledgments of God's superior majesty, which simultaneously also mention the reason for the praise. The D-stem of *šbḥ* can thereby be understood as declarative-estimative;[5] thus, the verb is more descriptive than confessional.

In 1QapGen 10:8, a call to praise, fragmentary, but apparently directed to the true God, a synonym, here *hll*,[6] rare in Aramaic, joins *šbḥ*. In contrast, 11Q10 14:5 (Job 29:11) employs it in reference to a human—Job himself, whom others once happily praised[7]—with no further terms. The possible emendation of a form of *šbḥ* in 4Q196 17 2:7 (Tob. 13:9), Tobit's song of praise, is uncertain because the verb may have also appeared in one of the numerous lacunae in the preceding section of lines.[8]

As a verb with no specific religious connotation, *šbḥ* therefore also occurs in the diction of the Palmyrene honorary inscriptions for meritorious citizens.[9] Even in later usage, it is not necessarily associated with praise of God, but can additionally represent "to recommend," "to praise," etc.[10]

---

2. T. Nöldeke, *Neue Beiträge zur semitischen Sprachwissenschaft* (Strassburg, 1910), 36.
3. *DUL*³, 112 (erroneously cited there as *ʾašbú*).
4. Cf. K. Koch, *Daniel 1–4*. *BK* XXII/1 (2005), 180.
5. Cf. Jenni, 216f.,246,248.
6. → *ydī* I.
7. For Hebrew *ʾšr.*
8. So *DSSStE*, 386f.; *ATTM*, 2, 184 suggests *rw*]*ḥy*.
9. *PAT* 0197.8; likewise, the adjective *šbyḥyt* "in praiseworthy manner" in *PAT* 1378.7, with *nhwryt* "brilliant," in the Greek version λαμπρῶς καὶ ἐνδόξως.
10. Cf. *DJPA*, 534; *DJBA*, 1101; *LexSyr*, 751.

III. "Praise." The noun *tšbḥh* "praise," first identifiable at Qumran, also belongs to religious diction and refers in hymnic contexts to the praise of God. Like the verb (→ II), other terms often supplement it, such as *brkh*[11] and *hdr*.[12] Qumran also attests it for entities near God such as truth or wisdom,[13] and proper behavior.[14] The latter three occurrences all stand in the admonitions of Enoch and Qahat, which have wisdom connotations; consequently, this noun seems to belong to the fixed vocabulary of ethico-religious paranesis.

Furthermore, in later texts one encounters the nouns *šbḥ*, *šbwḥ* or *šwbḥ* in other patterns, but with the same meaning.[15] The hypothesized reading *šbḥ* toward the beginning of the line in 1QapGen 11:13[16] is uncertain paleographically, however; consequently, *DSSStE*, 34f., refrains entirely from attempting to decipher it.

Gzella

---

11. 1QapGen 11:13, Noah's song of thanks after the flood and employed in reference to God.

12. 4Q201 1 2:10 par. 4Q204 1 1:29 (1 En. 5:1); in the subsequent clause then the call to praise with the verb *hll* "praise."

13. 4Q212 1 2:15 (1 En. 91:10); because of differences in the formulation of the parallel versions, the Aram. wording cannot be precisely reconstructed, but God himself may also be mentioned here.

14. 4Q542 1 1:11, in parallel with *dy'ṣ* "jubilation" (from the verb *dūṣ*, *ATTM*, 2, 373) and *ḥdw'* "joy" (→ *ḥdwh*).

15. *DJPA*, 533f.; *DJBA*, 1101f.; *LexSyr*, 750; in addition, Syriac knows various other nominal forms; *MdD*, 453.

16. So along with other editors, recently also D. A. Machiela, *The Dead Sea Genesis Apocryphon*. *STDJ* 79 (2009), 54.

שבט *šbṭ* /šabṭ/; חטר *ḥṭr* /ḥoṭr/

I. Etymology and Lexical Field. II. Noun "Stick," "Stem." III. Noun "Rod, Scepter."

I. Etymology and Lexical Field. As a term for "stick, staff," the masculine /šabṭ/,[1] in a few Aramaic languages secondarily revocalized as a *qitl*-form /šibṭ/, rarely *qutl* /šobṭ/,[2] is common Semitic. The characteristic figurative meaning "tribe" in Jewish literary texts[3] is borrowed from Hebrew; Aramaic otherwise employs the ethnic terms → *'m* "people" and *'mh* "tribe, clan" for population groups.

M. Becker, "*šbṭ*," *ThWQ*, III, 812-15 (Heb.); H.-J. Zobel, "שֵׁבֶט *šēḇeṭ*," *TDOT*, XIV, 302-11.

1. From the fifth century B.C.E. with anaptyxis /šabəṭ/.

2. *ATTM*, 700.

3. In older Aram. once for certain in Ezra and perhaps once in the Testament of Amram from Qumran.

In its literal use, /šabṭ/ overlaps with the likewise common Semitic masculine /ḥoṭr/[4] "rod, scepter." The evidence permits no certain conclusions concerning possible original semantic distinctions. Indeed, a few old non-Jewish instances employ /šabṭ/ in the sense of "(divine) rod," while, additionally, at least in Sam'alian, which has lexical affinities with Aramaic,[5] /ḥoṭr/ can denote "scepter,"[6] but the limited distribution makes it unclear whether these usages are actually representative of the specific semantics of the two lexemes.

II. Noun "Stick," "Stem." For earliest Aramaic, the literal meaning of *šbṭ* "stick" in the metaphorical expression *šbṭ dy nyrgl* "rod of Nergal" as a paraphrase for the plague (*mwtn*)[7] in the concluding curse formula of the Tell Fekheriye inscription[8] is assured. To the contrary, the description of the sin offering in Ezr. 6:17, in which twelve goats are sacrificed for the twelve tribes of Israel,[9] has connections with Hebrew conceptions; indeed, the conceptualization of ethnic identity as an alliance of tribes designated as such is known only for Israel. Finally, with respect to 4Q548 1 2-2:1 from Qumran, it remains unclear due to the fragmentary context whether it represents the nuance "stick" or "tribe."[10]

III. Noun "Rod, Scepter." In the earliest and only clear instance, *ḥṭr* also occurs in the context of upbringing through chastisement;[11] two additional specimens are too fragmentary for a closer determination.[12]

Gzella

4. From */ḫoṭr/; in Aram. then secondarily opened to /ḥoṭar/.
5. For its classification, see P. M. Noorlander, "Sam'alian in Its Northwest Semitic Setting," *Or* 81 (2012) 202-38.
6. *KAI* 214.9,15,20,25.
7. → *mūt* VI.
8. *KAI* 309.23.
9. → *'z* III.
10. So *ATTM*, 2, 120, on R 5:1; cf. C. Stadel, *Hebraismen in den aramäischen Texten vom Toten Meer* (Heidelberg, 2008), 62.
11. *TADAE* C1.1:176.
12. *TADAE* B8.5a:5; D4.26:5.

שׁבק *šbq*

I. Etymology, Lexical Field, and Constructions. II. Old and Imperial Aramaic. III. Biblical Aramaic. IV. Aramaic Texts from the Dead Sea.

I. Etymology, Lexical Field, and Constructions. The verb *šbq* "to let" represents a characteristic of the Aramaic lexicon and has no direct connections with other Semitic roots; at least in terms of phonetics, Arabic *sabaqa* "to prevent" would come into question,[1] but the semantic development in this case remains unclear.

Aramaic employs *šbq* in the transitive G-stem with a number of differing nuances, which, depending on the nature of the direct object and other complements, can be divided very roughly into "to allow someone to make something," "to leave something, to set aside" or "to forgive," and "to leave someone behind, to dismiss." For "to set free" of persons, Aramaic has the more rare → *ntr* in the C-stem and *pṭr*,[2] both of which occur in this meaning in Imperial Aramaic, or at Qumran *plṭ* in the D-stem.[3] In the Imperial Aramaic written tradition, *l-* often introduces an animate direct object, but *l-* can also indicate the indirect object "to someone" with the nuance "to cede," "to set aside," or "to forgive." Furthermore, the verb can take other adverbial expressions such as *byd* "in the hand." The extensive semantic overlap with the Hebrew verb *ʿzb* "to abandon" manifests itself in the Aramaic translation of *ʿᵃzaḇtānī* "you have abandoned me" (Ps. 22:2) with σαβαχθανι for /šabaqtānī/ in Mk. 15:34 and Mt. 27:46.[4]

The Gt-stem indicates the passive voice "to be ceded, to be set free, to be abandoned," as does, in the first pre-Christian millennium, the inner passive, which in the perfect, as attested through Qumran, and in the participle also emphasizes the result.[5] In any case, the two categories seem to be partially interchangeable already in Imperial Aramaic, cf. the variation in *TADAE* A6.7:9 and B3.6:9f.[6] Post-Christian Jewish Palestinian also employs the D-stem "to reject," generally in the context of divorce.[7] The *plurale tantum* of the noun *šbqyn* "divorce" (formation unknown), however, already occurs in private documents from the Judean wilderness;[8] Qumran attests the *qitl*-noun /šibq/ "open room, access balcony."[9]

II. Old and Imperial Aramaic. The first specimens of the verb *šbq* occur in the later Old Aramaic of the sayings of Aḥiqar. Already here, it appears in various usages: for "to let" with an article of clothing that an evildoer had snatched (*ʾḥd*), but which one had left in his hand and should bring his case before the sun god (who sees all and, thus, was regarded as the guardian of righteousness),[10] and with gold in the sense "to leave in

---

E. S. Gerstenberger, "עָזַב *ʿāzaḇ*," *TDOT* X, 584-92; H. Gzella, "*šbq*," *ThWQ*, III, 832-35; H.-P. Stähli, "עזב *ʿzb* to abandon," *TLOT*, 866-68.

1. Wehr⁵, 548; so also I. Kottsieper, *Die Sprache der Ahiqarsprüche. BZAW* 194 (1990), 233, but with reservations.
2. *TADAE* A3.9:7; t-passive A3.3:13.
3. → *nṣl* IV.2.
4. Regarding the form, see *ATTM*, 130.
5. Cf. *šbyqt* "I was left over" in 1QapGen 20:10.
6. On the disappearance of the inner passive in Aramaic, see *ATTM*, 152.
7. *DJPA*, 537.
8. *ATTM*, 702; 2, 487.
9. 2Q24 1:2 par. 4Q554 1 2:13 and 5Q15 1 1:1.
10. *TADAE* C1.1:107.

someone's care, to entrust,"[11] both with "in the hand";[12] it is attested for "to leave behind" of persons,[13] for "to let run" of an ass;[14] it also has the connotation "to let happen" or "to leave someone to themselves" in the sense of an antiauthoritarian upbringing, which, as is well-known, only leads to ruin.[15] In two additional passages, the constructions and precise meanings are not clear.[16] The Philistine prince Adon's plea for help, who asks the pharaoh to send him military assistance and not to abandon him,[17] stems from about the same period.

The occurrences from the Achaemenid period exhibit a similar spectrum of meaning: in the pre-Imperial Aramaic letters from Hermopolis for "to leave behind" of goods[18] and persons;[19] in Imperial Aramaic also of goods[20] and of asses for "to let run"[21] and of persons;[22] further, for "to abandon a post [*mnṭrh*]"[23] and with an infinitive as complement, permissively for "to allow to do, to permit."[24] In the juridical diction of the private document, in contrast, it can mean "to set free,"[25] perhaps also "to remit debts."[26] In a couple of additional instances, the context cannot be reconstructed exactly because of lacunae.[27] The official letters from Bactria employ the verb mostly of persons who are held in some way or hindered in their work,[28] and once supplemented with an infinitive for "to allow to do."[29]

The passive[30] generally corresponds to the usages also attested in the active voice. It represents "to be set free" of persons[31] and "to be abandoned" of land.[32] The context in *WDSP* 2:7 is unclear as is the nuance in *KAI* 319.18 (freedom from taxes?).

---

11. *TADAE* C1.1:192.
12. → *yd.*
13. *TADAE* C1.1:111.
14. *TADAE* C1.1:185.
15. *TADAE* C1.1:177.
16. *TADAE* C1.1:98,112.
17. *TADAE* A1.1:7
18. *TADAE* A2.2:15; 2.4:10.
19. *TADAE* A2.4:4.
20. *TADAE* D7. 18:2; 7.33:3.
21. *TADAE* A3.1 recto l. 6, cf. *TADAE* C1.1:185.
22. *TADAE* A3.8:11.
23. *TADAE* A4.5:1.
24. *TADAE* 4.7:23 par. 4.8:23; Segal, 26.3,5,8.
25. Of slaves *TADAE* B3.6:4; 8.5:9 perhaps of prisoners; with no further context also on a very brief ostracon from Idumea, see I. Eph'al and J. Naveh, *Aramaic Ostraca of the Fourth Century BC from Idumaea* (Jerusalem, 1996), no. 196, l. 2.
26. *TADAE* B4.7:5, but the context is fragmentary.
27. *TADAE* A3.1 verso l. 6; D1.17:4; Segal, 26.9.
28. J. Naveh and S. Shaked, *Aramaic Documents from Ancient Bactria (Fourth Century B.C.E.)* (London, 2012), A1,5,6,7,11, of camel herders who are extorted or harassed; 4,4f.; 6,10.
29. A1,2.
30. For the distribution of forms, → I.
31. *TADAE* A6.7:9; B3.6:9f.
32. *TADAE* A6.11:2,4.

III. Biblical Aramaic. Of the numerous uses of the verb already attested in Imperial Aramaic, Biblical Aramaic attests the nuances "to leave over" (Dnl. 4:12,20,23, of rootstock[33] in Nebuchadnezzar's dream and with the connotation "to spare") and "to allow" (Ezr. 6:7, of the work on the temple). Furthermore, in the Gt-passive stem it represents "to be delivered" (Dnl. 2:44, negated of the eternal kingdom of God that will be delivered to no other nation).

IV. Aramaic Texts from the Dead Sea. On one hand, the approximately twenty instances from Qumran continue the usage documented in Imperial Aramaic: *šbq* here denotes "to transfer property,"[34] "to free a prisoner,"[35] and in the passive "to be left to someone."[36] Much as in Dnl. 4, in Abraham's dream of the cedar and the date palm, it has the connotation "to spare."[37] Likewise, it is used of persons to mean "to let go"[38] and in the wisdom reworking of inheritance terminology, as known in private documents from the Judean wilderness,[39] the ethico-religious legacy of the patriarchs.[40]

On the other hand, decidedly theological uses also appear at Qumran. They include the wisdom motif of abandoning the proper path[41] and, especially, the connotation "to forgive sins."[42] The construction with the suffixed preposition *lh* in 4Q242 1-3:4, which involves the removal of King Nabonidus's guilt by a Jewish exorcist, is unclear; here the preposition may refer either, as an object particle, to the prepended direct object[43] or perhaps, as a *dativus ethicus*, to the subject and thus indicate ingressive action. In any case, this usage also rests on an originally juridical expression "to remit debts."[44] Additionally, it may underlie the petition "and forgive us our debt" in the Lord's Prayer (Mt. 6:12: ὀφειλήματα "debts"; Lk. 11:4: ἁμαρτίας "sins").[45]

The feminine passive participle appears once in a substantival usage in 11Q10 31:4 (Job 38:27) for "abandoned land."[46]

For a more thorough discussion of these and a few fragmentary examples from Qumran,[47] see Gzella.

Gzella

---

33. → *ʿqr* III.
34. 1QapGen 22:20.
35. 1QapGen 22:25.
36. 4Q196 2:2 (Tob. 1:20), of property.
37. 1QapGen 19:15f., both in the act. and the pass., as also in the reality described through the dream: 19:19; 20:10.
38. 4Q543 3:1 par. 4Q545 1a-b 2:17 par. 4Q546 2:3.
39. Cf. nV 2; 3; 7; instances in *ATTM*, 2, 487.
40. 4Q542 1 1:12.
41. 4Q213 4:5.
42. 4Q242 1-3:4; 11Q10 38:2 (Job 42:9 following LXX, contra MT).
43. So also *DJD*, XXII (1996), 90.
44. Cf. nV 42:26 in *ATTM*, 2, 245.
45. Cf. the extensive treatment in J. Luzarraga, *El Padrenuestro desde el arameo*. *AnBib* 171 (2008), 130f.
46. Heb. *mšʾh*.
47. 4Q243 33:1; 4Q546 24:2; 4Q556a 1 1:10; 4Q558 64:3.

שׁבשׁ *šbš*

I. Etymology and Lexical Field. II. Usage.

I. Etymology and Lexical Field. The etymology of the Aramaic verb *šbš*, in the Dt-stem a middle-passive "to be confused," "to fall into confusion," is uncertain, involving the rare identity of the first and third radicals.[1] It first occurs in the book of Daniel, which attests a rich psychological vocabulary, and then twice at Qumran, but continues to be productive in East Aramaic, which also attests it in the G-stem.[2] Its meaning overlaps with that of → *bhl* "to be terrified" (the two appear together in Dnl. 5:9). The lexical field includes *krī* "to be confused" (Dnl. 7:15); for additional terms → *ʿṣb* "to worry" and → *dḥl* "to fear."

II. Usage. In Dnl. 5:9, *šbš* denotes the terror of Belshazzar's court in view of the eerie flaming writing with the initially puzzling divine verdict and appears here as a synonym of → *bhl* for the reaction of the king himself. In 1QapGen 5:16, the context is too fragmentary for a more precise determination, but it, too, seems to stand in the context of a vision report (in 15:18, by contrast, one might perhaps read a form of *šmš* "to serve, to honor," as Beyer suggests in *ATTM*, 2, 98).[3] Finally, 4Q541 9 1:7 parallels *šbš* with *ṭʿī* "to stray."[4]

Gzella

1. Cf. *GesB*[18], 1538.
2. *DJBA*, 1106f.; *LexSyr*, 766; *MdD*, 448,457,470.
3. Contra D. A. Machiela, *The Dead Sea Genesis Apocryphon*. *STDJ* 79 (2009), 63, who is confident of the reading *mtšbšyn*, but the parallelism with → *plḥ* "to serve" would be unusual.
4. → *ḥṭī* V.

שׁגל *šgl* /šēgal/

I. Etymology and Lexical Field. II. Usage.

I. Etymology and Lexical Field. Aramaic borrowed *šgl* /šēgal/ "king's consort" from Akkadian; it is usually associated with *ša ekalli* "she of the palace."[1] It traveled further

S. A. Kaufman, *The Akkadian Influences on Aramaic*. *AS* 19 (1974).

1. Kaufman, 97; *ATTM*, 703; *GesB*[18], 1323; sometimes another derivation, from *issu ekalli*

into Hebrew, presumably through Aramaic (Ps. 45:10; Neh. 2:6). The precise status at court of the person so designated is unknown,[2] but the meaning "queen" is certain, at least for the loanword in Hebrew usage. Dnl. 5 (→ II) employs it in the plural along with that of *lḥnh* "lady of the court,"[3] which may imply a quite late devaluation from "queen" to "concubine." Dnl. 5:2,3,10 juxtaposes both groups with the *mlkh*,[4] although it remains unclear whether this term, not historically verified,[5] refers to the queen mother or the main wife.

II. Usage. In older Aramaic, *šgl* occurs only in Dnl. 5:2f.,23 and, in the plural in a stereotypical expression repeated three times, it indicates a group of women who, together with the *lḥnn* (→ I) and the *rbrbn* "nobles" of the king, participate in Belshazzar's decadent and blasphemous celebration as mere extras. The account distinguishes them from the *mlkh* in 5:10 (→ I), who avoids the revelry and only enters the hall after the appearance of the flaming letters on the wall with the divine verdict in order to direct Belshazzar to Daniel who, thanks to his gift of divine wisdom, could read the oracle (5:11f.). The original concept gives way to didactic typification: in foolhardy arrogance, the celebrating king with his entourage of concubines (*šgln*) and other courtesans[6] drinks himself to judgment, while, thanks to her own knowledge of events in the time of Nebuchadnezzar, Belshazzar's father,[7] the modest queen knows what to do and senses the divine power in Daniel.

Gzella

"woman of the palace," is suggested, cf. P. Mankowski, *Akkadian Loanwords in Biblical Hebrew. HSS* 47 (2000), 137f., with bib.; but it would presuppose a complicated phonetic development.

2. For extensive analysis of the state of the evidence, see B. Landsberger, "Akkadisch-hebräische Wortgleichungen," *Hebräische Wortforschung. FS W. Baumgartner. SVT* 16 (1967), 198-204.

3. → *lḥn.*

4. → *mlk* II.2.

5. Landsberger, 204.

6. *lḥnh* was later understood as "concubine."

7. Which would speak for an interpretation of *mlkh* as queen mother.

שׁוי *šwī*; שׁוה *šwh* /šawæ/

I. Etymology, Lexical Field, and Constructions. II. G-stem "to Resemble." III. D-stem "to Make Into." IV. Adjective "Suitable, Apt."

M. Sæbø, "שָׁוָה *šāwâ*," *TDOT*, VII, 330-45.

I. Etymology, Lexical Field, and Constructions. Because of the differentiated meanings in Aramaic as in Hebrew, forms of *šwī* divide synchronously into two homonymous routes, *šwī* I, in the G-stem "to be like," and *šwī* II, in the D-stem "to lay," but the categorization is not always clear[1] and the etymology remains unclear in both cases.

The G-stem of *šwī* I "to be like" can take a prepositional expression following *ʿm* "with" and is difficult to clearly distinguish semantically from the Gt-stem "to agree." Meanwhile, the D-stem "to make into" is doubly transitive, but forms of the corresponding t-passive have affinities with *šwī* II "to lay" and lexicographers sometimes assign them to it.[2] The adjective /šawæ/ "suitable, apt," which appears with various nuances, belongs to *šwī* I. Meanwhile, → *dmī* represents "to be similar, to resemble" and → *šnī* "to be different."

II. G-stem "to Resemble." The Gt-stem of *šwī* first appears in a contract concerning the apportionment of slaves among the heirs of a mother and means "to agree."[3] In Dnl. 5:21, *šwy* is pointed as a D-stem *šawwī*, which, because of the context, interpreters usually regard as an error for an original G-stem in the sense of an abbreviated comparison "(his heart) became like (that of the animals)."[4] *LexLingAram*, 164 and *GesB*[18], 1539 suspect an inner passive "to be equated," presuming a transitive G-stem; *ATTM*, 704 assumes an intransitive G-stem and suggests an active. The nuance "to correspond" in a formulaic expression in the astronomical book of Enoch about the light in reference to the course of the moon[5] is intransitive.[6]

III. D-stem "to Make Into." In contrast to the G-stem, the D-stem has the factitive meaning "to make it such that something becomes like," consequently "to make into." It has this meaning in Dnl. 3:29 regarding the edict of Nebuchadnezzar that threatens that the houses of blasphemers would be changed to ruins,[7] here in the t-passive (→ I). The active voice appears at Qumran, although the meaning and assignment to one of the two roots are controversial here, too. In 4Q242 1-3:3, one could accept a nuance "to consider to be equalized"[8] and in 4Q214a 2-3 1:4 "to give a name."[9] Other instances, however, remain entirely uncertain and, contra others, surely belong to *šwī* II "to lay," especially in descriptions of sacrifice[10] and the imposition of tribute.[11]

---

1. Cf. *ATTM*, 704, slightly different *GesB*[18], 1539.
2. So Dnl. 3:29 according to *GesB*[18], 1539, contra *LexLingAram*, 164 and *ATTM*, 704.
3. *TADAE* B2.11:2.
4. For the context → *lbb* II.
5. E.g., 4Q209 7 3:7.
6. See H. Drawnel, *The Aramaic Astronomical Book [4Q208-4Q211] from Qumran* (Oxford, 2011), 252f.
7. Cf. 2:5 with K. Koch, *Daniel 1–4. BK* XXII/1 (2005), 90.
8. *ATTM*, 2, 139,489; in *ATTM*, 704, in contrast, *šwī* II "to determine."
9. *ATTM*, 704.
10. 4Q156 1:3 [Lev. 16:13]; 11Q18 8:3; 13:3; cf. *ATTM*, 2, 489.
11. 1QapGen 21:26.

IV. Adjective "Suitable, Apt." Finally, the spectrum of the usage of the adjective *šwh* /šawǣ/ "like" is broad. In financial contexts, such as the dowry lists of Imperial Aramaic marriage contracts, it denotes "with a value of."[12] Various other nuances appear at Qumran: "sufficient"[13] or "symmetrical."[14] In Jason's grave inscription, it seems to denote "appropriate, worthy."[15]

Gzella

12. *TADAE* B2.6:8f.,11f.,13; 3.3:4f.; 3.8:7f.,10f.,12; 6.1:8.
13. 4Q196 13:1 (Tob. 6:5), in reference to provisions for a journey.
14. 4Q561 1 1:3, of teeth.
15. *ATTM*, 329, l. 3.

שור *šwr* /šūr/

I. Etymology and Lexical Field. II. Usage.

I. Etymology and Lexical Field. Aramaic indicates the wall of a city[1] with the masculine /šūr/, distinct from /kotl/ or /ʾeggār/,[2] the wall of a house. It already occurs in Hebrew in archaic poetry (Gen. 49:22; 2 S. 22:30 par. Ps. 18:30), and thus may be an old rare synonym for *gdr* "stone fence" and *ḥwmh* "wall," not an Aramaic loanword.

II. Usage. Old Aramaic already attests the word, which regularly designates a strong, attached wall: in Zakkur's list of accomplishments[3] and, in Imperial Aramaic, in a letter concerning the destruction of the Elephantine temple referring to a wall in the city itself.[4] In Ezra, it refers to the renovation of the city wall of Jerusalem in the report of the opponents of the reconstruction (4:12f.,16), and also in the new Jerusalem from Qumran.[5] On the other hand, 4Q196 1:1 (Tob. 1:17) intends the city wall of Nineveh and, figuratively, 4Q213 1-2 2:2 wisdom as a city that no one can conquer. In 4Q537 12:3 *šwr* also denotes the external wall of a city, as mostly at Hatra.[6]

Gzella

1. → *qryh.*
2. → *ktl.*
3. *KAI* 202 A 10.17; both of a city and also as part of a siege wall.
4. *TADAE* A4.5:5f.
5. 2Q24 8:2; 11Q18 6:2; 12 1:6.
6. H290:4; 336b:9; 343:6; 1027:2; in 272:1: "enclosure wall."

שחת *šḥt*

I. Etymology and Lexical Field. II. Verb and Adjective.

I. Etymology and Lexical Field. The root *šḥt* "to be deformed" has cognates in other West Semitic languages, but occurs much less often in Aramaic than in Hebrew. In Aramaic, the C-stem means "to annihilate." The participle /šaḥīt/ functions as an adjective "bad, ruined." The lexical field includes → *b'š*.

II. Verb and Adjective. In the earliest example, a saying of Aḥiqar, the verb appears in the C-stem "to annihilate," although without sufficient context.[1] The G-stem "to be deformed" occurs in 1QapGen 2:17 for the facial expression of a frightened person. The passive participle *šḥyt* /šaḥīt/ occurs three times in Biblical Aramaic denoting bad behavior, in Dnl. 2:9 a dream interpretation, false under the circumstances, and in 6:5, twice substantivally of the nonexistent error in Daniel's execution of office.[2]

Gzella

J. Conrad, "שָׁחַת *šāḥat*," *TDOT*, XIV, 583-95; T. Hansberger, "*šḥt*," *ThWQ*, III, 899-902.

1. *TADAE* C1.1:155.
2. → *'lh*.

שיזב *šyzb*

I. Etymology. II. Usage. 1. With a Human Subject. 2. With a Divine Subject.

I. Etymology. Aramaic borrowed the verb *šzb* from Neo-Assyrian in the eighth century B.C.E. at the latest. It occurs both in the framework narrative of Aḥiqar and in the proverbs;[1] in addition, around the middle of the seventh century B.C.E., the name *Nb(w)šzb* appears on

J. P. Hyatt, "The Deity Bethel and the OT," *JAOS* 59 (1939) 81-98, esp. 83f.; H. Ingholt, *Studier over Palmyrensk Skulptur* (Copenhagen, 1928), esp. no. 3:2; S. A. Kaufman, *The Akkadian Influences on Aramaic. AS* 19 (1974), esp. 105, no. 373; 123, no. 36; R. Zadok, *On West Semites in Babylonia During the Chaldean and Achaemenian Periods* (Jerusalem, ²1978), esp. 61; idem, *The Pre-Hellenistic Israelite Anthroponomy and Prosopography. OLA* 28 (1988), esp. 44,174,435.

1. *TADAE* C1.1:46,211.

Aramaic clay tablets.[2] Yet, these names can be read either as Aramaic ("Nabû has delivered") or as Akkadian ("Oh Nabû, deliver!"). One would expect the C-stem imperative of *ezēbu* (*ʿzb*),[3] the ground form in which the word was adopted, but the Neo-Babylonian imperative *šūzib* influenced its vocalization in Palmyrene,[4] Syriac, Mandean, Samaritan Aramaic, and Christian Palestinian (*šwzb*) while Jewish and Nabatean scribes retained the old orthography *šyzb*. The verbal form *šyzbh* functions uninflected as a substantive "place of refuge." It occurs in the Targums, e.g., *ʾtr qry šyzbh* "a place, a city of refuge,"[5] *qrwyʾ lšyzbʾ* "cities of refuge,"[6] *šyzbʾ lyt byh lršyʿyʾ* "there is no refuge in it for evildoers,"[7] *lʾ hwt lhwn šyzbwtʾ* "there was no refuge for them,"[8] and developed further in its meaning as a feminine substantive.

Furthermore, originally Aramaic verbs for "to deliver" include the C-stem of → *nṣl*[9] and the D-stem of *plṭ*[10] and constructed in the same manner, i.e., with a direct object and optionally supplemented with *mn* "from."

II. Usage.

1. With a Human Subject. On one hand, a human person can appear as the subject of the verb: e.g., Aḥiqar, who saved Nabû-sum-iskun,[11] Soados, who saved a caravan,[12] various individuals mentioned in private letters,[13] and a person mentioned in a fragmentary court record,[14] on the other, however, characters of a proverb,[15] of a poetic work[16] or of a vision.[17] In Nabatean royal titulature, the verb appears in the stereotypical epithets of King Rabbel II (70-106 C.E.): *dy ʾḥyy wšyzb ʿmh* "who kept alive and delivered his people."[18] According to Dnl. 6:15 King Darius tried to deliver Daniel.[19]

2. With a Divine Subject. In addition, God also frequently stands as the subject of *šzb*, as in private letters[20] or in the stories of the book of Daniel concerning wondrous deliverances

2. O. 3656:10; O. 3716:11: E. Lipiński, *SAIO* III. *OLA* 200 (2010), 153-65.
3. Cf. E. S. Gerstenberger, "עָזַב *ʿāzaḇ*," *TDOT*, X, 584-92.
4. Once: *PAT* 0197.9.
5. Targum Neofiti of Ex. 21:13.
6. Targum Onqelos of Nu. 32:31.
7. Targum Jonathan on Joel 2:3.
8. Targum on 2 Ch. 14:12.
9. Also in the same context as *šzb*.
10. → *nṣl* IV.
11. *TADAE* C1.1:46.
12. *PAT* 0197.9.
13. E.g., in Imperial Aramaic *TADAE* A3.1, recto l. 8; 4.3:5.
14. *TADAE* D2.33:2.
15. *TADAE* C1.1:211.
16. 11Q10 14:6 (Job 29:12).
17. 4Q537:1.
18. *CIS*, II, 183:4; cf. *Syria* 35, 1958, 227; *RÉS* 83, 12f.; 86 = 471:4; 468:5; 1434:6,12; 2058; *RB* 42 (1933) 408, ll. 2,5; *IEJ* 11 (1961) 135, l. 4; *IEJ* 13 (1963) 113, l. 4; Pap. Yadin 1:1,12,47; 2:1,5,18,24; 3:5,21,27; → *ḥyī* II.
19. On the context of the passage → *nṣl* III.
20. *TADAE* D1.24:2; 1.30:5; etc.

(Dnl. 3:15,17,28; 6:17,21,28). A large number of Assyrian and Babylonian personal names consist of a theophoric element and the preterite (*ušēzib*), imperative (*šēzib*, *šūzib*), participle (*mušēzib*), or verbal adjective (*šūzub*) of this verb. A few of them appear in Aramaic texts and could be regarded as Aramaic, at least when an Aramaic deity serves as the theophoric element, such as Bet-El, the divinized "House of God," in ^d*Ba-ti-il-še-zib*[21] or *Byt'lšzb*.[22] This name is attested since the sixth century B.C.E. Around 400 B.C.E., the name *ṣlmšzb* "the (deified) statue has delivered" appears in Tēma.[23] The interpretation of the name *Nb*(*w*)*šzb* as Aramaic is dubious, however, although it appears not just on Aramaic clay tablets (→ I), but also in Aramaic papyri from Egypt,[24] which typically abbreviate it *nbwšh* Nabûšē.[25] Palmyra employed the short form *nbwšy*.[26] The same doubt regarding Aramaic identity also remains in the case of *šzbnbw*,[27] paralleling Babylonian Šūzib-Marduk "Deliver, O Marduk!" and Šūzib-Adad "Deliver, O Adad!,"[28] or, more likely to be read as Šūzub-Adad and Šūzub-Marduk[29] "Delivered by Adad," "Delivered by Marduk," etc. The name *mšyzb'l* (Neh. 3:4; 10:22; 11:24) is Akkadian, however: Mušēzib-Il "The one who delivers is god."[30] Its Greek transcription as Μασεζεβηλ (Neh. 3:4) or Μεσωζεβηλ (Neh. 10:22) exhibits in the first case a secondary vocal *a* after a consonant pronounced with no subsequent vowel (*Mšēzib-Il) and in the second, a confusion of *y* and *w*. Furthermore, one observes a religious connotation in the expression "city of refuge" (→ I).

Lipiński

---

21. Hyatt.
22. *TADAE* A2.5:6; D9.10:7.
23. *KAI* 228 A 9,11,21; B 1; cf. *PEFQS* 70 (1938) 188f., tab. XIV,2.
24. *TADAE* A2.1:15.
25. *TADAE* A2.1:2,13; A2.2:2,6; A2.5:1,10.
26. Ingholt.
27. *TADAE* A3.1, verso l. 1.
28. *APN*, 227; *ANG*, 170.
29. *ANG*, 258.
30. *PNA*, 779.

שכב *škb*; משכב *mškb* /maškab/

I. Etymology, Lexical Field, and Constructions. II. Verb "to Lie (Down)." III. Noun "Bed."

I. Etymology, Lexical Field, and Constructions. In Aramaic, the common Semitic root *škb* "to lie (down)," which appears here rarely, but as elsewhere in the G-stem,

---

W. Beuken, "שָׁכַב *šāḵaḇ*," *TDOT*, XIV, 659-71; R. Telöken, "*škb*," *ThWQ*, III, 911-16.

denotes literally, on the one hand, lying down, usually in association with sleep (*šnh* /šenā/), and euphemistically, on the other, death. Further, it underlies the masculine /maškab/[1] "bed."

II. Verb "to Lie (Down)." The usage "to lie down (to die)" already occurs in the Old Aramaic Tell Dan stele.[2] In Levi's petitionary prayer from Qumran, it appears in the context of a vision.[3] In 11Q10 it translates the Hebrew *škb*,[4] *nḥt*[5] and *šūb* "to return to the dust."[6] The occurrence in 4Q569 2:6 has no context.

III. Noun "Bed." Aramaic attests the noun *mškb* "repository, bed" beginning with Daniel where it regularly occurs in the context of visions in a dream (2:28f.; 4:2,7,10; 7:1)[7] like the verb in 4Q213a 2:14 (→ II). 11Q10 22:10 (Job 33:15) has it for the Hebrew cognate *mškb*.

Gzella

1. Later revocalized as /miškab/.
2. *KAI* 310.3, together with *hūk* "to go"; → *hlk* II.
3. 4Q213a 2:14, along with → *ytb*.
4. 11Q10 11:10 (Job 27:19), of sleep.
5. 11Q10 1:3 (Job 17:16), of death.
6. 11Q10 24:9 (Job 34:15).
7. → *ḥlm*.

שכח *škḥ*; שכחה *škḥh* /šakaḥā/

I. Etymology, Lexical Field, and Constructions. II. In the Gt-stem "to Be Found." III. In the C-stem. 1. "To Find." 2. As a Modal Verb "to Be Able."

I. Etymology, Lexical Field, and Constructions. The highly productive root *škḥ*, in the Gt-stem "to be found," in the C-stem "to find," is a lexical peculiarity of Aramaic in comparison to other Semitic languages. It may, indeed, have a parallel in the Ugaritic *škḥ* "to meet," which occurs in a couple of letters,[1] yet the further etymology remains unclear. Verbs of finding took various forms in the individual Semitic languages, such

W. Schottroff, "שכח *škḥ* to forget," *TLOT*, 1322-26, esp. 1322; J. Screnock, "*škḥ*," *ThWQ*, III, 916-20.

1. See *DUL*³, 803.

as Hebrew *mṣ'* from "to arrive at."[2] No relationship to the root *škḥ*, which appears in Hebrew as "to forget,"[3] has been demonstrated.

Depending on context, the Gt-stem appears with either a gerundival or a middle nuance "to be found, to be located," as the semantics of the verb suggest,[4] although Aramaic usually expresses this notion with a nominal clause or → *hwī*, sometimes with the passive participle of → *śīm* "lying, located." Rarely, it has the evaluative sense "to be deemed something," which is otherwise indicated by → *ḥšb* "to recognize." Similarly, the C-stem, which serves here for the active voice, can appear figuratively as a modal verb "to be able," although always negated, thus "to be not in a position to." Normally, → *ykl* represents "to be able," both positively and negatively. The antonym of the meaning "to find" is → *bʿī* "to seek."

The Gt-stem with the meaning "to be found" and related nuances are intransitive and take various prepositional modifiers. Very widespread are locative expressions following *b-* "in, at" (e.g., Dnl. 5:11f.,14; 6:24; Ezr. 6:2) or with persons *ʿl* "with, against" (Dnl. 6:5); when the verb means "to be deemed something," the pertinent attributive accompanies it, like the adjective *ḥsyr* "(too) light" in Dnl. 2:35. It also occurs sporadically with *l-* "regarding, with reference to" (Dnl. 6:23). In the C-stem, *škḥ* is singly (e.g., Dnl. 2:25; 6:5) or doubly transitive, in the second case denoting "to find someone waiting for something" (e.g., Dnl. 6:12). Essentially the same prepositional modifiers can more closely define the location with the C-stem as with the Gt-stem, thus *b-* "in" (Ezr. 4:15) or "with reference to" (Dnl. 6:6) and *ʿl* "with, against" (Dnl. 6:6), as well as *qdm* "before" or an object clause following *dy* "that" (Ezr. 4:19). With the nuance "to be able," the verb takes an infinitive following *l-*.[5]

In a Nabatean contract, the rare feminine noun /šakaḥā/ "finding" refers to a mixed orchard.[6]

II. In the Gt-stem "to Be Found." In the Gt-stem for "to be found," *škḥ* often implies a test or a preceding examination. It first occurs in the later Old Aramaic of the sayings of Aḥiqar, namely in the literal sense of a thief who is found/discovered.[7] In similar fashion, it appears in an Imperial Aramaic letter in relation to burglars who are discovered and arrested.[8] Meanwhile, another letter employs it with the abstract subject *mḥbl* "damage, guilt":[9] the writers confirm that they have not left their posts during an uprising so that no guilt can be assigned, or damage attributed, to (*l-*) them.[10] There is a construction similar to that in Dnl. 6:23 (see above), but the nuance remains unclear because of the debatable meaning of *mḥbl* in this passage.

---

2. → *mṭī*.
3. Borrowed by Jewish Babylonian Aramaic: *DJBA*, 1144.
4. Cf. e.g., *se trouver* in French or *trovarsi* in Italian.
5. E.g., 1QapGen 21:13.
6. nV 1:27 in *ATTM*, 2, 205-8.
7. *TADAE* C1.1:173.
8. *TADAE* A4.4:6.
9. → *ḥbl* II.
10. *TADAE* A4.5:2; the verb also stands in isolation in l. 13.

Legal texts sporadically employ *škḥ* of goods found in the possession of a person.[11] Furthermore, it appears regularly in a formulaic entry in the list of import and export duties in *TADAE* C3.7 in the context of oil export,[12] that were "found," that is, on hand.[13] In the language of accountancy, therefore, it functions for the inventory.

Biblical Aramaic narratives employ the verb once with the nuance "to be discovered, to turn up," already known in Imperial Aramaic, in reference to an old scroll in the royal archive (Ezr. 6:2) that had been sought,[14] and with the nuance "to be on hand," negated of the totally annihilated statue (Dnl. 2:35).[15] It occurs mostly, however, of characteristics found in a person: the outstanding intellectual gifts of Daniel (Dnl. 5:11f.,14; with *b-* "with, in"); negated for the lack of any negligence in his execution of office (Dnl. 6:5, with *ʿl*);[16] and positively for the innocence he demonstrated (6:23).[17] Dnl. 6:24 employs it negated with → *ḥbl* "damage"; after Daniel climbed out of the lions' den, one could find no injury to him. The predicative use "to be found" in the interpretation of the "mene-tekel"[18] is rare: King Belshazzar was weighed and "found to be too light [*ḥsyr*]" (Dnl. 5:27). As is usual in Imperial Aramaic, the context here also presumes a test through an examination or inventory wherein *škḥ* "to be found" differs from a mere nominal clause "to be, to be located." The pair of instances from Qumran corresponds to the same circumstance: 4Q550 1:5f. of the discovery of a scroll as in Ezr. 6:2,[19] for "to be on hand" 4Q537 1+2+3:2 (negated of lies). It appears in reference to qualities of character (*ṭb*)[20] as with Daniel in a Palmyrene honorary inscription.[21]

III. In the C-stem. Most often, *škḥ* occurs in the C-stem "to find" and can, in this function, appear with a person, a thing, or an abstract entity as object, corresponding entirely to the use of the Gt-stem and essentially its active counterpart. In contrast, it only appears relatively rarely negated for "to be unable."

1. "To Find." The first examples appear in texts from Egypt in a variety of styles, mostly in private letters, and refer to the discovery of goods[22] and persons,[23] but also to characteristics like errors.[24] With an attributive, mostly a passive participle, the verb as

11. *TADAE* B4.6:11, context damaged; fragmentary also in the marginal subtext of 7.3, l. 2.
12. → *mšḥ* III.1.
13. Instances in *TADAE* C, p. liii.
14. → *bqr.*
15. → *ʿwr* II.
16. For the context → *šlī* III.
17. → *zkw* II.
18. → *mnī.*
19. Cf. 4Q243 6:4.
20. → *ṭīb.*
21. *PAT* 1421.3.
22. *TADAE* A2.2:15; 2.4:10; 3.8:3,7f.; 4.2:10; 4.3:9; D1. 20:2; 7.43:11; in a destroyed context probably also A3.11:2; from Bactria J. Naveh and S. Shaked, *Aramaic Documents from Ancient Bactria (Fourth Century B.C.E.)* (London, 2012), C5,8.
23. *TADAE* A2.1:9; 2.4:11; similarly in literary works: C1.1:34,76.
24. *TADAE* A4.3:7.

the second object means "to find something as, to encounter,"[25] and in analogy with the Gt-stem with the nuance "to be deemed something."[26] It can also involve an accidental find, however.

Contracts frequently utilize *škḥ* in the formulation "what you find" in reference to things in the context of an inventory of property in the form of various goods,[27] corresponding to the Gt-stem as its passive counterpart (→ II),[28] once in the sense of "to be on hand, to have at one's disposal."[29]

The usages of this comprehensive verb demonstrated by Imperial Aramaic diction continue in Biblical Aramaic even for the C-stem. Thus, it appears with persons (Dnl. 2:25), goods (Ezr. 7:16), characteristics like errors (Dnl. 6:5f.), and circumstances (6:12), in the latter case with the active participle in a predicative function "they found Daniel praying."[30] With regard to the detection or discovery of circumstances, an object clause after *dy* "that" can stand instead of the participle as in Ezr. 4:19.[31]

The texts from Qumran contain the same usages: with persons,[32] inanimate objects[33] and with a predicated double object with a participle or another nominal form.[34] As expected, 11Q10 employs *škḥ* in the C-stem for the Hebrew *mṣʾ*.[35] The phrase "to find grace" in 1QapGen 6:23 probably imitates the Hebrew;[36] cf. "to find mercy" in 4Q213a 1:15. 1QapGen 10:12; 4Q562 2:3 are fragmentary.

2. *As a Modal Verb "to Be Able."* Qumran attests *škḥ* negated as a modal verb "to be unable" (in an intellectual or physical respect) with a subsequent infinitive several times.[37] It occurs only rarely later in Jewish Palestinian.[38] Since Greek also uses εὑρίσκειν for "to have the opportunity, to be able,"[39] analogous formulations such as the one in Mt. 7:17 (Lk. 13:24: ἰσχύειν "to be able") need not trace back to Aramaic substrate influence.

Gzella

25. *TADAE* A2.1:4; 4.3:4; 4.7:14 par. 4.8:13; D7.9:6.
26. → II on Dnl. 5:27.
27. *TADAE* B3.1:9f.,17; 3.13:11.
28. *TADAE* B4.6:11.
29. *TADAE* B2.7:5.
30. Cf. H. Gzella, *Tempus, Aspekt und Modalität im Reichsaramäischen. VOK* 48 (2004), 277 with n. 25.
31. Paralleling → *ydʿ* "to learn," cf. 4:15; regarding the construction, cf. Gzella, 278f.
32. 1QapGen 2:23; 4Q196 2:12 (Tob. 2:2); 4Q549 2:3.
33. 4Q213 2-3 2:2, of places of refuge and reconstructed based on a Geniza manuscript; figuratively "branches of fire" 4Q529 1:2.
34. 1QapGen 21:19: *šlm* "undamaged"; 22:7: *šryn* "stored"; 4Q196 14 2:6 par. 4Q197 4 3:3 (Tob. 7:1): *ytb* "sitting"; apparently so also 4Q204 4:5 (1 En. 89:33): "blinded," to be reconstructed based on the parallel versions.
35. 11Q10 7A:3; 22:4 (Job 23:3; 33:10).
36. → *ḥnn* IV.
37. 1QapGen 21:13; 4Q201 1 2:2:8 (1 En. 4:1); 4Q530 2 2+6-12:13f.; 4Q531 22:5.
38. *DJPA*, 549f.
39. Cf. *ATTM*, 2, 492, with further bib.

שכן škn; משכן mškn /maškan/

I. Etymology and Lexical Field. II. Verb in the G-stem "to Dwell." III. D-stem "to Cause to Dwell." IV. Noun "Dwelling."

I. Etymology and Lexical Field. Aramaic attests the Semitic root *škn,* in the G-stem "to settle down, to dwell," significantly less than in Hebrew. At the same time, the few instances between Imperial Aramaic and Qumran reflect various uses. The G-stem "to dwell" can take God,[1] animals,[2] or an abstract entity like *brkh* "blessing"[3] as subject; the factitive D-stem "to settle" occurs in the pre-Christian era only once in Biblical Aramaic with God, who causes his name to dwell in the temple. In addition to a place name as an adverbial complement,[4] the G-stem can take prepositional phrases following *b-* "in" (Dnl. 4:18) or *ʿl* "on,"[5] and with an occurrence of the D-stem the local adverb *tmh* "there (in the temple)." The title → *sgn* is a loanword.

Furthermore, the masculine noun /maškan/ "dwelling" belongs to the root *škn.* It, however, has mostly religio-cultic connotations, in contrast to *mwtb*[6] "residence." The substantival passive participle *škynh* "indwelling" for the divine presence first appears in late antiquity in Jewish[7] and Christian[8] texts, but takes up the older usages of the verb for God's presence in the temple (→ II). Later phases of the language also attest additional nominal forms from the lexical field of "to dwell, to be present" or "to give."[9]

The meaning of the root *škn* overlaps with that of → *dūr* "to dwell," → *ytb* "to settle, to sit, to dwell," and → *šrī* in the sense of "to tarry." The distribution of the occurrences suggests that *škn* like *šrī*[10] referred more to a temporary stay and not to a permanent dwelling. Because of the overall only schematically formed lexical field for "to dwell" in older Aramaic, no obvious pair of opposites clearly accentuates this difference.

II. Verb in the G-stem "to Dwell." The earliest instance of the verb in the G-stem stems from the beginning of a private document from Elephantine and is a participle

---

A. Berlejung, *Die Theologie der Bilder. OBO* 162 (1998); M. Görg, "שָׁכַן *šāḵan,*" *TDOT,* XIV, 691-702; G. Holtz, "*škn,*" *ThWQ,* III, 920-30; A. R. Hulst, "שכן *škn* to dwell," *TLOT,* 1327-30; E. Jenni, *Das hebräische Piʿel* (Zurich, 1968).

1. *TADAE* B3.12:2.
2. Dnl. 4:18; 11Q10 33:9 (Job 39:28); in both cases birds.
3. 4Q542 1 2:3; → *brk* IV.
4. *TADAE* B3.12:2: "in Elephantine."
5. 4Q542 1 2:3.
6. → *ytb.*
7. *DJPA,* 550; *DJBA,* 1145a.
8. *LexSyr,* 776.
9. Cf. *LexSyr,* 776f. for Syriac.
10. Cf. 1QapGen 20:34 and 22:8,13 for its use of Abraham's camp.

describing the God Yaho as dwelling in Elephantine.[11] It appears in relation to the greater specification and identification of a member of the staff[12] of the same temple. It was regarded as the earthly dwelling of the God who transcends space and time who dwells there as he wishes, but was not statically settled there.[13]

In Biblical Aramaic, the same verb occurs in the tree vision of King Nebuchadnezzar in reference to the birds that nest in the branches of the mighty treetop (Dnl. 4:18). Here, too, it involves tarrying for a certain time, as also in the image of the eagle (*ʿwzʾ*) on the cliff (*kp*) in 11Q10 33:9 (Job 39:28). The wish for eternal blessing (*brkt ʿlmʾ*),[14] however, may intend the ingressive nuance "to settle down."

III. D-stem "to Cause to Dwell." The D-stem of *škn* "to settle" occurs in Ezr. 6:12 as an attributive referring to God who causes his name to dwell in the Jerusalem temple and, consequently, can destroy any who disturb this temple. Thus, the meaning corresponds to that of the G-stem as in *TADAE* B3.12:2 (→ II) and its usage is analogous to that of the same verb in Hebrew (e.g., Dt. 12:11 or Neh. 1:9):[15] it accents the gracious attention of God, not his permanent presence.

In post-Christian times, the D-stem of *škn* also appears with the meaning "to give";[16] it derives from the noun *mškn* "deposit" (→ IV).

IV. Noun "Dwelling." The noun *mškn* occurs beginning with Biblical Aramaic;[17] in the oldest known instance, Ezr. 7:15, it serves, in agreement with the verb (→ III), to describe God, who has his dwelling in Jerusalem, namely in the temple.

It occurs in 4Q156 2:4 from Qumran with the same meaning in *mškn zmnʾ* as the translation of *ʾhl mʿd* "tent of revelation" in Lev. 16:20; further in Enoch's animal vision corresponding to the Hebrew cognate for "tabernacle";[18] and once in a fragment without context.[19]

The word also appears in a cultic context at Hatra,[20] but once in the plural may also indicate "tents" in the quite general sense.[21]

In Palmyrene, *mškn* first appears in the meaning "deposit"[22] as also in later Aramaic languages. This meaning traces to Akkadian influence.[23]

Gzella

11. *TADAE* B3. 12:2.
12. → *lḥn* III.
13. See overall Berlejung; cf. Jenni, 92f.
14. 4Q542 1 2:3, Testament of Qahat.
15. See Jenni, 92f.
16. For Jewish Palestinian, cf. *DJPA*, 550f.
17. Vocalized *miškan.*
18. 4Q204 4:10 (1 En. 89:36); only the *m* is legible, but the emendation seems certain.
19. 4Q243 34:1.
20. H50.3; 79.10.
21. H281.3; for a discussion cf. *DNSI*, 702.
22. *PAT* 1981.8; 2775.10; *DNSI*, 702.
23. Cf. S. A. Kaufman, *The Akkadian Influences on Aramaic. AS* 19 (1974), 70.

שלח šlḥ; שדר šdr; אשתדור ʾštdwr /ʾāštedōr/

I. Etymologies. II. *šlḥ* "to Send." 1. Humans/Things. 2. *yd* "Hand." 3. Reports. III. *šdr*. 1. "Sending." 2. "Intervention." IV. *ʾštdwr*.

I. Etymologies. Ugaritic, Phoenician, Hebrew, and Aramaic attest the root *šlḥ* "to send"; in contrast, *šdr* "to send" is Aramaic.

II. šlḥ "to Send." The verb *šlḥ*, Old to Biblical Aramaic peal,[1] Qumran Aramaic pael,[2] takes a direct and an indirect object.[3]

1. Humans/Things. Old Aramaic attests *šlḥ* peal "to send" only with an animate direct object.[4] A nonhuman object appears in the curse of the Sefire inscription: *yšlḥn ʾlhn mn klmh ʾkl bʾrpd* "may the gods send any pest against Arpad."[5]

In Imperial Aramaic, *šlḥ* peal idiomatically denotes the sending of news (→ II.3), *yšr* aphel the sending of goods.[6] Persons stand as the object of *šlḥ* in *TADAE* C1.1:62 (*gbrn* "men"), C2.1:19 (*prsy* "a Persian"), l. 39 *ḥylʾ* "the army," Segal, 33.1:1 (*qryqn* "fugitive slaves [?]"). In the literary *TADAE* D23.5b:8, in the context of a war, one reads *ʾštʾ ʾšlḥ bhm* "I will send fire against them (fortifications?)."[7] Examples of the sending (*šlḥ*) of goods appear on ostraca[8] and may reflect a lower register of speech than *yšr* aphel, but also appear in late Achaemenid letters from subordinate (?) officials from Bactria,[9] not in the letters of the satrap himself.

Daniel 3:28; 6:23 explain God's intervention on behalf of the captives in the fiery

---

M. Delcor and E. Jenni, "שלח *šlḥ* to send," *TLOT*, 1330-34; H.-J. Fabry, "*šlḥ*," *ThWQ*, III, 942-47; J. A. Fitzmyer, *The Genesis Apocryphon of Qumran Cave 1 (1Q20)*. *BietOr* 18B ([3]2004); M. L. Folmer, *The Aramaic Language in the Achaemenid Period*. *OLA* 68 (1995); J. C. Greenfield, "Some Reflections on the Vocabulary of Aramaic in Relationship to the Other Semitic Languages," in P. Fronzaroli, ed., *Atti del secondo Congresso Internazionale di Linguistica Camito-Semitica* (Florence, 1978), 151-56; F.-L. Hossfeld and F. van der Velden, "שָׁלַח *šālaḥ*," *TDOT*, XV, 49-73; J. Naveh and S. Shaked, *Aramaic Documents from Ancient Bactria (Fourth Century B.C.E.)* (London, 2012); F. Rosenthal, *A Grammar of Biblical Aramaic*. *PLO* 5 ([7]2006).

1. In the passive ithpaal.
2. In the passive ithpaal.
3. To someone: *ʾl*, *l-* or *ʿl*; "against": *b-*.
4. *KAI* 224.8 *mlʾk* "messenger" with *ʾl* to someone; *KAI* 233.13 *ʿzr* "assistance"; *TADAE* A1.1:7 *lmšlḥ ḥyl* "to send an army," inf. peal; on *yd* and *lšn*, → II.2.
5. *KAI* 222 A 30; 3mp impf. with an indirect object following *b-*; regarding the curse, cf. Dt. 32:24; for 1QapGen 20:16 see below.
6. Folmer, 652-60.
7. 1s impf. with *b-* plus an indirect object.
8. *TADAE* D7.21:4: *lbšʾ* "the garment"; D7.33:6: *sptʾ* "the jug(?)"; D7.57:4f.: *ʿnz* "a goat."
9. Naveh and Shaked, B4,7; 4,3f.; 5,6.

furnace and on behalf of Daniel in the lions' den with the words *šᵉlaḥ malʾᵃkeh* "he sent his angel";[10] God helps, then, by means of his messenger.[11]

Qumran Aramaic attests *šlḥ* pael "to send"[12] only with an animate direct object, mostly people;[13] thus, in 1QapGen 20:23 pharaoh is urged that "he should send his wife (i.e., Sarah) away to her husband (Abraham)" (*yšlḥ ʾntth mnh lbʿlh*, elaborating Gen. 12:18-20). The verb also describes God's intervention in the world with the aid of various mediators. In 4Q558 51 2:4 (a free translation of Mal. 3:23), God announces: *lkn ʾšlḥ lʾlyh qd[m* "therefore, I will send Elijah befo[re."[14] The sending of prophets, idiomatic in Biblical Hebrew, occurs only here in Aramaic.[15] In 1QapGen 20:16, one finds *šlḥ lh ʾl ʿlywn rwḥ mkdš* "the Most High God sent him (pharaoh) a spirit of plague."[16] In 1QapGen 22:26 (of captives) and 11Q10 32:4 (Job 39:5),[17] *šlḥ* means "to set free, to send to freedom."

2. yd "Hand." The idiomatic *šlḥ yd* "to raise the hand" already occurs in Old Aramaic[18] as a hostile act in the Sefire Treaty inscriptions:[19] *bry [l]yšlḥ yd bbrk* "my son will [not] raise his hand against your son."[20] The expression *šlḥ lšn* "to send out the tongue," i.e., "to get involved"[21] in *KAI* 224.21: *ltšlḥ lšn bbyty* "you should not get involved in my house."[22]

Biblical Aramaic attests the usage in Ezr. 6:12 in the decree of King Darius in a comparable context. Any foreign king who *yišlaḥ yᵉḏeh lᵉhašnāyā* "raises his hand to alter (the decree)"[23] faces the threat of divine punishment. In contrast, one should understand *šᵉlîᵃḥ passā ḏī yᵉḏā* (Dnl. 5:24) in the interpretation of the flaming writing on the wall literally as "the palm of the hand was sent."[24]

3. Reports. The sending of reports occurs in Old Aramaic only in the Asshur ostracon *KAI* 233.19: *mlʾkty ʾšlḥ lk* "I send you my message."[25] In Imperial Aramaic, *šlḥ* peal in this meaning is frequent, less often the passive ithpaal,[26] in the context of official exchange of correspondence; the phraseology may manifest Akkadian influence.[27] The addressee follows

---

10. Pf. 3ms; cf. above on *KAI* 224.8.
11. → *mlʾk*; for the background in the history of religions, → *qdš* IV.2.
12. 4Q558 62:3: *l]šlḥwth* inf. pael(!) with 3ms suff.; Levi apocryphon 4Q541 9:2f.: ithpaal.
13. To or "after" someone: *l-*, 4Q530 9:11: *ʿl*.
14. Animate direct object with *l-*.
15. See above for the sending of angels.
16. See above on *KAI* 222 A 30; → *rwḥ* VI.
17. The same root in Heb.; of an ass.
18. "Against": *b-*, with a subsequent *w-* and an impf. *KAI* 222 B 27; → *yd* II.1.
19. *KAI* 222 B 25.
20. In addition, *KAI* 223 B 6:222 B 34f.; judging from the context, also *KAI* 202 B 21 and in Samʾalian in *KAI* 214.25.
21. Later *šdr* in the ithpaal represents this meaning, → III.2.
22. Negated 2ms impf., *b-* plus indirect object; also in ll. 17f.; → *lšn* II.
23. Impf. 3ms with inf.
24. → *yd* III.
25. Impf. peal 1s.
26. Sender: *mn*, *TADAE* A4.7:24.
27. Greenfield, 153.

l- or *ʿl*; explicit direct objects are the missives[28] and the greetings.[29] In accord with the potential direct objects, one should interpret elliptical formulations as "to send, communicate (a report)"[30] or "to send (instruction), to command."[31] The use of the verb with and without object in the letters from the Bactrian archive accord with these circumstances.[32]

Because of the verbal image, the singular form of the masculine singular pael participle with third-person feminine singular suffix in the saying of Aḥiqar C1.1:82, *ky ṣnpr hy mlh wmšlḥh gbr lʾ lb*[*b*] "for a word is (like) a bird, who sends it out: a man without understandin[g]," merits mention here.

Imperial Aramaic usage continues in Biblical Aramaic.[33] Except for one, specimens stem from the official Aramaic documents in Ezra that deal with the reconstruction of the Jerusalem temple. Direct objects are the writings *paršæḡæn ʾiggartā* "copy of the letter" (Ezr. 4:11; 5:6),[34] *piṯᵉḡāmā* "the communication" (4:17; 5:7), *nišṯᵉwānā* "the document" (4:18),[35] and in Ezr. 5:17 the written "will of the king" *rᵉʿūṯ malkā*.[36] Ezr. 6:13 has the elliptical *šᵉlaḥ dāryāwæš* "Darius commanded," similar to Dnl. 3:2, where the officials were called together for official purposes (*malkā šᵉlaḥ lᵉmiḵnaš laᵃḥašdarpᵉnayyā* "the king commanded the satraps to assemble").[37]

Qumran Aramaic does not attest this official Imperial Aramaic phraseology, but it echoes it in the expression *šlḥ qrʾ* "he sent, called/he had called."[38] Finally, 1QapGen 20:8f.: *wšlḥ lʿwbʿ dbrhʾ* "he sent in haste, he brought her/he had her bring quickly" is also comparable.

III. *šdr*.

1. "Sending." The verb *šdr* pael "to send"[39] is still rare in Imperial Aramaic. It appears in an ellipsis in the saying of Aḥiqar *TADAE* C1.1:101 [*sn*]*yʾ šdr lrmn*[ʾ] "the t[hornbush]

---

28. → *spr* "letter" (*TADAE* A2.3:5), *ʾgrh*/*ʾgrt* "letter" (A4.7:19; A6.13:2, ithpaal; → *spr* IV), *mlh* "word" (A6.11:3; → *mll*), *qbylh* "complaint" (A6.15:5,11; → *qbl* IV), → *ṭʿm* "instruction" (D7.48:8), → *ptgm* "communication" (D7.39:8; D1.32:15, ithpaal).

29. *šlm* "well-being" (A3.5:3; formulaic D7.21:2f. *šlm wḥyn* "well-being and life") and *brkh* "blessing" (D7.1:1f.; → *brk*).

30. Paired with *ydʿ* aphel, A4.7:29; often impv., A2.4:6, with indirect address D7.6:8-10: *šlḥ ly ʾmt tʿbdn psḥʾ* "tell me when you celebrate Pesach"; pf. with subsequent citation (also without explicit addressees, A6.2:6), A6.8:1 *šlḥ ʿly kn ʾmr* "he communicated to me and said thus."

31. With a subsequent *w-* and impf. A2.2:6f.: *šlḥy ʿl tby wtwšr lky ʿmr* "instruct Tabi that she send you wool"; with inf. D7.24:15f.: *šlḥt lh lmprš ly mltʾ* "I instructed him to explain the word to me," also l. 16f.

32. Naveh and Shaked, A2,1,4; 4,1,4; 6,1; B1,6f.; 2,3; 3,5f.; 4,2; 5,7; 10,2; pass. ptcp.: A1,5; 4,1; 6,5.

33. The addressee always follows *ʿl*, however; regarding Imperial Aramaic parallels for the word pair *šᵉlaḥnā wᵉhōḏaʿnā* "we sent and communicated" in Ezr. 4:14 see above.

34. → *pršgn*.

35. → *nštwn*.

36. → *rʿī*.

37. With inf.; so also Ezr. 7:14: *šᵉlīᵃḥ lᵉḇaqqārā* "sent to investigate," pass. ptcp. masc. sg.

38. To someone: *l-*; 1QapGen 20:18f.; 21:21; 4Q545 1a 1:8, once syndetic in the Testament of Amram, collated from 4Q543 1:5; 4Q545 1a 1:5; 4Q546 1:3; → *qrī* IV.

39. Segal, 69.1:1 with the direct object "oil," to someone: *l-*; 46:1 ithpaal.

sent (news) to [the] pomegranate tree," like *šlḥ* elsewhere (→ II.3), with subsequent verbatim speech. In the Bar Kokhba letter Pap. Yadin 55:4f.,6, it denotes the sending of people.[40] It is frequent in late Aramaic.[41]

2. *"Intervention."* In the ithpaal, *šdr* means "to step in/to bother, to intervene,"[42] as in Dnl. 6:15, where Darius *hᵃwā mištaddar lᵉhaṣṣālūṯeh* "sought to save him (Daniel),"[43] although he had violated the decree of the king and had prayed to his God.[44]

IV. *'štdwr.* The noun vocalized *'æštaddūr* "rebellion, war," which characterizes the inhabitants of the city in the letter to Artaxerxes protesting the reconstruction of Jerusalem (Ezr. 4:15) and in his written response (4:19),[45] could be associated with *šdr* ithpaal (→ III.2), but is probably a loanword from the Persian **āxštidrauga.*[46] Qumran Aramaic attests the word in 11Q10 31:1 (for Job 38:23, *milḥāmā*) and 33:6 in the phrase *z'qt 'štdwr* "war cry" (for Job 39:25, *tᵉrū'ā*), always paired with *qrb* "battle."[47]

Stadel

40. Direct object: *yt*; to someone: *l-*.
41. *DJPA*, 538b; *DJBA*, 1112f.; *LexSyr*, 759; *MdD*, 450.
42. With someone: *'m*, *TADAE* A4.3:4, Pap.Yadin 53.3f.; for the meaning → II.2.
43. Act. ptcp. masc. sg. with inf.
44. Regarding the context → *nṣl* III.
45. Paired with *mᵉraḏ* "uprising"; → *mrd.*
46. Rosenthal, 63.
47. → *qrb* V.

שלט *šlṭ*; שליט *šlyṭ* /šallīṭ/; שלטן *šlṭn* /šolṭān/

I. Root and Cognates. II. Imperial Aramaic. III. Biblical Aramaic. IV. Qumran.

I. Root and Cognates. The root *šlṭ* with the basic meaning "to have power" or "to exercise power" is typically Aramaic. Cognates in Arabic and Ethiopic can, thus, best

H. Gzella, "*šlṭ*," *ThWQ*, III, 949-54; S. A. Kaufman, *The Akkadian Influences on Aramaic. AS* 19 (1974); J. Naveh and S. Shaked, *Aramaic Documents from Ancient Bactria (Fourth Century* B.C.E.*)* (London, 2012); M. Sæbø, "שָׁלַט *šālaṭ*," *TDOT*, XV, 83-88; D. Schwiderski, *Die alt- und reichsaramäischen Inschriften*, vol. I: *Konkordanz. FSBP* 2 (2008); M. Wagner, *Die lexikalischen und grammatikalischen Aramaismen im alttestamentlichen Hebräisch. BZAW* 96 (1966).

be understand as Aramaic loans, just as in Hebrew[1] and Akkadian.[2] Ugaritic *šlyṭ*[3] is probably a name with an unclear etymology and can hardly be associated with the same root.[4] In addition to the verb in the G-stem for "to have power, control over,"[5] C-stem "to empower," the frequent adjective *šlyṭ* /šallīṭ/ "powerful," constructed similarly to the verb, is also attested, as is, furthermore, the masculine noun *šlṭn* /šolṭān/, usually "dominion" or "ruler." It is vocalized in Biblical Hebrew and twice in Biblical Aramaic (→ III) as *šilṭōn.*[6]

II. Imperial Aramaic. Old Aramaic does not yet attest the root *šlṭ*; the first instances are known from Imperial Aramaic. In the documentary texts from Egypt, one finds forms of *šlṭ* predominantly in private documents. The noun *šlṭn* appears only once; it means "legal authority": *wyntnwn ly šlṭn'* "that they give me authority," i.e., to sell the grain mentioned in the same written order.[7]

The adjective *šlyṭ* signifies the rights of the owner: according to *TADAE* B3.5:19, after the death of Ananis, his children should be *šlyṭn* "authorized to dispose of"[8] his portion. Line 20 of the same document adds that the other person *l' yšlṭ b-* "shall have no authority to dispose of (the house)."[9] At the same time, this is the sole Imperial Aramaic occurrence of the verb.

In contrast, numerous instances of *šlyṭ* occur, but all in the same legal sense as in the example discussed.[10] Three other cases have no preposition as in the passage mention above.[11] Various prepositional phrases complement the others. Most frequently, *b-* denotes the property, including slaves.[12] It occurs twenty-six times.[13] Then follows *l-* with the infinitive of the corresponding verb expressing the action for which someone is authorized (twelve times); in this usage, it also designates a specific command in an official letter from the Bactrian archive.[14] The combination of *b-* with the object of the authorization and the infinitive of the verb following *l-* also occurs (twice). For Palmyra, see *PAT*, p. 415.

---

1. Wagner, 114.
2. Kaufman, 98f.
3. The seven-headed monster in *KTU* 1.3 III 42: *šlyṭ d šbʿ rašm* and the corresponding parallel passages.
4. For the discussion, see *DUL*[3], 810.
5. *b-*, less often *ʿl*; in addition to "to do" with a verbal complement in the inf.
6. According to *BLA*, §lt.51z''' under Hebrew influence.
7. *TADAE* D7.56:12; followed by *l-* and an inf.
8. Masc. pl. in the abs. state with a predicative function.
9. Impf. 3ms.
10. See Schwiderski, 787f. for an overview; for a discussion of the terminological background, cf. A. F. Botta, "The Legal Function and Egyptian Background of the שליט Clause," *Maarav* 13 (2006) 193-209.
11. *TADAE* B3.12:23; 3.10:21; 3.11:9.
12. → *ʿbd* III.
13. Synonymous *ʿl* "over," however, only once.
14. Naveh and Shaked, A4,4.

III. Biblical Aramaic. Biblical Aramaic exhibits the root thirty-three times, of which all except for *šallīṭ* in Ezr. 4:20; 7:24 occur in Daniel; both as the verb *šlṭ* (seven times) and in the nouns *šolṭān* (fourteen times), *šilṭōn* (twice; on the form → I), and *šallīṭ* (ten times). One can compare the fifteen examples of the Hebrew cognate: as a verb (five times in the G-stem: Eccl. 2:19; 8:9; Est. 9:1 [2×]; Neh. 5:15; three times in the C-stem: Ps. 119:133; Eccl. 5:18; 6:2), as the noun *šilṭōn* (twice: Eccl. 8:4,8; cf. Sir. 9:13), and as the adjective *šallīṭ* (four times: Gen. 42:6; Eccl. 7:19; 8:8; 10:5; cf. Sir. 9:13) with the feminine form *šallæṭæṯ* (once in Ezk. 16:30, in pause); in contrast, *šolṭān* does not appear. Of these fifteen occurrences, nine appear in Qoheleth; the others also stem from the postexilic period, except for *hū haššallīṭ ʿal-hāʾāræṣ* in Gen. 42:6, which may, however, be a later explanatory gloss.

In the G-stem, the verb denotes the exercise of ruling power, as in Dnl. 2:39. Another person, such as an official authorized by the king, can also be in the position to exercise it (Dnl. 5:7,16). In the figurative sense, it denotes "to assume authority" in reference to fire (3:2) or lions (6:25). The C-stem means "to give power, to empower" and has the king (2:38) or a high functionary (2:48) as object. Other than this latter passage, all instances of the verb have the preposition *b-* as complement indicating over whom or where the power will be exercised.

The noun *šilṭōn* appears in Dnl. 3:2f. (twice) personified "ruler" as *šilṭōnē m^e^ḏīnāṯā*, i.e., the high officials who govern the provinces of the Persian empire (along with other official titles).

In contrast, the noun *šolṭān* functions as a verbal abstract in the sense of "power, dominion" in Dnl. 3:33; 4:19,31 (2×); 6:27 (2×); 7:6,12,14 (3×),26; 7:27 (2×). The plural in Dnl. 7:27 refers to the empires of the world. The word appears in context with other terms from the same lexical field: *malḵū* "dominion, ruling power"[15] in 3:33; 4:31; 6:27; 7:14,27; *r^e^ḇū* "majesty, grandeur"[16] in 4:19; 7:27; *y^e^qār* "honor, dignity"[17] in 7:14.

Furthermore, the form *šallīṭ* occurs ten times, two of them substantivally for "official" (Dnl. 2:15) or "ruler" (5:29).[18] In both cases it accompanies the preposition *b-* indicating the realm of dominion. Seven additional passages employ the word as an adjective "mighty" (Dnl. 2:10; 4:14,22,23,29; 5:21; Ezr. 4:20), all except for Dnl. 2:10 also with *b-* in the sense described. Finally, it occurs in an impersonal construction in Ezr. 7:24, *lā šallīṭ* followed by the infinitive meaning "it is not permitted to."

The theological use of *šallīṭ* is most clearly evident in the contrast between contingent secular power and the absolute dominion of God. As the holy ones[19] in Nebuchadnezzar's dream in Dnl. 4:14 explain, the supreme God rules over human power (*šallīṭ b^e^malḵūṯ ^a^nāšā*) and is free to bestow it upon whomever he will. The dream interpretation in Dnl. 4:22,23,29 then relates this statement to the king. An echo of the same theological conviction resounds in Dnl. 5:21. From this perspective, *šallīṭ* and *šolṭān* are part of the

---

15. → *mlk* IV.
16. → *rb*.
17. → *yqr*.
18. The parallel passages 5:7,16 employ instead the verb *šlṭ*.
19. → *qdš* IV.2.

theological vocabulary in Daniel that consistently describes God's superior dominion over human kingdoms and realms. In contrast to them, his dominion, as Dnl. 6:27 emphasizes, has no end.

Theodotion translates *šallīṭ* in Dnl. 4:22(25),29(32) with the verb κυριεύειν "to rule," but in Dnl. 4:14(17) has κύριος εἶναι "to be lord." The unrevised old translation (Old Greek [OG]) employs ἐξουσίαν ἔχειν "to have power" in Dnl. 4:14(17),29(32). In Dnl. 4:23, both versions (Theodotion 4:26; OG 4:27) read the noun /šolṭān/ for the plural absolute *šallīṭīn*, in the consonantal text spelled defectively *šlṭn*, and render it with ἐξουσία "power."

IV. Qumran. At Qumran, *šlyṭ* appears in eighteen passages.[20] As elsewhere in Aramaic, it means "to be empowered, to have power"; various prepositions complement it: *b-*, *ʿl* or *l-* with infinitive, the latter expressing the nuance "to be able."[21] A passage in Abraham's petition[22] illustrates the various constructions: *dy ʾnth mrh wšlyṭ ʿl kwlʾ* "for you are Lord and rule over everything," *wbkwl mlky ʾrʿʾ ʾnth šlyṭ lmʿbd bkwlhwn dyn* "and you have power over all the kings of the earth to execute justice against all of them." It also represents the power of God in 4Q542 1 1:2f. and 4Q550 7+7a:1, secular dominion in the vision of the four trees in 4Q552 1 2:6, and in the juridical sense "authority to dispose of" in 1QapGen 22:24 (→ II). The noun can also function in the sense of "owner," as in 11Q10 32:6 (Job 39:7), *wngśt šlyṭ lʾ yšmʿ* "and he (the wild ass) does not heed the goading of an owner."

The verb *šlṭ* in the G-stem generally has the meaning "to exercise power," so that its usage is very similar to that of *šlyṭ* although the verb gives clearer expression to the dynamic nuance "to exercise dominion" in contrast to "to be ruler" as the comparison of 1QapGen 20:13 (see above) and l. 15 *wʾl yšlṭ blylyʾ dn lṭmyʾ ʾntty* "so that he (pharaoh) is not able in this night to sully my wife" demonstrates. In addition to *l-* and the infinitive for "to be able," as here, the verb also finds usage like the adjective with the prepositions *ʿl* (six times) or *b-* (four times). As an astronomical term, the verb further denotes "to shine" in reference to stars.[23]

In the C-stem, it means "to empower someone, to allow to exercise power," as in the sense of the power to make political decisions ("to name") in 4Q196 2:5,8 (Tob. 1:21f.) and generally in 4Q213a 1:17 (T. Levi, here as a request to God, "let no opponent rule over me"). The inner passive *ʾšlṭt* "I was empowered" occurs in 4Q544 3:1, Amram's vision of the battle between the evil and the good angels, and alternates with the passive participle of the C-stem in 4Q544 1:11; 2:11,15 for the angels who have power over every human fate.[24]

Finally, the noun *šlṭn* /šolṭān/ occurs in fourteen passages[25] and has the basic meaning "dominion," as in *šlṭnh šlṭn ʿlm* "his dominion is an eternal dominion,"[26] explicitly in

---

20. Eight of which are partially emended.
21. Generally indicated by the modal verb → *ykl*.
22. 1QapGen 20:13.
23. E.g., 1 En. 73; 4Q209 7 3:4; 9:2; cf. Gen. 1:16; the noun *šlṭn* (see below) functions similarly in 4Q209 28:2 (1 En. 82:10).
24. On this and its theological implications, cf. the extensive treatment in Gzella, "*šlṭ* III."
25. Half of which, however, are partially emended.
26. 4Q246 1 2:9; for a discussion of this text in general → *br* IV.

the religious sense *šlṭn šmy' l'r'' nḥt* "the dominion of heaven came down to the earth" in the Book of Giants,[27] and generally *'bdy šlṭn'* for "rulers" in the Persian Empire in the court tale of the edict of Darius.[28] On the astronomical use in reference to stars in 4Q209 28:2, see above.

For a more detailed treatment of the usages sketched here and a discussion of the other pertinent instances, sometimes only preserved in fragments, see Gzella.

Gianto

27. 4Q530 2 2+6-12:16.
28. 4Q550 1:6f.

שלי *šlī*; **שלו** *šlw* /šalū/; **שלין** *šlyn* /šelyān/; **שלה** *šlh* /šalǣ/; **נוח** *nwḥ*; **ניח** *nyḥ* /nayāḥ/

I. Etymology, Forms, and Lexical Field. II. Verb "to Be Calm." III. Noun "Undisturbed Fortune," "Negligence." IV. Noun "Calm." V. Adjective "Calm, Carefree."

I. Etymology, Forms, and Lexical Field. Forms of the Semitic verbal root *šlī*[1] "to be calm, carefree" and its nominal derivatives occur in Aramaic and Hebrew, and also in Akkadian,[2] Ugaritic, and Arabic. Old Aramaic already attests it; along with the verb, older material already has the feminine /šalū/ "calm, negligence,"[3] the masculine /šelyān/ "calm," and the adjective "calm, carefree."

The root *šlī* with its various derivatives denotes internal calm and freedom from external disturbances, sometimes pejoratively for the associated carefreeness and negligence. Consequently, its opposite consists of verbs of internal agitation like → *bhl* or *krī* "to terrify" (in Dnl. 3:24)[4] and → *'ṣb* or *yṣp* "to be concerned" as well as more specific emotional states such as → *dḥl* or *zū'* "to be anxious." In contrast, older Aramaic has *nūḥ*[5] for external calm as the absence of motion. It is sometimes ingressive "to come to

K. Grünwald, "שָׁלָה *šālâ*," *TDOT*, XV, 9-13.

1. From **šlū*.
2. Where, however, *šlī* is borrowed from Aram.; cf. W. von Soden, "Aramäische Wörter in neuassyrischen und neu- und spätbabylonischen Texten," *Or* 37 (1968) 268, and *AHw*, III, 1211a.
3. Following the Hebrew, pointed *šᵉlēwᵉṯāḵ* in Dnl. 4:24 (*BLA*, §51y), but the consonantal spelling *šlwtk* probably represents /šalūtakā/, as *ATTM*, 710 suggests; → III for a discussion.
4. Also → *twh*.
5. Arisen from an original **nūḫ*.

a stop" as in the settling of the ark,[6] but also for the calm of the earth after the destruction of evil,[7] and with a similar connotation in the C-stem "to create calm."[8] The related masculine *nyḥ* /nayāḥ/ "calm" may, indeed, already occur in *TADAE* C1.1:92 figuratively for *bnyḥ* "in calm, satisfaction," but it is not entirely certain because of the possibility of lost letters at the end of the line.[9] In Jewish and Christian Aramaic languages of late antiquity, forms of this root occur regularly for the calm of death. For "to tarry," Aramaic employs instead → *šrī*, for "to dwell" → *ytb*,[10] or, rarely, → *škn*.

Apparently unrelated to the root *šlī*, the word *šlh* in Dnl. 3:29 erroneously appears in the pointing as *šālū*, but most likely intends the Akkadian loanword /šillā/ "impertinence, blasphemy" no longer known to the Masoretes.[11]

II. Verb "to Be Calm." As a verb, *šlī* "to be calm" appears only sporadically, but can already be identified in an Old Aramaic treaty of state from Sefire in a clause concerning fugitives. It prohibits one ally from accepting fugitive subjects of the other and saying to them: *šlw ʿl ʾšrkm* "remain calm in your place."[12] The connotation "to dwell without concern" may also shine through here, i.e., it involves not granting renegades a home, but the meaning may converge with that of → *ytb* "to dwell, to remain" in exactly the same context in ll. 6f.

On the other hand, the nuance in the Aramaic of late antiquity seems to have narrowed more to "to be negligent" probably under the influence of the nominal forms;[13] Syriac, e.g., attests it, however, in the meaning "to be calm, still."[14]

III. Noun "Undisturbed Fortune," "Negligence." The connotation "negligence, carelessness" of the feminine substantive *šlw* /šalū/ already manifests itself clearly in Biblical Aramaic: according to Dnl. 6:5, despite every effort, those who envy Daniel could discover no error in his reliable execution of office, neither *šālū* nor *š*ᵉ*ḥīṯā* "error,"[15] that would provide an occasion for an accusation.[16] The same meaning underlies the king's admonition in Ezr. 4:22 not to behave negligently in order to avert damage from the government,[17] and the expression *dī lā šālū* "without omission" in Ezr. 6:9. The word also appears late with this meaning.[18]

Consequently, it may be different in its usage in the otherwise atypical sense "calm, well-being" in Dnl. 4:24 and pointed on the pattern of the regular verb as a *qatilat* form

6. 1QapGen 10:12.
7. 4Q212 11 2:16 (1 En. 91:10).
8. 4Q246 1 2:4.
9. Cf. *DNSI*, 729f.
10. Lit., "to sit, to settle."
11. Bib. in *GesB*[18], 1540.
12. *KAI* 224.5.
13. *DJPA*, 553a; *DJBA*, 1148b.
14. *LexSyr*, 778.
15. Substantival pass. ptcp. of *šḥt*.
16. → *ʿlh*.
17. → *nzq*.
18. *DJPA*, 551b; *DJBA*, 1147a.

with a consonantal /w/ (→ I), as in Hebrew, since Hebrew *šālēw* "calm" and *šalwā* "calm" consistently have the connotation "carefree." Because it corresponds precisely to the meaning of the adjective *šlh* "calm" in Dnl. 4:1, however (→ V), and the transition from "carefree" to "negligent" is fluid, in any case, there are reasons to assume that this is also true of the noun and only the punctuation has distinguished the two nuances "calm" and "negligence" in two different forms. At the same time, the lexicographical tradition usually assumes two different lemmata.[19] In any case, *šlwtk* "your rest" in Daniel's interpretation of Nebuchadnezzar's dream in 4:24 alludes to *šlh* "peaceful, content" in 4:1: the king's good fortune will only endure if he acknowledges God as the true ruler and, as atonement for his arrogance, act justly.

IV. Noun "Calm." The masculine form *šlyn* /šelyān/ "calm" occurs in Aḥiqar's admonition not to allow oneself rest (*šlyn lnpšk ʾl tśym*) after assuming a debt (*hn tzp zptʾ*) until it is repaid,[20] and probably on an ostracon.[21] The same word, negated, appears in reference to a fire flickering turbulently in Enoch's vision;[22] the parallel versions enable the reconstruction of the context of the Aramaic fragment.

V. Adjective "Calm, Carefree." Finally, older Aramaic attests the related adjective *šlh* /šalǣ/ "calm, carefree" once (Dnl. 4:1). The parallelism with *rʿnn* /raʿnan/ "prosperous," literally "lush green, luxuriant" and probably adopted from Hebrew,[23] makes it clear that the positive connotation stands in the foreground here. Nonetheless, according to 4:27f, the king's self-satisfaction brings divine punishment because "pleasant rest" does not lead to "pure virtue" on its own.

Gzella

19. See J. Barth, *Die Nominalbildung in den semitischen Sprachen* (Leipzig, ^{2}1894); *LexLingAram*, 167; *KBL*^{3}, 1790; *GesB*^{18}, 1540.

20. *TADAE* C1.1:130.

21. H. Lozachmeur, *La collection Clermont-Ganneau*, vol. 1 (Paris, 2006), 233cv3.

22. 4Q205 1 11:5 (1 En. 23:3), here *šlyʾn* with a vowel letter for /-ā-/, as often in proximity with *w* or *y*; on the form, cf. *ATTM*, 241,710 and 410 for the orthography.

23. *ATTM*, 697; regarding the interpretation, which probably anticipates the tree vision, cf. P. W. Coxon, "The Great Tree of Daniel 4," in *A Word in Season. FS McKane. JSOTSup* 42 (1986), 91-111, esp. 97f.

שלם *šlm*; שָׁלֵם *šlm* /šalem/; שְׁלָם *šlm* /šalām/

I. Etymology and Lexical Field. II. G-stem "to Be Complete." III. D-stem "to Pay, to Repay." IV. C-stem "to Hand Over." V. Adjective "Whole, Undamaged." VI. Noun "Joy, Well-being."

I. Etymology and Lexical Field. In all the branches of the Semitic languages, verbal and nominal forms of the root *šlm* with the G-stem meaning "to be complete" are very productive. Individual nuances crystallize in context since the concept of completeness has other implications depending on the subject. With reference to objects, the connotation is "to be ready, finished," to persons "to be perfect, flawless,"[1] to numerical concepts "to be complete" and, to specific times and periods, "to be over, past." The transitive D-stem functions mostly as a financial term "to pay"[2] and the rarer C-stem denotes "to hand over, to deliver." Elements of the semantic spectrum of this verb have points of contact with that of → *mlī* "to be full," in the D-stem "to fill," while *bṭl* indicates the cessation of an activity.[3] "To return" is mostly the C-stem of → *tūb* or simply → *ytn*/*ntn* "to give." In official diction, furthermore, the lexicalized causative forms *šyṣ'* (Ezr. 6:15) and *škll* (Ezr. 4:12f.,16; 5:3,9,11; 6:14) probably adopted from or influenced by Akkadian denote "to complete."[4]

Of the two nominal forms in use, the adjective /šalem/ "whole, complete, undamaged" corresponds to the meaning of the verb in the G-stem and has a synonym in *gmyr* /gamīr/ "perfect, complete."[5] Its meaning in the introduction to the letter in Ezr. 7:12 is debated, however; presumably *šlm* must be supplied to attain the expression for "complete salvation."[6]

Finally, the masculine substantive /šalām/ "peace, well-being," which occurs primarily in the wish and the greeting formula, has a related, but independent semantic nuance. It may quite generally denote the well-being of an individual, including physical health and peace of mind. The analogous Hebrew form /šalōm/, perceptible in the plene spelling *šlwm*, serves to mark Jewish cultural identity and often appears as a farewell at the end of Jewish Palestinian grave and synagogue inscriptions.[7]

II. G-stem "to Be Complete." In the stative G-stem, *šlm* functions generally like the adjective (→ V) and sometimes takes *l*- "for" plus an indirect object. Only the usage of *tšlm* in *TADAE* B3.13:11 seems unusual. In context, it must mean "to be completely paid out" (with *b*- "in") and, thus, corresponds to the D-stem "to pay" employed elsewhere in the same contract (→ III);[8] consequently, some have suggested a passive form of this stem, perhaps a misspelled t-passive *tštlm*.[9]

M. G. Abegg, "*šlm*," *ThWQ*, III, 958-69; G. Gerleman, "שלם *šlm* to have enough," *TLOT*, 1337-48; K.-J. Illman, "שָׁלֵם *šālēm*," *TDOT*, XV, 97-105; J. Naveh and S. Shaked, *Aramaic Documents from Ancient Bactria (Fourth Century* B.C.E.*)* (London, 2012); D. Schwiderski, *Die alt- und reichsaramäischen Inschriften*, vol. I: *Konkordanz*. *FSBP* 2 (2008); F. J. Stendebach, "שָׁלוֹם *šālôm*," *TDOT*, XV, 13-49.

1. Although external and internal perfect are not clearly distinguished.
2. Later, as a derivative, also "to replace, to repay."
3. For this lexical field → *sūp*.
4. → *kll*.
5. Which belongs to the root *gmr* "to complete," attested as a verb only later.
6. So also *ATTM*, 544, for a discussion cf. *GesB*[18], 1479.
7. *ATTM*, 712; 2, 494.
8. *TADAE* B3.13:4,7.
9. Cf. *DNSI*, 1144.

Otherwise, the verb designates the state of completion and represents the end of construction (Ezr. 5:16, negated of the not yet finished temple), the immaculate beauty of a person,[10] and the "completion," i.e., "being past" of times.[11] In analogy to the latter usage, it can also appear with other numerical concepts when it means "to be complete."[12]

III. D-stem "to Pay, to Repay." The meaning of the D-stem "to pay, to repay" with that to be paid as the object, optionally complemented with *l-* for the indirect object and *b-* for the nature of the payment,[13] is more narrowly defined than that of the G-stem. It appears regularly since the Neo-Assyrian period in debt certificates corresponding to the Akkadian *šallumu.*[14] It appears with the same meaning in business letters[15] and a proverb concerning the repayment of a loan.[16] In an expansion of this usage, the verb can also mean "to replace, to requite."[17]

It appears figuratively for "to repay, to requite" in 11Q10 23:5 (Job 33:26)[18] and 24:5 (Job 34:11)[19] and in the passive in 23:6 (Job 33:27).[20] In addition, it serves in an astronomical context in a description of the phases of the moon as "to complete."[21]

IV. C-stem "to Hand Over." The C-stem of *šlm* appears only sporadically in older Aramaic. Besides the uncertain and partially emended instance in *KAI* 222 B 24, where the context requires the meaning "to fulfill" (of a contract),[22] it usually denotes "to give back" or "to hand over." Ezr. 7:19 utilizes it for the return of the temple implements to (*qdm*) God, Dnl. 5:26 for God's recall of Belshazzar's dominion.[23] Admittedly, the causative nuance of the G-stem "to make complete," i.e., "to end" could also stand in

10. 1QapGen 20:6 of Sarah's legs; probably, with *ATTM*, 711 a 3fp pf. since the adj. must have been *šlmn*; J. A. Fitzmyer, *The Genesis Apocryphon of Qumran Cave 1 (1Q20). BietOr* 18/B (^{3}2004), 195f., and others suspect an adj. with number disagreement, which, however, is less likely.

11. 1QapGen 6:9f.; 22:28; perhaps also in a corrupt context in 10:1; with inf. *'d mšlm* "until the completion" 4Q535 3:5 par. 4Q536 1:2.

12. So 4Q210 1 2:14 (1 En. 76:14) in a list.

13. Both, e.g., in *TADAE* B3.1:7,11,14.

14. Cf. E. Lipiński, *SAIO* III. *OLA* 200 (2010), 64; for Mesopotamia, see A. Lemaire, *Nouvelles tablettes araméennes* (Geneva, 2000), no. 16.1, and Lipiński, *SAIO* III, O. 3672:3f.; 3648:7; 3649:10; for contracts from Egypt *TADAE* B2.7:5; 3.1:7,11,14f.,16; 3.13:4f.,7f.,9; 4.2:3,5,7f.,10; 4.5:5(emend.),6; 4.6:5; fragmentary also Segal, 177.1; and for Samaria in Palestine *WDSP*, 1:9; 8:10; certainly to be reconstructed also in 4:11; 5:11; 18:6; furthermore, from a later period, in a divorce certificate from the Dead Sea (M 19:10,23 in *ATTM*, 307f.).

15. *TADAE* A3.8:2; D1.13:8; 1.17:5.

16. *TADAE* C1.1:131.

17. As in reference to the personal liability of subordinate state officials for possible damages resulting from misbehavior *TADAE* A6.15:8; Naveh and Shaked, A6,10; probably also "to replace" later in 1QapGen 7:5, although between lacunae.

18. For Heb. *šūb*.

19. For Heb. *šlm*.

20. For *šwī* "to be appropriate, sufficient."

21. Of the light of the full moon: 4Q210 1 3:5 (1 En. 78:6f.).

22. Cf. J. A. Fitzmyer, *The Aramaic Inscriptions of Sefire. BietOr* 19/A (^{2}1995), 108.

23. Ultimately, God installs and deposes kings: 2:21; → *mlk* IV.

the foreground,[24] since nothing is handed over, but is taken away. In 1QapGen 20:32, the verb refers to the return of Sarah, in 4Q542 1 1:4 to the heritage of the fathers (i.e., the religious law and its traditions), handed over to the descendants of the patriarchs. At Palmyra, too, it means "to hand over."[25]

V. Adjective "Whole, Undamaged." The adjective *šlm* /šalem/ "whole, complete, undamaged" first appears in Aramaic at Qumran, but because of the ambiguous spelling, the discussion also attributes a few instances to the noun "peace, well-being" (→ VI). Because of the meaning "complete," the use for light in an astronomical context[26] involves the adjective with substantial certainty, as does 11Q10 32:2 (Job 39:2).[27] Contrariwise, *ʿbd šlm* in 4Q246 1 2:6 can mean "to make whole"[28] or "to make peace." Similarly, the word in 4Q535 3:2 in the context of a birth could represent the adjective in the full sense "complete, undamaged, sound"[29] or the noun for "it goes well for him." If one reads the paleographically unclear passage 4Q242 4:2 as *šlm šl[m*,[30] it would involve a combination of noun and adjective "complete health," although the line breaks off thereafter. A few other instances are too fragmentary for a precise determination.

VI. Noun "Joy, Well-being." The root appears in the form of the noun *šlm* /šalām/ "well-being" since the earliest Aramaic. It can first denote "peace" as the well-being of an entire people.[31]

It usually refers, however, to personal well-being and is related semantically to the concept "life"[32] and the adjective /šarīr/ "healthy." One can ask for it for oneself and for others, through the dedication of a statue, for example,[33] or wish for it in the formalized greeting. Since the appearance of Aramaic letters in the later Old Aramaic period in official[34] or private correspondence,[35] therefore, it appears as part of various expressions in the prescript. The Aramaic documents from Egypt preserve dozens of instances;[36] now, the writings of lower officials from Bactria join them.[37] Scribal training transmitted these formulas. They divide into a concise version *šlm* PN (*mn* PN) "Well-being to PN (from

24. So *LexLingAram*, 169: *finivit*, similar to Theodotion's ἐπλήρωσεν and the *conplevit* of the Vulgate.
25. *PAT* 0322.4, with *ʿl ydwh* "into his hands."
26. 4Q209 7 3:7.
27. A simplified translation of a Heb. formulation with the D-stem of the verb *mlʾ* "to fill."
28. So *ATTM*, 2, 149,493.
29. Cf. *ATTM*, 2, 164.
30. With *ATTM*, 2, 139.
31. *KAI* 320.2, with the word *lḥmh* "war," unusual in Aramaic, as an antonym; otherwise → *qrb* has this meaning; perhaps also in *KAI* 224.8, but the reading is uncertain; see Fitzmyer, *Sefire*, 150.
32. → *ḥyī*.
33. *KAI* 309.8f., for the well-being of the king, his descendants, and his people.
34. First in *KAI* 233.1.
35. Attested since the Hermopolis papyri.
36. See Schwiderski, 789-91 for an overview.
37. Naveh and Shaked, B1,1; 2,1; 4,1f.; 6,1f.

PN)" as an address formula of the epistolary ostraca, whose tone is mostly matter-of-fact[38] and *šlm* (PN) "Well-being (to PN)" as the shortest variant[39] and several types of more extensive salutations and felicitations with *šlm* as the object of the verbs → *š'l*,[40] → *šlḥ*, or the C-stem of *yšr*,[41] or in the construct state with the name of a temple.[42] In combination with *b*-, the word also functions like an adverb "healthy," as in letters in the "reunion formula" with the verb → *ḥwī*.[43] Together with *l*- or *qdm*, it denotes "it is going well (for me, etc.)," perhaps expanded with *tnh* "here";[44] as the object of *š'l* with a human subject "to ask about the well-being," it means simply "to greet," even in narratives.[45] For an extensive taxonomy, cf. D. Schwiderski, *Handbuch des nordwestsemitischen Briefformulars. BZAW* 295 (2000), 107-11,115-54; similarly, Ezr. 4:17; 5:7; Dnl. 3:31; 6:26. A greeting can also stand at the end.[46] In the predication "PN is a well-being" it means "it goes well for PN."[47] "Healthy" appears often with verbs of travel,[48] as "in peace" of a good death.[49]

Gzella

38. E.g., *TADAE* D7.16:1; 7.20:1f.
39. So, besides many other examples, *TADAE* A2.1:3; 3.7:1f.
40. E.g., *TADAE* A3.7:1; 4.7:1f.
41. E.g., *TADAE* A6.3:1, together with *ḥyn* "life"; D7.21:2f., with *šrrt* "health."
42. Cf. *TADAE* A2.2:1.
43. E.g., *TADAE* A2.1:2.
44. Cf. TADAE A4.2:2.
45. → *š'l* III.1.; similarly in animal fables: *TADAE* C1.1:94,168.
46. Schwiderski, 231; Naveh and Shaked, B1.7; 3.5; 6.7.
47. 1QapGen 21:19; 4Q197 4 3:7 (Tob. 7:5); cf. 2 S. 20:9.
48. 4Q197 4 1:2 (Tob. 5:21); 4 3:4 par. 4Q196 14 2:7 (Tob 7:1); 4Q544 1:9.
49. 4Q196 18:12 (Tob. 14:2).

שׁם *šm* /šem/

I. Etymology, Form, and Grammatical Constructions. II. As an Identifying Characteristic. 1. Basics. 2. "Name" in the Written Witnesses. 3. Naming. III. Expanded for "Reputation." IV. Name of God. V. Fixed Expressions.

H.-J. Fabry, "*šm*," *ThWQ*, III, 969-79; K. Radner, *Die Macht des Namens. Santag* 8 (Wiesbaden, 2005); T. Ilan, *Lexicon of Jewish Names in Late Antiquity*, 4 vols. (Tübingen, 2002-2012); F. V. Reiterer, H. Ringgren, and H.-J. Fabry, "שֵׁם *šēm*," *TDOT*, XV 128-76; D. Schwiderski, *Die alt- und reichsaramäischen Inschriften*, vol. I: *Konkordanz. FSBP* 2 (2008), 793-96; A. S. van der Woude, "שֵׁם *šēm* name," *TLOT*, 1348-67; R. Zadok, *On West Semites in Babylonia during the Chaldean and Achaemenian Periods* (Jerusalem, ²1978).

I. Etymology, Form, and Grammatical Constructions. Common to all Semitic languages is the masculine substantive "name" /š-m/ with a vowel that varies in the individual languages between */i/[1] and */u/.[2] Probably under the influence of the labial /m/, the Aramaic ground form /šem/ was sometimes pronounced /šom/;[3] the word occurs rarely with a prosthetic glottal stop *ʾšm*.[4] The plural has the feminine ending, in the absolute /šemahān/, but behaves in agreement as a masculine. In addition to its function as an identifying characteristic, the name also refers to the person and one's reputation, in religious speech to the name of God as a sign of God's personal nature that makes it possible for people to address him and to find in him a counterpart. The word often appears with the verb → *qrī* "to name," but can also function as the object, e.g., of → *ḥbl* "to damage" or → *śīm* "to apply, to attach." In the designation of God's name, it regularly appears with verbs of address, praise, and honor. Furthermore, it is a component in compound expressions, especially *bšm* "in the name/at the commission of; relating to." The expression *šm* with *l-* means "to have a name"; *mn šmk* is "what is your name?"; and one usually replies "I PN" for "my name is," i.e., a nominal clause with a personal pronoun and the personal name.

II. As an Identifying Characteristic.

1. Basics. The name serves first to identify a person or a place. In reference to people, it sets the individual apart from the group and is therefore maximally definite in grammatical terms. It thereby represents the unalterable identity of a self-conscious subject throughout the subject's life and continues after death to be the anchoring point in the memory of others. At the same time, it is embedded in cultural traditions, can reflect a religious or political commitment or simply a preference of the name-givers (as a rule, primarily parents), or emphasize an external or internal trait perceived as characteristic.

Aramaic names have roots in the conservative West Semitic onomasticon[5] with its common stock of theophoric elements, divine names in nominal or verbal phrases, that express a trait of the respective deity or its relationship to the bearer,[6] in addition to certain abbreviations,[7] and through the addition of hypocoristic endings such as /-ā/[8] and single word names.[9] Within this stock, transmitted over centuries, sometimes millennia, Aramaic names, especially in consonantal spellings, are not always distinguishable from Canaanite or Arabic. A few lexical elements are typically Aramaic, however: *zbn* "to buy" or *yhb* "to give," patterns such as *qātōl*, or the gentilic affix /-āy/ as a hypocoristic ending.[10]

---

1. Hebrew, mostly in Aramaic, Arabic with metathesis *ism*.
2. E.g., Akkadian and Ugaritic.
3. *ATTM*, 712.
4. *KAI* 222 C 25; B 7.
5. Cf. Zadok.
6. Like /natan/ "has given" or /ḥanan/ "has shown mercy."
7. Usually as expressions of endearment.
8. E.g., Elna for Elnatan "El has given."
9. E.g., /kalb/ "dog" and other animal names or the time, circumstances, etc. of the desired or welcomed birth.
10. Instead of Arabic /-īy/.

In Aramaic texts, West Semitic names could also interchange with Mesopotamian, Egyptian, and beginning in the Achaemenid period, Iranian names. In the Hellenistic-Roman period, one can also find Greek, Latin, and Arabic names in Aramaic-speaking regions. Especially in bilingual and bicultural societies such as Roman Palmyra, persons sometimes had two names that may have translated one another, sounded alike, or were entirely unrelated.[11] Direct conclusions drawn from the language of a name concerning its bearer or his or her often imperceptible ethnicity are mostly impossible, but certain theophoric elements reflect a cultural affiliation, such as /Yō-/ or /-Yā/ as an abbreviation for the God of Israel in Jewish personal names.

The inventory of Aramaic names, including distribution and meaning, is available in specialized onomastic studies for the individual corpora of inscriptions.[12]

Besides people, divine beings, and animals, places, bodies of water, sometimes buildings,[13] and other things like stars[14] or abstract concepts like the letters of the alphabet,[15] the months and festivals have names, in fact even some objects do.

2. *"Name" in the Written Witnesses.* Name and existence interlink inextricably. In the representational culture of the Old Aramaic principalities in Syria, which produced the first textual witnesses, kings record their own names in history in the reports of their deeds; with them begins the self-introduction of the author at the beginning of the respective inscriptions. Consquently, it is also very important that this name be preserved; the introduction[16] of another name stands under a curse, therefore.[17] The treaties of state

11. H. Gzella, "Die Palmyrener in der griechisch-römischen Welt," *KLIO* 87 (2005) 445-58, esp. 453.

12. Cf. M. Maraqten, *Die semitischen Personennamen in den alt- und reichsaramäischen Inschriften aus Vorderasien. TStO* 5 (1988), for Old and Imperial Aramaic; *ATTM*, 729-41 and 2, 507-19 for the texts from the Dead Sea and Biblical Aramaic; J. K. Stark, *Personal Names in Palmyrene Inscriptions* (Oxford, 1971), with R. Degen, review of J. K. Stark, *Personal Names in Palmyrene Inscriptions, BiOr* 29 (1972) 210-16, for Palmyra; A. Negev, *Personal Names in the Nabatean Realm* (Jerusalem, 1991), with M. C. A. Macdonald, "Personal Names in the Nabataean Realm: A Review Article," *JSS* 44 (1999) 251-89, and F. al-Khraysheh, "Die Personennamen in den nabatäischen Inschriften des Corpus Inscriptionum Semiticarum" (diss., Marburg, 1986), for Nabatean; S. Abbadi, *Die Personennamen der Inschriften aus Hatra. TStO* 1 (1983), and K. Beyer, *Die aramäischen Inschriften aus Assur, Hatra und dem übrigen Ostmesopotamien* (Göttingen, 1998), 144-67, and idem, "Die aramäischen Inschriften aus Assur, Hatra und dem übrigen Ostmesopotamien (datiert 44 v. Chr. bis 238 n. Chr.) – Nachträge," *WO* 43 (2013) 50-55 for Hatra; a list of the names in Old Syriac inscriptions in H. J. W. Drijvers and J. F. Healey, *The Old Syriac Inscriptions of Edessa and Osrhoene. HO* 42 (1999), 275-80; more on Aramaic names, etc. in G. F. Grassi, *Semitic Onomastics from Dura Europos* (Padua, 2012), with H. Gzella, review of G. F. Grassi, *Semitic Onomastics from Dura Europos. AfO* 55 (2013) 457-63, and *ATTM*, 2, 323f.

13. → II.2 for the new Jersualem.

14. → *šmyn* IV.

15. M. Krebernik, "Buchstabennamen, Lautwerte und Alphabetgeschichte," in R. Rollinger et al., eds., *Getrennte Wege?* (Frankfurt, 2007), 108-75.

16. → *śīm*.

17. *KAI* 309.11f.; in l. 16 also of the name of the donor on cultic offerings.

from Sefire wish that the descendants[18] of an oath-breaker "inherit no name" (*'l yrt 'šm*).[19] Conversely, by nature, a coup d'etat involves destroying the name of the toppled prince.[20] (An additional instance of *šm* occurs in a highly damaged context in *KAI* 202 C 2, another royal inscription.)

With the appearance of private grave memorials, the quest for *memoria* in the time of ancient Near Eastern empires spread further among the upper class,[21] who looked to the forms of expression in the royal inscriptions and also wished for an enduring remembrance.[22] In the Roman Near East, this pursuit, with the added influence of the Hellenistic practice of publicly honoring private individuals, then became the driving force for the brisk production of epigraphy.[23] One must distinguish, however, between inscriptions honoring civil beneficence, as in Palymra and in late antiquity in Jewish Palestinian and Samaritan synagogues, and personal memorial, dedicatory, and grave inscriptions that continue an older practice.

Beginning with the Neo-Assyrian period, Aramaic written witnesses also document administrative practice. Here, the name serves primarily practical purposes: it identifies individual persons in correspondence and in legal affairs, and indicates the owner of slaves and objects. From the Achaemenid period on, official texts frequently employ the construction PN *šmh* "a certain PN,"[24] probably under Persian or Akkadian influence;[25] the same construction also appears in Ezr. 5:14. Thereby, the voices of individuals who make contracts[26] and file official petitions,[27] as well as the names of persons involved in penal proceedings[28] first become audible. In Ezr. 5:4,10, too, the opponents of the temple construction ask for the names of those responsible in order to report them (Ezr. 5:4: *mn 'nwn šmht gbry'* "what are the names of the men"; 5:10: → *š'l šm* "ask for the names").

3. Naming. The Aramaic sources rarely speak of the act of naming, which is of such theological significance in the OT, or of renaming after a decisive event. The new name of Daniel after his entry into royal service (Dnl. 2:26; 4:5,16; 5:12)[29] corresponds to the Mesopotamian custom of changing the name at the beginning of a new phase of life.[30] In the context of the book of Daniel, it represents the complex identity of people who

---

18. → *šrš*.

19. *KAI* 222 C 25.

20. *KAI* 223 B 7; → *'bd*.

21. Cf. H. Gzella, *A Cultural History of Aramaic*. *HO* 111 (2015), 144-47.

22. "May the name of one who desecrates a grave be eradicated": *KAI* 225.9f.; 228 A 14f.,21f.

23. Gzella, 212-80; → *dkr*.

24. Schwiderski, 794f. lists the many instances.

25. See *ATTM*, 2, 495.

26. Many examples in *TADAE* B and *WDSP*; cf. *TADAE* A6.11.

27. E.g., *TADAE* A4.10.

28. *TADAE* A6.3; 6.7.

29. Cf. in the Hebrew section 1:7.

30. Service in the temple, at court, or as a slave in the house of the owner, for women, divorce; see Radner, 27-35.

assert themselves in a foreign environment with all its possibilities, on the one hand, yet remain true to their religio-cultural traditions, on the other. One can understand the dual cultural identity of the Palmyrene elite similarly: in Aramaic, the participle of the Gt-stem of → *qrī*, "who was (also) called," indicates the second name, in Greek ὁ καί (cf. Acts 13:9). Qumran sporadically mentions naming (by the father) in the context of biographical details concerning the patriarchs.[31]

In some cases, the name itself suggests possible reasons for its choice. Papponymy, i.e., naming a child after its grandfather, widespread in Greco-Roman times, appears in genealogical information in Palmyrene inscriptions and related, at least originally, to the fact that the child was considered a substitute for the already deceased family member, which also finds expression in the so-called "substitute names."[32] If not pure convention, the choice of a theophoric element can express a religious commitment, as to Hadad or Baal in Syria or to the God of Israel in Palestine, and in the case of Nabatean basilophoric names, also to a certain king. Time or circumstances of the birth appear, e.g., in Haggai (/ḥaggāy/) or Shabbatai (/šabbatāy/) "the one born on a feast day/Sabbath," Silas (/šaʾīl/) "the one asked for," etc. Since bilingual Palmyrene inscriptions still sometimes translate name elements,[33] they were apparently considered significant.

In symbolic contexts, "to have a name" can also signify "to stand for something." Thus, the visionary of a historical allegory of four empires asks about the names (*mn šmk*) of the trees that symbolize these empires; the reply of the first tree is: "Babylon."[34] Further, the gates in the vision of the new Jerusalem bear the names of the tribes of Israel whom they represent.[35] Consequently, a nickname can also be included under the term *šm*, as the use with the verb *knī b-* in the D-stem "to call by a nickname"[36] indicates.[37]

III. Expanded for "Reputation." Because of the close connection of name and person, *šm* also represents a person's reputation. It is already a recurring theme in the Old Aramaic proverbial wisdom of Aḥiqar. Honoring one's parents demands taking pride in the name (*bšm*) of father and mother;[38] through shameful behavior, one soils the name of past and future generations of one's own family.[39] Therefore, in the presence of others, one must consider their regard.[40] Thus, the name determines not only the continued life of a person in the memory of others, but, above all, how one remembers this person. To acquire[41] a

31. 4Q204 5 1:26 (1 En. 106:1), with → *qrī* "to name"; 4Q546 9:3.
32. For a discussion, see, e.g., A. Schüle, *Die Syntax der althebräischen Inschriften. AOAT* 270 (2000), 226-28.
33. E.g., ἀντί for *ḥlp* in *PAT* 0377.
34. 4Q552 1 2:5.8 par. 4Q553 3+2 ii+4:4,6.
35. 4Q554 1 1:12,14,19; 1 2:6,8.
36. Etymologically related to "kunya" in Arabic.
37. In 4Q246 1 1:9, here a t-passive and paralleling *qrī*, the connotation can be deduced from the later material, cf. *LexSyr*, 334a; for a discussion of the text itself → *br* IV.
38. *TADAE* C1.1:138; regarding the form of the verb → *rīm* IV.
39. *TADAE* C1.1:180.
40. *TADAE* C1.1:141; the fragmentary l. 106 may deal with malicious gossip.
41. → *śīm*.

good name (*šm ṭb*) is a gift of the gods, just as is a long life.[42] In the religious literature from Qumran, this deeply rooted conception recurs at the surface of the Aramaic tradition: the mention of the name[43] in future generations guarantees continuity,[44] and the descendant's good reputation because of upright behavior is also a reason for the ancestors to rejoice;[45] conversely, the shame of the individual transfers to the family.[46] The topic of the king's fame echoes in a court novella.[47]

IV. Name of God. Just as the name of a person renders his individuality nameable and confirms his existence, the name of God enables access to his person. The statement that he causes his name to dwell in the temple (Ezr. 6:12)[48] refers to his presence, per se. Consequently, the concept of the name of God occurs regularly in the language of personal prayer, as evident in Biblical Aramaic and the texts from Qumran. The hymn of thanksgiving praises it (Dnl. 2:20),[49] it is holy[50] and revered,[51] thus bearing the very characteristics of God;[52] by sharing his "great"[53] name, God reveals himself to the believer and makes himself known;[54] he can therefore be addressed in prayer.[55] The same verbs and modifiers used of God also refer to his name. Similarly, *šm* can appear in relation to God with the nuance "reputation" when, in hymnic praise, it means the knowledge of God's great deeds across the generations.[56] In God's case, the naming of his name is already closely related to praise (as in other ancient cultures).[57]

The angels, called upon especially in later magical texts to protect against evil, also have names; older Aramaic transmits them primarily in the books of Enoch, as well as parts of Daniel, and, from Qumran, Tobit and the Testament of Amram.[58] The names of the fallen angels do not differ essentially from those of the holy ones since even the former once stood in God's service. Characteristic in most cases is the theophoric element El,[59] which clarifies the angels' alignment with God.

---

42. *KAI* 226.3.
43. → *qrī.*
44. 1QapGen 14:12.
45. See 4Q541 24 2:5; 4Q542 1 1:10; → *ḥdwh* IV.2.
46. 4Q213a 3-4:3,5f.; cf. 4Q196 6:10 (Tob. 3:15).
47. 4Q550 2:2.
48. → *škn* in the D-stem.
49. → *brk*; 1QapGen 21:2, *hll.*
50. → *qdš.*
51. → *yqr.*
52. 4Q196 6:7 (Tob. 3:11).
53. → *rb.*
54. 4Q542 1 1:1; C-stem of → *yd'* IV.1.
55. 1QapGen 21:2; with → *qrī b-*.
56. 4Q196 17 2:15 (Tob. 13:11); the reconstruction of the wording is not entirely certain.
57. S. Pulleyn, *Prayer in Greek Religion* (Oxford, 1997), 96-115.
58. Assembled in the catalog of names in *ATTM*, 729-41; 2, 507-19.
59. As, e.g., in Michael, Gabriel, Raphael, Uriel, and others.

V. Fixed Expressions. In addition to the expression *šm ṭb* for "a good reputation, fame" and the regular use of *šm* with certain verbs (→ I), the word appears frequently as part of fixed expressions that associate the name closely with a person. As *bšm* "in the name," it can mean "on behalf of" and refer both to people[60] and to God.[61] Especially in legal diction, however, it also means "in reference to," in which case it designates the subject of a contract[62] or a clause of one,[63] just like *ʿl dbr*.[64] While *bšm* and *ʿl dbr* characterize an action, *ʿl šm* means "in the name of";[65] *lšm* may function similarly for a city built in the name of God[66] and in contracts from the time of the second rebellion with the name of the rebel leader Bar-Kosiba in the sense of *nomine et auspiciis*.[67] In addition, other prepositional expressions with a similar meaning occur sporadically later.[68]

Gzella

60. As in legal matters: *TADAE* B2.2:14; 2.3:16; 2.10:12f.
61. As in the activity of prophets in Ezr. 5:1.
62. E.g., *TADAE* B2.3:12: land; B2.7:9; 3.4:13,17; 3.5:14; 3.11:15; 3.12:25,28f.; 5.4:7: a house; B2.8:8: property; B5.5:4f.,9f.: a sum of money.
63. *TADAE* B2.8:9: the oath.
64. Cf. the parallel formulation involving a house in *TADAE* B2.2:6,16; involving a slave: B2.11:8f.,11.
65. As in the branding of a slave: *TADAE* B5.6:3.
66. 4Q529 1:9.
67. V 49:1 and 50:1 in *ATTM*, 2, 252-54.
68. Instances in *ATTM*, 2, 495.

שמין *šmyn* /šamayn/; כוכב *kwkb* /kawkab/

I. Etymology, Form, and Lexical Field. II. As Part of the Visible World. III. 1. As the Dwelling Place of Divine Beings. 2. Visionary Journeys to Heaven. IV. Stars and Zodiac Signs.

I. Etymology, Form, and Lexical Field. Just as the ubiquitous heaven belongs among the universal human impressions, the word for it is also a common primary noun in the

R. Bartelmus, "שָׁמַיִם *šāmayim*," *TDOT*, XV, 204-36; R. E. Clements, "כּוֹכָב *kôḵāḇ*," *TDOT*, VII, 75-85; B. Ego, "Denkbilder für Gottes Ewigkeit, Herrlichkeit und Richtermacht—Himmelsvorstellungen im antiken Judentum," *JBT* 20 (2005) 151-88; H.-J. Fabry, "*šmym*," *ThWQ*, III, 985-93; T. Nicklas et al., eds., *Other Worlds and Their Relation to This World. JSJSup* 143 (2010); J. A. Soggin, "שָׁמַיִם *šāmayim* heaven," *TLOT*, 1369-72.

Semitic languages. Aramaic /šamayn/ traces back to a form of the *qalī* pattern in the dual[1] or *plurale tantum*.[2] No clear conceptual foundation for this variation in number is known. In Aramaic, the substantive behaves mostly as a masculine plural in agreement,[3] but can also occasionally, as e.g., sometimes in Syriac, function as a masculine or feminine singular. As a meteorological term, "heaven" designates the realm above and beyond the earth and, seamlessly, the sky above as the associated habitat of divine beings. Consequently, "heaven" functions as an antonym of → *ʾrʿ* "earth"; the two together constitute a pair repeatedly attested throughout the older phases of the language[4] as a figurative paraphrase of totality.[5] Aramaic does not attest an independent lexeme for "underworld."

In both nuances, /šamayn/ often appears in the construct state together with associated phenomena, on the one hand as "sky" with birds or certain meteorological phenomena such as winds or dew, and on the other as a title in the designation of God or of the angels, and extended metonymically for God himself. Furthermore, it combines with various prepositions to indicate direction: *l-*[6] or *ʿd*[7] "(reaching) to heaven," *mn*[8] "from heaven," or *tḥwt* "under heaven"[9] as a synonym of *ʿl ʾnpy ʾrʿ*[10] "on the surface of the earth."[10] The masculine *kwkb* /kawkab/[11] denotes "star." Sun[12] and moon[13] as once divine beings and the planets and zodiac signs[14] each had their own names.

II. As Part of the Visible World. As a visible part of the universe, heaven is distinct from the earth accessible to human beings (→ I). The earth can also occasionally divide into the habitable dry land, the sea,[15] and other areas such as the mountains;[16] cf. 1QapGen 7:1, but, because of a lacuna in the text, it is unclear whether the reference to zodiac signs, sun, moon, and stars in l. 2 constitutes a contrast. In contrast to earthly nature, it has undergone no alteration so that Aramaic also attests *kywmy šmyn* "like the days of heaven"[17] as an expression for eternal duration (cf. Dt. 11:21; Ps. 89:30); only a teleological perspective such as Mk. 13:31 associates "heaven and earth" as an expression for "everything" with transience.

---

1. As, e.g., in Aramaic and Hebrew.
2. As in Ugaritic as evidenced by the syllabic spelling *ša-mu-ma* (*DUL*[3], 814) for /šamūma/; the nominative dual would have had /ā/ instead of /ū/; *ATTM*, 713; 2, 495.
3. Consequently, it appears in Dnl. 4:23 with an accordingly declined predicate adj.
4. *KAI* 309.2; *KAI* 202 B 25; 222 A 26; *TADAE* A1.1:2; Jer. 10:11; Dnl. 6:28; 1QapGen 22:16,21.
5. For which, otherwise, the abstract term /koll/ is available, → *kll*.
6. Dnl. 4:8,19; 1QapGen 10:17.
7. 1QapGen 6:25.
8. Dnl. 4:10,20,28; 1QapGen 11:15.
9. Dnl. 7:27.
10. nV 1:33; *ATTM*, 2, 205-8.
11. And then /kōkab/.
12. → *šmš*.
13. *śhr* /śehr/, *ATTM*, 704; 2, 489.
14. Collective: *mzl* /mazzal/, 1QapGen 7:2.
15. → *ym*.
16. → *ṭwr*.
17. *TADAE* A1.1:3, in the wish for enduring dominion.

In the spatial sense, *šmyn* represents the habitat of birds.[18] Here, the word primarily means "air, sky," for which Semitic languagues originally had no independent word.[19] The "birds of heaven" in the collective expression *'wp šmy'* (Dnl. 2:38) or as a plural of individuality *ṣpry šmy'* (Dnl. 4:9,18) constitute a distinction within the animal world to the land animals (*ḥywt br'* "animals of the field");[20] together, they contrast with humanity. In royal ideology, *'wp šmy'* functions in Dnl. 2:38, on the one hand, as the object of Nebuchadnezzar's unlimited claim to power (admittedly, it does not mention the sea), and *ṣpry šmy'* (the birds that nest in the branches of the world tree) in 4:8,19, on the other, as a picture of the comprehensive protection that the king offers everything in his dominion. The tree that reaches to heaven (Dnl. 4:8,17,19)[21] represents Nebuchadnezzar himself and illustrates the ambivalence of all secular dominion with its majesty in the constant tension between ruling authority and ruinous hybris.

More often, *šmyn* appears in the context of various meteorological phenomena; to be sure, in the texts from the book of Daniel and from Qumran, in which they occur in concentration, they are always embedded in visions. The expression *ṭl šmy'* "dew of heaven,"[22] which recurs as a leitmotif in the account of Nebuchadnezzar's dream, its interpretation, and its realization (Dnl. 4:12,20,22,30; summarized in 5:21), may designate a basic provision of nature: the king, dehumanized in banishment, is indeed stripped of his majesty and shares the habitat of the animals of the field, but the dew and herbs[23]—both positively connoted terms for the nurturing aspect of the essentially good creation, attendant upon humanity—keep him alive so that at the end of his period of penance, as soon as he has recognized God as the supreme Lord, he is able to return to office.

In contrast, the images of the vision of Dnl. 7, loaded with mythical reminiscences, have cosmic connotations. The four animals as symbols of the four sequential empires ascend to an apocalyptic otherworldly landscape of the sea churned up[24] by the four winds of heaven (*'rb' rwḥy šmy'*; Dnl. 7:2), which may recall the hostile power of chaos associated with the sea in ancient Canaanite mythology.[25] The "son of man" constitutes the counterpart. He comes "together with the clouds of heaven" (*'m 'nny šmy'*) and, before the throne of a divine figure elevated above time and space, receives from this figure eternal dominion after the destruction of earthly powers (Dnl. 7:13). The myth of Baal, rider of the clouds, and his victory over chaos resounds here.[26]

At Qumran, the four winds of heaven also appear as a destructive power that defoliates and destroys the olive tree in Noah's vision.[27] In addition, 11Q10 13:2 (Job 28:21) has

---

18. → *ṣpr*.
19. Later *'wr* /'awēr/ is borrowed from Greek ἀήρ, see *ATTM*, 506; for the words for "breath" → *nšm*.
20. → *ḥyī* IV.
21. Regarding the nuances of the verb form → *mṭī* II.3.
22. → *ṭl*.
23. → *'šb*.
24. C-stem of *gūḥ*.
25. → *ym* IV.
26. → *'nn* II.
27. 1QapGen 13:16; the fragmentary text seems to combine motifs from Dnl. 2 and 4.

ṣpry šmy' for Hebrew *'wp hšmym*.[28] Otherwise, *šmyn* appears more often in astronomic contexts, either in the actually redundant phrase *kwkby šmy'* "stars of heaven"[29] or in the technical astronomical expression *m'ny šmy'* "heavenly bodies";[30] *mzlt šmy'* "zodiac signs of heaven"[31] is also a double expression (→ IV). These texts add precision, primarily in the written tradition, to the Aramaic lexical field "heaven."

In relation to the heavenly gates of the wind, the expression *rwḥy šmy'* serves in the literal sense for the "winds of heaven," on which the figurative meaning "cardinal directions" rests;[32] otherwise, *rwḥyn* without *šmy'* also serves this purpose.[33] Further, the stars exit the gates of heaven when they rise;[34] thus, they function as portals that link heaven, as sky, with the firmament above.[35] From them descend not only wind and rain, but through them, cries of lament and the fragrance of sacrifice also arise to God (→ III.1).

According to the teleological historical perspective of apocalypticism, however, heaven is also only preliminary: in a reversion of the old function of *šmyn* as an eternal concept,[36] according to the ten weeks apocalypse, at the dawn of the eschaton, a *šmyn qdmyn* "first heaven" will pass away.[37]

A few other examples from Qumran resist definition because of the lack of context.

III. *1. As the Dwelling Place of Divine Beings.* At the same time, heaven is also the dwelling place of divine beings, and, in the principalities of Syria, since Old Aramean times, gods were venerated who were linked with meteorological or astral phenomena.[38] With Attar or Ištar, who appeared as stars in heaven, and with the fertility god Hadad, whose voice was believed to be heard in thunder[39] and who was *gwgl šmyn w'rq* "irrigator of heaven and earth" because of his dominion over the rain,[40] the two aspects of heaven as a visible space above the earth and as the habitat of the gods fused. Old Aramaic inscriptions explicitly mention "gods of heaven";[41] a treaty of state from Sefire calls as witnesses heaven[42] along with previously mentioned gods, and then earthly powers such as springs

---

28. Aramaic also attests *'wp*, see above on Dnl. 2:38 and cf. 4Q531 2+3:4, but it was apparently more refined diction, however.
29. 4Q209 23:5 par. 4Q210 1 2:16 (1 En. 77:2).
30. 4Q209 23:7 (1 En. 77:3).
31. 1QapGen 7:2.
32. 4Q209 23:2 (1 En. 76:14).
33. 1QapGen 22:8; 11Q10 33:8 (Job 39:26); → *rwḥ* IV.
34. 4Q211 1 2:4 (1 En. 82:25); → *tr'*.
35. /raqīʿ/ adopted as a Heb. loanword, cf. *ATTM*, 697; no independent Aramaic lexeme is known.
36. *TADAE* A1.1:3, see above.
37. 4Q212 1 4:23f. (1 En. 91:16); cf. Mk. 13:31.
38. Cf. E. Lipiński, *SAIO* II (1994), 193-201.
39. → *ql*.
40. *KAI* 309.2.
41. *KAI* 202 B 25; the subsequent text may have had "gods of the earth," but the text is extremely fragmentary.
42. Presumably together with the earth in the subsequent lacuna.

and the cosmic phenomena day and night,[43] presumably based on a Hittite model.[44] In a somewhat later letter of the vassal prince Adon, "heaven and earth" probably serve to designate the area of dominion of a West Semitic deity mentioned in the preceding, now lost text.[45] The name of the West Semitic god Ba'alšamin, still venerated in Roman times,[46] is programmatic; the greeting formula of a pre-Imperial Aramaic private letter from Hermopolis attests the popular veneration of a *mlkt šmyn* "queen of heaven."[47] The writers of this letter belonged to a community of Aramaic-speaking Syrians who probably originally emigrated to Egypt. El, the chief god of the sayings of Aḥiqar, also has ties with heaven.[48]

Beginning in the Achaemenid period, the understanding of divine power expanded to include all-encompassing kingship.[49] In the greeting formulas of official letters from Elephantine in this period, in addition to *'lh šmy'* "god of heaven,"[50] one also finds the title *mr' šmy'* "lord of heaven."[51] Such neutral terms for the supreme god permit coming to agreement with the Persian government on a common basis in questions of religion,[52] but need not be of Iranian origin. Instead, they could also develop West Semitic theologoumena.[53]

Via the general understanding of heaven as God's dwelling place (Dnl. 2:28), Biblical Aramaic adapts this conception with its specifically mediating function ("God of heaven": Dnl. 2:18f.,37,44; Ezr. 5:11f.; 6:9f.; 7:12,21,23; "lord of heaven": Dnl. 5:23; additionally, *mlk šmy'* "king of heaven": 4:34). Thus, the proper commitment to the God of Israel can also be linked to the overarching veneration of a divine ruler even among other nations. Therefore, messengers from God come "from heaven" (Dnl. 4:10,20,28), one raises one's eyes to "heaven" in prayer (4:31).[54] The angels[55] constituted the heavenly host (Dnl. 4:32).[56] Under the influence of this close association, *šmy'* "the heaven" can also occasionally represent God himself (Dnl. 4:23).

The Aramaic texts from Qumran root in the same terminology; "Lord of heaven" appears especially in 1QapGen,[57] further also "King of heaven"[58] or simply "heaven,"[59]

---

43. *KAI* 222 A 11; the context of the word in B 7 is unclear.

44. Cf. J. A. Fitzmyer, *The Aramaic Inscriptions of Sefire. BietOr* 19/A (^{2}1995), 76, with bib.; so also, e.g., Dt. 4:26, etc.

45. *TADAE* A1.1:2.

46. H. Niehr, *Ba'alšamem. OLA* 123 (2003), 89-184.

47. *TADAE* A2.1:1, cf. Jer. 7:18; 44:25.

48. *TADAE* C1.1:79; an addition, yet unclear, instance of the word occurs in l. 189.

49. → *mlk* III.

50. *TADAE* A3.6:1; 4.3:3,5; 4.7:2,27f. par. 4.8:2,27; 4.9:3f.; → *'lh* II.2.

51. *TADAE* A4.7,15 par. 4.8,14; → *mr'* IV.1.

52. See already A. Vincent, *La religion des Judéo-Araméens d'Éléphantine* (Paris, 1937), 92-143.

53. On the discussion, see K. Koch, *Daniel 1–4. BK* XXII/1 (2005), 160-64.

54. Similarly 4Q196 6:8 (Tob. 3:12) and 4Q213a 1:8 from Qumran; → *nṭl*.

55. → *qdš* IV.2.

56. → *ḥyl* III.

57. 1QapGen 7:7; 12:17; with "and of the earth" 22:16,21; → *mr'* II.5.

58. 1QapGen 2:14.

59. 4Q541 9 1:3.

and "Ruler of heaven" (*šlṭn šmy'*).[60] The frequent reference to the angels accommodates the growing interests in angelology. They are called *bny šmyn* "heavenly beings,"[61] sometimes *'yry šmy'* "the watchers of heaven"[62] or *qdyšy šmy'* "the holy ones of heaven."[63] Likewise, a more precise conception appears, as in the meteorological realm: the fragrance of sacrifice can simply rise to "heaven,"[64] but as God's residence, gates seal[65] heaven, through them the cry of lament reaches God[66] and visionaries gain access (see below).

2. *Visionary Journeys to Heaven.* The desire to reach heaven may be the hidden root of all mythology. In this regard, however, the attempt to storm heaven in one's own power represents a sign of hybris that became proverbial in the tower of Babel, but also still echoes in the world tree of Nebuchadnezzar's night vision (Dnl. 4:8,19, → II). Insight into the heavenly world during their lifetimes opens only to particularly gifted individuals such as Enoch: Levi enters it in his vision through the "gates of heaven"[67] and an extensive report of revelation is associated primarily with the figure of Enoch (cf. already Gen. 5:24). He tells of high mountains and valleys and a paradisiacal landscape (1 En. 17–19; 21–36), the courses of the stars (73; 77–79; 82:22), the winds and seasons (76; 82); thus, he sees heaven as a whole. Qumran preserves fragments of a vision report. The new Jerusalem may also involve a heavenly vision, but none of the preserved fragments say so.

IV. Stars and Zodiac Signs. Terminologically, *kwkb* /kawkab/, which is also a common Semitic primary noun, distinguishes the stars from *šmš* /šamš/ "sun" and *śhr* /śehr/ "moon"; the latter two appear alone in lists such as 1QapGen 7:2; 13:11. Before Qumran, *kwkb* appears only in a comparison of the many unknown star names with people as unknown beings in a proverb of Aḥiqar.[68] In texts from Qumran, along with two passages translated directly from the Hebrew in 11Q10 9:8; 30:5 (Job 25:5; 38:7), the word appears mostly in the books of Enoch in various contexts: falling stars symbolize the fall of the angels at the beginning of the allegorical history of the world in the form of an animal vision;[69] the notion of stars as an angelic host (→ III.1) appears in the name Kokab-El;[70] the interpretation of stars *nḥšy kwkbyn* ("omen of the stars") belongs to the civilizing

60. 4Q530 2 2+6-12:6.
61. 1QapGen 2:5,16; 5:3f.; 6:11.
62. 4Q204 1 6:8 (1 En. 13:10); → *'yr*.
63. 4Q201 1 4:10 (1 En. 9:1); → *qdš* IV.2.
64. → *slq*, 1QapGen 10:17.
65. → *tr'*.
66. 4Q202 1 3:10 (1 En. 9:2); 4Q201 1 4:6 (1 En. 8:4), emended following *ATTM*, 236; without "gate": 4Q206 1 22:4 (1 En. 22:5).
67. 4Q213a 2:18.
68. *TADAE* C1.1:164.
69. 4Q207 1:1,4 (1 En. 86:1,3); 4Q206 4 1:11 (1 En. 88:3).
70. 4Q201 1 3:7 par. 4Q204 1 2:25.

capacities that the fallen angels shared with humanity;[71] in the astronomical book, the west is the direction the stars arrive after their exit from the gates of heaven[72] and their course.[73] Astronomical terminology refers to the stars further as *m'ny šmy'* "heavenly bodies."[74] Their fixed course is the "action [*'bd* /'obād/] of heaven";[75] it demonstrates the planned arrangement of creation.[76]

Already in Old Aramaic times, the individual stars had their own names, as *TADAE* C1.1:164 demonstrates (see above). All the names of the zodiac signs are first transmitted in Aramaic in a "brontologion," an astrological brontology, from Qumran.[77] In contrast to the umbrella term *mzl* /mazzal/ borrowed from Akkadian,[78] they completely accord with the known mosaics with captions in West Semitic, including Aries[79] and Pisces:[80] *dkr'* /dakarā/ "Aries,"[81] *twr'* /tawrā/ "Taurus,"[82] *t'wmy'* /to'āmayyā/[83] "Gemini," *srṭn'* /sarṭānā/ "Cancer," *'ryh* /'aryǣ/ "Leo,"[84] *btwlt'* /batūltā/ "Virgo," *mwzny'* /mawzenayyā/ "Libra,"[85] *'qrb'* /'aqrabā/ "Scorpio," *qšt'* /qaššātā/ "Sagittarius,"[86] *gdy'* /gadiyā/ "Capricorn," *dwl'* /dawlā/ "Aquarius," and *nwnj'* /nūnayyā/ "Pisces." The two divergences from Hebrew and the agreements with the Syriac tradition attested later prove these names to be genuinely Aramaic.

Gzella

71. 4Q201 1 4:3 par. 4Q202 1 3:3 (1 En. 8:3).
72. 4Q211 1 2:4 (1 En. 82:25); → *tr'*.
73. 4Q209 23:5 par. 4Q210 1 2:16 (1 En. 77:2), *kwkby šmy'*.
74. 4Q209 23:7 (1 En. 77:3); → *m'n* IV.
75. → *'bd* V.
76. 4Q204 1 1:18 (1 En. 2:1).
77. 4Q318.
78. From Babylonian *manzaltu*; cf. S. A. Kaufman, *The Akkadian Influences on Aramaic. AS* 19 (1974), 69f.
79. Hebrew *ṭlh* "lamb."
80. For which Hebrew has a different lexeme, /dag/; cf. *ATTM*, 2, 167.
81. → *dkr*.
82. → *twr*.
83. *ATTM*, 2, 501.
84. → *'ryh*.
85. → *tql* I.
86. → *qšṭ* I.

שמע *šm'*

I. Verbal Root and Etymology. 1. Common Semitic. 2. Common Aramaic. II. Biblical Aramaic. III. Qumran.

I. Verbal Root and Etymology.

1. Common Semitic. The verbal root *s_1m' is common Semitic and occurs in every branch of the Semitic family of languages.[1] The verb serves to denote auditory perception in the most general sense and often has connotations of "to obey" and "to understand" that result from pure hearing.[2] The root appears in the various languages either with the regular reflections of Semitic *s_1 or often with the loss of the voiced pharyngeal.[3] Reflections of the root in Semitic in unaltered form are Amorite *śm'* (*yiśma'*),[4] Ugaritic *šm'*,[5] Canaanite *šm'* (Hebrew *šāma'*;[6] Phoenician *šm'*),[7] Arabic *sami'a*, Sabaean *s_1m'*,[8] and North Ethiopic *sm'* (e.g., Classical Ethiopic *säm'a*).[9] The following languages exhibit the loss of the pharyngeal: Akkadian *išme* (*šemûm*),[10] Punic *šm*,[11] and Amharic *sämma*.[12] Modern South Arabian attests the transition from */s_1/ > /h/, e.g., Soqotri *h(y)émaḥ*;[13] the latter root also manifests the devoicing of the pharyngeal. Modern South Arabian also exhibits the loss of the nasal, to be replaced with the nasalization of the vowel, Jibbāli *šĩ'/yšũ'*. The presumptive base vowels are /i/ in the perfect[14] and /a/ in the imperfect.[15] The perfect, especially in Northwest Semitic, manifests the transition from /i/ > /a/.[16]

W. Arnold, *Das Neuwestaramäische: V. Grammatik* (Wiesbaden, 1990); A. F. L. Beeston et al., *Sabaic Dictionary (English-French-Arabic)* (Louvain-la-Neuve, 1982); G. Bergsträsser, *Introduction to the Semitic Languages*, trans. P. T. Daniels (Winona Lake, IN, 1983, orig. pub. 1928); C. Brockelmann, *Grundriss der vergleichenden Grammatik der semitischen Sprachen*, vol. 1 (Berlin, 1908); R. Degen, *Altaramäische Grammatik der Inschriften des 10.–8. Jh. v. Chr. AKM* 38,8 (1969); H.-J. Fabry, "*šm'*," *ThWQ*, III, 999-1005; I. J. Gelb, *Computer-Aided Analysis of Amorite. AS* 21 (1980); O. Jastrow, *Lehrbuch der Ṭuroyo-Sprache* (Wiesbaden, 1992); W. Leslau, *Comparative Dictionary of Ge'ez* (Wiesbaden, 1987); idem, *Lexique Soqoṭri (sudarabique moderne) avec comparaisons et explications étymologiques* (Paris, 1938); R. Macuch, *Grammatik des samaritanischen Aramäisch* (Berlin, 1982); C. Müller-Kessler, *Grammatik des Christlich-Palästinisch-Aramäischen. TStO* 6 (1991); T. Nöldeke, *Compendious Syriac Grammar*, trans. James A. Crichton (Winona Lake, IN, 2001); U. Rüterswörden, "שָׁמַע *šāma'*," *TDOT*, XV, 253-79; H. Schult, "שמע *šm'* to hear," *TLOT*, 1375-80.

1. See, e.g., Bergsträsser, 183.
2. Cf., e.g., Rüterswörden, 253ff.; *DNSI*, 1164ff.
3. Cf. in general Brockelmann, 120ff.
4. Gelb, 32.
5. *DUL*[3], 811f.
6. *KBL*[3], 1452.
7. *DNSI*, 1164.
8. Beeston et al., 127.
9. Leslau, *Ge'ez*, 501ff.
10. *AHw*, III, 1211; *CAD*, XVII, 277.
11. *DNSI*, 1164.
12. Leslau, *Ge'ez*, 502.
13. Leslau, *Soqoṭri*, 144.
14. Arabic *sami'a*, in pause Hebrew *šāme^{a}'*, *KBL*[3], 1452, Western Neo-Aramaic *išme'*, Arnold, 56 (if not borrowed from Arabic).
15. Old Akkadian, *AHw*, III, 1211; all West Semitic languages.
16. Hebrew, Aramaic.

2. Common Aramaic. The root is widespread in both older and modern Aramaic. Many varieties exhibit the loss or alteration of the pharyngeal. Unaltered as *šm'*, the root occurs in Old Aramaic,[17] Imperial Aramaic,[18] Nabatean and Palmyrene,[19] Syriac,[20] as well as Western Neo-Aramaic *išme'* [21] and Turoyo *šomī'*.[22] Mandaic *šma*[23] and various North-Eastern Neo-Aramaic languages[24] attest the loss of the pharyngeal and the shift to the root class III-*ī*. A few older varieties belong in this group, but offer historical orthography with '.[25] In several modern varieties ' has become '.[26]

The thematic vowel in the perfect is usually /a/,[27] in the imperfect also mostly /a/,[28] but also /u~o/.[29] The verb occurs primarily in the G-stem and the corresponding t-stem and less often in the D- or C-stem. The peculiar short imperfect of the Gt-stem *ytšm'* "may it be heard" without metathesis /tš/ > /št/ attested in Old Aramaic merits mention.[30]

A series of nominals derive from the root, e.g., Syriac *šem'ā* "news, report, obedience,"[31] *mašm'ā* "hearing"[32] or Mandean *šima* "faculty of hearing."[33]

Old Aramaic already attests the meaning "to obey" for the G-stem,[34] otherwise the verb denotes auditive perception per se:[35] for hearing prayers[36] or hearing a word (*mlh*);[37] similarly in Imperial Aramaic,[38] in private letters in reference to news,[39] similarly in official letters of reports.[40]

---

17. See Degen, 68; *DNSI*, 1165.
18. *DNSI*, 1165.
19. *DNSI*, 1165.
20. *LexSyr*, 786.
21. Arnold, 56.
22. Jastrow, 47.
23. *MdD*, 469.
24. Arbel *šmy;* G. Khan, *A Grammar of Neo-Aramaic. HO* 47 (1999), 558. Sulemaniyya/Ḥalabya *šame*; G. Khan, *The Jewish Neo-Aramaic Dialect of Sulemaniyya and Halabja. SSLL* 44 (2004), 36,115. Cf. Khabur-Assyrian *šame*; Koy Sanjaq *šame*.
25. Christian Palestinian *šm'* (Müller-Kessler, 43ff.), Samaritan *šm'* [*šǣmœ*] (Macuch, 175), Jewish Babylonian *šm'/ī*.
26. Amadiya *šm'*, Barwar *šm'*, Hertevin *šame'*, Qaraqosh *k-šamə'*.
27. Cf. Biblical Aramaic *šma'*, Dnl. 6:15; Syriac *šma'*, *LexSyr*, 786; contrast Western Neo-Aramaic *išme'* with /e/, Arnold, 56.
28. Biblical Aramaic *yišma'*, Dnl. 3:10; Syriac *nešma'*, Nöldeke, 111.
29. Christian Palestinian *tšmw'wn* (**tišmū'on*), Müller-Kessler, 157.
30. See Degen, 67; *DNSI*, 1166.
31. *LexSyr*, 786.
32. *LexSyr*, 787.
33. *MdD*, 462.
34. *KAI* 222 B 21; 223 B 3; Degen, 68; *DNSI*, 1165ff.
35. For the meaning of the t-stems of *šm'* → II, the treatment of Dnl. 7:27.
36. *KAI* 309.9; 201.4.
37. *TADAE* C1.1:188.
38. *TADAE* C1.1:29; 2.1:67 for "hearsay."
39. *TADAE* A3.3:13; 3.5:2; 3.6:2.
40. *TADAE* A6.10:3.

II. Biblical Aramaic. Biblical Aramaic exhibits *šmʿ* in nine verses exclusively in Daniel, eight times in the G-stem and once in the Dt-stem. Attested are the perfect forms of the peal *š*^{e}*maʿ* (6:15) and *šimʿe̱t* (5:14,16), the imperfect forms of the peal *yišmaʿ* (3:10) and *tišm*^{e}*ʿūn* (3:5,15), and the participle *šām*^{e}*ʿīn* (3:7; 5:23). Daniel 7:27 has the imperfect of the Dt-stem *yištamm*^{e}*ʿūn.*

In the peal, the verb essentially denotes the act of hearing per se. In four passages, the sound[41] of several musical instruments[42] stands as the object of the verb *šmʿ*: Dnl. 3:5 *b*^{e}*ʿiddānā dī-ṯišm*^{e}*ʿūn qāl* . . . "as soon as you hear the sound of . . . (you should bow down and pay homage to the golden statue that Nebuchadnezzar has erected)"; Dnl. 3:7 *beh-zimnā k*^{e}*ḏī šām*^{e}*ʿīn kol ʿammayyā qāl* . . . "as soon as all nations heard the sound of. . . . (all peoples, nations, and languages bowed down and paid homage to the golden statue that Nebuchadnezzar had erected)"; Dnl. 3:10 refers to the order and the king repeats it in 3:15.

In Dnl. 6:15, the object of hearing is a certain circumstance:[43] ^{xe}*ḏayin malkā k*^{e}*ḏī mill*^{e}*ṯā š*^{e}*maʿ* "when the king then heard of the situation (it displeased him greatly and he turned his attention to Daniel, in order to save him)." Daniel 5:23 employs the verb without object in relation to idols who have no faculty of hearing: . . . *dī lā ḥāzayin w*^{e}*lā šām*^{e}*ʿīn w*^{e}*lā yāḏ*^{e}*ʿīn šabbaḥtā* "(you and your nobles, your secondary wives and concubines, you have drunk wine from them, and the gods of silver, gold, bronze, iron, wood, and stone), who do not see and cannot heart and do not understand, you have praised."[44] Finally, the verb appears twice together with the preposition *ʿal* "regarding" in the meaning "to hear of/about": Dnl. 5:14 *w*^{e}*šimʿe̱t* ^{a}*lāk* [*K ʿlyk*] *dī rū*^{a}*ḥ* ^{xe}*lāhīn bāḵ* "I have heard of you that the spirit of gods is in you" and Dnl. 5:16 *wa*^{xa}*nā w*^{e}*šimʿe̱t* ^{a}*lāk* [*K ʿlyk*] *dī ṯikkul* [*K twkl*] *pišrīn l*^{e}*mip̄šar w*^{e}*qiṭrīn l*^{e}*mišrē* "I have heard of you that you give interpretations and can resolve difficult tasks."

The sole passage with the Dt-stem of the root *šmʿ* in the meaning "to obey" is Dnl. 7:27: . . . *w*^{e}*ḵol šolṭānayyā leh yip̄l*^{e}*ḥūn w*^{e}*yištamm*^{e}*ʿūn* "(his kingdom is an eternal kingdom) and all powers will serve and obey him." On the basis of the Jewish Aramaic *ʾištemaʿ*[45] *BLA*, §275q and *ATTM*, 714 prefer the Dt-stem to the Gt-stem. Yet this emendation, following *ʾištammaʿ*[46] and the Mandean Dt-stem[47] with the same meaning, does not seem necessary.

The LXX renders *šmʿ* in the peal with ἀκούω, in the ithpaal with ὑπακούω or πειθαρχῶ. The Peshitta employs the same root *šmʿ*. The Vulgate has *audio* for the peal, but *oboedio* for the ithpaal.

III. Qumran. Qumran also attests the uses of *šmʿ* known from Daniel, although, because of the many passages, more formal and syntactic phenomena occur that cannot be located in Biblical Aramaic. The not infrequently fragmentary state of the preservation of the texts often hinders unequivocal interpretation, however.

41. *qāl*; → *ql.*
42. → *zmr.*
43. *mill*^{e}*ṯā*; → *mll.*
44. For the context → *dhb* III.
45. Corresponding to Syriac *eštmaʿ*, *LexSyr*, 787.
46. = *ʾišt*^{e}*maʿ*; *DictTalm*, 1599.
47. *MdD*, 469.

An object usually follows the verb, most frequently the lexeme *mlh* "word," e.g., [*mny hwʾ kwl ʾnwš d*]*y ykl yšmʿ mly qdšʾ* [*rbʾ*] "everyone will come from me who hears the word of the great holy one"[48] or *wkdy šmʿ ḥrqnwš mly lwṭ ʾzl* "when Hyrcanos heard the word of Lot, he went away."[49] The statement *mʾ ʿṭr mlʾ nš*[*mʿ*] "how we hear (only) the whisper of a word!"[50] also belongs here. Other substantives as objects include → *ql* "voice," *šmʿtʾ qlh* "you heard a voice";[51] *tmhyn* "wonder,"[52] *tmhyn šmʿt* "I heard a wonder";[53] *ngśh* "urging," *wngśt šlyṭ lʾ yšmʿ* "and he did not hear the urgings of a powerful person";[54] *qbylh* "complaint," *wqbylt ʿnyn yšmʿ* "he will hear the complaint of the oppressed"[55] or a pronoun such as *lmšmʿ ʾdn šmʿtk* "just as an ear hears, I have heard you"[56] and *yšmʿnh* "(he prays to God and he) will hear him."[57]

Because of the state of preservation of the texts, the objects are unclear in 11Q10 19:5 (Job 31:29) or 4Q197 4 3:13 (Tob. 7:10), for example. Biblical Aramaic does not, but a few times Qumran attests a complementary clause with *dy* "that" as object, e.g.: *wšmʿt dy śbʿʾ śg*[*y bmṣryn* "Then I heard that a great abundance ruled in Egypt";[58] *wšmʿ mlk swdm dy ʾtyb ʾbrm* "the king of Sodom heard that Abraham had brought back. . . ."[59]

Prepositional objects also follow *šmʿ*. Qumran has *b*- with *ql* "voice" in *wšmʿ ʾlhʾ bqlh dy ʾywb* "and God heard Job"[60] and *l*- with a pronoun in [*wkʿ*]*n šmʿ ly ʾḥy* "Now hear me, too, my brother."[61] The addressees of imperative forms at Qumran include: God in *šmʿ nʾ wʾnh ʾmll ʾšʾlnk whtybny* "but hear, I will speak. I will ask you, so answer me!";[62] Noah in [*wkʿ*]*n ʾṣt wšmʿ ʾnth* "and now, listen and hear!"[63] and male descendants in [*š*]*mʿw bny* "hear, my sons."[64]

The meaning "to obey" for *šmʿ* in the G-stem with the preposition *l*- occurs in *whwʾ ʾmr yšmʿwn lh wʾzlyn lʿbdyhwn* "and he said: (The personified forces of nature) will obey him, and they go to their activities."[65] 4Q550 1:1 employs the t-stem known from Dnl. 7:27:[66] [*wmš*]*tmʿyn lptryzʾ ʾbwk* "and they obyed your father Patirēsā."[67]

---

48. 4Q212 1 5:16 (1 En. 93:11); emend. following *ATTM*, 249.
49. 1QapGen 20:24; cf. also, perhaps, 2:21 or 4Q197 4 2:19 (Tob. 6:19).
50. 11Q10 10:5 (Job 26:14).
51. 4Q530 2 2+6-12:23.
52. → *tmh* III.
53. 6Q8 1:6.
54. 11Q10 32:6 (Job 39:7).
55. 11Q10 25:4 (Job 34:28); → *qbl* V.
56. 11Q10 37:7 (Job 42:5).
57. 11Q10 23:3 (Job 33:26).
58. 1QapGen 19:10.
59. 11Q10 22:12; cf. 4Q546 14:4.
60. 11Q10 38:2 (Job 42:9, although MT differs).
61. 4Q196 14 1:9 (Tob. 6:16).
62. 11Q10 37:6 (Job 42:4).
63. 1QapGen 14:9.
64. 4Q539 2-3:2.
65. 11Q10 29,2 (Job 37,12).
66. For the discussion of the form, → II.
67. Reading with e.g., *DSSStE*, 1096 and now also *ATTM*, 2, 150; *ATTM.E* 113 has [*hww*] *šmʿyn*, a G-stem participle.

Otherwise, of the derived stems, Qumran has only the C-stem of *šm*ʿ in [*wm*]*šlḥt qdyš*ʾ *rb*ʾ *ly ql* ʾ*šm*ʿ "and the embassy of the great Holy One caused me to hear a voice."[68]

Waltisberg

68. 1QapGen 6:15; for the translation, see *ATTM*, 2, 93.

שמש *šmš* /šamš/ (< /śamš/)

I. Form. 1. Phonetic Shift. 2. Tiberian Pointing. 3. Gender. II. As a Heavenly Body. 1. Astronomical. 2. Various Fixed Expressions. 3. Sunlight. III. As a Heavenly Being. 1. Sun God. 2. "Sun of God." 3. "Daughter of the Sun."

I. Form.

1. Phonetic Shift. The monosyllabic root /śamš-/ of the Semitic word for "sun" underwent various phonetic shifts in Aramaic. In the fourth century B.C.E., the pronunciation of its phonemic sibilant /ś/, often represented by *lt* in Neo- and Late Babylonian, still differed from the fricative palato-alveolar /š/ as the cuneiform transcriptons ^{d}*Il-ta-mi-iš*, ^{d}*Il-te-meš* etc. of the corresponding theophoric elements, often abbreviated ^{d}*Tam-meš*,

J. Brümmer, "*šmš*," *ThWQ*, III, 1013-17; J. H. Charlesworth, "Les Odes de Solomon et les manuscrits de la Mer Morte," *RB* 77 (1970) 522-49, esp. 538-40; F. Cumont, *Fouilles de Doura-Europos. BAH* 9 (1926); C. H. Gordon, "Aramaic Incantation Bowls," *Or* 10 (1941) 116-41,272-84,339-60, esp. 127, l. 8; T. Hartmann, "שֶׁמֶשׁ *šemeš* sun," *TLOT*, 1384-92; I. Kottsieper, *Die Sprache der Aḥiqarsprüche. BZAW* 194 (1990); A. Lemaire, "Coupe astrale inscrite et astronomie araméenne," in *Michael. FS M. Heltzer* (Tel Aviv-Jaffa, 1999), 195-211, esp. 198; J. M. Lindenberger, *The Aramaic Proverbs of Ahiqar* (Baltimore, 1983); E. Lipiński, "Le culte du Soleil chez les Sémites occidentaux du Ier millénaire avant J.-C.," *OLP* 22 (1991) 57-72, esp. 58-61; idem, *Semitic Languages: Outline of a Comparative Grammar. OLA* 80 (^{2}2001); idem, "Shemesh," *DDD*, 764-68; idem, "שֶׁמֶשׁ *šemeš*," *TDOT*, XV, 305-13; J. T. Milik, *Dédicaces faites par des dieux (Palmyre, Hatra, Tyr) et des thiases sémitiques à l'époque romaine. BAH* 92 (1972), esp. 193; idem, "Parchemin judéo-araméen de Doura-Europos, an 200 ap. J.-C.," *Syr* 45 (1968) 97-104; J. Naveh, "A Nabatean Incantation Text," *IEJ* 29 (1979) 111-19, esp. 118f.; A. Negev, *Personal Names in the Nabatean Realm. Qedem* 32 (Jerusalem, 1991), esp. 65, no. 1161; J. Quaegebeur, *Le dieu égyptien Shaï dans la religion et l'onomastique. OLA* 2 (1975), esp. 231; C. Robin, "Les 'filles de Dieu' de Saba' à La Mecque," *Sem* 50 (2001) 113-92; S. M. Ruozzi Sala, *Lexicon nominum Semiticorum quae in papyris Graecis in Aegypto repertis ab anno 323 a.Ch.n. usque ad annum 70 p.Ch.n. laudata reperiuntur. Testi e documenti per lo studio dell'Antichità* 46 (Milan, 1974); J. Tubach, *Im Schatten des Sonnengottes* (Wiesbaden, 1986); J. Walker, "The Coins of Hatra," *Numismatic Chronicle* 18 (1958) 167-72; R. Zadok, *On West Semites in Babylonia During the Chaldean and Achaemenian Periods* (Jerusalem, ^{2}1978), esp. 39-42.

demonstrate.[1] At the same time, the shift /ś/ > /s/ already entered a few first milliennium B.C.E. Aramaic dialects in the event that the spellings *smš* in *TADAE* B3.6:9 from Elephantine (427 B.C.E.) and *sa-mi-iš* from Persepolis[2] do not merely distinguish between /ś/ and /š/. An additional possible example of /ś/ > /s/ from Elephantine is *sbrw* in *TADAE* A4.2:7. Palmyrene inscriptions, Biblical Aramaic, and manuscripts from Qumran attest the same shift very well as, e.g., *ysgyn* "they multiply" in 4Q201 (4QEn^{a}) and *stw'l* "winter of God" in 4Q204 (4QEn^{c}) from the first half of the second century B.C.E. or the late first century B.C.E., respectively, demonstrate. Somewhat later, an original /śaggī'/ "much" is spelled *sgy*[3] n Pap. Yadin 57.5,[4] "grain" *s'ryn* in Mur 8:1,[5] and "the hater" *sn'h* in Meg. Ta'anit 26 (thirteenth century C.E. MS).[6] The oldest Syriac examples for /ś/ > /s/ stem from the middle of the third century C.E. Pap. Dura 151, l. 15f.; the first example from Jewish Babylonian dates to the second century C.E. where the plural of the determined state of the word "grain" appears twice in the spelling *s'ry*.[7] This shift is regular in the Syriac and the Jewish Aramaic literary languages, although *šmš* represents an example that can by explained as the assimilation of the etymological /ś/ to the initial /š/ as in the parallel case of /šeršā/ < *śrš* "root."

In any case, this assimilation did not permeate spoken languages, as indicated, e.g., by *smš'l* "sun of god" on an eighth-century C.E. inscribed magic bowl found on the island of Biğān in Iraq.[8] Instead, *šmsy'* in Frahang I:11c assimilates the pronunciation of the word in Arabic. Also very widespread in spoken languages is the addition of a labial /b/ or /p/ between /m/ and the immediately following consonants.[9] This pronunciation explains the Greek transcription of the personal name Šamšay as Σαμψαι(ο)ς in the Jewish papyri of the first centuries B.C.E. and C.E.,[10] and also the classical Ethiopic spelling of the name of the fallen angel Šamši-El as Simipesi'el (1 En. 6:7; 69:2; with variants), in Greek Σαμψιηλ. It was transliterated in Classical Ethiopic spelling as *smps'l* and vocalized arbitrarily when the Ethiopic consonant signs were provided with obligatory vowel markings in the fourth century C.E. Neo- and Late Babylonian attest the shift /m/ > /w/ between or after vowels very well, as the Aramaic transcription *šwš* for Šamaš and the Greek spelling Σαος demonstrate. In contrast, the Middle and Neo-Assyrian shift from /w/ between vowels to a glottal stop and a long vowel led to the Aramaic spelling of the theophoric element Šamaš as *ss*, as in, e.g., *ssnwry* in *KAI* 309.7,[11] and later *ššy* for Šamšau.[12]

---

1. Zadok; Lipiński, *Semitic Languages*, §16.4.
2. R. T. Hallock, *Persepolis Fortification Tablets*. *OIP* 92 (1969), 675a.
3. → *śgī*.
4. A letter of Bar Kochba.
5. *DJD*, II (1961), 88; → *ś'r*.
6. → *śnī*.
7. Milik, "Parchemin judéo-araméen."
8. M. Gawlikowski, "Une coupe magique arameenne," *Sem* 38 (1990) 140, l. 2.
9. Lipiński, *Semitic Languages*, §11.9.
10. Ruozzi Sala, 37; Quaegebeur.
11. *SAIO* II, 57f.
12. Contra *SAIO* I, 188-90; cf. also *ATTM*, 102f.,715.

2. *Tiberian Pointing.* The monosyllabic ground form of the root had the vowel /a/, which the syllabic spelling m.d*Il-ta-mi-iš-ma-ḫir* from the fifth century B.C.E. still attests.[13] Instead, the Tiberian pointing as *šimšā* (Dnl. 6:15) indicates a pronunciation with [i] or [y], as in *Šimšōn*. Personal names from Dura-Europos in the second century C.E. such as Ιαβ-συμσος[14] and Αβιδ-σιμ-σ[ος][15] also attest this. They exhibit the loss of the short vowel /a/ in an unaccented syllable and the resulting indefinite quality of the vowel.[16] Furthermore, *šimšā* is the Mandaic form, *šemšā* the Syriac.

3. *Gender.* The noun *śmš* > *šmš* is gender-ambivalent in Aramaic. This alternation appears in the astronomical book of Enoch from Qumran (1 En. 72–82) in 4Q211 (4QEnastr^{d}) 1 1:3 from the second half of the first century B.C.E. It has *šmš* as the subject of the verbs *npq w'l* "goes forth and sinks," both in the masculine. Meanwhile, in 4Q209 (4QEnastr^{b}) from the beginning of the first century C.E., it stands as the subject of the feminine verb in *'lt šmš'* "the sun sinks," and the suffix in *ḥrtyh* "their sections" also appears as a feminine form. In contrast, the participle *mšrh* "beginning" and the stative *šry šmš'* "the sun begins" are masculine. In other passages, the gender depends on the reconstruction of the context. One may suspect the influence of the masculine gender of Šamaš in Akkadian since the astrological series Enūma Anu Enlil was the chief inspiration of the astronomical book of Enoch.[17] This assumption is quite plausible, but cannot be confirmed because of the scarcity of useful sources from older times. In any case, the numerous Aramaic masculine names from Mesopotamia with Šamaš as a theophoric element hardly point to an understanding of the sun as female nor do they attest feminine gender in syntactical agreement when this theonym constitutes the subject of a verbal clause. The name of a slave m.d*Šá-mas-im-mì* sold in 713 B.C.E. by an Aramean named Gabru constitutes an exception.[18] The word for "sun" is also only rarely a feminine in Syriac.

II. As a Heavenly Body.

1. *Astronomical.* The disk of the sun with seventeen rays and the inscription *šm[š]* appears on an eighth-century B.C.E. bronze bowl decorated with astral symbols.[19] The word "sun" also occurs often in the books of Enoch, e.g., in 4Q209 (4QEnastr^{b}) 6:9 which says that the moon will be *mṭmr 'm š[mš]* "concealed with the s[un]." This happens when the two come into conjunction, i.e., when they stand in the same heavenly degree of longitude. This temporal usage of *'m* also occurs in Dnl. 3:33; 4:31; 7:2; consequently, the translation "concealed by the s[un] is certainly incorrect (cf. 1 En. 73:7). The Deir 'Allā inscription alludes to a solar eclipse.[20]

13. *BM* 33935.17.
14. Cumont, no. 9c-d.
15. Cumont, no. 27.13.
16. Lipiński, *Semitic Languages*, §21.32.
17. H. Drawnel, "Moon Computation in the Aramaic Astronomical Book," *RevQ* 23 (2007) 3-41.
18. *SAA*, VI, 6, 1'.
19. Lemaire.
20. I:6f.(,8f.) = *KAI* 312, cf. *SAIO* II, 128f.

2. *Various Fixed Expressions.* The word *šmš* appears quite often in the fixed expressions *mwʿ(ʾ/h) šmš* "east,"[21] *mʿrb šmš* "sunset"[22] or "west,"[23] and *mdnḥ šmš* "east"[24] or *mʿly šmš*, "sunset" (Dnl. 6,15). The phrase *mn ṭlʾ lsmš* "from shadow to sun"[25] means "complete," as does *šmš wḥnh ṭll* "resting in sun and shadow" in Nabatean contracts.[26] The juxtaposition of sun and shadow indicates that the whole parcel of land is involved in the purchase: *ḥnh* is the active participle of the root *ḥnī*.[27]

3. *Sunlight.* The sayings of Aḥiqar mention the sun in a curse that wishes death upon those who do not honor their parents: "May the sun not shine [on him]."[28] An aphorism in the same collection compares the king with the sun: "The king is as beautiful to see as the sun [*kšmš*] and his rays are precious to those who walk the earth."[29] The same image recurs later in relation to God in the Syriac Odes of Solomon, which were presumably composed in an older Aramaic dialect: "The Lord is like the sun above the earth" (11:13; cf. 15:1f.). Ode 16:15f. describes the role of the sunlight: "The barn of the light is the sun, the barn of darkness is the night. // The sun works until the day is bright, the night brings darkness on the face of the earth."

III. As a Heavenly Being.

1. *Sun God.* The following already mention the sun god: Aramaic inscriptions from Syria,[30] Sam'alian,[31] and the Deir ʿAllā inscription[32] where the sun appears as a goddess, moreover the sayings of Aḥiqar,[33] an epistolary ostracon from Elephantine,[34] a few inscriptions from Wadi el-Hudi,[35] and perhaps the lengthy cave inscription from Sheikh Fadl.[36] Additionally, Aramaic inscriptions from Asia Minor, from Kesecek Köyük,[37] and from Gözne[38] mention Šamaš. Later, the sun deity appears in several Palmyrene inscriptions,[39] one dedicated to a "Šamaš, the god of your father's house,"[40] while three grave

---

21. *TADAE* B2.2:8; B2.3:6; B2.10:6; B3.4:9; B3.5:10; B3.10:3,8; B3.11:3; B3.12:7,9,15,17.
22. *TADAE* A4.1:7.
23. *TADAE* B2.2:9; B2.7:15; B2.10:7; B3.5:11; B3.10:11; B3.11:4; B3.12:7,15,18.
24. *TADAE* B3.7:7.
25. *TADAE* B3.6,9.
26. Pap. Yadin 1:5,31; 2:8,28; 3:8,31.
27. *DNSI*, 387; *ATTM*, 2, 399.
28. *TADAE* C1.1:138.
29. *TADAE* C1.1:92.
30. *KAI* 222 A 9; 202 B 24; 225.9.
31. *KAI* 214.2f.,11, 18; 215.22.
32. I:6(.8), → II.1.
33. *TADAE* C1.1:187f.
34. *TADAE* D7.30:3.
35. *TADAE* D22.47:4; (D22.48:1f.); D22.49:2.
36. *TADAE* D23.1.2:7; D23.1.3-4:2; D23.1.6:2.
37. *KAI* 258.5.
38. *KAI* 259.4.
39. *PAT* 0297.5; 0324.
40. *PAT* 0324.6.

inscriptions express a heavenly life with the sun deity after death: *wh' npš' dh mwly' bšmš* "and, in fact, this grave marker brings Šamaš near."[41] The participle *mwly'* belongs to the C-stem of the Arabic verb *waliğa* "to be near." In Hatra, the "rectangular" temple was dedicated to the sun god, who was identical with Maren "our Lord," the father in the Hatrene triad of deities consisting of Maren, Marten, and Bar-Maren. Thus, H107.6f. reads: *dy bn' brmryn lšmš 'bwhy* "which Bar-Maren built for his father Šamaš." A variety of the inscriptions also mention Šamaš. The legends of coins from Hatra read: *ḥṭr' dšmš* "Hatra (i.e., pens) of Šamaš."[42] Šamaš also appears as the theophoric element of many Aramaic personal names, whether written in alphabet or cuneiform script.

2. *"Sun of God."* An interesting pheneomon in the Jewish writings of the Persian period is the very prominent concept of a heavenly host, presumably developed under Iranian influence. They adopt the sun god under the name Šamši-El "sun of God" with the Hebrew theophoric element *'l* instead of the Aramaic *'lh*. He already appears in the oldest parts of the book of Enoch (1 En. 6:7; 8:3), whose earliest Aramaic manuscripts trace back to the third or second century B.C.E. He taught humanity the "signs of the sun" (*nḥšy šmš*), i.e., astronomy, and belongs, therefore, among the ten angelic teachers, but is also listed as the fifteenth fallen angel. Furthermore, Šamši-El appears in the Nabatean personal name *šmš'l-b'l* "the sun god is Lord," so far attested only once.[43] The Greek translation of the books of Enoch originally transcribed the name as Σαμψιηλ, which also served as the basis for the Classical Ethiopic version, but the ψ has fallen out in the archetype of the Greek versions of the Cairo manuscript 10759 (fifth/sixth century C.E.), as it has also in the Chronicle of Syncellus. There, the name of the angel appears as Σεμιηλ or Σαμιηλ, and the Greek text of the Apocalypse of Baruch 4:8 9:7 and the Christian versions of the Martyrdom of Isaiah 1:8; 2:1; 3:13; 5:15 adopt this corrupt form. The original name of this evil spirit was Malki-Ra' "evil king" (1:8); it appears further in a recension of the Testament of Solomon 7:1-8, the second Sibylline Oracle l. 215, the Greek original of the Slavonic book of Enoch, the Gnostic texts from Nag Hammadi, the document *Adversus haereses* by Irenaeus, Bishop of Lyon (second century C.E.), etc.[44] In rabbinic tradition, the name *šm'l* first appears in the statements by R. Jose, the fourth century Palestinian Amora in Targum Pseudo-Jonathan on Gen. 3:6 and, as an exception, on Amariac magic bowls.[45] The spelling *šm'l* apparently involves a transcription of the corrupt Greek name; its vocalization as *Samā'el* has nothing to do with the Jewish name Σαμάηλος attested in papyri.[46] It is a Greek transcription of Šama'-El "God has heard (the prayer)."

3. *"Daughter of the Sun."* A Nabatean incantation text, found about ten kilometers from Beersheba and dated to circa 100 B.C.E., mentions the female figurines of five incan-

41. *PAT* 1166.3-5; 1168.3f.; 1198; cf. Milik, *Dédicaces faites*.

42. Walker.

43. Negev.

44. Cf. E. Lipiński, review of A. H. Lange, K. E. Lichtenberger, and D. Romheld, eds., *Die Dämonen. BiOr* 61 (2004) 386f.

45. Gordon.

46. Ruozzi Sala, 34.

tation priestesses,[47] one addressed by the name "daughter of Šamaš,"[48] while three others are addressed as *brt'l* "daughter of El." Such figurines are well known; they were presumably deposited in sanctuaries in order to recall the symbolic dedication of a woman into the service of a deity, here Šamaš. The Koran alludes repeatedly to the faith of the pagan inhabitants of Mecca, who venerate deities of lesser rank as "daughters of Allah."[49]

Lipiński

47. Naveh.
48. *bršmš*, with the assimilation /tš/ > /šš/; cf. Lipiński, *Semitic Languages*, §27.3.
49. Sure 16:59; 17:42; 37:150,153; 43:15,18; 53:28; cf. Robin.

שמש *šmš*

I. Etymology and Lexical Field. II. Meaning.

I. Etymology and Lexical Field. Within the Semitic languages, the verbal root *šmš* "to serve" is only productive in Aramaic, but apparently has an Egyptian cognate.[1] The mediating path leading to this unexpected distribution has not been explained. In Aramaic, the verb appears in the transitive D-stem and finds very frequent usage in later phases on the language.[2] In addition to the corresponding t-stem "to utilize," they attest still other nuances such as "to pass time" or "to have marital intercourse." In the majority of the few older instances, however, it means cultic service and, thus, functions as a synonym of the better-attested root → *plḥ*.

II. Meaning. The earliest occurrences of the verb *šmš* appear in religious literature. In Dnl. 7:10, it occurs in the court scene for the "thousand times thousands" (*'lp 'lpym*) who serve the "ancient of days"[3] and the parallelism with *rb rbwn qdmwhy yqwmw* "a thousand times ten thousands stand before him" proves it to be a term for liturgical veneration. Of the certain instances from Qumran, 4Q246 1 1:8 refers to the world dominion of the "son of God," whom all serve,[4] while Dnl. 7:10 echoes in 4Q530 2 2+6-12:17 from the Book of Giants. The reading and interpretation of 1QapGen 15:18 are uncertain, especially since according to some editors, a form of → *šbš* may occur here.

1. For the discussion, cf. *GesB*[18], 1541.
2. *DJPA*, 559; *DJBA*, 1162; *LexSyr*, 788; *MdD*, 470.
3. → *'tyq* III.
4. Regarding the controversial identification → *br* IV.

Palmyrene honorific inscriptions employ *šmš* for both religious[5] and political[6] offices. At Hatra, the t-passive "to be served" also first appears.[7] In nV 7:28,62,[8] "to serve" refers to a wife's care. Later nominal forms are also attested.[9]

Gzella

5. *PAT* 0270.5; 2743.3.
6. *PAT* 0278.3; 0280.3.
7. H408.7, in the context of a cultic meal.
8. *ATTM*, 2, 218-23.
9. Cf. *DJPA*, 559b; *LexSyr*, 788b.

שנה *šnh* /šanā/; ירח *yrḥ* /yarḥ/; שבה *šbh* /šabbā/

I. Etymology and Lexical Field. II. Noun "Year." 1. Generally. 2. In Dates. III. Noun "Month." IV. Noun "Sabbath, Week."

I. Etymology and Lexical Field. The feminine Semitic primary noun *šnh* /šanā/ denotes the "year," regardless of the underlying calendrical order. It consists of twelve months, Aramaic *yrḥ* /yarḥ/ (→ III), which, in the Jewish tradition, in turn, each consist of four weeks, denoted by the feminine /šabbā/ (→ IV). Yet, according to the Babylonian calendar it numbers a total of 360 days, in the Jewish lunar calendar regularly 354,[1] and, according to the solar calendar at Qumran, 364 days.[2] It is unknown by what regular or more likely sporadic[3] intercalations Qumran dealt with the ten days difference between the lunar and solar calendars in order to keep the number in step with the duration of the earth's orbit of 365¼ which governs the change of seasons.

The terms /šanā/ "year" and /yarḥ/ "month," along with /yawm/ "day" mostly occur in dates in documentary texts, /šanā/ and /yawm/ also in literary writings to denote precisely or approximately a longer or shorter duration and /šanīn/ after /bar/ or /barat/[4] in the construct, literally "a son/daughter of," with a number indicating the age of a male or

C. Berner, *Jahre, Jahrwochen und Jubiläen. BZAW* 363 (2006); A. Grund, *Die Entstehung des Sabbats. FAT* 75 (2011); H. Gzella, "*šnh*," *ThWQ*, III, 1025-30; D. Schwiderski, *Die alt- und reichsaramäischen Inschriften*, vol. I: *Konkordanz. FSBP* 2 (2008); F. J. Stendebach, "שָׁנָה *šānâ*," *TDOT*, XV, 323-39.

1. With a periodic intercalation called /ʿebbūr/ (→ *ʿbr* IV) of a thirteenth month, then 384.
2. → *ywm*.
3. See *ATTM*, 359.
4. > /bat/; → *br*.

female person in years. Meanwhile, the month as a more general temporal term, which lies between these two units in length, plays only a subordinate role outside precise datings. With numbers or signs indicating a specific number of years, /šanīn/ appears, as is typical in Semitic languages, in the absolute state with a masculine ending, but agrees syntactically as a feminine (cf. Ezr. 5:11).

II. Noun "Year."

1. Generally. As a general term for age, *šnh* occurs as a suffixed plural "his years" along with the plural of *ywm* "his days" also common in this meaning already in the oldest known Aramaic inscription.[5] It states as the reason for the dedication of a statue the wish of the royal donor for a long life granted by the gods.[6] Figuratively for a long duration, the "seven years" in curse formulas in the Sefire treaties of state and the Bukān inscription intend the misfortune that an oath-breaker should encounter.[7]

As indications of age, *br šnn* (for men) and *bt šnn* (for women) first appears in Imperial Aramaic marriage contracts[8] and, in a clause concerning legal succession, mentions the death of a marital partner at the hypothetical age of one hundred years.[9] Likewise, Dnl. 6:1 employs the word for the age of King Darius at the beginning of his reign as do many grave inscriptions known from later times.[10]

Furthemore, *šn(y)n śgy'n* "many years" can denote an indefinitely long period[11] and *šnh bšnh* the distributive expression "year by year," as for certain, regularly recurring activities.[12]

Indications of time occur frequently in 1QapGen, where they give the accounts epic breadth,[13] and sporadically in a few other Aramaic texts from Qumran.[14] A few additional instances are severely fragmentary, but probably reflect the same usage.

2. In Dates. Hundreds of instances in Imperial and post-Imperial Aramaic sources, mostly legal and commercial texts, less often memorial inscriptions, employ *šnh* as part of dating formulas.[15] They have either *bšnt* in the construct with a subsequent cardinal number, or rarely in the absolute *bšnn* with a number,[16] sometimes with another

5. *KAI* 309.8.
6. *'rk* with days as the object parallels *kbr* and years here.
7. *KAI* 222 A 27; 223 A 5f.; 320.12.
8. *TADAE* B3.5:17f. (wife, husband); B3.7:18 (wife); B6.3:2 (husband).
9. Perhaps chosen as a euphemism; in *TADAE* B3.7:18; 6.3:2 not attained.
10. Instances in *DNSI*, 1172f.
11. *TADAE* A6.14:4; Ezr. 5:11.
12. *KAI* 228 A 21; 319.12f.,17; 4Q201 1 2:12 (1 En. 5:2).
13. 1QapGen 12:10,13,15; 19:23; 20:18; 21:26f.; 22:27.
14. 4Q201 1 2:6,14f. (1 En. 3:1; 5:5); 4Q242 1-3:3,7; 4Q246 1 2:2; in calendar calculations: 4Q530 2 2+3:4; in a prophecy: 4Q536 1:2f. par. 4Q535 3:5; for age in patriarchal biographies: 4Q545 1a i 2f.,6,8, similarly 4Q196 18:13 (Tob. 14:2); twice in translations from Heb. for the corresponding cognate in 11Q10 27:5; 28:4 (Job 36:11,26).
15. See Schwiderski, 802-8; *DNSI*, 1172; *ATTM*, 715f.; 2, 496f.
16. *TADAE* B1.1:1,4f.

preposition.[17] In the time of the empires, the enumeration follows the regnal year of the respective king, as first attested from Neo-Babylonian times with Nebuchadnezzar,[18] then very frequently in Achaemenid documents, and in Biblical Aramaic (Ezr. 5:13; 6:3; Dnl. 7:1); among the Nabateans, of their king. In the Hellenistic and Roman Near East, however, dates were otherwise often calculated after the Seleucid year from 312/311 B.C.E.[19] Occasionally, the dating could also be following an event, as an Old Aramaic comment on a temple offering from Hazael already dates in relation to a river crossing[20] or the gravestones from Zoar in late antiquity do in relation to the destruction of the Jerusalem temple.[21]

III. Noun "Month." In contrast to "year," *yrḥ* "month" is apparently restricted largely to dates in legal and commercial documents[22] and also appear on this model in Ezr. 6:15. As a unit of time like the twelve months between Nebuchadnezzar's warning dream and the self-satisfied walk of the king in Dnl. 4:26, the month is otherwise atypical and hardly occurs in literary texts such as those from Qumran: the two wisdom uses in 11Q10 5:3; 32:1 (Job 21:21, for *ḥdš*; 39:2, for *yrḥ*) translate the Hebrew; the usage for the phases of the moon in 4Q210 1 3:6 (1 En. 78:1) is specifically astronomical. Names typically designate the months; they are rarely enumerated.

In this regard, the old Semitic month names rooted in daily life and the cultic order continue in usage into the Hellenistic-Roman period: 1. *nysn* Nisan (March/April); 2. *ʾyr* Iyyar (April/May); 3. *sywn* Siwan (May/June); 4. *tmwz* Tammuz (June/July); 5. *ʾb* Ab (July/August); 6. *ʾlwl* Elul (August/September); 7. *tšry* Tishri (September/October); 8. *mrḥšwn* Marcheshwan (October/November); 9. *kslw* Kislev (November/December); 10. *ṭbt* Tebet (December/January); 11. *šbṭ* Shebat (January/February); 12. *ʾdr* Adar (February/March). The Jewish tradition intercalated a short-term, second month of Adar in order to synchronize the calendar once it became apparent that it had become too distant from the course of the seasons.[23] In contrast, there was probably no forecast yet. Unlike Hebrew, Phoenician, and Ugaritic, Aramaic does not employ the same basis for "moon"[24] as for "month,"[25] but an independent lexeme, *śhr* /śehr/.[26]

IV. Noun "Sabbath, Week." Aramaic does not have an indigenous word for "week"; /šabbā/ is borrowed from Hebrew and traces to /šabbat/ "Sabbath."[27] In contrast, the noun

17. Such as *ʿd* "until" in Ezr. 4:24 or in the genitive following *dy* "of such and so years," as in 6:15.

18. *KAI* 227.4f.

19. For bib. → *ywm*.

20. *KAI* 311; → *nhr* II.

21. → *ḥrb* V.

22. References are in Schwiderski, 375f.; *DNSI*, 469-71; *ATTM*, 600; 2, 412.

23. A rabbinic missive transmitted in the Talmud attests a decision to this end; see the text and the introductory remarks with bib. in *ATTM*, 359f.

24. Heb. *yārēᵃḥ*.

25. Heb. *yæraḥ*.

26. → *šmyn*.

27. E. Haag, "שָׁבַת *šāḇaṯ*," *TDOT*, XIV, 381-97.

/šabūʿ/[28] derived from the number "seven" may very well be an Aramaic form,[29] but the concept of the seven-day week in Aramaic texts from Qumran stands under Jewish influence. Festivals lasted seven days.[30] The loanword *šbh* appears at Elephantine.[31] Weekdays are enumerated from the Sabbath.[32]

Gzella

28. 1QapGen 6:18; 4Q212 1 4:15,19,25 (1 En. 91:12,14,17).
29. C. Stadel, *Hebraismen in den aramäischen Texten vom Toten Meer* (Heidelberg, 2008), 22f.; *ATTM*, 701 assumes a loanword here, too.
30. Such as the marriage in 4Q543 la-c:7 par. 4Q545 la 1:6.
31. *TADAE* D7.12:9; 7.16:2; probably also 7.28:4; 7.48:5.
32. → *ywm* II.1.

שׁני *šnī*

I. Etymology, Lexical Field, and Grammatical Constructions. II. G-stem "to Be Different," "to Change." III. D-stem "to Change." IV. C-stem "to Alter." V. In Legal Diction.

I. Etymology, Lexical Field, and Grammatical Constructions. Aramaic *šnī*, in the G-stem "to be different, to change," preserves a common Semitic root **šnū*. The intransitive G-stem has a middle nuance and can function both statively and ingressively. The transitive D-stem constitutes a factitive counterpart "to alter, to transform" whose passive forms[1] semantically approximate the G-stem again. Compare the variation between the two forms in Dnl. 5:9f.: the G-stem expresses the fact that "his face changed" in reference to Belshazzar turning pale, but the Dt-stem expresses the queen's encouragement in the following verse "may it not change." Likewise, Dnl. 7:7 employs the passive participle of the D-stem for "to be different," precisely like the perfect of the G-stem in 7:19,23f. In addition, the D-stem can mean "to violate (a law)" (Dnl. 3:23). Like the D-stem, the rarer C-stem denotes "to change (consciously/willingly)" once and, similarly, "to violate" sporadically (Ezr. 6:11f.). In this latter usage, one otherwise sometimes encounters → *ʿbr*. Regularly, *šnī* denotes alteration in the facial expression,[2] sometimes also in the mood,[3] of a person as a negative reaction to a frightening experience and, consequently, often

A. Justnes, "*šnh* II," *ThWQ*, III, 1022-24; T. Kronholm, "*šānâ*," *TDOT*, XV, 317-22.

1. Inner pass. and Dt-stem.
2. Dnl. 3:19; 5:6,9f.; 7:28; 1QapGen 2:12,17.
3. 1QapGen 2:2,11.

parallels other verbs of distress, especially → *bhl*. In this function, the verb belongs to the highly developed psychological vocabulary of the book of Daniel. In addition, it appears in visions. Meanwhile, instances of the verb in older Aramaic concentrate in Daniel, for the difference between reality, as it appears and as it truly is, belongs to the central themes of the book. In contrast, *hpk* in the Gt-stem better serves to denote a complete change.[4] Sometimes, the root also occurs as a term for "to alter" or "to differ."[5]

Regardless of its meaning, *šnī* can take as modifiers prepositional expressions with *mn* "from" with "to be different" in the G-stem or "to alter," passive "to be/become changed" in the D-stem, or with *ʿl* "in" relating to change in the appearance of feelings of a person, otherwise also generally *b*- "with reference to" (Dnl. 6:18; on contracts → V).

II. G-stem "to Be Different," "to Change." With a stative nuance, the G-stem of *šnī* first means, quite generally, "to be other, different" and often, but not solely, refers to visible differences. Thus, it appears in Dnl. 7:3,19,23 in the vision of the four animals as symbols of the four empires in reference to the different beings and, especially, the fourth that differs so from the others.[6] In parallel, the interpretation of the horns of this animal in 7:24 clearly further distinguishes the tenth, most horrifying from its predecessors with *šnī* (*whwʾ yšnʾ mn qdmyʾ*).

The ingressive connotation "to change" underlies the negated expression *wsrblyhwn lʾ šnw* "and their pants (or: cloaks) were unchanged" in Dnl. 3:27; the passage describes how the three condemned exited the fiery furnace unharmed. Likewise, it serves in 6:18 in the story of Daniel in the lions' den to explain the sealing of the stone:[7] nothing should change with regard to Daniel (*lʾ tšnʾ ṣbw bdnyʾl*), i.e., no one should secretly intervene and come to his assistance.

It specifically represents the alteration in the facial expression as a sign of terror in reference to Belshazzar's reaction to the initially incomprehensible divine verdict on the wall in Dnl. 5:6,9, in both instances with → *zyw* "radiance; fresh, sound skin tone" as subject.[8] In this meaning, the verb seems synonymous with the otherwise somewhat more frequent Dt-stem (→ III). It parallels → *bhl* to "terrify" in 5:6 for the shaking of the bones.[9]

In Qumran, the G-stem of *šnī* occurs, besides the usages for an alteration of the facial expression known from Daniel,[10] for "to be different" in reference to the trees in Enoch's vision[11] and in reference to an unpreserved physical characteristic in the prophecy of Noah's birth,[12] and once more in an entirely obscure context.[13]

---

4. Cf. 4Q204 4:10 (1 En. 89:36): the lamb changes and becomes a human.
5. For a discussion, → II.2.
6. The pf. expressing the state seems synonymous with the pass. ptcp. of the D-stem in 7:7, → III.
7. → *ḥtm*.
8. Following *wzywhy šnyn ʿlwhy* "the color of his face changed" in 5:9, 5:6 is also often corrected to *zywhy šn<yn ʿl>why*.
9. → *ḥrṣ* II.
10. 1QapGen 2:17; with → *ʾnp*.
11. 4Q206 1 27:2 (1 En. 32:3).
12. 4Q534 1 1:3.
13. 1QapGen 11:19.

III. D-stem "to Change." The D-stem represents the factitive counterpart of the G-stem and means "alter" with a view to the result, while the C-stem explicitly denotes a conscious and controlled alteration (→ IV). The D-stem can also designate a higher agency, as in Dnl. 4:13 in relation to Nebuchadnezzar's heart that one will change[14] and "to deform" in regard to the activity of evildoers in 4Q201 1 2:12 (1 En. 5:4). The active can also mean "to disdain, to transgress," as in Dnl. 3:28 and 4Q204 5 2:18 (1 En. 106:14), for which Ezr. 6:11f. has the C-stem.

Semantically, the passive forms overlap with the G-stem "to be different," as in the t-passive for a person in *TADAE* C1.1:200, four times in Dnl. 2:9, and frequently for the face or the attitude (→ II): Dnl. 3:19;[15] 5:10; 7:28 (→ IV); 1QapGen 2:2,11f. The passive participle can also function for "to be different," as in Dnl. 7:7 (→ II). Several fragments from Qumran contain still other instances that remain, for the most part, grammatically and semantically obscure, including *yšn'* in 11Q10 24:3 (Job 34:9), that could be either a G- ("to change") or C-stem ("to alter").[16]

IV. C-stem "to Alter." The relatively rare C-stem also means "to alter," but seems always to express a higher agency, and thus the subject's control, and to emphasize the action, thus with the sense "intentionally to alter." Negated, it refers to a law[17] that no one should alter (Dnl. 6:9,16), affirmatively with the change of the time periods that God, as the Lord over time, establishes (2:21), and for the insolence of the final, God-opposing ruler, to imitate God in this regard (7:25). Like the D-stem, however, the C-stem can also denote "to transgress" (Ezr. 6:11f.).

The Daniel manuscript 4Q112 14:9 reads for Dnl. 7:28, not the Dt-stem (→ III), but the C-stem *yhšnwn*, which is not used elsewhere, however, for an involuntary alteration of the complexion and probably results from a scribal error due to the semantic proximity of the two stems.

V. In Legal Diction. Finally, *šnī* occurs in legal diction. The few, mostly fragmentary instances from the Samaria papyri[18] involve the formulaic expression *'w hw yšnh b'sr' znh* "or if he alters something in this contract." By form, the verb could in principle be either the G- or the D-stem, but, since the independent personal pronoun seems to designate the acting subject and the preposition *b-* the affixed object,[19] the meaning here may be, not the intransitive "to differ," but the factitive "to alter," which, however, belongs in the active more to the D-stem based on known usages.[20]

14. Impersonal expression with no agency to emphasize that the alteration does not proceed from the king himself.

15. To be read as a plural with the consonantal text, *BLA*, §159s′.

16. *ATTM*, 716.

17. → *dt*.

18. Contained in full in *WDSP*, 2:5; in addition to the partial reconstructions in 6:7; 7:11; 15:13.

19. Paralleling the intransitive usage"to alter in" Dnl. 6:18.

20. For substantive parallels, cf. J. Dušek, *Les manuscrits araméens du Wadi Daliyeh et la Samarie vers 450-332 av. J.-C. CHANE* 30 (2007), 143f.

Contrariwise, a few Nabatean contracts from the Dead Sea mean "to differ from" as evidenced by the preposition *mn*,[21] so that the verb here can stand in the G-stem. Otherwise, the verb → *'dī* functions for "to differ," likewise with *mn* "from."

Gzella

21. nV 2:14,38; 3:17,44; 8:8; all in *ATTM* 2.

שעה *š'h* /šā'ā/

I. Etymology and Lexical Field. II. Usage.

I. Etymology and Lexical Field. Terms for smaller time units have no standard in nature like the day or the year, and therefore also differ in Semitic in the respective individual languages. The Aramaic feminine /šā'ā/ "moment, hour" may have a Canaanite cognate in a letter from Amarna,[1] but its etymology remains unclear. From Aramaic, it spread into Postbiblical Hebrew,[2] as well as Arabic and Ethiopic.[3] The plural has the masculine ending /šā'īn/, but agrees syntactically as a feminine. For "instant," Aramaic has → *zmn* and → *'dn*.

II. Usage. The first examples of *š'h* stem from the book of Daniel. There it means "moment" most generally, thus a subjectively perceived brief period of time. It functions mostly as an adverb *bh š't'* "in the same moment, immediately" for a sudden occurrence (Dnl. 3:6,15; 4:30; 5:5), and once as *š'h ḥdh* for "a moment long" in reference to Daniel's reaction to Nebuchadnezzar's disturbing dream. The Roman division of the day into twelve hours led to the chronological specification of *š'h* as "hour," so that Nabatean private documents can use the word for precisely defined irrigation periods.[4] It is understandable, then, that as *š'n śgy'n* in 1QapGen 13:13 it can denote "many hours," which would be contradictory with regard to the original meaning. For "immediately," Qumran attests *br š'thwn*[5] with a suffix corresponding to the person of the superordinate verb.[6] It is unclear whether *bh bšt'* "in the same year"[7] in 4Q550 1:3 should be emended to *bh*

1. EA 138.76.
2. Sir. 37:14; otherwise, Hebrew has *zmn* for "moment."
3. T. Nöldeke, *Neue Beiträge zur semitischen Sprachwissenschaft* (Strassburg, 1910), 44).
4. nV 3:25; 7:7,12,38,43f.,47; both in *ATTM*, 2.
5. 4Q549 2:5.
6. Later fixed as the unalterable *br š'th*; T. Nöldeke, *Compendious Syriac Grammar*, trans. James A. Crichton (Winona Lake, IN, 2001), 255f. §321b.
7. So also *DSSStE*, 1096.

bš<'>t' "immediately." A dedicatory inscription from Palmyra may have *š'h* for "time"[8] like the later "hour of need."[9]

Gzella

8. *PAT* 1928.2.
9. C. E. Morrison, "The 'Hour of Distress' in 'Targum Neofiti' and the 'Hour' in the Gospel of John," *CBQ* 67 (2005) 590-603.

שׁפל *špl*; שׁפל *špl* /šapel/; שׁפלו *šplw* /šapelū/

I. Etymology and Lexical Field. II. C-stem "to Humiliate." III. Adjective "Lowly." IV. Noun "Humiliation."

I. Etymology and Lexical Field. Of the common Semitic (with the exception of Ethiopic) root *špl* "to be lowly," Aramaic attests as a verb mostly C-stem "to humiliate," but Syriac also has the G- and the D-stems ("to humiliate").[1] The nuance "to run, lead downstream" in Jewish Babylonian[2] may represent a special development. The Dt-stem "to bow," however, may already appear in 4Q569 1-2:4, although in a fragmentary context and not entirely clear paleographically. Daniel first attests the adjective /šapel/ "lowly," Qumran the feminine /šapelū/ "humiliation." In both the literal and figurative senses, → *rīm* "to be high, arrogant," serves as an antonym, in addition to the frequent *g'h* "pride."[3]

II. C-stem "to Humiliate." All six known instances of the C-stem of *špl* in older Aramaic have the figurative meaning "to humiliate," said mostly of the arrogant: first in a proverb of Aḥiqar,[4] in Dnl. 4:34 of God's might,[5] in 5:19 of royal authority and in contrast to the C-stem of *rīm* "to elevate." With → *lbb* "heart, mind" as object, in contrast, it appears in 5:22 for "to be humble," which Belshazzar fails to be, in the interpretation of the vision of the four empires and the rise of the last potentate in 7:24 with the connotation "to topple (a ruler)."[6] In the political theology of the book of Daniel, then, it designates the fullness of royal power, which is nonetheless subordinate to God's omnipotence.

J. Brümmer, "*špl*," *ThWQ*, III, 1054-56 (Heb.); K. Engelken, "שָׁפֵל *šāpēl*," *TDOT*, XV, 442-48.

1. Cf. *LexSyr*, 795f.
2. *DJBA*, 1171f.
3. → *g'ī*.
4. *TADAE* C1.1:150, but without a broader context.
5. With "those who walk in pride" as object, → *g'ī* II.
6. In accord with the picturesque → *'qr* "to eradicate" in the vision itself.

11Q10 34:7 is a literal translation of Job 40:11, as is Dnl. 4:34 with *g'h* "the proud" as the object of "to humiliate." God challenges Job, in an ironic refraction, to do the same.

III. Adjective "Lowly." Like the verb, the adjective *špl* /šapel/ "lowly" in Dnl. 4:14 also has a figurative meaning. Here, it functions in the construct state with *'nšym*[7] as a superlative "the lowliest of people," whom God can elevate.[8] It probably also has a figurative intent in 1QapGen 0:7, but it appears there between lacuna. It is literally "to be low" in nV 7:13,49.[9]

IV. Noun "Humiliation." Older Aramaic attests the noun *šplw* /šapelū/ "humiliation" with certainty in 4Q542 1 1:6. It occurs in Qahat's admonition to subsequent generations to hold firm to the religious heritage of their fathers so that they do not experience humiliation and *nblw* "shame." *ATTM*, 2, 93 suspects an additional instance in 1QapGen 7:20, which lacks context, however, and the unclear remnants of letters may point more to the otherwise unattested form *śklw* "insight" from → *śkl*.[10]

Gzella

7. Hebrew pl. ending.
8. C-stem of → *rīm*.
9. *ATTM*, 2, 217-23.
10. D. A. Machiela, *The Dead Sea Genesis Apocryphon. STDJ* 79 (2009), 48.

שפר *špr*; שפיר *špyr* /šappīr/; שפר *špr* /šopr/; שפרפר *šprpr* /šaparpar/

I. Etymology. II. Old and Imperial Aramaic. III. Biblical Aramaic. IV. Qumran.

I. Etymology. Presumably, the root *špr* "to be beautiful" has a long history in West Semitic; its cognate in Amorite personal names at least suggests so.[1] Contrariwise, East Semitic (as represented by Akkadian) has no traces of this root with the same meaning. In Northwest Semitic, it is limited to Aramaic, although Hebrew borrowed it, cf. *šāp̄ᵉrā ʿalay* "(my heritage) is beautiful to me" in Ps. 16:6[2] and the feminine name *šip̄rā* in

H. Huffmon, *Amorite Personal Names in the Mari Texts* (Baltimore, 1965); M. Wagner, *Die lexikalischen und grammatikalischen Aramaismen im alttestamentlichen Hebräisch. BZAW* 96 (1966).

1. Huffmon, 252.
2. Wagner, 116.

Ex. 1:15.[3] The etymologies of (*rūḥō šāmayim*) *šip̄rā* in Job 26:13 and (*ʾimrē-*)*šāp̄er* in Gen. 49:21 are unclear.[4] No relationship exists with Hebrew *šōp̄ar* "horn"[5] and Ugaritic *špr* in *KTU* 1.108:10.

The adjective /šappīr/ "beautiful" and the masculine substantive /šopr/ "beauty"[6] occur as nominal forms.

II. Old and Imperial Aramaic. Old Aramaic attests the root only in the form of the adjective /šappīr/ (spelled *špr*) which functions as a synonym of the adjective *ṭb* "good":[7] [. . . *kl mh z*]*y špr wkl mh zy ṭ*[*b* . . .] "[everythin]g that is beautiful, and everything that is goo[d]."[8]

The same adjective occurs eight times in texts transmitted from the Achaemenid period. Papyri from Egypt preserve six of them in various nuances, especially in the (originally pre-Imperial Aramaic) sayings of Aḥiqar. It characterizes inner personal qualities and wisdom: *trtyn mln špyjrh* "two things are outstanding," i.e., sharing wine and the exercise of wisdom.[9] Another shading occurs in *špyr mlk lmḥzh* "The king is beautiful to see."[10] It refers similarly to a characteristic attitude, as in *ʾyš špyr mddh* "a man, whose character is excellent (and whose heart is good)."[11] *TADAE* C3.28:109, A2.2:12, and D 23.1.8:9 mention various beautiful things, but the fragmentary context complicates their identification. Two additional specimens stem from outside Egypt, the first of which appears in a second century B.C.E. grave inscription from Turkish Arebsun praising a queen as *špyrʾ ʾnt mn ʾlhn* "you are more beautful than goddesses";[12] the second stems from a second-century C.E. Aramaic-Greek diglot from Armazi in Georgia praising a women deceased at a young age as *ṭb wšpyr* "good and beautiful."[13]

Imperial Aramaic does not attest the verb *špr* "to please, to do something good," to be sure, but Palmyrene does quite frequently.[14] None of them employs it in the impersonal construction *špr l-/qdm* "it pleases" ("it is beautiful in the judgment of") as does Biblical Aramaic, however.

III. Biblical Aramaic. As a verb, the root appears three times in Biblical Aramaic; all instances stem from the book of Daniel. It occurs with various prepositions: *ʿal* in *malkā milkī yišpar ʿᵃlāḵ* "O king, may my counsel please you" (Dnl. 4:24); *qᵒḏām* in *šᵉp̄ar qᵒḏām daryāweš wahᵃqīm* "it pleased Darius and he installed" (6:2), i.e., Darius

3. *KBL*³, 1510; *GesB*¹⁸, 1406.
4. Cf. *KBL*³ and *GesB*¹⁸, s.v.
5. Aramaic employs → *qrn* for this.
6. After the middle of the fifth century B.C.E. expanded to /šopar/, see *ATTM*, 114.
7. → *ṭīb* III.1.
8. *KAI* 224.29.
9. *TADAE* C1.1:187.
10. In comparison to Šamaš, → *šmš* II.3; *TADAE* C1.1:92.
11. *TADAE* C1.1:95.
12. *KAI* 264.6.
13. *KAI* 276.9.
14. See *DNSI*, 1184 for the instances.

decided to install 120 satraps over the kingdom. Here, the complement appears in the form of an independent clause introduced syndetically with *wa-*; in Dnl. 3:32 *l-* with the infinitive follows instead: *šᵉp̄ar qᵒd̠āmay lᵉhaḥᵃwāyā* "it pleases me to make known," i.e., it seems appropriate to the speaker (King Nebuchadnezzar) to make known in the kingdom the signs and wonders that the supreme God had demonstrated to him. The use of the verb in these passages expresses a close connection between *špr* and that which is appropriate, suitable, and pleasing.[15]

The adjective occurs twice in the identical expression *ʿop̄yeh šappīr* "its foliage was beautiful" in reference to the tree in Nebuchadnezzar's dream that the king first reports in Dnl. 4:9 and to which Daniel refers in 4:18 when he gives the interpretation. These passages associate the concept of beauty with plenty and wealth.[16] Theodotion renders *šappīr* in 4:9,18 (enumerated with MT) with ὡραῖα "beautiful" (4:12) and εὐθαλῆ "blossoming" (4:21). He always translates the verb with ἀρέσκειν "to please" (4:27; 6:2). The unrevised Greek version has no equivalent in these cases. The noun /šaparpar/ "daybreak" appears in Dnl. 6:20; the unrevised version translates it with πρωί "early morning" and Theodotion expands it to τὸ πρωὶ ἐν τῷ φωτί "at daybreak."

IV. Qumran. Forms of the root appear in concentration in the passage with the song of praise to Sarah's beauty in 1QapGen 20:2-9, the adjective *špyr* four times, the verb twice, and the noun also four times: *špyr* "beautiful" was the appearance of her face (l. 2), her light complexion (l. 4), her arms (l. 4), and her feet (l. 5f.); no virgins or brides who enter the bridal chamber *yšprn* "are more beautiful" (l. 6)[17] than she; she *šprh* (l. 7)[18] "is more beautiful" than all women in *šwpr* "beauty"[19] and *šprh'* "her beauty"[20] surpasses them all (l. 7). Yet, with all this *špr'* "beauty" there is also much wisdom in her (l. 7). The last praise, then, fuses beauty and wisdom and thereby portrays Sarah as the ideal woman. When pharaoh saw her, he marveled at *šprh'* "her beauty" (l. 9).[21] The adjective *špyr* also occurs in 4Q197 4 1:17 and 4 2:1;[22] 4Q202 1 2:3;[23] 4Q213a 1:16;[24] 4Q561 1 1:2.[25] Traces of the adjective *špyr'* can still be perceived in 1QapGen 7:18,[26] and of the noun *špr'* in 4Q553 9:1, but because of the unclear context,

---

15. → *šwī* IV.
16. → *'yln* III; *śgī* V.1.
17. Vb. in the 3fp pf.
18. The same form in the sg.
19. Noun.
20. Suffixed noun.
21. Another suffixed noun; regarding this text, cf. G.-W. Nebe, "Das Lied von Sarais Schönheit in 1Q20 = Genesis-Apokryphon XX, 2-8 und die Anfänge der aramäischen Poesie," in *Der Christliche Orient und seine Umwelt. FS J. Tubach* (Wiesbaden, 2007), 59-86; M. Popović, *Reading the Human Body. STDJ* 67 (2007), 286f.
22. Both in reference to Sarah, Raguel's daughter.
23. Of the daughters of human beings, alluding to Gen. 6:1f.
24. Concerning deeds before God.
25. In an omen text in reference to someone's nose, → *ngd.*
26. See D. A. Machiela, *The Dead Sea Genesis Apocryphon. STDJ* 79 (2009), 48.

the meaning is uncertain. In 1QapGen 13:14, one probably finds an additional instance.[27] For instances in a legal formula in treaties from the Dead Sea, see *ATTM*, 2, 498f., for memorial inscriptions *DNSI*, 1184f.

Gianto

27. Of the fruit of a tree in a vision, Machiela, 58; for Dnl. 4 → III.

שרי *šrī*; משרי *mšry* /mašrī/

I. Etymology and Lexical Field. II. G-stem "to Loosen." 1. Literally. 2. Figuratively "to Interpret" and "to Linger." III. D-stem "to Begin." IV. Noun "Camp."

I. Etymology and Lexical Field. Admittedly, the root *šrī* "to loosen" has a common Semitic etymology, but, of the languages of Syria-Palestine, is apparently only productive in Aramaic. The one Ugaritic instance occurs in poetic language;[1] the one or two occurrences in Hebrew[2] may be either borrowings from Aramic or poetic archaisms.

Since the earliest period, Aramaic attests first forms of the verb. The G-stem can function literally and transitively for "to unbind," and figuratively and transitively for "to resolve"[3] and intransitively for "to settle, to camp, to tarry."[4] Only a small step leads from the literal nuance "to loosen a knot (or the like)" to the metaphorical "to solve a problem"; it occurs in Biblical Aramaic with → *qṭr* as object. The usage for "to camp" may have arisen from an abbreviation of "to loosen the field pack" or the like. The D-stem functions as an auxiliary verb "to begin" with the corresponding full verb in the infinitive following *l-*.[5] Dnl. 5:6 uses a participle of the t-stem with the meaning "to loosen" of shaking joints and points it as a Dt-stem *mištārayin*, but, semantically, it approximates the G-stem. It is unclear whether it involves an independent nuance or a pointing error because of otherwise unusual usage.

The texts from Qumran also first manifest the feminine verbal noun /mašrī/ "camp, dwelling." Antonyms of the literal meaning "to loosen" are → *'sr*, *kpt* or → *qṭr* "to bind," of "to tarry" → *ngd* "to set out," and of the D-stem "to begin," *bṭl* "to cease."[6]

H. Gzella, "*šrh*," *ThWQ*, III, 1075-78.

1. *KTU* 1.4 V 9; for a discussion, cf. *DUL*³, 833.
2. G-stem "to set free" in Job 37:3 and a D-stem of unclear meaning in Jer. 15:11, where the text is uncertain, however.
3. A task, like → *prš* and → *pšr*.
4. Synonymous with → *škn*.
5. As in post-Christian times sometimes with *ptḥ* "to open," cf. *DJBA*, 946.
6. → *sūp*.

II. G-stem "to Loosen."

1. Literally. Older Aramaic since the earliest attested phase of the language frequently utilizes the G-stem of *šrī* in the literal sense "to loosen (something bound)." In a treaty of state from Sefire, the probably negated form [*'l*] *tšryh* "do not let him loose" parallels the imperative *'srh* "bind him," i.e., "take him prisoner."[7] In Dnl. 3:25, the verb, a passive participle in an attributive function "unfettered," also refers to prisoners, namely the three young men in the fiery furnace, and in explicit contrast to the passive participle of *kpt* "to fetter" in 3:23f. The loosening of the fetters is part of the wonder of deliverance. The usage in Enoch's letter to the fallen angels in the Book of Giants has a theological nuance. It demands that they set free what they have captured,[8] here with the substantivized passive participle of *'sr* as the object.[9] In 11Q10 32:5 (Job 39:5), the verb represents the D-stem of the Hebrew verb *ptḥ;* the passage speaks literally of releasing a wild ass.

2. Figuratively "to Interpret" and "to Linger." Of the two figurative nuances, "to interpret" and "to camp," the first occurs initially in Dnl. 5:12,16. It involves Daniel's capacity for interpreting dreams, solving puzzles, and "knots"[10] in the obvious metaphorical sense of disentangling difficult questions, which predestines him to explain the mysterious writing on the wall after the king's scholars proved to be overwhelmed. In both passages, *šrī* constitutes a parallelism with → *pšr*; in 5:12, rather than the D-stem participle *m^{e}šārē* in MT and as in 5:16, one should probably read a G-stem infinitive and point it as *mišrē*.[11] If the pertinent emendation, so far without alternative, *'š*]*r'* "[I will interpr]et" in 4Q246 1 1:3 following *ATTM*, 2, 147 is correct, it involves the same usage with a vision (*ḥzw*)[12] as object.

Better attested is the usage for "to encamp, to tarry." Semantically, this intransitive construction approximates the middle-passive. Meanwhile, the form occurs in the oldest datable instance, an Imperial Aramaic hunting inscription from Cilicia, probably in the Gt-stem for "to picnic."[13] The participle with the meaning "to tarry" —of the light that dwells with God —in Dnl. 2:22 is pointed as a passive participle *š^{e}rē*, which one can easily explain semantically as an active usage "dwelling" for "released,"[14] but some assume an originally active form /šārǣ/.[15] In 1QapGen 20:34 and 22:8, the verb denotes "to pitch a tent, to camp" in reference to a person, in 4Q246 1 1:1 to the spirit of God who settled on a visionary, and in 4Q531 22:6 (Book of Giants) to the heavenly beings

7. *KAI* 224.18; a coup d'état constitutes the context.

8. 4Q203 8:14.

9. So, no doubt correctly, *ATTM*, 261; cf., in addition, L. T. Stuckenbruck, *The Book of Giants from Qumran. TSAJ* 63 (1997), 89.

10. → *qṭr*.

11. Cf. *BLA*, §89i; *GesB*[18], 1543; et al.

12. → *ḥzī* IV.

13. *KAI* 261.6, if one does not choose to read a Dt-stem with the Syriac translation of ἀριστᾶν in Lk. 11:37; cf. *LexSyr*, 805b.

14. See *BLA*, §297e.

15. So *ATTM*, 718.

who tarry "among the holy ones" (*bqdšy'*),[16] here paralleling → *ytb*. In contrast to the otherwise largely synonymous verb → *škn*, *šrī* is not apparently defined as a temporary stay. Because of the lacuna in the context, 4Q556 14:2 is unclear.

III. D-stem "to Begin." Further, *šrī* appears in the D-stem for "to begin" and is mostly complemented by the respective full verb in the infinitive after *l*-, rarely in the particple.[17] It can refer to a wide variety of verbal actions: the distribution of goods,[18] construction measures,[19] and at Qumran, also farming,[20] drinking,[21] verbs of speech[22] and of motion.[23] It occurs in the book of Enoch with remarkable frequency, namely for the beginning of the evil that the fallen angels and their descendants effected among human beings,[24] and in the animal allegory of world history;[25] as well as in reference to the beginning of the motion of the sun in the astronomical book of Enoch.[26] Two possibly synonymous instances of the Dt-stem in the Book of Giants[27] have been preserved without sufficient context.

In contrast, the participle in Dnl. 5:6, vocalized as a Dt-stem (→ I), is a middle-passive for "to loosen" in referent to Belshazzar's shaking hip joints (*qṭry ḥrṣh*)[28] and actually corresponds to the active meaning of the G-stems,[29] but has parallels in Syriac.[30]

IV. Noun "Camp." The feminine *mšry* /mašrī/ "camp, dwelling" first appears at Qumran. In 1QapGen 21:1, it denotes an encampment and three other times in fragments largely without context.[31] Additional nominal forms occur in later Aramaic languages, especially Syriac.[32] Of them, 4Q196 2:11 (Tob. 2:1) already attests the feminine *šrw* /šarū/[33] "meal."

Gzella

16. For a discussion of the form → *qdš* IV.2.
17. So *TADAE* D7.9:11.
18. *TADAE* D7.9:11.
19. Ezr. 5:2, with a redundant → *qūm* II.3.
20. 1QapGen 12:13.
21. 1QapGen 12:15.
22. 1QapGen 19:18; 11Q18 19:5.
23. 1QapGen 21:15.
24. 4Q202 1 2:18 (1 En. 7:1); 1 3:5 (1 En. 8:3).
25. 4Q206 4 1:17; 4 2:18; 4Q204 4:3,7 (1 En. 89:3,15,32,35).
26. 4Q209 7 3:2,5 (1 En. 73).
27. 4Q531 30:3, 4Q581 1:3.
28. → *ḥrṣ* II.
29. *ATTM*, 719 therefore suggests a Gt-stem; cf. J. A. Montgomery, *The Book of Daniel. ICC* (1927), 255.
30. *LexSyr*, 805b.
31. 4Q556 1:3; 4Q558 42:1; according to *ATTM*, 2, 499 also 11Q18 15:1.
32. See *LexSyr*, 803-5.
33. Secondarily mutated to /šerū/, cf. *ATTM*, 2, 499.

שׁרשׁ *šrš* /šorš/ (< /śorš/?)

I. Etymology, Form, and Lexical Field. II. Meaning.

I. Etymology, Form, and Lexical Field. Some assume an original form /śorš/ for the masculine primary noun *šrš* /šorš/ "root,"[1] whose initial /ś/ became not /s/, but under the influence of the final sibilant /š/ in accordance with the principles of phonetics;[2] some assume a similar development for → *šrš* "sun."[3] In a few post-Christian Aramaic languages, the word appears as a *qitl*-form.[4]

It appears from Old Aramaic times and occurs since regularly in obvious figurative expressions for the survival of individuals or their descendants. It differs semantically from → *ʿqr* III "rootstock," but sometimes occurs with it in the same context. Since no derivatives of *šrš* are yet known in older Aramaic, which uses *ʿqr* for "to eradicate" instead, *šᵉrōšī* in Ezr. 7:26 may be a misspelling of the Iranian loanword → *srwšy* "discipline."

II. Meaning. In the curse formula of an Old Aramaic inscription from Sefire, *šrš* already metaphorically represents "descendant," which should be denied the party who violates the treaty.[5] Otherwise, these treaties of state utilize *ʿqr* in clauses that also obligate dynastic successors. In a fragmentary, perhaps similar context, one should reconstruct *šrš* at the end of *KAI* 202 B 28. Daniel 4:12,20,23 uses it in the expression *ʿqr šršwhy* "his rootstock" symbolically for the foundation of Nebuchadnezzar's kingdom. In the dream of the cedar and the date palm,[6] it denotes the solidarity of Abraham and Sarah. Occurences in 4Q530 2 2+6-12:8; 4Q542 3 1:1; 4Q558 21a-b:2; 26:1; 6Q8 2:1 (dream) have no context.

Gzella

U. Dahmen, "*šwrš*," *ThWQ*, III, 886-88; J. Renz, "שֹׁרֶשׁ *šōreš*," *TDOT*, XV, 489-502.

1. From the second half of the first millennium B.C.E. expanded to /šorəš/.
2. Cf. *ATTM*, 102,719.
3. For the contested discussion, see, however, Renz, 489f.
4. *ATTM*, 115.
5. *KAI* 222 C 24f.; for parallels, see J. A. Fitzmyer, *The Aramaic Inscriptions of Sefire. BietOr* 19/A (²1995), 120.
6. 1QapGen 19:16.

שתי *štī*; משתה *mšth* /maštǣ/; משתו *mštw* /maštū/; שקי *šqī*; צבע *ṣbʿ*

I. Etymology, Lexical Field, and Grammatical Constructions. II. Drinking as an Everyday Activity. III. In the Context of Banquets. IV. Nouns "Drink, Drinking Bout."

I. Etymology, Lexical Field, and Grammatical Constructions. Since most branches of the Semitic languages attest the root *štī* "to drink," it may belong to the common basic lexicon, although *šrb* replaces it in Arabic. In Aramaic, the verb appears in the transitive G-stem, either absolutely with that drunk—mostly water (*myn*) or wine[1]—as object. A prepositional modifier with *b-* can indicate the drinking vessel.[2] Subjects are usually people. The form [*lmš*]*t*[ʾ] "to drink" in Enoch's animal allegory[3] is almost completely reconstructed.[4] Nothing contradicts the possibility that *štī*, as in Hebrew, could also apply to animals and plants. In reference to an angelic being, however, whose spiritual body assumes human form, one statement explicitly indicates that eating and drinking are only apparent.[5] Like a few other words that begin with a sibilant,[6] this verb can take a prosthetic glottal stop in the perfect. Daniel 5:3f. first attests this phenomenon that has parallels at Qumran[7] and occurs later in Syriac and Jewish Aramaic languages.[8]

Instead of *štī*, the root *šqī* "to give to drink, to water" in the C-stem[9] and once *yhb* "to give" with *myʾ* "water" as object[10] denote causative action; *nsk* "to pour out"[11] denotes "to make a libation" (usually with wine). The verb *ṣbʿ* occurs in the D-stem with the specific meaning "to moisten" (Dnl. 4:12,20,30; 5:21). If solely drinking is not meant, *štī* also occurs regularly with → *ʾkl* "to eat." These instances mostly involve depictions of banquets (→ III).

In addition, the root appears in the form of the masculine noun /maštǣ/, which designates either the object of drinking ("beverage") or as *pars pro toto* the event ("drinking bout," cf. the English *drinks*). The feminine /maštū/ "marriage celebration" also derives from *štī*.

J. Gamberoni, "שָׁתָה *šāṯâ*," *TDOT*, XV, 515-43; G. Gerleman, "שתה *šth* to drink," *TLOT*, 1407-10; C. Stadel, "*šth*," *ThWQ*, III, 1083-87.

1. → *ḥmr*.
2. *TADAE* A4.5:8; Dnl. 5:2f.,23.
3. 4Q206 5 3:18 (1 En. 89:28).
4. *ATTM*, 245 abstains from reconstructing.
5. 4Q196 17 1:2 (Tob. 12:19).
6. Especially the initial /št/ of the number "six."
7. 1QapGen 21:20.
8. See *ATTM*, 134 n. 3 and 438; *BLA*, §47q.
9. *TADAE* A4.5:7; 1QapGen 17:12; 4Q530 2 2+6-12:7.
10. 4Q206 4 3:18 (1 En. 89:28).
11. *KAI* 222 A 26; B 38; 224.5,7; *TADAE* C3.13:7; Dnl. 2:46; for the noun /nesk/ and other terms in sacrificial terminology → *mnḥh* III.2.

II. Drinking as an Everyday Activity. As an activity of everyday life, drinking first appears in a few proverbs of Aḥiqar. One describes the sharing (or libation?) of wine as a "beautiful," i.e., "noble," deed,[12] and another aphorism advises against drinking water entrusted to one so that one may enjoy even greater trust and may guard even gold.[13] The context of *TADAE* C1.2:6, a passage from the Bar-Puneš tale, is unclear.

Further, the verb occurs in a few Imperial Aramaic letters from Elephantine. A report concerning the destruction of a well[14] mentions drinking water (*my'*) in (*b-*) this well (*br'*) alongside the causative verb *šqī* "to give to drink" in relation to the provision of water for a garrison; drinking water typically came from wells or cisterns. The petitionary letter of the Elephantine community concerning the reconstruction of the temple emphasizes abstinence from wine as a gesture of mourning and fasting.[15] Similarly, in the context of religious prescriptions, one finds the prohibition against drinking something in another letter,[16] but the object of the verb has been lost with the text in the preceding lacuna. As evidenced by various commercial texts, wine was very widespread[17] and was used for pleasure as well as for cultic purposes, serving, thus, as a standard component of banquets (→ III), although it was not essential. Many deities also abstained: a Palmyrene dedicatory inscription is dedicated to a god "who drinks no wine [*dy l' št' ḥmr*]."[18] Diodorus Siculus states that the pre-Islamic Nabateans also did not consume wine (μήτε οἴνου χρῆσθαι).[19] In contrast, an ostracon with a writing exercise form Idumea explicitly mentions a group of persons who drank wine.[20]

III. In the Context of Banquets. In addition, the enjoyment of wine constitutes a hallmark of the depiction of banquets in narrative passages such as the court tales of Daniel and a few documents from Qumran. In Old Aramaic times, in contrast, only Sam'al attests funerary meals, which may reflect Anatolian influence; along with pictorial representations of such celebrations, an inscription from this region also contains the wish that the "soul" of the deceased be able "to drink" together with the gods.[21]

The oldest preserved portrayal of a banquet in Aramaic literature is Belshazzar's feast in Dnl. 5. The drunken king arrogantly blasphemes to an almost double degree in that, along with his court, he desecrated the holy vessels from the Jerusalem temple by

12. *TADAE* C1.1:187f.
13. *TADAE* C1.1:191; → *nṭr*.
14. *TADAE* A4.5:8.
15. *TADAE* A4.7:21 par. 4.8:20.
16. *TADAE* A4.1:6.
17. → *ḥmr* II.
18. *PAT* 0319.4f.
19. xix 94 3; cf. J. F. Healey, *The Religion of the Nabataeans. RGRW* 136 (2001), 143-47.
20. A. Lemaire, *Nouvelles inscriptions araméennes d'Idumée*, vol. 2 (Paris, 2002), no. 365, l. 7, pp. 181-85.
21. *KAI* 214.17,22, → *nšm* III.1; contrariwise, l. 9 has "eating and drinking" as an expression of the well-being of the people.

drinking from them (Dnl. 5:2f.)[22] and then praising the idols (5:4).[23] The introduction has the verb *štī* with *ḥmr* "wine" as object almost *pars pro toto* for the entire feast: "he celebrated" (5:1).[24] Thereby, the text clearly distinguishes Belshazzar as a degenerate ne'er-do-well from his father Nebuchadnezzar, a "noble pagan," whose fate, even during his festive mood, is sealed. In the same context, *bt mšth* denotes the location of the event (→ IV); the frequent repetition of forms of the same root *štī* elevates drinking here to a negatively connoted leitmotif.

In relation to regular banquets, in contrast, *štī* "to drink" usually appears together with *'kl* "to eat": Abraham's altar dedication[25] and the following celebration for his friends,[26] Raguel's hospitable entertainment of Tobias and the angel (→ I),[27] Usiel's marriage to Miriam,[28] the cultic meal in the new Jerusalem,[29] and in analogy to the noun *mšth* (→ IV) in relation to Abraham's feast for the Egyptian nobility,[30] and Melchizedek's entertainment of Abraham.[31] Meanwhile, at the "new wine festival" that Noah arranged after the first vintage, celebrants only drank.[32] The otherwise positively connoted combination of *'kl* and *štī* undergoes a perversion to the unnatural, however, in the report concerning the ruin that the giants produced on the earth by eating the flesh of living beings and drinking their blood.[33]

IV. Nouns "Drink, Drinking Bout." Of the two nominal derivatives of the root already attested in pre-Christian Aramaic, *mšth* /maštǣ/ occurs first alongside *m'kl* "food," for "drink" (→ III),[34] in the combination *bt mšth* "festival hall," and second representing the event (Dnl. 5:10). In the context of Belshazzar's banquet, it denotes a wicked place that honorable figures such as the queen and Daniel enter only in cases of extreme need. Qumran first attests the noun *mštw* /maštū/; both passages where it appears employ it explicitly for a marriage celebration.[35]

Gzella

22. → *m'n.*
23. → *šbḥ*; both mentioned together in the recapitulation 5:23, but as distinct actions.
24. Regarding the morphologically unequivocal, but syntactically difficult to explain participle in reference to the past at the beginning of the scene, cf. H. Gzella, *Tempus, Aspekt und Modalität im Reichsaramäischen. VOK* 48 (2004), 124f.
25. 1QapGen 21:20.
26. 1QapGen 21:22.
27. 4Q197 4 3:12 (Tob. 7:9); on 4Q196 17 1:2 (Tob. 12:19).
28. 4Q545 1a 1:6 par. 4Q543 1a-c:7.
29. 11Q18 25:6.
30. 1QapGen 19:27.
31. 1QapGen 22:15, following Gen. 14:18.
32. 1QapGen 12:15.
33. 4Q202 1 2:25a (1 En. 7:5).
34. 1QapGen 19:27; 22:15, there as object of the C-stem of → *npq* "to put on."
35. 4Q197 4 2:4 (Tob. 6:13); 4Q545 1a 1:6-8, here as the object of → *'bd*, cf. *'bd lḥm* in Dnl. 5:1.

תבר *tbr*

I. Etymology. II. Old and Imperial Aramaic. III. Biblical Aramaic. IV. Qumran.

I. Etymology. Derivatives of the root **θbr*, so Ugaritic,[1] also occur in Hebrew, Phoenician, Akkadian, and Ethiopic.

II. Old and Imperial Aramaic. The only Old Aramaic instances of the verb "to shatter" in the G-stem[2] appear in a curse formula in the Sefire inscription *KAI* 222 A 38f.: *w'yk zy tšbr*[3] *qšt' wḥṣy' 'ln kn yšbr*[4] *'nrt whdd* [*qšt mtʿ'l*] "As the bow and this arrow are broken, so may Inurta and Hadad break [the bow of Matiʿel]."[5] The Imperial Aramaic letter of the Jews from Elephantine reports the shattering of the stone columns of their temple.[6] The verb appears often in images and allegories (→ III and IV), as in the sayings of Aḥiqar: *rkyk lšn m*[*lk*] *wʿlʿy tnyn ytbr* "Soft is the tongue [of a kin]g, but it breaks the ribs of a dragon"[7] and *m'n ṭb ks*[*y*] *mlh blbbh whw z*[*y*]*tbyr hnpqh br'* "A good jug hol[ds] a word inside it, but [a]broken one lets it out."[8]

III. Biblical Aramaic. Biblical Aramaic only attests the G-stem as a participle passive feminine singular absolute in the interpretation of Nebuchadnezzar's dream (Dnl. 2:42). The toes of the statue, partly iron, partly clay, symbolize the fact that "the kingdom will be partly strong, partly fragile" (*min qᵉṣāṯ malkūṯā tæhᵆwē ṯaqqīpā*[9] *ūminnah tæhᵆwē ṯᵉḇīrā*). In the interpretation, Daniel combines two lexical fields: breaking of material (→ II), here clay, and of immaterial (→ IV), here the kingdom.[10]

IV. Qumran. Qumran Aramaic attests only the G-stem[11] and the passive Gt-stem. The verb appears in the material meaning only in Noah's vision of the olive tree in 1QapGen 13:16 when the four winds of heaven "strike off its branches and shatter it" (*mʿnpn lh*

A. Bledsoe, "*šbr*," *ThWQ*, III, 835-40; J. A. Fitzmyer, *The Genesis Apocryphon of Qumran Cave 1 (1Q20)*. *BietOr* 18B (³2004); B. Knipping, "שָׁבַר *šāḇar*," *TDOT*, XIV, 367-81.

1. Arabic *tbr* "to shatter," *ṯbr* "to destroy," the latter also in Old South Arabian.
2. With a direct object; in Old Aramaic spelled with *š* for the still preserved /θ/.
3. Impf. 3fs pass. Note that the form is singular despite the expected plural with a compound subject.
4. Impf. 3ms. Note that the form is singular despite the expected plural with a compound subject.
5. For the motif of the weapon-breaking God, cf. Hos. 1:5; Jer. 49:35.
6. *TADAE* A4.7:9: *tbrw hmw* "they shattered them," pf. 3mp.
7. *TADAE* C1.1:89f.; impf. 3ms; regarding the context → *ʿlʿ* II.
8. *TADAE* C1.1:93; ptcp. pass. masc. sg. abs.; → *m'n.*
9. Antonym, → *tqp*.
10. For the context → *dhb* II; for synonyms from the lexical field of destruction → *ḥbl*.
11. With a direct object, for the ptcp. *l*-.

wtbrn lh).[12] In the revision of Gen. 14, the verb means "to conquer": as in 1QapGen 21:32, *'tbr mlk swdwm w'rq* "the king of Sodom was conquered and fled";[13] and later in reference to Abraham's campaign against the Transeuphratenes, 1QapGen 22:8f., *hww' qṭl bhwn blyly' wtbr 'nwn* "he massacred them in the night and conquered them."[14] In 11Q10 34:7f. (Job 40:12), *kl rmt rwḥ ttbr whṭpy ršy'[yn tḥw]tyhwn* "All arrogance will be shattered, and he has extinguished all evil[doers amon]g them,"[15] the verb translates the Hebrew *kn'* in the C-stem. The form *mtbry'* in 4Q566 1:3 in a fragmentary context is ambiguous, although probably a participle masculine plural determined in the Gt-stem.

Stadel

12. Ptcp. act. fem. pl.
13. Pf. 3ms, Gt-stem; on Gen. 14:9f.
14. Pf. 3ms, act. G-stem, paraphrasing *wayyakkēm* in Gen. 14:15; regarding the construction → *hwī* II.
15. Impf. 3fs, Gt-stem.

תוב *tūb*; תוב(א) *twb(')* /tūbā/

I. Etymology, Lexical Field, and Grammatical Constructions. II. G-stem "to Return." III. C-stem "to Give Back." IV. Adverb "Again."

I. Etymology, Lexical Field, and Grammatical Constructions. Aramaic *tūb*, in the G-stem "to return," belongs to the Semitic verbal root **θūb*. Old Aramaic still retained the initial interdental and, in accordance with Old West Syrian orthography, spelled it with *š*, after its fusion with /t/ then, at the latest in Imperial Aramaic, consistently with *t*.[1] The intransitive G-stem, which occurs with persons and abstract subjects, literally means "to return" or figuratively "to diverge from, to turn,"[2] and appears in conjunction with an additional verb to mean "to do again." Further, the transitive C-stem "to give back" is extremely productive in Aramaic. In addition to material terms, it can also take abstract terms as object; it often appears with → *ptgm* "message"[3] for "to answer," for which Aramaic also has an independent verb in → *'nī* I.

Both G- and C-stems take various prepositional complements to express adverbial

H.-J. Fabry, "*šwb*," *ThWQ*, III, 861-78; A. Graupner and H.-J. Fabry, "שׁוּב *šûḇ*," *TDOT*, XIV, 461-522; J. A. Soggin, "שׁוּב *šûb* to return," *TLOT*, 1312-17.

1. *ATTM*, 99f.
2. Cf. Dutch *terugkomen* "to return" and *terugkomen op* "to change one's opinion."
3. And abbreviated then also absolutely.

relations: both frequently take *l*-, with the G-stem to indicate direction "toward" or "to," with the C-stem for the indirect object "to someone" and in the Imperial Aramaic tradition and later in East Aramaic also for the direct object; for persons, *ʿl*, mostly "to," also appears with both stems, but in the G-stem also for "on" or "against." With the G-stem as a verb of motion, furthermore, the ablative *mn* "from" can also appear, rarely *b*- "with."

The adverb /tūbā/ "again" or, in official style, "further," also derives from the same root.

II. G-stem "to Return." Old Aramaic already employs the G-stem of *tūb* "to return"[4] figuratively. In the conclusion of a treaty of state from Sefire, it occurs with a place name as subject and refers to the return of a region to (*l*-) the dynasty of a treaty partner.[5] Neo-Assyrian legal documents employ it with *ʿl* in the curse formula at the end for "to turn against someone."[6] It probably denotes withdrawal from an oath, although following a lacuna, also in Imperial Aramaic in *TADAE* B7.1:5 and perhaps in D2.25:4 (although entirely without context).

The three Biblical Aramaic examples all employ it in relation to the rehabilitation of Nebuchadnezzar, to (*ʿl*) whom, when at the end of his penance he acknowledged God as the supreme ruler, his mind (*mndʿ*, Dnl. 4:31,33)[7] as well as his dominion and royal dignity returned (4:33).[8]

Qumran first manifests the usage as a verb of motion, where, however, it is regular in journey reports.[9] It functions figuratively, e.g., in reference to evil that returns onto (*ʿl*) someone's (namely the transgressor's) head, as in 4Q550 7+7a:6, and in 11Q10 23:3 (Job 33:25)[10] for the return of youth. The nuance "to diverge from" already attested in older legal diction also appears.[11] Finally, as an auxiliary verb "to do again" with a syndetically appended similar form of a main verb, it first appears in reference to the regular course of the stars in the astronomical book of Enoch[12] and to Noah's renewed praise of God.[13] A few additional instances are unclear in terms of their contexts.

---

4. Spelled *šūb* here, → I.

5. *KAI* 224.25.

6. *KAI* 316.11; V. Hug, *Altaramäische Grammatik der Texte des 7. und 6. Jh. s v. Chr. HSAO* 4 (2003), 25; the same formulation also appears in A. Lemaire, *Nouvelles tablettes araméennes* (Geneva, 2001), no. 4, l. 16f., pp. 41-48; ibid., no. *6, l. 3, pp. 126-28; probably to be emended in no. 3, l. 5, pp. 33-41.

7. → *ydʿ* III.4.

8. On the impf. for a secondary action in the past, see H. Gzella, *Tempus, Aspekt und Modalität im Reichsaramäischen. VOK* 48 (2004), 136-42.

9. 1QapGen 21:19 (with a syndetically appended *ʾtī* and the ethical dative for punctiliar action "after my return, I arrived home"); 21:30 (absolutely); 22:29 (with *mn* "out of," which should probably be supplied in 4Q196 14 1:1 [Tob. 6:13]); 4Q196 2:9 (Tob. 2:1), 4Q204 4:6 (1 En. 89:34), 4Q543 15:1, and 4Q547 1-2 3:5.8 par. 4Q544 1:9 (all five with *l*- "to"); in 11Q10 32:3 (Job 39:4), as expected, for the Hebrew cognate *šūb* and in contrast to → *npq* "to go forth."

10. Likewise for *šūb*.

11. 4Q201 1 3:2 (1 En. 6:4); 11Q10 27:4; 33:4 (Job 36:10; 39:22); reversed, "to turn to (*l*-)" in 38:3 (Job 42:10).

12. 4Q209 7 3:2,5 (1 En. 73).

13. 1QapGen 11:13.

III. C-stem "to Give Back." The C-stem of *tūb* "to give back" also already appears in Old Aramaic texts. A treaty of state from Sefire employs it in a clause concerning the return of fugitives[14] and with a divine subject for the restoration of the dynasty of a treaty partner in relation to the return of a territory.[15] The Old Aramaic spelling *šūb* still appears here (→ I). The verb also occurs in the Asshur ostracon, now as *tūb*, for the return of prisoners.[16] A saying of Aḥiqar employs it figuratively; it warns against attacking[17] a righteous person with an arrow because he stands under the protection of the gods and they will redirect the arrow to (*ʿl*) the shooter.

Imperial Aramaic letters employ the verb in the literal sense for "to give back" with goods, whether stolen property[18] or property attained in some other illegal manner,[19] similarly in legal texts[20] and in sales contracts from Samaria specifically for the return of the sales price in the case of a legal dispute.[21]

The verb may already function for "to answer" in Segal, 59.4, which can not be verified because of the absence of a broader context; Biblical Aramaic first attests this usage with certainty. Here, the verb occurs several times with the Iranian nouns → *ptgm* "report" (Dnl. 3:16; Ezr. 5:11) or → *nštwn* "official letter" (Ezr. 5:5) as objects, which point to the roots of this expression in Achaemenid chancellery style. In this style, it appears in Dnl. 2:14 with *ʿṭʾ* "counsel"[22] and → *ṭʿm* "understanding" as objects, for a clever response by Daniel. In Ezr. 6:5, it literally represents the symbolically significant return of the temple implements[23] that inaugurates the reconstruction of the Jerusalem cultic center; as in *KAI* 224.24 (see above), this passage employs the verb to express historical continuity.

These usages grounded in Old Aramaic occur then in the texts from Qumran. Here, *tūb* appears in relation to the return of persons[24] and goods.[25] 11Q10 employs it often for "to answer,"[26] so possibly also 4Q550 5+5a:5.[27] Contracts from the Dead Sea attest the same semantic spectrum.[28]

---

14. *KAI* 224.6,20.
15. *KAI* 224.24, along with the G-stem, → II.
16. *KAI* 233.11.
17. *rkb* in the C-stem.
18. *TADAE* A4.4,8.
19. So *TADAE* A6:15,7,10.
20. *TADAE* B2.9:7; the fragmentary instances in B8.11:2 and D2.29b:2 may be comparable.
21. *WDSP* 4:10; 7:13.
22. → *yʿṭ* III.
23. → *mʾn* III.
24. 1QapGen 20:30; 21:3; 22:12,24 (prisoners, see above for the Old Aramaic evidence); 4Q198 1:9 (Tob. 13:5); 4Q204 4:8 (1 En. 89:35); in the inner pass. also 4Q196 2:10 (Tob. 2:1).
25. 1QapGen 22:24; paralleling → *yhb*.
26. For the instances with discussion → *ptgm* II.3.
27. With no object in the preserved text.
28. Return of goods: nV 17:41 in *ATTM*, 2, 231f.; in a marriage contract, the promise to free and return the wife, should she be taken prisoner: nV 10:11 in *ATTM*, 2, 226-28 and probably to be supplied at the beginning of the line with relative certainty; for the juridical terminology → *prq*.

IV. Adverb "Again." The related adverb /tūb(ā)/ occurs since Imperial Aramaic and appears in Achaemenid texts in the spellings *twb*[29] and *twb'*.[30] According to *ATTM*, 722, both represent the form /tūbā/, whose unaccented final adverbial ending /-ā/ was not always written at first. It may be that one should not exclude the possibility of a by-form */tūb/ without this ending, but the later body of occurrences do not evidence it, since an unaccented /-ā/ had fallen out again secondarily in the time of the vocalizations of Aramaic.[31] Furthermore, /tūbā/ could be expanded to /tūbān/.[32]

In the meaning "again,"[33] this adjective corresponds semantically with the verbal root, but it appears regularly at least in official texts as a pure particle of apposition "further."[34] This dual usage is still very frequent in post-Christian Aramaic,[35] where the word in the second sense often introduces a new narrative unit.

Gzella

29. *TADAE* B2.4:12; B5.1:7; D7.11:11.
30. *TADAE* A6.15:11; C1.1:44.
31. *ATTM*, 122-25.
32. *ATTM*, 149.
33. Thus clearly in *TADAE* A6.15:11, then at Qumran in ritual instructions in T. Levi: 4Q214b 2-6 i 8; and probably also in a prophecy: 4Q540 1:1f.
34. *TADAE* B2.4:12; 5.1:7; partially emended in a later contract from the Dead Sea, V 36:5 in *ATTM*, 2, 240f.; so also in literary prose: *TADAE* C1.1:44; and in building inscriptions: S 1:7 from East Mesopotamia, *PAT* 0042.8 and 0065.4 from Palmyra; the precise function in *TADAE* D7.11:11 cannot be determined.
35. *DJPA*, 576; *DJBA*, 1195f.; *LexSyr*, 817; *MdD*, 483.

תוה *twh*

I. Etymology. II. Meaning.

I. Etymology. The verbal root *twh* with the G-stem meaning "to terrify" is very rare in Aramaic; some conjecture an etymological relationship with → *tmh* "to astonish," which finds phonetic support in the readily explicable shift /m/ > /w/, but the nuances, at least in Biblical Aramaic, already seem distinct from one another.

II. Meaning. The sole occurrence of *twh* in older Aramaic is the reaction of Nebuchadnezzar to the wondrous scene in the fiery furnace (Dnl. 3:24).[1] Here, it appears

1. Regarding the form, cf. *BLA*, §46v′.

alongside → *bhl* "to terrify" and → *qūm* "to stand up,"[2] which points to a sudden, but not necessarily pleasant, stimulus. Later, the root also occurs in East Aramaic.[3]

Gzella

2. Ingressive "suddenly," as K. Koch, *Daniel 1–4. BK* XXII/1 (2005), 254, suggests, is unlikely, since *qm* would probably stand in first, not second, position.
3. *DJBA*, 1196b; *LexSyr*, 818; *MdD*, 485.

תור *twr* /tawr/; תורה *twrh* /tawrā/; עגל *'gl* /'egl/

I. Form and Meaning. II. Masculine "Cattle of Both Genders." III. "Steer" Figuratively. IV. Feminine "Cow." V. "Calf." VI. Derivatives.

I. Form and Meaning. The word */θawr/[1] is a Semitic and Indo-European (ταῦρος, *taurus*) primary noun, an old *Wanderwort* "cattle," in Arabic, Aramaic, and Indo-European only masculine in gender, but it can include female animals. Already in pre-Christian times, the Aramaic pronunciation changed in two respects from the original /θawr/: already before 800 B.C.E. /θ/ > /t/,[2] in contrast to Abyssinian > /s/, Akkadian and Canaanite also > /š/, and in second century B.C.E. Aramaic /aw/ > /ō/ initially in closed,[3] then in some of the Aramaic languages also in an open syllable,[4] and contrary to Akkadian throughout and Canaanite in part[5] since the beginning of the traditions. This results for Aramaic in the masculine singular absolute /θawr/ > /tawr/ > /tōr/, the determined /tawrā/ or /tōrā/, and the masculine plural absolute /tawarīn/ > /tawrīn/ > /tōrīn/.

II. Masculine "Cattle of Both Genders." The masculine means "cattle of either gender." In the story of Nebuchadnezzar's penitential period, it appears several times as

I. Eph'al and J. Naveh, *Aramaic Ostraca of the Fourth Century BC from Idumaea* (Jerusalem, 1996); I. Kottsieper, "Zum aramäischen Text der 'Trilingue' von Xanthos und ihrem historischen Hintergrund," in *Ex Syria et Mesopotamia Lux. FS M. Dietrich. AOAT* 281 (2002), 209-43; A. Lemaire, *Nouvelles inscriptions araméennes d'Idumée au musée d'Israel* (Paris, 1996); D. K. Sharpes, *Sacred Bull, Holy Cow* (New York, 2006); H-J. Zobel, "שׁוֹר *šôr*," *TDOT*, XIV, 546-52.

1. So still in Arabic and early Old Aramaic.
2. *ATTM*, 100; 2, 51: due to the lack of an independent letter, an old /θ/ is usually spelled, in accordance with the Phoenician consonant shift, with *š*, and rarely, in accordance with the phonetic similarity, with *s*.
3. Plutarch, *Sulla* 17:8, ca. 100 C.E.: θωρ.
4. *ATTM*, 116-20; 2, 54f.
5. Ugaritic /ṯōr/.

a grass-eater along with the king: Dnl. 4:22,29,30; 5:21; all in the plural absolute /tōrīn/. Elsewhere, it denotes cattle as sacrificial animals: the singular absolute *šwr*[6] in l. 3 of the Kuttamuwa inscription from Sam'al (eighth century B.C.E.);[7] Imperial Aramaic then in the spelling *twr TADAE* A4.10:10 (407 B.C.E.) along with "sheep" and "goats"; triglot from Xanthos, *KAI* 319.17 (fourth century B.C.E.; in the Greek text βοῦν); the singular determined *twr'* in the new/heavenly Jerusalem from Qumran 11Q18;[8] further in T. Levi according to a manuscript from the Cairo Geniza;[9] also in Palmyrene;[10] the plural absolute *twryn*: Ezr. 6:17; 7:17 along with rams and lambs; 11Q18;[11] *bny twryn* "young cattle": Ezr. 6:9; *pr twryn* "yearling" in T. Levi.[12]

III. "Steer" Figuratively. Additionally, "steer" also functions as an image: the singular determined *twr'* in the astrological brontology 4Q318[13] for the constellation of Taurus; in 1QapGen 17:10; 21:16[14] as a toponym *ṭwr twr'* "the mountain of the steer";[15] the plural determined *twry'* in Enoch's animal vision 4Q206[16] as an image of Noah and his sons.

IV. Feminine "Cow." The feminine "cow" occurs in the singular absolute after a number in an apparently widespread Old Aramaic curse formula: *KAI* 222 A 23 (Sefire; eighth century B.C.E.) much like *KAI* 320.5 (Bukān; eighth century B.C.E.) "May seven cows suckle to no effect!"; similarly *KAI* 309 (Tell Fekheriye; ca. 850 B.C.E.) in the Aramaic alphabet of the eleventh century B.C.E. with apparently twelve misspellings,[17] including in l. 20 after a number, where Old Aramaic rarely has the thing counted in the singular, but mostly in the plural, so that one would expect *swr<h/n>* /θawr<ā>/ or /θawar<ān>/ "may a hundred cows suckle to no effect!" Contrariwise, in the Sam'alian (→ II) inscription of Panammuwa (eighth century B.C.E.),[18] *šwrh*, along with other grains, apparently refers to "sorghum" (cf. Isa. 28:25). The singular determined *twrt'* appears on an ostracon from Idumea[19] (fourth century B.C.E.) denoting a sacrificial animal.

---

6. Corresponding to the determined state.
7. Text in D. G. Pardee, "A New Aramaic Inscription from Zinjirli," *BASOR* 356 (2009) 51-71; regarding the relationship to Aramaic, see H. Gzella, *A Cultural History of Aramaic. HO* 111 (2015), 72-77, esp. 76f.
8. *DSSStE*, 1222 (11Q18 13:2).
9. *DSSStE*, 52,54 (CT. Levi Bodleian d:6,21); in the same context as /parr/, → V.
10. *PAT* 2163.
11. *DSSStE* 1226 (11Q18 28:5).
12. xL 36:23; → V.
13. *ATTM*, 2, 167; *DSSStE*, 676 (4Q318 2 1:5,2 2:1).
14. *ATTM*, 171,179.
15. Ταῦρος ὄρος, the Amanus Mountains; → *ṭwr* II. Cf. *DSSStE*, 38f.,44f., which translates "the mountain of the Bull."
16. *DSSStE*, 426 (4Q206 5 1:19f. = 1 En. 89:5-6).
17. See *ATTM*, 2, 15.
18. *KAI* 215.6,9.
19. Eph'al and Naveh, no. 118.1.

V. "Calf." Semitic has an independent word for "calf," as a masculine /ʿegl/, as a feminine /ʿeglā/. In contrast, /parr/ "young cattle"[20] is Hebrew.

VI. Derivatives. Two derivates of *twr* "cattle" denote "cattle breeder," "cattle herder," "cattle plowman." They are formed either through the addition of the gentilic affix /-āy/[21] or through transition to the *qattāl* noun form.[22] They allow for the readings /tawrāyǣ/ or /tawwārayyā/ on the plural determined-state noun *twryʾ* on an ostracon from Idumea (fourth century B.C.E.).[23] Otherwise, there is a verb in the D-stem "to plow with cattle."[24]

Beyer

20. CT. Levi Bodleian d:23 in *DSSStE*, 54, → II.
21. As in Jewish Babylonian: *DJBA*, 1199b.
22. *DJBA*, 239b,1197a.
23. Lemaire, 104.4.
24. *LexSyr*, 819b.

תמה *tmh*; תמה *tmh* /temh/

I. Etymology, Lexical Field, and Grammatical Constructions. II. Verb "to Astonish." III. Noun "Wonder."

I. Etymology, Lexical Field, and Grammatical Constructions. Aramaic and Hebrew know the verbal root *tmh*.[1] In accordance with the middle meaning "to astonish," it occurs as a G- or Gt-stem, although no semantic difference is apparent. The basis of the astonishment usually appears in the prepositional expression following *ʿl*. There may be a relationship to → *twh* "to terrify" since the two share the same lexical field and, especially, since a shift from /m/ to /w/ can be explained phonetically with no problem.[2] The preserved Aramaic texts, however, employ *tmh* more for a wondrous, somewhat enduring astonishment, while *twh* in Dnl. 3:24 refers to a sudden terror. Common to both is the relationship with a sensory, more precisely, visual perception. They belong to the extremely differentiated psychological vocabulary in theological literature. Later, *tmh* also seems to denote "to be dim."[3] The masculine /temh/ (> /temah/) "wonder"[4] belongs to the root *tmh*.

U. Berges, "תָּמַהּ *tāmah*," *TDOT*, XV, 681-84.

1. With a consonantal /h/ as the final radical.
2. Cf. West Aramaic *ḥmī* "to see" and *ḥwī* "to show," → *ḥzī* I.
3. Cf. L. Prijs, "Ergänzungen zum talmudisch-aramäischen Wörterbuch," *ZDMG* 117 (1967) 286.
4. Mandean probably secondarily transformed into a *qutl* form with metathesis *tuhma*, *MdD*, 483.

II. Verb "to Astonish." As a verb, *tmh* first appears in religious literature from Qumran. Here, the G- and Gt-stems seem to have largely synonymous usage, the first twice in Noah's reaction to the vision of a luxuriant olive tree, once in a periphrastic construction with a durative nuance *hwyt tmh* "I stood rapt in astonishment"[5] and then again in the perfect;[6] further as a command "be not astonished!"[7] probably likewise after a vision, but in an extremely fragmentary context. The Gt-stem appears in the same text for pharaoh's reaction to Sarah's perfect beauty and, in contrast to the G-stem, could have the nuance that the desire of the king became immediately inflamed and had its object abducted immediately. The stems of the other two occurrences are not clear: 11Q10 10:2 (Job 26:11) has the verb in the image of the reverential trembling of heaven in view of God's omnipotence as a translation of the Hebrew *ytmhw* with *mn* and could be either an Aramaic G- or Gt-stem; 4Q205 1 12:8 (1 En. 26:6) involves Enoch's astonishment over the gigantic mountains that he saw on his journey to heaven (see above on 1QapGen 13:15); the verb can be emended either as a G-stem *t*]*mht* or as a Gt-stem *'t*]*mht*.

III. Noun "Wonder." Since the book of Daniel, Aramaic attests the noun *tmh* /temh/ "wonder." Daniel uses it twice for God's wondrous acts of deliverance, each time in the plural along with → *'t* "sign" and in a hymnic confession by the king who attained the recognition of the true God after the deliverance of the three young men from the fiery furnace (Dnl. 3:33) and of Daniel from the lion's den (6:28). At Qumran, in contrast, it occurs once in 11Q10 4:5 (Job 21:6) for the Hebrew *pallāṣûṯ* "terror, shuddering," and again in 6Q8 1:6 from the Book of Giants in relation to a giant's disbelief of a probably preceding but now lost vision report.[8]

Gzella

5. → *hwī* II.
6. 1QapGen 13:15.
7. 1QapGen 15:19.
8. Cf. L.T. Stuckenbruck, *The Book of Giants from Qumran. TSAJ* 63 (1997), 199.

תקל *tql*; תקל *tql* /teql/ (שׁקל *šql* /šeql/); מתקל *mtql* /matqāl/

I. Etymology and Grammatical Constructions. II. Verb "to Weigh." III. Noun "Shekel." IV. Noun "Weight."

I. Etymology and Grammatical Constructions. Aramaic *tql* "to weigh" arose from older Semitic **θkl* and appears in the transitive G-stem, which can be optionally supple-

P. B. Hartog, "*šql*," *ThWQ*, III, 1063-66.

mented with adverbial modifiers following *b-* "on (a scale)" or, with the nuance "to pay," *l-* "to someone," for example. As a verb, the root appears significantly less frequently, however, than the masculine substantive for the weight /teql/[1] ubiquitous in legal and commercial texts "shekel." The very frequent spelling *šql*, often abbreviated *š*, is probably borrowed from Akkadian /šeql/ as the historical orthography for the old */θekl/.[2] The "menetekel" of Dnl. 5 depends on a double entendre of verb and noun. The likewise masculine noun /matqāl/ "weight" belongs to the same root. Apparently no relationship to the homonymous verb *tql* "to stumble"[3] exists, however. "Scale" is /mawzen/.[4]

II. Verb "to Weigh." Legal and commercial texts for the Neo-Assyrian period first evidence the verb *tql* "to weigh," like the noun "shekel,"[5] then in Imperial Aramaic *WDSP* 17:3, and with the nuance "to pay (what has been weighed out)" *TADAE* B2.6:24.[6] Both nuances occur, in addition, in Aramaic treaties from the Dead Sea: "to pay" in V 36:6; 37:3,[7] the passive participle *tqylyn* "weighed out" in V 88:2.[8]

Overall, however, the verb is rather rare so that it is not recognizable as such in the puzzling oracular saying with the divine verdict on the blasphemer Belshazzar in Dnl. 5:25 *mn' mn' tql wprsyn* and, alongside the supposed, equally frequent noun "mene,"[9] appears to be a substantive, which it is also vocalized as in the transmitted text.[10] The passive perfect *t^eqīltā* "you will be weighed" in Daniel's interpretation according to 5:27 demonstrates, however, that *tql* is meant instead as a passive participle /taqīl/ "weighed"; V 88:2 attests such a form in the plural *tqylyn* (see above), which was, therefore, actually in use in contemporaneous Aramaic. The defective spelling *tql* instead of the customary *tqyl* makes it even more difficult, however, to choose the correct reading. Instead of the apparently capricious sequence of weights in the illogical order "mene," "shekel," "half-mene," therefore, it involves a nominal clause referring to the king "(you will be) paid out, weighed, and apportioned," announcing the end of the kingdom.

III. Noun "Shekel." Beginning in Neo-Assyrian times, in contrast, *tql/šql* "shekel" appears in hundreds of instances.[11] There can be no wonder, then, that Belshazzar's scholars thought of this, the most frequent form of the root in the unvocalized text of

1. After ca. 500 B.C.E. expanded to /teqəl/.

2. *ATTM*, 726.

3. 11Q10 25:6 (Job 34:30).

4. *TADAE* B2.6:24; 3.8:26; in Dnl. 5:27 in the pl. det. state spelled *m'zny'* with ' instead of *w* as in Isa. 40:12 following MT, cf. *ATTM*, 565.

5. *KAI* 316:6, also in V. Hug, *Altaramäische Grammatik der Texte des 7. und 6. Jh. s v. Chr. HSAO* 4 (2003), 25; further O. 3655, l. 8, in E. Lipiński, *SAIO* III (2010), 62-70.

6. *TADAE* C1.2:23 is unclear in context.

7. *ATTM*, 2, 240-42.

8. *ATTM*, 2, 260.

9. → *mnī*.

10. The orthographic convention requires consistent punctuation, even if the contemporary reader did not yet know this aid and it is detrimental to the literary point of the passage.

11. Cf. D. Schwiderski, *Die alt- und reichsaramäischen Inschriften*, vol. I: *Konkordanz*. *FSBP* 2 (2008), 817-21.

the writing on the wall, just as with the word "mene."[12] In contrast, thanks to his giftedness with divine wisdom, Daniel was in the position to extract the true message from the ambiguous text (→ II). The play with administrative terms such as weights and the verbs "to pay" and "to weigh" indicates the deep roots of Biblical Aramaic literature in Achaemenid administrative diction.[13] From Qumran, the noun also appears in 4Q535 2:3,[14] and without context in 4Q580 1 2:11.

IV. Noun "Weight." The noun *mtql* /matqāl/ "weight" with the apparently largely or entirely synonymous feminine *mtqlh* /matqālā/ is relatively rare. It refers to specific information, such as, in Imperial Aramaic, the feminine in the expression *bmtqlt* "according to the weight of" in reference to the respective standard[15] and probably the masculine at Qumran in 4Q535 3:3 of a certain, numerically specified weight (→ III).[16]

Gzella

12. → *mnī* IV and V.

13. See H. Gzella, *A Cultural History of Aramaic. HO* 111 (2015), 201-8, and idem, "Von der Kanzlei- zur Kultursprache: Die Anfänge der aramäischen Weltliteratur," *ThQ* 197 (2017) 107-32, esp. 124-31.

14. For the weight of a child between seven and eight pounds: *ATTM*, 2, 164.

15. *TADAE* A6.2:21; B2.11:11; 3.9:8.

16. The prefix there has been supplied, however: *m*]*tql*.

תקן *tqn*

I. Etymology and Lexical Field. II. Usage.

I. Etymology and Lexical Field. The verb *tqn* "to be/become firm" belongs to a common Semitic root. In addition to the intransitive G-stem, it appears in the transitive C-stem "to install" and D-stem "to prepare."

II. Usage. The G-stem occurs in 4Q206 4 2:4 (1 En. 89:8) for "to set up" of the ark in Enoch's animal vision, the C-stem "to install" in the passive in Dnl. 4:33 for the restoration of Nebuchadnezzar's kingship, and the D-stem "to prepare" in Palmyrene.[1]

Gzella

1. *PAT* 1787.4, of a grave.

תקף *tqp*; תֹּקף *tqp* /toqp/; תַּקִּיף *tqyp* /taqqīp/

I. Etymology. II. Old and Biblical Aramaic. III. Aramaic Texts from the Dead Sea.

I. Etymology. The root *tqp* occurs in Aramaic and as *ṯqf* in Arabic. It also appears in Hebrew, where it is usually considered to be an Aramaism, however.[1] Its meaning depends on the notion of power, either as such ("to be strong") or as a concrete phenomenon (Arabic and Hebrew "to overpower").

II. Old and Biblical Aramaic. The root *tqp* hardly appears before Biblical Aramaic. The Tell Dan stele may contain an instance of the adjective *tqyp* /taqqīp/ "strong" in l. 6,[2] but the passage is severely corrupt and preserves only remnants of two letters,[3] so that it supports no further conclusions.

Biblical Aramaic, however, has *tqp* as a verb in the G- and D-stems, as a noun, and as an adjective. In the form of the noun, the root appears in the determined state as *tqp'*[4] "strength, power," namely in Dnl. 2:37: *dy 'lh šmy' mlkwt' ḥsn' wtqp' wyqr' jhb lk* "for the God of heaven bestowed on you the kingship, power, strength, and honor." Dnl. 4:27, *hl' d' hy' bbl rbt' dy 'nh bnyth lbyt mlkw btqp ḥsny wlyqr hdry* "Is this not the grand Babylon that I built as a royal residence through the power of my might and to the honor of my majesty?" vocalizes the construct as *t^eqap̄*, perhaps an error for *t^eqop̄*.[5]

As an adjective, the root takes the form *tqyp* /taqqīp/, a formation that typifies the adjective in Aramaic and, accordingly, means "strong, mighty," as in Dnl. 2:40: *wmlkw rby'yh {rby''h} thw' tqyph kprzl'* "and a fourth kingdom will be as strong as iron";[6] likewise in Ezr. 4:20: *wmlkyn tqypyn hww 'l yrwšlm* "mighty kings ruled over Jerusalem." In Dnl. 3:33, *wtmhwhy kmh tqypyn* "and his wonders, how mighty they are!," this adjective expresses a feeling of trembling before the wonders of the Most High.[7]

Finally, as a verb in the G-stem, *tqp* means "to be/become strong," as in Dnl. 4:8: *rbh 'yln' wtqp* "the tree grew and became strong" and the corresponding interpretation of

---

J. A. Fitzmyer, *The Genesis Apocryphon of Qumran Cave 1 (1Q20). BietOr* 18B (³2004); H. Gzella, "*tqp*," *ThWQ*, III, 1158-62; S. A. Kaufman, *The Akkadian Influences on Aramaic. AS* 19 (1974); E. Kautzsch, *Die Aramaismen im Alten Testament* (Halle, 1902); J. T. Milik, *The Books of Enoch* (Oxford, 1976); T. Nöldeke, "Bemerkungen zu den aramäischen Inschriften von Sendschirli," *ZDMG* 47 (1893) 96-105; D. Schwiderski, *Die alt- und reichsaramäischen Inschriften*, vol. I: *Konkordanz. FSBP* 2 (2008); A. Yardeni, *Textbook of Aramaic, Hebrew and Nabatean Documentary Texts from the Judean Desert and Related Material*, 2 vols. (Jerusalem, 2000).

1. Nöldeke, 102; Kautzsch, 92.
2. Cf. the corresponding reconstruction suggested in Schwiderski, 840.
3. Most read *šb*]*'n* "seventy," so also *KAI* 310.6.
4. /toqpā/, regarding the abs. state /toqp/, then expanded to /toqəp/ or /toqop/, cf. *ATTM*, 112-15.
5. See *BLA*, §51e''.
6. For the context → *dhb* II.
7. → *tmh* III.

the image in Dnl. 4:19: *ʾnt{h} hwʾ mlkʾ dy rbyt wtqpt* "it is you, O King, who grew and became strong." Dnl. 5:20, *wkdy rm lbbh wrwḥh tqpt lhzdh*, literally, "and when his heart became haughty and his spirit became emboldened to behave arrogantly," supplements the verb *tqp* with a subsequent infinitive following *l-*. Finally, the D-stem has the factitive meaning "to make strong." It appears once in Dnl. 6:8: *ʾtyʿṭw kl srky mlkwtʾ . . . lqymh qym mlkʾ wltqph ʾsr* "all the high officials of the kingdom prepared . . . to issue the royal decree and to enforce a prohibition," in the figurative sense of "to make valid, to put into force," i.e., to make legally binding.

III. Aramaic Texts from the Dead Sea. The same verbal, substantival, and adjectival uses of the root *tqp* also appear in the Aramaic texts from the Dead Sea. There, the substantive *tqp* appears frequently with the meaning "strength, might," as in 1QapGen 22:30f.: *wʾhwh lk sʿd wtqp* "I will be support and strength for you." The spelling in the construct and absolute states varies since, in addition to *tqp*, the forms *tqwp* and *twqp* also occur, e.g., 4Q531 22:3 (Book of Giants): *mt*]*gbr wbtqwp ḥyl drʿy* "[I have] demonstrated [myself as mi]ghty and through the power of the strength of my arm";[8] *twqp*, in contrast, in 1QapGen 20:14: *dbrt ʾntty mny btwqp* "my wife was taken from me by force"; which suggests a dual morphological realization of the substantive as /tqop/ and /toq(V)p/ in this phase of Aramaic. The legal documents from Naḥal Ḥever employ the substantive *tqp* with the meaning "valid document,"[9] a specialized meaning also well known from Nabatean that can be traced, as an Akkadian loan translation, to Assyrian *dannatu* "valid tablet,"[10] in which the original significance of the Akkadian root *dnn* "strength" refers figuratively to juridical power, i.e., the legal efficacy of the treaty.[11]

The adjective *tqyp* occurs with the meaning "strong," e.g., in 1QapGen 1:22: *msyr tqyp* "a strong captive."[12] In 22:31, *wʾsprk lk ltqyp* "(and I will . . .) be for you a shield against any who is stronger than you," the meaning "to overpower" shines through the adjective in a substantival usage in reference to anyone who attempts to overpower Abraham. Finally, the adjective *tqyp* also expresses the strength, i.e., the intensity of an action, e.g., 1QapGen 2:8: *ʾdyn btʾnwš ʾntty bḥlṣ tqyp ʿmy mllt* "thereupon, my wife Bettenosh spoke to me with great ferocity"; 20:10f.: *wbkyt ʾnh ʾbrm bky tqyp* "and I, Abraham, cried bitterly (literally: a strong crying)." As in Daniel (→ II), it also denotes a feeling of shakiness, as in 4Q205 2 2:29 (1 En. 89:30): *wḥzyh tqyp wrb wd*[*ḥyl*] "and its appearance was mighty and great and fearsome."[13]

The verb *tqp* in the G-stem also appears frequently in the meaning "to be/become strong," supplemented with a prepositional expression following *ʿl* "over, against someone/something," as in 11Q10 2:1 (Job 19:11): [*wtq*]*p ʿly rgzh* "[and] his wrath against me

8. Milik, 307.

9. E.g., in sales contracts such as NḤ 2:24f. in Yardeni 279: [g]*ntm hy . . . wtqp wtbt wqšm* "that [gar]den . . . and according to a valid document, a firm document, and a portion?"

10. Kaufman, 46.

11. E. Lipiński, *SAIO* I, 1975, 142 n. 4.

12. Fitzmyer, 67; Beyer, *ATTM*, 2, 89, and others read *mswr tqyp* "a strong fetter," cf. H. Gzella, review of D. A. Machiela, *The Dead Sea Genesis Apocryphon*, *BiOr* 68 (2011) 376.

13. Milik, 223.

[became st]rong";[14] 1QapGen 20:18: *wlswp trtyn šnyn tqpw wgbrw ʿlwhy mktšyʾ wngdyʾ* "and at the end of two years, the plagues and blows became more ferocious and stronger for him." In disputes, "to be strong over against someone" developed into the meaning "to conquer someone," employed transitively in 4Q203 9:4 (Book of Giants): *wkwl ṣbw lʾ tqptkh* "and nothing conquered you";[15] 1QapGen 21:25f: *wtqp mlk ʿylm . . . lmlk swdm* "but the king of Elam . . . conquered the king of Sodom."[16] Similarly, the root *tqp* occurs in the C-stem and, together with the preposition *b*-, has the meaning "to grasp, to hold, to take possession of," either literally[17] or figuratively.[18]

Kuty

14. *DJD*, XXIII (1998), 91.
15. Milik, 316.
16. With the object marked by *l*-.
17. 4Q536 7:10: *bsyp mḥsnyk ʾtqp* "with a sword, he to possession of your property" (*DJD*, XXXI [2001], 167).
18. E.g., 4Q542 1:8: *wʾtqpw bdyny ʾbrhm* "hold fast to the prescriptions of Abraham!" (*DJD*, XXXI [2001], 268).

תרע *tr*ʿ /tarʿ/; תרע *tr*ʿ /tarrāʿ/; אסף *ʾsp* /ʾasopp/; בב *bb* /bāb/; דש *dš* /dašš/

I. Etymology and Lexical Field. II. Literally "Gate." III. Figuratively "at Court." IV. Astronomically. V. "Gatekeeper."

I. Etymology and Lexical Field. Behind the Aramaic masculine /tarʿ/ "gate" hides the common Central Semitic[1] noun */θaġr/ with metathesis /ġr/ > /rġ/ and then /ġ/ > /ʿ/, and then secondarily expanded to /taraʿ/.[2] It usually denotes a large, stable external gate of a building or a city, in an expansion of the usage for the palace gate, also "at court,"[3] and in astronomical contexts the "gates of heaven."

Its literal meaning overlaps with that of /dašš/ "door, wing of a door," borrowed from

H.-J. Fabry, "*šʿr*," *ThWQ*, III, 1038-44; E. Otto, "שַׁעַר *šaʿar*," *TDOT*, XV, 359-405; S. A. Kaufman, *The Akkadian Influences on Aramaic*. *AS 19* (1974); H. P. Rüger, "Das Tor des Königs," *Bib* 50 (1968) 247-50; H. Wehr, "Das 'Tor des Königs' im Buche Esther und verwandte Ausdrücke," *Der Islam* 39 (1964) 247-60.

1. Thus, excluding Akkadian and Ethiopic.
2. *ATTM*, 108,113.
3. As in common usage in the Near East on into Ottoman times, cf. Wehr.

Assyrian *dassu*, which supplanted native Aramaic */dalt-/.[4] Imperial Aramaic sometimes employs /dašš/ in relation to private houses[5] when it denotes "door"; in juxtaposition, it obtains its specific meaning "wing of a door."[6]

Sporadically, Imperial Aramaic exhibits /bāb/, also an Akkadian loanword, for the external gate of a building,[7] which also means "post, entry" in lists, corresponding to its meaning in Late Babylonian,[8] and survived in the East Aramaic languages.[9] The interchange of /tar'/ and /bāb/ in the same expression for "palace gate" in the framework narrative of Aḥiqar[10] demonstrates the extensive degree of synonymity. The word for the gate area, /'asopp/ (> /'asop/), also arose from Akkadian;[11] it is masculine in gender and finds usage in Aramaic often in the vision of the new Jerusalem.[12] An additional Akkadian loanword from the same semantic field is /('a)skoppā/ "threshold."[13]

Finally, the masculine *nomen professionis tr'* /tarrā'/ "gatekeeper" also derives from /tar'/.

II. Literally "Gate." In the literal sense, *tr'* first occurs in a late Aramaic proverb of Aḥiqar for the gates of a city of evildoers that is abandoned to plundering,[14] i.e., injustice will be repaid. The root of the verb *yṣ'wn* is disputed; it may involve a form of *ṣ'ī* "they (the gates) bow."[15] In legal documents from Elephantine, the word refers to the outer gate of a house,[16] in the letter concerning the destruction of the local temple to its stone doors (→ I).[17] The sole instance in Biblical Aramaic with a concrete meaning (on Dnl. 2:49 → III) designates the opening—perhaps a metal hatch—of the doubtless very large fiery furnace (Dnl. 3:26).

Both nuances recur at Qumran: with around sixty specimens (including dual occurrences and fragments without context), by far more of the passages refer to the twelve city gates named for the tribes of Israel[18] in the vision of the new Jerusalem,[19] sometimes

4. As in Canaanite; Kaufman, 45.

5. *TADAE* B3.10:13; 3.11:3; 3.12:13.

6. Cf. the stone gates of the Elephantine temple with their bronze wings in *TADAE* A4.7:10f.; similarly in the description of the new Jerusalem from Qumran: 4Q554 2 3:15,17; 5Q15 1 1:9 (along with *tr'*),11,17,19.

7. *TADAE* B3.11:3f.; in A4.4:6 for a city gate; in C1.1:17.23 and partially emended in l. 9 for the palace gate.

8. Thus regularly in *TADAE* C3.28.

9. Cf. Kaufman, 40f.

10. *bb hykl'*: *TADAE* C1.1:17,23; *tr' hykl'*: l. 44.

11. From *asuppu*, Kaufman, 38.

12. *ATTM*, 519; 2, 352.

13. Kaufman, 37; later Aramaic instances in *ATTM*, 646.

14. *TADAE* C1.1:104.

15. For the discussion, cf. M. Weigl, *Die aramäischen Achikar-Sprüche aus Elephantine und die alttestamentliche Weisheitsliteratur*. *BZAW* 399 (2010), 208.

16. *TADAE* B2.1:3,12,14; 3.10:15, here in relation to *trbṣ* "court, gateway" (*DNSI*, 1229f.); 3.12:21.

17. *TADAE* A4.7:9 par. 4.8:9.

18. → *šm*.

19. 4Q554, 5Q15 and 11Q18; citations in *ATTM*, 728; 2, 505.

more precisely defined with (*ʿl*) two wings (*dšyn*; → I).[20] The word also denotes the outer gate of a house[21] and the porthole of the ark.[22] The usage for "city gate" in 11Q10 14:1 (Job 29:7) accords with the Hebrew text. On the usage as an astronomical term, → IV. For additional instances of the meaning "gate," see *DNSI*, 1233.

III. Figuratively "at Court." Occasionally, *trʿ* stands as an abbreviation of *trʿ hyklʾ* "palace gate" with *b-* in tales from the royal court *pars pro toto* for service at the court, first in the framework narrative of Aḥiqar (→ I)[23] and then in Dnl. 2:49 (*btrʿ mlkʾ*; cf. Est. 3:2f.; 5:9,13; 6:10).

IV. Astronomically. As a technical astronomical term, *trʿ*[24] means the twelve gates of the western, northern, eastern, and southern quadrants through which the winds pass,[25] as do stars[26] when they appear in the firmament. The human appeal to God also enters[27] and one accesses heaven[28] through them.

V. "Gatekeeper." The professional designation *trʿ* /tarrāʿ/ "gatekeeper" appears without a proximate context in a few Imperial Aramaic commercial ostraca from Idumea.[29] In Ezr. 7:24, it stands in the middle of a list of temple personnel exempt from taxes sorted in descending status and at Hatra in the construct state with subsequent personal names.[30]

Gzella

---

20. 5Q15 1 1:9.
21. 4Q197 4 3:3 (Tob. 7:1).
22. 1QapGen 11:1.
23. *TADAE* C1.1:44.
24. In the pl.
25. 4Q210 1 2:4f.7 (1 En. 76:5f.7); 4Q209 23:2 (1 En. 76:14).
26. 4Q209 26:2 (1 En. 79:3); often in 1 En. 73.
27. 4Q202 1 3:10 (1 En. 9:2); 4Q201 1 4:6 (1 En. 8:4).
28. 4Q213a 2:18; probably also in the fragment 1QapGen 6:25.
29. Instances in D. Schwiderski, *Die alt- und reichsaramäischen Inschriften,* vol. I: *Konkordanz. FSBP* 2 (2008), 842.
30. H292i.k.

IRANIAN OFFICIAL TITLES IN BIBLICAL ARAMAIC

According to the original plan for this dictionary, all non-Aramaic administrative terms would be assigned to an appendix. But because they were integrated morphologically, quite normally, into the Aramaic lexicon—like, e.g., /rāz/ (→ *rz*)—the new editor included them alphabetically, as a rule, and restricted the corresponding appendix to Iranian official titles that comprise a closed, small group in terms of lexical field, function, and distribution. In Aramaic, most of them begin with *aleph* and, following the alphabetic principle, should have been treated in the first fascicle. Their forms, partially corrupted in the transmission of the biblical text, have assimilated to the likely reconstruction of the form in the headings and bodies of the respective articles. This decision should limit the interruption of the alphabetic sequence to the unavoidable cases, but not separate substantively related terms. For the English translation, it was determined to be best to leave these terms in this appendix along with this more general material about the terms.

Only terms that occur in Ezra and Daniel are included; several additional titles for workers in the Persian administration on quite different levels now appear in the texts from the Bactrian archive in J. Naveh and S. Shaked, *Aramaic Documents from Ancient Bactria (Fourth Century B.C.E.)* (London, 2012), with discussions of etymology and meaning: *ʾpdyt* "chief," *ywbr* "grain vendor,"[1] *srwšy* "taskmaster,"[2] *srkr* "leader, administrator," and *ptpkn* "distribution officer" (for the allocation of rations). Among the specific terms for the various kinds of servants,[3] the Bactrian texts attest, in addition to the perhaps generic *hnškrt*, the probably specialized functions *ʾsngšn*, *ḥštrkn*, and *rytkn*, and finally for contractually obligated shepherds *wzn* "goose keeper" and *dmydtknn*, perhaps "animal keeper." They should now be added to dictionaries such as *DNSI*.

The exact function of a certain official in the Achaemenid administrative hierarchy, however, is unknown in most cases. Therefore, the use of these titles in Biblical Aramaic—in the court narratives of Daniel, which primarily employs them for a certain official coloration, more than in Ezra—are only rarely precise. Remarkably, different official designations occur in Daniel and Ezra.

W. Hinz, *Altiranisches Sprachgut der Nebenüberlieferungen. GÖF* III/3 (1975); K. Koch, *Daniel 1–4. BK* XXII/1 (2005); J. Tavernier, *Iranica in the Achaemenid Period (ca. 550-330 B.C.). OLA* 158 (2007).

1. Cf. *ywdn* in *TADAE* A4.5:5.
2. → *srwšy*.
3. → *ʿbd*; *ʿlym*.

אדרגזר *'drgzr* for */'addarzagar/

So far, the title, to be reconstructed based on Iranian **handarzakara*[1] as /'addarzagar/, occurs only in Dnl. 3:2f. where it appears with metathesis and in the plural as *ᵃdargāzᵉrayyā* in a list of dignitaries whom King Nebuchadnezzar gathered to dedicate his statue. The noun **handarza* "instruction, commission" may underlie the word; it is also known in Imperial Aramaic.[2] Suggested translations vary between "counselor," "generals," or "tax collector."[3] If one assumes a list planfully constructed and essentially ordered by descending rank, this term, following the satraps,[4] prefects of provincial administration,[5] and governors,[6] introduces a second group of high officials in internal civil service.[7] Their area of responsibility cannot be determined, however.

1. Hinz, 115.
2. *TADAE* A6.13:3f.; 6.10:12; 6.13:4,7; 6.14:3; see Tavernier, 408 §4.4.3.4.
3. Koch, 246; *ATTM*, 505: "court counselor."
4. See below at *'ḥšdrpn*.
5. → *sgn*.
6. → *pḥh*.
7. Cf. Koch, 277.

אחשדרפן *'ḥšdrpn* /'aḥšadrapān/

The best-known of the Iranian official titles is *'ḥšdrpn* /'aḥšadrapān/. It designates the satraps (**xšaθrapāna*),[1] i.e., the supreme administrators of a major Achaemenid province.[2] It appears in Imperial Aramaic in the spelling *ḥštrpn* in the Xanthos triglot.[3] Yet, the official correspondence of the Egyptian satrap Aršama and that of the Bactrian governor Achvamazda (who presumably also held the rank of satrap) do not employ the official designations *'ḥšdrpn* or *ḥštrpn*, but the honorific *mr'y* "my lord."[4]

Biblical Aramaic employs the word in Dnl. 3:2f.,27 and 6:2f.,4f.,7f. Daniel 3:2f.,7 uses it at the beginning of a long and a shorter list of royal dignitaries;[5] in Dnl. 6:2f.,4f.,7f.,

1. Tavernier, 436.
2. For the backgrounds, see B. Jacobs, *Die Satrapienverwaltung im Perserreich zur Zeit Darius' III. TAVO.B* 87 (1994).
3. *KAI* 319.4.
4. → *mr'*.
5. Regarding the possible layered structure, see above at *'drgzr*.

it denotes the 120 satraps of the empire, to whom Daniel and two other high officials (*srkyn*)[6] were subordinate. The satraps confronted Daniel together with his two colleagues as their collective opposition in the story of the lions' den since they envied the foreigner, who even had another religion, his rapid ascent (which still occurs repeatedly in such closed milieus, just as sometimes in academics) and defamed him.

6. → *srk.*

אפרסך *'prsk* /'eprasak/

In Aramaic, the term *'prsk*, following Iranian **frasaka*[1] and the vocalization of the plural *ᵃparsᵉḵāyē* in Aramaic, should probably be reconstructed as /'eprasak/; only Ezr. 5:6 and 6:6 also attest it; however, in Akkadian it occurs as *iprasakku*.[2] Most understand it as "investigative official" or "justice official."[3] In the contexts of the two Biblical Aramaic passages, it refers to the officials from the province who reported to Darius concerning the construction work on the Jerusalem temple. Their letter has the character of an official report. The word is not identical with the designation *'prstk* (see below), but the Tiberian vocalization assimilates it, hence the long *ā*; it seems like a gentilic adjective which led erroneously to a translation as the name of a people (Αφαρσαχαιοι, *Apharsacei*) in the LXX and the Vulgate.

1. Hinz, 97; Tavernier, 420f.
2. *AHw*, I, 385.
3. Cf. the suggested translations in *GesB*[18], 1469.

אפרסתך *'prstk* /'eprastāk/

Only Ezr. 4:9 attests *'prstk*, following the Iranian **frastāka*,[1] probably originally /'eprastāk/. The word refers to administrative officials in Samaria and comes after "judge"[2] and before the unknown words *ṭrply'* and *'prsy'*, which probably mean "people from Tarpel"[3]

1. Hinz, 97.
2. → *dīn.*
3. But also regarded as an official title in the past; see the literature in *GesB*[18], 1498.

and "people from Sippar."[4] At the end of the verse stand three clear ethnicities: "people from Erech, Babel, and Susa." The asyndetic addition of *ṭrply'* after the syndectic connection between *dyny'* and *'prstky'* clarifies the shift from official to population designations, not further motivated in terms of content, but the combination of these different and largely unknown terms already led in the LXX and the Vulgate to an interpretation of the plural *'prstky'* as the name of a people (Αφαρσαθαχαιοι, *Apharsathei*) and apparently influenced the vocalization of the similar-sounding *'prsk* (see above).

Because of the etymology, W. Eilers[5] thinks that the function may have involved emissaries, but the context of Ezr. 4:9 suggests only that it involves staff members of the governor of Samaria.[6] Further conclusions about the precise meaning of this evidence are not currently possible.

4. Read *spry'*; regarding this much-discussed passage, see the extensive treatment in H. G. M. Williamson, *Ezra, Nehemiah. WBC* (1985), 54f.

5. *Iranische Beamtennamen in der keilschriftlichen Überlieferung. AKM* 25,5 (1940), 30-40.

6. Cf. Hinz, 97.

הדבר *hdbr* /hadabār/

The title *hdbr* /hadabār/, attested frequently in Daniel, traces to Iranian **hadabāra*, literally "cobearer."[1] In each case, it designates dignitaries at the royal court as a body and with no more precise indication of their function: summarily in Dnl. 3:24; in 3:27 in distinction to satraps, prefects, and governers, and is thus, perhaps, an umbrella term for the high officials in inner service of 3:2f.,[2] similarly in 6:8; in 4:33, it appears along with *rbrbyn* "nobles"[3] for Nebuchadnezzar's inner circle whom he seeks out in his rehabilitation at the end of his banishment. Since, on the one hand, the *hdbryn* differ from the provincial administrators and, on the other, appear with the possessive suffix except in 6:8 (3:24; 4:33) or in the construct state with *mlk* "of the king" (3:27), they apparently denote functionaries from the king's inner circle. A more precise definition is impossible, however, and the ancient translations already rendered these terms quite differently.[4]

1. Hinz, 109.

2. See above at *'drgzr*.

3. → *rb*.

4. Cf., e.g., the Vulgate: *optimates* in 3:24 and 4:33, but *potentes* in 3:27, and *senatores* in 6:8; the Greek versions are similarly diverse.

כרוז *krwz* /krōz/

The etymology of *krwz* /krōz/ "herald" was long disputed, but it is now generally traced to Iranian **xrausa* "crier."[1] In Dnl. 3:4, it denotes the royal herald who proclaims throughout the empire the order to fall before the statue of Nebuchadnezzar. The denominal verb *krz*, in the C-stem "to cry out," serves in Dnl. 5:29 for proclaiming Daniel third in the kingdom after the decipherment of the flaming script. The noun and the verb remained part of the lexicon in post-Imperial Aramaic times;[2] in the legal diction of Nabatean contracts from the Dead Sea, the noun serves for "dispossession,"[3] and the verb in the G-stem, analogously, for "to dispossess."[4]

1. *ATTM*, 609; Koch, 247.
2. *LexSyr*, 344a.
3. nV 1:24; 42:16f.,18,31; *ATTM*, 2, 205-8,244-47.
4. nV 42:16f.

תיפת *typt* /tīpat/

According to a supposed connection with the Iranian **tīpati*,[1] *typt* /tīpat/ may designate an officer in the bodyguard or a police commander.[2] Two instances, *TADAE* A4.5:9 and Dnl. 3:2f., employ the word along with judges,[3] i.e., probably for the executive.

Gzella

1. So Tavernier, 431, with discussion of other suggestions.
2. So the traditional translation: *ATTM*, 723; *GesB*[18], 1545.
3. → *dīn*.

NUMBERS

Cardinal numbers are sometimes written out; in documentary texts such as contracts or lists, however, they are often indicated through a system based on vertical lines for the ones and horizontal lines for the tens.[1] Beginning in the first century B.C.E., letters of the alphabet also appear in this function.

The cardinal number words for "one" and "two" originated as adjectives, the higher number words are substantives. Of these, the other ones from "three" to "ten" behave in terms of gender agreement (indicated in each case in the article heading) in reverse to the gender of the thing enumerated. The tens are formed with the plural of the corresponding one with a masculine ending, "two" and "two hundred" are dual forms.[2] Independent lexemes represent "hundred" (/me'ā/), "thousand" (/'alp/) and, as the largest independent word, "ten thousand" (/rebbō/).[3]

Qatīl forms of the cardinals with the gentilic /-āy/ denote the first ten ordinals; as in many other languages, the two ordinals "first" (/qadmāy/)[4] and "second" (/tenyān/)[5] in Aramaic diverge from this pattern.

The fractions "third" to "ninth" are substantives on the *qutl* or *qatīl* paradigm.[6] For higher fractions, one employs distributive terms.[7]

The individual languages form the cardinals between "eleven" and "nineteen" through various combinations of the one with the ten, either with a syndetically appended one (e.g., *'śrh wtryn* "twelve") or with a preceding one in the construct state (thus *try 'śr*, Dnl. 4:26; Ezr. 6:17). The older Aramaic languages already attest a variation here.[8] In composite cardinals over "twenty," the elements often descend, linked syndetically with /wa-/.

Old and Imperial Aramaic attest only some of the number words[9] and reach to "thousand." In contrast, the dimensions of the vision of the new Jerusalem and of the astronomical calculations of the book of Enoch from Qumran, which write them out because of the literary character of the text, attest them in abundance. Generally, dates have cardinal numbers.

---

1. Old and Imperial Aramaic instances of signs appears in D. Schwiderski, *Die alt- und reichsaramäischen Inschriften*, vol. I: *Konkordanz. FSBP* 2 (2008), 844-905; see also F. Rosenthal, *Die aramaistische Forschung seit Theodor Nöldeke's Veröffentlichungen* (Leiden, 1939), table 5.

2. Given the spelling *'śrn* "twenty" is a plural, however, since the expected spelling of the dual would be spelled **'śryn*.

3. → *rb*.

4. → *qdm*.

5. Alternatively /'oḥrān/ "another," → *'ḥr*.

6. With the independent lexeme /palg/ for "half," → *plg*.

7. Thus, e.g., "half a seventh" for "fourteenth"; *ATTM*, 460f. gathers the relevant examples from the calculations in the astronomical book of Enoch.

8. Cf. T. Muraoka and B. Porten, *A Grammar of Egyptian Aramaic. HO* 32 (^{2}2003), 87-90.

9. They appear in concentration in *TADAE* A6.2.

1 חד(ה) *ḥd(h)* /ḥad(ā)/

The form /ḥad/, as a feminine /ḥad(ā)/ with apharesis of the first syllable from an original Semitic */ʾaḥad/ "one," is typically Aramaic. In addition to the numerical use, the cardinal number also denotes "single,"[1] negated "not one,"[2] and as a pronoun "the same"[3] or as an indefinite article,[4] in fixed expressions such as *kwl ḥd wḥd* "each individual"[5] or *ḥd ḥd* "one another," regularly in multiplicative expressions for "times,"[6] and accordingly as a distributive "each."[7] Additionally, the adverb *kḥdh* or *kḥdʾ* /kaḥadā/ "together"[8] is rather frequent, sometimes supplemented by *ʿm* "with."[9] A subsequent *lḥdh* /laḥadā/ means "very,"[10] as otherwise /śaggī/[11] often functions. The etymologically unrelated word /qadmāy/[12] constitutes the pertinent ordinal, "first."

N. Lohfink and J. Bergman, "אֶחָד *ʾechādh*," *TDOT*, I, 193-201; G. Sauer, "אֶחָד *ʾeḥād* one," *TLOT*, 78-80; M. Sprungmann and B. Schlenke, "*ʾḥd*," *ThWQ*, I, 136-41.

1. Cf. *TADAE* A4.7:29: "in a single letter."
2. *TADAE* A4.7:19.
3. Cf. 1QapGen 20:8; *pm ḥd* "from the same mouth."
4. E.g., *ṣlm ḥd* "a statue" in Dnl. 2:31; *ʿrb ḥdh* "a ship" in 4Q206 4 1:14 (1 En. 89:1), followed by the det. *ʿrbʾ* "the ship"; likewise 1QapGen 19:14; 4Q197 4 1:6 (Tob. 6:2). The situation is more complicated in Syriac, though; cf. M. Waltisberg, "Einzelheiten der syrischen Grammatik," *Mediterranean Language Review* 24 (2017) 35-84, esp. 37-52.
5. 4Q204 1 6:1 (1 En. 13:6).
6. E.g., *TADAE* A4.7:3; Dnl. 3:19.
7. As in 4Q554 2 2:21 par. 5Q15 1 1:5: "four ells per street."
8. E.g., Dnl. 2:35; 1QapGen 19:15; 21:25.
9. 1QapGen 21:21; 22:1.
10. As, e.g., in 1QapGen 20:33; 22:32.
11. → *śgī*.
12. → *qdm*; cf. 1QapGen 12:14f. for a variation between cardinal in the date and a subsequent ordinal involving the construction.

2 תרין *tryn* /terayn/, תרתין *trtyn* /tertayn/

The Aramaic word for "two" /terayn/[1] also diverges from the ground form through the shift /n/ > /r/, singular in Northwest Semitic. It preserves the old dual, however. It

---

H.-J. Fabry, "*šnym*," *ThWQ*, III, 1030-34.

1. < */θ(e)nayn/; cf. R. D. Hoberman, "Initial Consonant Clusters in Hebrew and Aramaic," *JNES* 48 (1989) 25-29, for the possibility of an initial doubled consonant.

transformed into /tar-/ sometime after 200 B.C.E.[2] Suffixed, it denotes "(we, etc.) two."[3] Furthermore, it is part of the number *try ʿśr* "twelve," that designates the months of a year, for example, (Dnl. 4:26) or the tribes of Israel (Ezr. 6:17), and in agreement with this, the twelve gates of the new Jerusalem.[4] "Second" is either /tenyān/[5] or /ʾoḥrān/ "other";[6] "half" is the unrelated noun /palg/.[7]

---

2. Cf. *ATTM*, 107.
3. E.g., 1QapGen 19:16.
4. → *trʿ*.
5. Based on the older form with /n/.
6. → *ʾḥr*.
7. → *plg*.

3 (ה)תלת *tlt(h)* /talāt(ā)/

Aramaic /talāt/ "three" arose from the common Semitic */θalāθ-/ and is therefore spelled in Old Aramaic, which still retained */θ/, with *š*, after they fused with /t/ toward the end of the Old Aramaic period,[1] then, in accordance with the pronunciation, with *t*. Sometimes, "three" refers not to a precise number, but to "a few,"[2] as in the *tlt ʿlʿyn* "three ridges" in the mouth of the second animal in Daniel's vision Dnl. 7:5,[3] perhaps also of the pharaohs who sought for Abraham,[4] similarly, the three burdened Amorites[5] and the three days spent seeking Aḥiqar.[6] "Two or three" probably has the same significance.[7] Three is the precise number of the young men in the fiery furnace (Dnl. 3:23f.), likewise the world history;[8] the highest officials in the kingdom, superior even to the satraps as their supervisors, are a triad according to Dnl. 6:3.[9]

Substantivally, the determined state of the feminine form[10] /talāttā/ means "the three," thus "the number 3," in a list[11] or in reference to the position as "number three" in the

---

H.-J. Fabry, "*šlwš*," *ThWQ*, III, 939-42.

1. *ATTM*, 99f.
2. As in the English "two or three."
3. → *ʿlʿ*.
4. 1QapGen 19:24.
5. 1QapGen 21:21; cf. 22:23.
6. *TADAE* C1.1:39.
7. 4Q201 1 2:6 par. 4Q204 1 1:25 (1 En. 3:1), of years.
8. → *qrn*.
9. → *srk*.
10. I.e., with a masc. reference.
11. *TADAE* C1.1:187.

empire offered to Daniel (Dnl. 5:16,29), for which, however, the synonymous ordinal /talītāy/ can stand, even in the same text (Dnl. 5:7). Just as Dnl. 4:26 mentions "twelve months" instead of "one year," Dnl. 6:8,13 mentions "thirty days" (the period in which no one may direct a request to a god or person except the king).

4 ארבע(ה) *ʾrbʿ(h)* /ʾarbaʿ(ā)/

In Aramaic, the cardinal number /ʾarbaʿ/ "four," as in other Semitic languages, suitably retains its quadriradical ground form, while derived formations like the ordinal /rabīʿāy/ "fourth," the fraction /robʿ/ "fourth"[1] and various other forms such as the noun /marabbaʿ/ "quadrant"[2] with the loss of the first radical, then assimilated to the triconsonantal scheme dominant in the formation of words.

"Four" symbolizes completion, as the four directions[3] visibly express. Their designations vary: /garbǣ/,[4] /ʿellāy/[5] or /śamʾāl/[6] for "north"; /taḥtāy/[7] for "south"; /maʿrab/ "west";[8] and /madnaḥ/[9] or /mawʿǣ/[10] "east"; beginning with Qumran, also the Hebrew loanwords /ṣeppōn/ "north,"[11] /darōm/ "south,"[12] and /qadīm/ "east."[13]

In addition to space, vision reports also divide world history into four (ever more barbarous) empires until the dawn of the final judgment and the beginning of the kingdom of God: in Nebuchadnezzar's dream of the statue of four metals (Dnl. 2:31-35),[14] in Daniel's vision of the four monsters from the sea (Dnl. 7:1-28),[15] and in a fragmentarily preserved allegory of four trees from Qumran[16] that seems to combine motifs from Dnl. 2 and 7. For the other instances from Qumran, see Fabry, "*ʾrbʿ*," 281-83.

H.-J. Fabry, "*ʾrbʿ*," *ThWQ*, I, 277-83; idem, "*rbyʿy*," *ThWQ*, III, 604-6.

1. In Imperial Aramaic, very often as currency "quarter shekel," abbreviatred *r*, later "quarter sela"; cf. *ATTM*, 2, 354 regarding the change of the unit of weight.
2. 4Q554 2 2:13; 5Q15 1 2:5.
3. → *rwḥ*; *šmyn*.
4. 4Q210 1 2:6 (1 En. 76:6).
5. Lit. "above," → *ʿly* III.1.
6. Lit. "left"; 1QapGen 21:8; 22:10; 4Q210 1 2:1 (1 En. 76:3); 4Q554 2 3:20 par. 5Q15 1 2:2.
7. Lit. "below," → *ʿly* III.1.
8. Toward the sunset; e.g., *TADAE* A4.1:7; 1QapGen 17:8,10; 21:9.
9. Toward the sunset; e.g., *TADAE* B3.7:7; 1QapGen 21:9,12,16f.,20.
10. Frequent, especially in descriptions of real estate from Elephantine, e.g., *TADAE* B2.3:4f.
11. 1QapGen 16:10, etc.
12. E.g., 1QapGen 17:12.
13. 4Q210 1 2:4 (1 En. 76:5).
14. → *dhb* II.
15. → *gp*.
16. 4Q552-553.

5 (ה)חמש *ḥmš*(*h*) /ḥameš(ā)/

The Aramaic word /ḥameš/ "five" arose from an older */ḫameš/.[1] Five is the number of the sons and daughters of Noah;[2] five years pass from the planting of a vineyard to his first "wine festival" (12:15); for the same period, Sarah hid in Egypt until pharaoh's emissary sought Abraham's hospitality.[3] Several dimensions in the vision of the new Jerusalem are multiples of five.[4] "Five" does not occur in Biblical Aramaic.

H.-J. Fabry, "*ḥmš*," *ThWQ*, I, 1009-15.

1. In Syriac the masc. form *ḥammeš* became fem. *ḥamšā*, assimilating the syllable structure for the neighboring /'arba'/, /'arb'ā/ "four"; cf. W. Diem, "Syrische Kleinigkeiten," in *Studia Semitica necnon Iranica. FS R. Macuch* (Wiesbaden, 1989), 67-72.
2. 1QapGen 12,11.
3. 1QapGen 19:23.
4. 4Q554 1 1:12,15; 5Q15 1 2:6; cf. Fabry, 1015.

6 (ה)שת *št*(*h*) /šett(ā)/

The common Semitic */šedθ/ "six" became /šett/ (> /šet/) in Aramaic. No special usages are known, although the plural /šettīn/ occurs for the height in the dimensions of the statue of Nebuchadnezzar in Dnl. 3:1 (width six ells) and of the Jerusalem temple in Ezr. 6:3 (twenty ells wide). In Syriac, the feminine (*štā*) determined state assimilated to biradical nouns.[1]

---

1. A. Spitaler, "Das Femininum des Zahlworts für *zwei* im Hebräischen und für *sechs* im Syrischen," in *Semitic Studies. FS W. Leslau* (Wiesbaden, 1991), 2, 1497f.

7 (ה)שבע *šb'*(*h*) /šab'(ā)/

Originally, the Semitic word /šab'/ "seven"[1] is a *qatl* form that transformed in a few Aramaic languages into *qitl* (as in the Biblical Aramaic vocalization) or *qutl*

H.-J. Fabry and C. Stettler, "*šb'*," *ThWQ*, III, 823-32; E. Otto, "שֶׁבַע *šeḇa'*," *TDOT*, XIV, 336-67.

1. > /šaba'/.

forms.[2] While "four" symbolizes completion, "seven" represents a long time or a large amount. Both nuances already appear in stereotypical Old Aramaic curse formulas: whoever falls under the ban, famine will dominate his land for seven years[3] and not even a maximal commitment of seven cows, ewes, or wet nurses will satisfy a nursling.[4]

Nebuchadnezzar's seven-year period of penance stands in the same tradition (Dnl. 4:13,20,22,29)[5] as does his command, issued in anger, to heat the fiery oven seven times (*ḥaḏ šiḇʿā*) hotter than usual (Dnl. 3:19); the excess (*yattīrā* "very strong") is also evident in the fact that a darting flame killed the executioner's assistants (3:22). Similarly at Qumran, Abraham lived seven years in Egypt;[6] the demon in love with Tobias's bride Sarah murdered seven of her fiancés;[7] in the apocalypse of ten weeks, the "witnesses of the truth" are to receive seven-fold wisdom and knowledge.[8] Other heptads may also have symbolic significance: Ezr. 7:14 mentions "seven counsels" in the king's letter to Ezra; 4Q550 1:5 mentions a scroll of Darius sealed with seven seals. An observation of nature notes the seven delta distributaries of the Nile.[9] The seven days of the week[10] in the Jewish division of time begin with Sunday as the first day; the astronomical book of Enoch calculates the lunar phases by sevenths and fourteenths.[11]

"Seventy" intensifies the concept even more: the Tell Dan inscription, with its propagandistic rhetoric, mentions seven kings as a very high number of enemies;[12] the fallen angels will be fettered for seventy generations[13] until judgment,[14] thus a long time, difficult to conceive.

2. *ATTM*, 700.
3. *KAI* 320.12; 222 A 27; 223 A 5.
4. *KAI* 320.5f.,7; 222 A 22f., cf. 24; 223 A 1. *KAI* 309 has "100" in this formula.
5. Here *ʿiddānīn* "times," → *ʿdn* III; cf. 4Q242 1-3:3,7.
6. 1QapGen 22:28.
7. 4Q196 6:12 (Tob. 3:15).
8. 4Q212 1 4:3 (1 En. 93:10).
9. 1QapGen 19:12.
10. → *šnh* IV.
11. 4Q209 1 1:3; 7 2:11.
12. *KAI* 310.5f.
13. → *dūr* III.1, because of the *d*[before the lacuna, a rather certain emendation.
14. 4Q202 1 4:10 (1 En. 10:12).

8 תמנה *tmnh* /tamānæ/, תמניה *tmnyh* /tamāniyā/

In Aramaic, the foundational */θamānī/ "eight" appears as /tamānæ/ as a result of the fusion of /θ/ and /t/ at the end of the Old Aramaic period. According to the ten weeks apocalypse in the book of Enoch, the eighth week (/tamīnāy/)[1] is the one in which the evildoers will be delivered to the true ones for judgment.[2] Otherwise, ancient times yield no remarkable usages.

1. From */tamīniyāy/: *ATTM*, 725.
2. 4Q212 1 4:15 (1 En. 91:12).

9 תשע(ה) *tš'(h)* /teš'(ā)/

"Nine" occurs so rarely that it first appears only at Qumran. Besides the possible indications of dimensions and time, it denotes the "nine mountains" of which the archangel Michael reports in prehistorical conversation.[1]

1. 4Q529 1:3, extremely fragmentary.

10 עשר(ה) *'śr(h)* /'aśr/, /'aśarā/

Common Semitic /'aśr/,[1] before or after the ones, forms the numbers "11" to "19," in the plural "20." Otherwise, it appears sporadically: in reference to the ten horns of Dnl. 7:7,20,24,[2] the ten jubilees from Noah's birth to the flood,[3] and Abraham's ten-year wandering.[4] The verb *'śr* (pael) "to tithe"[5] derives from it.

H.-J. Fabry, "*'śr*," *ThWQ*, III, 233-40; R. North, "עֶשֶׂר *'eśer*," *TDOT*, XI, 404-9.

1. In Aramaic later > /'aśar/.
2. → *qrn.*
3. 1QapGen 6:10; 500 years after Gen. 5:32.
4. 1QapGen 22:27.
5. 4Q213b 1:4f.; cf. "to give a tenth" in 1QapGen 22:17.

100 מאה *m'h* /me'ā/

The feminine *m'h* /me'ā/ "hundred" is common Semitic and, except as the basis of the hundreds,[1] rare. In the curse formula *KAI* 309.20-22 it constitutes a variant for "seven" (see above); in Ezr. 6:17 it refers to the sacrifices to dedicate the temple (e.g., 100 steers, 200 rams).

B. Ziemer, "*m'h*," *ThWQ*, II, 545-53.

1. Counted with the ones: *tlt m'h* "300," etc., in the dual for "200."

1000 אלף *'lp* /'alp/

Masculine *'lp* /'alp/,[1] rare in Aramaic, denotes a large quantity: the seed disseminated for naught in *KAI* 309.19; members of Belshazzar's court in Dnl. 5:1; and the thousand times a thousand righteous ones in 7:10,[2] taken up in 4Q530 2 2+6-12:17.

Gzella

J. Duhaime, "*'lp*," *ThWQ*, I, 197-200.

1. > /'aləp/.
2. → *rb*.

HISTORICAL OUTLINE OF ARAMAIC GRAMMAR

The depiction of the linguistic data in the dictionary strives for a higher historical precision than in the typical grammars and lexica, which are mostly purely descriptive. Consequently, a brief outline should clarify the preliminary decisions made here (especially in phonetics and the reconstruction of the pronunciation of Imperial Aramaic based on them). At the same time, it introduces the foundations of Aramaic accidence and morphological syntax by disclosing very succinctly the linguistic terminology employed (as in reference to verbal forms and stems that play an important role for the differences of meaning throughout the individual articles) and the associated determinations of function. It is intended as a mere supplement to the textbooks in use: the definitive reference grammar for Biblical Aramaic continues to be *BLA*; as an introduction, the basically synchronic (and diachronically not always entirely accurate) presentation by F. Rosenthal, *A Grammar of Biblical Aramaic. PLO* 5 (^{7}2006), continues to be useful. To date, there is no modern scientific reference grammar of Old or Imperial Aramaic. For a start, see H. Gzella, "Language and Script," in H. Niehr, ed., *The Aramaeans in Ancient Syria. HO* 106 (2014), 71-107, for Old Aramaic, and idem, "Imperial Aramaic," in S. Weninger, ed., *The Semitic Languages* (New York, 2011), 574-86, for Imperial Aramaic.

1. Script and Spelling

With the shift in the scribal culture of Syria-Palestine from the cuneiform to the alphabetic script shortly after 1000 B.C.E., this new system spread from the Phoenicians also among the Arameans. Twenty-two letters served to notate the significantly different consonants; *plene* spellings with "vowel letters" (*matres lectionis*) also increasingly indicate long vowels, at first primarily at the end, later increasingly also internal to the word.[3] In post-Achaemenid times, e.g., at Qumran, such vowel letters also indicated short vowels in certain cases. The orthography of official texts, royal inscriptions, legal and commercial documents, as well as formal letters was firmly normed already from the beginning and became even more firmly unified in the Achaemenid chancellery. Texts at larger distances from such chancellery traditions (such as private letters) sometimes exhibit a less conventional and more phonetic spelling, but, in pre-Christian times, as a whole oriented around the administrative and literary diction prevalent at the time; see A. Millard, "The Alphabet," in H. Gzella, ed., *Languages from the World of the Bible* (New York, 2011), 14-27.

2. Phonology

The transmitted form of Biblical Aramaic texts stands under the influence of later linguistic developments, either through revisions leading to the final redaction (in the case of the book of Daniel ca. 165 B.C.E.) or through the altered pronunciation that rests on the pointing of the established synagogal recitation. If one wishes to position Biblical Aramaic in its historical context—that is, the Imperial Aramaic scribal tradition—it is advisable to establish the pronunciation of Achaemenid Imperial Aramaic of ca. 500

3. I.e., *w* for /ū/ (and later /ō/), *y* for /ī/ (and later /ē/), and *h* for /ā/ and /ǣ/.

B.C.E. as the common starting point, i.e., around the time when Imperial Aramaic arose as the binding standard. With no fixed vocalization, its pronunciation can only be approximated, but can be delimited through a combination of *plene* spellings, transcriptions in other alphabets, later vocalization traditions,[4] and comparative historical Semitics. Such a reconstruction creates a common framework for biblical and extrabiblical texts and is always indicated in the lemma headings. In this regard, the forward slashes (/. . ./) signify a "phonemic" abstraction, i.e., they indicate only the pure sounds that distinguish meaning (phonemes) without consideration for further variations in the actual pronunciation (allophones).

The oldest witnesses to the Aramaic language display twenty-seven consonants. One can group them by articulation point and manner as follows: the vocalic laryngeal /ʾ/[5] and its voiceless counterpart /h/, similarly the pharyngeal /ʿ/[6] and /ḥ/,[7] the velars /g/ and /k/, the sibilants /z/ and /s/,[8] the dentals /d/ and /t/, the interdentals /δ/[9] and /θ/,[10] the bilabials /b/ and /p/, the palatovelar /š/,[11] the lateral /ś/,[12] and a sound based on Semitic */ṣ́/, which was probably originally pronounced like /q/; furthermore, the "emphatic" counterparts of the voiceless velar, sibilant, dental, and interdental, thus /q/, /ṣ/, /ṭ/ and /θ̣/, whose pronunciation changed in the course of time from the /ʾ/-off glide (glottalization) to the /ʿ/-off glide (pharyngealization) or, as far as /q/ is concerned, velarization;[13] finally the lateral /l/, the "tongue"-/r/,[14] the dento-nasal /n/ and the bilabio-nasal /m/, and the semi-vowels /w/[15] and /y/. These distinctions are certain and can be demonstrated directly from Aramaic spellings; sometimes an additional distinction is made between /ḥ/ and /ḫ/[16] and between /ʿ/ and /ġ/,[17] although both are consistently spelled with *ḥ* and ʿ, respectively. The transcriptions of Aramaic do not take account of /ḫ/ and /ġ/, but the etymological derivations do. All of the consonants, even the laryngeals and pharyngeals (gutturals), could be lengthened, i.e., they were articulated longer between beginning and silence (traditionally, but imprecisely, called gemination). As phonemic vowels, short /a/, /e/ (from a Semitic */i/), and /o/ (from a Semitic */u/), long /ā/, /ī/, /ū/, and /ǣ/ (pronounced like a long *ä*, arisen secondarily from a final /-ī/),[18] and the semi-vowels /aw/ and /ay/ are directly, or at least indirectly, demonstrable.

---

4. Excluding secondary alterations such as, especially, the loss of unaccented short vowels in open syllables.
5. Glottal stop.
6. Laryngeal spirant.
7. Guttural *h*, as in the pronunciation roughly between *h* and German *ch* as in "ach!"
8. Perhaps still pronounced with a dental projection, i.e., /ᵈz/ and /ᵗs/.
9. As in English *this*.
10. English *thin*.
11. Like *sh* in English "ship."
12. Whose original pronunciation may have sounded like the hissing of a goose.
13. I.e., with elevation of the back part of the tongue against the palate.
14. Probably "rolled," i.e., pronounced as in Italian.
15. As in English *water*.
16. As between German "Loch" or "ach."
17. Spirantized *g*, as, e.g., in Modern Greek or Standard Dutch; see *ATTM*, 101f.
18. Cf. *ATTM*, 97.

Since the Phoenician alphabet adopted by the Arameans has only twenty-two different letters (here transliterated in italics), a few of them served in Old Aramaic to indicate multiple consonants: *š* for /š/, /ś/, and mostly /θ/,[19] *z* for /z/ and /δ/, *ṣ* for /ṣ/ and /θ̣/, and *q* for /q/ and the Aramaic counterpart of */ṣ́/.[20]

Between Old Aramaic and Achaemenid Imperial Aramaic, certain variations in spelling and sometimes transcription of different pronunciation changes are identifiable: undisputed is the fusion of the interdentals /θ/, /δ/, and /θ̣/ with the corresponding dentals /t/, /d/, and /ṭ/ prior to circa 700 B.C.E., since they are then spelled mostly with *t*, *d*, and *ṭ*,[21] and ca. 650 B.C.E. that of */ṣ́/ with /ʿ/, represented in spelling with ʿ instead of the older *q*.[22] Especially for the old */δ/ in the very frequent demonstrative pronoun and the relative particle, however, the historical spelling with *z* persisted on into post-Achaemenid times, thus *znh* for /denā/[23] and *zy* for /dī/ "that."[24] In Biblical Aramaic the phonetic spelling has been put into effect, consequently only *dnh* and *dy* appear there.

The first case of the loss of the syllable closing /ʾ/ with the lengthening of a preceding short vowel[25] may well have been even earlier. It led to the fusion of verbs III-ʾ[26] with verbs III-*ī*.[27] Because some historical spellings of corresponding forms with ʾ persisted for a long time, however, and phonetic spellings with *h* appear more frequently only beginning ca. 600 B.C.E.,[28] the precise window in time for the change remains uncertain. The lemma heading will indicate the original form of the root for these verbs.

Furthermore, Old Aramaic times probably also already saw the beginning of the shift from /h/ to /ʾ/ for the prefix of the C-stem, first in the imperfect with the loss of /-h-/ between vowels, then analogously, also at the beginning of the perfect and the imperative (/ha-/ > /ʾa-/), whereby the haphel became an aphel.[29] Historical spellings preserve forms with the etymological *h*, however. It cannot be ruled out that a monophthongization of /aw/ and /ay/ to /ō/ and /ē/, respectively, took place already at this time in parts of the language.[30]

Transcriptions of personal names in cuneiform suggest the beginning of two further developments around 500 B.C.E., the dissimilation of /a/ to /e/ in the prefix of the G-stem imperfect, first before the thematic vowel /a/[31] and the anaptyxis (syllable expansion) of a double consonant (i.e., two different consonants, not a long,

19. In contrast, the Tell Fekheriye inscription has *s* for /θ/.

20. Regarding *ḥ* as a possible representation also of /ḫ/ and ʿ also of /ġ/ see above.

21. *ATTM*, 100f.

22. H. Gzella, *A Cultural History of Aramaic. HO* 111 (2015), 38f.; formerly dated to ca. 600 B.C.E.

23. From */δenā/.

24. From */δī/.

25. With the typical Aramaic */-aʾ/ > /-ē/ (*ATTM*, 138: /-ǣ/).

26. I.e., with /ʾ/ as the third radical.

27. Ending in a vowel; *ATTM*, 104-6 dates this between the ninth and eighth century B.C.E.

28. Which probably also had to do with the beginning of a rather slow expansion of a less standardized orthography such as in private letters.

29. *ATTM*, 148.

30. Contra *ATTM*, 116-20.

31. I.e., the first step of the "Barth-Ginsberg law," *ATTM*, 109f.

or "geminate," consonant) at the end of a word with a helping vowel (ə) that then became a full vowel.[32] In post-Achaemenid times, because of the increasing use of vowel letters for short vowels, both developments become evident and also appear in the pointing of Biblical Aramaic. The lemma headings transcribe nouns[33] without the inserted vowel, although the section concerning etymology and form will refer to the phenomenon in relevant cases.

In contrast, the degeminating spelling characteristic of Imperial Aramaic[34] is probably not a phonetic, but an orthographic development: as in the other Semitic languages of Syria-Palestine, Aramaic also typically assimilates /n/ in the contact position.[35] In Achaemenid spelling, then, such long consonants appear with a prefixed *n*[36] that persisted for a period in post-Achaemenid times under the influence of the Imperial Aramaic chancellery tradition and also occurs in Biblical Aramaic.[37] The variation in spellings without *n* and the rapid extinction of this peculiarity with the erosion of Achaemenid orthography point, however, to a purely graphic peculiarity and not to a nasalized pronunciation. Therefore, the transliteration in the lemma headings employ a spelling with *n* and the reconstructed vocalization will assume assimilation.[38]

Even after the fall of the Achaemenid Empire, Aramaic remained the vernacular in large parts of Syria-Palestine and Mesopotamia so that it, under the surface of the Aramaic literary languages of the Greco-Roman period that still followed Achaemenid conventions, changed throughout the region where it was dispersed. The first reliably post-Achaemenid developments, which also underlie the pointing of Biblical Aramaic, but partly, however, continue older processes, are the expansion of the prefix vowel /e/ in the G-stem imperfect with all thematic vowels[39] and a regular separating vowel with previously word-ending double consonants.[40]

With a few additional phonetic changes, first evident in the post-Achaemenid period and therefore not considered in the reconstruction, Aramaic approaches its Tiberian form: ca. 200 B.C.E. /e/ before a root-ending /h/, /ḥ/, /ʿ/, or /r/ was generally assimilated with /a/,[41] before sibilants sometimes conversely /a/ > /e/,[42] and the monophthongizations /aw/ > /ō/ and /ay/ > /ē/ were finalized;[43] they may have already begun in some varieties even earlier. Furthermore, in the same period, long final consonants became short[44]

32. *ATTM*, 112.

33. Such as the *qatl*, *qitl*, and *qutl* paradigms.

34. Also called dissimilation of geminates.

35. Thus, e.g., /ʾáttā/ "you" from */ʾanta/, spelled *ʾt* in Old Aramaic; exceptions arise with /ḥ/ as in *mhnḥt* /mohanḥet/ "one who brings down" in *KAI* 309:2; → *nḥt*.

36. Like *ʾnt* "you."

37. *ATTM*, 89-95.

38. Like → *ḥnṭh* /ḥeṭṭā/ "wheat."

39. *ATTM*, 110f.

40. *ATTM*, 113-15; consequently, Biblical Aramaic also has segholates.

41. *ATTM*, 107f.

42. *ATTM*, 115f.

43. *ATTM*, 116-20.

44. → *gw*; *ATTM*, 120-22.

and the fusion of */ś/ with /s/, a process that probably did not follow a straight line of development, was finalized.[45] After 150 B.C.E., /ʾ/, /ʿ/, and /r/, even in internal positions, were no longer elongated, whereupon preceding vowels were mostly lengthened compensatorily.[46] Then, unaccented final vowels dropped out of spoken Aramaic,[47] but were partially retained in the traditional recitation of Biblical Aramaic, etc. and are therefore supplied with vowel signs there.[48] Furthermore, stops, already aspirated somewhat earlier in a weak articulation,[49] developed fricative allophones so that a *daghesh* marks plosive pronunciations of /b, g, d, k, p, t/ in Biblical Aramaic.[50] If /ḥ, ḫ/ and /ʿ, ġ/ were once still differentiated, they now fused together.

Even later, namely ca. 250 C.E., the loss of short, unaccented vowels in open syllables was finalized.[51] Only thereby did the Aramaic of the vocalized traditions acquire its characteristic phonetic form in comparison, e.g, to Hebrew or Arabic.

Finally, Biblical Aramaic pointing reflects a few even later changes: /-ūn/ > /-ōn/ with a suffix,[52] as in all Aramaic, and the diminishment of /e/ > /i/ and /o/ > /u/,[53] so that, e.g., the imperfect preformative here, contrary to the older Aramaic vocalization, is pointed *yi-*; in addition, /a/ > /e/ in closed, unaccented syllables.[54]

The accent falls mostly on the last syllable, although the evidence of individual languages is complicated by stress shifts.[55] Isolated pausal forms in Biblical Aramaic[56] were transferred from Hebrew and not original, nor, presumably, are sporadic cases of compensatory lengthening instead of the reduction of unaccented short vowels in open syllables.[57] Similarly, compensatory lengthening before internal, reduced /ʿ/ was often not executed.[58] The Tiberian pointing of Biblical Aramaic is thus even more heterogenous than that of Biblical Hebrew. Some fragments of the book of Daniel from Qumran are closer, however, to Imperial Aramaic spelling than to MT.

3. Morphology and Morphosyntax

The independent personal pronouns serve, as in other Semitic languages, to designate the subject in nominal clauses or for emphasis (in contrasts, for example: "I, however, . . .") in verbal clauses:

45. → *šmš* /šamš/; *ATTM*, 102f.
46. *ATTM*, 122.
47. *ATTM*, 122-25.
48. *ATTM*, 124f.
49. I.e., generally after a vowel.
50. *ATTM*, 125-28.
51. *ATTM*, 128-36.
52. According to *ATTM*, 136 ca. 400 C.E.
53. *ATTM*, 138-40: 7th-8th cent. C.E.
54. *ATTM*, 140f.
55. *ATTM*, 142-47.
56. Such as *ḥāyil* in Dnl. 3:4; Ezr. 4:23; → *ḥyl*.
57. E.g., *mārīm* "he raised" [→ *rīm*] in Dnl. 5:19.
58. Cf. *BLA*, §40g.

	Singular	**Plural**
first-person	*'nh* /'anā/ "I"	*'nḥn(h)* /'anáḥnā/ "we"
second-person masculine	*'nt* /'áttā/"you"	*'ntm* /'attūm/ "you"
second-person feminine	*'nty* /'áttī/ "you"	(*/'attenn/ "you")
third-person masculine	*hw* /hū/ "he"	*hm(w)* /hóm(ū)/ "they"
third-person feminine	*hy* /hī/ "she"	*hny* /hénnī/ "they"

Imperial Aramaic orthography spells the forms of the second person with *n*.[59] The same is true for Bibical Aramaic, where, however, *'nt(h)* is pointed *'ant* and was at least originally pronounced /'at/,[60] since /n/ regularly assimilates with following consonants and */'ant/ is unlikely. Imperial Aramaic differentiates in the third-person singular between *hw* and *hy*, while Old Aramaic has the spelling *h'* for both forms. In Biblical Aramaic, probably under Hebrew influence, the two appear graphically as *hw'* and *hy'*. Daniel has for the second- and third-person of the masculine plural, both of pronouns and the perfect endings (see below), /-n/ instead of /-m/ (*'attūn* in 2:8), like later phases of Aramaic, but also already in private letters from Hermopolis. In the vocalization of the same forms, the /e/ of the feminine is transferred to the masculine and diminished to /i/,[61] thus *himmō(n)* (Ezr. 5:4 *'innūn*). The unaccented final /-ā/ of the second-person masculine singular fell away in post-Imperial Aramaic,[62] but the /-ū/ of the third-person masculine plural was preserved because of the shift of accent to the ultima and, in Daniel, supplemented with /-n/. The third-person masculine plural appears in Biblical Aramaic as *'innīn* (Dnl. 7:17); Old and Imperial Aramaic do not yet attest the second-person feminine plural reconstructed from later evidence.

The demonstratives are *znh* /dénā/,[63] *z'* /dā/, and *'l(h)/'ln/*'ellǣ(n)/ "this/these" (masculine and feminine singular, common plural) and analogously *zk* /dek/, *zk* /dāk/, and *'lk* /'ellǣk/ "that/those";[64] /d/ here traces back to */δ/ and, in these frequent forms, is also spelled with *z* in Imperial Aramaic, as is also the relative particle *zy* /dī/. Meanwhile, Biblical Aramaic consistently has phonetic spellings with *d* and used, as already in Old Aramaic, the independent personal pronoun of the third person for the distant deixis "that" (Dnl. 2:32,44). The interrogatives are *mn* /man/ "who?" and *mh* /mā/ "what/?" Indefinite expressions often have *gbr* /gabar/ "someone"[65] and, beginning with the letters from Hermopolis, *mnd'm* /medde'm/ "something."[66]

Nominals, including the adjective, inflect according to gender (m/f), number (sg., pl., and remnants of the dual), and state (abs., det., const.), although not every feminine is

59. Old Aramaic attests only *'t* for the 2ms.

60. I.e., with a simplified /-t/ at the end (→ 2) and on analogy with the plural articulated as a plosive, as in Syriac.

61. Cf. *ATTM*, 138-40.

62. *ATTM*, 122-25.

63. Rarely spelled *dnh*, *zn(')* or *dn(')*.

64. With the by-forms *znk* or *zkm*/*dkm*, *zky* and *'lky*, Biblical Aramaic *dikkēn*.

65. → *gbr*.

66. → *yd'*.

externally marked, and sometimes the singular and the plural differ in gender (this will be indicated for the lemmata concerned). Individual attempts to identify the remnants of a productive case inflection in Aramiac have failed. Endings mark the three other dimensions:

	Singular	**Plural**	**Dual**
masculine absolute	/-Ø/	-(*y*)*n* /-īn/	/-ayn/
masculine construct	/-Ø/	-*y* /-ay/ (>/-ē/)	= pl.
masculine determined	-*ʾ* /-ā/ (<*/-āʾ/)	-*yʾ* /-ayyā/ (<*/-ayyāʾ/)	= pl.
feminine absolute	-*h* /-ā/ (<*/-at/)	-*n* /-ān/	/-tayn/
feminine construct	-*t* /-at/	-*t* /-āt/	/-tay/
feminine determined	-*tʾ* /-tā/ (<*/-tāʾ/)	-*tʾ* /-ātā/ (<*/-ātāʾ/)	-

For forms of the determined state, a phonetic spelling with *h* sometimes appears as early as Old Aramaic instead of the historical spelling with *ʾ*. The dual survives for the numbers "two" and "two hundred" and for natural pairs such as body parts. A few nominals employed adverbially preserve the old feminine ending */-at/, such as, e.g., *qblt* "as a complaint,"[67] *rḥmt* "voluntarily," (often),[68] or *ʾntt* "for the woman,"[69] perhaps through analogy with adverbs ending in /-īt/ and /-ūt/. The absolute state is the unmarked nominal that appears both in expressions of number and totality and as predicative adjectives, and is always cited in the lemma headings; the construct denotes a genitive relationship with the following word and can be paraphrased through *dy*; the determined state indicates the greatest degree of definiteness and, beginning in post-Christian East Aramaic, replaces the absolute state as the naming form. Gentilic adjectives with the ending /-āy/ (like names of nations) form the plural of the determined state with /-ǣ/ instead of /-ayyā/, which becomes the typical plural ending in East Aramaic. Nominals of the form *qatl*, *qitl*, and *qutl* probably have a two syllable plural basis /qVtal-/.

In addition to this type, very frequent in all Semitic languages, Aramaic also knows many further nominal forms with and without external augmentation.[70] Some of them are firmly associated with definite meanings, such as *qattīl* for adjectives[71] or *qattāl* for professional designations,[72] those with the prefix /ma-/[73] often for a location.[74]

Nominals of various paradigms exhibit a few peculiarities in inflection: feminines with the original endings */-āt/, */-īt/, and */-ūt/ lose the /-t/ in the absolute state in Aramaic, but retain the long vowel so that, in such cases, the naming form indicated is, e.g., /malkū/ (< */malkūt/) "kingdom." In the plural, meanwhile, the ending vowel extends

67. *TADAE* A6.8:3; → *qbl.*
68. → *rḥm.*
69. *TADAE* B3.8:22.
70. For an overview see *ATTM*, 425-45.
71. E.g., /ḥakkīm/ "wise," → *ḥkm.*
72. Such as /tarrāʿ/ "gatekeeper," → *trʿ.*
73. Later > /mi-/, as in Biblical Aramaic pointing.
74. Like /maškab/ "bed," → *škb.*

to a triphthong before vocalic endings, as with /-ā/ absolute /-awān/, construct /-awāt/, determined /-awātā/; with /-ī/ analogously /-iyān/, /-iyāt/, /-iyātā/; with /-ū/ then /-uwān/, /-uwāt/, /-uwātā/.[75] The nominals with */-ī/ (Aramaic > /-ǣ/) behave similarly, like e.g., the participles of roots III-*ī*: for the masculine in the singular absolute and construct /-ǣ/, determined /-iyā/, in the plural absolute /-ayn/, construct /-ay/, determined /-ayyā/; for the feminine singular absolute /-iyā/, construct /-iyat/, determined /-ītā/, for the plural absolute /-iyān/, construct /-iyāt/, determined /-iyātā/. Other individual nominals manifest additional peculiarities: /bayt/ "house"[76] behaves, at a no longer precisely definable moment, in the singular absolute like a feminine ending in a long vowel and /-t/, thus /bay/ (det. /baytā/), and in the determined state of the plural has the determined plural /bāttayyā/; /'ettā/ "woman"[77] takes the suppletive basis /nešīn/ for the plural;[78] /bar/ "son"[79] retains in the plural basis /ban-/ the old /n/; and, once again, others expand a biconsonantal basis with an extension like /'ab/ "father"[80] to /'abah-/ or reduplication like /rabb/[81] to /rabrab-/. For /'ab/ "father," /'aḥ/ "brother",[82] and /ḥam/ "father-in-law,"[83] forms with suffixes beginning with consonants (see below) preserve an old const. in /-ū/. Sporadic instances of the plural ending /-īm/ for the masculine absolute in Biblical Aramaic (Dnl. 4:14; 7:10; Ezr. 4:13) and at Qumran are Hebraisms. Akkadian, Iranian, Greek, and other loanwords are incorporated in differing degrees into the Aramaic inflection of nominals.

Pronominal suffixes can be added to the construct of a noun to indicate a possessive relationship ("my," "your," etc.), to prepositions for an adverbial relationship with a pronominal element ("as for you," "with us"), and to verbs for a pronominal direct object ("they wrote it," "I saw him," etc.). With a nominal basis ending with a consonant, as is generally the case in the masculine singular[84] and in the entire feminine, a linking vowel appears before a suffix beginning with a consonant[85] whose value seems essentially to correspond to that of the original vowel of the pertinent suffix:

	Singular	**Plural**
first-person	*-y* /-ī/	*-n(')* /-ánā/
second-person masculine	*-k* /-ák(ā)/	*-km*/*kn* /-okūm, -okūn/
second-person feminine	*-ky* /-ék(ī)/	*-kn* /-ekenn/
third-person masculine	*-h* /-eh/	*-h(w)m*/*hwn* /-ohūm, -ohūn/
third-person feminine	*-h(h)* /-áh(ā)/	*-hn* /-ehenn/

75. Cf. Biblical Aramaic const. *malḵwāṯ*, det. *malḵwāṯā*.
76. → *byt*.
77. → *'nth*.
78. In *KAI* 309.22f., in contrast, /nešawān/.
79. → *br*.
80. → *'b*.
81. → *rb*.
82. → *'ḥ*.
83. First attested in the post-Achaemenid period, cf. *PAT* 0117.3.
84. Except for /'ab/, /'aḥ/ and /ḥam/.
85. I.e., throughout, except for the 1s /-ī/ "my."

In contrast, the suffixes attach to the nominal basis of the plural masculine construct and of the dual masculine and feminine construct, all ending with /-ay/, with no linking vowel, and also in the cases of /ʾabū-/, /ʾaḥū-/ and /ḥamū-/ (see above),[86] one can distinguish two series of suffixes:[87]

	Singular	**Plural**
first-person	*-y* /-ayy/	*-yn*(ʾ) /-áynā/
second-person masculine	*-yk* /-áyk(ā)/	*-ykm*/*ykn* /-aykūm, -aykūn/
second-person feminine	*-yky* /-áykī/	*-ykn* /-aykenn/
third-person masculine	*-wh*(*y*) /-áwhī/	*-yh*(*w*)*m*/*yhwn* /-ayhūm, -ayhūn/
third-person feminine	*-yh*(*h*) /-áyh(ā)/	*-yhn* /-ayhenn/

In the third-person masculine, /-hī/ developed from */-hū/, /-aw-/ through dissimilation of the */-ay-/. Masculine suffixes of the second-/third-person plural with /-n/ occur in Daniel and later Aramaic. Biblical Aramaic pointing reflects the secondary shift /-ūn/ > /-ōn/.[88] With suffixes to a base ending in a vowel,[89] it has in the second-person masculine singular *-āḵ*,[90] in the third-person feminine *-ah*,[91] and in the first-person plural *-anā*,[92] otherwise the expected monophthongization /ay/ > /ē/ and in the third-person masculine singular /aw/ > /ō/, in the first-person singular the abbreviation /-ayy/ > /-ay/ (→ 2). Sometimes, the third-person feminine plural manifests a gender difference between the masculine form in the consonantal text and the feminine form in the vocalization (Dnl. 7:8,19).

Alterations in the syllable structure with the addition of suffixes or endings result in the retention of unaccented short vowels that otherwise drop out in an open syllable.[93]

Prepositions indicate spatial, temporal, or logical relationships. Most frequently encountered are /ba-/ "in," /la-/ "for, to," and /ka-/ "like," along with /ʾel/ "toward,"[94] /bayn/ "between," /men/ "from, out of," /ʿad/ "until," /ʿal/ "on, against," /ʿemm/ "with," and a few original nouns reduced in usage to prepositions, such as, e.g., /ḥalp/ "instead of,"[95]

86. Yet /ʾabī/ "my father."

87. Sometimes called sg. and pl. suffs., since the former occurs mostly with sg. and the latter with pl. bases.

88. *ATTM*, 136.

89. Pl. suffs.

90. In a consonantal text *-yk*.

91. Consonantal text *-yh*.

92. Consonantal text *-ynʾ*; *ATTM*, 153.

93. E.g. *ʿaḇḏōhī* "his servant" in Ezr. 5:11 from /ʿabadawhī/, as with other *qatl*-, *qitl*-, and *qutl*-nominals with an originally bisyllabic pl. base, which can still be observed in the spirantized *ḏ* in the vocalization; in contrast *ʿᵃḇeḏ* "servant" on the ground form /ʿabd/ after anaptyxis /ʿabəd/, spirantization, lengthening of the half-vowel to a full vowel, and the loss of a vowel.

94. In the course of time replaced by /ʿal/.

95. → *ḥlp*.

/qobl/ "before, according to,"[96] /qodām/ "before,"[97] or /taḥt/ "under." The suffixed forms /ʾel/, /bayn/, /ʿal/, /qodām/, and /taḥt/ have an expanded basis with /-ay/, i.e., they take the "plural suffixes" (see above). The respective articles note the functions of certain prepositional supplements with verbs. Very often, /la-/ indicates the indirect object, which developed in the Imperial Aramaic tradition into its use also as a marker for a(n often animate) direct object,[98] while the Old Aramaic languages of Syria employ the particle /ʾiyyāt/ for this purpose and West Aramaic uses the related form /yāt/.[99] Both object particles appear in Biblical Aramaic. Other ubiquitous function words are the conjunctions /wa-/ "and" and /ʾaw/ "or," the conditional particle /hen/ "if,'" and various subordinating conjunctions based on the relative particle /dī/ combined with a preposition like /ka-/ (e.g., *kzy* /kadī/ "when") or a prepositional expression with /qobl/.[100] Object clauses and other subordinate clauses also follow an introductory /dī/ 'that"; the respective articles note the construction with verbs.[101] The marker of existence /ʾīt(ay)/ "there is," negated /layt(ay)/ "there is not," employed with /la-/ denotes "to have," since Semitic languages have no independent verb for this. As negations, Aramaic has /lā/, and older Aramaic /ʾal/ in prohibitions. Furthermore, Aramaic employs deictic particles such as /hā/, /ʾarū/, or /(hā)lū/ "look!"[102] and adverbs such as /ʾayk/ "how?," /ʾān/ "where?," /ʾap/ "also," /ken/ "thus," /kaʿat/ "now," /tūb(ā)/ "again,"[103] and still others.

Verbal roots designate verbal actions. They always appear in a certain stem indicating kind of action (unmarked, factitive, and causative) and voice (active and nonactive, i.e., middle passive, passive, and the associated categories such as reflexive). All stems form finite conjugations and certain paradigmatic verbal nouns (participles and infinitives). The finite forms each conjugate according to person, gender, and number; the participles, like other nominals, decline. The unmarked stem (G-stem or peal) can differentiate between dynamic and stative verbs.

The finite conjugations indicate the semantic categories of tense (the temporal relation of a circumstance), aspect (internal contour), and mood (relationship of a statement to actual, possible, or desired reality). Tense distinguishes, first, between past and present-future, aspective between the subjective portrayal of an action as complete (or punctiliar) and incomplete (in process), and mood between epistemic (various nuances of possibility) and deontic (demands). These three basic semantic categories overlap so that, e.g., the present is always in process, the future generally uncertain and, thus, approximating mood, and a specific demand or an account of consecutive events is usually inclined toward the punctiliar mode of portrayal. Such

96. → *qbl.*
97. → *qdm.*
98. Also in later East Aramaic.
99. See H. Gzella, "Differentielle Objektmarkierung im Nordwestsemitischen als Konvergenzerscheinung," in *Nicht nur mit Engelszungen. FS W. Arnold* (Wiesbaden, 2013), 113-24.
100. → *qbl.*
101. E.g., → *ydʿ*; *šmʿ*.
102. Frequent in Biblical Aramaic in vision reports, → *ḥzī.*
103. → *tūb.*

relationships are evident throughout the language.[104] Since tense, aspect, and mood appear in only two or three verbal categories in Old Aramaic, one begins with broad and fluid spectra of function instead of simple basic meanings,[105] spectra that then become fixed in specific usages according to context into a clearer temporal, aspective, or modal nuance.[106]

In Old and Imperial Aramaic, including Biblical Aramaic, a perfect formed with affirmatives (also designated the affirmative or suffix conjugation) and an imperfect formed with pre- and affirmatives (prefix conjugation) are also productive, the second in a long (sometimes also simply called imperfect) and a short form (jussive). This short imperfect survived in post-Achaemenid Aramaic only at Qumran and thereafter disappears entirely throughout Aramaic; it differs from the long form by different endings in a few forms. The basis of both conjugations is already determined by the superordinate verbal stem; the pre- and affirmatives of the perfect and both the long and short perfect that appear on this basis are alike in all the stems. The perfect covers various shades of the past,[107] in the G-stem the vowel in the second syllable of the base form is lexical;[108] here is the paradigm for → *ktb*:

	Singular	**Plural**
first-person	*ktbt* /katáb-(ə)t/	*ktbn* /katáb-n(ā)/
second-person masculine	*ktbt* /katáb-t(ā)/	*ktbt*(*w*)*n* /katab-tūn/
second-person feminine	*ktbty* /katáb-tī/	*ktbtn* /katab-ten/
third-person masculine	*ktb* /katab-Ø/	*ktbw* /katáb-ū/
third-person feminine	*ktbt* /katáb-at/	*ktbw* /katáb-ū/

In Imperial Aramaic, the masculine form replaces the third-person feminine plural; so far, there are no Old Aramaic instances. Post-Imperial Aramaic, however, displays here an independent form *ktbh* /katab-ā/.[109] Biblical Aramaic preserves the unaccented final long vowel of the perfect; the loss of the short vowel and the shift /e/ > /i/ led in the first- and third-person singular to *kiṯbeṯ* "I wrote" and *kiṯbaṯ* "she wrote." Otherwise, the base is *kᵉṯaḇ*. This base, however, also appears in the third-person feminine singular (*bᵉṭelaṯ* "she stopped," Ezr. 4:24).

104. See H. Gzella, "Some General Remarks on Interactions between Aspect, Modality, and Evidentiality in Biblical Hebrew," *FO* 49 (2012) 225-32.

105. In outdated portrayals often traced back to relative phases of time or a binary aspect system.

106. See the extensive treatment in H. Gzella, *Tempus, Aspekt und Modalität im Reichsaramäischen. VOK* 48 (2004); for Daniel also, similarly, T. Li, *The Verbal System of the Aramaic of Daniel. SAIS* 8 (2009).

107. Without differentiating between punctiliar and durative, in addition to resultative, preformative ("Hereby. . ."), sometimes also in statements that are timelessly valid (gnomic) and in the protasis of conditional clauses for relative prior time.

108. Usually /a/ for action and /e/ for stative verbs.

109. Likewise in Biblical Aramaic pointing.

The long imperfect operates in the functional realm of present-future, duration/incompleteness, and epistemic modality. Here, too, the base in the G-stem has a lexical vowel, for verbs of action, mostly /o/:[110]

	Singular	**Plural**
first-person	*'ktb* /'a-ktob/	*nktb* /na-ktob/
second-person masculine	*tktb* /ta-ktob/	*tktb(w)n* /ta-ktob-ūn/
second-person feminine	*tktbyn* /ta-ktob-īn/	*tktbn* /ta-ktob-(ə)n, -ān/
third-person masculine	*yktb* /ya-ktob/	*yktbwn* /ya-ktob-ūn/
third-person feminine	*tktb* /ta-ktob/	*yktbn* /ya-ktob-ān/

It is questionable how long the old /a/ preformative vowel survived in Old and Imperial Aramaic and when /e/ (as in the later pointings) replaced it.[111] For the second-/third-person feminine plural, the vocalizations indicate /-ān/ on the analogy of the masculine instead of the original */-n(ā)/, but the moment of this shift is unknown.[112]

In contrast, the short imperfect for demands and wishes[113] differs in spelling from the long form only in the second-person feminine singular and the second-/third-persons plural:

	Singular	**Plural**
first-person	*'ktb* /'a-ktob/	*nktb* /na-ktob/
second-person masculine	*tktb* /ta-ktob/	*tktbw* /ta-ktob-ū/
second-person feminine	*tktby* /ta-ktob-ī/	*tktbn* /ta-ktob-(ə)n/
third-person masculine	*yktb* /ya-ktob/	*yktbw* /ya-ktob-ū/
third-person feminine	*tktb* /ta-ktob/	*yktbn* /ya-ktob-(ə)n/

In post-Imperial Aramaic, the long form replaced the short imperfect. In the Tell Fekheriye inscription, the preformative /l-/ instead of /y-/ of the nonnegated short imperfect already appears, in Biblical and Qumran Aramaic only with → *hwī*. East Aramaic generally has /l-/ or /n-/[114] instead of /y-/.

As a rule, the second persons of the short imperfect without preformative are identical with the imperative; the short imperfect negated with /'al/ functions as the negative imperative. At least since Imperial Aramaic, the active participle *ktb* /kāteb/ in a predicative function as a present or process form becomes increasingly integrated into the verbal system

110. Biblical Aramaic /u/, → 2.
111. → 2 regarding the Barth-Ginsberg Law.
112. *ATTM*, 147.
113. Negated with /'al/.
114. Which probably arose from /l-/.

and sometimes also serves as a historical present. Together with the perfect or imperfect of → *hwī*, it constitutes a periphrastic conjugation expressing duration or process in past and future. The passive participle *ktyb* /katīb/ has mostly resultative nuances and finds frequent usage as an adjective. Beginning with Imperial Aramaic, the infinitive is *mktb* /maktab/ (> /miktab/), which functions with the preposition /la-/ mostly as a verbal complement to auxiliary verbs; Old Aramaic also attests forms without the *m*-prefix (/ktab/?).

Except for the participle, the verbal forms could be complemented with a suffix to mark a pronominal object. The first person singular has /-nī/ "me,"[115] otherwise the suffixes are identical to those with the noun (see above), e.g., /yahabtā-hā/ "you have given her." Since Imperial Aramaic, the third-person plural independent person pronouns replaced the corresponding suffixes. Typically, suffixes attach to long imperfect forms without afformative through the energicus ending /-an/, which apparently has no function otherwise, with no linking vowel. In pronunciation, the /-n/ presumably assimilated to the /-k/ of the suffix, as in /yaśīmákkā/ "he places you" (< /yaśīm-án-kā/).

Derived stems only change the base, the D-stem (pael) for factitive nuances doubles the middle consonant of the root, and the C-stem (haphel/aphel, on which, → 2) takes the prefix /ha-/ (> /'a-/). The G-, D-, and C-stems each have a t-stem with infixed /-t-/ for middle-passive or reflexive nuances (ithpeel, ithpaal, and ittapal) and until the end of the first millennium B.C.E. an inner passive formed by a vowel shift on the basis of the active; afterward, the respective t-stems assumed their functions. The ground forms are:

	Perfect	**Imperfect**	**Participle**	**Infinitive**
Peal	/katab/	/yaktob/	/kāteb/	/maktab/
Ithpeel	/'etkateb/	/yetkateb/	/metkateb/	/'etkatābā/
Pael	/katteb/	/yakatteb/	/makatteb/	/kattābā/
Ithpaal	/'etkattab/	/yetkattab/	/metkattab/	/'etkattābā/
Aphel	/'akteb/	/yakteb/	/makteb/	/'aktābā/
Ittapal	/'ettakteb/	/yettaktab/	/mattaktab/	/'ettaktābā/

The meanings of verbs that form both a D- and a C-stem differ individually. The inner passive[116] first disappears in the imperfect, so that its t-stem already appears with a passive nuance. The perfect of the inner passive sometimes has a resultative meaning. A sibilant at the beginning of a root usually fuses with the /-t-/ of the t-stems via metathesis.[117] The infinitives of the derived stems manifest both diachronous and synchronous variations.[118]

Various verb classes manifest alterations resulting from unstable root letters: syllable-ending /'/ disappears with compensatory lengthening so that verbs III-' have fused with

115. With the auxiliary vowel /-anī/.

116. Peal: pf. /katīb/, impf. /yoktab/, ptc. /katīb/; pael: pf. /kotteb/, impf. /yakottab/, ptc. /makattab/; aphel: pf. /'okteb/, impf. /yoktab/, ptc. /maktab/.

117. With /-tz-/ > /-zd-/.

118. Cf. briefly *ATTM*, 150.

those III-*ī*; /n/ as the first consonant of the root is assimilated, as is /l/ in *lqḥ*,[119] and the imperative then has a biradical basis.[120] In the imperfect, various verbs with an initial /y/ lengthen the second consonant of the root[121] and also have a biconsonantal imperative;[122] the C-stem retains an original initial /w-/. Forms with preformatives and prefixes of verbs with a doubled second radical lengthen the first: /ʿallat/ "she entered," but /taʿʿol/ "you enter";[123] in ithpeel, pael, and ithpaal they behave regularly. Hollow roots with long middle vowels retain them in the long imperfect[124] and otherwise have the vowel corresponding to that of regular verbs.[125] Active G-stem participle and pael are regular, although a reduplicated stem sometimes occurs.[126] Verbs ending in vowels (III-*ī*) retain the etymological /-ī/ in the perfect and imperative,[127] but it becomes /-ǣ/ in the imperfect, participle, and G-stem infinitive. Many verbs, by contrast, have a perfect with /-ā/ instead of /-ī/.[128] Suffixed III-*ī* forms diphthongize the long vowel before the linking vowel.[129]

4. Syntax

In older Old Aramaic, the word order verb-subject-object dominated in verbal clauses and subject-predicate in nominal clauses.[130] Alterations of sentence structure, probably first in part under Akkadian, then Persian influence, at the latest from Imperial Aramaic, lead, however, to the erosion of the pattern of a fixed word order and a tendency to move the verb back and the direct object forward, a tendency notable also in Biblical Aramaic. The same influences resulted in the very typical proleptic suffixes such as *brh dy* PN "his son, the son of PN" = "PN's son." Other syntactical phenomena correspond, on the whole, to the Northwest Semitic evidence: coordination generally resolves double subordination; compound subjects, collectives, and passive predicates sometimes diverge from regular syntactical agreement.

---

119. → *nśī*.
120. E.g., /qaḥ/ "take!"
121. /yaddaʿ/ "he knows."
122. /hab/ "give!"
123. Often written degeminatively *tnʿl*.
124. Although shortened in the short form.
125. Thus, in the pf. /qām/, impf. /yaqūm/.
126. → *rīm*.
127. > /ay/ for affirmatives with /i/ and > /aw/ for those with /ū/.
128. > /-ay-/ before consonantal affirmatives occurs often, > /-āt/ in 3fs and /-aw/ in 3pl.
129. E.g., /haḥwiyán(ā)/ "he showed us."
130. Often with a personal pronoun as copula, e.g., Dnl. 2:38: "you are the head of gold."

Alphabetical Aramaic-English Word List

(Transcribed according to Imperial Aramaic Orthography)

'b /'ab/ "father"
'bd (v.) "perish"
'bdn /'abdān/ "demise" → *'bd*
'bl (v.) "mourn" → *'ṣb*
'bn /'abn/ "stone"
'gr /'eggār/ "wall" → *ktl*
'grh /'eggarā/ "letter" → *spr*
'dr /'edder/ "threshing floor" → *'wr*
'drgzr */'addarzagar/ official in the inner circle of civil service → Iranian Official Titles
'wṣr /'ōṣar/ "store(house)" → *mlk*
'zd /'azd/ "known"
'zl (v.) "go" → *hlk*
'ḥ /'aḥ/ "brother"
'ḥh /'aḥā/ "sister" → *'ḥ*
'ḥydh /'aḥīdā/ "puzzle"
'ḥr /'aḥar/ "after, then" → *'ḥry*
'ḥry /'aḥaray/ "after, behind"
'ḥrn /'oḥrān/ "other" → *'ḥry*
'ḥšdrpn /'aḥšadrapān/ "satrap" → Iranian Official Titles
'yln /'īlān/ "tree"
'ymh /'aymā/ (> /'ēmā/) "terror"
'kl (v.) "eat"
'lh /'elāh/ "god"
'lp (v.) "learn," "teach" (*pa*)
'lp /'alp/ "thousand" → Numbers
'm /'emm/ "mother" → *'b*
'mh /'amā/ "servant" → *'bd*
'mh /'ommā/ "tribe, clan" → *'m*
'mn (v.) "trust" (*ha*)
'mr (v.) "say" → *mll*
'mr /'emmer/ "lamb"
'nb /'ebb/ "fruits" → *'yln*
'ns (v.) "oppress, force"
'np /'app/ "nose," "face" (dual), "surface"
'nš /'enāš/ "human being"
'nth /'ettā/ "woman, wife"
'ntw /'ettū/ "marriage" → *'nth*
'sh /'asǣ/ "physician" → *'šp*
'swr /'asūr/ "fetter" → *'sr*
(')*skph* /(')a)skoppā/ "threshold" → *tr'*
'sp /asopp/ "gate area" → *tr'*
'sprnh /'osparnā/ "complete, precise"
'sr (v.) "bind, take captive"
'sr /'esār/ "prohibition" → *'sr*
'ʿ /'a'/ "wood, beam," "boards" (plural)
'prsk /'eprasak/ "investigative officer" → Iranian Official Titles
'prstk /'eprastāk/ "emissary"(?) → Iranian Official Titles
'ṣb' /'eṣba'/ "finger, toe" → *jd*
'rb' /'arba'/ "four" → Numbers
'rgwn /'argawān/ "(reddish) purple"
'rz /'arz/ "cedar" → *'yln*
'rḥ /'orḥ/ "path, street, lifestyle"
'ryh /'aryǣ/ "lion"
'ryk /'arīk/ "long"
'rk /'ork/ "length"
'rkh /'arakā/ "duration"
'rm /'aram/ "Aram" → *'m*
'rmy /'aramāy/ "Aramaic; pagan" → *'m*
'r' /'ar'/ "earth, ground"
'š /'oš/ "foundations" (plural)
'š' /'æššā/ "fire"
'šp /'āšep/ "incantation priest"
'šrn /'āšarn/ "woodwork, lumber"
'štdwr /'āštedōr/ "rebellion" → *šlḥ*
't /'āt/ "sign, wonder"
'twn /'attūn/ "oven" → *nwr*
'tī (v.) "come"
'tn /'atān/ "female ass" → *'rd*
'tr /'atar/ "place"

b'yš /ba'īš/ "evil, bad" → *b'š*
b'r /be'r / (> /bēr/) "well" → *štī*
b'š (v.) "be bad, displease"

b'š /bōš/ "(something) bad" → *b'š*
b(')tr /bātar/ "after, behind" → *'tr*
bb /bāb/ "gate" → *trʻ*
bbh /bābā/ "pupil" → *ʻyn*
bdr (v.) "scatter" (*pa*)
bhylw /bahīlū/ "haste" → *bhl*
bhl (v.) "hurry" (*itp*), "frighten" (*pa*)
bṭl (v.) "stop," "install" (*pa*) → *sūp*
bṭn /baṭn/ "belly, womb" → *rḥm*
byrh /bīrā/ "fortification"
byt /bayt/ (> /bēt/) "house"
bkī (v.) "cry" → *ʻṣb*
bl /bāl/ "spirit, mind"
blw /belō/ "income" (tribute) → *hlk, mndh*
blī (v.) "decay," "annihilate" (*pa*)
bnī (v.) "build"
bnyn /benyān/ "building" → *bnī*
bʻī (v.) "want, seek, request, be about to"
bʻw /baʻū/ "petition" → *bʻī*
bʻl /baʻl/ "lord, husband, owner, member"
bʻl (v.) "marry" (*ha*) → *bʻl*
bqr (v.) "examine, investigate" (*pa*)
br /bar/ "son"
br /barr/ "open field"
br' /barrā/ "outside" → *br* /barr/
brh /barā/ "daughter" → *br*
bry /barrāy/ "external" → *br* /barr/
brk (v.) "bless, praise" (*pa*)
brk /berk/ "knee" → *brk*
brk (v.) "kneel" → *brk*
brkh /barakā/ "blessing" → *brk*
bśr /baśar/ "flesh"
bšlm /ba-šalām/ "all right, in good order" → *šlm*

g'wh /ga'wā/ (> /gēwā/) "arrogance" → *g'ī*
g'ī (v.) "be grand, arrogant"
gb /gobb/ "hole"
gbwrh /gabūrā/ "strength" → *gbr*
gbr (v.) "be strong"
gbr /gabar/ "man" → *gbr*
gbr /gabbār/ "hero" → *gbr*
gbrw /gabbārū/ "strength" → *gbr*
gw /gaww/ "interior"
gūḥ (v.) "stir up" (*aph*) → *šmyn*
gwy /gawwāy/ "internal" → *gw*
gzyrh /gazīrā/ "determination, decision" → *gzr*
gzr (v.) "cut off, conclude"
gzr /gāzer/ (/gazzār/?) "soothsayer" → *gzr*
glw /galū/ "exile" → *glī* II
glī I (v.) "uncover, reveal"
glī II (v.) "emigrate," "deport" (*aph*)
gll (v.) "roll" → *gll*
gll /galāl/ a kind of stone
gmyr /gamīr/ "perfect, complete" → *šlm*
gnz /ganza/ "treasure"
gnzbr /ganzabār/ "treasurer" → *gnz*
gnyzh /ganīzā/ "storage, depot" → *gnz*
gp /gapp/ "wing"
gpn /gapn/ "grapevine" → *ḥmr*
grbh /garbǣ/ "north" → Numbers, 4
gšm /gešm/ "body"

d'b /de'b/ "wolf" → *db*
db /dobb/ "bear"
dbḥ (v.) "sacrifice"
dbḥ /debḥ/ "sacrifice" → *dbḥ*
dbḥ /dābōḥ/ "sacrificial priest" → *dbḥ*
dbq (v.) "cling, adhere, border on, arrive (rare)"
dbr (v.) "lead"
dbr /dabbār/ "driver" → *dbr*
ʻl dbr(t) /ʻal dabar(at)/ "because of, with regard to" → *dbr, mll*
dhb /dahab/ "gold"
dūṣ (v.) "rejoice" → *ql*
dūr (v.) "dwell"
dḥyl /daḥīl/ "frightful" → *dḥl*
dḥl (v.) "be afraid"
dḥlh /deḥlā/ "fear" → *dḥl*
dīn (v.) "judge"
dyn /dīn/ "court" → *dīn*
dyn /dayyān/ "judge" → *dīn*
dyr /dayr/ (> /dēr/) "pen, stall" → *dūr*
dkī (v.) "be clean, "cleanse" (*pa*) → *zkw*
dkr /dakar/ "male, ram"
dkr (v.) "remember"
dkrn /dokrān/ "memorandum, record" → *dkr*
dm /dam/ "blood"
dmw /damū/ "similarity" → *dmī*
dmī (v.) "be like, resemble"
dqn /daqan/ "beard" → *śʻr*
dqq (v.) "crush"
dr /dār/ "generation" → *dūr*
drg /darg/ "stairs" → *nḥt*

drh /dārā/ "court(yard)" → *dūr*
dr' /derā'/ "arm"" → *yd*
dš /dašš/ "wing of a door, door" → *tr'*
dt /dāt/ "law, royal edict"
dt' /datǣ/ "grass" → *'śb*

hdbr /hadabār/ a dignitary in the inner circle of civil service → Iranian Official Titles
hdr (v.) "ascribe majesty, praise" (*pa*) → *hdr*
hdr /hadar/ "majesty"
hwī (v.) "be"
hwn /hawn/ (> /hōn/) "mind, understanding, attention" → *śīm*
hykl /hēkal/ "palace, temple"
hymnw /haymānū/ (> /hēmānū/) "fidelity" → *'mn*
hūk (v.) "go"
hlk (v.) "walk"
hlk /helk/ "tax" → *hlk*
hmī (v.) "make noise" → *ql*

zbn (v.) "buy," "sell" (*pa*)
zhyr /zahīr/ "respectful, deliberate" → *zhr*
zhr (v.) "pay attention" (*itp*)
zūn (v.) "feed" → *'kl*
zū' (v.) "tremble, be afraid" → *dḥl*
zīd (v.) "be arrogant"→ *ḥṭī*
zyw /zīw/ "splendor"
zkw /zakū/ "innocence"
zkī (v.) "be innocent" → *zkw*
zky /zakkāy/ "innocent" → *zkw*
zmn (v.) "make an appointment" (*itpa*) → *zmn*
zmn /zemān/ "time"
zmr /zamūr/ "blue" → *zmr*
zmr (v.) "make music, sing"
zmr /zamār/ "music" → *zmr*
zmr /zammār/ "musician" → *zmr*
zmr (v.) "prune" → *zmr*
z'yr /zo'ayr/ (> /zo'ēr/) "small, few" → *śgī*
z'q (v.) "call"
z'qh /za'aqā/ "cry" → *z'q*
zqp (v.) "pile" → śīm
zr' (v.) "sow"
zr' /zar'/ "seed, crop" → *zr'*

ḥbb (v.) "love" → *rḥm*
ḥbwlh /habūlā/ "crime" → *ḥbl*
ḥbyb /ḥabbīb/ "beloved" → *rḥm*
ḥbl (v.) "ruin, annihilate" (*pa*)
ḥbl /habāl/ "annihilation" → *ḥbl*
ḥbr (v.) "bind, consort with" (*itpa*)
ḥbr /ḥaber/ "comrade, other" → *ḥbr*
ḥbr /ḥabr/ "incantation" → *ḥbr*
ḥd /ḥad/ "one; time" → Numbers
ḥdwh /ḥedwā/ "joy"
ḥdī (v.) "rejoice" → *ḥdwh*
ḥūb (v.) "owe" → *ḥṭī*
ḥwb(h) /ḥōb(ā)/ "guilt" → *ḥṭī*
ḥwī (v.) "communicate, show" (*pa, aph*)
ḥwr (v.) "whiten, bleach, cleanse" (*pa*) → *ḥwr*
ḥwr /ḥewwār/ "(something) white"
ḥwry /ḥewwāräy/ "white" → *ḥwr*
ḥzh /ḥāzǣ/ "seer" → *ḥzī*
ḥzh /ḥazǣ/ "useful, necessary" → *ḥzī*
ḥzw /ḥazū/ "sight, visibility" → *ḥzī*
ḥzw /ḥezū/ "dream vision, vision" → *ḥzī*
ḥzwn /ḥezwān/ "phenomenon" → *ḥzī*
ḥzī (v.) "see," "show" (rare) (*pa*)
ḥzy /ḥazī/ "sign, marking" → *ḥzī*
ḥzywn /ḥezyōn/ "dream vision, vision" → *ḥzī*
ḥṭ' /ḥeṭē/ "sin" → *ḥṭī*
ḥṭī (v.) "sin"
ḥṭy /ḥaṭāy/ "sin" → *ḥṭī*
ḥṭr /ḥoṭr/ "rod, scepter" → *šbṭ*
ḥy /ḥayy/ "alive" → *ḥyī*
ḥyb /ḥayyāb/ "guilty" → *ḥṭī*
ḥywh /ḥaywā/ (> /ḥēwā/) "animal, animals" → *ḥyī*
ḥyī (v.) "live"
ḥyyn /ḥayyīn/ "life" → *ḥyī*
ḥyl (v.) "strengthen" (*pa*) → *ḥyl*
ḥyl /ḥayl/ (> /ḥēl/) "power, host"
ḥk /ḥekk/ "palate" → *pm*
ḥkym /ḥakkīm/ "wise" → *ḥkm*
ḥkm (v.) "teach" (*pa*)
ḥkmh /ḥokmā/ "wisdom" → *ḥkm*
ḥlm (v.) "dream"
ḥlm /ḥelm/ "dream" → *ḥlm*
ḥlm II (v.) "become powerful" (*itp*), "heal" (*aph*) → *ḥlm*
ḥlp (v.) "follow, replace," "interchange" (*aph*)
ḥlp /ḥalp/ "replacement" → *ḥlp*
ḥlph /ḥelpā/ "sprout" → *ḥlp*

ḥlq (v.) "allocate"
ḥlq /ḥelq/, /ḥolāq/ "portion" → *ḥlq*
ḥmh /ḥemā/ "wrath"
ḥmī (v.) "see" (W. Aramaic)
ḥmr /ḥamr/ "wine"
ḥmr /ḥemār/ "ass" → *ʿrd*
ḥmrh /ḥemārā/ "female ass" → *ʿrd*
ḥmš /ḥameš/ "five" → Numbers
ḥn /ḥenn/ "favor, esteem" → *ḥnn*
ḥnṭh /ḥeṭṭā/ "wheat"
ḥnk (v.) "consecrate" → *ḥnkh*
ḥnkh /ḥanokā/ "consecration"
ḥnn (v.) "have mercy," "plead for mercy" (*itpa*)
ḥsyn /ḥassīn/ "strong" → *ḥsn*
ḥsyr /ḥassīr/ "few" → *ḥsr*
ḥsn (v.) "take possession of" (*aph*)
ḥsn /ḥosn/ "strength" → *ḥsn*
ḥsr (v.) "lack," "diminish" (*pa*), "loose" (*aph*)
ḥsrn /ḥosrān/ "lack" → *ḥsr*
ḥpr (v.) "dig" → *ʿmq*
ḥrb (v.) "be a wilderness," "be desolated" (*aph*)
ḥrbn /ḥorbān/ "destruction" → *ḥrb*
hrhr /harhūr/ "dream fantasy" → *ḥlm*
ḥrṭm /ḥarṭom/ "soothsayer" → *ʾšp*
ḥrṣ /ḥarṣ/ "loin, hip"
ḥšb (v.) "mean, consider"
ḥšbn /ḥošbān/ "calculation" → *ḥšb*
ḥšḥ (v.) "use"
ḥšḥw /ḥāšeḥū/ "need" → *ḥšḥ*
ḥšwk /ḥašōk/ "darkness" → *ḥšk*
ḥšyk /ḥaššīk/ "dark" → *ḥšk*
ḥšk (v.) "be dark"
ḥšl (v.) "smash"
ḥštrpn → *ʾḥšdrpn*
ḥtm (v.) "seal, close"
ḥtm /ḥātam/ "seal" → *ḥtm*

ṭʾb (v.) "go well" → *ṭīb/yṭb*
ṭb /ṭāb/ "good" → *ṭīb/yṭb*
ṭbw /ṭābū/ "good deed" → *ṭīb/yṭb*
ṭhr /ṭehr/ "midday" → *ywm*
ṭwb /ṭūb/ "blessed is/are . . . !" → *ṭīb/yṭb*
ṭwr /ṭūr/ "mountain"
ṭīb (v.) "be satisfied, please"
ṭl /ṭall/ "dew"
ṭl /ṭell/, /ṭoll/ "shadow" → *ṭll*
ṭlwl /ṭalūl/ "roof" → *ṭll*
ṭll (v.) "roof" (*pa*), "shade" (*aph*) → *ṭll*
ṭll /ṭelāl/ "shade"
ṭmr (v.) "be hidden" (of heavenly bodies) → *str*
ṭʿw /ṭaʿū/ "error" → *ḥṭī*
ṭʿwn /ṭaʿūn/ "burden" → *nśī*
ṭʿī (v.) "err" → *ḥṭī*
ṭʿm (v.) "taste," "determine" (*aph*)
ṭʿm /ṭaʿm/ "command, matter; attention, obedience" → *ṭʿm*
ṭʿn (v.) "load on" → *nśī*

yd /yad/ "hand"
ydī (v.) "acknowledge, praise" (*aph*)
ydʿ (v.) "know, perceive," "acknowledge" (*aph*)
yhb (v.) "give"
yhwd /yahūd/ "Judea"
yhwdy /yahūdāy/ "Judean, Jew" → *yhwd*
ywm /yawm/ (> /yōm/) "day"
yṭb → *ṭīb*
ykl (v.) "be able," "vanquish" (rare)
ym /yamm/ "sea"
ymī (v.) "swear"
yʿṭ (v.) "advise"
yʿṭ /yāʿeṭ/ "advisor" → *yʿṭ*
yṣb (v.) "consider certain, certify" (*pa*)
yṣbh /yaṣbā/ "certainty" → *yṣb*
yṣyb /yaṣṣīb/ "certain" → *yṣb*
yqd (v.) "burn" → *ʾšʾ*
yqdh /yaqedā/ "fire, blaze" → *ʾšʾ*
yqyr /yaqqīr/ "esteemed" → *yqr*
yqr /yaqār/ "honor"
yrḥ /yarḥ/ "month" → *šnh*
yrk /yarek/ "thigh" → *rgl*
yšr (v.) "send" (*aph*), Imperial Aramaic of goods → *šlḥ*
ytb (v.) "sit, settle, dwell"

kbš (v.) "compel" → *ykl*
kdb (v.) "lie"
kdb(h) /kadab(ā)/ "lie" → *kdb*
kdb /kaddāb/ "liar" → *kdb*
khl → *ykl*
khn /kāhen/ "priest"
khnw /kāhenū/ "priesthood" → *khn*

kwkab /kawkab/ (> /kōkab/) "star" → *šmyn*
kl /koll/ "all, each, every" → *kll*
kmr /komr/ "priest" (only pagan) → *khn*
knh /kenā/ "colleague"
knī (v.) "give a nickname" (*pa*) → *šm*
knš (v.) "gather"
ksī (v.) "conceal oneself," "cover" (*pa*) → *str*
ksp /kasp/ "silver, money" → *dhb*
kp /kēp/ "rock" → *ṭwr*
kp /kapp/ "palm of the hand, sole of the foot" → *yd*
krwz /krōz/ "herald"; "dispossession" → Iranian Official Titles
krz (v.) "dispossess," "call out" (*aph*) → Iranian Official Titles
krī (v.) "be saddened" (*itp*) → *bhl*, *ʿṣb*
krm /karm/ "vineyard" → *ḥmr*
krsʾ /korseʾ/ (> /korsæ/) "throne"
kśdy /kaśdāy/ "Chaldean, astrologer" → *ʾšp*
ktb (v.) "write, sign," "mark" (*pa*)
ktb /ketāb/ "writing, document" → *ktb*
ktbh /katobā/ "marriage contract," "marking" → *ktb*
ktwb /kātōb/ "scribe" → *ktb*
ktl /kotl/ "wall"

lbb /lebab/, *lb* /lebb/ "heart, mind"
lbwnh /lebōnā/ "incense" → *mnḥh*
lbwš /labūš/ "clothing" → *lbš*
lbš (v.) "put something on," "clothe" (*aph*)
lbš /lebāš/ "robe, dress" → *lbš*
lwy /lewāy/ "Levite" → *khn*
lḥh /laḥæ/ "bad" → *bʾš*
lḥm /laḥm/ "nourishment, bread"
lḥn /laḥen/ "temple employee"
lḥnh /laḥenā/ "court lady" → *lḥn*
lylh /laylæ/ (> /lēlæ/) "night"
lpm "according to" → *pm*
lqḥ (v.) "take" → *nśī*
lšn /leššān/ "tongue, language"

mʾh /meʾā/ "hundred" → Numbers
mʾn /maʾān/ "container, vessel"
mbqr "overseer"? "examiner"? → *bqr*
mglh /magallā/ "scroll" → *gll*
mgr (v.) "overthrow, topple" (*pa*)
mdbḥ /madbaḥ/ "altar" → *dbḥ*
mdbr /madbar/ "wilderness" → *dbr*
mdy /māday/ "Media"
mdy /mādāy/ "Mede" → *mdy*
mdynh /madīnā/ "province, region, city" → *dīn*
mdnḥ /madnaḥ/ "east" → Numbers, 4
mdr /madār/ "resting place" → *dūr*
mhmn /mahayman/ (> /mahēman/) "reliable" → *ʾmn*
mwzn /mawzen/ (> /mōzen/) "scales" → *tql*
mwmh /mawmæ/ (> /mōmæ/) "oath" → *ymī*
mwʿh /mawʿæ/ (> /mōʿæ/) "east" → Numbers, 4
mūt (v.) "die," "kill" (*aph*)
mwt /mawt/ (> /mōt/) "death" → *mūt*
mwtb /mawtab/ (> /mōtab/) "residence" → *ytb*
mwtn /mawtān/ (> /mōtān/) "plague" → *mūt*
mzwn /mazōn/ "food" → *ʾkl*
mzl /mazzal/ "zodiac" → *šmyn*
mḥwz /maḥōz/ "harbor" → *ḥzī*
mḥzh /maḥzæ/ "appearance" → *ḥzī*
mḥzy /maḥzī/ "mirror" → *ḥzī*
mḥī (v.) "smite, hit"
mḥlqh /maḥloqā/ "division" → *ḥlq*
mṭī (v.) "attain, enter, arrive at"
mṭl /meṭṭoll/ "because of" → *ṭll*
mṭll /maṭlal/ "roof" → *ṭll*
mṭr /maṭar/ "rain" → *ʿnn*
myn /mayn/ (> /mēn/) "water" → *štī*
myt /mīt/ "dead" → *mūt*
mlʾk /malʾak/ "messenger, angel"
mlh /malæ/ "full" → *mlī*
mlh /mellā/ "word, matter" → *mll*
mlḥ (v.) "salt"→ *mlḥ*
mlḥ /melḥ/ "salt"
mlī (v.) "be full," "fill" (also *aph*)
mlk (v.) "rule," "install as king" (*aph*) → *mlk*
mlk (v.) "advise" → *mlk*
mlk /malk/ "king"
mlk /melk/ "advice" → *mlk*
mlkh /malkā/ "queen" → *mlk*
mlkw /malkū/ "kingdom" → *mlk*
mll (v.) "speak"
mmll /mamlal/ "speech" → *mll*
mndh /maddā/ "tribute"
mndʿ /maddaʿ/ "knowledge, insight" → *ydʿ*
mnh /manā/ "portion" → *mnī*
mnh /manæ/ "mine" (weight) → *mnī*

mnḥh /manaḥā/ "grain offering"
mnṭrh /maṭṭarā/ "guard" → *nṭr*
mnī (v.) "number," "determine" (*pa*)
mnyn /menyān/ "quantity" → *mnī*
mntn(h) /mattan(ā)/ "gift" → *ntn*
msgd /masgad/ "cultic site" → *sgd*
mstr /mastar/ "hiding place" → *str*
mʿbd /maʿbād/ "deed"→ *ʿbd*
mʿbr /maʿbar/ "ford" → *ʿbr*
mʿyn /maʿyān/ "spring" → *ʿyn*
mʿyn /meʿayn/ (> /meʿēn/) "belly" → *rgl*
mʿl /maʿʿal/ "entrance" → *ʿll*
mʿrb /maʿrab/ "west" → Numbers, 4
mplh /mappalā/ "fall" → *npl*
mpq /mappaq/ "exit" → *npq*
mptḥ /mapteḥ/ "key" → *ptḥ*
mqdš /maqdaš/ "sanctuary" → *qdš*
mqm /maqām/ "status, position" → *qūm*
mrʾ /mārǣ/ "lord"
mrʾh /māreʾā/ "lady" → *mrʾ*
mrd (v.) "rebel"
mrd /merd/ "rebellion" → *mrd*
mrd /marrād/ "rebel" → *mrd*
mśgh /maśgǣ/ "mass" → *śgī*
mšḥ (v.) "anoint"
mšḥ II (v.) "measure" → *mšḥ*
mšḥ /mešḥ/ "oil" → *mšḥ*
mšyḥ /mašīḥ/ "anointed one, messiah" → *mšḥ*
mškb /maškab/ "bed" → *škb*
mškn /maškan/ "dwelling," "deposit" → *škn*
mšrwqy /mašrōqī/ "flute, pipe" → *zmr*
mšry /mašrī/ "camp, encampment" → *šrī*
mšth /maštǣ/ "drink, drinking bout" → *štī*
mštw /maštū/ "wedding celebration" → *štī*
mtql /matqāl/ "weight" → *tql*

nbʾ (v.) "appear as a prophet" (*itpa*) → *nbyʾ*
nbwʾh /nabūʾā/ "prophecy" → *nbyʾ*
nbzbh /nabizbā/ "gift" → *ntn*
nbyʾ /nabī/ "prophet"
nbʿ (v.) "bubble" → *ʿyn*
ngd (v.) "set out, move on"
ngd /negd/ "emissary" → *ngd*
ngh /nogh/ "daybreak"
ngyd /nagīd/ "cut severely" → *ngd*
ngydw /nagīdū/ "advance" → *ngd*
ndb (v.) "be willing," "give" (*itpa*)
ndd (v.) "flee"
ndr (v.) "promise" → *ndb*
nhwr /nahōr/ "light" → *nhr*
nhyr /nahhīr/ "bright" → *nhr*
nhr /nahar/ "river"
nhr (v.) "shine" (*aph*)
nūḥ (v.) "stand still," "create calm" (*aph*) → *šlī*
nūr (v.) "shine" (*aph*) → *nwr*
nwr /nūr/ "fire"
nzq (v.) "suffer damage," "damage" (*aph*)
nzq /nezq/ "damage" → *nzq*
nḥwḥ /nīḥōḥ/ "incense offering" → *mnḥh*
nḥš /noḥāš/ "copper, bronze" → *dhb*
nḥš /naḥš/ "soothsaying," "omen" (plural) → *šmyn*
nḥt (v.) "descend," "deposit" (*aph*)
nṭl (v.) "raise"
nṭr (v.) "preserve"
nyḥ /nayāḥ/ "rest" → *šlī*
nksyn /nekasīn/ "property"
nmr /nemr/ "leopard"
nsb (v.) "lift up, take" → *nśī*
nsk /nesk/ "libation" → *mnḥh*
npyl /napīl/ "giant" (mythological) → *npl*
npl (v.) "fall, fall to"
npq (v.) "exit," "bring out" (*aph*)
npqh /napaqā/ "spending, costs" → *npq*
npš /napš/ "soul, self," a kind of grave marker → *nšm*
nṣb (v.) "plant"
nṣb /naṣīb/ "stele" → *ṣlm*
nṣbh /neṣbā/ "planting" → *nṣb, ṣlm*
nṣḥ (v.) "win," "distinguish oneself" (*itpa*)
nṣl (v.) "snatch away, deliver," "demand back" (*aph*)
nqh /naqǣ/ "innocent" (rare) → *nqh*
nqh /neqǣ/ "sheep"
nqī (v.) "cleanse" (rare) (*pa*)
nśī (v.) "take," "rise" (rare) (*itpa*)
nšm (v.) "breathe"
nšm(h) /našam(ā)/ "breath" → *nšm*
nšp (also *nšb*) (v.) "blow" → *nšm*
nšr /nešr/ "vulture"
nštwn /neštāwan/ "decree, official letter"
ntyn /natīn/ "temple slave" → *ntn*
ntn (v.) "give"
ntr (v.) "fall out/off," "take away, set free," "peel off" (*aph*)

sbwl /sabūl/ "support, base" → *sbl*
sbl (v.) "carry," "support" (*pa*)
sgd (v.) "pay homage"
sgdh /segdā/ "veneration" → *sgd*
sgn /sagan/ "prefect," "leader"
sgr (v.) "close" → *ptḥ*
swmpnyh /sūmpōnyā/ "double flute"(?) → *zmr*
sūp (v.) "stop, disappear," "annihilate" (*aph*)
swp /sawp/ (> /sōp/) "end" → *sūp*
sypyn /sayāpīn/ "end, extremity" → *sūp*
skl /sakal/ "gate" → *ḥkm*; *śkl*
skph → *'skph*
skr (v.) "close" → *ptḥ*
slq (v.) "ascend," "offer" (*aph*)
smk (v.) "support" → *sbl*
ss /sās/ "moth" → *npl*
s'd (v.) "help" (also *pa*)
s'd /sa'd/ "help" → *s'd*
spr /sepr/ "document, book, literacy"
spr /sāper/ "scribe, secretary" → *spr*
srwšy /srōšī/ "discipline"
srk /sārak/ "administrator, treasurer"
srk /sirk/ "order" → *srk*
str (v.) "conceal"
str /setr/ "concealment" → *str*

'bd (v.) "make, do"
'bd /'abd/ "servant, slave" → *'bd*
'bd /'obād/ "deed" → *'bd*
'bwr /'abūr/ "grain" → *'br*
'bwr /'ebbūr/ "leap year" → *'br*
'bydh /'abīdā/ "work, service" → *'bd*
'br (v.) "cross," "lead over" (*aph*)
'br /'ebr/ "opposite side" → *'br*
'gl /'egl/ "calf" → *twr*
'dī (v.) "go away," "take away" (*aph*)
'dynh /'edyānā/ "pregnancy" → *'dī*
'dn /'eddān/ "moment, term," "year" (rare)
'dr /'edr/ "help" → *s'd*
'wz /'ōz/ or /'ūz/ "eagle" → *nšr*
'wyh /'awāyā/ "sin" → *ḥṭī*
'wyr /'awīr/ "blind" → *'yn*
'wl /'ōl/ "wrong" → *ḥṭī*
'wp /'awp/ (> /'ōp/) "bird" (collectively) → *ṣpr*
'ūr (v.) "blind" → *'yn*
'wr /'awār/ "blindness" → *'yn*
'wr /'ūr/ "chaff"
'z /'ezz/ "goat"
'zqh /'ezqā/ "signet ring"
'ṭh /'eṭā/ "advice" → *y'ṭ*
'yn /'ayn/ (> /'ēn/) "eye," "spring" (rare)
'īr (v.) "(a)waken" → *ndd*, *'yr*
'yr /'īr/ "guard"
'lh /'alā/ "burnt offering" → *mnḥh*
'lh /'ellā/ "grounds for an accusation, pretext"
'ly /'ellāy/ "above," "north"
'lyh /'elliyā/ "upper chamber" → *'ly*
'lym /'olaym/ (> /'olēm/) "lad, youth, fellow"
'll (v.) "enter," "lead in" (*aph*)
'll /'alāl/ "entrance, access" → *'ll*
'llh /'alalā/ "yield" → *'ll*
'lm /'ālam/ "eternity, world, era"
'l' /'ela'/ "rib"
'm /'amm/ "people"
'myq /'ammīq/ "deep" → *'mq*
'mq (v.) "be deep," "make deep" (*aph*)
'mq /'omq/ "depth" → *'mq*
'nb /'enab/ "grape" → *ḥmr*
'nh /'anǣ/ "lowly, poor" → *'nī* II
'nwh /'anwā/ "poverty" → *'nī* II
'nī I (v.) "lift, answer, hear"
'nī II (v.) "be lowly, poor"
'nn /'anān/ "cloud"
'np /'anap/ "branch" → *'yln*
'py /'opī/ "foliage" → *'yln*
'ṣb (v.) "be saddened" (*itp*)
'ṣyb /'aṣīb/ "saddened" → *'ṣb*
'qr (v.) "tear out, uproot"
'qr /'eqqār/ "rootstock" → *'qr*
'r /'arr/ "opponent" → *'rr*
'rd /'arād/ "onager, wild ass"
'rymw /'arīmū/ "insight" → *ḥkm*
'rm (v.) "be clever" → *ḥkm*
'rmn /'ormān/ "cleverness" → *ḥkm*
'rpl /'arapel/ "dark cloud" → *'nn*
'rq (v.) "flee" → *ndd*
'rr (v.) "raise an objection"
'rr /'arār/ "objection" → *'rr*
'rr (v.) "uncover" → *'rr*
'śb /'eśb/ "herbage"
'śr /'aśr/ "ten" → Numbers
'št (v.) "plan," "be considering" (*itp*)
'tyq /'attīq/ "old"
'tr /'otr/ "wealth" *'rr* II

pḥh /pāḥā/ "governor"
pṭr (v.) "release" → *šbq*
plg (v.) "divide"
plg /palg/ "half" → *plg*
plgn /palogān/ "divisions (of priests)" → *plg*
plgn /polgān/ "allocation" → *plg*
plḥ (v.) "work, serve, venerate"
plḥn /polḥān/ "worship service" → *plḥ*
plṭ (v.) "escape," "deliver" (*pa*) → *nṣl*
plṭh /paleṭā/ "deliverance" → *nṣl*
pm /pomm/ "mouth," "opening"
ps /pass/ "(back of the) hand" → *yd*
psntryn /psantērīn/ "harp" → *zmr*
przl /parzel/ "iron" → *dhb*
prs (v.) "divide" → *mdy*
prs /pars/ "demi-mine (weight)" → *mnī*
prs /pārs/ "Persia" → *mdy*
prsy /pārsāy/ "Persian" → *mdy*
prq (v.) "redeem, liberate"
prš (v.) "separate," less often "explain, interpret"
prš /parāš/ "interpretation" → *prš*
prš /paraš/ "horse" → *prš*
pršgn /parešagn/ "copy"
pšq (v.) "designate as a donation" → *ndb*
pšr (v.) "interpret"
pšr /pešr/ "interpretation" → *pšr*
ptgm /pategām/ "communication, edict"
ptḥ (v.) "open," "become sighted" (*itp*)
ptyḥ /patīḥ/ "open" → *ptḥ*

ṣbw /ṣabū/ "concern, matter" → *ṣbī*
ṣbī (v.) "want, seek"
ṣbyn /ṣebyān/ "favor" → *ṣbī*
ṣbʿ (v.) "moisten" → *ṭl*; *štī*
ṣdyq /ṣaddīq/ "righteous" → *ṣdq*
ṣdq (v.) "be in the right"
ṣdq /ṣedq/ "loyalty," later "justification" → *ṣdq*
ṣdqh /ṣadaqā/ "righteousness" → *ṣdq*
ṣwrh /ṣūrā/ "copy, figure" → *ṣlm*
ṣlw /ṣalō/ "payer" → *ṣlī*
ṣlḥ (v.) "advance, have success" (*aph*)
ṣlī (v.) "pray" (*pa*)
ṣlm /ṣalm/ "statue"
ṣmḥ (v.) "sprout" → *rb*
ṣpyr /ṣapīr/ "ram" → *ʿz*
ṣpn (v.) "be hidden," "hide" (*aph*) → *str*
ṣpr /ṣapr/ "morning" → *ywm*, *ngh*
ṣpr /ṣeppar/ "bird"

qbylh /qabīlā/ "complaint" → *qbl*
qbl (v.) "complain," "receive" (*pa*)
qbl /qobl/ "before" → *qbl*
qbl (II?) (v.) "darken" → *ḥšk*
qbl /qabl/ "darkness" (astronomical) → *ḥšk*
qdym /qadīm/ "east" → *qdm*
qdyš /qaddīš/ "holy," substantivally "god," "angel" → *qdš*
qdm (v.) "go ahead" (*pa*), "do first" (*aph*)
qdm /qodām/ "before" → *qdm*
qdmh /qadmā/ "former time, formerly" → *qdm*
qdmy /qadmāy/ "earlier, first" → *qdm*
qdš (v.) "sanctify" (*pa*)
qdš /qodš/ "holiness" → *qdš*
qdš /qodāš/ "earring" → *qdš*
qūm (v.) "stand (up), remain," "decree" (*pa*), "erect" (*aph*)
qwmh /qawmā/ (> /qōmā/) "stature, growth" → *qūm*
qṭl (v.) "kill"
qṭl /qaṭl/ "execution" → *qṭl*
qṭr (v.) "bind, knot"
qṭr /qeṭr/ "knot, joint, problem" → *qṭr*
qym /qayām/ "decree" → *qūm*
qym /qayyām/ "constant" → *qūm*
qytrs /qītāris/ "zither" → *zmr*
ql /qāl/ "voice, sound, tone"
qṣ /qeṣṣ/ "ends of the earth" → *qṣṣ*
qṣp /qaṣp/ "wrath" → *ḥmh*
qṣṣ (v.) "chop off" (*pa*)
qṣt /qaṣāt/ "part" → *qṣṣ*
qṣt /qaṣōt/ (plural) "ends" → *qṣṣ*
qrb (v.) "approach," "present" (*pa* and *aph*)
qrb /qarāb/ "battle, war" → *qrb*
qrbn /qorbān/ "offering" → *qrb*
qrī (v.) "call, name, invite, read"
qryh /qaryā/ "city, locality"
qryb /qarrīb/ "nearby," substantivally, "relative" → *qrb*
qrn /qarn/ "horn," "corner"
qrṣ (v.) "cut off" → *ʾkl*
qrṣ /qarṣ/ "cut-off piece" → *ʾkl*
qšṭ /qošṭ/ "truth, uprightness"
qšyš /qaššīš/ "senior" → *ʿtyq*

qšš "raise" (*aph*) → *rb*
qšt /qašt/ "bow" → *qšṭ*

r'š /rēš/ "head, top, point, leader, beginning, capital"
rb /rabb/ "large," substantivally "leader, commander, master"
rbh /rabǣ/ "officer" → *rb*
rbw /rabū/ "greatness" → *rb*
rbw /rebbō/ "ten thousand" → *rb*
rbī (v.) "grow," "make great" (*pa*)
rbn /rabbān/ "dignitary, leader, master" → *rb*
rbrb (v.) "boast" → *rb*
rgz /rogz/ "wrath, anger" → *ḥmh*
rgl /regl/ "foot," "time"
rgš (v.) "be angry," "behave anxiously, survey" (*pa*)
rwḥ /rūḥ/ "breath, puff, wind, spirit, demon"
rwm /rūm/ "height" → *rīm*
rz /rāz/ "puzzle, secret"
rḥym /raḥīm/ "beloved, darling" → *rḥm*
rḥyq /raḥḥīq/ "distant" → *rḥq*
rḥm (v.) "love, like, choose," "have mercy" (*pa*)
rḥm /rāḥem/ "friend" → *rḥm*
rḥm /raḥm/ "womb" → *rḥm*
rḥmyn /raḥmīn/ "mercy" → *rḥm*
rḥmn /raḥmān/ "merciful" → *rḥm*
rḥṣ (v.) "trust" (*itp*)
rḥṣn /roḥṣān/ "certainty" → *rḥṣ*
rḥq (v.) "be distant, refrain," "remove" (*pa*)
rḥš (v.) "creep" → *rb*
ryḥ /rēḥ/ "aroma"
rīḥ (v.) "smell" → *ryḥ*
rīm (v.) "rise (over), become arrogant," "raise" (*aph*), "praise" (*pawl*)
rm /rām/ "high" → *rīm*
rmh /rāmā/ "height" → *rīm*
rmī (v.) "throw, place upon"
rmš /ramš/ "evening" → *ywm*
rʿw /raʿū/ "pleasure, will" → *rʿī*
rʿī (v.) "appease, be unified"
rʿyn /reʿyān/ "thought, wish" → *rʿī*
ršyʿ /raššīʿ/ "evildoer" → *b'š*
ršm (v.) "write, engrave" → *ktb*
ršm /rošm/ "sign, mark" → *ktb*
ršʿ (v.) "do evil" → *b'š*
ršʿ /rašaʿ/ "crime" → *b'š*

śb /śāb/ "old," substantivally "old man, elder"
śbk /śabbok/ "sambuke" → *zmr*
śg' /śogǣ/ "mass" → *śgī*
śgī (v.) "be many," "multiply" (*aph*)
śgy' /śaggī/ "many; very" → *śgī*
śhd (v.) "witness to, attest" (*pa*)
śhd /śāhed/ "witness" → *śhd*
śhdw /śāhedū/ "witness" → *śhd*
śhr /śehr/ "moon" → *šmyn*
śybh /śēbā/ "(old) age" → *śb*
śīm (v.) "put, place, lay"
śymh /śīmā/ "treasure, treasury" → *śīm*
śkl (v.) "pay attention" (*itpa*)
śkltnw /śokltānū/ "insight" → *śkl*
śm'l /śam'āl/ "left" → Numerals, 4
śn' /śānē/ "enemy" → *śnī*
śn'h /śen'ā/ "hatred" → *śnī*
śnī (v.) "hate"
śʿr /śaʿr/ "hair," "barley"
śph /śapā/ "lip" → *pm*

š'l (v.) "ask, request"
š'lh /ša'elā/ "question," "demand" → *š'l*
š'r (v.) "remain"
š'r /šo'ār/ "remnant" → *š'r*
š'ry /šērī/ "remnant" → *š'r*
šbh /šabbā/ "sabbath, week" → *ywm*; *šnh*
šbḥ (v.) "praise" (*pa*)
šbṭ /šabṭ/ "staff, tribe"
šbī (v.) "take away captive" → *glī* II
šby /šebī/ "captivity" → *glī* II
šbyb /šabīb/ "flame" → *'š'*
šbʿ /šabʿ/ "seven" → Numbers
šbq (v.) "leave, abandon, set free, forgive"
šbq /šibq/ "access balcony" → *šbq*
šbš (v.) "become confused" (*itpa*)
šgl /šēgal/ "king's consort"
šdr (v.) "send" (*pa*) → *šlḥ*
šwh /šawǣ/ "suitable" → *šwī*
šwī (v.) "be like," "agree" (*itp*), "close" (*pa*)
šwī II (v.) "place, determine" (*pa*) → *šwī*
šwq /šūq/ "major commercial road" → *mlk*
šwr /šūr/ "wall"
šḥyt /šaḥīt/ "ruined" → *b'š*; *šḥt*
šḥt (v.) "be deformed," "destroy" (*aph*)
šyzb (v.) "deliver"
šyṣy' (v.) "complete" → *kll*

škb (v.) "lie down, lie"
škḥ (v.) "be found" (*itp*), "find, be able" (*aph*)
škḥh /šakaḥā/ "discovery" → *škḥ*
škll (v.) "complete" → *kll*
škn (v.) "dwell," "cause to dwell, settle" (*pa*)
škn /šekn/ "eyelid" → *ʿyn*
šlh /šalǣ/ "calm, carefree" → *šlī*
šlh /šillā/ "impertinence, blasphemy" → *šlī*
šlw /šalū/ "rest, leisure," "negligence" → *šlī*
šlḥ (v.) "send" (also *pa*), in Imperial Aramaic of reports
šlṭ (v.) "have/exert power," "empower" (*aph*)
šlṭn /šolṭān/ "dominion, ruler" → *šlṭ*
šlī (v.) "be calm"
šlyṭ /šallīṭ/ "powerful, empowered" → *šlṭ*
šlyn /šelyān/ "calm" → *šlī*
šlm (v.) "be complete," "count, repay" (*pa*), "hand over" (*aph*)
šlm /šalem/ "complete, undamaged" → *šlm*
šlm /šalām/ "peace, well-being" → *šlm*
šm /šem/ "name"
šmd (v.) "destroy" (*pa*) → *ʾbd*
šmyn /šamayn/ (> /šamēn/) "heaven"
šmʿ (v.) "hear, obey"
šmš /šamš/ (< /śamš/) "sun"
šmš (v.) "serve, venerate" (*pa*)
šn /šenn/ "tooth" → *pm*
šnh /šanā/ "year"
šnī (v.) "be different," "alter" (*pa* and *aph*)
šʿh /šāʿā/ "moment, hour"
špwlyn /šepōlīn/ "foot (of a mountain)" → *rgl*
špṭ (v.) "sue" → *dīn*
špyr /šappīr/ "beautiful" → *špr*
špl (v.) "humiliate" (*aph*)
špl /šapel/ "lowly" → *špl*
šplw /šapelū/ "humiliation" → *špl*
špr (v.) "be beautiful, please"
špr /šopr/ "beauty" → *špr*
šprpr /šaparpar/ "dawn" → *špr*
šq /šāq/ "leg" → *rgl*
šqī (v.) "give to drink, water" (*aph*) → *štī*
šql → *tql*
šrī (v.) "free, linger, settle down," "begin" (*pa*)
šryr /šarīr/ "sound" → *šlm*
šrš /šorš/ (< /śorš/?) "root, descendant"
št /šett/ "six" → Numbers
štī (v.) "drink, celebrate"

tbr (v.) "shatter"
tdyr /tadīr/ "lasting" → *dūr*
thwm /tehōm/ "primordial deep" → *ym*
tūb (v.) "return, diverge," "give back," "answer" (*aph*)
twb(ʾ) /tūbā/ "again, further" → *tūb*
twh (v.) "terrify"
twr /tawr/ (> /tōr/) "steer, cattle"
twrh /tawrā/ (> /tōrā/) "cow" → *twr*
twtb /tawtab/ (> /tōtab/) "sojourner" → *ytb*
tḥnwnyn /taḥnūnīn/ "request," "plead" → *ḥnn*
tḥty /taḥtāy/ "under," "south" → *ʿly*
typt /tīpat/ "police commander" → Iranian Official Titles
tlg /talg/ "snow" → *ʿnn*
tlt /talāt/ "three" → Numbers
tmh (v.) "be astonished" (also *itp*)
tmh /temh/ "wonder" → *tmh*
tmnh /tamānǣ/ "eight" → Numbers
tṣlw /taṣlū/ "prayer" (Old Aramaic) → *ṣlī*
tqyp /taqqīp/ "strong" → *tqp*
tql (v.) "weigh, pay"
tql /teql/ "shekel" → *tql*
tqn (v.) "be firm," "prepare" (*pa*), "install" (*aph*)
tqp (v.) "be strong, defeat," "strengthen, put in force" (*pa*)
tqp /toqp/ "strength, power" → *tqp*
tryn /terayn/ (> /terēn/) "two" → Numbers
trʿ /tarʿ/ "gate," "hatchway, opening" (rare)
trʿ /tarrāʿ/ "gatekeeper" → *trʿ*
tšbḥh /tašboḥā/ "praise" → *šbḥ*
tšʿ /tešʿ/ "nine" → Numbers

English-Aramaic Glossary

(Transcribed according to Imperial Aramaic orthography)

a certain PN *šmh* (→ *šm*)
abandon (v.) *šbq*
above *ʿly* /ʿellāy/
accept (v.) *qbl* (*pa*)
access *ʿll* /ʿalāl/ (→ *ʿll*)
access balcony šbq /šibq/ (→ *šbq*)
according to *lpm* (→ *pm*)
acknowledge (v.) *ydī* (*aph*)
administrator *srk* /sārak/
advance (v.) *ṣlḥ* (*aph*)
advance *ngydw* /nagīdū/ (→ *ngd*)
advice *mlk* /melk/ (→ *mlk*), *ʿṭh* /ʿeṭā/ (→ *yʿṭ*)
advise (v.) *yʿṭ*
advisor *yʿṭ* /yāʿeṭ/ (→ *yʿṭ*)
after *ʾḥr* /ʾaḥar/ (→ *ʾḥry*), *b(ʾ)tr* /bātar/ (→ *ʾtr*)
again (further) *twb(ʾ)* /tūbā/ (→ *tūb*)
age *śybh* /śēbā/ (→ *śb*)
agreeing (*k*)*pm ḥd* (→ *pm*)
air → breath → heaven (in the sense of the sky)
alive *ḥy* /ḥayy/ (→ *ḥyī*)
all *kl* /koll/ (→ *kll*)
altar *mdbḥ* /madbaḥ/ (→ *dbḥ*)
alter (v.) *šnī* (*pa* and *aph*)
ancestor → *ʾb*
angel *mlʾk* /malʾak/, *qdyš* /qaddīš/ (→ *qdš*) → Watchers
anger *ḥmh* /ḥemā/, *qṣp* /qaṣp/, *rgz* /rogz/ (→ *ḥmh*)
animal *ḥywh* /ḥaywā/ (> /ḥēwā/; → *ḥyī*)
annihilate (v.) *blī* (*pa*; → Supplement), *ḥbl* (*pa*), *sūp* (*aph*), *šḥt* (*aph*), *šmd* (*pa*; → *ʾbd*)
annihilation *ḥbl* /habāl/ (→ *ḥbl*)
annually *šnh bšnh* (→ *šnh*)
annul (v.) *šrī*
anoint (v.) *mšḥ* (→ *mšḥ*)
answer (v.) *ʿnī* I, *tūb* (*aph*)
to appear as prophet (v.) *nbʾ* (*itpa*; → *nbyʾ*)
appearance *ḥzwn* /ḥezwān/ (→ *ḥzī*), *mḥzh* /maḥzǣ/ (→ *ḥzī*)
appease (v.) *rʿī*
approach (v.) *qrb*
approximately *ytyr ʾw ḥsyr* (→ *ḥsr*)
Aram *ʾrm* /ʾaram/ (→ *ʿm*)
Aramaic *ʾrmy* /ʾaramāy/ (→ *ʿm*)
archive → treasury
arm *drʿ* /derāʿ/ (→ *yd*)
aroma *ryḥ* /rēḥ/
arrange (v.) *ʿbd*
arrive at (v.) *mṭī*, rarely *dbq*
arrogance *gʾwh* /gaʾwā/ (> /gēwā/; → *gʾī*)
as follows *lʾmr* /lēmar/ (→ *mll*)
ascend (v.) *slq*
ask (v.) *šʾl*
ass (female) *ḥmrh* /ḥemārā/, *ʾtn* /ʾatān/ (→ *ʿrd*)
ass (male) *ḥmr* /ḥemār/ (→ *ʿrd*), *ʿrd* /ʿarād/
astrologer *kśdy* /kaśdāy/ (→ *ʾšp*)
astrology *nḥšy kwkbyn* (→ *šmyn*)
at court *btrʿ* (→ *trʿ*)
attain (v.) *mṭī*
attention *ṭʿm* /ṭaʿm/ (→ *ṭʿm*)
awaken (v.) → waken (v.)

bad *bʾyš* /baʾīš/, *lḥh* /laḥǣ/ (→ *bʾš*)
banquet hall *bt mšth*
barley *śʿr* /śaʿr/
base *sbwl* /sabūl/ (→ *sbl*)
battle *qrb* /qarāb/ (→ *qrb*)
be (v.) *hwī*
be able (v.) *ykl*, *khl*, *škḥ* (*aph*)
be about to (v.) *bʿī*
be afraid (v) *dḥl*, *zūʿ* (→ *dḥl*)
be arrogant (v.) *zīd* (→ *ḥṭī*), *rīm*
be astonished (v.) *tmh* (also *itp*)
be beautiful (v.) *špr*

be called (v.) *qrī* (*itp*); Question: "What is your name?": *mn šm* (→ *šm*); Answer: "I am"
be calm (v.) *šlī*
be clean (v.) *dkī* (→ *zkw*)
be clever (v.) *'rm* (→ *ḥkm*)
be complete (v.) *šlm*
be dark (v.) *ḥšk*, astronomically: *qbl* (→ *ḥšk*)
be deep (v.) *'mq*
be deformed (v.) *šḥt*
be different (v.) *šnī*
be distant (v.) *rḥq*
be firm (v.) *tqn*
be found (v.) *škḥ*
be full (v.) *mlī*
be hidden (v.) *ṣpn*, of heavenly bodies also *ṭmr* (→ *str*)
be illiterate (v.) *l' yd' spr* (→ *spr*)
be incumbent on (v.) *hwī l-/'l*
be innocent (v.) *zkī* (→ *zkw*)
be like (v.) *dmī, šwī*
be lowly (v.) *'nī* II
be many (v.) *śgī*
be poor (v.) *'nī* II
be saddened (v.) *krī* (*itp*; → *bhl*), *'ṣb* (*itp*)
be satisfied (v.) *ṭīb/yṭb*
be strong (v.) *gbr, tqp*
be unified (v.) *r'ī*
be waste (v.) *ḥrb* (also *aph*)
be willing (v.) *ndb*
beam " /'a'/
bear *db* /dobb/
beard *dqn* /daqan/ (→ *ś'r*)
beautiful *špyr* /šappīr/ (→ *špr*)
beauty *špr* /šopr/ (→ *špr*)
because of *'l dbrt* /'al dabarat/ (→ *dbr*), E. Aramaic *mṭl* /meṭṭoll/
become (v.) *hwī*
become angry (v.) *rgš*
become confused (v.) *šbš* (*itpa*)
become powerful (v.) *ḥlm* II (*itp*; → *ḥlm*)
bed *mškb* /maškab/ (→ *škb*)
before *qbl* /qobl/ (→ *qbl*), *qdm* /qodām/ (→ *qdm*)
beginning *r'š* /rēš/
behave anxiously (v.) *rgš* (*pa*)
behavior *'rḥ* /'orḥ/
behind *'ḥry* /'aḥaray/, *b(')tr* /bātar/ (→ *'tr*)
belly *bṭn* /baṭn/ (→ *rḥm*), *m'yn* /me'ayn/ (> /me'ēn/; → *rgl*)
bind (v.) *ḥbr* (*itpa*), *'sr, qṭr*
bird *ṣpr* /ṣeppar/ (individually), *'wp* /'awp/ (> /'ōp/; collectively → *ṣpr*)
bless (v.) *brk* (*pa*)
blessing *brkh* /barakā/ (→ *brk*)
blind (v.) *'ūr* (→ *'yn*)
blind *'wyr* /'awīr/ (→ *'yn*)
blindness *'wr* /'awār/ (→ *'yn*)
blood *dm* /dam/
blow (v.) *nšp* (also *nšb*; → *nšm*)
blessed is/are . . . ! *ṭwb* /ṭūb/ (→ *ṭīb/yṭb*)
blue *zmr* /zamūr/ (→ *zmr*)
boards " /'a'/ (plural)
boast (v.) *rbrb* (→ *rb*)
body *gšm* /gešm/
book *ktb* /ketāb/ (→ *ktb*), *spr* /sepr/
border on (v.) *dbq*
bow *qšt* /qašt/ (→ *qšṭ*)
boy *'lym* /'olaym/ (> /'olēm/)
branch *'np* /'anap/ (→ *'yln*)
bread *lḥm* /laḥm/
breath *nšm(h)* /našam(ā)/ (→ *nšm*), *rwḥ* /rūḥ/
breathe (v.) *nšm*
bright *nhyr* /nahhīr/ (→ *nhr*)
brilliance *zyw* /zīw/
bring (down from) (v.) *nḥt* (*aph*)
bring out (v.) *npq* (*aph*)
bronze *nḥš* /noḥāš/ (→ *dhb*)
brother *'ḥ* /'aḥ/
bubble (v.) *nb'* (→ *'yn*)
build (v.) *bnī*
building *bnyn* /benyān/ (→ *bnī*)
burden *ṭ'wn* /ṭa'ūn/ (→ *nśī*)
burn (v.) *yqd* (→ *'š'*)
buy (v.) *zbn*

calculation *ḥšbn* /ḥošbān/ (→ *ḥšb*)
calendar → *šnh*
calf *'gl* /'egl/ (→ *twr*)
call (cry out) (v.) *z'q*
call (name) (v.) *qrī*
call out (v.) *krz* (*aph*; → Iranian Official Titles)
calm *šlh* /šalǣ/ (→ *šlī*)
camp (v.) *šrī*
camp *mšry* /mašrī/ (→ *šrī*)

capital *r'š* /rēš/
captivity *šby* /šebī/ (→ *glī* II)
carefree *šlh* /šalǣ/ (→ *šlī*)
carry (v.) *sbl*
cattle *twr* /tawr/ (> /tōr/)
cedar *'rz* /'arz/ (→ *'yln*)
celebrate (v.) *štī*
certainly *yṣyb* /yaṣṣīb/ (→ *yṣb*)
certainty *yṣbh* /yaṣbā/ (→ *yṣb*), *rḥṣn* /roḥṣān/ (→ *rḥṣ*)
certify (v.) *yṣb* (*pa*)
chaff *'wr* /'ūr/
Chaldeans *kśdy* /kaśdāy/ (→ *'šp*)
chop off (v.) *qṣṣ* (*pa*)
chronicle *spr dkrny'* (→ *dkr*)
city *qryh* /qaryā/, later also *mdynh* /madīnā/ (→ *dīn*)
city wall *šwr* /šūr/
claim *dyn* /dīn/ (→ *dīn*)
clan *'mh* /'ommā/ (→ *'m*)
cleanse (v.) *dkī* (*pa*; → *zkw*), rarely *nqī* (*pa*; → *nqh*)
cleverness *'rmn* /'ormān/ (→ *ḥkm*)
cling to (v.) *dbq*
close (v.) *sgr* (→ *ptḥ*), *skr* (→ *ptḥ*), *śīm*, *šwī* (*pa*)
clothe (v.) *lbš* (*aph*)
clothing *lbwš* /labūš/ (→ *lbš*)
cloud *'nn* /'anān/, *'rpl* /'arapel/ (→ *'nn*)
colleague *knh* /kenā/
come (v.) *'tī*
command *ṭ'm* /ṭa'm/ (→ *ṭ'm*); → edict
commander *rb* /rabb/
communicate (v.) *ḥwī* (*pa*, *aph*)
communication *ptgm* /pategām/
compel (v.) *kbš* (→ *ykl*)
complain (v.) *qbl*
complaint *qbylh* /qabīlā/ (→ *qbl*)
complete (v.) *škll*, *šyṣy'* (→ *kll*)
complete *gmyr* /gamīr/ (→ *šlm*)
completely *gmyr* /gamīr/ (→ *šlm*), *šlm* /šalem/ (→ *šlm*)
comrade *ḥbr* /ḥaber/ (→ *ḥbr*)
conceal (v.) *str*, *ṣpn* (*aph*; → *str*)
concealment *str* /setr/, *mstr* /mastar/ (→ *str*)
concern → matter
conscientious(ly) *'sprnh* /'osparnā/
consciousness → heart
consecrate (v.) *ḥnk* (→ *ḥnkh*)
consecration *ḥnkh* /ḥanokā/
consider (v.) *'št* (*itp*)
consort with (v.) *ḥbr* (*itpa*)
constant *qym* /qayyām/ (→ *qūm*)
constellations, names of → *šmyn*
contract *spr* /sepr/
copper *nḥš* /noḥāš/ (→ *dhb*)
copy *pršgn* /parešagn/, *ṣwrh* /ṣūrā/ (→ *ṣlm*)
corner *qrn* /qarn/
correct *ṭb* /ṭāb/ (→ *ṭīb*/*yṭb*)
cosmetics → spice
cost → spending
count (v.) *mnī*
course of the stars *'bd šmy'* (→ *šmyn*)
court *dyn* /dīn/ (→ *dīn*), *drh* /dārā/ (→ *dūr*)
court lady *lḥnh* /laḥenā/ (→ *lḥn*)
cover (v.) *ksī* (*pa*; → *str*)
cow *twrh* /tawrā/ (> /tōrā/; → *twr*)
creep (v.) *rḥš* (→ *rb*)
crime *ḥbwlh* /habūlā/ (→ *ḥbl*), *rš'* /raša'/ (→ *b'š*)
cross over (v.) *'br*
crush (v.) *dqq*
cry (v.) *bkī* (→ *'ṣb*)
cry *z'qh* /za'aqā/ (→ *z'q*)
cult site *msgd* /masgad/ (→ *sgd*)
cultic image *ṣlm* /ṣalm/
cut off (v.) *gzr*, *qrṣ* (→ *'kl*)
cut severely *ngyd* /nagīd/ (→ *ngd*)

damage (v.) *nzq* (*aph*)
damage *nzq* /nezq/ (→ *nzq*)
dark *ḥšyk* /ḥaššīk/ (→ *ḥšk*)
darkness *ḥšwk* /ḥašōk/, astronomically: *qbl* /qabl/ (→ *ḥšk*)
darling *ḥbyb* /ḥabbīb/ (→ *rḥm*), *rḥym* /raḥīm/ (→ *rḥm*)
date formulae → *ywm*; *šnh*
daughter *brh* /barā/ (→ *br*)
dawn *šprpr* /šaparpar/ (→ *špr*)
day *ywm* /yawm/ (> /yōm/)
dead *myt* /mīt/ (→ *mūt*)
death *mwt* /mawt/ (> /mōt/; → *mūt*)
decay (v.) *blī*
decision *gzyrh* /gazīrā/ (→ *gzr*)
decree (v.) *qūm* (*pa*)

deed *mʿbd* /maʿbād/ (→ ʿbd), *ʿbd* /ʿobād/ (→ *ʿbd*)
deep *ʿmyq* /ʿammīq/ (→ *ʿmq*)
defame (v.) *ʾkl qrṣ*
defeat (v.) *tqp*
deliberate *zhyr* /zahīr/ (→ *zhr*)
deliver (v.) *nṣl* (*aph*), *plṭ* (*pa*; → *nṣl*), *šyzb*
deliverance *plṭh* /paleṭā/ (→ *nṣl*)
demand (v.) *šʾl*
demand *šʾlh* /šaʾelā/ (→ *šʾl*)
demand back (v.) *nṣl* (*aph*)
demi-mine (weight) *prs* /pars/ (→ *mnī*)
demise *ʾbdn* /ʾabdān/ (→ *ʾbd*)
demon *rwḥ* /rūḥ/
deport (v.) *glī* II (*aph*)
deposit (v.) *nḥt* (*aph*)
deposit *mškn* /maškan/ (→ *škn*)
depot *gnyzh* /ganīzā/ (→ *gnz*)
depths *ʿmq* /ʿomq/ (→ *ʿmq*)
descend (v.) *nḥt*
descendant *šrš* /šorš/ (< /śorš/?)
desert *mdbr* /madbar/ (→ *dbr*)
designate as a donation (v.) *pšq* (→ *ndb*)
destruction *ḥrbn* /ḥorbān/ (→ *ḥrb*)
determination *gzyrh* /gazīrā/ (→ *gzr*), *mlk* /melk/ (→ *mlk*)
determine (v.) *ṭʿm* (*aph*), *mnī* (*pa*), *šwī* II (*pa*; *šwī*)
dew *ṭl* /ṭall/
die (v.) *mūt*
dig (v.) *ḥpr* (→ *ʿmq*)
diminish (v.) *ḥsr* (*pa*)
directions *rwḥyn*, *rwḥy šmyʾ* (→ *rwḥ*; *šmyn*); names of → Numbers, 4
discipline *srwšy* /srōšī/
discovery *škḥh* /šakaḥā/ (→ *škḥ*)
displease (v.) *bʾš*
dispossess (v.) *krz* (→ Iranian Official Titles)
dispossession *krwz* /krōz/ (→ Iranian Official Titles)
distant *rḥyq* /raḥḥīq/ (→ *rḥq*)
distinguish oneself (v.) *nṣḥ* (*itpa*)
diverge (v.) *tūb*
divide (v.) *ḥlq*, *plg*, rarely *prs* (→ *mdy*)
division *mḥlqh* /maḥloqā/ (→ *ḥlq*), *plgn* /palogān/ (plural; → *plg*)
do (v.) *ʿbd*
do evil *ršʿ* (→ *bʾš*)
do first (v.) *qdm* (*aph*)
do good (v.) *ṭʾb* (*aph*; → *ṭīb*/*yṭb*)
document *spr* /sepr/
dominion *mlkw* /malkū/ (→ *mlk*), *šlṭn* /šolṭān/ (→ *šlṭ*)
door *dš* /dašš/ (→ *trʿ*)
double flute *swmpnyh* /sūmpōnyā/(?; → *zmr*)
dream (v.) *ḥlm*
dream *ḥlm* /ḥelm/ (→ *ḥlm*)
dream fantasy *hrhr* /harhūr/ (→ *ḥlm*)
dress *lbš* /lebāš/ (→ *lbš*)
drink (v.) *šrī*
drink *mšth* /maštǣ/ (→ *štī*)
driver *dbr* /dabbār/ (→ *dbr*)
duration *ʾrkh* /ʾarakā/
dwell (v.) *dūr*, *ytb*, *škn*, *šrī*
dwelling *mškn* /maškan/ (→ *škn*)

each *kl* /koll/ (→ *kll*)
eagle *ʿwz* /ʿōz/ or /ʿūz/ (→ *nšr*)
earring *qdš* /qodāš/ (→ *qdš*)
earth *ʾrʿ* /ʾarʿ/
east *mdnḥ* /madnaḥ/, *mwʿh* /mawʿǣ/ (> /mōʿǣ/; → Numbers, 4), *qdym* /qadīm/ (→ *qdm*)
eat (v.) *ʾkl*
edict *dt* /dāt/, *ṭʿm* /ṭaʿm/ (→ *ṭʿm*), *nštwn* /neštāwan/, *ptgm* /pategām/
eight *tmnh* /tamānǣ/ (→ Numbers)
elder *śb* /śāb/
emigrate (v.) *glī* II
emperor *mlk mlkʾ* (→ *mlk*)
empower (v.) *ḥyl* (*pa*; → *ḥyl*), *šlṭ* (*aph*)
empowered *šlyṭ* /šallīṭ/ (→ *šlṭ*)
end (v.) *sūp* (*aph*)
end *swp* /sawp/ (> /sōp/; → *sūp*); spatially also *sypyn* /sayāpīn/ (→ *sūp*) or *qṣt* /qaṣōt/ (plural; → *qṣṣ*)
end of the world *qṣ* /qeṣṣ/ (→ *qṣṣ*)
enemy *ʿr* /ʿarr/ (→ ʿrr), *śnʾ* /śānē/ (→ *śnī*)
engrave (v.) *ršm*(?)
enter (v.) *ʿll*
enthrone (v.) *mlk* (*aph*; → *mlk*)
entourage → court lady → noble
entrance *mʿl* /maʿʿal/ (→ *ʿll*)
entry *ʿll* /ʿalāl/ (→ *ʿll*)
erect (v.) *qūm* (*aph*)
err (v.) *ṭʿī* (→ *ḥṭī*)

error *ṭʿw* /ṭaʿū/ (→ *ḥṭī*)
escape (v.) *plṭ* (→ *nṣl*)
esteemed *yqyr* /yaqqīr/ (→ *yqr*)
eternity *ʿlm* /ʿālam/
evening *rmš* /ramš/ (→ *ywm*)
evil *bʾyš* /baʾīš/ (→ *bʾš*)
evildoer *ršyʿ* /raššīʿ/ (→ *bʾš*)
exactly *ʾsprnh* /ʾosparnā/
examine (v.) *bqr* (*pa*)
execution *qṭl* /qaṭl/ (→ *qṭl*)
execution of office *mlkw* /malkū/ (→ *mlk*)
exile *glw* /galū/ (→ *glī* II)
exit (v.) *npq*
exit *mpq* /mappaq/ (→ *npq*)
explain (v.) *prš*
external *bry* /barrāy/ (→ *br* /barr/)
extremity *sypyn* /sayāpīn/ (→ *sūp*)
eye *ʿyn* /ʿayn/ (> /ʿēn/)
eyelid *škn* /šekn/ (→ *ʿyn*)

face *ʾnp* /ʾapp/ (dual), rarely *ṣlm* /ṣalm/
fall (v.) *npl*
fall *mplh* /mappalā/ (→ *npl*)
fall off (v.) *ntr*
fall to (v.) *npl*
fame *šm ṭb* (→ *šm*)
fate *ḥlq* /ḥelq/ (→ *ḥlq*)
father *ʾb* /ʾab/
favor (v.) *rḥm*
favor *ḥn* /ḥenn/ (→ *ḥnn*)
fear *dḥlh* /deḥlā/ (→ *dḥl*)
feast *mšth* /maštǣ/ (→ *štī*)
feed (v.) *zūn* (→ *ʾkl*)
fellow *ʿlym* /ʿolaym/
fetter *ʾswr* /ʾasūr/ (→ *ʾsr*)
fidelity *hymnw* /haymānū/ (> /hēmānū/; → *ʾmn*)
field (open) *br* /barr/
fight (v.) *ʿbd* qrb (→ *qrb*)
figure *ṣwrh* /ṣūrā/ (→ *ṣlm*)
fill (v.) *mlī* (also *aph*)
find (v.) *škḥ* (*aph*)
finger *ʾṣbʿ* /ʾeṣbaʿ/ (→ *yd*)
fire *ʾšʾ* /ʾæššā/, *yqdh* /yaqedā/ (→ *ʾšʾ*), *nwr* /nūr/
first *qdmy* /qadmāy/ (→ *qdm*)
flame *šbyb* /šabīb/ (→ *ʾšʾ*)
flee (v.) *ndd*, *ʿrq* (→ *ndd*)
flesh *bśr* /baśar/
flood *thwm* /tehōm/ (→ *ym*)
flute *mšrwqy* /mašrōqī/ (→ *zmr*)
foliage *ʿpy* /ʿopī/ (→ *ʾyln*)
follow (v.) *ḥlp*
food *lḥm* /laḥm/, *mzwn* /mazōn/ (→ *ʾkl*); → barley → wheat → oil → wine
fool *skl* /sakal/ (→ *ḥkm*; *śkl*)
foot *rgl* /regl/ (of a mountain: *špwlyn* /šepōlīn/, → *rgl*)
force (v.) *ʾns*
ford *mʿbr* /maʿbar/ (→ *ʿbr*)
forgive (v.) *šbq*, *šrī*
former, formerly *qdmh* /qadmā/ (→ *qdm*)
fortification *byrh* /bīrā/
foundation *ʾšyn* /ʾoššīn/
four *ʾrbʿ* /ʾarbaʿ/ (→ Numbers)
free (v.) *šrī*
friend *rḥm* /rāḥem/ (→ *rḥm*)
frighten (v.) *bhl* (*pa*), *twh*
frightful *dḥyl* /daḥīl/ (→ *dḥl*)
fruits *ʾb* /ʾebb/ (→ *ʾyln*)
full *mlh* /malǣ/ (→ *mlī*)

gate *trʿ* /tarʿ/, *bb* /bāb/ (→ *trʿ*)
gatekeeper *trʿ* /tarrāʿ/ (→ *trʿ*)
gate area *ʾsp* /asopp/ (→ *trʿ*)
gather (v.) *knš*
generation *dr* /dār/ (→ *dūr*)
giant *gbr* /gabbār/ (→ *gbr*), (mythological) *npyl* /napīl/ (→ *npl*)
gift *mntn*(*h*) /mattan(ā)/, *nbzbh* /nabizbā/ (→ *ntn*)
gifted *ḥkym* /ḥakkīm/ (→ *ḥkm*)
give (v.) *yhb*, *ndb* (*itpa*), *ntn*
give a nickname (v.) *knī* (*pa*; → *šm*)
give back (v.) *tūb* (*aph*)
give to drink (v.) *šqī* (*aph*; → *štī*)
go (v) *ʾzl*/*hūk* (→ *hlk*)
go ahead (v.) *qdm* (*pa*)
go away (v.) *ʿdī*
go well (v.) *ṭʾb* (→ *ṭīb*/*yṭb*), *šlm* /šalām/ (as a predicate in a nominal clause; → *šlm*)
goat *ʿz* /ʿezz/; male *ṣpyr* /ṣapīr/ (→ *ʿz*)
god *ʾlh* /ʾelāh/, rarely *šmyʾ* (→ *šmyn*)
gold *dhb* /dahab/
good *ṭb* /ṭāb/ (→ *ṭīb*/*yṭb*)
good deed *ṭbw* /ṭābū/ (→ *ṭīb*/*yṭb*)

governor *pḥh* /pāḥā/, *šlṭn* /šolṭān/ (→ *šlṭ*)
grace → favor
grain *ʿbwr* /ʿabūr/ (→ *ʿbr*); → barley → wheat
grape *ʿnb* /ʿenab/ (→ *ḥmr*)
grapevine *gpn* /gapn/ (→ *ḥmr*)
grass *dtʾ* /datǣ/ (→ *ʿśb*)
grave marker *npš* /napš/ (→ *nšm*)
greatness *rbw* /rabū/ (→ *rb*)
greet (v.) *šʾl šlm* (→ *šʾl*)
greetings! *šlm* /šalām/ (→ *šlm*)
ground *ʾrʿ* /ʾarʿ/
grounds for an accusation *ʿlh* /ʿellā/
grow (v.) *rbī*
grow up (v.) *rb* /rabb/
guarantee (v.) *mḥī yd*
guard (v.) *ʿīr* (→ *ndd*, *ʿyr*)
guard *mnṭrh* /maṭṭarā/ (→ *nṭr*)
guardian (angel) *ʿyr* /ʿīr/
guilt *ḥwb(h)* /ḥōb(ā)/ (→ *ḥṭī*), *ḥyb* /ḥayyāb/ (→ *ḥṭī*)

hair *śʿr* /śaʿr/
half *plg* /palg/ (→ *plg*)
hand *yd* /yad/
hand (back of the) *ps* /pass/ (→ *yd*)
hand over (v.) *šlm* (*aph*)
harbor *mḥwz* /maḥōz/ (→ *ḥzī*)
harp *psntryn* /psantērīn/ (→ *zmr*)
haste *bhylw* /bahīlū/ (→ *bhl*)
hate (v.) *śnī*
hatred *śnʾh* /śenʾā/ (→ *śnī*)
have mercy (v) *ḥnn*, *rḥm* (*pa*)
have/exercise power (v.) *šlṭ*
head *rʾš* /rēš/
healthy *bšlm* (→ *šlm*)
hear (v.) rarely *ʿnī* I, *šmʿ*
heart *lbb* /lebab/, *lb* /lebb/
heaven *šmyn* /šamayn/ (> /šamēn/)
heavenly bodies *mʾny* *šmyʾ* (→ *mʾn*)
height *rmh* /rāmā/ (→ *rīm*), *rwm* /rūm/ (→ *rīm*)
help (v.) *sʿd* (also *pa*)
help *sʿd* /saʿd/ (→ *sʿd*), *ʿdr* /ʿedr/ (→ *sʿd*)
herald *krwz* /krōz/ (→ Iranian Official Titles)
herbage *ʿśb* /ʿeśb/
hero *gbr* /gabbār/ (→ *gbr*)
high *rm* /rām/ (→ *rīm*)
hip → joint

hit (v.) *mḥī*
hole *gb* /gobb/
holiday *ywm ṭb* /yawm ṭāb/ (→ *ywm*)
holiness *qdš* /qodš/ (→ *qdš*)
holy *qdyš* /qaddīš/ (→ *qdš*)
honor *yqr* /yaqār/
horn *qrn* /qarn/
horse *prš* /paraš/ (→ *prš*)
host *ḥyl* /ḥayl/
hour *šʿh* /šāʿā/
house *byt* /bayt/ (> /bēt/)
humiliate (v.) *špl* (*aph*; → *špl*)
humiliation *šplw* /šapelū/ (→ *špl*)
hundred *mʾh* /meʾā/ (→ Numbers)
hurry (v.) *bhl* (*itp*)
husband *bʿl* /baʿl/

immediately *bh šʿtʾ*; *br šʿt-* (→ *šʿh*)
immigrant *twtb* /tawtab/ (> /tōtab/; → *ytb*)
impertinence *šlh* /šillā/ (→ *šlī*)
in the control of *byd* (→ *yd*)
in the judgment of *bʿyny* (→ *ʿyn*)
in the name of *bšm* (→ *šm*)
incantation *ḥbr* /ḥabr/ (→ *ḥbr*)
incantation priest *ʾšp* /ʾāšep/
incense *lbwnh* /lebōnā/ (→ *mnḥh*)
inner *gw* /gaww/; *gwy* /gawwāy/ (→ *gw*)
innocence *zkw* /zakū/
innocent *zky* /zakkāy/ (→ *zkw*), rarely *nqh* /naqǣ/ (→ *nqh*)
insight *ʿrymw* /ʿarīmū/ (→ *ḥkm*), *śkltnw* /śokltānū/ (→ *śkl*)
install (v.) *bṭl* (*pa*; → *sūp*), *śīm*, *tqn* (*aph*)
interchange (v.) *ḥlp* (*aph*), *yhb*/*ntn b-*
interpret (v.) *prš*
interpretation *pšr* /pešr/ (→ *pšr*); less often *prš* /parāš/ (→ *prš*)
investigate (v.) *bqr* (*pa*)
invite (v.) *qrī*
iron *przl* /parzel/ (→ *dhb*)

joint (anatomically) *qṭr* /qeṭr/ (→ *qṭr*)
joy *ḥdwh* /ḥedwā/
Judea *yhwd* /yahūd/
Judean, Jew *yhwdy* /yahūdāy/ (→ *yhwd*)
judge (v.) *dīn*
judge *dyn* /dayyān/ (→ *dīn*)
jump (v.) *dūṣ* (→ *ql*)

justification *ṣdq* /ṣedq/ (→ *ṣdq*)

key *mptḥ* /mapteḥ/ (→ *ptḥ*)
kill (v.) *mūt* (*aph*), *qṭl*
king *mlk* /malk/
king's consort *šgl* /šēgal/
kingdom *mlkw* /malkū/ (→ *mlk*)
knee *brk* /berk/ (→ *brk*)
kneel (v.) *brk* (→ *brk*)
knot *qṭr* /qeṭr/ (→ *qṭr*)
know (v.) *qṭr*
knowledge *mnd*ʿ /maddaʿ/ (→ *yd*ʿ)
known *'zd* /'azd/

lack (v.) *ḥsr*
lack *ḥsrn* /ḥosrān/ (→ *ḥsr*)
lady *mr'h* /māre'ā/ (→ *mr'*)
lamb *'mr* /'emmer/
lamp oil *mšḥ lnwr'* (→ *mšḥ*)
language *lšn* /leššān/
large *rb* /rabb/
lasting *tdyr* /tadīr/ (→ *dūr*)
law *dt* /dāt/
lead (v.) *dbr*
lead across (v.) *ʿbr* (*aph*)
lead in (v.) *ʿll* (*aph*)
leader *sgn* /sagan/, *r'š* /rēš/, *rb* /rabb/, *rbn* /rabbān/ (→ *rb*)
leap year *ʿbwr* /ʿebbūr/ (→ ʿbr)
learn (v.) *'lp*
leave (v.) *npq mn*, *šbq*
left *śm'l* /śam'āl/ (→ Numbers, 4)
leg *šq* /šāq/ (→ *rgl*)
leisure *šlw* /šalū/ (→ *šlī*)
length *'rk* /'ork/
leopard *nmr* /nemr/
letter *'grh* /'eggarā/ (→ *spr*)
Levite *lwy* /lewāy/ (→ *khn*)
liar *kdb* /kaddāb/ (→ *kdb*)
liberate (v.) *prq*
lie (v.) *škb*
lie *kdb* /kadab/ (→ *kdb*), *kdb*(*h*) /kadab(ā)/ (→ *kdb*)
life *ḥyyn* /ḥayyīn/ (→ *ḥyī*)
life force → breath → soul
lifestyle *'rḥ* /'orḥ/
lift (v.) *nṭl*, *nśī*
lift up (v.) *nsb* (→ *nśī*)
light *nhwr* /nahōr/ (→ *nhr*)
like (v.) *rḥm*
linger (v.) *šrī*
lion *'ryh* /'aryǣ/
lip *śph* /śapā/ (→ *pm*)
literacy *spr* /sepr/
little *zʿyr* /zoʿayr/ (> /zoʿēr/; → *śgī*), *ḥsyr* /ḥassīr/ (→ *ḥsr*)
live (v.) *ḥyī*
load on (v.) *ṭʿn* (→ *nśī*)
located *śym* /śīm/ (→ *śīm*)
loin *ḥrṣ* /ḥarṣ/
long *'ryk* /'arīk/
lord *bʿl* /baʿl/, *mr'* /mārǣ/
lose (v.) *ḥsr* (*aph*)
love (v.) *rḥm*, later also *ḥbb* (→ *rḥm*)
lowly *ʿnh* /ʿanǣ/ (→ *ʿnī* II), *špl* /šapel/ (→ *špl*)
loyalty *ṣdq* /ṣedq/ (→ *ṣdq*)
lumber *'šrn* /'āšarn/

magician *'šp* /'āšep/
maid *'mh* /'amā/ (→ *ʿbd*)
majesty *hdr* /hadar/
major commercial road *šwq* /šūq/ (→ *mlk*)
make (v.) *ʿbd*
make an appointment (v.) *zmn* (*itpa*; → *zmn*)
make deep (v.) *ʿmq* (*aph*)
make music (v.) *zmr*
make noise (v.) *hmī* (→ *ql*)
male *dkr* /dakar/
man *'nš* /'enāš/, *gbr* /gabar/ (→ *gbr*)
many, much *śgy'* /śaggī/ (→ *śgī*)
mark (v.) *ktb* (*pa*)
marking *ḥzy* /ḥazī/ (→ *ḥzī*), *ktbh* /katobā/, *ršm* /rošm/ (→ *ktb*)
marriage *'ntw* /'ettū/ (→ *'nth*)
marriage celebration *mštw* /maštū/ (→ *štī*)
marriage contract *ktbh* /katobā/ (→ *ktb*), *spr 'ntw* /sepr 'ettū/ (→ *spr*)
marry (v.) *bʿl* (*aph*) (→ *bʿl*), *lqḥ* (*aph*), *nśī* (Old and Imperial Aramaic), *nsb* (*aph*; → *nśī*, later)
mass *mśgh* /maśgǣ/ (→ *śgī*), *śg'* /śogǣ/ (→ *śgī*)
master *rb* /rabb/, *rbn* /rabbān/ (→ *rb*)
matter, concern *ṭʿm* /ṭaʿm/ (→ *ṭʿm*), *mlh* /mellā/ (→ *mll*), *ṣbw* /ṣabū/ (→ *ṣbī*)
measure (v.) *mšḥ* II (→ *mšḥ*)

Mede *mdy* /mādāy/ (→ *mdy*)
Media *mdy* /māday/
member *bʿl* /baʿl/, *br* /bar/
memorandum *dkrn* /dokrān/ (→ *dkr*)
menetekel → *mnī*
merciful *rḥmn* /raḥmān/ (→ *rḥm*)
mercy *rḥmyn* /raḥmīn/ (→ *rḥm*)
messenger *mlʾk* /malʾak/, rarely *ngd* /negd/ (→ *ngd*)
messiah *mšyḥ* /mašīḥ/ (→ *mšḥ*)
midday *ṭhr* /ṭehr/ (→ *ywm*)
mighty *šlyṭ* /šallīṭ/ (→ *šlṭ*)
million *ʾlp ʾlpyn* (→ Numbers)
mind *bl* /bāl/, *lbb* /lebab/, *lb* /lebb/; later *hwn* /hawn/ (> /hōn/; → *śīm*)
mine (weight) *mnh* /manǣ/ (→ *mnī*)
mirror *mḥzy* /maḥzī/ (→ *ḥzī*)
moisten (v.) *ṣbʿ* (→ *ṭl*)
moment *ʿdn* /ʿeddān/
moment *šʿh* /šāʿā/
money *ksp* /kasp/ (→ *dhb*)
month *yrḥ* /yarḥ/ (→ *šnh*)
month names → *šnh*
moon *śhr* /śehr/ (→ *šmyn*)
morning *ngh* /nogh/, *ṣpr* /ṣapr/ (→ *ywm*, *ngh*)
moth *ss* /sās/ (→ *npl*)
mother *ʾm* /ʾemm/ (→ *ʾb*)
mountain *ṭwr* /ṭūr/
mourn (v.) *ʾbl* (→ *ʿṣb*)
mouth *pm* /pomm/
multiply (v.) *śgī* (*aph*)
music *zmr* /zamār/ (→ *zmr*)
musician *zmr* /zammār/ (→ *zmr*)
muzzle *pm* /pomm/

name (v.) *qrī*, *šlṭ* (*aph*)
name *šm* /šem/
near *qryb* /qarrīb/ (→ *qrb*)
necessary *ḥzh* /ḥazǣ/ (→ *ḥzī*)
need *ḥšḥw* /ḥāšeḥū/ (→ *ḥšḥ*)
negligence *šlw* /šalū/ (→ *šlī*)
night *lylh* /laylǣ/ (> /lēlǣ/)
nine *tšʿ* /tešʿ/ (→ Numbers)
no one *lʾ gbr*
north *grbh* /garbǣ/ (→ Numbers, 4), ʿ*ly* /ʿellāy/, /śamʾāl/ (→ Numbers, 4)
nose *ʾnp* /ʾapp/
number *mnyn* /menyān/ (→ *mnī*)

oath *mwmh* /mawmǣ/ (> /mōmǣ/; → *ymī*)
obedient *ṭʿm* /ṭaʿm/ (→ *ṭʿm*)
obey (v.) *šmʿ*
objection *ʿrr* /ʿarār/ (→ *ʿrr*)
offer (v.) *slq* (*aph*), *qrb* (*pa* and *aph*)
offering *qrbn* /qorbān/ (→ *qrb*)
officer *rbh* /rabǣ/ (→ *rb*)
oil *mšḥ* /mešḥ/ (→ *mšḥ*)
old *ʿtyq* /ʿattīq/, *śb* /śāb/; of anagraphic age: for males *br šnn*, for females *bt šnn* (→ *šnh*)
old man *śb* /śāb/
olive oil *mšḥ zyt* (→ *mšḥ*)
on the instructions of *ʿl pm* (→ *pm*)
onager *ʿrd* /ʿarād/
one *ḥd* /ḥad/ (→ Numbers)
one another *ḥd ḥd* /ḥad ḥad/ (→ Numbers)
open (v.) *ptḥ*
open *ptyḥ* /patīḥ/ (→ *ptḥ*)
opening *pm* /pomm/
opponent → enemy
order *srk* /sirk/ (→ *srk*)
other *ʾḥrn* /ʾoḥrān/ (→ *ʾḥry*); *ḥbr* /ḥaber/ (→ *ḥbr*)
outside *brʾ* /barrā/ (→ *br* /barr/)
oven *ʾtwn* /ʾattūn/ (→ *nwr*)
overthrow (v.) *mgr*
owe (v.) *ḥūb* (→ *ḥṭī*)
owner *bʿl* /baʿl/

pagan *ʾrmy* /ʾaramāy/ (→ *ʿm*)
palace *hykl* /hēkal/
palate *ḥk* /ḥekk/ (→ *pm*)
palm of the hand *kp* /kapp/ (→ *yd*)
panther → leopard
parents → father → mother
part *qṣt* /qaṣāt/ (→ *qṣṣ*); → portion
path *ʾrḥ* /ʾorḥ/
pay (v.) *šlm* (*pa*), *šql*
pay attention (v.) *zhr* (*itp*), *śkl* (*itpa*)
pay homage (v.) *sgd*
peace *šlm* /šalām/ (→ *šlm*)
people *ʿm* /ʿamm/
perish (v.) *ʾbd*
Persia *prs* /pārs/ (→ *mdy*)
Persian *prsy* /pārsāy/ (→ *mdy*)
person → name → self
physician *ʾsh* /ʾasǣ/ (→ *ʾšp*)

picnic (v.) *šrī* (*itp*)
pile (v.) *zqp* (→ *śīm*)
pious *dḥl ʾlh*
place (v.) *śīm*, *šwī* II (*pa*; → *šwī*)
place *ʾtr* /ʾatar/
place upon (v.) *rmī*
plague *mwtn* /mawtān/ (> /mōtān/; → *mūt*)
plan (v.) *ʿšt*
plant (v.) *nṣb*
planting *nṣbh* /neṣbā/ (→ *nṣb*, *ṣlm*)
plea *tḥnwnyn* /taḥnūnīn/ (→ *ḥnn*)
plead for mercy (v.) *ḥnn* (*itpa*)
please (v.) *ṭīb*/*yṭb*; *špr*
pleasure *ṣbyn* /ṣebyān/ (→ *ṣbī*), *rʿw* /raʿū/ (→ *rʿī*)
point *rʾš* /rēš/
police commander *typt* /tīpat/ (→ Iranian Official Titles)
poor *ʿnh* /ʿanǣ/ (→ *ʿnī* II)
portion *ḥlq* /ḥelq/ (→ *ḥlq*), *mnh* /manā/ (→ *mnī*)
poverty *ʿnwh* /ʿanwā/ (→ *ʿnī* II)
power *ḥyl* /ḥayl/ (> /ḥēl/); → strength
praise (v.) *brk* (*pa*), *hdr* (*pa*; → *hdr*), *ydī* (*aph*), *rīm* (*pawl*), *šbḥ* (*pa*)
praise *tšbḥh* /tašboḥā/ (→ *šbḥ*)
pray (v.) *ṣlī* (*pa*)
prayer *ṣlw* /ṣalō/ (→ *ṣlī*), Old Aramaic also *tṣlw* /taṣlū/
prefect *sgn* /sagan/
pregnancy *ʿdynh* /ʿedyānā/ (→ *ʿdī*)
prepare (v.) *tqn* (*pa*)
preserve (v.) *nṭr*
pretense *ʿlh* /ʿellā/
pride *gʾwh* /gaʾwā/ (> /gǣwā/; → *gʾī*)
priest *khn* /kāhen/, *kmr* /komr/ (only pagan; → *khn*)
priesthood *khnw* /kāhenū/ (→ *khn*)
prince → king
problem *qṭr* /qeṭr/ (→ *qṭr*)
prohibition *ʾsr* /ʾesār/ (→ *ʾsr*)
promise (v.) *ndr* (→ *ndb*)
property *nksyn* /nekasīn/
prophecy *nbwʾh* /nabūʾā/ (→ *nbyʾ*)
prophet *nbyʾ* /nabī/
province *mdynh* /madīnā/ (→ *dīn*)
prune (v.) *zmr* (→ *zmr*)
pupil *bbh* /bābā/ (→ *ʿyn*)
purple *ʾrgwn* /ʾargawān/
put (v.) *śīm*
put in force (v.) *tqp* (*pa*)
put something on (v.) *lbš*
puzzle *ʾḥydh* /ʾaḥīdā/, *rz* /rāz/

queen *mlkh* /malkā/ (→ *mlk*)
question *šʾlh* /šaʾelā/ (→ *šʾl*)

rain *mṭr* /maṭar/ (→ *ʿnn*)
raise (v.) *rīm* (*aph*)
raise an objection (v.) *ʿrr*
ram *dkr* /dakar/
read (v.) *qrī*
rear (v.) *qšš* (*aph*; → *rb*), *rbī* (*pa*; → *rb*)
rebel (v.) *mrd*, rarely *nśī* (*itpa*)
rebel *mrd* /marrād/ (→ *mrd*)
rebellion *mrd* /merd/ (→ *mrd*), *ʾštdwr* /ʾāštedōr/ (→ *šlḥ*)
receive (v.) *qbl* (*pa*)
recognize (v.) *ydʿ*
record *dkrn* /dokrān/ (→ *dkr*)
redeem (v.) *prq*
refrain (v.) *rḥq*
regarding *ʿl dbr* /ʿal dabar/ (→ *dbr*), *bšm* (→ *šm*)
region *mdynh* /madīnā/ (→ *dīn*)
regulation *qym* /qayām/ (→ *qūm*)
rejoice (v.) *dūṣ* (→ *ql*), *ḥdī* (→ *ḥdwh*)
relative *qryb* /qarrīb/ (substantivally; → *qrb*)
release (v.) *pṭr* (→ *šbq*), *plṭ* (*pa*; → *nṣl*), *šbq*
reliable *mhmn* /mahayman/ (> /mahēman/; → *ʾmn*)
remain (v.) *qūm*
remember (v.) *dkr*
remnant *šʾr* /šoʾār/ (→ *šʾr*); *šʾry* /šērī/ (→ *šʾr*)
remove (v.) *rḥq* (*pa*)
repay (v.) *šlm* (*pa*)
replace (v.) *ḥlp*
replacement *ḥlp* /ḥalp/ (→ *ḥlp*)
reputation *šm*
request (v.) *bʿī*, *šʾl*
request *bʿw* /baʿū/ (→ *bʿī*)
resemble (v.) *dmī*
residence *mwtb* /mawtab/ (> /mōtab/; → *ytb*)
rest *šlw* /šalū/ (→ *šlī*), *šlyn* /šelyān/ (→ *šlī*)
resting place *mdr* /madār/ (→ *dūr*)
return (v.) *tūb*

reveal (v.) *glī* I
rib *ʿlʿ* /ʿelaʿ/
righteous *ṣdyq* /ṣaddīq/ (→ *ṣdq*)
righteousness *ṣdqh* /ṣadaqā/ (→ *ṣdq*)
rip out (eradicate) (v.) *ʿqr*
rise (to speak) (v.) *ʿnī* I
river *nhr* /nahar/
robe → clothing
rock *kp* /kēp/ (→ *ṭwr*)
rod *ḥṭr* /ḥoṭr/ (→ *šbṭ*)
roll (v.) *gll*
roof (v.) *ṭll* (*pa*; → *ṭll*)
roof *ṭlwl* /ṭalūl/, *mṭll* /maṭlal/ (→ *ṭll*)
root *šrš* /šorš/ (< /śorš/?)
rootstock *ʿqr* /ʿeqqār/ (→ *ʿqr*)
ruined *šḥyt* /šaḥīt/ (→ *bʾš*; *šḥt*)
rule (v.) *mlk* (→ *mlk*)

sabbath *šbh* /šabbā/ (→ *ywm*; *šnh*)
sacrifice (v.) *dbḥ*
sacrifice *dbḥ* /debḥ/ (→ *dbḥ*), *mnḥh* /manaḥā/ (grain offering), *nḥwḥ* /nīḥōḥ/ (incense offering), *nsk* /nesk/ (libation), *ʿlh* /ʿalā/ (burnt offering, → *mnḥh*)
sacrificial priest *dbḥ* /dābōḥ/ (→ *dbḥ*)
saddened *ʿṣyb* /ʿaṣīb/ (→ *ʿṣb*)
salt (v.) *mlḥ* (→ *mlḥ*)
salt *mlḥ* /melḥ/
sambuke *śbk* /śabbok/ (→ *zmr*)
sanctify (v.) *qdš* (*pa*)
sanctuary *mqdš* /maqdaš/ (→ *qdš*)
say (v.) *ʾmr* (→ *mll*)
scale *mwzn* /mawzen/ (> /mōzen/; → *tql*)
scatter (v.) *bdr* (*pa*)
scepter *ḥṭr* /ḥoṭr/ (→ *šbṭ*)
scholar *spr* /sāper/ (→ *spr*)
scribe *ktwb* /kātōb/ (→ *ktb*), *spr* /sāper/ (→ *spr*)
scroll *mglh* /magallā/ (→ *gll*)
sea *ym* /yamm/
seal (v.) *ḥtm*
seal *ḥtm* /ḥātam/ (→ *ḥtm*)
secret *rz* /rāz/
secretary *spr* /sāper/ (→ *spr*)
see (v.) *ḥzī* (W. Aramaic *ḥmī*)
see again (v.) *ḥzī ʾnpy*
seed *zrʿ* /zarʿ/ (→ *zrʿ*)
seek (v.) *bʿī*
seer *ḥzh* /ḥāzǣ/ (→ *ḥzī*)
self *npš* /napš/ (→ *nšm*)
sell (v.) *zbn* (*pa*)
send (v.) *šdr* (*pa*; → *šlḥ*), *šlḥ* (also *pa*), Imperial Aramaic of reports and *yšr* (v.) of goods (*aph*; → *šlḥ*)
senior *qšyš* /qaššīš/ (→ *ʿtyq*)
servant *ʿbd* /ʿabd/ (→ *ʿbd*), *ʾmh* /ʾamā/ (→ *ʿbd*)
serve (v.) *plḥ*, *šmš* (*pa*)
service *ʿbydh* /ʿabīdā/ (→ *ʿbd*)
set out, move on (v.) *ngd*, *npq*
settle (v.) *škn* (*pa*)
settle down (v.) *šrī*
seven *šbʿ* /šabʿ/ (→ Numbers)
shade (v.) *ṭll* (*aph*; → *ṭll*)
shadow *ṭll* /ṭelāl/, *ṭl* /ṭell/ (E. Aramaic /ṭoll/)
shatter (v.) *tbr*
sheep *nqh* /neqǣ/
shekel *tql* /teql/ (→ *tql*)
shine (v.) *nhr* (*aph*), *nūr* (*aph*; → *nwr*)
shoot → sprout
show (v.) *ḥwī* (*pa*, *aph*), rarely *ḥzī* (*pa*), *ydʿ* (*aph*)
sight *ḥzw* /ḥazū/ (→ *ḥzī*)
sign (v.) *ktb*
sign (wonder) *ʾt* /ʾāt/
sign → marking
signet ring *ʿzqh* /ʿezqā/
silver *ksp* /kasp/ (→ *dhb*)
similarity *dmw* /damū/ (→ *dmī*)
sin (v.) *ḥṭī*
sin *ḥṭʾ* /ḥeṭē/, *ḥṭy* /ḥaṭāy/, *ʿwyh* /ʿawāyā/ (→ *ḥṭī*)
sing (v.) *zmr*
sister *ʾḥh* /ʾaḥā/ (→ *ʾḥ*)
sit, settle (v.) *ytb*
six *št* /šett/ (→ Numbers)
slave *ʿbd* /ʿabd/ (→ *ʿbd*)
sleep (v.) *škb*
small *zʿyr* /zoʿayr/ (> /zoʿēr/; → *śgī*)
smash (v.) *ḥšl*
smell (v.) *rīḥ* (→ *ryḥ*)
smite (v.) *mḥī*
snatch away (v.) *nṣl* (*aph*), *ntr* (*aph*)
snow *tlg* /talg/ (→ *ʿnn*)
sojourner *twtb* /tawtab/ (> /tōtab/; → *ytb*)
sole of the foot *kp* /kapp/ (→ *yd*)
son *br* /bar/

soothsayer *ḥrṭm* /ḥarṭom/ (→ *'šp*); *gzr* /gāzer/ (→ *gzr*)
soothsaying *nḥš* /naḥš/ (→ *šmyn*)
soul (life force) *npš* /napš/ (→ *nšm*)
sound *ql* /qāl/; *šryr* /šarīr/ (→ *šlm*)
south *tḥty* /taḥtāy/ (→ *'ly*)
sow (v.) *zr'*
speak (v.) *mll*
speech *mlyn* (plural), *mmll* /mamlal/ (→ *mll*)
spending *npqh* /napaqā/ (→ *npq*)
spice, aromatic oil *mšḥ bśm* (→ *mšḥ*)
spirit *bl* /bāl/ (of humans), *rwḥ* /rūḥ/
spring *m'yn* /ma'yān/, rarely *'yn* /'ayn/ (> /'ēn/; → *'yn*)
sprout (v.) *ṣmḥ* (→ *rb*)
sprout *ḥlph* /ḥelpā/ (→ *ḥlp*)
staff *šbṭ* /šabṭ/, in the Jewish realm also "tribe of Israel"
stair *drg* /darg/ (→ *nḥt*)
stall *dyr* /dayr/ (> /dēr/; → *dūr*)
stand up (v.) *qūm*
star *kwkab* /kawkab/ (> /kōkab/; → *šmyn*)
statue *ṣlm* /ṣalm/
stature, growth *qwmh* /qawmā/ (> /qōmā/; → *qūm*)
status, position *mqm* /maqām/ (→ *qūm*)
steer *twr* /tawr/ (> /tōr/)
stele *nṣb* /naṣīb/ (→ *ṣlm*)
stem → rootstock
stir up (v.) *gūḥ* (*aph*; → *šmyn*)
stone *'bn* /'abn/, rarely *gll* /galāl/ (→ *gll*)
stop (v.) *sūp*, *bṭl* (→ *sūp*)
store(house) *'wṣr* /'ōṣar/ (→ *mlk*)
street *'rḥ* /'orḥ/
strength *gbwrh* /gabūrā/, *gbrw* /gabbārū/ (→ *gbr*), *ḥsn* /ḥosn/ (→ *ḥsn*), *tqp* /toqp/ (→ *tqp*); → power
strengthen (v.) *ḥyl* (*pa*; → *ḥyl*)
strong *ḥsyn* /ḥassīn/ (→ *ḥsn*), *tqyp* /taqqīp/ (→ *tqp*)
succeed (v.) *ṣlḥ* (*aph*)
suddenly *bh š't*; *br š't-* (→ *š'h*)
sue (v.) *špṭ* (→ *dīn*)
suffer damage (v.) *nzq*
suitable *šwh* /šawǣ/ (→ *šwī*)
sun *šmš* /šamš/ (< /śamš/)
support (v.) *sbl* (*pa*), *smk* (→ *sbl*)
support *sbwl* /sabūl/ (→ *sbl*)
surface *'np* /'app/
survey, scout (v.) *rgš* (*pa*)
survive (v.) *š'r*
swear (v.) *ymī*
Syria *'rm* /'aram/ (→ *'m*)
Syria-Palestine *'br nhr'* (→ *'br*)

take (v.) *lqḥ*, *nśī* (Old and Imperial Aramaic), *nsb* (→ *nśī*, later)
take away (v.) *'dī* (*aph*)
take possession of (v.) *ḥsn* (*aph*)
take prisoner (v.) *'sr*
taste (v.) *ṭ'm*
tax *hlk* /helk/ (→ *hlk*)
teach (v.) *'lp* (*pa*), rarely *ḥkm* (*pa*)
tell a lie (v.) *kdb*
temple *hykl* /hēkal/, *byt* /bayt/ (> /bēt/)
temple employee *lḥn* /laḥen/
temple slave *ntyn* /natīn/ (→ *ntn*)
ten *'śr* /'aśr/ (→ Numbers)
ten thousand *rbw* /rebbō/ (→ *rb*)
tent *mškn* /maškan/ (→ *škn*)
term (as period of time) *'dn* /'eddān/, *zmn* /zemān/; (as designation) *šm* /šem/
terror *'ymh* /'aymā/ (> /'ēmā/)
testify about, attest (v.) *śhd* (*pa*)
testimony *śhdw* /śāhedū/ (→ *śhd*)
then *'ḥr* /'aḥar/ (→ *'ḥry*)
thigh *yrk* /yarek/ (→ *rgl*)
think (v.) *ḥšb*
thought *r'yn* /re'yān/ (→ *r'ī*)
thousand *'lp* /'alp/ (→ Numbers)
three *tlt* /talāt/ (→ Numbers)
threshing floor *'dr* /'edder/ (→ *'wr*)
threshold (')*skph* /(')a)skoppā/ (→ *tr'*)
throne *krs'* /korse'/ (> /korsǣ/)
throw (v.) *rmī*
time *zmn* /zemān/; *ḥd* /ḥad/ (→ Numbers, 1), *rgl* /regl/
today *ywm' znh* (→ *ywm*)
toe *'ṣb'* /'eṣba'/ (→ *yd*)
tone *ql* /qāl/
tongue *lšn* /leššān/
tooth *šn* /šenn/ (→ *pm*)
top *r'š* /rēš/
topple (v.) *mgr*
transgress (v.) *šnī* (*pa* and *aph*)
treasure *gnz* /ganza/, *śymh* /śīmā/ (→ *śīm*)

treasurer *gnzbr* /ganzabār/ (→ *gnz*); *srk* /sārak/
treasury *byt gnzy*ʾ (→ *gnz*), *śymh* /śīmā/ (→ *śīm*)
tree *ʾyln* /ʾīlān/
tremble, be afraid (v.) *zūʿ* (→ *dḥl*)
tribute *blw* /belō/ (→ *hlk*), *mndh* /maddā/ (→ tax)
trust (v.) *ʾmn* (*aph*), *rḥṣ* (*itp*)
truth *qšṭ* /qošṭ/
two *tryn* /terayn/ (> /terēn/; → Numbers)

ugly *bʾyš* /baʾīš/ (→ *bʾš*)
uncover (v.) *glī* I, *ʿrr* (→ *ʿrr*)
undamaged *šlm* /šalem/ (→ *šlm*)
under *tḥty* /taḥtāy/ (→ *ʿly*)
upper chamber *ʿlyh* /ʿelliyā/ (→ *ʿly*)
uprightness *qšṭ* /qošṭ/
use (v.) *ḥšḥ*
usual *ḥzh* /ḥazǣ/ (→ *ḥzī*)

venerate (v.) *plḥ*
veneration *sgdh* /segdā/ (→ *sgd*)
verbatim *mprš* (→ *prš*)
very *śgy*ʾ /śaggī/ (→ *śgī*)
vessel *mʾn* /maʾān/
vineyard *krm* /karm/ (→ *ḥmr*)
vision *ḥzw* /ḥezū/, less often *ḥzywn* /ḥezyōn/ (→ *ḥzī*)
voice *ql* /qāl/
voluntarily *brḥmn* (→ *rḥm*)
vulture *nšr* /nešr/

walk (v.) *hlk* (*pa*)
wall *ktl* /kotl/, *ʾgr* /ʾeggār/ (→ *ktl*), *šwr* /šūr/ (city or external walls)
want (v.) *bʿī*, *ṣbī*; in legal diction also *rḥm*
war *qrb* /qarāb/ (→ *qrb*)
warn (v.) *zhr* (*aph*)
water *myn* /mayn/ (> /mēn/; → *štī*)
wealth *ʿtr* /ʿotr/ (→ *ʿnī* II)
week *šbh* /šabbā/ (→ *ywm*; *šnh*)
weigh (v.) *tql*
weight *mtql* /matqāl/ (→ *tql*)
well *bʾr* /beʾr/ (> /bēr/; → *štī*)
well-being *šlm* /šalām/ (→ *šlm*)
west *mʿrb* /maʿrab/ (→ Numbers, 4)
wheat *ḥnṭh* /ḥeṭṭā/
white *ḥwry* /ḥewwārāy/ (→ *ḥwr*)
white object *ḥwr* /ḥewwār/
whiten (v.) *ḥwr* (*pa*; → *ḥwr*)
wife *ʾnth* /ʾettā/
will *rʿw* /raʿū/ (→ *rʿī*)
win (v.) *nṣḥ*
wind *rwḥ* /rūḥ/
wine *ḥmr* /ḥamr/
wing *gp* /gapp/
wing (of a door) *dš* /dašš/ (→ *trʿ*)
wisdom *ḥkmh* /ḥokmā/ (→ *ḥkm*)
wise *ḥkym* /ḥakkīm/ (→ *ḥkm*)
wish (v.) → want
wish *rʿyn* /reʿyān/ (→ *rʿī*)
with one another *ḥd mn ḥd* /ḥad men ḥad/ (→ Numbers)
witness *śhd* /śāhed/ (→ *śhd*)
wolf *dʾb* /deʾb/ (→ *db*)
woman *ʾnth* /ʾettā/
womb *bṭn* /baṭn/ (→ *rḥm*), *rḥm* /raḥm/ (→ *rḥm*)
wonder *ʾt* /ʾāt/, *tmh* /temh/ (→ *tmh*)
wood *ʾʿ* /ʾaʿ/
woodwork *ʾšrn* /ʾāšarn/
word *mlh* /mellā/ (→ *mll*)
work (v.) *plḥ*
work *ʿbydh* /ʿabīdā/ (→ *ʿbd*)
world (cosmos) *šmyn wʾrʿ* (→ *šmyn*)
world (era) *ʿlm* /ʿālam/
worship *plḥn* /polḥān/ (→ *plḥ*)
write (v.) *ktb*, rarely *ršm*
writing, document *ktb* /ketāb/ (→ *ktb*)
wrong *ʿwl* /ʿōl/ (→ *ḥṭī*)

year *šnh* /šanā/, rarely *ʿdn* /ʿeddān/
yield *ʿllh* /ʿalalā/ (→ *ʿll*)
youth *ʿlym* /ʿolaym/

zither *qytrs* /qītāris/ (→ *zmr*)
zodiac sign *mzl* /mazzal/ (→ *šmyn*)

www.ingramcontent.com/pod-product-compliance
Lightning Source LLC
Chambersburg PA
CBHW032125010526
44111CB00033B/76
9780802883308